June 3-7, 2018
Fort Worth, TX, USA

Association for
Computing Machinery

Advancing Computing as a Science & Profession

JCDL 2018
Fort Worth, Texas

JCDL '18

Proceedings of the 18th ACM/IEEE

Joint Conference on Digital Libraries

Sponsored by:

ACM SIGWEB, ACM SIGIR, & IEEE TCDL

Supported by:

UNT College of Information, UNT Health Science Center, UNT Libraries, Emerald Publishing, Wuhan University School of Information Management, and Coalition for Networked Information (CNI)

Association for
Computing Machinery

Advancing Computing as a Science & Profession

The Association for Computing Machinery
2 Penn Plaza, Suite 701
New York, New York 10121-0701

ISBN: 978-1-4503-5178-2 (Digital)

ISBN: 978-1-4503-6153-8 (Print)

Additional copies may be ordered prepaid from:

ACM Order Department
PO Box 30777
New York, NY 10087-0777, USA

Phone: 1-800-342-6626 (USA and Canada)
+1-212-626-0500 (Global)
Fax: +1-212-944-1318
E-mail: acmhelp@acm.org
Hours of Operation: 8:30 am – 4:30 pm ET

JCDL 2018 General Chairs' Welcome

We are pleased to welcome you to JCDL 2018 - the 2018 ACM/IEEE-CS Joint Conference on Digital Libraries in Fort Worth, Texas. JCDL 2018 is hosted by three units of the University of North Texas (UNT) – the College of Information, the UNT Health Science Center, and the UNT Libraries. Its co-organizer also includes the School of Information Management at Wuhan University.

The theme of this year is *From Data to Wisdom: Resilient Integration Across Societies, Disciplines, and System.* We aim to bring researchers, practitioners, and students together to exchange their ideas and to share experiences on exploring strategies, technologies, and users in the broad area of digital libraries. In the era of big data, we will examine how data, information, knowledge, and wisdom interact with each other and impact our disciplines and communities.

We are delighted to have three outstanding keynote speakers:

- We Have Interesting Problems: Some Applied Grand Challenges from Digital Libraries, Archives and Museums, Dr. Trevor Owens, Library of Congress
- Improving Research Outcomes Leveraging Digital Libraries, Advanced Computing, and Data, Dr. Niall Gaffney, University of Texas at Austin
- Open Source Technology for Scholarly Communication: Why It Matters, Dr. Carly Strasser, Collaborative Knowledge Foundation

The three speakers will bring their perspectives on important issues relating to the future development of digital libraries. They will engage audience with their experiences and insights. Specifically Dr. Carly Strasser is the shared speaker with UNT Open Access Symposium.

We thank the whole organizing committee for their diligence and commitment to make this conference. Our committee members come from different disciplines and countries. Many of them have been experts in digital libraries. We especially thank the program co-chairs Edward Fox, Min-Yen Kan, and Vivien Petras for organizing the program committee and leading the effort to create an intriguing, high-quality program.

Fort Worth, Texas is the rustic and artistic threshold into the American West. It is an easily accessible city that is both affordable and full of western charm and hospitality. Known for its ranching heritage, Fort Worth is often referred to by the sobriquet "Cowboy town" and still features a daily cattle drive through the historic Stockyards district just minutes from downtown. Fort Worth is home to a thriving cultural district which includes the widely acclaimed Kimbell Museum and a lively downtown district. The JCDL 2018 conference will be held at UNT Health Science Center (HSC) in Fort Worth. UNT HSC provides top-notch equipped conference rooms and is close to Fort Worth Museum of Science and Technology. We especially thank Daniel Burgard and his library staff for their hard work on local arrangements for JCDL 2018.

We thank our sponsors: ACM SIGIR, ACM SIGWEB, and IEEE TCDL, and our supporters: UNT College of Information, UNT Health Science Center, UNT Libraries, Wuhan University School of Information Management, Emerald Publishing, and Coalition for Networked Information (CNI). Our sponsors and supporters enable the conference to support the student authors, keynote speakers, and doctoral consortium participants, and to award authors of the best papers.

JCDL 2018 will provide you opportunities to meet old and new friends, to experience Texas culture, and to enjoy wine and good food. Welcome to JCDL 2018!

Jiangping Chen, Marcos André Gonçalves, and Jeff M. Allen
Conference general co-chairs

JCDL 2018 Program Chairs' Welcome

Welcome to the 2018 ACM/IEEE-CS Joint Conference on Digital Libraries (JCDL) in Fort Worth, Texas!

It is our great pleasure to present the proceedings of the 18th JCDL. This year's conference theme -- *From Data to Wisdom: Resilient Integration across Societies, Disciplines, and Systems* -- reflects the progress of digital libraries into a mature research field. JCDL has always invited a broad range of reporting on research, development, and best practices, ranging across theories, systems, services, and applications in the field. This year's call focused on inviting contributions from many different disciplines (also newcomers and associated disciplines) and different stakeholders (researchers and practitioners), with the intent to showcase the diverse methods and research mix in the DL community.

We believe that this goal has been achieved. This year's sessions cover topics about different object types (e.g., text, multimedia), different domains (science, archives), different digital library development stages (collection building, indexing and access, use), and different analysis approaches (citation analysis, topic modelling, linking).

The call for papers attracted submissions from 29 countries on four continents. The program committee reviewed and accepted 26 full research papers (from 71 reviewed), 13 short research papers (from 38 reviewed), 4 tutorials, 5 workshops (from 7 reviewed), 45 posters and 3 demonstrations (from 68 reviewed). The doctoral consortium, which looks to assist and mentor young scholars in the investigation and research of digital libraries, received 20 submissions and accepted 11 for presentation at JCDL. This proceedings volume contains the full text of the papers, as well as abstracts of the keynotes, tutorials, workshops, panels, demonstrations, and posters.

All paper submissions went through a rigorous reviewing process with three individual reviewers on each paper and a meta-review by a fourth expert from the DL community, which prepared the discussion for the program committee meeting in February 2018. With over 160 PC committee members from three continents, the program committee met virtually to discuss all submitted papers and the conference schedule. Posters and demos were accepted in two rounds of submissions: first, in an open, public call, as well as a second, invitation-only round for converting longer submissions into poster form.

As in the past, we will be awarding three honors: the Vannevar Bush Best Paper Award, the Best Student Paper Award, and the Best Poster/Demo Award. During the opening session of the conference, the nominees for the two Best Paper Awards will be announced. The prizes will be presented at the banquet. We hope you will be inspired by the high quality and creativity of these award-winning papers.

The packed, two and a half day program will be presented in three parallel tracks, and feature three interactive panels and three keynote speakers (Dr. Trevor Owens, Dr. Niall Gaffney, and Dr. Carly Strasser). The final keynote will bridge the conference over to the second, allied event of the Open Access Symposium at The University of North Texas that will take place in the second half of the week.

To organize a conference takes a large number of people. Selecting papers involves careful analysis and dedicated work. We would like to thank all members of the program committee and their secondary reviewers who prepared reviews. We also are grateful for those who joined in the program committee meeting. We want to recognize exceptional reviewers, whose comments helped to refine their reviewed papers, helping achieve a higher level of excellence. To accomplish this, we will be awarding the title of Outstanding Paper Reviewer to such reviewers, each of whom will receive a certificate for their extraordinary service. A special thanks goes to those organizing the other parts of the conference: the doctoral consortium chairs Stephen Downie, Oksana Zavalina, and Sampath Jayarathna; tutorial chairs

Lillian (Boots) Cassel and Wei Jin; workshop chairs Zhiwu Xie and Kazunari Sugiyama; panel chairs Robert H. McDonald and Yohei Seki; and poster and demo chairs Richard Furuta, Daniel Alemneh, and Liangcai Gao. The publication chairs Daqing He, Dan Wu, and Faryaneh Poursardar worked tirelessly on producing these proceedings. A very special thank you goes to Michael Nelson, who -- as the continuity chair -- assured that we stayed true to the JCDL standards of excellence.

The local organization and planning for the conference is as important as the program: a very warm thank you goes to the local chairs Daniel Burgard and Mark Phillips, and particularly to the general chairs Jiangping Chen, Marcos André Gonçalves and Jeff M. Allen, for steering all of us towards our joint goal of offering a creative, innovative, enjoyable, and explorative conference.

Welcome to JCDL 2018!

Edward Fox, Min-Yen Kan, and Vivien Petras
Program Co-Chairs

Table of Contents

Session 2A: Collection Access and Indexing

Session 3A: Citation Analysis

Session 3B: Scientific Collections and Libraries I

Session 3C: Multimedia Retrieval

Session 4A: Quality and Preservation

Session 4B: Text Collections

Session 5A: Exploring and Analyzing Collections

Session 5B: Scientific Collections and Libraries II

Session 5C: Archiving

Session 6A: opic Modeling and Detection

Panels

Posters

Demonstrations

Tutorials

Workshops

Doctoral Consortium

JCDL 2018 Conference Organization

General Chairs: Jiangping Chen, College of Information, UNT, USA
Marcos André Gonçalves, Federal University of Minas Gerais, Brazil
Jeff M. Allen, College of Information, UNT, USA

Program Chairs: Edward A. Fox, Virginia Tech, USA
Min-Yen Kan, National University of Singapore, Singapore
Vivien Petras, Humboldt-Universität zu Berlin, Germany

Poster and Demo Chairs: Richard Furuta, Texas A&M University, USA
Daniel Alemneh, University of North Texas (UNT), USA
Liangcai Gao, Peking University, China

Panel Chairs: Robert H. McDonald, Indiana University Bloomington, USA
Yohei Seki, University of Tsukuba, Japan

Tutorial Chairs: Lillian (Boots) Cassel, Villanova University, USA
Wei Jin, Computer Science, University of North Texas (UNT), USA

Workshop Chairs: Zhiwu Xie, Virgina Tech Libraries, USA
Kazunari Sugiyama, National University of Singapore, Singapore

Doctoral Consortium Chairs: Stephen Downie, University of Illinois at Urbana-Champaign, USA
Oksana Zavalina, College of Information, UNT, USA
Sampath Jayarathna, California Polytechnic University, USA

Publication Chairs: Daqing He, University of Pittsburg, USA
Dan Wu, Wuhan University, China
Faryaneh Poursardar, Texas A&M University, USA

Continuity Chair: Michael Nelson, Old Dominion University, USA

Local Organization Chairs: Daniel Burgard, UNT Health Science Center Library, USA
Mark Phillips, University of North Texas (UNT) Libraries, USA

Publicity Chairs: Unmil Karadkar, University of Texas at Austin, USA
Mat Kelly, Old Dominion University, USA
Haihua Chen, University of North Texas, USA

Treasurers: Jeonghyun (Annie) Kim, College of Information, UNT, USA
Xiaozhong Liu, Indiana University Bloomington, USA

Volunteer Chairs: Brenda Reyes Ayala, College of Information, UNT, USA
Michele Whitehead, UNT Health Science Center Library, USA

Sponsorship Chairs: Abdulrahman Habib, College of Information, UNT, USA
Martin Halbert, University of North Texas (UNT) Libraries, USA

Program Committee (continued):

Edward Fox, Virginia Tech, USA
Luis Francisco-Revilla, The University of Texas at Austin, USA
Nuno Freire, INESC-ID, Portugal
Ingo Frommholz, University of Bedfordshire, UK
Richard Furuta, Texas A&M University, USA
Niloy Ganguly, Indian Institute of Technology Kharagpur, India
Daniela Gifu, Alexandru Ioan Cuza University of Iasi, Romanian Academy – Iasi Branch, Romania
C. Lee Giles, The Pennsylvania State University, USA
Bela Gipp, University of Konstanz, Germany
Vinay Goel, Internet Archive, USA
Dion Goh, Nanyang Technological University, Singapore
Swapna Gottipati, Singapore Management University, Singapore
Julie Griffin, Virginia Tech Libraries, USA
Jim Hahn, University of Illinois at Urbana-Champaign, USA
Kishaloy Halder, National University of Singapore, Singapore
Felix Hamborg, University of Konstanz, Germany
S.M. Shamimul Hasan, Oak Ridge National Laboratory, USA
Dafang He, The Pennsylvania State University, USA
Bradley Hemminger, The University of North Carolina at Chapel Hill, USA
Maureen Henninger, University of Technology, Sydney, Australia
Drahomira Herrmannova, Oak Ridge National Laboratory, USA
Annika Hinze, University of Waikato, New Zealand
Helen Hockx-Yu, University of Notre Dame, USA
Nick Homenda, Indiana University Libraries, USA
Xiao Hu, The University of Hong Kong, Hong Kong
Bill Ingram, Virginia Tech University Libraries, USA
Antoine Isaac, Europeana & VU University Amsterdam, Netherlands
Nabeela Jaffer, University of Michigan, USA
Kokil Jaidka, University of Pennsylvania, USA
Adam Jatowt, Kyoto University, Japan
Sampath Jayarathna, California State Polytechnic University Pomona, USA
Jacob Jett, University of Illinois at Urbana-Champaign, USA
Jaap Kamps, University of Amsterdam, Netherlands
Min-Yen Kan, National University of Singapore, Singapore
Sarantos Kapidakis, Ionian Uninversity, Greece
Unmil Karadkar, The University of Texas at Austin, USA
Mat Kelly, Old Dominion University, USA
Madian Khabsa, Apple, USA
Claus-Peter Klas, GESIS - Leibniz Institute for Social Sciences, Germany
Martin Klein, Los Alamos National Laboratory, USA
Petr Knoth, The Open University, UK
Alberto Laender, Federal University of Minas Gerais, Brazil
Jin Ha Lee, University of Washington, USA
Jonathan Leidig, Grand Valley State University, USA
Kun Lu, University of Oklahoma, USA
Clifford Lynch, Coalition for Networked Information (CNI), USA

Program Committee (continued):

Mirella M. Moro, Federal University of Minas Gerais, Brazil
Gary Marchionini, The University of North Carolina at Chapel Hill, USA
Byron Marshall, Oregon State University, USA
Catherine Marshall, Texas A&M University, USA
Philipp Mayr, GESIS - Leibniz Institute for Social Sciences, Germany
Robert H. McDonald, Indiana University Bloomington, USA
Dana McKay, The University of Melbourne, Australia
Norman Meuschke, University of Konstanz, Germany
Ian Milligan, University of Waterloo, Canada
Animesh Mukherjee, Indian Institute of Technology, Kharagpur, India
Uma Murthy, Amazon, USA
Federico Nanni, University of Mannheim, Germany
Wolfgang Nejdl, L3S & University of Hannover, Germany
Michael Nelson, Old Dominion University, USA
Erich Neuhold, University of Vienna, Austria
David Nichols, University of Waikato, New Zealand
Jean-Marc Ogier, University of La Rochelle, Laboratoire L3i, France
Denilson Pereira, Universidade Federal de Lavras, Brazil
Vivien Petras, Humboldt-Universität zu Berlin, Germany
Beth Plale, Indiana University Bloomington, USA
Simone Paolo Ponzetto, University of Mannheim, Germany
Faryaneh Poursardar, Virginia Tech, USA
Animesh Prasad, National University of Singapore, Singapore
Edie Rasmussen, University of British Columbia, Canada
Andreas Rauber, Vienna University of Technology, Austria
Sagnik Ray Choudhury, Pennsylvania State University, USA
Brenda Reyes, University of North Texas (UNT), USA
Thomas Risse, University Library Johann Christian Senckenberg, Germany
Horacio Saggion, Universitat Pompeu Fabra, Spain
Hany Salaheldeen, Old Dominion University, USA
Jacques Savoy, University of Neuchatel, Switzerland
Ralf Schenkel, Trier University, Germany
Christin Seifert, University of Twente, Netherlands
Yi Shen, Virginia Tech, USA
Frank Shipman, Texas A&M University, USA
Ali Shiri, University of Alberta, Canada
Sandipan Sikdar, Indian Institute of Technology Kharagpur, India
Gianmaria Silvello, University of Padova, Italy
David Smith, Northeastern University, USA
Joan Smith, Old Dominion University, USA
Min Song, Yonsei University, South Korea
Venkat Srinivasan, Virginia Tech, USA
Shigeo Sugimoto, University of Tsukuba, Japan
Kazunari Sugiyama, National University of Singapore, Singapore
Hussein Suleman, University of Cape Town, South Africa
Tamara Sumner, University of Colorado Boulder, USA
Nicholas Taylor, Stanford Libraries, USA
Pradeep Teregowda, IBM, USA

Program Committee (continued):

Alex Thurman, Columbia University, USA
Dominika Tkaczyk, Trinity College Dublin, Ireland
Ricardo Torres, University of Campinas, Brazil
Giannis Tsakonas, University of Patras, Greece
Douglas Tudhope, University of Glamorgan, UK
Herbert Van De Sompel, Los Alamos National Laboratory, Research Library, USA
Andre Vellino, University of Ottawa, Canada
Karin Verspoor, The University of Melbourne, Australia
Jenq-Haur Wang, National Taipei University of Technology, Taiwan
Peiling Wang, University of Tennessee, USA
Michele Weigle, Old Dominion University, USA
Nicholas Worby, University of Toronto, Canada
Mike Wright, University of Colorado Boulder, USA
Dan Wu, Wuhan University, China
Jian Wu, The Pennsylvania State University, USA
Iris Xie, University of Wisconsin-Milwaukee, USA
Zhiwu Xie, Virginia Tech, USA
Weijia Xu, The University of Texas at Austin, USA
Seungwon Yang, Louisiana State University, USA
Xiao Yang The Pennsylvania State University, USA
Masatoshi Yoshikawa, Kyoto University, Japan
Bei Yu, Syracuse University, USA
Zhiwei Zhang, Purdue University, USA
Maja Žumer, University of Ljubljana, Slovenia

Additional reviewers:

Sawood Alam
Seyed Ali Bahrainian
Anastasia Giachanou
Monica Landoni
Colin McRae
Jory Morrison
Alexander Nwala
Sozon Papavlassopoulos
Lahari Poddar
Marios Poulos
Jing Zhao

JCDL 2018 Sponsors & Supporters

Sponsors:

Supporters:

We Have Interesting Problems: Some Applied Grand Challenges from Digital Libraries, Archives and Museums

Trevor Owens
Library of Congress
trow@loc.gov

ABSTRACT

Libraries, Archives and Museums now have massive digital holdings. There is tremendous potential for library and information science, computer science and computer engineering researchers to partner with cultural heritage institutions and make our digital cultural record more useful and usable. In particular, there is a significant need to bridge basic research in areas such as computer vision, crowdsourcing, natural language processing, multilingual OCR, and machine learning to make this work directly usable in the practices of cultural heritage institutions. In this talk, I discuss a series of exemplar projects, largely funded through the Institute of Museum and Library Services National Digital Platform initiative, that illustrate some key principles for building applied research partnerships with cultural heritage institutions. Building on Ben Schniderman's The New ABCs of Research: Achieving Breakthrough Collaborations, I focus specifically on why the public purpose and missions of cultural heritage institutions are particularly valuable in establishing new kinds of collaborations that can simultaneously advance basic research and the ability for people of the world to engage with their cultural record.

BIOGRAPHY

Dr. Trevor Owens is a librarian, researcher, policy maker, and educator working on digital infrastructure for libraries. Owens serves as the first Head of Digital Content Management for Library Services at the Library of Congress. As part of this role, he directs studies and testing of digital library best practices and standards for management of digital content. In addition, he teaches graduate seminars in digital history for American University's History Department and graduate seminars and digital preservation for the University of Maryland's College of Information, where he is also a Research Affiliate with the Digital Curation Innovation Center. He previously worked as a senior program administrator at the United States Institute of Museum and Library Services (IMLS). At the IMLS, he led the establishment of the National Digital Platform initiative, which under his leadership, invested more than $30 million in 110 projects to advance digital infrastructure for libraries across the nation. Prior to that, he worked on digital preservation strategy and as a history of science curator at the Library of Congress. Before joining the Library of Congress, he led outreach and communications efforts for the Zotero project at the Center for History and New Media at George Mason University. Owens is the author of three books, the most recent of which, The Theory and Craft of Digital Preservation, is in press with Johns Hopkins University Press. His research and writing has been featured in: Curator: The Museum Journal, Digital Humanities Quarterly, The Journal of Digital Humanities, D-Lib, Simulation & Gaming, Science Communication, New Directions in Folklore, and American Libraries. In 2014 the Society for American Archivists granted him the Archival Innovator Award, presented annually to recognize the archivist, repository, or organization that best exemplifies the "ability to think outside the professional norm.

JCDL'18, June 3-7, 2018, Fort Worth, TX, USA.
ACM ISBN 978-1-4503-5178-2/18/06 021-1/17/06.
DOI: https://doi.org/10.1145/3197026.3197027

Title: Improving Research Outcomes Leveraging Digital Libraries, Advanced Computing, and Data

Niall Gaffney
Texas Advanced Computing Center
University of Texas at Austin
ngaffney@tacc.utexas.edu

ABSTRACT

With the advancements in data driven research ushered in with the "Big Data" era, many research fields from astrophysics to genomics have discovered previously impossible outcomes including exoplanet detection and precision medicine. As with many other rapid changes, challenges are emerging now in extending the reach of these technologies to less computationally savvy fields that often have even more challenging computational problems to address. In this talk, I will explore some of the ways the Texas Advanced Computing Center (TACC) and others are creating environments to simplify onboarding new communities both through simple yet powerful user interfaces that feature the ability to preserve and publish data, computational workflows, and outcomes as linked yet separate entities. By linking, preserving, and making discoverable these entitles, researchers new to these computational capabilities can more easily understand them often in a research context with which they are already familiar. By then seeing the details of how a result came from the data, they can more easily build upon the work of others or even begin new workflows tuned to their own research needs. I will talk out our collaboration with publishers and libraries to not only preserve and expose the links between these digital entities but allow for their recall into computational environments to either reproduce previous results or extend the research through additional data and/or new computational methods.

BIOGRAPHY

Dr. Niall Gaffney is the director of Data Intensive Computing at Texas Advanced Computing Center (TACC), The University of Texas at Austin. Dr. Gaffney's background largely revolves around the management and utilization of large inhomogeneous scientific datasets. Prior to join TACC in May 2013, Dr. Gaffney worked for 13 years in the role of designer and developer for the archives housed at the Space Telescope Science Institute (STScI), which hold the data from the Hubble Space Telescope, Kepler, and James Webb Space Telescope missions. He was also a leader in the development of the Hubble Legacy Archive, projects that harvested the 20+ years of Hubble Space Telescope data to create some of the most sensitive astronomical data products available for open research. Prior to his work at STScI, Dr. Gaffney worked as "the friend of the telescope" for the Hobby Eberly Telescope (HET) project at the McDonald Observatory in west Texas where he started working to create systems to acquire and handle the storage and distribution of the data the HET produced. Dr. Gaffney earned his B.A., M.A., and Ph.D. degrees in astronomy from The University of Texas at Austin.

JCDL'18, June 3-7, 2018, Fort Worth, TX, USA.
ACM ISBN 978-1-4503-5178-2/18/06.
DOI: https://doi.org/10.1145/3197026.3202665

Open Source Tech for Scholarly Communication: Why It Matters

Carly Strasser
Collaborative Knowledge Foundation (Coko)
carlystrasser@gmail.com

ABSTRACT

We can all agree that current publishing and dissemination modes for scholarly communication are not optimized for speed or utility and are often impediments to advancing ideas and knowledge. I will discuss the current landscape of publishing tech, and what the Collaborative Knowledge Foundation (Coko) and its partners are doing to shake things up.

BIOGRAPHY

Dr. Carly Strasser is the Director of Strategic Development for the Collaborative Knowledge Foundation (Coko). Coko builds open source software solutions for scholarly communication that foster openness, collaboration, and speed. Prior to Coko, Dr. Strasser was a Program Officer for the Data-Driven Discovery Initiative, an effort within the Moore Foundation's Science Program focused on promoting academic data science. She also worked as a Research Data Specialist at the California Digital Library, where she was involved in development and implementation of many of the University of California Curation Center's services and worked to promote data sharing and good data management practices among researchers. Dr. Strasser received a B.A. in Marine Science and a Ph.D. in Biological Oceanography from the MIT/WHOI Joint Program.

JCDL '18, June 3-7, 2018, Fort Worth, TX, USA.
ACM ISBN 978-1-4503-5178-2/18/06
DOI: https://doi.org/10.1145/3197026.3202666

Understanding the Position of Information Professionals with regards to Linked Data: A Survey of Libraries, Archives and Museums

Lucy McKenna
ADAPT Centre,
Trinity College Dublin,
Ireland
lucy.mckenna@adaptcentre.ie

Christophe Debruyne
ADAPT Centre,
Trinity College Dublin,
Ireland
christophe.debruyne@adaptcentre.ie

Declan O'Sullivan
ADAPT Centre,
Trinity College Dublin,
Ireland
declan.osullivan@cs.tcd.ie

ABSTRACT

The aim of this study was to explore the benefits and challenges to using Linked Data (LD) in Libraries, Archives and Museums (LAMs) as perceived by Information Professionals (IPs). The study also aimed to gain an insight into potential solutions for overcoming these challenges. Data was collected via a questionnaire which was completed by 185 Information Professionals (IPs) from a range of LAM institutions. Results indicated that IPs find the process of integrating and interlinking LD datasets particularly challenging, and that current LD tooling does not meet their needs. The study showed that LD tools designed with the workflows and expertise of IPs in mind could help overcome these challenges.

CCS CONCEPTS

• **General and reference → Surveys and overviews**; • **Information systems → Digital libraries and archives**; **Resource Description Framework (RDF)**; • **Human-centered computing →** *User studies*; User interface design; Usability testing;

KEYWORDS

Linked Data, Semantic Web, library, archive, museum, information professional, survey, questionnaire

ACM Reference Format:

Lucy McKenna, Christophe Debruyne, and Declan O'Sullivan. 2018. Understanding the Position of Information Professionals with regards to Linked Data: A Survey of Libraries, Archives and Museums. In *JCDL'18: The 18th ACM/IEEE Joint Conference on Digital Libraries, June 3–7, 2018, Fort Worth, TX, USA.* ACM, New York, NY, USA, 10 pages. https://doi.org/10.1145/3197026.3197041

1 INTRODUCTION

Through the use of Linked Data (LD), Libraries, Archives and Museums (LAMs) have the potential to expose their collections to a larger audience, increase the use of their materials, and allow for more efficient user searches [13].

JCDL'18, June 3–7, 2018, Fort Worth, TX, USA

ACM ISBN 978-1-4503-5178-2/18/06…$15.00
https://doi.org/10.1145/3197026.3197041

One might argue that LD for LAMs could be generated by technical experts or via crowd-sourcing, rather than by Information Professionals (IPs) such as librarians and archivists. However, as keepers of large amounts of data and as experts in the field of metadata creation and knowledge discovery, IPs are well positioned to play a leading role in the development of the Semantic Web (SW). As such, facilitating and supporting their engagement with LD is of particular value.

The aim of our research is twofold. Firstly, it investigates what IPs, both with and without experience in using LD, consider to be the benefits and barriers towards LAMs publishing and consuming LD. Secondly, it explores the idea of LD tooling designed for IPs as a means of facilitating the LAM community to engage with LD.

In light of the above, the objectives of our research were to investigate IPs':

(1) Knowledge of the Semantic Web and Linked Data
(2) Views on the benefits and challenges of using Linked Data.
(3) Experiences of using Linked Data.
(4) Usability of cataloguing and Linked Data interfaces.
(5) Views on Linked Data tools for Information Professionals.

Data was collected via a questionnaire which was distributed to IPs working in the LAM domain.

Results indicated that, while IPs consider LD to have many benefits for LAMs, such as improved resource discoverability and interoperability, they also find using LD to be fraught with challenges. Challenges reported included difficulties using LD tooling and difficulties interlinking LD resources. Participants indicated that LD tools designed specifically for IPs could make LD more accessible to the LAM domain.

Our study provides an up-to-date and broader perspective of LD for LAMs by including IPs, both with and without LD experience, from a range of institutions. Our study contributes to the LAM domain by exploring LD tooling designed for IPs as a means of increasing this group's engagement with LD.

Intended readers include Information Professionals, such as librarians, archivists, cataloguers and curators, and researchers in the field of Library and Information Science, the Semantic Web, and Linked Data.

The details of our research are discussed below in the following structure; Background, Related Work, Methodology, Findings, Discussion, Conclusions, and Future Directions.

2 BACKGROUND

The Semantic Web (SW) is an extension of the current Web where data is given well defined meaning and where the relationships between data, and not just documents, are defined in a common machine-readable format [4]. Linked Data (LD) describes a set of best practices for publishing and interlinking structured data on the SW, as per the principles defined by the World Wide Web Consortium (W3C) [3, 5]. These principles include the use of HTTP URIs (Uniform Resource Identifiers) as names for entities, such as works, people, places, and events, and also for retrieving data using the existing HTTP stack.

The Resource Description Framework (RDF) is a model, developed by the W3C, for representing and exchanging LD on the web as structured data [38]. An RDF statement takes the form of a triple, which consists of a subject, predicate (relationship) and object. RDF requires that URIs are used to identify subjects and predicates - allowing for the resulting data to be understood by computers. SPARQL is an RDF query language which allows for the retrieval and manipulation of data stored in RDF format via a SPARQL endpoint [8].

The SW and LD have the potential to transform the Web into a globally interlinked and searchable database rather than a disparate collection of documents [39]. This would allow for easier searching, querying, and processing of data by humans and machines alike - all of which would benefit the LAM domain.

2.1 Linked Data for LAMs

By freeing metadata from LAM's databases and sharing it on the SW, these institutions could increase the discoverability and re-usability of their resources [13]. Publishing records as LD also offers LAMs new opportunities to create meaningful links between objects across collections. Some of the benefits of LAMs becoming part of the SW are discussed below.

2.1.1 Interoperability and Re-Usability. Currently, a number of different metadata standards are being used across LAMs making metadata interoperability extremely challenging [1]. Publishing metadata as RDF would allow for the seamless sharing and re-use of metadata across institutions - increasing collaboration and reducing record duplication [1, 33]. As well as lowering costs, this would provide IPs with more time to focus on creating richer descriptions for local resources [13, 17].

2.1.2 Discoverability and Visibility. Many of the metadata standards employed by LAMs cannot be processed by search engines. As such, a significant amount of relevant content is not visible in search engine results [14, 31]. Data published in RDF, however, is easily processed by SW search engines [32]. As the Web is typically the first place users search for information, publishing metadata to the SW will provide LAMs with a way of enhancing the discoverability and visibility of their records [13, 26]. Not only will this make it easier for LAM patrons to find useful information; it will also provide LAMs with the opportunity to reach those who would not typically use their resources [12].

Additionally, as LD requires the use of URIs for identifying entities within and across resources, searching for specific terms will become more efficient and effective [13].

2.1.3 Interlinking and Integration. A vital component of LD is to provide links to other URIs so that users can discover related information [3]. LAM metadata that has been enriched with related links would allow users to navigate seamlessly between internal and external datasets [1, 9, 33]. By publishing resources as LD, LAMs have the potential to open up and share their metadata on the Web in ways that were previously restricted by metadata models [13].

2.1.4 Reliability and Authority Control. Since anyone can publish and interlink data on the SW, as the Web of Data grows there will be an increased need to identify who completed these tasks in order to establish data authenticity and accuracy. LAMs are typically well-established trusted sources of information, as such LD generated by IPs is likely to be treated with increased credibility over data generated by non-authoritative sources [24, 26, 34].

Additionally, IPs are experts in using controlled vocabularies for the consistent description of similar concepts and entities across records. A number of these vocabularies are already available as LD and could be used to consistently describe and link entities across the SW [26].

2.2 Linked Data Challenges for LAMs

The main successful examples of LD projects emerging from LAMs have been single-institution initiatives with limited interlinking, rather than Web-wide multi-institutional data integration projects [11, 19, 40]. As one of the fundamental prerequisites of the SW is the existence of large amounts of meaningfully interlinked resources [5], it is key that institutions not only publish RDF datasets but also interlink their data with others. These linking issues may be due to the fact that interlinking is one of the most challenging areas of LD and that few tools have been developed for users who are non-technical experts [1, 2, 34].

Other challenges faced by LAMs when attempting to participate in the SW include:

- Relatively few projects that demonstrate how implementing LD can benefit LAMs [17, 25].
- Most current LAM cataloguing software does not support LD requirements [7, 15, 25].
- Transforming existing records to RDF is time-consuming and challenging [32].
- Copyright and intellectual property issues [6, 32].

Despite the many benefits of publishing and using LD in LAMs discussed in 2.1, relatively few institutions have adopted the use of LD [17, 25]. We believe that this slow uptake is partially due to the challenges mentioned above, and also due to a 'chicken and egg' issue, whereby LAMs are likely to be reluctant to invest in LD projects without clear signs of success from other institutions, and without a variety of RDF datasets to interlink with.

3 RELATED WORK

The Online Computer Library Centre (OCLC) conducted an International LD Survey for Implementers in both 2014 and 2015, receiving responses from a total of 90 institutions across 20 countries [35]. Participating institutions, mostly libraries, were either publishing LD, consuming LD, or both. The questionnaire gathered data on the types of LD projects being implemented, the data being published and consumed, the rationale for implementing the project, and the barriers encountered.

The majority of projects were both consuming and publishing LD. The chief motivations and benefits of implementing the LD projects included increased discoverability of resources, improved data reusability, exposing resources to a larger audience, enhanced data quality, improved search accuracy, and enhanced Search Engine Optimisation (SEO).

In projects where LD was consumed, the most commonly used resources included the Virtual International Authority File (VIAF), DBPedia, the Library of Congress LD Service (id.loc.gov), and local resources. The main barriers to consuming LD included issues with data alignment issues, vocabulary mapping, unreliable or absent URIs, lack of authority control, and lack of dataset updates.

For LD publishing projects, the most commonly used RDF vocabularies and ontologies included the Simple Knowledge Organisation System (SKOS), Friend of a Friend (FOAF), DCMI Metadata Terms (DCTerms), the Dubin Core Metadata Element Set (DCE) and Schema.org. The most commonly used technologies were SPARQL, Java, XSLT, Zorba, Solr and Virtuoso Universal Server. The main barriers to LD publication included a steep learning curve for implementers, difficulties selecting ontologies, interlinking issues, a lack of documentation outlining how to build LD systems, and a lack of tooling.

The OCLC study provided a detailed overview of how LD is currently being used in libraries, as well as the benefits and challenges being experienced. However, one area that was not covered in the study was how IPs, who are not currently working with LD, view the role of the SW in the library domain. This perspective was investigated in a study by LaPolla [20], where an online questionnaire was distributed to academic cataloguers and technical-services professionals within the library domain. LaPolla's 22 question survey explored librarians' level of understanding and attitudes towards the SW, as well as their views on its role in the library.

LaPolla received 156 responses from librarians, 35% of whom rated themselves as "Very Familiar" with the SW, and 55% as "Somewhat Familiar". 42% of participants reported that their institution was already exploring the use of SW catalogues. Survey responses indicated that participants were interested in exploring the use of SW technologies within the library domain. Issues such as financial constraints, a lack of awareness of the SW, and a lack of SW best practices were reported as the main barriers to libraries engaging with the SW.

Overall, the results of LaPolla's study indicated that, while the majority of participants were knowledgeable and interested in the potential of the SW for the library domain, less than half of the represented institutions were actively exploring SW technologies due to a number of barriers.

Across both the OCLC and LaPolla studies, participants seemed to have a positive view of the use of LD in library domain with many benefits being listed. However, multiple barriers to its use were also identified. With IPs clearly having an interest in LD, the importance of investigating potential solutions to the identified barriers is of significant importance.

3.1 Contribution

Our study builds on and contributes to work in the area of LD for LAMs by:

(1) Taking into account the views of IPs, both with and without LD experience, from a variety of LAM domains.
(2) Evaluating the usability and utility of cataloguing and LD interfaces.
(3) Providing an up-to-date view of IPs knowledge of LD,how LD is currently being used in LAMs, and the benefits and challenges being experienced.
(4) Exploring the potential of dedicated LD tooling for IPs as a means of overcoming LD challenges.

4 METHODOLOGY

The primary means of data collection for our research was a questionnaire. The structure of this questionnaire is outlined below, and information on participation criteria and sampling is also provided.

4.1 Questionnaire

An online questionnaire[1] consisting of 50 questions was developed using Qualtrics[2]. In line with the aims and objectives of our study, the questionnaire was divided into six main Sections:

(1) Cataloguing Experience
(2) Usability of Cataloguing Tools
(3) Knowledge and Views on Linked Data
(4) Linked Data Project Experience
(5) Usability of Linked Data Tools
(6) Linked Data for Information Professionals

Questions in Section 1, 2, and 5 of the questionnaire aimed at gathering information on the usability of cataloguing and LD tools. Sections 3 and 4 of the questionnaire were designed to gather data on IPs' knowledge of LD, their experiences using LD, and the perceived benefits and challenges of using LD. Finally, Section 6 of the questionnaire collected information on participants' perceived usefulness of LD tooling.

Questions were mostly multiple choice, however some open-ended questions were also included. The questions were partially based on the results of the LD studies discussed in Section 3, as well as the results of two interviews exploring the benefits and challenges of using LD in libraries. These interviews were conducted with two academic librarians as part of a related study focusing on the development of an RDF-enabled cataloguing tool [22, 23].

For questions where participants were asked to choose from a proposed list of answer options, they also had the opportunity to add their own additional observations. This was done so as not to limit the range of responses, thus allowing for a more comprehensive view of participants' thoughts and opinions.

Included in Sections 2 and 5 of the questionnaire was the Computer System Usability Questionnaire (CSUQ) [21] which is used for measuring software usability and utility. The CSUQ was chosen over other usability questionnaires as it does not have to be completed directly after an interaction with a system and it was designed to be administered online or via mail [37].

[1] Available @ http://hdl.handle.net/2262/82670
[2] https://www.qualtrics.com

The CSUQ consists of 19 statements about which the user rates agreement on a seven-point scale from Strongly Agree (1) to Strongly Disagree (7) - thus lower scores indicate less usability issues. For the purpose of this questionnaire, a subset of nine statements, focusing on efficiency, efficacy, and ease of use, were used.

4.1.1 Participants. Participants in our questionnaire were primarily IPs with experience working in the LAM domain. IPs were encouraged to participate regardless of whether they had any prior experience working with the SW or LD. This was done in an attempt to recruit a broad range of participants, rather than just IPs who are highly experienced in LD. That being said, it is possible that many participants who completed the survey already had a prior interest in the SW and LD in order to be motivated to do so. Also recruited were a small number of Researchers and Academics with research experience in the LAM and LD domain. This was done so as to gain input on current SW and LD research for LAMs.

Non-probabilistic sampling methods were used to recruit participants [10]. IPs were recruited by contacting LAM institutions and associations with a request to distribute the questionnaire and by asking those who completed the questionnaire to forward it to other suitable candidates. Specific researchers and academics, known to the authors for having experience in the LAM and LD domain, were contacted directly via email. The types of institutions where the questionnaire was shared were large reputable universities, national libraries, archives and digital repositories, and also LAM related associations, conferences and research groups. The link to the questionnaire was also shared on Twitter[3] by the researchers, other IPs, and reputable LAM associations.

The questionnaire received over 230 responses. Of these, 185 were deemed suitable for analysis. The questionnaires removed from the study were eliminated on the basis that participants did not indicate that they had experience working as an IP or a researcher. Additionally, some questionnaires were removed due to repetitive answer patterns suggesting that the respondent may not have read the questions in their entirety.

Participants (Number of Participants (N) = 185) represented Europe (68%), North America (29%), Australia (2%), Asia (1%), Africa (1%) and South America (1%). Participants came from 20 different countries, with the majority coming from Ireland (28%), the USA (23%) and the UK (20%).

88% of participants had more than 4 years of experience working in the LAM or research domain, with the majority of participants (61%) having 10 or more years of experience.

Participants represented a variety of institutions including Academic Library (56%), Research Institution/University (7%), Public Library (7%), Special Library (6%), Archive (6%), National Library (5%), Museum (4%), and Special Archive (1%). As can be seen, the majority of participants came from an Academic Library setting. This is possibly due to the fact that, although the questionnaire was shared amongst libraries, archives and museums, the academic libraries in which in the questionnaire was distributed were very large. This likely resulted in greater participant numbers from this particular setting. As such, results are not generalisable across all domains, but they do offer an insight into LD for LAMs nonetheless.

[3]https://twitter.com

Tool	Technical Assistance Required				% of Participants (N = 173)
	Yes	No	Unsure	Total	%
Aleph	20	20	5	45	26%
Omeka	2	33	6	41	24%
DSpace	13	20	7	40	23%
Sierra	13	23	3	39	20%
Koha	5	18	2	25	18%
Fedora	12	8	7	27	16%
Voyager	8	12	4	24	14%
Filemaker	3	15	0	18	11%
Alma	9	20	9	20	11%
Millenium	3	9	4	16	10%

Table 1: Cataloguing Tools

5 FINDINGS

The results of the questionnaire are presented in the following paragraphs, and will be discussed and interpreted in corresponding Subsections of Section 6.

5.1 Cataloguing Experience

74% of participants (N = 132) reported being currently involved in the metadata cataloguing process of their workplace. When asked what metadata formats are used, this subgroup of participants mentioned a total of 41 formats with the most commonly cited being MARC 21 (73%), Dublin Core (43%), Encoded Archival Description (EAD) (20%), MARC XML (17%), Metadata Object Description Schema (MODS) (16%). Other reported formats used included BIBFRAME (5%), MODS-RDF (4%), the Metadata Authority Description Schema (MADS) (2%), and MADS-RDF (2%). A Discussion of these results is available in Section 6.1.

5.2 Usability of Cataloguing Tools

94% of participants (N = 173) reported having previous experience using a cataloguing tool. The most commonly reported tools can be seen in Table 1. Also included in Table 1 is the number of participants who indicated whether technical assistance was required when initially learning how to use the cataloguing tool. Participants also completed a CSUQ for each of the tools they reported having experience using - see Table 2. A Discussion of these results is available in Section 6.2.

5.3 Knowledge and Views on LD

Participants were asked to rate their prior knowledge of the SW and LD as either Extremely Knowledgeable (EK), Very Knowledgeable (VK), Moderately Knowledgeable (MK), Slightly Knowledgeable (SK) or Not at all Knowledgeable (NK). Table 3 provides an overview of these ratings, as well as a comparison between the ratings of participants with LD project experience (LDExp) (N = 54) and those with no LD project experience (NoLDExp) (N = 131).

Table 4 outlines the results for the question, "Do you think that publishing LAM metadata as LD could add value to the SW?". 81% of participants responded "Yes" to this question (N = 150). The

Tool	It was simple to use this tool	I could effectively complete my work using this tool	I was able to complete my work quickly using this tool	It was easy to learn how to use this tool	Whenever I made a mistake using the tool, I recovered easily and quickly	The organisation of information on the tool's screen was clear	The interface of this tool was pleasant	This tool had all the functions and capabilities I expected it to have	Overall, I was satisfied with this tool	Total Score	%
Aleph	4	2	3	4	4	4	4	3	3	31	49.21%
Omeka	3	2	3	2	3	3	3	4	3	26	41.27%
Dspace	3	2	3	3	3	3	4	4	3	28	44.44%
Sierra	3	3	3	3	3	3	4	4	3	29	46.03%
Koha	3	2	3	3	3	3	3	3	3	26	41.27%
Fedora	5	3	3	4	4	4	4	3	3	33	52.38%
Voyager	3	2	2	3	3	3	4	3	3	26	41.27%
Filemaker	3	2	3	3	3	3	3	3	3	26	41.27%
Alma	4	2	3	3	3	3	4	3	3	28	44.44%
Millenium	3	2	2	2	2	3	4	3	3	24	38.10%

Table 2: CSUQ for Cataloguing Tools

Topic	Rating	% of Participants (N = 185) LDExp	NoLDExp	Overall
Semantic Web	EK	5%	1%	6%
	VK	9%	5%	14%
	MK	14%	24%	38%
	SK	2%	25%	26%
	NK	0%	16%	16%
Linked Data	EK	5%	1%	6%
	VK	11%	9%	20%
	MK	11%	28%	39%
	SK	2%	23%	25%
	NK	0%	10%	10%

Table 3: SW and LD Knowledge Ratings

Question	Answer	% of Participants (N = 185) LDExp	NoLDExp	Overall
Publishing LAM metadata as LD could add value to the SW?	Yes	27%	54%	81%
	No	1%	1%	2%
	Unsure	2%	15%	17%
LAMs face barriers to publishing metadata as LD?	Yes	26%	41%	67%
	No	0%	1%	1%
	Unsure	3%	29%	32%
Consuming LD could benefit LAM domains?	Yes	28%	55%	83%
	No	0%	1%	1%
	Unsure	1%	15%	16%
LAMs face barriers to consuming LD?	Yes	24%	40%	64%
	No	0.5%	0.5%	1%
	Unsure	5%	30%	35%

Table 4: LD Publication and Consumption

most commonly reported benefits of publishing LAM metadata as LD were: Expose data to a larger audience (89%), Improve data accessibility (82%), Easier metadata sharing (81%), More efficient data searches (73%), Increased metadata openness (71%), Improved authority control on the SW (73%), Create a research environment (55%), and Improved Search Engine Optimisation (SEO) (51%).

Participants were also asked whether they thought LAMs faced barriers to publishing their metadata as LD - see Table 4. 67% of participants responded "Yes" (N = 124). The most commonly reported barriers were: Difficulty incorporating LD publication into cataloguing workflow (77%), Difficulty cleaning data (67%), Time consuming (66%), Steep learning curve (63%), Copyright issues (52%), Difficulty using LD tools (52%), Inadequate LD tools available (50%), Difficulty establishing links (43%), Difficulty using SPARQL endpoints (42%) and an Insufficient number of controlled vocabularies available as LD (41%).

Following this, participants were asked whether consuming LD could benefit LAM domains - see Table 4. 83% of participants responded "Yes" (N = 154). The most frequently reported benefits that consuming LD would offer LAMs were: Improved data discovery (85%), Interlinking across institutions (81%), Enriched bibliographic metadata (79%), Interlinking across datasets (75%), Harmonise data from multiple sources (73%), More efficient data searches (70%), Improved metadata quality (68%), Automated authority control (53%), and Reduced time spent cataloguing (52%).

Again, participants were asked whether they thought LAMs faced barriers to consuming LD - see Table 4. 64% of participants responded "Yes" (N = 119). The most significant barriers mentioned were: Difficulty ingesting into the catalogue (75%), Time consuming processes (71%), Issues with dataset reliability (58%), Difficulty using LD tools (55%), Authority control issues (53%), Lack of LD tools available (51%), Issues with data re-usability (49%), Difficulty establishing interlinks (45%), and Use of unstable URIs (45%). A Discussion of these results is available in Section 6.3.

5.4 LD Project Experience

Of the 185 participants, 29% (N = 54) stated that they had previously been directly involved in the implementation of a LD project or service - the LDExp subgroup. Of this subgroup of participants, 28 (51%) indicated that the project involved both the consumption and publication of LD, 22 (41%) indicated the LD was published only, and 4 (8%) indicated that LD was consumed only.

For projects where LD was consumed (N = 32), results indicate that the most frequently used datasets included the Art and Architecture Thesaurus (AAT) (55%), DBpedia (52%), VIAF (52%), Wikidata (26%), GeoNames (38%), Getty Thesaurus of Geographic Names (TGN) (35%), Library of Congress NACO Authority File (NAF) (29%), WorldCat.org (29%), and Europeana (26%).

In all projects where LD was published (N = 50), participants indicated that the most common types of data published were Bibliographic data (55%), Digital collections (55%), Authority Files (35%), Controlled vocabularies (32%), Ontologies (32%) and Holdings data (22%). Data was also gathered on the RDF Vocabularies and Ontologies that were used as part of these projects. The most frequently mentioned were Schema.org (50%), SKOS (45%), DCTerms (43%), DCE (37%), FOAF (33%) and Local vocabularies (31%). A Discussion of these results is available in Section 6.4.

5.5 Usability of LD Tools

The most commonly reported LD tools that the LDExp subgroup (N = 54) had experience using can be seen in Table 5. Also included in Table 5 are the number of participants who indicated whether or not they initially required the support of a technical person to use the tool. Participants also completed a CSUQ for each of the tools they reported having experience using - see Table 6. A Discussion of these results is available in Section 6.5.

5.6 LD for IPs

When participants (N= 185) were asked to provide their thoughts on the concept of LD tooling specifically for IPs, a number of common themes emerged. These included that such tools would:

- Enable more LAMs to become part of LD community.
- Allow LAMs to fully engage with LD.
- Make LD creation and usage more accessible for IPs.
- Enable LD to be incorporated into cataloguing workflows.
- Make it easier for IPs to understand the benefits of LD.
- Help reduce the technological barrier.

Requirements included that such a tool should be:

- Easily integrated with Library Management Systems.
- Incorporable into cataloguing workflows.
- Available in the public domain.
- Considerate of IPs point of view.
- Tuned to IPs working environment.
- Usable without having to understand LD technicalities or requiring the help of an IT professional.
- Standards compliant with a user-friendly interface.

Concerns raised were:

- The technologies and principles of LD are the same across different domains - LAMs require a knowledge of how to apply existing tools to their domain.
- Having bespoke tools may limit how LAMs could interact with allied communities not using these tools, potentially limiting the use of their work.
- Would tools be able to interact with closed vendor systems.
- If too bespoke it may be difficult to adapt the tool to the individual needs of specialised teams.
- Workflows and data processes differ across institutions.

As highlighted in Section 2.2, one of the main challenges with LAM LD projects is the process of interlinking LD resources. Table 7 outlines participants' responses when asked to rate the usefulness of a dedicated LD Interlinking Tool specifically for IPs. Participants also provided feedback on why they provided their selected rating - see Table 8. Unfortunately, participants who rated the tool as Useless did not provide feedback.

Participants were then asked to indicate which functions they thought such a tool should have. The most commonly stated functions included: Data enriching (61%), Awareness of common data sources (58%), Automatic linking to controlled vocabularies (54%), Configurable to the institution's workflow, (54%), Ability to integrate LD datasets into the catalogue (52%), Data cleaning (49%), Link validation (48%), Link discovery (46%), Review data source quality (43%), Vocabulary alignment/reconciliation (43%), Automatically link to ontologies (42%), Remove the need for understanding LD technicalities (40%), and to Create controlled vocabularies in SKOS (64%).

Tool	Technical Assistance Required				% of Participants (N = 54)
	Yes	No	Unsure	Total	%
OpenRefine	2	12	1	15	28%
Protégé	3	6	4	9	20%
Fedora	6	2	2	10	18%
Apache Fuseki	1	2	3	6	15%
RDF Refine	1	3	2	6	11%
Virtuoso	1	4	0	5	11%
Pubby	1	3	0	4	11%
Blazegraph	1	3	0	4	11%

Table 5: LD Tools

Tool	It was simple to use this tool	I could effectively complete my work using this tool	I was able to complete my work quickly using this tool	It was easy to learn how to use this tool	Whenever I made a mistake using the tool, I recovered easily and quickly	The organisation of information on the tool's screen was clear	The interface of this tool was pleasant	This tool had all the functions and capabilities I expected it to have	Overall, I was satisfied with this tool	Total Score	%
OpenRefine	4	2	3	4	4	4	4	3	3	31	49.21%
Protégé	4	3	3	3	2	3	3	3	3	27	42.86%
Fedora	5	3	4	4	4	4	3	3	3	33	52.38%
Apache Fuseki	5	3	3	4	4	4	3	3	3	32	50.79%
RDF Refine	3	2	3	3	3	3	3	3	3	26	41.27%
Virtuoso	4	3	4	4	4	5	5	4	3	36	57.14%
Pubby	3	2	2	3	3	3	4	3	3	26	41.27%
BlazeGraph	3	3	3	3	3	3	4	4	5	31	59.21%

Table 6: CSUQ for LD Tools

Rating	% of Participants (N = 185)		
	LDExp	NoLDExp	Overall
Extremely Useful	16%	24%	40%
Moderately Useful	5%	25%	30%
Slightly Useful	2%	5%	7%
Neither Useful nor Useless	14%	5%	19%
Slightly Useless	0%	0%	0%
Moderately Useless	.5%	.5%	1%
Extremely Useless	1.5%	1.5%	3%

Table 7: Usefulness of a Dedicated Interlinking Tool for IPs

Rating	Feedback
Extremely Useful	Reconciliation is one of LOD's greatest problems
Moderately Useful	IPs could establish connections as they create/interact with data
	More institutions would get involved if there were less barriers to entry
	Overcome the technical knowledge gap of content experts that create metadata
	Create potential for new interdisciplinary research opportunities
	Reduce the need for IPs to learn to use different interfaces, search strategies, and vocabularies
	A dedicated approach would be more appealing to IPs
	Time saving
Slightly Useful	A tool with awareness of the sources that IPs trust/prefer will be more efficient
	May have limited use within sectors that are similar to LAMs but are not cultural heritage institutions
	Need for automatic interlinking across collections
Neither Useful nor Useless	Need useful case study to be convinced
	Unsure of IPs' reaction to having roles changed
	More evidence required for financial investment

Table 8: Rationale for Usefulness Rating

Also documented were the LD datasets that participants would find most useful to interlink with. The most frequently selected datasets were: Workdcat.org (72%), id.loc.gov (59%), NAF (45%), ORCID (44%), British National Bibliography (BNB) (43%), VIAF (41%), AAT (40%), Europeana (40%), The British Museum's Semantic Web Collection (34%), and GeoNames (33%).

Finally, participants were asked to indicate what quality criteria they apply when using or searching for external data sources. These criteria were taken from a LD quality survey [41] which discussed

	% of Participants (N = 185)		
Criteria	**LDExp**	**NoLDExp**	**Overall**
Trustworthiness	44%	22%	66%
Interoperability	21%	30%	51%
Licensing Issues	17%	32%	49%
Completeness	9%	32%	41%
Understandability	13%	27%	40%
Provenance	13%	27%	39%
Timeliness	13%	25%	38%
Syntactic Validity	11%	25%	36%
Availability	13%	19%	32%
Conciseness	8%	15%	23%
Versatility	4%	7%	11%
Other	4%	2%	6%
None/Unsure	1%	8%	9%

Table 9: Criteria Used for Dataset Quality Evaluation

the metrics that are typically considered in a LD setting. The aim of this question was to analyse and understand what *fitness for use* means to IPs. Participants indicated that Trustworthiness (66%) was by far the most important criteria, followed by Interoperability (51%) and Licensing Issues (49%) - see Table 9. A Discussion of these results is available in Section 6.6.

6 DISCUSSION

A discussion and interpretation of the results from Section 5 has been provided in a corresponding Subsection below.

6.1 Cataloguing Experience

11% of particpants (N = 132) reported creating metadata in RDF format (BIBFRAME (5%), MODS-RDF (4%), and MADS-RDF (2%)), confirming that LD is not yet widely published by LAMs.

With the majority of participants coming from the library domain, unsurprisingly the most frequently reported metadata format used was MARC 21. As MARC does not inherently allow for linking, the standard is incompatible with LD. Converting MARC 21 to RDF, though possible, is extremely challenging [7]. Although MARC is still the most commonly used library metadata model, there seems to be a consensus that it is no longer the most effective means of encoding library metadata, however the future of the bibliographic record still remains unclear [18, 36].

One future possibility is BIBFRAME [29], a LOC initiative aimed at evolving bibliographic description standards to a LD model. With BIBFRAME currently in development, and with libraries having reservations about moving away from MARC and towards LD, one possible approach would be to use a schema that is compatible with both. One such format is MODS - an XML schema for a bibliographic element set that can be used for the purpose of cataloguing digital resources [28]. Being derived from MARC 21 and having a MODS-RDF ontology already [27], MODS could be a viable format for institutions wishing to move towards LD [23]. Interestingly, 16% of participants (N = 132) currently involved in the cataloguing process in their workplace reported using MODS, with 4% reporting using MODS-RDF.

6.2 Usability of Cataloguing Tools

Across all of the tools that participants mentioned they had experience using, in the majority of instances, participants did not require the support of a technical person in order to be able to use the tool. Looking at the individual tools presented in Table 1, only Fedora[4] had more participants requiring assistance, and only Aleph[5] had equal numbers across both groups. Interestingly, both Fedora and Aleph had the highest scores on the CSUQ, indicating the most usability problems. That being said, the overall scores for all tools indicated moderate usability issues.

Higher scores were noted on questions regarding the usability of the tool's interface, suggesting increased issues in this area. Also noted was that, while participants indicated that they could complete their work effectively using the tool, tools received higher scores on questions concerning their ease of use, learnability, and number of available functions.

6.3 Knowledge and Views on LD

Results show that the vast majority participants had some prior knowledge of the SW (84%) and LD (90%). With the majority rating themselves as at least Moderately Knowledgeable for both the SW (58%) and LD (65%) - see Table 3.

Looking at the individual subgroups, i.e. participants with (LDExp) (N = 54) and without LD project experience (NoLDExp) (N = 131):

- 95% of the LDExp group rated their knowledge of the SW as Moderately Knowledgeable or above, as compared with 44% of the NoLDExp group. 86% of the NoLDExp group rated themselves as Slightly Knowledgeable or above.
- 95% of the LDExp group rated their knowledge of LD as Moderately Knowledgeable or above, as compared with 54% of the NoLDExp group. 87% of the NoLDExp group rated themselves as Slightly Knowledgeable or above.
- Of all participants (N = 185), only 16% considered themselves to have no prior knowledge of the SW and only 10% rated themselves as having no prior knowledge of LD. All of these participants were part of the NoLDExp group.

These high knowledge ratings could allow for the results of our study to be treated with increased confidence. However, it is important to bear in mind that participants were asked to rate their own level of knowledge of the SW and LD, without having to demonstrate this knowledge, thus running the risk of participants being more or less knowledgeable than they rated themselves to be.

6.3.1 Benefits of LD. Results regarding the benefits of LAMs publishing and consuming LD aligned with previous research (See Sections 2.1 & 3). The overarching benefits reported were improved:

(1) Data Discoverability
(2) Data Accessibility
(3) Authority Control
(4) Metadata Enrichment
(5) Data Sharing and Interlinking
(6) Cataloguing Efficiency

[4] http://fedorarepository.org
[5] http://www.exlibrisgroup.com/category/Aleph

6.3.2 *Challenges of LD.*

With regards to the challenges of using LD, the results affirm those mentioned in Section 2.2. The overarching challenges to LAMs publishing and consuming LD were:

(1) Difficulty Integrating and Interlinking Datasets
(2) Issues with LD Tooling
(3) Insufficient LD Resources Available
(4) Quality Issues with Available LD Resources

A more in depth exploration of the Integration and Interlinking issue indicated that the main barriers lie in the area of data mapping. Barriers included difficulties:

- Mapping between LAM metadata formats and LD models
- Mapping controlled vocabularies
- Aligning controlled vocabulary terms that have been used differently, but correctly, across disparate datasets
- Managing spelling differences between datasets
- Managing differences in descriptive structures and practices across institutions

These barriers suggest that IPs are experiencing difficulties in the areas of link type selection and data provenance. Creating typed links between datasets is a known challenge of LD. Particularly challenging is the process of creating identity links, which involves determining whether two URIs refer to the same entity thus allowing for the use of the owl:sameAs property [16, 30]. It is apparent from our research that IPs are experiencing difficulties selecting the appropriate link type when interlinking datasets. Once cause of these difficulties appears to be a lack of provenance data. Decision making with regards to link generation could be made less challenging if metadata were enriched with provenance data explaining the descriptive practices and decisions of the metadata creator.

With regards to the barriers experienced with LD Tooling, participants specifically mentioned that tools are often challenging to learn and use, inadequate for use in LAMs, and difficult to incorporate into cataloguing workflows. The fact that all the LD tools reviewed in Section 6.5 were found to have moderate usability issues could be seen as evidence of this.

Finally, in relation to challenges experienced with LD resources, participants highlighted concerns with the reliability of currently available LD resources, as well as copyright issues.

Other concerns that were frequently mentioned included the cost, both financial and time-wise, of publishing and consuming LD. This included the time and cost of training staff on LD and hiring new IT staff. Participants indicated that in order to invest time and finances into LD, more useful examples of its applications would need to be seen.

6.4 LD Project Experience

Almost one third (29%) of participants had experience working on a LD project previously. The vast majority of these projects involved LD Publication (92%), with 59% involving LD Consumption. Judging by this discrepancy, it is possible that IPs are experiencing issues consuming and using LD resources that have already been published to the SW. This may be related to the integration, interlinking and data quality issues discussed in Section 6.3 above.

6.5 Usability of LD Tools

CSUQ scores across all tools suggested moderate usability issues. Participants indicated that they had mild-moderate difficulties completing their work effectively using the tools. Interface design, ease of use, error recovery and learnability received some of the highest scores, suggesting more severe usability issues in these areas. Despite this, in the majority of instances participants did not require the support of a technical person in order to be able to use the tools. Fedora[6] was the only tool where more participants stated that they required assistance. This suggests that, perhaps whilst not user-friendly, the tools were still usable for IPs.

6.6 LD for IPs

Participants had a generally positive response to the idea of LD tooling for IPs, and indicated that such tools could make LD more accessible for IPs. Participants suggested that, being more attuned to the needs and workflows of IPs, such tools could increase the number of LAMs engaging with LD.

Concerns with LD tooling for IPs were also raised, including the importance of ensuring such tools would be flexible and adaptable to the needs and processes of different institutions and teams. It was also highlighted that there are already existing LD Tools that LAMs could use. Whilst this is true, based on the data discussed in Section 6.3, it could be argued that LAMs find these tools challenging to use and adapt to their workflows.

When asked to rate the usefulness of a LD Interlinking Tool designed for IPs, the vast majority of participants (89%) indicated that they thought it to be a useful idea. When asked to explain why they rated the idea as useful, see Table 8, the most commonly cited reason was that a bespoke tool could help overcome the technical knowledge gap of IPs who find interlinking to be one of the most challenging areas of creating LD. Again, concerns regarding how adaptable such a tool would be to the individual needs of institutions were raised, as well as a need for useful case studies if time and finances were to be invested in using such tooling.

Also explored here were the quality criteria IPs apply when using or searching for external data sources. In Section 6.3.2 participants raised concerns regarding the quality of currently available LD datasets. Having a knowledge of the criteria that IPs use to select reliable resources would be useful when publishing to the SW.

7 CONCLUSION

Nowadays, with the Web being the first and often only place where users search for information, it is of great importance that LAMs make their data available online where it can be found by search engines and interact with other information resources. LD offers a means for LAMs to achieve this.

Our study highlighted the main challenges that IPs are facing in terms of engaging with LD. The processes of data integration and interlinking, specifically data mapping and link type selection, were found to be particularly problematic. The possibility of enriching metadata with provenance data as a means of aiding IPs with the link type selection process was discussed.

The results of our study also identified a need amongst IPs to make LD tooling more accessible and attuned to their workflows.

[6]http://fedorarepository.org

The response to the idea of a LD interlinking tool for IPs was positive, and a detailed set of requirements for such a tool was established - see Section 5.6. Developing this tool has the potential to facilitate increased engagement amongst IPs with LD, something which would benefit the LAM domain as a whole.

8 FUTURE DIRECTIONS

Following this study, the next step of our research will be to develop a LD interlinking framework specifically for IPs and the LAM community. This will be achieved by distilling a set of user requirements from the survey data. Thus far these requirements include:

- Enable provenance data enrichment
- Ability to map directly to LD models
- Ability to map controlled vocabularies
- Automated interlinking between controlled vocabularies
- Awareness of common data sources and authorities
- Ability to identify and rank trusted data sources and authorities

Further analysis of the LD Tools mentioned in our research will also be conducted in order to identify how these tools are used to create, share and consume LD. The CSUQ scores for these tools will also be further analysed in order to identify more specifically the difficulties IPs had when using them.

It is important to note that our research provides the LAM community with data outlining where the barriers lie in relation to IPs engaging with LD - see Section 6.3.2. While it is not within the scope of this research to address all of these issues, LAMs could use this information to address and provide potential solutions to other identified challenges.

ACKNOWLEDGMENTS

This study is supported by the Science Foundation Ireland (Grant 13/RC/2106) as part of the ADAPT Centre for Digital Content Platform Research (http://www.adaptcentre.ie/) at Trinity College Dublin.

REFERENCES

[1] G. Alemu, B. Stevens, P. Ross, and J. Chandler. 2012. Linked Data for Libraries: Benefits of a conceptual shift from library-specific record structures to RDF-based data models. *New Library World* 113, 11/12 (2012), 549–570.
[2] M. Bergman. 2014. A Decade in the Trenches of the Semantic Web. http://www.mkbergman.com/1771/a-decade-in-the-trenches-of-the-semantic-web/.
[3] T. Berners-Lee. 2006. Linked Data - Design Issues. https://www.w3.org/DesignIssues/LinkedData.
[4] T. Berners-Lee, J. Hendler, and O. Lassila. 2001. The Semantic Web. *Scientific American* 284, 5 (2001), 1–5.
[5] C. Bizer, T. Heath, and T. Berners-Lee. 2009. Linked Data - The Story So Far. *International Journal on Semantic Web and Information Systems* 5, 3 (2009), 1–22.
[6] G. Byrne and L. Goddard. 2010. The Strongest Link: Libraries and Linked data. *D-Lib Magazine* 16 (2010), 11–12.
[7] T.W. Cole, M.J. Han, W.F. Weathers, and E. Joyner. 2013. Library Marc Records Into Linked Open Data: Challenges and Opportunities. *Journal of Library Metadata* 13, 2-3 (2013), 163–196.
[8] K. Coyle. 2012. Semantic Web and Linked Data. *Library Technology Reports* 48, 4 (2012), 10–14.
[9] K. Coyle. 2013. Linked Data: An Evolution. *Italian Journal of Library, Archives and Information Science* 4, 1 (2013), 53.
[10] J. Daniel. 2011. *Sampling Essentials: Practical Guidelines for making Sampling Choices* (1st ed.). SAGE Publications Ltd., CA, Chapter Choosing Between Non-Probability Sampling and Probability Sampling, 66–80.
[11] C. Deliot. 2014. Publishing the British National Bibliography as Linked Open Data. *Catalogue and Index* 174 (2014), 13–18.
[12] T. Fons. 2016. Making Libraries Visible on the Web. *Library Journal* 141, 13 (2016), 44–46.
[13] B.M. Gonzales. 2014. Linking Libraries to the Web: Linked Data and the Future of the Bibliographic Record. *Information Technology and Libraries* 33, 4 (2014), 10–22.
[14] M. Guerrini and T. Possemato. 2016. From Record Management to Data Management: RDA and New Application Models BIBFRAME, RIMMF, and OliSuite/WeCat. *Cataloging and Classification Quarterly* 54, 3 (2016), 179–199.
[15] M. Hallo, S. Lujan Mora, and J. C. Trujillo Mondejar. 2014. Transforming library catalogs into Linked Data.. In *Proceedings of the 7th International Conference of Education, Research and Innovation.*
[16] H. Halpin, P.J. Hayes, J.P. McCusker, D.L. McGuinness, and H.S. Thompson. 2010. When owl:sameAs IsnâĂŹt the Same: An Analysis of Identity in Linked Data.. In *Proceedings of the 9th International Semantic Web Conference.*
[17] R. Hastings. 2015. Linked Data in Libraries: Status and Future Direction. *Computers in Libraries* 35, 9 (2015), 12–16.
[18] A. Kroeger. 2013. The Road to BIBFRAME: The Evolution of the Idea of Bibliographic Transition into a Post-MARC Future. *Cataloging and Classification Quarterly* 51, 8 (2013), 873–890.
[19] C. K. Lampert and S. B. Southwick. 2015. Leading to Linking: Introducing Linked Data to Academic Library Digital Collections. *Journal of Library Metadata* 13, 2-3 (2015), 230–253.
[20] F. LaPolla. 2013. Perceptions of Librarians Regarding Semantic Web and Linked Data Technologies. *Journal of Library Metadata* 13, 2-3 (2013), 114–140.
[21] R.J. Lewis. 1995. IBM computer usability satisfaction questionnaires: psychometric evaluation and instructions for use. *International Journal of HumanâĂŞComputer Interaction* 7, 1 (1995), 57–78.
[22] L. McKenna. 2017. Engaging Librarians in the Process of Interlinking RDF Resources. In *Proceedings of the 14th European Semantic Web Conference.*
[23] L. McKenna, M. Bustillo, T. Keefe, C. Debruyne, and D. O'Sullivan. 2017. Development of an RDF-Enabled Cataloguing Tool. In *Proceedings of the 21st International Conference on Theory and Practice of Digital Libraries.*
[24] E. Miller and M. Westfall. 2011. Linked Data and Libraries. *The Serials Librarian* 60, 1-4 (2011), 17–22.
[25] E.T. Mitchell. 2016. Library Linked Data: Early Activity and Development. *Library Technology Reports* 52, 1 (2016), 5–33.
[26] P. Neish. 2015. Linked data: what is it and why should you care? *The Australian Library Journal* 64, 1 (2015), 3–10.
[27] Library of Congress. 2013. MODS RDF Ontology: Primer. https://www.loc.gov/standards/mods/modsrdf/primer.html.
[28] Library of Congress. 2016. Metadata Object Description Schema: MODS. http://www.loc.gov/standards/mods/.
[29] Library of Congress. 2016. Overview of the BIBFRAME 2.0 Model. http://www.loc.gov/bibframe/docs/bibframe2-model.html.
[30] L. Papaleo, N. Pernelle, and F. SaÃŕs. [n. d.]. On evaluating the quality of RDF identity links in the LOD. In *Proceedings of IC'2014 Workshop.*
[31] O. Pesch and E. Miller. 2016. Using BIBFRAME and Library Linked Data to Solve Real Problems: An Interview with Eric Miller of Zepheira. *The Serials Librarian* 71, 1 (2016), 1–8.
[32] V. Schilling. 2012. Transforming Library Metadata into Linked Library Data. American Library Association. http://www.ala.org/alcts/resources/org/cat/research/linked-data.
[33] D. Seeman and L. Goddard. 2015. Preparing the Way: Creating Future Compatible Cataloging Data in a Transitional Environment. *Cataloging and Classification Quarterly* 53, 3-4 (2015), 331–340.
[34] P. Shvaiko and J. Euzenat. 2013. Ontology matching: State of the Art and Future Challenges. *IEEE Transactions on Knowledge and Data Engineering* 25, 1 (2013), 158–176.
[35] K. Smith-Yoshimura. 2016. Analysis of an International Linked Data Survey for Implementers. *D-Lib Magazine* 22, 7/8 (2016).
[36] A. Sprochi. 2016. Where Are We Headed? Resource Description and Access, Bibliographic Framework, and the Functional Requirements for Bibliographic Records Library Reference Model. *International Information and Library Review* 48, 2 (2016), 129–136.
[37] T. Tullis and W. Albert. 2013. *Measuring the User Experience, Second Edition: Collecting, Analyzing, and Presenting Usability Metrics* (2nd ed.). Morgan Kaufmann Publishers Inc., MA, Chapter Self-Reported Metrics, 121–161.
[38] W3C. 2014. RDF: Resource Description Framework. https://www.w3.org/RDF/.
[39] W3C. 2015. Semantic Web. https://www.w3.org/standards/semanticweb/.
[40] F. Zablith, M. Fernandez, and M. Rowe. 2015. Production and Consumption of University Linked Data. *Interactive Learning Environments* 23, 1 (2015), 55–78.
[41] A Zaveri, A. Rula, A Maurino, R. Pietrobon, J. Lehmann, and S. Auer. 2015. Quality Assessment for Linked Data: A Survey. *Semantic Web* 7, 1 (2015), 63–93.

The Role of Pre-Existing Highlights in Reader–Text Interactions and Outcomes

Samuel Dodson
University of British Columbia
dodsons@mail.ubc.ca

Luanne Freund
University of British Columbia
luanne.freund@ubc.ca

Rick Kopak
University of British Columbia
r.kopak@ubc.ca

ABSTRACT

Many digital information environments enable sharing of readers' highlights and other annotations, despite the lack of clear evidence of the effects on interaction behaviours and outcomes. We report on an experimental user study (n=15) of the impact of pre-existing highlights of varying quality on the digital reading process and outcomes of participants with different cognitive styles. We found that highlight quality affects surface level comprehension, but not deeper understanding. Participants were able to assess highlight quality and expressed different approaches to highlighting that influenced their interpretation of pre-existing highlights. Results regarding the impact of cognitive style were inconclusive.

CCS CONCEPTS

• **Information systems → Collaborative and social computing systems and tools; Users and interactive retrieval;** • **Applied computing → Collaborative learning;**

KEYWORDS

annotation, comprehension, highlighting, reading, social reading

ACM Reference Format:
Samuel Dodson, Luanne Freund, and Rick Kopak. 2018. The Role of Pre-Existing Highlights in Reader–Text Interactions and Outcomes. In *JCDL '18: The 18th ACM/IEEE Joint Conference on Digital Libraries, June 3–7, 2018, Fort Worth, TX, USA.* ACM, New York, NY, USA, 4 pages. https://doi.org/10.1145/3197026.3197066

1 INTRODUCTION

Annotation is widely considered to be an effective method to support active and effective reading [19], and highlighting, the most commonly used form of annotation [14], is available as a social, or shared, feature in many reading and learning platforms [7]. Within the digital library research community, there is more than two decades of research on annotation, and with much of that work focused on the conceptual and technical implementation [e.g., 1, 12].

Much less is known about the effects of shared and pre-existing highlighting on reading and learning. There is an assumption that sharing annotations can be useful for learning, as indicated by the development of social annotation systems for this purpose [e.g., 8], but the evidence is far from conclusive. It is unclear, for example, how shared highlights affect reading processes, particularly across different groups of readers. A recent study of the effects of pre-existing highlights on reading outcomes [3] found that highlights did not improve comprehension and may be a disadvantageous feature of the text. To better understand this phenomenon and to inform the design of social reading systems and digital libraries, this study addresses the following research questions: i) What is the impact of variable quality highlights (i.e., appropriate and inappropriate) on comprehension? ii) How are such highlights used and perceived by readers with different cognitive styles? iii) What factors affect the use and usefulness of highlights for readers?

2 PRIOR WORK

Given the central role of reading in learning, and the impact of reading comprehension on post-secondary education outcomes, it is essential to find ways to support effective reader–text interactions [17]. There has been a trend to increase readers' interactions with texts through active reading, where readers continuously evaluate the meaning of the text and its use for their task [21], or in deep reading, defined as reading with the aim of comprehension and long term retention [16]. A related goal is to facilitate social and collaborative reading and learning, through systems that enable multiple reader–text interactions, often through shared annotation capabilities, whether within private reading groups or public digital reading systems, such as Hypothesis (https://web.hypothes.is).

Though highlighting is one of the most commonly used reading strategies [14], existing studies of highlighting are inconclusive as to its benefits. Dunlosky et al. [4] carried out a review of a wide range of learning techniques employed by students, and concluded that highlighting, while widely practiced by students, was not found to be effective in improving outcomes. They suggest that these findings are limited, in that prior studies have not controlled for the amount of text highlighted or the quality of the highlights, nor has research focused on what the conditions for effective highlighting are. The majority of studies Dunlosky et al. reviewed were print based, and do not address the concerns raised by digital reading practices and the greater challenges in attention and deep reading.

The strongest effects of highlighting seem to be those for directing attention to particular words and for recall of facts, rather than for comprehending concepts. Fowler and Barker [5] found that pre-existing highlights can have a positive effect on recall. Similarly, Chi, Gumbrecht, and Hong [2] found that readers were able to answer reading questions faster and more accurately using a digital text with pre-existing highlights than without. Silvers and Kreiner [18] studied the effects of appropriate and inappropriate

JCDL '18, June 3–7, 2018, Fort Worth, TX, USA

ACM ISBN 978-1-4503-5178-2/18/06...$15.00
https://doi.org/10.1145/3197026.3197066

pre-existing highlighting on comprehension and found that comprehension levels were not improved by appropriate highlights but were significantly lower for inappropriate highlighting. Similar effects were found by [3] in a digital reading environment.

Reading depends on bottom-up and top-down cognitive processes [22]. Integrating a theory of comprehension into our study offers insight into the cognitive processes that influence how readers create and restructure mental representations of the text. Theories of comprehension that use an interaction of bottom-up and top-down processes, such as the Construction-Integration (CI) Model [9], "are currently considered the best frameworks for understanding individual differences in reading comprehension" [10]. Kintsch [9], for example, distinguishes between how readers generate representations of a text at different levels: the microstructure and macrostructure. The CI model shows that a reader can establish a microstructure representation of a text that is sufficient to answer some questions about the text without comprehending the deeper meaning of the text through the macrostructure.

Messick [13] defines cognitive style as the "strategies determining a person's typical modes of perceiving, remembering, thinking, and problem solving." One of the most studied cognitive styles is Field Dependence-Independence (FDI) [23]. Depending on their degree of FDI, individuals process, encode, and recall information differently. Field Dependents (FDs) use external cues when interacting with information, whereas Field Independents (FIs) rely on internal cues [24]. When reading, for example, FDs are more likely to use the pre-existing structure of a text than FIs, who tend ignore external cues. Wolfe [25] states, "annotations provide a critical scaffolding that can support students' critical thinking and argumentation activities." We posit that FDI may play a role in shaping how individuals perceive and use highlights.

3 METHODS

We conducted a within-subjects study in which each of 15 participants, undergraduate students recruited using a listserv, read two articles with pre-existing highlights. The study employed eye-tracking, questionnaires, and interviews for data collection. Participants were asked to read two articles from *Scientific American* [15, 20] containing highlights created by the authors. Their instructions asked them to read the articles as if they were assigned for an upcoming class, and noted that the highlights were left by previous readers. Articles were selected so as to be interesting to undergraduate students across disciplines, and texts of approximately 3,000 words were used, longer in comparison to those used by [18]. Participants read the texts using a twenty-four inch liquid-crystal display on a desktop computer equipped with a Tobii Pro X2-60 eye-tracker.

Articles were presented in two conditions, which we termed appropriate (APP) and inappropriate (INAPP) highlighting. In keeping with Kintsch's CI model of comprehension [9], APP highlights marked key concepts and themes important to understanding the overall gist or message of the article, and INAPP highlights marked content that was secondary or peripheral. To create these conditions, the three authors read the texts independently, highlighting appropriate content first, and on a second pass, highlighting inappropriate content. The three sets of highlights were aggregated and spans of text that were highlighted by at least two of the authors were selected to represent each condition. In the final versions of the articles, highlighting emphasized no more than fifteen percent of the text, in accordance with guidelines based on previous findings [11]. The instruments and highlights were identical to those used in a previous experiment [3], however, we eliminated the control condition (no highlighting) as our purpose was to compare the more specific effects of APP and INAPP highlights on reading.

The paper version of the Group Embedded Figures Test (GEFT) was administered to participants at the beginning of the study to identify their cognitive style. Participants were classified as FD or FI using the median split used in [3]. The response variables were participants' comprehension scores and eye fixations while reading the articles. Comprehension scores were determined using Term–Definition Matching, where participants were asked to match a term with one of nine possible definitions, and a modified Cloze test, where participants were asked to fill-in the blanks of a paragraph summary of each article. The quiz was designed to measure both shallow (surface level recall) and deep (conceptual understanding and gist) levels of comprehension, in accordance with the CI model.

Participants were given five minutes to read each article and seven minutes to complete the quiz, and they were informed of these contstraints in the instructions. Through pilot testing, we found this was enough time for participants to skim the articles while also encouraging use of the highlights. At the end of each session we asked participants to rate their level of prior topical knowledge, topical interest, and perceptions of the highlights on a 5-point scale. After completing the reading tasks, a 10 minute semi-structured interview was carried out to learn more about participants' task-related experiences, and their reading and highlighting practices more generally. Participants received a $20 honorarium.

4 RESULTS

Quantitative results are summarized first in three sections, followed by findings from the interview data. The assumptions necessary to run parametric tests were met, and an alpha value of .05 was used.

4.1 Comprehension Outcomes

Across all participants, scores were significantly higher in the APP than the INAPP condition for the Term–Definition Matching questions (Table 1). While the mean comprehension was also higher in APP for the Cloze questions, the difference was not significant. Within FDI groups, there were no significant differences between APP and INAPP comprehension scores, perhaps due to the smaller group sizes. A t-test showed no difference between FD and FI participants (t=-0.620, df=9.873, p=.550), indicating that the impact of the APP and INAPP conditions was similar across these groups.

4.2 Use and Perceptions of Highlights

A summary of the eye-tracking fixation data (Table 2) shows a higher mean time spent looking at highlights in the APP condition compared to INAPP. This difference is significant for the FD participants ($t(5)$=3.921, p=.011), but not for FIs ($t(8)$=2.180, p=.061). While mean times spent looking at highlights are higher for FDs than FIs in both conditions, t-tests indicate that differences are not significant: APP (t(6.801)=1.665, p=.141); INAPP (t(12.861)=0.353,

Table 1: Term–Definition Matching and Cloze score by FDI and condition.

		Term–Definition Matching			Cloze		
FDI	n	APP M (SD)	INAPP M (SD)	APP–INAPP	APP M (SD)	INAPP M (SD)	APP–INAPP
FD	6	6.33 (2.42)	4.50 (2.07)	$t(5)$=1.611, p=.168	3.50 (2.17)	3.83 (2.79)	$t(5)$=-0.415, p=.695
FI	9	7.22 (1.48)	5.56 (2.65)	$t(8)$=1.826, p=.105	4.11 (2.93)	3.56 (3.17)	$t(8)$=0.342, p=.741
all	15	6.87 (1.88)	5.13 (2.42)	$t(14)$=2.525, p=.024	3.87 (2.59)	3.67 (2.92)	$t(14)$=0.199, p=.845

p=.730). So, while there is some suggestion that FDs relied more heavily on the highlights, the impact of the conditions on both groups was similar in terms of their fixation times.

Table 2: Mean fixation duration (seconds) on highlights by FDI and condition.

FDI	n	APP M (SD)	INAPP M (SD)	Both
FD	6	117.18 (23.50)	88.00 (11.71)	102.59 (23.36)
FI	9	99.84 (12.13)	85.44 (16.34)	92.64 (15.81)
all	15	106.78 (18.94)	86.46 (14.25)	96.62 (19.44)

Results indicate that, overall, highlights did not attract a disproportionate amount of attention in comparison to non-highlighted text. Given that the Areas of Interest marking highlighted texts for the eye-tracking analysis constituted about a third of the content for each condition, the baseline fixation time would be 100 seconds of the total reading time of 300 seconds (5 minutes). Only the FDs in the APP condition exceeded this baseline (Table 2).

Participants' perceptions of the usefulness of highlights are summarized in Table 3. Overall, participants rated the usefulness of highlights significantly higher in the APP condition than the INAPP. These differences are not significant within the FDI groups.

Table 3: Mean usefulness scores of highlights by FDI and condition (5-point scale).

FDI	n	APP M (SD)	INAPP M (SD)	APP–INAPP
FD	5*	3.60 (0.89)	3.20 (0.84)	$t(4)$=1.000, p=.374
FI	9	3.89 (0.60)	3.22 (0.97)	$t(8)$=2.000, p=.081
all	14	3.79 (0.70)	3.21 (0.89)	$t(13)$=2.280, p=.040

*Data missing from one participant.

4.3 Role of Prior Knowledge and Interest

To investigate the association between comprehension and self-report measures we calculated nonparametric correlations. Results show significant positive correlations between interest and Cloze test scores in both the APP $r_s(12) = .564$, p=.036 and INAPP $r_s(12)$=.713, p=.004 conditions, with the strongest correlation observed in the latter. Prior knowledge and comprehension scores were not significantly correlated. This suggests that participants' level of interest in the content of the articles is a factor in their ability to grasp their overall meaning, or gist, as assessed through the Cloze test. This was particularly true in the INAPP condition.

4.4 Findings From Interviews

The interview data was coded inductively using QDA Miner. Responses provide further insights on uses and perceptions of highlights and factors that affect use. Two different approaches to highlighting emerged. One group, including many FIs, viewed highlights as a means to gain overall understanding: "the passages were too long, so what I did was to only read the highlights because they helped me get the main idea of the articles" [P12]. This was based on the idea that highlights convey "the gist of the paragraph" [P4].

Another group, primarily FDs, expected highlights to signal information or facts of significance. P11 noted, "I found the ones that were highlighting a certain word or something... like definitions, I found those really helpful." P5 clearly preferred such highlights: "in the first article... the highlights... skipped over the useful details that I would have personally highlighted and they went over the main statement of the topic being discussed." This preference may have been driven by the task (i.e. reading to prepare for a test), as P15 noted, "the more that [highlights] pertained to technical terminology as opposed to whatever the overall theme... the more I found it useful to answer the questions."

A theme that arose in the interviews is the tension between the value of highlights for focusing attention and the negative potential for distraction. P15 expressed this well: "[I] found it problematic because it would try and grab your attention to something that I would try and think, 'oh, that should be relevant. I should pay attention to this,' but it's in the middle of something that A) has no context — you don't have any frame of reference to try and understand that and B) it kind of disorients the natural flow of your reading, because you get drawn to this."

Participants identified intrinsic and extrinsic factors that affected highlight use. Chief among the former is the type of content highlighted, notably the distinction between thematic and fact-based highlighting. Other factors included location and coverage. Issues arose with highlights of partial sentences or those situated mid paragraph, due to a lack of context. Two extrinsic factors were noted: time, and prior knowledge. Many participants expressed that the usefulness of highlights increased under time pressure, when they "wouldn't have enough time to read the entire thing word for word" [P4]. P3 noted that highlights "really helped guide my attention to where, probably, the bulk of the information for the quiz was going to be." However, some were disappointed when they used this technique and the answers were not among the highlighted text. A small number of participants indicated that when they are more familiar with the content and vocabulary of a text, they would have less use for highlights as a guiding or structuring feature.

5 DISCUSSION & CONCLUSION

Results clearly indicate that there are negative effects of exposing readers to poor quality highlights in this type of time limited reading task. This adds evidence to earlier findings [18]. Comprehension scores were lower in the INAPP condition, although only the surface level test was affected. Given that the APP highlights were designed to focus attention on the main themes and concepts, we expected to see an effect on conceptual understanding as well, but this was not the case. Readers with higher levels of interest were better able to reach a deeper conceptual understanding, perhaps because the interest enabled them to focus their attention even in the face of inappropriate highlights. These results provide support for the conclusion in [4], that highlights serve better as signaling devices than as scaffolding for text comprehension.

We found that most participants were aware of the quality variation, and some clearly attended less to the INAPP highlights. This suggests that post-secondary readers have the capacity to recognize and ignore less useful highlights that they may encounter in social reading systems. The interview data suggests that ignoring such highlights was not always easy, and that the effort needed to assess and ignore distracting highlights might subtract from the effort available to engage in deep reading of challenging texts.

We expected highlights would have more value for FDs, who typically benefit from external structure. However, results show no clear differences between FD and FI readers. FDs did spend more time viewing highlights in the APP conditions than in the INAPP condition, while FIs did not spend any more time in the highlights than the rest of the text, perhaps because they had little need of them. This brings into question the hypothesis posed in [3] that FIs perform badly when faced with inappropriate highlights, because they spend valuable time trying to make sense of them. Interestingly, our initial analysis of the interview data suggests that FDs and FIs may have used highlights differently, with FDs using them predominantly to focus on factual information and FIs to gain a general conceptual understanding.

Clearly time is a key factor in the use of highlights, but more research needs to be done to determine the extent to which highlights can serve to increase reading efficiency, as suggested in [6]. A central finding of this work, is that for social highlighting to be effective, systems should support diverse approaches to highlighting. While the thematic and factual approached identified here are not new [e.g., 12], results suggest that there may be both personal and task-based reasons to adopt one or the other. We can conclude that in social reading systems, including digital libraries, there can be benefit in creating guidelines for shared highlighting, to maximize potential benefits.

Highlight quality was shown to affect surface level text comprehension, although readers were able to assess the quality of highlights and to adjust their reliance upon them accordingly. Results indicate that readers approach highlighting differently. As such, there is danger in adopting a one size fits all approach in which shared highlights are aggregated and displayed to readers. A task-based approach that adds information to highlights and allows readers to know why a highlight was created, by whom, or for what task, may be valuable, but the negative potential of distraction needs to be addressed. We fully acknowledge the limitations of this work, which is small-scale, lab-based and therefore non-naturalistic. The time constraint on readers was also quite severe and results may not generalize to more relaxed or lengthy reading tasks. Future work will move towards organic studies of social reading and learning systems in use in university courses to validate and extend these findings.

REFERENCES

[1] Maristella Agosti and Nicola Ferro. 2007. A formal model of annotations of digital content. *ACM Transactions on Information Systems* 26, 1 (2007), 244–255.

[2] Ed H Chi, Michelle Gumbrecht, and Lichan Hong. 2007. Visual foraging of highlighted text: an eye-tracking study. In *Human-Computer Interaction: HCI Intelligent Multimodal Interaction Environments.* Springer, Berlin, Germany, 589–598.

[3] Samuel Dodson, Luanne Freund, and Rick Kopak. 2017. Do highlights affect comprehension? Lessons from a user study. In *Proceedings of the 2017 Conference on Human Information Interaction and Retrieval.* ACM, New York, NY, 381–384.

[4] John Dunlosky, Katherine A Rawson, Elizabeth J Marsh, Mitchell J Nathan, and Daniel T Willingham. 2013. Improving students' learning with effective learning techniques: promising directions from cognitive and educational psychology. *Psychological Science in the Public Interest* 14, 1 (2013), 4–58.

[5] Robert L Fowler and Anne S Barker. 1974. Effectiveness of highlighting for retention of text material. *Journal of Applied Psychology* 59, 3 (1974), 358–364.

[6] Luanne Freund, Rick Kopak, and Heather O'Brien. 2016. The effects of textual environment on reading comprehension: implications for searching as learning. *Journal of Information Science* 42, 1 (2016), 79–93.

[7] Anis Kalboussi, Omar Mazhoud, and Ahmed Hadj Kacem. 2016. Functionalities provided by annotation systems for learners in educational context: an overview. *International Journal of Emerging Technologies in Learning* 11, 2 (2016).

[8] Nancy Kaplan and Yoram Chisik. 2005. In the company of readers: the digital library book as "practiced place". In *Proceedings of the 5th ACM/IEEE-CS Joint Conference on Digital Libraries.* ACM, New York, NY, 235–243.

[9] Walter Kintsch. 1998. *Comprehension: a paradigm for cognition.* Cambridge University Press, Cambridge, United Kingdom.

[10] Jacqueline Leighton and Mark Gierl. 2011. *The learning sciences in educational assessment: the role of cognitive models.* Cambridge University Press, Cambridge, United Kingdom.

[11] Robert F Lorch, Jr. 1989. Text-signaling devices and their effects on reading and memory processes. *Educational Psychology Review* 1, 3 (1989), 209–234.

[12] Catherine C Marshall. 2009. *Reading and writing the electronic book.* Morgan & Claypool Publishers, San Rafael, CA.

[13] Samuel Messick. 1976. *Individuality in learning.* Jossey-Bass Publishers, San Francisco, CA.

[14] Ilia A Ovsiannikov, Michael A Arbib, and Thomas H McNeill. 1999. Annotation technology. *International Journal of Human-Computer Studies* 50, 4 (1999), 329–362.

[15] Matthieu Ricard, Antoine Lutz, and Richard J Davidson. 2014. Mind of the meditator. *Scientific American* 311, 5 (2014), 38–45.

[16] Judith C Roberts and Keith A Roberts. 2008. Deep reading, cost/benefit, and the construction of meaning: Enhancing reading comprehension and deep learning in sociology courses. *Teaching Sociology* 36, 2 (2008), 125–140.

[17] Jean-Francois Rouet. 2006. *The skills of document use: from text comprehension to web-based learning.* Psychology Press, Hove, United Kingdom.

[18] Vicki L Silvers and David S Kreiner. 1997. The effects of pre-existing inappropriate highlighting on reading comprehension. *Literacy Research and Instruction* 36, 3 (1997), 217–223.

[19] Michele L Simpson and Sherrie L Nist. 1990. Textbook annotation: an effective and efficient study strategy for college students. *Journal of Reading* 34, 2 (1990), 122–129.

[20] Keith C Summa and Fred W Turek. 2015. The clocks within us. *Scientific American* 312, 2 (2015), 50–55.

[21] Craig Tashman and W Keith Edwards. 2011. Active reading and its discontents: the situations, problems and ideas of readers. In *Proceedings of the SIGCHI Conference on Human Factors in Computing Systems.* ACM, New York, NY, 2927–2936.

[22] Ludo Verhoeven and Charles Perfetti. 2008. Advances in text comprehension: model, process and development. *Applied Cognitive Psychology* 22, 3 (2008), 293–301.

[23] Herman A Witkin, R B Dyk, H F Fattuson, Donald R Goodenough, and S A Karp. 1962. *Psychological differentiation: studies of development.* Wiley, New York, NY.

[24] Herman A Witkin and Donald R Goodenough. 1977. Field dependence revisited. *ETS Research Bulletin Series* 1977, 2 (1977), i–53.

[25] Joanna Wolfe. 2008. Annotations and the collaborative digital library: Effects of an aligned annotation interface on student argumentation and reading strategies. *International Journal of Computer-Supported Collaborative Learning* 3 (2008), 141–164.

Evaluating Saccade-Bounded Eye Movement Features for the User Modeling

Sampath Jayarathna, and Sobiga Shanmugathasan
Computer Science, California State Polytechnic University
Pomona, CA 91768
(ukjayarathna,sobigas)@cpp.edu

ABSTRACT

This paper presents a foundation for an extensive framework expanding the use of eye movements as a source for user modeling. This work constructs a model of human oculomotor plant features during user's interactions with the goal of better interpreting user gaze data related to resource content. This work also explores the anatomical reasoning behind incorporating additional gaze features, the integration of the additional features into an existing interest modeling architecture, and a plan for assessing the impact of the addition of the features. The paper concludes with few observations regarding the promises of using OPF in a user modeling framework in studying search behavior.

CCS CONCEPTS

• **Information Systems → Novelty in Information Retrieval**

Keywords

User interest modeling; eye movements; oculomotor plant

ACM Reference format:

S. Jayarathna, and S. Shanmugathasan. 2018. SIG Proceedings Paper in word Format. In *Proceedings of Joint Conference on Digital Libraries, Fort Worth, Texas USA, June 2018 (JCDL'18)*, 4 pages. https://doi.org/10.1145/3197026.3197072

1. INTRODUCTION

Accurate models of user interest are valuable in personalizing the presentation of the often large quantity of information relevant to a query or other form of information request. We have previously developed and evaluated a software framework [14-16] for capturing user activity across multiple applications and combining this activity data in user interest models to aid personalized information delivery. Personalization in these models uses the information about a user or their task to adapt the presentation of resources. A user model is often the basis for such adaptation. A user model can be as simple as person's explicitly provided preferences or as complicated as a representations of the user's knowledge in different areas. In the context of a classroom setting, information in such user models could include the user's roles (teacher or student), their classes and grade levels, their preferences for how to view resources, and explicit ratings of or comments (semi-explicit) on resources they have provided, their past queries, and past resource access. The more information available about the user, the greater the potential for personalization.

ACM ISBN 978-1-4503-5178-2/18/06...$15.00
https://doi.org/10.1145/3197026.3197072

1.1 Motivation and Problem Statement

The motivation behind our work is that not all gazes are created equal. Thus, systems should not treat focus activity equally when using gaze information for user interest modeling. We hypothesize that the anatomical characteristics of the human eye may be utilized to estimate set of non-visible anatomical features called "*oculomotor plant features (OPF)*" that can then be used to aid personalization in user interest modeling techniques. This paper entails a comprehensive description of the OPF capturing process and an initial hypothesis to study what features will be of most use in conjunction with traditional implicit relevance feedback indicators. This study attempts to use eye movements and these OPF values to identify the relevance of resource content.

Our objective is to develop a user modeling framework for the personalization based on the non-visible anatomical structure and its characteristics of the human eye via OPF.

2. BACKGROUND

The human eye already provides a plethora of information useful for user modeling. Eye tracking has been employed in studying user attention on the web. Yarbus et al. show that visual behavior is closely correlated to the user task when looking at a visual scene [29]. A variety of uses of gaze data have been explored as a source of implicit relevance feedback for IR. Previous work has primarily focused on identifying visual attention to make user interest predictions [2, 4] and more recently to predict a target in search results [3, 11, 27, 30]. The

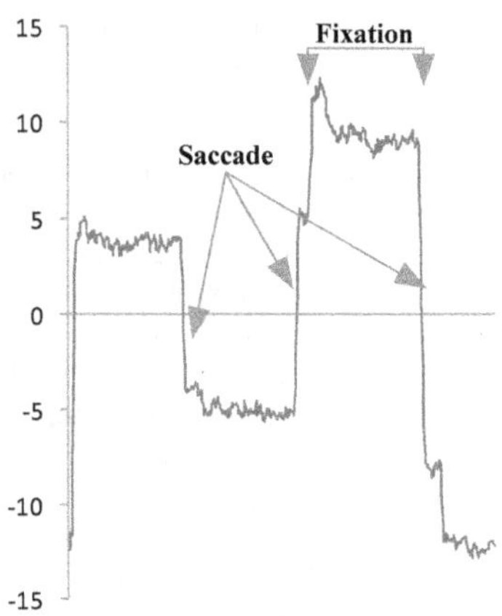

Figure 1: Sample raw eye movement signal before classification.

human-computer interaction and information retrieval communities have investigated trends and differences in user attention patterns and cognitive processing including correlations to the relevance of reading text [6], identifying pattern differences [9], tasks types [12], and user accuracy in alternative interfaces [25].

The human oculomotor plant (OP) consists of the eye globe and six extraocular muscles and its surrounding tissues, ligaments each containing thick and thin filaments, tendon-like components and liquids. In general there are six major eye movement types: fixations, saccades, smooth pursuits, optokinetic reflex, vestibule-ocular reflex and vergence [22]. An eye-tracker provides eye gaze position information as well as other gaze related parameters (pupil dilation etc.) so that algorithmic derivation in terms of two primary eye movements, *fixations* (relative gaze position at one point on the screen), and *saccades* (rapid eye movements of gaze from one fixation point to another) can be analyzed to derive the users attention patterns (see Figure 1). The retinal image is transmitted to the brain during fixations but not during saccades. The static and dynamic characteristics of the human OP are represented by the series elasticity, viscosity, active-state tension, length-tension and force-velocity relationships and the frequency characteristics of the neuronal control signal sent by the brain to the extraocular muscles and the speed of propagation of this signal.

We next present details of the underlying OPF, an existing interest modeling architectures and then how the features are expected to provide value during user modeling.

2.1 Oculomotor Plant Features (OPF)

The goal of the oculomotor plant model is to describe a system of equations capable of accurately reproducing the features of normal human eye movements in real-time, based on the set of properties of the extraocular muscles responsible for rotation of the eye globe. A number of previous models have been proposed generally representing the oculomotor plant linearly in one-dimension (horizontal) or non-linearly [26] in three dimension (horizontal, vertical, torsional). Linear one-dimensional models have thus far failed to reproduced the saccadic amplitude-peak velocity relationships present in normal human saccades, while non-linear three-dimensional models have received limited testing and are computationally complex, making them less suitable for real-time applications. More recently, our contributions [13, 19, 20] focused on the two-dimensional linear homeomorphic model of the oculomotor plant driven by twelve differential equations, and is capable of simulating saccades with properties resembling normal humans on a two-dimensional plane (horizontal and vertical).

Oculomotor plant features: We refer to the parameters of our oculomotor plant model as oculomotor plant features[17]. These parameters describe an important anatomical and neurological properties exhibited by the oculomotor plant system. In our model, each muscle is represented by a complex anatomical structure, the properties of which can be effectively described by: *series elasticity* – the elastic resistance to rapid changes in muscle length produced by active muscles; *passive elasticity* – the elastic resistance to rapid changes in muscle length produced by inactive muscles; *length-tension relationship* – the relationship between length of a muscle and the force it is capable of exerting during activation; *force-velocity relationship* – the relationship between velocity of muscle contraction/relaxation and the force it is capable of exerting;

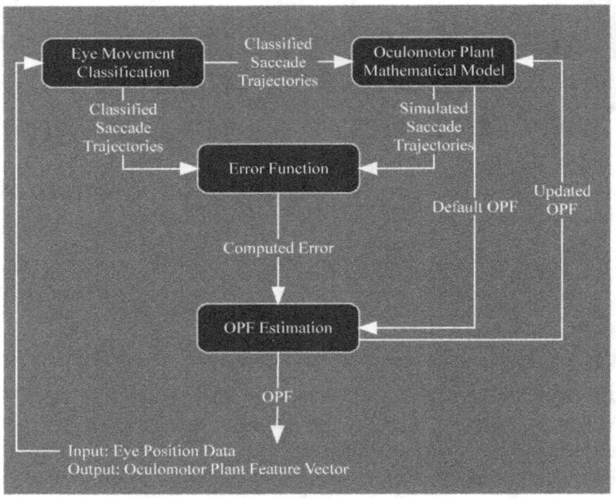

Figure 2: OPF optimization algorithm.

active-state tension – the tension developed as a result of muscle activation by the neuronal control signal. There is also the eye globe and the surrounding tissue which also produces passive elastic and viscous properties.

Saccade-Bounded OPF: In order to estimate OPF for a given saccade, the model is initiated with default parameters based on the relevant literature [1, 20] and then Nelder-Mead simplex algorithm [21] is employed as the absolute difference between the measured and simulated saccadic eye movement trajectory (see Figure 2). By estimating OPF via the recorded eye position signal and the simulated saccade trajectory, these saccade-bounded OPF values can help deduce how gaze data is incorporated into the evolving user interest model.

3. USER MODELING

User models can be developed by adapting the content consumed or produced by the user, and their specific task, background, history and information needs [28]. These models can be used to identify resources (documents) or to bring a user's attention to the more valuable content of a resource (document segments). User interest models can be developed based on explicit or implicit feedback. Explicit feedback is the most accurate indicator of user interest but rather difficult to obtain as users often cannot (or will not) express their interests. Implicit interest indicators, such as records of user activity, are easy to obtain but require more interpretation to infer user interests. Past research studies [8, 18] have shown that implicit feedback can be used to develop valuable user models.

Recognizing user interest based on observed user activity is confounded by idiosyncratic work practices. As a result, systems that aggregate evidence of user interest from a wide variety of sources are more likely to build a robust user interest model. A majority of past studies [7, 18, 24] have focused on monitoring implicit and explicit interest indicators present in a single application sources, e.g., implicit and explicit interactions with the user's web browser. Though relatively new, the idea to use eye movement data for estimating relevance has been approached [5, 10, 23]. However, these studies are operated on the raw gaze data to detect fixations, saccades and derived features from these eye movements. The proposed work differs in the use of complex anatomical structures of the human oculomotor system and dual aspect of physical and neurological components to identify relevance.

3.1 OPF-Aware User Modeling

Our interest modeling system [15, 16] incorporates user activity data from multiple applications within a personal profile server to support personalized information presentations. The user activity data collected includes a combination of implicit and semi-explicit interest information. It also shares the inferred user interests with registered applications that ask for it.

The profile server currently communicates with a web browser (Mozilla-Firefox) to present search results and also to visualize recommendations, and three other content reading and authoring applications: a PDF reader, Microsoft Word, and Microsoft PowerPoint. Records of user activity in PDF documents, Mozilla Firefox, MS Word and MS PowerPoint are stored in the server and drive the visualizations that the server generates for each of the applications registered for relevant notification request.

The design of oculomotor plant module is expected to provide insight into the user's assessment of content to the modeling system via the OPF values. The eye tracker provides a continuous eye movement signal during the user activity. An interest profile is then made up of the aggregated heterogeneous interest evidence collected from these different clients that is generated based on all the features, including the OPF values. By characterizing elements of the previously outlined OPF values, we will be able to assess how well the different designs could be used to create user interest models similar to the unification process introduced in our previous work [15, 16].

4. DATASET AND RESULTS

4.1 Apparatus, Participants and Eye Movement Invocation Task.

The eye tracking dataset used in the paper is compiled from our previous work [13, 19, 20], and is publicly available. Oculomotor behavior is recorded using the Tobii x120 eye tracker with accuracy 0.5^0, spatial resolution 0.2^0 and sampling frequency 120 Hz. 12 subjects' records were selected for the current study from the original dataset. The original data collection procedure is based on a stimulus presented as a white single "jumping point" on a black background with vertical coordinates fixed to the middle region of the screen. The sequence consists of 15 fixation points.

Next, the recorded eye movement signal from the 12 participant dataset is supplied to the *eye movement classification module* that classified these position signals into fixations and saccades. In our previous work [19], we found evidence that Velocity Threshold algorithm proves to be the better choice for systems measuring saccadic performance and utilized velocity-based model for eye movement classification with thresholds 70^0/s. The classified saccades trajectories represented by the onset and offset coordinates of the eye position and amplitude (length) of the saccade are used to generate simulated saccade trajectories based on the default OPF values. Each individual classified saccade is then compared with the simulated saccade and the corresponding saccade-bounded OPF values are extracted by minimizing the error in each pair.

Figure 3 presents six OPF values collected from the user study and the boxplot of the data including the default values (red dash-line). We acknowledge that the dataset is not necessarily based on an information task where the user engagement with information resources and "ground-truth" of user interest is not available due to the nature of stimulus invocation task. In this work, our main focus is to explore the OPF data and improve optimization methods used in the methodology to conduct further studies to collect "ground-truth" for evaluating the interest models. Results suggest that the few of default OPF values (series elasticity and passive viscosity) require further refinements due to the first quartile, median and third quartile data which deviate from the empirical default values.

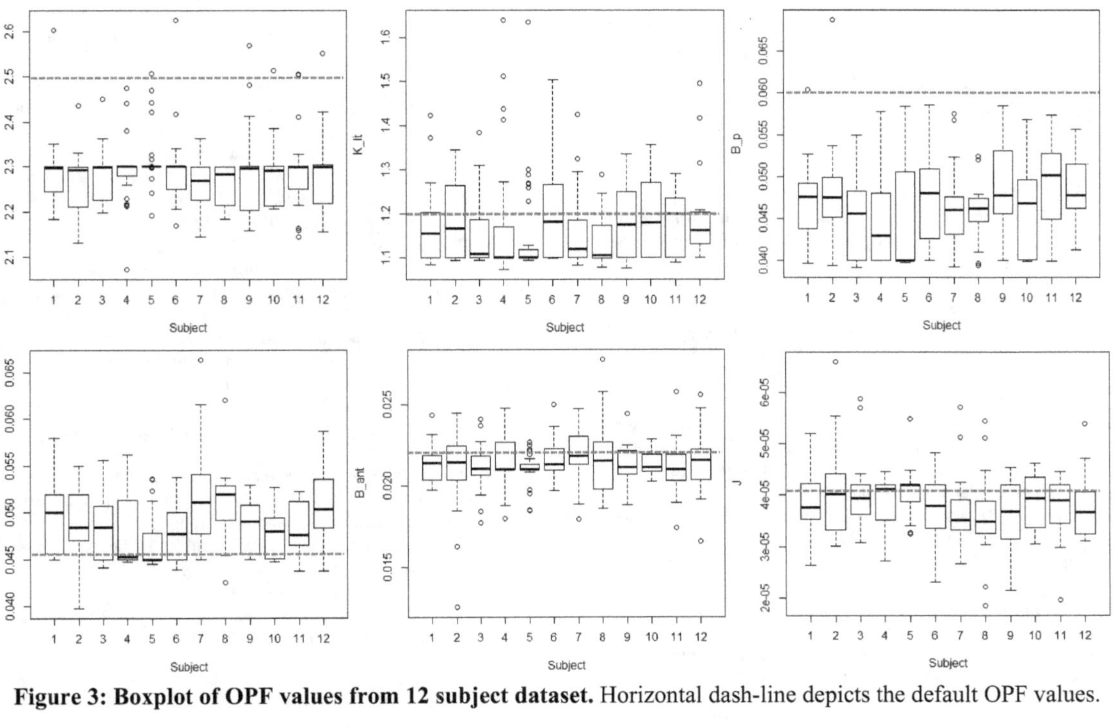

Figure 3: Boxplot of OPF values from 12 subject dataset. Horizontal dash-line depicts the default OPF values.

4.2 Future Work: Gathering OPF-Aware Data from Information Tasks

Saccades, fixations and OPF are integral parts of visual attention. Our framework and architecture incorporates saccade-bounded OPF data capture, storage and feature analysis techniques to explore the value of saccades, fixations and OPF in determining the relevance of encountered content.

The design and development of user interest models require variety of formative and summative evaluations. Results of this work will include algorithms for eye movement classification, aggregating saccade-bounded OPF and other relevant feature values and inferred user interest and development of visualization and interfaces for presenting interest-resource relationships. By giving the user a specific task and a set of resources of known relevance, we can explore the hypothesis that OPF data will be distinguishable between the relevant and non-relevant resources. The subjects' task will be to (1) read the task assigned and decide whether each resource associated with the task contains the content relevant to the task assignment, (2) Select the relevance score for each resource on a 5-point Likert-scale (1-non-relevent, 5-higly relevant) for content relevance assessment.

5. DISCUSSION AND CONCLUSION

The research outcomes are expected to provide an intuitive framework for user modeling by including oculomotor plant features during the use of eye tracking data. This will allow us to assess user behavior in relation to the relevance of resources in order to build and evaluate the possibility of using oculomotor plant features in various applications including *student learning difficulties*. We believe that understanding how the OPF values change over the course of user engagement with information resources will be valuable in the pursuit of developing more accurate interest models.

There are wide range of follow-on work related to the user modeling approach explored here. We limited our approach to features that could be computed from oculomotor plant data. Understanding how saccades relate to the fixations they precede is also an important part of moving towards a richer account of relevance learning in the context of user modeling. Most theories and models are based on fixation patterns that lack an understanding of how saccadic eye movements preceding these fixations are affected by the task environment.

6. REFERENCES

[1] Bahill, A Terry, "Development, validation and sensitivity analyses of human eye movement models," *CRC Critical Reviews in Bioengineering*, vol. 4, pp. 311-355, 1980.

[2] Borji, Ali and Itti, Laurent, "Defending Yarbus: Eye movements reveal observers' task," *Journal of vision*, vol. 14, p. 29, 2014.

[3] Borji, Ali, Lennartz, Andreas, and Pomplun, Marc, "What do eyes reveal about the mind?: Algorithmic inference of search targets from fixations," *Neurocomputing*, vol. 149, pp. 788-799, 2015.

[4] Borji, Ali, Sihite, Dicky N, and Itti, Laurent, "Probabilistic learning of task-specific visual attention," in *Computer Vision and Pattern Recognition (CVPR), 2012 IEEE Conference on*, 2012, pp. 470-477.

[5] Buscher, Georg, Dengel, Andreas, and Elst, Ludger van, "Eye movements as implicit relevance feedback," presented at the CHI '08 Extended Abstracts on Human Factors in Computing Systems, Florence, Italy, 2008.

[6] Buscher, Georg, Dengel, Andreas, and van Elst, Ludger, "Eye movements as implicit relevance feedback," in *CHI'08 extended abstracts on Human factors in computing systems*, 2008, pp. 2991-2996.

[7] Claypool, Mark, Le, Phong, Wased, Makoto, and Brown, David, "Implicit interest indicators," in *Proceedings of the 6th international conference on Intelligent user interfaces*, Santa Fe, USA, 2001, pp. 33-40.

[8] Goecks, Jeremy and Shavlik, Jude, "Learning users' interests by unobtrusively observing their normal behavior," in *Proceedings of the 5th international conference on Intelligent user interfaces*, 2000, pp. 129-132.

[9] Goldberg, Joseph and Helfman, Jonathan, "Eye tracking for visualization evaluation: Reading values on linear versus radial graphs," *Information visualization*, 2011.

[10] Gwizdka, Jacek, "News stories relevance effects on eye-movements," presented at the Proceedings of the Symposium on Eye Tracking Research and Applications, Safety Harbor, Florida, 2014.

[11] Haji-Abolhassani, Amin and Clark, James J, "A computational model for task inference in visual search," *Journal of vision*, vol. 13, p. 29, 2013.

[12] Iqbal, Shamsi T and Bailey, Brian P, "Using eye gaze patterns to identify user tasks," in *The Grace Hopper Celebration of Women in Computing*, 2004, pp. 5-10.

[13] Jayarathna, Sampath, "Two Dimentional Oculomotor Plant Mechanical Model (2DOPMM)," MS Thesis, Computer Science, Texas State University San Marcos, 2010.

[14] Jayarathna, Sampath, Patra, Atish, and Shipman, Frank, "Mining user interest from search tasks and annotations," in *Proceedings of the 22nd ACM international conference on Conference on information & knowledge management*, 2013, pp. 1849-1852.

[15] Jayarathna, Sampath, Patra, Atish, and Shipman, Frank, "Unified Relevance Feedback for Multi-Application User Interest Modeling," presented at the Proceedings of the 15th ACM/IEEE-CS Joint Conference on Digital Libraries, Knoxville, Tennessee, USA, 2015.

[16] Jayarathna, Sampath and Shipman, Frank, "Analysis and Modeling of Unified User Interests," in *IEEE 18th International Conference on Information Reuse and Integration*, San Diego, CA, 2017, pp. 298-307.

[17] Jayarathna, Sampath and Shipman, Frank, "Rationale and Architecture for Incorporating Human Oculomotor Plant Features in User Interest Modeling," in *Proceedings of the 2016 ACM on Conference on Human Information Interaction and Retrieval*, 2016, pp. 281-284.

[18] Kelly, Diane and Belkin, Nicholas J, "Reading time, scrolling and interaction: exploring implicit sources of user preferences for relevance feedback," in *Proceedings of the 24th annual international ACM SIGIR conference on Research and development in information retrieval*, New Orleans, USA, 2001, pp. 408-409.

[19] Komogortsev, Oleg V, Holland, Corey, and Jayarathna, Sampath, "Two-Dimensional Linear Homeomorphic Oculomotor Plant Mathematical Model," 2012.

[20] Komogortsev, Oleg V and Jayarathna, Ukwatta KS, "2D Oculomotor Plant Mathematical Model for eye movement simulation," in *BioInformatics and BioEngineering, 2008. BIBE 2008. 8th IEEE International Conference on*, 2008, pp. 1-8.

[21] Lagarias, Jeffrey C, Reeds, James A, Wright, Margaret H, and Wright, Paul E, "Convergence properties of the Nelder--Mead simplex method in low dimensions," *SIAM Journal on optimization*, vol. 9, pp. 112-147, 1998.

[22] Leigh, R John and Zee, David S, *The neurology of eye movements*: Oxford University Press, 2015.

[23] Loboda, Tomasz D., Brusilovsky, Peter, #246, and Brunstein, erg, "Inferring word relevance from eye-movements of readers," presented at the Proceedings of the 16th international conference on Intelligent user interfaces, Palo Alto, CA, USA, 2011.

[24] Oard, Douglas W and Kim, Jinmook, "Implicit feedback for recommender systems," in *Proceedings of the AAAI workshop on recommender systems*, 1998, pp. 81-83.

[25] Plumlee, Matthew D and Ware, Colin, "Zooming versus multiple window interfaces: Cognitive costs of visual comparisons," *ACM Transactions on Computer-Human Interaction (TOCHI)*, vol. 13, pp. 179-209, 2006.

[26] Quaia, Christian and Optican, Lance M, "Dynamic eye plant models and the control of eye movements," *Strabismus*, vol. 11, pp. 17-31, 2003.

[27] Rajashekar, Umesh, Bovik, Alan C, and Cormack, Lawrence K, "Visual search in noise: Revealing the influence of structural cues by gaze-contingent classification image analysis," *Journal of Vision*, vol. 6, p. 7, 2006.

[28] Renda, M Elena and Straccia, Umberto, "A personalized collaborative digital library environment: a model and an application," *Information processing & management*, vol. 41, pp. 5-21, 2005.

[29] Yarbus, Alfred L, Haigh, Basil, and Rigss, Lorrin A, *Eye movements and vision* vol. 2: Plenum press New York, 1967.

[30] Zelinsky, Gregory J, Peng, Yifan, and Samaras, Dimitris, "Eye can read your mind: Decoding gaze fixations to reveal categorical search targets," *Journal of vision*, vol. 13, p. 10, 2013.

Interaction on An Academic Social Networking Sites: A Study of ResearchGate Q&A on Library and Information Science

Shengli Deng
School of Information Management
Wuhan University
China
victorydc@sina.com

Jingjing Tong
School of Information Management
Wuhan University
China
JingjingTong@whu.edu.cn

Shaoxiong Fu
School of Information Management
Wuhan University
China
fu_shaoxiong@163.com

ABSTRACT

Online information interaction on academic social networking sites (ASNSs) has been increasingly popular in recent years. It is unclear whether these sites have satisfied scholars' needs for interaction. This study investigates what scholars ask about, what features the questions and answers convey, and what socio-emotional reactions during the interaction on ResearchGate Q&A. Bales' Interaction Process Analysis (IPA) was adopted to analyze 371 questions and 7530 answers on Library and Information Science from ResearchGate Q&A. Implications of results are discussed and suggestions for future study are made.

CCS CONCEPTS

• **Networks** → Network performance analysis; **Networks** → Social media networks

KEYWORDS

Academic social networks, interaction process analysis(IPA), ResearchGate, Library and Information Science(LIS)

ACM Reference format:

Shengli Deng, Jingjing Tong and Shaoxiong Fu. 2018. Interaction on An Academic Social Networking Sites: A Study of ResearchGate Q&A on Library and Information Science. In *Proceedings of JCDL '18 (JCDL '18)*. *ACM, New York, NY, USA, 4 pages.* https://doi.org/10.1145/3197026.3197062

1 INTRODUCTION

People are increasingly seeking information and advice in online communities [1]. With the widespread use of massive and instant tools, various academic activities can be fully launched online [2]. Along with the popular generic social network services, a variety of academic social networking sites (ASNSs) were established. The most popular academic social networking sites are ResearchGate (RG), Mendeley and Academia.edu. RG has almost doubled its population in a year [3], which has more than 13 million users by August 2017 (http://www.researchgate.net).

In recent years, ASNSs attract studies to investigate their user populations and functional characteristics [2]. Data from RG Q&A has been used to examine the interaction patterns between scholars [2] and evaluate academic answer quality [4]. For example, there is research that has identified the difference of information exchange across three distinct disciplines [2]. However, the study above was based on limited data and paid less attention to socio-emotions. In the current study, we investigate the interaction patterns based on a larger sample set with respect of questions, answers and socio-emotional reactions.

Bales' interaction process analysis (IPA) is an influential method for exploring the interaction between team members [5] and group moods during interaction [6]. It is the first and most frequently applied tool to investigate small group dynamics [7]. Therefore, in this study, we use IPA as the general framework to analyze and understand online interaction between scholars. In order to clarify whether these ASNSs have satisfied scholars' needs and provide suggestions for a better Q&A platform, this article explores the following three research questions:

Q1: What kinds of questions do scholars ask on RG Q&A on the topic of Library and Information Science?

Q2: What are the features of answers posted by different scholars in response to different question types?

Q3: What socio-emotional reactions do scholars express during the interaction?

2 LITERATURE REVIEW

2.1 Study on academic social networking sites

According to Elsayed [8], ASNSs are specialized platforms where researchers could take part in various activities. Previous research displays two differentiated trends. On one hand, many studies take a bibliometric approach [9] to demonstrate differences by discipline, country and various sites [10] and

JCDL '18, June 3–7 2018, Fort Worth, TX, USA
 978-1-4503-5178-2/18/06...$15.00
https://doi.org/10.1145/3197026.3197062

identified the conventional metrics and altmetrics of scientific impact [11].

On the other hand, ASNSs attract many scholars exploring user behavior on these platforms. The motivation that leads scholars to take part in these sites has been investigated due to the strong addition of researchers in a short time period. From a recent view, it could be noticed that there are a majority of scholars using ASNSs to share publications [8]. Also, the usage and utility of RG has been examined through an online survey and interviews [9].

2.2 Study on Interaction Online Between Scholars

There are three types interaction patterns including student and content, student and student, and student and teacher, which are often applied as a theoretical framework to explore online learning [12]. Fariza et al. [13] examined data collected from an online discussion boards to identify collaborative learning patterns including providing information, giving feedback, contributing and exploring, etc.

Interaction between students can be affected by many factors [2]. Castanomunoz et al. [14] found effectiveness of e-learning varies with degree of interaction intensity based on date from 17090 students. Also, to some degree, age and ethnicity statues play a role in interaction between online courses. It has been considered that online interaction is a key aspect of efficient e-learning and can enhance academic accomplishment [14].

3 Methods

In this study, we select RG as research site to explore the interaction among scholars due to the Q&A platform of RG for scholars to discuss.

3.1 Data Collection

A certain level of professional knowledge was needed to conduct content analysis. Therefore, this study chose "library and information science" as our object of study. The data for this study consists of 371 questions with 7530 answers. The time of data collection is between August 11, 2017 and August 14, 2017.

3.2 Data Analysis

The 4 functional areas of IPA incorporate questions, attempted answers, socio-emotional positive and socio-emotional negative. Table 1 addresses the functional areas with 8 specific categories adapted from the research of Nam et al. [5]. Some details of the description of questions were noticed, and we adopted coding scheme from Jeng et al. [2] to analysis the characteristics of descriptions. Table 2 provides justifications of each category.

Questions were classified by three steps. Firstly, the 371 questions and their descriptions were categorized by two coders working individually. Cohen' kappa values are 0.79 and 0.68 for the question-type and content feature respectively. Secondly, identification of socio-emotions was conducted based on the function of data exploration in NVivo 11. In this step, two coders examined all the answers with an overall agreement rate of 0.89 (Cohen' kappa). Finally, the difference was resolved with a discussion between a third researcher and coders.

Table 1: Interaction Categories

Functional Area	Category	Examples
Attempted answers	Giving suggestions	I suggest you read more books.
	Giving opinions	I think this movie is fun.
	Giving information	The movie starts at 9 pm.
Questions	Ask for information	When does the movie start?
	Ask for opinions	How do you think of the book?
	Ask for suggestions	How to learn English ?
Social emotions	Positive: shows solidarity, tension release, agreement	Thanks for your useful information.
	Negative: shows disagreement, tension, antagonism	I disagree with your opinions.

Table 2: Coding Category of Description

Content Feature	Justification
Providing resources	Sharing hyperlink, citations, files, research objects as sources
Providing contact information	Containing a responder's contact information such as an email address
Providing personal experience	Containing a user's self-disclosed information such as their work background, life experience
Providing factual information	Containing information based on facts

4 RESULTS

4.1 Asking Questions in RG Q&A

Questions raised for seeking information play a key role in RG Q&A, accounting for about 43.9% (n=163), followed by questions for opinions (n=137, 36.9%). We found that it was not often for scholars to look for suggestions directing task.

Table 3 shows the characteristics of questions' descriptive information. We found that 31 of 71 (43.7%) questions asking for suggestions were added with the information-seekers' personal experience, whereas we found only 26 of 137 (16%) questions asking for opinions with descriptions of personal experience. Only 4 users provided contact information, and all of them were seeking for information.

Table 3: Question Characteristics

Content Feature	Ask for information	Ask for opinions	Ask for suggestions
Providing resources	19 (11.7%)	14 (10.2%)	5 (7%)
Providing contact information	4 (2.5%)	0 (0.0%)	0 (0.0%)
Providing personal experience	55 (33.7%)	26 (16%)	31 (43.7%)
Providing factual information	17 (10.4%)	47 (28.8%)	15 (21.1%)

4.2 Providing Answers in RG Q&A

Table 4 summarizes the activities of answering. Response time of questions for opinions was significant longer. However, when it comes to the response time of first answer, questions for suggestions were answered in a timelier manner. Compared to questions for information, for each answer, the average length of answers for opinions and suggestions is much longer.

A one-way ANOVA test that compares the response time by types of questions indicated that there were significant differences in response time (F=277.2, P<0.001). However, no significant differences were observed, when it comes to the first response time among the three groups (F=0.44, P=0.645). There were also significant differences in the length of answers (F=7.33, P<0.001).

Table 4: Features of Answers

	Ask for information	Ask for opinions	Ask for suggestions
Average of response time (days)	115.8	314.9	195.6
Average of the first of response time (days)	40.2	33.7	17.4
Average of the length of answers (words)	58.0	67.5	67.0
Average of the No. of responses	7.8	36.5	17.9
Percentage of questions unanswered	14.1%	8.0%	8.5%

4.3 Socio-emotional Reactions in RG Q&A

Social reactions in questions and answers were displayed respectively in Table 5 and Table 6. Questions asking for opinions have received the most recommendations on average. We examined the descriptions of questions, only 55 of 371 (14.8%) questions containing expressions for appreciation. Additionally, the average of followers of questions asking for suggestions was more than twice as much as questions for information.

Table 5: Social Reactions in Questions

	Ask for information	Ask for opinion s	Ask for suggestions
Average followers of questions	11.1	19.0	23.3
Average recommendations of questions	1.1	2.7	2.2
The number of questions expressing appreciations	33 (2.0%)	11 (0.8%)	11 (1.5%)

The types of answers were identified by the kinds of questions. Among the 7530 responses, more than half the answers (4995, 66.33%) were classified to giving opinions. When examining recommendations in answers, it was found that responses for opinion questions were recommended more often. We also found that when exchanging opinions, scholar tend to express opinions directly with much more sentences of consensus building. However, when it comes to expressing appreciation, only 9.4% answers to opinion questions were included. In contrast, 20.3% responses for information questions contained expressions of appreciation.

A one-way ANOVA suggested there were significant differences in followers (F=3.61, P=0.028) and recommendations (F=3.04, P=0.049) among the three group of questions. Additionally, the result based on one-way ANOVA indicated that there were significant differences in recommendations of answers to different types of questions (F = 659.003, P<0.001).

Table 6: Social Reactions in Answers

	Answers to information questions	Answers to opinion questions	Answers to suggestion questions
Average of recommendations	0.25	3.31	0.35
Agreement with others	38(3.0%)	222(4.4%)	49(3.9%)
Disagreement with others	2(0.2%)	16(0.4%)	3(0.2%)
Expressing appreciation	257(20.3%)	472(9.4%)	176(13.9%)

5 DISSCUSSION

The findings of this study are discussed in this section by the three research questions.

Research Questions 1: What kinds of questions do scholars ask on RG Q&A on the topic of Library and Information Science?

In RG Q&A, there is an unbalance in the distribution of questions classified by intention of information-seekers. A large proportion of questions were raised for information, which is corroborated by Jeng et al. [2].

In regard to the characteristics of questions, it is found that scholars prefer adding a great deal of factual information to descriptions of opinion questions. The findings also suggest that scholars tend to describe their own experiences when asking for information and suggestions. It should be noted that when asking for information, scholars tend to provide their emails for further contact, which may increase their informational benefits [9].

Following the findings in questions, we propose several suggestions for improvement of Q&A platform. In order to reduce the number of questions unanswered, it may be useful to classify questions according to information-seekers' intention. Moreover, it seems effective that Q&A platforms provide questioners with a service of inviting other scholars to give response.

Research Questions 2: What are the features of answers posted by different scholars in response to different question types?

The analysis of responses to different questions revealed that scholars in RG prefer providing answers to opinion questions. Each question for opinions receives 36.5 responses on average, which is the potential reason for the longest time of average response. Additionally, advice questions on RG receive first response with a quickest speed for 17.42 days on average. However, this is surprising given that Jeng et al. [2] found means of the first of response time was no more than 137.21 hours. This could be possibly because Jeng et al. [2] collected only 33 questions about Library and Information Science in December 2013. In this study, many questions were answered more than two years after the question were raised.

Some actions should be taken to promote user participation according to the findings of answers. It is necessary to add a function of marking whether a question is answered satisfactorily and improve the recommendation mechanism. On the one hand, information questions should be recommended positively because one answer may solve these questions perfectly. On the other hand, it is useful to recommend questions to new users because these users have a strong intention to providing answers.

Research Questions 3: What socio-emotional reactions do scholars express between the interactions?

Based on the results of our study, some complex patterns about socio-emotional reactions were identified. Scholars prefer giving recommendations to expressions of users' view. Especially in answers, opinion answers receive recommendations on average is more than 9 times of the other two types of answers. Additionally, more expressions of appreciation can be found in questions for information and its answers, and more sentences for consensus building are used in answers of questions for opinions.

Thus, suggestions for improving socio-emotional experience are provided based the findings. We have observed that in the current design of RG Q&A there is only one way for scholars to evaluate the questions and answers. It may be ineffective to decide whether give recommendations to messages when exchange of views is required. Thumbs up and thumbs down could also be provided for scholars to express evaluations.

6 Conclusions

This research explored 371 questions with 7530 answers collected from RG Q&A about Library and Information Science. Using Bales' Interaction Process Analysis (IPA) as the general framework, this study provides a new perspective in understanding interaction between scholars.

In this research, we conclude interaction patterns between scholars on Q&A platform. We argue that ASNSs could reinforce interaction between scholars by promoting recommendation mechanism, classifying questions and strengthening emotional experience. These suggestions will help facilitate user engagement and user experience in the design of an effective Q&A platform.

However, there are some limitations in this study. First, not all questions about Library and Information Science are included due to the fact that RG does not provide all the question lists about specific topics. Second, the analysis of interaction is limited to a special ASNS. In the future, more research may address these limitations and explore other ASNSs with a larger sample for more generalizable findings.

REFERENCES

[1] Crawford, M. 2011. Biologists using social-networking sites to boost collaboration. Bioscience, 61(9), 736-736.

[2] Jeng, W., Goodwin, S., He, D. and Li, L. 2017. Information exchange on an academic social networking site: a multidiscipline comparison on researchgate q&a. Journal of the Association for Information Science & Technology, 68(3), 638-652.

[3] Ortega, J. 2017. Toward a homogenization of academic social sites: A longitudinal study of profiles in Academia.edu, Google Scholar Citations and ResearchGate. Online Information Review. 41(6), 812-825.

[4] Li, L., He, D., and Zhang, C. 2016. Evaluating academic answer quality: a pilot study on researchgate q&a. 3rd International Conference on HCI in Business, Government, and Organizations - eCommerce and Innovation. Lecture Notes in Computer Science, Vol. 9751. Toronto, Canada, 61-71. DOI: 10.1007/978-3-319-39396-4_6.

[5] Nam, C., B. Lyons, J., Hwang, H.-S. and Kim, S. 2009. The process of team communication in multi-cultural contexts: an empirical study using bales' interaction process analysis (ipa). International Journal of Industrial Ergonomics. 39(5), 771-782.

[6] Beck, S., A. Paskewitz, E., A. Anderson, W., Bourdeaux, R. and Currie-Mueller, J. 2016. The task and relational dimensions of online social support. Health Communication. 32(3), 347-355.

[7] Leung, L. and Law, N. 2016. Exploring the effectiveness of online role play simulations in tackling groupthink in crisis management training. International Journal of Gaming and Computer-Mediated Simulations. 8(3), 1-18.

[8] Elsayed, A. 2015. The use of academic social networks among arab researchers. Social Science Computer Review. 34(3), 378-391.

[9] Muscanell, N. and Utz, S. 2017. Social networking for scientists: an analysis on how and why academics use researchgate. Online Information Review. 41(5), 744-759

[10] Ortega, J. 2015. Disciplinary differences in the use of academic social networking sites. Online Information Review. 39(4), 520-536.

[11] Hoffmann, C., Lutz, C. and Meckel, M. 2015. A relational altmetric? network centrality on researchgate as an indicator of scientific impact. Journal of the Association for Information Science & Technology. 67(4), 1-11.

[12] Bernard, R., Abrami, P., Borokhovski, E., Wade, C.A., Tamim, R., A. Surkes, M. and Bethel, E. 2009. A meta-analysis of three types of interaction treatments in distance education. Review of Educational Research. 79(3), 1243-1289

[13] Fariza, N., Hamat, A. and Embi, M. 2012. Patterns of discourse in online interaction: seeking evidence of the collaborative learning process. Computer Assisted Language Learning. 25(3), 237-256.

[14] Duart, J., Castaño-Muñoz, J. and Sancho-Vinuesa, T. 2013. Online interaction in higher education: is there evidence of diminishing returns? International Review of Research in Open & Distance Learning. 14(5), 240-257.

Impact of Crowdsourcing OCR Improvements on Retrievability Bias

Myriam C. Traub
Centrum Wiskunde & Informatica
Amsterdam, The Netherlands
myriam.traub@cwi.nl

Thaer Samar
Centrum Wiskunde & Informatica
Amsterdam, The Netherlands
thaer.samar@cwi.nl

Jacco van Ossenbruggen
Centrum Wiskunde & Informatica
Amsterdam, The Netherlands
VU University Amsterdam
Amsterdam, The Netherlands
jacco.van.ossenbruggen@cwi.nl

Lynda Hardman
Centrum Wiskunde & Informatica
Amsterdam, The Netherlands
Utrecht University
Utrecht, The Netherlands
lynda.hardman@cwi.nl

ABSTRACT

Digitized document collections often suffer from OCR errors that may impact a document's readability and retrievability. We studied the effects of correcting OCR errors on the retrievability of documents in a historic newspaper corpus of a digital library. We computed retrievability scores for the uncorrected documents using queries from the library's search log, and found that the document OCR character error rate and retrievability score are strongly correlated. We computed retrievability scores for manually corrected versions of the same documents, and report on differences in their total sum, the overall retrievability bias, and the distribution of these changes over the documents, queries and query terms. For large collections, often only a fraction of the corpus is manually corrected. Using a mixed corpus, we assess how this mix affects the retrievability of the corrected and uncorrected documents. The correction of OCR errors increased the number of documents retrieved in all conditions. The increase contributed to a less biased retrieval, even when taking the potential lower ranking of uncorrected documents into account.

CCS CONCEPTS

• **Information systems → Query log analysis**; **Evaluation of retrieval results**;

KEYWORDS

Retrievability Bias, Digital Library, Data Quality, OCR

ACM Reference Format:

Myriam C. Traub, Thaer Samar, Jacco van Ossenbruggen, and Lynda Hardman. 2018. Impact of Crowdsourcing OCR Improvements on Retrievability Bias. In *JCDL '18: The 18th ACM/IEEE Joint Conference on Digital Libraries, June 3–7, 2018, Fort Worth, TX, USA,* Editor1, Editor2, and Editor3 (Eds.). ACM, New York, NY, USA, Article 4, 8 pages. https://doi.org/10.1145/3197026.3197046

JCDL '18, June 3–7, 2018, Fort Worth, TX, USA

ACM ISBN 978-1-4503-5178-2/18/06...$15.00
https://doi.org/10.1145/3197026.3197046

1 INTRODUCTION

Digitized collections are the foundation for services and research tasks that would be much more difficult (if not impossible) to perform on collections of physical items. Examples of such tasks are full-text search and quantification of changes in textual features over long time periods. Most of these services, however, rely on the use of retrieval systems.

How well these systems perform has been investigated with regard to many different aspects, such as precision and recall, and based on many different types of corpora, such as community-created TREC collections, digital libraries or Web archives. The *retrievability measure* as introduced by Azzopardi et al. [1] extends these evaluation measures by means to detect and assess bias when retrieving documents.

In a previous study, we used retrievability to investigate whether a retrievability bias influences access to a digitized collection of historic newspapers and to measure the extent of this bias [14]. We found a relation between document features, such as document length, and retrievability. In this study, we focus on the effects of OCR quality on retrievability and how a (partial) manual correction of the OCR errors impacts the accessibility of document. We investigate the following research questions.

• *RQ1: What is the relation between a document's OCR character error rate and its retrievability score?* By relating the retrievability scores of documents with the character error rates of their content, we investigate how the quality of OCR processing impacts a document's retrievability.

• *RQ2: How does the correction of OCR errors impact the retrievability bias of the corrected documents* (direct impact)*?* Assuming that the complete set of documents has been corrected, we investigate if the correction makes retrieval more or less biased in terms of retrievability, and how differences in retrievability scores are distributed over documents, queries and query terms.

• *RQ3: How does the correction of a fraction of error-prone documents influence the retrievability of non-corrected ones* (indirect impact)? Typically, only small fractions of a collection are corrected. We investigate how this affects the other documents in the collection by comparing the retrievability scores in a mixed collection where 50% of the collection has been corrected with those of an uncorrected only collection.

2 RELATED WORK

2.1 OCR Quality and Retrieval

In 2015, we conducted a series of interviews with digital humanities scholars on their use of digital archives for their research. All agreed that the (OCR) quality of digitized documents makes digital libraries unsuited for "distant reading" and other computational approaches [15]. Several studies investigated the applicability of crowdsourcing tasks to transcribe documents [7, 8] or the use of a tool that combines the search in a digitized corpus with correction of OCR errors [10]. While the results from these studies can help improve data quality more efficiently, it remains unclear how this correction affects a scholar's research.

Mittendorf et al. investigated how robust IR systems are toward OCR errors in digitized documents [9]. They found that longer documents describing a single topic redundantly have a better chance of retrieval than documents that are either short or discuss different topics.

Taghva et al. investigated the performance of the vector space model on OCRed documents [13]. They found that for their full text collection neither average precision, nor recall of the documents is affected by OCR errors. 674 documents were used in a OCR processed version and a manually corrected ground truth version. The character error rate was estimated to be around 10 – 20% and the average length of the documents is reported to be around 40 pages. This confirms the findings of Mittendorf et al. that the effect of OCR errors on long documents can be expected to be very low. Since our corpus is characterized by relatively short documents with a high estimated error rate, we expect a higher impact of OCR errors than in the studies of Mittendorf et al. and Taghva et al.

Ohta et al. studied whether the effect of OCR errors on document retrieval can be compensated by generating additional search terms based on a character confusion matrix [11]. They based their study on two collections of documents obtained from the *Elsevier Electronic Subscriptions* service and published between 1995 and 1996. The document collection in this case can therefore be expected to be very homogenous in terms of layout, fonts, document length, quality of the physical copy and as a consequence cause little variation in error rates and error types. In our case, documents vary strongly in all of these aspects and therefore errors are less systematic as in the documents of Ohta et al. A statistical approach would be difficult, as it could only be applied to subsets of very similar documents.

Chiron et al. investigated for the AmeliOCR project how OCR errors are distributed in a large and diverse digitized corpus [5]. They found that about 15% of the misspelled terms represent named entities and that even 80% of the top 500 queries contain at least a mention of one. In a manual inspection of the 100 most frequent terms in the query set we used for [14], we found that 56 were named entities. The frequency of named entities in the document collection, however, can be very low and they may not even be found in common dictionaries. This makes them particularly susceptible to OCR errors. This combination, i.e. terms that occur very frequently in queries, but very infrequently in documents, is the reason that OCR errors in these terms can have a disproportional effect on the retrieval results [5].

2.2 Retrievability Assessment

The foundation for the assessment of retrievability bias in document collections is the work by Azzopardi et al [1]. They introduced *retrievability* as an extension to traditional IR measures, one that does not require the availability of relevance judgments. It considers the number of results that a user is willing to examine (c). If the rank k_{dq} of a document d is retrieved within the cutoff value c, the utility/cost function f returns a score of 1, otherwise 0.

$$r(d) = \sum_{q \in Q} o_q \cdot f(k_{dq}, c)$$

o_q allows different weighting of queries according to their importance. We use $o_q = 1$ for all queries. To measure a potential bias among $r(d)$ scores, [1] suggested to use the Gini coefficient, which was introduced to measure inequalities in societies [6]. Wilkie et al. later compared it to other inequality measures and confirmed its aptitude for retrievability analyses [18].

Follow-up studies confirmed the applicability of the retrievability measure to assess bias in retrieval models [16] and its relatedness to retrieval effectiveness [3, 4]. Several studies found that Okapi BM25 induces the least bias and can therefore be considered to be the fairest retrieval model [14, 16, 17]. While [1] and most subsequent retrievability studies (e.g. [2, 4, 12, 18]) made use of *simulated user queries*, we follow the line of our previous study and use queries collected from real users of the digital library [14]. In [14], we investigated the applicability of the retrievability metric on a digitized newspaper collection and questioned the representativeness of simulated queries for the search behavior of real users. Our findings revealed significant differences in number of query terms used and the frequency of named entity queries.

The current study extends the findings of [14] in several aspects. Our first study was based on the complete archive which comprises more than 102 million documents. The relatively high *document - query ratio* (DQR) had a large impact on the inequality in the $r(d)$ scores because a large fraction of the documents was never retrieved. By focusing on a small subset of the newspaper collection in this study, we prevented a high DQR rate, and analyze an inversed scenario where the number of queries exceeds by far the number of documents. Finally, the availability of a ground truth data set enables us to investigate retrieval results on a corrected document collection, a collection containing errors, and a mixed collection.

3 APPROACH

To investigate whether and how errors in OCRed documents influence their retrievability, we performed a series of experiments that make use of the concept of *retrievability* as introduced by Azzopardi et al. [1]. For this, we used different subsets of a digitized newspaper collection and search queries that were collected from users of the online access portal of the archive.

The National Library of the Netherlands (KB)[1] made a ground truth data set available that contains the manually corrected versions of 100 newspaper issues. By comparing these documents with their original versions, we were able to assess the number of incorrect characters and compute the character error rates (*CER*) for each document. This allowed us to investigate a relation between the documents' quality and their retrievability scores (*RQ1*).

The manual correction of OCR errors *directly* impacts the retrievability of these documents. We investigated this effect with two retrievability experiments based on a small document collection and two versions of query sets that were originally collected from users of the digital archive. By comparing the *r(d)* scores, we investigate which documents and queries gained or lost *r(d)* scores through the correction and how this influences the total number of retrieved documents (*wealth*) and retrieval bias (*inequality*) of the results (*RQ2*).

Since correction of OCR errors is often performed manually, it is a costly process. As a consequence only relatively small fractions of a collection are corrected. The same document may score lower in a corpus consisting of only highly findable documents than it would as part of a collection of documents that are difficult to find. Therefore, we explored how the correction of only a part of the collection *indirectly* impacts the retrievability of documents that remain uncorrected (*RQ3*).

4 EXPERIMENTAL SETUP

The setup we used for our experiments follows the setup used in [1, 14], modifications are explicitly described in this section.

4.1 Document Collections

We use different subsets of the historic newspaper archive, a manually corrected ground truth subset and queries collected from the online users of the archive.

OCR Ground Truth Corpus (822_{GTcor}) For a small subset of the newspaper collection of the National Library of the Netherlands, the OCR text has been manually corrected. This subset covers 100 newspaper issues published between 14-06-1618 and 26-10-1624 (17th*century* subset) and between 04-10-1940 and 29-09-1944 (*WWII* subset). The 17th*century* sub-collection constitutes the part of the archive with the oldest documents. It is prone to OCR errors as the decay of the physical material, the layout and the (gothic) fonts make character recognition very difficult. The *WWII* collection includes illegal newspapers, printed secretly, often in non-professional settings. Some of these articles therefore have a lower OCR quality than pro-German papers of the same period with better print quality. Combined, they include a total of 822 newspaper items. Note that this corpus is very small compared to 100M item corpus used in our first study [14].

OCRed Corpus containing Errors (822_{GTerr}) We used the uncorrected versions of the articles in 822_{GTcor} to build the 822_{GTerr} corpus.

Mixed Documents Corpus (1644_{mix} and 1644_{err}) We extended 822_{GTcor} and 822_{GTerr} with an equal number of articles that originate from the same newspaper titles as in the 822_{GTerr} collection. We selected the 503 earliest articles from the KB collection and a random sample of 319 articles from the WWII period (822_{mixin}). These documents added to 822_{GTcor} yields the 1644_{mix} corpus, and added to 822_{GTerr} yields the 1644_{err} corpus.

4.2 Query Set

The queries we used were collected from the users of the library's Web interface (Delpher.nl) between March and July 2015. The data set comprises a total number of 1, 008, 915 queries from 162, 536 unique users with an average length of three terms. We removed stopwords[2] and terms shorter than three characters from the queries. The final, deduplicated, query set comprises 859, 716 *multi-term queries*. Additionally, we created a *single-term query set* by extracting all 259, 091 unique terms.

4.3 OCR Quality Assessment

We measured the OCR quality of 822_{GTerr} set using the OCRevalUAtion tool[3] developed by the IMPACT project. It allowed us to compute the character error rates (*CER*) for each article in 822_{GTerr}.

4.4 Setup for Retrievability Analysis

We investigated whether and how OCR quality impacts retrievability by comparing how retrievability scores ($r(d)$) differ between documents containing errors and their corrected versions. To compute the $r(d)$ score for each document, we issued all queries against the document collections using the Indri search engine[4] and BM25 as retrieval model. For each document we calculated how often it was retrieved in the top c results (for cut-off values of $c = 1, 10$ and 100) and how often it was retrieved at all ($c = \infty$).

The *wealth*, or the total sum of all *r(d)* scores, depends on the number of queries issued and the number of results taken into account (c). To assess differences between the results obtained from the different corpora we calculated the wealth for each corpus for all values of c. An increase or decline in retrieval bias is determined using the *Gini coefficient*, which is a measure developed to express inequalities in societies [6].

4.5 Impact Analysis

Assessment of Query Impact We investigated the *impact* each unique query *term* has on the total wealth of a document collection. For this, we issued all unique single query terms against the document collections and recorded the matching query - document pairs. We used these to assess, for every multi-term query - document pair, which of the terms in the query was responsible for retrieving the documents that appeared on the result list for said multi-term query. We then assigned each successful term a score of $\frac{1}{n_t}$ where n_t is the number of successful query terms t for a document - multi-term query pair. The sum of all of these scores for all occurrences of a query term is its *impact score* and the sum of all impact scores equals the total wealth of all $r(d)$ scores for a corpus.

Assessment of Direct Impact We investigated the differences in the retrievability of documents before (822_{GTerr}) and after

[1] www.kb.nl

[2] http://snowball.tartarus.org/algorithms/dutch/stop.txt

[3] http://www.digitisation.eu/training/succeed-training-materials/ocr-evaluation/ocrevaluation/the-ocrevaluation-tool/

[4] http://www.lemurproject.org/indri.php

(822_{GTcor}) error correction. For this, we evaluate the total number of documents retrieved (*wealth*), the equality of the *r(d)* scores' distribution, and we analyze qualitatively the documents and queries for which the differences between the experimental conditions are the largest. We measure the difference in inequality among the *r(d)* scores for the two versions of the document collection using the Gini coefficient. A high Gini coefficient indicates a large inequality in the distribution, a low Gini coefficient indicates a more equal and therefore less biased distribution. Then we investigate the difference in *r(d)* scores for each document in both versions. A gain in *r(d)* scores indicates that the document benefited from the correction of its content. A decrease in *r(d)* scores shows that its corrected version was retrieved by fewer queries than the original version. We manually assessed the documents with the largest differences and the queries that retrieved those documents to find out what caused the drop or increase in *r(d)* scores.

Assessment of Indirect Impact For this experiment we used the 1644_{mix} and the 1644_{err} data sets. Again, we evaluated differences in the overall wealth of distributed *r(d)* scores, the inequality between documents in terms of *r(d)* scores and the differences between documents in direct comparison. Differences in the results are caused by the interlace between the rankings of the corrected and unchanged documents. The analyses we perform for this section are similar to those of the *direct impact* experiments.

4.6 Limitations

Since relevance judgments are not available for this document collection, we were not able to explore how OCR errors correlate with precision and recall. In our mixed experiment, we only evaluated a correct/incorrect ratio of 50:50, other ratios are planned for future work.

5 RESULTS

5.1 OCR Quality versus Retrievability

First, we studied to what extent a document's OCR error rate and its *r(d)* score are related (*RQ1*).

QCR Quality We evaluated the OCR quality using the OCReval-UAtion tool[5]. The results showed that the mean character error rate (*CER*) of the collection is high: 29% (with a median CER of even 37%). We found a clear difference in the *CER* distributions of the two sub-collections (see Fig. 1). As expected, the more recent documents from *WWII* suffer from far fewer mis-recognized characters (median CER = 3.97%) than the documents from the 17th*century* (median CER = 42.00%).

Retrievability in 822_{GTerr} An analysis of the *r(d)* scores showed that we retrieved 4,521,030 documents from 822_{GTerr} ($c = \infty$) in total. The scores ranged from $r(d) = 0$ (16 documents, of which two are part of the *WWII* sub-collection and 14 are part of the 17th*century* sub-collection) to $r(d) = 65,347$. Most documents are in the lowest bin ($r(d) < 674$), as shown in the margin histogram on the right of Fig. 1. The median scores are

- $r(d) = 991$ for 822_{GTerr},
- $r(d) = 447$ for 17th*century*, and
- $r(d) = 8,237$ for the *WWII* sub-collection.

[5]https://github.com/impactcentre/ocrevalUAtion

Corpus	c = 1	c = 10	c = 100	c = ∞
822_{GTerr}	0.75	0.72	0.74	0.74
822_{GTcor}	0.68	0.59	0.61	0.61
1644_{err}	0.78	0.70	0.73	0.73
1644_{mix}	0.73	0.63	0.66	0.66

Table 1: Gini coefficients indicating to which extent the distribution of *r(d)* scores among documents for different *c*'s is biased (higher values indicate more bias).

This confirms the hypothesis that the *WWII* documents are easier to retrieve due to their better OCR quality.

We found a strong correlation between OCR quality and retrievability of a document for results with $c = \infty$. Documents with a low *CER* generally obtained higher *r(d)* scores (see Figure 1). The correlations of −0.57 (Pearson) and −0.61 (Spearman) were both strong and significant with $p < 0.001$. While this correlation may suggest that low $r(d)$ scores are *caused* by high OCR error rates, other explanations could be that our modern query set just better matches the *WWII* sub-collection, or that 17th*century* documents are harder to retrieve in general. To establish a causal relation, we study the direct impact of the crowd-sourced improvements on the *r(d)* scores in the next section.

5.2 Direct Impact Assessment

Next, we studied how the correction of OCR errors influences retrievability bias (*RQ2*). For this, we measure the direct impact of correcting OCR errors by comparing the $r(d)$ scores over 822_{GTcor} with the corresponding scores in 822_{GTerr}.

Wealth We found that more documents were retrieved from 822_{GTcor} than from 822_{GTerr} and that the relative difference increases for larger values of *c* (see Fig. 2). The total wealth at $c = 1$ indicates how many queries could be matched with at least one document. For $c = 1$, 8% more documents are retrieved from 822_{GTcor} than from 822_{GTerr}, which means that fewer queries retrieved no documents at all. For $c = \infty$ the total wealth increases by 34% (see Fig. 2). This suggests that for users willing to examine *all* search results (which is not uncommon in a research library) the impact of the error-correction is much larger. Correcting the OCR errors thus indeed leads to higher numbers of documents retrieved, even for small c's, and the effect increases when more results are taken into account.

Equality We computed and compared Gini coefficients for 822_{GTerr} and 822_{GTcor} to find out whether the increase in wealth contributed to a more equal or more biased distribution of *r(d)* scores (see Table 1). Gini coefficients for 822_{GTcor} are consistently lower than for 822_{GTerr} for all c's. The correction of the documents thus contributed to *less biased* retrieval for all c's. In contrast to other studies [1–3] and our earlier findings in [14], Gini coefficients do *not* show a clearly decreasing trend for larger cutoff values *c*. This suggests that in this experiment, ranking does not contribute much additional bias. This may be caused by the relatively small corpus size.

Increased retrieval per document We investigated how the changes of *r(d)* scores were distributed among documents, i.e. whether many documents gained a little or whether very few documents

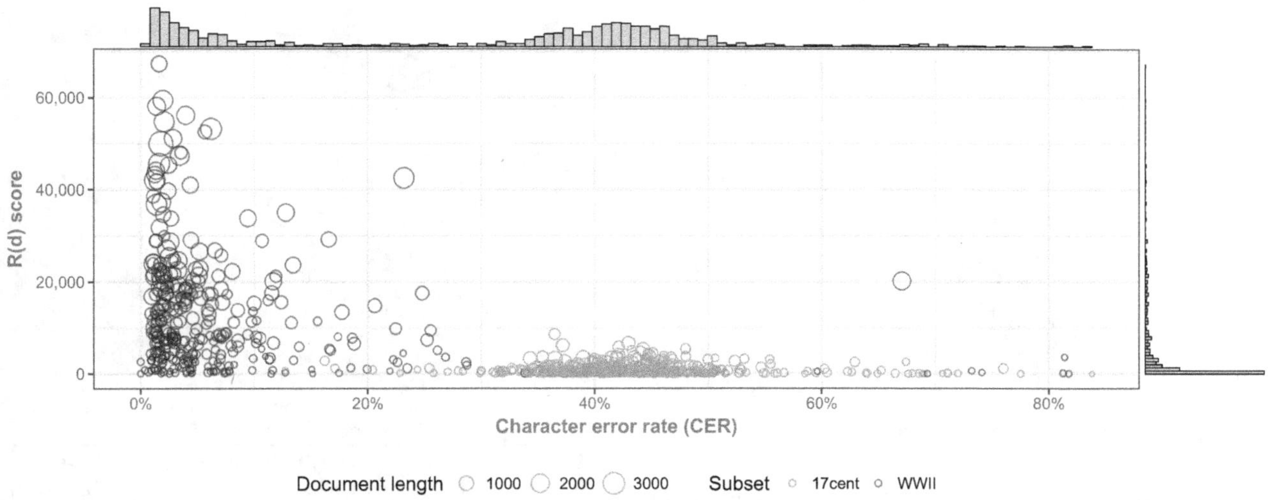

Figure 1: The 17th*century* collection has a higher character error rate (*CER*) than the *WWII* collection. The *r(d)* scores and *CER* for $c = \infty$ are strongly correlated: the higher the error rate, the less retrievable is a document.

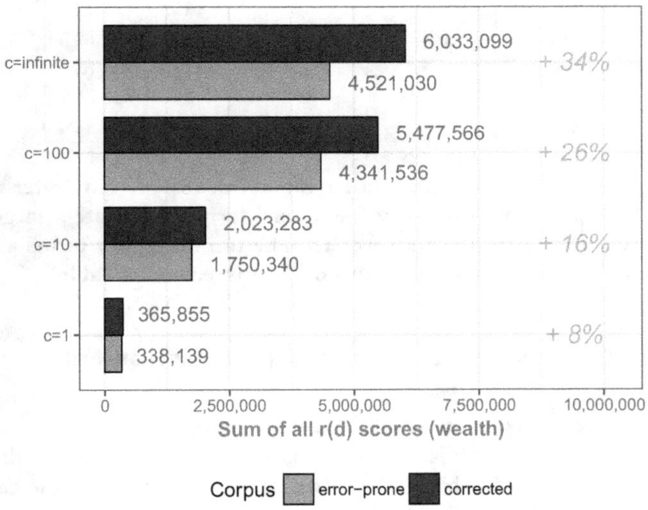

Figure 2: Difference in distributed wealth between the uncorrected and corrected corpus.

c	Min.	1st Qu.	Median	Mean	3rd Qu.	Max.
1	-5,039	-56	8	34	99	7,160
10	-7,124	-153	177	332	647	8,408
100	-7,040	24	652	1,382	1,941	25,647
∞	-7,019	275	912	1,840	2,292	27,926

Table 2: Summary statistics of differences in *r(d)* scores between the two corpora.

gained a lot. For Fig. 3 we ordered documents according to their difference in *r(d)* scores between 822_{GTerr} and 822_{GTcor}. We see a few documents on the left of the 0-axis, these documents had a

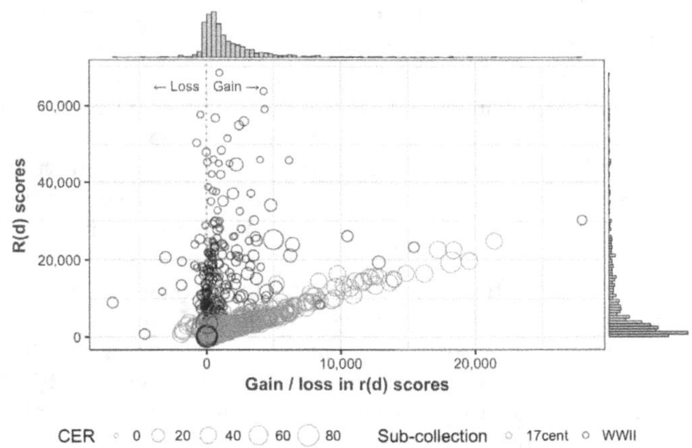

Figure 3: Documents ordered by their gain/loss in *r(d)* scores ($c = \infty$). The position on the y-axis represents their *r(d)* scores for 822_{GTcor}.

higher *r(d)* score in the uncorrected corpus. Closer inspection indicated that these were false positive matches *caused by* OCR errors. Their decreasing scores can therefore be interpreted as a potential improvement in precision. For most documents, OCR correction increased their *r(d)* score, and they are therefore found on the right of the 0-axis. This can be interpreted as a potential improvement in recall. We see clearly different patterns for the two corpora, with many 17th*century* documents improving more but scoring overall lower than the *WWII* documents. Several documents scored very low in 822_{GTerr}, but gained a lot from the correction. This is one explanation for why Gini coefficients for 822_{GTcor} show less bias than for 822_{GTerr}. Most documents, however, have a modest *r(d)* score and gained a modest amount, as shown in the margin

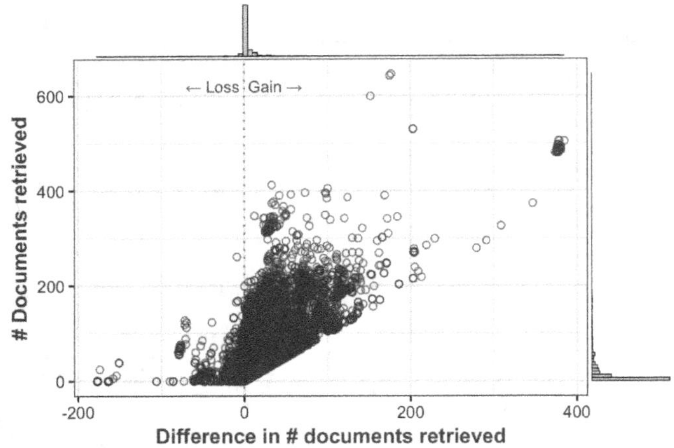

Figure 4: Queries ordered by their gain/loss in number of retrieved documents. The position on the y-axis represents the number of documents retrieved from 822_{GTcor}.

histograms. The distributions of the differences in *r(d)* scores in Table 2, show that for all cutoff values, the median of the differences is positive, and increases from 8 ($c = 1$) to 912 ($c = \infty$). The maximum loss and the maximum gain in *r(d)* scores increase for larger cutoff values c, the latter to a much larger extent. Note that for $c = 1$ and $c = 10$ the entire first quartile is filled with documents that scored *worse* in the corrected version. This shows that the competition in the top results makes the gain of some documents the loss of others.

Increased retrieval per query In a final step, we investigated how the changes of *r(d)* scores were distributed among the queries, i.e. if many queries contributed a little or if only a few queries that contributed a lot to the change in wealth. The large majority of queries does not match with any of the documents in our collection. Only 384, 486 out of 859, 716 queries retrieved at least one document from either of the document collections. This is due to misspellings from users, invalid words, numbers, words in foreign languages or simply queries that are unrelated to our (small) corpus. In Figure 4 we ordered these queries by how many more (or less) documents they retrieved in 822_{GTcor}. Note that despite the small corpus size, we still see outliers with very large gains (to over 400 documents more retrieved for some queries). Also note that some queries have a negative gain, which means that for these queries, the OCR errors caused more false positive matches than false negatives.

Finally, we were interested in finding out which query *terms* are responsible for most of the increase in wealth. Figure 5 shows that most of the increase can be attributed to *very few* query terms. The top ten queries[6] (see table adjacent to Fig 5) contribute 35% of the increase. This disproportionately large impact originates from a combination of the terms' high frequency in the users' queries and the large extent to which they are susceptible to errors in OCR processing.

[6]Translations: new, Amsterdam, end, Mister, died/dead, grand/large, Willem (name), two, three, old

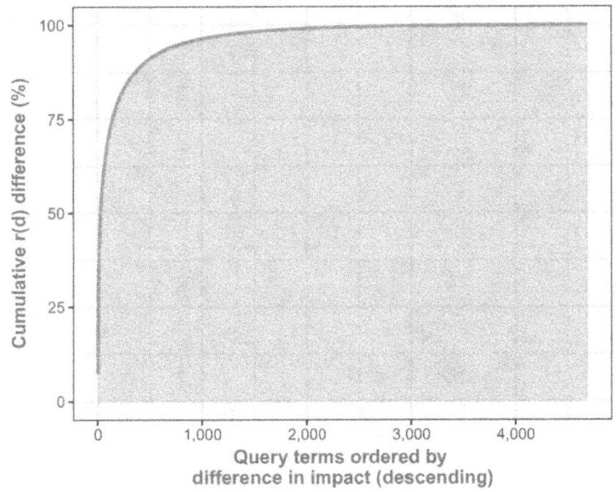

Query Term	Frequency in Queries	822_{GTerr}	822_{GTcor}	Cum. Impact
nieuwe	1,903	99	166	7.36%
amsterdam	7,885	41	57	14.65%
ende	185	103	480	18.69%
heer	826	20	89	21.99%
overleden	3,698	5	18	24.78%
groot	1,573	125	153	27.33%
willem	5,375	5	13	29.81%
twee	319	64	175	31.83%
drie	401	34	120	33.81%
oude	991	50	78	35.41%

Figure 5: The accumulated impact scores of single-term queries show that very few query term contribute a large fraction of the overall wealth. The top ten query terms account for more than a third of the increase (see Table).

5.3 Results of Indirect Impact Assessment

Finally, we investigated the influence of OCR error correction on the retrieval of documents that remain uncorrected (*RQ3*). We investigate for the typical case of a partial error-correction how the improved retrievability of the corrected documents impacts the *r(d)* scores of the documents that have not (yet) been corrected.

Wealth When looking at the *r(d)* scores of the mixed collection, we see that the correction of half the documents still leads to an increase in wealth for the complete corpus for all values of c (see Fig. 6). We first focused on the 822_{GTcor} documents within the mixed corpus. These are retrieved for the same queries as in the previous section. The mixed-in documents only cause differences in ranking. For $c = \infty$, we thus see identical *r(d)* scores and total wealth as in Section 5.2. For the lower c values, we see lower wealth due to competition in the ranking with the unaltered documents, but also large gains caused by the manual OCR correction.

In the remainder of this section, we focus solely on the documents that remain uncorrected, 822_{mixin}. In terms of distributed *r(d)* scores we found a decrease in wealth for the mixed-in documents for values of c from $c = 1$ to $c = 100$. This is because the corrected versions push many mixed-in documents to higher ranks that exceed the number of documents we take into account (c). This difference in wealth is largest for $c = 1$ (−13%), followed by $c = 10$

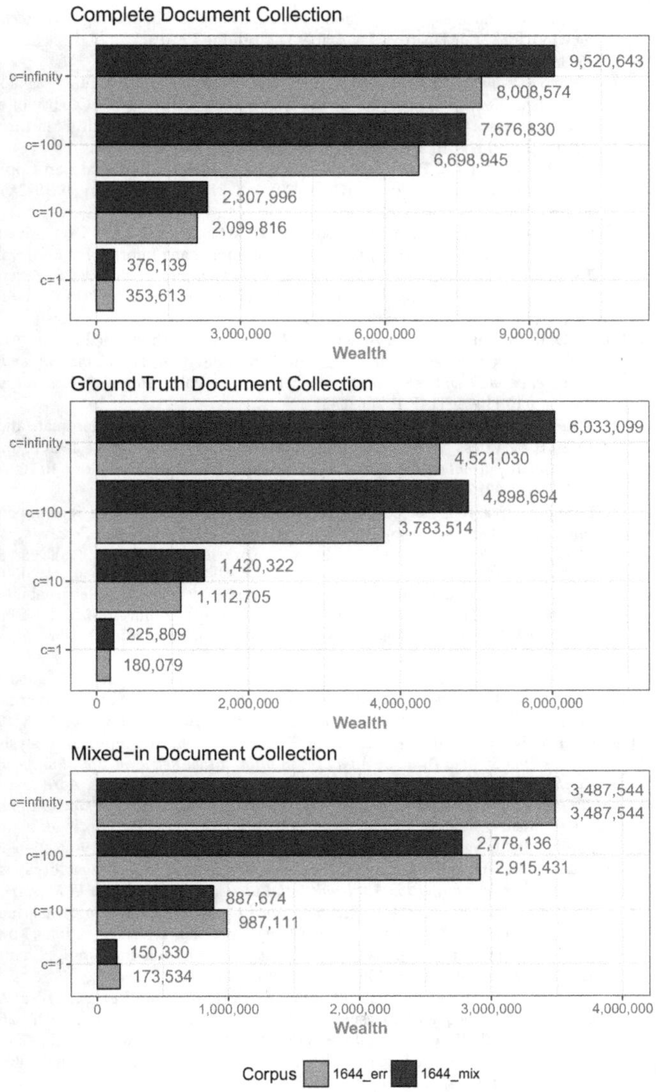

Figure 6: Wealth in *r(d)* scores for the complete collection (top), the 822_{GT} documents (middle) and the mixed in documents, 822_{mixin} (bottom).

(−10%) and c = 100 (−5%). For larger values the ranking does not take effect and the wealth remains the same.

Equality When we compare the Gini coefficients we obtained for different values of c, we see that they are lower for the corpus that was partially corrected, 1644_{mix}. Again, the correction of a part of the collection has reduced retrievability bias (see Table 1).

Retrieval per document The *r(d)* scores of most mixed-in documents changed very little after the correction of the other documents. Most documents' *r(d)* scores drop slightly (see Fig. 7), which could be expected as they now compete with corrected documents for low ranks. In total, 522 documents have lost in r(d) scores, of which 266 are from the *WWII* sub-collection and 256 from 17th*century*. We also see that 171 documents gain in *r(d)* scores, of which 8 are from *WWII* and 163 from 17th*century* (see Fig. 7). These documents profit from false positive matches that disappeared through the correction.

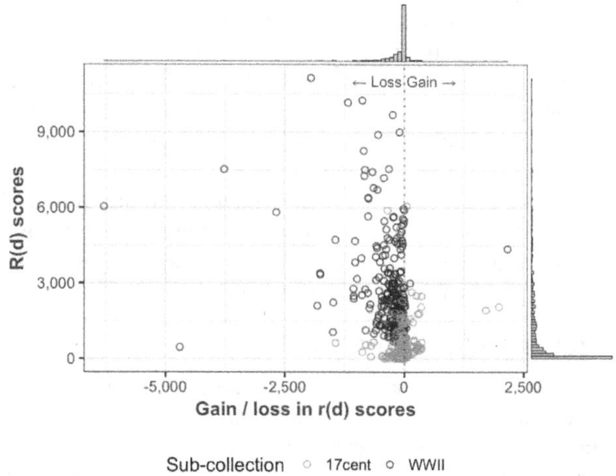

Figure 7: Documents ordered according to their difference in *r(d)* scores (non-GT documents at c = 10). Position on the y-axis indicated the *r(d)* score in the mixed condition. Documents in the left part of the graph lost *r(d)* scores.

Overall, we found that even in this mixed condition, the overall positive effect in improved retrievability for the corrected documents by far outweighs the slightly reduced retrievability of the unchanged documents. The net effect of the correction is still an overall *reduction of retrievability bias.*

6 CONCLUSIONS

Many text documents in digital libraries are affected by errors caused by OCR engines. It is therefore vital to understand how these errors and their (partial) correction impact retrieval tasks of digital library users. We investigated the relation between OCR quality of digitized newspaper articles and their retrievability and found a strong correlation: high error rates correlate with low retrievability scores. We compared the overall retrievability of a manually corrected ground truth document collection with the results obtained from the same documents but in their original, uncorrected version. Our analyses showed that error correction leads to both higher and more equally distributed retrievability scores.

The higher scores are mainly caused by a disproportionately small set of query terms, that are both very frequent in the query set and highly susceptible to OCR errors. This shows that for retrievability studies with real user queries, understanding the impact of a (biased) query set on the retrievability bias is important, while this is typically not considered in the literature, where synthetic query sets are more prevalent.

Our findings could be used for improving and evaluating automatic OCR-error correction techniques, or to improve query expansion techniques designed to deal with OCR-errors in uncorrected texts.

Furthermore, we looked at interference effects that the correction of a subset may have on documents that are excluded from the correction. We found that the reduced scores for the excluded documents do not outweigh the improved scores of the corrected version. The overall outcome is still a less biased retrieval result. Because we lack relevance judgments for this corpus, we cannot measure the improvement of the correction in terms of precision and recall. We can, however, conclude that the error correction has led to more documents being retrieved overall while reducing the retrievability bias in all experimental setups.

ACKNOWLEDGMENTS

We would like to thank the National Library of the Netherlands for their support and Alejandro Bellogín for his comments on an earlier version of the paper. This research is partly funded by the Dutch COMMIT/ program, the WebART project and the VRE4EIC project, a project that has received funding from the European Union's Horizon 2020 research and innovation program under grant agreement No 676247. Part of the analysis work was carried out on the Dutch national e-infrastructure with the support of the SURF Foundation.

REFERENCES

[1] Leif Azzopardi and Vishwa Vinay. 2008. Retrievability: An Evaluation Measure for Higher Order Information Access Tasks. In *Proceedings of the 17th ACM Conference on Information and Knowledge Management (CIKM '08)*. ACM, New York, NY, USA, 561–570. https://doi.org/10.1145/1458082.1458157

[2] Shariq Bashir. 2014. Estimating retrievability ranks of documents using document features. *Neurocomputing* 123, 0 (2014), 216 – 232. https://doi.org/10.1016/j.neucom.2013.07.011 Contains Special issue articles: Advances in Pattern Recognition Applications and Methods.

[3] Shariq Bashir and Andreas Rauber. 2014. Automatic ranking of retrieval models using retrievability measure. *Knowledge and Information Systems* 41, 1 (2014), 189–221. https://doi.org/10.1007/s10115-014-0759-6

[4] Shariq Bashir and Andreas Rauber. 2017. Retrieval Models Versus Retrievability. In *Current Challenges in Patent Information Retrieval*, Mihai Lupu, Katja Mayer, Noriko Kando, and Anthony J. Trippe (Eds.). Springer Berlin Heidelberg, 185–212. https://doi.org/10.1007/978-3-662-53817-3_7

[5] G. Chiron, A. Doucet, M. Coustaty, M. Visani, and J. P. Moreux. 2017. Impact of OCR Errors on the Use of Digital Libraries: Towards a Better Access to Information. In *JCDL 2017*. 1–4. https://doi.org/10.1109/JCDL.2017.7991582

[6] George Garvy. 1952. Inequality of income: Causes and measurement. In *Studies in Income and Wealth, Volume 15*. NBER, 25–48.

[7] Rose Holley. 2009. How Good Can It Get? Analysing and Improving OCR Accuracy in Large Scale Historic Newspaper Digitisation Programs. *D-Lib Magazine* 15, 3/4 (2009). https://doi.org/10.1045/march2009-holley

[8] Kimmo Kettunen, Timo Honkela, Krister Lindén, Pekka Kauppinen, Tuula Pääkkönen, Jukka Kervinen, et al. 2014. Analyzing and Improving the Quality of a Historical News Collection using Language Technology and Statistical Machine Learning Methods. In *80th IFLA General Conference and Assembly*.

[9] Elke Mittendorf and Peter Schäuble. 2000. Information Retrieval Can Cope with Many Errors. *Inf. Retr.* 3, 3 (Oct. 2000), 189–216. https://doi.org/10.1023/A:1026564708926

[10] Günter Mühlberger, Johannes Zelger, and David Sagmeister. 2014. User-driven Correction of OCR Errors: Combining Crowdsourcing and Information Retrieval Technology. In *Proceedings of the First International Conference on Digital Access to Textual Cultural Heritage (DATeCH '14)*. ACM, New York, NY, USA, 53–56. https://doi.org/10.1145/2595188.2595212

[11] M. Ohta, A. Takasu, and J. Adachi. 1997. Retrieval methods for English-text with missrecognized OCR characters. In *Proceedings of the Fourth International Conference on Document Analysis and Recognition*, Vol. 2. 950–956 vol.2. https://doi.org/10.1109/ICDAR.1997.620651

[12] Thaer Samar, Myriam C. Traub, Jacco van Ossenbruggen, Lynda Hardman, and Arjen P. de Vries. 2017. Quantifying retrieval bias in Web archive search. *International Journal on Digital Libraries* (18 Apr 2017). https://doi.org/10.1007/s00799-017-0215-9

[13] Kazem Taghva, Julie Borsack, and Allen Condit. 1996. Effects of OCR errors on ranking and feedback using the vector space model. *Information Processing & Management* 32, 3 (1996), 317 – 327. https://doi.org/10.1016/0306-4573(95)00058-5

[14] Myriam C. Traub, Thaer Samar, Jacco van Ossenbruggen, Jiyin He, Arjen de Vries, and Lynda Hardman. 2016. Querylog-based Assessment of Retrievability Bias in a Large Newspaper Corpus. In *Proceedings of the 16th ACM/IEEE-CS on Joint Conference on Digital Libraries (JCDL '16)*. ACM, New York, NY, USA, 7–16. https://doi.org/10.1145/2910896.2910907

[15] Myriam C. Traub, Jacco van Ossenbruggen, and Lynda Hardman. 2015. *Impact Analysis of OCR Quality on Research Tasks in Digital Archives*. Springer International Publishing, Cham, 252–263. https://doi.org/10.1007/978-3-319-24592-8_19

[16] Colin Wilkie and Leif Azzopardi. 2014. Best and Fairest: An Empirical Analysis of Retrieval System Bias. In *Advances in Information Retrieval: 36th European Conference on IR Research, ECIR 2014, Amsterdam, The Netherlands, April 13-16, 2014. Proceedings*, Maarten de Rijke, Tom Kenter, Arjen P. de Vries, ChengXiang Zhai, Franciska de Jong, Kira Radinsky, and Katja Hofmann (Eds.). Springer International Publishing, Cham, 13–25. https://doi.org/10.1007/978-3-319-06028-6_2

[17] Colin Wilkie and Leif Azzopardi. 2014. Efficiently Estimating Retrievability Bias. In *Advances in Information Retrieval: 36th European Conference on IR Research, ECIR 2014, Amsterdam, The Netherlands, April 13-16, 2014. Proceedings*, Maarten de Rijke, Tom Kenter, Arjen P. de Vries, ChengXiang Zhai, Franciska de Jong, Kira Radinsky, and Katja Hofmann (Eds.). Springer International Publishing, Cham, 720–726. https://doi.org/10.1007/978-3-319-06028-6_82

[18] Colin Wilkie and Leif Azzopardi. 2015. Retrievability and Retrieval Bias: A Comparison of Inequality Measures. In *Advances in Information Retrieval*, Allan Hanbury, Gabriella Kazai, Andreas Rauber, and Norbert Fuhr (Eds.). Lecture Notes in Computer Science, Vol. 9022. Springer International Publishing, 209–214. https://doi.org/10.1007/978-3-319-16354-3_22

Applying the Analytic Hierarchy Process to an Institutional Repository Collection

Pamela Andrews
University of North Texas
Denton, Texas
pamela.andrews@unt.edu

Karen Harker
University of North Texas
Denton, Texas
karen.harker@unt.edu

Ana Krahmer
University of North Texas
Denton, Texas
ana.krahmer@unt.edu

ABSTRACT

Building the collection of an institutional repository requires a complex understanding of both digital library infrastructure and staff resources, as well as the institution's faculty awareness and attitudes toward self-archiving. For collection development decisions, institutional repository (IR) managers weigh the influence of these factors when pursuing strategies to increase content and faculty participation. To evaluate strategies for collection development, the authors will apply the Analytic Hierarchy Process (AHP) to create a model through which collection development strategies can be evaluated based on the unique context of the institution.

CCS CONCEPTS

• **Information systems → Digital libraries and archives;** • **Applied computing → Decision analysis;**

KEYWORDS

institutional repository; analytic hierarchy processing; digital libraries

ACM Reference Format:
Pamela Andrews, Karen Harker, and Ana Krahmer. 2018. Applying the Analytic Hierarchy Process to an Institutional Repository Collection. In *JCDL '18: The 18th ACM/IEEE Joint Conference on Digital Libraries, June 3–7, 2018, Fort Worth, TX, USA.* ACM, New York, NY, USA, 4 pages. https://doi.org/10.1145/3197026.3197064

1 INTRODUCTION

The institutional repository collection often operates in tandem with an institution's other digital collections, functioning as a portion of the library specifically tailored to preserving and providing access to the scholarly output of an institution. With nearly 400 institutional repositories in the United States alone [8], many digital libraries have developed resources and policies to guide the development of these collections. However, while these collaborations help IR management by providing them numerous strategies to consider and implement, the highly contextual nature of the home institution plays a role in the level of success for these adapted strategies. Repository managers must consider variables such as the institution's unique faculty composition, the faculty members' attitudes toward self-archiving policies, institutional policies toward open-access initiatives, the technical infrastructure of the institutional repository, and their own staff resources when deciding upon a collection development strategy specifically for the IR. For the specific context of the IR, collection development is in large part accomplished through mediation practices dealing with the solicitation and collection of materials for the IR. The primary value of the method proposed in this paper lies in its ability to explore the relationship between these variables, making explicit the implied relationships, in a manner that can be understood by the repository's stakeholders, library administrators, and those external to the library.

ACM ISBN 978-1-4503-5178-2/18/06...$15.00
https://doi.org/10.1145/3197026.3197064

1.1 Literature Review

Analytic Hierarchy Process is a mathematical model for decision-making that is based on relative paired-comparisons. Developed in the 1970's by operations researcher Thomas Saaty, it has become a standard tool in engineering and business management. Only recently has it been applied to library and information science, mostly in Asia or Europe. The AHP model applies proportions of ratings of criteria in a square matrix to generate weighted scores of objects being evaluated. For example, Harshan, Chen and Shi assess the quality of library websites to identify attributes that prioritized improvements [4]. Xi, et al. employed AHP to evaluate interlibrary loan service [11]. The weights of the criteria were derived from scores by experts in the field; the measurements used for each of the levels or scores for these criteria were objective and not difficult to assess. For example, for the criterion of Condition of Library there were four attributes, one of which was Collection Quantity, for which there were seven mutually-exclusive and comprehensive levels, for which successively greater scores were applied: $< 1,000,000(2); 1.0 - 1.5M(3); 1.51M - 2.0M(4)..., > 3.51M$. The researchers then applied the aforementioned weights of the criteria to the scores, which were then produced in a cross-matrix, and finally, the sums of the subcriteria matrices were calculated for an overall quality score, Q. Based on the moderately extensive literature review, however, no applications of AHP were found within the library science and information subfields of archival studies or digital libraries.

AHP offers possibilities to institutional repository (IR) managers to solve vexing issues. The 2013 Confederation of Open Access Repositories (COAR) [7] environmental scan of open access repositories identified barriers to depositing works, including faculty awareness, motivation, time, and permissions. The authors of the report encouraged the adoption of sustainable practices to solve these: incentivization, repository integration at the institutional services, and assigning a full-time employee to oversee IR operations and assist faculty with deposit [7]. Since this report, the Coalition for Networked Information released a summary of a roundtable session rethinking the nature of institutional repositories, in response to the continual changing landscape of repository services, new platforms arising in competition with as well as complementary to IRs, and the position of IRs within broader open access strategies [3]. Solutions discussed by CNI acknowledged the variety of factors impacting how individual repositories operate. A large portion of the report acknowledges the difficulty of needing firmer strategic goals for the repository before a solution could be found to address how the IR functions within the broader open access and scholarly communication landscape, as well as how faculty needs may also shape what strategic directions are most desired by the institution's community. Local concerns drive a large number of decisions, yet the CNI roundtable reported that despite a large number of librarians present, "only a few institutions discussed assessment of repository programs and no institution present had stated goals or metrics for what constituted success" [3]. This omission points to a need among repository managers for tools to guide assessment and for formulating metrics of success. While both reports describe strategies for repositories, it is striking that the same issues exist four years after the first report, and that similar strategies are recommended in both discussions.

Shifting from the professional organizational level to individual repository managers, Ruth Tillman [10] and Ellen Dubinsky [2] conducted surveys of both repository managers and repositories respectively to examine the many variables associated with repository growth. Both studies imply that despite high-levels of IR manager outreach, faculty participation in the IR is low, and the implications demand further research into faculty buy-in and library retention in IR position. Additionally, the lack of faculty participation despite these efforts can lead to burnout or overall job dissatisfaction with repository management staff due to an increased workload with little results, and a feeling of a lack of control in increasing the effectiveness of IR services [1]. Repository staff can find support and control in their decision-making process by applying a systematic method of evaluating the multiple variables involved in developing the repository collection. The AHP decision-making model can also provide support in justifying a given decision to internal and external stakeholders. By requiring a stated goal as part of the model, repository staff are asked to specify a single goal by which these decisions can be evaluated. Stating the goal is also an essential part of establishing an assessment through by which their later efforts can be evaluated. By making tangible the often implicit factors that impact faculty participation, this model provides a method of gaining clarity regarding a repository staff's effectiveness. Applying AHP to decision-making processes in the evaluation and promotion of institutional repositories could enable repository managers to consider new ways to solicit faculty participation.

2 RESEARCH DESIGN

This project examines how the mediation practices for a repository manager's collection development strategy can be evaluated in a systematic way despite being based on multiple variables unique to the individual institution's context by adapting the AHP decision-making model for IR managers. This tests the feasibility of adapting AHP to the IR and sets a conceptual foundation for further studies to evaluate the model with a given institution and discuss its implementation. Building the AHP model consists of four processes:

(1) Deciding upon the goal which this decision should meet
(2) Selecting the criteria by which the goal will be measured for success as well as the alternative decisions that will be used to pursue the goal
(3) Weighting these criteria
(4) Comparing scores to determine the suitability of these options in meeting the overall goal.

To visually demonstrate the overall connections of the model, Figure 1 provides an example of the connections between the top-level goal, the criteria for determining a decision, and the alternative decisions available. The goal, which for the example is to prioritize the effect of mediation practices on the quality of the collection, is then broken down into measures of success as listed in Table 1 and used to score the alternative decisions listed in Table 2 in order to evaluate mediation practices against the individual institutional context so as to best meet the stated goal.

Figure 1: AHP Model Structure

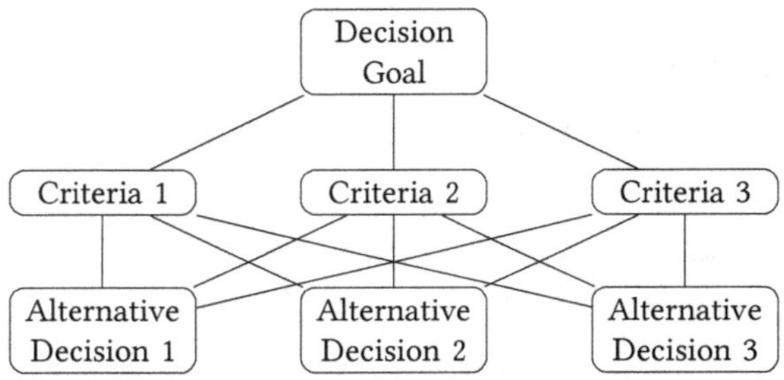

While the model for an institutional repository will have more criteria and alternative decisions than shown, Figure 1 demonstrates how each alternative is considered through each criterion listed rather than against the goal itself. In doing so, each decision is measured against the reality of its operation rather than the perception of its outcome.

For the purpose of building this model, the goal, criteria, and alternative decisions were initially derived from the authors' home institution and experiences with the institutional repository, then discussed and reframed against the broader context of recommendations for repository managers as reviewed previously. However, in adapting this model for other institutions, their own local context will guide the selection of the goal, criteria, and alternative decisions. For example, the metrics available through another institution's IR may limit or expand possible criteria for inclusion. While adapting the model will require strategic planning on the part of repository management staff at another institution, this model proves an example of what it would look like to employ this systematic process for evaluating decisions for IR collection development. Adapting the AHP model structure to fit the decisions and criteria considered by repository managers also pushes the translation of anecdotal data and qualitative landmarks of success into concrete, codified elements to be considered against each other. The goal of this project is to demystify AHP as a method for library use, and to provide a working example to ease the labor in translating IR strategies.

2.1 Criteria and Decision Selection

From the repository management perspective mediation practices are both informed by staff understanding of faculty attitudes and behavior, as well as by the technical infrastructure of the repository. As the example institution does not have a mechanism for faculty to self-submit items to the repository, instead sending items to the repository manager for preparation and uploading, mediation practices are primarily considered with processes for gathering materials for inclusion in the IR. The top level of the hierarchy is the decision goal for the repository. As stated previously, for this example the goal is to prioritize the effect of mediation practices on the quality of the collection. As reviewed previously, repository managers have a number of organizations and studies to consult for strategies to increase the repository collection. This process will allow for prioritizing strategies to understand how one might better fit the institution's context over another.

For the purpose of this example, quality was decided by the authors to consist of three criteria as seen in Table 1: dissemination of knowledge, impact on reputation, and efficiency. These criteria relate to the IR as a part of open access initiatives to increase access to knowledge, speak to the IR as a way to showcase the research output of a given institution, and include a pragmatic understanding of the technical infrastructure and human resources available for maintaining the IR, elements outlined in both the COAR and CNI reports.

Table 1: AHP criteria as measures of success for quality

AHP Level	Measure of Success
Criterion 1	Dissemination of knowledge
Sub-criterion 1.1	Rarity of items
Sub-criterion 1.2	Distribution of subjects
Sub-criterion 1.3	Direct uses
Criterion 2	Impact on reputation
Sub-criterion 2.1	Indirect use
Sub-criterion 2.2	Grant-funded research products
Criterion 3	Efficiency
Sub-criterion 3.1	Low cost per unit input

As these criteria are broad, sub-criteria have been included to further define how these criteria will be met. The dissemination of knowledge can further be understood by the rarity of items collected (whether they are only available in the repository or elsewhere, as well as risk of being lost due to technological obsolescence), whether this knowledge is highly specialized or has representation from the variety of subjects and disciplines studied by the institution, and direct uses of these items to understand their discoverability and usage. Impact on reputation focuses on the IR as a way to facilitate the application of collected items to further research, and was determined to be measured by indirect usage (such as by citations and links to items in other scholarship) as well as its relationship with facilitating funded research projects. The criterion of efficiency applies to whether a decision leads to the greatest outcomes for the least effort, particularly with the time and labor cost for item gathered.

Many repository managers and professional organizations recommend a combination of different tactics. However, including specific tactics (e.g. systematic review of faculty CVs for items to upload) as alternative decisions within the model places them in competition with each other. Specific tactics also require more specific criteria for evaluation that would crowd the model, making it less useful for broadly evaluating decisions against the overall goal. Instead, these tactics have been arranged around a leading emphasis to evaluate whether tactics in these groups would be more or less useful for meeting the goal. After evaluating the model and choosing the alternative decision, the repository manager then has a very targeted lens through which they can select tactics rather than being overwhelmed by the many recommendations. The areas of emphasis have been listed in Table 2 as alternative decisions.

Table 2: AHP alternative decisions for implementing mediation practices

AHP Level	Mediation Practice
Alternative Decision 1	System focused processes
Alternative Decision 2	Partner focused processes
Alternative Decision 3	Champion focused processes

Tactics that focus on leveraging the technical infrastructure or primarily shift the labor of gathering items onto the repository manager (such as a systematic review of all faculty CVs rather than relying on faculty to approach the repository manager) fall under system-focused processes. Strategies that involve leveraging institutional partners, such as items gathered by the Graduate School for electronic theses and dissertations or the Honors College for senior theses or honors capstone works, would fall under partner-focused processes. Champion-focused processes rely on recruiting selected individuals across campus and using this network to promote and gather items for the IR.

Stating each criterion's relationship to the goal also helps stakeholders understand how large a role it plays in measuring the value of the decision in relation to the goal. If the weights assigned to the criteria need to be adjusted during the consistency analysis, stakeholders will need to understand the relationship of the criteria to the goal and possibly consider whether the goal itself should be modified.

2.2 Implementation

After constructing the hierarchy, repository staff can weight the criteria to codify the relationships between hierarchy levels in the decision-making process. Following the approach of Nakatani and Chuang [6], AHP is implemented through the following steps:

(1) Create a pairwise comparison matrix with a scale of 1-9 to compare the criteria and/or subcriteria and assign a value demonstrating their importance in relation to the others in terms of meeting the goal.

(2) After completing all comparisons for the model, normalize the scores to obtain the eigenvector of the matrix.
(3) Repeat this process for the next level down, with an additional pair-wise comparison matrix comparing each alternative with respect to the sub-criterion at the next higher level.
(4) Once all comparisons have been weighted and calculated, synthesize these matrices to understand the overall priorities.

AHP itself is not a complicated procedure. The bulk of the work for repository staff is translating the context and resources of their own institution into hierarchical levels and then weighting the criteria as appropriate for their institution.

As this model contains a large degree of subjective judgment, some comparisons may seem inconsistent. Whereas one criteria, such the low cost per unit input, may be deemed more important than the rarity of the content collected, it may be less important than direct usage, but not necessarily by the same amount. In their summary of AHP, Mu and Pereyra-Rojas [5] recommend that users calculate consistency, using a consistency ratio in which the consistency index of the created matrix is compared to the consistency index of a random-like matrix. Saaty [9] has provided values for the random-like matrix, which is the average consistency index of 500 randomly filled matrices. A consistency ratio of 0.10 or less indicates a reasonably consistent matrix. Scores higher than 0.10 should be re-evaluated to locate areas of increased inconsistency [5].

Mu and Pereyra-Rojas [5] also recommend a sensitivity analysis to give further context to decisions made using AHP. For this analysis, another pair-wise comparison matrix is created, but with different weighted values to represent a what-if scenario. For example, all weighted values may be made the same to consider how the alternatives rank with all factors considered equal. This can be used to demonstrate to administration how the nature of an individual institution's context can influence values, particularly if the decision recommended with all factors weighted equally was determined to be unsuccessful in the past.

3 APPLICATIONS

The flexible nature of the criteria and alternative decisions allow this model to be applied in a number of different scenarios for repository management staff. While this project is concerned with collection development through mediation practices, it is not limited to these types of decisions. As more repository managers learn and share new methods for increasing collection engagement, the authors believe this will be a useful tool for testing the applicability of these methods at other institutions before expending the time and resources on implementation. As outlined here, this model can be used as constructed and recalculated according to another institution's priorities. However, it is also flexible enough to be repopulated with another institution's own criteria for their goal. For example, it could be re-purposed to evaluate marketing strategies suggested for increasing faculty awareness of the IR. After a decision has been implemented, its relative success or failure can also be used to adjust the AHP model. Ultimately, this model is recommended to aid repository staff in justifying their decisions through a systematic evaluation of the decisions available, and the strengths and weaknesses of the institution's existing resources.

4 CONCLUSIONS

Institutional repository managers require a complex understanding of both their own resources and the larger campus context to best to build the collection. The highly contextual nature of their work means that practices shared among managers are not likely to have consistent results at multiple institutions. Applying AHP to the multifaceted nature of repository collection building attempts to provide a standard procedure for how managers can make decisions for collection-planning and building based upon their context, rather than upon anticipated success based on a different institution's outcomes. AHP enables managers to balance, through weighted criteria, degrees of contexts and the goal of their respective institutions toward planning around needs and resources. The AHP approach, with weighted criteria, helps IR managers rank relevance of current strengths and desired goals toward repository planning and decision-making.

REFERENCES

[1] L. Christian. 2015. A Passion Deficit: Occupational Burnout and the New Librarian: A Recommendation Report. *The Southeastern Librarian* 62, 4 (2015), 2–11. https://digitalcommons.kennesaw.edu/seln/vol62/iss4/2/
[2] Ellen Dubinsky. 2014. A Current Snapshot of Institutional Repositories: Growth Rate, Disciplinary Content and Faculty Contributions. *Journal of Librarianship and Scholarly Communication* 2, 3 (2014). http://dx.doi.org/10.7710/2162-3309.1167
[3] Coalition for Networked Information. 2017. Rethinking Institutional Repository Strategies. (2017). https://www.cni.org/wp-content/uploads/2017/05/CNI-rethinking-irs-exec-rndtbl.report.S17.v1.pdf
[4] Ramanayaka Kokila Harshan, Xianqiao Chen, and Bing Shi. 2016. Analytic Hierarchy Process (AHP) based model for assessing performance quality of library websites. *Information Technology Journal* 16, 1 (December 2016), 35–43. https://doi.org/10.3923/itj.2017.35.43
[5] Enrique Mu and Milagros Pereyra-Rojas. 2017. *Practical Decision Making*. SpringerBriefs in Operation Research, Vol. 2. Springer International Publishing, New York, Chapter Understanding the Analytic Hierarchy Process, 7–22. https://doi.org/10.1007/978-3-319-33861-3_2
[6] Kazuo Nakatani and Ta-Tao Chuang. 2011. A web analytics tool selection method: an analytical hierarchy process approach. *Internet Research* 21, 2 (January 2011), 171–186. https://doi.org/10.1108/10662241111123757
[7] Confederation of Open Access Repositories. 2013. Incentives, Integration, and Mediation: Sustainable practices for populating repositories report. (2013). https://www.coar-repositories.org/news-media/publications/sustainable-practices-for-populating-repositories-report/
[8] Directory of Open Access Repositories. 2018. List of Repositories - United States. (2018). http://www.opendoar.org/countrylist.php?cContinent=North%20America#United%20States
[9] Thomas L. Saaty. 2012. *Decision Making for Leaders: The Analytic Hierarchy Process for Decisions in a Complex World* (third revised ed.). RWS Publications, Pittsburgh, PA.
[10] R. K. Tillman. 2017. Where Are We Now? Survey on Rates of Faculty Self-Deposit in Institutional Repositories. *Journal of Librarianship and Scholarly Communication* 5, 1 (December 2017), 1–27. https://doi.org/10.7710/2162-3309.2203
[11] Qingkui Xi, Qian Zhang, Feng Ni, Guiting Cha, and Ping Bao. 2015. Promoting ILL/DD within the Jiangsu Academic Library & Information System in China by small consortia. *Interlending & Document Supply* 43, 4 (August 2015), 182–188. https://doi.org/10.1108/ILDS-08-2015-0024

Computer-Assisted Crowd Transcription of the U.S. Census with Personalized Assignments for Better Accuracy and Participation

Douglas J. Kennard
Historic Journals
dougk@hjournals.com

ABSTRACT

Our *Open Genealogy Data* census transcription project is intended to make valuable census data more readily available to researchers, digital libraries, and others. We use automatic handwriting recognition to bootstrap our census database, facilitating searches even in the early stages of the project while manual transcription is underway. We provide a web-based interface for crowd-sourced transcription of the census to complete and correct the database.

In an effort to improve both volunteer participation and transcription accuracy, we provide default transcription assignments based on transcribers' own genealogical family lines or geographical locations to improve the likelihood that the transcribers will be familiar with the names and places in their assignments.

CCS CONCEPTS

• **Information systems** → **Crowdsourcing**; • **Applied computing** → Digital libraries and archives; Document analysis;

KEYWORDS

Collaborative transcription; census; open data; genealogy

ACM Reference Format:

Douglas J. Kennard. 2018. Computer-Assisted Crowd Transcription of the U.S. Census with Personalized Assignments for Better Accuracy and Participation. In *JCDL '18: The 18th ACM/IEEE Joint Conference on Digital Libraries, June 3–7, 2018, Fort Worth, TX, USA.* ACM, New York, NY, USA, 4 pages. https://doi.org/10.1145/3197026.3197067

1 BACKGROUND

U.S. Census data is used for a variety of research in many fields by numerous organizations, government agencies, and others. Census records are also valuable to individuals who are researching their own genealogy and family history. Access to census records and data would be a valuable addition to many existing digital libraries.

The National Archives and Records Administration (NARA) has released microfilm copies of each census conducted more than 72 years ago.[1] However, no complete digital transcription of any census has been provided by NARA due to the enormity of the task and the high costs associated with it. There can be millions of pages of records in even a single census. The 1930 census has 2,667 rolls of microfilm and a roll typically has more than 1,000 census pages. As seen in Figure 1, a single page holds up to 50 rows of handwritten information, and 32 columns of data may be filled for each row.

Some large, well-funded entities have gone to the expense of scanning the microfilm and transcribing the handwritten information into databases that can be searched online either for free or as part of paid subscription services.[2] Access to the data through these organizations' search portals is convenient and adequate for researching relatively small numbers of records, but for research or innovation that requires unfettered access to the entire corpus of census data, the search portals are not sufficient. Due to the high cost of creating a census database and the competitive advantage gained by having data others do not, it is understandable that the databases as a whole are not openly shared by these entities, and are available for use only with special permission and restrictions on their use that prevent dissemination of the data. However many digital libraries, researchers, organizations, businesses, and individuals could benefit from access to entire census databases.

The USGenWeb Census Project[3] was started in 1997 with the goal of transcribing census records directly from microfilm to make the digital transcriptions freely available, but after 21 years has only transcribed a fraction of the records.

In recent years, the Allen County Public Library in Indiana and the Internet Archive collaborated to scan census microfilms and make the digital images available. [10] However, no digital transcription of the census data contained within the images is available.

Clawson et al. [4] present work toward automatic processing of census images, and Clawson and Barrett [3, 5] developed a semi-automated, trainable census indexing tool prototype. However, these proof-of-concept systems have not been applied at production scale to actually transcribe the census and release a census database.

Some projects do exist for making census data available in other countries, for example the Netherlands and the United Kingdom[4].

2 OPEN GENEALOGY DATA PROJECT

The goal of our *Open Genealogy Data* project[5] is to make historical data that is relevant to genealogy more readily available to researchers, libraries, and others in digital format. In this paper, we discuss the first project, which is aimed at transcription of the U.S. Census, beginning with the census of 1930.

[1] The 1940 census was released as digital images scanned from microfilm

[2] Well-known examples include FamilySearch.org and Ancestry.com

[3] www.usgwcensus.org

[4] www.volkstellingen.nl and freecen.org.uk

[5] Our *Open Genealogy Data* project website is at URL OpenGenData.org

ACM ISBN 978-1-4503-5178-2/18/06...$15.00
https://doi.org/10.1145/3197026.3197067

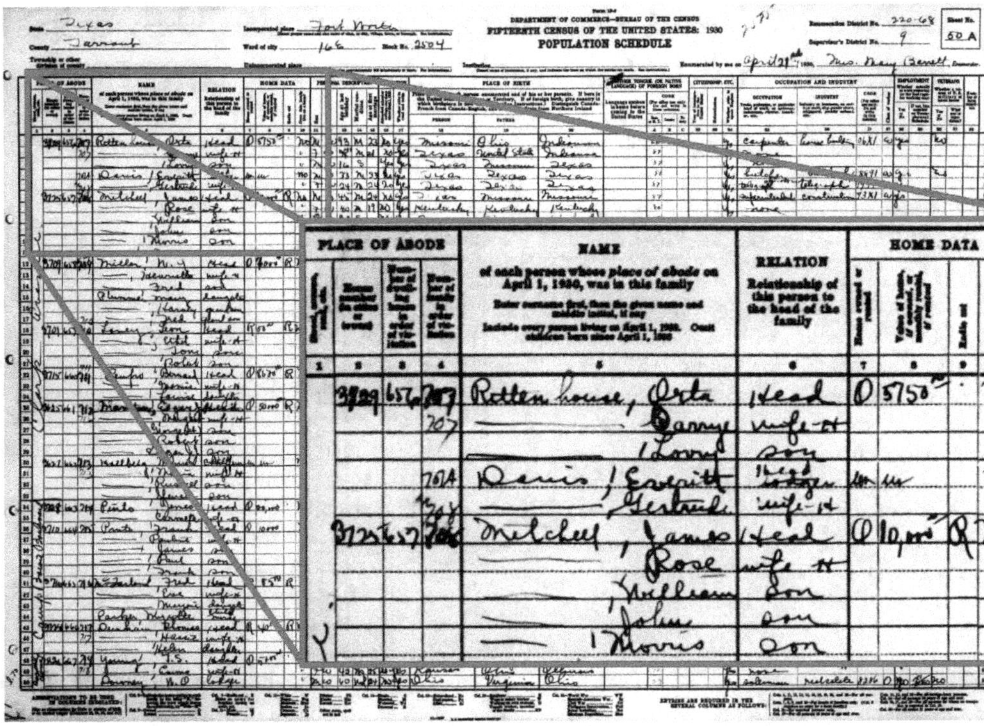

Figure 1: One of approximately 2.5 million page images from the 1930 census. 50 rows x 32 columns of handwritten data covering part of an area next to the UNT Health Science Center conference venue in Fort Worth, TX. Each row contains personal information for one individual (name, age, birth place, citizenship, occupation, etc.) and families or people dwelling in the same location are grouped. Other information such as street name and house number are also included.

2.1 Automatic Handwriting Recognition (HR)

In the past, automatic handwriting recognition (HR) accuracy was very low except in constrained tasks such as postal address [12] and bank check processing. However, HR accuracy has consistently improved, [1, 2, 7, 13] and significant advances have been made recently with the proliferation of deep learning methods. For example, Wigington et al. [14, 15] significantly improved accuracy with data augmentation in an HR system based on image-based sequence recognition work by Shi et al. [11]. Some HR work by Thibauld et al. [9] has been applied to census records, although resulting databases are not publicly available.

We use Censcript AI[6] document image processing and HR systems to preprocess census images, align the census fields (for both manual and automatic transcription), and to perform automatic HR to bootstrap our census database. While the HR does not yet reach human-level recognition accuracy, it allows us to provide a searchable— albeit not completely correct— database while manual transcription is still in its very early stages. Preliminary tests with a small amount of transcribed data suggest we can achieve 92% character recognition accuracy on names that are confidently transcribed by humans. Other more constrained fields (gender, relation, birth place, ...) will almost certainly be recognized with even higher accuracy. As transcription continues, we anticipate that the accuracy of the HR system will improve due to the additional data available for training the HR system. We also anticipate that improvements will continue in the HR technology itself.

[6]censcript.com (disclosure: the author is also affiliated with Censcript AI)

2.2 Crowd-Sourcing Census Transcription Tool

Our web-based tool for census transcription allows volunteers to begin immediately without long-term commitment or significant training. It divides transcription into small, focused assignments that can be prioritized. For example, instead of asking volunteers to transcribe all data on a page, we focus first on transcribing the columns most useful in training the HR system and in finding specific people within the census: Name, Relation, Sex, Age, and Age when married (Figure 2-a). Assignments for other columns can be given as needed or as the project progresses. Column-based assignments are in line with research by Clawson [5] that indicates there are benefits to working down columns instead of across rows.

For volunteers more fully-invested in the project, assignments include recording header information such as the enumeration district (ED) and sheet number for each page image on a microfilm roll (Figure 2-b).

In addition to allowing us to focus transcription efforts on the highest-priority information at any given time, small assignments also require less time to complete and less preliminary training, and are more easily adaptable for mobile devices. We anticipate that more volunteers will participate in the project with small tasks that are more convenient and less of a commitment.

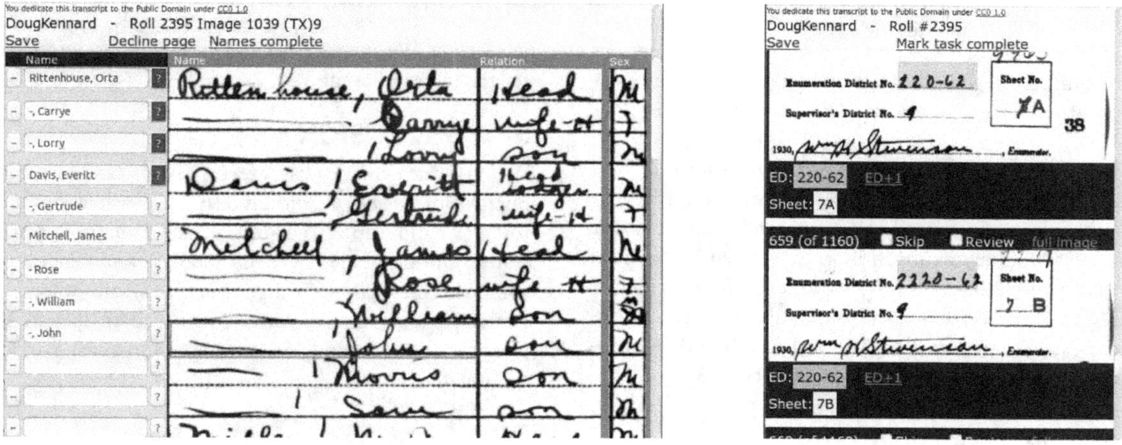

(a) (b)

Figure 2: Transcription assignments are split into smaller, prioritized tasks. a) Name, relation, sex, and age columns are high priority for finding individuals. Here we show name transcription in progress. b) Enumeration Districts and Sheet numbers are also important and are most often ordered incrementally, allowing the computer to do most of the work even though they are often written incorrectly.

Volunteers transcribe under the Creative Commons CC0 1.0 Public Domain Dedication. This prevents complications like those experienced by other projects such as OpenStreetMap[7] when they needed to change from one open license to another.

2.3 Computer-Assisted Transcription

Instead of requiring volunteers to type in all information, we reduce volunteers' workload for some tasks by predicting the values. For example, the sheet number (Figure 2-b) usually increments predictably within a given enumeration district. We automatically increment sheet numbers so the user can quickly look through the images, only making changes for sheets that do not follow the expected order. Similarly, enumeration districts are often in numerical order, so the user can just click on "ED+1" to designate the start of a new enumeration district instead of manually typing in the new enumeration district number.

We predict values for many other fields using automatic HR results. These predictions can be used to auto-suggest values, to autocomplete as the user types, or to highlight probable mistakes.

3 PERSONALIZED ASSIGNMENTS

It is easy to find records that are incorrectly transcribed in existing census search portals. This is the case even in databases for which multiple people were used to validate each transcription entry, because some census enumerators had very poor penmanship that makes it difficult to come to a consensus on what they wrote.

In the author's personal experience, it is easier to decipher poor penmanship for names that are familiar, and significantly easier when the transcriber has knowledge about the named people or places (apart from just the handwriting itself).

We allow transcribers the option to choose their own assignments, but default assignments are based on distance to the transcriber and on the transcriber's own ancestral lines (if available).

[7]openstreetmap.org

3.1 Location-Based Personalization

Many given names, surnames, and place names are more common in some areas than in others due to factors such as demographics, culture, and the predominant ancestry of the people who settled the area or moved there later. A person from one part of the country may be completely unfamiliar with a name that is quite in another part of the country. A Polish surname that is common in northern Indiana, for example, might be completely unfamiliar to a volunteer in Idaho.

We use browser location data (if the user allows) or rough geolocation estimates from IP addresses to provide transcription assignments as close to the transcriber as available. We assume that transcribers will, on average, be more familiar with names of people and places common in their own vicinity— and more likely to recognize names that are hard to read— than a random transcriber from a distant location would be. We also believe that users will tend to be more engaged and interested in transcribing data for locations that are near them. As the project progresses, it will be possible to use A/B testing to verify these assumptions.

3.2 Genealogy-Based Personalization

The Historic Journals project[8] allows users to archive digital artifacts such as scanned copies of personal diaries and letters of their ancestors, and create links between the artifacts and a genealogical database. [8] Users who have their genealogy available in the database often also have sources listed that document where information about their ancestors was found, such as which census record or death record contained the information.

For census transcribers who log in through the Historic Journals website and have their genealogy information available, we attempt to personalize transcription assignments by assigning census sheets that have the transcribers' own ancestors listed on them.

[8]The Historic Journals project started as a student project at Brigham Young University and now continues independently at URL hjournals.com

Currently we do this by checking for sources referencing the census. In the future we may also attempt to determine candidate census pages by comparing the automatic HR results directly with names and locations of ancestors and the ancestors' immediate family members who are listed in the genealogy database and were likely to be found in the same household as the ancestor.

Transcribers who know who their ancestors are should be able to recognize the names more easily and accurately than random transcribers, and will likely be much more interested in the transcription assignment. Personal experience and empirical evidence indicate that this is the case, but it will be possible to use A/B testing to verify these assumptions quantitatively as the project progresses, just like for the assumptions made in Section 3.1.

3.3 Search-Based Personalization

A final method of personalization that we propose is based on records that users explicitly search for through the search portal. When a user views a record that has only been indexed with automatic HR and has not yet been manually transcribed, we will offer the opportunity for the user to transcribe it or review it for necessary corrections. The fact that the user has searched for the record implies both an interest in its content and familiarity with the names used in the search query.

4 DISCUSSION

Hansen et al.[6] found that human census transcription accuracy is affected by the transcriber's native language in relation to the language being transcribed. They saw significantly lower accuracy for names and places transcribed from French Canadian census records by mostly English speakers. These findings seem to lend support to our own hypothesis that being familiar with names and places will generally improve accuracy. We have only recently begun manual transcription, but as we accumulate more data it will be possible to verify whether a similar trend of lower accuracy holds for distant locations within the U.S. as we believe it will.

Hansen et al.[6] also found that accuracy improves as the experience (number of completed transcriptions) of a volunteer increases. If we are successful in our efforts to provide our volunteers with assignments that are more engaging to them (their own ancestors, locality, or areas of interest), an added benefit may be that users transcribe more, resulting in higher accuracy due to the additional experience, besides any improvements due to the advantage of contextual knowledge they may have about their specific assignments.

While the primary goal of our project is simply to make census data more readily available, the reason behind the goal is to facilitate further innovation using the data. We know that it will result in a massive amount of labeled handwriting examples written by tens of thousands of different people, which can be used to train handwriting recognition systems. That in itself will be useful for future automatic transcription of additional records and datasets.

Once the census database is complete, it will likely be possible to match much of the population from one census to the next, providing a resource for more detailed studies of population migration, economic changes, or other types of research.

While we anticipate these few possible uses for the census data, it is hard to predict the broader impact that the data may have as others use it for research and innovation in fields that we have not guessed at. We are eager to find out what other uses may be found for the data in the future.

5 CONCLUSION

We introduce the crowd-sourced census transcription project of our *Open Genealogy Data* initiative. We use a combination of automatic handwriting recognition and computer-assisted manual transcription to build a census database and make it more readily available to researchers, digital libraries, and others. We also personalize transcribers' assignments based on factors such as their location and genealogy in an effort to increase participation and accuracy.

REFERENCES

[1] Roman Bertolami and Horst Bunke. 2008. Hidden Markov Model-Based Ensemble Methods for Offline Handwritten Text Line Recognition. *Pattern Recognition (PR)* 41, 11 (2008), 3452–3460.

[2] Horst Bunke. 2003. Recognition of Cursive Roman Handwriting- Past, Present and Future. In *7th International Conference on Document Analysis and Recognition (ICDAR 2003)*, Vol. 1. Edinburgh, Scotland, 448–459.

[3] Robert Clawson and William Barrett. 2015. Intelligent Indexing: A Semi-Automated, Trainable System for Field Labeling. In *Document Recognition and Retrieval XXII (DRR 2015)*. SPIE IS&T Electronic Images, Vol. 9402 94020A-1, San Francisco, California.

[4] Robert Clawson, Kevin Bauer, Glen Chidester, Milan Phontsch, Douglas Kennard, Jongha Ryu, and William Barrett. 2013. Automated Recognition and Extraction of Tabular Fields for the Indexing of Census Records. In *Document Recognition and Retrieval XX (DRR 2013)*. SPIE IS&T Electronic Images, Vol. 8658 86580J, San Francisco, California.

[5] Robert T. Clawson. 2014. *Intelligent Indexing: A Semi-Automated, Trainable System for Field Labeling.* Master's thesis. Brigham Young University, Provo, Utah.

[6] Derek L. Hansen, Patrick J. Schone, Douglas Corey, Matthew Reid, and Jake Gehring. 2013. Quality Control Mechanisms for Crowdsourcing: Peer Review, Arbitration, & Expertise at FamilySearch Indexing. In *Conference on Computer Supported Cooperative Work (CSCW 2013)*. San Antonio, Texas, 649–660.

[7] Douglas J. Kennard. 2013. *Warping-Based Approach to Offline Handwriting Recognition.* Ph.D. Dissertation. Brigham Young University, Provo, Utah.

[8] Douglas J. Kennard, William B. Lund, and Bryan S. Morse. 2009. Improving Historical Research by Linking Digital Library Information to a Global Genealogical Database. In *Joint Conference on Digital Libraries (JCDL 2009)*. Austin, Texas.

[9] Thibauld Nion, Farès Menasri, Jérôme Louradour, Cédric Sibade, Thomas Retornaz, Pierre-Yves Métaireau, and Christopher Kermorvant. 2013. Handwritten Information Extraction from Historical Census Documents. In *12th IAPR International Conference on Document Analysis and Recognition (ICDAR 2013)*. Washington, DC.

[10] Alexis Rossi. 2010. 1790-1930 U.S. Census Records Available Free. https://blog.archive.org/2010/12/22/1790-1930-u-s-census-records-available-free/. (2010).

[11] Baoguang Shi, Xiang Bai, and Cong Yao. 2015. An End-to-End Trainable Neural Network for Image-based Sequence Recognition and Its Application to Scene Text Recognition. *CoRR* abs/1507.05717 (2015).

[12] Sargur N. Srihari and Edward J. Kuebert. 1997. Integration of Hand-Written Address Interpretation Technology into the United States Postal Service Remote Computer Reader System. In *4th International Conference on Document Analysis and Recognition (ICDAR 1997)*, Vol. 2. Ulm, Germany, 892–896.

[13] Alessandro Vinciarelli, Samy Bengio, and Horst Bunke. 2004. Offline Recognition of Unconstrained Handwritten Texts Using HMMs and Statistical Language Models. *IEEE Transactions on Pattern Analysis and Machine Intelligence (TPAMI)* 26, 6 (jun 2004), 709–720.

[14] Curtis Wigington. 2017. Geometric Distortion for Handwriting Recognition. In *BYU Family History Technology Workshop (FHTW 2017)*. Provo, Utah.

[15] Curtis Wigington, Seth Stewart, Brian Davis, Bill Barrett, Brian Price, and Scott Cohen. 2017. Data Augmentation for Recognition of Handwritten Words and Lines using a CNN-LSTM Network. In *14th IAPR International Conference on Document Analysis and Recognition (ICDAR 2017)*. Kyoto, Japan, P2–14.

Prioritizing and Scheduling Conferences for Metadata Harvesting in dblp

Mandy Neumann
Philipp Schaer
TH Köln
firstname.lastname@th-koeln.de

Christopher Michels
Ralf Schenkel
Trier University, dblp
(michelsc,schenkel)@uni-trier.de

ABSTRACT

Maintaining literature databases and online bibliographies is a core responsibility of metadata aggregators such as digital libraries. In the process of monitoring all the available data sources the question arises which data source should be prioritized. Based on a broad definition of information quality we are looking for different ways to find the best fitting and most promising conference candidates to harvest next. We evaluate different conference ranking features by using a pseudo-relevance assessment and a component-based evaluation of our approach.

KEYWORDS

Bibliography, dblp, digital libraries, metadata harvesting, ranking, pseudo-relevance, scheduling

ACM Reference Format:
Mandy Neumann, Christopher Michels, Philipp Schaer, and Ralf Schenkel. 2018. Prioritizing and Scheduling Conferences for Metadata Harvesting in dblp. In *JCDL '18: The 18th ACM/IEEE Joint Conference on DigitalLibraries, June 3–7, 2018, Fort Worth, TX, USA.* ACM, New York, NY, USA, 4 pages. https://doi.org/10.1145/3197026.3197069

1 INTRODUCTION

Monitoring and maintaining databases and data sources are core responsibilities of metadata aggregators such as digital libraries. Metadata provided by publishers at specific intervals might be overdue which needs to result in some notification. Similarly, self-sufficient metadata harvesting relies on scheduling or event tracking and prognosis, for example. Integrating such heterogeneous sources is naturally error-prone. The various data sources involved need to be continuously monitored and maintained.

The database publisher *dblp computer science bibliography* (dblp) provides approx. 4 million publication records originating from more than 4,000 conferences and 1,500 journals. These records are provided by sources varying from emminent commercial publishers to isolated alternating web sources (as of 01/2018). Acquiring metadata from this extent of sources mainly involves data provided by publishers as well as highly customized harvesting software, so-called wrappers. However, data sets might be provided at arbitrary intervals or wrappers might not be successful in retrieving the expected metadata. Several questions arise from these problems: 1) Which data are expected next and when? 2) Are they missing and overdue? 3) Which source usually provides the metadata? 4) Is there an alternative source? 5) Is there a ready solution for harvesting the data? 6) Which are the most urgent? These questions illustrate the expected costs of finding a solution to missing data in the acquisition process.

Simply crawling every possible data source every night is no solution as the conceptional and technical costs are too high. At the scale of dblp, filtering data deliveries, leveraging metadata harvesting, and other challenges of database maintenance require some form of automated prioritization in order to be more efficient: Which missing data from which data source are the most urgent?

A similar issue is known for web crawlers where it is crucial to prioritize and rank the most promising web pages for the following web crawling process. Different strategies have been proposed, such as pre-calculating a PageRank and sorting the crawling candidates according to [2]. Other approaches include temporal web link-based rankings to estimate a better time-dependent web page authority compared to PageRank [3]. While these strategies help to achieve the objective of crawling important pages early in the process, applying these strategies for the use case of dblp does not work as we miss the necessary information, such as the linking between conferences. Recent work on dblp data has implemented conference recommenders which cluster and rank conferences based on author-conference similarities and co-authorship networks [4].

The research question is to find a prioritization mechanism for conference series in order to get a ranked list with regard to their expected urgency for the data acquisition process. A highly ranked conference in this list is a conference which the dblp editorial staff should include in the next data harvesting or import routine. The need for smart, prioritized metadata harvesting is most prominent with conference series and their dynamic event structure in comparison with journals or other publication venues.

Based on a broad definition and idea of information quality and the question which features are necessary to measure the goodness or quality of a data source [1, 6] we are looking for different ways to find the best fitting and most promising conference candidates. We evaluate different conference ranking features by using a pseudo-relevance assessment and a component-based evaluation of our approach.

2 RANKING OF CONFERENCE CANDIDATES

Prioritizing which conference is checked next for new proceedings worth adding to a literature database at a given date is a typical

JCDL '18, June 3–7, 2018, Fort Worth, TX, USA

ACM ISBN 978-1-4503-5178-2/18/06...$15.00
https://doi.org/10.1145/3197026.3197069

ranking problem: the set of conferences needs to be ranked in descending order according to their relevance for the database.

The following notations pertain to the description and evaluation of all scoring factors for the ranking of conferences: We consider the set of conferences C, where a conference (JCDL, SIGIR, etc.) $c \in C$ is a set of conference events (events) $E(c) = \{e_1, \dots, e_n\}$ archived in the bibliography. The date of an event is denoted by $d(e)$. Dates $d = (m, y)$ are represented as pairs of a month m (numeric) and a year y. The difference of two dates is the number of months between the dates. Adding δ months to a date yields a date that is δ months later. The function $year(d)$ yields the year, $month(d)$ yields the month of date d. The current date is denoted by NOW.

For each conference, the characteristic interval $\delta_{year}(c)$ is estimated as the median of distance of the years of the five most recent subsequent events in $E(c)$ (or of all events if c has less than five events). Additionally, we define the month $m(c)$ in which events usually take place as the most frequent (mode) $month(d(e))$ of all events in $E(c)$. Finally, we determine the characteristic delay $\delta_{month}(c)$ of a conference as the median of the delays in months between the conference event and the entry of its proceedings into the database. By analogy with $\delta_{year}(c)$, we use up to the five most recent events in $E(c)$ for calculation.

2.1 Scoring Conference Candidates

In order to score and rank the inclusion candidates for conference events, we define the following intuitive and comprehensible criteria. Determining the relevance of a conference to a bibliography depends to a large extent on the fact that conference events usually occur on a regular basis. Consequently, observing and evaluating historical data of database maintenance is crucial to a relevance-based ranking for conferences. Additionally, external regional conference ratings, the internationality of a conference, a citation score, and a prominence score are integrated as boosting factors in the relevance ranking for conferences, whereas presumably discontinued conferences receive a penalizing factor. We describe in section 3 how these scores can be computed for dblp. Note that not all information necessary for these factors might be available for a given bibliographic database.

Delay. From the entry date $d_n(c)$ of the last known event of a conference, we can estimate the expected entry date of the next event in this series $d_{n+1}(c) = (m(c), year(d_n(c)) + \delta_{year}(c)) + \delta_{month}(c)$. For any given point in time, we can then determine $\Delta(c) = \text{NOW} - d_{n+1}$ to see if and how long the conference c is already presumably overdue. We derive the following base scoring factor $w_{delay}(c)$ from $\Delta(c)$, ranking conferences with a smaller delay, for which the expected next entries are more recent, higher than those with a greater delay.

$$w_{delay}(c) = \begin{cases} 4 & 0 \leq \Delta(c) \leq 3 \\ 3 & 4 \leq \Delta(c) \leq 7 \\ 2 & 8 \leq \Delta(c) \leq 11 \\ 1 & 12 \leq \Delta(c) \\ 0 & \Delta(c) < 0 \end{cases} \quad (1)$$

To calculate the score for a conference, this base scoring factor is multiplied by one of the following weighting factors.

Conference ratings. Existing conference ratings such as *CORE Computing Research & Education*[1] (CORE) rate conferences to model their importance for the research communities involved. Such external ratings might not cover the entire set of conferences for a given database because they are usually subject to a specific regional, scientific, or other type of focus. Regardless of their scope, combining these ratings serves the purpose of boosting the most important conferences for all rating-specific perspectives. If possible, existing rating classes are integrated and mapped to numeric classes. Conferences without any rating values are attributed to the residue class 0. Then, $r(c)$ is the average of all numeric rating values attributed to c, with the corresponding weighting factor:

$$w_r(c) := 1 + \frac{r(c)}{max_C r(c)} \quad (2)$$

Internationality. We define the internationality of a conference $i(c)$ as the number of distinct countries where the conference has taken place. The idea of this factor is that it reflects how often the conference venue is changing locations across countries. We argue that conferences which are more international in this sense should be prioritized against local ones. By analogy with the rating factor $w_r(c)$, we put $i(c)$ in relation to the whole collection to obtain the internationality weighting factor:

$$w_i(c) := 1 + \frac{i(c)}{max_C i(c)} \quad (3)$$

Discontinued conferences. The development of conferences and their respective events over time constitutes a dynamic process. Conferences might have been merged, or co-located with others, or they might be discontinued entirely. Database publishers might have dismissed particular conferences, i.e., due to a change of scope. In either case, it is impractical to rank these conferences high because they are dozens of months overdue. Consequently, suspended conferences are reflected by the penalizing weighting factor:

$$w_d(c) := \left(1 + \frac{\#years\ since\ last\ entry}{\delta_{year}(c)}\right)^{-2} \quad (4)$$

Citations. In the same way incoming links account for the popularity of a web page [6], the number of papers by which a given paper is cited can be used to measure its influence on the research community. With $cit(e, y)$ denoting the number of incoming citations in year y to all papers from event e as well as the number of papers $p(e)$ for the same event, we compute the average number of citations per paper across the events of a conference $E(c)$ with $Y = \{y | \exists e \in E(c) : y = year(d(e)) \wedge y < year(\text{NOW})\}$:

$$w_{cit}(c) = 1 + \frac{cit(c)}{max_C cit(c)}, \ cit(c) = \sum_{y \in Y} \sum_{e \in E(c)} \frac{cit(e, y)}{p(e)} \quad (5)$$

Author Prominence. An authors' scientific prominence is commonly measured by the number of their publications. Thus, events with many frequently published scientists are preferred over events which have published rather unknown authors. For each event e we may know its number of distinct authors $a(e)$ and $p(a, y)$ as the number of records per author a until year y. Equation 6 shows how the prominence score is computed for an individual event.

[1] http://portal.core.edu.au/conf-ranks

Table 1: Example values for conference features used in the rankings, computed for December 2016.

c	$\Delta(c)$	w_{delay}	w_r	w_i	w_d	w_{cit}	w_{prm}
jcdl	3	4	1.88	1.192	0.250	1.029	1.312
tpdl	0	4	1.63	1.577	0.250	1.024	1.352
icadl	0	4	1.75	1.385	0.250	1.009	1.347
dl	146	1	1.00	1.039	0.004	1.091	1.445

We define the author prominence weighting factor as in 7. Events with less than 10 publications are excluded due to too much noise, resulting in the subset $\overline{E}(c) = \{e_i | e_i \in E(c) \wedge p(e_i) >= 10\}$ of $E(c)$.

$$prm(e) = \frac{1}{a(e)} \sum_{i=1}^{a(e)} p(a_i, year(\text{NOW}) - 1) \quad (6)$$

$$w_{prm}(c) = 1 + \frac{prm(c)}{max_C prm(c)}, \; prm(c) = \frac{1}{|\overline{E}(c)|} \sum_{e \in \overline{E}(c)} prm(e) \quad (7)$$

3 DATA SETS

The evaluation of these scoring factors for the conferences of dblp is based on the following data sets. A different literature database might require additional, compatible sources of information in order for the scoring factors above to be applied. We explain how external ratings and a citation graph have been consolidated with the dblp database to perform and evaluate the conference candidate scoring described above.

dblp. For each modification of a record the updated metadata is persisted in dblp with a timestamp. Thus, the entry date for each proceedings record is obtained from its earliest modification date. Our analyses are based on the dblp as of 2018/01/04, containing more than 4 million distinct records (excluding author homepages). Of those, about 36,000 records are proceedings of approx. 4,300 different conferences. As the conferences' coverage varies among the computed weighting factors, a conference which is not covered by a specific factor receives the neutral weight 1 for that factor.

Additional information for the evaluation of the weighting factors can be acquired from dblp records. All forms of the function $p()$ and $a()$ above constitute simple queries based on person, record, and conference indentifiers as well as time-range restrictions. The country of an event is parsed from the geographical information[2] in the titles of proceedings. Similarly, the date $d(e) = (m, y)$ of an event is extracted from its title if possible. As this date information is crucial to our scorings, we filter the available data sets to retain only those 4,129 conferences where this information is available for at least one event record.

Conference ratings. The Australian rating CORE in 2008 and 2017 as well as the results of the conference rating in [5] from 2008 serve as the basis for the conference rating weighting factor. Their combined rating classes are $\{A*, A, B, C, Other\}$. For $r(c)$ the rating values across the 3 ranked lists are mapped to their equivalent from the numeric rating classes $\{4, 3, 2, 1, 0\}$. Thus, $r(c)$ is higher than 0 for 824 conferences.

Citations. To enhance the dblp data set with citation information, 166,192,182 publication records from the *Microsoft Academic Graph*[3] (MAG) and their relationships are mapped to their equivalents in dblp. About 3.6 million records occurring in MAG were successfully matched based on their DOIs and titles. To compute $cit(e, y)$ for 4,210 conferences with matching records in dblp and MAG, the incoming citations are counted for each conference and each year of citation starting from 1970. These numbers are based on the MAG as of 2017/06/09.

4 EVALUATION

In order to evaluate the performance of our rankings, relevance judgments for all conferences are needed. As it is impossible to get human judgments for thousands of conferences, we resorted to pseudo-relevance. Our graded pseudo-relevance is interval-based, inverted and takes into account only the delay between the entry month of the latest record and the current month which we refer to as $\delta_{month}(c)$. Conferences where the newest event had been added more recently to the dataset (small delay) receive a higher relevance rating than those with a larger delay. The pseudo-relevance scores $rel_p(c)$ are assigned in the same way as the delay-based scoring factor $w_{delay}(c)$, see eq. 1, with $\delta_{month}(c)$ instead of $\Delta(c)$.

After establishing the relevance judgments, we perform a leave-out evaluation. First, all the latest entries of 2016 are ignored. For each month of 2016 and each conference, the base scoring factor $w_{delay}(c)$ is weighted by one of the five features discussed above. Then, a priority ranking to indicate which conferences should be added next is predicted by sorting them by score in descending order. A sliding window over the months of 2016 is used to calculate the qrels and ranking scores for each month, averaging the results over the year afterwards. Performance measurements are carried out by the standard trec_eval evaluation procedure. Since we have a graded relevance scale we compute the normalized Discounted Cumulative Gain (ndcg) on different cut-off levels. As our evaluation year $year(\text{NOW})$ is set to 2016, all weighting factors discussed in section 2.1 are calculated taking into account all events and records up to and including $year(\text{NOW}) - 1$ (in this case 2015). Table 1 shows some examples of the available data for scoring.

4.1 Results

The results of the evaluation are shown in tables 2 and 3. Table 2 gives an overview on all computed ndcg-100 values for each month of the evaluation year and the year's average. A hundred documents is a typical amount of conferences the dblp editors can handle in one month. The raw delay $\Delta(c)$ of a conference constitutes the baseline. We can see that each ranking factor outperforms our baseline, conference rating and the discontinuity being the best-performing factors. Over the months of the year, we observe some fluctuation, which might be attributed to certain time slots where the number of simultaneous conference events peak. In the beginning of the year, the ndcg values are remarkably low. The values peak in September and decline towards the end of the year.

[2]For parsing geographical information, the Python library geotext (https://pypi.python.org/pypi/geotext) by Yaser Martinez Palenzuela was used.

[3]MAG is a part of the Open Academic Graph by AMiner (https://aminer.org/open-academic-graph)

Table 2: Overview on ndcg-100 values for each month and the year's average.

system	jan	feb	mar	apr	may	jun	jul	aug	sep	oct	nov	dec	avg
baseline	0.240	0.338	0.353	0.434	0.510	0.505	0.566	0.601	0.690	0.632	0.581	0.605	0.505
conf. rating	0.230	0.378	0.524	0.627	0.682	0.781	0.783	0.769	0.758	0.725	0.746	0.736	0.645
internationality	0.226	0.331	0.507	0.610	0.639	0.679	0.735	0.758	0.716	0.681	0.732	0.679	0.608
discontinued	0.291	0.411	0.615	0.727	0.686	0.673	0.702	0.676	0.779	0.743	0.707	0.711	0.643
citations	0.225	0.333	0.442	0.517	0.546	0.583	0.621	0.634	0.741	0.714	0.652	0.643	0.554
prominence	0.248	0.423	0.568	0.637	0.601	0.621	0.671	0.682	0.752	0.678	0.718	0.696	0.608

Table 3: Comparison of ndcg values on different cut-offs. Statistical differences to the baseline tested with two-sided t-test ($*** = p < 0.001$, $** = p < 0.01$, $* = p < 0.05$).

system	ndcg-10	ndcg-20	ndcg-100	ndcg-200
baseline	0.530	0.545	0.505	0.439
conf. rating	0.739**	0.716**	0.645***	0.597***
internationality	0.616	0.632	0.608***	0.575***
discontinued	0.713**	0.686***	0.643***	0.594***
citations	0.588	0.575	0.554***	0.548***
prominence	0.681**	0.662**	0.608***	0.577***

Nevertheless, the overall trend regarding the individual ranking factors is quite stable over the year.

Table 3 also shows that differences between the rankings and the baseline are always highly significant for discontinued and conference rating factors. These two factors are also performing best in all observations. While for low cut-off values the differences between the rankings are high, they are lower for high cut-offs. This pattern is plausible as divergences between different rankings balance out in the long tail of the ranked list.

5 DISCUSSION AND FUTURE WORK

The idea of utilizing quality metrics in information retrieval systems is not new. Most of these metrics target the goodness of web sources [2]. In this work we transfer this idea to the question which of the missing metadata in a literature database needs to be included next.

From a synoptic, philosophical perspective [1], the most prominent features of information quality are accuracy, completeness, currency, compactness, usability, consistency, and credibility. These seven facets also permeate the perspectives of other scientific fields, such as information and computer science. Similar to [6], we propose several features of conference metadata to improve the quality and maintenance of literature databases. Our features operationalize the following quality metrics: *currency*, through the delay of expected data and our proposed discontinuity factor; *popularity* via citation, internationality and prominence scores; and *credibility* via the conference ratings. We have proposed an evaluation framework to evaluate the effectiveness of these operationalized features for the problem of ranking data sets according to their expected urgency for a data acquisition process. We were able to show that the baseline ranking, which only takes the raw delay into account, can be outperformed by a number of semantically plausible factors. When it comes to create a priority ranking of conference data sets, currency expressed through penalizing a delay with a measure for discontinuity, and credibility of a conference seem to be the best-performing factors.

We had to make some compromises to perform our analyses. For a number of conferences, not all desirable information was available. For example, if no venue is mentioned in the title of proceedings, or no citation numbers are available from MAG, we will ignore this data for scoring. Our definition of internationality also needs to be revised to account for conferences which do not change locations frequently but still are of international relevance. For further investigations, we will also need to separate conferences from workshops co-located with them. In the current setting they are bundled together, which may add some noise to our data.

Our evaluation framework allows to perform follow-up investigations, for example by employing additional ranking factors that relate to the remaining quality metrics. We also want to combine factors to come up with the best-performing solution for a specific use case. In future work, we consider additional evaluation metrics to enhance our ranking.

ACKNOWLEDGMENTS

This work was supported by the DFG (Project ID: 217852844). We thank Hendrik Adam for his contribution to the implementations of the different ranking factors and the evaluation framework.

REFERENCES

[1] Brenda Reyes Ayala. 2017. We need new names: Applying existing models of Information Quality to web archives. *TCDL Bulletin* 13, 1 (2017). http://www.ieee-tcdl.org/Bulletin/v13n1/papers/reyes.pdf

[2] Ricardo A. Baeza-Yates, Carlos Castillo, Mauricio Marín, and M. Andrea Rodríguez. 2005. Crawling a country: better strategies than breadth-first for web page ordering. In *Proceedings of the 14th WWW 2005, Chiba, Japan, May 10-14, 2005.* ACM, 864–872. https://doi.org/10.1145/1062745.1062768

[3] Na Dai and Brian D. Davison. 2010. Freshness Matters: In Flowers, Food, and Web Authority. In *Proceeding of the 33rd ACM SIGIR 2010, Geneva, Switzerland, July 19-23, 2010.* ACM, 114–121. https://doi.org/10.1145/1835449.1835471

[4] Grettel García, Bernardo Pereira Nunes, Giseli Rabello Lopes, Marco Antonio Casanova, and Luiz André P. Paes Leme. 2017. Techniques for comparing and recommending conferences. *J. Braz. Comp. Soc.* 23, 1 (2017), 4:1–4:14. https://doi.org/10.1186/s13173-017-0053-z

[5] Waister Silva Martins, Marcos André Gonçalves, Alberto H. F. Laender, and Gisele L. Pappa. 2009. Learning to assess the quality of scientific conferences: a case study in computer science. In *Proceedings of the JCDL 2009, Austin, TX, USA, June 15-19, 2009.* ACM, 193–202. https://doi.org/10.1145/1555400.1555431

[6] Xiaolan Zhu and Susan Gauch. 2000. Incorporating quality metrics in centralized/distributed information retrieval on the World Wide Web. In *Proceedings of the 23rd ACM SIGIR 2000, Athens, Greece, July 24-28, 2000.* ACM, 288–295. https://doi.org/10.1145/345508.345602

Entity-Aspect Linking: Providing Fine-Grained Semantics of Entities in Context

Federico Nanni, Simone Paolo Ponzetto
Data and Web Science Group
University of Mannheim
Germany
federico,simone@informatik.uni-mannheim.de

Laura Dietz
Department of Computer Science
University of New Hampshire
U.S.A.
dietz@cs.unh.edu

ABSTRACT

The availability of entity linking technologies provides a novel way to organize, categorize, and analyze large textual collections in digital libraries. However, in many situations a link to an entity offers only relatively coarse-grained semantic information. This is problematic especially when the entity is related to several different events, topics, roles, and – more generally – when it has different aspects. In this work, we introduce and address the task of entity-aspect linking: given a mention of an entity in a contextual passage, we refine the entity link with respect to the aspect of the entity it refers to. We show that a combination of different features and aspect representations in a learning-to-rank setting correctly predicts the entity-aspect in 70% of the cases. Additionally, we demonstrate significant and consistent improvements using entity-aspect linking on three entity prediction and categorization tasks relevant for the digital library community.

KEYWORDS

entities, entity-aspects, wikification, information retrieval, knowledge bases

ACM Reference Format:

Federico Nanni, Simone Paolo Ponzetto and Laura Dietz. 2018. Entity-Aspect Linking: Providing Fine-Grained Semantics of Entities in Context. In *Proceedings of The 18th ACM/IEEE Joint Conference on Digital Libraries (JCDL '18)*. ACM, New York, NY, USA, 10 pages. https://doi.org/10.1145/3197026.3197047

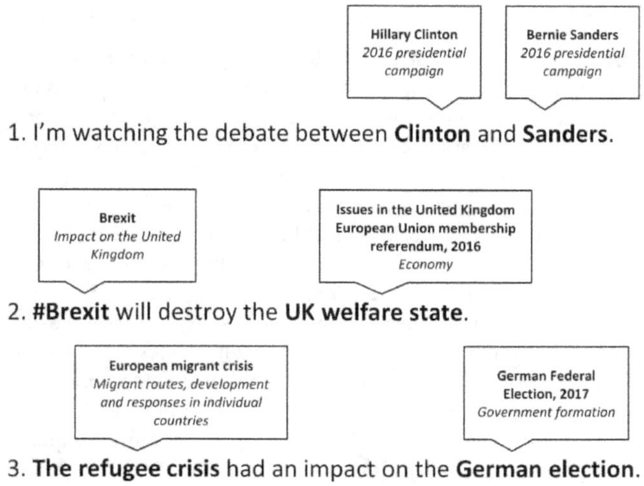

Figure 1: Example of entity-aspect linking: Boldface indicates entity links, italics presents the related aspects.

1 INTRODUCTION

The ability of enriching a collection of documents with entity-link (EL) annotations is a major advancement achieved in recent years by the natural language processing (NLP) community and a great improvement to the accessibility of large-scale digital library (DL) collections, from historical documents,[1] over newspaper corpora [43, 44] to web archives [11, 18].

Knowing that the mentions "Clinton" and "Sanders" presented in the first example in Figure 1 refer to the DBpedia [2] entities Hillary_Clinton and Bernie_Sanders, and not to Bill_Clinton or Sarah_Huckabee_Sanders, can support several downstream applications, such as entity-centric information retrieval [9], question answering [6] as well as corpus exploration and collection-building [19, 27], which are staple tasks of the fields of Digital Humanities and Computational Social Science [28, 39, 44].

Current limitations. Although entity-linking systems such as TagMe [12] or DBpedia spotlight [22] have recently brought several benefits to the research community, the coarseness of entity-link annotations limits their adoption in many digital library tasks. For instance, if we consider the first example in Figure 1, we can notice that detecting whether a sentence mentions the entity Hillary_Clinton might not be enough for a digital librarian who wants to organize documents in different event-collections (e.g., the different U.S. Presidential campaigns – as the Internet Archive aims to do[2]). As a matter of fact, a mention of Hillary_Clinton might refer to her role as First Lady of the United Stated during the Bill Clinton presidency, as the Senator of the state of New York (2001-2009), as the opponent of Barack Obama in the 2008 Democratic Primary race, as the Secretary of State during the first Obama administration or as the Democratic presidential candidate for the 2016 Presidential Elections. While state-of-the-art entity linking technologies [12, 22] can identify that the mention "Clinton" refers to Hillary_Clinton, they do not provide further information on the aspect of the entity that is most related to the context.

[1] See the Europeana Entity API: https://pro.europeana.eu/resources/apis/entity

[2] https://archive-it.org/collections/8118

ACM ISBN 978-1-4503-5178-2/18/06...$15.00
https://doi.org/10.1145/3197026.3197047

The same issue emerges in social-science and humanities applications. Imagine a researcher examining the different angles from which the entity Brexit has been mentioned on social media messages (as the tweet presented in Figure 1) [21] or a scholar studying in which discourses the entity European_Migrant_Crisis emerges in relation to the vote for the 2017 German federal elections (Figure 1, example 3) [29]: in both cases the simple linking of a mention to an entry in a knowledge base will not capture the specificity of the context. For all these reasons and in order to support digital librarians in offering collections that are even more semantically enriched, we present the task of entity-aspect linking (EAL).

The task. Given an entity-mention in a specific context (e.g., in a tweet, a sentence or a paragraph), our goal is to link it to one from a set of predefined aspects that captures the addressed topic. In our setting, we assume that each of these *entity-aspects* is accompanied by a textual description and a heading. While our approach is general and applies to any source of predefined aspects, from biomedical catalogs[3] to historical knowledge resources [39, 43], in this work we exclusively focus on predefined aspects extracted from Wikipedia. Each top-level section of an entity's Wikipedia page defines a single aspect (i.e., a specific entity sub-topic), which comes with heading, textual content and entity links. The mention "Clinton" presented above would therefore be linked to the aspect 2016_Presidential_Campaign, from Hillary Clinton's Wikipedia page. The idea of using sections and the definition of "aspects" comes from previous work on automatic Wikipedia enrichment and entity recommendation [1, 13, 36, 37].

Advantages. The outcome of this task is a refined entity link, which provides richer information about the entity and enables the user to choose the granularity appropriate for the task at hand. In Figure 1, we present a series of examples where, together with the linked entities, we offer the heading of the most relevant section, given the context of the mention.

Aspects vs. types vs. properties. On the one hand, this definition of aspects has similarities to entity types, which however refer to groups of semantically equivalent entities and are therefore coarser than the definition of an entity [8, 30]. For instance, Hillary_Clinton in the first example in Figure 1 will be assigned to the types "debater", "politician", or "person", depending on the vocabulary of types. These are some of the types that are currently associated to Hillary_Clinton on DBpedia: "First Lady", "Lawyer", "Senator", "Human Being", and "Grammy Award Winner". In contrast, our definition of an aspect refers to a list of events, topics, or roles that are specific to the given entity. It is therefore more fine-grained than the definition of an entity: In the example above, the relevant aspect of Hillary_Clinton is the one referring to her participation in the 2016 presidential race.

On the other hand, our definition of aspects has similarities with properties, which describe specific attributes of an entity, such as height or date-of-birth. However, as properties are generally not accompanied with textual descriptions, we do not consider them in our work. Nevertheless, we are aware that the boundaries between types, properties, and aspects are often fluid.

[3]For instance MeSH: https://www.nlm.nih.gov/mesh/

Explicit vs. implicit aspect representations. In this paper, we present and address the entity-aspect linking task in particular to meet the demands of the fields of Digital Humanities and Computational Social Science [15, 34]. These communities often employ entity-linking as a semantically explicit alternative to Latent Dirichlet Allocations (LDA) [3, 4] for corpus exploration and topic-based document selection [19, 31], as latent topics detected by LDA are often difficult to interpret and evaluate [7, 24, 45]. To satisfy the need of fine-grained interpretable topics, we have developed a system that adopts and provides explicit representations of pre-defined entity-aspects harvested from Wikipedia. As a future step for supporting the exploration of digital library collections, we envision the possibility to associate each entity in each document with its aspect, which will offer rich information on the topics addressed.

Our contribution. We present a method that employs learning-to-rank on a tailored set on lexical and semantic features in order to perform the newly introduced entity-aspects linking task, with both minimal and noisy contextual information (i.e., from a sentence to a section). The system outperforms several established baselines on a set of new datasets.[4] In addition, we show the usefulness of EAL for three different tasks that are relevant for the digital library community: Query- and event-based entity-ranking and collection organization.

Outline. The rest of the paper is organized as follows. First of all, we offer an overview of related work on the topic. Next, we present the proposed method in detail. Then we describe how the entity-aspect dataset has been created. A quantitative evaluation of the different approaches follows, together with an error analysis of the different systems. Finally, we present three different applications of entity-aspects in digital library tasks.

2 RELATED WORK

In this section we offer an overview of the task of entity linking, which serves as a starting point for the entity-aspect linking task. Next, we describe previous works that have focused on identifying entity-aspects.

Entity linking. Also known as entity resolution, the task of linking textual mentions to an entity in a knowledge base is called entity linking [35]. As an information extraction task, it involves the ability to recognize named entities in text (such as people, locations, organizations, as well as products and events), to resolve coreference between a set of mentions that could refer to the same entity (e.g. "Hillary Clinton" and "Mrs. Clinton") and to disambiguate the entity by linking it to a specific entry in a knowledge base such as DBpedia [2], Yago [41] or Freebase [5]. The disambiguation process is the most challenging step of any entity linking pipeline, as mentions of an entity in text can be ambiguous (as in the "Clinton" and "Sanders" examples presented in the introduction). For this reason, entity linking systems such as TagMe! [12], DBpedia Spotlight [22] or Babelfy [23] examine the mention's context to precisely disambiguate it. For instance, in the expression "the debate between Clinton and Sanders", "Clinton" is more likely to refer to the DBpedia entity Hillary_Clinton than to Bill_Clinton. However, in the expression "Clinton vs. Bush debate", the mention "Clinton"

[4]All the resources used in this paper are available at: https://federiconanni.com/entity-aspect-linking/

is more likely to refer to Bill_Clinton. In recent years, EL has been tackled with approaches based on artificial neural networks, which have been employed both for producing embedding representations of entities from text and knowledge graphs [17, 38, 46], and for entity-disambiguation and linking [47].

In this paper, we address what we envision as the further fine-grained step in entity-linking, namely to identify which specific section (i.e., aspect) in the Wikipedia page of the entity is relevant, given its mention in context. In building our pipeline, we test both established approaches from the entity-linking task and we also examine the usefulness of both word and entity embeddings.

Sections as entity-aspect. The formalization of entity-aspect that we adopt in our work is derived by Fetahu et al. [13]. In their paper, the authors enrich Wikipedia sections with news-article references. They do so in two steps: *a)* article-entity placement and *b)* article-section placement. While the authors do not explicitly use the word "aspect" in their paper, they consider – as we do – each section as a different sub-topic. In a similar way, Banerjee and Mitra [1] enrich Wikipedia stubs by assigning content retrieved from the web to the specific section. Following these works, Reinanda et al. [37] recently adopted the definition of "aspect" of an entity referring to its section; in their paper the authors use aspect-features to identify relevant documents for long tail entities. Unfortunately, the datasets used in these works are not available to the research community (we will expand on this in the Dataset section).

Our work differs from these studies in a few ways: *1)* we develop a system able to deal with both short and long snippets of text, and not only with long documents, as in previous work [1]. This is because we believe that the research community will benefit from such approach in order to analyze different types of digital collections, from historical archives to datasets of social media messages; *2)* we build a system that is applicable to any entity mention in a context, and not only to the most salient entities in text (as opposed to Fetahu et al. [13]); *3)* we do not adopt any type of feature that is specific to a particular Wikipedia category (as in Banerjee and Mitra [1]), in order to present a pipeline that is completely domain-independent and can be used to link any type of entity; *4)* finally, we present a fine-grained entity-linking tool to be used in digital library applications for supporting research in the humanities and social sciences. While our approach could be adopted to enrich Wikipedia sections with new snippets (i.e., the focus of previous papers on entity aspects), the long-term goal of our work is a system that could directly be used by digital librarians for creating topic-specific collections from large archives, for instance by retrieving all mentions of Hillary_Clinton related to the 2016 Election Campaign from the Internet Archive.

Other ways of obtaining "aspects". While in our paper we use sections to describe different aspects of an entity, there are other ways to detect them: for instance, by extracting information from large-scale query logs [32, 36, 48], or by conducting entity profiling in order to generate salient content about an entity from a given corpus [20, 42]. Even though these two types of approaches could be useful in many contexts, they strongly depend on the corpus under study and cannot be extended to, for example, long-tail entities that do not frequently appear in the collection, as we would like to do in our work.

3 APPROACH

In order to assign a mention m of the entity e in context cx to the most relevant aspect a of its Wikipedia page w (see Figure 2), we test different aspect representations and ranking strategies and combine them together in a learning-to-rank (L2R) system.

As opposed to previous work [1, 13], this method can be applied to any entity mention, regardless of its entity-type or prominence in a context. Moreover, in the evaluation section we provide evidence of the usefulness of this approach with text of different length.

While the methodology here described relies on Wikipedia, it can be adapted to any knowledge resource which provides textual descriptions of entity "sub-topics".

3.1 Aspect Representations

We consider three different ways of representing the entity-aspect in order to detect its similarity to the mention in context:

Header. We compare the similarity of the mention (m) in context (cx) and the header (h) of each section in the Wikipedia page (w) and rank aspects based on that. We do so, because often headers are very short summaries of the content of their section (as 2016_Presidential_Campaign, regarding the example in Figure 1).

Content. We measure the similarity between the mention in context (cx) and the content (co) of each section of the Wikipedia page of the entity and rank aspects based on that, as already done in previous work [1, 13].

Entity. We compare the entities (el) mentioned in cx and co. This follows the intuition that referring to similar entities should be an additional signal on the relation between the two texts. For detecting entities we used TagMe [12] with standard parameters.

3.2 Features

We employ two types of feature-vectors for ranking aspects.

3.2.1 *Word Vector Models.*

These features consider symbolic representations of each word as a single token. We employ them to rank aspects using header, content and entity representations:

tf-idf (cs). We compute the cosine similarity (cs) between the tf-idf (logarithmic, L2-normalized variant) vector of contextual mention and aspect. We tested both lemmatization and stemming as pre-processing steps during the experimental phase; as lemmatization has always offered better performance we report these results in the paper. We excluded numbers and stopwords[5].

BM25. We rank aspect representations given the contextual mention as a query using Okapi BM25 with k_1=2 and b=0.75. As in the previous approach, we adopt lemmatization and we remove numbers and stopwords.

3.2.2 *Distributional Semantic Models.*

The following features consider the representations of each word/entity as a vector in an embedding space. We employ word embeddings for ranking aspects with header and content representations, while we use entity-embeddings with the entity representation of each aspect:

w-emb (cs). We compute the cosine similarity between the mention in context and the aspect using the pre-trained word embeddings

[5] Based on the NLTK English stopword list: https://www.nltk.org/

Table 1: Type of features generated from each aspect-representation.

Representation	Features
Header	tf-idf (cs), BM25, w-emb (cs)
Content	tf-idf (cs), BM25, w-emb (cs)
Entity	tf-idf (cs), BM25, ent-emb (cs)

GloVe [33] of 300 dimensions. As in previous work [16, 25], every word w in cx and co is represented as a K-dimensional vector $\vec{w}$. A vector representation $\vec{v}$ for the whole text d is then obtained by a weighted element-wise average of word vectors $\vec{w}$ in the text. To give more attention to infrequent word, we additionally use the tf-idf of each word w to weight:

$$\vec{v} = \frac{1}{|d|} \sum_{w \in d} \text{tf-idf}(w) \cdot \vec{w}$$

ent-emb (cs). As in previous work [26, 27], we obtain latent vector representations $\vec{el}$ of each linked entity el appearing in cx and co using pre-computed RDF2Vec 500 dimensions entity embeddings [38]. A vector representation $\vec{v}$ for the whole text d is then computed as a weighted element-wise average of entity vectors $\vec{el}$. By casting mentions in context and aspects as bag-of-entities we adapt tf-idf to entity links (link statistics from DBpedia 2015-04 [2]):

$$\vec{v} = \frac{1}{|\{el \in d\}|} \sum_{el \in d} \text{tf-idf}(el) \cdot \vec{el}$$

3.3 Machine Learning

For measuring the similarity between every entity in context and aspect, the features presented above generates a vector of length 9, as summarized in Table 1.

Aspects are then ranked with a list-wise learning-to-rank (L2R) approach implemented in RankLib.[6] The weight parameter is learned by optimizing for the precision at 1 (P@1) using coordinate ascent with linear normalization. We then conduct a feature-ablation study by applying L2R on held-out test data using 5-fold cross-validation. In the experimental section we provide evidence on the usefulness of the selected features.

4 ENTITY-ASPECT DATASET

Given the fact that the resources employed in previous works [1, 13, 37] were too general for our task (they consider only certain type of entities and context sizes) and are not available anymore,[7] we decided to build a new collection of entity-aspect links to evaluate the presented method, based upon human-curated Wikipedia section links.

Wikipedia section links. As described in Wikipedia's Manual of Style and Linking,[8] "if an existing article has a section specifically about the topic" Wikipedia contributors are encouraged to point hyper-links directly to it. This should be done by suffixing the article name with a # and the name of the section (e.g., "Hillary_Clinton #2016_presidential_campaign).

We derived a collection of these section-links from the recently released TREC Complex Answer Retrieval dataset,[9] where organizers have processed a large amount of articles from Wikipedia, organizing them in sections, subsections, paragraphs and disambiguating entity-links [10].[10] From this dataset, we have retrieved a set of 201 entity-section links and for each of them we have manually reassessed the existence of a relation between the mention of the entity in context and the linked section.

Aspect structure. For each of these links, we consider the top level section heading as the associated aspect. Each aspect has therefore a name, which is the heading of the section, and a content, comprising all text included in the section (both textual descriptions and sub-headings).

Gold standard. We additionally provide a set of negative section-candidates for each correct section-link, which are extracted from the same Wikipedia page. The number of candidates, depending on the Wikipedia page under study, varies between 2 and 29, with an average of 6 potentially relevant aspects for each section-link. Generating this type of natural gold standard leads to a total of 1274 entity-section pairs.

If we reconsider the first example in Figure 1, together with the section 2016_presidential_campaign, we also present the sections 2008_presidential_campaign, U.S._Secretary_of_State, Email_ controversy, and so on.

4.1 Different Types of Context

For each entity-aspect link, we examine the performance of our system considering different types of context (statistics in Table 2).

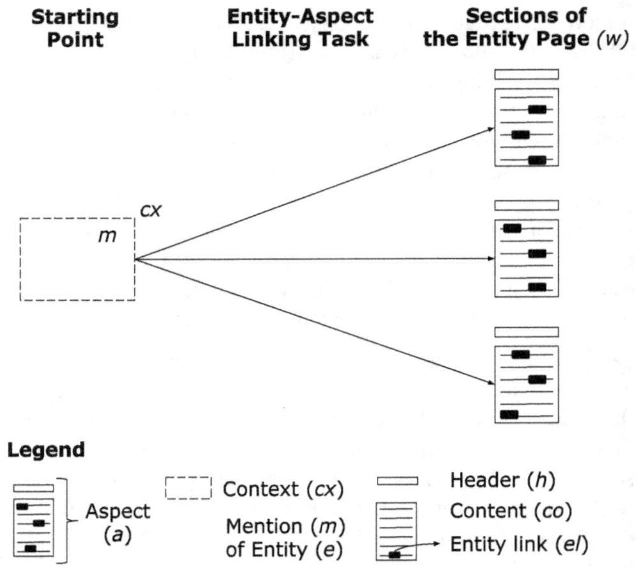

Figure 2: Graphical representation of the task.

[6]https://sourceforge.net/p/lemur/wiki/RankLib/

[7]The dataset from Fetahu et al.[13] is the only resource still available online; however, this collection reflects only a sub-part of the dataset used in their paper. This issue impeded us from employing it in our work. More information here: https://federiconanni.com/aspect-linking-previous-dataset/

[8]https://en.wikipedia.org/wiki/Wikipedia:Manual_of_Style/Linking

[9]http://trec-car.cs.unh.edu/

[10]We used the unprocessed_train file, version 1.5.

Table 2: Statistics of the dataset: number of tokens, depending on the context.

Context	Min.	Avg.	Max.
sentence	5	27	102
paragraph	5	94	318
section	48	19478	1259176

Sentence. The first type of context we test is the sentence in which the entity is mentioned. While this context should be highly relevant for the mentions, its brevity allows to simulate entity-aspect linking in situations where more contextual information is lacking (e.g., on social media platforms).

Paragraph. The second type of context is the paragraph in which the entity is mentioned. Paragraphs are taken from the Trec-CAR paragraph corpus [10] and are generally composed of 3–4 sentences, offering richer context to the mention.

Section. We additionally consider the section in which the entity is mentioned. This will allow us to test EAL, given a large context (which could simulate, for example, the length of a newspaper article). As opposed to previous work [13], we do not filter entities based on whether they are salient for the context or not; for this reason the task is very challenging, as already pointed out [27].

5 EXPERIMENTAL EVALUATION

We present a quantitative evaluation of our system on the new entity-aspect dataset described in the previous section. These experiments aim to answer the following research questions:

- **RQ1**. To which extent is it possible to link an entity-mention in context to the most appropriate aspect?
- **RQ2**. Does the combination of different representations of aspects (header, entity) improve the performance, over the use of content features?
- **RQ3**. Do different context sizes have an impact on the performance of the proposed method?
- **RQ4**. If yes, what is the best context setting for performing entity aspect-linking?

We begin by introducing the set of baselines we tested in our work, then we offer an overview of our system setting. We evaluate both baselines and our approach in terms of Precision at 1 (P@1) and mean average precision (MAP) using trec-eval.[11] We conclude this section with a discussion of the results.

5.1 Baselines

Inspired by previous work [1, 13, 37] and by the literature on entity linking [23, 35], we test a variety of standard approaches and heuristics for performing entity-aspect linking.

5.1.1 Simple Heuristics. The following baselines test a few simple heuristics:

- **size.** We consider the length of each section (in number of tokens) and we link the entity-mention to the longest.
- **content overlap.** We measure the overlap between tokens in the context of the mention and the section. Words have been tokenized, lemmatized and we excluded numbers and stopwords.
- **entity overlap.** We measure the overlap between entities in the context of the mention and in the section.

5.1.2 Text Similarity Baselines. The second group of baselines considers each aspect representation and ranking strategy presented in the Approach section as an independent system, for example: **tf-idf (cs)** with header representation, **BM25** with content representation, etc.

5.1.3 Learning To Rank Baselines. This third group of baselines uses all ranking features from each single aspect representation:

- **L2R (Header).** All the features generated by the comparison between the mention in context and the header of the section.
- **L2R (Content).** All the features generated by the comparison between the mention in context and the content of the section. This approach is supposed to be a very hard-to-beat baseline.
- **L2R (Entity).** All the features generated by the comparison between the entities mentioned in the context and the entities mentioned in the section.

This final group of baselines will tell us whether considering only a single type of aspect representation (e.g., only the content) is sufficient for performing the task.

5.2 Our Models

For what concerns the learning-to-rank approach proposed in this paper for entity-aspect linking (EAL), we present the results adopting two different settings:

- **EAL (All).** This setting adopts all features presented in the Approach section (denoted with † in the results).
- **EAL (Selected).** This setting employs a tailored set of features (denoted with ⋄ in the results), namely: tf-idf (header, content and entity), BM25 (content) and w-emb (content). We have identified them by conducting a series of ablation studies in the different test settings, using an additional validation set. We refer to this as EAL (Selected) in the rest of the paper .

5.3 Aspect-Linking with Sentence Context

The first experiment we present is on linking the correct aspect (a) of an entity (e), when only a sentence is given as a context cx. An example could be the following sentence (entity mention in boldface):

I'm watching the debate between ***Clinton*** *and Sanders.*

As it can be seen by the results presented in Table 3,[12] the use of a simple heuristics that checks the content overlap between the sentence and the section is already a good indicator for the entity-aspect linking task. On the other hand, the use of header features by themselves rarely provide good results. Adopting entity features alone does not lead to good performance either; this is due to the fact that a section often mentions a very large number of entities

[11] Version 8.1: http://trec.nist.gov/trec_eval/

[12] In tables, * marks improvements statistically significant (p-value lower than 0.10; paired Student's t-test) over all other baselines.

Table 3: Precision at 1 (P@1) and mean average precision (MAP) on aspect-linking using sentence context.

Model	P@1	MAP
random baseline	0.16	0.41
Simple Heuristics		
size	0.39	0.60
content overlap	0.57	0.72
entity overlap	0.50	0.69
Header		
tf-idf (cs) †⋄	0.44	0.63
BM25 †	0.42	0.62
w-emb (cs) †	0.32	0.54
L2R (Header)	0.44	0.63
Content		
tf-idf (cs) †⋄	0.62	0.76
BM25 †⋄	0.60	0.74
w-emb (cs) †⋄	0.54	0.70
L2R (Content)	0.65	0.77
Entity		
tf-idf (cs) †⋄	0.50	0.69
BM25 †	0.54	0.71
RDF2Vec (cs) †	0.49	0.68
L2R (Entity)	0.57	0.73
Our Approach		
EAL (All) †	0.66	0.79
EAL (Selected) ⋄	***0.70**	***0.81**

Table 4: Precision at 1 (P@1) and mean average precision (MAP) on aspect-linking using paragraph context.

Model	P@1	MAP
random baseline	0.16	0.41
Simple Heuristics		
size	0.39	0.60
content overlap	0.55	0.72
entity overlap	0.53	0.71
Header		
tf-idf (cs) †⋄	0.42	0.62
BM25 †	0.41	0.62
w-emb (cs) †	0.31	0.53
L2R (Header)	0.42	0.62
Content		
tf-idf (cs) †⋄	0.62	0.76
BM25 †⋄	0.58	0.74
w-emb (cs) †⋄	0.53	0.69
L2R (Content)	0.58	0.75
Entity		
tf-idf (cs) †⋄	0.53	0.70
BM25 †	0.55	0.70
RDF2Vec (cs) †	0.49	0.66
L2R (Entity)	0.53	0.70
Our Approach		
EAL (All) †	0.63	0.77
EAL (Selected) ⋄	**0.65**	**0.78**

and only a small fraction of them is relevant to the topic. The use of content features in L2R leads to good performance, strongly improving over the simple use of content overlap.

For what concerns the apporaches introduced in this paper, our tailored selection of features and aspect representations, named EAL (Selected), achieves a statistically significant improvement over all baselines, both for P@1 and MAP. This is due to the fruitful combination of features derived from different aspect representations. Our EAL (All) approach also shows very good performance, significantly outperforming the majority of the baselines.

Take-Away. Linking an entity to its most relevant aspect given a sentence of context is often possible, as our EAL-Selected system shows by reaching a P@1 of 0.70 (**RQ1**). In particular, our experiments reveal that for facing the scarce amount of contextual information available in a sentence, it is often necessary to combine features derived from the content with header and entity representation of the aspect (**RQ2**).

5.4 Aspect-Linking with Paragraph Context

Next, we tackle the task of entity-aspect linking at paragraph-level. In the following example, the mentions (in boldface) of the entity Bernie_Sanders point to the section 2016_Presidential_Campaign on its Wikipedia page. This is evident, thanks to the words "Trump", "general election", "Democratic National Committee", etc., which appear in the surrounding text:

> *Although* ***Sanders*** *had not formally dropped out of the race, he announced on June 16, 2016, that his main goal in the coming months would be to work with Clinton to defeat Trump in the general election. On July 8, appointees from the Clinton campaign, the Sanders campaign, and the Democratic National Committee negotiated a draft of the party's platform. On July 12,* ***Sanders*** *formally endorsed Clinton at a rally in New Hampshire, appearing with her.*

Our starting hypothesis was that having more context surrounding the mention would support the different models, as it provides additional information. However, we discovered that the overall topic of the paragraph is not always relevant for disambiguating the referred aspect, as the entity is often mentioned on a side.

As it can be noticed by looking at Table 4, there is in particular a drop in performance for the supervised approaches, in comparison to the results with sentence context. This is mainly due to two reasons: *a)* often different unsupervised models produce very similar rankings and therefore provide no new information to the L2R systems; *b)* moreover semantic features, which capture the meaning of the paragraph, tend to add noise to the model.

Take-Away. Having more context surrounding the mention often hurts the performance of the tested approaches, as the topic of the paragraph is not always relevant for the linking task (**RQ1**). While both our methods outperform all other L2R approaches, they do not

Table 5: Precision at 1 (P@1) and mean average precision (MAP) on aspect-linking using section context.

Model	P@1	MAP
random baseline	0.16	0.41
Simple Heuristics		
size	0.39	0.60
content overlap	0.46	0.66
entity overlap	0.52	0.70
Header		
tf-idf (cs) †⋄	0.41	0.62
BM25 †	0.37	0.59
w-emb (cs) †	0.27	0.49
L2R (Header)	0.41	0.62
Content		
tf-idf (cs) †⋄	0.53	0.70
BM25 †⋄	0.50	0.69
w-emb (cs) †⋄	0.45	0.64
L2R (Content)	0.49	0.68
Entity		
tf-idf (cs) †⋄	0.51	0.67
BM25 †	0.52	0.69
RDF2Vec (cs) †	0.48	0.65
L2R (Entity)	0.48	0.66
Our Approach		
EAL (All) †	0.55	0.72
EAL (Selected) ⋄	**0.57**	**0.73**

significantly improve the performance of their strongest feature, namely tf-idf (cs) with content representation of the aspect (**RQ2**).

5.5 Aspect-Linking with Section Context

The final set of experiments we conduct on our new dataset adopts an entire section as a context for the EAL task. As already remarked at paragraph level, during our experiments we noticed that most of the time the entity is not central to the context of the section. For this reason, as we do not perform any entity-filtering (as opposed to previous work [13]), the surrounding text adds a large amount of noise to the linking task. To better understand this issue, consider the following example, where Barack Obama is mentioned in the description of the attempt of the city of Chicago in organizing the 2016 Summer Olympics.

> ***President*** *and First Lady traveled to Denmark to support Chicago's bid for the 2016 Summer Olympics.*

While the sentence highlights the aspect of the entity Barack_Obama that is most related to the mention (in boldface), i.e., its presidency, the rest of the surrounding context is not relevant if not misleading for the task. For instance, the city "Chicago" – which is often mentioned in the section – is relevant for another aspect of the entity which is only slightly related, namely the fact that Obama studied and worked in the city, and was senator of Illinois.

The impact of this can be noticed by looking at the results in Table 5, which show a drastic drop in performance for the majority of the approaches (**RQ1,3**). In an in-depth study we noticed in

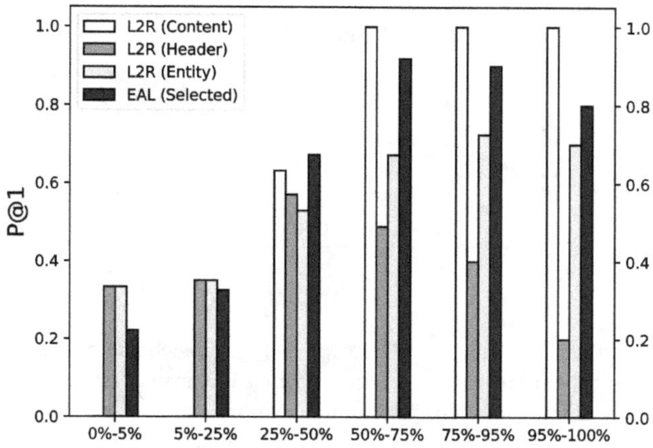

Figure 3: Difficulty-test for P@1, comparing L2R (Content) to other learning to rank systems with sentence context.

particular how semantic features derived from the content become drastically less informative in cases of large contexts.

Take-Away. Nevertheless, the two settings of our EAL system both outperform all other L2R baselines. This shows again the advantages of fruitfully combining the different types of features and aspect representations in a learning-to-rank setting (**RQ2**). However, it is also important to remark that, in this very noisy setting, a simple heuristics such as measuring the overlap between the entities provides already good results.

5.6 Discussion

In this experimental section we have shown how it is possible to link entity mentions in context to the correct aspect, reaching in certain settings high performance (both in terms of MAP and P@1 - **RQ1**). The use of content features by themselves for performing entity-aspect linking is a very strong baseline; however to deal with complex scenarios (from sentence to section levels), the combination of these features with the ones derived from other types of aspect representations often enables to our EAL systems to significantly improve the performance (**RQ2**). To better understand the benefit of this, we present in Figure 3 an additional test where we have divided all queries into different levels of difficulty according to the performance (P@1) achieved by the L2R (Content) at sentence level: the 5% most difficult queries for this method are to the left, the 5% easiest queries to the right. By comparing the performance of the L2R (Content) to the other L2R methods in the different bins it emerges that whenever it is difficult to perform the task with content features, other features derived from the heading and the entity support our learning-to-rank system.

It is also important to remark on the fact that different context-sizes have a serious impact on the performance of all methods (**RQ3**); due to this fact our error-analysis suggests that a good strategy is to employ as context only the most relevant one to three sentences surrounding each mention (**RQ4**). This take-away is not only important for the entity-linking task presented in this paper, but could be relevant also to the researchers interested in automatic Wikipedia enrichment [1, 13]: the relation between documents and

Table 6: MAP and P@5 regarding entity ranking for web queries on Robust04 and ClueWeb12.

	Robust04		ClueWeb12	
Model	**MAP**	**P@5**	**MAP**	**P@5**
REWQ [40]	-	0.79	-	**0.84**
Fusion [14]	0.57	0.85	0.39	0.82
EAL	**0.73**	**0.93**	**0.57**	0.74

entity sections may be better captured by considering only a few relevant sentences surrounding the mention, instead of using the entire document as contextual information.

Given the promising results achieved at sentence-level, in the next section we additionally test the performance of our EAL system in a few downstream applications relevant for the digital library community, from query-expansion to tweet classification.

6 EAL: DOWNSTREAM APPLICATIONS

After presenting the results of our experiments, we now examine a series of applications of the obtained entity-aspects in digital libraries, derived with our **EAL (Selected)** approach.

6.1 Predicting Latent Entities for a User Query

As a first type of application, we explore the usefulness of entity-aspects for the task of ranking latent relevant entities, given a user query. This task supports both the suggestion of named entities related to a search and the expansion of the query with semantic information from a knowledge base such as DBpedia.

Approach. In this setting, we rank each candidate entity, based on its most related section to the user query.

Dataset. We conduct experiments for measuring the usefulness of this approach on the two datasets for the task presented by Schuhmacher et al. [40] and extended by Foley et al. [14] (Robust04 and ClueWeb12). In these resources, each user-query is associated with a list of entities. For example the query "oic balkans 1990s" is associated with the relevant entities Bosnia-Herzegovina and Organisation_of_Islamic_Cooperation.

Comparison. In Table 6 we report the results of the currently two best systems for the task in terms of MAP and precision at 5 (P@5): REWQ [40] employs a learning-to-rank approach based upon features of entities linked in pseudo-relevant documents; The Fusion approach presented by Foley et al. [14] also employs learning-to-rank but, instead of relying on entity linking annotations, uses lexical features in a minimal linguistic resource setting. Since we adopt the extended version of the dataset created by Foley et al., for REWQ we are able to report only the precision at 5.

Results. The results of our system (EAL), presented in Table 6, show the usefulness of employing aspects for ranking entities, given a user query. In fact, we obtain a drastic improvement on the Robust04 dataset compared to the state-of-the-art approaches, and our method also shows good performance on ClueWeb12, outperforming Fusion [14] in term of MAP.

Table 7: MAP and P@5 regarding entity ranking for named events using dataset from Nanni et al. [27].

Model	MAP	P@5
RDF2Vec (cs)	0.65	0.80
EAL (EvAsp)	0.74	0.73
EAL (EntAsp)	**0.82**	**0.90**

6.2 Predicting Relevant Entities for an Event

Another relevant task that could be addressed through the use of entity-aspects is to suggest relevant entities, given a specific named event. Knowing which entities are the most relevant supports the creation of comprehensive event collections by capturing even the documents that do not explicitly mention the event name [26].

Approach. The system we present for this task follows the intuition that only a few aspects (i.e., sections) of an entity will be related to an event and vice-versa.

We rank entities in two different ways. First, by the similarity between the entity-name and all sections on the Wikipedia page of the event. We call this approach **EvAsp**, as it employs event-aspects. Second, by the event-name and all sections on the Wikipedia page of the entity, which we call **EntAsp**. While it is important to remark that our EAL approach has not been designed for dealing with such small context (i.e., only the name of the event/entity is given), our intention is to assess whether it could benefit from its combination of lexical and semantic features.

Dataset. We adopt the event-entity dataset introduced in our previous work [27], where global events such as the Orange Revolution are associated with a set of potentially relevant entities, which have to be ranked.

Comparison. In our previous work [27], we evaluated different approaches and found that ranking by the cosine similarity of pre-computed RDF graph embedding representations [38] of entities and events is an efficient solution for the task. However, we suspect that using pre-computed vector representations is not always an ideal approach, as new and long-tail entities are not present in the entity embeddings vocabulary. We evaluate the performance of the systems in terms of MAP and p@5.

Results. As can be seen in Table 7, the use of aspects reveals to be an efficient solution also for ranking entities, given a named event. As a matter of fact, in the EntAsp setting, this approach significantly outperforms RDF2Vec both for what concerns MAP and P@5. This boost in performance is given in particular by the use of semantic features (word embeddings) for measuring the relatedness between the event name and the content of the entity sections.

6.3 Predicting Event-Aspects for Tweets

As the last downstream application tested in this paper, we examine the use of entity aspects to improve the organization and navigation of topic-based collections. In our previous work [27], we focused on how to help digital librarians in the creation of event-collections, by automatizing the building process; we addressed in particular how to obtain a comprehensive coverage of each event analyzed by also capturing their premises and consequences. We envision the integration of these two technologies as the next step of our work.

We adopt for this experiment the large-scale collection that Zhang et al. [49] have recently created and made available to the research community regarding the Brexit referendum. It comprises around 12 million tweets and 240,000 news articles related to the event, crawled starting from 30 days before the vote. The researchers have entity-linked each tweet and assigned it to a DBpedia category that should capture the most relevant sub-topic of the event, such as Category:Immigration_to_Europe or Category:European_Union_Law.

However, while examining the dataset, we noticed that the associated categories often identify very general themes and are not useful for structuring the collection in sub-topics (for instance, many tweets are associated with Category:Euroscepticism_in_the _United_Kindgom). For this reason, in this final application we explore whether the use of entity aspects could be an alternative approach for describing the topics of the tweets and for facilitating the exploration of the collection.

Approach. To represent the topic Brexit, we consider the eight aspects of the entity Issues_in_the_United_Kingdom_European_ Union_Membership_Referendum,_2016 as they describe the event and offer a clear overview of the major stories discussed during the campaign (see Table 8). Our EAL approach is then used to assign each tweet to one of the different aspects.

Dataset. We took a sample of 750 tweets in English, randomly selected from the Brexit collection [49]. For each tweet, we asked three human experts to assign it, when possible, to the most related section of the page. We obtained a good agreement between the annotators with an inter-annotator agreement measured in Cohen's kappa of 0.66. Annotators also flagged tweets that were too general (270) for the task or not related to the event (106), for example:

The end is near ***#brexit***

Congrats!!! ICELAND 2-1 ***Brexit*** *in Euro 2016*

This analysis already indicates the complexity of organizing tweets in event sub-topics: in fact, almost half of the messages are too general to be classified or not related to the event. We decided to remove these tweets from the dataset when conducting the final evaluation, which left us with 372 tweets, each of them assigned to a specific section depending on the aspect of the event Brexit that was most relevant.

Comparison. We test the quality of our approach in comparison with two types of baselines:

- **Ranking Approaches.** We report the results of two of the best performing baselines from the entity-aspect linking task, namely: BM25 and word-embedding (cosine similarity) between the tweet and the content of the section;
- **Classification Approaches.** As additional hard-to-beat baselines, we treat this problem as a classification task, where each tweet is associated with a label (i.e., the section-heading). We compare two types of classifiers (Naive-Bayes and Support Vector Machine) with different features (tf-idf and word embeddings) in a 10-fold cross validation setting.

Table 8: Statitics on the annotation of Brexit aspects.

Topic	# Tweets
Economy	155
Immigration	52
Sovereignty and influence	50
Security, law enforcement and defense	3
Risk to the Unity of the United Kingdom	30
Transatlantic Trade and Investment Partnership	5
Enlargement of the European Union	12
Proposed consequences of a vote to leave	65
Total	372
Excluded	
General	270
Out-of-topic	108

Table 9: Precision at 1 on Brexit-aspect dataset.

Model	P@1
random baseline	0.12
Ranking Approaches	
Content - BM25	0.37
Content - w-emb (cs)	0.36
EAL	**0.42**
Classification Approaches	
Naive Bayes (tf-idf)	0.27
SVM (tf-idf)	0.27
Naive Bayes (w-emb)	0.38
SVM (w-emb)	0.37

Results. As can be seen in the results reported in Table 9, the performance of all approaches reveal the high complexity of the task, where it is necessary to identify the topic of a political message, which is often conveyed in just a few words. Nevertheless, our EAL approach outperforms all other methods and in particular the classifiers trained with in-domain data. Once again, it is important to remark that this is due to the fact that our learning-to-rank system combine both lexical and semantic features and different representation of aspects. These initial results motivate us in further exploring the use of aspects for structuring event collections in explicit sub-topics and in improving our system for addressing these specific challenges.

7 CONCLUSION

In this paper we presented and addressed the task of entity-aspect linking. Given a mention of an entity in a context, we developed a method to link it to its most related Wikipedia section. We showed how our method significantly outperforms several established baselines and delivers good results in different contexts (a sentence, a paragraph, or a section). When applying entity-aspect links to a series of relevant tasks for the digital library community – query- and event-based entity-ranking and sub-topics collection organization – we achieve state-of-the-art improvements. This demonstrates that our method, which can be applied to large-scale corpora, provides an effective way to gain detailed topical insights into a text collection. Refining entity-links in text with aspect information opens now the way to the next step of our research, which will be focused on combining the linked aspects of multiple entities in the same context for generating an explicit description of the topic addressed in text. This type of output will be useful for digital librarians who intend to offer semantically richer collections and will also support the adoption of advanced computational approaches in the humanities and social sciences.

Acknowledgements

This work was funded in part by a scholarship of the Eliteprogramm for Postdocs of the Baden-Württemberg Stiftung (project "Knowledge Consolidation and Organization for Query-specific Wikipedia Construction"). Furthermore, this work was partially funded by the Junior-professor funding programme of the Ministry of Science, Research and the Arts of the state of Baden-Württemberg (project "Deep semantic models for high-end NLP application").

REFERENCES

[1] Siddhartha Banerjee and Prasenjit Mitra. 2015. WikiKreator: Improving Wikipedia Stubs Automatically.. In *Proc. of ACL*. 867–877.
[2] Christian Bizer, Jens Lehmann, Georgi Kobilarov, Sören Auer, Christian Becker, Richard Cyganiak, and Sebastian Hellmann. 2009. DBpedia - A Crystallization Point for the Web of Data. *Journal of Web Semantics* 7, 3 (2009), 154–165.
[3] David M Blei. 2012. Topic modeling and digital humanities. *Journal of Digital Humanities* 2, 1 (2012), 8–11.
[4] David M. Blei, Andrew Y. Ng, and Michael I. Jordan. 2003. Latent dirichlet allocation. *Journal of Machine Learning Research* 3 (2003), 993–1022.
[5] Kurt Bollacker, Colin Evans, Praveen Paritosh, Tim Sturge, and Jamie Taylor. 2008. Freebase: a collaboratively created graph database for structuring human knowledge. In *Proc. of SIGMOD*. 1247–1250.
[6] Antoine Bordes, Sumit Chopra, and Jason Weston. 2014. Question answering with subgraph embeddings. *Proc. of EMNLP* (2014).
[7] Jonathan Chang, Sean Gerrish, Chong Wang, Jordan L Boyd-Graber, and David M Blei. 2009. Reading tea leaves: How humans interpret topic models. In *Advances in Neural Information Processing Systems*. 288–296.
[8] Luciano del Corro, Abdalghani Abujabal, Rainer Gemulla, and Gerhard Weikum. 2015. Finet: Context-aware fine-grained named entity typing. In *Proc. of ACL*.
[9] Jeffrey Dalton, Laura Dietz, and James Allan. 2014. Entity query feature expansion using knowledge base links. In *Proc. of SIGIR*.
[10] Laura Dietz and Ben Gamari. 2017. TREC CAR: A Data Set for Complex Answer Retrieval. Version 1.5. http://trec-car.cs.unh.edu
[11] Pavlos Fafalios, Helge Holzmann, Vaibhav Kasturia, and Wolfgang Nejdl. 2017. Building and Querying Semantic Layers for Web Archives. In *Proc. of JCDL*, Vol. 2017.
[12] Paolo Ferragina and Ugo Scaiella. 2010. TagMe: on-the-fly annotation of short text fragments (by Wikipedia entities). In *CIKM*. 1625–1628.
[13] Besnik Fetahu, Katja Markert, and Avishek Anand. 2015. Automated news suggestions for populating wikipedia entity pages. In *Proc. of CIKM*. 323–332.
[14] John Foley, Brendan O'Connor, and James Allan. 2016. Improving Entity Ranking for Keyword Queries. In *Proc. of CIKM*. 2061–2064.
[15] Francesca Frontini, Carmen Brando, and Jean-Gabriel Ganascia. 2015. Semantic web based named entity linking for digital humanities and heritage texts. In *First International Workshop on the Semantic Web for Scientific Heritage at ESWC-15*.
[16] Goran Glavaš, Federico Nanni, and Simone Paolo Ponzetto. 2017. Unsupervised cross-lingual scaling of political texts. In *Proc. of EACL*.
[17] Hongzhao Huang, Larry Heck, and Heng Ji. 2015. Leveraging deep neural networks and knowledge graphs for entity disambiguation. *arXiv preprint arXiv:1504.07678* (2015).
[18] Nattiya Kanhabua, Philipp Kemkes, Wolfgang Nejdl, Tu Ngoc Nguyen, Felipe Reis, and Nam Khanh Tran. 2016. How to search the internet archive without indexing it. In *Proc. of TPDL*. Springer, 147–160.
[19] Anne Lauscher, Federico Nanni, Pablo Ruiz Fabo, and Simone Paolo Ponzetto. 2016. Entities as topic labels: combining entity linking and labeled LDA to improve topic interpretability and evaluability. *IJCol-Italian journal of computational linguistics* 2, 2 (2016), 67–88.
[20] Peng Li, Yinglin Wang, Wei Gao, and Jing Jiang. 2011. Generating aspect-oriented multi-document summarization with event-aspect model. In *Proc. of EMNLP*. 1137–1146.
[21] Julio Cesar Amador Diaz Lopez, Sofia Collignon-Delmar, Kenneth Benoit, and Akitaka Matsuo. 2017. Predicting the Brexit Vote by Tracking and Classifying Public Opinion Using Twitter Data. *Statistics, Politics and Policy* 8, 1 (2017), 85–104.
[22] Pablo N Mendes, Max Jakob, Andrés García-Silva, and Christian Bizer. 2011. DBpedia spotlight: shedding light on the web of documents. In *Proc. of Semantic Systems*. ACM, 1–8.
[23] Andrea Moro, Alessandro Raganato, and Roberto Navigli. 2014. Entity linking meets word sense disambiguation: a unified approach. *Transactions of the Association for Computational Linguistics* 2 (2014), 231–244.
[24] Federico Nanni, Hiram Kümper, and Simone Paolo Ponzetto. 2016. Semi-supervised Textual Analysis and Historical Research Helping Each Other: Some Thoughts and Observations. *International Journal of Humanities and Arts Computing* 10, 1 (2016), 63–77.
[25] Federico Nanni, Bhaskar Mitra, Matt Magnusson, and Laura Dietz. 2017. Benchmark for Complex Answer Retrieval. *Proc. of ICTIR* (2017).
[26] Federico Nanni, Simone Paolo Ponzetto, and Laura Dietz. 2016. Entity relatedness for retrospective analyses of global events. In *NLP+CSS Workshop at WebSci*.
[27] Federico Nanni, Simone Paolo Ponzetto, and Laura Dietz. 2017. Building entity-centric event collections. In *Proc. of JCDL*. IEEE, 1–10.
[28] Federico Nanni, Yang Zhao, Simone Paolo Ponzetto, and Laura Dietz. 2017. Enhancing Domain-Specific Entity Linking in DH. *Digital Humanities* (2017).
[29] Fabian G Neuner and Christopher Wratil. 2017. The myth of the boring election: populism and the 2017 German election. *LSE European Politics and Policy (EUROPP) Blog* (2017), 1–5.
[30] Andrea Giovanni Nuzzolese, Anna Lisa Gentile, Valentina Presutti, Aldo Gangemi, Darío Garigliotti, and Roberto Navigli. 2015. Open knowledge extraction challenge. In *Semantic Web Evaluation Challenge*. Springer, 3–15.
[31] Alex Olieman, Kaspar Beelen, Milan van Lange, Jaap Kamps, and Maarten Marx. 2017. Good Applications for Crummy Entity Linkers? The Case of Corpus Selection in Digital Humanities. *Proc. of Semantic Systems* (2017).
[32] Patrick Pantel, Thomas Lin, and Michael Gamon. 2012. Mining entity types from query logs via user intent modeling. In *Proc. of ACL*. 563–571.
[33] Jeffrey Pennington, Richard Socher, and Christopher D Manning. 2014. Glove: Global Vectors for Word Representation.. In *Proc. of EMNLP*, Vol. 14.
[34] Thierry Poibeau and Pablo Ruiz. 2015. Generating navigable semantic maps from social sciences corpora. *Digital Humanities* (2015).
[35] Delip Rao, Paul McNamee, and Mark Dredze. 2013. Entity linking: Finding extracted entities in a knowledge base. In *Multi-source, multilingual information extraction and summarization*. Springer, 93–115.
[36] Ridho Reinanda, Edgar Meij, and Maarten de Rijke. 2015. Mining, ranking and recommending entity aspects. In *Proceedings of the 38th International ACM SIGIR Conference on Research and Development in Information Retrieval*. ACM, 263–272.
[37] Ridho Reinanda, Edgar Meij, and Maarten de Rijke. 2016. Document filtering for long-tail entities. In *Proc. of CIKM*. ACM, 771–780.
[38] Petar Ristoski and Heiko Paulheim. 2016. Rdf2vec: Rdf graph embeddings for data mining. In *Proc. of ISWC*. Springer.
[39] Marco Rovera, Federico Nanni, Simone Paolo Ponzetto, and Anna Goy. 2017. Domain-specific named entity disambiguation in historical memoirs. In *Proc. of Clic-IT*.
[40] Michael Schuhmacher, Laura Dietz, and Simone Paolo Ponzetto. 2015. Ranking Entities for Web Queries Through Text and Knowledge. In *Proc. of CIKM*.
[41] Fabian M Suchanek, Gjergji Kasneci, and Gerhard Weikum. 2007. Yago: A core of semantic knowledge. In *Proc. of WWW*. 697–706.
[42] Bilyana Taneva and Gerhard Weikum. 2013. Gem-based entity-knowledge maintenance. In *Proc. of CIKM*. ACM, 149–158.
[43] Theo van Veen, Juliette Lonij, and Willem Jan Faber. 2016. Linking Named Entities in Dutch Historical Newspapers. In *Proc. of MTSR*. Springer, 205–210.
[44] Piek Vossen, Rodrigo Agerri, Itziar Aldabe, Agata Cybulska, Marieke van Erp, Antske Fokkens, Egoitz Laparra, Anne-Lyse Minard, Alessio Palmero Aprosio, German Rigau, et al. 2016. Newsreader: Using knowledge resources in a cross-lingual reading machine to generate more knowledge from massive streams of news. *Knowledge-Based Systems* 110 (2016), 60–85.
[45] Hanna M Wallach, Iain Murray, Ruslan Salakhutdinov, and David Mimno. 2009. Evaluation methods for topic models. In *Proc. of ICML*. ACM, 1105–1112.
[46] Ikuya Yamada, Hiroyuki Shindo, Hideaki Takeda, and Yoshiyasu Takefuji. 2016. Joint learning of the embedding of words and entities for named entity disambiguation. *Proc. of CoNLL* (2016).
[47] Ikuya Yamada, Hiroyuki Shindo, Hideaki Takeda, and Yoshiyasu Takefuji. 2017. Learning Distributed Representations of Texts and Entities from Knowledge Base. *Transactions of the Association for Computational Linguistics* (2017).
[48] Xiaoxin Yin and Sarthak Shah. 2010. Building taxonomy of web search intents for name entity queries. In *Proc. of WWW*. ACM, 1001–1010.
[49] Lei Zhang, Maribel Acosta, Michael Färber, Steffen Thoma, and Achim Rettinger. 2017. BreXearch: Exploring Brexit Data Using Cross-Lingual and Cross-Media Semantic Search. In *Proc. of ISWC*.

Investigating Entity Linking in Early English Legal Documents

Gary Munnelly
Adapt Centre
Dublin, Ireland
gary.munnelly@adaptcentre.ie

Séamus Lawless
Adapt Centre
Dublin, Ireland
seamus.lawless@adaptcentre.ie

ABSTRACT

In this paper we investigate the accuracy and overall suitability of a variety of Entity Linking systems for the task of disambiguating entities in 17th century depositions obtained during the 1641 Irish Rebellion. The depositions are extremely difficult for modern NLP tools to work with due to inconsistent spelling, use of language and archaic references. In order to assess the severity of difficulty faced by Entity Linking systems when working with these documents we use the depositions to create an evaluation corpus. This corpus is used as an input to the General Entity Annotator Benchmarking Framework, a standard benchmarking platform for entity annotation systems. Based on this corpus and the results obtained from the General Entity Annotator Benchmarking Framework we observe that the accuracy of existing Entity Linking systems is limited when applied to content like these depositions. This is due to a number of issues ranging from problems with existing state-of-the-art systems to poor representation of historic entities in modern knowledge bases. We discuss some interesting questions raised by this evaluation and put forward a plan for future work in order to learn more.

CCS CONCEPTS

• **Applied computing** → **Digital libraries and archives**; • **Information systems** → *Content analysis and feature selection*;

KEYWORDS

Named Entity Disambiguation, Digital Humanities, Cultural Heritage

ACM Reference Format:
Gary Munnelly and Séamus Lawless. 2018. Investigating Entity Linking in Early English Legal Documents. In *JCDL '18: The 18th ACM/IEEE Joint Conference on Digital Libraries, June 3–7, 2018, Fort Worth, TX, USA.* ACM, New York, NY, USA, 9 pages. https://doi.org/10.1145/3197026.3197055

1 INTRODUCTION

In this paper we present an evaluation of the performance of Entity Linking (EL) systems when applied to a collection of 17th century depositions. The corpus is comprised of interviews with Irish citizens regarding alleged crimes committed against them during the 1641 Irish Rebellion. They are of interest to numerous parties for a variety of reasons, but the challenging nature of their content, discussed further in Section 3.1, makes them difficult for scholars to explore.

We wish to investigate how well state-of-the-art EL systems perform in the task of automatically linking spotted entities in the depositions with a suitable referent. This referent may be used to resolve multiple mentions of entities throughout the collection, or even to build links between disparate collections based on mutual entities. Ideally the application of EL would facilitate the imposition of a semantic structure on the depositions, allowing historians to execute more complex queries on the collection's content and enabling the provision of more sophisticated search, discovery and personalisation services.

This paper is concerned exclusively with the EL problem. While Named Entity Recognition (NER) is a related and similarly important task, given the challenging nature of the depositions' content we consider it to be a separate problem which requires a dedicated study of its own. The inconsistent nature of language in the depositions means that NER tools introduce too much noise for us to be able to investigate the positive and negative properties of the EL algorithms themselves.

We perform our investigation by first manually annotating a subset of the depositions with referent URIs taken from DBpedia. We observe that only a small percentage of mentions in the text can be linked with a suitable referent, demonstrating the severe penalty introduced to an EL system's performance if the referent knowledge base provides insufficient coverage for the chosen collection. This is a common problem observed when working with EL systems in Cultural Heritage (CH) [1, 22]. We evaluate the performance of various EL systems with respect to this ground truth using a standard benchmarking framework.

2 BACKGROUND

In this section we will provide a high level description of EL, what it is and how it works. This is not intended to be a thorough state-of-the art review, nor is it a detailed tutorial on how to perform EL. For parties seeking more information we refer to the work of Shen et al. [16]. We will, however, discuss some previous efforts to employ EL in solving Digital Humanities (DH) problems.

2.1 A Brief Introduction to Entity Linking

Entity Linking (also called Named Entity Disambiguation) is a problem in computational linguistics whereby an automated process attempts to determine the specific subject of a reference to an entity found in free text. The input to an EL system is usually a series of entity mentions and a body of text from which the mentions were sourced. The program produces as output a corresponding

JCDL '18, June 3–7, 2018, Fort Worth, TX, USA

ACM ISBN 978-1-4503-5178-2/18/06...$15.00
https://doi.org/10.1145/3197026.3197055

list of referents for each mention in the input set. For example, given the input text, "*The said deponent then fled to the County of Dublin*" and the entity mention "*County of Dublin*" extracted from the text, an EL system might return a DBpedia URI which identifies http://dbpedia.org/page/County_Dublin as the referent entity. The set of URIs which identify referents is obtained from a knowledge base that is part of the EL system. This knowledge base is usually derived from popular linked data repositories such as DBpedia or YAGO.

Given a suitable knowledge base, the EL system identifies a number of candidate entities to which the mentions in the source text might be referring. Taking again the example of Dublin, we could be referring to a city in Ireland, a community in America, a village in Belarus or something else[1]. It is the task of the EL system to look at the evidence available to it and establish which entities in its knowledge base are the most suitable referents for the mentions it received as input. If no suitable referent can be established then the system may label the mention as NIL, meaning it could not identify an appropriate referent.

There has been much research into the development of EL systems with methods ranging from simple string lookups [15] to more sophisticated methods which perform a lexical comparison between the context of a mention and a source text which describes an entity [26]. Many methods also make the assumption that entities which are mentioned in the same context are likely related by some common theme [20, 25]. Therefore the system can combine the evidence from multiple entities to establish sensible referents.

EL systems face a number of challenges when applied to CH collections. One of the most immediately identifiable problems is the quality of the knowledge base.

If an entity does not exist in the knowledge base then the EL system cannot know about it. Given the highly specialised nature of many CH collections, this is a serious problem as a large proportion of entities that are important to the collection itself are either poorly represented or even entirely omitted from knowledge bases that are based on DBpedia or similar Wikipedia derived resources. An ongoing challenge is to deal with the problem of Emerging Entities (EE), those entities which might appear multiple times in text but do not have a referent in the knowledge base. In the absence of a solution to the EE problem, methods of compensating for gaps in the knowledge base need to be established.

EL systems are also taxed by the prevalence of evolving entities in collections which span broad periods of time. For example, titles such as the "King of England" or the "Bishop of Meath" are passed from person to person as new people take on a particular role over time. It is extremely difficult to establish precisely which individual holds a given title based solely on contextual information derived from the content of a source text. Similarly it can be challenging to deal with entities whose names and titles change over time. A common example might be a soldier who receives a promotion. Such an individual may be referred to with the title "Lieutenant" in earlier texts, but "Captain" in later ones. Alternatively, a woman who marries will often change her family name to match her husband's. Capturing these evolving entities is extremely difficult as they are rarely well documented in the knowledge base.

[1]https://en.wikipedia.org/wiki/Dublin_(disambiguation)

With respect to the linking process itself, certain assumptions made by the linking algorithm are not upheld when applied to CH collections. For example, it is common to compare the context in which an entity mention is found with the context from which the candidate referent in the knowledge base was extracted. This assumes that both sources of information use language in the same manner. This is obviously a problem, as language is an evolving thing. When dealing with older collections, a contextual similarity measure based on co-occurring words, word embeddings or other similar measures is often an unreliable feature as the language of the knowledge base is usually obtained from more modern resources.

To provide an alternative example of problematic assumptions made by entity linkers, some systems make use of a candidate probability prior derived from the popularity of a candidate entity in the knowledge base (where "popularity" can be determined by a variety of different methods). The intuition is that the most popular referent for a given surface form will be the correct referent for the majority of instances of the surface form in text. For CH collections, popular entities are not necessarily good candidates and this prior can actually mislead the linking process by encouraging it to favour more popular modern entities over more sensible candidates that are relevant to the collection.

The range of challenges faced by EL systems when dealing with CH is broad. Careful consideration must be given to the nature of the collection, the methods employed by the EL system and the quality of information obtained from the knowledge base in order to ensure that the annotations provided by the entity linker are reliable.

2.2 Related Work

A number of interesting efforts have been made to investigate the applications of EL for DH problems.

Work by Van Hooland et al. [22] attempted to assess the suitability of NER and EL tools for use in DH. They experimented with three disambiguation services – Alchemy API, DBpedia Spotlight and Zemanta. They raised some interesting points regarding what exactly *is* the correct URI for an entity in any given context. This is an extremely important question, particularly when trying to disambiguate entities through the lens of history. To take an example from our own research, if we see a reference to "Ireland" in a 17th century document, is the most appropriate disambiguation the landmass that forms the island of Ireland, the Kingdom of Ireland (which is probably most appropriate for the time) or the Republic of Ireland (which is a more modern reference)? Ultimately Van Hooland et al. suggested that perhaps the "best" referent is the one on which the majority of annotation sources can agree. Nevertheless, he calls for caution, awareness and education on the part of those who would employ such tools to ensure that we are not too trusting of what the machine tells us.

Work by De Wilde also sought to investigate the usefulness of EL for digital archives [24]. He investigated the applications of EL on German and Dutch documents ranging from the early 19th century to the mid-20th century. His texts had been digitised through a method involving Optical Character Recognition (OCR), meaning there is likely to have been some noise in the resulting data. De Wilde used a simple disambiguation method based on dictionary lookups and SPARQL queries. Where there was more than one possible referent for an entity, De Wilde chose the longest match. This approach was extremely simple but achieved impressive results which matched the state of the art. De Wilde was very enthusiastic about his results and planned to integrate the output from his EL software into the search interface for the "Historische Kranten" project. He also suggested that the noise introduced by OCR might not have too severe an effect on the quality of EL.

One of the more considered efforts to address the challenge of EL in CH is by Carmen Brando, Francesca Frontini and Jean-Gabriel Ganascia [2]. Their work focused on the problem of poor entity coverage in common knowledge bases. They developed a method which can disambiguate with respect to multiple knowledge bases simultaneously. Their method allows for specialised knowledge bases such as BnF[2] to be integrated with more general sources such as DBpedia. The general knowledge base can compliment the specialised one by providing additional information which can be used by the linking process.

Given a set of entity mentions as input, REDEN [2] begins by retrieving a set of candidate referents from an index built on one the knowledge bases. The knowledge base used for candidate retrieval should be the one that is most representative of the collection being linked. References to the same candidates are then retrieved from the supporting knowledge bases using *owl:sameAs* and *skos:exactMatch* properties. Entities retrieved from all knowledge bases are then fused into a single unified graph representation of each candidate referent. Once the fusion process is complete REDEN applies a graph centrality measure to determine the correct referent for each mention.

REDEN is an extremely interesting example of an attempt to perform EL in CH. It does not rely on language similarity as one of its features, as this is known to be unreliable in CH. Instead it focuses purely on the graph structure. It also provides mechanics for limiting what parts of the knowledge base are indexed so that only entities from a particular geographic region or time period may be considered for linking. This is often noted as potentially useful behaviour by those who have attempted to perform EL on CH collections [9].

3 CORPUS

In this section we introduce the 1641 depositions which form the basis of our evaluation corpus. We present some of the history behind the documents and explain why they present a challenge for Computer Scientists. We will also explain how the depositions were prepared for use as part of this paper's experiment. Those interested in learning more about the depositions are referred to the 1641 website[3] or the Cultura project[4].

3.1 The 1641 Depositions

The 1641 Depositions are a collection 8,000 depositions or witness statements, examinations and associated materials, amounting to 19,010 pages and bound in 31 volumes. They document the various losses, military actions, attacks and transgressions inflicted on numerous individuals during the 1641 Irish Rebellion. In spite of some controversy surrounding the accuracy of certain witness statements, the depositions provide an fascinating window into the lives of people in 17th century Ireland.

Through a painstaking process which spanned a number of years the depositions have been digitised and annotated in TEI format preserving all aspects of the source manuscripts including the original spelling, deletions, margin notes, etc. A team of scholars manually examined the depositions to extract references to locations and people whilst simultaneously tagging the documents with the nature of their contents (murder, theft, etc). The result is an extremely data rich historical digital corpus.

Linguistically the depositions are challenging to work with as English was still a developing language in 1641. The documents are rife with features which make them difficult to interpret for a modern English speaker. Among the most striking of these features are the vast array of spelling inconsistencies and a severe lack of punctuation. Often a deposition is comprised of a continuous run-on sentence with the phrase "and further saith that" seemingly being substituted for a full-stop. The extract below from the *Examination of Elizabeth Williams* provides an example of these qualities:

> The rest of this deponents husbands goods Garrett mc Eohee and Donell mc Cabe kept & detained from him they being in the possession of them at the begining of the insurreccion And this Examinate further saith that she her husband together with their whole family was remoued into the Towne, where they had of their owne goods onely two steares and one Barrell of oates dureing the whole tyme of 17 weekes And further saith that on the seccond of January 1641 the Rebells came abroad into the Towne and tooke her husband (Mr William Williams) Mr Gabriell Williams (her brother in law) Mr Ithell Jones her sisters husband together with a Scotchman one Thomas Tran & hanged them all in a Barne in the backsyd of their lodgings where they were in prison, That day suffered besides these fower about fowerteen or fifteene whoe were all hanged or stabbed or both in the Towne

These peculiarities mean that the depositions have the capacity to confound some of the most basic off-the-shelf NLP tools including part-of-speech taggers, sentence chunkers and NER tools. Previous work by Mitankin et al. [12] tackled the problem of normalising spelling in the depositions with great success, while the Cultura project [18] also ambitiously attempted to provide a personalised search experience over the depositions with entity-based approaches being core to a number of services. Yet a suitable, automatic method of resolving and disambiguating multiple mentions of entities has not yet been found.

Performing EL on the depositions is challenging for a number of reasons. Setting aside the problem of language structure, the very nature of the entities themselves presents a problem. The vast majority of people mentioned in the depositions are common folk who have no representation in popular knowledge bases like DBpedia. Even seemingly significant figures (e.g. Florence Fitzpatrick, who is accused of committing a number of atrocities in County Offaly), are often not present.

[2]http://www.bnf.fr/en/tools/a.welcome_to_the_bnf.html
[3]http://1641.tcd.ie
[4]http://cultura-project.eu

In many cases people of great significance are referred to by title rather than by name, e.g. the "kinge of Spaine". This can be problematic as there is currently a king of Spain – Filipe VI – who, from the perspective of a naive disambiguation tool, is likely a much better referent than our intended target – Philip IV.

It is also worth noting (although we do not consider this problem in this paper) that some entities are referenced by lineage rather than by name, e.g. "The son of Lord Mountgarret".

Locations also present an issue. Land borders have changed over time, meaning that some locations no longer exist (e.g. the Barony of Upper Ossory) or have been divided into new sub-regions, e.g. Talbotstown is now split into upper and lower Talbotstown. This makes it hard to establish a suitable referent in modern knowledge bases. In some instances the appropriate action is simply to not annotate those locations if the modern equivalent is too different from the historic one.

Sometimes resolving an entity is difficult simply because of how different the historical spelling is from the modern one, e.g. "Barony of Fassadinin" has been transcribed as "Barrony of ffassa and Dyninge" in the depositions.

Hence performing any sort of automatic analysis on a collection like the depositions is extremely difficult for a variety of reasons. Considering EL in isolation is challenging enough in this context largely due to problems with popular knowledge bases and the under-representation of the entities in which we are interested.

3.2 Corpus Preparation

From the complete collection of depositions we sampled 16 documents to use for our evaluation. We chose documents that were approximately 800 words in length as we felt this would provide enough content per deposition that they would be interesting yet not be too onerous to annotate. Depositions were chosen randomly from geographically distributed counties across Ireland.

While the purpose of this corpus in the context of this experiment is to assess how well EL works, in future we would like to expand it for use in assessing a more complete pipeline including NER and some of the more fundamental NLP tools (tokenizers, chunkers, etc).

To help with this, we performed some basic pre-processing that we would expect an appropriate library to perform in practice. We removed content from the files that was contained in the margins or that had been crossed out by the original scribe (these were marked by `<note>` and `<del>` tags in the original TEI files). We also broke the depositions into approximate sentences as, again, this is an operation that we would expect a suitably implemented tool to perform.

Using WebAnno [5], a human annotator read the selected depositions and attached a DBpedia URI to each identified entity. The focus was on locations and people. Where no suitable URI could be identified, the entities were given an appropriate NIL label:

```
http://aksw.org/notInWiki/<entity_text>
```

where `entity_text` was the surface form of the entity with spaces removed. This format conformed with the annotation suggested by the GERBIL wiki[5].

[5]https://github.com/dice-group/gerbil/wiki/URI-matching#consequences

The annotated corpus contains 480 annotated instances of people and locations. These were found to refer to 283 unique entities of which only 64 were found to have a suitable referent in DBpedia. The remaining 219 were assigned a suitable NIL label.

4 EXPERIMENT

Given the human-annotated depositions, the purpose of the experiment was to assess how well annotations provided by an EL system would match those of a human annotator. In order to perform this comparison we made use of the General Entity Annotator Benchmarking Framework (GERBIL) [21] as an experimentation platform.

GERBIL was developed to provide a simple, consistent, reproducible means of assessing the performance of EL systems on different datasets. Users of the platform can configure an experiment by selecting a set of EL systems, an evaluation dataset and an evaluation method. Gerbil executes the experiment under the given conditions and returns the results in tabulated format. We will discuss the metrics by which these results are compared in Section 5.

As new EL systems are developed, their creators can register their API with GERBIL so that their technology may be used in future experiments. At the time of writing the platform has 17 registered annotation systems and 32 evaluation datasets.

The experiment configuration interface also allows users to upload custom datasets in NLP Interchange Format (NIF) as well as providing a hook for custom implementations of EL systems.

In our setup we chose to use *Disambiguate to Knowledge Base* (D2KB) as our experiment type. Under this configuration the EL systems are provided with the source text of each deposition and the already extracted entities. The only task which the EL systems need to perform is the assignment of URIs to each mention. This simplifies the experiment as the EL systems do not need to perform NER on the source text. We chose to run the experiment in this manner because our interest is in the ability of the system to accurately identify entities, rather than its ability to process the challenging language of the depositions. Resolving unconventional or archaic entity references to a modern referent is challenging enough.

It is also worth noting that some of the EL systems provided by GERBIL cannot perform NER and would need be omitted from an experiment if NER was a requirement.

The depositions described in Section 3 were uploaded as a custom dataset to GERBIL and the experiment was configured to evaluate all available annotation systems against the collection. Under these conditions GERBIL ran the experiment.

5 RESULTS

Under our experiment configuration, GERBIL returns a vast array of statistics which must be interpreted. We have organised and presented these results across Tables 1, 2, 3, 4 and 5. Of the 17 annotation systems tested, 9 failed to finish due to internal errors. Problems like this usually occur because the service is offline and cannot respond to the experiment requests. Hence we have only reported the statistics from the 8 annotators which successfully completed annotating the depositions [3, 7, 10, 13, 17, 20, 23?]. A

Table 1: Results of D2KB evaluation obtained from GERBIL

Annotator	Macro F1	Macro Precision	Macro Recall	Micro F1	Micro Precision	Micro Recall
AGDISTIS	**0.5979**	0.5979	**0.5979**	**0.6052**	0.6052	**0.6052**
Babelfy	0.1299	0.2941	0.0833	0.1130	0.3348	0.0743
DBpedia Spotlight	0.1449	0.4767	0.0854	0.1281	0.4970	0.0774
Dexter	0.1082	0.3333	0.0646	0.0933	0.3536	0.0580
FOX	0.4051	**0.6327**	0.2979	0.4054	**0.6791**	0.2999
FREME NER	0.1012	0.3118	0.0604	0.1045	0.3076	0.0694
KEA	0.1466	0.3358	0.0938	0.1363	0.3384	0.0923
PBOH	0.4250	0.4250	0.4250	0.4266	0.4266	0.4266

Table 2: Results of D2KB evaluation obtained from GERBIL considering InKB

Annotator	Macro F1	Macro Precision	Macro Recall	Micro F1	Micro Precision	Micro Recall
AGDISTIS	**0.3395**	0.4589	0.3063	**0.3557**	0.4040	0.3177
Babelfy	0.2229	0.3348	0.1858	0.2439	0.2941	0.2083
DBpedia Spotlight	0.2667	**0.4970**	0.1959	0.2950	**0.4767**	0.2135
Dexter	0.1865	0.3536	0.1444	0.2175	0.3333	0.1615
FOX	0.3189	0.5176	0.2604	0.3077	0.4000	0.2500
FREME NER	0.2025	0.3076	0.1837	0.2035	0.3118	0.1510
KEA	0.2518	0.3384	0.2373	0.2761	0.3358	0.2344
PBOH	0.2696	0.2203	**0.3834**	0.2799	0.2292	**0.3594**

Table 3: Results of D2KB evaluation obtained from GERBIL considering EE

Annotator	Macro F1	Macro Precision	Macro Recall	Micro F1	Micro Precision	Micro Recall
AGDISTIS	**0.7189**	0.6858	**0.7840**	**0.7326**	0.6869	**0.7847**
Babelfy	0.0000	0.0000	0.0000	0.0000	0.0000	0.0000
DBpedia Spotlight	0.0000	0.0000	0.0000	0.0000	0.0000	0.0000
Dexter	0.0000	0.0000	0.0000	0.0000	0.0000	0.0000
FOX	0.4557	**0.9050**	0.3261	0.4822	**0.8962**	0.3299
FREME NER	0.0000	0.0000	0.0000	0.0000	0.0000	0.0000
KEA	0.0000	0.0000	0.0000	0.0000	0.0000	0.0000
PBOH	0.5565	0.7561	0.4612	0.5782	0.7542	0.4688

Table 4: Results of D2KB evaluation obtained from GERBIL considering GSInKB

Annotator	Macro F1	Macro Precision	Macro Recall	Micro F1	Micro Precision	Micro Recall
AGDISTIS	0.3063	0.3063	0.3063	0.3177	0.3177	0.3177
Babelfy	0.2571	0.5373	0.1779	0.2879	0.5278	0.1979
DBpedia Spotlight	0.3026	**0.7382**	0.1959	0.3361	**0.7885**	0.2135
Dexter	0.2096	0.4900	0.1444	0.2480	0.5345	0.1615
FOX	0.3743	0.7215	0.2604	0.3569	0.6234	0.2500
FREME NER	0.2469	0.4306	0.1837	0.2397	0.5800	0.1510
KEA	0.3042	0.6085	0.2164	0.3281	0.6562	0.2188
PBOH	**0.3834**	0.3834	**0.3834**	**0.3594**	0.3594	**0.3594**

Table 5: Performance statistics and configurations

Annotator	Errors	avg millis/doc	Threshold
AGDISTIS	0	6,049.6875	0.0000
Babelfy	0	4,288.4375	0.0607
DBpedia Spotlight	0	155.3125	0.0000
Dexter	0	2,734.1250	0.0000
FOX	0	23,157.5625	0.0000
FREME NER	0	347.5625	0.0000
KEA	1	9,240.3333	0.4833
PBOH	0	1,930.6875	0.0000

brief summary of the methods employed by the EL systems which successfully completed the task is given below, followed by an explanation of how GERBIL computes the values in each of the tables.

5.1 Entity Linking Systems

AGDISTIS is a graph based EL system which uses the well known HITS algorithm to select referent entities [20]. A set of candidates is retrieved from the knowledge base and a breadth first search is executed on candidate outbound links in order to construct a graph. HITS is executed on the graph and the candidate with the highest combined authority/hub score for each mention is selected as the referent.

Babelfy combines the tasks of Word Sense Disambiguation (WSD) and EL in order to present a unified method of semantically annotating text. During a pre-processing stage, a set of semantic signatures is generated for all concepts present in the knowledge base. After these signatures have been generated, an arbitrary input text may be processed for linking. Candidates for all mentions in the text (both entities and words) are retrieved and a graph is constructed with edges being added between candidates which have similar semantic signatures. A dense subgraph is then computed to determine the appropriate referents for all input mentions.

DBpedia Spotlight uses the Vector Space Model (VSM) in order to choose an appropriate referent for each surface form [10]. Every entity in the knowledge base is assigned a contextual description comprised of the concatenation of all paragraphs that reference the entity. DBpedia Spotlight also weights terms in this contextual aggregate according to how many entity contexts they are associated with. The EL process itself is essentially executed as an Information Retrieval problem. The similarity between an input mention (and the contextual text surrounding the mention) is compared with all of its candidate referents using cosine similarity. The candidate with the highest similarity score is chosen as the referent.

Dexter is an NER and linking framework which implements three different EL methods from the literature – TagME [6]: a vote based method which uses the Wikpedia-Link Based Measure between candidates combined with the probability that a given anchor text points to a candidate entity; Collective Linking [8]: a graph based method which assigns weights to candidate entities based on a combination of importance of the mention to the surrounding context, compatibility of the candidate with the mention and coherence of the candidate with respect to other candidates; and WikiMiner [11]: a machine learning method which uses the probability that a surface form refers to a given candidate combined with the relatedness of the candidate to the surrounding context using the Wikipedia-Link Based Measure.

FOX is actually a NER tool which incorporates EL as one of its outputs [17]. In order to perform EL, it uses its own deployment of AGDISTIS (described above).

FREME treats the problem of mapping surface forms to URIs as an Information Retrieval problem. The surface forms are executed as queries against a search index of entities which acts as the knowledge base. The top ranked entity for each surface form is chosen as the referent. The service also provides the option to re-rank the results from the search engine based on surface form similarity between the mention and the candidate referent's surface form, but this is not the default behaviour and is not part of this evaluation.

KEA implements a four stage EL process. At each stage in this four step process, if KEA believes it has found the correct referent for any given entity then it will commit to that referent and will not proceed to the next step.
From the set of candidates a graph is generated based on links between entities. Links are only created between candidates which are not competing directly with each other. First the algorithm considers connected components in the graph. The assumption is that the correct referents will form a long chain of connections. Next the algorithm checks to see how many of the candidates co-occur on each others' Wikipedia pages. After this a ranking algorithm such as PageRank or HITS is applied to find authoritative candidates. Lastly, if all else fails, a "negative context" step is applied which discards any candidates that do not fit with any referents that were chosen earlier in the disambiguation process [19].

Probabilistic Bag Of Hyperlinks (PBOH) learns a probability distribution based on the likelihood of a candidate being the correct candidate given the surface form by which it is referenced, the context obtained from the surrounding text and the joint probabilities of all candidates appearing together [7]. This problem is NP-hard, hence the resulting probabilities are approximated in practice using loopy belief propagation [14].

5.2 Evaluation Metrics

GERBIL is based on the BAT framework [4], which was designed to provide a consistent and fair means of assessing the relative performance of different EL systems. The BAT framework defines a number of different entity annotation problems on which an evaluation might be based, a vocabulary for describing EL systems and a set of metrics for assessing the output of said systems.

GERBIL adopts the evaluation metrics suggested by BAT, namely micro and macro precision (P), recall (R) and $F1$. Definitions for these are provided in the original paper [4], but we provide them below for clarity. In the context of EL P, R and $F1$ are computed using the number of true/false positives and true/false negatives. These may be defined as:

- True Positives (tp): The number of correctly annotated entities.
- True Negatives (tn): The number of correctly ignored entities (these values are not actually used, but we have included it for completeness).
- False Positives (fp): The number of entities which were annotated when they should have been ignored.
- False Negatives (fn): The number of entities which were ignored when they should have been annotated.

Given these definitions, the standard formulae for computing the values of P, R and $F1$ may be expressed as:

$$P = \frac{|tp|}{|tp| + |fp|}$$

$$R = \frac{|tp|}{|tp| + |fn|} \quad (1)$$

$$F1 = \frac{2 \times P \times R}{P + R}$$

Micro and macro P, R and $F1$ evaluate the annotators by taking two different perspectives on the collection.

Micro considers the entire collection as a single disambiguation problem. The total scores for tp, fp and fn are calculated across the entire collection and used to compute P_{micro}, R_{micro}. This, of course, lends greater weight to longer documents which are comprised of more entities. $F1_{micro}$ is then computed as the harmonic mean of P_{micro} and R_{micro}. The formulae for these values are given below:

$$P_{micro} = \frac{\sum_{d \in D} |tp_d|}{\sum_{d \in D} |tp_d| + |fp_d|}$$

$$R_{micro} = \frac{\sum_{d \in D} |tp_d|}{\sum_{d \in D} |tp_d| + |fn_d|} \quad (2)$$

$$F1_{micro} = \frac{2 \times P_{micro} \times R_{micro}}{P_{micro} + R_{micro}}$$

Macro treats each document as an individual disambiguation problem and then produces final evaluation scores by averaging the performance of the system on each document. In other words, P and R are calculated for each document using the formulae given in Equation 1. The values of P_{macro} and R_{macro} are the average of P and R scores obtained for each document. $F1_{macro}$ is then computed as the harmonic mean of P_{macro} and R_{macro}. The formulae for these values are given below:

$$P_{macro} = \frac{\sum_{d \in D} P_d}{|D|}$$

$$R_{macro} = \frac{\sum_{d \in D} R_d}{|D|} \quad (3)$$

$$F1_{macro} = \frac{2 \times P_{macro} \times R_{macro}}{P_{macro} + R_{macro}}$$

In the event of a division by zero in any of Equations 1, 2, 3, GERBIL responds in one of two ways. If all tp, fp and fn values are zero, then P, R and $F1$ are assigned the value 1. Alternatively, if tp is zero but fp or fn are non-zero then P, R, and $F1$ are zero. This behaviour is documented on the GERBIL wiki[6].

Values for micro and macro P, R and $F1$ are computed for each annotator under four different experiment conditions, the results of which are displayed in Tables 1, 2, 3, and 4.

Table 1 presents the results for a standard evaluation. All tp, fp and fn results are considered for all entities in the collection. This is an overall summary of how well each annotator performed.

Table 2 presents the results when we only consider responses from the annotators which are contained in the knowledge base (in this case, DBpedia). This essentially considers how well the annotator performed if we ignore Emerging Entities.

Table 3 presents the results of the experiment when only Emerging Entities (EE) are considered. Emerging Entities are entities that are not in the knowledge base. In the case of this experiment, anything which could be termed an Emerging Entities was given a NIL label in the gold standard. Hence this score can be considered a measure of how often an annotator correctly abstained from applying a label to a document entity.

Table 4 presents the results if we only consider entities in the gold standard that are present in the knowledge base. Again, this eliminates emerging entities, but we also only consider URIs returned by the annotators if the URI is applied to an entity in the gold standard whose correct annotation is contained in the knowledge base. Essentially if we only consider the entities that the annotator *should* have annotated and *did* annotate, then we count how many of those annotations were correct.

Table 5 is included to report some performance and configuration information for the annotators while the experiment was being run. Errors is a total count of errors reported by the annotation system. Avg millis/doc is the average number of milliseconds taken to annotate each document in the gold standard. Finally, some annotators have a confidence threshold. If the confidence of an annotator in its selected URI is below this threshold then the annotator will not apply the given URI to the corresponding mention. We had no control over the threshold value, but we wish to report it for the sake of completeness.

6 DISCUSSION

Looking at the results in Table 1, the annotator which seems to clearly stand out above the rest is AGDISTIS. However, a closer

[6] https://github.com/dice-group/gerbil/wiki/Precision,-Recall-and-F1-measure

examination of the results shows that it achieved the best performance in the EE task but actually performed quite poorly in the InKB task (albeit still better than the other annotators). This suggests that AGDISTIS' stellar performance is largely because it abstained from annotating most of the entities in the depositions. Because NILs comprise about 77% of the unique entity mentions, this was sufficient to increase its score immensely as demonstrated by the reported scores in Table 3. FOX (which is built on AGDISTIS) and PBOH also exhibit relatively appreciable overall performance for the same reason.

It is interesting that other annotators do not seem to succeed at abstaining and always apply a URI to a surface form. This, overzealous, approach to annotating entities may be extremely problematic if these systems were deployed in practice. Scholars who would use tools such as EL systems (or services built on top of the outputs they produce) need to know that they can trust the data with which they are being presented. If an annotation system is prone to annotating a collection with inaccurate links then it is of little use to history scholars.

The results of the InKB and GSInKB evaluation show that no single annotator is particularly suited to identifying the correct referent where one exists, although AGDISTIS does still perform better than the other EL systems considered. DBpedia Spotlight's performance warrants note as its EL method is based on comparing the context of the mention with known entity contexts in DBpedia using a VSM. This approach is obviously hobbled by the inconsistent language of the depositions, yet it still performs better than Babelfy, FREME, KEA and Dexter.

While none of the results for the annotation tasks on the InKB and GSInKB problems are especially good, certain graph based approaches appear to be more robust against the anomalies that we see in the depositions. AGDISTIS which uses HITS, and PBOH which builds probability distribution based on links between pages, seem to perform relatively well when compared with other systems. This suggests that being able to exploit the relationships between candidates when selecting a referent may be an important consideration when choosing an EL system for collections such as the depositions. Yet Babelfy uses a dense subgraph approach while KEA uses connected components, neither of which appear to have resulted in particularly accurate annotations.

A statistic which is not reported by GERBIL is how often the correct referent was considered as a candidate and then ultimately rejected by the EL method, as opposed to the situation where the correct candidate was not identified as a potential candidate in the first place. It would be interesting to see how much of the inaccuracy of the surveyed systems can be ascribed to the candidate retrieval process as opposed to the EL method.

Clearly a large problem that we face is the lack of representation for the deposition entities in popular knowledge bases. Of the 283 unique entities which were manually annotated in the gold standard, only 64 (23%) were found to have a referent in DBpedia. One possible solution is to identify alternative, specialised sources of knowledge which can work in tandem with more common knowledge bases, much like Brando's approach. An alternative (and likely more sustainable) approach would be to focus on the Emerging Entities problem. Given the ad hoc nature of the entities encountered in the depositions (often servants or soldiers), this probably makes more sense, as identifying an all-encompassing knowledge base will be difficult.

We acknowledge that a fundamental weakness in our method is the lack of annotators involved in creating the evaluation corpus. Unfortunately, due to the specialised nature of the depositions, finding annotators with the prerequisite knowledge to annotate the entities is challenging. We are presently working with historians to improve the quality of the evaluation corpus.

Ultimately we would like to produce a corpus that is comprised of a more representative number of depositions, a minimum of 64: two documents for each county in Ireland. Alternatively it has been suggested that greater benefit may be derived from focusing on a specific county as this will help to constrain the problem that the corpus represents. However this seems like an unrealistic constraint as choice of county could have a drastic effect on the difficulty of the resulting corpus. This is because some counties are likely to have better representation in knowledge bases than others. For example, there are DBpedia entries for specific streets in Dublin City whilst some towns in the neighbouring County Meath have little-to-no representation.

7 CONCLUSIONS

Overall we believe that this research has raised some interesting questions about the properties of a "good" EL system for CH. There is still much work to be done. We will proceed by expanding and enhancing the gold standard 1641 depositions so that we can perform more rigorous evaluations. We will continue to work with historians to ensure its integrity.

We will also continue to seek answers to the problem of dealing with poor representations of entities in knowledge bases. This is undeniably our greatest challenge. The depositions provide many excellent examples of the obstacles faced when dealing with niche collections.

Finally we will work to discern the traits and qualities possessed by the tested annotation systems which resulted in their success (or otherwise) during this evaluation.

We believe that finding concrete answers to the questions raised by this paper will allow us to create powerful EL tools which will help to build meaningful links within and across archives.

ACKNOWLEDGMENTS

This research is supported by the Science Foundation Ireland (Grant 13/RC/2106) and the ADAPT Centre (www.adaptcentre.ie) at Trinity College, Dublin.

REFERENCES

[1] Eneko Agirre, Ander Barrena, Oier Lopez De Lacalle, Aitor Soroa, Samuel Fern, and Mark Stevenson. 2012. Matching Cultural Heritage items to Wikipedia. In *LREC.* 1729–1735.

[2] Carmen Brando, Francesca Frontini, and Jean-Gabriel Ganascia. 2016. REDEN: Named Entity Linking in Digital Literary Editions Using Linked Data Sets. *Complex Systems Informatics and Modeling Quarterly* 7 (July 2016), 60 – 80.

[3] Diego Ceccarelli, Claudio Lucchese, Salvatore Orlando, Raffaele Perego, and Salvatore Trani. 2013. Dexter: an open source framework for entity linking. In *Proceedings of the sixth international workshop on Exploiting semantic annotations in information retrieval.* ACM, 17–20.

[4] Marco Cornolti, Paolo Ferragina, and Massimiliano Ciaramita. 2013. A framework for benchmarking entity-annotation systems. In *Proceedings of the 22nd international conference on World Wide Web.* ACM, 249–260.

[5] Richard Eckart de Castilho, Eva Mujdricza-Maydt, Seid Muhie Yimam, Silvana Hartmann, Iryna Gurevych, Anette Frank, and Chris Biemann. 2016. A web-based tool for the integrated annotation of semantic and syntactic structures. In *Proceedings of the Workshop on Language Technology Resources and Tools for Digital Humanities (LT4DH)*. 76–84.

[6] Paolo Ferragina and Ugo Scaiella. 2010. Tagme: on-the-fly annotation of short text fragments (by Wikipedia entities). In *Proceedings of the 19th ACM international conference on Information and knowledge management*. ACM, 1625–1628.

[7] Octavian-Eugen Ganea, Marina Ganea, Aurelien Lucchi, Carsten Eickhoff, and Thomas Hofmann. 2016. Probabilistic bag-of-hyperlinks model for entity linking. In *Proceedings of the 25th International Conference on World Wide Web*. International World Wide Web Conferences Steering Committee, 927–938.

[8] Xianpei Han, Le Sun, and Jun Zhao. 2011. Collective entity linking in web text: a graph-based method. In *Proceedings of the 34th international ACM SIGIR conference on Research and development in Information Retrieval*. ACM, 765–774.

[9] Hugo Manguinhas, Nuno Freire, Antoine Isaac, Juliane Stiller, Valentine Charles, Aitor Soroa, Rainer Simon, and Vladimir Alexiev. 2016. Exploring comparative evaluation of semantic enrichment tools for cultural heritage metadata. In *International Conference on Theory and Practice of Digital Libraries*. Springer, 266–278.

[10] Pablo N Mendes, Max Jakob, Andrés García-Silva, and Christian Bizer. 2011. DBpedia spotlight: shedding light on the web of documents. In *Proceedings of the 7th international conference on semantic systems*. ACM, 1–8.

[11] David Milne and Ian H. Witten. 2008. Learning to Link with Wikipedia. In *Proceedings of the 17th ACM Conference on Information and Knowledge Management (CIKM '08)*. ACM, New York, NY, USA, 509–518.

[12] Petar Mitankin, Stefan Gerdjikov, and Stoyan Mihov. 2014. An Approach to Unsupervised Historical Text Normalisation. In *Proceedings of the First International Conference on Digital Access to Textual Cultural Heritage (DATeCH '14)*. ACM, New York, NY, USA, 29–34. https://doi.org/10.1145/2595188.2595191

[13] Andrea Moro, Alessandro Raganato, and Roberto Navigli. 2014. Entity linking meets word sense disambiguation: a unified approach. *Transactions of the Association for Computational Linguistics* 2 (2014), 231–244.

[14] Kevin P Murphy, Yair Weiss, and Michael I Jordan. 1999. Loopy belief propagation for approximate inference: An empirical study. In *Proceedings of the Fifteenth conference on Uncertainty in artificial intelligence*. Morgan Kaufmann Publishers Inc., 467–475.

[15] Felix Sasaki, Tatiana Gornostay, Milan Dojchinovski, Michele Osella, Erik Mannens, Giannis Stoitsis, and Phil Ritchie. 2015. Introducing FREME: Deploying Linguistic Linked Data. In *MSW@ESWC*. 59–66.

[16] Wei Shen, Jianyong Wang, and Jiawei Han. 2015. Entity linking with a knowledge base: Issues, techniques, and solutions. *IEEE Transactions on Knowledge and Data Engineering* 27, 2 (2015), 443–460.

[17] René Speck and Axel-Cyrille Ngonga Ngomo. 2014. Named Entity Recognition using FOX. In *International Semantic Web Conference 2014 (ISWC2014), Demos & Posters*.

[18] Christina M Steiner, Maristella Agosti, Mark S Sweetnam, Eva-C Hillemann, Nicola Orio, Chiara Ponchia, Cormac Hampson, Gary Munnelly, Alexander Nussbaumer, Dietrich Albert, et al. 2014. Evaluating a digital humanities research environment: the CULTURA approach. *International Journal on Digital Libraries* 15, 1 (2014), 53–70.

[19] Nadine Steinmetz and Harald Sack. 2013. Semantic multimedia information retrieval based on contextual descriptions. In *Extended Semantic Web Conference*. Springer, 382–396.

[20] Ricardo Usbeck, Axel-Cyrille Ngonga Ngomo, Michael Röder, Daniel Gerber, Sandro Athaide Coelho, Sören Auer, and Andreas Both. 2014. AGDISTIS-graph-based disambiguation of named entities using linked data. In *International Semantic Web Conference*. Springer, 457–471.

[21] Ricardo Usbeck, Michael Röder, Axel-Cyrille Ngonga Ngomo, Ciro Baron, Andreas Both, Martin Brümmer, Diego Ceccarelli, Marco Cornolti, Didier Cherix, Bernd Eickmann, et al. 2015. GERBIL: general entity annotator benchmarking framework. In *Proceedings of the 24th International Conference on World Wide Web*. ACM, 1133–1143.

[22] Seth Van Hooland, Max De Wilde, Ruben Verborgh, Thomas Steiner, and Rik Van de Walle. 2015. Exploring entity recognition and disambiguation for cultural heritage collections. *Digital Scholarship in the Humanities* 30, 2 (2015), 262–279.

[23] Jörg Waitelonis and Harald Sack. 2016. Named Entity Linking in #Tweets with KEA. In *#Microposts*. 61–63.

[24] Max De Wilde. 2015. Improving Retrieval of Historical Content with Entity Linking. In *New Trends in Databases and Information Systems (Communications in Computer and Information Science)*, Tadeusz Morzy, Patrick Valduriez, and Ladjel Bellatreche (Eds.). Springer International Publishing, 498–504.

[25] Mohamed Amir Yosef, Johannes Hoffart, Ilaria Bordino, Marc Spaniol, and Gerhard Weikum. 2011. AIDA: An online tool for accurate disambiguation of named entities in text and tables. *Proceedings of the VLDB Endowment* 4, 12 (2011), 1450–1453.

[26] Stefan Zwicklbauer, Christin Seifert, and Michael Granitzer. 2016. Robust and Collective Entity Disambiguation through Semantic Embeddings. ACM Press, 425–434.

An Analysis of Cross-Document Linking Mechanisms

Ahmed A.O. Tayeh and Beat Signer
Web & Information Systems Engineering Lab
Vrije Universiteit Brussel
Pleinlaan 2, 1050 Brussels, Belgium
atayeh, bsigner@vub.be

ABSTRACT

Physical and digital documents do often not exist in isolation but are implicitly or explicitly linked. Previous research in Human-Computer Interaction and Personal Information Management has revealed certain user behaviour in associating information across physical and digital documents. Nevertheless, there is a lack of empirical studies on user needs and behaviour when defining these associations. In this paper, we address this lack of empirical studies and provide insights into strategies that users apply when associating information across physical and digital documents. In addition, our study reveals the limitations of current practices and we suggest improvements for associating information across documents. Last but not least, we identify a set of design implications for the development of future cross-document linking solutions.

CCS CONCEPTS

• **General and reference → Surveys and overviews;** • **Human-centered computing → Pointing; User centered design; Empirical studies in interaction design;**

KEYWORDS

Cross-document linking; linking mechanisms; user linking behaviour; reading and writing; hypertext; annotation

ACM Reference Format:
Ahmed A.O. Tayeh and Beat Signer. 2018. An Analysis of Cross-Document Linking Mechanisms. In *JCDL '18: The 18th ACM/IEEE Joint Conference on Digital Libraries, June 3–7, 2018, Fort Worth, TX, USA*. ACM, New York, NY, USA, 10 pages. https://doi.org/10.1145/3197026.3197053

1 INTRODUCTION

As already mentioned by Vannevar Bush in 1945, documents do not exist in isolation but are often related to other documents [6]. This has also been confirmed by HCI research investigating the user behaviour while reading and writing physical and digital documents. For example, Marshal [11] stated that users use highlights or underlines as anchors while reading to explicitly associate (link) information within a single document. Some other research in the domain of Personal Information Management (PIM) identified that users use digital and physical folders for organising and relating (associating) information across documents [9].

A number of solutions have been proposed in order to help users in associating information within and across documents. For instance, the majority of recent digital document formats support simple forms of mostly unidirectional linking features. Furthermore, various open hypermedia and annotation solutions have been introduced to allow users to link and annotate documents in order to create explicit associations. Moreover, some recent solutions [2, 5] enable the use of annotations for associating information across documents.

Even though there exist some general findings regarding the user behaviour when linking information within and across documents, to the best of our knowledge there are no studies aiming to understand a knowledge worker's behaviour when associating information across physical as well as digital documents. As a result of the lack of such empirical studies, the development of most existing linking systems has been solely motivated by limitations of their predecessors or new features to be supported, rather than on a clear understanding of the needs and requirements of end users [17]. We believe that only a better understanding of the user behaviour in linking and associating documents as well as the user requirements for cross-document linking will lead to more advanced and usable linking solutions. In this paper, we therefore provide a detailed investigation of user needs and behaviour when associating information across physical and digital documents. Our approach is based on a multi-case design approach consisting of an online survey and interviews with some of the participants of the online survey in order to investigate their cross-document linking behaviour as well as their feedback about existing solutions. The insights that we gained from the presented user study further enabled us to formulate a number of design implications for future cross-document link services.

We begin in Section 2 by highlighting previous research results. In Section 3, we discuss the methodology used for our study, whilst the results of the study are presented in Section 4. In Section 5 we critically discuss the study results and provide a number of design implications for future cross-document link services, before providing some concluding remarks in Section 6.

JCDL '18, June 3–7, 2018, Fort Worth, TX, USA

ACM ISBN 978-1-4503-5178-2/18/06...$15.00
https://doi.org/10.1145/3197026.3197053

2 BACKGROUND

There have been a number of studies in different domains revealing some interesting findings regarding the user behaviour when associating information within and across digital and physical documents. In the digital world, some studies have stated that system folders, which are used to organise documents, are a way of associating "entire" documents [9]. Besides the use of folders, previous studies have shown that users make use of annotations in order to create associations between parts of documents. In the physical world, the filing, piling and mixing organisational strategies [10, 19] are used to organise relevant documents.

Previous studies in HCI that aimed to understand and analyse a user's reading and writing activities have stated that users perform a *cross-document referencing* task in order to integrate and associate information from one or multiple documents. According to Adler et al. [1], this cross-document referencing task forms a major part of the reading and writing activity. The work by O'Hara et al. [13, 14] revealed that readers of digital or physical documents tend to use different kinds of annotations (e.g. marginal notes or underlines) to define references between documents. In her work 'Toward an Ecology of Hypertext Annotation' [11], Marshall stated that some user annotations in physical books are an emulation of *hypertext patterns*, such as creating and referring to anchors within a book. For example, readers used highlights or underlines as anchors in a printed book in order to refer to them from another part of the same book. They also tend to use annotations to explicitly make references to entire chapters or sections within the same book.

The literature within the field of Personal Information Management is mainly focusing on how people organise and retrieve information artefacts. Despite the fact that Whittaker et al. [20] have noted the lack of empirical research in PIM, there are some interesting findings that are relevant in the context of our research. Jones et al. [9] stated that folders are used to summarise, organise and associate information that is relevant for a specific user task (e.g. a planned project or some course material). Another study by Boardmann et al. [4] revealed that some users use a consistent folder naming convention for relating resources to each other. According to the same study, users create so-called *overlapping folders* (folders with the same name) by using different tools (e.g. Outlook and the file system) in order to organise resources that are related to the same production activity. A user might, for instance, create a folder named 'marriage' in an email client to store all emails concerning their marriage plan and at the same time create a system folder with the same name for storing other related documents.

We believe that the existing findings regarding the user behaviour in associating information across documents are not sufficient for building future linking solutions. In the presented user study we therefore thoroughly investigated the user behaviour in linking and associating information across physical and digital documents.

3 METHODOLOGY

We have chosen a qualitative approach using a multi-case design to explore different users' cross-document information association behaviour [21]. Our study relies on a mixed methods approach consisting of an online survey combined with interviews with participants of the online survey. The participants of our study were informed that the collected data would be used for scientific research as well as in scientific publications. Furthermore, they were ensured that their data would be treated confidentially and be fully anonymised if used in any publication.

3.1 Data Collection

3.1.1 Online Survey. For the purpose of this study, we designed an online questionnaire (for details about the questions see [17]) which focuses on investigating whether users associate information in both, the physical and digital media, which mechanisms they use to associate information, why they create these associations and whether they are happy with the mechanisms that they currently use to define these associations. Our online survey allowed us to collect data from a much larger number of participants than it would have been feasible through alternative methods such as observations or think aloud experiments [21].

In order to identify the reasons for associating information as well as potential problems, we first needed to find out whether users had ever felt the need to link or associate information in a particular way (further referred to as a scenario). A negative reply to this question implies that it is rather unlikely that a user has ever engaged in this type of linking activity, whereas a positive reply indicates that they are likely to have engaged in associating information or experienced an inability to do so. In the case of a negative reply, the survey therefore immediately moved on to the next scenario. In case of a positive answer, participants were asked for more information about their behaviour in associating information or any difficulties preventing them from creating associations.

The survey contained both open-ended questions as well as quantitative questions using a 5-point Likert scale. The open-ended questions enabled participants to freely describe their previous activities in associating information within and across documents. It is worth mentioning that some of the survey questions investigated the information association mechanisms that have already been identified by previous research, including the use of digital folders and annotations. The survey was conducted using the LimeSurvey[1] online tool and contained four groups of questions:

(1) Questions related to a participant's demographic information such as gender, country of residence, education and age;
(2) Questions related to a participant's behaviour in associating information in the physical space. These questions differentiated between two main scenarios:

[1] https://www.limesurvey.org

(a) single physical (SP) (b) multiple physical (MP) (c) single digital (SD) (d) multiple digital same (MDS) (e) multiple digital different(MDD) (f) digital physical (DP)

Figure 1: Different scenarios of linking and associating information

- Associating information within a single **p**hysical document (**SP**) (e.g. between two different sections or chapters of a printed book)
- Associating information across **m**ultiple **p**hysical documents (**MP**). An annotation in a printed document that declares the existence of a relationship to (parts of) another printed document is an example for this scenario.

(3) Questions about a participant's behaviour in associating information within and across digital documents. The questions differentiated between three main scenarios:
- Associating information within a single **d**igital document (**SD**);
- Associating information across **m**ultiple **d**igital documents of the **s**ame document type (**MDS**);
- Associating information across **m**ultiple **d**igital documents of **d**ifferent document types (**MDD**).

(4) Questions about a participant's behaviour in associating information across **d**igital and **p**hysical documents (**DP**).

Note that the scenario names and their abbreviations (illustrated in Figure 1) are extensively used in the remainder of this paper. At the end of the survey, the participants were invited to upload any screenshots or images of associations they have created in the past and we received 15 images in total. Finally, the participants were also invited to provide their email address if they were willing to potentially extend their participation in the form of an interview. As an incentive, participants who provided their email address could win a 30 Euro Amazon voucher.

3.1.2 Interviews. In addition to the online survey, we interviewed some of the survey participants in order to further investigate their answers and gain detailed insights about their information association behaviour. We used unstructured open questions to obtain descriptions of interesting mechanisms for associating information or clarifications of vague answers given during the survey. The interviews were performed either face-to-face or via Skype, lasted 15 minutes on average and were recorded. In addition to the recordings, the researchers also collected some notes during the interviews. The interviews and notes were later transcribed in a Word document in order to facilitate the data analysis.

3.2 Population

The link to our online survey has been distributed internationally via email to researchers from various research fields. Given the focus of our study, we chose to recruit participants from a population of researchers as they represent a group of *knowledge workers* who frequently use documents and can be expected to engage in document linking. It is worth mentioning that other user groups such as secretaries could also be considered as knowledge workers since they frequently use documents. However, we believe that researchers are more engaged in associating information especially when reading and writing scientific articles. In total, 238 people completed the survey. Our sample includes Master's students (n = 23), PhD students (n = 169) and researchers holding a PhD degree (n = 46). The 238 participants consisted of 82 female and 156 male participants, ageing from 21 to 60 years. While 97 participants have provided us their email addresses, we only selected 12 participants for a follow-up interview based on their answers. Note that given the population, the results of our study might be generalised for the community of researchers but not necessarily for other knowledge workers.

3.3 Data Analysis

The collected quantitative data was analysed using descriptive statistics, while the qualitative data was analysed using an informal coding. During the qualitative analysis, the written comments of participants, the notes of the interviewer as well as the received images and screenshots were all taken into account. First, the qualitative data was carefully checked in search of common association mechanisms used by the participants. Based on this assessment, a list of association mechanisms was compiled for every scenario presented to the participants (i.e. SP, MP, SD, MDS, MDD and DP). Second, we identified the characteristics and limitations of each mechanism and calculated how many participants applied that particular mechanism.

4 RESULTS

Our study shows that *most knowledge workers are either occasionally or frequently associating information across documents* as highlighted in Figure 2. Users are associating information during both, reading and writing activities, which confirms the findings presented in [1, 9, 13]. As shown in Table 1, users apply different linking mechanisms to associate information in the different scenarios. Please note that in Table 1, association mechanisms that have been already identified in previous research are written in normal font, whereas the mechanisms that we have discovered are emphasised in

Mechanism		SP	MP	SD	MDS	MDD	DP
Annotations & highlights	B1	24.2%	28.7%	35.8%	30.2%	28.9%	21.7%
	B2	30.5%	29.4%	27.6%	20.1%	19.3%	24.8%
	U1	31%	22.6%	35%	45.6%	48.2%	25.5%
	U2	31%	42.4%	34.3%	33.5%	34.4%	35.6%
Line & arrow drawings		11.8%	—	—	—	—	—
Common symbols		2.2%	—	—	—	—	—
Separate documents		2.2%	7.5%	3.3%	12.7%	12.4%	4.6%
Physical folders		—	3.4%	—	—	—	—
Post-it notes		1.1%	1.3%	—	—	—	0.7%
Physical counterparts		—	—	2.8%	3.3%	3.4%	3.8%
Copy & paste		—	—	2.2%	1.3%	1.3%	—
Digital folders		—	—	—	63%	66%	—
External applications		—	—	—	3.3%	2.7%	—
Writing physical parts into a digital document		—	—	—	—	—	2.3%
Scanning physical documents		—	—	—	—	—	3.1%

Table 1: Linking mechanisms used in the different information association scenarios

italics. Further, the percentages presented in Table 1 are relative to the number of participants who associate information in the given scenario as illustrated in Table 2.

4.1 Linking Information in Physical Documents

As shown in Table 2, many participants (74.3%) indicated that they associate information in a single physical document, with 11 participants (6.2%) doing this very frequently (see Figure 2). In the case of MP, 61.3% of the participants indicated that they have faced situations where they had to associate information across two or more physical documents, with only 6 of them (4.1%) doing this very frequently. This difference in terms of frequency might be caused by various factors. As discussed later, some users apply simple and trivial mechanisms to associate information in SP that cannot be applied in MP (e.g. drawing a simple line between the associated parts). Furthermore, sometimes the closeness of the associated parts in SP (e.g. information on the same page) helps users to easily associate information.

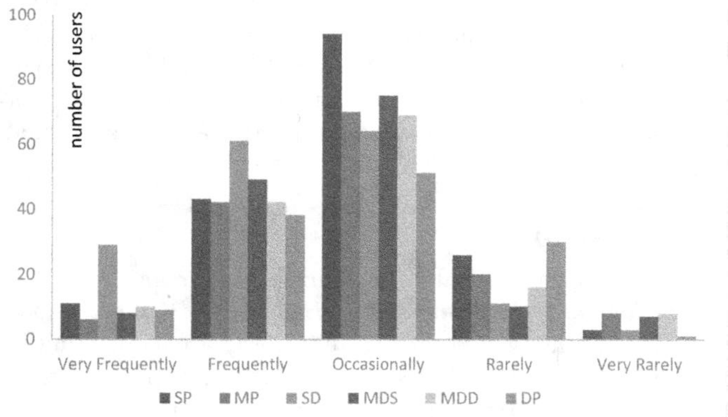

Figure 2: Linking frequency in the different scenarios

Our investigation revealed that participants are applying different mechanisms to create associations between pieces of information in both physical scenarios. Most of the participants use annotations (e.g. comments, arrows or highlights) in order to explicitly associate information. This seems to confirm the findings presented in [11, 13, 14]. The use of annotations as well as highlights enables participants to *establish associations at any level of granularity* since participants are able to highlight and annotate any part of a document such as a chapter, a section, a paragraph or a single word. Annotations and highlights also yield to different types of *bidirectional* and *unidirectional* associations.

Scenario	Size of the subsample relative to the total number of participants
SP	74.3%
MP	61.3%
SD	70.5%
MDS	62.6%
MDD	60.9%
DP	54.2%

Table 2: Relative size of the subsample of participants who associate information in a particular scenario

Our study identified two main types of bidirectional associations resulting from using annotations and highlights as illustrated in Figure 3. For the first type (B1), the bidirectionality is established by highlighting the different parts and writing annotations with references to each other next to these parts. For the second type (B2), participants only write annotations next to each part without any highlighting. In a bidirectional association, participants write down references to all the linked parts in order to help them later in information refinding tasks. The B1 associations mimic the creation of hypertext anchors since participants explicitly highlight the exact text anchors to be linked with each other. This confirms Marshall's findings [11] that participants create anchors in a printed book in order to refer to them from another part in the same document.

In the SP scenario, B1 associations are used by 24.2% of the participants, whereas 28.7% use them in the MP scenario.

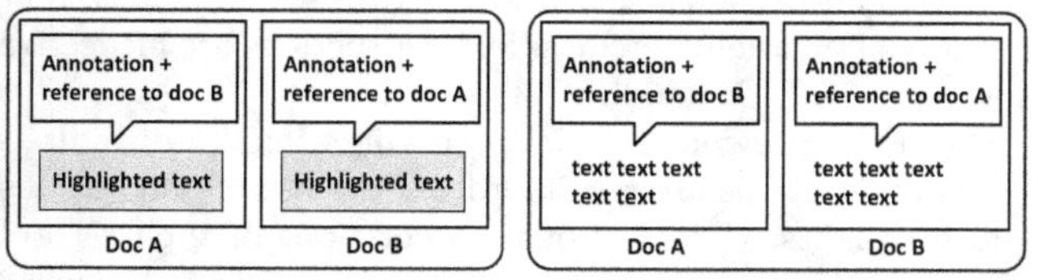

(a) B1 (b) B2

Figure 3: Two main types of bidirectional associations using annotations and highlights

The B2 associations are used by 30.5% of the participants in the SP scenario and by 29.4% in the MP scenario. We also discovered other interesting bidirectional association patterns. One important pattern emerges in a single document scenario where the parts are close to each other (e.g. on the same page). In this case, 11.8% of the participants indicated that they would normally draw arrows or lines between the associated parts. Moreover, four participants (2.2%) indicated that they use common symbols or numbers in order to match the different pieces in the single document scenario. The use of line drawings and common symbols as association mechanisms illustrates the flexibility in the SP scenario.

We further discovered that many participants are creating *unidirectional associations* between the intended pieces of information. Two main types of unidirectional associations resulting from using annotations and highlights were identified. As illustrated in Figure 4, in the first type (U1), the unidirectionality is established by highlighting the different parts and by writing annotations next to one of the parts. In the second type (U2), annotations are written next to one of the parts without any highlighting. The U1 associations are used by 31% of the participants in scenario SP and by 22.6% of the participants in scenario MP. U2 associations are used by 31% of the participants in the SP scenario and by 42.4% in the MP scenario. The collected data from the survey and the interviews shows that participants prefer to have bidirectional associations due to the advantages in re-finding the linked parts.

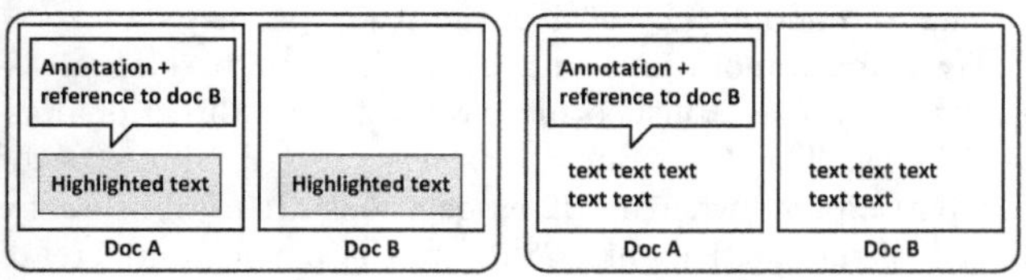

(a) U1 (b) U2

Figure 4: Two main types of unidirectional associations using annotations and highlights

Another interesting finding is that numerous participants tend to use a *separate document* in order to explicitly create associations, in particular in the MP scenario. In the SP scenario, 2.2% of the participants indicated that they use a separate document (digital or physical) in order to note, summarise or copy and paste the different parts. On the other hand, in the MP scenario, 7.5% of the participants are using a separate document to explicitly indicate the association.

Other association mechanisms applied by participants include the use of physical folders, ring binders as well as paper stacks in order to associate information across multiple physical documents (MP). These mechanisms result in the filing and piling organisational strategies that are well known in the PIM literature [10]. Finally, the use of post-it notes was mentioned for associating information in both, the SP and MP scenarios.

4.2 Linking Information in Digital Documents

In general, most participants are applying numerous mechanisms to associate information in the different digital scenarios. From the participants who associate information, 7.7% in the SD scenario, 3.3% in the MDS scenario and 3.4% in the MDD scenario have indicated their inability to create associations between the intended parts. In general, the lack of a suitable linking tool as well as the necessary effort to create associations between the intended parts are the main reasons that prevented participants from creating these associations.

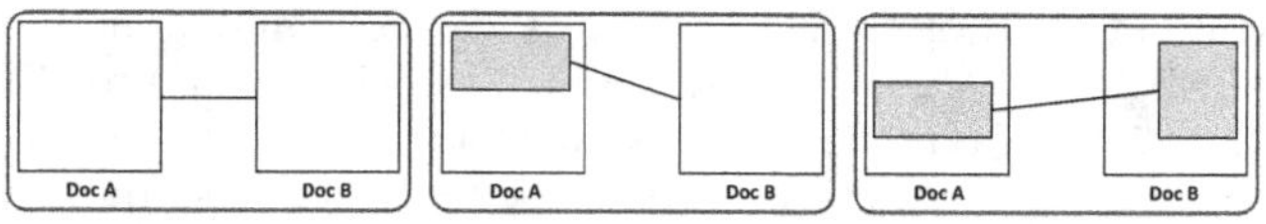

(a) (b) (c)

Figure 5: Associations between digital documents are created to link entire documents (a), parts of a document with an entire document (b) or different parts of the documents (c)

As illustrated in Figure 5, associations across different digital documents are created at *different levels of granularity* to link entire documents (a), parts of a document with another document (b) or different parts of two documents (c). In the context of the MDS scenario, 75.1% of the participants who associate information create associations between the different parts of documents (c). In the same scenario, 57% of the participants associate information between parts of a document and another document (b) and 48.3% of the participants create associations between entire documents (a). In the MDD scenario, 46.2% of the participants associate information between entire documents (a), 80% between parts of different documents (c) and 61.3% between parts of a document with another document (b).

4.2.1 Single Digital Document. In the SD scenario, 70.5% of the participants indicated that they have faced situations where they associated information within a single document. While 82.3% of those participants use annotations as well as highlights to explicitly create the associations, another 10% of the participants have adopted various other interesting mechanisms to create the associations between the different parts.

As mentioned earlier, the remaining 7.7% of the participants are not able to create the intended associations.

The annotation features provided by the different document viewers and applications such as Foxit Reader[2] have enabled the majority of the participants to create the associations using annotations and highlights not only in the SD scenario but also in the other digital MDS and MDD scenarios. This is an interesting finding since it contradicts to some extent some findings of a previous study carried out by O'Hara et al. [13] which compared participants' reading activities of physical and digital documents. In their study, the majority of participants did not prefer to annotate digital documents. According to O'Hara et al., the difficulty of annotating documents and the inflexibility of interaction techniques via mouse and keyboard were the main reasons that prevented participants from annotating digital documents. The discrepancy between our findings and these earlier study findings might be explained in different ways. For example, in the study of O'Hara et al., participants were obliged to use a specific document viewer (Microsoft Word 6.0) for reading their documents and some participants might not have been familiar with the offered annotation features.

By using the annotations and highlights mechanism to create associations, participants tend to create bidirectional and unidirectional associations between the different parts. Out of the 82.3% of the participants who use annotations and highlights, 35.8% create bidirectional associations of type B1 and 27.6% of type B2. Unidirectional associations of type U2 are established by 34.3%, whereas U1 associations are used by 35% of the participants.

As mentioned before, other interesting association mechanisms are used. Various users (3.3%) tend to use separate documents to summarise or copy and paste the associated parts. According to numerous participants, *"the new document that was used to describe the different associations served as a database of related information or as a starting point to remember some content of the linked documents at a later stage"*. Five participants (2.8%) mentioned that they prefer to read printed versions of the documents and associate information in physical counterparts. Two of them have explicitly indicated the flexibility in annotating physical documents compared to digital documents and four participants (2.2%) mentioned that they *"copy one part and paste it next to the other"*.

4.2.2 Different Documents of the Same Document Type.

In this scenario, 62.6% of the participants have adopted various mechanisms to create associations between pieces of information in different documents of the same document type. These mechanisms include storing the linked documents in the same digital folder, using annotations and using separate documents for describing the intended associations.

Participants are mainly using the digital folder mechanism (63%) in order to create associations between entire documents. This confirms the finding of Jones et al. [9] stating that participants use folders to organise related information. It is worth mentioning that previous research has shown that traditional digital hierarchical folder structures are ineffective and cognitively demanding [3].

As in the previous scenarios, unidirectional and bidirectional associations are resulting from the use of annotations and highlights. Unidirectional associations of type U1 are created by 45.6% of the participants while the ones of type U2 are applied by 33.5%. Bidirectional associations of type B1 are established by 30.2% and of type B2 by 20.1% of the participants.

Some other mechanisms are applied by 22.6% of the participants. The use of a separate document to associate information is adopted by quite a large percentage of the participants with 12.7% of the participants using separate documents to summarise, describe or copy and paste the parts.

The use of the physical counterpart mechanism has been applied by five participants (3.3%). They prefered to associate information in the printed version of the intended documents. *"I prefer to work on printed material which I can also easily sort physically in addition to storing the files in the same folders"*, one participant justified their strategy. Three other participants (2%) rely on their memories to remember associations but according to them, over time they tend to forget their associations.

Five of the participants (3.3%) have indicated the use of some external applications (e.g. Evernote[3] and Zotero[4]) to create associations between entire documents of the same digital type. Bibliography reference managers such as Zotero are used by participants to make associations between entire documents in order to facilitate the creation of citations and bibliography while writing scientific reports. Most of the interviewees (12) did not indicate the use of bibliography reference managers in the online survey. Nevertheless, in the interviews, all of them confirmed the use of these systems during scientific writing activities. Further, most of the interviewees did not consider the bibliography reference managers as association and linking tools.

4.2.3 Different Documents of Different Types.

In this scenario, 60.9% of the participants associate information across two or more documents. As in the previous scenario, storing associated documents in the same folder is the dominant mechanism adopted by 66% of the study participants.

By using annotations and highlights, unidirectional associations are established more often than bidirectional associations. The U1 associations are created by 48.2% of the participants whereas U2 associations are established by 34.4% of the participants. 28.9% of the participants create B1 associations whereas 19.3% establish B2 associations.

Another 20.8% of the participants are applying various other mechanisms similar to the ones presented earlier for the MDS scenario. They form a subset the participants who have mentioned the use of various association mechanisms other than the folder and annotations mechanisms in the previous MDS scenario.

[2] https://www.foxitsoftware.com/pdf-reader/

[3] https://evernote.com

[4] https://www.zotero.org

Mechanism	Directionality		Granularity	
	Unidirectional	Bidirectional	Entire document	Any level
Annotations & highlights	✓	✓	✓	✓
Line & arrow drawings	✗	✓	✗	✓
Common symbols	✓	✓	✓	✓
Separate documents	✓	✓	✓	✓
Physical folders	✗	✗	✓	✗
Post-it notes	✓	✓	✗	✓
Physical counterparts	✓	✓	✓	✓
Copy & paste	✓	✓	✗	✓
Digital folders	✗	✗	✓	✗
External applications	✗	✗	✓	✗
Writing physical parts into a digital document	✓	✗	✗	✓
Scanning physical documents	✗	✗	✓	✓

Table 3: Characteristics of the resulting associations

4.3 Linking Physical and Digital Documents

More than half of the participants (54.2%) indicated that they have associated information across digital and physical documents. The collected data reveals that participants are using different mechanisms to associate information across digital and physical documents. By using annotations and highlights, they tend to create either unidirectional or bidirectional associations. Out of the 54.2% of the participants who associate information in the DP scenario, 21.7% tend to create bidirectional associations of type B1. Furthermore, bidirectional associations of type B2 are created by 24.8% of the participants. Unidirectional associations of type U1 are created by 25.5% and of type U2 by 35.6% of the participants.

Another 16.3% of the participants mentioned the use of a wide range of mechanisms to associate the intended parts. Some of them (3.8%) indicated that they tend to print the digital document in order to have flexibility in annotating and archiving. Other users (2.3%) prefer to write the information of the physical part into the digital document and 4.6% indicated the use of the separate document mechanism to associate information across digital and physical media. While one of them uses a separate physical document, the rest use separate digital documents. Four other participants (3.1%) mentioned that they scan the physical document or take a photo of it with their smartphones. The scanned document or photo is then stored in the same digital folder as the digital document. It is obvious that those four participants are also using the same folder strategy in combination with the scanning mechanism. Finally, one participant (0.7%) mentioned the use of post-it notes on physical documents for creating associations.

4.4 Details of Information Linking Mechanisms

Most of the association mechanisms identified by our study are a result of different work practices. Moreover, each of them produces different types of associations (e.g. unidirectional or bidirectional). Furthermore, participants have different levels of satisfaction regarding their adopted association mechanisms.

4.4.1 Characteristics of the Links. We have already discussed some characteristics (bidirectionality and unidirectionality) of associations resulting from the use of annotations and highlights in the different scenarios. Two important aspects should be kept in mind while investigating the nature of an association; *the granularity of the associated parts* (e.g. fragments or entire documents) as well as *the attached references to the associated parts.* A bidirectional association enables a user to navigate from a source to a target document and vice versa. On the other hand, a unidirectional association only allows them to navigate from a source to a target document. Finally, some associations, such as the ones created by the folder mechanism, do not imply any traversal. A summary of the characteristics of the resulting associations is provided in Table 3.

The use of the annotations and highlights mechanism enables users to create all types of associations at any level of granularity. Annotations written next to two linked parts in a bidirectional association should contain references to each other in order to enable a user to easily navigate between the linked documents. If annotations in one linked part do not contain reference(s) to the other part(s), the created association is categorised as a unidirectional association. Different document viewers enable users to write annotations at any place in a document. Users can further highlight almost any part of a document and thereby associate information at the word, paragraph, section or chapter level as well as define links between entire documents.

The drawing mechanism (i.e. lines and arrows) that is used to connect parts of close-by information produces bidirectional associations. Users are able to see all endpoints of the resulting associations. The fact that "most" of the drawings are attached to a single document limits the possibilities to create associations at some levels of granularity. With the drawing mechanism users can, for example, not establish associations between two chapters of a document. As with drawings, the common symbols mechanism would normally produce bidirectional associations. In contrast to the drawing mechanism, common symbols support the linking at any level of granularity. Users are able to associate different chapters, sections or even entire documents with the common symbols as long as they attach the right references to the linked parts.

The use of separate physical or digital documents for associating information enables the creation of unidirectional and bidirectional associations at any level of granularity. Some users write the correct references to all the linked documents which results in a bidirectional association. On the other hand, a unidirectional association is established by not writing a reference to one of the linked parts. Note that some users create associations between entire documents by summarising all the linked documents or by only writing down the titles of the linked documents.

The use of the system folder as well as bibliography reference managers enables users to create undirected associations between entire documents. The traversal between documents is not defined for both of these mechanisms. A system folder visualises its documents in a way (e.g. a list) that enables users to navigate to any document. Most bibliography reference managers do not enable the navigation between documents but from a document to the corresponding system folder.

The associations resulting from physical archives (folders) as well as the scanning mechanism have more or less the same characteristics as the associations resulting from the use of system folders. The scanning of documents implies that the linked documents are stored in the same folder, whereas the system folders are an emulation of the physical archives. The use of the printed versions of digital documents mechanism to associate information implies the use of annotations or physical archives for associating information. Thereby, the associations have similar characteristics as the associations resulting from using annotations or physical archives. Last but not least, the associations resulting from the copy and paste, the writing of physical parts into digital documents and the post-it notes mechanisms depend on the recording of references to the associated documents as well as the granularity of the information part that has been noted down or copied.

4.4.2 User Satisfaction with the Used Linking Mechanisms. Figure 6 summarises the study participants' satisfaction with their used mechanisms in the three different digital scenarios as well as across digital and physical documents. Note that the percentages presented in Figure 6 are relative to the number of participants associating information in the corresponding scenario (see Table 2). It is clear that many participants (57.7%) are satisfied with the mechanisms they use for associating information in a single document (SD). In contrast to the SD scenario, the majority of participants are not happy or uncertain about the way they create associations in the other three scenarios. For the MDS scenario, 31.6% of the participants have indicated that they are not satisfied with the used mechanisms and 32.2% are uncertain about the way they create associations. In the MDD scenario, 40% and 28.3% are not satisfied or uncertain, respectively. Finally, in the DP scenario, 59.7% are not satisfied with the used mechanisms.

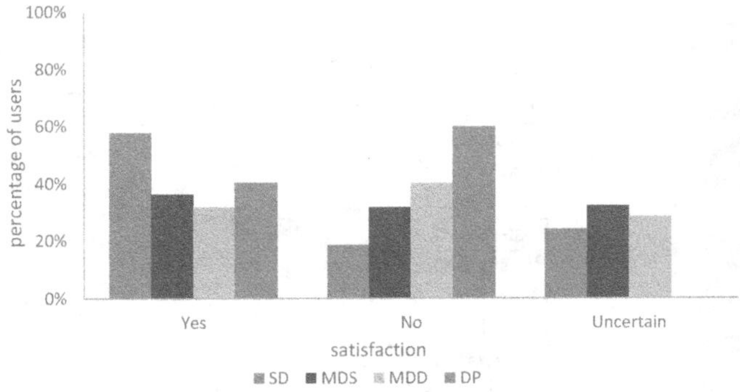

Figure 6: User satisfaction when associating information in digital documents and across digital and physical documents

Participants have given us numerous reasons for not being satisfied with their currently used association mechanisms. Some participants, in particular those reporting difficulties to create associations in different scenarios, have given us general complaints such as: *"I cannot create it"* and *"It is not intuitive how to make the associations"*.

In the context of the different digital scenarios, most participants who use annotations and highlights to associate information complained about the *"wasted time in creating and refinding an association"* between documents. Many of the participants who adopted the organisation of related documents within system folders have given numerous reasons for not being satisfied with this mechanism. Some of their complaints were: *"common folder is not the most accurate"* and *"the structure [of the folders] is unclear, it is not organised well enough, causing confusion and waste of time"*. Last but not least, participants who use separate documents as well as the copy and paste mechanism were mainly concerned about the wasted time.

In the DP scenario, participants were complaining about the time wasted in creating associations as well as the retrieval and tracking of the linked documents. We think that most of the used association mechanisms in the DP scenario require an effort from users in creating annotations in the two different media (digital and physical) or scanning and archiving documents.

4.4.3 The Need for a Linking Tool. After asking the survey participants about potential issues with their used mechanisms, they were questioned whether there is a need for a tool or a mechanism to facilitate the linking (associating) of information in the different scenarios. Most participants (179) indicated a need for a tool that easily supports the creation of associations between parts of digital documents as well as the navigation between these document parts.

In the digital scenarios, 25.1% out of the 179 participants shared their thoughts and suggestions for a suitable tool for associating information. 35 participants emphasised that a tool must support the creation of hyperlinks. One of them mentioned: *"It comes natural to me that such a system would resemble the mechanism of the Web"*. Some participants were concerned about the usability of any future linking tool: *"It should be extremely quick and easy"*.

Some participants were concerned about the inclusion of essential features in any future linking tool and two of them about the integration of the linking mechanism in their workflow. One participant mentioned: *"It would be dreamable if the linking mechanism would be available in the native document viewing program, and not that we are forced to use another application to link documents"*. Another participant who complained about the searching and refinding of associations stated: *"[...] allowing me to link and then search for the associations"*.

In the DP scenario, 20% out of the 59.7% who are not satisfied with the used mechanisms have shared their thoughts and suggestions for a better linking mechanism across digital and physical documents. One of the participants who is familiar with the recent Anoto[5] digital pen and paper technology suggested to exploit this technology in realising future cross-media linking solutions. Other participants suggested the use of QR codes and RFID tags. Another participant suggested a totally different idea of *"automatically scanning physical documents and do text recognition on them. Then collect keywords from them to organise them on the computer together with the digital files"*.

4.4.4 User Work Practices. Most of the interviewees have mentioned the use of multiple documents while reading and writing, not only in the physical space but also in the digital space. The use of multiple screens for multi-document viewing and associating information is a very common work practice for most of the interview participants. These findings are consistent with previous research findings [13]. According to the study participants, the simultaneous use of multiple documents enables them to easily annotate related information or to summarise it in a separate document.

The annotation features of different document viewers are an important manner to establish associations by using annotations and highlights. Nevertheless, as raised by different participants, while users are able to create different kinds of annotations within their documents, they are not offered the necessary functionality to search, re-find or manage their annotations. According to various participants, most of the time they are forced to open their documents and search within them to recall and find the previously created associations.

Another interesting work practice that we have discovered is the limited use of bibliography reference managers in reading activities. Participants are mainly using these applications for some scientific writing activities. We discovered that most users are not aware of the many interesting features (e.g. to relate documents to each other) offered by these applications. Indeed, as most of the interviewees have indicated, these systems are not primarily linking tools, but they can be seen as a layer on top of the system folder where users can group documents of different system folders into one unified collection.

[5]http://www.anoto.com

Last but not least, recent advancements in the resolution of embedded smartphone cameras enabled various participants to scan and take photos of physical documents while associating information in the DP scenario. According to two interviewees, this practise does not require much effort in taking the photo, but it needs an effort for archiving and storing the photo. According to one of them, the required effort depends on the installed smartphone applications as well as the synchronisation of the smartphone with a user's desktop or laptop computer.

5 DESIGN IMPLICATIONS

Our study revealed a number of interesting and important findings. Participants have adopted various mechanisms to associate information in digital and physical space at any level of granularity, including the document, chapter, section, paragraph or even word level.

In most of the investigated scenarios, users are mainly using annotations, folders and separate digital or physical documents to explicitly create the associations between documents. Some of the association mechanisms used in the physical space (SP and MP) are emulated with or similar to other mechanisms in the digital space (SD, MDS and MDD). The use of a physical folder mechanism (e.g. filing cabinets) in the physical space is, for example, emulated via the digital folder mechanism in digital space. The use of separate documents to associate information is a common mechanism for both, digital and physical media.

In addition, our study shows that users tend to create different types of associations (i.e. bidirectional, unidirectional and undirected associations) between associated parts. Nevertheless, regardless of the nature of the created associations, most users are not satisfied with their used mechanisms. In the following, we outline a number of design implications (D1-D5) for future linking solutions, that we have derived from the collected data as well as from issues and suggestions mentioned by the study participants.

D1: Granularity of the associations: As mentioned earlier, the associations between documents exist at any level of granularity and a user should therefore be able to establish "hyperlinks" at any level of granularity. The fact that document formats have different logical structures and document models (e.g. tree or linear structures) [8] should not create any barrier in supporting this feature in a future linking solution and an application should rather support different fragment identifiers (selectors or anchors) for different document formats.

D2: Bidirectional associations: Many users prefer bidirectional associations over unidirectional associations. A future association and linking tool should not only enable the creation of bidirectional associations, but also allow users to seamlessly navigate these associations in both directions. We believe that users who are used to create unidirectional or undirected associations will not complain about the support of bidirectional hyperlinks after experiencing their advantages. Unidirectional hyperlinks are often criticised since they cannot be navigated in both directions [16, 18]. An update or delete operation on one endpoint of a unidirectional hyperlink normally produces a broken or dangling hyperlink. Bidirectional hyperlinks are less exposed to such inconsistencies when updating or deleting endpoints since an application can ensure the consistency of both endpoints.

D3: Side-by-side documents: The use of multi-document viewing enables users to easily associate information across documents. It is worth mentioning that many systems have been built based on the side-by-side reading and annotation of documents [7]. A future linking tool should enable the side-by-side visualisation of documents to offer users some flexibility in creating "hyperlinks" between the visualised documents by using simple drag-and-drop interactions.

D4: Linking across digital and physical: It is not sufficient to build applications that support the associating of information in digital media only but we should think about possibilities to support the information integration and association across physical and digital media [12, 15] based on digital pen and paper or other technologies. A future linking application should overcome the limitations of existing cross-media applications by supporting the seamless integration of printed materials and arbitrary digital media.

D5: Management of the associations Giving users the possibility to create associations between different documents should come along with the possibility to manage their associations. As discussed before, a future linking solution should have an integral management component that helps users in managing and searching their associations. An optimal link management component should go beyond the simple search mechanism for associations. Instead, users should be able to filter and sort their associations based on various dimensions, including the types of the associated documents, the context of associations or the time when they were created.

6 CONCLUSION

We have presented the first study mainly investigating the user behaviour when associating information within as well as across digital and physical documents. Our study revealed twelve different linking mechanisms and their characteristics, which are adopted by participants when associating information in digital and physical documents. Furthermore, our study demonstrated that there is a need for an efficient and suitable information and cross-document linking solution in order to help users in creating and finding their associations. Based on the study participants' feedback about the limitations of the used linking mechanisms, their suggestions for better solutions as well as our interpretation of the collected data, we finally proposed a number of design implications for future cross-document linking solutions.

ACKNOWLEDGEMENTS

We would like to thank all the survey and interview participants for their valuable contribution.

REFERENCES

[1] Annette Adler, Anuj Gujar, Beverly L. Harrison, Kenton O'Hara, and Abigail Sellen. 1998. A Diary Study of Work-Related Reading: Design Implications for Digital Reading Devices. In *Proceedings of CHI 1998*. Los Angeles, USA. https://doi.org/10.1145/274644.274679

[2] Maristella Agosti and Nicola Ferro. 2005. A System Architecture as a Support to a Flexible Annotation Service. In *Proceedings of the 6th DELOS Workshop*. Cagliari, Italy. https://doi.org/10.1007/11549819_10

[3] Deborah K. Barreau. 1995. Context as a Factor in Personal Information Management Systems. *Journal of the American Society for Information Science* 46, 5 (1995). https://doi.org/10.1002/(SICI)1097-4571(199506)46:5<327::AID-ASI4>3.0.CO;2-C

[4] Richard Boardmann, Robert Spence, and Angela M. Sasse. 2003. Too Many Hierarchies? The Daily Struggle for Control of the Workspace. In *Proceedings of HCI 2003*. Crete, Greece.

[5] Paolo Bottoni, Roberta Civica, Stefano Levialdi, Laura Orso, Emanuele Panizzi, and Rosa Trinchese. 2004. MADCOW: A Multimedia Digital Annotation System. In *Proceedings of AVI 2004*. Gallipoli, Italy. https://doi.org/10.1145/989863.989870

[6] Vannevar Bush. 1945. As We May Think. *Atlantic Monthly* 176, 1 (1945).

[7] Nicholas Chen, Francois Guimbretiere, and Abigail J. Sellen. 2013. Graduate Student Use of a Multi-Slate Reading System. In *Proceedings of CHI 2013*. Paris, France. https://doi.org/10.1145/2470654.2466237

[8] Richard Furuta. 1989. *Structured Documents*. Cambridge University Press, Chapter Concepts and Models for Structured Documents.

[9] William Jones, Ammy J. Phuwanartnurak, Rajdeep Gill, and Harry Bruce. 2005. Don't Take My Folders Away! Organizing Personal Information to Get Things Done. In *Proceeding of CHI 2005*. Portland, USA. https://doi.org/10.1145/1056808.1056952

[10] Thomas W. Malone. 1983. How People Organize Their Desks? Implications for the Design of Office Information Systems. *ACM Transactions on Office Information Systems* 1, 1 (1983). https://doi.org/10.1145/357423.357430

[11] Catherine C. Marshall. 1998. Toward an Ecology of Hypertext Annotation. In *Proceedings of Hypertext 1998*. Pittsburgh, USA. https://doi.org/10.1145/276627.276632

[12] Moira C. Norrie and Beat Signer. 2003. Web-Based Integration of Printed and Digital Information. In *Proceedings of the Di-Web CAiSE 2002 Workshop*. 200–219. https://doi.org/10.1007/3-540-36556-7_17

[13] Kenton O'Hara and Abigail Sellen. 1997. A Comparison of Reading Paper and On-Line Documents. In *Proceedings of CHI 1997*. Atlanta, USA. https://doi.org/10.1145/258549.258787

[14] Kenton O'Hara, Fiona Smith, William Newman, and Abigail Sellen. 1998. Student Readers' Use of Library Documents: Implications for Library Technologies. In *Proceedings of CHI 1998*. Los Angeles, USA. https://doi.org/10.1145/274644.274678

[15] Beat Signer. 2008. *Fundamental Concepts for Interactive Paper and Cross-Media Information Spaces*. Books on Demand GmbH.

[16] Beat Signer. 2010. What is Wrong with Digital Documents? A Conceptual Model for Structural Cross Content Composition and Resuse. In *Proceedings of ER 2010*. Vancouver, Canada. https://doi.org/10.1007/978-3-642-16373-9_28

[17] Ahmed A.O Tayeh. 2016. *A Dynamically Extensible Cross-Document Link Service*. Ph.D. Dissertation. Vrije Universiteit Brussel.

[18] Ahmed A.O Tayeh and Beat Signer. 2014. Open Cross-Document Linking and Browsing based on A Visual Plug-in Architecture. In *Proceedings of WISE 2014*. Thessaloniki, Greece. https://doi.org/10.1007/978-3-319-11746-1_17

[19] Sandra Trullemans and Beat Signer. 2014. From User Needs to Opportunities in Personal Information Management: A Case Study on Organisational Strategies in Cross-Media Information Spaces. In *Proceedings of DL 2014*. London, UK. https://doi.org/JCDL.2014.6970154

[20] Steve Whittaker, Loren Terveen, and Bonnie A. Nardi. 2000. Let's Stop Pushing the Envelope and Start Addressing it: A Reference Task Agenda for HCI. *Human Computer Interaction* 15, 2 (2000). https://doi.org/10.1207/S15327051HCI1523_2

[21] Robert K. Yin. 2009. *Case Study Research: Desing and Methods*. Sage Publications.

Putting Dates on the Map: Harvesting and Analyzing Street Names with Date Mentions and their Explanations

Jannik Strötgen
Max Planck Institute for Informatics
Saarbrücken, Germany
jannik.stroetgen@mpi-inf.mpg.de

Rosita Andrade
Max Planck Institute for Informatics
Saarbrücken, Germany
randrade@mpi-inf.mpg.de

Dhruv Gupta
Max Planck Institute for Informatics
Saarbrücken, Germany
dhgupta@mpi-inf.mpg.de

ABSTRACT

Street names are not only used across the world as part of addresses, but also reveal a lot about a country's identity. Thus, they are subject to analysis in the fields of geography and social science. There, typically, a manual analysis limited to a small region is performed, e.g., focusing on the renaming of streets in a city after a political change in a country. Surprisingly, there have been hardly any automatic, large-scale studies of street names so far, although this might lead to interesting insights regarding the distribution of particular street name phenomena.

In this paper, we present an automated, world-wide analysis of street names with date references. Such *temporal streets* are frequently used to commemorate important events and thus particularly interesting to study. After applying a multilingual temporal tagger to discover such street names, we analyze their temporal and geographic distributions on different levels of granularity. Furthermore, we present an approach to automatically harvest potential explanations why streets in specific regions refer to particular dates. Despite the challenges of the tasks, our evaluation demonstrates the feasibility of the street extraction and the explanation harvesting.

KEYWORDS

computational history; street name analysis; temporal tagging; explanation harvesting; collective memory

ACM Reference Format:
Jannik Strötgen, Rosita Andrade, and Dhruv Gupta. 2018. Putting Dates on the Map: Harvesting and Analyzing Street Names with Date Mentions and their Explanations. In *JCDL '18: The 18th ACM/IEEE Joint Conference on Digital Libraries, June 3–7, 2018, Fort Worth, TX, USA.* ACM, New York, NY, USA, 10 pages. https://doi.org/10.1145/3197026.3197035

1 INTRODUCTION

When strolling the *Avenida 9 de Julio* in Buenos Aires or the *Straße des 17. Juni* in Berlin, chances are high that one either already knows the reason behind the naming of the street or that locals can tell tourists what is commemorated by the street name: Argentina's Independence Day on July 9, 1816 and the uprising of East German workers on 17th of June, 1953, when several protesting workers were shot. However, what about all the streets in Brazil that refer to 362 distinct days of the year? And what about the more than 40,000 streets across the world that are named in a similar way, i.e., with a date mention? Knowing the reasons behind such street names could not only be interesting for a travel enthusiast, but also for social scientists, historians, and other researchers as the history behind a street name says a lot about a country and its culture.

In social science and geography, the commemorative power of street names has often been subject of analysis (e.g., [8]), and it is well known that street names are not only used as parts of addresses but are often markers of historical events for a region. In these research areas, manual studies typically focus on the naming or renaming of streets in a limited region and during a particular time [9, 10, 26, 27] or on a particular personality after which streets are named [3–5]. In contrast, in the context of natural language processing (NLP) and geographic information retrieval (GIR), street names are processed automatically. Here, they are a special – and due to the high ambiguity particularly challenging – type of toponyms, which need to be detected and grounded [12, 25, 39].

Interestingly, though being of interest for the extraction and disambiguation in NLP and GIR for address geo-coding [25], and despite their importance in social science due to serving as important commemorative landscape for remembering the past [3], street names have hardly been analyzed automatically and on a large scale so far. Two exceptions are an analysis of the distribution of male and female names in street names in seven major cities as a blog post [32] and our own preliminary work [6]. A reason for the lack of more prior work is that several challenges are involved, e.g., a high number of languages has to be considered and determining the reason behind a street name is often difficult.

We perform, to the best of our knowledge, the first world-scale analysis of street names and make the following contributions:

- we extract all street names from a map provider grouped by region, determine the language(s) spoken in each region, and automatically detect all street names with date references, i.e., *temporal streets* (Section 2),
- we develop a model to automatically gather region-level explanations for the naming of *temporal streets* (Section 3),
- we perform an in-depth temporal and geographic analysis of *temporal streets* to study the distribution across regions and to detect which dates do most frequently occur in street names, in general and in particular regions (Section 4), and
- we evaluate both, the extraction and the explanation harvesting processes (Section 5).

All data sets and a link to an online tool (Section 6) to explore *temporal streets* are available at: http://ts.wannauchimmer.de/. Related work is finally surveyed in Section 7.

JCDL '18, June 3–7, 2018, Fort Worth, TX, USA

ACM ISBN 978-1-4503-5178-2/18/06...$15.00
https://doi.org/10.1145/3197026.3197035

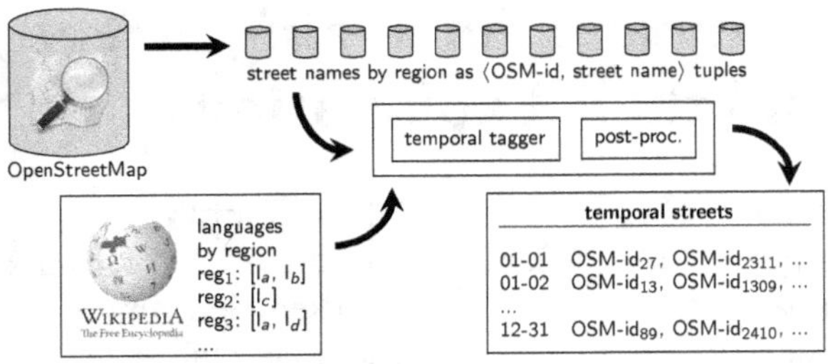

Figure 1: Pipeline to extract *temporal streets*.

2 EXTRACTION OF TEMPORAL STREETS

In this section, we explain what types of temporal expressions we want to extract from street names. Then, we describe our extraction pipeline, which is depicted in Figure 1.

2.1 Temporal Expressions of Interest

Following the temporal markup language TimeML [31], a temporal expression te_i is of a type $t \in \mathcal{T}$, with $\mathcal{T}$ = {DATE, TIME, DURATION, SET}. Time and date expressions refer to points in time of different granularities $g \in \mathcal{G}$, with $\mathcal{G} = \{..., \mathcal{G}_{part\text{-}of\text{-}day}, \mathcal{G}_{day}, \mathcal{G}_{week}, ...\}$, so that $\mathcal{G}_{part\text{-}of\text{-}day} <_\mathcal{T} \mathcal{G}_{day} <_\mathcal{T} \mathcal{G}_{week}$, etc. It is defined that $t(te_i) \in$ TIME if $g(te_i) <_\mathcal{T} \mathcal{T}_{day}$ and $t(te_i) \in$ DATE if $g(te_i) \geq_\mathcal{T} \mathcal{T}_{day}$. Date expressions can be further classified as explicit, implicit, relative, and underspecified [35]. Examples are shown in Table 1.

In texts, temporal expressions are realized as strings (e.g., "November 23, 2016") and can be normalized to a value in standard format (e.g., 2016-11-23). They can thus be formally defined as:

Definition 2.1. A *temporal expression te* is a five-tuple ⟨*s, l, t, g, v*⟩ realized as a string *s* in a language *l* (*l* ∈ {English, Spanish, ...}), is of type *t* (*t* ∈ {DATE, ...} and granularity $g \in \{\mathcal{G}_{day}, ...\}$, and can be normalized to a value *v* in standard format.

In contrast to other natural language texts, street names are extremely short and there is no space for any kind of context information. In addition, street names are often used to commemorate important events in a region's history. Thus, as our analysis will confirm, date expressions are much more frequent than duration, set, and time expressions, but implicit and relative date expressions are infrequent in street names compared to explicit and underspecified ones. Reasons are that relative expressions could not be resolved due to missing context, and implicit expressions are often named after an entity or event so that a street would more likely be named after the entity or event rather than the respective date expression, e.g., "Columbus Street" instead of "Columbus Day Street".

To refer to important events of the history of a particular region, date expressions often occur with a granularity of day – either explicitly, i.e., with year information, to directly refer to the date of the event, or underspecified, i.e., without year information, to commemorate the event by referring to the yearly anniversary. Thus, the focus of our analysis will be on so-called *temporal streets*.

Definition 2.2. A *temporal street s* is a street with a name $n(s)$ containing a temporal expression *te*, with $t(te) \in$ DATE and $g(te) \in \mathcal{G}_{day}$, realized either explicitly (i.e., with year information) or underspecified with day and month, but without year information.

Table 1: Temporal expressions as defined in [31] and [35].

duration	three years / 20 days
set	twice a week / yearly
time	9 pm / the morning of the 1st of May
date, explicit	November 23, 2016 / May 2017
date, implicit	Columbus Day / Good Friday
date, relative	two years ago / the following day
date, underspecified	March / September 13

2.2 Map Data and Street Name Extraction

To get access to street names all over the world, there are several map providers available, e.g., Google Maps, Bing Maps, and OpenStreetMap (OSM). We rely on OSM [19] as it is publicly available for query and download and there are APIs to access the data.[1]

The conceptual model of OSM contains *nodes* to define points in space, *ways* to define linear or polygonial boundaries, and *relations* to define how elements relate to each other. All elements can have associated tags of key-value pairs, e.g., to specify the type of a *way* element or to set another attribute such as a name of a street.

As potential languages for all street names are needed for further processing, we organize all streets in region buckets. Using Geofabrik[2] and Gisgraphy[3], OSM data excerpts are available on region level, and we create a data bucket for each region with an own country code.[4] For all buckets, we extract all *way* elements containing a *highway* key with any value such as "primary" or "pedestrian", and keep all elements which also contain a *name* attribute. The streets are stored as ⟨*OSM-id, street name*⟩ tuples. Details about a *temporal street* (e.g., its city) can later be accessed via its *OSM-id.*

The total number of street elements, which we extracted from OpenStreetMap is 29,109,428. Initially, there had been 250 region buckets with OSM data. However, as some very small islands are assigned own country codes, OSM does not contain any street information about them and some of the buckets have been empty, e.g., those of Tokelau and Bouvet Island. Out of the initial 250 region buckets, 243 contain at least one street in our data set and thus contribute to the total of more than 29 million street elements.

2.3 Assigning Languages to Regions

Street names occur in various languages. For example, street names in Germany are typically in German, whereas street names in Spain are typically either in Spanish, Catalan, Basque, or Galician. Using the Wikipedia article[5] *List of official languages by country and territory,* we assign to all region buckets all official languages spoken in respective areas. This information is then used to run a multilingual temporal tagger with respective language settings.

In addition, we process all street names with English, as in some countries, English is used for naming streets although it is not an official language. For instance, there is the *14th October Street* in Yemen, although Yemen's official language is Arabic.

[1] https://www.openstreetmap.org/
[2] https://www.geofabrik.de/geofabrik/geofabrik.html
[3] https://download.gisgraphy.com/openstreetmap
[4] https://en.wikipedia.org/wiki/ISO_3166-1
[5] https://en.wikipedia.org/wiki/List_of_official_languages_by_country

2.4 Temporal Tagging of Street Names

Temporal tagging is the NLP task of extracting and normalizing temporal expressions from texts [35]. Detected expressions are assigned *type* and normalized *value* information (cf. Definition 2.1).

Normalizing the Local Semantics. For the disambiguation of relative and underspecified date expressions, context information is required. For instance, without further information, the underspecified "September 13" cannot be normalized to a specific year. However, as street names typically do not contain context information, we normalize only the local semantics of temporal expressions (e.g., "September 13" receives the value XXXX-09-13) – similar as the formalism for local semantics of temporal expressions in [30].

Temporal Tagger Selection. While there are some temporal taggers available, e.g., SUTime [14], UWTime [24], and HeidelTime [34], we are faced with highly multilingual data so that the main criterion for selecting a temporal tagger is its support for multiple languages. SUTime and UWTime both support English only, and HeidelTime comes with manually developed resources for 13 languages. In addition, it was automatically extended to cover more than 200 languages [34]. Thus, for languages with manually created resources, we use those, and for all other languages, we use HeidelTime with the automatically developed resources.

Note that the expected variety of temporal expressions occurring in street names is rather limited compared to other types of texts, and our particular interest lies on *temporal streets* (cf. Definition 2.2). Thus, although HeidelTime's automatically created language resources are less sophisticated than the manually developed ones, they can be expected to work fine for our purpose for many languages. Nevertheless, to decrease the number of missed temporal expressions, we apply some post-processing (cf. Section 2.5).

To normalize all temporal expressions with respect to their local semantics, we set HeidelTime's *domain type* parameter to *narrative* and process each street name as a single document to avoid that information about any other street name is used as context information for normalizing underspecified expressions.

Temporal Tagging Output. After processing the street names with HeidelTime for all determined languages, we filter streets with temporal expressions. Due to using multiple languages, some streets might have overlapping matches. In such cases, we keep the longest match as it will have the most precise temporal information. For instance, in *Rambla 25 de Agosto de 1825,* Spanish HeidelTime matches *25 de Agosto de 1825* and English HeidelTime matches *1825.*

The output of this processing are street elements as six-tuples $\langle OSM\text{-}id, n, s, l, t, v\rangle$, i.e., an identifier *OSM-id,* the street name n, the extracted string s, the language l used for extraction, a type t, and a normalized value v, e.g., ⟨444578101, *Rambla 25 de Agosto de 1825,* "25 de Agosto de 1825", *Spanish,* DATE, 1825-08-25⟩.

After normalization, temporal expressions are term- and language-independent and our analysis can be performed for all *temporal streets* of the world simultaneously and in an identical manner.

2.5 Post-processing of Street Names

A first inspection of the tagging output revealed three main issues: (i) Italian data processed with English contained temporal expressions which were not extracted with the Italian resources, (ii) with some of the automatically developed resources, HeidelTime missed parts of temporal expressions, and (iii) same street names occurred multiple times in particular for rather long streets. For this, we performed the following adaptations and post-processing steps.

Adapting Italian Resources. HeidelTime's Italian resources contain a negative rule to avoid the extraction of temporal expressions within street names. Though this might sound surprising, according to the TimeML specifications, phrases that are part of proper names (e.g., titles of books) should not be extracted as temporal expressions [13, 15]. Despite that specification, only HeidelTime's Italian resources contain such a negative rule, probably due to the occurrence of a not-annotated date in a street name in the EVALITA training data, which was used to develop the Italian HeidelTime resources [28]. Obviously, we removed that negative rule.

Refining Normalized Information. For some languages with automatically created resources, we identified that parts of temporal expressions have been missed by HeidelTime. For instance, a Bulgarian street name with the string 8-ми март 1948 (8th of March, 1948) was matched as март 1948 and normalized to 1948-03, i.e., the "8th" (8-ми) was not part of the extracted expression.

We thus ran the following post-processing strategy to detect missing day information: street names without day but with month information (determined via the normalized value) were checked for numbers between 1 and (29|30|31) depending on the normalized month information. If such a number was detected, the value attribute was modified to the respective day granularity value.

Duplicate Removal. For many countries, identical street names occurred several times in the temporal tagging output. Obviously, identical street names can be used to refer to different streets, e.g., within a country, but it is rather likely that spatially proximate streets with identical names are parts of the same street.

To detect duplicates, we used the Nominatim tool[6] for reverse geo-coding. We stored for each OSM-id available information about the suburb, district, postal code, city, state, and country. Although latitude/longitude information could be used to determine if streets are spatially close to each other, a proximity threshold would have been required. Instead of using a difficult to determine and manually set parameter, we assume that streets with identical names occurring in the same postal code, suburb, or district (depending on which information is available) are considered as duplicates. In contrast, streets with distinct OSM-ids and identical names that are located in the same city, state, or country but with different postal code, suburb, or district information are assumed to be distinct.

2.6 Detected Temporal Expressions

Table 2 shows the number of street elements with HeidelTime matches as well as the frequencies of the four types of temporal expressions. Out of the more than 29 million street elements extracted from OSM, HeidelTime detected temporal expressions in 392,446 of them. That is, a significant percentage of about 1.35% of all street elements extracted from OSM have a name with an extracted temporal expression. About 97% of these expressions are of type DATE. While there are also few DURATION expressions (1.98%)

[6] https://wiki.openstreetmap.org/wiki/Nominatim

Table 2: Number of street elements with temporal expressions as detected by HeidelTime.

total	Date	Duration	Time	Set
392,446	380,667	7,778	3,883	118
	97.00%	1.98%	0.99%	0.03%

Table 3: Number of temporal streets after duplicate removal.

total	with year information	without year information
41,179	7,100 (17%)	34,079 (83%)

and Time expressions (0.99%), there are almost no Set expressions (0.03%) detected. The following list shows one example per type, with temporal expressions highlighted in italics.

- date: "Rambla *25 de Agosto de 1825*" (Spanish, Street of the 25th of August 1825), Montevideo, Uruguay
- duration: "*Nine Days* Lane", Redditch, England
- time: "*Sunday Morning* Lane", near Leesburg, Virgina (USA)
- set: "Route de *l'Annuelle*" (French, Route of the Annual) near Saint-Claude, France

Note that not all types of temporal expressions are equally likely to be extracted correctly. A first look into the street names with extracted temporal expressions for some languages we are familiar with showed that there are quite some false positives or cases which are difficult to decide without local knowledge due to ambiguities. That is, words in street names may or may not refer to a date, time, duration, or set. An example is the French street "Rue du Midi" – in which "Midi" was extracted as "noon", but "le Midi" is also used to refer to the South of France.

Obviously, due to the lack of context information and the high number of languages, a full evaluation of streets across the world is not feasible, and the numbers reported in Table 2 should be interpreted with that in mind. However, in the following, we focus on *temporal streets*, i.e., street names which are frequently used to commemorate important events in a region's history. *Temporal streets* are likely to be extracted correctly due to the joint mention of day and month (and year) information. Thus, we assume that not many false positives are part of the set of streets that our analysis is based on – as we will also show in our evaluation in Section 5.

2.7 Extracted Temporal Streets

As defined above, *temporal streets* contain in their names date expressions referring to days, either with or without year information. Besides occurring quite frequently (as will be shown below) and the high likelihood of being extracted correctly, such street names are likely to commemorate important events in a country's or region's history and are thus particularly interesting to study.

As summarized in Table 3, out of the 392,446 street elements with any type of date expression of any granularity (cf. Table 2), we found after duplicate removal 41,179 streets with names containing references to days. 83% of them occurred as underspecified expressions without year information in the name, and 17% were explicit expressions containing day, month, and year information.

Table 4: Harvested explanations by method.

street-page	country-page	holiday-list	event-mentions	dense-region
≈ 700	≈ 5,500	≈ 14,000	≈ 2,000	≈ 1,000

3 EXPLANATION HARVESTING

To harvest explanations for the extracted *temporal streets*, we make heavy use of Wikipedia to generate candidate explanations. Formally, the goal is to harvest explanations as defined in the following:

Definition 3.1. An *explanation* e is detected by a method m as a potential reason why a temporal street s located in a region r is assigned a name n referring to a particular day normalized as value v by the applied temporal tagger.

3.1 Candidate Pages

To be able to extract possible explanations for the naming of *temporal streets*, we need to either find pages about a particular street directly, or co-occurrences of the date mentioned in the name (n) and the region (r) in which the street is located. For this, we process the full English Wikipedia[7] with HeidelTime and index all normalized values of the extracted temporal expressions, in addition to the title and the terms of the pages. These indexes are then exploited by several methods m. Table 4 shows the number of harvested explanations after the successive applications of these methods.

3.2 Wikipedia Pages on Particular Streets

If a street is a major landmark in the city or even country, in which it is located, there might exist a Wikipedia page about the street. In these cases, chances are high that an explanation behind the reason of the street name is also provided, which we try to extract using a pattern matching approach searching for sentences containing phrases such as "named", "renamed", "commemorates" etc. (m="street-page"). For instance, the "Straße des 17. Juni" in Berlin has its own page,[8] from which we extract the explanation:

> In 1953, West Berlin renamed the street Straße des 17. Juni, to commemorate the uprising of the East Berliner workers on 17 June 1953, when the Red Army and GDR Volkspolizei shot protesting workers.

Explanations of famous streets in a particular city are inherited to streets with identical names in the same region (typically on country level). For instance, few further streets and places in Germany refer to the 17th of June, e.g., in Hamburg and Leipzig.

3.3 Wikipedia Pages on Countries

All sentences in articles about a country and containing a date expression are extracted as potential explanations for *temporal streets* referring to these dates in respective regions (m="country-page"). Note that independent of the language of the street name, temporal expressions can be matched due to the normalized values in the street names and the Wikipedia pages.

[7]We focus on English Wikipedia as estimating the explanation harvesting quality based on evaluating samples for all involved languages would be infeasible.
[8]https://en.wikipedia.org/wiki/Stra%C3%9Fe_des_17._Juni

For instance, the article on France[9] contains several such mentions, e.g., a sentence with an expression normalized to 1789-07-14 describes the Storming of the Bastille, an event that later resulted in the creation of a public holiday. This explanation can thus be used for streets in France containing the normalized values 1789-07-14 and XXXX-07-14.

3.4 Wikipedia List of Public Holidays

We also used the Wikipedia page about holidays grouped by countries[10] and extracted for each country all dates and holiday names as potential explanations for streets in respective countries (m="holiday-list"). The idea is that holidays are typically on days when important events took place so that the naming of a street referring to the same date has the same explanation as the holiday. For instance, the street "18th November street" in Muscat, Oman can be explained by the fact that the 18th November is a public holiday to commemorate the Sultan's birthday.[11]

3.5 Wikipedia Pages Mentioning Events

Using our pre-processed and indexed English Wikipedia dump, we also searched for all ⟨date, region⟩ combinations potentially describing events happening at the specific date in the specific region. That is, given a street with value v_i extracted from region r_i, $\langle v_i, r_i \rangle$ co-occurrences in Wikipedia sentences are harvested as potential explanations for that street (m="event-page"). For instance, a street in Saarland, Germany is named "Straße des 13. Januar" and we are able to harvest the explanation on the Wikipedia page[12] about the Saar referendum in 1935, in which the following sentence describes what happened on that day in Saarland:

> A referendum on territorial status was held in the Territory of the Saar Basin on 13 January 1935, over 90% voters opted for reunification with Germany [...]

However, due to the high risk of extracting false explanations with this rather general approach, this method was only applied for such ⟨date, region⟩ combinations, which contain explicit date mentions in street names, i.e., date mentions with year information.

3.6 Temporally Dense Regions

As a final method, we tried to detect regions in which many *temporal streets* are located (m="dense-region"). Such regions might be an evidence that not specific events are commemorated, but the date mentions are just used for organizing the street names in specific areas – similar to the usage of enumerated streets and avenues in many cities, e.g., in the US. For this, we calculate the distance of a street to the closest x *temporal streets* within a distance θ.

Based on observations in the data, we set the parameter θ to "one kilometer" and x to 10. We found that in many areas five *temporal streets* occur within one kilometer – however, then for most of the streets explanations have been harvested using any of the above mentioned methods. Thus, we increased the parameter x to 10, which reflects the goal that this method is only considered as fallback option and only in very temporally dense regions.

[9]https://en.wikipedia.org/wiki/France
[10]https://en.wikipedia.org/wiki/List_of_holidays_by_country
[11]https://en.wikipedia.org/wiki/Public_holidays_in_Oman
[12]https://en.wikipedia.org/wiki/Saar_status_referendum,_1935

Table 5: Distribution of *temporal streets* on continent level.

Europe	S. America	N. America	Asia	Africa	Oceania
50.62%	31.04%	12.45%	5.30%	0.57%	0.02%

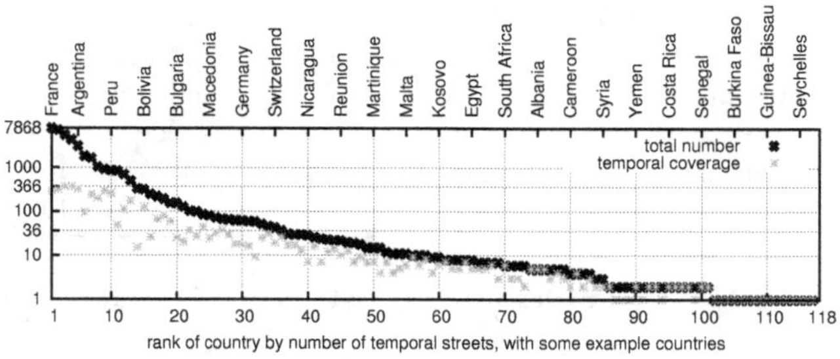

Figure 2: Distribution of temporal streets across countries and the temporal coverage per country [log scale].

3.7 Summary

Using the above methods, we harvested potential explanations for about 62% of the temporal streets in our data set (cf. Table 4).

4 ANALYSIS OF TEMPORAL STREETS

We now analyze *temporal streets* w.r.t. their temporal references, their geographic distributions, and the languages of their names.

4.1 Country- and Region-based Analysis

We started the street extraction process from OSM with 250 countries (region buckets). 243 had at least one street, and 187 had at least one street with a name from which a temporal expression was extracted. However, not all of them contain *temporal streets*.

Distribution across Continents. Table 5 shows the distribution of *temporal streets* on continent level (with Russia as Asia). As can be observed, *temporal streets* are particularly frequent in European and (Latin) American countries.

Number of Temporal Streets across Countries. The more than 41,000 *temporal streets* are spread across 118 countries in a very unbalanced way. The distribution across countries is shown in Figure 2, and all countries with 100 or more *temporal streets* are listed in Table 6.[13] We can observe that France, Italy, and Brazil have the highest numbers of *temporal streets*, and that five further countries have still above 1,000 such streets. In contrast, 60 countries have at least one but less then ten *temporal streets*.

Temporal Coverage across Countries. As the total number of temporal streets, the diversity of referenced dates also differs across countries. Besides the distribution, Figure 2 also shows the temporal coverage of all countries. In addition, countries with references to more than 40 days are listed in Table 7. Although the coverage of some countries is very high, there is no single country with a street for each day of the year. While there are twelve countries covering more than 100 dates, only six more cover at least 40 dates. Overall,

[13]High resolution plots with all country names: http://ts.wannauchimmer.de/.

Table 6: Countries with highest number of *temporal streets*.

≥ 1,000		≥ 300		≥ 100	
France	7,868	Ecuador	925	Belarus	250
Italy	7,166	Peru	861	Dom. Rep.	221
Brazil	5,550	Romania	854	Paraguay	195
Mexico	4,376	Uruguay	704	Venezuela	157
Argentina	3,132	Chile	507	Bulgaria	156
Russia	1,827	Hungary	332	Moldova	129
Portugal	1,678	Bolivia	318	Turkey	104
Spain	1,042			Cuba	100

Table 7: Countries with highest temporal coverage.

≥ 275		≥ 100		≥ 40	
Brazil	362	Peru	255	Russia	95
Mexico	358	Portugal	235	Paraguay	81
Argentina	317	Spain	195	Dom. Rep.	67
Italy	306	Chile	172	Venezuela	59
Ecuador	286	Bolivia	126	Romania	48
France	284	Uruguay	110	El Salvador	44

streets of 43 countries refer to at least ten different days, i.e., 75 countries cover at least one but less than ten dates.

Brazil covers 362 dates of the year and only misses streets referring to February 22, 23, and 26 and to June 14. With Brazil, Mexico, and Argentina, three American countries have the highest coverage of the year although the total number of temporal streets is higher for Italy and France (cf. Table 6). Particular low coverages despite many temporal streets have Russia (1,827 vs. 95), Romania (854 vs. 48), Hungary (332 vs. 15), and Belarus (250 vs. 26).

Most Frequent Dates in particular Countries. Obviously, not all dates are equally important for a country or region so that we can hypothesize that in particular countries few important dates occur particularly frequent in the street names. In Table 8, we list the three most frequent dates in street names of countries with at least 500 *temporal streets*. In addition, we show the percentage of the overall number of temporal streets covered by these dates.

European countries tend to have a much higher ratio of *temporal streets* covered by the most frequent dates. For instance, May 8 and March 8 cover 30.3% and 38.1% of the *temporal streets* in France and Russia, respectively (though Russia can be considered as part of Europe or Asia). With the exception of Spain, European countries with more than 500 *temporal streets* (France, Italy, Russia, Portugal, Romania) have at least a 20% and 50% coverage with the most frequent and the three most frequent days, respectively. In contrast, in Ecuador, Peru, and Brazil, the most frequent date does not even cover 10%, and only Uruguay and Argentina cover more than 40% of their temporal streets with the three most frequent dates. All other Latin American countries (Brazil, Mexico, Ecuador, Peru, and Chile) have a coverage of less than 30%.

While most of the dates mentioned in Table 8 do only occur in one of the countries, the 1st of May is among the three most frequent dates in eight of the 13 countries.

Distribution among Covered Dates. Figure 3 shows the distribution of *temporal streets* among all covered dates for countries with more than 500 *temporal streets*. As for the three most frequent dates, the overall distribution per country shows a similar picture: European countries (incl. Russia) have few very frequent dates while the distribution across dates is more balanced in the street names of the Latin American countries. Most notable are Ecuador, where the 50 most frequent days do not even cover 60% of all *temporal streets*, and Romania and Russia, where 97% and 94% of all *temporal streets* are covered by streets referring to the 25 most frequent dates.

4.2 Language-based Analysis

Figure 4 shows the distribution of temporal streets across languages. Most streets have been extracted by the main languages used in the countries with most temporal streets, i.e., Spanish, French, Portuguese, Italian, and Russian. These are five of the 13 languages, for which HeidelTime contains manually developed resources.

However, the next three most frequent languages are Romanian, Hungarian, and Bulgarian – which are contained in HeidelTime's set of automatically developed language resources (cf. Section 2.4). These "auto-languages" are even responsible for the extraction of more *temporal streets* than the English HeidelTime resources, which have been applied to process the street names of all countries. In general, there are many temporal streets, which have been extracted with one of HeidelTime's "auto-languages". Further examples are Turkish, Catalan, Macedonian, and Azeri. In Section 5, we will evaluate the quality of the detected *temporal streets* and also discuss the performance of the "auto-languages".

An interesting finding is that not only individual languages have been successfully used for specific countries, but processing a country's streets with multiple languages (cf. Section 2.3) is a good strategy. For instance, not only Spanish, but also Catalan and Galician contributed to the extraction of temporal streets in Spain with 88 and 7 streets, respectively. Overall, 12 of the 13 languages with manually developed HeidelTime resources (all except of Chinese) and 19 "auto-languages" successfully detected *temporal streets*.

4.3 Time-centric Analysis

The temporal distribution across granularity levels is analyzed next.

Distribution across Days of the Year. In Figure 5, we show the overall distribution of *temporal streets* across the days of the year, i.e., for all countries jointly. Eight date references occur in almost or more than 1,000 street names with May 1, May 8, and March 19 being the most frequent ones. Combining this information with the numbers shown in Table 8 reveals that some days occur frequently in street names of several countries, as will be further detailed next.

Coverage of Dates in Countries. Figure 6 shows for each day of the year the coverage across countries. By far the highest coverage is reached by May 1, which is referred to by temporal streets in 55 countries (probably because it is the International Workers' Day in many countries). Further well covered dates are mostly the ones which also occur frequently in total (cf. Figure 5), namely March 8 in 32 countries and April 25, May 8, and November 11 (15 countries).

However, there are also some dates, which occur in many countries but not very often in any of them: while May 9 is the third

Table 8: Three most frequent dates, their frequency and ratio of temporal streets covered by them for countries with more than 500 temporal streets. Dates occurring only once within the top-3 of these countries are highlighted.

	France	Italy	Brazil	Mexico	Argentina	Russia	Portugal	Spain	Ecuador	Peru	Romania	Uruguay	Chile
date	**05-08**	**11-04**	**09-07**	**05-05**	**07-09**	03-08	04-25	05-02	**08-10**	**07-28**	**12-01**	**07-18**	**05-21**
freq.	2,383	1,483	526	487	583	696	360	155	61	79	221	117	65
ratio	30.3%	20.7%	9.5%	11.1%	18.6%	38.1%	21.5%	14.9%	6.6%	9.2%	25.9%	16.6%	12.8%
date	**03-19**	04-25	**11-15**	**09-16**	**05-25**	05-01	05-01	05-01	**05-24**	05-02	05-01	**08-25**	**09-18**
freq.	1,689	1,183	318	406	549	376	267	154	48	61	181	103	45
date	**11-11**	05-01	**05-13**	**11-20**	05-01	**01-09**	**10-05**	03-08	05-01	05-01	**05-09**	**04-19**	**04-05**
freq.	1,402	963	293	320	220	168	218	71	37	38	85	90	31
cum.	69.6%	50.6%	20.5%	27.7%	43.2%	67.9%	50.4%	36.5%	15.8%	20.7%	57.0%	44.0%	27.8%

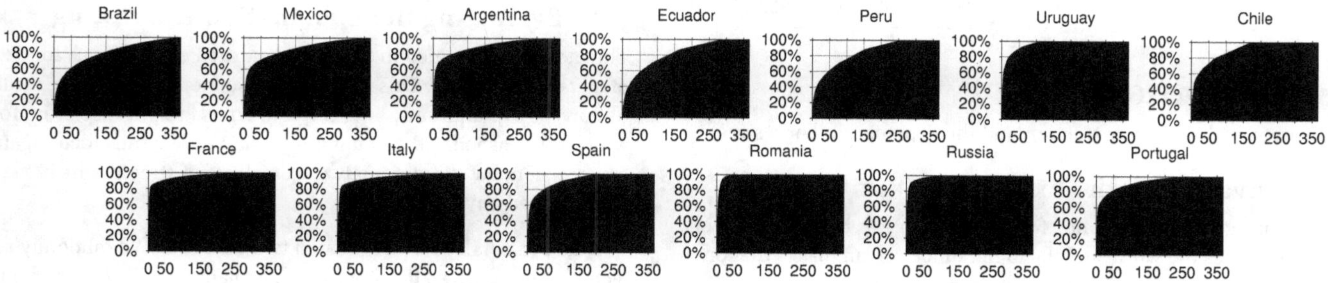

Figure 3: Coverage distribution; the 366 dates are ordered by frequency; America (top) vs. Europe (bottom).

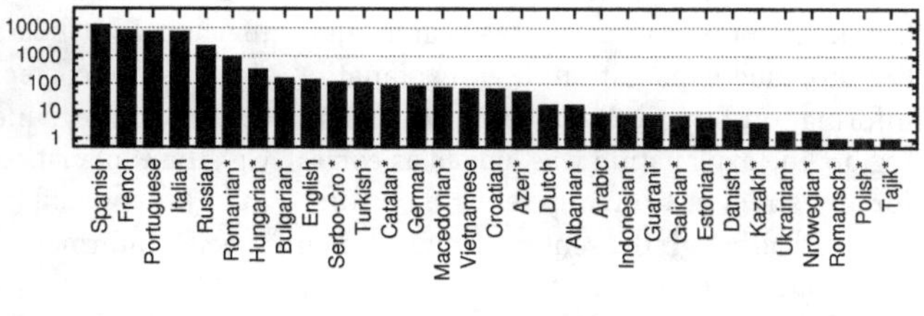

Figure 4: Coverage of dates across languages [log scale]; HeidelTime's "auto-languages" are marked with *.

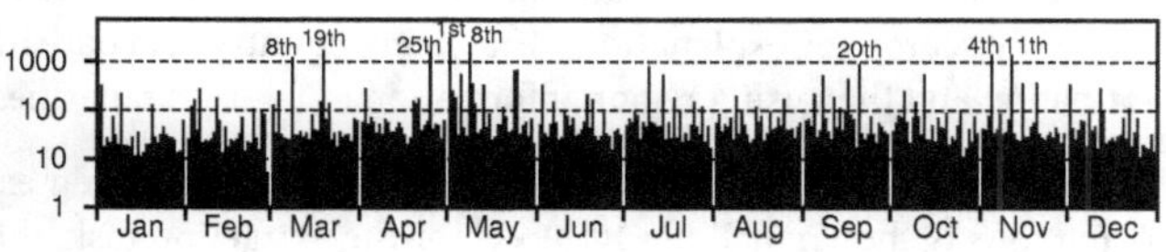

Figure 5: Distribution across the year [log scale].

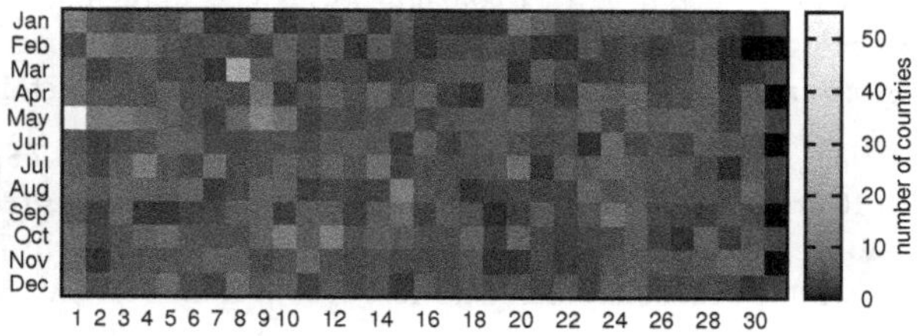

Figure 6: Coverage of dates in countries.

Table 9: Percentage distribution across months.

Jan	Feb	Mar	Apr	May	Jun	Jul	Aug	Sep	Oct	Nov	Dec
3.1	4.1	11.1	8.7	25.3	4.9	7.6	4.3	9.1	5.7	11.9	4.2

most frequent date in Romania, October 10 and 12, August 15, and July 4 all occur in 21 or 20 countries but are not within the three most frequent dates in any of the countries listed in Table 8.

Distribution across Months. Table 9 shows *temporal streets* accumulated on month granularity. Dates in May, November, and March are most frequent, dates in January occur least often.

Interestingly, May has also been the month with the highest number of references to days in literary texts although in them, most of the references have been used to anchor fictitious events [17].

Distribution of Explicit Years. So far, we did not distinguish between temporal streets with underspecified and explicit dates. Figure 7 shows the distribution of temporal streets with explicit year information for all countries jointly for the years between 1780 and 2010. In addition, we mark the occurrences in particular countries if a year occurs explicitly in more than five street names.

Obviously, events during World War II are most frequently commemorated with explicit year information, in particular in Italy and France. Events during World War I, in particular in 1918, are often commemorated in France, Romania, and Italy. Furthermore, 1789 (French Revolution) and 1962 (end of Algerian War) are very frequent in France and 1989 in Romania and Moldova.

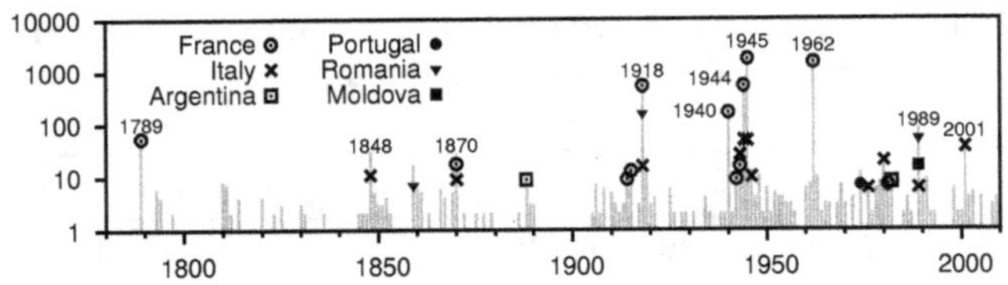

Figure 7: Explicit date expressions across years [log scale].

Table 10: Evaluation results.

a) Extraction.

	TP	FP	prec
TS_{100}	97	3	97.00%
TS_{118}	110	8	93.22%

b) Explanation harvesting.

	TP	FP	prec
EH_{100}	99	1	99.0%
EH_{98}	94	4	95.9%

5 EVALUATION

We now evaluate the extraction and the explanation harvesting.

5.1 Evaluating the Extraction Task

Evaluating the recall is not feasible due to the high number of streets across the world and the high number of languages that one would have to be familiar with. Thus, we focus on precision.

Note, however, that due to the use of automatically created HeidelTime resources for several languages, it is likely that areas exist, in which we failed to extract *temporal streets*, e.g., in regions with morphologically rich languages. Further reasons for missed *temporal streets* might also be errors or missing streets in OpenStreetMap.

Data Sets. We created two *temporal street* (*TS*) data sets: TS_{100} with 100 randomly selected of the total of 41,179 *temporal streets*. Due to the unequal distribution across countries, we further created TS_{118} with one randomly selected street of each of the 118 countries.

The manual analysis was done by two annotators who were given the following instructions: A street is correct if (i) the street truly exists in the country, (ii) the street contains a date reference, and (iii) the extracted normalized value matches the date in the street name. To determine if the street truly exists, the annotators made use of the Nominatim API. To check if the detected normalized value matches the date mentioned in the street name, the annotators were asked to use Google Translate for languages they were not familiar with. Both annotators judged all streets identically.

Results and Error Analysis. The results of the evaluation are shown in Table 10(a). With 97% precision, the extraction quality on the whole set of extracted streets is very high. Even if the streets are not selected randomly on the full set but on country level, the precision is still at over 93%. This drop allows the conclusion that the precision is higher for countries with many streets. However, we found no evidence that HeidelTime's auto-languages resulted in more errors than the languages with manually developed resources.

The perfect inter-annotator agreement also suggests that temporal tagging of street names is less challenging than other types of text, in particular when focusing on temporal street style date expressions. Due to the multilinguality, however, processing street names on world scale is nevertheless challenging.

Some of the false positives were indeed not even due to incorrect temporal tagging but due to date mentions in the OSM street name attribute although they are not part of the name. For example, a street name is succeeded with "closed until May 2, 2010". Further errors were detected in street names containing numbers in date format instead of names of months. Examples are "10-01 Forest Service Road" and "Highway 6/10". Extracting only street names with month names could increase the precision.

Another curiosity, which we detected independent of the evaluation is the street "31 de Junio" in Ecuador[14] although the month of June has only 30 days. Obviously, it is impossible to judge without local knowledge whether this street is incorrectly named in OSM or whether this name is indeed assigned to the (quite remote) street. In Google Maps, this street had no name information at all.

5.2 Evaluating the Explanation Harvesting

The methods explained in Section 3 returned explanations for 62% of all *temporal streets*. This number is the upper bound for the recall of correct explanations, but *temporal streets* might also exist for which the reason for the naming is unknown. We thus focus again on precision, but we also analyze a small set of streets, which were not assigned any explanation.

Data Sets. As above, we created two data sets. We randomly selected streets from all the streets with explanations (EH_{100}) and one random street per country for which at least one explanation was harvested (EH_{98}). The annotator was expected to judge the correctness based on the provided explanation, but, in case of difficulties, the annotator was asked to use a search engine to manually validate the provided explanation. If an explanation contains the correct information for another street with the same name in the same region, the explanation was judged as correct, e.g., the explanation for any street in Germany referring to the 17th of June would be accepted although the sentence might contain specific information on the most famous street in Berlin (cf. Section 3.2).

A further data set (EH_{20}) was created to determine the difficulty of harvesting explanations for street names for which our approach did not generate suggestions. We randomly selected 20 *temporal streets* without explanations, and the annotator was expected to manually search for explanations, first using country and date information and then using region information of finer granularities.

Results and Error Analysis. The precision of the harvested explanations is shown in Table 10(b). As for the extraction task, the precision is very high on both data sets but a bit lower on the data set covering streets from all countries with explanations.

The analysis of the EH_{20} data set showed the following findings: (i) For six streets, we could not find convincing explanations, (ii) explanations for nine streets were found within a minute, and (iii) explanations for five streets were found within three minutes.

For six streets, results were determined by querying the country name and the date in English. For the remaining explanations, we used a combination of country, date, and region information (city or district or state). However, several explanations were only detected on pages in languages other than English and several good explanations were not among the top search results.

[14]http://www.openstreetmap.org/way/290165263

Above observations suggest that for famous combinations of dates and country names, explanations can be found on other websites, which we do not consider, yet. On the other hand, detecting suitable explanations is a non-trivial task even for humans.

6 EXPLORATION

Our Web-based application DATE-ROME[15] (*Date References On Maps with Explanations*) can be used to explore *temporal streets*. The user chooses a date on the calendar and is shown (i) a hierarchically ordered list organized by continents and countries with *temporal streets* for that day, and (ii) a map on which all these street are anchored. The list items and the pins on the map can be selected to receive information about the region and potential explanations for the street name. In addition, for each temporal street, we link to the closest streets referring to the previous and next days of the year so that the user can travel the wold in a year chronologically.

7 RELATED WORK

To the best of our knowledge, our work is the first automatic, world-scale analysis of street names. However, there has been a long history in manually analyzing street names, temporal taggers have been used to analyze diverse text types, and studying collective memories through text mining has recently gained a lot of attention.

Studies on the Naming of Streets. There have been some works on manually studying the naming or renaming of streets [3–5, 8–10, 26, 27]. Most of them focus on particular regions and time periods. Azaryahu [8] discusses the role of street names as "participants in the cultural production of shared past" and determines their commemorative power. In [9], he analyzes the renaming of East Berlin streets as an aspect of the German reunification and "investigates the ideological dispositions and political configurations that [...] directed the process" to eliminate East Berlin's communist past from the commemorative landscape. Light et al. [26] study the role of renaming streets "to legitimate [...] the ideology of revolutionary socialism" focusing on Bucharest, Romania during 1948–1965 when many streets were renamed to commemorate "a wide variety of events and personalities from the history of Romanian and Soviet Communism". In [27], the same phenomenon of post-socialist change was analyzed, considering renamed streets in Bucharest in 1990–1997. The renaming of streets in Arab-Palestinian localities (pre- and post-1948) as an aspect of an official identity-formation procedure that reflects ideological premises is studied in [10], where the authors conclude that street names "offer historical orientation [...] as well as an official version of historical heritage".

An alternative restriction to perform a manual study that allows to enlarge the region and time period under analysis is to focus on particular street names, e.g., streets named after a particular person. For instance, there have been detailed works on the challenges of (re-)naming streets after Martin Luther King Jr. [3–5].

The only automatically performed study that we are aware of is an automatic gender study of street names in seven cities, which revealed that more streets are named after men than women and streets named after men are more centrally located [32].

Distribution of Temporal Expressions in Texts. The primary domain in which temporal expressions have been studied are news articles. These are typically written in standard language and are published at a specific time, which can often be used to normalize underspecified and relative expressions [35]. In [11], occurrence types of temporal expressions in the TimeBank corpus (manually annotated news articles) were analyzed. In [29], temporal expressions in manually annotated Wikipedia articles about wars are analyzed. In such narrative-style texts, the reference time for normalizing underspecified and relative expressions has to be detected in the text, which is often challenging.

Colloquial texts were subject of analysis in the form of short messages [33] and tweets [38], and a general overview of domain-sensitive temporal tagging is provided in [35]. An analysis if tweets refer more frequently to the past or future is presented in [21], where the tweets' temporal expressions are analyzed accordingly.

While these works all analyze temporal expressions in particular types of documents, none addresses street names or other texts with such limited context. The probably most similar approach is an analysis of date references (with explicit day and month information) in literary texts [17]. The focus has been on fictitious happenings and not on date mentions to commemorate important events as in our work. A further challenge in our work is the high number of languages, which was never tackled in any study before.

Text Mining on Collective Memories. Collective memories (*mémoire collective*) introduced in sociology by Halbwachs [20] can be considered as collective view of the society on the past. Due to large amounts of diachronic and dynamic corpora, several text mining approaches have been suggested to study this topic on a large scale. By extracting year references from large amounts of news articles for various countries, [7] studies how the past is remembered w.r.t. these countries. An exploratory analysis of history-related tweets is performed in [37] by analyzing time periods referred to on websites shared via such tweets. In [22], contemporary and history-related information from Wikipedia was exploited to analyze historical persons and to estimate their importance based on temporal aspects of Wikipedia's link structure.

Suchanek and Preda coined the term *semantic culturomics*: the idea is to exploit knowledge bases to semantically annotate and analyze large (newspaper) corpora for discovering trends that shaped society and history [36]. An approach to detect important events in the past, present, and future is described in [1]. Based on frequent itemset mining and semantic annotations in large document collections, identified events are ranked based on mutual information.

In [23], the negotiation and construction process of collective memories is studied through an analysis of the long-term dynamics of event-related Wikipedia pages. An earlier study [16] analyzed the collective memory building process by example of North African uprisings starting in 2010, i.e., focusing on traumatic and controversial events. Finally, in the context of the "Collective Memory in the Digital Age" project, an analysis of Wikipedia page views revealed the cascading effects between recent and past events [18].

8 CONCLUSIONS

In this paper, we studied the phenomenon of street names with date references and showed that *temporal streets* occur in many countries. Some countries even make heavy use of them, in particular in Europe and Latin America. We also harvested explanations why

[15]http://ts.wannauchimmer.de/

streets in specific regions refer to particular dates. Though our evaluation showed high quality for both tasks, it is sometimes challenging to determine correct explanations, even for humans.

For 132 countries (or regions), we identified no temporal streets – which might either be because such streets do not exist or the temporal tagging was erroneous. While we recognized that for morphology-rich languages, the automatically created HeidelTime resources do not perform well enough, it is also known that areas exist – in particular in developing countries – in which nameless streets occur frequently [2]. However, in some countries, date references in street names to commemorate important events seem to just not be an option, e.g., in Australia.

REFERENCES

[1] Abdalghani Abujabal and Klaus Berberich. 2015. Important Events in the Past, Present, and Future. In *Proceedings of the 24th International Conference on World Wide Web (WWW '15 Companion)*. ACM, New York, NY, USA, 1315–1320. https://doi.org/10.1145/2740908.2741692

[2] Dirk Ahlers. 2013. Where the Streets Have No Name: Experiences in GIR for a Developing Country. In *Proceedings of the 7th Workshop on Geographic Information Retrieval (GIR '13)*. ACM, New York, NY, USA, 47–48. https://doi.org/10.1145/2533888.2533937

[3] Derek H. Alderman. 2002. Street names as Memorial Arenas: The Reputational Politics of Commemorating Martin Luther King Jr. in a Georgia County. *Historical Geography* 30, 1 (2002), 99–120.

[4] Derek H. Alderman. 2006. Naming Streets for Martin Luther King, Jr.: No Easy Road. *Landscape and Race in the United States* (2006), 213–236.

[5] Derek H. Alderman and Joshua Inwood. 2013. Street Naming and the Politics of Belonging: Spatial Injustices in the Toponymic Commemoration of Martin Luther King Jr. *Social & Cultural Geography* 14, 2 (2013), 211–233.

[6] Rosita Andrade and Jannik Strötgen. 2017. All Dates Lead to Rome: Extracting and Explaining Temporal References in Street Names. In *Proceedings of the 26th International Conference on World Wide Web Companion (WWW '17 Companion)*. International World Wide Web Conferences Steering Committee, 757–758. https://doi.org/10.1145/3041021.3054249

[7] Ching-man Au Yeung and Adam Jatowt. 2011. Studying How the Past is Remembered: Towards Computational History Through Large Scale Text Mining. In *Proceedings of the 20th ACM International Conference on Information and Knowledge Management (CIKM '11)*. ACM, New York, NY, USA, 1231–1240. https://doi.org/10.1145/2063576.2063755

[8] Maoz Azaryahu. 1996. The Power of Commemorative Street Names. *Environment and Planning D: Society and Space* 14, 3 (1996), 311–330.

[9] Maoz Azaryahu. 1997. German Reunification and the Politics of Street Names: the Case of East Berlin. *Political Geography* 16, 6 (1997), 479–493.

[10] Maoz Azaryahu and Rebecca Kook. 2002. Mapping the Nation: Street Names and Arab-Palestinian Identity: Three Case Studies. *Nations and Nationalism* 8, 2 (2002), 195–213.

[11] Branimir Boguraev and Rie Kubota Ando. 2005. TimeBank-driven TimeML Analysis. In *Dagstuhl Seminar Proceedings*. Schloss Dagstuhl-Leibniz-Zentrum für Informatik.

[12] Davide Buscaldi and Bernardo Magnini. 2010. Grounding Toponyms in an Italian Local News Corpus. In *Proceedings of the 6th Workshop on Geographic Information Retrieval (GIR '10)*. ACM, New York, NY, USA, 15:1–15:5. https://doi.org/10.1145/1722080.1722099

[13] Tommaso Caselli and Rachele Sprugnoli. 2014. *EVENTI Annotation Guidelines for Italian. V. 1.0.* Technical Report.

[14] Angel X. Chang and Christopher D. Manning. 2012. SUTime: A Library for Recognizing and Normalizing Time Expressions. In *Proceedings of the 8th International Conference on Language Resources and Evaluation (LREC '12)*. ELRA, 3735–3740. http://www.lrec-conf.org/proceedings/lrec2012/summaries/284.html

[15] Lisa Ferro, Laurie Gerber, Inderjeet Mani, Beth Sundheim, and George Wilson. 2005. *TIDES 2005 Standard for the Annotation of Temporal Expressions.* Technical Report.

[16] Michela Ferron and Paolo Massa. 2011. Collective Memory Building in Wikipedia: The Case of North African Uprisings. In *Proceedings of the 7th International Symposium on Wikis and Open Collaboration (WikiSym '11)*. ACM, New York, NY, USA, 114–123. https://doi.org/10.1145/2038558.2038578

[17] Frank Fischer and Jannik Strötgen. 2015. When Does German Literature Take Place? - On the Analysis of Temporal Expressions in Large Corpora. In *Proceedings of the Digital Humanities Conference (DH '15)*.

[18] Ruth García-Gavilanes, Anders Mollgaard, Milena Tsvetkova, and Taha Yasseri. 2017. The Memory Remains: Understanding Collective Memory in the Digital Age. *Science Advances* 3, 4 (2017). https://doi.org/10.1126/sciadv.1602368

[19] Mordechai Haklay and Patrick Weber. 2008. Openstreetmap: User-generated Street Maps. *IEEE Pervasive Computing* 7, 4 (2008), 12–18.

[20] Maurice Halbwachs. 1950. *On Collective Memories.* Heritage of Sociology Series, University of Chicago Press, Chicago, Illinois.

[21] Adam Jatowt, Émilien Antoine, Yukiko Kawai, and Toyokazu Akiyama. 2015. Mapping Temporal Horizons: Analysis of Collective Future and Past Related Attention in Twitter. In *Proceedings of the 24th International Conference on World Wide Web (WWW '15)*. International World Wide Web Conferences Steering Committee, 484–494. https://doi.org/10.1145/2736277.2741632

[22] Adam Jatowt, Daisuke Kawai, and Katsumi Tanaka. 2016. Digital History Meets Wikipedia: Analyzing Historical Persons in Wikipedia. In *Proceedings of the 16th ACM/IEEE-CS Joint Conference on Digital Libraries (JCDL '16)*. ACM, New York, NY, USA, 17–26. https://doi.org/10.1145/2910896.2910911

[23] Nattiya Kanhabua, Tu Ngoc Nguyen, and Claudia Niederée. 2014. What Triggers Human Remembering of Events?: A Large-scale Analysis of Catalysts for Collective Memory in Wikipedia. In *Proceedings of the 14th ACM/IEEE-CS Joint Conference on Digital Libraries (JCDL '14)*. IEEE Press, Piscataway, NJ, USA, 341–350. http://dl.acm.org/citation.cfm?id=2740769.2740828

[24] Kenton Lee, Yoav Artzi, Jesse Dodge, and Luke Zettlemoyer. 2014. Context-dependent Semantic Parsing for Time Expressions. In *Proceedings of the 52nd Annual Meeting of the Association for Computational Linguistics (ACL '14)*. ACL, 1437–1447. http://www.aclweb.org/anthology/P14-1135

[25] Jochen L. Leidner and Michael D. Lieberman. 2011. Detecting Geographical References in the Form of Place Names and Associated Spatial Natural Language. *SIGSPATIAL Special* 3, 2 (July 2011), 5–11.

[26] Duncan Light, Ion Nicolae, and Bogdan Suditu. 2002. Toponymy and the Communist City: Street Names in Bucharest, 1948–1965. *GeoJournal* 2, 56 (2002), 135–144.

[27] Duncan Light and Craig Young. 2014. Habit, Memory, and the Persistence of Socialist-Era Street Names in Postsocialist Bucharest, Romania. *Annals of the Association of American Geographers* 104, 3 (2014), 668–685. https://doi.org/10.1080/00045608.2014.892377

[28] Giulio Manfredi, Jannik Strötgen, Julian Zell, and Michael Gertz. 2014. HeidelTime at EVENTI: Tuning Italian Resources and Addressing TimeML's Empty Tags. In *Proceedings of the Forth International Workshop EVALITA*. Pisa University Press, Pisa, Italy, 39–43.

[29] Pawel Mazur and Robert Dale. 2010. WikiWars: A New Corpus for Research on Temporal Expressions. In *Proceedings of the 2010 Conference on Empirical Methods in Natural Language Processing (EMNLP '10)*. ACL, 913–922. http://www.aclweb.org/anthology/D10-1089

[30] Pawel Mazur and Robert Dale. 2011. LTIMEX: Representing the Local Semantics of Temporal Expressions. In *1st International Workshop on Advances in Semantic Information Retrieval (ASIR '11)*. IEEE, 201–208. http://ieeexplore.ieee.org/document/6078263/

[31] James Pustejovsky, Kiyong Lee, Harry Bunt, and Laurent Romary. 2010. ISO-TimeML: An International Standard for Semantic Annotation. In *Proceedings of the 7th International Conference on Language Resources and Evaluation (LREC '10)*. ELRA, 394–397. http://www.lrec-conf.org/proceedings/lrec2010/summaries/55.html

[32] Aruna Sankaranarayanan. 2015. Mapping Female versus Male Street Names. https://www.mapbox.com/blog/streets- and-gender/. (2015).

[33] Jannik Strötgen and Michael Gertz. 2012. Temporal Tagging on Different Domains: Challenges, Strategies, and Gold Standards. In *Proceedings of the 8th International Conference on Language Resources and Evaluation (LREC '12)*. ELRA, 3746–3753. http://www.lrec-conf.org/proceedings/lrec2012/summaries/425.html

[34] Jannik Strötgen and Michael Gertz. 2015. A Baseline Temporal Tagger for All Languages. In *Proceedings of the 2015 Conference on Empirical Methods in Natural Language Processing (EMNLP '15)*. ACL, 541–547. http://aclweb.org/anthology/D15-1063

[35] Jannik Strötgen and Michael Gertz. 2016. *Domain-sensitive Temporal Tagging.* Synthesis Lectures on Human Language Technologies, Morgan & Claypool Publishers, San Rafael, CA. https://doi.org/10.2200/S00721ED1V01Y201606HLT036

[36] Fabian M. Suchanek and Nicoleta Preda. 2014. Semantic Culturomics. *Proc. VLDB Endow.* 7, 12 (Aug. 2014), 1215–1218. https://doi.org/10.14778/2732977.2732994

[37] Yasunobu Sumikawa, Adam Jatowt, and Marten Düring. 2017. Analysis of Temporal and Web Site References in History-related Tweets. In *Proceedings of the 2017 ACM on Web Science Conference (WebSci '17)*. ACM, New York, NY, USA, 419–420. https://doi.org/10.1145/3091478.3098868

[38] Jeniya Tabassum, Alan Ritter, and Wei Xu. 2016. TweeTime: A Minimally Supervised Method for Recognizing and Normalizing Time Expressions in Twitter. In *Proceedings of the 2016 Conference on Empirical Methods in Natural Language Processing (EMNLP '16)*. ACL, 307–318. https://aclweb.org/anthology/D16-1030

[39] Xiao Zhang, Baojun Qiu, Prasenjit Mitra, Sen Xu, Alexander Klippel, and Alan M. MacEachren. 2012. Disambiguating Road Names in Text Route Descriptions Using Exact-All-Hop Shortest Path Algorithm. In *Proceedings of the 20th European Conference on Artificial Intelligence (ECAI'12)*. IOS Press, Amsterdam, The Netherlands, 876–881. https://doi.org/10.3233/978-1-61499-098-7-876

Contextualised Browsing in a Digital Library's Living Lab

Zeljko Carevic
GESIS – Leibniz Institute for the Social Sciences
Cologne, Germany
Zeljko.Carevic@gesis.org

Sascha Schüller
GESIS – Leibniz Institute for the Social Sciences
Cologne, Germany
Sascha.Schueller@gesis.org

Philipp Mayr
GESIS – Leibniz Institute for the Social Sciences
Cologne, Germany
Philipp.Mayr@gesis.org

Norbert Fuhr
University of Duisburg-Essen
Duisburg, Germany
fuhr@uni-duisburg.de

ABSTRACT

Contextualisation has proven to be effective in tailoring search results towards the users' information need. While this is true for a basic query search, the usage of contextual session information during exploratory search especially on the level of browsing has so far been underexposed in research. In this paper, we present two approaches that contextualise browsing on the level of structured metadata in a Digital Library (DL), (1) one variant bases on document similarity and (2) one variant utilises implicit session information, such as queries and different document metadata encountered during the session of a users. We evaluate our approaches in a living lab environment using a DL in the social sciences and compare our contextualisation approaches against a non-contextualised approach. For a period of more than three months we analysed 47,444 unique retrieval sessions that contain search activities on the level of browsing. Our results show that a contextualisation of browsing significantly outperforms our baseline in terms of the position of the first clicked item in the result set. The mean rank of the first clicked document (measured as *mean first relevant - MFR*) was 4.52 using a non-contextualised ranking compared to 3.04 when re-ranking the result lists based on similarity to the previously viewed document. Furthermore, we observed that both contextual approaches show a noticeably higher click-through rate. A contextualisation based on document similarity leads to almost twice as many document views compared to the non-contextualised ranking.

ACM Reference Format:
Zeljko Carevic, Sascha Schüller, Philipp Mayr, and Norbert Fuhr. 2018. Contextualised Browsing in a Digital Library's Living Lab. In *JCDL '18: The 18th ACM/IEEE Joint Conference on Digital Libraries, June 3–7, 2018, Fort Worth, TX, USA.* ACM, New York, NY, USA, 10 pages. https://doi.org/10.1145/3197026.3197054

JCDL '18, June 3–7, 2018, Fort Worth, TX, USA

ACM ISBN 978-1-4503-5178-2/18/06...$15.00
https://doi.org/10.1145/3197026.3197054

1 INTRODUCTION

Exploratory search in a DL, especially on the level of browsing, is a frequent strategy when looking for related content [8], [6], [22]. Due to structured metadata that annotate the content of scholarly DLs, users are able to explore the content based on shared characteristics like keywords, classifications, or author information. These paths to start exploratory search in a DL are referred to as *Stratagems* [3] or search stratagems. Although stratagems are encouraging the user for further exploration, the system support on this level is rather low. Modern DLs support stratagem search as simple boolean filters that disregard information about the present user, his or her information need, and session activities. One way to enhance browsing on the level of stratagems is to integrate the users' search context and thus, tailor search results based on previous search activities [29]. Instead of filtering the documents based on shared characteristic as it is the current state-of-the-art in many DLs, we propose a contextualised stratagem search that extends the basic filtering by re-ranking the results with respect to the users' search context. We develop two short-term contextualisation approaches on the level of stratagems for DLs by utilising implicit user feedback. The goal of our contextualisation approach is to tailor search results on the level of stratagems towards the users' current search task.

Integrating the users' search context to personalise search results has provided large benefits during information seeking. While this is true for ad hoc search, the usage of contextual session information during exploratory search especially on the level of *browsing* has so far been underexposed in research.

Following [13], we understand browsing as a search activity that leads to a pre-defined group of information items sharing a particular metadata, while searching produces ad hoc collections of information that have not been gathered together before.

In this paper, we present two short-term contextualisation approaches that integrate the users' search context in exploratory search. A) A contextual feature that re-ranks documents based on their similarity to the previously viewed document and B) a contextual ranking feature that re-ranks documents based on the users' search activities (e.g. the previously entered query terms and viewed documents) in the current retrieval session.
In this study, we aim to answer the following research question:

- Can we improve the **effectiveness** of exploratory search on the level of browsing by using contextual ranking features in comparison to a non-contextual ranking feature?

One of the major challenges in the evaluation of contextualisation approaches is that large scale log data is usually hard to obtain. For this reason, we evaluate our approaches using the real life DL's living lab for the social sciences *Sowiport* and compare them against a non-contextualised ranking of exploratory search. Using an A/B/C testing, each user is randomly assigned to one approach for the entire session. To evaluate the effectiveness of each approach we measure: a) the position of the first clicked item which we refer to as "mean first relevant" (MFR) b) the click-through rate and c) the usefulness in terms of implicit relevance feedback.

Between September/12/2017 and December/20/2017 we analysed 607,109 sessions of transaction logs provided by our living lab. Our results show that contextualising search activities on the level of browsing significantly improved the retrieval quality in terms of MFR [12].

In modern DLs the most common feature to narrow down search results based on certain document features are *facets* which are widely implemented nowadays. Facets are described as a "set of meaningful labels organized in such a way as to reflect the concepts relevant to a domain" [14]. Although empirical studies identified various beneficial aspects of faceted browsing [10], they usually operate on the level of simple Boolean retrieval. Furthermore, facets require the user to interact with the result lists and to select each filter criterion one after another. In contrast to facets, our contextualisation approach tailors search results on the level of stratagems based on the users' previous interactions without additional effort by the user. In other words: our approach re-ranks documents that result from stratagem search with respect to the users' search context while the advantages of faceted browsing remain unaffected and can still be utilised by the user.

The paper is structured as follows. In the following Section we present the use case of our living lab study. In Section 2 an overview on related work is provided. Our contextualisation approaches and the baseline are presented in Section 3. In Section 4, we describe the metrics used to evaluate the effectiveness of our approach followed by a presentation of the results in Section 5. In Section 6, we discuss the results. Insights into the strengths and weaknesses of our living lab study are presented in Section 7.

Living Lab Use Case

The idea of a living lab is to understand information seeking behaviour in situ involving and integrating users within the research process and providing a context for testing and evaluating of IR models, methods and systems [2]. In general, a living lab is an environment in which researchers are facilitated to test their approaches in real life applications with real life users interacting with the system. One example of a living lab evaluation campaign was initially provided by the CLEF initiative and is now continued as *TREC - Open Search*[1] .

[1]http://trec-open-search.org/

We evaluate our contextual ranking features in *Sowiport*, a Digital Library for the social sciences [16] that is based on VuFind 2 with an Apache Solr 5.3 index. For the present study we utilised Sowiport as a Living Lab environment in which we injected our re-ranking based on contextualisation. Sowiport comprises about 9.7 mio. literature references from 23 different databases covering topics from social and political sciences. On a weekly basis, Sowiport reaches around 20,000 unique users. A document in Sowiport usually covers information about the author(s), keywords, classifications, source information (journal or conference proceedings). All these document properties are implemented as hyperlinks and when employed, a result list of documents that share that particular metadata is generated.

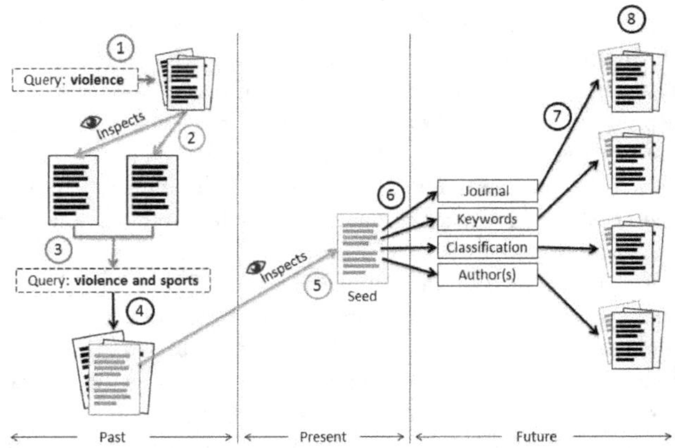

Figure 1: Schematic visualisation of contextualised stratagem searching.

A schematic visualisation of our contextualisation approach can be found in Figure 1. In this example, we have a user who is seeking information on the topic *violence and sports*. After entering a query (1), inspecting two documents (2) and refining the query (3), the user has found a document of interest in a result set (4: highlighted green in the figure) that he inspects in detail (5 and 6). To seek further related content the user could for instance look at the journal the document was published in or select a certain keyword that is contained in the current document. Each of these interactions (7) leads to a new result list containing documents that shares the same attribute with the seed document which is also part of the result list (8). Our approach is to re-rank these result lists based on contextual information about the users search sessions.

A more practical example is displayed in Figure 2a and 2b. In this example a document with the title "*Football in Southeastern Europe: ...*" has been retrieved via the query for "violence and sports". To perform a stratagem search a user could select a keyword, the name of the author, or the journal (*Südosteuropäische Hefte – Southeastern Europe Magazine*). Each of these interactions would lead to a result list of documents containing that particular filter criterion. Such a result list is displayed in Figure 2b which was generated by selecting the keyword *sport* from the seed document. In this example, the

Figure 2: Example of a keyword search in Sowiport.

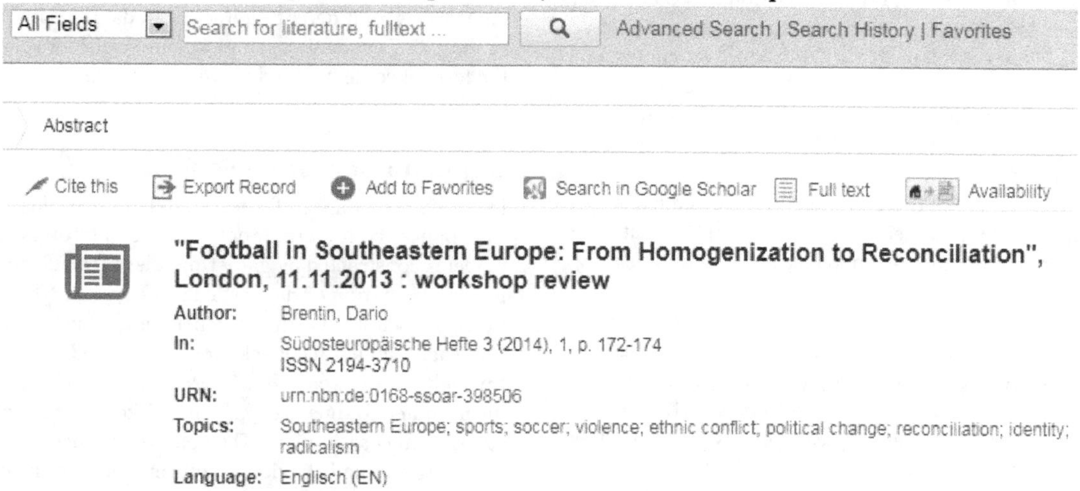

(a) Example document from Sowiport retrieved via a query search for "violence and sports".

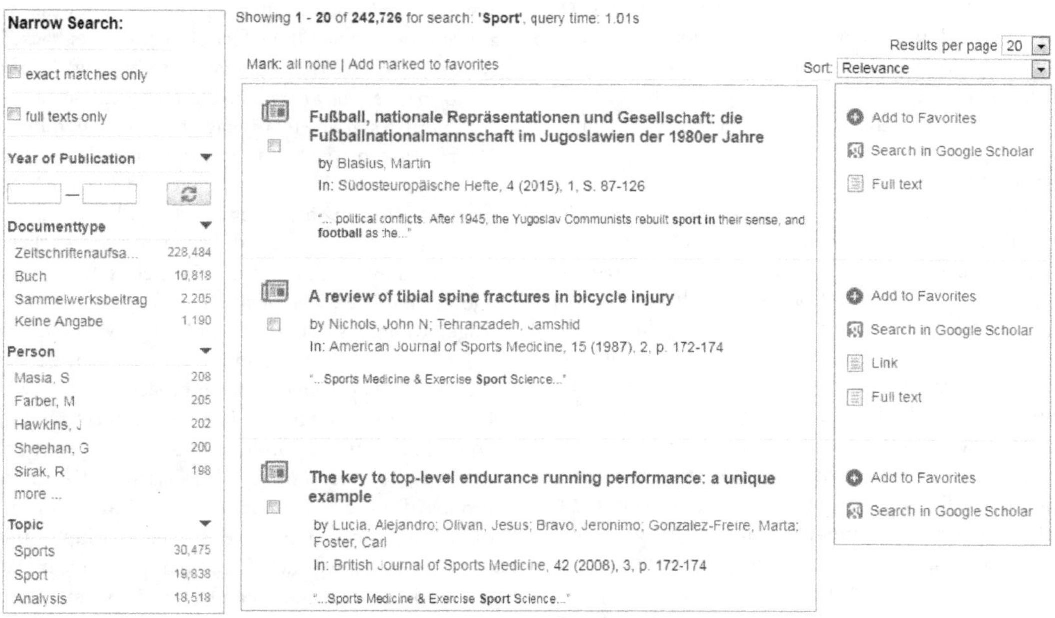

(b) Example result list after a stratagem search for the keyword "sports".

ranking has been contextualised towards the similarity of each document in the result set to the seed document. The displayed result list contains various characteristics worth noticing: One can see that the top ranked document is highly related to football in the former Republic of Yugoslavia which shows a topical relatedness to the seed document. Furthermore, one can see that the result list contains documents from different languages. In this case the top ranked document is in German. A click on a document in the result list leads to a detailed view of that particular document. It is important to notice that we did not modify the interface of the result list but rather only re-rank the results towards their similarity to the seed document. Thus, the user is still able to use features like facets or to narrow down the search results based on the year of publication. This is displayed in the left box of Figure 2b.

For each document a bookmarking feature, a lookup functionality in Google Books and Google Scholar, and a check for the availability in the local library is placed next to each record as well as a link to the full text of that record, if available. This is displayed in the right box of Figure 2b.

2 RELATED WORK

In the early 2000s, Lagoze et al. [19] and Smeaton and Callan [29] made a first move to put the concept of *context* into the perspective of DL research. They postulate that a DL "should be contextual, expressing the expanding web of inter-relationships and layers of knowledge" [19]. In this sense, they called for *proactive* [29] or *collaborative* [25] or *adaptive* [11] DLs. Since that time, state-of-the-art DLs have not changed much and remain often in the "simple catalog model" [19]. Personalisation and recommender systems have evolved and found their way into modern DLs, but deep contextual system support and user guidance are often still missing.

Exploratory search tasks usually comprise search activities on the level of learning and investigating that go beyond simple look up tasks such as known item search [20]. Due to the complexity of exploratory search tasks, various search activities on the level of moves, tactics, and stratagems are typically involved [6]. To date numerous studies have been conducted that aim to understand users' search behaviour and search activities during exploratory search. Ellis [9] studied the search behaviour of social scientists and identified six generic features: *Starting* (e.g. to identify a paper to start with), *Chaining* (e.g. to follow references in a certain paper), *Browsing* (e.g. to browse all papers by a certain author), *Differentiating* (e.g. to judge a source based on their nature), *Monitoring* (e.g. to subscribe to an alerting service) and *Extracting* (e.g. to identify material in a well-known journal).

Contextualisation (in web search more commonly referred to as personalisation) has drawn a lot of attention in web search, e.g. ([30], [21], [27]) and is distinguished between short-term (the current session) and long-term (over many user sessions) personalisation. While short-term personalisation provides better results for recent search interests, it lacks support of the users' long-term interests. Long-term personalisation on the other hand is suitable to capture the users' long-term interests but may not represent recent shifts in search interests [5]. In this paper, we focus on short-term personalisation which we refer to as contextualisation.

Constructing the user context can be done in various ways like as per explicit (a user explicitly providing feedback information) or implicit feedback which utilises all the information available about the current user, like for instance the viewed/skipped documents or the set of query (re-)formulations. A comparison between implicit and explicit feedback is presented in [34]. In total, 16 participants were asked to solve 16 tasks that were taken from the TREC-10 interactive track. In their experiment two interfaces were developed that connect to the Google search engine: one that uses implicit and one that uses explicit relevance feedback. The results showed no significant difference in terms of search effectiveness between the usage of implicit and explicit relevance feedback with regards to viewed result pages, task completion, and task time.

In the *TREC session track* [18] which ran from 2010 to 2014, the main goal was to consider the session history for (re-)ranking the output for subsequent queries. The TREC session track combines a given corpus, topics, queries and relevance judgments with retrieved results, click data and dwell times from crowd workers conducting searches within a session. Similar is the *INEX Interactive Track* [24] where different tasks of real users are conducted (see an overview of different interactive IR data sets in [4]). In contrast to the TREC evaluation setup, we only consider specific queries in the form of contextualised browsing, and we evaluate our approach in a living lab.

Implicit relevance feedback

In [31] various implicit feedback models are evaluated each aiming to enhance the representation of a user's information need. Each model is constructed by gathering relevance information from the user's exploration of the particular IR system. The different variations are evaluated using searcher simulations. The authors show that each implicit feedback model increased search effectiveness through query expansion. In [26] implicit relevance feedback is incorporated for query expansion and to select new terms that are added to the user's query. The authors conducted five experiments on incorporating behavioural information into the process of relevance feedback with 30 participants and 6 tasks. They observed the overall search behaviour, search effectiveness and the subjects perception of the different systems. The results indicate that search behaviour can be utilised in the process of relevance feedback. In [28] the authors studied the effect of implicit feedback, including query history and click-through history to improve information retrieval performance. They developed four context-sensitive language models that use statistical language models which incorporate context information into a basic retrieval model. Their experiments showed that the retrieval performance could be substantially improved without requiring any user effort. In [27] a long-term personalisation approach is developed that incorporated click behaviour into the document ranking. The approach is evaluated with data from the *Personalized Web Search Challenge* organised by Yandex and Kagell where researchers are able to provide their own solution to a personalisation task on Yandex log data. White et al. [32] developed a task-based personalisation approach that utilises session history from other users with similar tasks referred to as *groupisation.* A contextualisation approach aiming to support browsing in a local web site is presented in [1]. Based on the implicit feedback of groups of users, a document summarisation for browsing is developed. By matching all queries from a group of users a document summarisation was developed that performs on two levels: single document summarisation and a multi document summarisation, i.e. a summary that is generated from a collection of related documents.

Previous Work

The present paper is part of a large scale investigation on the usage of stratagems in exploratory search. In a position paper, we discussed the idea of contextual exploratory search [7]. We presented a concept for bibliometric enhanced stratagem searches that contextualises search activities and integrates further re-ranking features like co-citation analysis and author centrality. In [8] we presented a first approach on gathering a deeper understanding on the usage of stratagems by conducting an online survey with 128 respondents from twelve different fields of research. Our survey showed a general need for a contextual ranking in exploratory search which we tested using a journal run scenario in which the respondents were asked to arrange the content of a journal run based on two contextual features and four non-contextual features like date or title. The results of the survey showed that the respondents assess the ranking features based on contextualisation noticeably higher than the four non-contextual features. In a recent study [6] on exploratory search in a DL, we showed that the majority of search activities were performed on the level of browsing in comparison to queries and the usage of recommendations. A similar observation can be found in [33] in which the authors showed that less than one third of the interactions belonged to search result pages while the remainder belongs to pages that lie on the hyperlink trail from a search result page.

3 CONTEXTUALISED RE-RANKING APPROACH

We compare three methods for the ranking of exploratory search results. The first approach is the default ranking of Sowiport while the other two approaches are developed to support contextual browsing. We apply contextualised browsing on the level of stratagems and, thus, need a seed document to start with. From a set of documents $D = \{d_1, ..., d_n\}$ the seed document d_s is defined as the document which is currently opened and examined by a user and contains a set of possible browsing activities (*BrowsAct*) which are defined as follows:

$$BrowsAct(d_s) = \{Keywords_{d_s}, Authors_{d_s}, Classifications_{d_s}, Journal_{d_s}\}$$

where $Keywords_{d_s} = \{k_1, .., k_j\}$ is a set of keywords, $Authors_{d_s} = \{a_1, .., a_k\}$ is a set of authors, $Classifications_{d_s} = \{c_1, .., c_l\}$ is a set of classifications in d_s and $Journal_{d_s}$ is the journal the seed document d_s was published in. For all three approaches we excluded the seed document from the result set ($d \neq d_s$) to prevent a potential click bias towards the previously inspected document[2].

3.1 Default Ranking

In this section we describe the default ranking of Sowiport which we use as baseline. The default ranking is based on SOLR and can be formalised as follows:

$$DR : Q \times D \rightarrow \mathbb{R} \quad (1)$$

A filter query q (selected by the user) is submitted to an expansion function which takes the filter query and expands it with synonyms and corresponding translations (see conceptual model in [23]). If, for instance, a user clicks on the keyword "violence", this keyword is first expanded with synonyms and different translations. Furthermore, the filter type "keyword" is expanded to related metadata fields. The actual ranking is then provided by boosting the results based on the contained metadata field type. The boosting order is predefined by the DL which assumes that different metadata fields are of higher value than others (e.g. keywords > free keywords). The resulting list of ranked documents in this approach has no connection to the previous search activities of the user and is basically a simple Boolean filter which is extended by a boosting on particular metadata fields. We decided to utilise the described Sowiport default ranking as a baseline although an out-of-the-box VuFind-Solr configuration which performs a simple Boolean filter would decrease the complexity and allow a better reproducibility of our results. The main reason for this decision is that we want to compare our contextualisation approach to a realistic real life DL ranking which also provides us with a strong and established baseline.

A simplified example query for the default ranking is displayed in Listing 1. Again, we utilise our fictitious example of a user who is looking at a document about "Football in Southeastern Europe". In this example, the user selected the keyword "violence". One can see that the baseline approach not only performs a Boolean query on the keyword level but extends the query to related fields like in this case the metadata field "keyword_free" which is an alternative and less formal descriptor for keywords. Furthermore, one can see that the term violence is translated into the German word "Gewalt". The ranking of the retrieved documents is based on TF*IDF whereby the weighting of the fields is taken into account. In our example it can be seen that the metadata field "keyword" is boosted by a higher factor than the "keywords_free" field.

Listing 1: Example query for the default ranking

```
q => keyword:((violence OR "Gewalt")^400 OR
keyword_free:((violence OR "Gewalt"))^250
```

In the following two sections, we describe our contextualisation approach which is then compared against the baseline.

3.2 Re-Ranking based on Document Similarity

In this approach we perform a re-ranking of the result list based on the similarity of each document in the result set compared to the seed document.

This is described formally as follows:

$$SR : Q \times D \times D_s \rightarrow \mathbb{R} \quad (2)$$

The ranking function *SR* is an extension to the default ranking *DR*. The ranking function takes the filter query and the seed document (D_s) as input to produce a ranked list of documents. In a first step, the documents are filtered correspondingly to the default ranking. Instead of only boosting the documents based on field types containing the filter query, the ranking is extended by a similarity score of each document compared to the seed document. To estimate the similarity of each document compared to the seed document we utilise the *MoreLikeThis (MLT)* query parser[3] built in SOLR which is usually employed to provide related documents to a given seed document. An example query for the re-ranking based on document similarity is provided in Listing 2. One can see that the query is based on the default ranking described in Section 3.1 but uses the *MLT* query parser. The seed document is specified by the *DocID* parameter. To compute the similarity of all documents to the seed document we use the keywords, journal information, the abstract (in different languages if available), and the author names of the seed document. These are specified in the *qf* parameter in Listing 2.

[2]During a pretest, we observed an extraordinary high click rate on the duplicate entry of the result list.

[3]http://archive.apache.org/dist/lucene/solr/ref-guide/apache-solr-ref-guide-5.3.pdf

Listing 2: Example query for the re-ranking based on document similarity

```
q => {!mlt}DocID
keyword:((violence OR "Gewalt")^400 OR
keyword_free:((violence OR "Gewalt"))^250
qf=authors,keywords,journal,abstract
```

3.3 Re-Ranking based on Session Details

In this approach, the re-ranking is performed based on the user's session context which is derived from a set of actions the user has performed during the current search session.
This is described formally as follows:

$$CR : Q \times D \times U_c \rightarrow \mathbb{R} \quad (3)$$

where

$$U_c = \{Keywords(U), Categories(U), Queries(U)\}$$

The ranking function CR is again an extension to the default ranking DR. The function takes the filter query and the user's search context (U_c) as input to produce a ranked list of documents. Again, the first step is to filter all documents corresponding to the default ranking. The re-ranking based on the user's search activities is then provided by boosting the filtered documents using the user's session context (U_c) which consists of three features: keywords, categories and the queries a user U has submitted.

We create the keyword and category features from two sources: a) each keyword/category is considered that was contained in the list of documents the user has seen during the session, b) each keyword/category is considered that was contained in documents within a result set during the session. We then sort the list of keywords and categories based on the number of their occurrences within the session. If a certain keyword has appeared five times in the list of viewed documents and four times in documents within the result list, the score for that particular keyword is nine. To reduce noise, we limit the number of keywords and categories to the top three for each feature and normalise the count to range between zero and one. Regarding the queries, we did not create a threshold as we assume that all queries are equally important to describe the user's information need and do not contain any noise. An example session context could be described as shown in Listing 3:

Listing 3: Example session context

```
{"query":"violence sports","rank":1},
{"keyword":"Football","rank":1},
{"keyword":"Radicalism","rank":0.5},
{"keyword":"Ethnic Conflict","rank":0.5},
{"category":"Political Sociology","rank":1},
{"category":"Decision Making","rank":0.66},
{"category":"Sociology","rank":0.66}}
```

In this example, the user has submitted the query *violence sports*. From the corresponding result set and the viewed document, the categories and keywords are derived with a rank that represents the normalised frequency of that term in the result list and the viewed document. It may happen that we have an overall occurrence count of 1 resulting in a rank of 1 for each keyword and classification, which is the case when a user enters our DL from a web search engine and goes straight to the detailed view of a document. In this case, we use each keyword and classification from the seed document as session context.

The actual boosting is performed in the following order: by the entered query terms, the keywords, and the classifications each multiplied by their normalised rank (see Listing 3).

An example query for the re-ranking based on session details is displayed in Listing 4. The session context in this example is derived from the example session context in Listing 3. The first part of the query is based on the default ranking which is extended by a boosting parameter *bq*. In line 5, it can be seen that we look for the previously entered query term *violence sports* in the title field which is also the metadata field with the highest boosting value. In the lines 6 to 8 we boost documents that contain the most frequent keywords in the session context and boost each keyword with a decreasing factor depending on the keywords' frequency in the session context. In line 9 to 11 we boost documents that contain the category terms from the session context.

Listing 4: Example query for the re-ranking based on session details

```
1  q =>
2  keyword:((violence OR "Gewalt")^400 OR
3  keyword_free:((violence OR "Gewalt"))^250
4  [bq]=
5  (title:violence sports^1700) OR
6  (keyword:Football^1200 OR
7   keyword:Radicalism^1080 OR
8   keyword:Ethnic Conflict^1080) OR
9  (category:Political Sociology^800 OR
10  category:Decision Making^560 OR
11  category:Sociology^560 )
```

4 METHODOLOGY

At the beginning of a session each user is assigned one ranking method for the entire duration of a session. As most users click only on one suggested document, we use the rank position of the first clicked document as quality criterion. The most obvious metric to be used for this case would be mean reciprocal rank, but it has been argued in [12] that this metric is not on an interval scale, and thus the mean cannot be applied. Instead, we used the proposed alternative *mean first relevant (MFR)* which takes the rank position of the first clicked document in a result set and computes the arithmetic mean for all result sets that were generated using a stratagem search. This measure is proportional to the effort a user has to invest in finding the first relevant document in a result list: An MFR value of x represents the x-fold effort in comparison to the ideal value of 1. As the number of documents in a result set varies, it may happen that a result set only contains a small number of documents. One typical example is the search for other documents of a certain author or the search for a highly specific keyword. In this case, the MFR is usually rather low and might bias our results. Therefore, we additionally measured the MFR≥20 for all result sets that contain at least 20 documents which is the default number of documents on the first result page in Sowiport. Due to potential outliers that may distort our results, we furthermore disregard document views that were performed on the third page of a result set (first relevant > 40) when measuring MFR.

Besides the MFR values, we measure other session-related features like session length, number of document views, session duration, and usefulness of stratagems. To measure the usefulness of stratagems, we apply a measure previously described in [15] in which different interaction signals within a session can be used to estimate the success of a search session. For instance, if a user bookmarks a certain document one can consider this document as relevant. The list of implicit relevance signals considered to measure the usefulness is displayed in Table 1.

Short	Description
Add to favourites	Bookmark a single or multiple records to favourites
Goto Google Scholar	Search a record in Google Scholar
Goto Google Books	Search a record in Google Books
Goto Fulltext	View the full text of the record
Goto local availability	Check availability in the local library
Export record	Export the record in different citation styles or via e-mail

Table 1: List of implicit relevance feedback signals

To estimate if and how useful a stratagem was for the outcome of a search session, we measure the usefulness by observing the number of positive signals in the log file after the usage of a stratagem on two levels:

- Local usefulness
  The local usefulness counts the total number of implicit relevance signals on a document that was contained in the result set immediately after a stratagem run. For a visual example of implicit relevance feedback on a result set see the right box in Figure 2b.
- Global usefulness
  For each session, we count the total number of implicit relevance signals contained in the entire session after the first usage of a stratagem.

Using the local usefulness we determine the "immediate" relevance of a document in a result set after a stratagem search. The global usefulness on the other hand measures the usefulness of a stratagem search for the entire session.

5 RESULTS

In total, we analysed 607,109 unique sessions during our living lab study.

Descriptive statistics on the overall usage of stratagems can be found in Table 2. During our experiment, all three approaches were nearly equally distributed among the users (see column 2). Users applied a stratagem search 77,036 times from which 5,839 documents were clicked from the result lists. In column 5, we measured the mean dwell time starting from the first usage of a stratagem until the end of the session. When looking at the dwell time, we identified numerous outliers. We therefore removed all sessions that exceeded a dwell time of more than 20 minutes when measuring the average dwell time. On average, the users continued their search for 2.1 minutes after the first stratagem usage. All three approaches show a similar dwell time. Users that were assigned approach A or C continued their search for 123 seconds while approach B was continued for 133 seconds. In column 4, the mean number of interactions for all sessions containing a stratagem search is displayed. It can be seen that the number of interactions do not differ between the three approaches. In column 3, the number of document views from stratagem usage per approach is displayed. Both contextualised approaches have a considerably higher number of document views from stratagem search in comparison to the non-contextualised approach. Using the baseline, only 1,985 documents were viewed while the contextualisation based on similarity received more than 3,200 document views from stratagem searches. The contextualisation based on the session context also clearly outperforms the baseline with 2,627 document views. This tendency can also be seen in the click-through rates which are discussed later on in this section.

To estimate the effectiveness of the contextual ranking features in comparison to the non-contextualised baseline, we utilised the mean first relevant metric (MFR) as described in Section 4: the idea of the MFR metric is to take the position of the first clicked document in the result set. In Table 3, the MFR values for all sessions are displayed. The contextualisation based on similarity to the seed document performed best with an MFR of 3.10. The contextualisation based on session details received an MFR of 3.62 while the non-contextualised ranking performed the worst with an MFR of 4.66[4]. Besides the better results in terms of MFR, we can observe a higher click-through rate (denoted as N) for both contextualised approaches. For the contextualisation based on similarity, we observed nearly twice as many first relevant clicks (N=1999) compared to the baseline (N=1078).

The contextualisation based on the session context also clearly outperforms the baseline with 1,571 first relevant clicks.

Due to highly skewed data, we utilised a non-parametric Mann-Whitney U-Test to seek for significant differences in the results with a Bonferroni corrected $p^* = 0.016$. We see that both contextualised ranking features significantly outperform the non-contextualised ranking with A > B, p^*=0.001 r=0.13 and A > C, p^*=0.014 r=0.04. Furthermore, we see that the contextualisation based on similarity significantly outperforms the overall session context with (B > C, p^*=0.001 r=0.04).

As we may have different result set sizes, we furthermore measure the MFR≥20 for all result sets that contain at least 20 documents. The MFR≥20 values are displayed in column 4 of Table 3. The MFR≥20 values for all three approaches increased with a stronger impact on approach A and C. We can observe that the MFR for the non-contextualised approach increased from 4.66 to 6.47. However, we can not observe a substantial difference when

[4] In addition to MFR, we calculated mean reciprocal rank (MRR) values for all three approaches. MRR showed the same tendency as MFR, so we decided not to report MRR separately in this paper.

Approach	Total stratagem usage	Document views from stratagem search	Mean interactions per session	Mean dwell time (s)
(A) Baseline	25,426	1,985	7.61	123.79
(B) Similarity	25,475	3,212	7.91	134.98
(C) Session Context	26,135	2,627	7.76	123.27

Table 2: Descriptive statistics for the period of the study

Approach	MFR	SD	MFR ≥20	SD
(A) Baseline	4.66 (N=1078)	6.45	6.47 (N=607)	7.74
(B) Similarity	3.10* (N=1999)	4.41	3.39* (N=1528)	4.81
(C) Session context	3.62* (N=1571)	4.74	4.30* (N=1097)	5.33

Table 3: Mean first relevant

comparing MFR and MFR>20. The contextualisation based on document similarity still performs best while both contextualisation approaches still outperform the baseline significantly.

The efficiency of approach C highly depends on how rich the interaction of the user was before performing a stratagem search. If a user just entered the DL without any previous interaction we have a cold start problem. Therefore, we compared the MFR for different history sizes (defined as the number of interactions prior to the stratagem usage) to evaluate whether the usage of a stratagem later on in a session has any influence on the performance of the approaches. In Table 4, the MFR values for 3 different history sizes are displayed.

The results in Table 4 show that with a growing history size the MFR values of all three approaches increase. Looking at the non-contextualised approach the MFR at early stages of the session is 4.52 while increasing to 5.06 after a history size > 5. If we compare sessions with a history size ≥ 10, we can observe that the MFR for all approaches further increases (A=5.49, B=3.59, C=3.80). The differences between the MFR values get even more evident if we look at the percentage increase between the different history sizes. For a history size of $H \in [11, \infty]$ the MFR values of the baseline increased by 21.46% compared to a history size of $H \in [2, 5]$ while the contextualisation based on session context only increased by 6.14%. However, the number of sessions with a history size ≥ 10 is comparably low with only 487 sessions. Having a larger sample size would improve the reliability of these observations.

To measure the usefulness of the contextualisation in comparison to the baseline, we utilise implicit relevance signals which can be found in Table 1. In general, we measure the usefulness by observing the number of positive signals in the log file after the first usage of a stratagem on two levels: a) the local usefulness b) the global usefulness.

To exclude outliers from this experiment, we only considered sessions with a total of implicit relevance signals ≤ 10 . The results of this experiment are displayed in Table 5.

Approach	Local usefulness	Global usefulness
(A) Baseline	232	5,385
(B) Similarity	628	5,684
(C) Session Context	334	5,294

Table 5: Usefulness of stratagem browsing per session

Regarding the number of local usefulness signals displayed in column 2, we can observe that the contextual ranking (B=628,C=334) again outperforms the non-contextualised baseline (A=232). Regarding the global session usefulness, the results show only marginal differences between the contextual approaches and the non-contextual baseline. The similarity approach again performs best with 5,684 implicit relevance signals in total after the first usage of a stratagem search. However, the results for the global usefulness show only marginal differences between the contextual approaches and the non-contextual baseline.

6 DISCUSSION

By measuring the position of the first relevant document in the result set (MFR), we showed that both contextualisation approaches lead to significantly better results in comparison to the baseline. Besides the better results of the MFR we see a considerably higher click-through-rate of the contextualisation (B=1999, C=1571) compared to the baseline (A=1078). Both, the MFR and the click-through rates are strong indicators for a better effectiveness of the contextualised approaches in comparison to the non-contextualised baseline.

When limiting the MFR measure to all result sets that contain at least 20 documents we observed an increase of the MFR for all three approaches. The non-contextualised baseline for instance increased from an MFR of 4.66 to 6.47.

The results for MFR and the higher click-through rate do not include information about the relevance of the clicked documents but rather about a topical relatedness to the users search interests.

To overcome this problem and to get an insight into the perceived relevance, we additionally utilised the usefulness metric that takes implicit relevance signals into account. This analysis was carried out on two levels: a) the local usefulness of a search result after a stratagem run and b) the global usefulness which measures the implicit relevance signals for the entire session. The results for the local usefulness are in line with the results of the MFR. Both

Approach	MFR H ∈ [2, 5]	MFR H ∈ [6, 10]	MFR H ∈ [11, ∞]
(A) Baseline	4.52 (N=802)	5.06 (+11.94%, N=276)	5.49 (+21.46%, N=112)
(B) Similarity	3.04 (N=1491)	3.29 (+8.22%, N=508)	3.59 (+18.09%, N=215)
(C) Session context	3.58 (N=1201)	3.77 (+5.30%, N=370)	3.80 (+6.14%, N=160)

Table 4: Mean first relevant for different history sizes (H)

contextualised approaches outperform the baseline. The contextualisation based on document similarity gathered more than twice as many direct relevance signals as the baseline while the contextualisation based on the session context was also considerably higher (A=232,B=628,C=334). This underpins the assumption that the contextualised approaches provide a more effective topical relatedness to the users search interests. By utilising the global usefulness, we measured the number of implicit relevance signals after the first stratagem usage for the entire session. For the global usefulness, we identified only minor differences in the overall success of the sessions. This may be an indicator for a rather equal performance of the three approaches in terms of satisfying the users information need.

For the session context approach we identified a typical cold start problem. A majority of users visit Sowiport via a web search engine which indexes the detail view of a document. Users employing a stratagem for further exploration are very common in the transaction logs. However, in this case we have no information about the users information need and therefore, only little information can be used for contextualisation. The more interactions a user performs the more detailed the session context of the user can be modeled. This was also indicated by the results of our segmentation into different sets of window sizes in Table 4. We observed an increase in terms of MFR for larger history sizes. We assume that the performance of the session context depends on the complexity of the search task. If a session contains various interactions this is also an indication for the complexity of a search task. We assume that sessions with a higher number of interactions also have greater demands on the quality of a result list as all three approaches performed worse when the number of interactions increased.

We observed a general tendency for an improved performance of the session context with growing history sizes. The MFR values for the contextualisation based on similarity increased by 18.09% for larger history sizes in comparison to a history size of $H \in [2.5]$. The contextualisation based on session details only increased by 6.14%. The non-contextualised approach had the largest increase with 21.46%. Unfortunately, the number of sessions with a history size ≥ 10 is comparably low with only 487 sessions. Having a larger sample size would improve the reliability of these observations.

To overcome the cold start problem a hybrid approach could be implemented that contextualises browsing based on document similarity at the beginning of a session while longer sessions are contextualised based on session details. As the majority of search sessions in *Sowiport* comprises (1 to 5) interactions we can not generalise the results of our session context approach (C). We assume that for highly interactive search sessions the results of the re-ranking will differ and lead to a better performance.

Surprisingly, other session related measures like the dwell time or the number of interactions did not differ substantially between the approaches.

7 STRENGTHS AND LIMITATIONS OF THE STUDY

The results of the transaction log study provide insights towards a general usefulness of contextualised ranking features in exploratory search. Both, short-term and long-term ranking features outperform the baseline. While the baseline describes the general behaviour of many DLs it may not be suitable for comparison with more sophisticated approaches like the ones that are presented in this paper.

One downside of the present paper lies in the nature of transaction log studies. Our results indicate a significantly better ranking in terms of MFR on the level of contextual ranking features. However, we are not able to interpret our results in the light of quality and overall relevance. A similar argumentation is provided in [17] where a presentation bias in click-through data is observed. To gain a more qualitative view on the usage of contextual ranking features a user study could be conducted that gives insights into the relevance of documents and particular reasons for regarding or disregarding certain documents.
We used implicit relevance ratings to measure the overall success of each session. Although the implicit relevance ratings had previously been used to measure the usefulness of DL features [15], they are not evaluated entirely. Thus, the results for this observation are influenced by our subjective relevance ratings of search activities. However, they provide a suitable measure to estimate the usefulness of search results.

One downside of the present approach is that the user is not aware of the contextual ranking features. In a first attempt, we provided the users with an information box which aimed to give some information on the ranking mechanism and the ability to disable the contextualised ranking. After running a pretest we decided to remove all information about the ranking features on the user interface as this led to confusion and distorted results.

By assigning each user one approach for the entire session, we kept the overall usage balanced. In this way, we eliminated seasonal effects like the start of a university semester or weekends. On the other hand, we ignored potential shifts in the users' search interest during the session. A more sophisticated approach would be to identify session boundaries.

Another advantage of the present study is that it can be easily reproduced by other researchers and DL developers. As we relied on the MLT query parser which is a standard similarity function build in SOLR one can reproduce our approach in its own environment. The re-ranking based on the session context uses SOLR boost functions which also can be reproduced as long as a suitable user model can be derived.

8 CONCLUSION

In this paper, we have introduced two contextualisation approaches on the level of browsing in a DL: a) a contextualisation based on document similarity and b) a contextualisation based on implicit feedback about the users' search activities. Using a living lab environment, we evaluated our experiment on 47,444 sessions that contained browsing activities. Our results show that a contextualisation of browsing in DLs significantly outperforms the baseline in terms of MFR. Furthermore, we observed an increase in the click-through rate for our contextualisation approaches in comparison to the baseline. Other session related factors like dwell time or the total number of interactions per session did not differ between the approaches. As we utilised basic SOLR functions like the *More Like This* query parser to contextualise stratagem searches, our approach can easily be reproduced by other researchers and DL developers.

Although our contextualisation approach outperforms the baseline, a further investigation is necessary as our living lab study can not give insights into the overall relevance of the viewed documents. To tackle this problem we measured the local and global usefulness which take implicit relevance feedback into account. The results of our local usefulness analysis show that the contextualisation had a strong impact in terms of topical relatedness when selecting a document from the result set. Again, both contextualised approaches outperform the non-contextualised baseline. The global usefulness for the entire session, however, did not show significant differences between the contextualised and the non-contextualised re-ranking. Thus, we can state that the contextualised ranking features performed significantly better in terms of MFR, click-through rate and local usefulness. However, insights on the usefulness of our feature with regards to the users information need can not be derived from our living lab study. The increase in terms of the click-through rate and the significantly better MFR values, however, provide us with a strong indication that users could benefit from contextualised ranking features on the level of stratagems and that further research in this area could be of benefit for the DL community. Future work will be to conduct a user study that provides us with qualitative feedback on the effectiveness of our contextualisation approaches.

REFERENCES

[1] Azhar Alhindi, Udo Kruschwitz, Chris Fox, M Albakour, et al. 2015. Profile-based summarisation for web site navigation. *ACM Transactions on Information Systems (TOIS)* 33, 1 (2015), 4.

[2] Leif Azzopardi and Krisztian Balog. 2011. Towards a living lab for information retrieval research and development. In *International Conference of the Cross-Language Evaluation Forum for European Languages*. Springer, 26–37.

[3] Marcia J Bates. 1990. Where should the person stop and the information search interface start? *Information Processing & Management* 26, 5 (1990), 575–591.

[4] Nicholas J. Belkin, Daniel Hienert, Philipp Mayr, and Chirag Shah. 2017. Data Requirements for Evaluation of Personalization of Information Retrieval - A Position Paper. In *Working Notes of CLEF 2017 - Conference and Labs of the Evaluation Forum*. CEUR-WS.org, Dublin, Ireland. http://ceur-ws.org/Vol-1866/paper_193.pdf

[5] Paul N Bennett, Ryen W White, Wei Chu, Susan T Dumais, Peter Bailey, Fedor Borisyuk, and Xiaoyuan Cui. 2012. Modeling the impact of short-and long-term behavior on search personalization. In *35th SIGIR conference*. ACM, 185–194.

[6] Zeljko Carevic, Maria Lusky, Wilko van Hoek, and Philipp Mayr. 2017. Investigating exploratory search activities based on the stratagem level in digital libraries. *International Journal on Digital Libraries* (2017), 1–21. http://link.springer.com/10.1007/s00799-017-0226-6

[7] Zeljko Carevic and Philipp Mayr. 2015. Extending search facilities via bibliometric-enhanced stratagems. (2015), 40–46. http://ceur-ws.org/Vol-1344/paper5.pdf

[8] Zeljko Carevic and Philipp Mayr. 2016. Survey on High-level Search Activities based on the Stratagem Level in Digital Libraries. In *International Conference on Theory and Practice of Digital Libraries*. Springer, 54–66. http://link.springer.com/10.1007/978-3-319-43997-6_5

[9] David Ellis. 1989. A behavioural approach to information retrieval system design. *Journal of Documentation* 45, 3 (1989), 171–212.

[10] Jody Condit Fagan. 2010. Usability studies of faceted browsing: A literature review. *Information Technology and Libraries* 29, 2 (2010), 58.

[11] Enrique Frias-Martinez, Sherry Y. Chen, and Xiaohui Liu. 2009. Evaluation of a Personalized Digital Library Based on Cognitive Styles: Adaptivity vs. Adaptability. *Int. J. Inf. Manag.* 29, 1 (Feb. 2009), 48–56.

[12] Norbert Fuhr. 2017. *Some Common Mistakes In IR Evaluation, And How They Can Be Avoided*. Technical Report. University of Duisburg-Essen, Germany.

[13] Marti Hearst. 2009. *Search user interfaces*. Cambridge University Press.

[14] Marti A Hearst. 2006. Clustering versus faceted categories for information exploration. *Commun. ACM* 49, 4 (2006), 59–61.

[15] Daniel Hienert and Peter Mutschke. 2016. A usefulness-based approach for measuring the local and global effect of IIR services. In *Proceedings of the 2016 ACM Conference on Human Information Interaction and Retrieval*. ACM, 153–162.

[16] Daniel Hienert, Frank Sawitzki, and Philipp Mayr. 2015. Digital library research in action: supporting information retrieval in Sowiport. *D-Lib Magazine* 21, 3 (2015), 8. https://doi.org/10.1045/march2015-hienert

[17] Thorsten Joachims et al. 2003. Evaluating Retrieval Performance Using Click-through Data. (2003).

[18] Evangelos Kanoulas, Ben Carterette, Mark Hall, Paul Clough, and Mark Sanderson. 2011. Overview of the TREC 2011 Session Track. In *TREC 2011*. NIST.

[19] Carl Lagoze, Dean B. Kraft, Sandy Payette, and Susan Jesuroga. 2005. What Is a Digital Library Anyway?: Beyond Search and Access in the NSDL. *D-Lib Magazine* 11, 11 (Nov. 2005). https://doi.org/10.1045/november2005-lagoze

[20] Gary Marchionini. 2006. Exploratory search: from finding to understanding. *Commun. ACM* 49, 4 (2006), 41–46.

[21] Nicolaas Matthijs and Filip Radlinski. 2011. Personalizing web search using long term browsing history. In *Proceedings of the fourth ACM international conference on Web search and data mining*. ACM, 25–34.

[22] Philipp Mayr and Ameni Kacem. 2017. A Complete Year of User Retrieval Sessions in a Social Sciences Academic Search Engine. (2017), 560–565. https://doi.org/10.1007/978-3-319-67008-9_46

[23] Philipp Mayr and Vivien Petras. 2008. Cross-concordances: terminology mapping and its effectiveness for information retrieval. In *74th IFLA World Library and Information Congress*. IFLA, Quebec, Canada. http://www.ifla.org/IV/ifla74/papers/129-Mayr_Petras-en.pdf

[24] Nils Pharo, Thomas Beckers, Ragnar Nordlie, and Norbert Fuhr. 2011. Overview of the INEX 2010 Interactive Track. 227–235.

[25] M.Elena Renda and Umberto Straccia. 2005. A personalized collaborative Digital Library environment: a model and an application. *Information Processing & Management* 41, 1 (Jan. 2005), 5–21. https://doi.org/10.1016/j.ipm.2004.04.007

[26] Ian Ruthven, Mounia Lalmas, and Keith Van Rijsbergen. 2003. Incorporating user search behavior into relevance feedback. *Journal of the Association for Information Science and Technology* 54, 6 (2003), 529–549.

[27] Anna Sepliarskaia, Filip Radlinski, and Maarten de Rijke. 2017. Simple Personalized Search Based on Long-Term Behavioral Signals. In *European Conference on Information Retrieval*. Springer, 95–107.

[28] Xuehua Shen, Bin Tan, and ChengXiang Zhai. 2005. Context-sensitive information retrieval using implicit feedback. In *28th SIGIR conference*. ACM, 43–50.

[29] Alan F. Smeaton and Jamie Callan. 2005. Personalisation and recommender systems in digital libraries. *International Journal on Digital Libraries* 5, 4 (01 Aug 2005), 299–308. https://doi.org/10.1007/s00799-004-0100-1

[30] Jaime Teevan, Daniel J Liebling, and Gayathri Ravichandran Geetha. 2011. Understanding and predicting personal navigation. In *Proceedings of the fourth ACM international conference on Web search and data mining*. ACM, 85–94.

[31] Ryen White, Joemon Jose, C van Rijsbergen, and Ian Ruthven. 2004. A simulated study of implicit feedback models. *Advances in Information Retrieval* (2004), 311–326.

[32] Ryen W White, Wei Chu, Ahmed Hassan, Xiaodong He, Yang Song, and Hongning Wang. 2013. Enhancing personalized search by mining and modeling task behavior. In *22nd international conference on World Wide Web*. ACM, 1411–1420.

[33] Ryen W White and Steven M Drucker. 2007. Investigating behavioral variability in web search. In *Proceedings of the 16th international conference on World Wide Web*. ACM, 21–30.

[34] Ryen W White, Joemon M Jose, and Ian Ruthven. 2002. Comparing explicit and implicit feedback techniques for web retrieval: Trec-10 interactive track report. In *Proceedings of the Tenth Text Retrieval Conference (TREC-10)*. 534–538.

Machine Learning vs. Rules and Out-of-the-Box vs. Retrained: An Evaluation of Open-Source Bibliographic Reference and Citation Parsers

Dominika Tkaczyk
ADAPT Centre, School of Computer Science and Statistics
Trinity College Dublin, Ireland
Dominika.Tkaczyk@adaptcentre.ie

Andrew Collins
ADAPT Centre, School of Computer Science and Statistics
Trinity College Dublin, Ireland
Andrew.Collins@adaptcentre.ie

Paraic Sheridan
ADAPT Centre, School of Computer Science and Statistics
Trinity College Dublin, Ireland
Paraic.Sheridan@adaptcentre.ie

Joeran Beel
ADAPT Centre, School of Computer Science and Statistics
Trinity College Dublin, Ireland
Joeran.Beel@adaptcentre.ie

ABSTRACT

Bibliographic reference parsing refers to extracting machine-readable metadata, such as the names of the authors, the title, or journal name, from bibliographic reference strings. Many approaches to this problem have been proposed so far, including regular expressions, knowledge bases and supervised machine learning. Many open source reference parsers based on various algorithms are also available. In this paper, we apply, evaluate and compare ten reference parsing tools in a specific business use case. The tools are Anystyle-Parser, Biblio, CERMINE, Citation, Citation-Parser, GROBID, ParsCit, PDFSSA4MET, Reference Tagger and Science Parse, and we compare them in both their out-of-the-box versions and versions tuned to the project-specific data. According to our evaluation, the best performing out-of-the-box tool is GROBID (F1 0.89), followed by CERMINE (F1 0.83) and ParsCit (F1 0.75). We also found that even though machine learning-based tools and tools based on rules or regular expressions achieve on average similar precision (0.77 for ML-based tools vs. 0.76 for non-ML-based tools), applying machine learning-based tools results in a recall three times higher than in the case of non-ML-based tools (0.66 vs. 0.22). Our study also confirms that tuning the models to the task-specific data results in the increase in the quality. The retrained versions of reference parsers are in all cases better than their out-of-the-box counterparts; for GROBID F1 increased by 3% (0.92 vs. 0.89), for CERMINE by 11% (0.92 vs. 0.83), and for ParsCit by 16% (0.87 vs. 0.75).

CCS CONCEPTS

• **Information systems** → **Information systems applications**; *Digital libraries and archives*

KEYWORDS

bibliographic reference parsing, citation parsing, machine learning, sequence tagging

ACM Reference format:

D. Tkaczyk, A. Collins, P. Sheridan, J. Beel. 2018. Machine Learning vs. Rules and Out-of-the-Box vs. Retrained: An Evaluation of Open-Source Bibliographic Reference and Citation Parsers. In *Proceedings of ACM JCDL '18*, June 3–7, 2018, Fort Worth, TX, USA, 10 pages.
DOI: https://doi.org/10.1145/3197026.3197048

1 INTRODUCTION

Within the past decades there has been exponential increase in the volume of available scientific literature [1]. This has resulted in a scientific information overload problem, which refers to challenges related to consuming enormous amount of information by interested readers. Scientific information systems and digital libraries help researchers to tackle the scientific information overload problem by providing intelligent information retrieval and recommendation services. These services need machine-readable, rich bibliographic metadata of stored documents to function correctly, but this requirement is not always met in practice. As a consequence, there is a huge demand for automated methods and tools able to extract high-quality machine-readable bibliographic metadata information directly from scientific unstructured data.

Reference parsing is one important task in this research area. In reference parsing, the input is a single reference string, usually formatted in a specific bibliography style (Figure 1). The

JCDL '18, June 3–7, 2018, Fort Worth, TX, USA

ACM 978-1-4503-5178-2/18/06...$15.00
https://doi.org/10.1145/3197026.3197048

output is a machine-readable representation of the input string, typically called a parsed reference (Figure 2). Such parsed representation is a collection of metadata fields, each of which is composed of a field type (e.g. "volume" or "journal") and value (e.g. "12" or "Nature").

Dominika Tkaczyk, Pawel Szostek, Mateusz Fedoryszak, Piotr Jan Dendek and Lukasz Bolikowski. CERMINE: automatic extraction of structured metadata from scientific literature. In International Journal on Document Analysis and Recognition, 2015, vol. 18, no. 4, pp. 317-335, doi: 10.1007/s10032-015-0249-8.

Figure 1: An example bibliographic reference string on the input of the reference parsing algorithm.

author: Tkaczyk, Dominika
author: Szostek, Pawel
author: Fedoryszak, Mateusz
author: Dendek, Piotr Jan
author: Bolikowski, Lukasz
title: CERMINE: automatic extraction of structured metadata from scientific literature
journal: International Journal on Document Analysis and Recognition
year: 2015
volume: 18
issue: 4
first page: 317
last page: 335
doi: 10.1007/s10032-015-0249-8

Figure 2: An example output of the reference parsing task, which is a machine-readable representation of the reference string from Figure 1. This representation is a collection of metadata fields, each composed of a field type and value. For this reference, the following metadata field types were extracted: author, title, journal, volume, issue, first page, last page, year and doi.

Bibliographic reference parsing is important for tasks such as matching citations to cited documents [2], assessing the impact of researchers [3, 4], journals [5, 6] and research institutions [7, 8], and calculating document similarity [9, 10], in the context of academic search engines [11, 12] and recommender systems [13, 14].

Reference parsing can be viewed as reversing the process of formatting a bibliography record into a string. During formatting some information is lost, and thus the reversed process is not a trivial task and usually introduces errors.

There are a few challenges related to reference parsing. First, the type of the referenced object (a journal article, a conference publication, a patent, etc.) is typically not known, so we do not know which metadata fields can be extracted. Second, the reference style is unknown, thus we do not know where in the string specific metadata fields are present. Finally, it is common for a reference string to contain errors, introduced either by humans while adding the references to the paper, or by the process of extracting the string itself from the scientific publication. These errors include for example OCR errors, unexpected spaces inside words, missing spaces, typos and errors in style-specific punctuation.

The most popular approaches to reference parsing include regular expressions, template matching, knowledge bases and supervised machine learning. There also exist a number of open source reference parsers ready to use. It is unknown, however, which approaches and which open source parsers give the best results for given metadata field types. What is more, some of the existing parsers can be tuned to the data of interest. In theory, this process should increase the quality of the results, but it is also time consuming and requires training data, which is typically expensive to obtain. An important issue is then how high an increase in the quality should be expected after retraining. These aspects are important for researchers and programmers developing larger information extraction systems for scientific data, as well as digital library practitioners wishing to use existing bibliographic reference parsers within their infrastructures.

In this study we apply, evaluate and compare a number of existing reference parsing tools, both their out-of-the-box and retrained versions, in the context of a real business project involving data from chemical domains. Specifically, we are interested in the following questions:

1. How good are reference parsing tools for our use case?
2. How do the results of machine learning-based approaches compare to the results of more static, non-trainable approaches, such as regular expressions or rules?
3. How much impact does retraining the machine learning models using project-specific data have on the parsing results?

In the following sections, we describe the state of the art, give the larger context of the business case, list the tools we evaluated, describe our evaluation setup and report the results. Finally, we discuss the findings and present conclusions.

2 RELATED WORK

Reference parsing is a well-known research problem, and many techniques have been proposed for solving it over the years, including regular expressions, template matching, knowledge bases and supervised machine learning.

Regular expressions are a simple way of approaching the task of reference parsing. This approach is typically based on a set of manually developed regular expressions able to capture single or multiple metadata fields in different reference styles. Such a strategy works best if the reference styles to process are known in advance and if the data contains little noise. In practice, it can be challenging to maintain a regular expressions-based system, constantly adapting the set of used regular expressions to changing data.

Regular expressions are often combined with other techniques, such as hand-crafted rules or knowledge bases. In knowledge-based approaches, at the beginning the system is populated with knowledge extracted from available data and/or existing external sources, such as digital libraries. During the actual parsing, fragments of the input reference string are matched against the information in the knowledge base. This approach works best in the case of fields which values tend to form closed sets, such as journal titles or last names.

Gupta *et al.* [15] propose a combination of regular-expression based heuristics and knowledge-based systems for reference parsing. In addition, their approach is able to match inline citations to their corresponding bibliographic references.

Constantin *et al.* [16] describe a rule- and regular expressions-based system called PDFX. PDFX is in fact a large system able to extract the logical structure of scholarly articles in PDF form, including parsed bibliography.

Day *et al.* [17] employ a hierarchical knowledge representation framework called INFOMAP for extracting metadata from reference strings. They report 92.39% accuracy for extracting author, title, journal, volume, issue, year, and page from references formatted with six major reference styles.

Finally, Cortez *et al.* [18] present FLUX-CiM, a method for reference parsing based on a knowledge base automatically constructed from an existing set of sample metadata records, obtained from public data repositories. According to their results, FLUX-CiM achieves precision and recall above 94% for a wide set of metadata fields.

In template matching approaches, references are first matched against a database of templates and then template-specific rules or regular expressions are used.

For example, Hsieh *et al.* [19] propose a reference parsing algorithm, in which the matching is based on sequence alignment. They report a 70% decrease in the average field error rate (2.24% vs. 7.54%) in comparison to a widely used machine learning-based approach.

Chen *et al.* [20] describe a tool called BibPro, which is able to extract metadata from reference strings using a gene sequence alignment tool (Basic Local Alignment Search Tool).

The most popular approach to reference parsing is supervised machine learning. In this approach training data is used to learn a so-called model, which is used during actual parsing to extract metadata from the input string. Such an approach requires little expert knowledge, as patterns are learned directly from the training data. Maintainability is also an important concern in a machine learning-based approach, however, it is comparatively easy to make sure the models are up to date by repeatedly retraining them on newer data.

In a supervised machine learning-based approach, reference parsing is usually formally defined as a sequence tagging problem. In a sequence tagging problem, on the input there is a sequence of objects represented by features, and the goal is to assign a corresponding sequence of labels, taking into account not only the features themselves, but also the dependencies between direct and indirect neighboring labels in the sequence.

For a sequence tagger to be useful for a reference parsing task, first the input reference string has to be transformed into a sequence of smaller fragments, typically called tokens. Tokenization can be performed in many different ways, for example it can be based on punctuation characters, or spaces. After tokenization, each token is assigned a label by a supervised sequence tagger. The labels usually correspond to the sought metadata field types, and a special label "other" is used for tokens that are not a part of any metadata field. Sometimes separate labels are used for the first token of a metadata field. After assigning labels to tokens, neighboring tokens with the same label are concatenated to form the final metadata fields.

It is important to note that in order to train a supervised sequence tagger for reference parsing, a specific representation of a reference string, composed of labeled tokens is required (Figure 3). In practice, training data is usually stored in an XML-based format, which can be easily transformed to the sequence of labelled tokens (Figure 4).

[AU-FN]Dominika [AU-SN]Tkaczyk [OTH], [AU-FN]Pawel [AU-SN]Szostek [OTH], [AU-FN]Mateusz [AU-SN]Fedoryszak [OTH], [AU-FN]Piotr [AU-FN]Jan [AU-SN]Dendek [OTH]and [AU-FN]Lukasz [AU-SN]Bolikowski [OTH]. [TITLE]CERMINE [TITLE]: [TITLE]automatic [TITLE]extraction [TITLE]of [TITLE]structured [TITLE]metadata [TITLE]from [TITLE]scientific [TITLE]literature [OTH]. [OTH]In [JOURNAL]International [JOURNAL]Journal [JOURNAL]on [JOURNAL]Document [JOURNAL]Analysis [JOURNAL]and [JOURNAL]Recognition [OTH], [YEAR]2015 [OTH], [OTH]vol [OTH]. [VOL]18 [OTH], [OTH]no [OTH]. [ISSUE]4 [OTH], [OTH]pp [OTH]. [FPAGE]317 [OTH]- [LPAGE]335 [OTH], [OTH]doi [OTH]: [DOI]10 [DOI]. [DOI]1007 [DOI]/ [DOI]s [DOI]10032 [DOI]- [DOI]015 [DOI]- [DOI]0249 [DOI]- [DOI]8 [OTH].

Figure 3: An example of a reference string represented as a sequence of labelled tokens. In this case a single token can be either a sequence of letters, a sequence of digits, or a single other character. The labels are given in square brackets.

```
<citation>
  <author><fn>Dominika</fn> <sn>Tkaczyk</sn></author>,
  <author><fn>Pawel</fn> <sn>Szostek</sn></author>,
  <author><fn>Mateusz</fn> <sn>Fedoryszak</sn></author>,
  <author><fn>Piotr Jan</fn> <sn>Dendek</sn></author> and
  <author><fn>Lukasz</fn> <sn>Bolikowski</sn></author>.
  <title> CERMINE: automatic extraction of structured metadata
        from scientific literature</title>.
  In <journal>International Journal on Document Analysis and
        Recognition</journal>,
  <year>2015</year>,
  vol. <volume>18</volume>,
  no. <issue>4</issue>,
  pp. <fpage>317</fpage>-<lpage>335</lpage>,
  doi: <doi>10.1007/s10032-015-0249-8</doi>.
</citation>
```

Figure 4: An example of a reference string, represented in XML-based format. Given the tokenization strategy, there is a 1-1 mapping between this representation and the sequence of labelled tokens.

Many machine learning algorithms have been applied to problem of reference parsing, including Support Vector Machines (SVM) [21, 22], Hidden Markov Models (HMM) [23, 24, 25], and Conditional Random Fields (CRF) [21, 22, 26, 27, 28, 29, 30]. SVM is a general-purpose classification technique, while both HMM and CRF can be directly employed as sequence taggers.

Hetzner [23] proposes a simple HMM-based solution for extracting metadata fields from references. Yin *et al.* [24] employ a modification of a traditional HMM called a bigram HMM, which considers words' bigram sequential relation and position information. Finally, Ojokoh *et al.* [25] explore a trigram version of HMM, reporting overall accuracy, precision, recall and F1 measure of over 95%.

By far the most popular machine learning algorithm for reference parsing is Conditional Random Fields. Councill *et al.* [26] describe ParsCit, one of the best known, widely used open source CRF-based systems for extracting metadata from references.

GROBID, created by Lopez [27], is another example of a CRF-based system able to parse bibliographic references. GROBID is also a larger tool, able to extract the metadata and logical structure from scientific papers in PDF. The author reports metadata field-level accuracy of 95,7%.

CERMINE, proposed by Tkaczyk *et al.* [28], is also a large system able to extract metadata and structure, including parsed bibliography, from scientific papers in PDF format. CERMINE's reference parsing functionality is also based on CRF technique. In 2015 CERMINE won Semantic Publishing Challenge [31, 32], which included tasks requiring accurate extraction of title and year information from bibliographic references.

Matsouka *et al.* [33] also propose a CRF-based reference parsing method, which uses lexical features as well as lexicons.

Finally, Zhang *et al.* [30] applied CRF algorithm for the task of extracting author, title, journal and year information from reference strings, reporting an overall 97.95% F1 on PubMed Central data.

Some researchers also compare various approaches to bibliographic reference parsing. For example, Zou *et al.* [21] compare CRF and SVM, achieving very similar overall accuracies for both approaches: above 99% accuracy at the token level, and over 97% accuracy at the metadata field level.

Zhang *et al.* [22] propose structural SVM with contextual features, and compare it to conventional SVM and CRF. They also report similar accuracies for all three approaches: above 98% token classification accuracy and above 95% for field extraction.

Finally, Kim *et al.* [29] describe a system called BILBO and compare it to other popular reference parsing tools (ParsCit, Biblio, free_cite and GROBID), using previously unseen data. According to their study, the best results were obtained by BILBO (F1 0.64), followed closely by GROBID (F1 0.63).

A number of reference parsers are also available as open source tools. They can be divided into two categories: tools that are solely reference parsers, and tools with wider functionality.

Pure reference parsers include:

- Anystyle-Parser [2] (a CRF-based tool written in Ruby)
- Biblio[3] (a Perl library based on regular expressions)
- BibPro[4] [20] (based on sequence alignment)
- Citation[5] (a parser written in Ruby, uses regular expressions and additional rules)
- Citation-Parser[6] (a rule-based parser written in Python)
- Free_cite[7] (a CRF-based parser written in Ruby)
- Neural Parscit[8] (a parser based on LSTM, the only deep learning-based tool we found)
- Reference Tagger[9] (a CRF-based parser written in Python)

Apart from tools providing only reference parsing functionality, there exist a few larger systems able to extract much more information from scientific documents. It is possible, however, to employ them only for the task of reference parsing. These are:

- CERMINE[10] [28]
- GROBID[11] [27]
- ParsCit[12] [26]
- PDFSSA4MET[13]
- Science Parse[14]

Table 1 summarizes the techniques employed by each parser and gives details about the extracted metadata fields.

3 BUSINESS CASE

Some details related to the business case are left out on purpose, as we are not allowed to publish them.

In the business project, the input is a collection of 506,540 scientific documents in PDF format, mostly from chemical domains. The goal of the project is to extract machine-readable bibliographies from the input documents in order to identify all documents cited by each paper. More specifically, for each input document we require all bibliographic items (journal papers, conference proceedings, web pages, etc.) listed in the document. Every extracted bibliographic item should be in the form of a parsed bibliographic reference.

The input documents vary in quality. Some of them are native PDF files, with all characters correctly present in the PDF content stream, while others contain the results of a separate OCR process, with typical OCR errors.

The following metadata fields are required by the client of the project as output from the reference parsing process:

- author: the first author of the referenced document, formatted as "Lastname, Initial_of_the_first_name" (e.g. "Tkaczyk, D"),
- source: the source of the referenced document, this can be the name of the journal or the conference, URL or identifier such as ArXiv id or DOI,
- year,
- volume,

[2] https://github.com/inukshuk/anystyle-parser
[3] http://search.cpan.org/~mjewell/Biblio-Citation-Parser-1.10/
[4] https://github.com/ice91/BibPro
[5] https://github.com/nishimuuu/citation

[6] https://github.com/manishbisht/Citation-Parser
[7] https://github.com/miriam/free_cite
[8] https://github.com/opensourceware/Neural-ParsCit
[9] https://github.com/rmcgibbo/reftagger
[10] https://github.com/CeON/CERMINE
[11] https://github.com/kermitt2/grobid
[12] https://github.com/knmnyn/ParsCit
[13] https://github.com/eliask/pdfssa4met
[14] https://github.com/allenai/science-parse

- issue,
- page: the first page of the pages range,
- organization: the organization, which is an author of the referenced document, the "corporate author".

Unlike the typical reference parsing task, the title of the referenced document is not required by our client. In chemistry, information about the title is often missing from the reference string, as the information about the authors, source and numbers (volume, issue, pages) are sufficient to identify a cited paper.

For the task of extracting machine-readable bibliography metadata from a scientific paper, we employ a workflow composed of three stages (Figure 5):

1. First, the PDF file is parsed and the regions containing bibliography are recognized.
2. Next, the content of these bibliography regions is split into a list of individual reference strings.
3. Finally, we perform reference parsing for each reference string separately.

For the first two stages we employed the open source tool GROBID [27]. It uses supervised machine learning to find bibliography regions within a document and split their contents into a list of reference strings.

The third stage of the workflow is in fact reference parsing task. Since there are a lot of open source bibliographic reference parsers available (including the GROBID system itself), we decided to perform a comparative study to find out which parsers perform the best. This paper focuses solely on the third, final stage of the workflow.

4 METHODOLOGY

4.1 Evaluated Tools

In our study, we include only open source reference parsers: Anystyle-Parser, Biblio, BibPro, CERMINE, Citation, Citation-Parser, Free_cite, GROBID, Neural Parscit, ParsCit, PDFSSA4MET, Reference Tagger and Science Parse.

We were not able to evaluate three tools, due to installation errors or missing resources: BibPro, Free_cite and Neural ParsCit.

As mentioned before, not all evaluated tools extract all needed metadata fields. Also, in some cases the tools extract only a subset of a metadata field (for example, Anystyle-Parser extracts journal name, but not URL or DOI, which constitutes only part of the "source" field). Table 2 shows the matching between the fields extracted by all evaluated tools and the desired metadata fields.

4.2 Data

We had access to a collection of 9,491 pairs: PDF document + a list of parsed references, provided by our client. The collection contained 371,656 parsed references and 1,886,174 metadata fields in total. The data was manually curated and contains occasional minor errors (e.g. typos). For the purpose of the study we assume it is 100% correct.

Table 1: Summary of extracted metadata fields and techniques employed by each open source reference parser.

Tool	Approach	Extracted fields
Anystyle-Parser	CRF	authors, booktitle, date, DOI, edition, editor, genre, ISBN, journal, location, pages, publisher, title, URL, volume
Biblio	regular expressions	authors, date, editor, genre, issue, pages, publisher, title, volume, year
BibPro	template matching	authors, editor, institution, issue, journal, pages, volume, year
CERMINE	CRF	authors, DOI, issue, pages, title, volume, year
citation	regular expressions + rules	authors, title, URL, year
Citation-Parser	rules	authors, booktitle, issue, journal, pages, publisher, title, volume, year
free_cite	CRF	authors, booktitle, date, editor, institution, journal, location, pages, publisher, title, volume
GROBID	CRF	authors, date, editor, issue, journal, organization, pages, title, volume
Neural ParsCit	LSTM	authors, booktitle, date, editor, institution, journal, issue, location, pages, publisher, volume
ParsCit	CRF	authors, booktitle, date, editor, institution, journal, issue, location, pages, publisher, volume
PDFSSA4MET	regular expressions	pages, title, volume, year
Reference Tagger	CRF	authors, issue, journal, pages, title, volume, year
Science Parse	CRF	author title, volume, year, journal

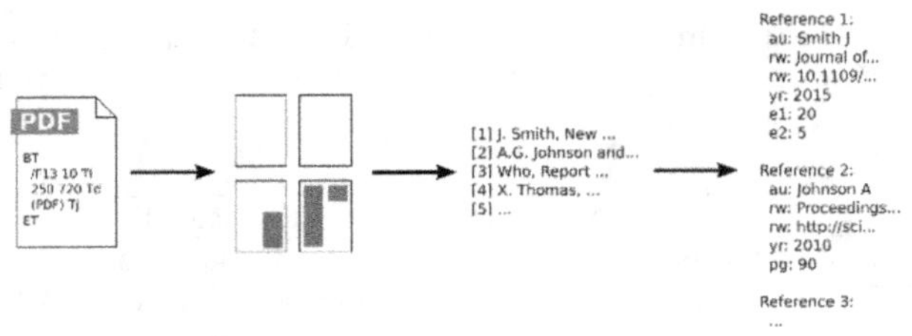

Figure 5: The workflow of extracting machine-readable bibliography metadata from a document in PDF format. The workflow is composed of three stages: 1) recognizing the bibliography regions in the document, 2) splitting the bibliography into individual references, and 3) parsing each reference string in isolation.

Table 2: The matching between the output of all evaluated tools and the metadata fields required in our project.

Tool	author	source	year	vol	issue	page	Org
Anystyle-Parser	+ [15]	+ [16]	+	+	-	+	-
Biblio	+ [17]	+	+	+	+	+	-
CER-MINE	+	+ [18]	+	+	+	+	-
citation	-	+ [19]	+	-	-	-	-
Citation-Parser	+	+ [20]	+	+	+	+	-
GROBID	+	+	+	+	+	+	-
ParsCit	+ [14]	+ [19]	+	+	+	+	-
PDFSSA-4MET	-	-	+	+	-	+	-
Reference Tagger	+	+ [15]	+	+	+	+	-
Science Parse	+ [16]	+ [15]	+	+	-	+	-

The data was divided in the following way: roughly 67% of the dataset (6,306 documents) were used for manual exploratory analyses and training the tools, and the remaining 33% (3,185 documents) were used for testing and comparing the tools, both their out-of-the-box and retrained versions. The test set contains 64,495 references in total, which is large enough for a fair comparison.

To be useful for the evaluation and training, the data needed additional preprocessing.

For the evaluation we needed pairs: reference string + parsed reference. One problematic issue was that the client did not provide reference strings directly, but they were buried in PDF files. To obtain them, we processed the PDFs automatically using the implementation of the first two steps of our workflow (Figure 5). Unfortunately, this process is not error-free and in some cases results in strings missing or incorrect strings present on the output. As a result, the number of extracted reference strings does not even have to be equal to the number of ground truth parsed references provided by the client, and we cannot simply use the order of the lists to decide which string corresponds to which ground truth reference. For example, the fifth reference string might correspond to the seventh parsed reference, because the first two strings are missing. To solve this problem, we used a separate process based on dynamic programming and fuzzy term matching to automatically infer correspondence between extracted strings and parsed references. This resulted in generating pairs needed for evaluation: reference string, parsed reference.

For training we needed the references in a format preserving both reference string and token tags, as explained in Section 2 (Figure 3 and Figure 4). To obtain such a representation, we matched the ground truth field values against the extracted strings, which allowed us to find substrings corresponding to the metadata fields. In some cases, this process failed to find a suitable substring (for example if the string was extracted erroneously or if it contains noise). Such references were discarded and not used for training.

4.3 Comparison Procedure

For a given tool and a given reference, the ground truth metadata fields are compared with the fields extracted by the tool from the string. The field values are subject to simple normalization and cleaning steps (transformation to lowercase, normalization of hyphen-like characters, cleaning fragments like "'" and "&"). After cleaning, every extracted metadata field is marked as correct or incorrect. A correct field is a field with both type and value equal to one of the fields in the ground truth parsed reference.

For a given metadata field type, we calculate precision, recall and F1 measure. Precision is the ratio of the number of correctly extracted fields (over the entire reference set) to the number of all extracted fields. Recall is the fraction of correctly extracted fields to the number of expected fields (fields in the ground truth data). F1 measure is the harmonic mean of precision and recall.

In practice, the tools vary in the field types and their meaning, and in each case careful mapping from the tool's output to our desired collection of fields was needed. For example, URL, DOI and journal name are usually present as three separate metadata field types, while in our project they are treated as one field "source". The tools also differ with respect to how the authors are extracted. Some tools (e.g. Anystyle-Parser) extract the entire author list as one field, while others split the author names. Some tools (e.g. Biblio, ParsCit, Science Parse) extract the entire author fullname as one string, while others mark additionally firstname, middlename and/or surname. In our

[15] Entire author list only
[16] Journal name only
[17] Author fullnames only
[18] Journal name and DOI only
[19] URL only
[20] Journal name and book title only

case, the surname and first name of the first author was needed. For the systems which do not include this information, we employ additional simple heuristics on top of their output.

4.4 Training Procedure

Some of the tools, in particular those based on machine learning, are trainable, which means that they are able to automatically learn custom parsing "rules" from the training data. Their out-of-the-box versions already contain trained models, which are used by default for parsing. However, we do not know whether the default models were trained on similar data as used in our project, or whether reference styles typical for chemical domains even appeared in the training sets used by the authors of the tools. As a result, we cannot be sure that the default models contain all needed information useful for parsing chemical references. For these reasons we decided to investigate whether retraining the parsers on the data specific for our project improves the parsing results.

We retrained the three most promising tools, that is, tools with the best average results obtained by their out-of-the-box versions: GROBID, CERMINE and ParsCit. For the training we used 10,000 references randomly chosen from the documents in the training set. We did not use more training data for performance reasons.

Even though all machine learning-based tools are trainable, it is important to note that they vary a lot in how easy it is to train them. For example, Anystyle-Parser, CERMINE, GROBID and ParsCit contain specific training procedures and instructions, while in other cases retraining is more difficult due to a lack of documentation.

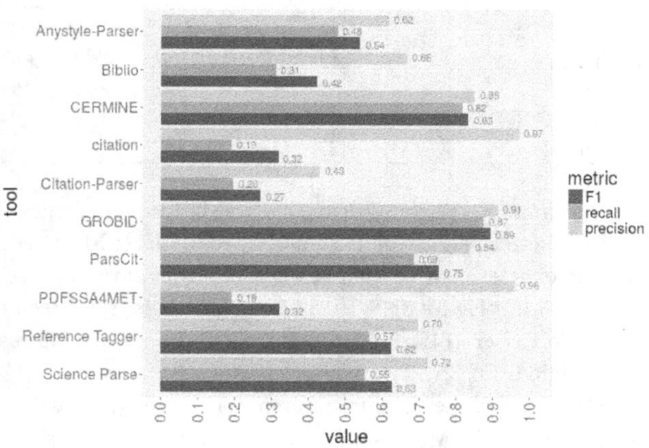

Figure 6: The overall precision, recall and F1 values for out-of-the-box systems.

5 RESULTS

Figure 6 presents the overall results of the comparison of the out-of-the-box systems and Table 3 presents the evaluation results broken down by metadata field type. Each cell in the table gives precision, recall and F1 values, respectively. For each combination (metadata type, metric) the best result is bolded. We do not give the results for organization, as none of the systems is able to extract this field.

Measured with F1, the best performing out-of-the-box tools are: GROBID (F1 0.89), followed by CERMINE (F1 0.83) and ParsCit (F1 0.75). All these tools implement CRF-based reference parsers. The worst performing systems are: Citation-Parser (F1 0.27), Citation (F1 0.32) and PDFSSA4MET (F1 0.32). All those tools are based on rules and/or regular expressions.

Table 3: Results of the evaluation of out-of-the-box tools. Each cell gives precision, recall and F1 values, respectively. For each category the best result is bolded.

Tool	author	source	year	vol	issue	page
Anystyle-	.62	.69	.74	.29	-	.76
Parser	.74	.44	.54	.27		.69
	.58	.54	.62	.28		.73
Biblio	.74	.29	.91	.81	.11	**.99**
	.65	.11	.51	.14	.14	.18
	.69	.16	.65	.24	.12	.30
CERMINE	.81	.75	.96	.91	.51	.93
	.81	.61	.96	.92	**.83**	.82
	.81	.67	.96	.92	.63	.87
citation	-	.47	**.99**	-	-	-
		.01	.95			
		.03	.97			
Citation-	.48	.09	.92	.45	.77	.67
Parser	.49	.06	.34	.07	.10	.03
	.48	.07	.50	.11	.18	.06
GROBID	**.86**	**.88**	.97	**.96**	**.91**	.90
	.82	**.82**	.95	**.93**	.82	**.89**
	.84	**.85**	.96	**.94**	**.86**	**.90**
ParsCit	**.86**	75	.98	.92	.91	.67
	.84	55	.84	.65	.42	.62
	.85	63	.91	.76	.57	.65
PDFSSA4M	-	-	.95	**.96**	-	**.99**
ET			.75	.05		.20
			.84	.10		.34
Reference	.69	.63	.97	.51	.58	.76
Tagger	.57	.53	.63	.47	.52	.66
	.62	.67	.76	.49	.55	.71
Science	**.86**	.62	.98	.43	-	.59
Parse	.62	.52	**.98**	.28		.45
	.72	.57	**.98**	.34		.51

Measured by recall, results are the same. GROBID (0.87), CERMINE (0.82), and ParsCit (0.69) perform best. Citation (0.19), PDFSSA4MET (0.19), and Citation-Parser (0.20) perform worst.

However, measured with precision, this ranking changes. Citation (0.97), PDFSSA4MET (0.96), and GROBID (0.91) perform best, while Citation-Parser (0.43), Anystyle-Parser (0.62) and Biblio (0.66) perform worst.

In general, for all tools precision is higher than recall, with the difference ranging from 0.03 (CERMINE, 0.82 and 0.85) to 0.78 (Citation, 0.19 and 0.97). Interestingly, the difference between precision and recall is smaller in the case of machine learning-based tools (average difference 0.11) than in the case of regular expressions- or rule-based systems (average difference 0.53).

The following three systems were retrained: GROBID, CERMINE and ParsCit. These are the systems achieving the best results in the previous experiment. Figure 7 and Table 4 show the results.

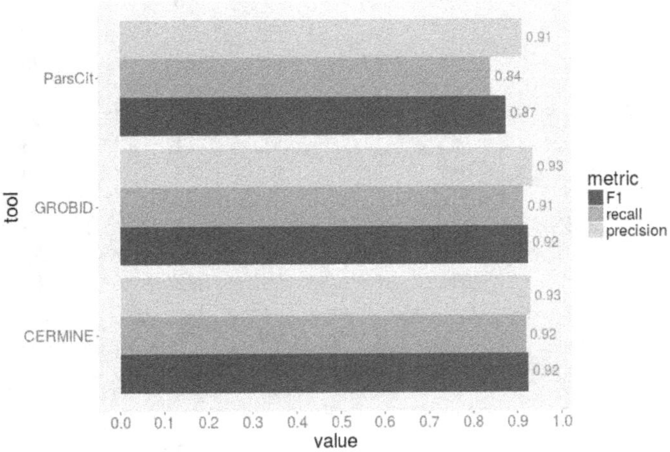

Figure 7: The overall precision, recall and F1 of the retrained tools.

Table 4: Evaluation results for retrained tools, broken down by metadata field types. Each cell contains precision, recall and F1, respectively.

Tool	author	source	year	vol	issue	page	org
CER-MINE	.91	.84	.98	.96	.94	.96	.55
	.91	.83	.97	.95	.87	.96	.31
	.91	.84	.98	.96	.90	.96	.39
GRO-BID	.93	.89	.99	.97	.92	.91	.54
	.92	.85	.98	.95	.87	.89	.52
	.92	.87	.98	.96	.90	.90	.53
Pars-Cit	.74	.88	.99	.97	.96	.97	-
	.71	.75	.97	.89	.78	.92	-
	.73	.81	.98	.93	.86	.72	-

Both retrained CERMINE and GROBID achieved the same F1 of 0.92, and ParsCit was a bit worse with F1 of 0.87. The results of CERMINE and GROBID broken down by metadata types (Table 4) are similar with the exception of source (CERMINE: 0.84, GROBID: 0.87), page (CERMINE: 0.96, GROBID: 0.90) and organization (CERMINE: 0.39, GROBID: 0.53). All three systems achieved very similar high results for year. ParsCit did not extract organization at all, which suggests the training process did not pick it up from the training data.

6 DISCUSSION

At the beginning, we stated the following questions:

1. How good are the results of existing reference parsing tools for previously unseen data?
2. How do the results of machine learning-based approaches compare to the results of more static, non-trainable approaches, such as regular expressions or rules?
3. How does retraining the machine learning models using project-specific data affect the results?

Question 1. The evaluated systems vary greatly in the quality of the results. The out-of-the-box tool achieving the best F1 is GROBID with F1 of 0.89, followed by CERMINE (F1 0.83) and ParsCit (F1 0.75). The tools with the worst F1 are: Citation-Parser (F1 0.27), Citation (F1 0.32) and PDFSSA4MET (F1 0.32). Table 5 shows the final ranking of out-of-the-box systems, ordered by decreasing F1.

Table 5: Final ranking of out-of-the-box tools, ordered by F1.

Tool	F1	precision	recall
GROBID	.89	.91	.87
CERMINE	.83	.85	.82
ParsCit	.75	.84	.69
Science Parse	.63	.72	.55
Reference Tagger	.62	.70	.57
Anystyle-Parser	.54	.62	.48
Biblio	.42	.31	.66
Citation	.32	.97	.19
PDFSSA4MET	.32	.96	.19
Citation-Parser	.27	.43	.20

Question 2. Machine learning-based systems achieve on average better results (precision: 0.77, recall: 0.66, F1: 0.71) than regular expressions- or rule-based tools (precision: 0.76, recall: 0.22, F1: 0.33) (Figure 8). What is more, the worst ML-based tool, Anystyle-Parser (F1 0.54) outperforms the best non-ML-based tool, Biblio (F1 0.42).

The main cause of this difference is recall (Figure 8). The average recall for ML-based tools (0.66) is three times as high as non-ML-based tools (0.22). At the same time, the difference in average precisions is small (0.77 for ML-based tools vs. 0.76 for non-ML-based tools). The reason for this might be that it is relatively easy to achieve good precision of manually developed rules and regular expression, but it is difficult to have a high enough number of rules, covering all possible reference styles.

Question 3. For all three retrained systems (CERMINE, GROBID, ParsCit), retrained versions are better than out-of-the-box versions. The relative increase in F1 vary: GROBID 3% (increase from 0.89 to 0.92), CERMINE 11% (increase from 0.83 to

0.92), ParsCit 16% (increase from 0.75 to 0.87). Figure 9 compares the F1 before and after retraining for each system. In addition, in Table 6 we present the exact values for all metrics.

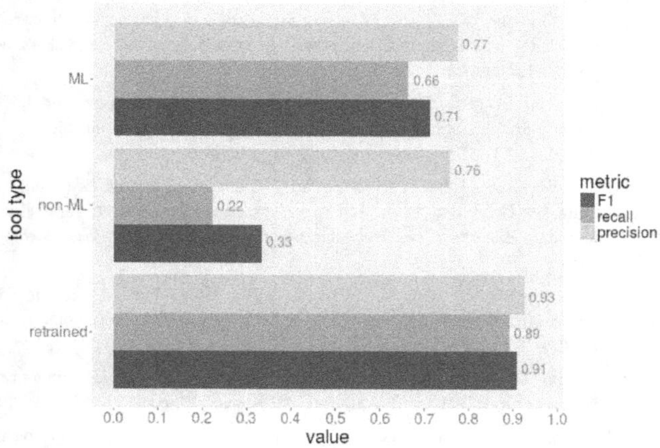

Figure 8: Overall precision, recall and F1 aggregated by system type (ML, non-ML and retrained). The values are averaged over all tools in the respective category.

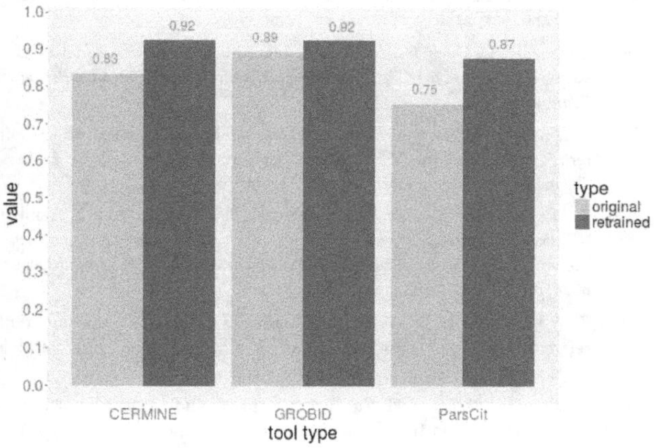

Figure 9: Comparison of F1 for the out-of-the-box, and retrained versions of systems: CERMINE, GROBID, ParsCit.

This effect is not surprising. We expect the retrained models to perform better, since they had an opportunity to analyze the training data and find specific "rules", as well as typical terms, useful for parsing chemical references.

We obtained the highest increase in the results in the case of ParsCit, which was the weakest system (of the three retrained) before retraining. On the other hand, in the case of GROBID the increase was the smallest. After retraining, the results of the three systems were much more similar to each other than before.

Table 6: Comparison of precision, recall and F1 between out-of-the-box versions of tools and retrained versions.

tool	metric	out-of-the-box	retrained	relative difference
GROBID	Precision	.91	.93	2%
	Recall	.87	.91	5%
	F1	.89	.92	3%
CERMINE	Precision	.85	.93	9%
	Recall	.82	.92	13%
	F1	.83	.92	11%
ParsCit	Precision	.84	.91	9%
	Recall	.69	.84	23%
	F1	.75	.87	16%

In general, our results suggest that if the pretrained version of a ML-based tool performs poorly (e.g. ParsCit), we can gain a lot by retraining the system. On the other hand, if a system already performs well (GROBID), we should still expect increase in the quality, but the magnitude of the increase might be lower.

7 SUMMARY AND FUTURE WORK

In this paper we study the problem of reference parsing in the context of a real business use case. We applied and compared ten reference parsing tools: Anystyle-Parser, Biblio, Citation, Citation-Parser, Reference Tagger, CERMINE, GROBID, ParsCit, PDFSSA4MET and Science Parse. We investigated the differences between tools that use rules or regular expressions and machine learning-based tools. We also checked, how important training machine learning-based tools is and how it affects the results.

According to our results, the best performing out-of-the-box tool is GROBID with F1 of 0.89, followed by CERMINE (F1 0.83) and ParsCit (F1 0.75). On average, machine learning-based systems achieve better results than rule-based systems (F1 0.71 vs. 0.33). While ML-based and non-ML-based tools achieve similar precisions (0.77 and 0.76, respectively), ML-based tools have three times higher recall than non-ML-based tools (0.66 vs. 0.22).

Our study also confirms that it is worth retraining the models using task-specific data, especially if initial results appear low. For all three retrained systems (CERMINE, GROBID, ParsCit), retrained versions are better than out-of-the-box versions, with the relative differences in F1 varying from 3% (GROBID, increase from 0.89 to 0.92), through 11% (CERMINE, increase from 0.83 to 0.92), to 16% (ParsCit, increase from 0.75 to 0.87).

It is important to note some limitations of our study. First, in our business project a very specific metadata type set was required by the client and only those types were present in the ground truth data. As a result, we did not evaluate the extraction of important metadata such as the title of the referenced document or the names of all the authors. Second, we limited our study to reference parsers fully implemented and made available on the Internet, rejecting also three systems which we could not install and use due to errors. As a result, the list of evaluated parsers does not include, for example, tools that use template matching. Finally, only the three best systems were retrained.

In the future, we plan to retrain all the available ML-based tools, and perform a similar study using other available datasets and including more metadata field types, in particular the title of the referenced paper and the names of all the authors. We also plan to experiment with building intelligent reference parsing ensembles.

ACKNOWLEDGMENTS

This publication has emanated from research conducted with the financial support of Science Foundation Ireland (SFI) under Grant Number 13/RC/2016. The project has also received funding from the European Union's Horizon 2020 research and innovation programme under the Marie Skłodowska-Curie grant agreement No 713567.

REFERENCES

[1] M. Khabsa and C. L. Giles, "The Number of Scholarly Documents on the Public Web," *PLoS ONE*, 2014.

[2] M. Fedoryszak, D. Tkaczyk and L. Bolikowski, "Large Scale Citation Matching Using Apache Hadoop," in *International Conference on Theory and Practice of Digital Libraries (TPDL)*, 2013.

[3] J. E. Hirsch, "An index to quantify an individual's scientific research output that takes into account the effect of multiple coauthorship," *Scientometrics*, vol. 85, no. 3, pp. 741-754, 2010.

[4] S. Alonso, F. J. Cabrerizo, E. Herrera-Viedma and F. Herrera, "h-Index: A review focused in its variants, computation and standardization for different scientific fields," *J. Informetrics*, vol. 3, no. 4, pp. 273-289, 2009.

[5] T. Braun, W. Glänzel and A. Schubert, "A Hirsch-type index for journals," *Scientometrics*, vol. 69, no. 1, pp. 169-173, 2006.

[6] B. González-Pereira, V. P. Guerrero Bote and F. de Moya Anegón, "A new approach to the metric of journals' scientific prestige: The SJR indicator," *J. Informetrics*, vol. 4, no. 3, pp. 379-391, 2010.

[7] J.-F. Molinari and A. Molinari, "A new methodology for ranking scientific institutions," *Scientometrics*, vol. 75, no. 1, pp. 163-174, 2008.

[8] D. Torres-Salinas, J. G. Moreno-Torres, E. D. López-Cózar and F. Herrera, "A methodology for Institution-Field ranking based on a bidimensional analysis: the IFQ2A index," *Scientometrics*, vol. 88, no. 3, pp. 771-786, 2011.

[9] P. Ahlgren and C. Colliander, "Document-document similarity approaches and science mapping: Experimental comparison of five approaches," *J. Informetrics*, vol. 3, no. 1, pp. 49-63, 2009.

[10] J. Beel, *Virtual Citation Proximity (VCP): Calculating Co-Citation-Proximity-Based Document Relatedness for Uncited Documents with Machine Learning [Proposal]*, 2017.

[11] J. Wu, K. M. Williams, H.-H. Chen, M. Khabsa, C. Caragea, S. Tuarob, A. Ororbia, D. Jordan, P. Mitra and C. L. Giles, "CiteSeerX: AI in a Digital Library Search Engine," *AI Magazine*, vol. 36, no. 3, pp. 35-48, 2015.

[12] C. Xiong, R. Power and J. Callan, "Explicit Semantic Ranking for Academic Search via Knowledge Graph Embedding," in *WWW*, 2017.

[13] J. Beel, A. Aizawa, C. Breitinger and B. Gipp, "Mr. DLib: Recommendations-as-a-Service (RaaS) for Academia," in *JCDL*, 2017.

[14] J. Beel, B. Gipp, S. Langer and C. Breitinger, "Research-paper recommender systems: a literature survey," *Int. J. on Digital Libraries*, vol. 17, no. 4, pp. 305-338, 2016.

[15] D. Gupta, B. Morris, T. Catapano and G. Sautter, "A new approach towards bibliographic reference identification, parsing and inline citation matching," in *International Conference on Contemporary Computing*, 2009.

[16] A. Constantin, S. Pettifer and A. Voronkov, "PDFX: fully-automated pdf-to-xml conversion of scientific literature," *ACM Symposium on Document Engineering*, pp. 177-180, 2013.

[17] M.-Y. Day, R.-H. Tsai, C.-L. Sung, C.-C. Hsieh, C.-W. Lee, S.-H. Wu, K.-P. Wu, C.-S. Ong and W.-L. Hsu, "Reference metadata extraction using a hierarchical knowledge representation framework," *Decision Support Systems*, vol. 43, no. 1, pp. 152-167, 2007.

[18] E. Cortez, A. S. da Silva, M. A. Gonçalves, F. de Sá Mesquita and E. S. de Moura, "A flexible approach for extracting metadata from bibliographic citations," *JASIST*, vol. 60, no. 6, pp. 1144-1158, 2009.

[19] Y.-L. Hsieh, S.-H. Liu, T.-H. Yang, Y.-H. Chen, Y.-C. Chang, G. Hsieh, C.-W. Shih, C.-H. Lu and W.-L. Hsu, "A Frame-Based Approach for Reference Metadata Extraction," in *Technologies and Applications of Artificial Intelligence*, 2014.

[20] C.-C. Chen, K.-H. Yang, C.-L. Chen and J.-M. Ho, "BibPro: A Citation Parser Based on Sequence Alignment," *IEEE Trans. Knowl. Data Eng.*, vol. 24, no. 2, pp. 236-250, 2012.

[21] J. Zou, D. X. Le and G. R. Thoma, "Locating and parsing bibliographic references in HTML medical articles," *IJDAR*, vol. 13, no. 2, pp. 107-119, 2010.

[22] X. Zhang, J. Zhou, D. X. Le and G. R. Thoma, "A structural SVM approach for reference parsing," *BMC Bioinformatics*, vol. 12, no. S-3, p. S7, 2011.

[23] E. Hetzner, "A simple method for citation metadata extraction using hidden markov models," in *Joint Conference on Digital Libraries*, Pittsburgh, 2008.

[24] P. Yin, M. Zhang, Z.-H. Deng and D. Yang, "Metadata Extraction from Bibliographies Using Bigram HMM," in *International Conference on Asian Digital Libraries*, 2004.

[25] B. A. Ojokoh, M. Zhang and J. Tang, "A trigram hidden Markov model for metadata extraction from heterogeneous references," *Inf. Sci.*, vol. 181, no. 9, pp. 1538-1551, 2011.

[26] I. Councill, C. Giles and M.-Y. Kan, "ParsCit: an open-source CRF reference string parsing package," in *International Conference on Language Resources and Evaluation*, 2008.

[27] P. Lopez, "GROBID: combining automatic bibliographic data recognition and term extraction for scholarship publications," *Research and Advanced Technology for Digital Libraries*, pp. 473-474, 2009.

[28] D. Tkaczyk, P. Szostek, M. Fedoryszak, P. Dendek and L. Bolikowski, "CERMINE: automatic extraction of structured metadata from scientific literature," *International Journal on Document Analysis and Recognition*, vol. 18, no. 4, pp. 317-335, 2015.

[29] Y.-M. Kim, P. Bellot, J. Tavernier, E. Faath and M. Dacos, "Evaluation of BILBO reference parsing in digital humanities via a comparison of different tools," in *ACM Symposium on Document Engineering*, 2012.

[30] Q. Zhang, Y. Cao and H. Yu, "Parsing citations in biomedical articles using conditional random fields," *Comp. in Bio. and Med.*, vol. 41, no. 4, pp. 190-194, 2011.

[31] D. Tkaczyk and L. Bolikowski, "Extracting Contextual Information from Scientific Literature Using CERMINE System," in *Semantic Web Evaluation Challenges - Second SemWebEval Challenge at ESWC*, 2015.

[32] A. Di Iorio, C. Lange, A. Dimou and S. Vahdati, "Semantic Publishing Challenge - Assessing the Quality of Scientific Output by Information Extraction and Interlinking," in *SemWebEval@ESWC*, 2015.

[33] D. Matsuoka, M. Ohta, A. Takasu and J. Adachi, "Examination of effective features for CRF-based bibliography extraction from reference strings," in *International Conference on Digital Information Management*, 2016.

Linked Open Citation Database: Enabling Libraries to Contribute to an Open and Interconnected Citation Graph

Anne Lauscher
University of Mannheim
Mannheim, Germany
anne@informatik.uni-mannheim.de

Kai Eckert
Stuttgart Media University
Stuttgart, Germany
eckert@hdm-stuttgart.de

Lukas Galke
ZBW – Leibniz Information Centre for Economics
Kiel, Germany
L.Galke@zbw.eu

Ansgar Scherp
ZBW – Leibniz Information Centre for Economics
Kiel, Germany
A.Scherp@zbw.eu

Syed Tahseen Raza Rizvi
DFKI – German Research Center for Artificial Intelligence
Kaiserslautern, Germany
syed_tahseen_raza.rizvi@dfki.de

Sheraz Ahmed
DFKI – German Research Center for Artificial Intelligence
Kaiserslautern, Germany
sheraz.ahmed@dfki.de

Andreas Dengel
DFKI – German Research Center for Artificial Intelligence
Kaiserslautern, Germany
andreas.dengel@dfki.de

Philipp Zumstein
Mannheim University Library
Mannheim, Germany
philipp.zumstein@bib.uni-mannheim.de

Annette Klein
Mannheim University Library
Mannheim, Germany
annette.klein@bib.uni-mannheim.de

ABSTRACT

Citations play a crucial role in the scientific discourse, in information retrieval, and in bibliometrics. Many initiatives are currently promoting the idea of having free and open citation data. Creation of citation data, however, is not part of the cataloging workflow in libraries nowadays.

In this paper, we present our project Linked Open Citation Database, in which we design distributed processes and a system infrastructure based on linked data technology. The goal is to show that efficiently cataloging citations in libraries using a semi-automatic approach is possible. We specifically describe the current state of the workflow and its implementation. We show that we could significantly improve the automatic reference extraction that is crucial for the subsequent data curation. We further give insights on the curation and linking process and provide evaluation results that not only direct the further development of the project, but also allow us to discuss its overall feasibility.

CCS CONCEPTS

• **Information systems → Digital libraries and archives**; *RESTful web services*; *Resource Description Framework (RDF)*; *Search interfaces*; *Link and co-citation analysis*; • **Applied computing →** *Optical character recognition*;

JCDL '18, June 3–7, 2018, Fort Worth, TX, USA

ACM ISBN 978-1-4503-5178-2/18/06...$15.00
https://doi.org/10.1145/3197026.3197050

KEYWORDS

citation data; library workflows; linked open data; editorial system; automatic reference extraction

ACM Reference Format:
Anne Lauscher, Kai Eckert, Lukas Galke, Ansgar Scherp, Syed Tahseen Raza Rizvi, Sheraz Ahmed, Andreas Dengel, Philipp Zumstein, and Annette Klein. 2018. Linked Open Citation Database: Enabling Libraries to Contribute to an Open and Interconnected Citation Graph. In *JCDL '18: The 18th ACM/IEEE Joint Conference on Digital Libraries, June 3–7, 2018, Fort Worth, TX, USA.* ACM, New York, NY, USA, 10 pages. https://doi.org/10.1145/3197026.3197050

1 INTRODUCTION

Originally, libraries cataloged their holdings only on the level of physical objects, mostly books, with the primary purpose to identify them and locate them on the shelves. Resources like conference proceedings, collections or journals are in the catalogs, too, but only on the level of a book or volume – the physical, bound book that is put somewhere on a shelf. The single papers in a conference proceeding, collection or journal, in which the patrons are usually most interested, are not captured in traditional library catalogs. This has changed since many libraries have introduced Resource Discovery Systems (RDS) that combine the classical content of the library catalog with large indexes of article data. These indexes are dominantly in the hand of commercial providers [2], but there are also library based approaches like the K10plus-Zentral index[1] that is curated by a library service center and at least partly contains article data produced by libraries. While libraries start to catch up on the indexing of articles, the database providers often already include another data source: citations extracted from the lists of references in the articles. Although such citation data gives a great functionality for a single database and allows to examine the referenced article as well as the articles referencing the current one, the

[1] https://verbundwiki.gbv.de/display/VZG/K10plus-Zentral

same data usually cannot be used in another database. The information which article cites a given article is extremely helpful during literature research [22] and allows a versatile ranking, not only of articles, but also authors, journals, conferences, and institutions, depending on the level of aggregation. [13]

Many libraries spend a lot of money for the big commercial citation databases like Web of Science (WoS) or Scopus. These databases have a focus on journal articles, although they have started some years ago to include other forms of scientific output as well, e.g. Book Citation Index, Data Citation Index. A comparative study from 2016 showed that the journal coverage of WoS and similarly for Scopus in Social Sciences is quite low and "English-language journals are favored to the detriment of other languages" [14]. It is not possible for libraries to extend the coverage of these databases by cataloging some missing resources. Moreover, there are restrictions about what you are allowed to do with the data, which exclude sharing the data in larger chunks with other researchers. This, however, is exactly what we would expect today from an open science perspective. For a transparent and replicable bibliometric or scientometric analysis we need open citation data.

Our project Linked Open Citation Database (LOC-DB)[2] aims to prove that a distributed infrastructure for the cataloging of citations in libraries is possible. We want to create a citation database within libraries, where the resulting citation data is available as linked and open data (under a CC0 waiver) using the OpenCitations data model to foster collaboration and sharing. Therefore, we develop a workflow (Section 3) that is embedded into the actual cataloging workflow of a library. The technical architecture (Section 4) is designed to distribute the workload across many participating libraries. At the core is the database back end (Section 4.1) that integrates components like the automatic reference extractor (Section 4.2) and various data sources for link suggestion. All data and links are curated in the front end editorial system (Section 4.3). All these components including the workflow need to be optimized to make the curation of the citation data feasible. We are particularly interested in the time that is needed to curate the citations and the quality of the resulting data that can be achieved. In Section 5, we present results of our initial evaluation after the first prototype implementation. This enables us to discuss some first estimations (Section 6) regarding our main question: how much would it cost, with respect to resources, if libraries cataloged everything and curated the citation graph?

2 RELATED WORK

Citation indexes in science first have been introduced by Garfield in 1955 [7] which lead to the development of the commercial database Web of Science owned now by Clarivate Analytics. Another big company with large influence in bibliometric analyses is Google which runs Google Scholar.[3] While Google Scholar is open for everyone to search and examine the citations in there, the data is not openly shared and cannot be used in other contexts or for large bibliometric analyses. Competing search engine providers have similar products, as Microsoft Academic[4] and Baidu Scholar.[5]

Other citation projects originate from academic institutions, like CiteSeer, that started in 1998 and since then was renamed to CiteSeerX,[6] hosted today by the Pennsylvania State University. They use a web crawler and a fully automated workflow for processing publicly available full-text documents in order to extract the citations [8], which sometimes leads to low quality citation data [9]. Their data can be reused under a CC-BY-NC-SA license.[7] The software is reused in CitEC - Citations in Economics[8] which analyzes full-text documents in economics and provides their data to the RePEc services. A similar fully automated pipeline based on the full-text of publicly available publications is run for Semantic Scholar[9] by the Allen Institute for Artificial Intelligence since 2015.

The OpenCitations project[10] has also a fully automated workflow but based on structured data, mainly from Europe PubMed Central. The references are then processed and provided as RDF-formatted data openly with a SPARQL end point. [16, 18] LOC-DB has adopted the OpenCitations data model, and is in close contact with the directors of OpenCitations to explore the possibilities for further cooperation.[11]

A mixture of automatic additions and manual edits is possible in the collaborative knowledge base Wikidata[12], which includes publication data and citation data mainly because of the recent WikiCite[13] initiative, with a focus on the automated extraction from electronic publications. [20]

OpenCitations and WikiCite are also among the funding organizations of the Initative for Open Citations (I4OC),[14] with the goal to promote the unrestricted availability of scholarly citation data. Several publishers already joined this initiative and provide their reference data openly via Crossref.[15] ExLibris includes this data into its commercial database Primo Central, that drives the Primo Discovery Service, since May 2016.[16] And of course we also use it in our workflow wherever possible.

From all these projects and products it can be seen that citation data is highly important and created by various means and from various sources, in varying quality. We believe that libraries should play a main role in providing this data for the public, and that fully automatic methods are not reliable enough considering the importance of the data. This is especially true for older publications which are not available in an electronic format. Hence, we reuse existing data and combine state-of-the-art reference extraction

[2]https://locdb.bib.uni-mannheim.de/
[3]https://scholar.google.com/

[4]https://academic.microsoft.com/, with a paid API https://azure.microsoft.com/en-us/services/cognitive-services/academic-knowledge/.
[5]http://xueshu.baidu.com/
[6]http://citeseerx.ist.psu.edu/
[7]http://csxstatic.ist.psu.edu/about/data
[8]http://citec.repec.org/
[9]https://www.semanticscholar.org/. They provide their data for download, but restrict the reuse on non-commercial research and non-commercial educational purposes: http://labs.semanticscholar.org/corpus/corpus/legal.
[10]http://opencitations.net
[11]https://opencitations.wordpress.com/2018/03/23/early-adopters-of-the-opencitations-data-model/
[12]https://www.wikidata.org/
[13]https://meta.wikimedia.org/wiki/WikiCite
[14]https://i4oc.org/
[15]https://www.crossref.org
[16]https://knowledge.exlibrisgroup.com/Primo/Product_Documentation/Highlights/047Primo_May_2016_Highlights, section Citation Trails

techniques with the knowledge of domain-experts, in an efficient system with distributed workflows.

3 LIBRARY WORFKLOW AND DATA

The capturing of citations in libraries can be integrated in the standard workflow for new acquisitions, or performed systematically in projects processing specific collections that might be of special interest. All possible publication formats, i.e. print and electronic, must be covered. For the LOC-DB project, a part of the social sciences collection of Mannheim University Library has been chosen to implement the workflow for the retrospective cataloging of citations. It consists of 522 print books and collections acquired by the library in 2011, and the articles that were published during the same year in 101 (mostly electronic) journals.[17] Apart from that, the new print acquisitions of the social sciences branch library are also processed regularly from July 2017 on.

The LOC-DB workflow builds on the traditional library cataloging work: Books, collections and journals already come with high quality metadata that can be retrieved in MARC21 format from a library union catalog. For collections and journals, the metadata of chapters and articles contained in them have to be captured next, in order to precisely identify the citing resources. All metadata of citing resources are saved to the LOC-DB database in a standardized, structured format that is fit for sharing and reuse in Linked Open Data contexts (see Section 4.1.2). Then, the references themselves can be ingested. If the citing resource is in print, the reference section is scanned and processed by the Automatic Reference Extractor of the LOC-DB system (see Section 4.2). If it is electronic, either the reference data can be retrieved from external sources (see Section 4.1.3) or the electronic text of the reference section is processed by the Automatic Reference Extractor. In any case, the output is a list of separate references (the "bibliographic entries"). They can be in a more or less structured or completely unstructured form, so they have to be "resolved", i. e., linked to a record in the standard LOC-DB format (a "bibliographic resource"). If possible, this is done by retrieving the metadata for the item from appropriate external databases (see Section 4.1.3). We take care to store the identifiers of the source databases (for example Crossref DOIs or union catalog IDs for books) in order to foster a possible future integration of the LOC-DB data into these databases.

3.1 Print Books

The set of 522 books consists of 330 monographs and 192 collections, for which a student assistant scanned the reference lists – usually one larger list at the end of a monograph or several shorter ones after each chapter of a collection. The average extent of a reference list in our set was 26 pages (see Table 1).

A standard book scanner has been used to create the scans. Comparable scanners are already available for patrons in many libraries, so there would be no need to purchase new hardware to do the workflow in many places.

For the new acquisitions, the relevant books are already marked with a special note in the acquisition process. When the books arrive,

Table 1: Printed books in social sciences purchased 2011 by Mannheim University Library with the number of pages in the list of references.

	monographs	collections	total
no. of books	330	192	522
pages overall	6,690	6,860	13,550
pages avg.	20	36	26

they pass through the normal cataloging workflow and other work steps of the library. For the collections, the librarians copy the table of contents, which will become handy later in the process. The books are then placed in a special location in our offices for the scanning process. If the item is not immediately requested by a patron, the scanning is done when a student assistant is available - this can take one or two days. Urgently needed books are of course provided to the patrons first, and the scanning is done later.

3.2 Electronic Journals

Most journals provide some alerting services like an RSS feed for newly published articles or issues. For the remaining journals, the library can actively monitor them on a regular time base. The bibliographic metadata for most journal articles itself can be found in Crossref, although we do some additional work trying to connect to some library databases as well. The citation data on the other hand can be in a lot of forms, which all have to be considered:

- citation data is already available in LOD, e.g. by OpenCitations project
- citation data is available as open data (structured or unstructured), e.g. by Crossref
- publisher provides some API for structured article data in XML, e.g. JATS-XML or Springer's A++ format
- full-text including the references is available as HTML
- full-text including the references is only available as PDF

We so far focused on the second case which is already quite frequent, thanks to the Initiative for Open Citations. A first assessment of the quality of the relevant data in Crossref showed that although there is a considerable amount of public, structured references available, many of these references are missing important data fields (like DOI, title, and first-page), which makes the identification of these publications really hard.[18] Thus, in order to provide high-quality data this then still needs further processing, which we do in our editorial system.

4 LOC-DB ARCHITECTURE

Our workflows are supported by three infrastructure components which we develop in our project: The central LOC-DB component, i.e. the back end (Section 4.1), the automatic reference extraction (Section 4.2), and the editorial system, i.e., the graphical user interface exposed to the librarians (Section 4.3). An overview of

[17] An electronic version of all these journals exists, but in two cases, Mannheim University Library doesn't have access to it, so that the print version has to be used for the project.

[18] E.g. among the relevant references for LOC-DB in Crossref only 35% have a DOI and only 43% have a year. For the detailed analysis, see the Data Quality section in https://github.com/locdb/locdb-journal-analysis/blob/master/locdb-journals.ipynb.

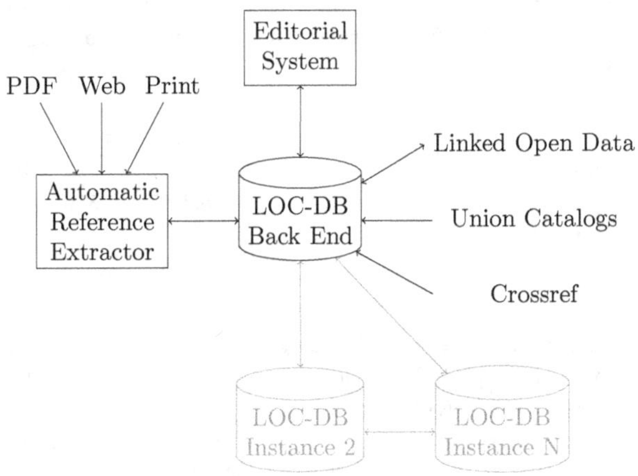

Figure 1: The infrastructure components of the LOC-DB project.

this infrastructure can be seen in Figure 1. The whole system is designed to work distributed, with independent instances of LOC-DB, communicating with each other to provide lookup services.[19]

4.1 Database and Back End

The back end of our system acts as a distributed central hub, which is responsible for saving files and data, ensuring the communication between all three components as well as for retrieving metadata from a variety of external sources. In the following, we will first describe the general architecture, then the provisional data model and last how we derive metadata from external sources.

4.1.1 Layered Design. The central LOC-DB component has two layers, the storage layer and the web-based Application Programming Interface (API). As data base in the storage layer we use MongoDB,[20] which we combine with an Elasticsearch[21] index in order to efficiently provide internal suggestions for matching bibliographic resources for a given citation to the user. Furthermore, we save files, such as uploaded scans of reference pages, in the file system. On top of that we expose several HTTP end points to the front end, which we implemented using Node.js.[22] These end points provide user management, basic `Create`, `Read`, `Update`, `Delete` (CRUD) functionalities as well as triggers for more sophisticated services such as the automatic reference extraction or the retrieval of external suggestions. A Swagger[23] interface which serves as interactive documentation describing the current status of the HTTP end points[24] as well as our source code[25] is available online.

4.1.2 Data Model. In order to ensure the sustainability of the data we generate and a seamless integration in the linked open data cloud, we adapt the OpenCitations metadata model [17] for our purposes. The model is aligned with the Semantic Publishing and Referencing (SPAR) Ontologies [15] for creating machine-readable metadata describing citations in Resource Description Framework (RDF) format. The main bibliographic entities of the OpenCitations data model are the following:

- Bibliographic Resource: A bibliographic resource, e.g. a monograph, which is cited by or cites another bibliographic resource.
- Resource Embodiment: The embodiment of a bibliographic resource, which can be print or digital.
- Bibliographic Entry: An entry in a reference list of a bibliographic resource, i.e. a citation.
- Responsible Agent: An agent, who is responsible for a bibliographic resource, e.g. a person.
- Agent Role: The role of an agent, e.g. author or publisher.

We extend the data model mainly in two parts: First of all, a property `scan` is added to resource embodiments, which saves links from an embodiment of a bibliographic resource to files that hold references belonging to that resource. This way, given a bibliographic resource, one can retrieve the original references pages of that resource at any time. Secondly, we add a link from each bibliographic entry to the scan it appears on, if available. The two extensions of the model ensure that we can not only automatically extract references from PDF files or image scans, but also that we are able to present the original page to the librarians when they check the data and create the links.

4.1.3 External Metadata Retrieval. Acting as a central hub, we implement back end services to extract metadata from a variety of external sources. Ideally, we get high-quality structured data this way which clearly speeds up the curation process. Another aspect is the creation of links which is automatically done whenever the librarian accepts a match. For the creation of bibliographic resources, we build upon the already existing cataloging infrastructure. For example, when a print monograph arrives in the library, it has been already assigned a union catalog identifier and also the metadata for that item has been already curated in the library union catalog. We reuse the cataloged metadata and retrieve it using existing end points, e.g. Search/Retrieve via URL (SRU)-interfaces, convert it, e.g., from MARC21, into our data model, and keep the original identifier to link back to the catalog.

For the cited bibliographic resources, where metadata might not yet be in our database, the user receives matching external suggestions, as stated above. The user ideally just has to select the suggestions that fit in order to create metadata for the target bibliographic resource, where links are created back to all matching resources. We encourage users to select all matching resources to increase link coverage. There is, however, also an immediate benefit when more resources are selected, as the metadata is created by combining all matched resources. This way, missing information can be filled and in case of differences in the data, ranking approaches can be applied to improve the data quality.

External sources for metadata include Crossref, the OpenCitations SPARQL endpoint, Google Scholar, or more domain-specific bibliographic databases. Candidates are generated using a query

[19]The software components we develop in our project are going to be available with an OpenCitations approved open source license.
[20]https://www.mongodb.com/
[21]https://www.elastic.co/de/products/elasticsearch
[22]https://nodejs.org/en/
[23]https://swagger.io
[24]https://locdb.bib.uni-mannheim.de/demo/docs/
[25]https://github.com/locdb/loc-db

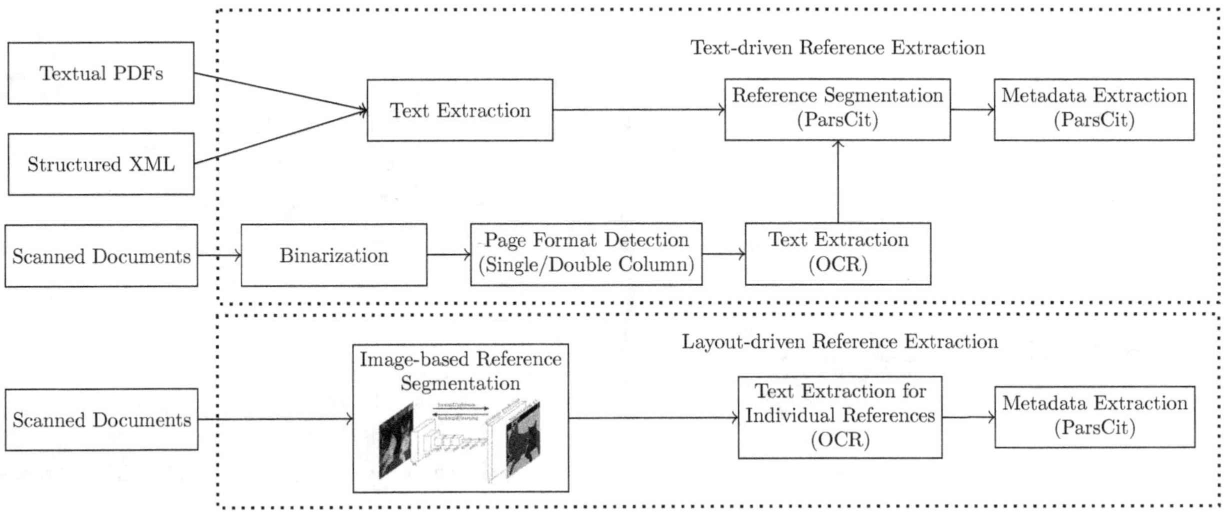

Figure 2: Automatic Reference Extraction Pipeline.

string based on the data we already have. In a second step, the candidates are weighted using the Dice similarity coefficient (DSC) [6]. The user can specify a threshold above which he or she wants to see the results or use the current default value of $DSC = 0.45$, which we observed to be a useful starting point in our user studies. We plan to further adapt this default value in order to provide optimal linking assistance and to conduct experiments with other measures of string similarity, e.g. Levensthein distance [11].

With this procedure, we want to ensure that the user does neither need to search manually for matching metadata in multiple metadata provider catalogs nor to enter all the metadata manually.

4.2 Automatic Reference Extraction

For the extraction of references, we use an automated approach that processes the pages with references, which might be scanned or born-digital.

Figure 2 provides an overview of the automatic reference extraction pipeline, which consists of two sub components: Text-driven Reference Extraction and layout-driven reference extraction.

4.2.1 Text-driven Reference Extraction. This method uses textual information to detect bibliographic references from a given document and is highly dependent on the referencing style of the document. Text-based extraction can be used for different electronic resources (born digital PDFs, structured xml, etc.) and scanned documents. For electronic resources, the document is passed directly to a text extraction module followed by reference segmentation and metadata extraction, i.e. to classify elements like author, title, journal, etc. For reference segmentation and metadata extraction, ParsCit [5] is used. ParsCit is an open source package for detecting and labeling citations strings from text. It is based on Conditional Random Fields (CRF) along with sophisticated heuristics to detect and segment citations strings.

For processing a scanned document image, it is firstly preprocessed by performing binarization (converting an RGB image to a binary image). The preprocessed document is further classified into a single column or double column layout document during page format detection phase. Once classified, the image is then passed to an optical character recognition (OCR) process for text extraction. We use OCRopus [3] which is an open source OCR software using Long Short-Term Memory (LSTM) networks [4]. Similar to electronic resources, the text obtained from OCR is then passed to the reference segmentation module to identify the reference and extract metadata out of the detected string. Both segmentation as well as metadata extraction is performed using ParsCit.

Text-driven extraction alone has several drawbacks. First, it depends heavily on the quality of OCR. If the text is not correctly recognized by OCR, then whole references can be missed. Second, for detecting and segmenting references, this approach relies on ParsCit. While ParsCit can be seen as state-of-the-art, it sometimes is unable to detect some references or it merges multiple references together and classifies them as a single reference. We therefore seek to improve the process by complementing the text-driven extraction with layout-driven extraction.

4.2.2 Layout-driven Reference Extraction. In contrast to the text-driven extraction, the layout-driven reference extraction uses only the layout information to localize each reference string in the document image. The method is inspired by how humans interpret a document. In this approach, the goal is to use layout information to localize each reference string region and then that region is passed to OCR for text extraction. To do so, a deep learning-based approach [1] is used to train a model for segmentation of individual references based on the graphical layout. Therefore, during training and application, all the text lines are blurred so that the content is no more readable. The trained model is then used to segment reference regions from new unseen scanned images. OCR is performed on detected reference areas of the image. Once the OCR is completed, all the text of the reference string is passed to the ParCit for metadata extraction.

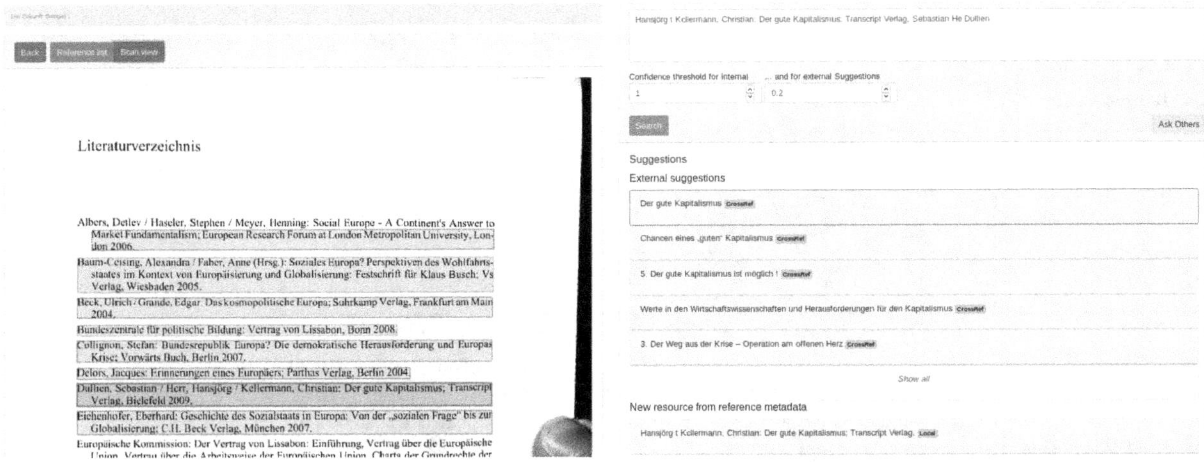

Figure 3: Reference linking in the editorial system. On the left: the reference list of the citing document. On the right: metadata of the candidate target resource.

4.3 Editorial System

The main goal of the editorial system is to provide a graphical user interface for librarians, wrapping the functionality of the LOC-DB back end as well as the automatic reference extractor. We developed the editorial system according to the principles of Interaction Design [19]. We created wireframes to mock the key words and visual representations of the interaction elements while taking the typical working environment of librarians into account. After discussing these wireframes with librarians from both ZBW and University Library of Mannheim, we implemented a prototype for continuous testing. This way, we could already identify and resolve early usability issues and proceed to continuously enhance the editorial system in accordance with the librarians.

4.3.1 Ingestion. The editorial system is split into two major visual components. On the one hand, there is a data ingestion component which allows uploading electronic documents, scanned documents, as well as providing an identifier to ingest metadata from external sources. When any kind of data is ingested, the resource metadata is retrieved (see Section 4.1.3) and the automatic reference extraction is triggered (see Section 4.2). On the other hand, the reference linking component offers the functionality to inspect the reference list of the source document and assign a matching target bibliographic resource for each of the citations.

4.3.2 Reference Linking. Resolving a citation link is a complex process that requires viewing the reference list of the source document along with the metadata of candidate target documents. We tackle this challenge by splitting the user interface into two columns (see Figure 3). On the left, the reference list of the source document is presented. On the right, the metadata of possible citation targets is displayed. To ensure that resolving a scientific reference can be performed in reasonable time, the editorial system presents the suggestions for matching resources generated by the back end (Section 4.1.3). The suggestions comprise data from the internal database as well as external data sources. In this context, internal means that a matching record has already been inserted into the LOC-DB earlier. External refers to those suggestions that come from external data sources. When only external suggestions are selected as a citation target, the metadata will get copied to the internal database, such that it can be edited if necessary. Hence, the formerly external resource will then be available as an internal suggestion. To avoid duplicate records, identifying a matching internal record is crucial and has the highest priority. In the worst case, neither internal nor external suggestions offer a match to the currently processed entry of the reference list. In this case, the LOC-DB system is still able to use the structured data which was extracted from the reference in the source document as a starting point for a new resource record. The front end needs to reflect this process of first looking for internal duplicates, then finding as many external references as possible and finally, as a last resort, providing the means to create a new record from scratch.

The editorial system needs to be capable of dealing with scanned documents, electronic documents, as well as metadata from external sources. An appropriate display of the reference lists is required for each of the three cases. For scanned documents and electronic documents, the reference list is displayed as an image with bounding boxes indicating automatically identified references. On the other side, sole citation metadata from external sources can only be displayed in structured format. Since the reference extraction process (see Section 4.2) also yields structured metadata for both electronic and scanned print documents, the structured reference list view is also available for these cases.

4.3.3 Metadata Editing. So far, the editorial system is intended to be the only front end for the LOC-DB. Thus, it needs to cover a set of certain classical operations of a database management system [12]. These operations comprise a minimum of CRUD operations for all considered data structures. Not only the links between resources, i.e. citations need to be inserted, but also the resources' metadata occasionally needs to be updated by the librarian. To this extent, dedicated forms targeting the editing process are necessary. On top of the four basic operations which directly use the services provided by the back end (see Section 4.1.1), we can enhance the user experience by offering interfaces for more complex operations. For instance, consider the functionality of committing a citation link between two resources. The librarian has selected an entry of the reference list in the source resource and is about to commit the link to the selected target resource. By design, the target resource might come from either an internal suggestion, an external suggestion or from the extracted metadata. When the resource was not present in the internal database before, a new resource gets automatically created. Potential changes to metadata of resources coming from external suggestions are kept locally in the editorial system until a citation link pointing to this specific resource is committed. In case the reference entry was pointing to another resource before, not only the link itself but also the higher-level `cites` property of the citing resource is updated.

On the whole, we created an editorial system comprising the functionality of data ingestion, reference linking, along with both mandatory and convenient database management operations. An interactive demo of the front end is available online[26] and the source code is available openly on GitHub[27].

5 USER STUDY AND QUANTITATIVE EVALUATION

As our final goal is to answer the question whether libraries could manage to catalog citations when provided with the right tools and processes, a constant evaluation of all software components and steps in our workflow is needed. To obtain a full picture, we use a mixed method design [10]. More specifically, we perform a qualitative user study as well as a quantitative evaluation.

5.1 User Study

Central to early-stage development of the LOC-DB platform are formative evaluations with our stakeholders [10]. Here, we applied several methods including prepared mock-ups and early user interface prototypes, and discussed them in interview sessions with domain experts. In addition, we have conducted a public workshop of LOC-DB for information professionals.[28] The domain experts acknowledged the complexity of resolving the citation link between two bibliographic resources and agreed on the abstraction of a bibliographic resource that disregards concrete embodiments for the purpose of storing citation data. They highlighted that the three tasks of scanning print documents, cataloging the document's metadata and resolving ambiguities are typically performed by different person groups. For resolving a citation link, the domain experts feel comfortable with receiving suggestions from the union catalogs and pointed out that these suggestions help to minimize the time required for each citation link, which is in turn crucial for the overall feasibility. In the podium discussion of the public workshop, there was consensus that citation data is a new, but important task for libraries. Questions about who should be responsible for storing and distributing the data were discussed as well as how to integrate the information into current systems and data formats [21].

[26]https://locdb.bib.uni-mannheim.de/demo-frontend/
[27]https://github.com/locdb/locdb-frend
[28]https://locdb.bib.uni-mannheim.de/blog/en/workshop-2/

Table 2: Comparison between the Text-driven vs. the Layout-driven Reference Extraction Method [1].

Method	Total References Extracted	Extracted %age
Text-driven	3,645	71.7%
Layout-driven	4,323	84.9%

5.2 Quantitative Evaluation

For the quantitative evaluation, we constantly monitor the whole process and collect usage data. The most important questions that can be answered in a quantitative way is how much time executing our workflow for indexing citations actually takes. In order to answer this question, we focused on finding appropriate measures for three major steps in our current process.[29]

5.2.1 Scanning. In case we are dealing with print resources, the reference pages need to be scanned (see above). As part of our study, we measured the amount of pages a student assistant can scan using standard library scanners. We found that scanning can be done at a rate of at least 100 pages per hour per person, largely depending on the person. This is of course really slow, but it gives us an upper bound of around 15 minutes for scanning from an average book with 26 pages of references (Table 1). More importantly, we found that the additional scanning time, when done by student assistants whenever time permitted it, did not significantly affect other processes in the library. This is hard to measure, but we estimate that the additional scanning prolongs the processing of a book on average by only 3 minutes.

5.2.2 Automatic Reference Extraction. The quality of the automatic extraction of references is crucial for the overall performance of our system. The better the reference extraction, the easier it is for our users to find correct matches and the more efficient is the linking process in the end. Therefore, we evaluate the text-driven vs. the layout-driven reference segmentation we presented above. In order to do so, the same image was processed through both approaches. Figure 4a and Figure 4b represent the reference detection output from the text-driven and the layout-driven approach respectively.

It can be clearly observed that the text-driven approach was unable to detect some references and has also classified multiple references as a single reference. On the other hand, the layout-driven approach worked very well and, at least in this example, it detected all references clearly, despite of the fact that it did not take any textual information into account.

A comprehensive evaluation [1] of both approaches with a total of 5,090 references from 286 scanned documents (Table 2) showed that the layout-driven segmentation performed almost 13 percentage points better than the text-driven approach, i.e., ParsCit, which is used in many projects applying automatic citation extraction.

[29]We also plan to add more metrics regarding other questions, such as the completeness and quality of the generated data. For now, we assume human-level quality as the data only gets stored when the librarians checked it for correctness and completeness.

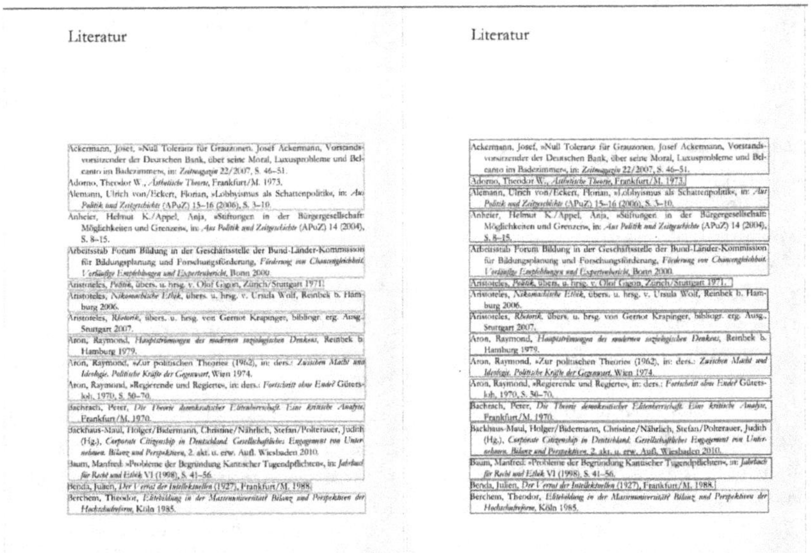

(a) Text-driven Detection Output

(b) Layout-driven Detection Output

Figure 4: Comparison between Text-driven and Layout-driven Reference Detection using a Sample Reference Page.

5.2.3 Reference Linking. One of the most valuable insights we are trying to obtain from the project is, which features of our infrastructure must be improved to decrease the reference linking time. The goal is that in the end we can ensure optimal support of the user in the reference linking step.

To this end, we added a logging mechanism to our graphical user interface and to our back end and defined a series of events which we log in order to trace how the user is interacting with the system. These events, e.g. the user selected a resource or the suggestions from external sources arrived, allow us to calculate several measures, which we define as follows.

- Citation Linking Time: The overall time needed to link a reference of a source bibliographic resource to a target bibliographic resource.
- Suggestion Retrieval Time: The amount of time needed to retrieve suggestions and display them to the user. We distinguish here between internal and external suggestions.
- Number of Searches performed per Reference: The number of searches performed in order to retrieve a matching reference.

Figure 5 visualizes all cases we obtained for citation linking. It can be seen that from 300 seconds on the times start to increase drastically, which is due to the fact that we do not (yet) have a pause button in the system. Sometimes people get distracted or forget to close the editorial system. We therefore decided to exclude all cases with a time larger than 600 seconds, to be precise: 87 cases with times up to 6 days.

Table 3 lists minimum, maximum, and median time in seconds for the remaining 444 cases that we used for this report.

On the one hand, we can see that the median reference linking time is currently about 89 seconds. This is a good starting point for a first prototype in an early stage, in which the internal data base is not populated yet. Here is clearly potential for improvement.

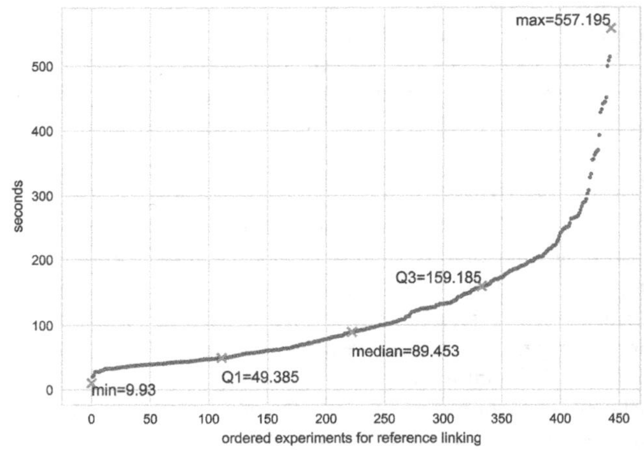

Figure 5: All 444 samples with their reference linking time ordered.

Table 3: Minimum, maximum, and median time in seconds for the reference linking step with a sample size of 444.

Criterion	Min	Max	Median
Citation Linking (s)	9.93	557.195	89.453
Internal Sug. Retrieval (s)	0.015	0.537	0.057
External Sug. Retrieval (s)	0.498	95.652	0.886
# Searches per Reference	1	36	2

On the other hand, when looking at the histogram (Figure 6), it can be seen that many links are resolved within one minute, with a minimum time of under 10 seconds. A deeper analysis showed that

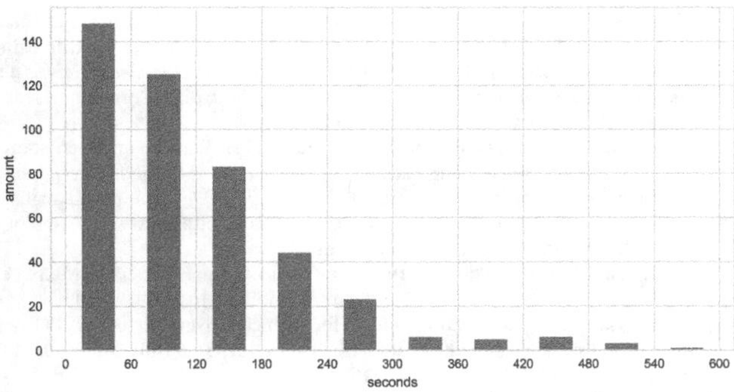

Figure 6: Histogram of reference linking times.

in those cases the metadata of the resource matching the reference was already in our internal database and that therefore the user only had to select the matching, internal suggestion. We can thus assume that the linking process will become much faster with a growing database.

Table 3 also shows the times that are needed to retrieve suggestions from internal and external sources. While the internal suggestions arrive usually within 60 ms, with a rare maximum of 10 seconds, the user has to wait significantly longer for the external ones, where the maximum time even reached 96 seconds until they arrive (average: 4 seconds).

We learn from these results that this step might slow down the user when working with our infrastructure. Therefore, we plan to pre-compute the external suggestions once we have extracted the reference strings. The user could then re-trigger the retrieval of external suggestions only if the pre-computed ones are not good enough, usually after editing the metadata. This way, the overall citation linking time can be decreased easily.

However, as the number of searches per reference indicates, currently usually the user has to search twice to get a correct suggestion. Only for 4.5% of all references, we could immediately provide the correct suggestion. This illustrates how crucial the original data extraction is for the performance. But also the matching process needs to be improved constantly to further reduce the number of searches.

6 DISCUSSION

We developed a distributed, semi-automated system to create and store citation data which is designed for usage in digital libraries. We have shown that the required additional resources for operating this semi-automated system in a distributed manner are affordable. Plus, not only digitally available resources but also scanned print documents may be processed using the LOC-DB system.

While we do not doubt that fully-automated citation extraction tools such as ParsCit [5] can be employed in many cases to get reasonable results, we believe that our semi-automated approach is doable in libraries. In contrast to the automated extraction, it guarantees a human-level quality for the curated citation data, which we deem important particularly for applications like scientometrics, where careers are at stake depending on the results.

Table 4: Estimation about the number of full-time employees needed to process all literature of social sciences bought in 2011 by Mannheim University Library, depending on the time t in seconds to resolve a reference.

t	1	5	10	20	30	60	120
employees	0.1	0.5	1	2	3	5.9	11.9

The LOC-DB system was developed in close collaboration with two libraries, namely the Mannheim University Library as well as ZBW – Leibniz Information Centre for Economics. The key requirements of the librarians could therefore be addressed early in the development process. We invited the German library community for a public workshop for evaluation of the LOC-DB system. Except for minor usability issues, the feedback considering the system itself and the general concept was thoroughly positive. We can therefore expect our findings to generalize to other digital, scientific libraries.

So, how much would it take to actually maintain LOC-DB? Based on our experience so far, we would like to ponder on some rough estimations. We deliberately chose the corpus in our project to be a complete year (2011) of incoming literature in a field where the Mannheim University Library has a strong focus, the social sciences. If LOC-DB is possible at all, it has to be possible to deal with all incoming relevant publications.

How many people would have been needed in Mannheim in 2011 to maintain LOC-DB for the social sciences? From our experience with the already scanned books we see that most books have less than 20 references on a single book page and hence we use this as the average number of references on a single book page. This leads to 271.000 references from all the books pages (cf. Table 1). Moreover, we identified 101 electronic journals in social sciences for which we want to resolve all articles published in 2011. An analysis of the subset of all journals in Crossref shows that there are 67 articles per journal on average (upper bound) and an article has 44 references on average.[30] This leads to 298, 000 references for all journal articles, so in sum we have around 570, 000 references overall which we need to resolve. Table 4 lists the number of full-time employees needed, depending on the required time to curate a reference.[31] At our current rate, Mannheim would need between 6 and 12 people just to maintain LOC-DB for social sciences. With a growing database, more openly available data and further improvements in our system, we can expect to reduce the time to at least 30 seconds. In our public workshop, we also asked the participants what they think is realistic for a library to invest in LOC-DB, with respect to people maintaining it. Answers varied, but half a full-time position was considered reasonable by many. This means: If many libraries join LOC-DB and collaborate, it should be possible to cover all the literature hold by these libraries. Some German libraries have already expressed their interest to test and possibly implement LOC-DB to improve their services.

[30] These estimations are made with the help of the Crossref API as shown in this Jupyter Notebook: https://github.com/locdb/locdb-journal-analysis/. The number of articles is based on registered DOIs per journal, which is an upper bound as sometimes DOIs are registered, but not actually used.

[31] For estimating the number of full-time employees, we assume that one employee works 200 days a year and 8 hours a day, resulting in 5, 760, 000 seconds a year.

7 CONCLUSION

Citations are a major resource in scientific discourse, information retrieval, and in bibliometrics. Recently, more and more initiatives are highlighting the importance of citations and propagating the idea of making reference data freely available.

We think that the responsibility of curating citation data and making it publicly available should be transferred to libraries in a distributed manner. The need to solely rely on citation data offered by publishers would be alleviated. This would directly affect the whole scientific community since funding and employment heavily depends on this citation data and the corresponding scientometrics.

In this paper, we presented our project Linked Open Citation Database (LOC-DB), which aims to prove that with well-designed processes and a distributed infrastructure the efficient cataloging and curation of the citation graph by librarians is possible. This way, we can overcome the current limitations in state-of-the art methods for automatic reference extraction and provide high-quality citation data integrated in the Linked Open Data cloud. In order to do so, we combine qualitative and quantitative evaluation methods. Here, we presented results from our development and public workshops as well as a first series of experiments, which focus on three important steps in our workflow: scanning reference pages of printed resources, automatically extracting references from various formats, and finally linking the references. The numbers reveal interesting insights: First of all, we have seen that scanning reference pages on standard library scanners is only a minor overhead to the daily work in the library. Secondly, we presented results of our automatic reference extraction, where we significantly improved the segmentation of references by using an image-based approach. Finally, we also analyzed the user interaction with our system in the citation linking step and showed that for many cases, the user already can efficiently find matching bibliographic resources for reference strings from internal and external suggestions. We are aware that our current evaluation is only a first step. Further studies are required and planned to obtain more detailed and reliable information about the practical applicability of our approach.

Therefore, we continuously evaluate and improve our workflow, with a focus on the reference extraction and the matching process, where we expect the highest impact on the overall performance.

While we do this, more and more citation data in the domain of social science is going to be generated by our librarians, which is going to be published as open data in the RDF-format. More data will be available thanks to all initiatives for open citations. As a final thought, we therefore would like to extend our question slightly: What if libraries cataloged everything and curated the citation graph? Let us find out.

REFERENCES

[1] Akansha Bhardwaj, Dominik Mercier, Andreas Dengel, and Sheraz Ahmed. 2017. *DeepBIBX: Deep Learning for Image Based Bibliographic Data Extraction*. Springer International Publishing, Cham, 286–293. https://doi.org/10.1007/978-3-319-70096-0_30

[2] Marshall Breeding. 2015. Future of Library Discovery Systems. *Information Standards Quarterly* 27, 1 (2015), 24. https://doi.org/10.3789/isqv27no1.2015.04

[3] Thomas M. Breuel. 2008. The OCRopus open source OCR system. In *Document Recognition and Retrieval XV, part of the IS&T-SPIE Electronic Imaging Symposium, San Jose, CA, USA, January 29-31, 2008. Proceedings (SPIE Proceedings)*, Berrin A. Yanikoglu and Kathrin Berkner (Eds.), Vol. 6815. SPIE, 68150F. https://doi.org/10.1117/12.783598

[4] Thomas M. Breuel, Adnan Ul-Hasan, Mayce Ibrahim Ali Al Azawi, and Faisal Shafait. 2013. High-Performance OCR for Printed English and Fraktur Using LSTM Networks. In *2013 12th International Conference on Document Analysis and Recognition, Washington, DC, USA, August 25-28, 2013*. IEEE Computer Society, 683–687. https://doi.org/10.1109/ICDAR.2013.140

[5] Isaac Councill, C. Lee Giles, and Min-Yen Kan. 2008. ParsCit: an Open-source CRF Reference String Parsing Package. In *Proceedings of the Sixth International Conference on Language Resources and Evaluation (LREC-08)*. European Language Resources Association (ELRA), Marrakech, Morocco. http://www.lrec-conf.org/proceedings/lrec2008/summaries/166.html

[6] Lee R. Dice. 1945. Measures of the Amount of Ecologic Association Between Species. *Ecology* 26, 3 (1945), 297–302. https://doi.org/10.2307/1932409

[7] Eugene Garfield. 1955. Citation Indexes for Science: A New Dimension in Documentation through Association of Ideas. *Science* 122, 3159 (July 1955), 108–111. https://doi.org/10.1126/science.122.3159.108

[8] C. Lee Giles, Kurt D. Bollacker, and Steve Lawrence. 1998. CiteSeer: An Automatic Citation Indexing System. In *Proceedings of the Third ACM Conference on Digital Libraries (DL '98)*. ACM, New York, NY, USA, 89–98. https://doi.org/10.1145/276675.276685

[9] Annette Klein. 2017. Von der Schneeflocke zur Lawine: Möglichkeiten der Nutzung freier Zitationsdaten in Bibliotheken. *o-bib. Das offene Bibliotheksjournal* 4, 4 (Dec. 2017), 127–136. https://doi.org/10.5282/o-bib/2017H4S127-136

[10] Jonathan Lazar, Jinjuan Feng, and Harry Hochheiser. 2017. *Research Methods in Human-Computer Interaction*. Morgan Kaufmann.

[11] Vladimir I. Levenshtein. 1966. Binary Codes Capable of Correcting Deletions, Insertions and Reversals. *Soviet Physics Doklady* 10, 8 (February 1966), 707–710.

[12] James Martin. 1981. Managing the data base environment. (1981).

[13] John Mingers and Loet Leydesdorff. 2015. A review of theory and practice in scientometrics. *European Journal of Operational Research* 246, 1 (2015), 1–19. https://doi.org/10.1016/j.ejor.2015.04.002

[14] Philippe Mongeon and Adèle Paul-Hus. 2016. The journal coverage of Web of Science and Scopus: a comparative analysis. *Scientometrics* 106, 1 (Jan. 2016), 213–228. https://doi.org/10.1007/s11192-015-1765-5

[15] Silvio Peroni. 2014. The Semantic Publishing and Referencing Ontologies. In *Semantic Web Technologies and Legal Scholarly Publishing*. Springer, Cham, 121–193. https://doi.org/10.1007/978-3-319-04777-5_5

[16] Silvio Peroni, Alexander Dutton, Tanya Gray, and David Shotton. 2015. Setting our bibliographic references free: towards open citation data. *Journal of Documentation* 71, 2 (2015), 253–277. https://doi.org/10.1108/JD-12-2013-0166 arXiv:https://doi.org/10.1108/JD-12-2013-0166

[17] Silvio Peroni and David Shotton. 2016. *Metadata for the OpenCitations Corpus*. Technical Report. https://dx.doi.org/10.6084/m9.figshare.3443876

[18] Silvio Peroni, David M. Shotton, and Fabio Vitali. 2017. One Year of the OpenCitations Corpus - Releasing RDF-Based Scholarly Citation Data into the Public Domain. In *The Semantic Web - ISWC 2017 - 16th International Semantic Web Conference, Vienna, Austria, October 21-25, 2017, Proceedings, Part II (Lecture Notes in Computer Science)*, Vol. 10588. Springer, 184–192. https://doi.org/10.1007/978-3-319-68204-4_19

[19] Yvonne Rogers, Helen Sharp, and Jenny Preece. 2012. *Interaction Design - Beyond Human-Computer Interaction, 3rd Edition*. Wiley.

[20] Dario Taraborelli, Lydia Pintscher, Daniel Mietchen, and Sarah Rodlund. 2017. WikiCite 2017 report. (Dec. 2017). https://figshare.com/articles/WikiCite_2017_report/5648233 DOI: 10.6084/m9.figshare.5648233.v3.

[21] Christian Wilke and Regina Retter. 2017. Zitationsdaten extrahieren: halbautomatisch, offen, vernetzt. Ein Workshopbericht. *Informationspraxis* 3, 2 (Dec. 2017). https://doi.org/10.11588/ip.2017.2.43235

[22] Dietmar Wolfram. 2015. The symbiotic relationship between information retrieval and informetrics. *Scientometrics* 102, 3 (2015), 2201–2214. https://doi.org/10.1007/s11192-014-1479-0

ACKNOWLEDGMENTS

This work is funded by the German Research Foundation (DFG) under project number 311018540 (Linked Open Citation Database).

We thank Kirsten Jeude and Sarah Gatz from ZBW – Leibniz Information Centre for Economics for their participation and insightful comments during the development workshops, Fabian Steputath for helping with the front end development, and Sylvia Zander and Laura Erhard for extensive testing, identifying problems and helping to improve the overall system.

Building a Theoretical Framework for the Development of Digital Scholarship Services in China's Universities

Lihong Zhou
School of Information Management
Wuhan University, China
L.zhou@whu.edu.cn

Xinyu Lu
School of Information Management
Wuhan University, China
xinyu.Lu@whu.edu.cn

Tim Zijlstra
University of Derby, UK
tim.zijlstra@gmail.com

ABSTRACT

The provision of digital scholarship services (DSS) in China's university is very unsystematic and fragmented. This paper reports on a literature review that aims to develop a comprehensive theoretical framework, which can serve as a practical guide for the development of DSS in China's university libraries. The framework was developed through systematically searching, screening, assessing, coding and aggregating DSS as reported in the existing body of literature. Academic literature, both in Chinese and English, as well as relevant professional reports are carefully searched, selected and analysed. The analysis of the literature pointed to 25 DSS in six categories: supporting services, formulating research ideas, locating research partners, proposal writing, research process, and publication. This paper focuses on the development of DSS in China's university libraries, but the research findings and the framework developed can provide useful insights and indications that can be shared across international borders.

CCS CONCEPTS

• **General and reference→Surveys and overviews•** Applied computing→Digital libraries and archives

KEYWORDS

Digital scholarship, Digital scholarship services, Theoretical framework, University libraries

ACM Reference format:

Lihong Zhou, Xinyu Lu and Tim Zijlstra. 2018. Building a Theoretical Framework for the Development of Digital Scholarship Services in China's Universities. In *Proceedings of JCDL '18 (JCDL '18) In JCDL '18: The 18th ACM/IEEE Joint Conference on Digital Libraries, June 3–7, 2018, Fort Worth, TX, USA. ACM, New York, NY, USA, 4 pages.* https://doi.org/10.1145/3197026.3197060

JCDL '18, June 3–7, 2018, Fort Worth, TX, USA

ACM ISBN 978-1-4503-5178-2/18/06...$15.00
https://doi.org/10.1145/3197026.3197060

1 INTRODUCTION

Digital scholarship is probably one of the trendiest words in the field of library and information sciences [1]. In fact, as identified by the Association of College and Research Libraries [2], digital scholarship is one of the twelve major trends of development in the field and in particular for academic libraries.

For centuries, libraries have played an important role in supporting research and knowledge creation in all subjects and disciplines [3]. DSS can be seen as a natural extension of traditional services in libraries in facilitating knowledge creation and transfer [4]. DSS can range from creating virtual or physical spaces for learning and research, providing technical support and administration, to assisting interdisciplinary research teams working on big data or longitudinal studies [1]. At present, many university libraries have actively supported and created digital scholarship centres. According to centerNet [5], an international network of digital humanities centres, there are more than 200 digital scholarship centres around the world, the majority of which are located in North America and Europe. Tzoc and Millard [1] stress that this is an emerging service model, which brings together researchers, students, technologists and librarians together in university libraries to develop digital project collaboratively through the provision of a variety of scholarly support and research services. Therefore, the number of these digital scholarship centres is continuously growing.

In China, the awareness of the importance of providing DSS in university libraries has been greatly influenced by scholars and colleagues from the West [6,7]. Zhou [8] claims that developing DSS is an unavoidable and important step for the growth and advancement of China's university libraries. Shao [9] asserts that the development of DSS respond to the new user requirements and challenges emerged from the digital age. Digital scholarship and humanities have been extensively discussed and confirmed as one of the top-key directions for China's library development during the "13th Symposium of Library Frontier and Problems", organized in Shanghai in 2016[6].

Nevertheless, DSS development in China's university libraries are merely at an early, exploring stage [10]. Shao [9] claims that some faculties in China's universities are unclear how DSS can help them, question the value of DSS considering the level of investment of financial and human resources, as well as lacking comprehension of how DSS are different from traditional services. Many researchers point out that this could be the result of the fact that the existing DSS provided are overly fragmented to support university research and innovation activities [11–13].

Thus, as advocated by a large number of scholars and library professionals, it is pressing to develop and implement systematic and well-structured DSS to support a diverse variety of research activities carried out by university faculties, staff and students [14]. In order to do so, it is perceived that DSS should be able to facilitate, support and collaborate with researchers in all activities along a research project lifecycle, from the beginning to publishing and disseminating research results. This view, however, is currently missing both in the DSS practice in Chinese university libraries and in the literature published by Chinese researchers.

This paper reports on a national-level research project sponsored by the National Social Science Fund of China. This project aims to establish a comprehensive theoretical framework for the development of DSS in China's university libraries. This paper presents the research findings drawn from a literature review as the first stage of research in this project and focuses on developing a framework by identifying DSS as reported in the literature and organsing them according to a research project lifecycle. The DSS framework is expected of practical value to Chinese university libraries, as well as can serves as a theoretical base for the remainder research.

2 REVIEW METHODS AND PROCESS

According to the aim of this literature review, the following review questions were formulated to orient the practice of literature selection and analysis:

(1) What DSS should be provided in China's university libraries?
(2) How DSS can support research activities along the research project life cycle?
(3) How DSS can be grouped to form a framework?

Under the light of the review questions, the literature review was carried out in two stages. A general review of existing literature was performed as the first stage, which aimed to provide a theoretical and contextual basis for more systematic literature retrieval and analysis in the second stage. To be more specific, there are two main aims at this stage: (1) to obtain a holistic understanding of the emergence and development of digital scholarship and the latest development of DSS provision in library environment; (2) to gain a general view of DSS provided in China's university libraries.

In stage two, a more structured and systematic literature review was performed. In this stage, academic works both in English and Chinese were retrieved and analysed. It is perceived, and thus decided accordingly, that the inclusion of relevant English and Chinese academic articles can be particularly useful not only to establish a comprehensive DSS framework, but also to ensure that the framework can be "contextually sensitive" and hence applicable to university libraries in China.

Therefore, two sets of academic databases were selected and systematically searched. The first set included three international academic databases: Web of Science, ScienceDirect and Emerald. As the second set, three Chinese academic databases were searched: CNKI, Wanfang and CQVIP. The database search was performed in early October 2017, using the search strategy presented below:

("digital scholarship" or "digital humanities" or "research support") and librar*

The search strategy was designed to be broad and inclusive to include as many relevant articles as possible. The database search returned a total of 426 articles, including 112 articles in English and 314 articles in Chinese. All these retrieved articles were carefully screened and selected using the following strategies: (1) remove duplicated articles from different databases and languages; (2) remove articles which are not focusing on library services; (3) remove articles which can be categorised as subjective opinion presentation; (4) remove articles which lacking adequate theoretical support. As a result, overall 79 articles were included in the literature analysis.

Moreover, a set of relevant professional reports was included in the analysis. These reports are shown in Table 1 below:

Table 1: Professional reports included in the literature analysis

Report Names	Organisations
Supporting Digital Scholarship SPEC Kit 350	Association of Research Libraries (ARL)
Digital Scholarship Support Profiles	Association of Research Libraries (ARL)
Survey of Digital Scholarship Centers Final Report	Association of College and Research Libraries (ACRL)
Building Expertise to Support Digital Scholarship: A Global Perspective	Council on Library and Information Resources (CLIR)
Working Together or Apart: Promoting the Next Generation of Digital Scholarship	Council on Library and Information Resources (CLIR)
Report of a One-Day Seminar on Promoting Digital Scholarship	Council on Library and Information Resources (CLIR)
Digital Scholarship Centers: Trends & Good Practice	Coalition for Networked Information (CNI)
Planning a Digital Scholarship Center	Coalition for Networked Information (CNI)
International advances in digital scholarship	Joint Information Systems Committee (JISC) and Coalition for Networked Information (CNI)

A thematic analysis approach as proposed by King and Horrocks [15] was adopted for the literature analysis. According to Zhou and Nunes [16], a thematic analysis is widely used approach of coding and representing qualitative data. In this study, data refer to the literature selected. Coding represents the processes of identifying, verifying and labelling DSS in the literature. Representation means the production of a theoretical narrative that summarises, describes and discusses DSS identified and organises them in a meaningful and useful manner.

Moreover, throughout the literature analysis, the DSS identified are expected to be organised along individual stages and processes in a research lifecycle. Thus, the research lifecycle model developed by JISC [17] in the UK was adopted as a preliminary theoretical framework used to orient the processes of coding. The research lifecycle model consists of five incremental research stages: ideas, partners, proposal writing, research process, and publication. These stages were employed in the literature analysis to frame the practice of coding.

3 RESULTS AND DISCUSSION

A total of 25 DSS have emerged from the literature analysis in six different themes: supporting services, formulating research ideas, locating research partners, proposal writing, research process, and publication. The research findings are demonstrated in Table 2:

Table 2: A demonstration of the research findings

Supporting Services	Digital scholarship IT infrastructure
	Digital and physical spaces for collaboration
	Teaching and training services
	Consulting services
Formulating research ideas	Hypothesis/question development
	Background literature search
	Bibliometric services
Locating research partners	Identifying potential collaborators
	Contacting potential partners
	Recruiting research team
Proposal writing	Grant seeking
	Grant proposal development
	Project planning
	Data management planning
Research process	Digital project management
	Data curation and management
	Data analysis and visualization
	Digitisation and preservation
	Embedded research services
Publication	Publication guidelines
	Digital and open publishing
	Copyright and fair use expertise
	Digital repository
	Research dissemination
	Research impact measurement

Of these main themes, "supporting services" are essentially the core provision for library DSS – supporting the five other themes in the framework. The literature analysis identified several DSS, which although are not directly related to the individual stages in the research lifecycle, these services provide necessary and indispensable supports to the provision of DSS throughout the research lifecycle. These DSS are strongly overlapping with traditional academic library services and consist of four services: digital scholarship IT infrastructure, digital and physical spaces for collaboration, teaching and training services, consulting services.

"Formulating research ideas" is emerged as the first stage in the research lifecycle. Three DSS have emerged: hypothesis/question development, background literature search, bibliometric services. According to the literature analysis, these three types of DSS are truly very often considered as basic and traditional research supports from the university libraries [18]. Whilst faculties and students can seek guidance on formulating and revising research hypothesis or questions [19], bibliometric services are extremely useful at this research stage and have been widely offered in a large number of university libraries around the world [20–22].

Through the literature analysis, "locating research partners" emerged as the second stage in a research cycle. After formulating and validating research ideas, researchers often expect to talk to colleagues, who are in the related fields and who are probably more experienced in research, about the struggles they are facing in their research [13,23,24]. Specifically, three DSS were identified in the analysis: identifying potential collaborators, contacting potential partners, recruiting research team.

Moreover, as stated in Cox [25] and Huang and Wang [26], library professionals are an invaluable asset when developing a research proposal, or applying a research grant. Thus, "proposal writing" was identified as the third stage in a research cycle. Four DSS should be provided in this stage: grant seeking, grant proposal development, project planning, data management planning.

The "research process" stage focuses on the provision of DSS in supporting the management, gathering, analysis, sharing and preservation of data. Specifically, the literature analysis pointed to five DSS: digital project management, data curation and management, data analysis and visualization, digitisation and preservation, embedded research services. According to the Chinese literature included, embedded services are highly valued and widely provided in university libraries in China [27]. Nevertheless, Lu [28] claims that these embedded services are actually rarely used by faculties and students. On one hand, Si and Xing [27] report that this could be resulted by the fact that these researchers are often unaware this type of services. On the other hand, Lu [28] points out a sheer lack of trust toward digital scholarship librarians. Many of them, as asserted by Lu [28], are inadequately trained and skilled, as well as insufficiently encouraged and motivated to outreach to potential users.

Finally, the "publication" stage focuses on systematically reporting the entire research process as well as the research findings. Through the literature analysis, six DSS have emerged: publication guidelines, digital and open publishing, copyright and fair use expertise, digital repository, research dissemination, research impact measurement. This stage is often considered as the last steps in a research project. Many consider that this is the ending stage of a research cycle [29,30]. However, publishing research results provides opportunities to generate new research ideas, identify new research partners, and articulate innovative visions and perspectives for future research.

4 CONCLUSIONS

In summary, this paper reports on a literature review, which aimed to formulate and propose a framework that can guide the development of DSS in China's university libraries. Through an analysis of relevant academic articles and professional reports in both English and Chinese, the framework is developed consisting of 25 DSS, which are grouped in six themes: supporting services, formulating research ideas, locating research partners, proposal writing, research process, and publication. The DSS framework developed in this literature review can be used for the development of DSS in China's university libraries, as well as can inform the articulation of relevant strategies and decision-making. However, the framework proposed in this article require further development, validation and verification through collecting and analysing empirical data (both qualitative and quantitative) gathered in the field.

ACKNOWLEDGMENTS

This work was supported by The National Social Science Fund of China (17CTQ042).

REFERENCES

[1] E. Tzoc, J. Millard. 2017. An on-demand, and cloud-based digital scholarship applications dashboard. Journal of Library Administration. 57(5), 563-576.
[2] Association of College and Research Libraries. 2016. 2016 top trends in academic libraries. College & Research Libraries News. 77(6), 274-281.
[3] Y. Zhao. 2009. Changing of library services under e-research environment. Electronic Library. 27(2), 342-348.
[4] B. Sinclair. 2014. University library as incubator for digital scholarship. Retrieved October 20, 2017 from https://er.educause.edu/articles/2014/6/the-university-library-as-incubator-for-digital-scholarship.
[5] Alliance of Digital Humanities Organizations. 2017. Retrieved October 20, 2017 from http://dhcenternet.org/about.
[6] R. Xie, W. Liu. 2017. Digital scholarship and citizen science: the new environment to reborn digital libraries - summary on the 13th advanced digital library seminar. Journal of Academic Library. 35(1), 6-10.
[7] L. E. 2017. The digital scholarship support of some university libraries in America and its enlightenment. Library and Information Service. 61(10), 74-80.
[8] Q. Zhou. 2015. Academic library service innovation oriented to digital humanities. Journal of Library Science. 37(6), 92-94.
[9] W. Shao. 2017. Research on the information service model in libraries with the aim of digital humanities. The Library Journal of Henan. 37(5), 89-91.
[10] Y. Xiang, J. Lai, N. Ding. 2013. Exploration of scientific data management service in university libraries – taking Wuhan University Library's practice in social science data management for example. Information Studies: Theory & Application. 36(12), 89-93.
[11] X. Zeng. 2014. The library under the digital humanities background: functions and services. Library & Information. 34(4), 111-113.
[12] Y. Lai. 2016. The study of the scientific research support service of library oriented to digital humanities. Library Work and Study. 38(10), 28-32.
[13] B. Zhu, H. Nie. 2017. Interaction and coexistence: digital humanities and historical research - conference review for "the 2n Peking University Digital Humanities Forum". Journal of Academic Libraries. 35(4), 18-22.
[14] L. Gu. 2016. Data governance: opportunity for the library. Journal of Library Science in China. 42(5), 40-56.
[15] N. King, C. Horrocks. 2010. Interviews in Qualitative Research. Sage Publications Ltd, London.
[16] L. Zhou, M. Nunes. 2016. Barriers to knowledge sharing in Chinese healthcare referral services: an emergent theoretical model. Global Health Action. 9(1), 29964. Retrieved October 20, 2017 from www.globalhealthaction.net/index.php/gha/ article/view/29964.
[17] Joint Information Systems Committee. 2017. Retrieved October 20, 2017 from http://webarchive.nationalarchives.gov.uk/20140702225057/http://www.jisc.ac.uk/whatwedo/campaigns/res3/jischelp.aspx
[18] T. Chitty, D. McRostie. 2016. Better together: the ESRC in the university research library of the twenty-first century. Australian Library Journal. 65(3), 157-166.
[19] Association of Research Libraries. 2017. Retrieved October 20, 2017 from http://www.arl.org/focus-areas/scholarly-communication/digital-scholarship/digital-scholarship-support.
[20] S. Petersohn. 2014. Bibliometric services in research evaluation: a new task area strengthening the jurisdiction of academic librarians. IATUL. Helsink.
[21] Y. Sun. 2014. Bibliometric service practices of academic libraries in Europe and implications. Journal of the National Library of China. 23(1), 90-96.
[22] F. Kang. 2017. Study on the application of academic social media in libraries' research services: a case of ResearchGate. Library Work in Colleges and Universities. 37(4), 86-89,96.
[23] M. K. Hensley, S. J. Bell. 2017. Digital scholarship as a learning center in the library: building relationships and educational initiatives. College & Research Libraries News. 78(3), 155-158.
[24] F. Nie. 2016. Design of scientific research services model based on research scientific teams' life cycle. Library. 44(9), 87-91.
[25] J. Cox. 2016. Communicating new library roles to enable digital scholarship: a review article. New Review of Academic Librarianship. 22(2-3), 132-147.
[26] Y. Huang, Y. Wang. 2017. Research on digital humanistic process embedded library scientific research data service. Information and Documentation Services. 38(6), 84-89.
[27] L. Si, W. Xing. 2012. Strategy selection of embedded services of academic libraries in China. Documentation, Information & Knowledge. 30(4), 46-52.63.
[28] J. Lu. 2015. A literature review on embedded services of university library. Digital Library Forum. 11(5), 51-54.
[29] M. Miao, Z. Liu. 2016. Study on open access publishing service of domestic libraries. Journal of the National Library of China. 25(2), 60-65.
[30] W. Xia, Y. Liu, Y. Zhao. 2017. A comparative study of research support services in domestic and foreign academic libraries. Journal of the Library Science Society of Sichuan. 39(3), 25-28.

Formula Ranking within an Article

Ke Yuan*, Liangcai Gao*✉, Zhuoren Jiang†, Zhi Tang*✉
*Peking University
†Sun Yat-sen University
{yuanke,glc}@pku.edu.cn,jiangzhr3@mail.sysu.edu.cn,tangzhi@pku.edu.cn

ABSTRACT

With the ever-increasing volume of formulae on the Web, formula retrieval has drawn much attention from researchers. However, most of the existing researches on formula retrieval treat each formula within an article equally, while different formulae in the same article have different importance to the article. In this paper, we address the issue to rank formulae within an article based on their importance. To evaluate the importance of each formula within an article, a formula citation graph is firstly built in a large scale corpus. And the inter-articles features of formulae are extracted by the link topology analysis of formulae based on the graph. Then the word embedding model is explored to extract the inner-article features by mining the semantic relevance between a formula and the corresponding article. Finally, we leverage learning to rank technique for formulae ranking within an article based on those features. The experimental results demonstrate that the proposed features are helpful for formula ranking and our approach yields better performance compared with other state-of-the-art methods.

KEYWORDS

Formula Importance, Formula Ranking, Formula Citation Graph

ACM Reference Format:
Ke Yuan*, Liangcai Gao*✉, Zhuoren Jiang†, Zhi Tang*✉. 2018. Formula Ranking within an Article. In *JCDL '18: The 18th ACM/IEEE Joint Conference on Digital Libraries, June 3–7, 2018, Fort Worth, TX, USA.* ACM, New York, NY, USA, 5 pages. https://doi.org/10.1145/3197026.3197061

1 INTRODUCTION

Formulae, which have gradually accumulated more and more valuable information, are used to present the knowledge of publications in mathematics and engineering. Research about formulae has gained more and more attention in recently years, as witnessed by math retrieval tasks at the NTCIR conferences [1, 17].

Although the previous research has achieved good performance in many formula exploration tasks, however, nearly all the research treat the formulae in the same article equally, which make it difficult for users to access the formula in which they are interested. Moreover, in one article, some formulae may play more important roles, such as the formulae describing main findings while others play auxiliary roles to the main formulae. In information retrieval case, the user reading an article may be more interested in the formula that describes the central topic of the article. For instance, if a user is searching for the concept "Bayes' theorem", the user find an article which contains the formula "$P(A|B) = \frac{P(B|A)P(A)}{P(B)}$" and "$P(A \cap B) = P(A|B)P(B)$", he/she may have more interests in the former formula, since the former one is more representative, which also means the former formula is more important in this article. Based on this consideration, Wang et al. propose that formula ranking in an article should be done according to their importance [15]. But how to effectively measure the importance of each formula within an article is a challenge. In Wang's method [15], they just consider little explicit information of formulae, leading to a limited improvement of performance.

In this paper, we address the challenge and explore the issue of how the formulae within an article should be ranked according to their importance. We design multi-dimensional features to evaluate the importance, including formula-based, inner-article and inter-article features. In our approach, the features about the properties of formula are defined as formula-based features. The word embedding [9] is explored for extracting the inner-article features (i.e., semantic relevance) to address the gap between formulae and text. Meanwhile, a formula citation graph is firstly designed and built to extract the inter-articles features, which are used to store the link topology information of formulae in a large scale dataset. Finally, we integrate multi-dimensional features under the learning to rank framework for formulae ranking within an article. The experiments show that this approach outperforms the state-of-the-art methods.

In summary, the main contributions of our work are as follows.

- We propose and explore a novel problem: To rank the formulae within an article based on their importance in the corresponding article.
- We propose and extract the semantic relevance between formulae and articles based on a word embedding model.
- We firstly design and built a *Formula Citation Graph* based on quantitative analysis of the link topology information between formulae in a large scale dataset.

2 RELATED WORK

The importance of retrieving formulae has motived much research in the area of Mathematical Information Retrieval (MIR). Miller and Yossef first study the math expressions retrieval in [10]. Afterwards many MIR systems have been proposed [4, 13, 14, 16, 18]. But almost all methods hypothesize that all formulae within an article are equal. This is unreasonable due to different formulae within an article often play different roles, some of which describe the main findings

JCDL '18, June 3–7, 2018, Fort Worth, TX, USA

ACM ISBN 978-1-4503-5178-2/18/06.
https://doi.org/10.1145/3197026.3197061

while others just play supportive roles. Therefore, formulae in an article are supposed to be distinguished by their importance in MIR.

Formula ranking within an article is a meaningful task for MIR systems. Up to now, the most related work is Wang et al. method [15], in which formulae within an article are ranked by their formulae importance. However, in this work, they only consider four type features of the formulae (the formula position, the cited number of the formula in a document, the length of the context of formulae, the number of formulae existing in a single document) and neglect much salient information (e.g., implicitly semantics, link information). However, discovering the implicit information of formulae is quite challenging. To address this problem, a formula citation graph and word embedding model are explored.

3 PROPOSED METHOD

Figure 1 illustrates the workflow of the proposed method, including two core modules: *Preprocessor* and *Feature Extractor*. The blue lines denote the offline workflow. Firstly, a formula citation graph is designed and built according to the citations which exist in the context of formulae in the Wikipedia. We extract the context using the method which is proposed in literature [15]. Secondly, the word embedding is constructed on the dump of Wikipedia. Finally, the ranking model is learned from training data.

The red lines indicate how the workflow ranks the formulae within a new article: we extract features about formulae which are exist in the article and score the formulae using a learning to rank (LTR) model which is trained in the offline workflow.

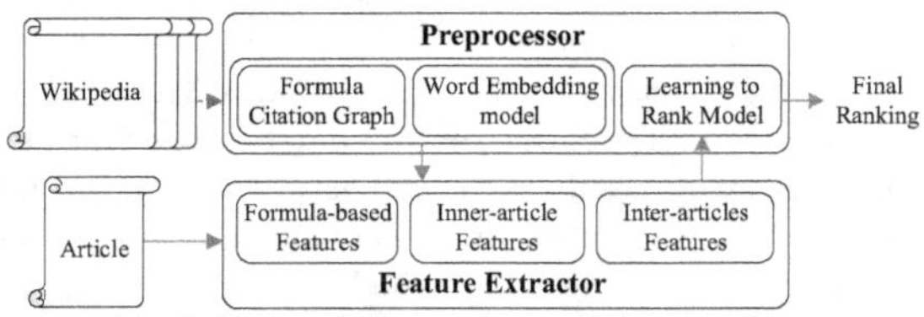

Figure 1: Workflow of formula ranking within an article. The blue line denotes the offline workflow and the red lines denote the online workflow

3.1 Preprocessor

The Preprocessor is comprised of formula citation graph, word embedding model, and learning to rank model. Details of the three parts are described as follows:

3.1.1 Formula Citation Graph. A citation is a quotation from or reference to an entity (article) in a network, for the purpose of acknowledging the relevance of the works of others to the topic of discussion at the spot where the citation appears [6]. In Wikipedia, a formula in one article often cites other article in its textual descriptions if the formula is detailedly described in the cited article. It implies that the formula has a high probability to represent the concept of the cited article. Thus, we build a formula citation graph to store the relation between formulae and articles. In the graph, the article titles are the vertices, the citations (hyperlinks) which exist in the textual descriptions of formulae, including the citing relations (out-links) and cited relations (in-links), are the edges between vertices. The edges will be used to extract the inter-article features (Section 3.3).

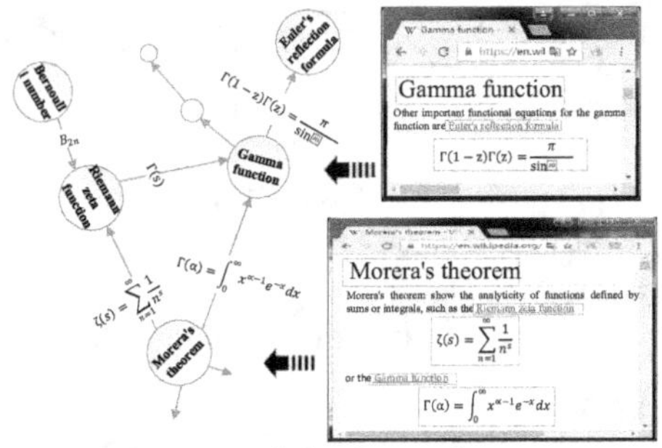

Figure 2: The part of the formula citation graph

As shown in Figure 2, formula "$\Gamma(\alpha) = \int_0^\infty x^{\alpha-1}e^{-x}dx$" exists in page "Morera's theorem" and page "Gamma function" with the citation "Morera's theorem" $\xrightarrow{cite}$"Gamma function", while formula "$\Gamma(1-z)\Gamma(z) = \frac{\pi}{\sin(\pi z)}$" exists in page "Euler's reflection formula" and page "Gamma function" with the citation "Euler's reflection formula" $\xrightarrow{cite}$"Gamma function". Given a Wikipedia page, "Gamma function", according to the citations, the former formula is clearly more representative than "$\Gamma(1-z)\Gamma(z) = \frac{\pi}{\sin(\pi z)}$", because it has a high probability to represent the meaning of "Gamma function" and "$\Gamma(1-z)\Gamma(z) = \frac{\pi}{\sin(\pi z)}$" has a high probability to represent the meaning of "Euler's reflection formula" (supplementary or extended concept of "Gamma function").

3.1.2 Word Embedding Model. The distributed word representation by word embedding model captures semantic similarities through vector arithmetic [9]. In this work, we train a skip-gram model to bridge the vocabulary gap between context-article pairs. The training data of word2vec model is the non-stopwords of the 2016-7-22 dump of Wikipedia[1], which contains more than 3 billion words, and the dimension of word vector is set to 300.

3.1.3 Learning to Rank Model. For predicting ranking scores, we adopt learning to rank technique to rank formulae within an article in this paper. To date, various learning to rank algorithms have been proposed in the information retrieval filed, such as RankSVM [7], ListNet [3], etc. Without loss of generality, we adopt ListNet for this task which has been successfully used in many applications.

ListNet is a listwise approach for learning to rank. It minimizes a direct loss between two permutation probability distributions derived from the gold standard ranking and system predicted ranking. We use the Ranklib[2] in our experiments.

3.2 Features Extractor

We explore the particular features for the task, and investigate three groups of features as follow. There are a total of 11 features, each feature corresponds to a value normalized in [-1,1].

3.2.1 Formula-based Features. The specific characteristics of formulae are explored as follows.

Length of Formula: The longer formula usually contains more information. For instance, the length of the formula "x^2" is 2.

[1] http://en.wikipedia.org/wiki/
[2] https://sourceforge.net/p/lemur/wiki/RankLib/

Numerical Position: It is a feature to denote the numerical position where a formula appears in an article. For instance, the value for the first formula is 1.

Position: The position feature reflects whether the formula occupies a whole line by itself. For an article, the leading formulae are usually on more important positions than embedded ones.

3.2.2 Inner-Article Features. The intuitive features are implicitly semantic similarities between formulae and articles. The semantics of formulae can be captured from the surrounding text [8]. Therefore, we propose several criteria to obtain the semantic relevance between formulae and articles.

Cited Number: The cited number is used to indicate the frequency of a formula in the article. If a formula is cited more in an article, it may play a more important role in the article.

Semantic Relevance to article: We speculate that the more important a formula is, the more possible it can be the central topic of an article. The article of Wikipedia is well-structured, and its lead paragraph often gives a good brief description of the article [11]. Therefore, In this paper, an article is represented by its **title** and **lead paragraph**. Then we calculate the semantic relevance between the title, lead paragraph of article with textual descriptions of the formula, respectively. The vectors of title, leading paragraph and the textual descriptions of the formula are the average vectors of words according to the word embedding model, and the similarity between them is the cosine similarity.

Semantic Relevance to Keywords: We leverage the *tf-idf* model [12] to extract top-5 keywords of the article, then treat the cosine similarity between extracted keywords and the descriptions of formulae as the semantic relevance.

Link: We hypothesize more stronger association between a formula and others is, the more important the formula is. The cosine similarity between formula (descriptions) pair is used to evaluate.

3.2.3 Inter-Article Features. In order to obtain the impact of the formulae citations, we explore the inter-articles features from the formula citation graph.

Frequency: The occurrence number of the formula in Wikipedia.

In-Formula: The in-formula feature is used to find whether the formula in an article is cited by other articles according to the formula citation graph. If the formula in an article is cited by other articles, the formula usually plays a more important role than other formulae in the original article, meanwhile the formula plays a supportive role in other articles.

Out-Formula: The out-formula feature is used to find whether the formula in an article cites other articles according to the formula citation graph. If the formula cites other articles in its textual descriptions, the formula often plays a supportive role in this article, and plays a important role in the cited article.

4 EXPERIMENTAL RESULTS

4.1 Dataset

To the best of our knowledge, there does not exist off-the-shelf datasets for evaluating formula contribution. Therefore we have to build a new dataset for this study. We randomly select 332 articles which contain more than one formulae from the 2016-7-22 dump of Wikipedia. These articles include 2384 formulae. The Figure 3 illustrates the distribution of articles with different number of formulae. It shows that most articles contain less than 10 formulae in the dataset.

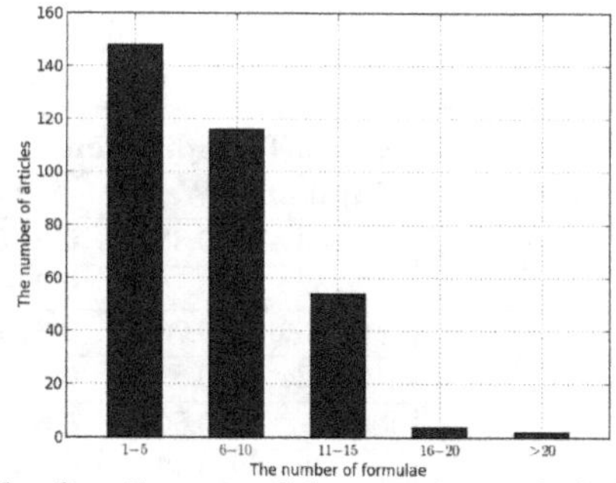

Figure 3: The distribution of the articles with different number of formulae

In the dataset, the contribution values of formulae within an article are annotated by six undergraduates, who are recruited from the major of mathematics and computer science. For each formula within an article, a participant gives a contribution value ($0 \sim 4$). 0 denotes the formula is irrelevant, and $1 \sim 4$ indicates the importance between formula and the article, where higher *value* indicates greater importance. Then the average value of annotated values are used as the importance value of the formula. In addition, the dataset is randomly spilted, according to the proportion of 2:1:1, as training set, validation set and test set, respectively.

4.2 Evaluation Metrics

In this paper, the average precision (P_k) and normalized discount cumulative gain (*NDCG*) [5] are used to evaluate the performance of our approach. The P_k characterizes ranking behavior as the important one ranked more near the front. In this paper, k is set to 3 and 5. *NDCG*, a widely used evaluation criteria in information retrieval and in the learning to rank community [2].

4.3 Compared Baseline Methods

The comparison of the proposed system and several baselines are described as below:

Random: The random model is implemented as a lower-bound. We repeat 50 times for random permutation of formulae in the same article, and average the performance to evaluate this model.

Wang: We re-implement the method proposed by Wang el at.[15].

FLW: We adopt the implementation (ListNet) in [3] for the formula ranking task as our method. The learning rate is set to 0.1, the iteration number is 260.

4.4 Comparison with Baseline Methods

Table 1 and Table 2 show the performance of different methods. The **Random** method obtains 0.7787 of *NDCG*, showing that most formulae in the articles are not "Unimportant" to the corresponding article. The **Wang** method, which only considers few explicit features obtains a little improvement than the weakest model. Our method (**FLW**) achieves the best performance, while consider three novel groups of features, since our approach is able to learn the explicit and implicit features between formulae and articles.

Table 1: The NDCG results of different methods

Method	NDCG
Random	0.7787
Wang	0.8057
FLW	**0.9085**

Table 2: Average Precision(P) of different methods

System		Random	Wang	FLW
Score > 0	P_3	0.8809	0.8815	**0.9547**
	P_5	0.7623	0.7628	**0.9380**
Score > 1	P_3	0.6869	0.7032	**0.8267**
	P_5	0.5924	0.5960	**0.7729**
Score > 2	P_3	0.4918	0.5094	**0.6258**
	P_5	0.4301	0.4312	**0.5682**
Score > 3	P_3	0.2760	0.2846	**0.3780**
	P_5	0.2381	0.2452	**0.3283**

4.5 Feature Validation

Different groups of features may play different roles in LTR models. In order to validate the impact of different groups of features, we conduct experiments with different combinations by removing each group of features respectively. Table 3 and Table 4 show the results, with "w/o" means experiments without the corresponding group of features.

Table 3: *NDCG* of different group feature

Features	NDCG
w/o Formula Based	0.9006
w/o Inner-Article Based	0.8542
w/o Inter-Articles Based	0.8973
All Features	**0.9085**

Table 4: Average Precision(P) of different group feature

Feature		w/o For.	w/o Inn.	w/o Int.	All
Score > 0	P_3	0.9536	0.9448	0.9536	**0.9547**
	P_5	**0.9347**	0.9300	0.9380	0.9380
Score > 1	P_3	0.8269	0.8004	**0.8311**	0.8267
	P_5	0.7669	0.7590	**0.7729**	**0.7729**
Score > 2	P_3	0.6214	0.5993	**0.6302**	0.6258
	P_5	0.5615	0.5523	**0.5682**	**0.5682**
Score > 3	P_3	0.2853	0.3471	0.2853	**0.3780**
	P_5	0.2892	0.3137	0.2892	**0.3283**

We can observe that all features contribute useful information for learning to rank model. Inner-Article based features are play an indispensable role for our task, since the more similar the semantics is, the more important the formula is. This also suggests that the Inner-Article based features are good indicators of formulae being the central point of the current article.

Mixed trends are found for the other two categories. The inter-articles based features and the formula based features are shown to be helpful to identify the most important formulae ($Rel > 3$) with the value of P_3 and P_5. Formula based features give little impact to the overall ranking performance (i.e. $NDCG$), as removing them, since they only consider few explicitly features.

5 CONCLUSIONS AND FUTURE WORK

In this paper, we study a novel task to measure the contribution value of formulae within an article. We develop a system based on learning to rank models with several novel features. A formula citation graph is firstly designed and built to extract the features of formulae through the link topology analysis of formulae in Wikipedia. The word embedding model is explored to extract the features by mining the implicitly semantic relevance between a formula and the corresponding article. Experimental results demonstrate that our proposed methods are effective.

In the future, we will integrate our approach into MIR to improve its performance. Besides, we think that our approach is applicable for ranking other graphical forms including figures, tables etc. Thus, we also plan to apply this approach to these tasks.

ACKNOWLEDGMENTS

This work is supported by the projects of National Natural Science Foundation of China (No. 61472014 and 61573028), which is also a research achievement of Key Laboratory of Science, Technology and Standard in Press Industry (Key Laboratory of Intelligent Press Media Technology).

REFERENCES

[1] Akiko Aizawa, Michael Kohlhase, Iadh Ounis, and Moritz Schubotz. 2014. NTCIR-11 Math-2 Task Overview. In *NTCIR*.

[2] Chris Burges, Tal Shaked, Erin Renshaw, Ari Lazier, Matt Deeds, Nicole Hamilton, and Greg Hullender. 2005. Learning to rank using gradient descent. In *ICML*. ACM, 89–96.

[3] Zhe Cao, Tao Qin, Tie Yan Liu, Ming Feng Tsai, and Hang Li. 2007. Learning to rank:from pairwise approach to listwise approach. In *International Conference on Machine Learning*. 129–136.

[4] Kenny Davila and Richard Zanibbi. 2017. Layout and Semantics: Combining Representations for Mathematical Formula Search. In *International Conference on Research and Development in Information Retrieval*. 1165–1168.

[5] Kalervo Järvelin and Jaana Kekäläinen. 2002. Cumulated gain-based evaluation of IR techniques. *TOIS* (2002), 422–446.

[6] Zhuoren Jiang, Xiaozhong Liu, and Yan Chen. 2016. Recovering Uncaptured Citations in a Scholarly Network: A Two-step Citation Analysis to Estimate Publication Importance. *J. Assoc. Inf. Sci. Technol.* 67 (2016), 1722–1735.

[7] Thorsten Joachims. 2002. Optimizing search engines using clickthrough data. In *SIGKDD*. ACM, 133–142.

[8] Giovanni Yoko Kristianto, Goran Topić, and Akiko Aizawa. 2017. Utilizing dependency relationships between math expressions in math IR. *Information Retrieval Journal* 20 (2017), 132–167.

[9] Tomas Mikolov, Ilya Sutskever, Kai Chen, Greg Corrado, and Jeffrey Dean. 2013. Distributed Representations of Words and Phrases and their Compositionality. *Advances in Neural Information Processing Systems* 26 (2013), 3111–3119.

[10] Bruce R Miller and Abdou Youssef. 2003. Technical aspects of the digital library of mathematical functions. In *AAAI*. Springer, 121–136.

[11] Hao Peng, Jing Liu, and Chin Yew Lin. 2016. News Citation Recommendation with Implicit and Explicit Semantics. In *ACL*. 388–398.

[12] Gerard Salton and Michael J McGill. 1986. Introduction to modern information retrieval. (1986).

[13] Bingjun Sun, Qingzhao Tan, Prasenjit Mitra, and C Lee Giles. 2007. Extraction and search of chemical formulae in text documents on the web. In *WWW*. ACM, 251–260.

[14] Abhinav Thanda, Ankit Agarwal, Kushal Singla, Aditya Prakash, and Abhishek Gupta. 2016. A Document Retrieval System for Math Queries. In *NTCIR*.

[15] Yuehan Wang, Liangcai Gao, Simeng Wang, Zhi Tang, Xiaozhong Liu, and Ke Yuan. 2015. WikiMirs 3.0:A Hybrid MIR System Based on the Context, Structure and Importance of Formulae in a Document. In *JCDL*. 173–182.

[16] Ke Yuan, Liangcai Gao, Yuehan Wang, Xiaohan Yi, and Zhi Tang. 2016. A mathematical information retrieval system based on RankBoost. In *JCDL*. 259–260.

[17] Richard Zanibbi, Akiko Aizawa, Michael Kohlhase, Iadh Ounis, Goran Topic, and Kenny Davila. 2016. NTCIR-12 MathIR Task Overview. In *NTCIR*.

[18] Richard Zanibbi, Kenny Davila, Andrew Kane, and Frank Wm Tompa. 2016. Multi-Stage Math Formula Search:Using Appearance-Based Similarity Metrics at Scale. In *SIGIR*. 145–154.

Ranking Scientific Papers and Venues in Heterogeneous Academic Networks by Mutual Reinforcement

Fang Zhang and Shengli Wu*
swu@ujs.edu.cn
School of Computer Science, Jiangsu University, Zhenjiang, China

ABSTRACT

Evaluating papers and venues objectively and fairly is a vital and challenging task for scientists, research organizations, and research funding bodies alike. Recently, heterogeneous networks have been used to evaluate papers, authors and venues separately or simultaneously. However, most of the approaches treat all the papers in the citation network equally and ignore the prestige of citing venues and citation time intervals. In this paper, we propose a new framework, MR-Rank, which ranks papers and venues iteratively in a mutually reinforcing way. Several factors including citation time interval, recent performance of a venue, and contribution of a paper to its venue are considered at the same time. Based on the ACL dataset, our experiments show that MR-Rank outperforms other models in terms of ranking effectiveness and efficiency.

KEYWORDS

Citation network; mutual reinforcement; heterogeneous network

ACM Reference format:

Fang Zhang and Shengli Wu. 2018. Ranking Scientific Papers and Venues in Heterogeneous Academic Networks by Mutual Reinforcement. In Proceedings of the Joint Conference on Digital Libraries, Fort Worth, TX, June 2018 (JCDL 2018), 4 pages. DOI: https://doi.org/10.1145/3197026.3197070

1 INTRODUCTION

With the gradual institutionalization of scientific research activities, the assessment and evaluation function of publications has become increasingly prominent. Citation plays an important role in the evaluation of journals and papers. Those citation count-based metrics such as IF and SIF- [10] are attractive, because they are single-valued and easy to interpret. However, many such classical metrics are based on the assumption that all the citations of a paper are equally important. This may be questionable according to some researchers [9, 15]. Citations from prestigious venues should be accorded greater weighting than from peripheral ones [6]. Papers that are cited shortly after their publication should also be given greater weight [11]. Furthermore, mutual association between papers and venues should lead to mutual reinforcement [13].

In this paper, we present a framework, MR-Rank (Mutual Reinforcement Ranking), to rank papers and venues simultaneously through an iterative process in heterogeneous networks. The heterogeneous networks consist of three sub-networks: the paper citation network, venue citation network, and the bipartite network that connects papers to venues.

Our approach is novel in several aspects as follows:

(1) Rather than assigning a flat weight for every citation, we consider the citation time interval in the paper sub-network. Greater weights are given to papers that are cited shortly after they were published;

(2) A paper obtains scores from two sources: the citation it obtains from other papers and the venue in which it is published;

(3) The score that a paper obtains from a venue is related to the past performance of the venue;

(4) All venues are evaluated separately on an annual basis.

We compare our approach with PageRank and HITS. Experiments on the ACL (Association for Computational Linguistics Anthology Network) dataset [7] show that our approach is more effective and efficient than both of them.

2 RELATED WORK

For the evaluation of journals, the most common metric is the impact factor, which is the yearly average of citations to the papers published in that journal. Many other metrics have also been proposed [3,10].

PageRank [1] is a well-known algorithm, initially used for assessing the authority of web pages, though it has found numerous other applications since, thanks to its versatility. However, a naïve application of PageRank in the context of academic citation networks suffers from two major drawbacks. Firstly, PageRank favors papers that have been published for longer because they have had more time to garner more citations. Secondly, for any citation, the credit goes to all those cited papers evenly. Consequently, considerable effort has been dedicated to addressing these two problems [8,11].

Some scholars rank authors, papers, and journals in heterogeneous networks. Zhou et al. propose a PageRank-like framework which ranks authors and papers at the same time [14]. Meng et al. propose another method for ranking papers and authors [5]. Yan and Ding propose an indicator, P-Rank, to score

JCDL '18, June 3–7, 2018, Fort Worth, TX, USA

ACM ISBN 978-1-4503-5178-2/18/06...$15.00
https://doi.org/10.1145/3197026.3197070

papers [12]. For each citation, the impact of the citing paper, the citing authors and the citing journal are considered. Liu et al. propose a graph-based framework Tri-Rank, which is able to rank authors, papers, and journals simultaneously [4]. Apart from the impact of the citing paper, the citing authors and the citing journal, they also consider the ordering of authors and the self-citation problem.

Among all the work that has been conducted, the work done by Liu et al. [4] is the most relevant to ours. In both cases heterogeneous networks are used. However, there are significant differences between our work and theirs in [4]. We believe that the quality of both venues and journals vary over time and it is more accurate to assess their impact year by year. In order to accommodate this, we use two measures in our approach. They are citation time interval and past performance of a venue. Both of them do not appear in [4].

3 THE MR-RANK FRAMEWORK

3.1 Preliminaries

The heterogeneous networks of papers and venues can be represented as $G = (V, E)$, where V denotes the set of nodes and E denotes the set of edges. There are two types of nodes: paper and venue, and there are three types of edges: citations between papers, citations between venues, and the publication of a paper in a venue. G can be divided into three sub-networks G_P=(V_P, E_{PP}), G_V=(V_V, E_{VV}), and G_{PV}=(V_{PV}, E_{PV}). Next let us discuss them one by one.

G_P=(V_P, E_{PP}) is a directed, weighted citation network of papers, where V_P denotes papers and E_{PP} denotes citation between papers. Let k be a paper and t_k be the year in which k is published, then the weight of the citation i to j is set as:

$$W_{PP}(i,j) = e^{-\tau(t_i - t_j)} \tag{1}$$

$W_{PP}(i,j)$ decreases exponentially with the citation time interval. τ is a parameter that can be adjusted to control the rate of decrease.

G_V=(V_V, E_{VV}) is a weighted directed citation network of venues, where V_V is the set of venues, and E_{VV} is the set of citations between venues. If a paper i published in venue v_i cites paper j published in venue v_j, then there is an directed edge (v_i, v_j) in E_{VV}. This is referred to as a citation relation between v_i and v_j. The more times venue v_j is cited by venue v_i, the more likely the quality of venue v_j is recognized by v_i. So the weight of edge (v_i, v_j) is set as

$$W_{VV}(v_i, v_j) = \frac{|cited(v_i, v_j)|}{|ref(v_i)|} \tag{2}$$

where $ref(v_i)$ is the set of papers that are cited in v_i, $cited(v_i, v_j)$ is a subset of $ref(v_i)$ referring to those published in v_j, and $|x|$ represents the size of set x.

G_{PV}=(V_{PV}, E_{PV}) is a bipartite graph, where $V_{PV} = (V_P \cup V_V)$ and E_{PV} is the set of edges. Each edge $E(i, v_i)$ in E_{PV} denotes the publication of a given paper i in a given venue v_i. Its weight is defined as

$$W_{PV}(i, v_i) = \begin{cases} 1 & E(i, v_i) \in E_{PV} \\ 0 & otherwise \end{cases} \tag{3}$$

3.2 The Ranking Algorithm

Rule 1: The total score of a paper is a linear combination of the score from publication and the score from citation.

$$Ps(i) = \alpha \times AVE\_VS_{(v_k)} + (1 - \alpha) \times inPs(i) \tag{4}$$

where $Ps(i)$ represents the score of paper i. Each paper obtains its scores from two types of sources: the venue in which it is published ($AVE\_Vs(v_k)$) and the papers which cite it ($inPs(i)$). More specifically, $AVE\_Vs(v_k)$ is defined as the average score that venue v_k obtains in the last three years[1]. α is an adjustable parameter whose value ranges from 0 to 1. Furthermore, we have

$$inPs(i) = \sum_{j \to i} W_{PP}(j, i) \times Ps(j) \tag{5}$$

Rule2: The score of a venue is the linear combination of the score of the venues that cite it and the average score of the papers published in the venue.

$$Vs(v_i) = \beta \times inVs(v_i) + (1 - \beta) \times outVs(v_i) \tag{6}$$

where $Vs(v_i)$ is the score of venue v_i, $inVs(v_i)$ denotes the average score of papers which are published in venue v_i, and $outVs(v_i)$ denotes the scores from other venues which cite venue v_i.

$$outVs(v_i) = \sum_{v_j \to v_i} W_{VV}(v_j, v_i) \times Vs(v_j) \tag{7}$$

$$inVs(v_i) = \frac{\sum_{i \in v_i} W_{VP} \times Ps(i)}{|E(i, v_i)|} \tag{8}$$

where $|E(i, v_i)|$ denotes the number of papers published in venue v_i. Algorithm 1 summarizes the ideas above.

ALGORITHM 1: MR-Rank

Input: Node sets V_P, V_V, edge sets E_{PP}, E_{PV}, E_{VV}, weight matrixes W_{PP}, W_{PV}, W_{VV}, and parameters α, β, τ, ε
Output: the scores of all the papers and venues Ps and Vs

```
Initialization: Ps(i) ← PageRank(i), Vs(vi) ← PageRank(vi),
        Normalize Ps(i) and Vs(vi) ;
while Δ > ε do
    Update paper score Ps(i) based on Equation (4);
    Update venue score Vs(vi) based on Equation (6);
    Normalize Ps(i) and Vs(vi);
    for i ∈ V_P and v_i ∈ V_V
        Δ = Σ_{i∈P_P}|Ps(i)^t − Ps(i)^{t−1}| + Σ_{v_i∈V_V}|Vs(v_i)^t − Vs(v_i)^{t−1}|
    end for
end while
```

[1] If a venue does not have data for all of the past three years, then the available data for a shorter period of time (0, 1, or 2 years) are used.

In Algorithm 1, we can see that all the papers and venues are set the initial scores which are from the PageRank algorithm, and then all of them go through the re-scoring process repeatedly. At each step, all the scores need to be normalized. More specifically, at each iteration step, we

1) update the scores of all the papers by using Rule 1, and
2) update the scores of all the venues by using Rule 2.

4 EXPERIMENTS

4.1 Dataset and Settings

In this experiment, we use the ACL dataset [7] which was constructed from the papers published in natural language processing venues (including journals, conferences and workshops from 1965 to 2015). There are a total number of 23,056 papers, 670 venues[2] and 124,710 citations in the corpus.

The ranking algorithms used for comparison are as follows:

a. MR-Rank: Our proposed algorithm uses all available information (citation, citation time interval, average performance score of a venue in the last three years).

b. MRB: A variant of our proposed algorithm which only uses citation and average performance score of a venue in the last three years.

c. MRW: A variant of our proposed algorithm which only uses citation and citation time interval.

d. MRN: A variant of our proposed algorithm which only uses citation.

e. PageRank

f. HITS

For those parameters, ε is set to 1e-3 for all the algorithms; τ is set to 0.117, which is the same as in [11]. α=0.4 and β=0.9 are used in MR-Rank and all of its variations, because such a setting is good for performance prediction of papers.

4.2 Ranking of Papers and Venues

4.2.1 Paper Ranking. We study the similarity between MR-Rank and the other two conventional methods (i.e. PageRank and HITS). The Pearson correlation coefficient between PageRank and MR-Rank is 0.424, while the coefficient between HITS and MR-Rank is 0.078. The correlation between MR-Rank and the other two ranking algorithms is relatively low, mainly because both PageRank and HITS favor old papers, while our algorithm is more balanced between old and new papers.

Table 1 shows the Top 10 papers and venues obtained by our algorithm MR-Rank. In this table, 5 out of 10 top-ranked papers (in bold) are published in 4 out of 7 top venues (in bold). This result confirms that the best performing papers and top venues are mutually reinforcing.

4.2.2 Venue Ranking. We adopt the modified impact factor (mIF) [13] and P@N to evaluate the quality of venue ranking. mIF is defined as $mIF_X = C/D$, where C is the times that all the papers published in venue X are cited, and D is the total number of papers in X. P@N is defined as P@N=|E ∩ F|/N, where E denotes the top N venues obtained from one method A, and F are the top N venues obtained from another method B. $P@N$ can be used to compare the similarity between these two methods.

We compare the similarity of rankings obtained by mIF and every one of the six methods. Fig. 1 shows the result with precision at three different levels: $P@50$, $P@80$, and $P@100$. From Fig. 1, we can see that MR-Rank performs better than PageRank. The performance of MRB is almost the same as MR-Rank, and this phenomenon shows that citation time interval has little impact on venue ranking. In all three cases, HITS obtains the lowest precision value.

Table 1: Top 10 papers and venues

Rank	Top Venues	Top Papers
1	**CL, 1993**	**J93-2004 (CL, 1993)**
2	**CL, 1996**	**J93-2003 (CL,1993)**
3	CL, 1995	P03-1021(ACL,2003)
4	CL, 1998	A88-1019 (ANLP,1988)
5	CL,1994	**P02-1040 (ACL, 2002)**
6	**CL, 1990**	A00-2018(ANLP-NAACL, 2000)
7	**ACL, 2002**	N03-1017(HLT-NAACL, 2003)
8	CL, 1997	**J90-2002(CL, 1990)**
9	CL, 2003	P97-1003(ACL, 1997)
10	CL, 2004	**J03-1002(CL, 1996)**

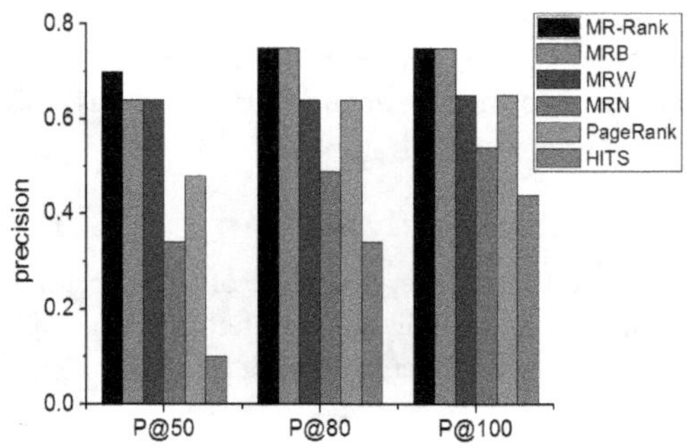

Figure 1: Venue ranking result

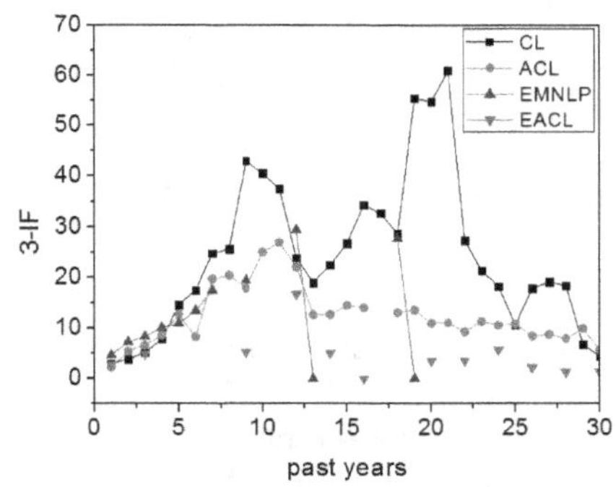

Figure 2: Variation of four venues' performance over 30 years

[2] In this paper we further distinguish between the different years of a venue. Therefore, we have 670 year-venues instead of 340 initial venues.

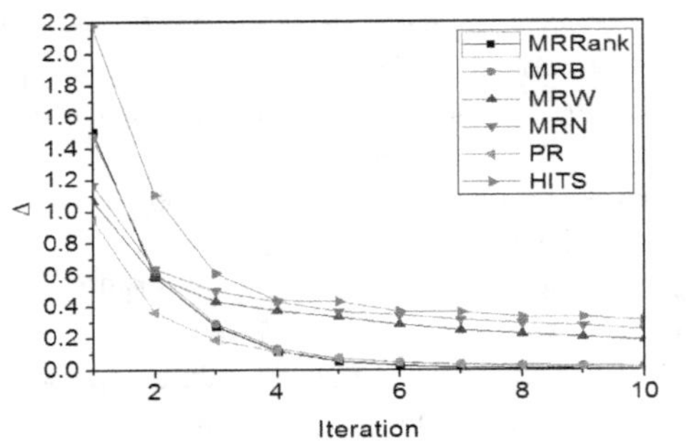

Figure 3: Convergence rate of the six algorithms

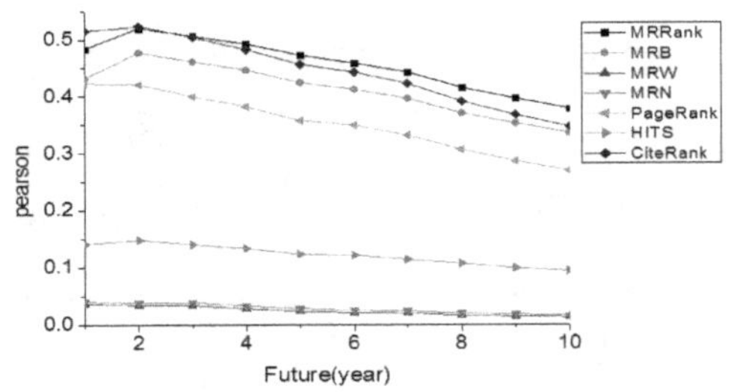

Figure 4: Precision of seven paper performance prediction methods

One major property of MR-Rank is that we evaluate each venue's performance on an annual basis. Fig. 2 shows the variation of four selected venues' performances over 30 years. We can see that all four venues' performances vary considerably from one year to next. Among them, CL has the largest variations over the years.

4.3 Convergence Analysis

In order to test the convergence rate of our algorithms, we use threshold ε to control the times of iteration. The difference between two consecutive iterations is defined as

$$\Delta = \sum_{i \in P_P} |Ps(i)^t - Ps(i)^{t-1}| + \sum_{v_i \in V_V} |Vs(v_i)^t - Vs(v_i)^{t-1}| \quad (9)$$

If Δ is less than ε, then the algorithm stops.

Fig. 3 shows the convergence rates of all six algorithms involved. We can observe that MR-Rank converges faster than the other five algorithms.

4.4 Paper Performance Prediction

For all the paper in the ACL data set, we use those papers published between 1997 and 2002 to predict their performance between 2003 and 2012. Apart from all six algorithms mentioned above, we also include CiteRank [8]. We observe that α=0.4, β=0.9 is the best option for MR-rank and all its three variations. Therefore, such a setting is used in this experiment. Fig. 4 shows the results. HITS, MRW and MRN are not as good as the others. On average, MR-Rank is better than CiteRank. However, a closer inspection shows that CiteRank is more accurate than MR-Rank in 2003, their performances are close in the next two years 2004 and 2005, and then MR-Rank is better than CiteRank in the next 7 years.

5 CONCLUSIONS

Objectively measuring papers and venues is a challenging task. This paper has proposed a ranking framework (MR-Rank) which is able to rank venues and papers at the same time. In this framework, we evaluate all the venues' performance year by year and allocate higher score to those papers that have shorter citation intervals and are published in prestigious venues. Experiments on a real world dataset ACL show that our approach is more effective and efficient than alternative models.

As our future work, we would consider author information and time-awareness in the framework. This will allow us to evaluate papers, venues, and authors at the same time. We expect that more accurate prediction of papers is achievable.

REFERENCES

[1] Sergey Brin and Lawrence Page. 1998. The Anatomy of a Large-scale Hypertextual Web Search Engine. *Comput. Netw. ISDN Syst.* 30, 1-7, 107–117.

[2] P. Dorta-González and M.I. Dorta-González. 2013. Impact maturity times and citation time windows: The 2-year maximum journal impact factor. *J. Informetr.* 7, 3 (July. 2013), 593–602.

[3] Borja González-Pereira, Vicente P. Guerrero-Bote, and Félix Moya-Anegón. 2010. A new approach to the metric of journals' scientific prestige: The SJR indicator. *J. Informetr.* 4, 3, 379–391.

[4] Zhirun Liu, Heyan Huang, Xiaochi Wei, and Xianling Mao. 2014. Tri-Rank: An Authority Ranking Framework in Heterogeneous Academic Networks by Mutual Reinforce. In *26th IEEE International Conference on TOOLS with Artificial Intelligence* (ICTAI2014). IEEE COMPUTER SOC, Washington, DC, 493-500.

[5] Qinxue Meng and Paul J. Kennedy. 2013. Discovering influential authors in heterogeneous academic networks by a co-ranking method. In *Proceedings of the 22nd ACM international conference on Conference on information & knowledge management* (CIKM '13). ACM, New York, NY, 1029–1036.

[6] Gabriel Pinski and Francis Narin. 1976. Citation influence for journal aggregates of scientific publications: Theory, with application to the literature of physics. *Inf. Process. Manage.* 12, 5, 297–312.

[7] Dragomir R. Radev, Pradeep Muthukrishnan, and Vahed Qazvinian. 2013. The ACL Anthology Network Corpus. In *Proceedings of the 2009 Workshop on Text and Citation Analysis for Scholarly Digital Libraries,* (NLPIR4DL '09). Association for Computational Linguistics, Stroudsburg, PA, 54–61.

[8] Dylan Walker, Huafeng Xie, Koon-Kiu Yan, and Sergei Maslov. 2007. Ranking scientific publications using a simple model of network traffic. *J. Stat. Mech-Theory. E.* 6, 6, P06010.

[9] Xiaojun Wan and Fang Liu. 2014. Are all literature citations equally important? automatic citation strength estimation and its applications. *J. Assoc. Inf. Sci. Tech.* 65, 9, 1929–1938.

[10] Fang Xu, Wenbin Liu, and Ronald Rousseau. 2015. Introducing Sub-impact Factor (SIF-) Sequences and an Aggregated SIF-indicator for Journal Ranking. *Scientometrics* 102, 2, 1577–1593.

[11] Erjia Yan and Ying Ding. 2010. Weighted citation: An indicator of an article's prestige. *J. Am. Soc. Inf. Sci. Technol.* 61, 8, 1635–1643.

[12] Erjia Yan, Ying Ding, and Cassidy R. Sugimoto. 2011. P-Rank: An Indicator Measuring Prestige in Heterogeneous Scholarly Networks. *J. Am. Soc. Inf. Sci. Technol.* 62, 3, 467–477.

[13] Su Yan and Dongwon Lee. 2007. Toward alternative measures for ranking venues: A case of database research community. In *Proceedings of the 7th ACM/IEEE-CS Joint Conference on Digital Libraries* (JCDL '07). ACM, New York, NY, 235–244.

[14] Ding Zhou, Sergey A. Orshanskiy, Hongyuan Zha, and C. Lee Giles. 2007. Co-ranking authors and documents in a heterogeneous network. In *Proceedings of the 2007 Seventh IEEE International Conference on Data Mining* (ICDM '07). IEEE Computer Society, Washington, DC, 739–744.

[15] Xiaodan Zhu, Peter Turney, Daniel Lemire, and André Vellino. 2015. Measuring academic influence: Not all citations are equal. *J. Assoc. Inf. Sci. Tech.* 66, 2, 408–427.

An Adaptive Image-based Plagiarism Detection Approach

Norman Meuschke, Christopher Gondek, Daniel Seebacher,
Corinna Breitinger, Daniel Keim, Bela Gipp
Department of Computer and Information Science
University of Konstanz, Germany
{first.last}@uni-konstanz.de

ABSTRACT

Identifying plagiarized content is a crucial task for educational and research institutions, funding agencies, and academic publishers. Plagiarism detection systems available for productive use reliably identify copied text, or near-copies of text, but often fail to detect disguised forms of academic plagiarism, such as paraphrases, translations, and idea plagiarism. To improve the detection capabilities for disguised forms of academic plagiarism, we analyze the images in academic documents as text-independent features. We propose an adaptive, scalable, and extensible image-based plagiarism detection approach suitable for analyzing a wide range of image similarities that we observed in academic documents. The proposed detection approach integrates established image analysis methods, such as perceptual hashing, with newly developed similarity assessments for images, such as ratio hashing and position-aware OCR text matching. We evaluate our approach using 15 image pairs that are representative of the spectrum of image similarity we observed in alleged and confirmed cases of academic plagiarism. We embed the test cases in a collection of 4,500 related images from academic texts. Our detection approach achieved a recall of 0.73 and a precision of 1. These results indicate that our image-based approach can complement other content-based feature analysis approaches to retrieve potential source documents for suspiciously similar content from large collections. We provide our code as open source to facilitate future research on image-based plagiarism detection.

CCS CONCEPTS

• **Information systems** → **Specialized information retrieval**;

KEYWORDS

Image Analysis, Plagiarism Detection, Academic Publishing

ACM Reference Format:

Norman Meuschke, Christopher Gondek, Daniel Seebacher, Corinna Breitinger, Daniel Keim, Bela Gipp. 2018. An Adaptive Image-based Plagiarism Detection Approach. In *JCDL '18: The 18th ACM/IEEE Joint Conference on Digital Libraries, June 3–7, 2018, Fort Worth, TX, USA*. ACM, New York, NY, USA, 10 pages. https://doi.org/10.1145/3197026.3197042

JCDL '18, June 3–7, 2018, Fort Worth, TX, USA

ACM ISBN 978-1-4503-5178-2/18/06...$15.00
https://doi.org/10.1145/3197026.3197042

1 INTRODUCTION

Academic plagiarism has been defined as "the use of ideas, concepts, words, or structures without appropriately acknowledging the source to benefit in a setting where originality is expected" [4]. Forms of academic plagiarism vary in their degree of obfuscation ranging from unaltered copies (copy&paste), to slightly altered forms of plagiarism, such as interweaving text passages from multiple sources (shake&paste), to disguised forms of plagiarism, including paraphrases, translations, and idea plagiarism [27], and even the plagiarism of academic data [11].

The easily identifiable copy&paste-type plagiarism is more prevalent among students [14], while heavily modified plagiarism is more characteristic of researchers, who have strong incentives to avoid detection by skillfully disguising unoriginal content [2]. Research on plagiarism detection (PD) has yielded mature systems employing text retrieval to find similar documents. These systems reliably retrieve documents containing copied text, but often fail to identify disguised forms of academic plagiarism [27].

As we briefly explain in Section 2, several approaches have been introduced to complement text-matching methods and to improve the detection capabilities for disguised forms of plagiarism. Compared to the many sophisticated text-based retrieval approaches that have been proposed for PD, analyzing images to detect academic plagiarism has attracted little research. In this paper, we examine the use of image similarity detection techniques as a promising method for plagiarism detection when textual similarity is lacking.

For our use case, we define 'images' as the visual representations of data, e.g., in the form of bar charts, scatter plots, graphs, etc., as well as of concepts in the form of figures showing the schematic representations of entities and their relations, e.g., flow charts, organigrams, and component diagrams. Our definition also includes photographs and photo-realistic renderings.

Images enable conveying much information in a compressed format, and they represent this information differently from the information conveyed in text. These characteristics make images a promising feature to examine when assessing the semantic similarity present in academic documents. Identifying semantic similarity is crucial for detecting translated plagiarism and idea plagiarism. In some cases, even the plagiarism of data becomes detectable if the data values can be reconstructed from graphs.

The paper is structured as follows. In Section 2, we briefly present general PD approaches and previous work on image-based PD. We then begin Section 3 by informing our image-based PD approach through an investigation of image similarities found in documents that have been accused of constituting academic plagiarism. The remainder of Section 3 introduces the methods we developed and subsequently integrated into an adaptive and scalable image-based

PD approach capable of targeting the identified types of image similarity. In Section 4, we evaluate the image-based PD approach with respect to the types of image similarity we defined. We discuss our findings and present future work to be investigated in Section 5, before summarizing our work in Section 6.

2 RELATED WORK

2.1 Plagiarism Detection Approaches

Plagiarism detection is a specialized Information Retrieval (IR) task with the objective of comparing an input document to a large collection and retrieving all documents exhibiting similarities above a predefined threshold. PD systems typically follow a two-stage process consisting of candidate retrieval and detailed comparison [24]. For candidate retrieval, the systems commonly employ efficient text retrieval methods, such as n-gram fingerprinting or vector space models [15, 26]. For the detailed comparison, the systems typically apply exhaustive string matching. However, such approaches are limited to finding near copies of a text. To detect disguised forms of academic plagiarism, researchers have proposed a variety of mono-lingual text analysis approaches employing semantic and syntactic features, as well as cross-lingual IR methods [2].

Researchers also showed that hybrid approaches, i.e., the combined analysis of text and other content features, improve the retrieval effectiveness for PD tasks. Alzahrani et al. combined an analysis of text similarity and structural similarity [1]. Gipp and Meuschke showed that the combined analysis of citation patterns and text similarity improves the identification of concealed academic plagiarism [5, 16]. Pertile et al. confirmed the positive effect of combining citation and text analysis and devised a hybrid approach using machine learning [20]. Recently, Meuschke et al. demonstrated the benefit of analyzing the similarity of mathematical expressions [17] and patterns of semantic concepts [18] for improving the identification of academic plagiarism.

2.2 Image Analysis for Plagiarism Detection

Few studies have investigated the analysis of image similarity for PD. Hurtik and Hodakova use higher degree F-transform to provide a highly efficient and reliable method to identify exact copies of photographs or cropped parts thereof [8]. However, the method does not consider image alterations aside from cropping.

Iwanowski et al. evaluate the suitability of well-established feature point methods, such as SIFT, SURF, and BRISK, to retrieve exact and visually altered copies of photographs [9]. Srivastava et al. address the same task using a combination of SIFT features extracted using SIFT and perceptual hashing [23].

Feature point methods identify and match visually interesting areas of a scene. The methods are insensitive to affine image transformations, such as scaling or rotation, and relatively robust to changes in illumination or the introduction of noise.

Perceptual hashing describes a set of methods that map perceived content of images, videos, or audio files to a hash value (pHash) [7]. Images perceived as similar by humans also result in similar pHash values, in contrast to cryptographic hashing, in which a minor change in the input results in a drastically different hash value. Thus, the similarity of images can be quantified as the similarity of their pHash values. If image components, such as shapes, are re-arranged, both feature point methods and perceptual hashing often fail.

Iwanowski et al. mention that the effectiveness of the feature point approaches they tested decreases if the test images consist of multiple sub-images. We also observed this limitation in our tests. For example, the two compound images shown in Figure 10 in Appendix A consist of six and four sub-images, respectively. The image in the later document omits two of the sub-images present in the compound image from the source document. Applying the combination of SIFT feature extractor and MSAC feature estimator to compare these two compound images correctly identifies a high similarity between the two sub-images at the top in both compound images, but does not establish a similarity for the other sub-image pairs. This problem can be solved by decomposing the compound image into sub-images and applying near duplicate detection methods, such as perceptual hashing, as we show in our evaluation (cf. Case 6 in Table 1, Section 4).

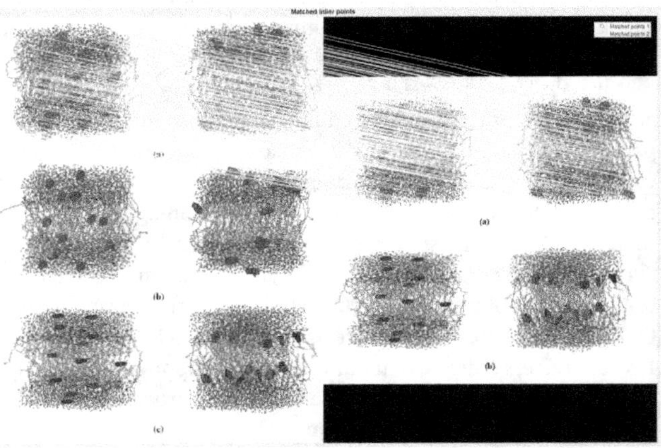

Figure 1: Comparison of compound images using SIFT+MSAC. The approach can only establish a similarity for some of the sub-images.

Feature point methods and perceptual hashing typically also fail to establish meaningful similarities for images primarily containing text, e.g., tables inserted as images. Typically, the feature points for individual letters are matched to multiple letters occurring in different places in the comparison document, which prevents identifying meaningful clusters of matching features.

In summary, prior research on image-based PD proposed methods that reliably retrieve exact and cropped image copies and images that underwent affine transformations. These methods focus on photographs, for which they achieve good results even if photo quality is reduced or modified, e.g., by blurring.

For images that underwent other modifications, such as rearranging shapes in the image, redrawing components of the image, or for images that consist primarily of text, the proposed methods often fail. Compound images should be split into meaningful sub-images before applying feature point methods or perceptual hashing to achieve the best retrieval performance. Identifying other types of image similarity than the comparably modest alterations detectable with the approaches we presented in this section requires additional use-case-specific analysis approaches.

3 ADAPTIVE IMAGE-BASED PD

The studies on image-based PD presented in Section 2.2 focused on providing reliable and computationally efficient methods to identify exact copies and cropped image copies, as well as affine image transformations. Our goal is to offer an efficient detection approach capable of identifying a larger subset of potentially suspicious image similarities. Specifically, we seek to enable the detection of similar images found in academic documents. To derive the requirements for such a detection approach, we examined alleged and confirmed cases of plagiarism, as we explain in the following section.

3.1 Types of Image Similarity

We used the VroniPlag collection[1] as a source for real-world cases of similar images in academic documents. The VroniPlag project (based in Germany) is a crowd-sourced effort investigating plagiarism allegations. Most of the examined works are doctoral dissertations written in German or English. Each document has been manually examined for potential plagiarism and has been annotated by several users according to a standardized workflow.

The project documents all findings, discussions, and other information pertaining to each examined case in the form of a wiki. Each passage of the analyzed document, for which similarities to a source document have been identified, is documented as a 'fragment' using a dedicated page in the wiki. Each fragment has been independently examined by a minimum of two users. Each work contains anywhere from a few dozen to several hundred fragments.

The analyses by the VroniPlag project yield a high-quality annotated dataset, which is continuously being expanded with new cases. At the time of writing, the dataset was composed of 196 academic works containing alleged instances of plagiarism[2]. For most cases, the responsible universities confirmed breaches of academic integrity resulting in the withdrawal of doctorates or other sanctions, such grade reduction or a formal reprimand. In several cases, official investigations are pending. In 14 cases, no official investigation has been initiated, e.g., because the statute of limitation for the alleged offense had passed[3].

Using a targeted Web crawler, we retrieved all pages of the VroniPlag wiki documenting fragments that involve the use of similar images. Hereafter, we describe and classify into broader categories the types of image similarity we observed during our review of these fragments.

3.1.1 Exact Image Copies. We define two images as exact copies if they have identical dimensions and the values and positions of their pixels match. This type of image similarity is very rare, since authors who reuse images are usually not able to access the original image file. In our investigation of the VroniPlag collection, no cases of exact copies were found. Image cropping or changes that are inadvertently introduced when authors reuse images from a PDF or print version of the source document are the main reason why exact image copies are extremely rare. Copying digital images from a PDF document will typically re-compress the images, resulting in rearranged pixels and the loss of information.

[1] http://de.vroniplag.wikia.com/wiki/Home
[2] http://de.vroniplag.wikia.com/wiki/VroniPlag_Wiki:Statistik
[3] http://de.vroniplag.wikia.com/wiki/VroniPlag_Wiki:Aberkennungen

3.1.2 Near Image Copies. We classify images as near copies if they share the large majority of their visual content, yet exhibit minor differences introduced by *i)* removing non-essential content (e.g., numeric labels or watermarks), *ii)* cropping or padding, *iii)* performing affine transformations (e.g., scaling or rotation), *iv)* changing the resolution, contrast or color space. Especially changes of the categories *iii)* and *iv)* can be introduced inadvertently by extracting and reusing images from a PDF or printed document.

We frequently encountered near image copies in our investigation. Figure 5 in Appendix A is a representative example. The author reused an illustration of a kidney from Wikipedia[4] without attribution. Some lines that connect labels to points in the illustration have been removed in the reused image.

3.1.3 Altered Image Reuse. We define altered image reuse as containing differences that required purposeful actions to visually change the reused image. Altered image reuse is hard to classify conclusively given the virtually infinite possibilities for modifying a visual representation. Given our observations, we distinguish three broad levels of alteration.

i) Weakly altered images typically reuse parts of an original image as near copies. Figure 10 in Appendix A shows an example in which sub-images of a compound image were reused.

ii) Moderately altered images typically reuse most or all the visual components of the original image, yet significantly rearrange the components. Figure 12 in Appendix A shows a typical example for moderately altered image reuse.

iii) Strongly altered images are typically completely redrawn versions of the source with significant changes made to the arrangement and/or visual appearance of image components. Figure 14 in Appendix A shows an example of this type of alteration. The two technical drawings show construction plans with identical dimensions, yet the arrangement of the sub-images and the placement of the labels and measurements differ.

3.1.4 Visualizing Reused Data. Reusing data or the visualizations of data without correct attribution may constitute plagiarism or data fabrication if the data presented was not collected. Figure 18 and Figure 19 in Appendix A show near-identical bar charts and line charts in the VroniPlag collection. We found no cases in which reused data was visualized differently. However, given that misuse of data is a well-known problem in academia [11], we hypothesize that such cases do exist, and we believe that our image-based PD analysis will contribute to making them identifiable.

3.2 Requirements Analysis

Given the types of image similarity we observed in the VroniPlag collection, we derive the following requirements for methods to detect such similarities.

Most similar images we observed fell into the category of near copies. This result was to be expected, since investigations of plagiarism allegations exhibit a known bias towards identifying less obfuscated, hence easier to spot, forms of content reuse [21]. The effort necessary to detect disguised forms of content reuse and the lack of tools to support users with that task result in a lower probability of discovering disguised plagiarism instances.

[4] https://commons.wikimedia.org/wiki/File:Kidney_PioM.png

Retrieving near copy images requires methods to reliably identify and efficiently match visually apparent features. Obtaining a semantic understanding of the image composition and underlying data, e.g., by incorporating knowledge about the image type, is typically unnecessary. Robustness against minor, potentially unintentional variations in image quality and dimensionality are important. Another requirement is computational efficiency, since the PD task requires comparing documents to large collections.

The task of retrieving slightly altered images can often be reduced to identifying near copies of image sections. For such cases, methods for identifying sub-images are key to achieving a high retrieval effectiveness. Detecting moderately and strongly altered images often requires obtaining a deeper semantic understanding of the data being visualized. Since the visual appearance of the data differs, additional features, such as labels, as well as information from the text surrounding the images, should be considered.

Employing image analysis to identify data reuse is a challenging retrieval task, since it requires bridging the semantic gap between the visual representation and the underlying data. We expect that identifying visually different representations of (near) identical data requires methods tailored to analyzing specific types of visualizations, such as bar charts, box plots, line graphs, or scatter plots. Similarly to the way in which humans interpret data visualizations, the methods should consider all available information, e.g., size, shape, color, and position of data points, axes scales, as well as the content and position of labels and legend entries.

Due to the variety of possible image similarities, we regard a combination of multiple analysis methods as most promising for covering the spectrum of similarities. The next section describes the detection approach we developed to address these requirements and the insights from prior work (cf. Section 2).

3.3 Overview of the Detection Process

Figure 2 illustrates the adaptive image-based detection process, for which we describe the key components in the following subsections.

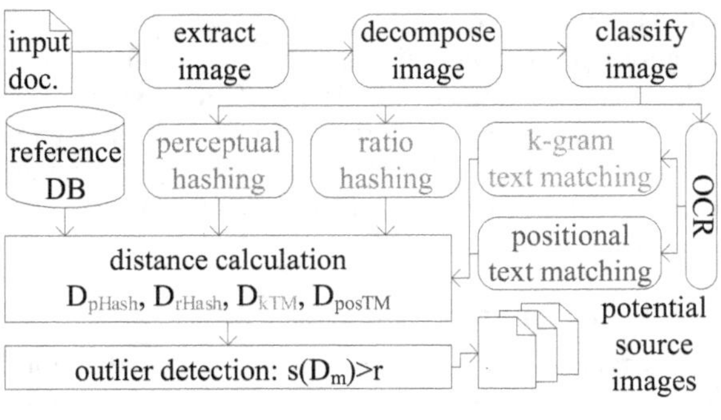

Figure 2: Overview of adaptive image-based PD approach.

The input to the process is a PDF, from which we extract the contained images and check whether they contain meaningful sub-images (cf. Section 3.4). To reduce the computational load for the system, we use the convolutional neural network (CNN) described in Section 3.5. The CNN classifies images according to their suitability for being analyzed using the different analysis methods.

Currently, our approach includes four analysis methods to identify potentially suspicious image similarity. We employ perceptual hashing as a well-established, fast, and reliable method to find highly similar images (cf. Section 3.6). To improve the identification of disguised image similarity, we employ two approaches that perform text-matching for the text extracted from images using Optical Character Recognition (cf. Section 3.7 for our OCR approach). The first approach, k-gram text matching (cf. Section 3.8), is a well-established, text-based PD method. The second approach, positional text matching (cf. Section 3.9), is a contribution of this paper. Another contribution is the ratio hashing approach (cf. Section 3.10), which we propose to identify highly similar bar charts. Ratio hashing is a first, specialized method to identify data reuse.

All analysis methods are applied independently of each other. The methods compute method-specific feature descriptors, which they compare to the method-specific feature descriptors for all documents of the reference collection. We use a relational database to store feature descriptors. The comparisons of feature descriptors yield separate lists of distance scores D_m for each analysis method m. The lists are ordered in ascending order of the distance scores and provided as the input to an outlier detection process (cf. Section 3.11). The outlier detection process computes method-specific suspiciousness scores $s(D_m)$ that indicate whether clear outliers exist within the lists of method-specific distance scores. The process then returns as potential sources for an image in the input document all images for which at least one method-specific suspiciousness score $s(D_m)$ is larger than a reporting threshold r.

We implemented the detection process as an Python 2.7 application that handles all inputs and outputs via a command line interface. This setup allows for easy integration of the application into existing IR systems as a loosely coupled module. The code is open source and available at:

www.purl.org/imagepd

3.4 Image Extraction and Decomposition

To extract the images contained in the input documents, we use poppler[5], an open source library for PDF processing. To reduce storage requirements, all images are converted to JPEG. To reduce computational effort and avoid false positives, we discard JPEG images with a file size below 7,500 bytes. This threshold reflects our observation that images with less than 7,500 bytes typically contain single characters, logos, or decorative elements that are of little value for identifying potential instances of plagiarism.

To decompose compound images, such as Figure 10 in Appendix A, we devised a heuristic process based on two assumptions. First, we assume that white pixels separate sub-images. Second, we assume that sub-images are rectangular and aligned horizontally or vertically within the compound image. Although these assumptions exclude some images, we consider the approach a reasonable trade-off between accuracy and computational effort. If successful, image decomposition can increase the detection performance for sub-images (cf. Section 2.2). However, compound images, for which image decomposition fails, are still analyzable.

The decomposition process includes the following steps: *i) conversion to grayscale* to reduce runtime; *ii) padding with white pixels* to remove a potential border; *iii) binarization using adaptive thresholding* to obtain a black and white image; *iv) dilation* to ensure

[5]https://poppler.freedesktop.org/

black pixels are connected; *v) floodfill* of white areas with black pixels; *vi) subtract original image*; *vii) invert image*; *viii) blob detection* using the algorithm of Suzuki and Abe [25]; *ix) estimate bounding box* by looking for large contours aligned along the image axes; *x) crop and store the identified sub-images in the reference database.*

3.5 Image Classification

We use a deep convolutional neural network to distinguish photographs and bar charts from other image types. Ratio hashing is exclusively applied to bar charts. Photographs are exclusively analyzed using perceptual hashing, since they typically contain too little text to apply OCR text-matching. All other image types are analyzed using perceptual hashing and OCR text matching.

The CNN implements the AlexNet architecture [13]. We used the Caffe framework [10] to train the CNN. Manually checking 100 classified images showed that the CNN achieves an accuracy of 92% for photographs and 100% for bar charts.

3.6 Perceptual Hashing

We include perceptual hashing in the detection process, since prior research demonstrated the suitability of the approach to reliably retrieve near copy images [7, 23]. In the experiments of Srivastava et al., perceptual hashing achieved an accuracy of 0.84, which was the second best result following SIFT, which achieved an accuracy of 0.95. Given that SIFT required approx. four times longer runtime than perceptual hashing, and perceptual hashing outperformed other prominent feature point methods, such as SURF, FREAK and KAZE [23], we consider the approach to be a reasonable trade-off between accuracy and computational complexity.

We tested different variants of perceptual hashing. We found that using a Discrete Cosine Transform (DCT) and comparing pHash values using their hamming distance achieved the best accuracy. The hamming distance of two pHash values is the number of bits that differ in the hashes. We precompute the pHash values for all images of the reference collection and store the pHash values in the reference database. In its current state, our prototype employs pairwise comparisons of the pHash for an input image to all pHash values in the reference database. To enable comparing an image to very large collections, the pairwise comparisons can be replaced with a locality sensitive hashing approach to speed up the process, as demonstrated by Srivastava et al. [23].

3.7 OCR Preprocessing

Including textual features in the similarity analysis requires a preprocessing step to extract the text from images. Research on OCR has provided a wide range of approaches for this task. We chose the open-source OCR engine Tesseract [22], because it allows extracting both characters and words, including their positions. Tesseract is widely-used, actively maintained, and repeatedly outperformed proprietary OCR engines in recognizing English texts [19].

Prior to applying Tesseract, the image is normalized to a height of 800 pixels while maintaining the aspect ratio, which significantly improves recognition. OCR is computationally expensive and processing times vary greatly depending on the input image. We extract the text for each image in the reference collection once and store the information in the reference database.

3.8 k-gram Matching

Determining textual similarity by analyzing matching word or character k-grams is a well-established IR approach. Numerous PD approaches employ variable-size or fixed-size k-grams [2, 15, 26]. For regular texts, k-grams with lengths corresponding to 3-5 words, i.e., approx. 15-30 characters, are used most frequently [3, 6, 12].

To choose a k-gram size for analyzing text in figures extracted using OCR, two use-case specific factors should be considered. First, images typically contain smaller text fragments, such as labels or bullet points. Second, we extract the text content of images using OCR, which is likely to introduce noise, i.e., wrongly recognized characters. Such recognition errors can significantly reduce the accuracy, especially for word k-gram approaches.

To account for the likelihood that incorrectly recognized characters occur, we chose a comparably fine-grained k-gram resolution of three characters. Given the typically sparse presence of text in figures, we retain all k-grams identified for an image as an unordered set that forms the k-gram descriptor of that image. Typically, k-gram-based PD approaches that analyze entire documents employ some form of k-gram selection [2, 15, 26]. We form the k-gram descriptor for all images of the reference collection during preprocessing and store the descriptors in the reference database.

Currently, our prototype performs pairwise comparisons of the k-gram descriptor of an input image to all k-gram descriptors of the reference collection. To scale the image-based detection approach to very large collections, an additional filtering step can easily be introduced, e.g., by indexing individual k-grams and requiring a minimum k-gram overlap to perform the full comparison of the k-gram descriptors. To quantify the distance d of two k-gram descriptors K_1 and K_2, we use the set-based distance function $d = \frac{K_1 \ominus K_2}{K_1 \cap K_2}$, in which $\ominus$ represents the symmetric difference.

3.9 Position-aware Text Matching

As explained previously, OCR errors are a serious threat to the retrieval performance of text-matching approaches. This problem is further aggravated by the typically sparse amount of text present in academic images. To improve the robustness of similarity assessments examining textual content in images, we propose including positional information as an additional feature of the analysis. Specifically, we suggest to only consider text matches for computing the similarity of two images if the matching text occurs in broadly similar regions in both images.

Figure 3 illustrates the approach. We assume an input image (left) and a comparison image (right) that have been scaled to the same height or width while maintaining the individual aspect ratio of the images. The markers A, B, C and D in Figure 3 symbolize text identified by the OCR engine, e.g., characters, words, or k-grams. Each text fragment identified in the input image is considered the center point around which a proximity region is defined. In Figure 3, a fixed-size circle is used as the proximity region, however other shapes and dynamic sizing of the shape, e.g., dependent on the length of the text fragment, are also possible. The proximity regions of the input image are projected into the comparison image. To compute the similarity score, only the text matches that also occur in corresponding proximity regions (A and D) are considered.

Text matches that occur outside of a defined proximity region (B) and non-matching text (C and X) are disregarded.

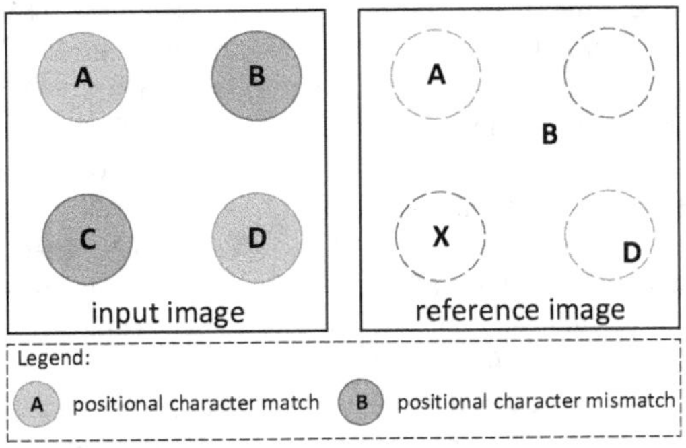

Figure 3: Illustration of position-aware text matching.

Our current prototype implements position-aware text matching using the following approach. Images are rescaled to a common height of 800px while maintaining their aspect ratio. We use single characters as the center points around which a fixed-size circular proximity region of 50px is defined. The distance function considers the number of position-aware text matches divided by the number of characters in the longer of the two OCR texts. This normalization reflects the assumption that two images are less likely to be similar if their amount of textual content differs strongly.

The pairwise comparison of position-aware text matches is computationally more expensive than the set-based k-gram comparison. For this initial study, we employ no filtering of candidate images except for the classification described in Section 3.5. To scale the approach, filtering heuristics, such as setting a minimum threshold for matching k-grams (cf. Section 3.8), can be added.

3.10 Ratio Hashing

To demonstrate a possible approach to target the plagiarism of academic data and results, we propose ratio hashing to identify semantically similar, yet visually differing bar charts. Due to the diversity of chart types, each type must be treated with a different approach. Since bar charts are very common in academic publications, ratio hashing is geared towards them. The idea of ratio hashing is to compute a hash value from the relative heights of bars compared to the height of the largest bar.

To extract the bar heights from an input image, we process the image as follows: *i) convert to grayscale*; *ii) binarize* using global thresholding to obtain a black and white image with sharp contours; *iii) pad image with white pixels* to ensure bars can be filled; *iv) clean artifacts* of black pixels using a threshold on the relative area covered by the pixels; *v) remove image border*; *vi) floodfill with black pixels and invert*; *vii) find candidates for bars* by determining the lengths of all vertical lines of black pixels, *vii) determine bars* by clustering vertical lines, remove noise from whiskers, labels, and legend entries, then assume the average height of the lines in a cluster as the bar height. Once the bar heights have been determined, we sort the bars by decreasing order of their height to speed up the comparison of two ratio hashes. We then calculate the relative bar heights and store the ratio hash, i.e., the sequence of relative bar heights, in the reference database.

To determine the distance between two ratio hashes, we compare the components of the hash, i.e., the relative bar heights, in decreasing order and calculate the sum of the differences of the bar heights. We currently compare the ratio hash of an input bar chart to all ratio hashes in the reference database. In the future, the computational effort of the approach can be reduced by indexing ratio hashes and implementing filtering steps. For our initial evaluation, we limited computational effort by requiring bar charts to have the same number of bars. However, the comparison approach can easily be changed to more exhaustive comparisons that consider the best fit between sets of different sizes if the analysis scope is reduced through prior filtering steps.

3.11 Outlier Detection

Each of the four analysis methods described in the previous subsections returns the method-specific distances of the input image to all images in the reference collection as an ordered list D_m. To quantify how suspicious, i.e., how indicative of potential image reuse, these distances are, we make two assumptions.

First, we assume that the input image can only be suspicious of being derived from (an)other image(s) in the collection if it exhibits *comparably strong similarities*, i.e., small distances, to a small number c of other images. Small distances of the input image to other images alone are not necessarily suspicious. The input image could be a logo that the preprocessing step missed to exclude. Such images would exhibit small distances to many other images in the collection. Therefore, we additionally require that the input image exhibits small distances to fewer than c other images. The cutoff parameter c is set to 10 in our system. In essence, c is a filter for false positives that accounts for potential deficits of the detection process or the collection, e.g., common images or multiple versions of documents not eliminated during preprocessing. The parameter should be chosen large enough to rule out any reasonable possibility that strong similarities to more than c documents are not false positives. We consider $c = 10$ a conservative estimate to ensure this property even for large collections.

Second, we assume that image similarities are comparably strong if *a clear separation* is observable in the distance scores for the $k < c$ images most similar to the input image and the distance scores of the remaining images in the collection. In other terms, images with strong similarities to the input images must be outliers. If that requirement is not fulfilled, the input image is either genuine or too dissimilar to a potential source for being detected. Alternatively, the reference collection may not contain the source image or the analysis method failed to determine a meaningful distance.

Given these assumptions, we detect outlier distances as depicted in Figure 4 and described hereafter. For each analysis method m, the absolute distances $d_i, 1 \leq i \leq n$ of the input image to all n images of the reference collection are stored as a list $D_m = (d_1, d_2, ...d_n)$ in ascending order of d_i. Each method-specific list of absolute distances D_m is transformed to a list D'_m of the relative deltas d'_i between d_i and d_{i+1} as follows: $d'_i = \frac{(d_{i+1} - d_i)}{d_i}$, $0 < i < |D_m|, i \in N$.

To find outliers, i.e., elements in D'_m that exhibit a clear separation to succeeding elements, we sequentially scan through D'_m and

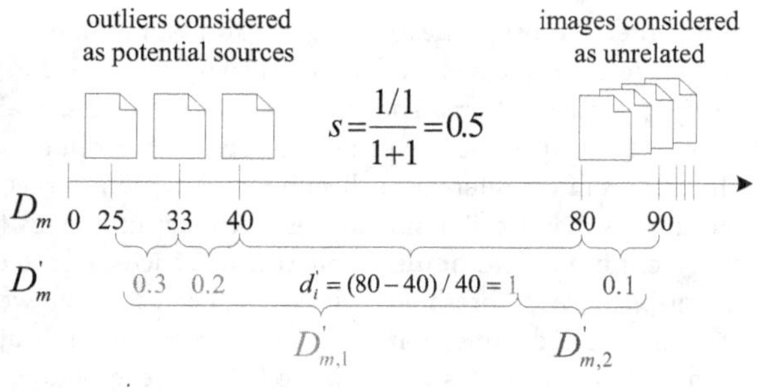

Figure 4: Illustration of the outlier detection process.

check for elements d'_i that exceed a threshold t. The threshold is customizable and set to $t = 1$ for all methods except for k-gram matching, where we found a threshold of $t = 2$ to yield better results. In other terms, we require that a pair of distances (d_i, d_{i+1}) exists, for which d_{i+1} is at least twice as large as d_i and three times as large as d_i in the case of k-gram matching. If an d'_i exceeds these thresholds, D'_m is split into $D'_{m,1}$ and $D'_{m,2}$ at the largest d'_i, where $d'_i \in D'_{m,1}$. If $D'_{m,1}$ has less than c elements, the corresponding images are considered potential sources of the input image.

The final suspiciousness scores $s(D_m)$ for each method-specific list of distances D_m are calculated as $s = \frac{\bar{d}}{1+\bar{d}}$ where $\bar{d} = \frac{\max(d'_i \in D'_{m,1})}{t}$. In other terms, s considers the relative delta in the distances that separates a previously determined group of outliers (in our case at most $c - 1 = 9$ images) from the remainder of the collection. We use the function $y = \frac{x}{x+1}$ to normalize the score s to $[0, 1]$. The sublinear normalization function assigns a weight of 0.5 if the image in the outlier group that is least similar to the input image is separated from the remainder of the collection by a margin that is as large as the absolute distance of this least similar outlier to the input image. For all analysis methods, we set $s = 0.5$ as the threshold to consider an image potentially suspicious and a score $s > 0.75$ as highly suspicious. For the case $s = 0.75$, the least similar outlier has a distance margin to the next similar image that is three times as large as its absolute distance to the input image.

4 EVALUATION

To evaluate the adaptive image-based PD process, we selected 15 image pairs from documents in the VroniPlag collection. We chose images that reflect the spectrum of image similarities we observed in the collection (cf. Section 3.1). We list the test cases, most of which are from the life science domain, in Appendix A. To create a realistic test collection, we obtained 4,500 random images contained in life science publications from the open access repository PubMed Central[6]. We hid the 15 known source images among the 4,500 obtained images and created the reference database by classifying each image and computing the applicable feature descriptors. After precomputing the reference database, we used each of the 15 reused images individually as input for the detection process.

Table 1 shows the method-specific suspiciousness scores $s(D_m)$ for each input image computed from the distance scores D_m of the four analysis methods, perceptual hashing (pHash), character tri-gram matching (OCR k-grams), position-aware character matching (OCR Pos.) and ratio hashing (rHash).

#	Image Type	Alteration	pHash	OCR k-grams	OCR Pos.	rHash
1	Illustration	near copy	**0.86**	< 0.5	< 0.5	-
2	Illustration	near copy	**1.00**	0.79	0.77	-
3	Illustration	near copy	**0.87**	< 0.5	< 0.5	-
4	Micr. Image	near copy	< 0.5	< 0.5	< 0.5	-
5	Table	near copy	< 0.5	< 0.5	< 0.5	-
6	Illustration	low	**0.78**	< 0.5	< 0.5	-
7	Illustration	low	**0.57**	< 0.5	< 0.5	-
8	Illustration	medium	< 0.5	**0.87**	< 0.5	-
9	Table	medium	0.62	**0.71**	0.55	-
10	Illustration	high	< 0.5	< 0.5	< 0.5	-
11	Table	high	< 0.5	**0.79**	< 0.5	-
12	Table	high	< 0.5	**0.92**	< 0.5	-
13	Line Chart	high	< 0.5	**0.70**	< 0.5	-
14	Bar Chart	near copy	0.62	0.64	0.77	**0.92**
15	Line Chart	near copy	< 0.5	< 0.5	< 0.5	-

Table 1: Suspiciousness scores for input images.

#	Image Type	Alteration	pHash	OCR k-grams	OCR Pos.	rHash
1	Illustration	near copy	1	> 10	> 10	-
2	Illustration	near copy	1	1	1	-
3	Illustration	near copy	1	> 10	> 10	-
4	Micr. Image	near copy	1	> 10	> 10	-
5	Table	near copy	> 10	> 10	> 10	-
6	Illustration	low	1	> 10	> 10	-
7	Illustration	low	1	> 10	> 10	-
8	Illustration	medium	1	1	> 10	-
9	Table	medium	1	1	1	-
10	Illustration	high	1	> 10	> 10	-
11	Table	high	> 10	1	> 10	-
12	Table	high	1	1	> 10	-
13	Line Chart	high	> 10	1	> 10	-
14	Bar Chart	near copy	1	1	1	1
15	Line Chart	near copy	> 10	> 10	> 10	-

Table 2: Ranks at which source images were retrieved.

Table 2 complements Table 1 by showing the ranks at which each of the four analysis methods retrieved the source image for an input image. Note that the system would not return any results for input images with a score below 0.5, as no similarities that form clear outliers were identified in such cases. To verify the appropriateness of this threshold, we retrieved for each of the input images having scores below 0.5 the 10 images identified as most similar and checked whether this set contained the source image. Limiting the set to 10 images is a heuristic that assumes a reviewer might be willing to browse through ten results, although none of them has been identified as clearly suspicious.

As shown in Table 1, scores above the reporting threshold of 0.5 were determined by at least one analysis method for 11 of the 15 input images, thus achieving a recall of 0.73. The cases 4, 5, 10, and 15 are false negatives, although pHash retrieved the source images for cases 4 (a microscope image) and 10 (a visually sparse sketch

[6]https://www.ncbi.nlm.nih.gov/pmc/tools/openftlist/

exclusively using basic geometric shapes) at the top rank. For these two cases, pHash computed similarities to many unrelated images of the same types. However, the low score assigned to the pHash distances shows that the identified similarities are not clear outliers. For case 5, the low quality of the input image caused insufficient OCR results to detect the nearly copied text in the table. The line chart in case 15 is visually too sparse to be detected by pHash. Little textual content and low image quality also caused the OCR-based methods to fail for this case.

As shown in Table 2, the true source images were retrieved at the top rank for all input images with a score above 0.5. For cases in which the method-specific score was lower than 0.5, no source image was retrieved among the top-ten most similar images. This result shows that the outlier detection process effectively eliminated all false positives, resulting in a precision of 1. A high precision is important for PD approaches to avoid false suspicion.

For near copies and weakly altered images, perceptual hashing in combination with sub-image extraction worked well, yielding suspiciously high scores for six of the nine cases falling into these categories. Text analysis utilizing OCR performed better than perceptual hashing for moderately and strongly altered images if the quality of the image was high enough to perform OCR reliably and if sufficient text content is present. The OCR-based approaches identified three of the four cases that involved tables (cases 9, 11, 12), for which they yielded clearly suspicious scores (0.71, 0.79, and 0.92, respectively). While k-gram matching performed better than the position-aware text matching for most cases, the position-aware text matching was more robust to low OCR quality. Combining both approaches therefore allows to process a larger number of input images in a real-world setting.

The test dataset contains only one case (14), in which a bar chart was reused. For this case, ratio hashing clearly outperformed all other methods (s=0.92), although the bar chart was rotated and slightly altered. Clearly, additional evaluations must be conducted to reliably determine the performance of ratio hashing.

Creating the reference database for the 4,515 images took around two hours using a desktop computer with a 2.70 GHz Intel Core i5-6400 CPU, 8 GB of main memory and a GeForce GTX960 GPU, which was used to accelerate the CNN classifier. Executing the analysis methods took between 1-3 seconds for perceptual hashing and ratio hashing and between 2 to 16 seconds for the OCR-based methods using the same computer. This time includes classifying the input images, computing the feature descriptors, and comparing the descriptors to all other descriptors in the database.

5 DISCUSSION & FUTURE WORK

Our results demonstrate that an adaptive image-based PD approach enables the identification of a wide range of suspicious image similarities in academic work. While the suitability of analysis methods strongly depends on the individual images, the combination of analysis methods achieved a good recall of 0.73 in our experiments. The proposed outlier detection process performed particularly well in our experiments. Using restrictive thresholds, our approach eliminated false positives and achieved a precision of 1.

While these results are promising, our small test collection, in which images from life science publications were overrepresented, limits the generalizability of our results. Future experiments must show whether the properties we require to assume that image similarities form suspicious outliers will also be observable in significantly larger collections. The outlier detection process mainly depends on the distribution of distances between an input image and the images in the reference collection. In large collections, unrelated images may exhibit similarities to the input images that prevent identifying clear outlier similarities. In such cases, reducing the suspiciousness threshold may become necessary and would likely result in the identification of false positives. Since the outlier detection process operates on a simple list of precomputed distance scores, adjusting the threshold at runtime is feasible. Hence, a frontend application could allow users to interactively adjust the threshold to determine the number of results (including potential false positives) the user is willing to examine.

Our approach is well suited to be scaled for an evaluation on much larger collections. All preprocessing steps can be executed in parallel. In the current implementation of the approach, only the time required for the comparison of feature descriptors depends on collection size. We described several easily implementable options to decrease the linear runtime requirement of this step by adding feature indexing and feature selection approaches.

However, an inherent challenge to conclusive, large-scale evaluations of PD approaches is the difficulty of compiling test collections. A widely accepted solution is to use collections containing artificially created plagiarism instances. For image plagiarism, such collections do not yet exist. Even if they existed, it would be questionable whether they are representative of the real-world plagiarism that is committed by experienced researchers with a strong incentive to hide their misconduct. For this reason, we opted to use real-world cases of image reuse in our experiments.

A technical challenge to the detection effectiveness of the proposed PD approach in the real-world detection settings we imposed for our experiments is OCR effectiveness. The OCR-based analysis methods showed the best results for medium to high-level alterations of images. However, poor image quality, especially for older digitized academic papers, reduces OCR performance. Perceptual hashing often performed poorly for visually sparse images. A dilation step might help achieve better results. Although our approach to sub-image extraction performed well for most cases, sometimes it failed to correctly extract overlapping sub-images. Specialized post-processing procedures could improve the results.

Aside from improving the analysis methods already included in the approach, adding specialized analysis methods for image types, such as line graphs, scatter plots, and photographic images, can further augment the detection capabilities of the approach.

6 CONCLUSION

We introduced an image-based plagiarism detection approach that adapts itself to forms of image similarity found in academic work. The adaptivity of the approach is achieved by including methods that analyze heterogeneous image features, selectively employing analysis methods depending on their suitability for the input image, using a flexible procedure to determine suspicious image similarities, and enabling easy inclusion of additional analysis methods in the future. To derive requirements for our approach, we examined images contained in the VroniPlag collection. This real-world collection is the result of a crowd-sourced project documenting alleged and confirmed cases of academic plagiarism. From these cases, we introduced a classification of the image similarity types that we observed. We subsequently proposed our adaptive image-based PD approach. Our process integrates perceptual hashing, for which we extended the detection capabilities by including an extraction procedure for sub-images. Since textual labels are common in academic images, we devised and integrated two approaches using OCR to extract text from images and use the textual features for similarity assessments. To address the problem of data reuse, we integrated an analysis method capable of identifying equivalent bar charts. To quantify the suspiciousness of identified similarities, we presented an outlier detection process. The evaluation of our PD process demonstrates reliable performance and extends the detection capabilities of existing image-based detection approaches. We provide our code as open source and encourage other developers to extend and adapt our approach.

REFERENCES

[1] Salha Alzahrani, Vasile Palade, Naomie Salim, and Ajith Abraham. 2011. Using Structural Information and Citation Evidence to Detect Significant Plagiarism Cases in Scientific Publications. *JASIST* 63(2) (2011).
[2] Salha M. Alzahrani, Naomie Salim, and Ajith Abraham. 2012. Understanding Plagiarism Linguistic Patterns, Textual Features, and Detection Methods. In *IEEE Trans. Syst., Man, Cybern. C, Appl. Rev.*, Vol. 42.
[3] Yaniv Bernstein and Justin Zobel. 2004. A Scalable System for Identifying Co-derivative Documents. In *Proc. SPIRE*. LNCS, Vol. 3246. Springer.
[4] Teddi Fishman. 2009. "We know it when we see it"? is not good enough: toward a standard definition of plagiarism that transcends theft, fraud, and copyright. In *Proc. Asia Pacific Conf. on Educational Integrity*.
[5] Bela Gipp. 2014. *Citation-based Plagiarism Detection - Detecting Disguised and Cross-language Plagiarism using Citation Pattern Analysis*. Springer.
[6] Cristian Grozea and Marius Popescu. 2011. The Encoplot Similarity Measure for Automatic Detection of Plagiarism. In *Proc. PAN WS at CLEF*.
[7] Azhar Hadmi, William Puech, Brahim Ait Es Said, and Abdellah Ait Ouahman. 2012. *Watermarking*. Vol. 2. InTech, Chapter Perceptual Image Hashing.
[8] Petr Hurtik and Petra Hodakova. 2015. FTIP: A tool for an image plagiarism detection. In *Proc. SoCPaR*.
[9] Marcin Iwanowski, Arkadiusz Cacko, and Grzegorz Sarwas. 2016. Comparing Images for Document Plagiarism Detection. In *Proc. ICCVG*.
[10] Yangqing Jia, Evan Shelhamer, Jeff Donahue, Sergey Karayev, Jonathan Long, Ross Girshick, Sergio Guadarrama, and Trevor Darrell. 2014. Caffe: Convolutional Architecture for Fast Feature Embedding. In *Proc. Multimedia*.
[11] H.F. Judson. 2004. *The Great Betrayal: Fraud in Science*. Harcourt.
[12] Jan Kasprzak and Michal Brandejs. 2010. Improving the Reliability of the Plagiarism Detection System. In *Proc. PAN WS at CLEF*.
[13] Alex Krizhevsky, Ilya Sutskever, and Geoffrey E Hinton. 2012. ImageNet Classification with Deep Convolutional Neural Networks. In *Proc. NIPS*.
[14] Donald L. McCabe. 2005. Cheating among College and University Students: A North American Perspective. *IJEI* 1, 1 (2005).
[15] Norman Meuschke and Bela Gipp. 2013. State-of-the-art in detecting academic plagiarism. *IJEI* 9, 1 (2013).
[16] Norman Meuschke and Bela Gipp. 2014. Reducing Computational Effort for Plagiarism Detection by using Citation Characteristics to Limit Retrieval Space. In *Proc. JCDL*.
[17] Norman Meuschke, Moritz Schubotz, Felix Hamborg, Tomas Skopal, and Bela Gipp. 2017. Analyzing Mathematical Content to Detect Academic Plagiarism. In *Proc. CIKM*.
[18] Norman Meuschke, Nicolas Siebeck, Moritz Schubotz, and Bela Gipp. 2017. Analyzing Semantic Concept Patterns to Detect Academic Plagiarism. In *Proc. Int. WS on Mining Scientific Publications at JCDL*.
[19] Chirag Patel, Atul Patel, and Dharmendra Patel. 2012. Optical Character Recognition by Open source OCR Tool Tesseract: A Case Study. *Int. J. of Computer Applications* 55, 10 (2012).
[20] Solange de L. Pertile, Viviane P. Moreira, and Paolo Rosso. 2016. Comparing and combining Content- and Citation-based approaches for plagiarism detection. *JASIST* 67, 10 (2016).
[21] Martin Potthast, Benno Stein, Alberto Barrón Cedeño, and Paolo Rosso. 2010. An Evaluation Framework for Plagiarism Detection. In *Proc. COLING*.
[22] Ray Smith. 2007. An Overview of the Tesseract OCR Engine. In *Proc. ICDAR*.
[23] Siddharth Srivastava, Prerana Mukherjee, and Brejesh Lall. 2015. imPlag: Detecting image plagiarism using hierarchical near duplicate retrieval. In *Proc. INDICON*.
[24] Benno Stein, Sven Meyer zu Eissen, and Martin Potthast. 2007. Strategies for Retrieving Plagiarized Documents. In *Proc. SIGIR*.
[25] Satoshi Suzuki and Keiichi Abe. 1985. Topological Structural Analysis of Digitized Binary Images by Border Following. *CVGIP* 30, 1 (1985).
[26] K. Vani and Deepa Gupta. 2016. Study on Extrinsic Text Plagiarism Detection Techniques and Tools. *J. Engin. Sc. & Techn. Review* 9, 5 (2016).
[27] Debora Weber-Wulff. 2014. *False Feathers: A Perspective on Academic Plagiarism*. Springer.

A TEST CASES

Figures 5-19 show the test cases of our study. Each case shows the source image on the left and the reused image on the right. Due to space limitations, we only cite the identifier of the investigation in the VroniPlag collection. The identifier consists of the case id, e.g., Ry, followed by the page number where the fragment appears in the later document. Appending the identifier to the base URL de.vroniplag.wikia.com/wiki/ shows each case and allows identifying its source http://de.vroniplag.wikia.com/wiki/Ry/073.

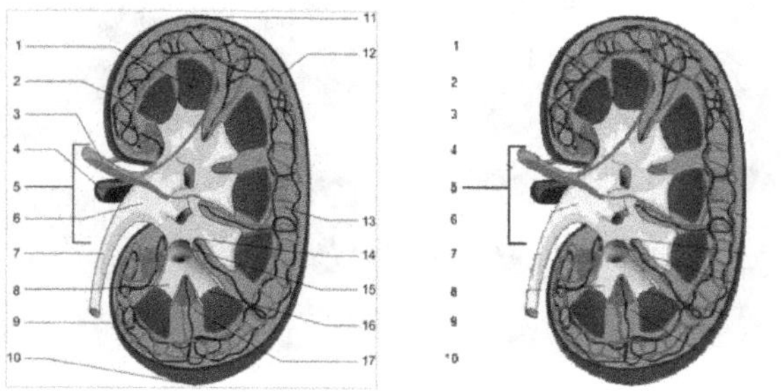

Figure 5: Case 1 - near copy illustration [Dsa/014].

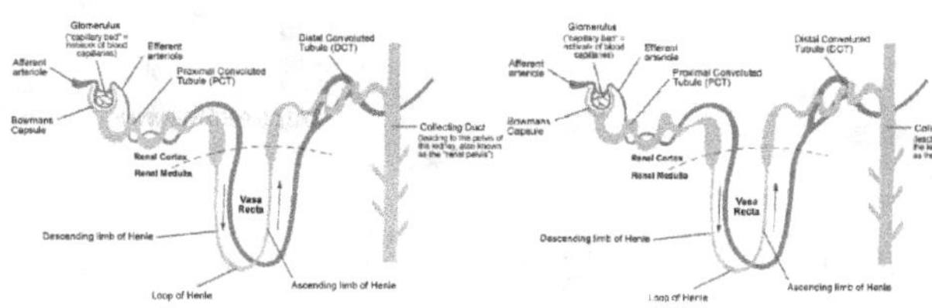

Figure 6: Case 2 - near copy illustration [Dsa/015].

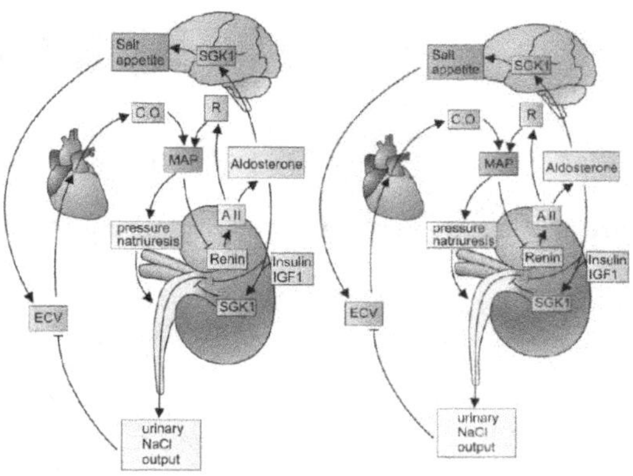

Figure 7: Case 3 - near copy illustration [Dsa/025].

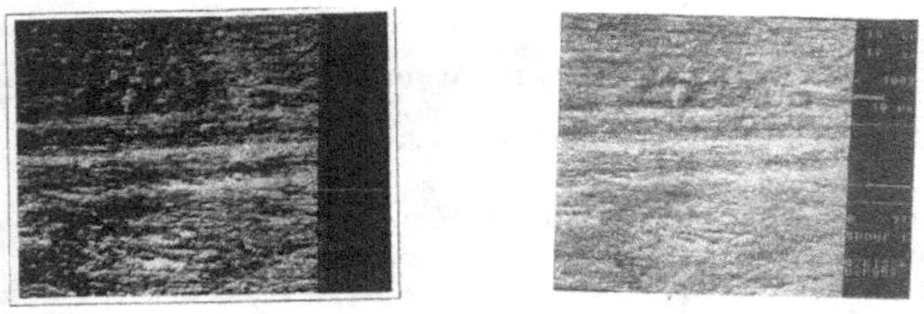

Figure 8: Case 4 - near copy microscope image [Cz/048].

Vertikale Auflösung	5 Å
Horizontale Auflösung	500 Å
Digitale Rauschunterdrückung	möglich
Meßbereich vertikaler Strukturen	100 Å - 655.000 Å

Vertikale Auflösung	5 Å
Horizontale Auflösung	500 Å
Digitale Rauschunterdrückung	möglich
Meßbereich vertikaler Strukturen	100 Å - 655.000 Å

Figure 9: Case 5 - near copy table [Cz/039].

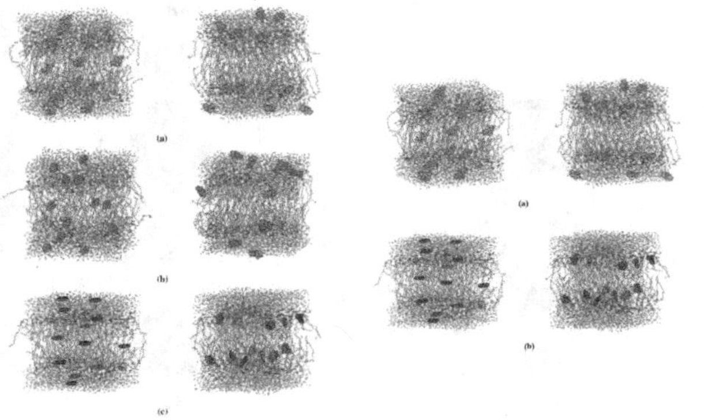

Figure 10: Case 6 - weakly altered illustration [Ry/073].

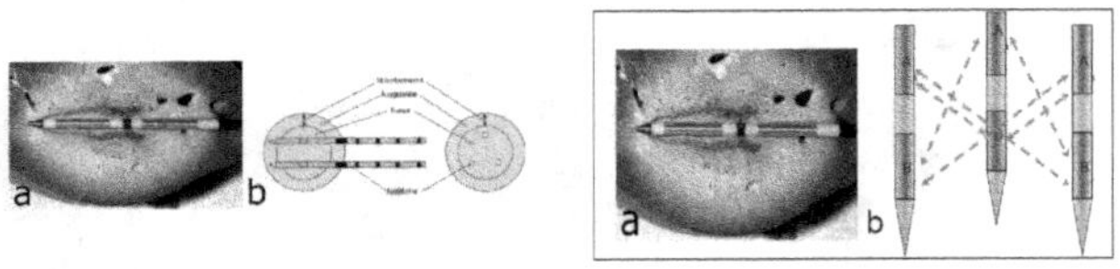

Figure 11: Case 7 - weakly altered illustration [Chh/005].

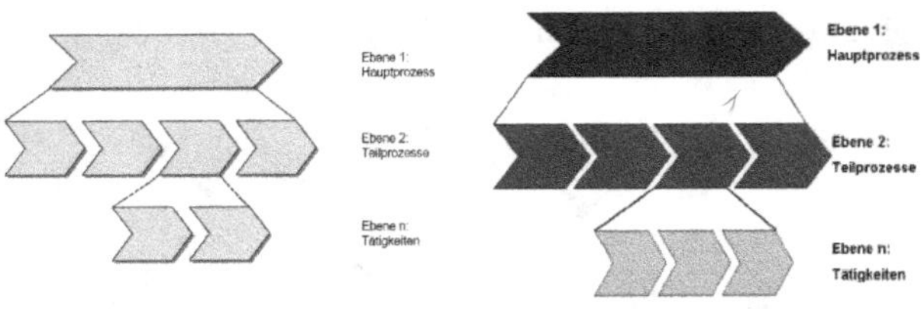

Figure 12: Case 8 - moderately altered figure [Ab/017].

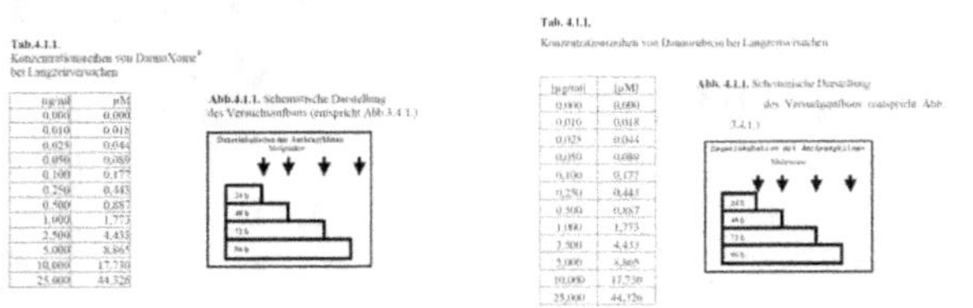

Figure 13: Case 9 - moderately altered table [Jus/029].

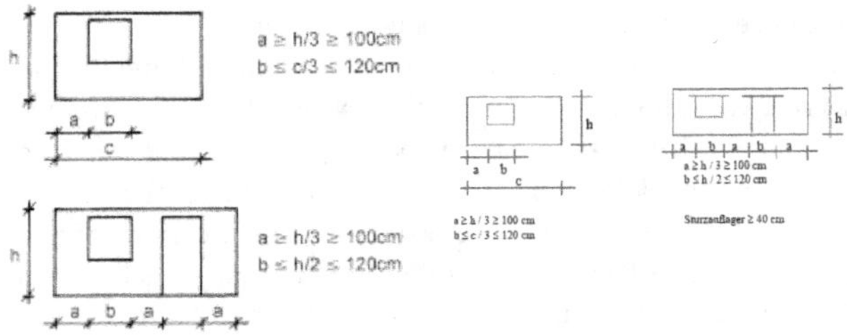

Figure 14: Case 10 - strongly altered sketches [Aos/193].

Figure 15: Case 11 - strongly altered table [Cz/035].

Zelllinie	Verdopplungszeit in der exponentiellen Wachstumsphase
Cado ES-1	ca. 32 Stunden
STA-ET-1	ca. 48 Stunden
STA-ET-2.1	ca. 76 Stunden
VH-64	ca. 20 Stunden

Zelllinie	Verdopplungszeit in der exponentiellen Wachstumsphase
Cado ES-1	ca. 32 Stunden
STA-ET-1	ca. 48 Stunden
STA-ET-2.1	ca. 76 Stunden
VH-64	ca. 20 Stunden

Figure 16: Case 12 - strongly altered table [Jus/022].

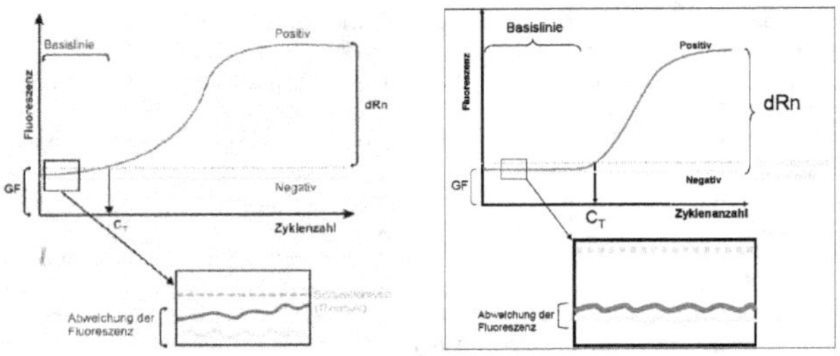

Figure 17: Case 13 - strongly altered line chart [Ad/068].

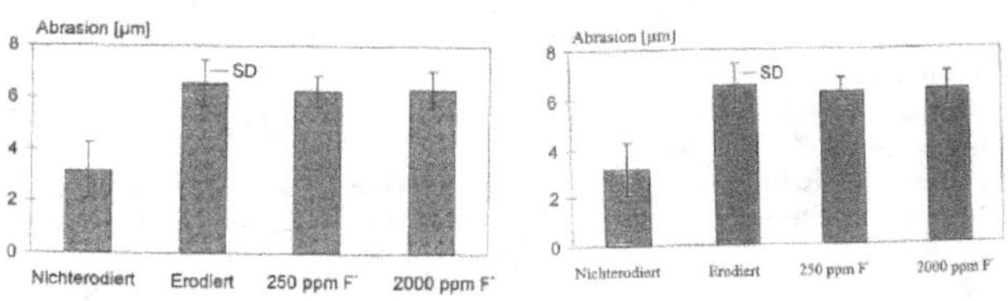

Figure 18: Case 14 - near copy bar chart [Cz/047].

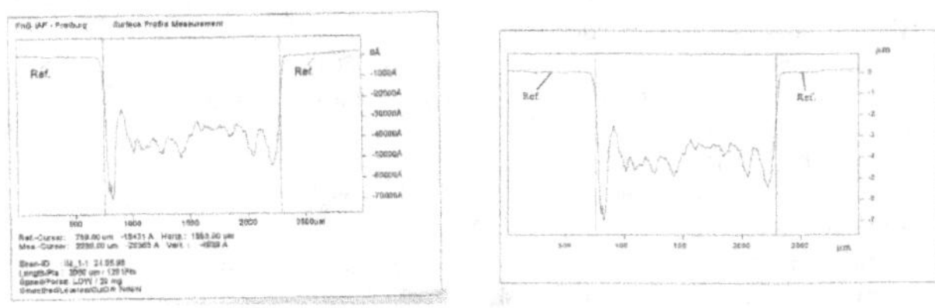

Figure 19: Case 15 - near copy line chart [Cz/044].

Extending Multiple Diagram Navigation with Internal Diagram and Collection Connections

Hisham Benotman
Portland State University
Portland, Oregon
benotman@pdx.edu

David Maier
Portland State University
Portland, Oregon
maier@pdx.edu

ABSTRACT

Multiple diagram navigation (MDN) uses multiple diagrams, maps, or charts to navigate a document collection. To support exploratory search scenarios, MDN provides unconventional overviews for the content and introduces novel navigational queries. In a Diagram-to-Content query, a user clicks on diagram elements to retrieve related collection documents. Diagram-to-Diagram queries allows users to select diagram element(s) to see related elements highlighted in other diagrams. Content-to-Diagram queries highlight diagram elements related to document(s) selected by the user. MDN depends on manually created connections between diagram elements and collection documents. Therefore, only a small portion of the targeted collection might be accessible from the diagrams. In this paper, we extend the domain of MDN diagram-to-content queries to reach related collection documents not directly connected to the diagrams. We focus on Wikipedia as a case study and a class of diagrams with specific characteristics. We exploit the Wikipedia hyperlink graph and internal diagram structures to provide a diagram-influenced ranking of Wikipedia pages. We tested different settings for our ranking algorithm using 12 diagrams from six domains. The results showed the strong influence of diagrams on ranking and reasonably high similarity between diagram elements selected by the user and the top-10-ranked pages.

KEYWORDS

Exploratory Search; Diagrams; Wikipedia; Faceted Search.

ACM Reference Format:
Hisham Benotman and David Maier. 2018. Extending Multiple Diagram Navigation with Internal Diagram and Collection Connections. In *JCDL '18: The 18th ACM/IEEE Joint Conference on Digital Libraries, June 3–7, 2018, Fort Worth, TX, USA.* ACM, New York, NY, USA, Article 4, 4 pages. https://doi.org/10.1145/3197026.3197071

1 INTRODUCTION

Multiple Diagram Navigation (MDN) [3] allows content authors to superimpose different diagrams over a collection, such as Wikipedia, by connecting elements in the diagrams to related documents in the collection. For example, consider the two diagrams in the domain of World languages shown in Figure 1; the top map organizes languages by countries where they are spoken while the bottom forest groups languages by trees and branches. *Visual elements* in the diagrams such as 'Dinka', 'Nilo-Saharan', and 'Zarma' are manually connected to their related *content elements* (Wikipedia pages). These connections are shown as dashed lines in Figure 1.B.

To support exploratory search [9], MDN provides three types of queries using the aforementioned connections. In a *Diagram-to-Content* (D2C) query, a user clicks on element(s) in a diagram to retrieve related page(s). An example of D2C is shown in Fig. 1.A. The opposite query, *Content to Diagram* (C2D) is when a user selects page(s) and sees related elements highlighted in the diagrams. The third query is *Diagram to Diagram* (D2D), where selecting an element in a diagram highlights related elements in other diagrams. These queries can be helpful in exploratory search scenarios [3].

Previous research in digital libraries provided overviews for collections using specific visualization tools such as timelines [2] and maps [7]. By accepting any type of diagram (in SVG or image format), MDN can provide interesting overviews different from those that a visualization tool could induce from a collection. However, MDN currently lacks the ability to access documents not directly connected to the diagrams. Our goal is to access such documents by utilizing internal structures of both diagrams and collections. Our approach depends on collection structures that connect related documents. Examples include hyperlinks and the category hierarchy in Wikipedia; similarity and recommendation connections in online shopping websites; metadata and bibliographic citations in digital libraries; and tags in social-bookmarking websites.

In this paper, we focus on a sub-problem with the following three characteristics: **(1)** We use Wikipedia as a case study. We take advantage of the Wikipedia hyperlink graph and category hierarchy as well as diagram internal connections (both shown as solid lines in Figure 2.B). We chose Wikipedia for its rich internal structures, diverse content, and high likelihood for being a destination for exploratory searchers. **(2)** We focus on MDN D2C queries with a single selected element. We extend the query range to retrieve related Wikipedia pages not directly connected to the diagrams. We also provide a *diagram-influenced ranking*. Since MDN can present different aspects (using multiple diagrams), we can incorporate the user's favored aspect in the ranking process. For example, a user may wish to retrieve languages spoken in the same country ('South Sudan') by clicking on 'Dinka' on the map. On the other hand, selecting 'Dinka' on the forest returns languages in the same tree and branch. **(3)** We study a specific class of diagrams that instantiate a common diagram model. We explain this model in Section 2.

ACM ISBN 978-1-4503-5178-2/18/06...$15.00
https://doi.org/10.1145/3197026.3197071

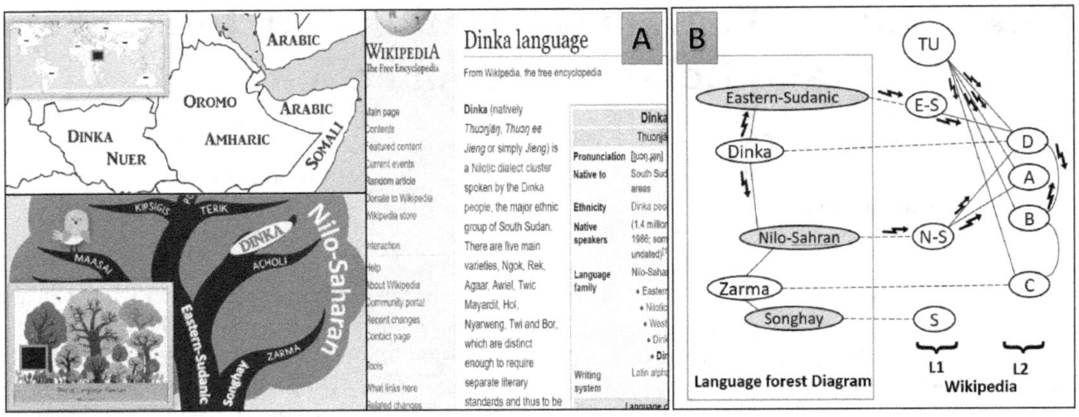

Figure 1: A: a Diagram-to-Content (D2C) query. A user clicks Dinka language in the forest [1]; MDN [3] displays Dinka Wikipedia page. B: Previously used connections between diagrams and Wikipedia [3] in dashed lines. Additional internal diagram and Wikipedia connections used in this paper in solid lines. Electric arrows illustrate energy spreading in the query in part A.

In the following three sections, we introduce our approach to retrieve and rank collection documents. In the last two sections, we report on our experiments to evaluate our approach.

2 ITEMS & ATTRIBUTES DIAGRAM MODEL

Diagrams can present different aspects of a domain by including similar sets of elements (e.g., the diagrams in Fig. 1 share many languages). Providing diagram-influenced ranking in this case is challenging. Two D2C queries from two of these diagrams will access similar sets of Wikipedia pages. Moreover, traversing to related pages is more likely to arrive at the same pages in each query producing similar query results. For these pairs (or groups) of diagrams, we observed that a specific diagram model is common which we term *Items and Attributes* (I&A). In Fig. 1, items represent languages in both diagrams; attributes represent countries in the map and language families in the forest. When multiple diagrams focus on the same items but use different attributes, they can show different perspectives of those items. This model can be observed in different domains. For example, attributes can represent actors, directors, and genres for movies; dates and locations for historic events; ingredients and manufacturers for candy bars. In this paper, we focus on I&A diagrams. In our experiments, we use 12 different diagrams in six different domains[2] [3]. The diagrams span different types, including a geographic map, a timeline, and a subway map.

The I&A model can also be noticed in Wikipedia. Items usually have links to their attributes. This property was noticed and used in Facetedpedia [8], a Wikipedia faceted-search interface. Furthermore, items are usually grouped in categories and lists. For example, there are categories or lists for chocolate bars, world languages, and the American civil war battles. In our ranking algorithm, we direct queries to pages linked by those categories and lists. We call such pages the *Target Universe* (TU). A future implementation can allow a user to change his or her target universe. For example, a user might query languages, countries, or ethnic groups related to languages in the forest shown in Fig. 1.A.

3 ENERGY SPREADING

Energy spreading ES (or *spreading activation* [4]) has been used in information retrieval (IR) since the early 1980s [4]. The ES method represents documents in a collection or terms in a thesaurus as nodes in a graph (or an *associative network* [4]); edges in the graph can represent relationships between the nodes such as bibliographic citations or thesaurus-like relationships [4]. To retrieve related nodes, ES sends energy from a node or nodes of interest and then ranks the relevance of the other graph nodes by the total energy each receives. Recent research has used ES methods on various tasks in IR including movie recommendation [5] and concept relatedness [6]. The latter used the graph of Wikipedia hyperlinks.

To expand the range of MDN queries, we send energy from both an I&A diagram (from the selected item) and from the categories and lists that link to same-type items. We hypothesize that by doing so we can get a diagram-influenced ranking of related items. For example, in Figure 1.B, we send energy from 'Dinka' to 'Nilo-Sahran' and 'Eastern-Sudanic' then to 'N-S' and 'E-S' pages. We also send energy from the list of languages *TU*. We predict that languages in the same language family will get more energy by virtue of their hyperlinks to the energy sources. To simplify our experiments by reducing the number of required diagram-to-Wikipedia connections, we do not send energy directly from diagram items to their Wikipedia pages (e.g., from 'Dinka' to 'D' page in Fig. 1.B).

Links between pages in Wikipedia can be outgoing, incoming, or reciprocal. The latest increases the confidence about the relationship between two pages as each page has an outgoing link to the other. Agirre et. al. [1] reported that using only reciprocal links in Wikipedia increased performance of their work regarding word relatedness and entity disambiguation. In an MDN setting, we think links between items and attributes can be reciprocal or non-reciprocal but reciprocal links should be given some preference. We experimented with giving non-reciprocal links less conductance (i.e., weaken energy sent through non-reciprocal links). When a

[1] Source: http://eurotalk.com/blog/tag/language-family/
[2] The diagrams used in this study can be retrieved from: https://goo.gl/RWzbx9
[3] Permission to use the diagrams has been requested for all diagrams and acquired for some of them.

page p sends its energy e to a page q and p has a non-reciprocal (incoming or outgoing) link to q, page q receives the energy $e * nRcp$. We tested four values for *nRcp*: 1, 0.7, 0.4, and 0. For reciprocal links we used the value 1 for conductance. Notice that *nRcp*= 1 treats reciprocal and non-reciprocal links equally, *nRcp* = 0.7 or 0.4 gives a preference to reciprocal links, and *nRcp* = 0 uses only reciprocal links. We report on this optimization in Section 6.

To compute final node energies (scores) from received energies (REs), we needed a function that rewards nodes with both high REs and a high number of REs (i.e., connectivity to many relevant nodes). Averaging REs, for example, does not reward high number of REs. For example, consider the nodes a and b with REs $(1, 1)$ and $(1, 1, 0.7)$, respectively. Averaging REs results in node a having a higher energy than b even though b has an additional RE. Summing on the other hand can reward nodes with low REs. Consider node c having 21 REs with each equal to 0.1. Summing REs ranks node c higher than node a even though c is only connected to marginal nodes. To overcome this problem, we introduce *Series Adjusted Summation* (SAS). We use a decreasing series such as the geometric series $S1 = \{\frac{1}{2}, \frac{1}{4}, \frac{1}{8}, ..., \frac{1}{2}^{20}\}$. For a list of received energies $LRE = (e_1, e_2, ..., e_n)$, where LRE is in a non-increasing order, and a decreasing series $S = (t_1, t_2, ..., t_n)$, $SAS(LRE, S) = e_1 * t_1 + e_2 * t_2 + ... + e_n * t_n$. SAS discounts low REs by multiplying them with the small terms in the series tail. We truncate the SAS computation after some point n (loss of precision is relatively low given that tails of both S and LRE contain relatively smaller numbers). Using $S1$ in the previous example yields the ranking: b, a, then c, with scores 0.84, 0.75, and 0.1, respectively. This ranking is a better estimate of the connectivity to relevant nodes in our view. We can tune the computation of SAS by using different series. For example, using $S1$ leads to only the top REs to have a significant effect on the node energy. However, using a gradually declining series $S3 = (\frac{20}{210}, \frac{19}{210}, \frac{18}{210}, ..., \frac{1}{210})$ distributes the effect over more REs. For an intermediate behavior we can use S2, where each term in $S2$ is the average of the terms at the same position in both $S1$ and $S3$. We evaluate the differences of using these three series in our experiments.

4 D2C-QUERY RANKING ALGORITHM

Inputs: **(1)** A diagram with items and attributes, each item is connected to one or more attributes. **(2)** Connections between Wikipedia pages and the diagram's attributes. **(3)** A set *CL* of category or list pages that link to items. **(4)** Selected item r. **(5)** Greediness factor F (described later). **(6)** A decreasing series S. **(7)** A non-reciprocal link conductance *nRcp*.

Output: A list of Wikipedia pages ranked by their relevance to r.

Preparation: **(1)** Represent (or combine) the set *CL* as one page *TU* (Target Universe) that links to all items. Remove duplicate hyperlinks to the same item. **(2)** Level one ($L1$) contains the *TU* and all attribute pages while level two ($L2$) contains the item pages. **(3)** $\forall p_2 \in L2$, keep a list of size 15. The list keeps the highest 15 energies received by each node sorted in a non-increasing order (new received energies may lead lowest energies to be removed from the tail of the list). This list is used in SAS. The size 15 was considered sufficient in early experiments.

Steps:

(1) Send full energy from the selected item r to its attributes in the diagram; the same energy propagates to the attribute pages. Also, assign full energy to *TU*. For example, in Figure 1.B, the *TU*, 'E-S' and 'N-S' pages are assigned full energy. Note that SAS is not used in this step.
(2) $\forall p_1 \in L1, \forall p_2 \in L2, p_1$ energy is e, and p_1 has a link k to p_2, if k is reciprocal then p_2 receives the energy $e * 1$, otherwise p_2 receives the energy $e * nRcp$.
(3) $\forall p \in L2$, compute (temporary) p energy from received energies using the SAS method described in Section 3.
(4) Sort the nodes in $L2$ in a non-increasing order by their temporary energies.
(5) For efficient energy spreading in $L2$, we used a greedy approach to process only the pages with high energies in $L2$ (save time by limiting the number of pages we process in $L2$). We compute *Threshold* = $F*$ highest node energy in $L2$. Only $L2$ pages with energies $\geq$ Threshold can send and receive energy. For example, Assuming $F = 0.9$ and page D in Figure 1.B has the highest energy in $L2$, then D could exchange (send and receive) energy with node B. However, pages B and C had energies below Threshold and therefore no energy exchange was done between them. In our experiment, we tested three values for F: 1.1, 0.9, and 0.75. Using $F = 1.1$ means that no energy exchange happens in $L2$; energy only spreads from $L1$ to $L2$. Using $F = 0.9$ allows fewer pages in $L2$ to exchange energies (relative to $F = 0.75$).
(6) $\forall p \in L2$, compute final energy at p from received energies using the SAS method.
(7) Sort $L2$ pages in a non-increasing order and return the list as the query result.

5 EVALUATION METHOD

We conducted an experiment to find answers to the following questions: **(RQ1)** Does our algorithm return pages (items) similar to a selected diagram item? **(RQ2)** Is the ranking influenced by the diagram used in the query? **(RQ3)** What are the best choices for the parameters *nRcp*, F, and S (the series used in the SAS computation)?

We used 12 diagrams in six domains (chocolate bars, American civil war battles, world languages, database platforms, cheeses, and cars) with two diagrams in each domain. We ran approximately 20 queries in each domain (10 for each diagram). For the most part, we used items that exist in the two diagrams to compare how diagrams influence the ranking process. We chose the selected item randomly and made sure the selected items activate different sets of attributes. For each query, we ran the ranking algorithm 36 times using 36 settings (all combinations for four *nRcp* values (1, 0.7, 0.4, and 0), three series ($S1$, $S2$, and $S3$), and three F values (1.1, 0.9, and 0.75).

The used lists and categories linked to the following numbers of items: 140 chocolate bars, 385 Civil War battles, 211 database platforms, 1243 World languages, 620 cheeses, and 1100 cars. To get only items whose type matches the items in the diagrams, we used CSS selectors to extract hyperlinks from specific parts of the list and category pages. However, hyperlinks to few odd pages (e.g., regions and ethnic groups related to languages) were also retrieved which negatively affected the ranking precision.

For the Wikipedia hyperlink graph, we extracted hyperlinks (graph edges) from Wikipedia pages and stored these edges in a

Ranking w. lang_forest	lbl	Ranking w. lang_map	lbl
Nuer	1	Dinka	1
Dinka	1	Nuer	1
Niger_Congo	3	Arabic	1
Maasai	1	Bari	1
Kuliak	1	English	1
Teso	1	Swahili	1
Murle	1	Zande	1
Luo_dialect	1	Murle	1
Meroitic	2	Lingua_frnc.	3
Luo	1	Spanish	1

Table 1: Top 10 Wikipedia pages with similarity ratings when selecting Dinka language on the forest (left) vs. the map (right). Pages were quite similar based on the used diagram; languages in the same family (left) vs. languages spoken in the same country (right).

MYSQL table for subsequent experiments. We discarded hyperlinks in templates (tables of hyperlinks usually placed in the bottom of Wikipedia articles). Templates can shift the topic of a page to a broader subject. For example, a chocolate bar page may include a manufacturer template with manufacturer-specific hyperlinks. In such cases only one hyperlink to the manufacturer is included. If the same template was found in the manufacturer page then all hyperlinks in the template are included.

A CS graduate student labeled the top ten pages for each query-setting using the following rating scale: 1 for a result similar to the selected item, 2 for a slightly similar result, and 3 for a dissimilar result. For example, in the query in Fig. 1.A, languages in the same branch (e.g., 'Eastern-Sudanic') as the selected language are considered similar, languages in the same tree are slightly similar, and languages in different trees are dissimilar. The first author reviewed the labeled data and discussed conflicts to reach an agreement.

Srs	nRcp	F	Rtng	Srs	nRcp	F	Rtng	Srs	nRcp	F	Rtng	Srs	nRcp	F	Rtng
2	0.7	0.9	1.23	3	0.7	0.75	1.25	3	1	0.9	1.39	2	0	0.9	1.55
3	0.4	0.75	1.23	1	0.4	0.75	1.27	2	1	0.9	1.40	3	0	0.75	1.55
3	0.7	0.9	1.24	1	0.4	0.9	1.27	3	1	0.75	1.40	3	0	0.9	1.55
3	0.4	0.9	1.24	3	0.7	1.1	1.27	1	1	0.9	1.40	2	0	0.75	1.55
1	0.7	0.9	1.24	2	0.7	1.1	1.28	1	1	0.75	1.40	1	0	0.9	1.56
1	0.7	0.75	1.24	3	0.4	1.1	1.28	2	1	0.75	1.42	1	0	0.75	1.56
2	0.7	0.75	1.24	1	0.4	1.1	1.28	1	1	1.1	1.49	1	0	1.1	1.61
2	0.4	0.75	1.25	1	0.7	1.1	1.28	2	1	1.1	1.49	2	0	1.1	1.61
2	0.4	0.9	1.25	2	0.4	1.1	1.28	3	1	1.1	1.49	3	0	1.1	1.61

Table 2: Avg. similarity rating (per setting) for top 10 pages in all queries. Parameters: Series (Srs), non-reciprocal-link conductance (nRcp), greediness factor (F), and avg. rating (Rtng) (1 to 3). Sorted by Rtng. A moderate decrease of nRcp (0.7 or 0.4) had the best performance (Rtng close to 1).

6 RESULTS AND DISCUSSION

RQ1: Table 2 shows the average similarity rating (Rtng) per setting computed for the top 10 pages returned from all queries on all diagrams. In Table 3.A, we show the same average for only the best setting in Table 2, ($S2$, 0.7, 0.90) computed for each diagram. In general, similarity rating was fairly good; based on the diagram used, the top 10 pages were mostly similar to the selected element.

RQ3: In Table 2, the first 18 settings (the best group) used $nRcp$ = 0.7 or 0.4 with $1.23 \leq Rtng \leq 1.28$. The second group used $nRcp$ = 1 (9 settings) with worse $Rtng$ (1.39 to 1.49). The group with worst performance used $nRcp = 0$ (i.e. use only reciprocal links) with $Rtng$ between 1.55 and 1.61. These differences based on $nRcp$ indicate that for A&I diagrams, both reciprocal and non-reciprocal links should be used but with some preference for reciprocal links. In all of the three groups, energy spreading in $L2$ (F = 0.9 or 0.75) had a slight positive effect on $Rtng$ compared to spreading energy only from $L1$ to $L2$ (F = 1.1). In addition, processing more nodes in $L2$ (F = 0.75) did not enhance $Rtng$ indicating that greediness reduced execution time without harming the ranking. Using different series ($S1$, $S2$, and $S3$) did not have a large impact.

Domain_diagram	A	B
Car_make	1.01	158
Cheese_map	1.07	169
Civilwar_timeLine	1.09	70
Chocolate_company	1.10	39
Language_map	1.10	102
Cheese_animalMilk	1.13	97
Civilwar_map	1.22	106
Language_forest	1.27	90
Database_features	1.38	65
Database_model	1.38	68
Car_size	1.47	219
Chocolate_ingredient	1.52	36

Table 3: Col. A: avg. similarity rating for top 10 pages per domain-diagram using the top setting in Table 2. Col. B: given top 10 pages when selecting an item on the diagram in the left col., we show avg. position of those 10 pages if the same item was selected in the other diagram. Avg=5.5 means top 10 pages were the same using the two diagrams.

RQ2: Table 1 shows an example of the different rankings returned when selecting the same element ('Dinka') in each diagram shown in Fig. 1.A. The two rankings were influenced by the diagram used as they contained mostly different languages. To provide an overview of the influence of diagrams on ranking in all domains, we used the best setting ($S2$, 0.7, 0.90) to compute the following. For a query (e.g., selecting 'Dinka' on the forest) we retrieved the top 10 pages and computed their average position when selecting the same element in the other diagram (e.g., selecting 'Dinka' on the map). Getting an average close to 5.5 means that both diagrams had similar pages in the top 10 and therefore diagrams had little or no influence on ranking. However, the high numbers shown in column B in Table 3 (average of averages for all queries) indicate that A&I diagrams had a strong impact on the ranking process.

REFERENCES

[1] Eneko Agirre, Ander Barrena, and Aitor Soroa. 2015. Studying the wikipedia hyperlink graph for relatedness and disambiguation. *arXiv preprint arXiv:1503.01655* (2015).

[2] Omar Alonso, Ricardo Baeza-Yates, and Michael Gertz. 2007. Exploratory search using timelines. In *SIGCHI 2007 Workshop on Exploratory Search and HCI Workshop*. 1–4.

[3] Hisham Benotman, Lois ML Delcambre, and David Maier. 2016. Multiple diagram navigation (MDN). In *Proceedings of the Third International Workshop on Exploratory Search in Databases and the Web*. ACM, 19–24.

[4] Fabio Crestani. 1997. Application of spreading activation techniques in information retrieval. *Artificial Intelligence Review* 11, 6 (1997), 453–482.

[5] Lubos Demovic, Eduard Fritscher, Jakub Kriz, Ondrej Kuzmik, Ondrej Proksa, Diana Vandlikova, Dusan Zelenik, and Maria Bielikova. 2013. Movie recommendation based on graph traversal algorithms. In *Database and Expert Systems Applications (DEXA), 2013 24th International Workshop on*. IEEE, 152–156.

[6] Stephan Gouws, GJ Rooyen, and Herman A Engelbrecht. 2010. Measuring conceptual similarity by spreading activation over Wikipedia's hyperlink structure. In *Proceedings of the 2nd Workshop on The People's Web Meets NLP: Collaboratively Constructed Semantic Resources*. 46–54.

[7] Mark Hall and Paul Clough. 2013. Exploring large digital library collections using a map-based visualisation. In *Research and Advanced Technology for Digital Libraries*. Springer, 216–227.

[8] Chengkai Li, Ning Yan, Senjuti B Roy, Lekhendro Lisham, and Gautam Das. 2010. Facetedpedia: dynamic generation of query-dependent faceted interfaces for wikipedia. In *Proceedings of the 19th international conference on World wide web*. ACM, 651–660.

[9] Gary Marchionini. 2006. Exploratory Search: From Finding to Understanding. *Commun. ACM* 49, 4 (April 2006), 41–46. https://doi.org/10.1145/1121949.1121979

Evaluation of Conformance Checkers for Long-Term Preservation of Multimedia Documents

Nicola Ferro
University of Padua, Italy
ferro@dei.unipd.it

Gianmaria Silvello
University of Padua, Italy
silvello@dei.unipd.it

Erik Buelinckx
Royal Institute for Cultural Heritage
KIK-IRPA, Belgium
erik.buelinckx@kikirpa.be

Boris Doubrov
Dual Lab, Belgium
boris.doubrov@duallab.com

Antonella Fresa
Promoter, Italy
fresa@promoter.it

Magnus Geber
Swedish National Archives
Riksarkivet, Sweden
magnus.geber@riksarkivet.se

Klas Jadeglans
Swedish National Archives
Riksarkivet, Sweden
klas.jadeglans@riksarkivet.se

Börje Justrell
Swedish National Archives
Riksarkivet, Sweden
borje.justrell@riksarkivet.se

Bert Lemmens
Center of Expertise in Digital
Heritage, PACKED, Belgium
bert@packed.be

Jerôme Martinez
MediaArea, France
jerome@mediaarea.net

Víctor Muñoz
Easy Innova, Spain
victormunoz@easyinnova.com

Sònia Oliveras
Records Management, Archives and
Publications Service
Girona City Council, Spain
soliveras@ajgirona.cat

Claudio Prandoni
Aedeka, Italy
prandoni@aedeka.com

Dave Rice
MediaArea, France
dave@dericed.com

Stefan Rohde-Enslin
Institute for Museum Research
Prussian Cultural Heritage
Foundation, SPK, Germany
s.rohde-enslin@smb.spk-berlin.de

Xavi Tarrés
Easy Innova, Spain
xavitarres@easyinnova.com

Erwin Verbruggen
Sound and Vision, The Netherlands
everbruggen@beeldengeluid.nl

Benjamin Yousefi
Swedish National Archives
Riksarkivet, Sweden
Benjamin.Yousefi@riksarkivet.se

Carl Wilson
Open Preservation Foundation, UK
carl@openpreservation.org

ABSTRACT

We develop an evaluation framework for the validation of conformance checkers for the long-term preservation. The framework assesses the correctness, usability, and usefulness of the tools for three media types: PDF/A (text), TIFF (image), and Matroska (audio/video). Finally, we report the results of the validation of these conformance checkers using the proposed framework. In general, the presented framework is a high-level tool that can be quite easily employed in other preservation related tasks.

CCS CONCEPTS

• **Information systems → Digital libraries and archives**;

KEYWORDS

long-term preservation, conformance checking, evaluation

ACM Reference Format:
Nicola Ferro, Gianmaria Silvello, Erik Buelinckx, Boris Doubrov, Antonella Fresa, Magnus Geber, Klas Jadeglans, Börje Justrell, Bert Lemmens, Jerôme

JCDL '18, June 3–7, 2018, Fort Worth, TX, USA

ACM ISBN 978-1-4503-5178-2/18/06...$15.00
https://doi.org/10.1145/3197026.3197037

Martinez, Víctor Muñoz, Sònia Oliveras, Claudio Prandoni, Dave Rice, Stefan Rohde-Enslin, Xavi Tarrés, Erwin Verbruggen, Benjamin Yousefi, and Carl Wilson. 2018. Evaluation of Conformance Checkers for Long-Term Preservation of Multimedia Documents. In *JCDL '18: The 18th ACM/IEEE Joint Conference on Digital Libraries, June 3–7, 2018, Fort Worth, TX, USA*. ACM, New York, NY, USA, 10 pages. https://doi.org/10.1145/3197026.3197037

1 INTRODUCTION

"Digital preservation is about more than keeping the bits [...] It is about maintaining the semantic meaning of the digital object and its content, about maintaining its provenance and authenticity, about retaining its interrelatedness, and about securing information about the context of its creation and use" [28, p. 45]. Since preservation aims at capturing the very essence of digital objects it is often associated with life cycles [27], preservation actions, and overall preservation frameworks and there is often the need to evaluate them and choose among them [3, 4, 19].

Memory institutions, in Europe and elsewhere, are facing a situation when transfers of electronic documents or other electronic media content for long term preservation are continuously increasing. Data are normally stored in specific file formats for documents, images, sound, video etc. that are produced by software from third-party providers controlled neither by the institution that produces the files, nor by the one holding the archive. There is a risk that data objects meant for preservation, passing through an uncontrolled generative process, can put at risk the whole preservation exercise.

PREFORMA[1] is an EU co-funded *Pre-Commercial Procurement (PCP)* project, whose main objective is to give memory institutions full control of the process for testing the conformity of files to be ingested into their archives for long-term preservation.

PCP operates by clustering together stakeholders in a given domain – memory institutions in our case – which group together in order to face a common technological challenge. The stakeholders consortium is in charge of describing the expected technological solution, specifying its needed features and characteristics, and defining how alternative approaches will be compared and assessed in order to understand their pros and cons. The consortium is responsible for monitoring the progress of the suppliers work towards the first product testing and for evaluating the final solution developed by the suppliers in order to understand which one best fits with their actual needs.

The main objective of PREFORMA is the development and deployment of an open source software licensed reference implementation for file format standards aimed for any memory institution (or other organisation with a preservation task) wishing to check conformance with a specific standard. This reference implementation, called the *conformance checker* consists of a set of modular tools which, in this paper, we validate against specific implementations of specifications of standards relevant to memory institutions for preserving their different kind of data objects.

A conformance checker:

- verifies whether a file has been produced according to the specifications of a standard file format, and hence,
- verifies whether a file matches the acceptance criteria for long-term preservation by the memory institution,
- reports in human and machine readable format which properties deviate from the standard specification and acceptance criteria, and
- performs automated fixes for simple deviations in the metadata of the preservation file.

The conformance checker software developed by PREFORMA is intended for use within the *Open Archival Information System (OAIS)* Reference Framework [22] and development is guided by the user requirements provided by the memory institutions that are part of the PREFORMA consortium. The conformance checker facilitates memory institutions to obtain sufficient control of the information in an OAIS Archive, provided to the level needed to ensure long-term preservation [33]. In particular, the conformance check enables implementation of the following OAIS functions [33]: *Quality assurance* at ingestion, validating the successful transfer of the *Submission Information Package (SIP)* to the temporary storage area; *Generate AIP* at ingestion, transforming one or more SIPs into one or more *Archival Information Packages (AIPs)* that conform to the Archive's data formatting standards and documentation standards; and, *Archival Information Update* at ingestion, providing a mechanism for updating (repackaging, transformation) the contents of the Archive.

The media types addressed by PREFORMA are: (i) *text* for establishing a reference implementation for PDF/A [23–25]; (ii) *images* for establishing a reference implementation for uncompressed TIFF [20, 21]; and, (iii) *audio-video* for establishing a reference implementation for an audiovisual preservation file, using FFV1, [2] Dirac [3] or JPEG2000 [26] for encoding video or moving image, uncompressed LPCM [18] for encoding sound and MKV [4] or OGG [5] for wrapping audio- and video-streams in one file.

This paper described the evaluation framework which has been developed for validating the PREFORMA conformance checkers. It consists of three phases: the first one is quantitative and system-oriented: the second one is qualitative and focuses on usability; and, the third one is also qualitative and targets usefulness.

The paper is organized as follows: Section 2 discusses related works; Section 3 describes our evaluation framework; Section 4 introduces the experimental collections we have developed; Section 5 presents the results of the three phases of the evaluation applied to the conformance checkers developed in PREFORMA; finally, Section 6 draws some conclusions and outlooks future work.

2 RELATED WORK

The idea of benchmarking tools for preservation is gaining more and more traction recently [7] and we share a similar approach with [9], who identify the main components of a digital preservation benchmark as:

- *motivating comparison* defines the comparison to be done and the benefits that comparison will bring in terms of the future research agenda;
- *task sample* is a list of tests that the subject, to which a benchmark is applied, is expected to solve;

[1] http://www.preforma-project.eu/

[2] http://www.ffmpeg.org/~michael/ffv1.html

[3] http://diracvideo.org/

[4] http://www.matroska.org/

[5] https://xiph.org/ogg/

- *performance measures* are qualitative or quantitative measurements taken by a human or a machine to calculate how fit the subject is for the task.

Creating a benchmark for complex tasks as long-term preservation, is expensive and requires to overcome multiple issues as highlighted by [10] for evaluating text extraction tools; they pointed out that the lack of proper datasets and related ground truth is the main obstacle for evaluating these tools. The construction of an experimental collection for these tasks is difficult because of the complex input space and the costs related to ground truth creation. Hence, [10] opted for developing a completely synthetic dataset, whereas we develop an experimental collection which follows the main principles of the Cranfield framework as [10] does, but it is composed of both real and synthetic files. Moreover, we extend this framework by adding two more phases to better assess usability and usefulness aspects of the evaluated tools.

In [6] the main scope of the PREFORMA project was described along with the challenges that it has to overcame to carry out the selection of three conformance checkers for text, images and audio/video. In [12], the selection process and methodology has been described as well as the main ideas for evaluating the selected tools; in particular, the evaluation as a classification task was defined in that paper, but there are no details about the overall evaluation framework composed of the three phases and the experimental results we describe and discuss in this paper.

3 EVALUATION FRAMEWORK

The framework we adopted to evaluate the conformance checkers is composed of three phases as summarized in Figure 1; each phase evaluates a different aspect of the conformance checkers: *correctness*, *usability* and *usefulness*. This framework is inspired by the triptych model [17] proposed to evaluate digital libraries where performance, usability and usefulness are evaluated holistically by considering systems, content and users. This framework can be also a further means to augment the reproducibility of the evaluated tools [13], the possibility to cite the data produced by the tools and by the evaluation process [30] and their overall quality in the broader context of the digital library quality model [11, 15].

The evaluation framework is built around a close collaboration between technical and domain experts and each evaluation phase instructs, in a continuous feedback fashion, the developers which improve the tools and address the detected issues.

3.1 Phase 1: Correctness

The first phase evaluates the correctness of the conformance checkers and it is aimed at understanding if these softwares respect the respective standards for long-term preservation, as described in [12] we briefly summarize here. Hence, the focus is on the systems and we relied on a Cranfield-like methodology [8]. The Cranfield paradigm makes use of experimental collections composed of a collection of documents of interest, a set of topics and a ground-truth which, given a document in the collection and a topic, determines the relevance of the document with respect to the considered topic.

We instantiate the Cranfield-based evaluation as a classification task, where we consider a set of classes, say C, as topics and the ground-truth is given by the correct labels assigned to each document for a given class [29]. Since the goal of the conformance checkers is to validate documents against their respective standards, we can determine, for each document, whether it is compliant, it suffers from issue 1, issue 2, and so on. Therefore, documents are labeled according to their characteristics and each label (compliant, issue 1, issue 2, ...) is a class C_i, representing the conformance of or an issue with a document.

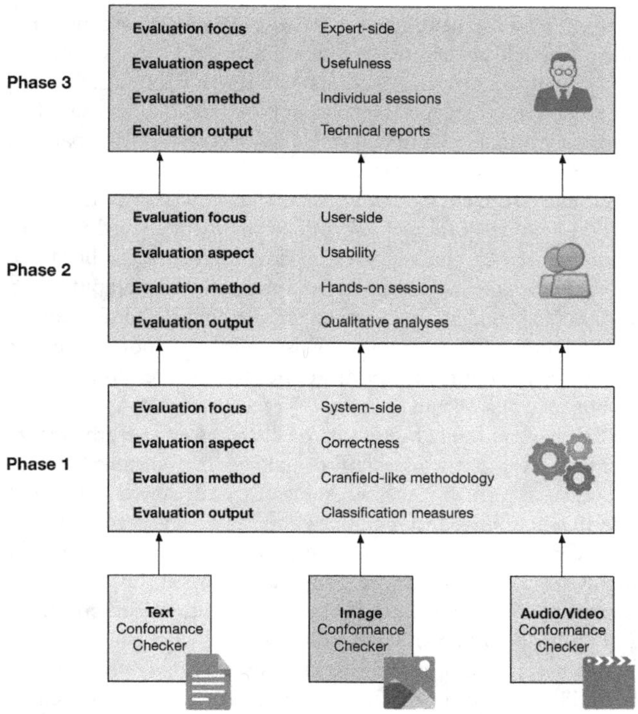

Figure 1: The evaluation framework capturing three aspects of the conformance checkers: correctness, usability and usefulness.

In general, classes may intersect, since a document may suffer from multiple issues at the same time, but the compliant class must be a separate one, since you cannot have documents that are compliant and not compliant at the same time.

In terms of the approach proposed by [9], we have that: the *motivating comparison* is given by the need of assessing conformance checkers; the *task sample* is defined by the identified classes $C_i \in C$, the gathered documents, and the ground-truth.

The preparation of the collection of documents to be used for assessing the performances of a conformance checker is a critical task that needs to be driven by domain experts. Documents must be representative of the different classes C_i against which we need to evaluate conformance checkers. In particular, we cannot have empty classes, i.e. classes without documents in the experimental collection, and the cardinality of each class, i.e. the number of documents belonging to that class, should make sense from two points of view. Firstly, it should have a size, relative to the other classes, which is proportional to the frequency of the issue represented by the class in real world settings; in other terms, there are issues that happen more frequently and there are issues which are more rare and this should be reflected by the cardinality of the classes, in order to confront conformance checkers with realistic settings. Secondly, we should not introduce any bias in the evaluation measurement and process due to an uncontrolled and excessive discrepancy in the cardinality of the classes.

Ground-truth creation is a demanding activity since it requires a great amount of human effort to be conducted. For this reason, a lot of research concentrated on how to reduce the burden of ground-truth creation ranging from the utopian attempt to eliminate assessments at all [31] to crowdsourcing [1]. Unfortunately, in the context of reference, crowdsourcing it is not a viable option since real domain experts are needed to carefully judge the compliance of a document to its reference standard.

Two issues need to be considered during ground-truth creation. The first one is that, to assess the compliance of a document, domain experts will probably also use some of the already existing tools and this may introduce circularity and bias. The second issue is to understand inter-assessor agreement and see whether on this highly specialised task it will have similar ratios as those for ad-hoc retrieval [34], i.e. in the range 30%–50%, or whether discrepancies from previously known tasks will arise.

Evaluating conformance checkers is not a binary process, i.e. it is not like going through a long check-list and if any of the items in the list is missing or incorrect, the conformance checker is rejected. Indeed, we quantified the extent a conformance checker is able to spot deviations from its reference standard.

Considering that we frame conformance checking as a classification task, it becomes natural to evaluate it according to the confusion matrix [32]. In our context each class C_i represents a possible mis-conformance with respect to a reference standard with the sole exception of the class C_0 which represents documents fully conforming to the standard. Thus, we define as *True Positve (TP)* the set of documents that a conformance checker has correctly labeled as belonging to class C_i; *True Negative (TN)* as the set of documents correctly labeled as not belonging to class C_i; *False Positive (FP)* as the set of documents incorrectly labeled as belonging to class C_i; and, *False Negative (FN)* as the set of documents incorrectly labeled as not belonging to class C_i.

Note that the meaning of the confusion matrix changes when considering C_0 – the class of compliant documents – or a generic C_i, $i \neq 0$, i.e. a class representing an issue within a document. In the case of C_0, TP_0 is the set of compliant documents correctly identified as compliant; TN_0 is the set of not compliant documents correctly identified as not compliant; FP_0 is the set of not compliant documents incorrectly identified as compliant; and, FN_0 is the set of compliant documents incorrectly identified as not compliant. In the case of C_i, $i \neq 0$, TP_i is the set of not compliant documents because of issue i correctly identified as suffering from issue i; TN_i is the set of documents correctly identified as not suffering from issue i; FP_i is the set of documents incorrectly identified as suffering from issue i; FN_i is the set of not compliant documents because of issue i, but incorrectly identified as not suffering from issue i.

Note that the impact of FP and FN is different in the case we are considering C_0 or a generic C_i, $i \neq 0$. In the case of C_0, FPs are the worst error for a conformance checker, since they are not conforming documents marked as compliant and thus allowed to proceed in the preservation chain, possibly causing issues in the long term; on the other hand, FNs are a less sever error, since they are compliant documents marked as not compliant which will require some additional work for further checks and fixes (actually not necessary) but, eventually, they will have a chance to go ahead in the preservation chain.

Therefore, we rely on two main evaluation measures able both to give a general account of conformance checkers performances and to deal with this duality between FNs and FPs: *Accuracy* and *Area under the curve (AUC)*.

Accuracy measures the overall effectiveness [32] of a conformance checker as

$$\text{Accuracy}_i = \frac{|TP_i| + |TN_i|}{|TP_i| + |TN_i| + |FP_i| + |FN_i|} \tag{1}$$

AUC measures the ability of a conformance checker to avoid false classification [32] as

$$\text{AUC}_i = \frac{1}{2}\left(\frac{|TP_i|}{|TP_i| + |FN_i|} + \frac{|TN_i|}{|TN_i| + |FP_i|}\right) \tag{2}$$

In order to obtain a single score for each conformance checker across all the categories C_i, we use a *macro-averaging* approach [29], which computes the arithmetic mean of the above measures over all the categories C_i.

Moreover, since a document cannot be compliant and not compliant at the same time, the class C_0 of the compliant documents must be separate from any other class C_i representing a possible issue of a document, i.e. $C_0 \cap C_i = \emptyset \, \forall i, \, i \neq 0$.

Therefore, we can introduce an additional overall performance measure, called *consistency*, which assesses the ability of a conformance checker to adhere to the above constraint of separation of C_0 from the other classes:

$$\text{Consistency}_i = 1 - \frac{|C_0 \cap C_i|}{|C_i|} \tag{3}$$

Note that consistency is different from the evaluation measures typically used in classification or clustering and serves the specific purpose of assessing the degree of separation between the compliant and not-compliant classes. This measure has been extensively used as a tool for refining the experimental collection while building it as we discuss below.

3.2 Phase 2: Usability

The second phase evaluates the usability of the conformance checkers. These tools are thought for memory institutions where domain experts have to decide if a given document – i.e. a text document, an image or an audio/video file – is compliant with the current standards for long-term preservation. To this end, usability is evaluated by means of user studies/focus groups with domain experts from different memory institutions.

The user studies have the form of hands-on sessions where the conformance checkers are described to the domain experts in order to get them to know the basic functionalities and how they work. In a second phase, the experts are divided into groups, usually one per conformance checker, and are asked to download, install and use the softwares by testing some files from their institutions. The files to be tested are selected by the experts themselves and so the hands-on session organizers have no control over the files to be tested; this guarantees that the user studies are unbiased and as close as possible to a real-world work scenario.

The usability of the conformance checkers is evaluated by assessing specific functionalities of the tools such as installation complexity, user interface, interpretation of the results, documentation and difference between desktop and web-based version of the checkers. Furthermore, after the use on the tools, other aspects such as the potential for innovation, ease of use, scalability, extensibility and interoperability are assessed by the domain experts.

The participants to the user studies are asked to compile questionnaires composed of several questions to be answered with a number from 1 (very poor) and 5 (very good) and other questions requiring a short textual answer.

3.3 Phase 3: Usefulness

The third phase is carried out by an evaluation committee composed of selected domain and technical experts that assess the final version of the conformance checkers. Moreover, the developers of the conformance checkers produce a final report where the results of the evaluation and all the fixes and improvements required by the experts are described.

The domain experts collect the files provided by some selected external institutions and validate them with the right conformance checker. Then, they verify if any issue arise and assess the XML and HTML report produced by the tool. Finally, they write a report describing the weaknesses of the tested tool, which is then used by the developers to improve their product. The technical experts verify if the tool compiles and can be used with different operating systems, if the installation process prompts any problems as well as if the validation process works correctly. At the end, they also produce a report describing possible problems to be fixed.

The report written by the developers comprises considerations about the files used for testing, the improvements made during the evaluation phases, the innovative aspects of the tools with respect to other existing tools, standardization efforts, dissemination activities, the partaken open-source approach, future plans for improvements and additional information, if any.

This evaluation phase allows us to further review the conformance checkers, to improve and fix some remaining issues and to produce a thorough documentation to be used as reference for future developments of the tools also by third-party agents.

4 EXPERIMENTAL COLLECTIONS

We created three shared and publicly available experimental collections, one for each media type targeted by PREFORMA, based on the Cranfield framework – i.e. a corpus of documents, a set of test classes of conformance and a ground truth created by experts.

The experimental collections we defined have a two-fold goal: *training*: the collections are used as a development tool to check the conformance checker functionalities while they are under construction in order to get immediate feedback and correct the issues that may arise; *testing*: the collections are used to evaluate the correctness of the checkers by a third-party organization not involved in their development, thus providing an unbiased assessment of the tools.

4.1 Corpora

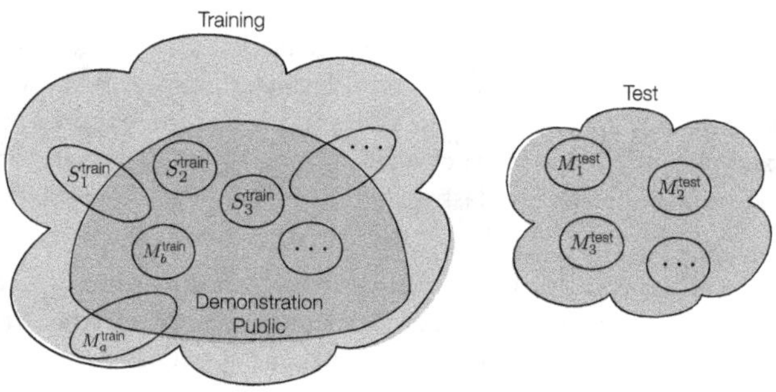

Figure 2: The training and test document corpora.

Figure 2 shows the structure of the document corpora we defined and made available for the development and the evaluation of the conformance checkers. The main distinction is between:

- *training dataset*: aimed at driving and facilitating the design and development of the conformance checkers, as well as show casing their functionalities.
- *test dataset*: aimed at evaluating and testing the tools.

Test and training datasets are kept as two distinct datasets, i.e. there is no intersection, in order to avoid overfitting the tools to be tested on datasets and to ensure fair and unbiased assessment of them.

Both training and test dataset are associated with ground-truth specifying the correct labels for the documents in the dataset but the ground-truth associated with the test data set will not be shared ahead, because it is needed for carrying out the final testing phase in an unbiased way.

More in detail, the test dataset is constituted by representative test data M_j^{test} provided by memory institutions providing the documents. The training dataset is constituted by two parts: a *demonstration* one, which can be used to show casing the tools; a *private* part, which is used internally by each developer for designing, developing, and testing its own system.

An orthogonal distinction on the datasets is between *synthetic* and *real* data. The former are data created with the specific purpose of pinpointing some specific compliance problem or critical issue for a given preservation format, as proposed also by [2]. The latter are data actually managed by memory institutions for their preservation duties. Both the training and the test datasets comprise both synthetic and real data.

4.2 Classes and Ground-Truth

For each media type a domain expert group has been established and was in charge of defining the list of classes. Each domain expert group is constituted as follows:

- one evaluation expert, i.e. an expert of organization of evaluation activities according to the Cranfield paradigm who oversees the classes definition process and facilitates the discussion within the group;
- two experts from memory institutions;
- one expert from developers.

For each class it is specified a unique identifier, a short name and a brief description. The class definition process was two-fold. Firstly, the experts defined the classes on the basis of the standard and in a second moment they revised them by removing the classes for which there were not enough files belonging to them, were not correctly specified or were too generic. Here we report a few examples of classes for each media type [14] – *TC* is a for text classes, *IC* is for image classes, and *AV* is for audio/video classes:

- Class *TC*015 – **Import/Link to External Resource**
  - *description*: Has links to an external resource (rather than embedding it) such as external File specifications and reference XObjects.
  - *PDF/A version*: 1-3
- Class *TC*024 – **Action Hide**
  - *description*: Has action to hide annotations or outlines. Actions are associated with annotations (including interactive forms) or outlines (bookmarks).
  - *PDF/A version*: 1-3
- Class *TC*042 – **Device dependent**
  - *description*: Does not have a Device dependent color space. The device colour spaces (DeviceCMYK, DeviceGray, DeviceRGB) enable a page description to specify colour values that are directly related to their representation on an output device (see PDF reference, sec. 8.6.4.1).
  - *PDF/A version*: 1-3
- Class *IC*003 – **Incorrect tag type**
  - *description*: TIFF with a Tag with incorrect type but still readable (TIFF readers should accept BYTE, SHORT, or LONG values for any unsigned integer field. [Section 2, page 15]
- Class *IC*009 – **Incorrect page number**
  - *description*: A TIFF multipage document (NewSubFileType values 2,3,6 or 7) with incorrect page number (page numbers must range from zero to the number of images, missing pages, duplicat pages, inconsistent number of pages) [Section 12, page 55]
- Class *IC*034 – **Bad Ascii7 format**
  - *description*: Tags with Ascii format containing non-7 bits ascii, Ascii without null character termination,More than one null between strings [Section 2, page 15]
- Class *AVC*013 – **EBML vint efficiency**
  - *description*: Section 2.2 IDs are always encoded in their shortest form e.g. 1 is always encoded as 0x81 and never as 0x4001." The bits following the Element ID's Length Descriptor are not more than (8 - $bit-length-of-length-descriptor) successive 0 bits i.e. vint is expressed as efficiently as feasible." [EBML/EBML-VINT-EFF]
- Class *AVC*015 – **Element Size 0x7F Reservation**
  - *description*: Note that the shortest encoding form for 127 is 0x407f since 0x7f is reserved." If Element Size is set to 0x11111111 but element size is actually 127 bytes provide a warning." [EBML/EBML-ELEM-SIZE-7F]
- Class *AVC*033 – **Missing header**
  - *description*: Version 2 and later files use a global header." If version is 2 or more, there should be a global header in the container private data" [FFV1/OUTOFBAND-HEADER-MISSING]

The experimental collection for text initially contained 88 classes that after a refinement were reduced to 78; 10 classes have been removed. The remaining classes verify if the PDF/A standard is met by the test files; for instance, they check if they contain annotations (e.g. sound, movies, 3D objects), use any denied compression (e.g. LZW), contain interpolated images, content layers, transparencies, executable scripts, action forms, javascript and so on.

The experimental collection of images initially contained 44 classes of which only one was removed after the refinement process.Among other things, the other classes verify the size of the TIFF offset, tag type, channels error, dimensions error, resolution error, TIFF signature, byte order, photometric interpretation, color tags, lossy compression and size of the uncompressed TIFF-file.

Finally, the experimental collection of audio/video initially had 69 classes, reduced to 56 after refinement that removed generic classes and classes targeting deprecated features of the Matroska standard (still under revision at the time of writing). Classes target files element data size length, element size byte length limit, non-Ascii data in string, missing header, coder type and so on.

4.3 Resources

All the resources required to reproduce the results presented in this paper as well as the source code of the tested conformance checkers are publicly available. The experimental collections for text, image and audio/video for both training and testing are available in the PREFORMA GitHub repository: http://github.com/preforma.

The source code of the conformance checkers is available at the following URLs:

- text conformance checker (veraPDF) source code: http://github.com/verapdf
- image conformance checker (DPF Manager) source code: http://github.com/EasyinnovaSL/DPFManager
- audio/video conformance checker (MediaConch) source code: http://github.com/MediaArea/MediaConch_SourceCode/

The evaluation was conducted by using the open source MATTERS library: http://matters.dei.unipd.it/.

5 EXPERIMENTAL RESULTS

5.1 Phase 1: Correctness

The Cranfiled-based evaluation framework has been iterated several times with the purpose of spotting issues and improving the tools until the performances reached a high level of correctness.

The tested tool for the text media type was the text conformance checker developed by VeraPDF. [6] In Table 1 we can see the values of accuracy, AUC and consistency averaged over all the text classes. The results are pretty good since accuracy is very close to the maximum value, whereas AUC could be further improved [16].

As we can see the text conformance checker reports some misclassification for the files within the class `TC000` which is the class with "correct files"; this means that the checker returns some false negative that would need a further check before being accepted for long-term preservation by a memory institution. The classes which

[6] http://verapdf.org/home/

Table 1: Average values of accuracy, AUC and consistency for text, image and audio/video media types. The minimum value is 0 and the maximum is 1.

Media type	Accuracy	AUC	Consistency
Text	0.9812	0.8495	1.0000
Image	1.0000	1.0000	1.0000
Audio/Video	0.9977	0.9621	1.0000

contain more mis-classified files are TC010 (image encoded interpolation), TC016 (has attachment of any kind of resource), TC017 (document non-PDF/A attachment), TC040 (has spacings around keywords 'obj', 'endobj', 'stream', 'end- stream', 'xref') and TC064 (does not have functionality required for Conformance Level U).

For images the tested conformance checker was DPF manager TIFF conformance checker. [7] As we can see from Table 1, this checker gets 100% accuracy, AUC and consisntecy for all the classes.

For audio/video the tested conformance checker was MediaConch [8] for Matroska, FFV1 and PCM. From Table 1, we see that this chacker behaves pretty well on average; the two classes failing to obtain 100% accuracy are AV001 (The first Element ID must equal 0x172351395 (EBML Header) [EBML/EBML-ELEM-START]) and AV061 (MKV is not at least version 4 [Matroska/MKV-V4+]).

5.2 Phase 2: Usability

Since when the tools have been completed and stabilized, a series of hands-on sessions and training seminars have been organized with the goal to explain to the participants what does conformance checking mean, why is file format validation so important in long-term digital preservation, how to create their own policy profiles and how to download, install, configure and use the conformance checker to analyze their files.

These workshops/seminars invited archivists/conservators/librarians to bring their files and analyze them with the conformance checkers under exam. At the end of the workshop, they understood which are the main issues related to digital preservation and file formats validation at many memory institutions, checked whether their files conform to the specifications of the standards, and learnt how to create a policy profile that allows them to verify if their files are compliant with the acceptance criteria for their digital repository.

5.2.1 User study. We organized two hands-on sessions with a total of 21 participants that tested the tools; fourteen participants were interested in the text format, sixteen in the images and thirteen in the audio/video format (of course there were participants interested in more than one media type). The participants were asked:

- "Is there any other file format for which you would be interested in having a conformance checker, besides those already covered in PREFORMA (PDF/A, TIFF, Matroska/FFv1)?"
  The vast majority answered "No", three wanted also the TXT format to be covered and one wanted also the JPEG format to be covered.
- How would you envisage to use the results of the open source projects in your legacy environment and/or in your digital archiving and preservation initiatives?
  Three answered "Web", two (from the cultural heritage domain) "Integration to legacy tools", eight "Integration in legacy system" and six "Standalone service via web".
- Do you expect that the PREFORMA's results will have a positive impact on the workflow of your institution/organisation?
  Seven answered "yes" because "It could improve the workflow, and relations with other institutions and agencies", "To test the tools and to find a possible integration with our system", "to increase the awareness of the issue" and "to increase discussion about policies and standardisation"; one answered "no" (i.e. the electronic adm. consultant) and all the others answered "too early to say".

All the participants tested all the conformance checker and we asked how they would rate their experience in using the tool(s) in terms of performance, usability, potential and other related aspects. The opinion were expressed with a number from 1 (very poor) to 5 (very good) and with a free text. The answers are reported in Table 2. We see that the user evaluation is quite good for all the considered aspects, even though they had difficulties at assessing the quality of documentation, scalability, interoperability and licenses. These features are hard to assess without enough time, long use of the tools and the required technical expertise; these aspects were further targeted in phase 3 of the evaluation.

Another question was: "How would you rate your experience in using the tool(s) in terms of specific functionality?" The answers are reported in Table 3 (one person did not answer).

To the question "What's the one single thing that you learnt today?", the most common answers were:

- The importance of some details, too often forgotten.
- Creating policies.
- How to create policy for audio/video.
- There is a good and interesting tool which deserves to be analysed and tested deeper.
- You can implement your own checking rules.
- There is a community working to answer my doubts.
- Application of correct parameters for the long-term preservation.
- More consciousness of the obsolescence.
- The digital preservation could be possible because we knew the right tools.
- Identifying and fix file formats and know a new software to do that.
- There is a software that can help to the administrations to know better their TIFF files for digital preservation.
- Using DPF Manager to check TIFF files.

5.2.2 Focus groups. In addition to the user study presented above, also two focus groups were organized. The first one was focused on the text media format and it was composed of 21 people:

- 12 came from state agencies and organisations, including 2 from public museums and archives and 3 from the offices of the Swedish Parliament and of the Swedish Government;

[7] http://dpfmanager.org/
[8] https://mediaarea.net/MediaConch/

Table 2: How would you rate your experience in using the tool(s) in terms of performance, usability, potential and other related aspects? From 1 (very poor) to 5 (very good) with a 0.5 step.

	Innovation potential	Performance	Usability	Documentation	Scalability	Interoperability	Licenses
User 01	4	4	4	4	-	-	4
User 02	4	4	3	3	4	3	-
User 03	4	4	5	4	4	-	-
User 04	4	5	5	5	5	5	5
User 05	-	-	5	5	-	-	-
User 06	4	5	5	4	4	4	4
User 07	5	5	4	4	4	4	4
User 08	5	4	4	4	-	-	-
User 09	4	5	5	5	5	5	5
User 10	-	-	5	5	-	-	-
User 11	4	4	4	4	-	-	-
User 12	5	5	4	-	-	-	-
User 13	5	4	4	2	4	4	5
User 14	4	2	4	2	4	4	4
User 15	5	2.5	3	-	-	-	5
User 16	3	2	2	2	3	-	-
User 17	4	3	4	3	-	-	-
User 18	4	5	4	-	-	2	-
User 19	4	4	3	-	-	-	4
User 20	2.5	3	2	-	-	-	-
User 21	2.5	3	4	-	-	4	-
Avg.	4.05	3.86	3.95	3.73	4.11	3.88	4.44
Std. Dev.	0.76	1.03	0.92	1.10	0.60	0.93	0.53

Table 3: How would you rate your experience in using the tool(s) in terms of specific functionality? From 1 (very poor) to 5 (very good) with a 0.5 step.

	Installation and configuration	User Interface	Command Line Interface	Conformance checking	Policy creation and checking	Results interpretation	Metadata fixing	Documentation	Web-based version
User 01	3	5	-	5	4	4	-	3	-
User 02	5	4	-	-	5	-	5	-	-
User 03	3.5	4.5	-	5	5	4	-	4	-
User 04	5	5	5	5	5	4	4	-	-
User 05	5	4	-	-	5	4	-	4	-
User 06	4	-	-	-	-	-	-	-	-
User 07	1	4	4	4	3	3	-	-	-
User 08	2	4	4	3	2	4	3	2	4
User 09	-	-	-	-	-	-	-	-	-
User 10	4	2	2	2	1	3	-	-	-
User 11	3	4	4	4	4	4	-	-	-
User 12	3.5	4.5	-	5	5	5	-	-	5
User 13	2	3	3	4	2	4	-	-	-
User 14	3.5	3	-	2	2	2.5	-	-	-
User 15	4	4	-	4	5	3	-	-	-
User 16	4	4	4	4	4	4	4	4	4
User 17	4	4	4	5	4	3	5	3	3
User 18	5	5	4	5	4	5	5	4	5
User 19	5	5	5	5	5	5	5	5	5
User 20	5	4	4	-	5	5	-	5	5
Avg.	3.76	4.06	3.91	4.13	3.89	3.91	4.43	3.78	4.43
Std. Dev.	1.71	0.78	0.83	1.06	1.32	0.80	0.79	1.00	0.80

- 5 came from communal agencies, 3 from local and 2 from regional ones:
- 3 came from small-medium enterprises targeting IT and archiving;
- 1 came from a private archival institution.

The focus group started with a presentation about what is conformance checking and what we mean with policy checking. Afterwards, there was a brief overview of the PDF/A format. All participants were to some extent familiar with the format, so this was more of an update and to equalize their knowledge.

All participants had to bring with them their own laptops (with Java and veraPDF version 1.4.6 installed) and examples of PDF/A files from their organisations. It was explained to the participants: how to read reports and failure messages, how to identify and interpret failures, possible actions to solve failures, how to formulate a policy and how to test a policy.

Each item was explained by means of a demonstration and was followed by practical exercises, where the participants used their own files or test files downloaded from Internet.

The focus group ended with a discussion to evaluate the day. The expectations expressed in the beginning of the seminar were mainly focusing on learning more about PDF/A in order to better understand its "pros and cons" but also to learn about validation and the text conformance checker. The feedback from the participants was very positive. Some commented that conformance checking requires knowledge about the format that most curators of digital object do not have today. More "fixers" was also asked for; the metadata fixer could be complemented with more simple fixing.

The second focus group was focused on the the image media type and composed of 22 participants mainly from small/medium-sized museums comprising directors, curators and some IT-people. At the beginning, there was a general introduction into file-formats for digital preservation. Four participants brought a laptop and some TIFF-files along to be tested. There was no problem in downloading and installing the software, but many of the participants were convinced that the IT-people responsible for their museum would have troubles installing the software. This impression was not supported by any evidence, but it has to be taken into account in order to simplify as much as possible the download and installation of the tools.

After the installation of the image conformance checker (DPF-Manager), the functionalities available in the windows version were explained; the participants were able to understand "conformance", "policy", etc. Most functionalities worked smoothly. Some functioning issues came up when using MS Windows as operating system.

There was some disappointment when the participants got the reports for their TIFF files: All were helpless, what to do and how to interpret the messages in purely technical English. What to do if a file was marked as not conforming? After some explanation we agreed that in any case it is good to know if a file is conform to the defined requirements or not.

At the end the participants agreed that the DPF-Manager is a valuable tool for their digitization-work, not only for digital preservation but also to be used when checking image-files produced by external companies in the framework of a digitization project of the museum. There was room for improvement: The messages should be in multilingual (German in this case) or at least there should be the possibility to set up languages other than English. It might be good to have some hints on software tools to correct found errors.

In general, it took some time to make clear, that conformance to baseline-TIFF is necessary for digital preservation. But after this was clarified, participants were eager to use the DPF-Manager tool.

5.3 Phase 3: Usefulness

The issues highlighted by the user study and the focus groups were analysed by the developers that improved the conformance checker tools accordingly. In particular, the documentation of the tools has been improved and the download and installation procedures have been simplified. Afterwards, the tools have been evaluated by some technical and domain experts that provided three final reports (one per media type) with the overall evaluation and additional suggestions for improving the tools.

5.3.1 Text Media Type. The domain expert underlined that it was a beneficial experience to test the veraPDF software since many national libraries are currently looking to develop digital archives which will need to have tools to validate their content. After an internal testing phase with some PDF/A files, no issues have been detected and the output of the conformance checker was consistent with the one of another checker. The tool works as expected, produces XML and HTML reports and saves them as it should. Nevertheless, the reports could be more user friendly for non-technical users.

The technical expert highlighted no problems with the download, compilation, installation and use of the conformance checker. Moreover, the expert highlighted that some previous issues have been resolved and documented by the developer.

5.3.2 Image Media Type. The domain and technical experts highlighted that this tool has been tested with the intention of using it in a high-volume automated productions system, hence the GUI is less important for them with respect to the command line. The DPF Manager worked well and fast enough and the experts thought that it should be made part of digital preservation workflows in museums. But, they discovered that it is also a useful tool for digitization projects. Often digitization in museums is done by external companies; hence, with DPF Manager the museums are enabled to check the quality of the work of these companies.

The domain expert wrote that he was very happy with the program and with the fast reaction when asking for some updates (e.g., to be able to check a certain additional policy-feature, the addition of basic identification metadata and the statistic module).

The technical expert tried out DPF Manager for both Windows and Linux Ubuntu platforms. Nevertheless, the instructions for installing in non-GUI-Linux systems were still missing in the documentation. Overall, the experts underlined that the software (both GUI and command line) should be made easier and more intuitive because even they, as expert users, find it hard to understand how to use the checker in a more detailed or specialized way, especially when they wanted to ignore errors in selected tags.

A future development plan should account for an interface to provide easily translations of massages and reports in languages other than English.

5.3.3 Audio/Video Media Type. The domain expert stated that the main issue with MediaConch is that, to him, it is a tool for professionals. To work well for users that do not have a good technical knowledge it will have to be completed with, perhaps a knowledge base and a guide (guidance) on how to interpret conformance errors. As for now the tool provides an error with a technical detail but no guidance on how this error could be interpreted or corrected. The expert pointed out that the software should benefit from adding a knowledge base to the software or the platform on Internet. The knowledge base should cover references to common errors and guidance on how to correct common errors. It could also include hints about how to deal with a more complex type of errors. This should probably make the software available to a broader public and increase its user base. In addition, an issue with the licensing has been covered within the evaluation of the final report.

The technical expert pointed out that that the standardization process for audio/video is ongoing and this fact created problems to the developers. As long as the standardization is ongoing, the conformance checking of the standard is no serious matter. However, the other areas of checking, such as the profiles (as presets or individually defined), still make sense. Overall, the conformance checker has been tested and it works quite well.

6 CONCLUSIONS AND FUTURE WORK

This paper discussed the overall evaluation framework we developed, in the context of the PREFORMA EU project, to validate the conformance checkers for the long-term preservation of PDF/A (text), TIFF (image), and Matroska (audio/video) files. The framework assesses three aspects of the conformance checkers: (i) correctness, in a quantitative system-oriented way; (ii) usability, in a qualitative user-oriented way; and, (iii) usefulness, in a qualitative domain and technical expert oriented way. The developed framework, besides its application in the PREFORMA project context, is a general tool which can be used for evaluating also other preservation related tasks, provided that the definition of the classes and the ground-truth are tailored to the case at hand.

The paper described the three experimental collections, one for each media type, we developed and which are open source available, the results of the conformance checkers evaluation using these collections, and the outcomes for usability and usefulness gathered with user hands-on sessions and domain experts focus groups. Overall, all these types of validation indicate that the PREFORMA conformance checkers are ready to be shared open source with the memory institution community at large.

Future work will concern the refinement of the framework by introducing a notion of severity for the classes to be used to weight the impact of each mis-conformance and to obtain a more fine-grained validation of the tools. Furthermore, we plan to extend the defined classes with a new set based on policies and best practices of the memory institutions and not only on strict conformance to the standards.

ACKNOWLEDGMENTS

The reported work has been partially supported by the PREFORMA project, as part of the 7th Framework Programme of the European Commission, grant agreement no. 619568, and the CDC STARS-StG project of the University of Padua, Italy.

REFERENCES

[1] O. Alonso. Implementing crowdsourcing-based relevance experimentation: an industrial perspective. *Information Retrieval*, 16(2):101–120, April 2013.

[2] C. Becker and K. Duretec. Free Benchmark Corpora for Preservation Experiments: Using Model-Driven Engineering to Generate Data Sets. In *Proc. 13th ACM/IEEE-CS Joint Conference on Digital Libraries (JCDL 2013)*, pages 349–358. ACM Press, New York, USA, 2013.

[3] C. Becker, K. Duretec, and A. Rauber. The Challenge of Test Data Quality in Data Processing. *ACM Journal of Data and Information Quality (JDIQ)*, 8(2), 2016.

[4] C. Becker and A. Rauber. Decision Criteria in Digital Preservation: What to Measure and How. *Journal of the American Society for Information Science and Technology (JASIST)*, 62(6):1009–1028, 2011.

[5] D. Calvanese, D. De Nart, and C. Tasso, editors. *Digital Libraries on the Move – Proc. 11th Italian Research Conference on Digital Libraries (IRCDL 2015)*. Communications in Computer and Information Science (CCIS) 612, Springer, Heidelberg, Germany, 2016.

[6] L. Cappellato, N. Ferro, A. Fresa, M. Geber, B. Justrel, B. Lemmen, C. Prandoni, and G. Silvello. The PREFORMA Project: Federating Memory Institutions for Better Compliance of Preservation Formats. In Calvanese et al. [5], pages 86–91.

[7] J.-P. Chanod, M. Dobreva, A. Rauber, S. Ross, and V. Casarosa. Issues in Digital Preservation: Towards a New Research Agenda. In J.-P. Chanod, M. Dobreva, A. Rauber, and S. Ross, editors, *Report from Dagstuhl Seminar 10291: Automation in Digital Preservation*, Dagstuhl Reports, pages 1–14. Schloss Dagstuhl–Leibniz-Zentrum für Informatik, Germany, 2010.

[8] C. W. Cleverdon. The Cranfield Tests on Index Languages Devices. In K. Spärck Jones and P. Willett, editors, *Readings in Information Retrieval*, pages 47–60. Morgan Kaufmann Publisher, Inc., San Francisco, CA, USA, 1997.

[9] K. Duretec, A. Kulmukhametov, A. Rauber, and C. Becker. Benchmarks for Digital Preservation Tools. In *Proc. 11th International Conference on Preservation of Digital Objects (iPRES 2015)*, 2015.

[10] K. Duretec, A. Rauber, and C. Becker. A Text Extraction Software Benchmark Based on a Synthesized Dataset. In *2017 ACM/IEEE Joint Conference on Digital Libraries, JCDL 2017*, pages 109–118. IEEE Computer Society, 2017.

[11] N. Ferro. Quality and Interoperability: The Quest for the Optimal Balance. In I. Iglezakis, T.-E. Synodinou, and S. Kapidakis, editors, *E-Publishing and Digital Libraries: Legal and Organizational Issues*, pages 48–68. IGI Global, USA, 2010.

[12] N. Ferro. Proposal for an Evaluation Framework for Compliance Checkers for Long-term Digital Preservation. In *Digital Libraries and Multimedia Archives – Proc. 12th Italian Research Conference on Digital Libraries (IRCDL 2016)*, pages 125–136. Communications in Computer and Information Science (CCIS) 701, Springer, Heidelberg, Germany, 2016.

[13] N. Ferro. Reproducibility Challenges in Information Retrieval Evaluation. *ACM Journal of Data and Information Quality (JDIQ)*, 8(2):8:1–8:4, January 2017.

[14] N. Ferro, E. Buelinckx, B. Doubrov, K. Jadeglans, B. Lemmens, J. Martinez, V. Muñoz, C. Prandoni, D. Rice, S. Rohde-Enslin, X. Tarrés, E. Verbruggen, B. Yousefi, and C. Wilson. Deliverable D8.1R2 – Competitive Evaluation Strategy. PREFORMA PCP Project, EU 7FP, Contract N. 619568, October 2016.

[15] N. Ferro and G. Silvello. Towards a Semantic Web Enabled Representation of DL Foundational Models: The Quality Domain Example. In Calvanese et al. [5], pages 24–35.

[16] N. Ferro, G. Silvello, E. Buelinckx, B. Doubrov, M. Geber, K. Jadeglans, J. Martinez, V. Muñoz, D. Rice, S. Rohde-Enslin, X. Tarrés, E. Verbruggen, B. Yousefi, and C. Wilson. Deliverable D8.6 – Testing Report. PREFORMA PCP Project, EU 7FP, Contract N. 619568, October 2017.

[17] N. Fuhr, G. Tsakonas, T. Aalberg, M. Agosti, P. Hansen, S. Kapidakis, C.-P. Klas, L. Kovács, M. Landoni, A. Micsik, C. Papatheodorou, C. Peters, and I. Sølvberg. Evaluation of Digital Libraries. *International Journal on Digital Libraries*, 8(1):21–38, 2007.

[18] IEC 60958. Digital audio interface - Part 1: General. Standard IEC 60958-1 Ed. 3.1 b:2014, 2014.

[19] P. Innocenti, S. Ross, E. Maceviciute, T. Wilson, J. Ludwig, and W. Pempe. Assessing Digital Preservation Frameworks: The Approach of the SHAMAN Project. In N. Spyratos, E. Kapetanios, and A. Traina, editors, *Proc. ACM International Conference on Management of Emergent Digital EcoSystems (MEDES 2009)*, pages 412–416. ACM Press, New York, USA, 2009.

[20] ISO 12234-2. Electronic still-picture imaging – Removable memory – Part 2: TIFF/EP image data format. Recommendation ISO 12234-2:2001, 2001.

[21] ISO 12639. Graphic technology – Prepress digital data exchange – Tag image file format for image technology (TIFF/IT). Recommendation ISO 12639:2004, 2004.

[22] ISO 14721. Space data and information transfer systems – Open archival information system (OAIS) – Reference model. Recom. ISO 14721:2012, 2012.

[23] ISO 19005-1. Document management – Electronic document file format for long-term preservation – Part 1: Use of PDF 1.4 (PDF/A-1). Recommendation ISO 19005-1:2005, 2005.

[24] ISO 19005-2. Document management – Electronic document file format for long-term preservation – Part 2: Use of ISO 32000-1 (PDF/A-2). Recommendation ISO 19005-2:2011, 2011.

[25] ISO 19005-3. Document management – Electronic document file format for long-term preservation – Part 3: Use of ISO 32000-1 with support for embedded files (PDF/A-3). Recommendation ISO 19005-3:2012, 2012.

[26] ISO/IEC 15444. Information technology – JPEG 2000 image coding system: Core coding system. Recommendation ISO/IEC 15444-1:2004, 2004.

[27] S. T. Kowalczyk. Before the Repository: Defining the Preservation Threats to Research Data in the Lab. In P. Logasa Bogen II, S. Allard, H. Mercer, and M. Beck, editors, *Proc. 15th ACM/IEEE-CS Joint Conference on Digital Libraries (JCDL 2015)*, pages 215–222. ACM Press, New York, USA, 2015.

[28] S. Ross. Digital Preservation, Archival Science and Methodological Foundations for Digital Libraries. *New Review of Information Networking*, 17(1):43–68, 2012.

[29] F. Sebastiani. Machine Learning in Automated Text Categorization. *ACM Computing Surveys (CSUR)*, 34(1):1–47, March 2002.

[30] G. Silvello. Theory and practice of data citation. *JASIST*, 69(1):6–20, 2018.

[31] I. Soboroff, C. Nicholas, and P. Cahan. Ranking Retrieval Systems without Relevance Judgments. In D. H. Kraft, W. B. Croft, D. J. Harper, and J. Zobel, editors, *Proc. 24th Annual International ACM SIGIR Conference on Research and Development in Information Retrieval (SIGIR 2001)*, pages 66–73. ACM Press, New York, USA, 2001.

[32] M. Sokolova and G. Lapalme. A Systematic Analysis of Performance Measures for Classification Tasks. *Information Processing & Management*, 45(4):427–437, July 2009.

[33] The Consultative Committee for Space Data Systems (CCSDS). Reference Model for an Open Archival Information System (OAIS). Magenta Book, Issue 2. Recommended Practice CCSDS 650.0-M-2, http://public.ccsds.org/publications/archive/650x0m2.pdf, June 2012.

[34] E. M. Voorhees. Variations in relevance judgments and the measurement of retrieval effectiveness. *Information Processing & Management*, 36(5):697–716, September 2000.

Ranking Archived Documents for Structured Queries on Semantic Layers

Pavlos Fafalios
L3S Research Center,
Leibniz University of Hannover
Hannover, Germany
fafalios@L3S.de

Vaibhav Kasturia
L3S Research Center,
Leibniz University of Hannover
Hannover, Germany
kasturia@L3S.de

Wolfgang Nejdl
L3S Research Center,
Leibniz University of Hannover
Hannover, Germany
nejdl@L3S.de

ABSTRACT

Archived collections of documents (like newspaper and web archives) serve as important information sources in a variety of disciplines, including Digital Humanities, Historical Science, and Journalism. However, the absence of efficient and meaningful exploration methods still remains a major hurdle in the way of turning them into usable sources of information. A semantic layer is an RDF graph that describes metadata and semantic information about a collection of archived documents, which in turn can be queried through a semantic query language (SPARQL). This allows running advanced queries by combining metadata of the documents (like publication date) and content-based semantic information (like entities mentioned in the documents). However, the results returned by such structured queries can be numerous and moreover they all equally match the query. In this paper, we deal with this problem and formalize the task of *"ranking archived documents for structured queries on semantic layers"*. Then, we propose two ranking models for the problem at hand which jointly consider: i) the relativeness of documents to entities, ii) the timeliness of documents, and iii) the temporal relations among the entities. The experimental results on a new evaluation dataset show the effectiveness of the proposed models and allow us to understand their limitations.

CCS CONCEPTS

• **Information systems** → *Probabilistic retrieval models*;

KEYWORDS

Semantic Layers; Archived documents; Ranking; Probabilistic modeling; Stochastic modeling

ACM Reference Format:

Pavlos Fafalios, Vaibhav Kasturia, and Wolfgang Nejdl. 2018. Ranking Archived Documents for Structured Queries on Semantic Layers. In *JCDL '18: The 18th ACM/IEEE Joint Conference on Digital Libraries, June 3–7, 2018, Fort Worth, TX, USA.* ACM, New York, NY, USA, 10 pages. https://doi.org/10.1145/3197026.3197049

ACM ISBN 978-1-4503-5178-2/18/06...$15.00
https://doi.org/10.1145/3197026.3197049

1 INTRODUCTION

Despite the increasing number of digital archives worldwide (like news and web archives), the absence of efficient and meaningful exploration methods still remains the major bottleneck in the way of turning them into usable information sources [6]. Semantic models try to solve this problem by offering the means to describe and publish metadata and semantic information about a collection of archived documents in the standard RDF format. A repository of such data, called Semantic Layer [11], allows running advanced queries which combine metadata of the documents (like publication date) and content-based semantic information (like entities mentioned in the documents). For example, we can access a Semantic Layer over a newspaper archive and find articles of a specific time period discussing about a specific category of entities (e.g., *philanthropists*) or about entities that share some characteristics (e.g., *lawyers born in Germany*), while we can also integrate information coming from other knowledge bases like DBpedia. Such advanced information needs can be directly expressed through structured (SPARQL) queries or through user-friendly interactive interfaces which transparently transform user interactions to SPARQL queries (e.g., Faceted Search-like browsing interfaces [39]).

However, the results returned by such queries can be numerous and moreover they all equally match the query: there is no relevance ranking like in the case of keyword-based information retrieval. Thus, there arises the need for an effective method to rank the returned results for discovering and showing to the users the most important ones. For instance, when requesting articles from a news archive published within a specific time period and mentioning one or more query entities, important documents may be those whose main topic is about an important event related to the query entities during the requested time period. Thus, an effective ranking method should consider the different factors that affect the importance of documents to the query, while at the same time relying only on the data available in the semantic layer (there is no access to the full contents of the documents).

Although there is a plethora of works on ranking archived documents for keyword-based temporal queries, the problem of ranking such documents for the case of structured queries on knowledge graphs has not yet been recognized and studied. In this paper, we address this gap by first introducing and formalizing this type of problem. Then, to cope with this problem, we propose two ranking models, a probabilistic one and a Random Walk-based one, which jointly consider the following aspects: i) the *relativeness* of a document to the query entities, ii) the *timeliness* of a document's publication date, iii) the temporal *relatedness* of the query entities to other entities mentioned in the documents. The idea is to promote documents that mention the query entities many times, that have been published in important (for the query entities) time periods, and that mention many other entities co-occurring frequently with the query entities in important time periods. Such an approach is widely applicable since it exploits the least amount of metadata.

In a nutshell, in this paper we make the following contributions:

- We formulate and formalize the problem of ranking archived documents for structured queries over semantic layers.
- Due to lack of evaluation datasets for this problem, we have created a new ground truth dataset for a news archive which we make publicly available.
- We propose two ranking models for the problem at hand: a probabilistic one and a stochastic one (Random Walk with restart).
- We present the results of an experimental evaluation which illustrate the effectiveness of the proposed models. We also analyze problematic cases for understanding when and why the models fail to provide good rankings.

The rest of the paper is organized as follows: Section 2 presents the required background and related literature. Section 3 defines the problem and describes a new evaluation dataset. Section 4 introduces the probabilistic model. Section 5 introduces the stochastic model. Section 6 presents evaluation results. Section 7 concludes the paper and discusses interesting directions for future research.

2 BACKGROUND AND RELATED WORKS

2.1 Semantic Layers

A Semantic Layer is an RDF repository (RDF graph) of structured data about a collection of archived documents [11]. Structured data includes not only metadata information about a document (like publication date), but also *entity annotations*, i.e., disambiguated entities mentioned in each document extracted using an entity linking system [34]. Figure 1 shows an example of (a part of) a Semantic Layer describing metadata and annotation information for a news article. We notice that the document was published on 6 January 2012 and mentions the entity name "Giuliani" at character position 512, which probably (with confidence score 0.9/1.0) corresponds to the known American lawyer and former politician Rudy Giuliani.

A semantic layer allows running advanced, entity-centric queries that can also directly integrate information from other knowledge bases like DBpedia. Listing 1 shows an example of a SPARQL query that can be answered by a semantic layer over a collection of old news articles. The query requests articles of 1989 mentioning New York lawyers born in Brooklyn. By accessing DBpedia at query-execution time, the query retrieves the entities that satisfy the query as well as additional information, in particular the birth date of each lawyer. We see that, using the entity URIs and type/category information, we can find documents about entities even if we do not know the names of the entities, or without needing to specify a long list of all the entity names. Moreover, using the SPARQL operators `COUNT` and `GROUP BY`, and exploiting the expressive power of SPARQL, we can aggregate information related to documents and entities.

As shown in [11], a semantic layer can answer information needs that existing keyword-based systems (like Google news) are not able to sufficiently satisfy. Such advanced (but also common) information needs can be directly expressed through SPARQL queries or by exploiting a user-friendly interface that transforms user interactions to SPARQL queries, like Sparklis [14] or SemFacet [2]. Since the results returned by such structured queries can be numerous and have no ranking, in this paper we study how we can rank them based on their importance to the query entities.

2.2 Related Works

We report works on the related problems of *time-aware document ranking* and *ranking in knowledge graphs*, and we discuss the commonalities and differences of these research areas to our problem.

2.2.1 Time-aware Document Ranking. The impact of *time* on information retrieval has received a large share of attention in the last decade. The surveys in [8] and [23] provide a comprehensive categorization and overview of temporal IR approaches and related applications. As regards time-aware *ranking*, existing works are classified into two different types based on two main notions of relevance with respect to time [8, 23]: 1) recency-based ranking, and 2) time-dependent ranking. Since recency-based ranking methods promote documents that are recently created or updated (this preference of freshness is common in general web searching), below we discuss only time-dependent ranking methods which are useful when searching archived collections of documents.

Jin et al. [22] proposed a ranking algorithm to sort results by applying a linear interpolation of text similarity, temporal information, and page importance (based on PageRank), where temporal similarity is the ranking score of temporal relevance based on the set of intersection conditions between the temporal query and the temporal expressions found in the web page. Arikan et al. [3] and Berberich et al. [5] introduced approaches that integrate temporal expressions extracted from the documents into language modeling frameworks. Metzler et al. [27] proposed a time-dependent ranking model to adjust the document scores based on an analysis of web query logs and a set of document fields to estimate the time of both the query and the document. The work by Perkio et al. [9] automatically detects topical trends and their importance over time within a news corpus using a statistical topic model and a simple variant of TF-IDF. These trends are then used as the basis for temporally adaptive rankings. Dakka et al. [10] consider the publication time of documents to identify the important time intervals that are likely to be of interest to an implicit temporal query. Then, time is incorporated into language models to assign an estimated relevance value to each time period. Aji et al. [1] proposed a term weighting model that uses the revision history analysis of a document to redefine the importance of terms which is then incorporated into BM25 and statistical language models. Kanhabua and Nørvag [24] proposed a time-sensitive ranking model based on learning-to-rank techniques for explicit temporal queries. To learn the ranking model, temporal and entity-based features are applied.

Regarding more recent works, Singh et al. [36] introduced the notion of *Historical Query Intents* and modeled it as a search result diversification task which intends to present the most relevant results from a topic-temporal space. For retrieving and ranking historical documents like news articles, the authors propose a retrieval algorithm, called HistDiv, which jointly considers the dimensions

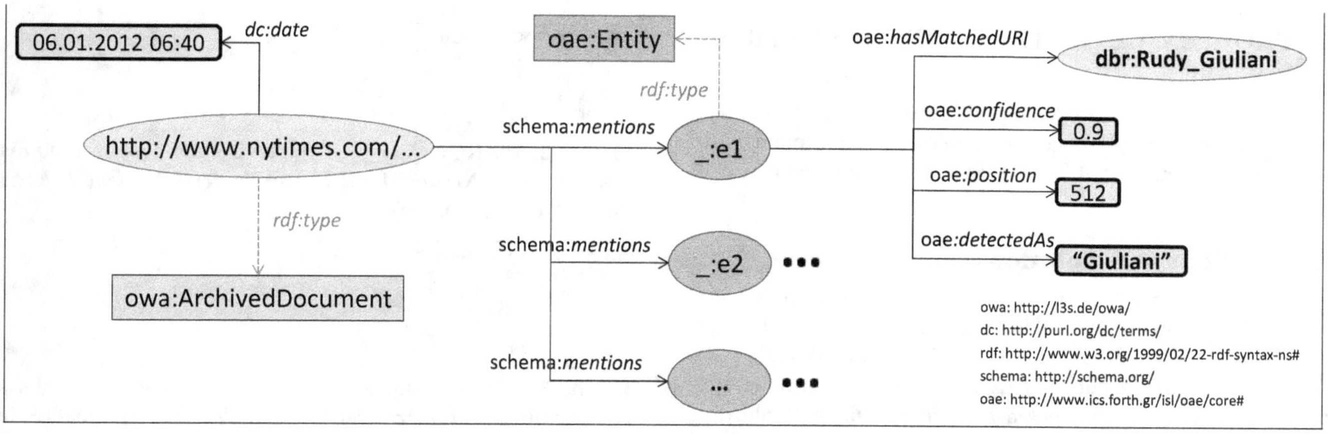

Figure 1: A part of a Semantic Layer describing metadata and entity annotations for a news article.

```
SELECT ?article ?title ?date ?nylawyer ?bdate ?abstr WHERE {
  SERVICE <http://dbpedia.org/sparql> {
    ?nylawyer dc:subject dbc:New_York_lawyers ; dbo:birthPlace dbr:Brooklyn .
    OPTIONAL { ?nylawyer dbo:birthDate ?bdate } }
  ?article dc:date ?date FILTER(year(?date) = 1989) .
  ?article schema:mentions ?entity .
  ?entity oae:hasMatchedURI ?nylawyer .
  ?article dc:title ?title
} ORDER BY ?nylawyer
```

Listing 1: Example SPARQL query over a Semantic Layer of a collection of old news articles. The query requests articles of 1989 discussing about New York lawyers born in Brooklyn.

of aspect and time. Expedition [35] is a time-aware search system for scholars which allows users to search articles in a news collection by entering free-text queries and choosing from four retrieval models: Temporal Relevance, Temporal Diversity, Topical Diversity, and Historical Diversity. Tempas [19] is a search system for web archives that exploits a social bookmarking service (Delicious) for temporally searching an archive by indexing tags and time. The new version of Tempas [20] exploits temporal link graphs and the corresponding anchor texts. The authors show how temporal anchor texts can be effective in answering queries beyond purely navigational intents, like finding the most central web pages of an entity in a given time period.

Difference of our case. Similar to the above works, our objective is to rank documents for a user information need. However, our case has the following three distinctive characteristics:

i) The full contents of the documents are not available and there are no term-based indexes on top of them. We have access only on the RDF triples existing in the semantic layer, i.e., on metadata about the documents and on the entities mentioned in the documents. Moreover, these entities have been extracted using automated entity linking systems and thus are prone to disambiguation errors.
ii) The information needs are expressed through structured SPARQL queries, not keywords. These SPARQL queries request documents of a specific time period mentioning one or more specific entities, while these query entities are specified through URIs which means that there is no ambiguity about them.
iii) We already know the documents that match the query, however there are no relevance scores, i.e., all documents *equally* match the query. Our objective is to identify (and rank higher) the documents that discuss important information about the entities given in the query.

2.2.2 Ranking in Knowledge Graphs. There is a plethora of works on ranking entities, concepts and resources in knowledge graphs [7, 18, 30], as well as on ranking the results returned by SPARQL queries [15, 25, 29]. The majority of these works exploits the structure of the graph and applies some variation of a popular link analysis algorithm. The survey in [32] formalizes and contextualizes the problem of ranking in the Web of Data and provides an analysis and contrast of the similarities, differences and applicability of the different approaches.

An interesting related line of research tackles the problem of *ad-hoc object retrieval* [31, 37]. In this problem, the input is a keyword query and the output is one or more resources (entity URIs) that satisfy the corresponding information need. To tackle this kind of problem, Pound et al. [31] propose an adaptation of TF-IDF, while Tonon et al. [37] combine an inverted index with entity graph traversal. In the same context, the SemSearch challenge [16] focused on finding the entity identifier of a specific entity described by a user query, while the TREC entity track [4] studied two related search tasks: i) finding all entities related to a given entity, and ii) finding entities with common properties given some examples.

Difference of our case. In all these works, the result is a ranked list of *well-structured* RDF resources (like entities, properties, or triples). On the contrary, in our problem the units of retrieval represent unstructured (textual) documents returned by structured (SPARQL) queries. These works operate over knowledge graphs like DBpedia, where entities are described through properties and associations with other entities. A semantic layer is a special kind of a knowledge graph that represents metadata and annotation information about a collection of textual documents like news articles. Given a non-ambiguous SPARQL query and its result (the documents that match the query), our aim is to identify those documents that discuss important information about the query entities in the requested time-period by exploiting only the contents of the semantic layer.

3 PROBLEM DEFINITION AND EVALUATION DATASET

In this section, we formalize the problem of ranking documents returned by structured queries and describe a new ground truth dataset for the problem at hand. First we introduce the required notions and notations.

3.1 Notions and Notations

Entities. In our problem, an *entity* is anything with a separate and meaningful existence that also has an identity expressed through a reference in a knowledge base (e.g., a Wikipedia/DBpedia URI). This does not only include persons, locations, organizations, etc., but also events (e.g., *US 2016 presidential election*) and more abstract concepts such as *democracy* or *abortion*. Let E be a finite set of entities, e.g., all Wikipedia entities, where each entity $e \in E$ is associated with a unique URI in the reference knowledge base.

Documents and extracted entities. Let D be a set of documents (e.g., a set of news articles) published within a set of time periods T_D of fixed granularity Δ (e.g., day). For a document $d \in D$, let $t_d \in T_D$ be the time period of granularity Δ in which d was published, while for a time period $t \in T_D$, let $docs(t) \subseteq D$ be the set of all documents published within t, i.e., $docs(t) = \{d \in D \mid t_d = t\}$. Let also $ents(d) \subseteq E$ be all entities mentioned in d extracted using an entity linking system [34]. Inversely, for an entity $e \in E$, let $docs(e) \subseteq D$ be all documents that mention e, i.e., $docs(e) = \{d \in D \mid e \in ents(d)\}$.

3.2 Problem Definition

Given a corpus of documents D, a set of entities $E_D \in E$ mentioned in documents of D, and a SPARQL query Q requesting documents from D published within a *time period* $T_Q \subseteq T_D$ and related to one or more query entities $E_Q \subseteq E_D$ with logical AND (mentioning all the query entities) or OR (mentioning at least one of the query entities) semantics, the problem is how to rank the documents $D_Q \subseteq D$ that match Q.

Listing 2 shows an example SPARQL query requesting documents published in 1990 discussing about the entities *Nelson Mandela* and *Frederik Willem de Klerk* (logical AND semantics), while the query in Listing 3 requests articles of 1990 discussing about *state presidents of South Africa* (logical OR semantics). Our objective is to rank the results returned by such SPARQL queries.

3.3 Evaluation dataset

Due to the lack of benchmark datasets for our problem, and to enable empirical evaluations, we have created a new ground truth dataset. We used the New York Times (NYT) annotated corpus [33] as the underlying document collection. The corpus contains over 1.8 million articles published by NYT between 1987 and 2007. We used Babelfy [28] for extracting DBpedia entities from each article, using a configuration proposed by the Babelfy developers[1]. We tested this configuration in the AIDA/CONLL-Test B ground truth dataset [17] and got the following evaluation scores: micro precision: 0.818, micro recall: 0.684, micro F1: 0.745 (the accuracy is

```
SELECT DISTINCT ?article WHERE {
  ?article dc:date ?date FILTER(year(?date) = 1990) .
  ?article oae:mentions ?entity1, ?entity2 .
  ?entity1 oae:hasMatchedURI  dbr:Nelson_Mandela .
  ?entity2 oae:hasMatchedURI  dbr:F._W._de_Klerk }
```

Listing 2: SPARQL query for retrieving articles of 1990 discussing about *Nelson Mandela* and *Frederik Willem de Klerk* (logical AND semantics).

```
SELECT DISTINCT ?article WHERE {
  SERVICE <http://dbpedia.org/sparql> {
    ?p dc:subject dbc:State_Presidents_of_South_Africa> }
  ?article dc:date ?date FILTER(year(?date) = 1990) .
  ?article oae:mentions ?entity .
  ?entity oae:hasMatchedURI  ?p }
```

Listing 3: SPARQL query for retrieving articles of 1990 discussing about *state presidents of South Africa* (logical OR semantics).

almost the same with the one reported in the Babelfy paper for the same dataset [28]). Based on these annotations, we constructed a semantic layer following the process described in [11]. Then, we created 24 SPARQL queries, each one requesting articles published in a specific *time period* and mentioning one or more *entities*. The queries are grouped into 4 categories:

- **Single-entity queries (Q1-Q6):** 6 queries requesting articles related to 1 entity (e.g., articles of 1990 discussing about *Nelson Mandela*).
- **Multiple-entity AND queries (Q7-Q12):** 6 queries requesting articles related to 2 or more entities with logical AND semantics (e.g., articles of 1990 discussing about *Nelson Mandela* and *F.W. de Klerk*).
- **Multiple-entity OR queries (Q13-Q18):** 6 queries requesting articles related to 2 or more entities with logical OR semantics (e.g., articles of 1990 discussing about *Nelson Mandela* or *F.W. de Klerk*).
- **Category queries (Q19-Q24):** 6 queries requesting articles related to entities belonging to a DBpedia category (e.g., articles of 1990 discussing about *presidents of South Africa*[2]). This category is a special case of multiple-entity OR queries where the number of entities can be very large (hundreds or even thousands).

We manually evaluated all the results returned by these queries (773 results totally) using a graded relevance scale (from 0 to 3), following the criteria described below:

- **Score 0**: The document has almost nothing to do with the query entities.
- **Score 1**: The topic of the document is **not** about the query entities, however the query entities are related to the document context.
- **Score 2**: The topic of the document is **not** about the query entities, however the query entities are important for the document context.
- **Score 3**: The topic of the document is about the query entities and discusses something important about them.

Table 1 shows the number of results per relevance score for each of the queries. The semantic layer, the SPARQL queries, and

[1] The configuration is available at: https://github.com/dice-group/gerbil/blob/master/src/main/java/org/aksw/gerbil/annotator/impl/babelfy/BabelfyAnnotator.java

[2] Entities that have the value <http://dbpedia.org/resource/Category:Presidents_of_South_Africa> in their subject property (<http://purl.org/dc/terms/subject>).

Table 1: Number of results per relevance score for each query of the evaluation dataset.

Query	Total number of results	Score 0 results	Score 1 results	Score 2 results	Score 3 results
1	65	13	13	4	35
2	28	20	5	1	2
3	28	24	2	0	2
4	23	15	3	1	4
5	38	18	6	7	7
6	24	16	4	1	3
7	29	13	6	8	2
8	61	10	27	15	9
9	42	14	10	10	8
10	28	17	4	6	1
11	27	13	10	4	0
12	24	13	2	8	1
13	30	21	1	4	4
14	37	15	8	8	6
15	27	18	5	2	2
16	23	5	14	2	2
17	21	13	2	2	4
18	25	6	4	9	6
19	41	24	4	8	5
20	22	11	8	3	0
21	29	16	5	5	3
22	47	33	7	3	4
23	31	18	3	8	2
24	23	14	3	3	3

the relevance scores (together with explanations for the provided scores) are publicly available[3].

4 PROBABILISTIC MODELING

The question is: *"what makes an archived document important given a time period and one or more query entities"?* We focus on an approach that makes use of the least amount of metadata information about the archived documents. This includes the *publication date* and the *extracted entities* of each document. Given this data, we have identified the following aspects that can affect the importance of a document to a query:

- the *relativeness* of a document with respect to the query entities (the document should talk about the query entities, ideally as its main topic).
- the *timeliness* of a document with respect to its publication date (the document should have been published in a time period which is important for the query entities).
- the *relatedness* of a document with respect to its reference to other entities (the document should discuss the relation of the query entities with other entities that are important for the query entities in important time periods).

The idea is to promote documents that: i) mention the query entities many times in their contents (because then, the topic of the document may be about these entities), ii) have been published in important (for the query entities) time periods, and iii) mention many other entities that co-occur frequently with the query entities in important time periods. For example, in case we want to rank articles of 1990 discussing about *Nelson Mandela*, we want to favor articles that i) discuss about *Nelson Mandela* as their main topic, ii) have been published in important (for *Nelson Mandela*) time periods (e.g., February of 1990 since during that period he was released from prison), and iii) mention other entities that seem to be important for Nelson Mandela during important time periods (e.g., *Frederik Willem de Klerk* who was South Africa's State President in 1990).

[3]http://l3s.de/~fafalios/jcdl/evaluation_dataset.zip

4.1 Relativeness

We consider that if the query entities are mentioned multiple times within a document, the document should receive a high score since the document's topic may be about these entities. The term frequency (in our case entity frequency) is a classic numerical statistic that is intended to reflect how important a word (entity) is to a document [26].

We first define a *relativeness* score of a document $d \in D_Q$ based on the *frequency* of the query entities in d. First, let $count(e, d)$ be the number of occurrences of e in document d. For the case of AND semantics ("$\wedge$"), the score is defined as:

$$score^f_\wedge(d, E_Q) = \frac{\sum_{e \in E_Q} count(e,d)}{\sum_{e' \in ents(d)} count(e',d)} \quad (1)$$

Notice that the score of a document will be 1.0 if it contains the query entities and no other entity. For the case of OR semantics ("$\vee$"), we can also consider the number of query entities mentioned in the document (since a document does not probably contain all the query entities as in the case of AND semantics). In this case, the *relativeness* score can be defined as follows:

$$score^f_\vee(d, E_Q) = \frac{\sum_{e \in E_Q} count(e,d)}{\sum_{e' \in ents(d)} count(e',d)} \cdot \frac{|ents(d) \cap E_Q|}{|E_Q|} \quad (2)$$

where $\frac{|ents(d) \cap E_Q|}{|E_Q|}$ is the percentage of query entities discussed in the document. The score of a document will be 1.0 if it contains all the query entities and no other entity. This formula favors documents mentioning many of the query entities multiple times.

Now, the probability of a retrieved document $d \in D_Q$ given only the query entities can be defined as:

$$P(d|E_Q) = \frac{score^f(d, E_Q)}{\sum_{d' \in D_Q} score^f(d', E_Q)} \quad (3)$$

4.2 Timeliness

Previous works on searching document archives have shown that, considering the fraction of documents published in a time period and mentioning the query entities can improve the effectiveness of document retrieval (compared to an approach that assumes equal distribution) [36]. In a similar way, and for the case of AND semantics, we define the following importance score of a *time period* $t \in T_Q$:

$$score^t_\wedge(t) = \frac{|docs(t) \cap D_Q|}{|D_Q|} \quad (4)$$

This scoring formula favors time periods in which there is a large number of documents discussing about the query entities.

For the case of OR semantics, in a time period t there may be a large number of documents discussing only for one of the query entities, while in another time period t' there may be a smaller number of documents discussing though for many of the query entities. For also taking into account the number of query entities discussed in documents of a specific time period, we consider the following formula:

$$score^t_{\vee}(t) = \frac{|docs(t) \cap D_Q|}{|D_Q|} \cdot N(E_Q, t) \quad (5)$$

where, $N(E_Q, t)$ is the average percentage of query entities discussed in articles of t, i.e.:

$$N(E_Q, t) = \frac{\sum_{d \in docs(t) \cap D_Q} \frac{|ents(d) \cap E_Q|}{|E_Q|}}{|docs(t) \cap D_Q|} \quad (6)$$

Now, the probability of a retrieved document $d \in D_Q$ given only its publication date t_d can be defined as:

$$P(d|t_d) = \frac{score^t(t_d)}{\sum_{d' \in D_Q} score^t(t_{d'})} \quad (7)$$

4.3 Relatedness

Recent works have shown that the co-occurrence of entities in documents of a specific time period is a strong indicator of their relatedness during that period [38, 40]. We also consider that entities that are co-mentioned frequently with the query entities in important time periods are probably important for them. However, there may be also some general entities that co-occur with the query entities in almost all documents (independently of the time period). Thus, we should also avoid over-emphasizing documents mentioning such "common" entities.

For the case of AND semantics, we consider the following *relatedness* score for an entity $e \in E_D \setminus E_Q$:

$$\begin{aligned} score^r_{\wedge}(e) &= idf_{\wedge}(e) \cdot \sum_{t \in T_Q} (score^t_{\wedge}(t) \cdot \frac{|docs(t) \cap D_Q \cap docs(e)|}{|docs(t) \cap D_Q|}) \\ &= idf_{\wedge}(e) \cdot \sum_{t \in T_Q} \frac{|docs(t) \cap D_Q \cap docs(e)|}{|D_Q|} \end{aligned} \quad (8)$$

where $idf_{\wedge}(e)$ is the inverse document frequency of entity e in the set of documents discussing about the query entities in the entire corpus, which can be defined as follows:

$$idf_{\wedge}(e) = 1 - \frac{|docs(e) \cap (\cap_{e' \in E_Q} docs(e'))|}{|\cap_{e' \in E_Q} docs(e')|} \quad (9)$$

The formula considers the percentage of documents in which the entity co-occurs with the query entities in important time periods.

For the case of OR semantics, the above formula does not consider the number of different query entities discussed in documents together with the entity e. To also handle this aspect, we consider the following *relatedness* score for the case of OR semantics:

$$\begin{aligned} score^r_{\vee}(e) &= idf_{\vee}(e)\, N(E_Q, e) \sum_{t \in T_Q} (score^t_{\vee}(t) \frac{|docs(t) \cap D_Q \cap docs(e)|}{|docs(t) \cap D_Q|}) \\ &= idf_{\vee}(e)\, N(E_Q, e) \sum_{t \in T_Q} (N(E_Q, t) \frac{|docs(t) \cap D_Q \cap docs(e)|}{|D_Q|}) \end{aligned} \quad (10)$$

where $N(E_Q, e)$ is the average percentage of query entities discussed in articles together with entity e, i.e.:

$$N(E_Q, e) = \frac{\sum_{d \in docs(e) \cap D_Q} \frac{|ents(d) \cap E_Q|}{|E_Q|}}{|docs(e) \cap D_Q|} \quad (11)$$

Now the inverse document frequency $idf_{\vee}(e)$ includes documents mentioning at least one of the query entities, i.e.:

$$idf_{\vee}(e) = 1 - \frac{|docs(e) \cap (\cup_{e' \in E_Q} docs(e'))|}{|\cup_{e' \in E_Q} docs(e')|} \quad (12)$$

This formula favors related entities that i) co-occur frequently with many of the query entities, ii) are discussed in documents published in important (for the query entities) time periods.

Now, the probability of a document $d \in D_Q$ given only other entities mentioned in the retrieved documents (E_{D_Q}) can be defined as:

$$P(d|E_{D_Q}) = \frac{\sum_{e \in ents(d) \setminus E_Q} score^r(e)}{\sum_{d' \in D_Q} \sum_{e' \in ents(d') \setminus E_Q} score^r(e')} \quad (13)$$

4.4 Joining the Models

We can now combine the different models in a single probability score:

$$P(d|E_Q, t_d, E_{D_Q}) = \frac{P(d|E_Q)P(d|T_Q)P(d|E_{D_Q})}{\sum_{d' \in D_Q} P(d'|E_Q)P(d'|T_Q)P(d'|E_{D_Q})} \quad (14)$$

where the denominator can be ignored as it does not influence the ranking.

5 STOCHASTIC MODELING

Here we model the problem as a *random walker* on the graph (*Markov chain*) defined by the query-entities E_Q, the returned documents D_Q, and the entities mentioned in the documents E_{D_Q}. Then, we propose a biased (personalized-like) PageRank algorithm for analyzing the graph and scoring its nodes. Similar modeling and scoring methods have been applied for the problems of *results re-ranking* [13] and *enrichment* [12] in information retrieval.

5.1 The Transition Graph

The walker starts from a query-entity and can move either to a document mentioning the entity or to a related entity that co-occurs with the query-entity in at least one document. From a document, the walker can move to an entity mentioned in it, while from a no query-entity, the walker can only move to a document mentioning that entity.

In the case of logical AND semantics, the query-entities are connected with all documents, while in the case of OR semantics, each query-entity is connected with at least one document. Figure 2 shows an example of a transition graph for the case of OR semantics. In this example, the query-entities are two (the black nodes), while we notice that three of the documents mention both query-entities (d_2, d_3 and d_4).

5.2 The Transition Probabilities

From query-entities to documents or related entities. When the walker lies at a query-entity $e \in E_Q$, he can either move to a document d mentioning the entity or to a related entity e'. When

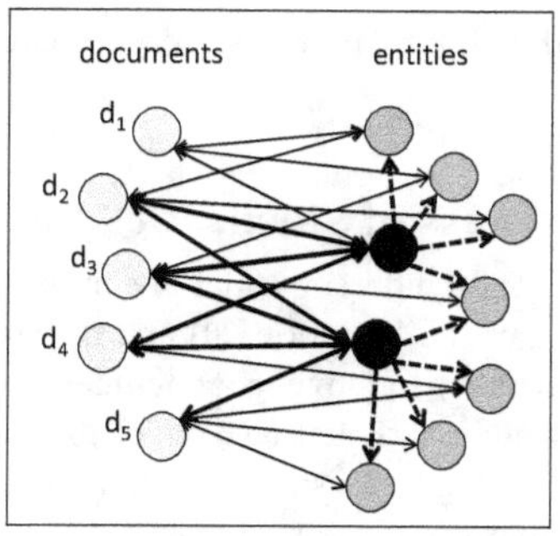

Figure 2: An example of the considered transition graph for the case of logical OR semantics (with the query-entities being the black nodes).

moving to a document, we consider its *relativeness* and *timeliness* scores as introduced in the previous section. Specifically, the weight of the edge from a query-entity e to a document d is defined as:

$$weight(e \longrightarrow d) = \frac{score^f(d, E_Q) \cdot score^t(t_d)}{\sum_{d' \in docs(e) \cap D_Q}(score^f(d', E_Q) \cdot score^t(t_{d'}))} \quad (15)$$

For moving from a query-entity e to a related entity e', we consider the *relativeness* score of e':

$$weight(e \longrightarrow e') = \frac{score^r(e')}{\sum_{e'' \in out(e)}(score^r(e''))} \quad (16)$$

where $out(e)$ is the set of nodes connected to e through outgoing edges starting from e.

However, the weights of the outgoing edges of a single node represent transition probabilities and must sum to 1. Thus, the weight of the edge from a query-entity e to a connected node n (that can be either a document or a related entity) is defined as:

$$weight(e \longrightarrow n) = \begin{cases} p_1 \cdot weight(e \longrightarrow d) & n \in D_Q \\ (1 - p_1) \cdot weight(e \longrightarrow e') & n \in E_{D_Q} \end{cases} \quad (17)$$

where $p_1 \in [0, 1]$ is the probability that the walker selects to move to a document node.

From documents to entities. For moving from a document d to an entity e mentioned in d, it is more likely that the walker moves to an entity that is mentioned many times within its contents. Thus, we simply consider the normalized frequency of e in d. Specifically:

$$weight(d \longrightarrow e) = \frac{count(e, d)}{\sum_{e' \in ents(d)}(count(e', d))} \quad (18)$$

From no query-entities to documents. Likewise, when moving from a no query-entity e to a document d, it is more likely that the walker moves to a document that mentions e many times. Thus, we again consider the normalized frequency of e in d. Specifically:

$$weight(e \longrightarrow d) = \frac{count(e, d)}{\sum_{d' \in docs(e) \cap D_Q}(count(e, d'))} \quad (19)$$

5.3 The Stochastic Analysis (Random Walk with Restart)

For analyzing the transition graph, we follow a PageRank-like algorithm. The walker starts from the query-entities and can either follow an edge or perform a "restart", i.e., jump to a query-entity and start again the traversal . Formally, the score of a graph node n is defined as:

$$r(n) = d \cdot Jump(n) + (1 - d) \cdot \sum_{n' \in in(n)} (weight(n' \longrightarrow n) \cdot r(n')) \quad (20)$$

where $d \in [0, 1]$ is the probability that the walker performs a restart, $Jump(n)$ is the probability the walker to restart by jumping to node n, $in(n)$ is the set of nodes connected to n through incoming edges, and $weight(n \longrightarrow n')$ (as defined in Formulas 15-19) is the probability that the walker visits n when being at node n' connected to n (there should be an edge from n' to n).

As regards the *restart*, we allow equiprobable jumps only to query entities, i.e.:

$$Jump(n) = \begin{cases} 1/|E_Q| & n \in E_Q \\ 0 & n \notin E_Q \end{cases} \quad (21)$$

Regarding the initial scores of the graph nodes, we assign the same score to the query entities ($1/|E_Q|$), while the score of all other entities is zero. Finally, the algorithm must iteratively run to convergence.

6 EVALUATION

We evaluated the performance of the proposed models using the ground truth dataset described in Section 3.3 and two evaluation measures: *Normalized Discounted Cumulative Gain (NDCG)* at positions 5, 10, full list, and *Precision (P)* at 5 and 10 (precision for full list is the same in all cases). Precision is the fraction of relevant results among the top retrieved results, while NDCG uses a graded relevance scale and measures the usefulness, or gain, of a document based on its position in the result list [21]. For precision, we consider a document as relevant if its relevance score is either 2 or 3 and irrelevant if it is either 0 or 1. As regards timeliness, we considered *day* granularity. We also tested the case of random rankings of the results. In this case, we computed 10 different random lists for each query and considered the average NDCG and precision scores.

6.1 Effectiveness of Probabilistic Models

We investigated the performance of each model described in Section 4 as well as their combinations.

6.1.1 Overall Results. Table 2 shows the average NDCG and precision scores for all queries. We notice that joining all three models provides the best results. The improvement of the top-5 results compared to *relativeness* is about 17% in NDCG and 18% in precision, which is statistically significant (paired t-test, $p \leq 0.05$). Note that *relativeness* can be considered a baseline model for our problem since it considers entity frequency which is a classic numerical statistic [26]. The results also show that *relatedness* performs very well, outperforming the joined models for P@10. This means that considering other entities that co-occur frequently with the query entities in important time periods has a positive effect on the ranking.

6.1.2 Detailed results per query type. Tables 3-6 show the results per query type.

Regarding *single entity queries* (Table 3), we observe that combining relativeness with relatedness has almost the same performance with the case of joining all models. This means that timeliness seems to have a minor negative effect on the rankings. For this query type, query 4 has the best performance on the joined model with NDCG@5 = 1.0 and NDCG@10 = 0.97. On the contrary, query 5 does not perform well with NDCG@5 = 0.29 and NDCG@10 = 0.37 (this query returns several "headlines" articles summarizing what is inside today's paper, which may confuse our modeling).

As regards *multiple-entity AND queries* (Table 4), we observe that joining relativeness with timeliness seems to perform better with small difference compared to the case of joining of all models, which means that here timeliness has a positive effect on the ranking. We also notice that all models perform worst compared to the single-entity case. For this query type, the NDCG@10 score of all queries ranges from 0.35 (for query 8) to 0.67 (for query 12).

The case of *multiple-entity OR queries* (Table 5) is very similar to the case of *single entity queries* where timeliness seems to have a minor negative impact. Here almost all queries have very good performance with NDCG@10 score > 0.55.

As regards *category queries* (Table 6), it is very interesting that the performance of relativeness is very low, while relatedness performs very well and timeliness has a positive impact especially for the top-5 lists. By thoroughly checking the results of queries that perform very bad in relativeness (like queries 19 and 22), we noticed that the reason for this bad performance is the presence of a large number of disambiguation errors in the returned documents. A characteristic of this type of queries is the big number of query entities which in turn increases the probability of disambiguation errors. Note that relativeness favors documents containing many instances of the query entities. However, if an irrelevant document contains many instances of entity names that have been wrongly linked to query entities, this document will receive a high relativeness score (since it contains many "false positive" query entities). For example, query 19 in our dataset has a very bad performance in relativeness (NDCG@5 = 0.02, NDCG@10 = 0.10). This query requests articles mentioning NASA civilian astronauts, however many instances of the entity name *Armstrong* have been incorrectly linked to the American astronaut Neil Armstrong (like the referee Hank Armstrong or the company Armstrong World Industries). Likewise, in query 22 several instances of the entity names *Teresa* and *Theresa* are incorrectly mapped to Mother Teresa. Nevertheless, we see that *relatedness* somehow fixes this problem. This model considers the co-occurrence of entities in important time periods and favors documents that contain many instances of other important entities. The probability that many false positive cases co-occur with the same related entities in many documents is very low, and thus considering entity associations has a positive effect on the ranking. In query 19, for example, the incorrect instances of the query entity Neil Armstrong co-occur with entities that do not exist in the documents in which Neil Armstrong has been correctly identified, and thus the relatedness score (Equation 10) of these entities is low.

6.2 Effectiveness of Stochastic Model

We run experiments for different values of d probability (probability to perform a restart, cf. Equation 20) and different values of p_1 probability (probability to move to a document node when being at a query-entity node, cf. Equation 17). For the restart probability, we tested the following 5 cases: $d = 0.0, 0.2, 0.4, 0.6, 0.8$. Note that testing $d = 1.0$ does not make sense, since the walker will never reach document nodes. Regarding the p_1 probability, we tested 6 cases ($p_1 = 0.0, 0.2, 0.4, 0.6, 0.8, 1.0$). Empirically, $d = 0.2$ provides the best results independently of the p_1 value. Thus, all the results reported below correspond to $d = 0.2$. Moreover, in all experiments, we set the number of iterations to 30.

Tables 7-10 show the results per query type and for different values of p_1 probability. For the first three types of queries, we observe that $p_1 = 1.0$ provides the best results and that, as the probability gets lower, the results get worse. Using $p_1 = 1.0$, the walker can move only to document nodes. This means that for small values of p_1 probability, the algorithm overemphasizes the association between the entities resulting in worst performance. Thus, the results show that reaching documents through related entities affects negatively the rankings for these types of queries.

Compared to the results of the probabilistic modeling, we see that: i) the performance of the two models is almost the same for single-entity queries, while the stochastic model outperforms the best probabilistic model for multiple-entity AND queries, and ii) the best probabilistic model outperforms the stochastic model for multiple-entity OR queries. Regarding (ii), this failure of the stochastic model is probably due to the fact that the graph in the case of OR queries is not as well-connected as in the case of AND queries (for OR queries, the graph may contain disconnected components, e.g., in cases where there are no documents mentioning all query entities).

However, for the category queries (Table 10), we see that $p_1 = 1.0$ provides the worst results, while $p_1 = 0.4$ performs better. This means that, for this type of queries, considering the associations of the query entities with other entities mentioned in the retrieved documents affects positively the results. However, at the same time, we see that we should not give too much emphasis to this (by giving very low value to p_1). Notice that this is in correspondence to the evaluation results of the probabilistic models for the same type of queries. Moreover, we notice that the stochastic model for $p_1 = 0.4$ performs better than the best probabilistic model, providing better rankings and more relevant results in the top positions.

6.3 Synopsis of Evaluation Results

Based on the evaluation results, we can conclude that:

- *Category queries* is a special case where the number of query entities can be very large and this makes the results more susceptible to disambiguation errors of the used entity linking system. Thereby, for this type of queries one should select a model which considers the associations between the query-entities and other entities mentioned in the returned

Table 2: Average NDCG and Precision of the probabilistic models for all queries.

Measure	Random ranking	Relativeness [A]	Timeliness [B]	Relatedness [C]	[A][B]	[A][C]	[B][C]	[A][B][C]
NDCG@5	0.26	0.48	0.27	0.41	0.53	0.52	0.45	**0.56**
NDCG@10	0.33	0.52	0.36	0.50	0.55	0.56	0.51	**0.58**
NDCG@all	0.68	0.79	0.69	0.76	0.80	0.81	0.76	**0.82**
P@5	0.27	0.44	0.28	0.48	0.48	0.50	0.45	**0.52**
P@10	0.29	0.38	0.30	**0.45**	0.37	0.42	0.41	0.41

Table 3: Average NDCG and Precision of the probabilistic models for single-entity queries (Q1-Q6).

Measure	[A]	[B]	[C]	[A][B]	[A][C]	[B][C]	[A][B][C]
NDCG@5	0.66	0.30	0.40	0.68	0.69	0.45	**0.70**
NDCG@10	0.69	0.38	0.51	0.70	**0.71**	0.51	0.70
NDCG@all	**0.88**	0.67	0.75	0.87	**0.88**	0.72	0.87
P@5	0.57	0.23	0.50	0.57	**0.60**	0.40	**0.60**
P@10	0.40	0.27	**0.45**	0.40	0.40	0.38	0.40

Table 4: Average NDCG and Precision of the probabilistic models for multiple-entity AND queries (Q7-Q12).

Measure	[A]	[B]	[C]	[A][B]	[A][C]	[B][C]	[A][B][C]
NDCG@5	0.34	0.28	0.31	**0.42**	0.35	0.38	0.40
NDCG@10	0.43	0.33	0.40	0.46	0.45	0.46	**0.47**
NDCG@all	0.76	0.71	0.75	**0.78**	0.76	0.77	0.77
P@5	0.43	0.33	0.30	**0.50**	0.47	0.43	**0.50**
P@10	0.50	0.32	0.42	0.48	**0.53**	0.47	0.50

Table 5: Average NDCG and Precision of the probabilistic models for multiple-entity OR queries (Q13-Q18).

Measure	[A]	[B]	[C]	[A][B]	[A][C]	[B][C]	[A][B][C]
NDCG@5	0.68	0.24	0.44	0.70	**0.72**	0.46	0.71
NDCG@10	0.69	0.36	0.55	0.69	0.72	0.54	**0.73**
NDCG@all	0.87	0.69	0.79	0.87	**0.88**	0.79	**0.88**
P@5	0.60	0.27	0.57	0.60	**0.63**	0.43	**0.63**
P@10	0.42	0.30	**0.48**	0.40	0.45	0.42	0.45

Table 6: Average NDCG and Precision of the probabilistic models for category queries (Q19-Q22).

Measure	[A]	[B]	[C]	[A][B]	[A][C]	[B][C]	[A][B][C]
NDCG@5	0.22	0.27	0.48	0.34	0.34	**0.52**	0.41
NDCG@10	0.28	0.37	**0.53**	0.36	0.38	**0.53**	0.43
NDCG@all	0.66	0.68	**0.78**	0.70	0.71	0.77	0.73
P@5	0.17	0.27	**0.53**	0.23	0.30	**0.53**	0.33
P@10	0.20	0.30	**0.45**	0.20	0.28	0.37	0.28

Table 7: Average NDCG and Precision of the stochastic model for single entity queries (Q1-Q6).

Measure	p_1=0.0	p_1=0.2	p_1=0.4	p_1=0.6	p_1=0.8	p_1=1.0
NDCG@5	0.09	0.27	0.48	0.63	0.65	**0.67**
NDCG@10	0.18	0.35	0.54	0.69	0.72	**0.74**
NDCG@all	0.60	0.68	0.77	0.85	**0.87**	**0.87**
P@5	0.07	0.23	0.43	0.47	0.53	**0.60**
P@10	0.12	0.23	0.33	0.37	0.42	**0.43**

Table 8: Average NDCG and Precision of the stochastic model for multiple-entity AND queries (Q7-Q12).

Measure	p_1=0.0	p_1=0.2	p_1=0.4	p_1=0.6	p_1=0.8	p_1=1.0
NDCG@5	0.29	0.29	0.32	0.31	0.37	**0.48**
NDCG@10	0.36	0.36	0.40	0.45	0.47	**0.52**
NDCG@all	0.72	0.73	0.74	0.75	0.78	**0.80**
P@5	0.27	0.27	0.27	0.30	0.37	**0.57**
P@10	0.30	0.30	0.38	0.45	0.47	**0.50**

Table 9: Average NDCG and Precision of the stochastic model for multiple-entity OR queries (Q13-Q18).

Measure	p_1=0.0	p_1=0.2	p_1=0.4	p_1=0.6	p_1=0.8	p_1=1.0
NDCG@5	0.20	0.30	0.32	0.38	0.45	**0.59**
NDCG@10	0.27	0.38	0.42	0.51	0.52	**0.65**
NDCG@all	0.66	0.71	0.72	0.75	0.76	**0.84**
P@5	0.27	0.33	0.33	0.37	0.47	**0.53**
P@10	0.30	0.33	0.35	0.42	0.42	**0.45**

Table 10: Average NDCG and Precision of the stochastic model for category queries (Q19-Q24).

Measure	p_1=0.0	p_1=0.2	p_1=0.4	p_1=0.6	p_1=0.8	p_1=1.0
NDCG@5	0.43	0.47	**0.53**	0.50	0.46	0.23
NDCG@10	0.48	0.54	**0.55**	0.52	0.54	0.36
NDCG@all	0.74	0.77	**0.79**	0.77	0.77	0.68
P@5	0.57	0.57	**0.60**	**0.60**	**0.60**	0.23
P@10	0.42	**0.43**	0.40	0.40	**0.43**	0.28

documents, since this limits the negative impact of this problem. Finally, a stochastic model with $p_1 = 0.4$ outperforms the best probabilistic model (relatedness).

- For the other types of queries, a model which considers both *relativeness* and *relatedness* should be selected, while *timeliness* does not seem to significantly affect the rankings. For single-entity and multiple-entity AND queries, one may select the stochastic model which seems to perform better than the probabilistic models, however for multiple-entity OR queries where the graph is not so well connected, one may opt for a probabilistic model.

7 CONCLUSIONS

We have formalized the problem of ranking archived documents for structured (SPARQL) queries on semantic layers, i.e., on RDF graphs describing metadata and annotation information about the documents. To cope with this problem, we have proposed two ranking models, a probabilistic one and a stochastic one, which jointly consider the following aspects: i) the *relativeness* of the documents to the query entities, ii) the *timeliness* of the documents, and iii) the temporal *relatedness* of other entities mentioned in the documents to the query entities. To evaluate our approach, and due to lack of evaluation datasets for the problem at hand, we carefully created a new ground truth dataset which we make publicly available for fostering further research on similar problems. The evaluation results showed that the proposed models can identify important - for the query entities - documents, achieving high NDCG and precision scores and outperforming a classic, frequency-based baseline model. The results also showed that *relatedness*, i.e., considering the temporal association of the query entities with other entities mentioned in the results, has a high positive impact on the ranking and can limit the negative effect caused by disambiguation errors of entity linking.

Regarding future work, we plan to study the applicability of similar models on other types of archives, like web archives where much more noisy (and probably spam) data exists and the archived documents (web pages) contain multiple similar or identical versions. Another interesting direction is the study of diversity-aware ranking methods that can reflect the diversity of the retrieved documents. We also plan to build user-friendly interfaces on top of semantic layers which will make use of the proposed ranking models and will allow end-users to easily explore the archives.

ACKNOWLEDGMENTS

The work was partially funded by the European Commission for the ERC Advanced Grant ALEXANDRIA (No. 339233).

REFERENCES

[1] Ablimit Aji, Yu Wang, Eugene Agichtein, and Evgeniy Gabrilovich. 2010. Using the past to score the present: Extending term weighting models through revision history analysis. In *19th CIKM*. ACM.

[2] Marcelo Arenas, Bernardo Cuenca Grau, Evgeny Kharlamov, Sarunas Marciuska, Dmitriy Zheleznyakov, and Ernesto Jimenez-Ruiz. 2014. SemFacet: semantic faceted search over yago. In *International Conference on World Wide Web*. ACM.

[3] Irem Arikan, Srikanta Bedathur, and Klaus Berberich. 2009. Time Will Tell: Leveraging Temporal Expressions in IR. In *2nd ACM International Conference on Web Search and Data Mining*. ACM.

[4] Krisztian Balog, Pavel Serdyukov, and Arjen P De Vries. 2010. Overview of the trec 2010 entity track. In *In TREC 2010*.

[5] Klaus Berberich, Srikanta Bedathur, Omar Alonso, and Gerhard Weikum. 2010. A Language Modeling Approach for Temporal Information Needs. In *European Conference on Information Retrieval*. Springer, 13–25.

[6] Karen Calhoun. 2014. *Exploring digital libraries: foundations, practice, prospects*. Facet Publishing.

[7] Stéphane Campinas, Renaud Delbru, and Giovanni Tummarello. 2012. Effective retrieval model for entity with multi-valued attributes: Bm25mf and beyond. In *International Conference on Knowledge Engineering and Knowledge Management*. Springer, 200–215.

[8] Ricardo Campos, Gaël Dias, Alípio M Jorge, and Adam Jatowt. 2015. Survey of temporal information retrieval and related applications. *ACM Computing Surveys (CSUR)* 47, 2 (2015), 15.

[9] Mario Cataldi, Luigi Di Caro, and Claudio Schifanella. 2010. Emerging topic detection on twitter based on temporal and social terms evaluation. In *Proceedings of the tenth international workshop on multimedia data mining*. ACM, 4.

[10] Wisam Dakka, Luis Gravano, and Panagiotis Ipeirotis. 2012. Answering general time-sensitive queries. *IEEE Transactions on Knowledge and Data Engineering* 24, 2 (2012), 220–235.

[11] P. Fafalios, H. Holzmann, V. Kasturia, and W. Nejdl. 2017. Building and Querying Semantic Layers for Web Archives. In *ACM/IEEE-CS Joint Conference on Digital Libraries (JCDL'17)*. Toronto, Ontario, Canada.

[12] P. Fafalios and Y. Tzitzikas. 2014. Post-Analysis of Keyword-based Search Results using Entity Mining, Linked Data and Link Analysis at Query Time. In *2014 IEEE Eighth International Conference on Semantic Computing (ICSC 2014)*. IEEE, Newport Beach, California, USA.

[13] Pavlos Fafalios and Yannis Tzitzikas. 2017. Stochastic reranking of biomedical search results based on extracted entities. *Journal of the Association for Information Science and Technology* 68, 11 (2017), 2572–2586.

[14] Sébastien Ferré. 2014. Sparklis: a sparql endpoint explorer for expressive question answering. In *ISWC Posters & Demonstrations Track*.

[15] Azam Feyznia, Mohsen Kahani, and Fattane Zarrinkalam. 2014. COLINA: A Method for Ranking SPARQL Query Results through Content and Link Analysis.. In *International Semantic Web Conference (Posters & Demos)*. 273–276.

[16] Harry Halpin, Daniel M Herzig, Peter Mika, Roi Blanco, Jeffrey Pound, Henry S Thompson, and Thanh Tran Duc. 2010. Evaluating ad-hoc object retrieval. In *International Workshop on Evaluation of Semantic Technologies, IWEST*. Citeseer.

[17] Johannes Hoffart, Mohamed Amir Yosef, Ilaria Bordino, Hagen Fürstenau, Manfred Pinkal, Marc Spaniol, Bilyana Taneva, Stefan Thater, and Gerhard Weikum. 2011. Robust disambiguation of named entities in text. In *Conference on Empirical Methods in Natural Language Processing*.

[18] Aidan Hogan, Andreas Harth, Jürgen Umbrich, Sheila Kinsella, Axel Polleres, and Stefan Decker. 2011. Searching and browsing linked data with SWSE: the semantic Web search engine. *Web Semantics: Science, Services and Agents on the World Wide Web* 9, 4 (2011), 365–401.

[19] Helge Holzmann and Avishek Anand. 2016. Tempas: Temporal Archive Search Based on Tags. In *International Conference on World Wide Web*.

[20] Helge Holzmann, Wolfgang Nejdl, and Avishek Anand. 2017. Exploring Web Archives Through Temporal Anchor Texts. In *Proceedings of the 2017 ACM on Web Science Conference*. ACM, 289–298.

[21] Kalervo Järvelin and Jaana Kekäläinen. 2002. Cumulated gain-based evaluation of IR techniques. *ACM Transactions on Information Systems (TOIS)* 20, 4 (2002), 422–446.

[22] Peiquan Jin, Jianlong Lian, Xujian Zhao, and Shouhong Wan. 2008. Tise: A temporal search engine for web contents. In *Intelligent Information Technology Application, 2008. IITA'08. Second International Symposium on*, Vol. 3. IEEE.

[23] Nattiya Kanhabua, Roi Blanco, Kjetil Nørvåg, et al. 2015. Temporal information retrieval. *Foundations and Trends® in Information Retrieval* 9, 2 (2015), 91–208.

[24] Nattiya Kanhabua and Kjetil Nørvåg. 2012. Learning to rank search results for time-sensitive queries. In *Proceedings of the 21st ACM international conference on Information and knowledge management*. ACM, 2463–2466.

[25] Sara Latifi and Mohammadali Nematbakhsh. 2014. Query-independent learning to rank RDF entity results of SPARQL queries. In *Computer and Knowledge Engineering (ICCKE), 2014 4th International eConference on*. IEEE.

[26] Jure Leskovec, Anand Rajaraman, and Jeffrey David Ullman. 2014. *Mining of massive datasets*. Cambridge University Press.

[27] Donald Metzler, Rosie Jones, Fuchun Peng, and Ruiqiang Zhang. 2009. Improving search relevance for implicitly temporal queries. In *32nd international ACM SIGIR conference on Research and development in information retrieval*. ACM, 700–701.

[28] Andrea Moro, Alessandro Raganato, and Roberto Navigli. 2014. Entity linking meets word sense disambiguation: a unified approach. *Transactions of the Association for Computational Linguistics* 2 (2014).

[29] Kunal Mulay and P Sreenivasa Kumar. 2011. SPRING: Ranking the results of SPARQL queries on Linked Data. In *Proceedings of the 17th International Conference on Management of Data*. Computer Society of India, 12.

[30] Axel-Cyrille Ngonga Ngomo, Michael Hoffmann, Ricardo Usbeck, and Kunal Jha. 2017. Holistic and Scalable Ranking of RDF Data. In *2017 IEEE International Conference on Big Data*.

[31] Jeffrey Pound, Peter Mika, and Hugo Zaragoza. 2010. Ad-hoc object retrieval in the web of data. In *19th international conference on World wide web*. ACM.

[32] Antonio J Roa-Valverde and Miguel-Angel Sicilia. 2014. A survey of approaches for ranking on the web of data. *Information Retrieval* 17, 4 (2014), 295–325.

[33] Evan Sandhaus. 2008. The new york times annotated corpus. *Linguistic Data Consortium, Philadelphia* 6, 12 (2008).

[34] Wei Shen, Jianyong Wang, and Jiawei Han. 2015. Entity linking with a knowledge base: Issues, techniques, and solutions. *IEEE Transactions on Knowledge and Data Engineering* 27, 2 (2015), 443–460.

[35] Jaspreet Singh, Wolfgang Nejdl, and Avishek Anand. 2016. Expedition: A Time-Aware Exploratory Search System Designed for Scholars. In *SIGIR conference on Research and Development in Information Retrieval*.

[36] Jaspreet Singh, Wolfgang Nejdl, and Avishek Anand. 2016. History by diversity: Helping historians search news archives. In *ACM Conference on Human Information Interaction and Retrieval*.

[37] Alberto Tonon, Gianluca Demartini, and Philippe Cudré-Mauroux. 2012. Combining inverted indices and structured search for ad-hoc object retrieval. In *ACM SIGIR*. ACM, 125–134.

[38] Nam Khanh Tran, Tuan Tran, and Claudia Niederée. 2017. Beyond Time: Dynamic Context-Aware Entity Recommendation. In *European Semantic Web Conference*.

[39] Yannis Tzitzikas, Nikos Manolis, and Panagiotis Papadakos. 2016. Faceted exploration of RDF/S datasets: a survey. *Journal of Intelligent Information Systems* (2016), 1–36.

[40] Lei Zhang, Achim Rettinger, and Ji Zhang. 2016. A Probabilistic Model for Time-Aware Entity Recommendation. In *International Semantic Web Conference*.

Preserving Author Editing History Using Blockchain Technology

Muhammad Syafiq Mohd Pozi
Universiti Tenaga Nasional
Selangor, Malaysia
syafiq.pozi@uniten.edu.my

Gopinath Muruti
Universiti Tenaga Nasional
Selangor, Malaysia
gopinathmuruti@gmail.com

Asmidar Abu Bakar
Universiti Tenaga Nasional
Selangor, Malaysia
asmidar@uniten.edu.my

Adam Jatowt
Kyoto University
Kyoto, Japan
adam@dl.kuis.kyoto-u.ac.jp

Yukiko Kawai
Kyoto Sangyo University
Kyoto, Japan
kawai@cc.kyoto-su.ac.jp

ABSTRACT

Authorship contribution is often taken for granted. Internally, the contribution rate is usually known among all the authors of a given paper. However, this rate is hard to be verified by external parties, as the measurement of the authors' contribution is still not common and the way to measure it is unclear. In this paper, we propose a new blockchain based framework to assess the contribution of all authors of any scientific paper. Our framework can be implemented by anyone who is directly or indirectly involved in the publication of the paper, such as a principal researcher, grant funder, research assistant or anyone from relevant external bodies.

CCS CONCEPTS

• **Information systems** → **Digital libraries and archives**; *Trust*; • **Applied computing** → Document analysis;

KEYWORDS

Authorship contribution; blockchain; history preservation;

ACM Reference Format:

Muhammad Syafiq Mohd Pozi, Gopinath Muruti, Asmidar Abu Bakar, Adam Jatowt, and Yukiko Kawai. 2018. Preserving Author Editing History Using Blockchain Technology. In *JCDL '18: The 18th ACM/IEEE Joint Conference on Digital Libraries, June 3–7, 2018, Fort Worth, TX, USA.* ACM, New York, NY, USA, 4 pages. https://doi.org/10.1145/3197026.3197068

1 INTRODUCTION

Many universities and research institutes evaluate researcher performance and significance based on the total number and quality of his/her publications. Those publications are typically assessed by the prestige level associated with the name of the proceedings or journal, conference rating or impact factor. What is also considered is the fact whether the publications were written by the researcher himself or herself only, or whether they were rather co-authored.

With the current methodologies however, one cannot determine non-contribute works, such as ones with "gift and guest authors" [1], that is authors who are listed as co-authors, even though they may have not contributed at all or who may have contributed to a limited extent to paper writing. It is difficult also to verify the fact that other non-authors (e.g., research assistants or under/graduate students) might have actually contributed much more to the paper compared to the work of the listed authors [9]. Even though there are authorship guidelines available such as ones in [14], politics still play an important role in authoring publications (e.g., pressure from a senior faculty member or grant holder). After all, everyone has his/her own interests.

Many metrics have been proposed to measure general author performance, from simple citation count to h−index [7], or g−index [4]. However, these metrics cannot provide proof-of-work for each author listed in a paper and they generally assume equal contribution of all listed co-authors. Yet, as stated before, in some cases, an author can, without any grounds, claim his/her contribution in regards to a paper, especially, when he or she is a senior researcher.

Motivated by these we propose a new authorship proof-of-work model based on blockchain technology [11]. Originated from Bitcoin [8], blockchain is used to verify every transaction that occurs on the network. Unlike traditional transactions, which are centralized and directed to one main server, blockchain verification involves large amount of users, known as "miners". These "miners" continue performing the verification process as long as there is some incentives for doing so. The blockchain paradigm as described using Ethereum platform [15] can be expressed as follows:

$$\sigma_{t+1} \equiv \Upsilon(\sigma_t, T) \quad (1)$$

where T is a transaction, Υ is the Ethereum state transition function, which covers components used to perform arbitrary computation; and σ is embracing components used to store arbitrary state between transactions. Each valid transaction is collated into blocks. These blocks are chained together, hence the name blockchain expressed as follows:

$$\sigma_{t+1} \equiv \Pi(\sigma_t, B) \quad (2)$$

$$B \equiv (\ldots, (T_0, T_1, \ldots)) \quad (3)$$

$$\Pi(\sigma, B) \equiv \Omega(B, \Upsilon(\Upsilon(\sigma, T_0), T_1)\ldots) \quad (4)$$

where Ω is the block-finalization state transition function (a function that rewards a nomination party); B is this block, consisting of a series of transactions and Π is the block-level state-transition function. Generating a new block is secured by cryptopuzzles, where each peer must expend effort in order to "win" the right to generate a block. The party that produces the longest chain, such as in Equation 2, 3, 4 will be selected by the network as the winner.

JCDL '18, June 3–7, 2018, Fort Worth, TX, USA

ACM ISBN 978-1-4503-5178-2/18/06...$15.00
https://doi.org/10.1145/3197026.3197068

Each transaction needs to be verified by every node in the network, which can been seen by the public. Henceforth, various applications such as asset registries [2] or domain registries [12] have been developed on top of blockchain technology to reap the benefit of cheap storage without jeopardizing the data integrity.

In this paper, we propose an authorship statistical aggregation model for, but not limited to, the scenarios of writing academic papers. This model could be adopted to other fields such as the medical one besides the academic field, where each medical prognosis can be viewed easily by other doctors across the world. Currently, the proposed model is adopted to enhance the integrity of a document, and at the same time, preserve the contributions of document's authors. In this paper, we attempt to record document authorship in a multi-author scenario.

The reminder of this paper is as follows: Section 2 highlights the related approaches done using the blockchain technology and is followed by Section 3 which details the proposed author contribution verification model as well as the overall functioning of the model's mechanisms. Section 4 describes our implementation, while Section 5 discusses model limitations. Finally, the last section contains conclusion and future work.

2 RELATED WORKS

Communication-based constructs such as transactions, contracts, agreements, and records protect various entities' interests. However, nowadays, due to large number of communication activities resulting from significant development in communication technology, these constructs and tools cannot be approached from an offline perspective only. For example, a valid transaction should have some witnesses in order to be trusted, however, it is hard to ensure the presence of witnesses when performing online transaction. Blockchain solves this key issue, that is the requirement for maintaining good trust level, as the description of a particular transaction is verified by large number of users. Hence, there is very strong guarantee on data integrity.

Various data-oriented domains have started to adopt blockchain into their operations. For example, privacy preservation model using blockchain has been proposed in [16] to store decentralized health-focused data permanently in the network. Typically health care data should not be modified as well as controlled by third, unrelated parties. Any breach on the integrity of data could result in serious consequences such as violation of user privacy as well as mistaken medical diagnosis. The later could even result in fatality. Hence, a trusted mechanism for preserving such data is necessary.

In the academic domain, researchers have introduced a concept of an intellectual currency that can represent scholarly reputation based on educational records [10]. However, its implementation is still in an infancy stage, despite quite ambitious objectives. The authors, though, has already established good infrastructure to facilitate the process[1].

Academic world revolves around scientific publications which are typically the basis for evaluating academic merit and achievement. The average number of co-authors of scientific publications have increased quite much throughout the last century [5] making the task of determining and recording the scope of individual's contribution more necessary. Moreover, anyone can be involved in the process of preparing an academic paper, even people from outside of academia. Thus we need an effective way of ensuring that co-authors are credited in a fair way. Our work is one of the first attempts towards this goal taking advantage of novel and trusted technology of Blockchain.

3 AUTHOR CONTRIBUTION VERIFICATION MODEL

Our proposed author contribution verification model must adhere to the following requirements:

(1) **Affordability**: Utilizing blockchain is actually expensive, since every transaction costs money. Hence, it is not practical to send data very frequently, such as whenever a change is made into a paper. It also depends on how large data is to be transfered, and how fast does a user wish the blockchain to verify the transaction. As a result, the cost may increase accordingly. Therefore, an effective model should be designed to send the data into the blockchain at the suitable time in order to avoid increased amount of transaction fees until the completion of the paper.

(2) **Privacy**: From the paper creation until the camera-ready version, every step should be kept private. This is important in order to protect the novelty of the paper, as well as the character of collaboration, challenges met during the paper preparation, etc. In some cases, the authors would even feel uncomfortable to reveal the problems or mistakes they made during the paper writing process, the misconceptions they held, the way they communicated or even the way they argued that could be guessed from the editing pattern.

The high level view of the proposed model is illustrated in Fig. 1. From left to right, each author contributes some content writing or editing the paper. Each revision of the paper is logged based on a user level. Then, at a certain threshold level of revision counts, all the accumulated revisions are encrypted and are sent to the blockchain network. Finally, the contribution rate of each author is calculated based on the revisions stored in the blockchain network. Anybody can download the data transaction records and perform calculation based on the contribution rate model.

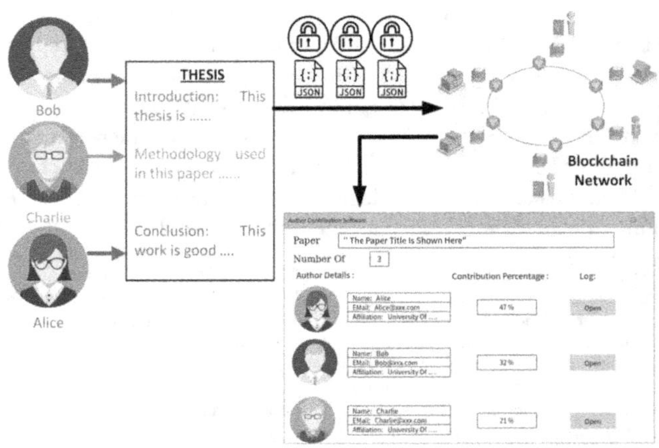

Figure 1: Proposed author contribution verification model.

[1] http://www.open.edu/openlearn/get-started/badges-come-openlearn

3.1 Privacy Preservation Logging Mechanism

A document D can be represented as a tuple of changes (changeset), $C = (c_1, c_2, c_3, \ldots, c_n)$ such that:

$$D = (\ell \rightarrow \ell')(c_1, c_2, c_3, \ldots, c_n), \bigcap_{i=1}^{n} c_i = \{\varnothing\} \tag{5}$$

where ℓ and ℓ' are the lengths of the document before and after the application of the changeset, respectively. $c_1 \in C$ is assumed to be the first change done on a blank document. Note that, c_i ($0 \leq i \leq \ell'$) is either character or an integer. Character represents the insertion of a new character while integer represents the retained character in the document. For example, in Eq. 6, X, Y and Z represent three changesets in one document done by three different users, which result in "ohayo gozaimasu Adam-sensei" appearing in the document. To simplify, document D can be represented as $(X \cdot Y) \cdot Z$ or $(XY)Z$, that is a document is a composition of $(XY)Z$. Changesets are closed under composition.

$$\begin{aligned} X &= (0 \rightarrow 5)(\text{"}ohayo\text{"}) \\ Y &= (5 \rightarrow 22)(0-4, \text{"}\ gozaimasu\ Adam\ sensei\text{"}) \\ Z &= (22 \rightarrow 22)(0-15, \text{"}-\text{"}, 17-21) \end{aligned} \tag{6}$$

The resulting document is: *"ohayo gozaimasu Adam-sensei"* (note the hyphen added as a result of the last changeset). Briefly, when a set of users, $U = \{u_1, u_2, u_3, \ldots\}$ make changes to the document, then, $u_i \rightarrow C$. All these changesets are recorded in local memory before being sent to the server.

At a specific time interval t, user will sent his changeset to the server as a record in revision records R. A revision record r is defined as a tuple such that $r = (C, u_i, r_j)$, where r_j is the revision counter. The revision records will be compressed and symmetrically encrypted before being submitted to the blockchain network. The encryption is needed to satisfy the privacy requirement. This process is described in Algorithm 1.

Algorithm 1: Logging mechanism

```
Data: document revisions, R, e.g. R = {r1, r2, r3, ..., rn}
Result: encrypted revisions in the blockchain network
initialization;
key, k;
i = 1;
maximum number of revisions, s;
current revision, r = ri;
R' ← r;
while i ≤ n do
    r = ri+1;
    R' ← r;
    if getSize(R') ≥ s then
        R' ← R' \ ri;
        r = ri-1;
        R'' ← Co(R');        // Compression function, Co
        R''' ← E(k, R'');    // Encryption function, E
        /* Here, send to blockchain network        */
        R' ← {ri};
    end
end
```

In Algorithm 1, s is the number of revisions that will be sent to the blockchain (should be less than the blockchain maximum transaction size such as gas limit in Ethereum). The revisions will only be sent to the blockchain network if the size of revisions is equal to maximum size s. This is to ensure the overall data size is not over the blockchain limit as well as for reducing the overall data transaction cost for the whole project.

All these data will be sent to one blockchain account, where each account represents one project, e.g. one academic paper. Hence, when collecting the data for performing data aggregation, one can simply refer to the corresponding account, and start retrieving it from the initial record.

3.2 Contribution Rate Calculation Model

Once the project is complete and all the contributions of authors are recorded, anyone can access the paper history from blockchain. It becomes then easy to assess the contribution rate of each author of the paper. For example, one could use a simple revision counter model to automatically measure the author contribution rate. For example, based on the number of changesets of an author, his or her contribution rate α, can be defined as follows:

$$\alpha_i = \frac{C_i}{\sum_{i=1}^{n} C_i} * 100 \tag{7}$$

where n is total number of authors of the paper. However, a loafing author could potentially easily abuse this model by simply repetitively editing the paper, for example, by adding and removing the same content. Hence, we introduce other metrics as complement.

Let the transformation of a string from string a to b be defined by a function $d(a, b)$, also known as edit distance. The edit distance $d(a, b)$ is the minimum-weight series of edit operations (e.g., character removal, addition) that transforms a into b. In this paper, the edit distance is measured based on two consequent user changesets, and/or between a changeset and the entire document.

The author's average edit distance, $\bar{u}$, is calculated based on the series of his/her changesets, such as follows:

$$\bar{u} = \frac{1}{n} \sum_{i=1}^{n} d(c_{i-1}, c_i) \tag{8}$$

$\bar{u}$ can then be used to reflect the average importance of each user's changesets. Note also that in addition, one could measure the importance of a particular changeset. For a given document at time t edited by user X and user Y, we could compute the distance function of each changeset of a given user to $D = XY$, such as follows:

$$\begin{aligned} u_X &= d(X, XY) \\ u_Y &= d(Y, XY) \end{aligned} \tag{9}$$

where in this context, $u_X < u_Y$ could mean for example that u_X changeset is more closer to the current document D relative to u_Y (i.e., the contribution of author u_X is less important than the one of u_Y in this round). Eq. 9 can be used to precisely measure author's contribution at a particular document state.

We note that various other simple models have been previously proposed to measure and view contribution rate of document authors. The approach used in [3] assumes that if 50% of author X's sentence has been retained in the next revision, after being edited by author Y, the sentence still "belongs" to author X. In [6], the authors proposed Gini coefficient to be used in every revision to measure authorship distribution in current revision. In [13], several visualization methods were proposed to identify malicious authorship in Wikipedia (e.g., vandalism) using temporal edit patterns, based on the assumption that if an edit renders a document version 90% smaller than the previous one, it is considered mass deletion.

4 IMPLEMENTATION

The framework implementation is based on NEM smart asset platform[2]. For simplicity, we downloaded NEM wallet to manage multiple accounts facilitating both incoming and outgoing data. Every account created in the wallet can be used to represent one project (i.e., one document). Hence, a wallet W can be represented as a set of mutable projects $\{p_1, p_2, p_3, \ldots, p_n\}$ (or, in other words, documents) such that $W = \{p_1, p_2, p_3, \ldots, p_n\}$.

We used NEM testnet network as it provides free XEM coin to facilitate the data transaction. The maximum transaction message, s, is limited to 1024 characters. Hence, to ensure that we do not exceed the maximum number of characters (after compression and encryption), as well as for the reasons of simplicity, we assume that one data transaction corresponds to one revision.

The authorship contribution rate, for this paper, is based on the following account on NEM testnet network: TDNWNC - X6HQZC - I7RVCM - BHJC6C - VPVCZ4 - Z33A6I - J5R3[3]. The rate distribution is as follows: {Author W: 50%, Author X: 7%, Author Y: 40%, Author Z: 3%}. Every data transaction is encrypted (the author identity is masked) in order to preserve and protect the authors' privacy[4].

5 DISCUSSION

This paper presents a work in progress in designing author contribution model on top of a blockchain network. There are several weak points that need to be further considered such as privacy and overall cost. In a typical blockchain network, everybody in the network would have the copy of the entire data that make the blockchain. This of course would cause privacy issues. Imagine, for example, the case when a reputable author such as a professor in a prestigious university makes silly mistakes during paper editing. They could be seen by the public after downloading the entire blockchain into a local storage. Therefore, data that will be sent to the blockchain network must be encrypted and/or filtered as well as carefully organized.

Encryption can be used to protect the privacy, but it also puts additional overhead into the data. Hence, it should be used in conjunction with other techniques such as compression, as blindly encrypting random data will not only increase the data size, but also increase the overall cost. However, one needs to keep in mind that, likely, any encryption can be eventually broken in the future, due to the increasing computing power over time.

Using existing blockchain platforms such as Ethereum and NEM could be expensive in the long run compared to running the system on a private blockchain network. This is because, currently, the economic scale of blockchain might not be affordable for smaller research institutes or users in developing countries, primaly, due to data transaction fees that need to be paid for each transaction. Hence, a community should decide either to setup a private blockchain network, which is easier nowadays, or use the existing network. It should be however noted that a private blockchain network must consist of large enough number of nodes to enforce the trust, especially in relation to data integrity. Furthermore, data should be processed accordingly in order to ensure that each author privacy is preserved and cost of data transaction is feasible before sending it to the blockchain network. For future work, a mechanism to control which data need to be sent to blockchain, and how it should be sent must be formulated, to assure the author privacy as well as to optimize the data transaction costs.

Finally, one should keep in mind that the actual contribution of a researcher may go beyond actions related to paper writing (e.g., proposing research topic, sketching research idea or method, or collecting data). However, this is obviously difficult to quantify and agree on among collaborating researchers as well as it is specific to the type of research and domain of science.

6 CONCLUSIONS AND FUTURE WORK

In this paper we present a blockchain based framework for preserving author contributions and measuring author contribution rate by public. Our solution offers a basic facility for various entities to measure each author contribution rate. In the future, we would like to formulate the weight calculation model to every revision made by each author. For example, equations and paraphrasing, should have more carefully assigned edit weight. In addition, author privacy should be better preserved and protected as data in the blockchain is available to the public.

ACKNOWLEDGMENTS

The work was supported in part by Grant MEXT Grantin-Aid #17H01828, Grant MIC SCOPE #171507010, and Grant TNB Seed Fund #U-TD-RD-17-02.

REFERENCES

[1] Tim Albert and Elizabeth Wager. 2010. How to handle authorship disputes: a guide for new researchers. (2010).
[2] Saifedean Hisham Ammous. 2016. Blockchain Technology: What is it good for? *Browser Download This Paper* (2016).
[3] Ofer Arazy and Eleni Stroulia. 2009. A Utility for Estimating the Relative Contributions of Wiki Authors.. In *ICWSM*.
[4] Leo Egghe. 2006. An improvement of the h-index: The g-index. ISSI.
[5] Daniele Fanelli and Vincent Larivière. 2016. Researchers' individual publication rate has not increased in a century. *PloS one* 11, 3 (2016), e0149504.
[6] Fabian Flöck and Andriy Rodchenko. 2012. Whose article is it anyway?–Detecting authorship distribution in Wikipedia articles over time with WIKIGINI. *Online proceedings of the Wikipedia Academy* (2012).
[7] Jorge E Hirsch. 2005. An index to quantify an individual's scientific research output. *Proceedings of the National academy of Sciences of the United States of America* 102, 46 (2005), 16569.
[8] Satoshi Nakamoto. 2008. Bitcoin: A peer-to-peer electronic cash system.
[9] Richard B Primack, John A Cigliano, and ECM Parsons. 2014. Coauthors gone bad; how to avoid publishing conflict and a proposed agreement for co-author teams. *Biological conservation* 176 (2014), 277–280.
[10] Mike Sharples and John Domingue. 2016. The blockchain and kudos: A distributed system for educational record, reputation and reward. In *European Conference on Technology Enhanced Learning*. Springer, 490–496.
[11] Melanie Swan. 2015. *Blockchain: Blueprint for a new economy*. " O'Reilly Media, Inc.".
[12] An Binh Tran, X Xu, I Weber, M Staples, and P Rimba. 2017. Regerator: a registry generator for blockchain. In *CAiSE Forum and Doctoral Consortium Papers*. 81–88.
[13] Fernanda B Viégas, Martin Wattenberg, and Kushal Dave. 2004. Studying cooperation and conflict between authors with history flow visualizations. In *Proceedings of the SIGCHI conference on Human factors in computing systems*. ACM, 575–582.
[14] Elizabeth Wager. 2009. Recognition, reward and responsibility: why the authorship of scientific papers matters. *Maturitas* 62, 2 (2009), 109–112.
[15] Gavin Wood. 2014. Ethereum: A secure decentralised generalised transaction ledger. *Ethereum Project Yellow Paper* 151 (2014).
[16] Xiao Yue, Huiju Wang, Dawei Jin, Mingqiang Li, and Wei Jiang. 2016. Healthcare data gateways: found healthcare intelligence on blockchain with novel privacy risk control. *Journal of medical systems* 40, 10 (2016), 218.

[2] nem.io/NEM_techRef.pdf
[3] http://bob.nem.ninja:8765
[4] The rate distribution is based on draft version of the paper

Using Deep Learning for Title-Based Semantic Subject Indexing to Reach Competitive Performance to Full-Text

Florian Mai
Kiel University
stu96542@informatik.uni-kiel.de

Lukas Galke
Kiel University
lga@informatik.uni-kiel.de

Ansgar Scherp
Kiel University
asc@informatik.uni-kiel.de

ABSTRACT

For (semi-)automated subject indexing systems in digital libraries, it is often more practical to use metadata such as the title of a publication instead of the full-text or the abstract. Therefore, it is desirable to have good text mining and text classification algorithms that operate well already on the title of a publication. So far, the classification performance on titles is not competitive with the performance on the full-texts if the same number of training samples is used for training. However, it is much easier to obtain title data in large quantities and to use it for training than full-text data. In this paper, we investigate the question how models obtained from training on increasing amounts of title training data compare to models from training on a constant number of full-texts. We evaluate this question on a large-scale dataset from the medical domain (PubMed) and from economics (EconBiz). In these datasets, the titles and annotations of millions of publications are available, and they outnumber the available full-texts by a factor of 20 and 15, respectively. To exploit these large amounts of data to their full potential, we develop three strong deep learning classifiers and evaluate their performance on the two datasets. The results are promising. On the EconBiz dataset, all three classifiers outperform their full-text counterparts by a large margin. The best title-based classifier outperforms the best full-text method by 9.4%. On the PubMed dataset, the best title-based method almost reaches the performance of the best full-text classifier, with a difference of only 2.9%.

CCS CONCEPTS

• **Information systems** → **Digital libraries and archives**; • **Computing methodologies** → **Neural networks**; *Natural language processing*;

KEYWORDS

Text classification; deep learning; digital libraries

ACM Reference Format:
Florian Mai, Lukas Galke, and Ansgar Scherp. 2018. Using Deep Learning for Title-Based Semantic Subject Indexing to Reach Competitive Performance to Full-Text. In *JCDL '18: The 18th ACM/IEEE Joint Conference on Digital Libraries, June 3–7, 2018, Fort Worth, TX, USA.* ACM, New York, NY, USA, 10 pages. https://doi.org/10.1145/3197026.3197039

ACM ISBN 978-1-4503-5178-2/18/06...$15.00
https://doi.org/10.1145/3197026.3197039

1 INTRODUCTION

Semantic annotations are crucial for users of digital libraries as they enhance the search of scientific documents. Given the large amount of new publications, automatic annotation systems are a useful tool for human expert annotators working at digital libraries to classify the publications into categories from a (hierarchical) thesaurus. However, providing automated recommendations for subject indexing in such systems is a challenging task. This is partly due to the data from which recommendations may be generated. Often neither the full-text of a publication nor its abstract may be available. For instance, the digital library EconBiz contains only for 15% of the documents an abstract. Even when the content can be legally provided by the library to the end users, copyright laws or regulations of the publishers may prevent text mining. Moreover, collecting and processing PDFs where it is possible, e. g., for some Open Access documents, adds high computational requirements to the library. This puts annotation methods on demand that are based on data with better availability, such as the title. Previous work by Galke et al. [4], however, has shown that title-based methods considerably fall behind full-text methods in terms of performance when the number of samples for training is equal. If our classifier was a human expert, this would not be a surprising result. A full-text contains more information and therefore also more indication of the publication's topic. A human expert will always make better annotations based on the full-text. In fact, the annotations that are used as gold-standard for automated subject indexing experiments are often created based on the full-text.

However, we argue that machine learning algorithms work differently than a human. In contrast to a human, they often require hundreds of thousands or even millions of training data to yield satisfactory models [1]. These amounts of data are not always available in the real world. One common reason is that human expertise is required for creating a large enough gold standard, which is expensive. For semantic subject indexing, the availability issues mentioned above do not only come into play at prediction time, i.e., when a machine learning model is used in a productive system, but also during training. In effect, methods based on the full-texts have drastically less training data available than methods based on titles. This raises the question if title-based methods can potentially narrow the performance gap to full-text methods by fully incorporating all training data available.

In this paper, we address this question. Formally, semantic indexing is framed as a multi-label classification problem, where a (commonly small) subset of labels has to be selected from a (relatively large) set of labels. From two digital libraries of scientific literature, PubMed and EconBiz, we have compiled an English full-text dataset and an English title dataset. Our compiled datasets are quite different with respect to their size. From PubMed, we extracted 12.83 million titles. For 5% of these a full-text is available (646k). From EconBiz, we extracted 1.06 million titles, of which approximately 7% have a full-text (71k). In order to fully utilize these large amounts of data, we develop and compare three different classifiers that have emerged from the deep learning community in recent years. Deep learning has advanced the state-of-the-art in many fields, such as vision, speech, and text [18]. These techniques are known to shine when a lot of training data is available. For text classification in particular, recent work [43] suggests that deep learning starts to outperform strong traditional models when 650k or more training samples are available. The number of full-text in PubMed is right at the edge of this number, whereas EconBiz has far less full-texts, making these datasets an interesting and revealing choice. In natural language processing, different types of neural networks have been successfully employed on different tasks, but it is an open question whether convolutional neural networks (CNNs), recurrent neural networks (RNNs), or multi-layer-perceptrons (MLPs) are superior for text classification tasks. Therefore, we employ a representative of each type in our study. We compare them against another strong MLP baseline (*Base-MLP*), which has previously been shown to also outperform traditional bag-of-words classifiers such as SVMs, Naive Bayes, and kNN [4]. Since the label space in our datasets is very large, our study can be understood as *eXtreme Multi-Label Classification* (XMLC). Here, only few studies have leveraged deep learning techniques to tackle the considerably harder problem when the label space is large [19, 42]. Hence, with our study, we contribute to the knowledge in this field, as well.

The results of our study indicate that title-based methods can match or even outperform the full-text performance when enough training data is available. On EconBiz, the best title classifier (MLP) performs on par with the best full-text classifier (MLP) when training with only 8× as many titles as there are full-texts available. When all available titles are used (approximately 15× more than full-texts), the title-based MLP outperforms its full-text counterpart by 9.4%. On the PubMed dataset, the best title method is the RNN, and it almost reaches the best full-text performance produced by an MLP. The gap is only as small as 2.9%. When using the same number of titles as full-texts are available, the gap in classification performance is 10.7%, indicating a considerable benefit from leveraging all title data. Generally, the MLP performs well, outperforming RNN and CNN in three out of the four combinations of the two datasets and title/full-text. It also consistently outperforms the baseline when all titles or full-texts are used. Moreover, our analysis suggests that our proposed classifiers are well-chosen for our study, because they benefit from increasing amounts of training data better than the baseline. The RNN performs rather poor on full-text, but shows strong performance on titles. While also yielding reasonably good results with CNN, it performs clearly below the other classifiers in all cases. This is a surprise, because a lot of the recent literature on large-scale text classification has focused on CNNs (e.g. [2, 17, 43], also see Section 2). Thus, our results indicate that it may be worth it to shift the research focus more towards other types of neural networks for text classification.

Our contributions can be summarized as follows:

- For the first time, we study the question whether title-based methods can reach the performance of full-text-based methods by exploiting the surplus of available training data.
- We demonstrate that title-based methods are on par or even outperform full-text methods when the number of training samples is sufficiently large.
- We develop and compare three strong classifiers for (extreme) multi-label text classification, contributing to the debate on which type of neural network is superior for text classification.

The remainder of the paper is structured as follows. In the subsequent section, we review relevant work on the comparison of short texts and full-text and on deep learning for text classification. In Section 3, we describe our deep learning models. We introduce the datasets and experimental setup in Section 4, and present the results in Section 5. We analyze and discuss the results in Section 6, before we conclude.

2 RELATED WORK

In this section, we review previous literature relevant to our study. First, we discuss papers that compare performance on titles with performance on full-text. Next, we briefly discuss methods for multi-label text classification other than deep learning. Finally, we discuss current deep learning methods for text classification.

Title versus Full-Text. The work directly related to our study is the one by Galke et al. [4]. The authors compare titles with full-texts for multi-label text classification on four datasets. Two datasets consist of scientific publications and are therefore comparable to the datasets in this study. In their experiments, the authors used the same number of samples for the title-based methods and the full-text methods. They found that the title-based methods can yield reasonably good performance. However, the difference between title and full-text on the two scientific datasets is still 10% and 20% in favor of the full-text, respectively. The first dataset is from the economics domain, and it is an earlier version of the one used in this study. The second dataset is from the political sciences. In their comparison of classifiers, an MLP to which in this study we refer as *Base-MLP*, outperforms all other (non-neural) classifiers in 7 out of 8 combinations. All the presented classifiers are based on the bag-of-words (BoW) feature representation, a traditionally strong baseline for text classification that disregards word order. Due to clearly superior performance, Base-MLP can also be considered the best representative of traditional BoW models. We therefore report its performance as our baseline for all subsequently developed models.

The comparison of metadata vs. full-texts has also been studied for tasks other than document classification. Nascimento et al. [25] studied how well queries for web search can be generated from title, abstract, or body, respectively. These queries are then issued to Web information sources to retrieve papers for recommendation. In their experiments, abstracts yielded the best queries, closely followed by the body. The title clearly performs worse. On the contrary, Nishioka and Scherp [26] have demonstrated that competitive paper recommendations to researchers based on their Twitter profile can be made by using only the title of the paper. This is achieved by their novel profiling method HCF-IDF, which is able to extract sufficient conceptual information from the title through spreading activation over a hierarchical knowledge base. Galke et al. [5] use text embedding techniques for the information retrieval task and compare how well these techniques perform when the index is built upon the title, abstract, or full-text of the documents. Here, titles have demonstrated a clear advantage over abstract and full-text. Lastly, Hemminger et al. [10] compare full-text search with metadata search in the PubMed database, where full-text search yields better results.

Multi-label Text Classification. Text classification is a well-studied problem. k-Nearest-Neighbors and SVM are common choices for text classification (see e.g. [8, 14, 28]). However, kNN's complexity grows in the number of training samples, which is problematic for the training sample sizes we consider in our study. SVMs do not provide a natural adaptation for multi-label classification. A binary relevance classification scheme, however, is impractical when the number of labels is large.

An active field of multi-label text classification research is the MeSH indexing community. This area is concerned with annotating PubMed articles with medical subject headings. BioASQ [33] is a challenge that recently finished its 5th iteration. It has the goal to advance the state-of-the-art in MeSH indexing, and to this end provides large datasets for training. We acknowledge the significance of the MeSH indexing community, and in our study, we include the dataset from the latest iteration of the BioASQ challenge. However, many of the approaches successful at this challenge, including learning to rank [12, 20, 21] and pattern matching [23], make use of features tailored to the biomedical domain. Since in this paper, we study domain-independent methods for subject indexing in digital libraries, these methods are not appropriate.

Deep Learning for Text Classification. Some early works leverage neural networks for multi-label text classification. In order to capture label inter-dependencies, Zhang and Zhou [40] employ a pairwise ranking loss function for text classification. Nam et al. [24] show that replacing the ranking-loss with cross-entropy leads to faster convergence and overall better prediction performance. Furthermore, they are the first to incorporate some of the milestone advancements from the deep learning era like rectified linear units, dropout, and the smart optimizer AdaGrad.

In recent years, neural networks have become the state-of-the-art in multi-class text classification, outperforming traditional linear BoW models, in particular on very large datasets. On a diverse set of text classification datasets of rather small scale (up to 10.7k samples), neural networks have shown their capability to perform well. These include CNNs [15, 37] and RNNs [31], as well as a combination of both [41].

Zhang et al. [43] were the first to introduce several large-scale multi-class text classification datasets ranging from 120k to 3.6 million training samples. The number of classes ranges from two to 14. Zhang et al. proposed a deep, character-based convolutional neural network and compared it with a number of traditional models, including multinomial logistic regression based on bag-of-ngrams with TF-IDF, and deep learning models such as a Long Short-Term Memory network (LSTM) and word-based CNNs. The finding most relevant to our study is that traditional models tend to outperform the neural network architectures on the four relatively small datasets with 560k training samples or less, whereas on the remaining four datasets with 650k training samples or more their neural network approach is superior. Although these numbers may vary depending on the dataset and classification task at hand, this result is the main reason why we choose to employ deep learning techniques in our study.

Several studies employing deep learning on these datasets have followed. Conneau et al. [2] draw inspiration from the computer vision community and improve the performance of character-based CNNs by increasing the depth. Le et al. [17] put these results into perspective by demonstrating that a shallow, word-based CNN performs on par with these models or better. Therefore, we have limited our study to shallow, word-based CNNs. For text classification, it is an open question whether CNNs or RNNs are superior [36]. Consequently, LSTMs had also some success on these large-scale datasets [35, 38], as well as hybrid approaches [34]. Joulin et al. [6] demonstrated that even a linear MLP classifier can yield results competitive with non-linear deep learning methods while maintaining computational efficiency.

To the best of our knowledge, each of the neural network types MLP, CNN, and LSTM provide the current state-of-the-art on at least one of these large-scale datasets (as shown in the work by Le et al. [17]). Hence, with our study we would like to contribute to this discussion by employing a representative of each of the neural network types.

Finally, due to the number of labels in our datasets, our study may be classified as XMLC. To the best of our knowledge, only two papers studied the application of deep learning to this setting [19, 42], from which we draw some inspiration for our models, which are described below.

3 METHODS

In this section, we present three neural network architectures for text classification used in our study. In the design phase, we aimed at carefully developing the strongest representative of each of the most common types of neural networks, MLPs, CNNs, and RNNs[1]. Here, we only present the final architectures which are used in the experiments presented in Section 4. These architectures may differ depending on the dataset and type of text (title or full-text) they operate on. This is necessary to avoid a bias for either of the datasets or types of text. The output layer as well as the training procedure in our neural networks are the same for all neural network architectures presented here.

Below, we describe the training procedure, before we go into each neural network architecture up to the last hidden layer. For brevity, we omit a formal mathematical description of the models here.

3.1 Training Procedure

The semantic annotation task is formally a *multi-labeling problem*, where instead of belonging to exactly one class, each publication is assigned a set of labels. This is an important difference to most of the previous literature on text classification with large datasets. *Binary Relevance* is a common technique to adapt a classifier for a

[1]For transparency, intermediate results of the design phase can be found in an extended version of the paper provided at https://github.com/florianmai/Quadflor.

multi-labeling problem. However, this is a costly technique when the number of labels is high because it requires to train as many classifiers as there are labels. Neural networks have a more natural way to deal with multi-label classification, which is also made use of by Galke et al. [4]. For multi-class text classification, the softmax activation function is used at the output layer to obtain a probability distribution over the classes. For multi-label classification, however, the sigmoid activation can be employed to determine a probability p_l for each label l whether it should be assigned or not. The difference is that softmax regards all labels at once, while sigmoid makes an independent decision for each label. Finally, the binary decision whether label l is assigned is made by checking whether p_l exceeds a threshold θ.

Using Adam [16], the networks are trained as to minimize the sum of all binary cross-entropy losses over all labels. This has shown to be superior to a ranking-based loss on multi-label text classification [19, 24]. Training is executed in mini-batches of size 256. We employ early stopping for regularization and as criterion to terminate training. The performance on the validation set is evaluated in terms of the sample-based F_1-measure. Training is terminated when the validation score has not improved over the best reported score for 10 consecutive evaluations.

Since the output of the sigmoid activation function can be interpreted as the probability whether a label should be assigned, a typical choice for the threshold is $\theta = 0.5$. However, depending on the evaluation metric, dataset, or model that generates the assignment probabilities, this value does not necessarily yield optimal results. Unfortunately, finding a good value for θ can be computationally expensive, especially when the datasets are very large. Therefore, we use a heuristic that continuously adjusts the threshold *during* training. To this end, the evaluation on the validation set used for early stopping is also used to optimize θ.

Formally, we initially set $\theta_0 := 0.2$, which Galke et al. [4] found to be a better threshold value than 0.5. After each validation step i, where the classifier predicts a probability for each of the $|L|$ labels and each of the n samples in the validation set, accumulated in $P_i \in (0,1)^{n \times |L|}$, we set

$$\theta_i := \underset{\tilde{\theta} \in \{-k*\alpha+\theta_{i-1}, \ldots, k*\alpha+\theta_{i-1}\}}{\arg\max} F_1(P_i; \tilde{\theta})$$

where $\alpha > 0$ is the step size and k controls the number of threshold values to check. This heuristic is based on the observation that the optimal choice for θ_i is in most cases in close proximity to the optimal choice of the previous evaluation step, θ_{i-1}. Since computing the F_1 score can be costly, we set $k = 3$ and $\alpha = 0.01$ to trade off granularity with speed.

In our preliminary experiments, this way of optimizing the threshold consistently yields good results, sometimes even better than when it is optimized manually.

3.2 Multi-Layer-Perceptron

Our baseline is a multi-layer-perceptron (MLP) described by Galke et al. [4]. It has one hidden layer with 1,000 units and rectifier activation and it takes a TF-IDF [29] bag-of-unigrams as input. The bag-of-unigrams only contains the 25,000 most common unigrams, which we determined to be sufficient for the multi-labeling task. For regularization, dropout [30] is applied after the hidden layer with a keep probability of 0.5. We will refer to this baseline as *Base-MLP*.

We extend the MLP from Galke et al. [4] by incorporating some techniques inspired from recent deep learning literature. The MLP architecture introduced in this study can be viewed as an adaptation of fastText [6] for multi-label classification. FastText is a linear BoW model enhanced with a feature sharing component (a hidden layer with identity activation) and local word order information (bigrams). We adopt this model by adding the 25,000 most common bi-grams in addition to the 25,000 most common unigrams. However, we found that omitting the non-linearity at the hidden layer rather hurts the classification performance considerably. Therefore, we keep the rectifier as a non-linear activation at the hidden layer.

In the introduction, it was mentioned that deep neural networks excel when the number of training samples is very large. This is because the representational power of neural networks increases as the number of parameters increases. This can be obtained by adding more layers or by adding more units to the existing layers. Additionally, deeper networks may be able to learn hierarchical representations of the input, as can be observed in the vision domain [9]. However, deep networks are generally harder to train due to the vanishing and exploding gradient problems. We apply Batch Normalization [13] to our deep MLPs to alleviate those.

In summary, MLP differs from Base-MLP in that it incorporates bi-grams and uses multiple layers and Batch Normalization where appropriate.

3.3 Convolutional Neural Network

We present a CNN architecture whose core was introduced by Kim [15] for sentence classification and has since been repeatedly adopted and enhanced upon. We adopt and combine some of these enhancements for our model.

The CNN operates on word embeddings, which are initialized with a pretrained model but finetuned during training. As in Kim's model, our CNN applies a 1D-convolution by sliding a window over the text in order to extract features at each position. These outputs are then transformed by a non-linear activation function (the detector). Commonly, the most salient position is selected by applying max-pooling after the detector stage. However, Liu et al. [19] instead split the output of the convolution into p nearly equal chunks, and perform max-pooling on each chunk. Afterwards, the outputs of the pooling stages are concatenated. For $p = 1$, this is identical to Kim's architecture.

Commonly, this process is repeated for multiple window sizes. The outputs of these processes are then concatenated before passing them to the next layer. For example, Kim's CNN uses window sizes 3, 4, and 5, while Liu et al. use 2, 4, and 8. We experimentally determined that using 2, 3, 4, 5, and 8 yields to even better results.

In Kim's model, the concatenated output of the pooling stages is directly propagated to the output layer. Liu et al. argue, however, that it is better to have an additional fully-connected layer with n_b units, called the *bottleneck layer*, because it adds more representational power to the network through the increased depth.

Considering the complexity of our datasets and the number of training samples available, the question of increased capacity arises with CNNs. Similar to MLPs, an increase in capacity can be achieved either through wider convolutions (larger feature-map) or additional stacked layers of convolutions. Since a recent study by Le et al. [17] has shown that depth does not yield improvement over shallow nets, we only consider the former approach.

3.4 Recurrent Neural Network

The Recurrent Neural Network (RNN) is a family of neural networks that was specifically designed for sequential input data. By maintaining a hidden state, the network is able to keep track of previous inputs. However, the vanilla RNN has difficulties keeping track of inputs that are far in the past. The LSTM [11] was designed to alleviate this by explicitly modeling the control over whether the current hidden state shall be forgotten, updated, or kept. For this study, initially we use an LSTM that has already achieved good results for text classification in a study by Zhang et al. [43]. This LSTM is the "vanilla" version described in [7]. Our final model, however, incorporates two techniques which have proven useful for NLP tasks in recent years, attention and bidirectionality [39].

Since any RNN produces an output at every time step, the outputs have to be aggregated after processing the entire sequence, in order to pass a vector of fixed size to the next layer. We experimented with choosing the last output, computing the sum, computing the average, and computing a weighted average where the weights are determined by an attention mechanism as used by Yang et al. [35]. While the benefit over the other aggregation methods is not large for titles, the attention mechanism consistently performs best. On full-texts, on the other hand, the difference is considerable. This is intuitive, because there is less need to focus on specific parts of the input if the input is as short as in a title.

In the same fashion as Yang et al. [35], we incorporate bidirectionality into our LSTM by concatenating at each time step the output of an LSTM that reads the input sequence from left to right, and an LSTM that reads the sequence in reverse order. This is a common technique to make the model aware of the entire sequence at every time step, and commonly boosts performance in text applications.

Again, we made some effort to investigate an increase in the capacity of the LSTM to account for the large number of training samples in our datasets. In the past, both increasing the memory cell size (the width) and stacking LSTMs on top of each other has been successful in some NLP tasks. For text classification, this has not been the case. The results of our experiments support this, where wider LSTMs are superior to stacked LSTMs, even when variational dropout [3] is used.

4 EXPERIMENTAL SETUP

4.1 Datasets

We built English datasets from two digital libraries of scientific publications. EconBiz[2] is a search portal for economics and business studies. Currently, it contains 2,485,000 English publications, out of which 615k are open access. Many publications are annotated by experts with a variable number of subject headings (so-called subject indexing) taken from a standardized set, the "Thesaurus for Economics" (STW)[3]. From all 2,485,000 English publications, we filtered the ones that have annotations and extracted their title. After deleting duplicates, 1,064,634 publications with annotations remain. Out of the 615k open access publications, the number of publications that have annotations and whose full-text can be downloaded and processed reduces to 70,619, which is 6.63% of all publications.

PubMed[4] is a search engine for biomedical and life science literature provided by the US National Library of Medicine. The publications found on PubMed are annotated with "Medical Subject Headings" (MeSH)[5] by human curators. We obtained a dataset consisting of millions of publication metadata, including title and MeSH annotations, from the training set of the semantic indexing task of the BioASQ challenge 2017 [33], which are all in English language. PubMed Central[6] is an archive of full-texts of biomedical and life science literature provided by the US National Library of Medicine. It comprises 4.3 million publications, which can be accessed freely and which are mostly English. However, only 1.5 million are open access and therefore allow text mining. From this dataset, we computed the intersection with the publications obtained from the BioASQ challenge. After removing duplicates, 12,834,026 titles and 646,513 full-texts with respective annotations remain. Hence, 5.04% of the samples have a full-text.

Table 1 lists some characteristics of the two datasets, EconBiz and PubMed. In terms of combinatorial complexity, the PubMed dataset is a harder problem because the number of labels out of which to pick the annotations for a publication is much higher. Yet, due to the relatively large number of labels and small number of samples per label on average, both datasets can be considered as XMLC problems[7]. The titles in PubMed contain on average more words than the publications' titles in EconBiz. However, this fact is put into perspective considering that the titles in PubMed have on average more labels to be predicted than there are words in the title. Regarding the full-texts, the ratio of words/labels is approximately the same in both datasets. Another fact worth noting is that the titles corpora have on average one label less than the full-texts. This suggests that the label distributions in the title dataset and full-text dataset are quite different.

Please note that on both datasets, the set of titles is a superset of the set of full-texts.

4.2 Experiments

In order to assess how the title-based methods behave as more and more titles are considered for training, we create sub-datasets of the title datasets by iteratively adding more data. This is illustrated in Figure 1.

For a fair comparison of title and full-text performance, the trained model must be evaluated on the same data. To this end, we split the set of publications where a full-text is available into ten folds, and perform a 10-fold cross-validation. In each iteration, nine folds are selected for training, and one is selected for testing. From this training set, we randomly select 20% for the validation set for early stopping and adjusting the threshold, as described in Section 3.1. These comprise the data used for our experiments on

[2]https://www.econbiz.de/
[3]http://zbw.eu/stw/version/latest/about
[4]https://www.ncbi.nlm.nih.gov/pubmed/
[5]https://www.nlm.nih.gov/mesh/meshhome.html
[6]https://www.ncbi.nlm.nih.gov/pmc/
[7]An overview of datasets commonly considered XMLC can be found at http://manikvarma.org/downloads/XC/XMLRepository.html.

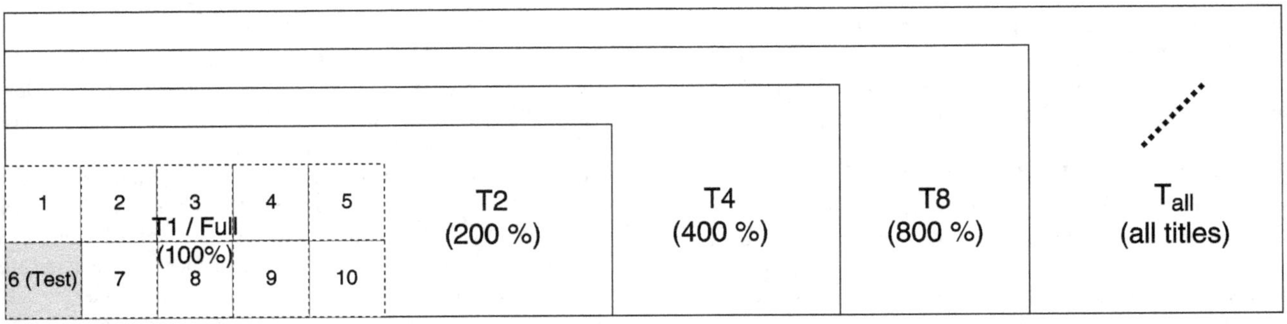

Figure 1: We organize our dataset in several sub-datasets to perform an iterative evaluation. T1 and Full comprise of the same set of publications (all samples where a full-text is available), and is split into 10 folds in order to perform the same 10-fold cross-validation with titles and full-texts for a fair comparison. For T2, T4, T8, increasingly more titles that do not have a full-text are added for training, but are in each cross-validation step evaluated on the same test samples (highlighted in green for exemplification). T_{all} includes all title samples.

Table 1: Characteristics of EconBiz and PubMed datasets. $|D|$ denotes the sample size, $|L|$ denotes the number of labels used in the dataset, d/l is the average number of publications a label is assigned to. l/d is the average number of labels assigned to a publication. $|V|$ is the size of the vocabulary and w/d denotes the average number of words per document.

	EconBiz (STW)		PubMed (MeSH)	
	Title	Full-Text	Title	Full-Text
$\|D\|$	1,064,634	70,619	12,834,026	646,513
Size	78.8MB	6.27GB	1.32GB	20.06GB
$\|L\|$	5661	4849	27773	26276
d/l	819.1	75.8	5852.3	331.0
l/d	4.4	5.3	12.6	13.5
$\|V\|$	91,505	1,502,336	660,180	6,774,130
w/d	6.88	6694.4	9.6	2533.4

full-text, and will be abbreviated as EconBiz Full and PubMed Full, respectively.

For the experiments on titles, the same publications from the 10-fold cross-validation are used for testing. However, the training set is iteratively extended with more samples from the titles dataset, so that the total number of training samples is always a power of two of the number of samples in the full-text experiment. In total, we conduct experiments on five title sub-datasets per domain: T1, T2, T4, T8, and T_{all}. Here, Tx means that x times as many title samples are used for training as there are full-text samples in the dataset. Lastly, T_{all} contains all title samples from the dataset.

We run each of the four classifiers Base-MLP, MLP, CNN, and LSTM on all of the sub-datasets. In total, we run 48 cross-validations. Following Galke et al. [4] who argue that the sample-based F_1-metric best reflects how subject indexers work, we use this metric to report the results. We also use this metric for early stopping and threshold adjustment on the validation set. The sample-based F_1-measure calculates the harmonic mean of precision and recall for each sample individually, and averages these scores over all samples.

4.3 Choice of Hyperparameters and Training

Since there are a lot of tunable hyperparameters involved in deep learning, tuning multiple hyperparameters at the same time can be very expensive, especially when the datasets are very large. On the other hand, fixing hyperparameters across all datasets and models would not be a fair approach in our study because the datasets and model architectures are very different and therefore may require very different hyperparameter settings. As a compromise, we decided to tune the hyperparameters for full-texts and titles separately in an incremental fashion on one fold. Here, we tuned one hyperparameter at a time and selected the locally best solution for full-text and titles, respectively. It is important to note that the parameters for titles were determined based on the performance on T_{all}, and were adopted for all other title sub-datasets. On the one hand, this alleviates a lot of the computational cost and allows to compare the performance between title sub-datasets. On the other hand, especially the performance of smaller sub-datasets might be suboptimal due to overfitting. This must be kept in mind for analysis.

In our experiments involving the MLP, we use a one-layer MLP with 2,000 units and dropout with a keep probability of 0.5 after the hidden layer for all experiments. Only for the experiments on the PubMed titles, we use a two-layer MLP with 1,000 units each, and apply no dropout. Instead, we use Batch Normalization after each hidden layer. In all cases, the initial learning rate for Adam is set to 0.001.

In the CNN experiments, we use $p = 3$ chunks and $n_b = 1,000$ units at the bottleneck layer [19] for both full-text experiments. On titles, we do not perform chunking ($p = 1$), and use a bottleneck layer size of $n_b = 500$. The size of the feature map is set to 400 in all experiments except for PubMed Full, where we use 100. The keep probability is set to 0.75 in all cases, and the initial learning rate is 0.001.

We use a single-layer LSTM for all experiments. For both datasets, we determined 1,536 to be the best size for the memory cell when using titles. 1,024 units and 512 are used for PubMed Full and EconBiz Full, respectively. The keep probability is set to 0.75 in all experiments except for PubMed on titles, where we set it to 0.5. The initial learning rate is 0.01 for EconBiz Full and 0.001 in all other cases. Training is done with backpropagation through time by unrolling the LSTM until the end of the sequence.

We adopt the preprocessing and tokenization procedure of Galke et. al [4]. For the LSTM and CNN, we use 300-dimensional pre-trained word embeddings obtained from training GloVe [27] on Common Crawl with 840 billion tokens[8]. Out-of-vocabulary words are discarded. The maximum sequence length is limited to the first 250 words. Longer sequences were harmful in preliminary experiments.

For implementation of our neural network models, we used the deep learning library TensorFlow[9] and integrated them within the multi-label classification framework "Quadflor"[10]. All experiments are run either on an NVIDIA TITAN or on a TITAN Xp GPU which both have 12GB of RAM.

5 RESULTS

The results of our experiments are shown in Table 2. In addition, we plot the performance of each method as a function of the number of samples used for training the title model. These are shown in Figure 2.

EconBiz. On the EconBiz dataset, the best results on both titles and full-texts are obtained by MLP. The title-based method is on par with the full-text method when eight times as many titles as full-texts are used. When all titles are used, the title-MLP outperforms its full-text counterpart by 9.4%, achieving an F_1-score of 0.500. In contrast, when the same number of samples for full-text and titles is used, the gap between the best title method (Base-MLP) and the best full-text method (MLP) is 16.9% in favor of the full-text.

The MLP seems to benefit the most from additional titles. Initially, when as many titles as full-texts are used for training, all our proposed methods, i. e., MLP, CNN, and LSTM, perform within 0.007 points in F_1-score from each other, but MLP performs worst. However, the relation flips as more titles are added. In Figure 2 (a), we can observe that MLP has the steepest curve of improvement out of all methods, in particular when considering the improvement from T1 to T2. With twice as many titles as full-texts, MLP is already the best performing classifier out of the ones we have proposed. The gap to the other methods only gets wider as more data is added for training. Overall, the MLPs performance on T_{all} improves over the performance on T1 by 40.1%. The other methods also improve continuously as more training data is added. However, the CNN and LSTM improve by only 17% and 29.4% with respect to T1, respectively. Still, this is enough to surpass their full-texts counterparts by 10.1% and 28.4%, respectively.

When using as many titles as full-texts, Base-MLP outperforms our proposed methods clearly by 0.027 points in F_1-score. However, Base-MLP does not benefit as much from additional training data. Its overall improvement is only 20.7%, so when all titles are used for training, it is outperformed by MLP by a margin of 5.9%. On the full-text, MLP has an advantage of 3.6% over the baseline. Yet, the baseline still has a large advantage over LSTM and CNN, both on titles and full-texts.

PubMed. On PubMed, MLP shows the best full-text performance, whereas LSTM yields the best results on titles. However, even when all titles are used for training, that is almost 20 times as many titles as full-texts, the LSTM still lacks behind the full-text MLP by 2.9%. However, this is a considerably smaller gap than when the same number of samples are used. Base-MLP, the best performing method on PubMed T1, achieves 10.7% lower scores than the best method on PubMed Full, which is MLP.

The MLP and the LSTM show very similar behavior when more training data is added. This can be seen from Figure 2 (b), where the lines of the MLP and LSTM are almost parallel. However, the overall improvement from T1 to T_{all} is slightly higher for the MLP than for the LSTM. The former improves by 12.3%, whereas the latter improves by 10.8%. The CNN does not seem to benefit from additional data at all. Initially, on T1, the CNN performs relatively close to the other methods, lacking behind the LSTM by 5.7%. However, as more data is added for training, the CNN demonstrates a worse classification performance than with fewer training samples. Only when all available titles are used, the CNN barely outperforms itself on T1 by a very slim margin of 0.5%. Consequently, the CNN has the largest difference to its full-text counterpart out of all proposed methods. It scores 9.8% lower on T_{all} than on PubMed Full, whereas the gap is 5.2% for the MLP and 1.8% for the LSTM.

By a considerable margin, the baseline is the best method on T1, where relatively few samples are used for training. However, despite using 20 times as many training samples, the performance on T_{all} is only 1.3% better, which is a difference to the MLP and LSTM of 3.9% and 6.2%, respectively. As it is the case on the EconBiz dataset, the full-text performance of BaseMLP is the second best and gets as close to the MLP as 0.8%.

6 DISCUSSION

The main question of our study is to which extent title-based methods can catch up to the performance of full-text-based methods by increasing the amount of title training data. On EconBiz, the best title-based method outperforms the best full-text method by 9.4% when all title training data is used. Considering that the difference is 16.9% in favor of the full-text when the sample sizes are equal, this is an impressive improvement. On PubMed, the improvement is less astounding. However, the title-based method is close to competitive to the full-texts, as the difference in score (less than 3%) is small. Considering that the gap is much larger for equal sample sizes (10.7%), we must acknowledge that current machine learning techniques in combination with large quantities of data are able to obtain just as good classification performance by merely using the titles.

However, in order to utilize title-based methods in a particular application, it is important to understand why there is such a large difference between the EconBiz and PubMed datasets regarding the benefit of employing title-based methods with large amounts of data. A possible explanation for that difference lies in the absolute numbers of full-texts available for training. As we have pointed

[8]This pretrained model can be downloaded at https://nlp.stanford.edu/projects/glove/.
[9]https://www.tensorflow.org/
[10]To increase the reproducibility of our study, we made the source code and the title datasets available at https://github.com/florianmai/Quadflor.

Table 2: Results of experiments in terms of sample-based F_1-measure. The best performing method on each sub-dataset is printed in bold font.

Method \ Dataset	EconBiz F_1 scores						PubMed F_1 scores					
	Full-Text	T1	T2	T4	T8	T_{all}	Full-Text	T1	T2	T4	T8	T_{all}
Base-MLP	0.441	**0.391**	**0.419**	**0.442**	0.451	0.472	0.526	**0.479**	**0.478**	0.475	0.465	0.485
MLP	**0.457**	0.357	0.396	0.432	**0.453**	**0.500**	**0.530**	0.449	0.456	0.464	0.465	0.504
CNN	0.387	0.364	0.382	0.400	0.407	0.426	0.483	0.438	0.437	0.431	0.419	0.440
LSTM	0.363	0.360	0.392	0.417	0.435	0.466	0.524	0.465	0.470	**0.477**	**0.481**	**0.515**

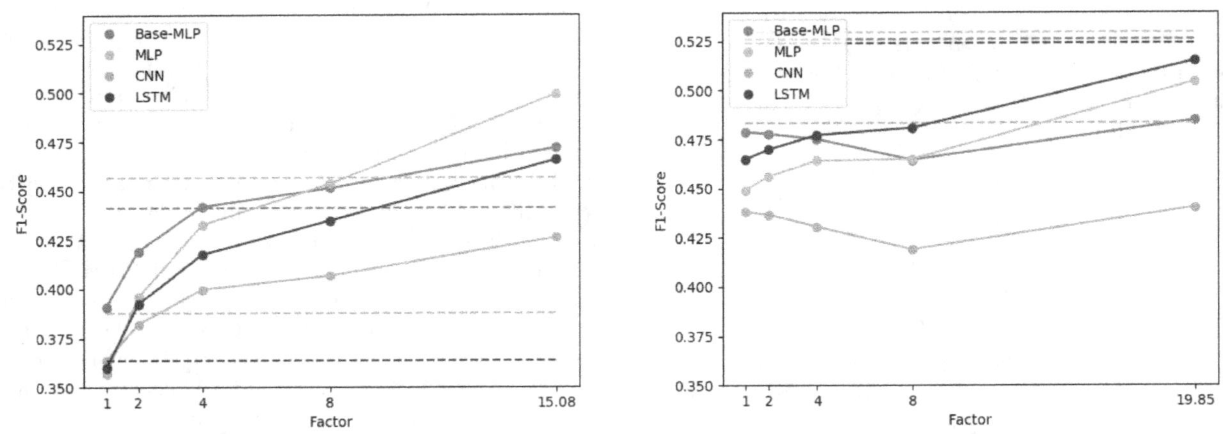

(a) (b)

Figure 2: The figures show the performance of each classifier on titles as a function of the sample size relative to the number of full-texts as a solid line on EconBiz (a) and PubMed (b). The dashed horizontal lines represent the respective classifier's performance on the full-text.

out, previous literature suggests that deep learning models require around 650,000 samples to outperform more traditional approaches. On EconBiz, this number of full-texts is far from being reached. Due to this lack of enough training data, our deep learning models may not do so well with full-texts, in absolute numbers. The models based on titles on the other hand may be able to achieve their impressive results because there is just enough data to unleash the power of deep learning models. In fact, our MLP, which was optimized for large sample sizes, starts to outperform the baseline when eight times as many titles as full-texts are used, which nets to approximately 560,000 training samples. On the PubMed dataset, there are almost 650,000 full-text samples available. Here, the deep learning models can already work well on full-text. This may explain why the LSTM performs so much better on PubMed's full-texts than on EconBiz's full-texts. These findings support the claim from previous literature that deep learning models work well for text classification only when the sample size is several hundred thousands. Furthermore, since our datasets have large label spaces, we can state that this observation extents to XMLC, which is arguably a harder task than single-label classification.

In order to push the limits of text classification based on titles, our strategy was to develop and employ methods that can make use of the vast amount of data available for training. Our results suggest that this strategy was largely successful. On both datasets, some of our methods surpass the performance of the baseline as they are given more and more data for training. BaseMLP on the other hand cannot make such good use of the additional training data. This becomes particularly apparent on the PubMed dataset, where it improves by only 1.3% even when it has 20 times more training data. Our methods on the other hand improve considerably the more data is used for training. To be fair, it is clear that part of the much larger gain compared to the baseline is due to overfitting on the small title datasets such as T1. Recall that our methods are optimized towards their performance on T_{all}. This design decision in our study was made to be able to fairly assess the development of the performance as the sample size increases. We observed that the capacity of the resulting models is likely too large for smaller datasets, which results in overfitting. This can be seen by the fact that BaseMLP, which has considerably lower capacity, outperforms our proposed methods on both PubMed and EconBiz. Yet, on T_{all}, MLP outperforms Base-MLP by a wide margin on both datasets. LSTM is close to Base-MLP on EconBiz and outperforms it drastically on PubMed. Again, this indicates the success of our strategy. The only exception is the CNN, which does not benefit as much from additional data as our other proposed methods, although its capacity is large compared to other architectures recently proposed in the literature. It is particularly interesting that the performance of CNN (and Base-MLP, too) actually has a drop on PubMed as more title samples are used for training. We explain this by the fact that in T2 to T8 more than 1,300 new labels that do not occur in T1 are introduced. Hence, the models have to account for these new labels even though they never appear in the test set, reducing their capacity to learn to classify the labels relevant to the test set.

Considering the amount of attention CNNs have received in recent years for their performance in text classification (cf. Section 2), the results of our CNN is rather underwhelming. This is true for both full-text, and titles. In neither case is this due to overfitting. Our preliminary experiments showed that the CNN benefits from increasing the feature map size a lot. Yet, the CNNs do not benefit from additional training data in the same way LSTMs and MLPs do. On PubMed, no benefit at all can be observed. On EconBiz, the rate of improvement is comparable to MLP and LSTM only up to a factor of four times the number of full-texts. After that, the improvement is relatively marginal. In conclusion of our findings, we think it would be good if future research shifted its focus more towards MLPs and LSTMs, as they have demonstrated to be serious competitors for CNNs in text classification.

The goal of this study is to investigate to which extent a model trained on vast amounts of sample titles can compensate for the lack of information in comparison to the full-text. Thus, it is not the aim to achieve results beyond the state-of-the-art performance on, e. g., full-texts. Yet, the models we use are based on and also enhance recently proposed models. As described in Section 3.1, the MLP is at its core a non-linear version of the popular fastText. The CNN is based on recent advances from the domain of text-based XMLC, but was improved by integrating more fine-grained window sizes and larger feature maps. Finally, we present a strong bidirectional LSTM with attention over the outputs that does not assume a hierarchical structure of the document and therefore also works for short text snippets, in contrast to previous work by Yang et al. [35]. Therefore, our methods are good candidates for researchers to also adopt for single-label text classification.

A common problem in machine learning research and in deep learning in particular is that models are very sensitive to the choice of hyperparameters. However, examining the whole hyperparameter space is very difficult due to its combinatorial complexity. Recently, this has called the validity of deep learning results into question, for example in language-modeling [22] or even text classification [17]. This problem persists in our study as well. However, instead of simply assuming values for our parameters or manually tuning them in a somewhat arbitrary fashion, we took an incremental tuning approach that in the end led to an improvement over initial base models from the literature in all cases. This gives us reason to believe that our results are largely reliable.

In this study, we have compared three deep learning methods. We did not compare against linear models such as logistic regression, and we did not compare against other non-linear approaches such as kNN or SVMs. However, as described in Section 2, there is evidence that traditional linear methods are inferior to non-linear ones when the training data is large. More importantly, we compared against a non-linear baseline by Galke et al. [4] that was shown to outperform not only linear models, but also other non-linear, non-parametric models like kNN and SVMs on a diverse set of datasets and by a wide margin on both titles and full-texts.

For comparability, our proposed models were chosen such that they can be employed to titles and full-texts uniformly. This prohibits that certain strengts of the full-text can be made full use of. For instance, full-text models might benefit greatly from a hierarchical model as proposed by Yang et al. [35]. On the other hand, we tried our best to tap the full potential of full-texts. For instance, in our CNN we employ dynamic max-pooling with $p = 3$ for full-texts although this does not have any beneficial effect on titles.

In our study, we have examined two datasets from digital libraries of scientific content. We argue that these results are likely to generalize to other datasets of scientific publications as well. In consent with previous text classification research, we found our deep learning methods to require approximately 550,000 samples to outperform the previous baseline (EconBiz T8). While this number of titles can certainly be reached in domains other than economics and biomedicine, not many scientific domains will reach this number of full-texts. This can be seen by considering the fact that the availability of full-texts is generally tied to their open access rate. The rate of open access journals in academia is approximately 7% as reported by Teplitskiy et al. [32]. This number closely matches the rate of 5 to 6.5% of available full-texts in our datasets. Moreover, Teplitskiy et al.'s study also suggests that the corpus of publications from the medical domain are among the largest. Therefore, we think it is likely that in other domains at least the relatively small gap of less than 3% between titles and full-texts can be achieved as well. However, in many other domains where only few full-texts are available, training models on titles may actually be much better, as we demonstrated for the economics domain.

Our results are of great practical importance for automatic semantic indexing in digital libraries. Considering the large amount of new literature published every year, subject indexers rely on the assistance of machines. It is desirable to have algorithms that produce good annotation suggestions by using only the title as textual input instead of the abstract or full-text. This is because the title is easy to obtain and free to use in text mining applications, whereas the full-text and even the abstract are often either not available or may not be processed automatically due to legal restrictions. For instance, in EconBiz only approximately 15% of the documents have an abstract and 7% have a full-text available. Furthermore, the task of downloading and processing the full-text is cumbersome, where one has tens of gigabytes of data. In contrast, as Table 1 shows, titles only comprise up to a few gigabytes of data. Thus, the full-text are by an order of magnitude larger. Thanks to the vast amount of data available for training title-based deep learning models, our study demonstrates that in a realistic scenario deep learning algorithms are able to satisfy the demand for sufficiently strong title-based classification methods. Engineers of (semi-)automatic semantic indexing algorithms should therefore consider shifting their focus from full-text-based classification to title-based classification in order to maximize the applicability of automatic semantic indexing systems.

7 CONCLUSION

In this paper, we have successfully answered the question if a semantic indexing system based on the title can reach the performance of a system based on the full-text if the number of samples for training the title-based method is much larger than the number of full-text samples. To this end, we developed three deep learning methods and evaluated them on two scientific datasets of different size. We found that in one case such a system is competitive with the full-text system, and in the other case it even yields considerably better scores. These results have important implications for automatic semantic indexing systems in digital libraries of scientific content.

In the future, we want to push the limits of classification based on large amounts of titles even further, and we would like to encourage the community to do the same. To this end, we published the title datasets, the source code, and an extended version of this paper on GitHub[11].

ACKNOWLEDGMENTS

This research was co-financed by the EU H2020 project MOVING (http://www.moving-project.eu/) under contract no 693092. We would like to thank Tamara Pianos and Tobias Rebholz from ZBW for providing helpful information on the EconBiz dataset.

REFERENCES

[1] Damien Brain and G Webb. 1999. On the effect of data set size on bias and variance in classification learning. In *Australian Knowledge Acquisition Workshop, AI'99*. 117–128.

[2] Alexis Conneau, Holger Schwenk, Loïc Barrault, and Yann Lecun. 2017. Very deep convolutional networks for text classification. In *ECACL*, Vol. 1. 1107–1116.

[3] Yarin Gal and Zoubin Ghahramani. 2016. A Theoretically Grounded Application of Dropout in Recurrent Neural Networks. In *NIPS*. 1019–1027.

[4] Lukas Galke, Florian Mai, Alan Schelten, Dennis Brunsch, and Ansgar Scherp. 2017. Using Titles vs. Full-text as Source for Automated Semantic Document Annotation. In *K-CAP*. 9.

[5] Lukas Galke, Ahmed Saleh, and Ansgar Scherp. 2017. Word Embeddings for Practical Information Retrieval. In *INFORMATIK*. 2155–2167.

[6] Edouard Grave, Tomas Mikolov, Armand Joulin, and Piotr Bojanowski. 2017. Bag of Tricks for Efficient Text Classification. In *EACL*. 427–431.

[7] Klaus Greff, Rupesh K Srivastava, Jan Koutník, Bas R Steunebrink, and Jürgen Schmidhuber. 2017. LSTM: A search space odyssey. *IEEE TNNLS* (2017).

[8] Gregor Große-Bölting, Chifumi Nishioka, and Ansgar Scherp. 2015. A comparison of different strategies for automated semantic document annotation. In *K-CAP*. ACM, 8.

[9] Kaiming He, Xiangyu Zhang, Shaoqing Ren, and Jian Sun. 2016. Deep residual learning for image recognition. In *CVPR*. 770–778.

[10] Bradley M Hemminger, Billy Saelim, Patrick F Sullivan, and Todd J Vision. 2007. Comparison of full-text searching to metadata searching for genes in two biomedical literature cohorts. *JASIST* 58, 14 (2007), 2341–2352.

[11] Sepp Hochreiter and Jürgen Schmidhuber. 1997. Long short-term memory. *Neural computation* 9, 8 (1997), 1735–1780.

[12] Minlie Huang, Aurélie Névéol, and Zhiyong Lu. 2011. Recommending MeSH terms for annotating biomedical articles. *JAMIA* 18, 5 (2011), 660–667.

[13] Sergey Ioffe and Christian Szegedy. 2015. Batch Normalization: Accelerating Deep Network Training by Reducing Internal Covariate Shift. In *ICML*. 448–456.

[14] Thorsten Joachims. 1998. Text Categorization with Support Vector Machines: Learning with Many Relevant Features. In *ECML*. Springer-Verlag, 137–142.

[15] Yoon Kim. 2014. Convolutional Neural Networks for Sentence Classification. In *EMNLP*. 1746–1751.

[16] Diederik Kingma and Jimmy Ba. 2014. Adam: A method for stochastic optimization. *arXiv:1412.6980* (2014).

[17] Hoa T Le, Christophe Cerisara, and Alexandre Denis. 2018. Do Convolutional Networks need to be Deep for Text Classification?. In *Proceedings of the AAAI-18 Workshop on Affective Content Analysis, New Orleans, Louisiana, United States, February 3rd.*

[18] Yann LeCun, Yoshua Bengio, and Geoffrey Hinton. 2015. Deep learning. *Nature* 521, 7553 (2015), 436–444.

[11] https://github.com/florianmai/Quadflor

[19] Jingzhou Liu, Wei-Cheng Chang, Yuexin Wu, and Yiming Yang. 2017. Deep Learning for Extreme Multi-label Text Classification. In *SIGIR*. ACM, 115–124.

[20] Ke Liu, Shengwen Peng, Junqiu Wu, Chengxiang Zhai, Hiroshi Mamitsuka, and Shanfeng Zhu. 2015. MeSHLabeler: improving the accuracy of large-scale MeSH indexing by integrating diverse evidence. *Bioinformatics* 31, 12 (2015), i339–i347.

[21] Yuqing Mao and Zhiyong Lu. 2017. MeSH Now: automatic MeSH indexing at PubMed scale via learning to rank. *J. of Biomedical Semantics* 8, 1 (2017), 15.

[22] Gábor Melis, Chris Dyer, and Phil Blunsom. 2017. On the state of the art of evaluation in neural language models. *arXiv:1707.05589* (2017).

[23] James G Mork, Dina Demner-Fushman, Susan Schmidt, and Alan R Aronson. 2014. Recent Enhancements to the NLM Medical Text Indexer.. In *Working Notes for CLEF*. 1328–1336.

[24] Jinseok Nam, Jungi Kim, Eneldo Loza Mencía, Iryna Gurevych, and Johannes Fürnkranz. 2014. Large-Scale Multi-label Text Classification - Revisiting Neural Networks. In *ECML*. 437–452.

[25] Cristiano Nascimento, Alberto HF Laender, Altigran S da Silva, and Marcos André Gonçalves. 2011. A source independent framework for research paper recommendation. In *JCDL*. ACM, 297–306.

[26] Chifumi Nishioka and Ansgar Scherp. 2016. Profiling vs. Time vs. Content: What does Matter for Top-k Publication Recommendation based on Twitter Profiles?. In *JCDL*. ACM, 171–180.

[27] Jeffrey Pennington, Richard Socher, and Christopher D. Manning. 2014. Glove: Global Vectors for Word Representation. In *EMNLP*. 1532–1543.

[28] Timothy N Rubin, America Chambers, Padhraic Smyth, and Mark Steyvers. 2012. Statistical topic models for multi-label document classification. *JMLR* 88, 1 (2012), 157–208.

[29] Gerard Salton and Christopher Buckley. 1988. Term-weighting approaches in automatic text retrieval. *Information processing & management* 24, 5 (1988), 513–523.

[30] Nitish Srivastava, Geoffrey E Hinton, Alex Krizhevsky, Ilya Sutskever, and Ruslan Salakhutdinov. 2014. Dropout: a simple way to prevent neural networks from overfitting. *JMLR* 15, 1 (2014), 1929–1958.

[31] Kai Sheng Tai, Richard Socher, and Christopher D. Manning. 2015. Improved Semantic Representations From Tree-Structured Long Short-Term Memory Networks. In *ACL*. 1556–1566.

[32] Misha Teplitskiy, Grace Lu, and Eamon Duede. 2017. Amplifying the impact of open access: Wikipedia and the diffusion of science. *JASIST* 68, 9 (2017), 2116–2127.

[33] George Tsatsaronis, Georgios Balikas, Prodromos Malakasiotis, Ioannis Partalas, Matthias Zschunke, Michael R Alvers, Dirk Weissenborn, Anastasia Krithara, Sergios Petridis, Dimitris Polychronopoulos, Yannis Almirantis, John Pavlopoulos, Nicolas Baskiotis, Patrick Gallinari, Thierry Artieres, Axel Ngonga, Norman Heino, Eric Gaussier, Liliana Barrio-Alvers, Michael Schroeder, Ion Androutsopoulos, and Georgios Paliouras. 2015. An overview of the BIOASQ large-scale biomedical semantic indexing and question answering competition. *BMC Bioinformatics* 16 (2015), 138.

[34] Yijun Xiao and Kyunghyun Cho. 2016. Efficient character-level document classification by combining convolution and recurrent layers. *arXiv:1602.00367* (2016).

[35] Zichao Yang, Diyi Yang, Chris Dyer, Xiaodong He, Alexander J. Smola, and Eduard H. Hovy. 2016. Hierarchical Attention Networks for Document Classification. In *NAACL-HLT*. 1480–1489.

[36] Wenpeng Yin, Katharina Kann, Mo Yu, and Hinrich Schütze. 2017. Comparative Study of CNN and RNN for Natural Language Processing. *arXiv:1702.01923* (2017).

[37] Wenpeng Yin and Hinrich Schütze. 2015. Multichannel Variable-Size Convolution for Sentence Classification. In *CoNLL*. 204–214.

[38] Dani Yogatama, Chris Dyer, Wang Ling, and Phil Blunsom. 2017. Generative and discriminative text classification with recurrent neural networks. *arXiv:1703.01898* (2017).

[39] Tom Young, Devamanyu Hazarika, Soujanya Poria, and Erik Cambria. 2017. Recent trends in deep learning based natural language processing. *arXiv:1708.02709* (2017).

[40] Min-Ling Zhang and Zhi-Hua Zhou. 2006. Multilabel neural networks with applications to functional genomics and text categorization. *IEEE TKDE* 18, 10 (2006), 1338–1351.

[41] Rui Zhang, Honglak Lee, and Dragomir R. Radev. 2016. Dependency Sensitive Convolutional Neural Networks for Modeling Sentences and Documents. In *NAACL-HLT*. 1512–1521.

[42] Wenjie Zhang, Liwei Wang, Junchi Yan, Xiangfeng Wang, and Hongyuan Zha. 2017. Deep Extreme Multi-label Learning. *arXiv:1704.03718* (2017).

[43] Xiang Zhang, Junbo Zhao, and Yann LeCun. 2015. Character-level convolutional networks for text classification. In *NIPS*. 649–657.

Social Tagging: Organic and Retroactive Folksonomies

Chris Holstrom
The Information School, University of Washington
Seattle, WA
cholstro@uw.edu

ABSTRACT

To develop a richer understanding of how folksonomies and social tagging differ from and are similar to professional indexing languages, the following paper presents preliminary analysis of over 2 million keyword tags on the community blog MetaFilter and its companion question-and-answer site Ask MetaFilter. Most of the tags in these narrow folksonomies were created by users when they published a post, but some tags were retroactively created for old posts by a small group of volunteers. Both organic and retroactive tags on MetaFilter and Ask MetaFilter followed a power law distribution, which is expected for folksonomies. Based on tag distribution, use of organization tags, and avoidance of synonyms, however, retroactive taggers did not tag like professional indexers. Instead, they tagged using similar practices to organic taggers, even actively accommodating the broader community's use of synonyms. These findings suggest that folksonomies remain a distinctly different approach to knowledge organization.

CCS CONCEPTS

• **Human-centered computing → Social tagging**;

KEYWORDS

Folksonomy, social tagging, MetaFilter, classification, indexing languages, online communities, categorization

ACM Reference Format:

Chris Holstrom. 2018. Social Tagging: Organic and Retroactive Folksonomies. In *JCDL '18: The 18th ACM/IEEE Joint Conference on Digital Libraries, June 3–7, 2018, Fort Worth, TX, USA.* ACM, New York, NY, USA, 4 pages. https://doi.org/10.1145/3197026.3197065

1 INTRODUCTION

Folksonomies and social tagging became popular on sites like Flickr and del.icio.us when Web 2.0 pushed the web toward increased interactivity and community participation in the mid 2000's. Users could tag resources like web pages or photographs with keywords, and then they and other users could use the tags to sort and find materials. The collected result of these social tags came to be known as folksonomies, a portmanteau of "folk" and "taxonomy" [19].

JCDL '18, June 3–7, 2018, Fort Worth, TX, USA

ACM ISBN 978-1-4503-5178-2/18/06...$15.00
https://doi.org/10.1145/3197026.3197065

Tagging proponents noted that folksonomies "directly reflect the vocabulary of users" [14], "reflect the population's conceptual model of the information" [16], support browsing and discovery, are inclusive, stay current, and have many other advantages [12]. Also, tagging is simpler than classifying, especially formal classification, and can provide much of the same value [14].

However, folksonomies have faced criticisms, even from proponents [11, 14, 16]. Critics cited the orthographic and semantic limitations of folksonomies in comparison to professionally curated indexing languages with controlled vocabularies. For example, social tagging might produce orthographic variations among tags like `cat`, `cats`, `feline`, and even a misspelling like `felime`, whereas a controlled vocabulary would standardize one term, such as `feline`. Another criticism of social tagging is that "because users are not under a centralized controlling vocabulary, no coherent categorization scheme *can emerge at all* from collaborative tagging" [10, emphasis in original].

The community blog MetaFilter and its companion question-and-answer site Ask MetaFilter have used social tagging since 2005 [17]. MetaFilter community members have actively engaged in tagging, creating over 2 million tags and regularly discussing tagging features and best practices [2]. MetaFilter also has tag-based information retrieval features like tag search, tag clouds, related tag lists, and subscription and filtering tools.

MetaFilter tagging history affords a unique opportunity to compare tagging done when posts were created—what I call *organic tagging*—with tagging done after the fact by a small group of volunteers—what I call *retroactive tagging*. MetaFilter launched in 1999 but did not implement tagging until 2005. Instead of leaving old posts untagged, a small group of MetaFilter community members volunteered to retroactively tag all of the old posts to improve retrieval. The top 10 volunteers tagged 59.7% of old posts [5].

Despite not organizing themselves as a monolithic indexing team with rigid tagging guidelines [4], we might expect the motivations, demographics (many librarians), and situation of the retroactive taggers to produce folksonomies more similar to professionally designed indexing languages. Professionally designed indexing languages have a shorter-tail distribution of terms or tags because they use a controlled vocabulary. They also employ more "organizing" terms to support a hierarchal categorization and avoid synonyms by selecting preferred terms. By analyzing how closely organic tags and retroactive tags match these expectations, we can better understand the differences and similarities between folksonomies and professionally designed indexing languages.

2 RELATED WORK

Previous work by Mathes predicted that folksonomy tags would be distributed according to a power law, with a small set of heavily used terms and a long tail of terms that are used only once or twice [14]. This prediction has proven true across numerous studies [6, 7, 10, 11, 13, 15] for both broad folksonomies (where many users tag the same entity) and narrow folksonomies (where the creator of an object tags the object) [18]. We can expect to see a similar distribution for MetaFilter and Ask MetaFilter.

Related to the power law distribution, both Kipp and Campbell as well as Halpin, et al., found that taggers arrive at consensus keywords or tags for a resource [10, 11]. Halpin, et al., found that del.icio.us users "developed some consensus about which tags best describe a site and those tags are used most often" [10]. This finding is specific to broad folksonomies, where many users tag the same resource, but it suggests that tagging patterns are generally consistent and that taggers follow predictable patterns.

These consistent tagging patterns form "tag correlation networks," which have some similarities to ontologies and categorization schemes [10]. Peter Mika found clusters of related tags or emergent ontologies based on the co-occurrence of tags on del.icio.us [15]. These emergent ontologies show that folksonomies can have properties similar to professionally developed ontologies and taxonomies, even relationships between broader and narrower terms. However, Mika's work focused on "only the 100 strongest associations in each network" to compare with ontologies.

Golder and Huberman identified kinds of tags in folksonomies [7]. These kinds of tags can be further simplified to two main types of tags: *organization tags* and *identification tags*. If social taggers create more organization tags, they are working more like professional indexers. We can expect taggers to create organization tags for social benefit [6, 13], and we can expect retroactive taggers to create organization tags at a higher rate because their motivations are more focused on social benefit.

Finally, both Kipp and Campbell as well as Guy, et al., found that tagging inconsistencies, including orthographic errors and semantic issues like synonyms, follow predictable patterns [9, 11], which suggests that "tagging supports and enhances traditional ways of classifying and indexing documents."

This paper aims to build on those findings by 1) analyzing narrow folksonomies (most studies have analyzed broad folksonomies) and previously unstudied folksonomies in MetaFilter and Ask MetaFilter, by 2) analyzing millions of tags instead of the thousands of tags that previous studies were limited to, and by 3) comparing the organic tagging that has been previously studied with retroactive tagging.

3 METHODS

To analyze organic and retroactive tags for narrow folksonomies, I downloaded MetaFilter and Ask MetaFilter tagging data [1] and analyzed all tags for posts created between July 15, 1999, and October 29, 2017. MetaFilter and Ask MetaFilter tags came in separate files and each tagging entry contained a tag ID, post ID, timestamp, and tag keyword. For example:

```
591412  147554 Mar 4 2010 12:55:29:853PM  kittens
```

If a post had more than one tag, the data set included an entry for each tag, with the same post ID for each entry. MetaFilter tags are space-separated, so `musichistory` and `music-history` are one tag each, but `music history` is two separate tags.

In total, there were 988,170 tags on MetaFilter and 1,315,013 tags on Ask MetaFilter. I used community discussions and a test post [3] to identify the date (January 18, 2005) when organic tagging started on MetaFilter and Ask MetaFilter and divided the tags into four data sets, as shown in Table 1.

Table 1: Total tag count and unique tags (tags used only once) in each of the four data sets. Organic tags were entered by the post creator at the same time as the post. Retroactive tags were created for old posts by a small team of taggers after tagging was implemented on January 18, 2005.

Data Set	Total Tags	Unique Tags
Organic MetaFilter	806493	216573
Retroactive MetaFilter	181677	48221
Organic Ask MetaFilter	1269485	168393
Retroactive Ask MetaFilter	45528	16755

To analyze and characterize the overall tag mass of each tag set, I used Google BigQuery [8], which supports SQL queries on large non-relational data sets, to calculate values like standard deviation of tag frequency and to create output text files with the total instances of each tag. For example, below is a BigQuery query to find the count for tags in the Organic MetaFilter data set and the results for the five most popular tags:

```
SELECT tag_name, COUNT(*) AS magnitude
FROM [Table] WHERE post_id > 38715
GROUP BY tag_keyword ORDER BY magnitude DESC

music,6963
art,5506
history,3631
video,3444
photography,3088
```

To understand how well these tag distributions matched expected distributions for folksonomies as predicted by Mathes, I fit each to a power law equation using Microsoft Excel. I then compared how quickly tag frequency diminished for organic and retroactive folksonomies to see if retroactive folksonomies made heavier use of a controlled set of terms, which would be more similar to indexing languages with controlled vocabularies.

Next, I coded the top 100 tags in each data set as either organization tags or identification tags. Organization tags are broad terms that appear at the top of hierarchies, like `music`, `art`, `history`, and `politics`. Identification tags are narrower terms for specific entities like `Canada`, `Obama`, and `Twitter`. Identification tags do not necessarily provide the hierarchical structure that you expect to see in a professionally designed indexing language.

Finally, to understand how prevalent synonyms were in both organic folksonomies and retroactive folksonomies I analyzed within the top 100 tags for synonyms. For example, I looked for variants of George W. Bush (`georgebush`, `georgewbush`, `gwb`, `bush`, `presidentbush`, `gwbush`, etc.), who was a common topic of discussion during his presidency. I also analyzed how often these synonyms were used to tag the same post (for example one post with both `georgebush` and `gwb`) to determine whether taggers were intentionally introducing synonym redundancy to support information retrieval.

4 RESULTS AND DISCUSSION

4.1 Power Law Distribution and "Steepness" Measures

All four tagging data sets were graphed with tag count on the $\log_{10}$ y-axis and tag rank on the x-axis, and fit to the power law distribution. Figure 1 shows this graph for organic tags on MetaFilter.

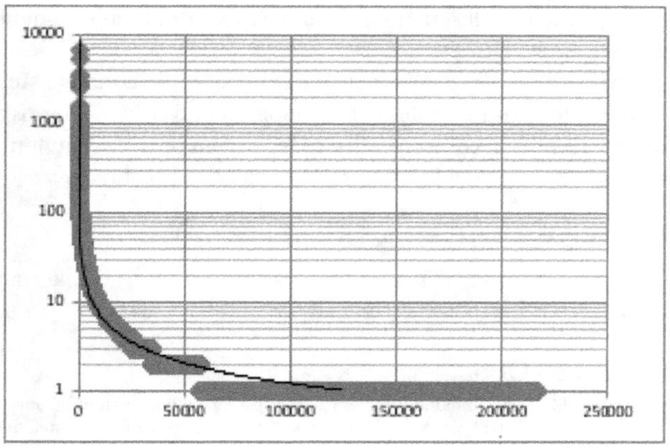

Figure 1: Distribution of organic tags for MetaFilter (*n*=806,493), fit to a power law distribution of $y=9305x^{-0.775}$ with a R-square value of 89.1%. The y-axis is $\log_{10}$ and represents the number of times each tag was used. The most-used tag (music, *n*=6963) is at the top left, and the tags that were used only once form the long tail to the right.

Similar graphs were created for all four data sets. Table 2 shows that all four data sets closely matched the expected power law distribution, with the following R-squared values.

Table 2: R-squared values from 89.1% to 92.5% show strong fits to power law curves for all four data sets.

Data Set	R-squared	n
Organic MetaFilter	89.1%	806493
Retroactive MetaFilter	91.0%	181677
Organic Ask MetaFilter	92.5%	1269485
Retroactive Ask MetaFilter	91.0%	45528

To understand whether retroactive tagging exhibited properties more similar to professionally designed indexing languages, I calculated three "steepness" values: percentage of tags used only once in the data set, standard deviation of tag frequency distribution, and the exponent for the power law distribution of the data set, as shown in Table 3.

Other than a slightly higher standard deviation for the distribution of retroactive tags, MetaFilter tags were largely similar for organic and retroactive tagging. Organic and retroactive taggers produced similarly "steep" distributions, which suggests that for MetaFilter retroactive tagging is not similar to professional indexing using a controlled vocabulary.

Table 3: Three "steepness" measures for all four tag data sets: percentage of tags that were used only once, standard deviation of tag frequency distribution, and the exponent for the power law distribution.

Data Set	Unique	SD	Exponent
Organic MetaFilter	26.9%	34.34	-0.775
Retroactive MetaFilter	26.5%	42.48	-0.802
Organic Ask MetaFilter	13.3%	63.02	-1.008
Retroactive Ask MetaFilter	36.8%	8.53	-0.719

Ask MetaFilter tags reveal more differences between organic and retroactive tags. Retroactive tags for Ask MetaFilter are much more likely to be used only once (36.8% to 13.3%), which is not what was expected for an approach similar to a controlled vocabulary. The standard deviation of tag distribution for organic Ask MetaFilter tags (63.02) is much larger than that for retroactive Ask MetaFilter tags (8.53), confirming the unexpected longer-tail distribution for retroactive tagging. The exponents of the power law distributions for Ask MetaFilter suggest that organic tags have a "steeper" slope, which does fit the hypothesis. Overall, these "steepness" results are inconclusive.

4.2 Organization and Identification Tags

I analyzed and coded the top 100 tags in all four data sets as organization tags or identification tags. A higher percentage of organization tags tells us that taggers are using more tags similar to those used by professional indexers to create a hierarchal structure. Table 4 shows the percentage of organization tags for each data set.

Table 4: Percentage of top 100 tags in each data set that were coded as organization tags.

Data Set	Organization Tags
Organic MetaFilter	61%
Retroactive MetaFilter	50%
Organic Ask MetaFilter	46%
Retroactive Ask MetaFilter	41%

Both MetaFilter and Ask MetaFilter had a higher percentage of organization tags for organic tagging, which does not match the hypothesis that predicts a higher percentage for retroactive tagging. Retroactive taggers are actually slightly less likely to use organization tags and more likely to use identification tags, although not significantly: χ^2 (1, *N*=100)=2.025, *p*=n.s. for MetaFilter and χ^2 (1, *N*=100)=0.326, *p*=n.s. for Ask MetaFilter.

4.3 Synonym Tags and Synonym Co-Occurrence

I analyzed how many synonyms (i.e., `television` and `tv`) existed within the top 100 tags of each data set and whether those synonyms co-occurred on the same post, as shown in Table 5.

Table 5: Percentage of top 100 tags in each data set that were synonyms of each other and percentage of those synonyms that co-occurred on the same post.

Data Set	Synonyms	Co-Occurring
Organic MetaFilter	33%	28.5%
Retroactive MetaFilter	34%	33.2%
Organic Ask MetaFilter	26%	15.2%
Retroactive Ask MetaFilter	27%	18.2%

Professional indexing languages with controlled vocabularies choose preferred terms to avoid synonyms, so we would expect retroactive taggers to use a lower percentage of synonyms if they were tagging more like professional indexers. What we see, however, is that the use of synonyms is slightly higher for organic and retroactive tagging for both MetaFilter and Ask MetaFilter, although not significantly: χ^2 (1, N=100)=0, p=n.s.

The higher than expected rate of synonyms for retroactive taggers might be explained by the higher rate of co-occurring synonyms. These co-occurring synonyms represent an effort on the tagger's part to accommodate the community's use of synonyms and the lack of synonym support in MetaFilter and Ask MetaFilter's tag search by using all or many of the popular tags for the topic. For example, instead of choosing between `cat` and `cats`, the tagger intentionally uses both tags. That retroactive taggers used co-occurring synonyms more than organic taggers suggests that while retroactive taggers did not restrict synonym use like professional indexers using a controlled vocabulary, they may have used synonyms intentionally to mimic organic tagging practices and maintain consistency for indexing and retrieval.

5 CONCLUSIONS AND FUTURE WORK

I found that both organic and retroactive folksonomies on MetaFilter and Ask MetaFilter followed a power law distribution, which is for folksonomies. Based on tag distribution, use of organization tags, and avoidance of synonyms, I did not, however, find that retroactive taggers tagged like professional indexers. Instead, they tagged much more like organic taggers.

These findings suggest that tagging might be a distinct activity from professional indexing, whether done at the moment of posting by the poster or done after the fact, by a dedicated tagger, to improve information retrieval; and that folksonomies remain a distinctly different approach to knowledge organization.

Folksonomies have not been studied intensely since their initial rise in popularity, which means that MetaFilter and Ask MetaFilter are just two of many unexplored folksonomies on the internet today. For example, future studies should examine Stack Engine communities, including Stack Overflow, because of the emphasis on tags in their navigation structure, the careful moderation of synonyms in their community, and the large number of communities using the same site design.

A future qualitative study of MetaFilter and Ask MetaFilter might serve as a companion the current study and help to better explain the motivations behind retroactive tagger's tagging choices. For example, retroactive taggers might explain when they tried to tag like professional indexers and when they tried to mimic existing tagging behaviors and conventions. Some of their choices and methods are discussed on MetaFilter discussion boards [4] and many retroactive taggers are still active community members and might be available to answer questions.

MetaFilter does not use autosuggest or autocomplete for tags like many other social tagging tools, which might have a significant effect on tag distribution and use of synonyms [10]. A future study should compare folksonomies with these features to folksonomies without these features.

Finally, it would also be valuable to take more concrete steps toward automatically building folksonomies into clustered terms or taxonomies using co-occurrence of terms and organization terms as broad terms, possibly using machine learning techniques.

ACKNOWLEDGMENTS

Thank you to Joseph T. Tennis, Nicholas Weber, Alexis Hiniker, and Jevin D. West for their help and advice on this research.

REFERENCES

[1] [n. d.]. MetaFilter Infodump. ([n. d.]). http://stuff.metafilter.com/infodump/
[2] [n. d.]. MetaTalk: Posts tagged with tags. ([n. d.]). https://metatalk.metafilter.com/tags/tags
[3] 2005. MetaFilter: test. (2005). https://www.metafilter.com/38715/test
[4] 2007. MetaTalk: Remembering Retrotagging. (2007). https://metatalk.metafilter.com/14245/Remembering-Retrotagging
[5] 2009. MetaTalk: Five years in the making and finally complete! (2009). https://metatalk.metafilter.com/18464/Five-years-in-the-making-and-finally-complete
[6] E. Angus, M. Thelwall, and D. Stuart. 2008. General patterns of tag usage among university groups in Flickr. *Online Information Review* 32, 1 (2008), 89–101. https://doi.org/10.1108/14684520810866001 arXiv:https://doi.org/10.1108/14684520810866001
[7] S. Golder and B. Huberman. 2005. *The Structure of Collaborative Tagging Systems.* Technical Report. HP Labs.
[8] Google. 2018. Google BigQuery. (2018). https://cloud.google.com/bigquery/docs/
[9] M. Guy and E. Tonkin. 2006. Folksonomies: Tidying Up Tags? *D-Lib Magazine* 12, 1 (January 2006).
[10] H. Halpin, V. Robu, and H. Shepherd. 2007. The Complex Dynamics of Collaborative Tagging. In *Proceedings of the 16th International Conference on World Wide Web (WWW '07).* ACM, New York, NY, USA, 211–220. https://doi.org/10.1145/1242572.1242602
[11] M. Kipp and D. Campbell. 2006. Patterns and Inconsistencies in Collaborative Tagging Systems: An Examination of Tagging Practices. In *Annual General Meeting of the American Society for Information Science and Technology.* Austin, Texas (US).
[12] E. Kroski. 2005. The Hive Mind: Folksonomies and User-Based Tagging. (2005). http://web20bp.com/13f1b6019/wp-content/uploads/2013/03/The-Hive-Mind-Folksonomies-2005.pdf
[13] Cameron Marlow, Mor Naaman, Danah Boyd, and Marc Davis. 2006. HT06, Tagging Paper, Taxonomy, Flickr, Academic Article, to Read. In *Proceedings of the Seventeenth Conference on Hypertext and Hypermedia (HYPERTEXT '06).* ACM, New York, NY, USA, 31–40. https://doi.org/10.1145/1149941.1149949
[14] A. Mathes. 2004. Folksonomies - Cooperative Classification and Communication Through Shared Metadata. (2004). http://adammathes.com/academic/computer-mediated-communication/folksonomies.html
[15] P. Mika. 2005. Ontologies Are Us: A Unified Model of Social Networks and Semantics. In *The Semantic Web – ISWC 2005*, Yolanda Gil, Enrico Motta, V. Richard Benjamins, and Mark A. Musen (Eds.). Springer Berlin Heidelberg, Berlin, Heidelberg, 522–536.
[16] E. Quintarelli. 2005. Folksonomies: Power to the people. In *Proceedings of ISKO Italy-UniMIB meeting.* Milan, Italy.
[17] D. Terdiman. 2005. Folksonomies Tap People Power. (February 2005). https://www.wired.com/2005/02/folksonomies-tap-people-power/
[18] T. Vander Wal. 2005. Explaining and Showing Broad and Narrow Folksonomies. (February 2005). http://www.vanderwal.net/random/entrysel.php?blog=1635
[19] T. Vander Wal. 2007. Folksonomy Coinage and Definition. (February 2007). http://vanderwal.net/folksonomy.html

A Query Algebra for Temporal Text Corpora

Jens Willkomm
Karlsruhe Institute of Technology
Department of Informatics
jens.willkomm@kit.edu

Christoph Schmidt-Petri
Karlsruhe Institute of Technology
Department of Humanities and Social Sciences
christoph.schmidt-petri@kit.edu

Martin Schäler
Karlsruhe Institute of Technology
Department of Informatics
martin.schaeler@kit.edu

Michael Schefczyk
Karlsruhe Institute of Technology
Department of Humanities and Social Sciences
michael.schefczyk@kit.edu

Klemens Böhm
Karlsruhe Institute of Technology
Department of Informatics
klemens.boehm@kit.edu

ABSTRACT

Researching the evolution of the concepts represented by words, like "peace" or "freedom", named conceptual history, is an important discipline in the humanities, but still a laborious task. It normally consists of reading and interpreting a large number of carefully selected texts, without however always having a comprehensive knowledge of all the potentially relevant material. Thus, our objective is to design a query algebra to access temporal text corpora. It shall comprehensively allow domain experts to formalize hypotheses on how concepts manifest in large-scale digital text corpora targeting at the complete works of Reinhart Koselleck, a highly prominent researcher in conceptual history. In cooperation with domain experts, we first determine the primary information types used in conceptual history, such as word usage frequency or sentiment. Based on this, we define database operators formalizing these types, which can be combined to formulate arbitrarily complex queries representing hypotheses. The result is a novel query algebra that enables researchers in conceptual history to access large text corpora and extensively analyze word behaviors over time in a comprehensive way. In a proof of concept, we demonstrate how to use our algebra resulting in the first novel insights. This proves the suitability of our algebra.

KEYWORDS

Query algebra; temporal text corpora; database operators; conceptual history

ACM Reference Format:

Jens Willkomm, Christoph Schmidt-Petri, Martin Schäler, Michael Schefczyk, and Klemens Böhm. 2018. A Query Algebra for Temporal Text Corpora. In *JCDL '18: The 18th ACM/IEEE Joint Conference on Digital Libraries, June 3–7, 2018, Fort Worth, TX, USA.* ACM, New York, NY, USA, 10 pages. https://doi.org/10.1145/3197026.3197044

JCDL '18, June 3–7, 2018, Fort Worth, TX, USA

ACM ISBN 978-1-4503-5178-2/18/06...$15.00
https://doi.org/10.1145/3197026.3197044

1 INTRODUCTION

The digitization of large time-labeled bibliographies has resulted in corpora such as the Google Ngram data set. Such corpora capture how words are used over time in a comprehensive way. As a result, they are expected to reveal novel insights into the history of how language and thus also how society evolved. This however requires that adequate analysis systems are available. Providing a query algebra that allows domain experts to formalize complex hypotheses is therefore a key factor to successfully unlock this potential. The case of conceptual history serves as our example. In conceptual history, researchers examine the evolution of concepts represented by words such as "peace" or "freedom". In exploring the history of a concept, scholars commonly make use of, but are not restricted to, word-usage frequencies, word contexts, sentiment analysis, how words refer and relate to and contrast with each other, or they look for word pairs or word families whose usage is correlated [2, 15]. As an example, think of conceptual history researchers who examine whether the words *Osten* and *Westen* (German for East and West) change from cardinal directions to a political meaning and their use in political contexts after 1945.

Existing query algebras, like the one for the Structured Query Language (SQL), have proven their worth, but do not feature specific support for analyses in this spirit. Other approaches from the literature, e. g., the Contextual Query Language [12], the Corpus Query Language [6], or the ANNIS Query Language [20], have similar issues.

In this paper, we propose a query algebra for empirical analysis for temporal text corpora. A *temporal text corpus* in our sense is a set of words and word chains, i. e., ngrams, together with their usage frequency at various points of time. In the humanities, approaching large amounts of texts using information systems is known as *Distant Reading* [9] and is contrasted with the conventional human close reading of individual texts. There now is the need for an approach that (1) is useful for domain experts, i. e., is descriptive and complete, and (2) bears optimization potential to allow fast query processing on large data sets. The ideal of *completeness* represents the ambition to provide an algebra that can match all actual and potential hypotheses of conceptual history. We address the problem of designing such a query algebra and examine its suitability. We focus on an algebra inspired by conceptual history, as exemplified by the work of Reinhart Koselleck [13]. Koselleck is the founding father of German conceptual history and one of the most frequently cited researchers in this field. This paper is part of an interdisciplinary collaboration between philosophers working on conceptual history and computer scientists.

1.1 Challenges

We have to solve two challenges: data characteristics and showing the completeness of our query algebra. We describe these challenges in more detail in the following.

Data Characteristics. Koselleck has given intuitive definitions of his concept types that are more concrete for some concept types and more abstract for others. In contrast, when working with real data, we need observable data characteristics that specify the behavior of individual words.

Completeness. To guarantee that domain experts can examine the whole conceptual history using our query algebra, we must show its completeness. We call our query algebra complete when one can formalize all potential hypotheses regarding Koselleck's conceptual history.

1.2 Contributions

In this work, we present a set of algebra operators that forms our CHQL algebra. It allows analyzing conceptual history related to arbitrary words and addresses the aforementioned challenges as follows.

We need to overcome the gap between the philosophical descriptions of information types and their implementation. Therefore, we define a set of data characteristics. Such a data characteristic is a concrete and quantifiable piece of information, e. g., how often has a word been used in a specific year, or which words are used around this word. The philosophical part is to propose data characteristics that allow to realize all of Koselleck's information types. The computer scientists part is to offer data characteristics and suggest alternative realizations. Our algebra is mostly based on these characteristics. We realize every data characteristic with one algebra operator. For example, our operator *surroundingwords* creates a set of words used around a target word. Another example is our *sentiment* operator. It maps every word to an integer that represents the sentiment value of this word.

Our completeness criterion is to cover all of Koselleck's hypotheses. We argue that using his hypotheses is a suitable and meaningful criterion, given his academic standing in the field. To show the completeness of our algebra in turn, we show that it completely covers the information types to analyze conceptual history.

Finally, we arrive at first novel insights from experimenting with a proof-of-concept implementation.

2 RELATED WORK

Developing methods (and systems) allowing to analyze large text corpora, e. g., from a linguistic or philosophic perspective, is a current trend that has created the *digital humanities.* We now review solutions from this field and declarative query languages in general.

Work in digital humanities mainly consists of data processing and the analysis of text corpora [3, 18]. For example, *distant reading* is a known idea for text analysis [9]. Existing solutions focus on linguistic and reflective properties as well as their evolution, i. e., changes over time, such as [4, 5, 14]. Respective systems cannot output the required information to conduct research on conceptual history in a comprehensive way. In addition, such systems do not provide a sufficiently abstract interface, a reason why experts are reluctant in using them [3].

A very common query algebra is the relational algebra [1, 8]. However, it does not contain sufficiently specific operators, e. g., temporal or linguistic operators. There are extensions to add temporal operators [16, 17], but not linguistic operators. To query relation between words, there are special-purpose query languages. For example, SQWRL is a language to query an ontology [11]. Querying word relations, e. g., from an ontology, does not include all linguistic relationships needed. Further, ontologies do not provide temporal information. SQWRL does not contain any temporal operator. – All of these algebras have in common that they do not cover both linguistic and temporal operators required for research on conceptual history.

3 CONCEPTUAL HISTORY FUNDAMENTALS

In this section, we explain fundamental terms of conceptual history. In the second part, we describe Koselleck's information types.

3.1 Terms of Conceptual History

Here we describe the meaning of important terms of conceptual history.

Concept A concept is a word with a wide range of social and political meanings. This wide range makes it ambiguous. This ambiguousness creates space for interpretation [21].

Concept Type A concept type is a group of concepts having a similar behavior. The objective of conceptual history is to determine which concept type a particular concept has fallen under during a particular period. For example, a *parallel concept* is a concept type containing concepts with a similar role in a particular discourse, such as "love" and "peace".

Information Type Koselleck distinguishes a number of concept types by various criteria. His criteria are for example changes in the sentence structure or changes in a word's linguistic context. We denote Koselleck's criteria as information types. We describe a full list of Koselleck's information types in Section 3.2.

3.2 Koselleck's Information Types

Koselleck does not explicitly give a set of information types he uses for his research. However, experts in this field have extensive knowledge about the information Koselleck uses, and how he argues. We, and the philosophers in particular, now assemble all information types Koselleck considers in his work, as follows.

Geography What is the geographical dispersion of words? In which country are specific words used, and which are not?

Conceptual Design Conceptual design means that words can be used as proxies for a more complex topic than their literal meaning. For instance, when talking about the topic war, one often does not mean the single word war but also words that belong to war, like soldiers and death.

Context The context refers to the linguistic context. A linguistic context is the set of words that are used around a target word. The context is of special interest for concepts and ambiguous words. Considering the context of a word allows to detect its meanings. This is not restricted to ambiguous words. For distinct words, the context might describe a different view on the same circumstance. Take the word *ecology*: It is used at least in political as well as in economic contexts. It has the same meaning, but triggers different targets, namely to take care of people's health – and a restriction to maximize the profit.

Sentence Structure The arrangement of words and phrases define the structure of a sentence. Keeping track of changes in the arrangement of phrases is an indicator of a social change. For example, the phrase *the history of the farmers* changed to *the history of the trade*. This might mean that trade has now taken the role agriculture used to have.

Neologisms A neologism is a word or phrase that either is completely new to a language or is used with a new meaning. It is not necessarily part of the mainstream language. A revolution usually goes along with new words to describe and categorize the new conditions.

World Affairs Conceptual history and the ability to interpret a concept and its meaning require knowledge about world affairs, e. g., changes of economic, political or social circumstances. Such historical events often trigger a social change which is reflected in the language.

Coverage in the Query Algebra. We decide to not deal with geographical information in our algebra. Using a certain language data set, e. g. the British English or the German one, implicitly contains important geographical information already. We also do not explicitly model world affairs, for two reasons. First, the user needs extensive knowledge about world affairs to correctly interpret the results. Second, a user may be looking for special world affairs and its impact on language. When we explicitly model some events, we would only facilitate the investigation of known events.

4 FROM CONCEPT TYPES TO OPERATORS

In this section, we describe how one can search for concept types with the operators which we formally define in Section 6. We show that one can search for concept types that follow the definitions of Koselleck [2]. We explain completeness in three steps, which Figure 1 illustrates. In Section 3.2, we show that Koselleck has come up with a relationship between concept types and a set of information types. In this section, since Koselleck's specifications of information types are rather abstract, we describe an interpretation of his information types. This interpretation is an original contribution of this article, based on the expert knowledge of the philosophers in the team of authors. As part of this step, we also describe a mapping of those types to so-called data characteristics. A data characteristic is a quantitative feature either explicitly present in the data, e. g., the usage frequency of word "peace" in 1969, or a derived piece of information, e. g., the difference between the usage frequency of words "peace" and "war" in 1941. In principle, we can create numerous data characteristics from a temporal text corpus. Hence, in the second step we describe which data characteristics are needed to simulate Koselleck's information needs. In the third step we explain our realization of all data characteristics and their implementation as operators.

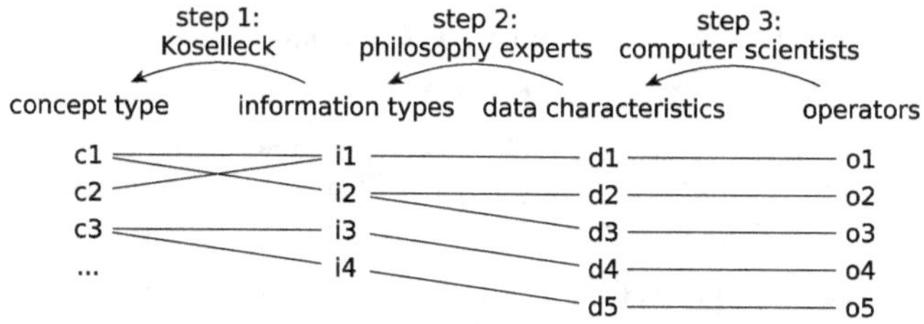

Figure 1: The relationship between concept types, information types, data characteristics and operators

4.1 Step 1: Relationship between Concept Types and Information Types

One of Koselleck's assumptions is that any concept type has its specific characteristic, i. e., any concept type can be described as a combination of information types. For example, words that form a parallel concept might have a significant number of equal surrounding words. However, for most concept types he does not specify this relationship explicitly. This means that we cannot directly look for concept types. We need to define operators to find the information types that are indicators for concept types.

EXAMPLE 4.1. *We illustrate a relationship between concept types and information types, using counter concepts as example. Counter concepts shape an asymmetric relation between "us" and "them" [21]. – Examples that are part of the following subsections will continue this example and say what concept types and information types are in this specific case. We use counter concepts as a running example in this section wherewith we illustrate each of the three steps.*

4.2 Step 2: Relationship between Information Types and Data Characteristics

Every concept type has its own characteristics, e. g., roles and functions in text. Koselleck's information types are a set of such characteristics. If Koselleck's theory holds, one can describe every concept type c as a combination of information types which characterizes c. This combination always is a subset of all of Koselleck's information types. We therefore strive for a system that finds these information types in large corpora. To this end, we need a formal definition of any information type which is observable and quantifiable. We call such a definition *data characteristic*. Our philosophy experts define a mapping from information types to data characteristics. Before defining all our data characteristics, here is an example for Step 2.

EXAMPLE 4.2. *This example continues Example 4.1. Words that are often used either near the word "us" or "them" potentially are counter concepts. Well-known counter concepts [21] are:*

- *the bourgeois opposing to the proletarian*
- *the socialist opposing to the liberal*
- *the West opposing to the East*
- *the Protestant opposing to the Catholic*

Hence, one must consider the context of the information type to find indications for counter concepts.

Our Data Characteristics. We now describe our data characteristics which identify each of Koselleck's information types. In Section 6, we define one operator for each of these characteristics.

Conceptual Design Words can have single or multiple meanings, i. e., be ambiguous. We realize finding conceptual design by checking whether a word describes a topic additionally to its own meaning. A topic is a group of words that are used to write about the same issue, e. g. politics or economy. Our experts define the data characteristic of conceptual design as the sum of the usage numbers of all words that belong to a topic. Hence, we propose an operator *topicgrouping* that groups words by its topic and sums their usage numbers. If a word has multiple topics, we sum it into all of these topics.

Context To determine a word's context in Koselleck's spirit requires two data characteristics: (1) a set of surrounding words for a target word, i. e., the linguistic context, and (2) the sentiment for this context, by summing up the sentiment values of the words of the context. Our *surroundingwords* operator and *sentiment* operator implement this.

Sentence Structure One needs to consider two data characteristics: (1) the function of a word, i. e., differentiate between the parts of speech, and (2) completing phrases, i. e., search for missing words in a phrase. The first data characteristic is implemented by our operator *pfilter*. We implement the second one as a pattern-matching operator which we call *textsearch*.

Neologisms The data characteristic of a neologism is an increasing word-usage frequency over time. To find this characteristic, we propose an operator *time series-based selection* that compares the time-series values with a constant. To allow for a temporal restriction, we also provide a *subsequence* operator that limits the selection to an arbitrary time interval. The combination of both operators facilitates the search for neologisms.

4.3 Step 3: Finding Data Characteristics with Operators

In the third step, we implement operators to find the specified data characteristic in a large text corpus. This allows to search for any of Koselleck's information types.

EXAMPLE 4.3. *This example continues Example 4.2. To find potential counter concepts, we apply the* surroundingwords *operator to our data. It returns a set of surrounding words for every word in the corpus. We now use our* textfilter *operator to search these sets of surrounding words for words like "us" or "them". The more often one of these words is found, the stronger is the indication that this word is part of a counter concept.*

If our operators can identify all data characteristics, one can search for any of Koselleck's information types. This means that one can formalize and test all hypothetical relationships between information and concept types. Hence, we claim that our set of operators is complete with respect to the set of possible hypotheses.

w^1	p^1	ts^3		
		1980	1981	1982
Begriffsgeschichte	∅	70	54	58
peace	NOUN	312,031	330,389	295,867
war	NOUN	875,479	878,696	873,246
soldier	NOUN	70,196	72,941	72,587

(a) Example elements of set G_1

w^2	p^2	ts^3		
		1980	1981	1982
Reinhart Koselleck	∅ ∅	65	24	19
conceptual history	∅ ∅	37	31	27
modern history	∅ ∅	3,074	3,165	3,459
history modern	∅ ∅	1	6	4
history books	∅ ∅	2,248	2,205	2,333

(b) Example elements of set G_2

Table 1: Example sets for $gram_n$

5 DATA MODEL

In this section, we define the data model behind our query algebra. We then describe additional data sources which would be necessary to realize all information types described in Section 4. In the last part of this section, we describe notation shorthands and our data sources.

5.1 Ngram

There are three elementary types: words, parts of speech and time series. We use w to represent an individual word and W for a set of words, e. g., $W = \{\emptyset, peace, war, soldier, \ldots\}$. $\vec{w} \in W^n$ is a vector of n words. For example, $W^2 = \{(conceptual, history), \ldots\}$. A part of speech p is an element of $P = \{\emptyset, NOUN, VERB, ADJ, ADV, PRON, DET, ADP, NUM, CONJ, PRT, X\}$. $\vec{p} \in P^n$ is a vector of parts of speech of length n. For example $P^2 = \{(ADV, VERB), \ldots\}$. A time series $\vec{ts} \in \mathbb{Z}^T$ is a vector of integer values of length T. Using these basic types, we now define $gram_n$.

Definition 5.1. A $gram_n$ is a tuple $(\vec{w}, \vec{p}, \vec{ts}) \in W^n \times P^n \times \mathbb{Z}^T$ consisting of a vector of n words, a vector of n parts of speech and a time series of length T. We abbreviate a set of $gram_n$ as G_n.

Parts of speech are classes of words with similar grammatical properties, e. g., nouns or verbs. The part of speech elements are intuitive, e. g., NOUN denotes a noun, VERB a verb. A full description of the part of speech elements is in [7]. Table 1 shows example elements of sets G_1 and G_2.

Projecting on Single Elements. We define functions that project a $gram_n$ tuple to its components. To access the word vector we have function *projwords* of type $G_n \rightarrow W^n$, as follows:

$$\text{projwords}(gram_n) := \vec{w} \quad (1)$$

To access the parts of speech of a $gram_n$ tuple, we have function *projpos* of type $G_n \rightarrow P^n$:

$$\text{projpos}(gram_n) := \vec{p} \quad (2)$$

w_1	sentiment
peace	+1
war	-1

Table 2: An example of sentiment information

w_1	category
war	military
soldier	military
military	military

Table 3: An example of category information

To access the time series, we have function *projts* of type $G_n \rightarrow \mathbb{Z}^T$:

$$\text{projts}(gram_n) := \vec{ts} \tag{3}$$

5.2 Notation Shorthands

We write $gram_n.w$ as shorthand for projwords($gram_n$), to access the word vector $\vec{w}$. We use $gram_n.p$ and $gram_n.ts$ to project on the parts of speech element and the time series, respectively. We use the notation w_i to access the ith element of vector $\vec{w}$. The same holds for p_i and vector $\vec{p}$. We additionally define two shorthands to access time-series values. The first one ts_y projects a time series to its value of a specific year y. The second notation maps a time series $\vec{ts}$ to a subsequence $\mathbb{Z}^T \rightarrow \mathbb{Z}^t$ where $0 \leq t \leq T$. The access to a subsequence from year y_s to year y_e inclusively is as follows.

$$\vec{ts}[y_s, y_e] := \begin{cases} \text{subsequence from } y_s \text{ to } y_e & \text{if } y_s < y_e \\ ts_{y_s} & \text{if } y_s = y_e \\ \text{empty subsequence} & \text{else} \end{cases} \tag{4}$$

5.3 Sentiment and Category

To realize all the information types, we need to combine information from different sources. We need to consider two additional kinds of information: the sentiment value of a word and its category. A word sentiment can be positive, negative or neutral. To implement such a contrast-word rating, we use a binary word-classification mechanism. A category is a group of words that are used in the same topic, such as religion or economy. To realize this, we need the information which category a word belongs to. We now define both kinds of additional information, the sentiment and the category.

Sentiment. In conceptual history, it is important to investigate the relations between concepts, e. g., differences in positive and negative sentiments, or their orientation towards the past or the future. Signal words typically make these differences explicit. To illustrate, in the phrase *the hope for peace* the word "hope" is a word that signals a positive phrasing of the sentence. The additional information is the knowledge about signal words and its positive or negative classification. To define the sentiment value for a word, we define a function *wordsentiment*: $W^n \rightarrow \mathbb{Z}$. The function maps single words as well as word vectors to a sentiment value. For example, the single word "power" is a positive word and may have a sentiment value of +1. The 2-gram "electrical power" in turn does neither have a positive nor a negative sentiment value. The sentiment value for a neutral rating is 0. *wordsentiment* returns integer values to allow modeling different grades of positive and negative sentiment. Table 2 lists example words and their sentiments.

Category. A category is a word that is used as proxy for a more complex topic than its literal meaning, e. g., the category military includes the word "war" as well as "soldiers" and others. To implement information type "conceptual design", we need to model the relationship between words and its categories. We define *category* as a function of type $W^n \rightarrow C$ that maps words to the category they belong to, where $C \subset W^1$ is a set of categories. Every category in C is described as a single word of the set of all words W^1. For example, the word "military" is a word ($military \in W^1$) and a category ($military \in C$). The word "soldier" in turn is a word $soldier \in W^1$, but does not describe a category $soldier \notin C$. Table 3 shows an example of such a category grouping.

Information Sources. We store the sentiment information as well as the category information independent of one specific source. Therefore, we are able to use every source that contains this information and also to replace a source if a better one is available. Due to their informedness regarding text and word interpretation, the philosophers in our team have decided for the following sources. We extract the sentiment information from the LIWC list [19]. This list is a common reference in computerized text analysis. We use the OpenThesaurus[1] database [10] for the mapping between words and categories.

6 QUERY OPERATORS

Section 3 lists a complete set of information types to analyze conceptual history. We now propose a corresponding set of query operators. Some operators realize an entire information type, while one needs a combination of operators to realize other, more complex types. This section introduces the operators, gives their definitions and shows how they implement the information types.

6.1 Topic Grouping Operator

We realize information type *conceptual design* by defining a topic grouping operator. To realize this abstraction, this operator groups all words from the same topic. The groups have names consisting of one word. Thus, the result is of type $gram_1$. This allows us to define word categories e. g., *military* or *religious*, and analyze or compare their developments over time. We first define the set of occurrence topics for a given set of words and afterwards we define our *topicgrouping* operator.

Definition 6.1. C_G is the set of categories that appear in set G.

$$C_G := \bigcup_{g \in G} \{\text{category}(g.\vec{w})\} \tag{5}$$

[1] https://www.openthesaurus.de

w^1	p^1	ts^3		
		1980	1981	1982
military	∅	945,675	951,637	945,833

Table 4: Example result set of the topic grouping operator

Definition 6.2. *topicgrouping* is an operator of type $\mathcal{P}(G_n) \rightarrow \mathcal{P}(G_1)$. It has the following semantics:

$$\text{topicgrouping}(G) := \bigcup_{c \in C_G} (c, \emptyset, \sum_{\{g \in G | \text{category}(g.\vec{w})=c\}} g.\vec{ts}) \quad (6)$$

The topicgrouping operator groups all ngrams by their topic and sums together their time series.

Example. This example, as well as the ones that follow, use the data in Tables 1, 3 and 2. *topicgrouping* sums up the time series of all words belonging to category military. The result is a time series with the number of times authors have written about a military topic. For our example data, the operator yields the result in Table 4.

6.2 Surrounding Words Operator

When computing the context of words, a *target word* is the word we determine the context for, whereas *context words* are the words used around the target word. Before defining the operator, we define two auxiliary functions. The first one maps a word vector to the set of words of the vector. The second function maps a word vector to a word vector of a higher dimensionality that includes the same elements as the original word vector. We first define the help function *split* and secondly use this function to define our *expandwords* operator.

Definition 6.3. *split* is a function of type $W^n \rightarrow \mathcal{P}(W^1)$.

$$\text{split}(w \in W^n) := \{w_1, w_2, \ldots, w_n\} \quad (7)$$

split maps a vector of n words to a set of n words.

Definition 6.4. *expandwords* is a function of type $\mathbb{N} \times W^n \rightarrow \mathcal{P}(W^m)$ with $n < m; n, m \in \mathbb{N}$.

$$\text{expandwords}(m, \vec{q} \in W^n) :=$$

$$\left\{ (w_1, w_2, \ldots, w_m) \in W^m \,\middle|\, \exists o : \bigwedge_{i=1}^{n} w_{i+o} = q_i \right\} \quad (8)$$
$$\text{with } 0 \leq o \leq m - n$$

expandwords maps a vector of words to a set of vectors that are of higher dimensionality and contain the original word vector. This includes word vectors with new words in the front or in the back or both. Parameter m defines the dimensionality of the target vectors. Function *expandwords* adds $m - n$ words to the input vector. For example, we expand the word vector "history" of length $n = 1$ to a word vectors of length $m = 2$. A partial result are the word vectors "the history", "conceptual history", or "history of".

w^1	p^1	ts^3		
		1980	1981	1982
conceptual	∅	75,586	78,319	84,518
modern	∅	523,599	510,492	532,338
books	∅	447,885	436,655	462,202

Table 5: Example result set of *surroundingwords*

Definition 6.5. *surroundingwords* is an operator of type $\mathbb{N} \times G_n \rightarrow \mathcal{P}(G_1)$. It has the following semantics:

$$\text{surroundingwords}(m, g \in G_n) :=$$

$$\bigcup_{i \in \text{expandwords}(m, g.\vec{w})} \bigcup_{j \in \text{split}(i)} \{\text{projwords}^{-1}(j)\} \quad (9)$$

The *surroundingwords* operator returns a set of context words occurring together with at least one of the target words in a window of size m. We split the description into three steps. First, we filter all multigrams of size m for those that contain at least one target word vector. Second, we split these multigrams into single words and third, we add the corresponding usage-frequency time series to the context words.

Here are the three steps in more detail.

(1) The help function *expandwords* selects all word vectors of size m which contain the target word vector $\vec{q}$, no matter at which position of the window it occurs. *expandwords* returns a set of word vectors.
(2) Having the set of word vectors that contain the target word vector, we split these word vectors into single words. To perform this splitting we need function *split*. This results in a set of single words.
(3) To return elements of type $gram_1$ instead of single words, we use function projwords^{-1} to get the $gram_1$ elements that contain the corresponding word. We do this for every single word that function *split* returns. The result is the union over all $gram_1$ elements of all surrounding words.

Example. Suppose that we want all surrounding words for the word *history* within a window of size $m = 2$. Then we get the result shown in Table 5.

6.3 Sentiment Operator

Another important information for conceptual history is a word's sentiment, i. e., the positive or negative emotions associated with a word. This operator can be used to determine the sentiment for a single word or for a set of context words. This operator is the second part to completely cover the *context* information types from Section 3.

Definition 6.6. *sentiment* is an operator of type $G_n \rightarrow G_n$. It has the following semantics:

$$\text{sentiment}(g \in G_n) := (g.\vec{w}, g.\vec{p}, g.\vec{ts} \cdot \text{wordsentiment}(g.\vec{w})) \quad (10)$$

This operator multiplies the usage frequency of a word by the word's sentiment value. This multiplication takes both into account, the word's sentiment value and the word's usage frequency in the

w^1	p^1	ts^3		
		1980	1981	1982
peace	NOUN	+312,031	+330,389	+295,867
war	NOUN	-875,479	-878,696	-873,246

Table 6: Example result set of the sentiment operator

w^2	p^2	ts^3		
		1980	1981	1982
history modern	∅ ∅	1	6	4
history books	∅ ∅	2,248	2,205	2,333

Table 7: Example result set of the textsearch operator

w^1	p^1	ts^3		
		1980	1981	1982
peace	NOUN	312,031	330,389	295,867
war	NOUN	875,479	878,696	873,246

Table 8: Example result set of the pfilter operator

w^1	p^1	ts^3		
		1980	1981	1982
peace	NOUN	312,031	330,389	295,867
war	NOUN	875,479	878,696	873,246

Table 9: Example result set of the time series-based selection

text. The sentiment operator changes the meaning of the time-series values. The time-series values then no longer stand for the usage frequency of the word, but its sentiment over time. More precisely, the time-series values represent the sentiment value of a ngram over time.

The sentiment operator is defined for all lengths of ngrams. However, it only matches the same ngram length that is specified in the sentiment mapping, but not shorter or longer ones. For instance, the sentiment for *war* only matches the 1-gram *war*, but not the 2-gram *civil war*. This allows a fine-grained definition of sentiment values, as it becomes possible to have different sentiment values for *War, Civil War, First World War, Second World War* and *Cold War*.

Example. Table 6 shows an example result of *sentiment*.

6.4 Text Search Operator

Having a large set of words, a fundamental need is to search for the words conceptual historians might be interested in which matches some pattern *pt*. *Pt* is short for a set of patterns. $Z = \{\exists, \forall\}$ is the set of standard quantifiers.

Definition 6.7. textsearch is an operator of type $Pt \times Z \times \mathcal{P}(G_n) \rightarrow \mathcal{P}(G_n)$. It maps its input as follows:

$$\text{textsearch}(pt, \zeta, G_n) := \{g \in G_n \mid \zeta i : g.w_i \text{ matches } pt\} \quad (11)$$

The operator selects all tuples that satisfy the given condition with $\zeta \in \{\exists, \forall\}$ as quantifier and *pt* as a search pattern. The quantifier controls whether all words need to match *pt* or just one.

Example. When searching for the Pattern "histo.*" the *textsearch* operator returns the set in Table 7.

6.5 Part of Speech Filtering

Analyses in conceptual history often only refer to specific parts of speech such as nouns. So we propose a filter to keep only ngrams having a specific parts of speech, e. g., it allows to select all nouns.

Definition 6.8. pfilter is an operator of type $P^n \times Z \times \mathcal{P}(G_n) \rightarrow \mathcal{P}(G_n)$. It maps its input as follows:

$$\text{pfilter}(p, \zeta, G_n) := \{g \in G_n \mid \zeta i : g.p_i = p\} \quad (12)$$

Like in the definition of the textsearch operator, we use the quantifier $\zeta \in \{\exists, \forall\}$ to match the part of speech for at least one element or for all elements. In contrast to the textsearch operator, we can only search for part of speech tags.

Example. Selecting all nouns returns a set like the one in Table 8.

6.6 Time Series-based Selection

We may want to exclude words with extreme time-series values from our analysis, e. g., very rarely used words, because they might falsify our results. So we need a filter for time-series characteristics. $\Theta = \{<, \leq, =, \neq, \geq, >\}$ is the set of standard comparison operators.

Definition 6.9. cond is a tuple $(\zeta, \theta, v) \in Z \times \Theta \times \mathbb{Z}$ of conditions *Cond*.

Definition 6.10. $F_{cond} \subseteq \mathbb{Z}^T$ is a set of time series that fulfill condition *cond*.

$$F_{(\zeta,\theta,v)} := \{\vec{ts} \in \mathbb{Z}^T \mid \zeta i : ts_i \, \theta \, v\} \quad (13)$$

Definition 6.11. tsselection is an operator of type $Cond \times \mathcal{P}(G_n) \rightarrow \mathcal{P}(G_n)$. It maps its input as follows:

$$\text{tsselection}(cond, G_n) := \{g \in G_n | g.\vec{ts} \in F_{cond}\} \quad (14)$$

The time series-based selection operator selects $gram_n$ elements based their time-series properties.

Example. Condition $cond = (\forall, >, 1000)$ is the condition to select all ngrams whose usage frequency is larger than 1,000 for every available year. The resulting set is shown in Table 9.

6.7 kNN Operator

Another information that is of interest for analyzing conceptual history is to find words with a similar evolution of usage frequency, sentiment or surrounding words. This leads us to the definition of a kNN operator, which returns the *k* ngrams having the most similar time series to a given ngram. This information type is part of analyzing the *grammatical structure*.

w^2	p^2	ts^3		
		1980	1981	1982
conceptual history	NULL NULL	37	31	27

Table 10: Example result set of the kNN operator

w^2	p^2	ts^2	
		1980	1981
Reinhart Koselleck	∅ ∅	65	24
conceptual history	∅ ∅	37	31

Table 11: Example result set of the subsequence operator

w^2	p^2	ts^3		
		1980	1981	1982
peace	NOUN	+312,031	+330,389	+295,867
war	NOUN	+875,479	+878,696	+873,246

Table 12: Example result set of the absolute operator

integer value
3

(a) Example result of the count operator

ts^3		
1980	1981	1982
−563, 448	−548, 307	−577, 379

(b) Example result of operator sumup

Table 13: Example results of the operators count and sumup

Definition 6.12. kNN is an operator of type $\mathbb{N} \times G_n \times \mathcal{P}(G_n) \rightarrow \mathcal{P}(G_n)$. It maps its input as follows:

$$\text{kNN}(k, q, G_n) := \underset{\{S \in \mathcal{P}(G_n): |S|=k\}}{\arg\min} \; \max_{s \in S} \left\| s.\vec{ts} - q.\vec{ts} \right\|_2 \tag{15}$$

Our kNN operator implements a kNN search based on the time-series values of the $gram_n$ elements. Input k defines the number of resulting elements, i. e., the number of nearest neighbors to search for. q defines the target $gram_n$ to search the neighbors for. Input set G_n defines the search space, i. e., the set of possible results. The kNN operator can be used with different distance measures. For example, our implementation currently supports the Euclidean distance and dynamic time warping (DTW).

Example. Searching for the $k = 2$ nearest neighbors of the target word "Reinhart Koselleck" yields the result in Table 10.

6.8 Subsequence Operator

Most time-specific information have a specific start or end date or are in a specific temporal range of historical events, e. g., in the period from 1945 to 1990. However, the operators above work over the whole time range. Hence, we need an operator that reduces time series to a certain time interval.

Definition 6.13. subsequence is an operator of type $G_n \times \mathbb{N} \times \mathbb{N} \rightarrow G_n$. It maps its input as follows:

$$\text{subsequence}(g, y_s, y_e) := (g.\vec{w}, g.\vec{p}, g.\vec{ts}[y_s, y_e]) \tag{16}$$

The subsequence operator has three parameters: the $gram_n$ element g, the start year y_s and the end year y_e. It takes the input ngram element and reduces its time series to the time window $[y_s, y_e]$.

Example. When applying function *subsequence* to consider only the years from 1980 to 1981, the result looks like the set in Table 11.

6.9 Absolute Value Operator

Using the sentiment operator allows generating positive and negative time-series values representing positive or negative word emotions. For some investigations of conceptual history one needs to quantify word's emotions, no matter whether they are positive or negative. To archive this, we first apply the sentiment operator and secondly the absolute value operator that maps all sentiment values to positive values, i. e., the absolute value of the sentiment value.

Definition 6.14. tsabs is a function of type $\mathbb{Z}^T \rightarrow \mathbb{N}_0^T$, as follows:

$$\text{tsabs}(\vec{ts}) := (|ts_1|, |ts_2|, \ldots, |ts_T|) \tag{17}$$

tsabs maps every value of a given time series to its absolute value.

Definition 6.15. absolute is an operator of type $G^n \rightarrow G^n$. It maps its input as follows:

$$\text{absolute}(g) := (g.\vec{w}, g.\vec{p}, tsabs(g.\vec{ts})) \tag{18}$$

The absolute value operator turns every time-series value of a $gram_n$ element into its absolute value. Function *tsabs* maps the values for every single year to its absolute value and creates a new time series with absolute values.

Example. Applying this operator to the previous set yields the result in Table 12.

6.10 Count Operator

When working with huge data sets, which is preferred for statistical analysis, for many queries a human user simply cannot look at all elements or count them manually. The count operator counts the number of elements of a given set.

Definition 6.16. count is an operator of type $\mathcal{P}(G_n) \rightarrow \mathbb{N}$. It maps its input as follows:

$$\text{count}(G \in \mathcal{P}(G_n)) := |G| \tag{19}$$

Given an input set, *count* counts its elements and returns the number of containing elements.

Example. When we want to count the number of nouns in our data set in Table 1, we first filter for nouns, using the *pfilter* operator, followed by the *count* operator. Table 13a shows the result.

6.11 Sumup Operator

There is often the need to sum up the time series of ngrams, e. g., to compare the frequency of all nouns or adjectives. The sumup operator gets a set of ngrams, sums up their time series and returns the resulting time series. In comparison to the topicgrouping operator, the sumup operator does not group the elements, but sums up all received time series.

Definition 6.17. *sumup* is an operator of type $\mathcal{P}(G_n) \rightarrow \mathbb{Z}^T$. It maps its input as follows:

$$\text{sumup}(G \in \mathcal{P}(G_n)) := \sum_{g \in G} g.\vec{ts} \tag{20}$$

The sumup operator iterates over the given set of ngrams and sums together their time series. In the case of summing up sentiment time series, the operator may return a time series containing negative values.

Example. The result set when applying this operator to the example set from the sentiment operator looks like the one in Table 13b.

6.12 Set Operators

Since we are working on sets, we are able to use the set operators intersection (∩), union (∪) and minus (\). The key on which these operators work is a combination of the word vector w and the corresponding part of speech, i. e., vector p. The time-series attribute of the result set is taken from the left input set.

6.13 Algebraic Expressions

So far, we have introduced individual operators. In order to formulate complex hypotheses revealing novel insights for conceptual history, one generally needs to combine operators. For instance, in case one wants to find the k nearest nouns to some given ngram in a specific time period, we can combine the existing operators to formulate an expression to compute the desired result. Operators are compatible if the output of the first operator is of the same type as the input of the second operator. Most of our operators result in a set of ngram tuples, but not all of them. There are two operators that do not result in such a set: *count* and *sumup*. Both operators yield a single value. These operators usually are the final operation in an algebraic expression, e. g., summing up the input tuples. How to come from a philosophical hypothesis to concrete queries, and how example results may look like is the topic of the next section.

7 PROOF OF CONCEPT

Our query algebra allows (1) hypothesis testing and (2) hypotheses engineering. We explain both in this section.

7.1 Hypothesis Testing

Hypothesis testing enables scholars to empirically test existing hypotheses regarding properties of different concept types. For example, scholars want to test a hypothesis that characterizes parallel concepts. This consists of the following steps: First, they formalize their hypothesis, i. e., translate it to an algebraic expression. Second, they let a machine evaluate it on a huge corpus. Third, they interpret the results. To illustrate, think of the two hypotheses:

Hypothesis H1 The words "Osten" and "Westen" (German for East and West) have acquired a political meaning, i. e,. a political context, during the Cold War, while the words "Norden" and "Süden" (German for North and South) have not changed their merely geographical meaning.

Hypothesis H2 The two words "Osten" and "Westen" have developed into contrasting classes, i. e., have changed from parallel concepts to counter concepts.

Formalizing Hypothesis H1. To formalize Hypothesis H1, we use several operators, see Figure 2a for the operator tree. First, we need the text-search operator for occurrences of the four cardinal directions. We then generate the common context of "Osten" and "Westen" as well as the one of "Norden" and "Süden". To remove the context words related to cardinal directions, we subtract the common context of "Norden" and "Süden" from the one of "Osten" and "Westen". This leads to the context of "Osten" and "Westen" that is not related to cardinal directions. In a final step, we categorize the remaining context words. Figure 2b visualizes the result of computing this operator tree.

Formalizing Hypothesis H2. Given the validation of Hypothesis H1 that the words "Osten" and "Westen" become a political context, in Hypothesis H2 we check whether the semantics of the context for these two words develop into contrasting directions, i. e., if one word gets a positive context while the other one gets a negative one. We again start using our text-search operator to select the appropriate occurrences. We then separately generate the context for "Osten" and for "Westen" and perform a sentiment analysis. The operator tree to test Hypothesis H2 is shown in Figure 3a. Figure 3b visualizes the result. The result shows that the word "Westen" is used in a context mainly consisting of positive words while the words around "Osten" sum up to a negative sentiment. There can be two reasons for this: (1) The word "Westen" has more positive surrounding words that overcome the negative ones, or (2) the word "Osten" misses some surrounding words that the word "Westen" has and therefore sums to a negative sentiment. One can test these two possible reasons with a corresponding expression in our algebra.

7.2 Hypotheses Engineering

Hypotheses engineering means developing criteria and hypotheses to distinguish between concept types, i. e., speculating about their differences, formalizing and executing algebraic expressions, and interpreting the result. We, especially the philosophers team, are interested in checking hypothesis to get a better understanding of the differences between parallel and counter concepts. From close reading, they already have some hypotheses regarding the characteristics of parallel concepts. These hypotheses relate to the usage frequency, the surrounding words and the sentiment values of words. We have formalized and tested all these hypotheses, with the outcome that we could not confirm any of them. Our conceptual history experts then have had a closer look at the results of the expression. They have observed that some queries produce better results than others, i. e., contain more parallel concepts. This confirms that our approach gives way to important information for conceptual history experts, to develop new hypotheses. At the end

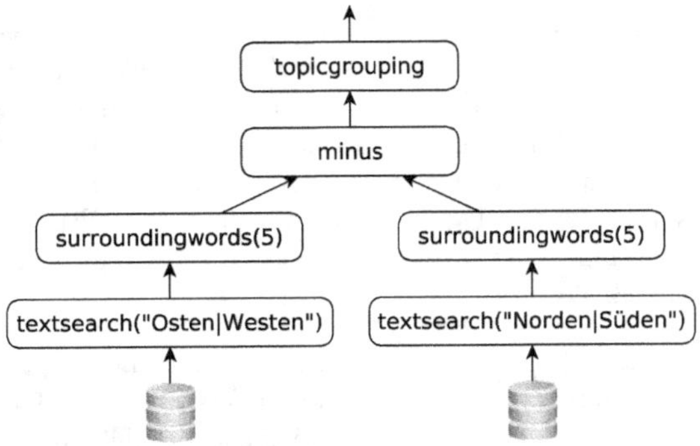

(a) The operator tree to realize the expression to test Hypothesis H1

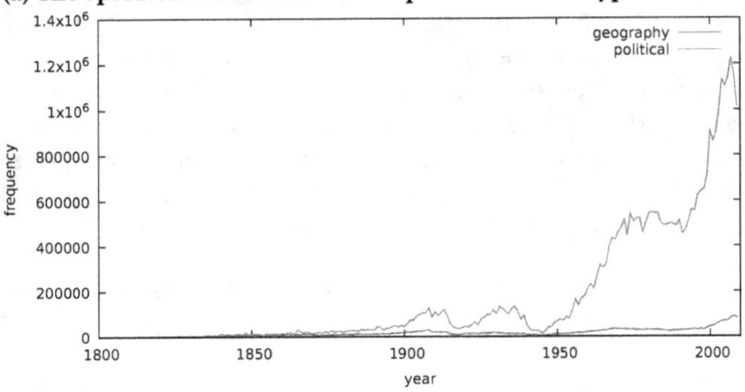

(b) Result when executing operator tree to test Hypothesis H1

Figure 2: Testing Hypotheses H1

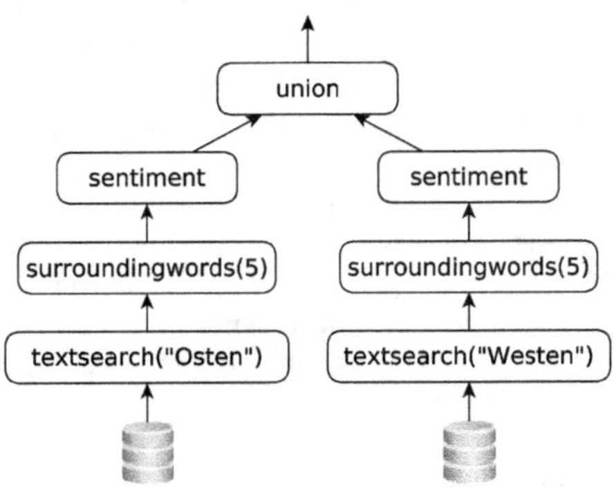

(a) The operator tree to realize the expression to test Hypothesis H2

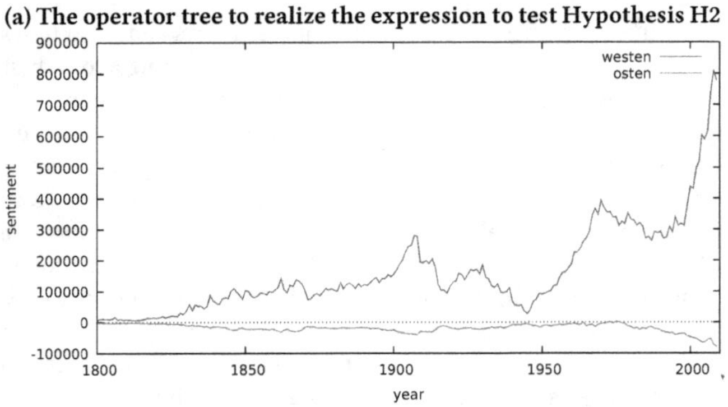

(b) Result when executing operator tree to test Hypothesis H2

Figure 3: Testing Hypotheses H2

of this process, our experts have been able to identify important information types of a parallel concept, as follows: A parallel concept features two concepts whose surrounding words have a similar sentiment, and they share numerous surrounding words. As part of our future work, we want to confirm this more rigidly, with a lot of close reading.

8 CONCLUSIONS

In this paper we propose the CHQL query algebra that supports exploring and understanding conceptual history. We have shown that our algebra completely covers all information types used by the pioneer of conceptual history, Reinhart Koselleck. We have demonstrated the usefulness of the algebra by formalizing two important hypotheses in conceptual history and testing it on Google's ngram data.

REFERENCES

[1] Serge Abiteboul, Richard Hull, and Victor Vianu. 1995. *Foundations of Databases: The Logical Level.* Addison-Wesley.
[2] Otto Brunner, Werner Conze, and Reinhart Koselleck. 2004. *Geschichtliche Grundbegriffe.* Vol. 1–8. Klett-Cotta.
[3] Shalin Hai-Jew. 2017. *Data Analytics in Digital Humanities.* Springer.
[4] William L. Hamilton, Jure Leskovec, and Dan Jurafsky. 2016. Cultural Shift or Linguistic Drift? Comparing Two Computational Measures of Semantic Change. In *Empirical Methods in Natural Language Processing.*
[5] William L. Hamilton, Jure Leskovec, and Dan Jurafsky. 2016. Diachronic Word Embeddings Reveal Statistical Laws of Semantic Change. (2016). arXiv:1605.09096v4
[6] Miloš Jakubíček, Adam Kilgarriff, Diana McCarthy, and Pavel Rychlý. 2010. Fast Syntactic Searching in Very Large Corpora for Many Languages. In *Pacific Asia Conference on Language, Information and Computation (PACLIC).*
[7] Yuri Lin, Jean-Baptiste Michel, Erez Lieberman Aiden, Jon Orwant, Will Brockman, and Slav Petrov. 2012. Syntactic Annotations for the Google Books Ngram Corpus. In *Annual Meeting of the Association for Computational Linguistics (ACL).* 169–174.
[8] David Maier. 1983. *Theory of Relational Databases.* Computer Science Press.
[9] Franco Moretti. 2013. *Distant Reading.* Verso Books.
[10] Daniel Naber. 2005. OpenThesaurus: Ein offenes deutsches Wortnetz. In *Sprachtechnologie, mobile Kommunikation und linguistische Ressourcen: Beiträge zur GLDV-Tagung 2005 in Bonn.* 422–433.
[11] Martin O'Connor and Amar Das. 2009. SQWRL: a Query Language for OWL. In *OWL: Experiences and Directions (OWLED).*
[12] The Library of Congress. 2013. The Contextual Query Language. (2013). https://www.loc.gov/standards/sru/cql/
[13] Niklas Olsen. 2012. *History in the Plural: An Introduction to the Work of Reinhart Koselleck.* Berghahn Books.
[14] Vinodkumar Prabhakaran, William L. Hamilton, Dan McFarland, and Dan Jurafsky. 2016. Predicting the Rise and Fall of Scientific Topics from Trends in their Rhetorical Framing. In *Annual Meeting of the Association for Computational Linguistics (ACL).* 1170–1180. https://doi.org/10.18653/v1/p16-1111
[15] Joachim Ritter, Karlfried Gründer, and Gottfried Gabriel. 2007. *Historisches Wörterbuch der Philosophie.* Vol. 1–13. Schwabe.
[16] Richard Snodgrass. 1987. The temporal query language TQuel. *ACM Transactions on Database Systems* 12, 2 (1987), 247–298. https://doi.org/10.1145/22952.22956
[17] Richard T. Snodgrass (Ed.). 1995. *The TSQL2 Temporal Query Language.* Springer.
[18] Claire Warwick. 2012. *Digital Humanities in Practice.* Facet Publishing.
[19] Markus Wolf, Andrea B. Horn, Matthias R. Mehl, Severin Haug, James W. Pennebaker, and Hans Kordy. 2008. Computergestützte quantitative Textanalyse. *Diagnostica* 54, 2 (2008), 85–98. https://doi.org/10.1026/0012-1924.54.2.85
[20] Amir Zeldes, Anke Lüdeling, Julia Ritz, and Christian Chiarcos. 2009. ANNIS: a search tool for multi-layer annotated corpora. In *Proceedings of Corpus Linguistics.* https://doi.org/10.18452/13437
[21] Niels Åkerstrøm Andersen. 2003. *Discursive Analytical Strategies: Understanding Foucault, Koselleck, Laclau, Luhmann.* Policy Press.

How it Happened: Discovering and Archiving the Evolution of a Story Using Social Signals

Omar Alonso
Microsoft
omalonso@microsoft.com

Vasileios Kandylas
Microsoft
vakandyl@microsoft.com

Serge-Eric Tremblay
Microsoft
sergetr@microsoft.com

ABSTRACT

Social networks like Twitter and Facebook are the largest sources of public opinion and real-time information on the Internet. If an event is of general interest, news articles follow and eventually a Wikipedia page. We propose the problem of automatic event story generation and archiving by combining social and news data to construct a new type of document in the form of a Wiki-like page structure. We introduce a technique that shows the evolution of a story as perceived by the crowd in social media, along with editorially authored articles annotated with examples of social media as supporting evidence. At the core of our research, is the temporally sensitive extraction of data that serve as context for retrieval purposes. Our approach includes a fine-grained vote counting strategy that is used for weighting purposes, pseudo-relevance feedback and query expansion with social data and web query logs along with a timeline algorithm as the base for a story. We demonstrate the effectiveness of our approach by processing a dataset comprising millions of English language tweets generated over a one year period and present a full implementation of our system.

ACM Reference format:
Omar Alonso, Vasileios Kandylas, and Serge-Eric Tremblay. 2018. How it Happened: Discovering and Archiving the Evolution of a Story Using Social Signals. In *Proceedings of The 18th ACM/IEEE Joint Conference on Digital Libraries, Fort Worth, TX, USA, June 3–7, 2018 (JCDL'18)*, 10 pages.
https://doi.org/10.1145/3197026.3197034

1 INTRODUCTION

Over the past couple of years, social networks like Twitter and Facebook, have seen phenomenal growth, making them one of the largest sources of public opinion and real-time information on the Internet. Trending topics and hashtags provide a very strong signal for important events that later would be covered in news articles, while, at the same time, controversial news articles trigger more discussion on social networks. If the event is of general interest, it is highly likely that it would eventually have its own Wikipedia article. This information flow, from social posts to a final encyclopedia-like entry through a series of news articles offers new opportunities to capture the main reactions as the event story evolves.

JCDL'18, June 3–7, 2018, Fort Worth, TX, USA

ACM ISBN 978-1-4503-5178-2/18/06...$15.00
https://doi.org/10.1145/3197026.3197034

Social posts provide real-time information but, at the same time, can be overwhelming for two reasons: there is no context for the uninformed user and there is a lot of noise for the informed user looking for the latest update. Compared to social posts, news articles are less frequent but provide more context and are ranked by topicality and freshness by a search engine. Wikipedia articles are curated documents by volunteers that describe the topic to a certain extent but do not always capture the progression of an event. From a data size perspective, the many thousands of posts derive into hundreds of news articles and, finally, a single Wikipedia page. Or, in other words, from the voice of the planet, to some journalists and editors, and to Wikipedians. While one could argue that editorial content and Wikipedia pages contain the best information, many other perspectives are left behind due to attention, bias, and human scalability. Would it be possible to combine the crowd activity and associated behavioral data with editorial news and create a Wiki-like page for events and related topics?

We use human sensing on social networks as a large distributed human computation crawler where links are constantly shared and annotated. This large scale link selection can be seen as a collaboratively retrieved set of documents for a query as expressed by a hashtag. By algorithmically improving the selection from social data, an initial sketch for the story can be devised. We provide an algorithm that uses social behavioral data as relevance surrogates to generate an informative timeline in conjunction with the entities to produce the story. Stories are updated given the frequency of the event, which is indicated by their trending activity in social data. We hypothesize that a system that captures the evolution of a story as perceived by the crowd in social media along with editorially produced articles, provides a new way of consuming and archiving information on a topic with diverse perspectives.

In this paper we describe a number of techniques that support the creation of a new document for events by algorithmically generating the core of the story as it evolves over time by using selected relevant content derived from social data and news articles. We define a story as a document that contains relevant text fragments that describe a concept or elaborate on certain specifics, relevant named entities, and temporal information that anchors a salient matter in time. This new data asset is a new type of document that is dynamic to the many data components of the story, always up-to-date, and constructed in a fashion that allows different aggregations and applications. Figure 1 shows an overview of our approach: extracting an initial set of relevant document links from Twitter, re-ranking them with a number of proposed techniques, and producing the final document.

We make the following contributions: (1) we propose a vote data structure that is used for weighting terms, (2) we introduce extensions to pseudo-relevance feedback and query expansion, so that

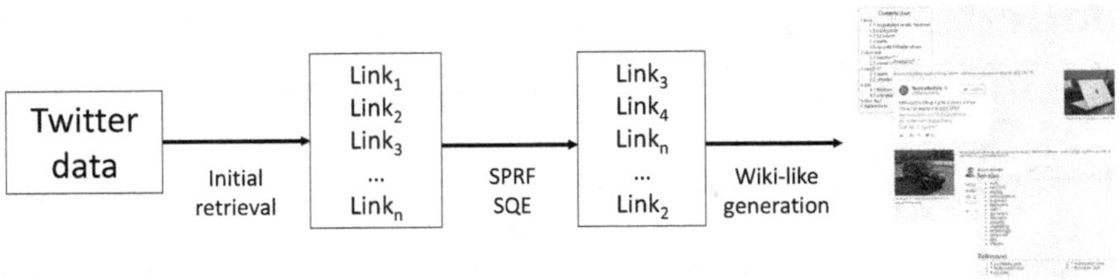

Figure 1: Overview of our proposed approach. After the initial retrieval of links for a topic from Twitter, the links are re-ranked using social pseudo-relevance feedback (SPRF) and social query expansion (SQE) techniques. A final automatic step produces a Wiki-like document that provides the evolution of a story along with related topics.

they include aggregated social information extracted from a social networking site, (3) we design a timeline generation algorithm using judgment aggregation, and (4) we show the construction of a Wiki-like document that describes the evolution of a story.

2 RELATED WORK

In this section we review some of the related work especially in the areas of Twitter data mining, story generation, and extensions to automatic query expansion and relevance feedback.

Microblog summarization is an active area of research and has recently received a lot of attention. Some of the techniques include phrase reinforcement introduced by Sharifi et al. [25] and clustering developed by Inouye et al. [12]. However their evaluation suffers from a similar bias towards noise-free content and they do not discuss the quality of their output when processing noisy content. The work by Ren et al. [19] presents a more personalized solution to the summarization problem. Martins et al. [16] describe a learning to rank framework that uses Wikipedia, Twitter, and news articles.

There has been previous work on using Wikipedia as external resource for query dependent pseudo-relevance feedback (PRF) [31]. Efron et al. [8] proposes document expansion using a temporal profile. Early work by Whiting et al. [29] proposes a method based on temporal profiles of ngrams extracted from the top relevance feedback tweets using a graph model. Classic PRF strategies are described in [11]. A two-step extension to PRF that contains a manual tweet selection and query-document temporal relevance model is described in [18]. There are similarities to the local context analysis described in [30], however, we rely on social data for term extraction and weights without manual intervention.

Query expansion using anchor text has been studied by [7] and [14]. We also use anchor text derived as a form of social anchor text for extracting candidate terms. The survey by [5] provides more information of the many techniques for automatic query expansion.

There is exciting work on building narratives, stories, and digests from different communities making it difficult to summarize related work. The work by [28] describes socially informed timelines. An integer linear programming approach for generating an event digest is introduced in [17]. Other work includes linking online news and social media [27], extracting relationships and threads between documents [10], creating story graphs from a collection of photo streams [13], and generating event storylines from microblogs [15]. A temporal intention resource sharing study is described in [20].

Our research is similar in spirit to the work on information cartography [24] and information maps [23] where the goal is to automatically connect the dots and discover hidden connections. Our work uses social and news data, in contrast to only news articles. The work by AlNoamany et al. [1] proposes a framework for integrating social media and web data for generation of stories. In terms of Wikipedia-like content generation, Sauper and Barzilay [21] analyze human-authored text to automatically induce a domain-specific template for the topic structure. A supervised approach for recommending news articles for entity Wikipedia pages is described by Fetahu et al. [9]. Finally, Soulier and Tamine surveys collaborative information retrieval [26].

3 METHODS

Intuitively, links shared in social media can be seen as a large set of manually selected documents for a query or topic tagged with a hashtag. If we restrict the selection for a specific time period like a day and repeat over time, we could have daily relevant content for a topic. As pointed out by [8], tweets tend to be about a single topic. Thus, we can envision harvesting the most relevant link documents over time and derive the progression of such a topic.

We introduce a voting scheme that captures behavioral data in a way that can be later used for term weighting. We introduce extensions to pseudo-relevance feedback with terms and weights extracted from social data that can be included on query expansion by re-ranking the document links already retrieved. We also derive new potential expansion terms from search query logs for a more global view on similar queries. Figure 1 shows the flow of data extracted from Twitter and how Social Pseudo-Relevance Feedback (SPRF) and Social Query Expansion (SQE) are used for generating the Wiki page.

3.1 Social Signatures and Contextual Vectors

A social signature is a high level representation of a web page from a social media perspective, that is, a list of ngrams associated with the link. For computing a social signature, we use the text of the tweets that share the link (after clean-up) using techniques introduced in [2]. For each link URL u_j, we generate a document d_j which aggregates all the social anchor text around that link from different users. In the case of Twitter, the social anchor text comprises the text in tweet, excluding the Twitter user profile handles. A score $score_g$ is calculated for each candidate social signature using $lm(TF_g, DF_g, TFIDF_g, \prod t_{u \in g} TFIDF_u, TF_g/max_u(TF_u), DF_g/max_u(DF_u))$, where $lm()$ is a linear combination of the features and u ranges over the unigrams that make up the ngram g.

A contextual vector represents a ranked list of ngrams for a set of tweets related to a hashtag or entity. For producing the list of ngrams, we first aggregate all the tweets related to a particular hashtag over the time period of consideration . The computation of the contextual vectors is similar to that of the social signatures. The main difference is that contextual vectors are computed for hashtags or entities instead of links. Small differences in the computation account for the different characteristics of hashtags and entities vs. links. The main differences are that only unigrams and bigrams are used for contextual vectors and the scoring weights are different.

3.2 Vote Data Structure

We generate a variety of aggregate counts for several elements of tweets and the connections between them. We compute how often hashtags, ngrams, and links appear in tweets and also how often combinations of hashtags and links or ngrams and links co-occur in a tweet. To deal with spammers and advertisers we use a voting scheme in addition to simple frequency counts. The problem with frequencies is that spam and advertising accounts (and sometimes overly zealous normal accounts) tend to post multiple tweets per day that contain the same information. For example, a company account might include a link to the company website in every tweet, or political supporters may add a hashtag about their favorite party in all their tweets. These behaviors can make links, hashtags, etc. artificially popular, when in fact most of their popularity comes from a small number of accounts.

$$\begin{Bmatrix} hashtag \\ ngram \\ link \\ hashtag-link \\ ngram-link \end{Bmatrix} \times \begin{Bmatrix} TweetFrequency \\ RetweetFrequency \\ TotalFrequency \\ TweetVotes \\ RetweetVotes \\ TotalVotes \end{Bmatrix}$$

Figure 2: The 30 frequency and vote counts used.

We therefore assign a single vote to each account per time period, so that one account cannot skew the frequency of an element or connection. Note that sometimes using a frequency is preferred over a vote. For instance, some hashtags can be used repeatedly by the same account, but they do not correspond to a single topic, such as a news account may be using the hashtag `#BreakingNews` for different links. In this case, we would not want to use a vote of 1 for `#BreakingNews` from that account, but a frequency of how many breaking news links were posted. We thus compute a set of counts that capture the importance of various elements (ngrams, hashtags, links) and their connections (hashtag-link, ngram-link):

Frequencies: These count the total number of times an element or connection has appeared anywhere in the data. It applies to:

- Tweets: The total number of times an element or connection appeared in an original tweet.
- Retweets (RTs): The total number of times an element or connection (that appeared in original tweets) was retweeted.
- Total: The sum of the previous two frequencies.

Votes: these count the number of individual users who posted tweets, where the element or connection appeared. They apply to:

- Tweets: The number of individuals who posted original tweets containing the element or connection.
- Retweets: The number of individual users who retweets tweets that contain the element or connection.
- Total: The number of individual users who tweeted or retweeted tweets containing the element or connection. This differs from the sum of the previous two votes, as some users could have tweeted *and* retweeted tweets so they would appear in both original tweets and retweets votes, but the users would be counted only once in the total votes.

For each hashtag, therefore, we compute the following counts: `hashtagTweetFrequency`, `hashtagRetweetFrequency`, `hashtagTotalFrequency`, `hashtagTweetVotes`, `hashtagRetweetVotes`, and `hashtagTotalVotes`. Similar counts are computed for the other elements and connections besides hashtags, as shown in Figure 2.

The element counts give the popularity of the element in the whole data set and the connection counts give the popularity of the connection, or in other words, the popularity of the first element given the second. For example, `hashtagTotalVotes` gives the overall popularity of the hashtag, whereas `HashtagLinkTotalVotes` gives the popularity of the hashtag with respect to the link, i.e. in the set of tweets that contain the link. The 30 frequency and vote counts that are computed create a vote record for each hashtag. This record describes all aspects of the hashtag we are considering and is used in the algorithms described later to compute various scores using different ways of combining the counts.

3.3 Hashtag Index

Using the Twitter firehose, we produce a different data structure with the new aggregations described so far, called hashtag index, that is used as main input. The hashtag index gives relevant links and other information about every selected hashtag. It provides a connection between a hashtag and all the links associated with it. To generate the hashtag index, we take all the selected hashtags and their information (the various hashtag scores and the hashtag context vector) and find all the links that appeared with each hashtag. For each hashtag-link combination we add all the hashtag-link scores we described in Section 3.2.

For each link, besides the link metadata like title, description and associated link scores, we also find all the ngrams and hashtags that are associated with the link. Specifically we select the top 20 most popular ngrams and hashtags that appeared together with the link in tweets (or RTs) and annotate them with their respective ngram-link or hashtag-link scores. We also include the social signature ngrams for the link and their scores. An extra addition is a set of 10 tweets (and the users who authored them), through which the link was shared. The tweets are selected according to a combination of metrics, such as tweet quality, author authority, etc. This information is not used by the algorithm, but is available for presentation purposes and, if needed, to provide the user with the provenance of the links. We therefore do not pick any RTs, but only original tweets. Table 1 shows a simplified example for the hashtag index with some data for contextual vectors and social signatures.

Date	Contextual vector	Social signature	Related hashtags	Link url
2-Dec	jill stein, donald trump, michigan recount	judge denies quick, federal judge denies, federal judge	#AuditTheVote #WIRecount	http://jsonline.com/story/news/politics/elections/2016/12/02/walker-considers-change-recount-law/94798548
2-Dec	jill stein, donald trump, michigan recount	fraud total waste, halt recount, michigan attorney	#Recount #Trump #theResistance	http://politico.com/story/2016/12/michigan-attorney-general-files-lawsuit-to-halt-recount-232114
2-Dec	jill stein, donald trump, michigan recount	voter fraud, homeland security, largest voter fraud	#CrossCheck	http://esquire.com/news-politics/politics/news/a48232/kris-kobach-voter-suppression
3-Dec	jill stein, croix county, county wisconsin	blocking, attorney, michigan, michigan attorney	#AudittheVOTE #michigan	http://act.demandprogress.org/sign/tell-michigan-attorney-dont-block-recount
3-Dec	jill stein, croix county, county wisconsin	statewide election recount, pennsylvania recount	#PA #PresidentTrump	http://pittsburgh.cbslocal.com/2016/12/03/green-party-drops-statewide-pennsylvania-recount
3-Dec	jill stein, croix county, county wisconsin	press conference, pennsylvania	#pennsylvania #PArecount	http://jill2016.com/recountpa

Table 1: Hashtag index simplified example for the hashtag #recount2016 during 2016. Note that the contextual vectors differ for the two consecutive days, even though they are on the same topic. Social signatures are link specific and they can be different or similar to other signatures. Related hashtags to #recount2016 provide alternative topics.

3.4 Clustering Similar Queries

In order to increase the number of keywords we need to find other queries similar to the original one. String similarity methods could be used but they mainly help with very similar or mistyped queries. To find conceptually similar but string-wise different queries (e.g., Xbox and Kinect) we need to use a different methodology. The key idea we use is to build groups of related keywords from the Bing search query logs. Take two different users who entered two different queries. If the logs show that they clicked on the same search result links, then the queries are probably related.

We build a query graph, where each node is a query and each edge weight measures the distance between the two queries. Edge weights are computed as the cosine of the angle between the two query vectors, where a query vector consists of the number of clicks the various links received when the query was searched. After computing the graph, we use modularity clustering to find groups of similar queries. Similar to hierarchical agglomerative clustering, we start with each query being its own cluster and we merge clusters based on achieving the largest modularity gain. Modularity-based clustering partitions a graph G into p components $C_1, \ldots, C_p$ such that the total modularity of the partitioning $Mod(C_1, \ldots, C_p) = Sum_{i=1..p} Mod(C_i)$ is maximized. The modularity of a component C is based on the number of edges m_C within C: $Mod(C) = m_C - E[m_C]$, where the expected number of edges $E[m_C]$ is computed based on the vertex degrees of the graph. More details can be found in [22].

3.5 Social Pseudo-Relevance Feedback

We assume a vector space model where the similarity $sim(q, d)$ between query q and document link d is computed as $sim(q, d) = \sum_{t \in q \cap d} w_{t,q} \cdot w_{t,d}$, where $w_{t,q}$ and $w_{t,d}$ are the weights of term t in query q and document link d respectively according to user engagement via RT, likes, and shares. Each title is then re-ranked by this new score.

Pseudo-relevance feedback is a very effective mechanism for improving retrieval without any user interaction in contrast to relevance feedback that requires users to mark documents that are relevant or not to a given query. As already mentioned, contextual vectors are derived from tweets and we can think of those ngrams as explicit terms selected by users in aggregate. Similar to pseudo-relevance feedback, ranking document links extracted from tweets by votes indicate that the top-k links are relevant to a given query (i.e., hashtag) on a specific time period, usually daily.

Using the vote record data structure, we now describe the weighting scheme that is computed for all elements in a contextual vector and social signature. As example, we present the formulas for hashtag and ngram. Each hashtag has an associated vote record that allows fine tuning to produce the final weight, denoted as counter c, for a hashtag ht_c.

$$\begin{aligned} \text{ht}_c = &(\log(\text{ht.tTweetVotes} * p_w) + \log(\text{ht.tRetweetVotes} * rt_w)) * v_w + \\ &(\log(\text{ht.ltTweetVotes} * p_w) + \log(\text{ht.ltRetweetVotes} * rt_w)) * l_w \end{aligned}$$

Similarly, the counter for an ngram, ng, is computed:

$$\begin{aligned} \text{ng}_c = &(\log(\text{ng.tTweetVotes} * p_w) + \log(\text{ng.tRetweetVotes} * rt_w)) * v_w + \\ &(\log(\text{ng.ltTweetVotes} * p_w) + \log(\text{ng.ltRetweetVotes} * rt_w)) * l_w \end{aligned}$$

where tweet weight $p_w = 0.8$, re-tweet weight $rt_w = 0.2$, vote weight $v_w = 0.35$, and link weight $l_w = 0.5$. That is, an original term in a tweet has more weight than a re-tweet and a document link has more weight than a regular vote. Compared to [30], we rely on a contextual vector for candidate expansion terms instead of extracting them from a list. With SPRF we have concentrated on using social signals for selecting and ranking document links. Similarly, we can also use social signals for selecting terms for query expansion. An early implementation of SPRF is described in [3].

3.6 Social Query Expansion

We now describe a number of expansions that we perform using social data in conjunction with the query clusters derived from a web search engine's query logs that contribute to different scores used in the final computation.

A problem with a hashtag as query for retrieving documents is that it can potentially miss similar hashtags that may contain other potential good documents and other terms. For example, #SuperBowl and #SB50 are related because they occur at the same point in time and they are used in social media to describe the same event. Our solution for finding similar hashtags is to use contextual vectors as hashtag signatures and use a SimHash-based technique to find

Query	Date	Hashtag 1	Contextual Vector 1	Hashtag 2	Contextual Vector 2
clinton	31-Jul	#hillaryclinton	blasts clinton delusional families hillary misunderstood office public victims	#benghazi	blasts clinton delusional families hillary misunderstood pat smith victims
	27-Sep	#clintonemailscandal	agent email fbi james owned private server	#comeyresignation	agent email fbi owned private server
trump	4-Aug	#trumptrain	america des governor iowa maine moines portland safer	#maga	des gloating governor iowa iranian maine moines portland
	16-Sep	#trumpnation	automatically construction contact democrat feel free industry volunteers vote	#trumparmy	automatically contact democrat feel free ohio presidency volunteers vote
bernie	2-Oct	#bernieorbust	bernie clinton gary hillary johnson sanders slams	#millenials	bernie clinton gary hillary johnson sanders slams urges
	11-Nov	#shouldvebeenbernie	bernie chamber echo hillary liberal lonely progressives sanders supporters	#stillsanders	bernie chamber echo liberal living lonely progressives sanders
rogueone	30-Oct	#rogueone	rogue star tomorrow wars win winner	#starwars	darth star tomorrow vader wars win winner
	26-Dec	#rogueone	carrie darth fisher leia mads mikkelsen princess star vader wars	#ripprincess	carrie fisher leia princess rip shell star swear wars

Table 2: Examples of the output of the SimHash-based technique to find similar hashtags within the same day.

similar contextual vectors. If we can find similar contextual vectors, we can identify similar hashtags for query expansion and, at the same time, potentially collect new links. This extra information is useful for discovering connections between related stories allowing users to explore different perspectives. Algorithm 1 shows an overview of the SimHash-based approach.

```
Data: Hashtagindex for time t
Result: Similar hashtags
extract hashtags and contextual vectors ;
foreach cv in ContextualVectorSet do
    hs = generateShingles(cv) ;
    foreach s in hs do
        computeHash(s);
        Add(S,s) ;
    end
    vector = generateVector(S) ;
    computeHash(vector) ;
end
Sort all vectors ;
foreach v in vectors do
    Compute Hamming distance(v_i,v_{i+1});
    Compute Jaccard distance(v_i,v_{i+1}) ;
    print hashtag pairs + Hamming + Jaccard ;
end
```

Algorithm 1: SimHash-based algorithm overview.

Table 2 shows a few examples of similar hashtags. We can observe that at the end of October, #rogueone is similar to #starwars, which is expected as the movie Rogue One belongs to the Star Wars franchise. By Christmas Holidays, while the movie was still at theaters, the actress that portrays an iconic character on the series passed away and therefore #ripprincess is a similar hashtag for #rogueone on 26-December-2016. The table also shows other examples for some events in the US Elections. This technique improves the link recall, which is useful for detecting more document links for the story. The new ranked retrieval consists of matching how similar the query q is to document title, web page description, and file name description after link normalization and clean up.

For query expansion, we use the contextual vector to re-rank the links based on how similar the links' titles are to the terms in the contextual vector. Because all these links have been tagged by users with a hashtag with a high vote, our hypothesis is that they belong to the same topic. We expand the title matching by also including related hashtags and query clusters. Overall, when computing the title similarity, each expansion contributes a specific score:

$$\text{htTitleScore} = \text{sim}(\text{title}, \text{q} + \text{ngrams})$$
$$\text{rtTitleScore} = \text{sim}(\text{title}, \text{q} + \text{relatedHashtags})$$
$$\text{ceTitleScore} = \text{sim}(\text{title}, \text{q} + \text{clusterExpansion})$$

The above scoring formulas are also applied to description and file name. We then take the max score from title, description, and file name on the element's dimension (e.g., hashtag, ngram, etc.): htScore $=$ max(htTitleScore $* t_w$, htDescScore $* d_w$, htFileScore $* f_w$), where title weight $t_w = 0.45$, description weight $d_w = 0.45$, and filename weight $f_w = 0.1$. That is, more weight on title and description and less on the link file name. The final score is a linear combination of the number of the different expansions already presented, multiplied by other link vote counters.

$$\text{score} = (\text{titleScore} + \text{descScore} + \text{fileScore} + \text{rtScore} + \text{htScore} + \text{ceScore} + \text{deScore}) * (\log(\text{otherCounters} + 1))$$

where the prefix "desc" stands for description, "ce" for query clusters, "ht" for hashtag & ngram, and "rt" for related hashtag respectively. The bottom-up approach for constructing these many scores allows parameter debugging and fine tuning.

3.7 Query Generation

With all the information gathered so far, it is possible to automatically generate potential queries for a particular entry in the story. We first use a modification of the Longest Common Subsequence (LCS) between title and description that returns a list of ranked set of ngrams sorted by size. That is, two-term queries have precedence over three-term queries and so forth. The contextual vectors are used to identify which ones match in either a title or description as alternatives (we do not discriminate the ngram size on the contextual vector). We finally, compute similarity between each pair of the query candidates derived from LCS and the matched ngrams. The final list contains the pairs ranked by score. The outline for the algorithm is presented in Algorithm 2.

```
Data: Hashtagindex for time t
Result: Queries relevant for entry t
extract title, description, contextual vector;
foreach t in timestamp do
    foreach ht in HashTagSet do
        queryList = LCS(title, description);
        matchedNgrams = FindNgram(cv, title, description);
        /* similarity between queryList and matchedNgrams pairs */ ;
        queries = sim(queryList_i, matchedNgrams_j);
    end
    foreach q in queries do
        print q, score;
    end
end
```

Algorithm 2: Query generation algorithm

4 STORY EVOLUTION ALGORITHM

Now that we have all the relevant document links, the problem is then how to select the best candidates per day and use them to generate a timeline. For generating the evolution of the story, we rely on a timeline algorithm that uses the methods described in the previous section to identify the most relevant document link titles according to a query. Information extracted from document link titles forms the base for the generation of the timeline. The intuition is that links that are from well-known domains are likely to be authoritative and contain a title that is well-written in English. By including a sample of tweets associated with a link as supporting evidence, the particular entry on the story shows provenance that can help clarify opinions and confirm facts.

Both contextual vectors and SPRF are local operations because they process the data set given a specific temporal window. The timeline generation is a global operation that needs to ingest a data set composed of many occurrences of a hashtag and associated contextual vectors over a much larger time window (e.g., weeks or months). The algorithm takes as input a set of timestamped hashtags and their contextual vectors, associated links, social signatures, and voting data. The data is used for query expansion and re-ranking of links. The output is a single document that contains a temporal order of link titles that are relevant to a topic. The overview of the algorithm is presented in Algorithm 3. The algorithm works well and has been tested in production with real data. There are, though, a few open issues that are part of future work. For example,

```
Data: Hashtagindex
Result: Timeline in chronological order for ht
timeline[] = empty;
find similar hashtags using SimHash-based technique;
group similar links;
find similar clusters for query expansion (section 3.4);
select top ngram;
foreach timestamp in ht do
    q = ht;
    /* query expansions for title */
    htTitleScore = sim(title, q + ngrams) ;
    rtTitleScore = sim(title, q + relatedHashtags) ;
    ceTitleScore = sim(title, q + clusterExpansion) ;
    /* query expansion for description *
    ...
    /* query expansion for filename */
    ...
    /* combines all expansions into a single score */
    ds = rank documents by score ;
    j = 0;
    if ds[j] not in timeline then
        add ds[j] to timeline;
    else
        repeat
            j++;
            select ds[j] ;
        until ds[j] is not in timeline;
        add ds[j] to timeline;
    end
end
foreach e in timeline do
    print timeline[e] ;
end
Select Related Hashtags;
Generate queries (Algorithm 2);
```

Algorithm 3: Story evolution algorithm

the algorithm could misplace links depending on link creation time vs. post creation time and over-population of good links for a single day. Our story evolution technique is not based on traditional summarization or NLP techniques. The goal is not to show the summary of an event but, instead, the evolution of the story over time according to information that, in aggregate, the crowd selected as important and relevant. We see traditional summarization as complementary to story evolution.

5 WIKI PAGE CONSTRUCTION

The final step is to combine the techniques presented so far and automatically generate a Wiki-like page that describes the story in a temporal order using a Wikipedia page structure. Instead of a single Wikipedia page edited by a few Wikipedians, we present a Wiki-like page constructed using editorially-written content that is selected by the crowd and ranked and refined by our algorithm.

Figure 3 shows the main structure of the Wiki-like page. The page structure contains four main sections: table of contents (TOC), story evolution, related stories, and references. For building the TOC, we use a standard hit-list clustering approach that takes the link titles and descriptions, and populates a trie data structure [4].

The top level entries are selected for the TOC based on relevance scores. The story evolution part contains the bulk of the timeline algorithm described in the previous section. Related stories are basically the pivots to the main story that enable exploration and increase the coverage and diversity of viewpoints about the story, and are computed using a combination of query suggestions and TOC. Finally, the references are the link domains used to construct the story that serve as the ultimate sources. A slider allows the user to limit the size of the story (for those that are quite lengthy).

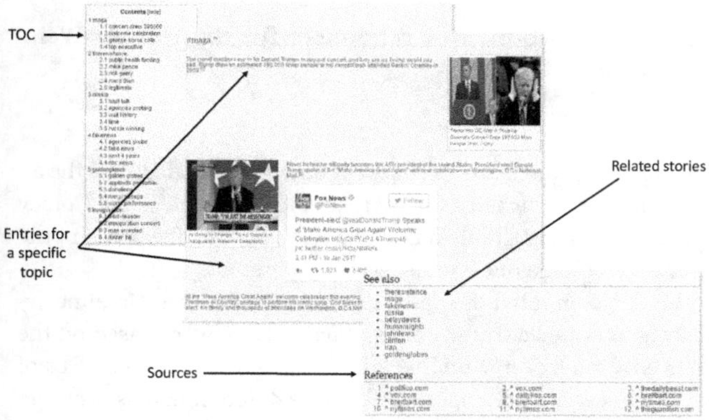

Figure 3: Wiki-like page generated for the US Elections 2016 using the same structure as a standard Wikipedia page. Link article titles and descriptions are selected by the techniques presented in Section 3. Entries are annotated with a tweet as social context and supporting evidence.

The complete back-end data pipeline and algorithms have been implemented in SCOPE [6] and run continuously on a distributed cluster (Cosmos). It is possible to archive long running stories over time and therefore provide different views.

The generated Wiki-like document is a new data asset that is then used to extract specific items from a story. For example, we can select the timeline and make it available as part of the search results for relevant queries in Bing. These stories have been released in production as part of the Bing News vertical and featured on the search engine result page for specific events. Figure 4 shows an example of how a story is placed next to the featured news article, presenting more context to the user who can also scroll down to examine the evolution of the story over time.

6 RESULTS AND EVALUATION

Due to confidentiality, we cannot disclose user engagement or other behavioral metrics. Instead, we describe three evaluation strategies: 1) an offline defect rate for stories, 2) a temporal comparison against Wikipedia articles in terms of precision and recall, and 3) the diversity of domains used in the story.

6.1 Offline Evaluation

We conducted an offline evaluation with an internal crowdsourcing tool for collecting labels using in-house editors for two different data sets, D1 and D2, consisting of 1K hashtags selected at random.

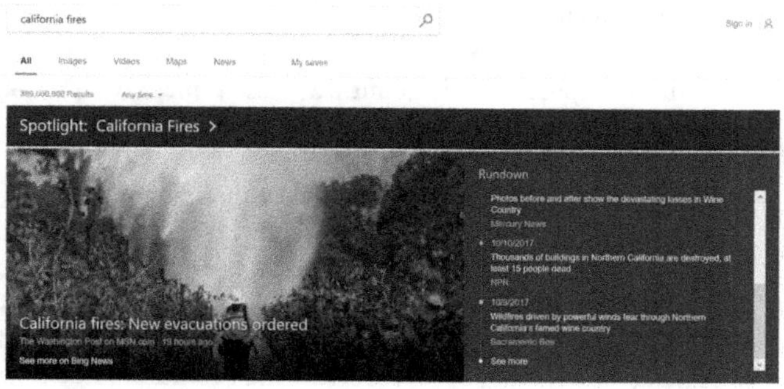

Figure 4: Timeline presented as a spotlight answer in Bing.

D1 was labeled in October 2016 by two editors and D2 was labeled using crowdsourcing (5 workers, majority label) on January 2017 using the evaluation template shown in Figure 5. In the case of D1, we consider an entry a defect if both editors agree that it is not relevant. For D2, if the majority vote says that the entry is not relevant, then there is a defect. We observe that for a story that contains 10 entries, editors report a 5.63% defect rate and the crowd slightly higher (7.09%). Results are presented in Table 3.

Instructions: the following task consists of a hashtag and associated timeline. Please help us evaluate the quality of the entries in the timelines by marking the ones that you think are not correct.

Task: please mark the entries that you think are not related to the topic or hashtag that describes the topic
Topic: "#thehashtag"

t1 [link] [] relevant [] somewhat [] no
...
tn [link] [] relevant [] somewhat [] no

Figure 5: Offline task relevance evaluation template.

# of entries in timeline	D1 Defect rate	D2 Defect rate
5	5.47%	8.72%
6	5.29%	7.69%
7	7.66%	9.69%
8	7.23%	5.78%
9	5.54%	11.94%
10	5.63%	7.09%

Table 3: Defect rates for stories with more than 5 entries.

6.2 Wikipedia Evaluation

We also compared the output of our timelines algorithm versus Wikipedia articles. The goal was to see how good the timelines generated by our algorithm were, both in terms of comprehensiveness and of quality of coverage.

In evaluating comprehensiveness, we are looking if the timelines are missing key events or dates. Regarding quality of coverage, the timelines in the stories should not contain events that are not relevant to the topic or not important enough to be included. To do this, we decided to compare the timeline we generated for a topic with the Wikipedia article about the same topic. The Wikipedia article is considered to contain all the events that are important for a timeline and only them.

There were some issues we faced with this approach. First, very few Wikipedia articles contain an explicit timeline. From the Wikipedia articles selected about topics at the time of writing this paper, only one contained an explicit timeline. Some have a History section, where the event is described in free-form text. Second, the Wikipedia articles do not just describe the evolution or history of an event, but other aspects as well, such as the causes, an analysis of the consequences, the public reactions, different opinions expressed and so on. Ideally, one would have to read the Wikipedia article, decide which information there should be part of a timeline and then construct the timeline. This is a very labor-intensive job, considering that most articles about popular topics are many pages long. We therefore did not use the timeline or history section of the Wikipedia article and instead followed a different evaluation strategy described later. Third, in some cases there are multiple Wikipedia articles related to the topic (e.g., there is an article about Harvey Weinstein and another one about the sexual abuse allegations). This last case is simpler to deal with, by choosing the most relevant article to the timeline topic (in the example, the sexual abuse allegations article).

The Wikipedia policy is that all the information in an article is based on the sources mentioned in the references, so instead of reading and parsing the articles, we decided to use the references in the articles as proxies of events that should be part of a timeline. Similarly, we use the references in our timelines, which, in our case, are much more directly connected to the timeline. The evaluation was then a matter of comparing the references in both our timeline and the Wikipedia article. Extracting and parsing references and dates is a much more automatable job than understanding the text of the Wikipedia article and extracting events from it. The evaluation process was as follows:

(1) We selected popular topics from 2017 and the associated Wikipedia articles and most relevant hashtags about them.
(2) From the Wikipedia articles we extracted the URLs of their reference and their respective dates.
(3) From our timeline on the same topic, we selected the URLs of the pages used to construct the timeline and their respective dates.
(4) We matched the URLs by date and compared how many URLs appear in our timeline and the Wikipedia article for each day.

We computed the distribution of references across time. Due to limited space, we show the distribution for three topics in figures 6, 7, and 8. In terms of the dates covered and the amount of coverage per date, our timelines track the Wikipedia articles quite closely. For suddenly breaking topics, such as the Harvey Weinstein scandal (Figure 6) and the Manchester arena bombing (Figure 7), our timelines begin earlier than Wikipedia. We think this is because our timelines are based on social media, where it is very easy and fast to share an article, whereas the Wikipedia articles require more

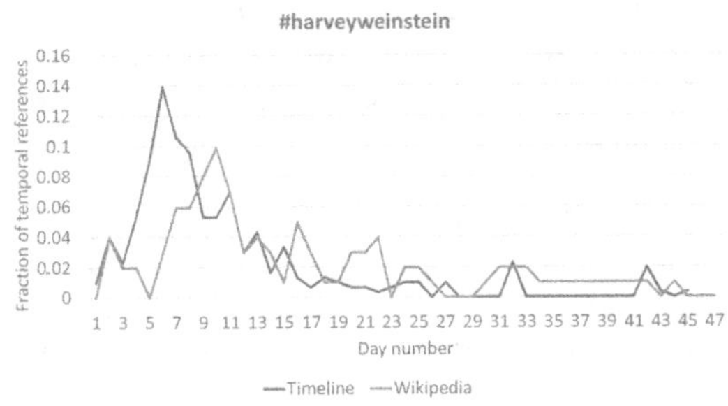

Figure 6: Distribution of references for the Harvey Weinstein scandal.

time for the wikipedians to choose their sources and author the article. For other topics that are more predictable, such as the Comey dismissal (Figure 8), both Wikipedia and our timeline agree in the respective volume of coverage across dates.

We also computed the precision and recall for our timeline, by treating Wikipedia as the gold standard. They were based on the dates covered by our timeline and Wikipedia. The exact URLs of the references are not important, because different news sites cover the same event, so the references do not need to be exactly the same. Also, the number of references per day is also not important, because for our timelines, this number is controlled by a threshold which dictates how many references to choose. We therefore computed precision and recall based only on the coverage of a date in our timeline only, Wikipedia only or both. We define Precision = $\frac{\#\text{dates appearing in both}}{\#\text{dates appearing in timeline}}$ and Recall = $\frac{\#\text{dates appearing in both}}{\#\text{dates in Wikipedia}}$.

The results are shown in Table 4. Recall is generally high, which is encouraging because it shows that important dates for the topic are covered in our timelines. Precision is usually low to average, which indicates that our timelines include articles from more dates than Wikipedia. As figures 6, 7, and 8 show, this is mainly an artifact of how we compute precision. For many days where Wikipedia has zero references, our timeline has a very small number (1 or 2), which being non-zero leads to a low precision. Another reason for the discrepancies has to do with the fact that many of these topics are recent or still evolving. Some Wikipedia articles contain annotations that some information is missing or they need to be updated (marked with an asterisk in Table 4). As more information is added to Wikipedia, it is likely that the precision of our timelines will increase. In Figure 9 we present a visual comparison of our generated Wiki-like page against a Wikipedia article for the Sonoma fires event. We can observe that both timelines are nearly identical.

6.3 Diversity Evaluation

When generating our timelines, we gave special attention to address an important aspect, that of the diversity of references. Given the recent focus on fake news and information bubbles, we believe that combining and showing information from a diverse set of sources is necessary for a well-rounded and less biased result. To measure this aspect of the timelines we computed the diversity of the sources (the domains of the URLs) used in the timelines and in the Wikipedia articles, using Simpson's index of diversity D:

Topic	Dominant hashtag	Wikipedia article	Wikipedia timeline	Precision	Recall
Catalonia election	catalonia	https://en.wikipedia.org/wiki/Catalan_independence_referendum,_2017 (*)	No	0.27	0.71
Tax reform	taxreform	https://en.wikipedia.org/wiki/Tax_Cuts_and_Jobs_Act_of_2017 (*)	No	0.28	0.88
DACA	daca	https://en.wikipedia.org/wiki/Deferred_Action_for_Childhood_Arrivals (*)	No	0.07	0.73
Harvey Weinstein scandal	harveyweinstein	https://en.wikipedia.org/wiki/Harvey_Weinstein_sexual_abuse_allegations	No	0.80	0.65
Hurricane Irma	irma	https://en.wikipedia.org/wiki/Hurricane_Irma	No	0.53	0.87
Hurricane Harvey	hurricaneharvey	https://en.wikipedia.org/wiki/Hurricane_Harvey	No	0.48	0.91
Manchester attack	manchesterarena	https://en.wikipedia.org/wiki/Manchester_Arena_bombing	No	0.56	0.31
James Comey	comey	https://en.wikipedia.org/wiki/Dismissal_of_James_Comey	No	0.18	0.97
Sonoma fires	sonomafires	https://en.wikipedia.org/wiki/Tubbs_Fire	Yes	0.66	0.75

Table 4: List of selected topics with their dominant hashtags and Wikipedia articles and the precision/recall at the date level of the generated timeline compared against Wikipedia. Except one, no Wikipedia article contains an explicit timeline for a direct comparison. An asterisk (*) in a Wikipedia article means it has a "Needs update" or similar label as of January 2018, which may result in artificially low precision.

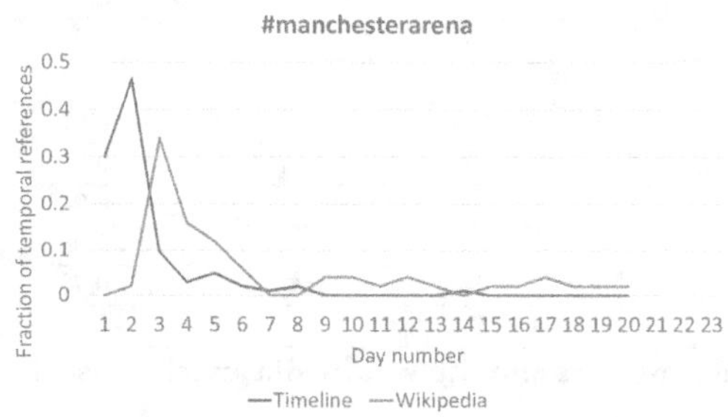

Figure 7: Distribution of references for the Manchester Arena Attack.

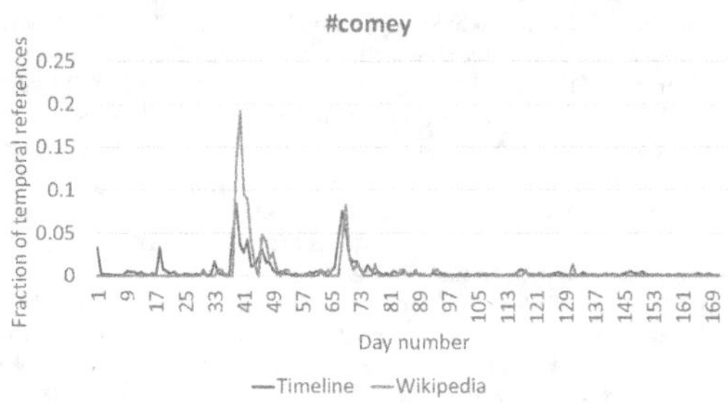

Figure 8: Distribution of references for the dismissal of James Comey.

$D = 1 - \left(\frac{\sum_{i=1}^{N} n_i(n_i-1)}{N(N-1)} \right)$, where n_i is the number of links belonging to the ith domain type and N is the total number of domains in the dataset. This index takes values between 0 and 1 and measures the degree of concentration when individuals are classified into types.

Table 5 shows, for each topic, the number of unique domains selected for constructing our timeline and appearing in Wikipedia and their respective diversity indices. The diversity index is high for Wikipedia, but even higher for our timelines, showing a wider selection of source domains.

7 CONCLUSION AND FUTURE WORK

In this paper, we study the problem of deriving the evolution of a story by combining social data with news articles and present the outcome as a Wiki-like page. A central part of our approach is to construct temporally sensitive contexts in the form of vectors that contain the chatter on social media for a specific time period. We introduce a vote data structure that captures information about hashtags, links, ngrams, and their connections. These votes are then used in the computation of social pseudo-relevance feedback. Contextual vectors and social signatures derived from Twitter with similar queries extracted from a commercial query log are also used for query expansion.

We evaluated our research from three different angles. Offline evaluation shows that stories have a promising defect rate. A comparison against Wikipedia articles reports high recall numbers showing that our techniques cover the important dates of the story. Finally, the diversity of the sources that we use for constructing the timelines are more diverse that the ones used by Wikipedia.

Future work includes learning the weights for SPRF and SQE and enhancements for query generation and TOC. The coherence of a story is something that requires more work as it involves NLP techniques that were not covered in the current version. Finally, we would like to explore different thresholds for optimizing different story length documents.

8 ACKNOWLEDGMENTS

Omar Alonso thanks Prof. Doug Oard for suggestions on different evaluation strategies.

REFERENCES

[1] Yasmin AlNoamany, Michele C. Weigle, and Michael L. Nelson. 2017. Generating Stories From Archived Collections. In *Proc. of WebSci.* 309–318.

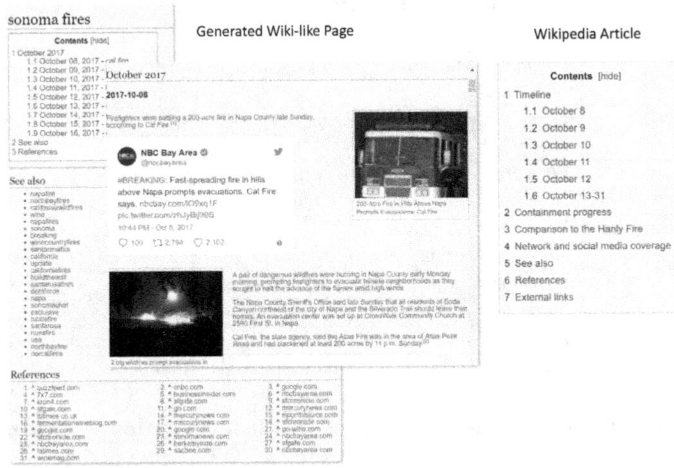

Figure 9: The TOC for Sonoma fires compared against the Wikipedia article shows how similar the timelines are.

Topic	Timeline (# unique domains)	Timeline D index	Wikipedia (# unique domains)	Wikipedia D index
Sonoma fires	130	0.95	111	0.90
Harvey Weinstein scandal	90	0.96	52	0.94
Catalonia election	130	0.96	111	0.98
Hurricane Irma	376	0.99	158	0.99
Hurricane Harvey	374	0.99	158	0.98
Manchester attack	64	0.98	48	0.94
Comey	288	0.98	70	0.96
DACA	339	0.98	74	0.98
Tax reform	149	0.98	78	0.95

Table 5: Diversity index and number of unique domains for the generated timelines and the Wikipedia articles associated with a topic.

[2] Omar Alonso, Sushma Bannur, Kartikay Khandelwal, and Shankar Kalyanaraman. 2015. The World Conversation: Web Page Metadata Generation from Social Sources. In *Proc. of WWW*. 385–395.

[3] Omar Alonso, Serge-Eric Tremblay, and Fernando Diaz. 2017. Automatic Generation of Timelines from Social Media. In *Proc. of WebSci*.

[4] Claudio Carpineto, Stanislaw Osinski, Giovanni Romano, and Dawid Weiss. 2009. A Survey of Web Clustering Engines. *ACM Comput. Surv.* 41, 3 (2009), 17:1–17:38.

[5] Claudio Carpineto and Giovanni Romano. 2012. A Survey of Automatic Query Expansion in Information Retrieval. *ACM Comput. Surv.* 44, 1 (2012), 1:1–1:50.

[6] Ronnie Chaiken, Bob Jenkins, Per-Åke Larson, Bill Ramsey, Darren Shakib, Simon Weaver, and Jingren Zhou. 2008. SCOPE: Easy and Efficient Parallel Processing of Massive Data Sets. *PVLDB* 1, 2 (2008), 1265–1276.

[7] Van Dang and W. Bruce Croft. 2010. Query Reformulation Using Anchor Text. In *Proc. of WSDM*. 41–50.

[8] Miles Efron, Peter Organisciak, and Katrina Fenlon. 2012. Improving Retrieval of Short Texts Through Document Expansion. In *Proc. of SIGIR*. 911–920.

[9] Besnik Fetahu, Katja Markert, and Avishek Anand. 2015. Automated News Suggestions for Populating Wikipedia Entity Pages. In *Proc. of CIKM*. 323–332.

[10] Jennifer Gillenwater, Alex Kulesza, and Ben Taskar. 2012. Discovering Diverse and Salient Threads in Document Collections. In *Proc. of EMNLP-CoNLL*. 710–720.

[11] Donna Harman. 1992. Relevance Feedback Revisited. In *Proc. of SIGIR*. 1–10.

[12] David I. Inouye and Jugal K. Kalita. 2011. Comparing Twitter Summarization Algorithms for Multiple Post Summaries. In *Proc. of PASSAT/SocialCom*. 298–306.

[13] Gunhee Kim and Leonid Sigal. 2015. Discovering Collective Narratives of Theme Parks from Large Collections of Visitors' Photo Streams. In *Proc. of KDD*. 1899–1908.

[14] Reiner Kraft and Jason Y. Zien. 2004. Mining Anchor Text for Query Refinement. In *Proc. of WWW*. 666–674.

[15] Chen Lin, Chun Lin, Jingxuan Li, Dingding Wang, Yang Chen, and Tao Li. 2012. Generating Event Storylines from Microblogs. In *Proc. of CIKM*. 175–184.

[16] Flávio Martins, João Magalhães, and Jamie Callan. 2016. Barbara Made the News: Mining the Behavior of Crowds for Time-Aware Learning to Rank. In *Proc. of WSDM*. 667–676.

[17] Arunav Mishra and Klaus Berberich. 2016. Event Digest: A Holistic View on Past Events. In *Proc. of SIGIR*. 493–502.

[18] Taiki Miyanishi, Kazuhiro Seki, and Kuniaki Uehara. 2013. Improving Pseudo-relevance Feedback via Tweet Selection. In *Proc. of CIKM*. 439–448.

[19] Zhaochun Ren, Shangsong Liang, Edgar Meij, and Maarten de Rijke. 2013. Personalized Time-aware Tweets Summarization. In *Proc. of SIGIR*. 513–522.

[20] Hany SalahEldeen and Michael L. Nelson. 2013. Reading the Correct History?: Modeling Temporal Intention in Resource Sharing. In *Proc. of JCDL*. 257–266.

[21] Christina Sauper and Regina Barzilay. 2009. Automatically Generating Wikipedia Articles: A Structure-Aware Approach. In *Proc. of ACL*. 208–216.

[22] Thibault Sellam, Martin Hentschel, Vasilis Kandylas, and Omar Alonso. 2016. e#: Sharper Expertise Detection from Microblogs. In *Proc. of EDBT*. 563–572.

[23] Dafna Shahaf, Carlos Guestrin, and Eric Horvitz. 2012. Trains of Thought: Generating Information Maps. In *Proc. of WWW*. 899–908.

[24] Dafna Shahaf, Carlos Guestrin, Eric Horvitz, and Jure Leskovec. 2015. Information Cartography. *Commun. ACM* 58, 11 (2015), 62–73.

[25] Beaux Sharifi, Mark-Anthony Hutton, and Jugal K. Kalita. 2010. Summarizing Microblogs Automatically. In *Proc. of NAACL-HLT*. 685–688.

[26] Laure Soulier and Lynda Tamine. 2017. On the Collaboration Support in Information Retrieval. *Comput. Surveys* (2017).

[27] Manos Tsagkias, Maarten de Rijke, and Wouter Weerkamp. 2011. Linking Online News and Social Media. In *Proc. of WSDM*. 565–574.

[28] Lu Wang, Claire Cardie, and Galen Marchetti. 2015. Socially-Informed Timeline Generation for Complex Events. In *Proc. of NAACL*. 1055–1065.

[29] Stewart Whiting, Iraklis A. Klampanos, and Joemon M. Jose. 2012. Temporal Pseudo-relevance Feedback in Microblog Retrieval. In *Proc. of ECIR*. 522–526.

[30] Jinxi Xu and W. Bruce Croft. 2000. Improving the Effectiveness of Information Retrieval with Local Context Analysis. *ACM Trans. Inf. Syst.* 18, 1 (2000), 79–112.

[31] Yang Xu, Gareth J. F. Jones, and Bin Wang. 2009. Query Dependent Pseudo-relevance Feedback Based on Wikipedia. In *Proc. of SIGIR*. 59–66.

Effective Unsupervised Author Disambiguation with Relative Frequencies

Tobias Backes
GESIS - Leibniz-Institute for the Social Sciences
tobias.backes@gesis.org

ABSTRACT

This work addresses the problem of author name homonymy in the Web of Science. Aiming for an efficient, simple and straightforward solution, we introduce a novel probabilistic similarity measure for author name disambiguation based on feature overlap. Using the researcher-ID available for a subset of the Web of Science, we evaluate the application of this measure in the context of agglomeratively clustering author mentions. We focus on a concise evaluation that shows clearly for which problem setups and at which time during the clustering process our approach works best. In contrast to most other works in this field, we are skeptical towards the performance of author name disambiguation methods in general and compare our approach to the trivial single-cluster baseline. Our results are presented separately for each correct clustering size as we can explain that, when treating all cases together, the trivial baseline and more sophisticated approaches are hardly distinguishable in terms of evaluation results. Our model shows state-of-the-art performance for all correct clustering sizes without any discriminative training and with tuning only one convergence parameter.

CCS CONCEPTS

• **Information systems → Entity resolution**;

KEYWORDS

Author Disambiguation; Probabilities; Agglomerative Clustering

ACM Reference Format:
Tobias Backes. 2018. Effective Unsupervised Author Disambiguation with Relative Frequencies. In *JCDL '18: The 18th ACM/IEEE Joint Conference on Digital Libraries, June 3–7, 2018, Fort Worth, TX, USA.* ACM, New York, NY, USA, 10 pages. https://doi.org/10.1145/3197026.3197036

1 INTRODUCTION

Documents have authors. This information is almost always available on a document and in the document's metadata. However, it is crucial to distinguish an author name mentioned on a specific document from the author itself. Usually, the author is *referred to* by a string of characters that is given with the document. This concept introduces two types of ambiguity:

(1) *Name synonymy*: One author is referred to by different strings, perhaps due to misspelling, language-specificity, different conventions for name specification, etc.
(2) *Name homonymy*: One string refers to different authors. With the the collection size the chance increases that two authors in the collection have the same name.

In general, both problems have to be addressed simultaneously, i.e. in a constrained clustering setup. This allows to establish that for example *DOE, J* can be *DOE, JW* or *DOE, JH* but not both. In this contribution, we focus on name homonymy and simplify the problem by considering that all initials are always given (assuming that *DOE, J*, *DOE, JW* and *DOE, JH* are different persons). In that case, *Author(ship/name) disambiguation* decides for a set of *author mentions* with the same name, which of them belong to the same author and which do not. This is a clustering problem over author mentions. Each cluster is considered an author. More formally:

- For each collection, there is a set $\mathfrak{N}$ of *names name* $\in \mathfrak{N}$
- For each name *name*, there is a set $\mathfrak{C}$ (also referred to as a *clustering*) of authors $C \in \mathfrak{C}$ (also referred to as a *cluster*) and a set of mentions $x \in X$
- Each author $C \subseteq X$ is a set of *mentions* $x \in C$
- For each mention x, there is a bag of *features* $f \in F(x)$, each with a frequency $\#(f, x)$ of occurrence with x

If a name is not disambiguated, we have no information about the belonging of single mentions. This state can either be expressed by putting all mentions in the same cluster $C = X$ such that $\mathfrak{C} = \{\{x \mid x \in X\}\}$, or by assigning each mention x its own cluster $C = \{x\}$, such that $\mathfrak{C} = \{\{x\} \mid x \in X\}$. The task of author disambiguation is then to suggest a *system* clustering $\mathfrak{C}_{sys}$ that is as close to the correct clustering $\mathfrak{C}_{cor}$ as possible. In the training/tuning and evaluation case, we have both $\mathfrak{C}_{sys}$ and $\mathfrak{C}_{cor}$ present and optimize some evaluation score $eval(\mathfrak{C}_{sys}, \mathfrak{C}_{cor})$. We can safely assume that this score measures the similarity between the system- and the correct clustering. In practice, we disambiguate one name at a time. This is referred to as *blocking* [15], where each name defines one *block*, that is a separate problem set.

Many different approaches have been proposed to solve the problem of author disambiguation. Although it is often not indicated as clearly, most of these approaches can be viewed within the framework and terminology described above. Despite the large number of proposed methods, we find that a straightforward, simple and sound, easy-to-implement – yet well performing – baseline is

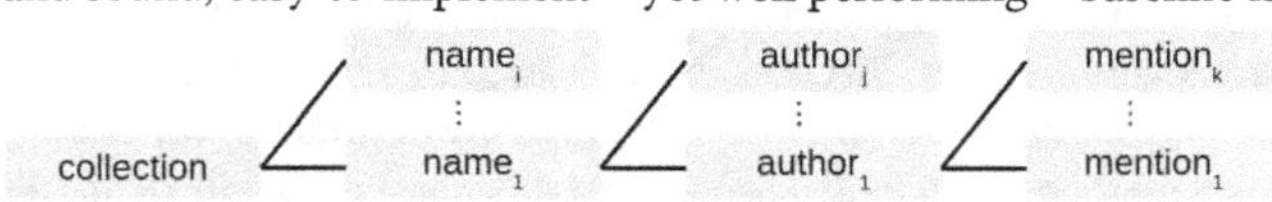

Figure 1: Author disambiguation problem structure

JCDL '18, June 3–7, 2018, Fort Worth, TX, USA

ACM ISBN 978-1-4503-5178-2/18/06...$15.00
https://doi.org/10.1145/3197026.3197036

still lacking. Existing solutions are either complicated to understand and implement, require training steps or are based on a number of rather arbitrary decisions. Normally, performance is not compared against the most primitive conceivable baseline [9]. Therefore, in this work, we elaborate on the following research questions:

RQ1 Can we deploy well-behaved, straightforward probabilities to establish a conceptionally simple, fast and reliable method for author name disambiguation that shows state-of-the-art performance?

RQ2 How difficult is the problem of author name disambiguation in general and separately for different problem sizes? How good are the most primitive baselines and how does our approach compare to them?

We structure the rest of the paper as follows. In section 2, we review the related work. In section 3, we describe the probabilistic model that we designed as a proof-of-concept for RQ1. In section 4, we explain the evaluation setup, including simple baselines and the separation of different problem sizes. This allows us to test our approach regarding RQ1 and gather insights towards the more general RQ2. We summarize the most prominent findings regarding these two research questions in section 5.

2 RELATED WORK

In this section, we give a brief overview over the most cited literature on author disambiguation that relates to our approach:

The Problem of Author Disambiguation. Ferreira et al. [2] give an overview of author disambiguation, distinguish author grouping (*synonymy*) vs. author assignment (*homonymy*) and different types of features for the latter. Smalheiser and Torvik [11] go into more detail, but to some extend also concerning their own project; Harzing [6] analyses the top 1% cited academics from Thompson Reuters Essential Science Indicators and contributes some details of the ambiguity problem in different languages. She shows that the extent of ambiguity has a direct influence on the scientific performance indicators measuring a scientist's academic output. Strotmann and Zhao [13] investigate the application of author disambiguation to citation networks. They show that one of the reasons for researchers being top-ranked is in fact a lack of author name disambiguation. Kramer, Momeni and Mayr [7] give an overview of the quantity of author gold annotation in the Web of Science. They conclude that the Web of Science researcher-ID used in this paper is a good source of author identity information, in contrast to other sources. Milojevic [9] analyzes the accuracy of name blocks built by considering all available initials of an author (and his last name). On the small sample used, this accuracy introduces a very high baseline.

Probabilistic Approaches, Topic Models. Han et al. [5] present a probabilistic Naive Bayes mixture model to disambiguate a small set of highly ambiguous author names. They compare to K-means and find that their model performs significantly better. However, they use a very long product, which can lead to extreme swings and the EM algorithm, a computationally and conceptionally rather complex method. Tang et al. [14] suggest a general probabilistic model based on Markov Random Fields to exploit a variable set of features for author disambiguation. They evaluate their approach on a small set of highly ambiguous names and compare the results to more basic clustering techniques, claiming significant improvements. With ~89% F1, their results are indeed impressive, but considerable effort is required to understand and implement the method. Torvik et al. [16] present a probabilistic model that compares pairs of authors based on various features such as terms, affiliations or venues. Torvik and Smalheiser [15] apply an improved version of this previous approach to the Medline data set and reach ~95% F1 for the one name reported. Their work is one of the most cited state-of-the-art methods in this field. Generally speaking, their experience allows the group to hard-code a lot of knowledge into their methods, but not all decisions can be easily comprehended by others. Although they use some probabilities in their formulas, it seems the final similarities are not normalized. Song et al. [12] present a probabilistic graphical topic model for hierarchical clustering of author names and compare their approach to other standard clustering approaches. They find their model performs better than for example DBSCAN. Although the good performance of ~90% F1 seems to justify the additional complexity, like Han et al., they introduce long products and inference steps on a 'detour' via topic assignments.

The Web of Science, Training Techniques. Like us, Gurney et al. [4] work on the Web of Science and use a very similar set of features. They deploy another group's method for clustering and the Taminoto coefficient for similarity. They report F1>90% for a number of names. Their approach is the one most similar to our proposal, but neither does it use feature-specificity nor return probabilities. Levin et al. [8] present a semi-supervised approach to author disambiguation on the Web of Science data set. The evaluation of their approach shows solid performance (but under 90% F1) and proves that the method scales to very large collections. As they do pairwise classification of author mentions, they make the problem harder than it needs to be. Overall, their work is very detailed but also quite difficult to reproduce. Ferreira et al. [3] present a semi-supervised classifier evaluated on DBLP and BDBComp data sets. Their model outperformed the other methods compared. Depending on supervision and rules, their model introduces a number of (dataset-specific) parameters. Recently, this group has updated their method to allow for incremental disambiguation by comparing not author mentions but mentions to clusters of mentions. [10] This is very practical but more difficult. In another paper focusing on training aspects, Culotta et al. [1] present a special similarity function and combine error-driven sampling with learning-to-rank. They also give an overview of other training approaches. They find that their approach can be beneficial in terms of performance. Similar to Ferreira et al., this approach requires training and uses specific similarity measures for different feature types.

3 METHOD DESCRIPTION

We intent to define a simple, yet effective probabilistic method for author disambiguation. Using the blocking paradigm, our method disambiguates one name at a time. It clusters all mentions of that name based on features extracted from the collection. We note that for each mention x, there is exactly one document $d(x)$ in which this mention appears. However, for each document, there can be multiple mentions that appear on it.

3.1 Features

Features $F(x)$ assigned to a mention x can be extracted (1) from $d(x)$ in general or (2) specifically for x on d. In the first case, the features $F(x)$ are the same as the features $F(\dot{x})$ of a mention $\dot{x}$ that appears on d as well. In the following, we will distinguish different *feature-types*, some of which are *unspecific* for x and some of which are *specific*. We train and test our approach on the Web of Science, as it is the major source of scientific documents annotated with actual author IDs (*researcher-ID*). The following information is used:

(1) *Terms* $F_{term}(x)$: All words considered relevant in the document and their frequency of occurrence in $d(x)$
(2) *Affiliations* $F_{aff}(x)$): All affiliations given for x on $d(x)$ – usually just one
(3) *Categories* $F_{cat}(x)$: All categories assigned to $d(x)$, where we consider categories to be relatively general terms picked from a relatively small vocabulary / thesaurus. The frequency of one category for a document d is usually 1
(4) *Keywords* $F_{key}(x)$: All keywords assigned to $d(x)$, where we consider keywords to be relatively specific terms that are picked from a relatively large vocabulary or only with respect to the current document. The frequency of one keyword for a document d is usually 1
(5) *Coauthornames* $F_{co}(x)$: All names of the coauthors of x on $d(x)$. Unless more than one author of d have the same name, the frequencies are 1
(6) *Refauthornames* $F_{ref}(x)$: All author names from documents d' in the collection such that d references d'. Frequencies larger than 1 will occur often, for example if multiple documents by the same author are referenced
(7) *Emails* $F_{email}(x)$: All email addresses given for x on $d(x)$ – usually just a single email address with a frequency of 1
(8) *Years* $F_{year}(x)$: A bag of years f given for $d(x)$. Like Levin et al. [8], we model $\#(f,x)$ as a Gaussian with the publication year of x as mean. This models temporal proximity.

While there are many details related to the question of which and how features are extracted and normalized, the focus of our research was not to investigate specific features but to develop a method that can provide satisfying results independent of the exact set of features and feature-types.

3.2 Agglomerative clustering

We apply a method of agglomerative clustering as we consider it the most straightforward approach. This means that we start with the initial state where each mention x is in its own cluster $C = \{x\}$. Then, pairs $(C, \dot{C})$ of clusters are merged. If no stopping criterion is applied, this will ultimately result in a state where all mentions are in the same cluster $C = X$. For this reason, we need to compute the score $score(C, \dot{C})$ of a pair $(C, \dot{C})$ of clusters to be merged. Furthermore, we deploy a *quality limit* l, that tells us whether the score can be considered good or not. In our approach, $score(C, \dot{C})$ is not dependent on the score of any other pair of clusters. Neither is the quality limit. This means that in each iteration of the clustering process, we merge all pairs $(C, \dot{C})$, such that (1) $\neg\exists\ddot{C} \in \mathfrak{C} : score(C, \ddot{C}) > score(C, \dot{C}) \wedge \neg\exists\ddot{C} \in \mathfrak{C} : score(\ddot{C}, \dot{C}) > score(C, \dot{C})$ and at the same time, (2) $score(C, \dot{C}) > l$. In other words, we evaluate all disjoint pairs $(C, \dot{C}) \in \mathfrak{C} \times \mathfrak{C}$; for each of these pairs, we check

Algorithm 1: Our agglomerative clustering (no evaluation)

Input: *name* with X and C as well as $N, \#(f), \lambda, \epsilon, l$
while $|C| > 1$ **do**
  $score \leftarrow NULL$;
  foreach $(C, \dot{C}) \in C \times C$ **do**
    $score(C, \dot{C}) \leftarrow \sum_{ftype} \lambda_{ftype} \cdot p_{ftype}(C|\dot{C})$;
  $merges \leftarrow \{\}$;
  foreach $(C, \dot{C}) \in C \times C$ **do**
    if $\neg\exists\ddot{C} \in C : score(C, \ddot{C}) > score(C, \dot{C})$ **and** $\neg\exists\ddot{C} \in C : score(\ddot{C}, \dot{C}) > score(C, \dot{C})$ **and** $score(C, \dot{C}) > l$ **then**
      $merges \leftarrow merges \cup (C, \dot{C})$;
  if $|merges| = 0$ **then** break ;
  else
    foreach $(C, \dot{C}) \in merges$ **do**
      $merge((C, \dot{C}))$;

whether (1) and (2) hold true. If yes, the pair is saved for merging. See algorithm 1 for a more formal description. At the end of each iteration, all saved pairs are merged. A new system clustering is obtained and the next iteration begins. This process converges if no pairs are saved for merging. For evaluation purposes, we can continue to merge with moves that are below the limit, but we will elaborate on this in the experiments section.

3.3 Probabilistic similarity

The main contribution of our approach is the similarity used to define $score(C, \dot{C})$. In the following, we will define and explain the probability that inspires the score. We say that the score of a pair of clusters can be seen as their *joint probability* $p(C, \dot{C}) = p(\dot{C}, C) = p(C|\dot{C}) \cdot p(\dot{C})$. Remember $\#(f,x)$ denotes the frequency of f in the set $F(x)$ of all features in x ($F = \bigcup_{x \in X} F(x)$). Consider $\#(f,x) = 0$ if $f \notin F(x)$. We define:

$$p(C|\dot{C}) = \sum_{(x,\dot{x}) \in C \times \dot{C}} p(x|\dot{x}) \cdot \frac{\#(\dot{x})}{\#(\dot{C})} \qquad p(C) = \sum_{x \in C} p(x)$$

$$p(x|\dot{x}) = \sum_{f \in F} \frac{\#(f,x) \cdot \#(f,\dot{x})}{\#(f) \cdot \#(\dot{x})} \qquad p(x) = \frac{\#(x)}{\#(.)}$$

$$\#(C) = \sum_{x \in C} \#(x) \qquad \#(x) = \sum_{f \in F} \#(f,x)$$

$$\#(f) = \sum_{x \in X} \#(f,x) \qquad \#(.) = \sum_{x \in X} \#(x)$$

To prevent division by zero, we apply *add*ϵ smoothing. This modifies $p(C|\dot{C})$, $p(\dot{x})$ and $p(x|\dot{x})$:

$$p(C|\dot{C}) = \sum_{(x,\dot{x})} p(x|\dot{x}) \cdot \frac{\#(\dot{x}) + \epsilon}{\#(\dot{C}) + |C| \cdot \epsilon} \qquad p(x) = \frac{\#(x) + \epsilon}{\#(.) + |X| \cdot \epsilon}$$

$$p(x|\dot{x}) = \frac{1}{\#(\dot{x}) + \epsilon} \cdot \left(\left(\sum_{f \in F} \frac{\#(f,x) \cdot \#(f,\dot{x})}{\#(f)} \right) + \frac{\epsilon}{|X|} \right)$$

3.4 Variations

So far, we have considered the clustering to be fully enclosed in the current name block. While still treating each name as a separate clustering problem, we can say that X is not only the set of mentions for the current name, but for the entire collection. This increases $\#(f)$, $\#(.)$ and obviously $|X|$. We find that the performance is considerably better if this approach is taken, which can be explained with less sparsity for $\#(f)$. However, this poses the question, what the 'collection' is that we take these counts from. Basically, we are simply looking for a realistic distribution of the frequency of features f independent of the mention they occur with. In an application scenario, this distribution can be taken from the data to be clustered itself. As $\#(f)$, $\#(.)$ and $|X|$ are available even for the data we cluster, in our evaluation scenario, we obtain them from the union of the training and testing portion.

In our preferred variant, we only use $p(C|\dot{C})$ in $score(C,\dot{C})$. This conditional probability does in fact perform much better than the joint probability. Intuitively, $p(C)$ favours large clusters for merging, which does not make sense as it introduces a tendency that reinforces itself. It does not matter that $p(C|\dot{C}) \neq p(\dot{C}|C)$ as merging is symmetric and the clustering procedure we described above will simply use $max(p(C|\dot{C}), p(\dot{C}|C))$ unless there is a third cluster that matches even better (or the limit is not met). In this case, $p(\dot{x})$ is never applied, so that we do not need $\#(.)$. Collecting $\#(f)$ over the entire collection, we then only need the number N of mentions in the collection. Therefore, X still denotes the set of mentions for one single name block. Furthermore, we tested a variant where we replace the sum of products with a maximum of products:

$$\tilde{p}(C|\dot{C}) = \max_{(x,\dot{x}) \in C \times \dot{C}} p(x|\dot{x}) \cdot \frac{\#(\dot{x})}{\#(\dot{C})}$$

Obviously, the value $\tilde{p}$ inspired by single-link clustering is not a probability anymore. This variant performed slightly different than the conditional probability.

3.5 Feature-type weights

All the probabilities shown above are obtained *separately* for each feature-type. Consider that each probability p should actually be denoted p_{ftype} where $ftype$ is either *term, aff, cat, key, co, ref, email* or *year*. For better readability, we drop the subscript where it is not necessary. We perform a simple linear combination with feature-type weights λ to obtain the final score:

$$score(C,\dot{C}) = \sum_{ftype} \lambda_{ftype} \cdot p_{ftype}(C|\dot{C})$$

Ideally, we would like to avoid all training so as to keep our method as simple as possible. Still, to allow for comparison, weights λ are trained on the training portion of our data. We sample pairs (x, C) and $(x, \dot{C})$ such that $x \in C \wedge x \notin \dot{C} \wedge |C| = |\dot{C}| \wedge C \cup \dot{C} \subseteq X$, where X is the set of mentions for a *single* name. All possible values for $|C| = |\dot{C}|$ are considered in order to create a more or less realistic binary classification scenario, where we are asked to assign x to a correct cluster C or an incorrect cluster $\dot{C}$. The classifier (*logistic regression* performed well) receives probabilities $p_{ftype}(x|C)$ and $p_{ftype}(x|\dot{C})$ for each $ftype$ together with the class 'correct' or 'incorrect'. It then learns feature-type weights λ_{ftype} in order to

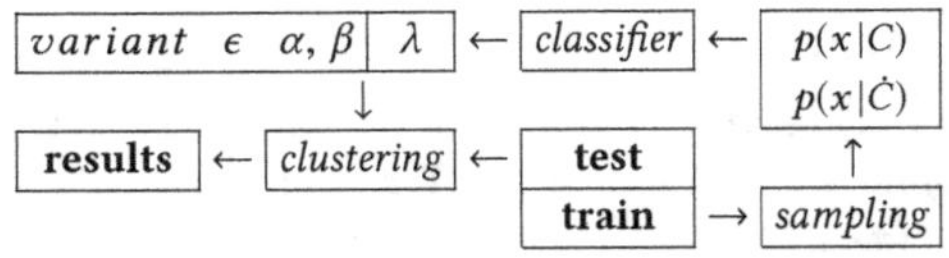

Figure 2: Setup for clustering, evaluation and training λ

optimize the classification outcome. While this is not the same scenario as the one that the weights are finally applied in, we hope that nevertheless, we gather some insight into the importance of single feature-types.

3.6 Convergence

Above, we have introduced a quality limit l on the scores for moves during clustering. In order to account for different problem sizes (and corresponding smaller probabilities), we define l as follows:

$$l = \alpha + |X| \cdot \beta$$

where $|X|$ is the number of mentions for the current name. Fortunately, when they are normalized such that $\sum_{ftype} \lambda_{ftype} = 1$, l is relatively independent of λ. Another pleasant finding was that it is sufficient to tune one parameter depending on whether we use the sum-of-products or the maximum-of-products variant. While we optimize both parameters, results were best if in the first case $\beta = 0$ and in the second $\alpha = 0$.

3.7 Implementational Details

Our approach as presented in previous sections can be implemented in an efficient and conceptionally simple way by means of matrix multiplication. In a first step, we calculate the matrix $\overline{p(x|\dot{x})}$ containing values $p(x|\dot{x})$ for all pairs $(x, \dot{x}) \in X \times X$. This is based on the $|X| \times (|F| + 1)$ count matrix $\overline{\#(x, f)}$, the feature count vector $\overrightarrow{\#(f)}$, and the mention count vector $\overrightarrow{\#(x)}$. For smoothing, $\overline{\#(x, f)}$ is extended by one column $\langle \epsilon \dots \epsilon \rangle^T$.

$$\overline{p(x|\dot{x})} = \overline{p(x|f)} \cdot \overline{p(f|\dot{x})} \qquad \overline{p(x|f)} = \frac{\overline{\#(x,f)}}{\overrightarrow{\#(f)}^T}$$

$$\overline{p(f|\dot{x})} = \frac{\overline{\#(x,f)}}{\overrightarrow{\#(x)}} \qquad \forall i : \overline{\#(x,f)}_{i,|F|+1} = \epsilon$$

Here, $\cdot$ denotes matrix multiplication (*matrix- or dot product*). During each iteration, we calculate the $|\mathfrak{C}_{sys}| \times |\mathfrak{C}_{sys}|$ matrix $\overline{p(C|\dot{C})}$ from $\overline{p(x|\dot{x})}$ and the current clustering as a $|X| \times |\mathfrak{C}_{sys}|$ matrix $\overline{\mathfrak{C}_{sys}}$:

$$\overline{p(C|\dot{C})} = \overline{\mathfrak{C}_{sys}}^T \cdot \left(\overline{p(x|\dot{x})} \cdot \overline{p(\dot{x}|C)}\right) \qquad \overrightarrow{\#(C)} = \overrightarrow{\#(x)}^T \cdot \overline{\mathfrak{C}_{sys}}$$

$$\overline{p(\dot{x}|C)} = \left(\left(\overrightarrow{\#(x)} + \epsilon\right) \cdot \frac{1}{\overrightarrow{\#(C)} + |\mathfrak{C}_{sys}|\epsilon}\right) \circ \overline{\mathfrak{C}_{sys}}$$

Here, $\circ$ denotes component-wise multiplication (*Hadamard product*), ensuring $p(x|C) = 0$ if $x \notin C$. For the *max* variant, all sums in the matrix products are replaced by a maximum function.

4 EXPERIMENTAL EVALUATION

In the following we describe the experimental setup used to train, tune and test our approach. This is also depicted in figure 2.

4.1 Data

We use the *Web of Science* (*WoS*) collection as a source of metadata and annotated authorship information. In a preprocessing step, we extract features for the feature-types mentioned in the previous section. We normalize author names as LASTNAME, INITS, where I, N, I, T, S are all the initials for each first name of the author mention. Thereby, on the one hand, we make the problem harder as we drop the full name information (increasing the problem size, i.e. *John Doe* = *Jack Doe*) and on the other we make it simpler as we treat mentions of the same author where his first names are given with varying completeness as separate problems (reducing the problem size, i.e. *John Doe* ≠ *John W. Doe*). We extract terms and their frequency from the title and abstract of the metadata. Title terms are weighted three times higher than abstract terms. Some stop words are omitted and all words are lower-cased. Furthermore some basic lemmatization from the *Natural Language Toolkit* (*NLTK*) is applied. Affiliations are already normalized in the WoS. Categories and keywords are taken as they are in the WoS. Co- and referenced author names are normalized as described above. Emails are not normalized, but we plan to lowercase them in the future. From the publication date, we only pick the year.

After extracting features for the entire WoS with more than 100 million documents, we create a database containing the features related to each single mention with a researcher-ID. For each name, we use all the mentions that are given a researcher-ID and we use all the authors that contain at least one such mention. As stated earlier, we consider each researcher-ID a distinct author. Names are ordered randomly and separated into training and testing portions. We use 25% names for training.

4.2 Test setup

In contrast to work by most other groups, we are specifically interested in evaluating the performance of our model in relation to the problem size. If this has been done in the literature, it is usually regarding the number $|X|$ of mentions with the same name (i.e. in Gurney et al. [4]). However, we sort our name blocks by the correct number of clusters that would need to be detected in order to achieve perfect results (the size $|\mathfrak{C}_{cor}|$ of the cluster*ing*). We compare a maximum of 1000 names for all $|\mathfrak{C}_{cor}| \in \{1..10\}$. Of this selection, 25% are used for training. Clustering sizes are distributed according to Zipf's law. For the sizes 1 to 4, more than 1000 names are available. See table 1 for exact number of names for each clustering size. We evaluate our approach for each size separately. Doing so, we are basically balancing our data in an artificial way. We find this is necessary, as the Zipf distribution of $|\mathfrak{C}|$ leads to a (usually unobserved) preference of models that create very few clusters. Furthermore, in order to view the actual behavior of our method, we carefully monitor the development of precision, recall and F1 measure with each iteration of the clustering process. We also monitor how the clustering would have continued if there were no limit l on the score of possible merges. So for each iteration in the clustering process, we record the following information:

(1) **Precision** of current system clustering
(2) **Recall** of current system clustering
(3) Current **number of clusters** in system clustering
(4) Whether the current iteration is before **convergence**

$\lvert\mathfrak{C}\rvert$	1	2	3	4	5	6	7	8	9	10	Σ
train	*255*	*250*	*250*	*250*	*215*	*139*	*80*	*65*	*43*	*35*	*1582*
test	*767*	*751*	*750*	*750*	*645*	*418*	*242*	*195*	*131*	*106*	*4749*
train+test	*1022*	*1001*	*1000*	*1000*	*860*	*557*	*322*	*260*	*174*	*141*	*6331*
all	*229653*	*14108*	*3630*	*1657*	*860*	*557*	*322*	*260*	*174*	*141*	*251362*
% used	*0.45*	*7.10*	*27.55*	*60.35*	*100*	*100*	*100*	*100*	*100*	*100*	*2.52*

Table 1: The number of names found or used with a correct clustering size $|\mathfrak{C}_{corr}| \in \{1..10\}$ in the WoS data

During the clustering process, we continuously apply the quality limit l to merges. Once an iteration is reached where no possible merge exceeds the limit, the following iterations are only hypothetical and all possible merges are applied if and only if no merge exceeds the limit. Note that this means that even during hypothetical iterations, there might be a limit-based selection of merges. As there is always at least one possible merge, all clusters are finally merged into one and we can evaluate the development of precision and recall as well as the point of convergence. This is particularly interesting if one has certain preferences towards precision or recall and would like to find a good stopping point for the clustering process. Figure 6 shows how we plot the recorded information.

4.3 Evaluation measures

In order to evaluate the performance of our approach, we use two popular evaluation measures for clustering: (1) *pairwise F1* (*pairF1*) and (2) *bCube*. Both measures define *precision* (*P*) and *recall* (*R*) when comparing two clusterings $\mathfrak{C}_{sys}$ and $\mathfrak{C}_{cor}$. F1 is defined as usual as $2 \cdot \frac{P \cdot R}{P+R}$. Except for one aspect, we use the definition by Levin et al. (2012) [8]:

$$pairs(\mathfrak{C}) = \bigcup_{C \in \mathfrak{C}} \{\{x, \dot{x}\} \mid x, \dot{x} \in C \land x \neq \dot{x}\}$$

$$P_{pairF1} = \frac{pairs(\mathfrak{C}_{cor}) \cap pairs(\mathfrak{C}_{sys})}{pairs(\mathfrak{C}_{sys})}$$

$$R_{pairF1} = \frac{pairs(\mathfrak{C}_{cor}) \cap pairs(\mathfrak{C}_{sys})}{pairs(\mathfrak{C}_{cor})}$$

$$C_{sys}(x) = C \in \mathfrak{C}_{sys} : x \in C$$

$$P_{bCube} = \frac{1}{|X|} \cdot \sum_{x \in X} \frac{|C_{sys}(x) \cap C_{cor}(x)|}{|C_{sys}(x)|}$$

$$R_{bCube} = \frac{1}{|X|} \cdot \sum_{x \in X} \frac{|C_{sys}(x) \cap C_{cor}(x)|}{|C_{cor}(x)|}$$

We note that the above shown P_{pairF1} and R_{pairF1} are not defined if in the first case $\mathfrak{C}_{sys}$ and in the second $\mathfrak{C}_{cor}$ are $\{\{\{x\} \mid x \in X\}\}$. Therefore we modify $pairs(\mathfrak{C}) = \bigcup_{C \in \mathfrak{C}} \{\{x, \dot{x}\} \mid x, \dot{x} \in C\}$. This increases the values for pairF1 slightly.

One important question with regard to these evaluation measures is on which subset of the problem they are applied. It is understood from the above formula, that there is a distinct precision and recall value for each clustering problem, that is for each name. However, one could also consider the pairs to be taken over the entire test data:

$$pairs_{cor}(\mathfrak{N}) = \bigcup_{name \in \mathfrak{N}} \bigcup_{C \in \mathfrak{C}_{cor}^{name}} \{\{x, \dot{x}\} \mid x, \dot{x} \in C \land x \neq \dot{x}\}$$

In that case one would calculate one value of precision and recall over all correct and incorrect pairs in the test data. From these two values, F1 could be calculated. If we calculate precision and recall for each name separately, we have to average over the results that we get for each single name. This weights each name equally (independent of the number $|X|$ of mentions with that name). We can then calculate F1 from the average precision and average recall over all names. We use this approach to obtain a final score for each correct number $|\mathfrak{C}|$ of clusters. We do not report a final score over all $|\mathfrak{C}_{cor}|$ as we aim to establish a more precise evaluation for the different cases that are possible. However, in table 1 we report the number of names that were found in the WoS data for each $|\mathfrak{C}_{cor}|$, from which one can approximate the performance over the whole collection. As the performance of our approach does not vary to any relevant extend between using *pairF1* or *bCube*, we show only plots for *bCube*.

4.4 Experiments

In our experiments, we use the setup and the measures described above in combination with different parameters, hyper-parameters and variants. Our model has the following variants:

(1) *within* / *overall*: $\#(f)$ only within one name or over all
(2) *pc_on* / *pc_off*: using $p(C, \dot{C})$ or using $p(C|\dot{C})$
(3) *prob* / *max*: sum-of-products or maximum-of-products

As indicated earlier, for most variants, results show that only one of the two options was worth further investigation. We choose the following setup based on first experiments on the training data: (1) *overall* and (2) *pc_off*. The difference between (3) *prob* and *max* was not as clear. We decided that the *max* variant is worth further investigation but focused mostly on the *prob* variant as it could be implemented to run much faster and first results also gave a better F1 score. Our model has the following (hyper-) parameters:

(1) Smoothing hyper-parameter ϵ
(2) Feature-type weights λ
(3) Convergence parameters α and β

So far, we have tried only one very small smoothing parameter $\epsilon = .0001$ to avoid division by zero. We train the feature-type weights over the union of training portions for all clustering sizes and approximate the results as shown in table 2. This table also shows all other feature-type weights examined. Observing stopping size vs. correct size, we tuned the limit parameters in a manual grid-search on the training data and found that a good choice is to set $\alpha = .0005$ for the *max* variant and $\beta = .000075$ for the *prob* variant. Our plots include a histogram of the clustering sizes $|\mathfrak{C}_{cor}|$ where the system clustering converged. All plots are given for the training data as they have been part of the parameter tuning process.

4.5 Results

As mentioned above, we record a number of measurements during the clustering process in order to understand the behavior of our method and the effect of different versions, stopping limits and feature-type weightings. Table 3 shows the final results with tuned parameters on the test portion. In addition to that, we present our measurements in two types of plots. Referring to figure 6 as an example, we briefly explain how to read the more comprehensive type:

	train	*opp.*	*unif.*	*select*			*leaving-one-out*			*author*	*doc.*
term	.15	.12	.125	1		0	0		.143	0	.2
aff	.2	.03	.125	0		0	.143		.143	0	0
cat	.18	.1	.125	0		0	.143		.143	0	.2
key	.03	.2	.125	0	⋱	0	.143	⋱	.143	0	.2
co	.2	.02	.125	0		0	.143		.143	.5	.2
ref	.12	.15	.125	0		0	.143		.143	.5	0
email	.1	.18	.125	0		0	.143		.143	0	0
year	.02	.2	.125	0		1	.143		0	0	.2

Table 2: Feature-type weights considered in our experiments

The y-axis displays the interval [0, 1], onto which precision, recall and F1 are mapped. The x-axis gives the number of clusters in a clustering iteration. For a single block, clustering starts somewhere on the left of the plot with very low recall and maximal precision. As the process continues to merge clusters, recall increases and precision decreases. Over all blocks, we see the same development, but averaged for each problem size (standart deviation shown). In a perfect method, precision would remain constant until the correct number of clusters, shown as a solid vertical line, is reached. In figure 6, we see that for the *max* variant, F1 peaks exactly at this point, while a bit later for the *prob* variant. For both variants, the empirical stopping size (our method does not know the correct number of clusters) for $|\mathfrak{C}| = 5$ peaks where F1 is maximal. The offset of this empirical distribution is tuned with the stopping parameters α and β. We can see in figure 7 that there is still room for improvement of the stopping limit l, as for $|\mathfrak{C}| = 10$ our method generally stops later than it should.

As preliminary tests on the training data clearly favour one combination of variants and the stopping parameters are easily tuned for to these two options, the most interesting comparison is between different feature-type weightings. As a first choice, trained weights from the classifier are used and give satisfying results (see fig. 3). The *max* variant performs worse in terms of F1, but precision is higher (see fig. 4). Detailed plots (fig. 6) of the clustering process suggest that the *prob* variant can sometimes gain relatively much recall in early stages of the clustering, while the *max* variant has particularly regular behavior with smaller deviations from the mean. It is also interesting to see that the *max* variant is able to gain the maximal F1 at the correct number of clusters, while the *prob* variant achieves higher values of F1 (due to better recall) but peaks at a clustering size larger than the correct one. The average maximum recall (*'max rec.'*) at perfect precision (which is independent of the stopping parameters) shown in figures 3 and 4 is much higher with the *prob* variant, which supports the notion that the *prob* variant has its strengths in a high recall. On the other hand, the average maximum precision (*'max prec.'*) at perfect recall is slightly higher for the *max* variant, suggesting that in general it can keep precision higher until the end. We also show precision and F1 for the baseline of putting all mentions into the same cluster (*'base prec.'* and *'base f1'*). Obviously, recall is 1 here.

The trained feature-type weighting is contrasted with a uniform weighting of feature-types. Results are almost identical as can be seen in figure 10, suggesting that equal weighting of all feature-types is a good choice. However, this does not mean that feature-type weighting has no influence on the performance. In

bCube			$\lvert\mathfrak{C}\rvert$	1	2	3	4	5	6	7	8	9	10
prob	$\alpha = 0$	trained	P	*100*	*95*	*95*	*96*	*97*	*96*	*94*	*96*	*95*	*94*
			F	***98***	***93***	***93***	***92***	***91***	***90***	***91***	***91***	***90***	***89***
			R	*97*	*91*	*90*	*88*	*86*	*85*	*87*	*87*	*86*	*84*
		uniform	P	*100*	*95*	*95*	*97*	*97*	*97*	*95*	*96*	*96*	*95*
			F	***98***	***93***	***93***	***92***	*90*	***90***	*90*	*90*	*89*	***89***
			R	*97*	*91*	*90*	*87*	*84*	*84*	*85*	*85*	*83*	*84*
max	$\alpha = .0005$	trained	P	*100*	*96*	*96*	*97*	*96*	*95*	*92*	*92*	*91*	*88*
			F	*96*	*92*	*91*	*91*	*90*	***90***	*89*	*89*	*89*	*88*
			R	*93*	*88*	*87*	*86*	*84*	*85*	*87*	*86*	*87*	*88*
		uniform	P	*100*	*96*	*96*	*97*	*96*	*95*	*92*	*92*	*91*	*88*
			F	*96*	*92*	*91*	*91*	*89*	***90***	*89*	*89*	*88*	*88*
			R	*92*	*88*	*87*	*86*	*83*	*85*	*86*	*86*	*85*	*88*

pairF1			$\lvert\mathfrak{C}\rvert$	1	2	3	4	5	6	7	8	9	10
prob	$\beta = .000075$	trained	P	*100*	*95*	*95*	*96*	*96*	*96*	*94*	*95*	*94*	*93*
			F	***99***	***94***	***93***	***92***	***92***	***91***	***92***	***92***	***91***	*90*
			R	*97*	*92*	*92*	*89*	*88*	*87*	*90*	*89*	*88*	*87*
		uniform	P	*100*	*95*	*95*	*96*	*97*	*96*	*94*	*96*	*94*	*94*
			F	***99***	***94***	***93***	***92***	*91*	*91*	*91*	*91*	*90*	***91***
			R	*97*	*92*	*91*	*89*	*86*	*85*	*88*	*87*	*85*	*87*
max	$\beta = 0$	trained	P	*100*	*96*	*96*	*97*	*96*	*95*	*92*	*90*	*89*	*87*
			F	*97*	*92*	*92*	*92*	*90*	*90*	*89*	*88*	*88*	*88*
			R	*94*	*89*	*88*	*87*	*84*	*85*	*87*	*86*	*86*	*89*
		uniform	P	*100*	*96*	*96*	*97*	*96*	*94*	*91*	*91*	*89*	*87*
			F	*97*	*92*	*92*	*91*	*89*	*89*	*89*	*85*	*87*	*88*
			R	*93*	*89*	*87*	*86*	*83*	*85*	*87*	*88*	*84*	*89*

Table 3: Results of the tuned method on the test portion, using bCube and pairF1 measure

order to investigate the influence of feature-type weighting, we test an 'opposed' weighting where the feature-type with the previously smallest weight is assigned the previously biggest weight, the feature-type with the previously biggest weight is assigned the previously smallest weight, and so on (see table 2). Results are clearly worse (see fig. 5), which shows that feature-type weighting is not completely irrelevant (in the sense that there are also counterproductive weightings). Furthermore, we use feature-type weighting to investigate the effect of single feature-types by on the one hand leaving them out (setting their weight to zero) and on the other using them exclusively (setting all others to zero). This analysis shows that most feature-types can be dropped (if they are the only one to be dropped) with the exception of co-authors (see fig. 11) and ref-authors. It is therefore interesting to see the results if only these two feature-types are used (see fig. 12). Performance is solid. The most important coreference indicators are co-author names, which might even be used alone (see fig. 9) . In a last experiment, we also test a weighting that selects only basic features of the document $d(x)$ (no features associated with the author mention x itself and no referenced authors). Results (fig. 13) are acceptable: F1 is not as good as before, but precision is high.

4.6 Discussion

A direct comparison of our experimental results to those obtained by other researchers is not possible. In fact such a comparison would almost certainly not be fair as evaluation results depend heavily on so many different factors that reproducibility is close to impossible under normal circumstances:

(1) *Dataset*: size, distribution of authors, version of data set, domain, availability of features, completeness of author name specification, hand-selected?, quality and amount of gold-annotation
(2) *Blocking scheme*: average size of blocks, unassigned names, overlapping blocks?
(3) *Evaluation measure*: general choice of measure, micro/macro average?, recall only inside block?, pair- or element-wise comparison?, counting pairs of equal mentions?, evaluated for different problem sizes?

It is therefore more than desirable to have a benchmark dataset with a framework that distinguishes clearly between *data*, *annotation*, *blocking*, *disambiguation* and *evaluation*. As a such benchmark is not available at a realistic scale like the Web of Science, we promote the paradigm to evaluate different problem sizes (number of clusters that need to be found) separately. This makes our results relatively robust against changes to many (not all) of the above mentioned factors. Unfortunately, this kind of evaluation can not be referenced from other publications that have worked on the Web of Science. Therefore, we base the assessment of the AD method proposed in this work on the fact that we were able to achieve results of more than 90% F1 for problem sizes of at least ten authors, which we find promising. Closely related work by Levin et al. [8] or Gurney et al. [4] does not report much higher values even though they do not separate the problems sizes so rigorously – which generally improves the results. However, we must note that Levin et al. cluster blocks of surname and first initial, while we use *all* initials. Therefore, they work with much larger problem sizes, which is computationally challenging and leads to more realistic estimation of recall, even if measured only within blocks. We hope that reporting results for individual problem sizes minimizes these distortions in the comparison.

5 CONCLUSIONS

In the following, we briefly summarize the main findings of our research: The best variant is using $p(C|\dot{C})$ instead of $p(C, \dot{C})$ with $\#(f)$ over the whole collection. Using maximum-of-products instead of sum-of-products constitutes a serious alternative. There are some hints that it might be even more precise (*'max prec.'* is slightly higher). Certainly, it runs significantly slower in our implementation, which is why we have not yet fully investigated potential gains of fine-tuning this variant. When tuning an appropriate stopping parameter, our method can deliver state-of-the-art results although being conceptionally simple. Even though feature-type weights learned in the classification scenario are quite heterogeneous, when applied in the clustering application, they do not perform better than uniformly distributed weights. We view this as a benefit of our model, as its score works well independent of any training. We hypothesize that the probabilities filter out unspecific features, thereby implicitly controlling feature weighting without any discriminative training. The stopping criterion needs to be tuned on some training set, but it is only a single variable per variant that needs to be fitted. This quality limit does remarkably well at finding an appropriate number of clusters to converge. Leaving out one feature-type at a time in the clustering score, we find that co-author names are the most important features. Apart from this, our method's performance is not dependent on the presence of specific feature-types. For example, a weighting where only the co-author names and the referenced author names are used performs well. Recording the results for each system clustering size $|\mathfrak{C}_{sys}|$ separately allows to precisely monitor the behavior of the clustering process. The plots created in this work also allow tuning precision vs. recall. This might be particularly interesting for digital libraries, as they might prefer precision over recall. Separate evaluation for each correct clustering size $|\mathfrak{C}_{cor}|$ shows how high the baseline of putting all mentions in a single cluster is for the frequent cases of $|\mathfrak{C}_{cor}| = 1$ or $|\mathfrak{C}_{cor}| = 2$. We conclude that, with larger problems not separated, an approach could easily be considered satisfying although only approximating this primitive baseline.

ACKNOWLEDGMENTS

This work was supported by the EU's Horizon 2020 programme under grant agreement H2020-693092, the MOVING project.

REFERENCES

[1] Aron Culotta, Pallika Kanani, Robert Hall, Michael Wick, and Andrew McCallum. 2007. Author disambiguation using error-driven machine learning with a ranking loss function. In *Sixth International Workshop on Information Integration on the Web (IIWeb-07), Vancouver, Canada.*

[2] Anderson A Ferreira, Marcos André Gonçalves, and Alberto HF Laender. 2012. A brief survey of automatic methods for author name disambiguation. *Acm Sigmod Record* 41, 2 (2012), 15–26.

[3] Anderson A Ferreira, Adriano Veloso, Marcos André Gonçalves, and Alberto HF Laender. 2010. Effective self-training author name disambiguation in scholarly digital libraries. In *Proceedings of the 10th annual joint conference on Digital libraries.* ACM, 39–48.

[4] Thomas Gurney, Edwin Horlings, and Peter Van Den Besselaar. 2012. Author disambiguation using multi-aspect similarity indicators. *Scientometrics* 91, 2 (2012), 435–449.

[5] Hui Han, Wei Xu, Hongyuan Zha, and C Lee Giles. 2005. A hierarchical naive Bayes mixture model for name disambiguation in author citations. In *Proceedings of the 2005 ACM symposium on Applied computing.* ACM, 1065–1069.

[6] Anne-Wil Harzing. 2015. Health warning: might contain multiple personalities - the problem of homonyms in Thomson Reuters Essential Science Indicators. *Scientometrics* 105, 3 (2015), 2259–2270.

[7] T. Kramer, F. Momeni, and P. Mayr. 2017. Coverage of Author Identifiers in Web of Science and Scopus. *ArXiv e-prints* (March 2017). arXiv:cs.DL/1703.01319

[8] Michael Levin, Stefan Krawczyk, Steven Bethard, and Dan Jurafsky. 2012. Citation-based bootstrapping for large-scale author disambiguation. *Journal of the American Society for Information Science and Technology* 63, 5 (2012), 1030–1047.

[9] Staša Milojević. 2013. Accuracy of simple, initials-based methods for author name disambiguation. *Journal of Informetrics* 7, 4 (2013), 767–773.

[10] Alan Filipe Santana, Marcos André Gonçalves, Alberto HF Laender, and Anderson A Ferreira. 2017. Incremental author name disambiguation by exploiting domain-specific heuristics. *Journal of the Association for Information Science and Technology* 68, 4 (2017), 931–945.

[11] Neil R Smalheiser and Vetle I Torvik. 2009. Author name disambiguation. *Annual review of information science and technology* 43, 1 (2009), 1–43.

[12] Yang Song, Jian Huang, Isaac G Councill, Jia Li, and C Lee Giles. 2007. Efficient topic-based unsupervised name disambiguation. In *Proceedings of the 7th ACM/IEEE-CS joint conference on Digital libraries.* ACM, 342–351.

[13] Andreas Strotmann and Dangzhi Zhao. 2012. Author name disambiguation: What difference does it make in author-based citation analysis? *Journal of the American Society for Information Science and Technology* 63, 9 (2012), 1820–1833.

[14] Jie Tang, Alvis CM Fong, Bo Wang, and Jing Zhang. 2012. A unified probabilistic framework for name disambiguation in digital library. *IEEE Transactions on Knowledge and Data Engineering* 24, 6 (2012), 975–987.

[15] Vetle I Torvik and Neil R Smalheiser. 2009. Author name disambiguation in MEDLINE. *ACM Transactions on Knowledge Discovery from Data (TKDD)* 3, 3 (2009), 11.

[16] Vetle I Torvik, Marc Weeber, Don R Swanson, and Neil R Smalheiser. 2005. A probabilistic similarity metric for Medline records: A model for author name disambiguation. *Journal of the American Society for information science and technology* 56, 2 (2005), 140–158.

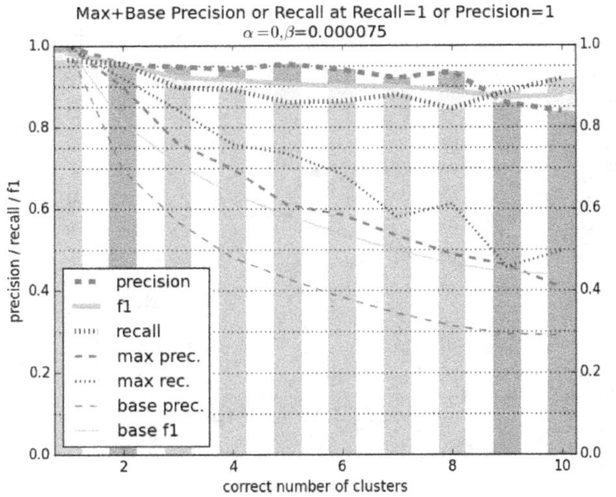

Figure 3: Results for trained weights λ;using *prob* variant

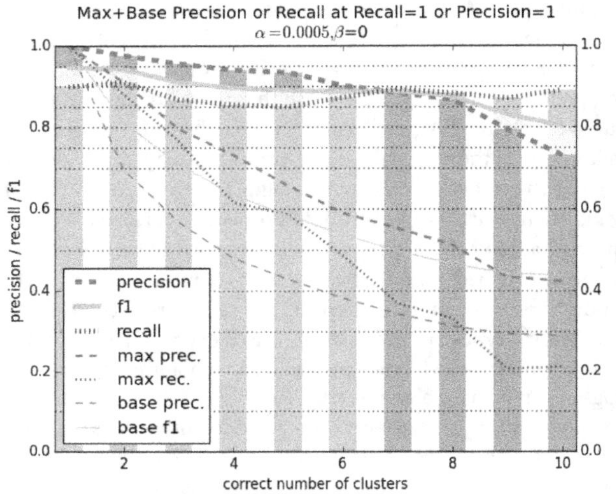

Figure 4: Results for trained weights λ; using *max* variant

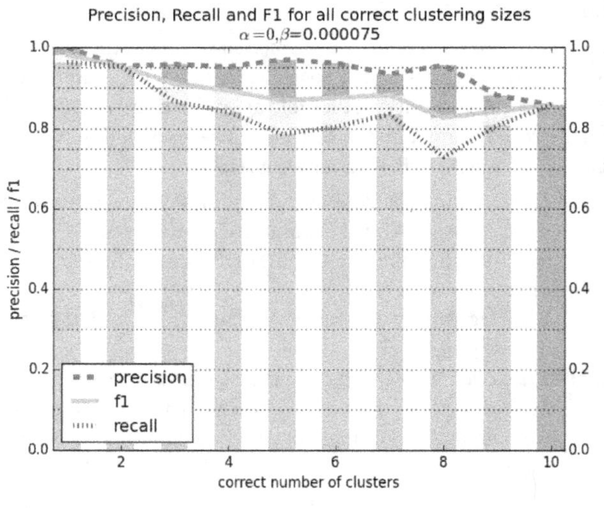

Figure 5: Results for opposed weights (compare figure 3)

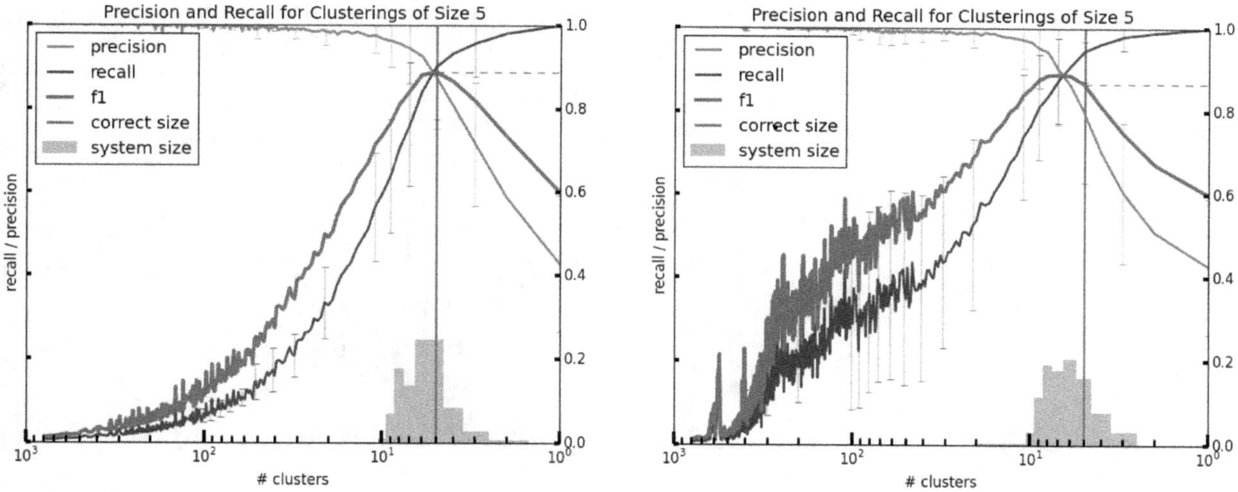

Figure 6: The clustering process visualised for trained weights λ; comparing *max* and *prob* variant; $|\mathfrak{C}| = 5$

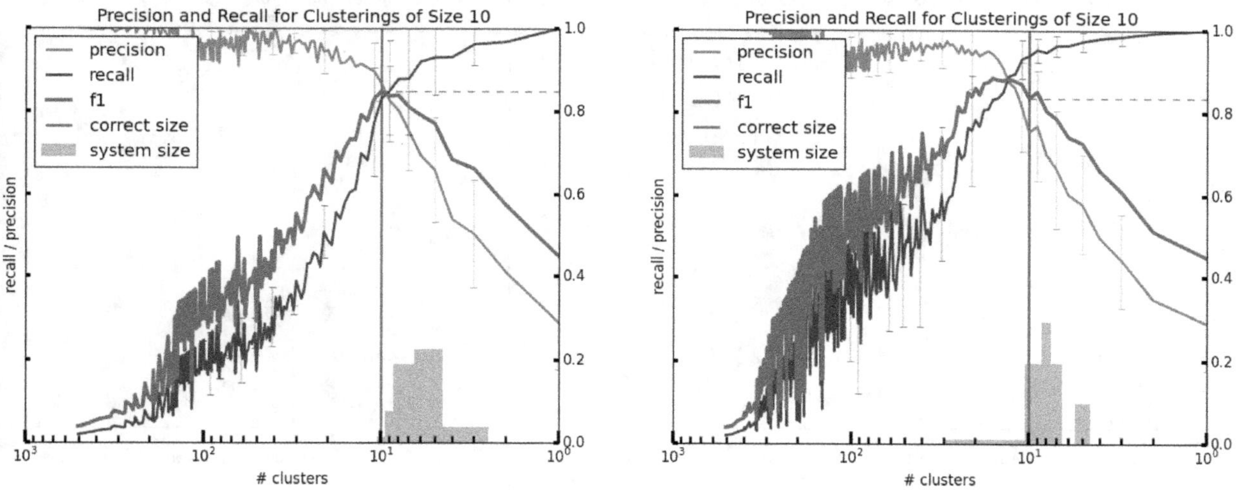

Figure 7: The clustering process visualised for trained weights λ; comparing *max* and *prob* variant; $|\mathfrak{C}| = 10$

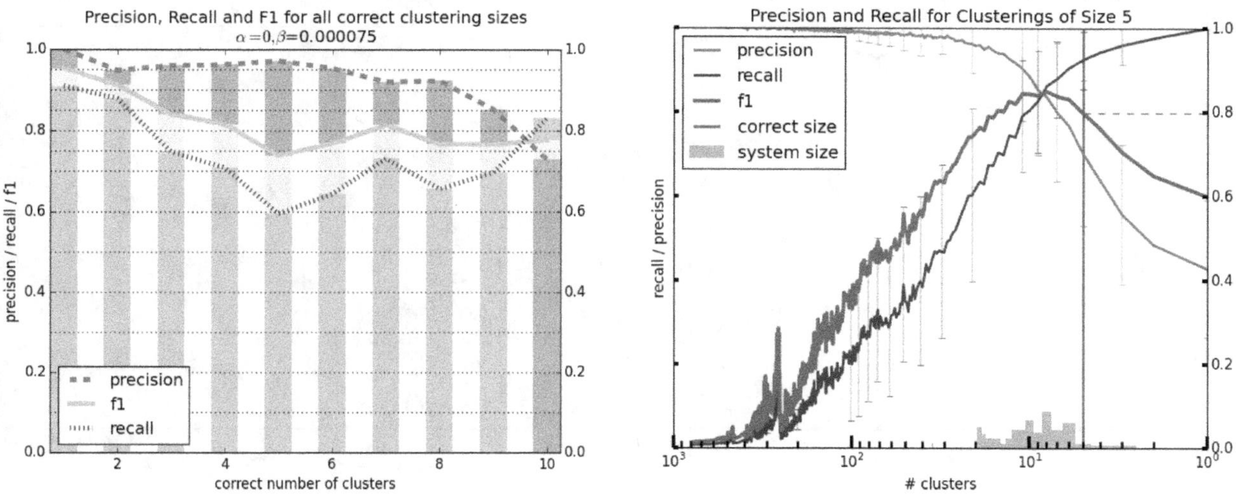

Figure 8: Selecting only terms as features; results and details of the clustering process for $|\mathfrak{C}| = 5$

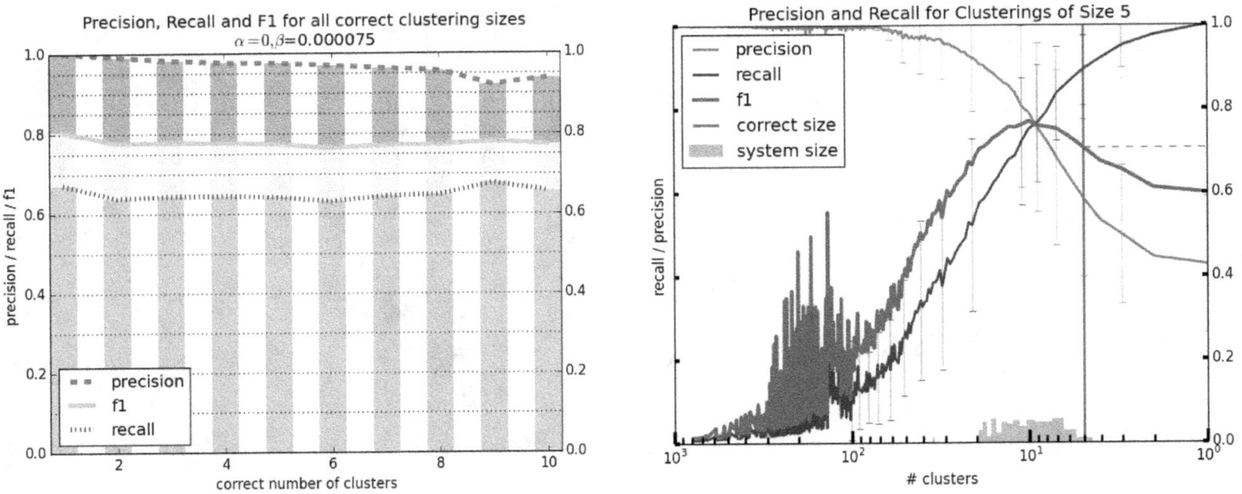

Figure 9: Selecting only co-authors as features; results and details for $|\mathfrak{C}| = 5$

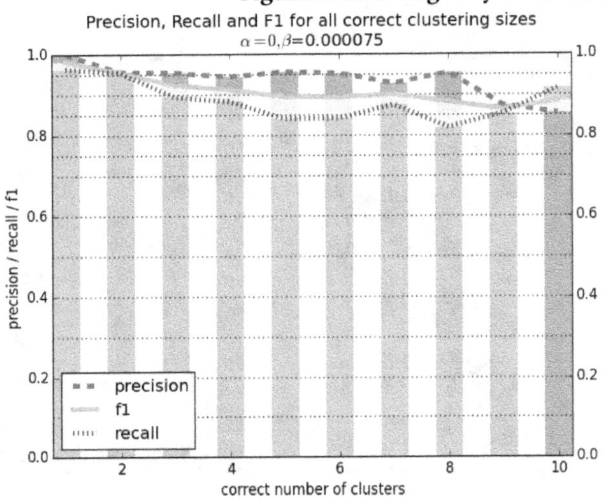

Figure 10: Results for uniform weights (compare figure 3)

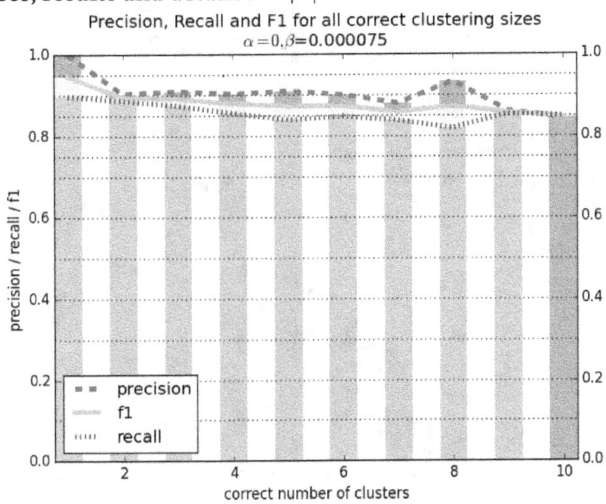

Figure 12: Only co- and referenced authors (compare fig. 3)

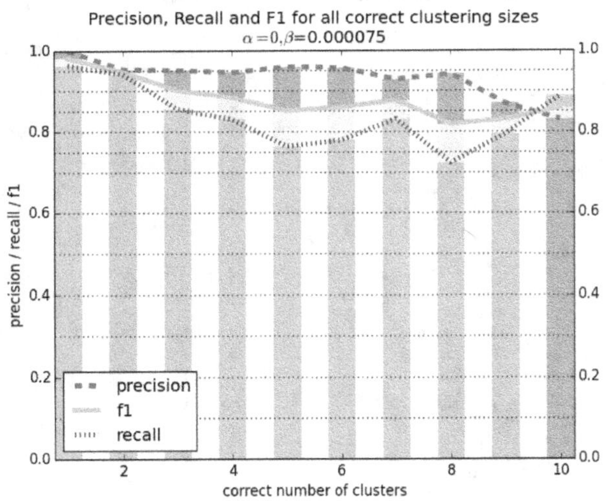

Figure 11: Leaving out co-authors (compare figure 3)

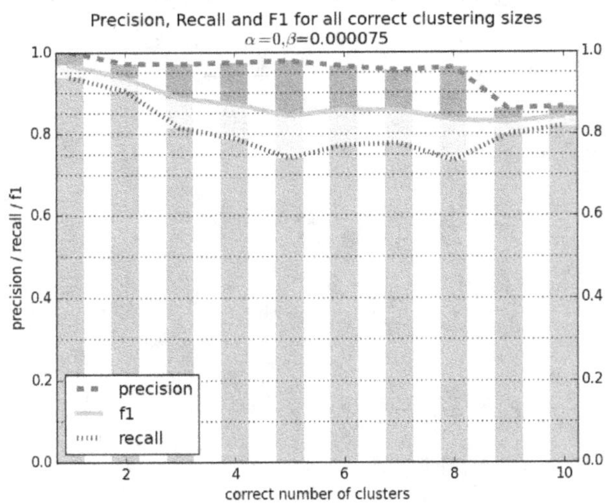

Figure 13: No author-specific features (compare figure 3)

Digital History meets Microblogging: Analyzing Collective Memories in Twitter

Yasunobu Sumikawa*
University Education Center,
Tokyo Metropolitan University
ysumikawa@acm.org

Adam Jatowt
Dept. of Social Informatics,
Kyoto University
adam@dl.kuis.kyoto-u.ac.jp

Marten Düring
Luxembourg Centre for
Contemporary and Digital History
marten.during@uni.lu

ABSTRACT

Microblogging platforms can offer good opportunities to study how and when people refer to the past, in which context such references appear and what purposes they serve. However, this area still remains unexplored. In this paper we report the results of a large scale exploratory analysis of history-focused references in microblogs based on 11-months long snapshot of Twitter data. Besides understanding the nature of history-focused content sharing in microblogs, the results of this study can be used for designing content recommendation systems and could help to improve time aware search applications.

KEYWORDS

social media analysis; history; collective memory; Twitter

ACM Reference Format:
Yasunobu Sumikawa, Adam Jatowt, and Marten Düring. 2018. Digital History meets Microblogging: Analyzing Collective Memories in Twitter. In *JCDL '18: The 18th ACM/IEEE Joint Conference on Digital Libraries, June 3–7, 2018, Fort Worth, TX, USA.* ACM, New York, NY, USA, 10 pages. https://doi.org/10.1145/3197026.3197057

1 INTRODUCTION

Having good knowledge and comprehension of history is important for a variety of reasons: History is commonly believed to play significant roles in our society: First, to help us understand the processes which shape the present and thereby enable us to actively take part in contemporary society. Second, to be the basis for the development of coherent identities. Third, as a means to give meaning and orientation with regard to the past. Others argue that history opens up perspectives for the future and provides support for decision making [1, 10]. As such, history remains one of the fundamental subjects taught from elementary schools onwards.

Social media has been commonly utilized to study public attitudes towards real time events such as the US American elections [19]. Yet, similarly to other media, microblogs are also used for sharing and finding information related to the past, sometimes to distant past. This offers unique opportunities for computational studies on explicit references to past events and opens up novel perspectives for the study of collective memories as well as the pursuit of public history.

While computational collective memory studies have already been conducted on news articles [2, 6] and Wikipedia [8, 9, 15, 16], with regard to microblogging, so far we are only aware of one ongoing project which focuses on the First World War [5] and compares commemorative cultures across countries. We then attempt at filling this gap by focusing on Twitter as a common social media platform frequently used in the computational social science. Our analysis has exploratory character and aims to provide initial and broad investigation of history-related content sharing in social networks.

Among others our study is guided by the following questions:

(1) How do people refer to history in microblogs?
(2) What is the time horizon of history-related references?
(3) How are collective memories expressed in Twitter?
(4) What are the key remembered events and entities?

We approach these and other questions by investigating portions of tweet messages generated from March 2016 to February 2017 and tagged with hashtags which indicate a strong relation to historical events. In particular, we apply a bootstrapping approach to discover related hashtags, which allowed us to collect close to 1 million tweets with explicit references to past events and entities.

Based on the collected data we investigate the distinguishing characteristics of tweets which are related to the past. Among the aspects we research are time horizons, concerned entities and popularities of hashtags. Furthermore, we propose a novel categorization scheme of hashtags as well as perform deeper investigation of the characteristics of the hashtag categories (Sec. 5). By this we try to organize and provide structure to the portion of user activities that relate to referencing, appreciating and sharing information on historical events and entities in social network services.

Besides being a novel approach towards the general question on how the past relates to our lives, our investigations can be beneficial to several applications. First, the *construction of specialized content detection and recommendation systems* can be informed by the reported results. The objective of such systems would be to facilitate sharing of historical knowledge. Historical content recommendation based on social media offers an interesting and informal environment for learning history. Understanding the types of popular shared content and the context of sharing can be helpful for designing effective recommendation systems. Indeed several projects already use social platforms like Twitter to stimulate interest in history and for teaching exercises [1].

*This research was performed while the first author was at Tokyo University of Science, Japan.

[1] https://twitter.com/RealTimeWWII, https://twitter.com/civilwarwp, https://twitter.com/1948War, https://twitter.com/samuelpepys

JCDL '18, June 3–7, 2018, Fort Worth, TX, USA

ACM ISBN 978-1-4503-5178-2/18/06...$15.00
https://doi.org/10.1145/3197026.3197057

Automatic content creation, especially, in the form of *conversing history-focused chatbots* could be another appealing idea. Tweets thanks to their short content and the effective means of measuring their popularity or attractiveness (e.g., retweet counts and analysis of user responses) are useful source of data for such systems.

Many history- and memory-focused tweets are triggered by current events or entities. Studying their formation and fluctuations of their popularity could be useful for understanding the conditions and circumstances for enabling "*historification*" of present texts. This means offering *access to relevant historical references and grounding for the present events and topics.*

To sum up we make the following contributions in this paper:

(1) To the best of our knowledge we are the first to study how users refer to history in microblogging based on large scale analysis.
(2) We provide novel findings which offer a better understanding of how collective memories are maintained and formed in microblogging.
(3) We propose new categorization of historical references in Twitter.
(4) We outline novel research directions and potential applications that can utilize history-related content in microblogs.

The remainder of this paper is structured as follows. In the next section we present related work. In Section 3 we describe the data collection and processing. Section 4 provides the findings of the general analysis, while the following section proposes our novel categorization of hashtags and details the results of the related study. We then include discussions in the Section 6. Finally, the last section concludes the paper and outlines future work.

2 RELATED WORK

The concept of *collective memory* (*social memory*) popularized by Halbwachs [11, 12] describes the shared reflection of the past within social groups. Collective memory can be contrasted with the concept of *collective amnesia* defined by Jacoby [14] as forceful or unconscious suppressions of memories, especially, those related to disgraceful or inconvenient events. In a similar fashion to personal memory [7], social memory is known to thin out over time and to be subject to temporal variations following the occurrence of memory triggers such as sudden events or anniversaries [2, 16, 17]. Studies of collective memory can help us to understand the mechanisms of forgetting and remembering as well as explain the role of the history and the past in our lives. In addition, they have direct implications on the archival selection by memory institutions such as national or dedicated archives [17]. Traditionally, research on collective memory has been based on small-scale investigations of personal accounts and the activities of political and cultural institutions. There is little literature on the use of computational approaches for the quantification of the characteristics of social memory over large text datasets. Cook *et al.* [6] investigated the decay of fame over time on the basis of the collection of news articles that spans 20th century. Au Yeung and Jatowt [2] have studied memory decay and the way in which past years are remembered based on the dataset of English news articles spanning 90 years. When it comes to other document genres, Ferron and Massa [8] and Kanhabua *et al.* [16] proposed to use Wikipedia as a global memory space. However, differently to our work they focused on memory triggers that cause forgotten or vaguely remembered events to be brought back into social attention. Anniversaries are natural examples of memory triggers. In another case, current events may also serve as triggers of the memories of similar, past events. Our work can be seen as complementary to the above mentioned researches.

Table 1: Dataset statistics.

Number of history-related hashtags	147
Number of tweets	888,251
Period of timestamps	8 Mar. 2016 – 24 Feb. 2017
Period of time references	8156 BC – 2029
Number of tweets with time references	357,682
Number of users	390,106
Number of URLs	204,075
Number of tweets with URLs	404,136

To the best of our knowledge only one work focuses on microblogging scenarios in which commemoration of the First World War [5] is studied in relation to diverse countries. In contrast, we use relatively large size data (at least, when it comes to history-related studies) and we investigate many unknown aspects ranging from the types of references, intensity of remembering, key entities, dates, temporal patterns and so on.

3 DATA COLLECTION

This section describes the data collection and preprocessing procedures as well as general statistics of the dataset used for analysis. The key statistics of the collected data are summarized in Tab. 1.

Collecting hashtags and tweets. To collect tweets that refer to the past or are related to collective memory of historical events/entities, we performed hashtag based crawl together with bootstrapping procedure. At the beginning, we gathered several historical hashtags selected by experts (e.g. `#history`, `#WmnHist`, `#HistoryTeacher`) [2]. In addition, we prepared several hashtags that are commonly used when referring to the past: `#onthisday`, `#throwbackthursday`, `#historicalevent`, `#thisdayinhistory`, `#otd`. We then collected tweets that contain these hashtags by using Twitter's official API[3].

The collected tweets were issued from 8 March 2016 to 24 February 2017. To increase the coverage, we applied bootstrapping to search for other hashtags frequently used with the seed hashtags. The tweets tagged by such hashtags were then included into the seed set after the manual inspection of all the discovered hashtags as of their relation to the history. In total, we gathered 147 history-related hashtags which allowed us to collect 888,251 tweets [4]. We show the complete list of the hashtags in Tab. 6.

Extracting time-references. We extracted *time-references* from tweet content. Two categories of temporal references are typically distinguished based on the common distinction of temporal expressions in IR and NLP [4]: *explicit* and *implicit* temporal expressions. The former one is a concrete time point or time period, such as "1945" or "1980s", while the latter is a relative temporal expression such as "yesterday" or "two years ago". We use both types of temporal references in our study and, so, we convert all implicit (relative)

[2]http://blog.historians.org/2013/08/history-hashtags-exploring-a-visual-network-of-twitterstorians/
[3]https://dev.twitter.com/rest/public
[4]Ids of tweets analyzed in this paper are available in http://tk2-222-20713.vs.sakura.ne.jp/jcdl_2018_target_tweet_ids.txt

temporal expressions to the explicit (absolute) ones. To extract both the types of time references, we use Heideltime [18], which is a temporal tagger with a specialized option for tweet processing. Heideltime outputs normalized temporal expressions according to the TIMEX3 annotation standard. In total, we have found over 357k tweets with temporal expressions which represents 40% of the dataset. [5]

4 GENERAL ANALYSIS

In this section, we first investigate characteristic features of history-related tweets based on three data types: time expressions, entities and hashtags.

4.1 Temporal Analysis

> Q. What is the character of memory decay?
> Q. Which years are strongly remembered in particular?

We first analyze which time periods users are interested in by investigating time references included in tweets. We map all the extracted temporal expressions on timeline as shown in Fig. 1. We call the curve in Fig. 1, the *remembering curve* as it reflects the strength of the collective attention of users towards different time periods of history. To plot such a curve, we converted the extracted temporal references to probability distributions over their corresponding timespans using year level granularity. In other words, for a given time reference (e.g., 1960s) with t_b denoting its start year (1960) and t_e indicating its end year (1969) we set the probability distribution with zero values for $t < t_b$ and for $t > t_e$ (e.g., before 1960 and after 1969) and with non-zero values for $t_b \leq t \leq t_e$ that sum to 1 (e.g., 1/10 for each year from 1960 to 1969). We then combined for every year all the computed probability distributions based on all the tweets in our dataset. The formal definition of the probability distribution for a year y is given in Eq. (1).

$$S(y) = \sum_{[t_b, t_e] \in T} \delta(y, [t_b, t_e]) * \frac{1}{t_e - t_b + 1} \quad (1)$$

where T includes all the extracted time references, and the function δ returns 1 if the first argument is included in the second argument; otherwise, it returns 0.

Looking at Fig. 1 (especially, at the zoomed out plot in the inner graph), we can see that the number of time references is usually rapidly increasing towards the present (neglecting short-term disturbances caused by key events to be discussed later). In general, *the recent past is referred to more than the distant past, and the memory decay is fastest in the recent years.* This is intuitive and correlates with the corresponding study conducted on news articles related to different countries [2].

Several significant peaks are visible in Fig. 1 which represent two key events in the last century: WWI and WWII, and year 2016. Two dates common for WWII are: 1941 denoting the Pearl Harbor attack and the subsequent participation of USA in the war, and 1945 which is related to the Normandy landing and the end of the war. While

[5]Note that some tweets contain abbreviated temporal expressions (e.g., 6/11/16 or 3/19/88). As Heideltime adds for such expressions "00" at the head of year information (e.g., 0016, 0088) we converted "00" to "19" or to "20" depending on whether the last two digits are less (conversion to 20) or more than 17 (conversion to 19).

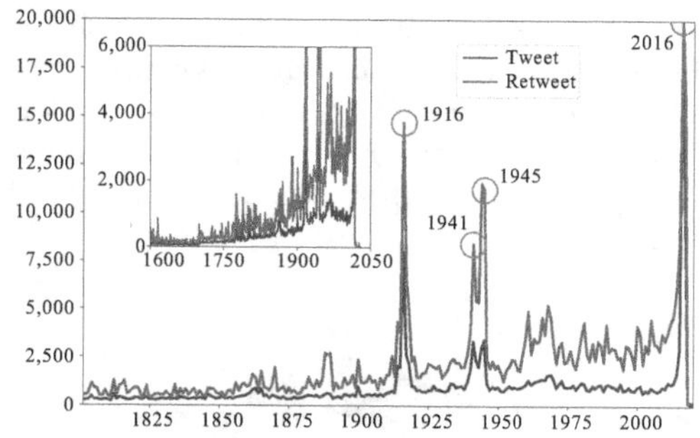

Figure 1: Distribution of time references in tweets. The peaks are in years 1916, 1941, 1945 and 2016.

WWII started in fact earlier with the Nazi invasion on Poland in 1939, many history-related tweets in our dataset originate from USA and Canada due to the chosen English hashtags resulting in the focus on the North American involvement in the war. This can be confirmed when looking at Fig. 2 that shows the most common entities corresponding to the peaks and at Fig. 4 which lists the top entities in our dataset. In this work we employ AIDA [13] - an annotation tool linking phrases in short text with their corresponding Wikipedia articles - for detecting entities.

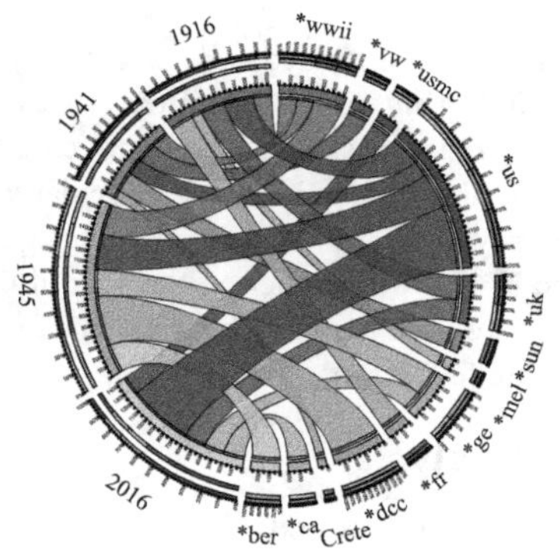

Figure 2: Top entities associated with the four peaks of Fig. 1. "*" is used to denote abbreviations made for saving space (*wwii: World War II , *vw: Virginia Woolf, *usmc: United States Marine Corps, *us: United States, *uk: United Kingdom, *sun: The Sun News-Pictorial, *mel:Melbourne, *ge: Germany, *fr: France, *dcc: Dachau Concentration Camp, *ca: Canada, * ber: Berlin).

Fig. 3 shows the most common hashtags used with content containing the peak years of Fig. 1. We can notice that 1916 and 1941, 1945 have strong connection with hashtags `#ww1` and `#wwii` as the two events were held during these respective years. Interestingly, Fig. 3 shows that there are many mentions of 2016 with `#ww1`. This is because 2016 marked the 100th anniversary of the Battle of Verdun which is especially remembered due to its estimated nearly 1 million casualties. In the same year (1916) another remarkable event occurred - the British Army suffered its worst day with the loss of 19,240 men in the Battle of Somme (hence, the hashtag `#somme100`).

These events together with the Easter Rising of Irish republicans against British occupation in Dublin are ones of the primary causes for the strong remembrance of 1916. The round anniversary in 2016 especially amplified this remembering; hence, the corresponding peak in Fig. 1 is even higher than the subsequent peaks associated with WWII.

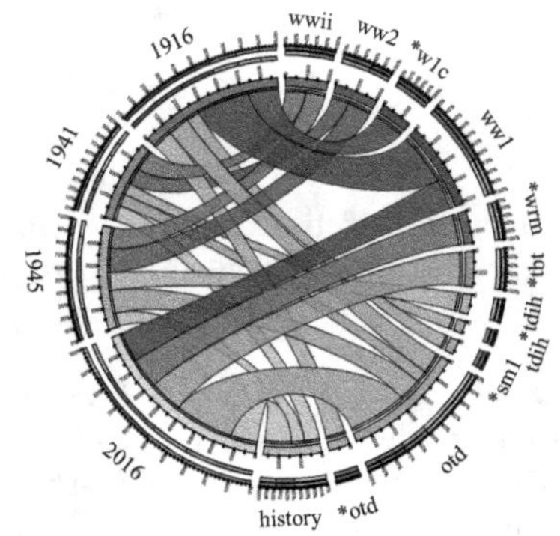

Figure 3: Top hashtags associated with the four peaks of Fig. 1. "*" is used to indicate abbreviations made for saving space (*w1c: #ww1centenary, *wrm: #weremember, *tbt: #throwbackthursday, *tdih: #thisdayinhistory, *sm1: #somme100, *otd: #onthisday).

Finally, as shown in Fig. 3 #otd and #onthisday are commonly used labels for indicating historical content that occurred on the same calendar day in the past. Past-to-present connection through the reference to a calendar day is in fact a popular way of recalling past events and is typically used in newspapers (e.g., sections about events reported in "our newspaper on this day in the past"). #otd and #onthisday are hashtag-based mechanisms for indicating this type of connection in Twitter.

4.2 Entity Analysis

> Q. Which types of entities and which entities in particular tend to be remembered?
> Q. Which past and present entities are compared or mentioned together?

We now look into entities referred to in tweets as, often, a particular entity such as a person or an event is what society remembers strongly from the past.

4.2.1 Entity Popularity and Type. We first count the number of times a given entity is mentioned in tweets. Fig. 4 lists the top frequent 30 entities overall. In these top 30 entities, there are 22 countries, regions, or cities, two historical events (WWI and WWII), three persons (Adolf Hitler, Abraham Lincoln, and Donald Trump), and three other kinds of entities. Location entity type tends to be then most frequently mentioned within the group of the top common entities. This is because places are key constructs helping to locate the occurrence of events, indicate locations of historical buildings or areas where famous people lived, as well as they form a kind of a "bridge" between the past and the present by existing across long time periods.

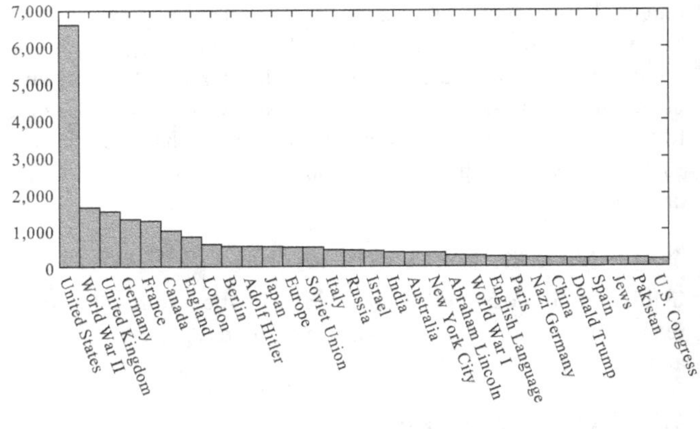

Figure 4: Top 30 entities mentioned in the dataset.

To thoroughly investigate entities and their types, we next automatically map all the entities into DBpedia [3] to obtain their type assignments. We then divide all the entities into five major types (Person, Group, Place, Event, and Others), and show their rates in Fig. 5. It can be noticed that *persons, places and groups tend to be frequently mentioned in history-focused tweets and the person category is especially common.* Note that while places were the most common entity type in the set of the top frequently mentioned entities as indicated in Fig. 4, they are actually less common than persons when all the entities in our dataset are concerned.

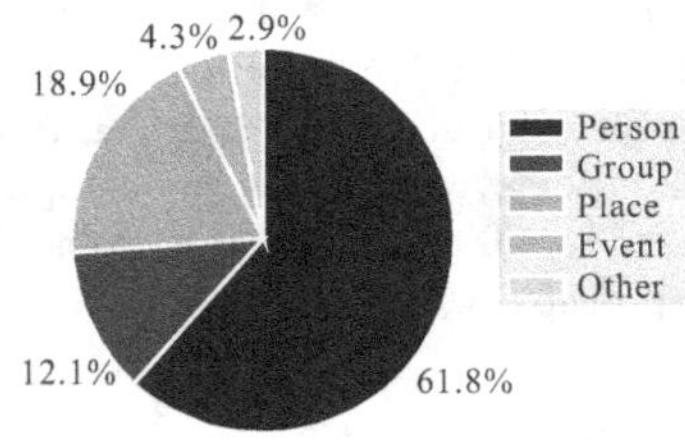

Figure 5: Rate of different types of entities.

To give some examples of entities, Tab. 2 lists the top 10 entities for the Person, Group and Event types[6]. As most of the tweets were posted in 2016 when the United States presidential election was held, the names of the five US presidents (Abraham Lincoln, Donald Trump, Bill Clinton, Barack Obama, and George Washington) appear within the top 10 persons. As for the events, wars and battles are the prevailing type. Interestingly, groups include many military units (e.g., U.S. Army, Royal Air force), *which also suggest the significant focus on wars and conflicts from the past.*

4.2.2 Connection of Past and Present Entities. The issue of connecting present and past entities is especially interesting as it relates to the notion of "usable history". Historical entities can be used for a variety of reasons, for example, for comparison with present entities or present context, for emphasizing analogy, making predictions and so on. To analyze the way in which past entities are utilized in connection to the present ones we first need to distinguish present from past entities, which is of course not straightforward. We apply

[6] Location examples can be seen in Tab. 5.

Table 2: Top 10 entities of persons, groups, and events.

Person	Group	Event
Adolf Hitler	Jews	World War II
Abraham Lincoln	U.S. Congress	World War I
Donald Trump	Royal Navy	Vietnam War
Sharon Corr	U.S. Army	Battles of Saratoga
Bill Clinton	U.S. House of Representatives	Battle of Verdun
Alan Evans	Luftwaffe	American Revolutionary War
Barack Obama	Royal Air Force	Korean War
Napoleon	U.S. Navy	Omaha Beach
George Washington	BBC	Cinco de Mayo
Jerrard Tickell	Federal Bureau of Investigation	Battle of Gettysburg

a simple division rule, according to which, an entity is regarded as a *past entity* if the end of its lifetime[7] (e.g., life, event duration) falls within the last millennium. We are aware that this may be seen arbitrary, yet, we had to set some threshold to carry out the analysis, and the turnover of the millennium seemed like a good choice for a temporal landmark. Entity lifetimes were collected from DBpedia [8].

First, in Tab. 3, we compare the sizes of the past and present entity sets extracted from our dataset. We can observe that the number of unique past entities extracted by AIDA and typed by DBpedia is relatively large constituting roughly half of that of the present entities. This confirms that our dataset is specifically focused on history.

Table 3: Sizes of the past and present entity sets.

	Total	Person	Group	Place	Event
Size of the past entity set	8,262	6,368	1,257	746	637
Size of the present entity set	16,355	10,858	4,723	340	774

We plot in in Fig. 6 conditional probabilities based on the studied entity types to understand how often the different types appear given another entity of a given type. We can observe that *present places tend to co-occur with entities of any other type. Especially, many past entities tend to appear together with present places.* Furthermore, $P(PresentPerson|PresentEvent)$ has relatively high value which is understandable. Finally, if a past place, such as "Nazi Germany" and "Holy Roman Empire", is in a tweet, past persons or past events tend to occur as well. This is also expected. Interestingly, past places are often mentioned with present places as well (supposedly for emphasizing place continuity, spatial relations or for place-oriented comparisons).

Next, in Tab. 4 we take the top 5 common present persons (column "Entity" in the top part of the table), the top 5 common past persons (column "Entity" in the middle part of the table), and the top 5 common past events (column "Entity" in the bottom part of the table). We then output in columns "1", "2" and "3" their top 3 most often co-occurring entities from the opposite time frame. In particular, if the "Entity" column contains past entities then in columns "1", "2" and "3" we show their top co-occurring present entities. Otherwise, we show past entities. When looking at past persons and past events, one can observe that indeed present places commonly co-occur with them. For example, for the top 5 past persons, their most common co-occurring entities contain 8 countries and 1 city, while for the past events the corresponding number of locations is 12. Apparently, when recalling past persons and past events users tend to also mention where the persons lived or where the events occurred, thus, "grounding" them in spatial dimension.

Finally, Tab. 5 lists past entities co-occurring with the top frequent locations, from where again the significance of WWII in relation to collective memories of many countries can be observed.

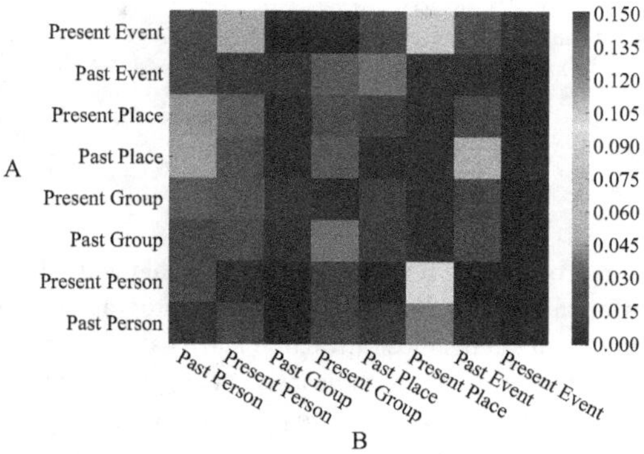

Figure 6: Conditional probabilities $P(B|A)$ of entity type on x axis (in column) given the presence of entity type on y axis (in row).

Table 4: Top 5 present, top 5 past persons and top 5 past events (given in "Entity" column) with their top 3 co-occurring past/present entities of any type. "-" denotes cases when no corresponding entity can be found.

	Rank	Entity	1	2	3
Present person	1	Donald Trump	Adolf Hitler	Abraham Lincoln	Nazi Germany
	2	Sharon Corr	-	-	-
	3	Bill Clinton	Charles Frankel	Nazi Germany	World War II
	4	Barack Obama	Muhammad Ali of Egypt	Adolf Hitler	-
	5	Elizabeth II	James II of England	George Washington	-
Past person	1	Adolf Hitler	Germany	Donald Trump	United States
	2	Abraham Lincoln	United States	Donald Trump	Israel
	3	Alan Evans	-	-	-
	4	Napoleon	France	United Kingdom	Italy
	5	George Washington	United States	Philadelphia	Martin Scorsese
Past event	1	World War II	United States	United Kingdom	France
	2	World War I	United States	Canada	United Kingdom
	3	Vietnam War	United States	CBS	Canada
	4	Battles of Saratoga	United States	-	-
	5	Battle of Verdun	France	Germany	United Kingdom

4.3 Hashtag Analysis

Q. What are the most popular hashtags?

In this section we investigate popularity patterns of hashtags. Hashtags are commonly used to indicate specific themes of tweets allowing others to find them. First, Fig. 7 (a) shows the top frequently used hashtags based on their tweet counts. We also list the top hashtags ranked by the retweet count in Fig. 7 (b) and by the number of Twitter accounts from which the tweets originate in Fig. 7 (c). From these data, we can observe that `#throwbackthursday`,

[7] For currently valid entities such as currently alive persons the end of their lifetimes is set to the current year.

[8] We use "birthDate" and "deathDate" for person entities, "formationDate" and "dissolutionDate" for groups, and "foundingDate" and "dissolutionDate" for locations.

Table 5: Top 10 locations and their top 3 co-occurring past entities of any type. The abbreviated names of entities are for: Helen Farnsworth Mears (H. F. Mears) and Dominion of Newfoundland (Dom. of Newfoundland).

Rank	Present locations	1	2	3
1	United States	World War II	Battles of Saratoga	Soviet Union
2	United Kingdom	World War II	James II of England	Soviet Union
3	Germany	Adolf Hitler	John Cudahy	Soviet Union
4	France	World War II	Napoleon	Louis XIV of France
5	Canada	World War II	World War I	Dom. of Newfoundland
6	Japan	World War II	H. F. Mears	Hideki Tojo
7	Italy	Holy Roman Empire	World War II	Battle of Monte Cassino
8	Russia	World War II	Catherine the Great	Nicholas I of Russia
9	Israel	World War II	Nazi Germany	Vichy France
10	India	Vasco Da Gama	Edwin Lutyens	World War II

which is representative for a trend among social media sites including Twitter and Facebook to post own past photographs (often from one's childhood), gains most attraction across all these dimensions of popularity. The tweets with hashtag `#throwbackthursday` and similar ones predominantly refer to personal experiences and these hashtags are used by large number of users. Another observation is that *Fig. 7 (a) shows that* `#onthisday`, `#otd` *are present in a relatively large number of tweets and retweets, yet, they are used by fewer accounts. Unlike* `#throwbackthursday`, *these hashtags tend to be used by specialists (often historians and scientists from related areas) who select and disseminate interesting content about the past.* This content then triggers relatively *high engagement from other users as evidenced by the high retweet popularity of* `#onthisday`, `#otd` *in Fig. 7 (b).* We note that the demographics analysis should provide many more interesting insights regarding typical profiles of posting users, and is going to form the part of our future work.

5 CATEGORY BASED ANALYSIS

Q. How can past-related tweets be categorized and arranged?
Q. What kinds of semantic categories hashtags can be grouped into?
Q. What are the characteristics of these categories?

5.1 Definitions

In this section we introduce our categorization scheme of hashtags. The objective is to determine key types of history references. Based on the proposed categories automatic classifiers could be built to allocate tweets into different classes. Automatically labeling tweets could be then used for improving content retrieval, recommendation or for further analysis that would lead to better understanding of history-related interest and content sharing. Based on manual investigation of a large sample of tweets, we propose the following categories:

1. **General History** : hashtags used in general to broadly identify history-related tweets that do not fall into any specific type (e.g., `#history`, `#historyfacts`).
2. **National or Regional History** : hashtags annotating tweets which describe national or regional histories, for example, `#canadianhistory` or `#ushistory` including also past names of locations (e.g., `#ancientgreece`).
3. **Facet-focused History** : hashtags which relate to particular thematic facets of history (e.g., `#sporthistory`, `#arthistory`).
4. **General Commemoration** : hashtags that contain tweets commemorating or recalling a certain day or period (often somehow related to the day of tweet posting), or unspecified entities, such as `#onthisday`, `#otd`, `#todayweremember`, `#4yearsago` and `#rememberthem`.
5. **Historical Events** : hashtags related to particular events in the past (e.g., `#wwi`, `#sevenyearswar`).
6. **Historical Entities** : hashtags denoting references to specific entities such as persons, organizations or objects (e.g., `#stalin`, `#napoleon`).

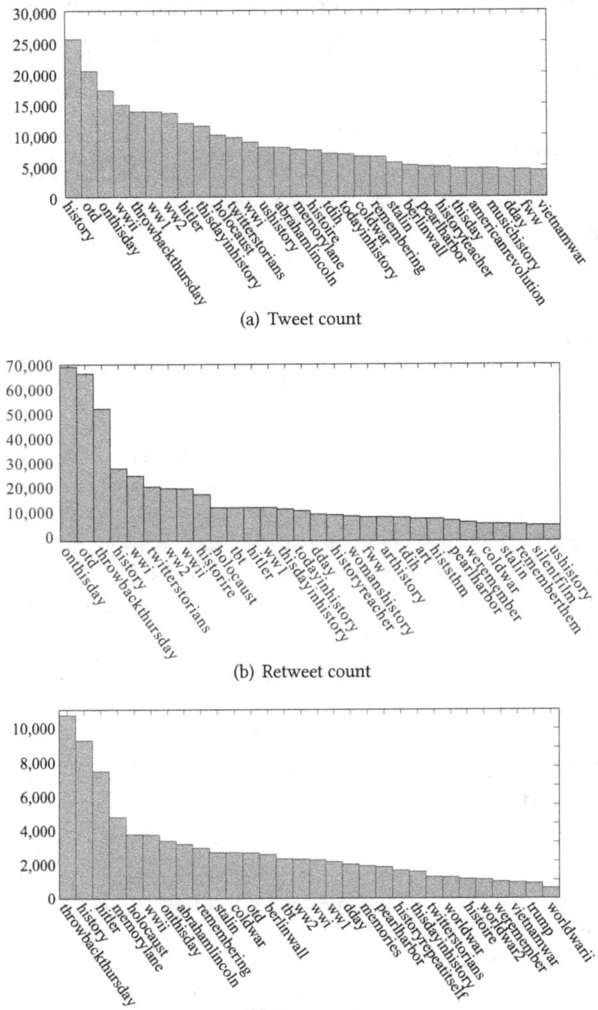

(a) Tweet count

(b) Retweet count

(c) User count

Figure 7: Top 30 popular hashtags by counts of tweets, retweets and users.

Tab. 6 shows our assignment of all the history-related hashtags found within the dataset into these categories. Note that hashtags

Table 6: Collected hashtags and their categories.

Category	Hashtags
General History	history, historyfacts, oldpicture, historyteacher, memorylane, histoire, twitterstorians, historicalcontext, colorization, memories, oldphoto, earlymodern, historicalevent, worldhistory, twitterstorian, historynerd, histedchat, historyfeed, archives, historymatters
National or Regional History	canadianhistory, ushistory, histoireducanada, jewishhistory, nazigermany, ottoman, cdnhistory, dchistory, cdnhist, thirdreich, tohistory, mdhistory, bchist, abhistory, vthistory, britishhistory, ancientchina, ancientegypt, ancientgreece, americanhistory, thisiscanadashistory, ottomanempire, ontariohistory, earlyamhistory, japanhistory, japanesehistory, chinesehistory, localhistory
Facet-focused History	blackfacts, histoiremiliterre, wmnshist, arthistory, sporthistory, womenshistory, navalhistory, presidentialhistory, musichistory, militaryhistory, blackhistory, envhist, histmed, wmnhist, todayintennishistory, todayinblackhistory, ibhistory, u2history, historythroughcoins, histSTM, silentfilm, historyscience, histsci, digitalhistory, foodhistory, histmonast, histnursing, histgender, histtech
General Commemoration	onthisday, otd, otdh, thisdayin, thisdayinhistory, todayinHistory, tdih, onthisdayinhistory, otdih, 100yearsago, thisday, lessthan100yearsago, todayweremember, titanicremembranceday, weremember, 100yearsago, remembering, wewillrememberthem, rememberthem, remembranceday, historyrepeatsitself, throwbackthursday, tbt
Historical Events	1ww, gulfwar, ColdWar, ww2, ww1, worldwar, worldwarii, vietnamwar, worldwar2, worldwartwo, veday, worldwarone, greatwar, battleofmidway, holocaust, frenchrevolutionarywar, wwii, wwi, sevenyearswar, firstworldwar, coldwarhist, gulfwar, battleofokinawa, dday, berlinwall, ddayoverlord, operationoverlord, fww, pearlharbor, americanrevolution, 6juin44, sww, june61944, victoryineuropeday, dday72, neverforget84, warof1812, ww1politics, ww1centenary,ww1economy, cw150
Historical Entities	stalin, hitler, abrahamlincoln, rudolfhess, napoleon

concerning particular dates or time periods such as #june61944 could be considered as a separate category or could be made a part of **General Commemoration.** We decided however to place them under the **Historical Events** category as they tend to be used to refer to particular events by their occurrence dates (e.g., #june61944 referring to the Normandy landings).

In Fig. 8 we show the rate of each category based on the count of tweets in our dataset. **Facet-focused History** appears to be quite common category followed by **General History** and **General Commemoration.** This suggests *relatively significant amount of specialized history-related content besides broad and general history related content.*

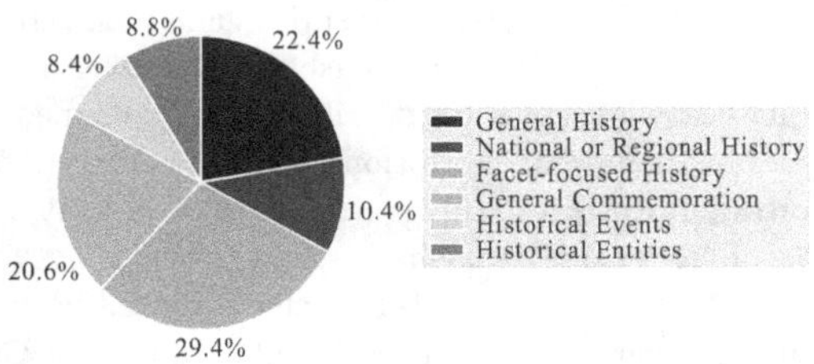

Figure 8: Distribution of categories.

5.2 Inter-category Similarity

To better understand characteristics of the proposed categories, we now investigate inter-category affinity by measuring the co-occurrence values between the categories. We use Jaccard coefficient computed as follows:

$$Score(A, B) = \frac{|\ T_A \cap T_B\ |}{|\ T_A \cup T_B\ |} \tag{2}$$

where: $|\cdot|$ is the size of a set. T_A and T_B are the numbers of tweets that include hashtags classified in category A and B, respectively.

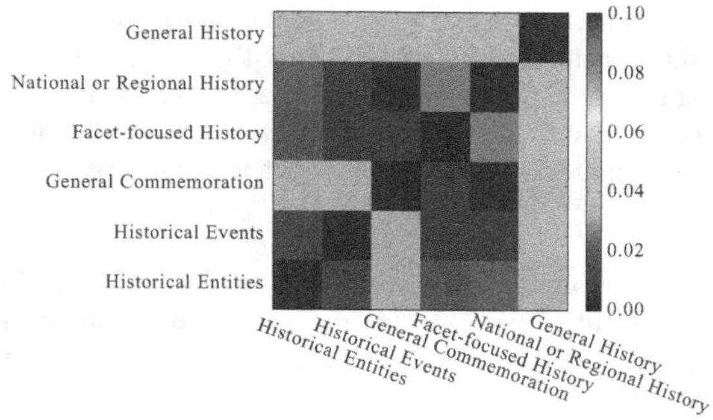

Figure 9: Category co-occurrence.

Fig. 9 plots the obtained co-occurrence values between the categories. We can see that the *category **General History** is truly "general" since the hashtags in this category tend to highly co-occur with hashtags in the other categories.* This is the only category that has relatively high similarity with every other category. Another observation is that the co-occurrence value between **Historical Events** and **Historical Entities** is quite high. This is because many famous entities in our dataset were involved in key events (e.g., Stalin, Hitler in WWII). Similarly, when users refer to the past as a general commemoration they tend to focus on particular well-known past events and key persons. Hence, **General Commemoration** and **Historical Entities/Historical Events** hashtags are sometimes used together. On the other hand, **National or Regional History** and **Facet-focused History** have rarely co-occurring hashtags with the hashtags of other categories (except for **General History**). This indicates that they tend to be assigned to relatively unique and specialized content.

5.3 Temporal Category Analysis

We now investigate temporal references in tweets in relation to their categories. Our interest is in understanding how similar are time references included within tweets annotated with the hashtags of the same category (or in other words, whether tweets under the same category tend to mention similar or rather different years).

We compute such temporal coherence for each category by comparing the vectors of hashtags in a given category. These are built based on temporal expressions associated with the hashtags. In particular, for each hashtag, we construct a vector representing year scores derived from temporal references within tweets labeled by this hashtag. We first map all the temporal references to the year level granularity and then compute year scores using Eq. 1. Such vectors reflect commonly mentioned years for each hashtag. Pairwise similarities of hashtags falling into the same category are then computed by using cosine similarity measure and are averaged to give the final scores displayed in Tab. 7.

Tab. 7 shows that the time-based similarities of hashtags in **Historical Entities** and **General History** are relatively high (when compared to the average value for the entire data shown in the last row). Though, we should keep in mind that many tweets under these hashtags lack time references as indicated by their ratio values being lower than the average values (see the 4th column). Nevertheless, hashtags under these two categories tend to be relatively similar to each other in terms of the focused time periods. This actually is not surprising for the **Historical Entities** category since several its hashtags represent entities with overlapping lifetimes (at least this is the case in our dataset). Yet for **General History** it would mean that there is a good level of agreement in the question of the most important historical periods and events (e.g., WWI and WWII).

Table 7: Average cosine similarity for each category based on years (2nd column), standard deviation of the similarities (3rd column) and the rate of tweets including time references (4th column).

Categories	Similarity	Std. dev.	Ratio
General History	0.75	0.29	0.19
National or Regional History	0.58	0.35	0.20
Facet-focused History	0.57	0.32	0.32
General Commemoration	0.54	0.34	0.55
Historical Events	0.47	0.31	0.18
Historical Entities	0.81	0.12	0.09
Total	*0.56*	*0.33*	*0.29*

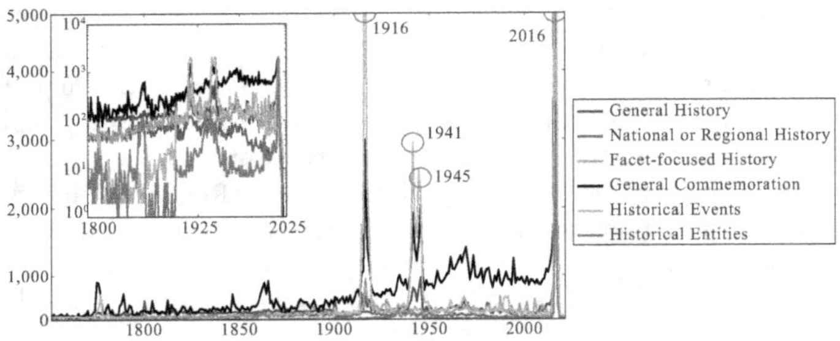

Figure 10: Distributions of time references in the categories (small inner graph shows the plots in log scale).

We next plot in Fig. 10 the distributions of time references extracted from tweets in each category. Naturally, all the categories have strong relation to the present (e.g., to the current events or present entities) since year 2016 is characterized by a high peak for all the plots. **Historical Events** category is strongly focused on the two critical events of the last century: WWI and WWII. While **General Commemoration** has also strong focus on the two wars, it features actually a very different time plot when compared to the ones from other categories. Since the common reason for commemorating events are their anniversaries (e.g., #otd) rather than external triggers such as ongoing events, the *tweets under **General Commemoration** relate to many diverse years in the past. The pattern of tweeting under this category reflects thus smaller selectivity (or higher diversity) of the collective attention towards time periods of history.*

5.4 Entity-focused Category Analyses

Next, we look into entity distributions to investigate their coherence in each category. In a similar way to the above-discussed temporal analysis, we first count how many times each entity is mentioned with a given hashtag in order to create hashtag's entity vector. We then calculate pairwise similarities between hashtags in each category by comparing their vectors and we average these similarities to give the final score per each category.

Table 8: Average cosine similarity for each category based on entities (2nd column), its standard deviation (3rd column) and the rates of: entities, past entities and present entities, displayed respectively in the last three columns.

Categories	Sim.	Std. dev.	All	Past	Present
General History	0.13	0.19	0.15	0.03	0.05
National or Regional History	0.05	0.16	0.16	0.03	0.08
Facet-focused History	0.12	0.16	0.19	0.05	0.07
General Commemoration	0.19	0.25	0.35	0.09	0.14
Historical Events	0.11	0.18	0.20	0.05	0.08
Historical Entities	0.12	0.12	0.09	0.02	0.03
Total	*0.10*	*0.17*	*0.14*	*0.05*	*0.08*

In Tab. 8 we show per each category the average similarities, their standard deviations as well as we output the rates of all the entities, the rate of past entities and the ones of present entities. The entity-focused similarities are in general relatively low indicating that hashtags of the same category tend to refer to different entities. Interestingly, when looking at Tab. 8 we can observe that all the values of **General Commemoration** are higher than the average values for the entire dataset (see the last row). Over one third of tweets under this category contain entities (see 4th column in Tab. 8), while more than half of its tweets contain time references as shown in Tab. 7. Thus, *compared with other categories, users tend to include more entity names and more temporal expressions into tweets tagged with the hashtags from **General Commemoration** category. This may be distinguishing characteristic of commemorating activity.*

5.5 Analysis of Entity and Time Reference Dispersions

Finally, we study the dispersions of entities and time expressions for each category. Fig. 11(a) places hashtags according to their entropy values calculated over the distributions of contained entities and mentioned temporal expressions. We can observe that **General Commemoration** hashtags (e.g., `#otd`, `#thisday`, `#otdih`) and some of **General History** hashtags (e.g., `#twitterstorians`, `#history`, `#colorization`) are often characterized by high values of entropy over time references. Hashtags under the **General Commemoration** category tend to also have relatively high values of entropy over entities (e.g., `#otd`, `#throwbackthursday`, `#tdih`). On the other hand, **Historical Events** and **Historical Entities** categories have on average low values of the entropy over temporal references, which is understandable given that they focus on relatively short-lasting events (e.g., `#ww1politics`, `#ww1economy`, `#june61944`). For the same reason, these categories also achieve low values of entity-based entropy. Furthermore, **National or Regional History** hashtags (e.g., `#britishhistory`) tend to have less varying entities compared to other categories.

Lastly, in the remaining two figures (Figs. 11(b) and (c)) we look into the relation between the entropy of user distributions and the entropy of entity distributions as well as the relation between the entropy of user distributions and the entropy of temporal references, respectively.

The right hand side corner of Fig. 11(b) is occupied by both ***General Commemoration*** *and* ***General History*** *hashtags suggesting that many different users tweet with these hashtags and the users tend to include references to many different entities.* **Historical entities** in our dataset like `#stalin` and `#hitler` tend to be referred to by large number of users and, interestingly, they also have relatively high values of entity entropies. In Fig. 11(c), **General Commemoration** tweets contain both many diverse dates and are issued by many users.

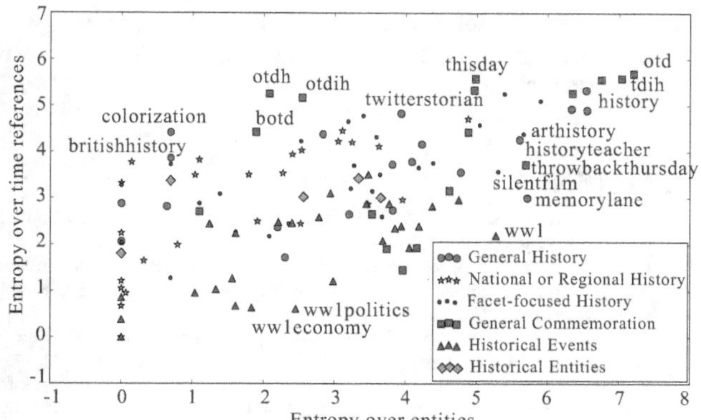

(a) Named entities (x axis) vs. time references (y axis)

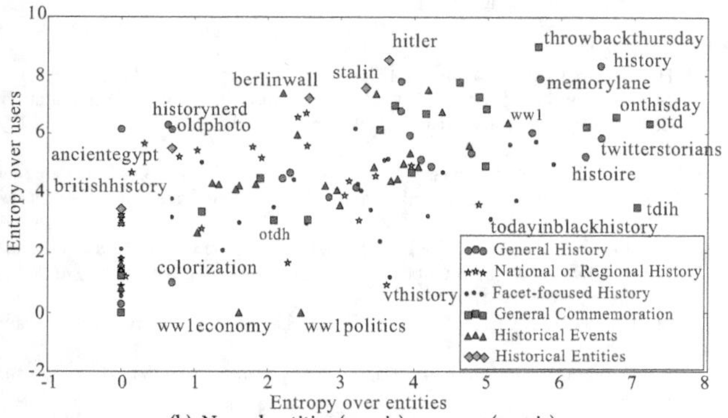

(b) Named entities (x axis) vs. users (y axis)

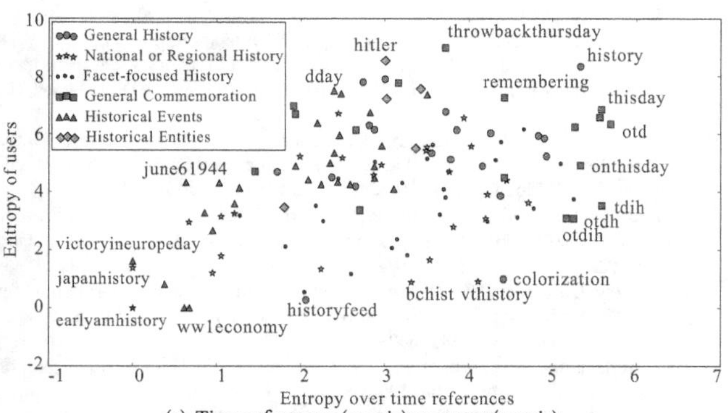

(c) Time references (x axis) vs. users (y axis)

Figure 11: Entropies related to different categories.

6 DISCUSSIONS

6.1 Limitations

Data Collection. We note that the data collection method that we relied on naturally misses the portion of tweets not tagged by any history-related hashtags. We list here two other approaches that could be used to collect history-related data: (1) *collecting content with temporal expressions pointing to the past*, and (2) *collecting content that contains past entities*. Every approach is however not without its shortcomings. The first method was used in [2] for extracting past references in news articles and relied on the presence of temporal expressions in text. This however is not always guaranteed for history-related tweets. Indeed, as it can be seen in Tab. 1 the rate of tweets with temporal expressions is 40%, hence, about 4 tweets out of 10 contain tweets any time reference. Thus, this approach would miss many relevant tweets resulting in rather low recall. Similarly, history-related tweets may not mention any past entity. Indeed, from Tab. 8 (see the column "Past" and the last row) we can actually notice that the rate of tweets containing at least one past entity, which can be recognized by the state-of-the-art tools, is only 0.05 for our dataset. Furthermore, some entities, especially, more obscure ones may not be even present in any knowledge base or may not be detectable using standard tools.

We thus assumed in this work an approach that relies on extracting explicit history-focused hashtags and on subjecting them to the manual analysis of tagged content. While such a choice is likely characterized by a high precision, it may obviously suffer from lowered recall as discussed before. Yet, in the view of the reported statistics, we still believe it is superior than collecting tweets based on contained dates or historical entities. Future work should nevertheless explore more refined approaches for extracting implicit past-related content; ideally, ones making use of the combination of all the signals (hashtags, past entities, temporal expressions, etc.). We also note that while we put great effort into the manual verification of used hashtags as for their relevance to the history, there is always chance that some might not be fully devoted to the past, or, in general, their selection may cause certain biases.

Different Languages. In the current study we have mainly focused on English tweets. Further exploration should involve different languages (e.g., French, Japanese) as well as the cross-comparison of the obtained results. Our current aim is however not to look into particular aspects and specificities related to different countries but to rather uncover general tendencies. The focus on English was a natural decision for this initial study due to the international role and ubiquity of this language.

Fine-grained Analysis. The present study is quantitative aiming to provide first glimpse into the issue of historical-references in SNS and to conduct broad exploratory analysis. Qualitative exploration should be later carried for obtaining fine-grained comprehension of the way in which users refer to the past. For example, the future analysis could examine why some entities are (or are not) popular as well as could apply sentiment analysis to identify tendencies in polarity towards particular past events or entities. Another research direction could be the detailed analysis of contexts in which the past entities or past years are mentioned. These would necessarily require some sort of manual and qualitative exploration of tweet content.

User-focused Analysis. Our study has exploratory character and focuses on the shared content first. However, a very interesting question is about the type of users who share or are interested in historical content in social network services. Due to the time and space constraints, we have left however the user-focused analysis for the future work.

Studying Temporal Data Snapshots. Subsequent work should investigate portions of data collected over different time frames in order to verify which of the results are specific to the particular time frames of data generation and which are of general character. We are currently in the process of collecting more data to perform such comparative investigation (aiming at the comparison of results based on tweets from 2016 with ones based on tweets issued in 2017).

6.2 Potential Applications

Finally, we list here several example applications that could be potentially constructed based on the history-related content shared in Twitter:

(1) *Recommending past-related content for readers interested in studying history.* This could be, for example, popular and interesting content or the content that matches particular user interests such as tweets under hashtags of the Facet-focused category that a user is interested in. Through this analysis and other forthcoming ones we could better understand what kind of history-related content at what time periods is becoming attractive to many users.
(2) *Creating history-focused chatbots for disseminating historical knowledge and for entertaining users.*
(3) *Finding, summarizing and explaining past entities which are mentioned in relation with the popular present entities to provide analogy and a novel, potentially interesting context for the latter.*
(4) *Automatically summarizing and comparing history-related opinions and popular topics across different regions.*
(5) *Automatically suggesting hashtags for tweets based on included entities, years and based on the predicted hashtag categories.*

7 CONCLUSIONS & FUTURE WORK

In this paper we have for the first time studied how people explicitly refer to the history in microblogging and in which contexts such references occur. As mentioned before, history-focused content recommendation should offer opportunities for the dissemination of interesting and trendy recollections by pushing them to users.

Our analysis does an initial groundwork in establishing how microbloggers conceive of, share and refer to history-related content such as one on past events and persons. Through this promising study we hope to shed more light on the way in which history-related content is used and shared in microblogging, and by this to encourage subsequent research and development of systems aiming at educating history. We perform basic study on a coarse level, providing initial observations, identifying several interesting research directions and suggesting potential applications. Our analysis is nevertheless conducted from multiple perspectives.

Future work will identify (a) *differences between general and personal histories as well as will look into what makes tweets about personal history appear interesting.* Social media provide novel opportunities to create such personal connections which can help raise an interest in the significance of historical knowledge beyond the personal experience. Future work will also include (b) *geographical analysis of tweets which may point to different cultural practices with regard to references to the past.* As currently most of the tweets in our dataset originate from the English-speaking part of the world we should contrast these results with ones obtained on data collected in different languages. Next, we plan also to (c) *explore the interdependence between present-day events, their function as triggers for references to history and the latter's effect on the interpretation of the present.* Finally, as mentioned before, (d) *we plan to study in detail the characteristics of users sharing history-related content in Twitter* such as their demographics, characteristics of their followers and followees, and their interaction patters.

Acknowledgments. This work was supported in part by MIC SCOPE (#171507010) and MEXT Grant-in-Aids (#17H01828 and #17K12792).

REFERENCES

[1] R. P. Abelson and A. Levi. 1985. Decision Making and Decision Theory, Handbook of Social Psychology. 231–309.
[2] C.-m. Au Yeung and A. Jatowt. 2011. Studying How the Past is Remembered: Towards Computational History Through Large Scale Text Mining. CIKM '11, Glasgow, Scotland, UK, 1231–1240.
[3] S. Auer, C. Bizer, G. Kobilarov, J. Lehmann, R. Cyganiak, and Z. Ives. 2007. DBpedia: A Nucleus for a Web of Open Data. ISWC'07/ASWC'07, Busan, Korea, 722–735.
[4] R. Campos, G. Dias, A. M. Jorge, and A. Jatowt. 2015. Survey of temporal information retrieval and related applications. *ACM Computing Surveys (CSUR)* 47, 2 (2015), 15.
[5] F. Clavert, B. Majerus, and N. BeauprÃĪ. [n. d.]. #ww1. Twitter, the Centenary of the First World War and the Historian.
[6] J. Cook, A. D. Sarma, A. Fabrikant, and A. Tomkins. 2012. Your Two Weeks of Fame and Your Grandmother's. WWW '12, Lyon, France, 919–928.
[7] H. Ebbinghaus. 1913. *Memory: A Contribution to Experimental Psychology.*
[8] M. Ferron and P. Massa. 2011. Collective Memory Building in Wikipedia: The Case of North African Uprisings. WikiSym '11, Mountain View, California, USA, 114–123.
[9] R. G.-Gavilanes, A. Mollgaard, M. Tsvetkova, and T. Yasseri. 2017. The memory remains: Understanding collective memory in the digital age. *Science Advances* 3, 4 (2017).
[10] T. Gilovich. 1981. Seeing the Past in the Present: The Effect of Associations to Familiar Events on Judgments and Decisions. *Journal of Personality and Social Psychology* 40, 5 (1981), 797.
[11] M. Halbwachs. 1950. *La Memoire Collective.* Les Presses universitaires de France, (in French).
[12] C. Hoerl and T. McCormack. 2001. *Time and Memory: Issues in Philosophy and Psychology.*
[13] J. Hoffart, S. Seufert, D. B. Nguyen, M. Theobald, and G. Weikum. 2012. KORE: Keyphrase Overlap Relatedness for Entity Disambiguation. CIKM '12, Maui, Hawaii, USA, 545–554.
[14] R. Jacoby. 1997. *Social Amnesia: A Critique of Contemporary Psychology.*
[15] A. Jatowt, D. Kawai, and K. Tanaka. 2016. Digital History Meets Wikipedia: Analyzing Historical Persons in Wikipedia. JCDL '16, Newark, New Jersey, USA, 17–26.
[16] N. Kanhabua, T. N. Nguyen, and C. Niederée. 2014. What Triggers Human Remembering of Events?: A Large-scale Analysis of Catalysts for Collective Memory in Wikipedia. JCDL '14, London, United Kingdom, 341–350.
[17] N. Kanhabua, C. NiederÃľe, and W. Siberski. 2013. Towards Concise Preservation by Managed Forgetting: Research Issues and Case Study. iPres'13, Lisbon, Portugal.
[18] E. Kuzey, J. Strötgen, V. Setty, and G. Weikum. 2016. Temponym Tagging: Temporal Scopes for Textual Phrases. WWW '16 Companion, Republic and Canton of Geneva, Switzerland, 841–842.
[19] A. Tumasjan, T. O. Sprenger, P. G. Sandner, and I. M. Welpe. 2010. Predicting Elections with Twitter: What 140 Characters Reveal about Political Sentiment. ICWSM'10, Washington, DC, USA.

Extracting Scientific Figures with Distantly Supervised Neural Networks

Noah Siegel*
Allen Institute for Artificial Intelligence
Seattle, Washington
siegeln@uw.edu

Nicholas Lourie
Allen Institute for Artificial Intelligence
Seattle, Washington
nicholasl@allenai.org

Russell Power
Allen Institute for Artificial Intelligence
Seattle, Washington
russell.power@gmail.com

Waleed Ammar
Allen Institute for Artificial Intelligence
Seattle, Washington
waleeda@allenai.org

ABSTRACT

Non-textual components such as charts, diagrams and tables provide key information in many scientific documents, but the lack of large labeled datasets has impeded the development of data-driven methods for scientific figure extraction. In this paper, we induce high-quality training labels for the task of figure extraction in a large number of scientific documents, with no human intervention. To accomplish this we leverage the auxiliary data provided in two large web collections of scientific documents (arXiv and PubMed) to locate figures and their associated captions in the rasterized PDF. We share the resulting dataset of over 5.5 million induced labels—4,000 times larger than the previous largest figure extraction dataset—with an average precision of 96.8%, to enable the development of modern data-driven methods for this task. We use this dataset to train a deep neural network for end-to-end figure detection, yielding a model that can be more easily extended to new domains compared to previous work. The model was successfully deployed in Semantic Scholar,[1] a large-scale academic search engine, and used to extract figures in 13 million scientific documents.[2]

KEYWORDS

Figure Extraction, Distant Supervision, Deep Learning, Neural Networks, Computer Vision

*Now at DeepMind.
[1]https://www.semanticscholar.org/
[2]A demo of our system is available at http://labs.semanticscholar.org/deepfigures/, and our dataset of induced labels can be downloaded at https://s3-us-west-2.amazonaws.com/ai2-s2-research-public/deepfigures/jcdl-deepfigures-labels.tar.gz. Code to run our system locally can be found at https://github.com/allenai/deepfigures-open.

JCDL '18, June 3–7, 2018, Fort Worth, TX, USA

ACM ISBN 978-1-4503-5178-2/18/06...$15.00
https://doi.org/10.1145/3197026.3197040

ACM Reference format:
Noah Siegel, Nicholas Lourie, Russell Power, and Waleed Ammar. 2018. Extracting Scientific Figures with Distantly Supervised Neural Networks. In *Proceedings of The 18th ACM/IEEE Joint Conference on Digital Libraries, Fort Worth, TX, USA, June 3–7, 2018 (JCDL '18)*, 10 pages.
https://doi.org/10.1145/3197026.3197040

1 INTRODUCTION

Non-textual components (e.g., charts, diagrams and tables) provide key information in many scientific documents. Previous research has studied the utility of figures in scientific search and information extraction systems; however, the vast majority of published research papers are only available in PDF format, making figure extraction a challenging first step before any downstream application involving figures or other graphical elements may be tackled. While some venues (e.g., PubMed) provide figures used in recently published documents, it remains a problem for older papers as well as many other venues which only publish PDF files of research papers.

Recent years have seen the emergence of a body of work focusing on use cases for extracted figures (see Section 2). All of these downstream tasks rely upon accurate figure extraction. Unfortunately, the lack of large-scale labeled datasets has hindered the application of modern data-driven techniques to figure and table extraction.[3] Previous work on this task used rule-based methods to address the problem in limited domains. In particular, [6] extract figures in research papers at NIPS, ICML and AAAI, and [7] extend their work to address papers in computer science more generally; however, stylistic conventions vary widely across academic fields, and since previous methods relied primarily on hand-designed features from computer science papers, they do not generalize well to other scientific domains, as we show in section 5.

Our main contribution in this paper is to propose a novel method for inducing high-quality labels for figure extraction in a large number of scientific documents, with no human intervention. Our technique utilizes auxiliary data provided in two large web collections of scientific documents (arXiv and PubMed) to locate each figure and its associated caption in the rendered PDFs. The resulting dataset consists of 5.5 million induced labels with an average precision of 96.8%. The size of this dataset is three orders of magnitude

[3]For brevity, we use *figure extraction* to refer to the extraction of both figures and tables in the remainder of the paper.

larger than human-labeled datasets available for figure extraction in scientific documents.

To demonstrate the value of this dataset, we introduce *DeepFigures*, a deep neural model for detecting figures in PDF documents, built on a standard neural network architecture for modeling real world images, ResNet-101. Comparison to prior rule-based techniques reveals better generalization across different scientific domains. Additionally, we discuss a production system for figure extraction built on DeepFigures that is currently deployed in a large-scale academic search engine (Semantic Scholar)[4] which covers multiple domains, illustrating the practical utility of our proposed approach.

Our main contributions are:

- We propose a novel method for inducing high-quality labels for figure extraction in large web collections of scientific documents.
- We introduce, to the best of our knowledge, the first statistical model for figure extraction, using a neural network trained exclusively on our dataset with no human labels.
- We release our figure extraction data, tool, and code for generating the datasets and extracting figures locally to facilitate future research in graphical information understanding in scientific documents.

2 RELATED WORK

In this section, we discuss two lines of related work in the literature. The first line focuses on extraction and understanding of figures in scientific documents, which motivate this work. The second line reviews related neural models which we build on.

2.1 Scientific Figures

Recent years have seen the emergence of a body of work focusing on applications involving figures in scholarly research papers. Researchers have considered a range of tasks from extracting the underlying data from plots [5, 20], to the use of figures in search engines and broader information extraction systems [4, 24, 26].

Figures are also a common topic of interest in medical domains, where they often contain graphical images such as radiology imaging. In [26], researchers introduced the system PDFMEF, which incorporated figures into its extracted information. In [24], researchers classified figures of brain images in order to provide more relevant information to doctors studying Alzheimer's Disease. In [4], researchers present a search engine for figures in chemistry journals, allowing scientists to more easily locate information that may not be expressed in text. Shared tasks such as ImageCLEF [9, 10] also helped drive more attention to compound figure detection [29], compound figure separation [23], medical image annotation [17], among other tasks related to medical images.

All of these downstream tasks rely upon accurate figure extraction. Previous work on this task has focused only on limited domains; [6] focused only on 3 AI conferences, and [7] concentrated on papers only within computer science. Stylistic conventions vary widely across academic fields, and as we show in section 5, features hand-designed for computer science papers do not generalize well across other scientific domains.

[4]https://www.semanticscholar.org

Our method for inducing figure extraction labels can be viewed as an application of distant supervision, a popular approach for generating noisy labels in natural language processing tasks. The key idea is to project known labels from an existing resource to related, unlabeled instances. For example, [18] used relations between entities in Freebase [1] to induce labels between pairs of corresponding entity mentions in unlabeled text, making the strong assumption that the Freebase relation is described in each sentence where both entities are mentioned. As will be discussed in the following section, the method we propose does not require making such strong assumptions.

2.2 Neural Models for Computer Vision

The model architecture we use for figure extraction in this paper leverages the great success of convolutional neural networks on a variety of computer vision tasks including object recognition and detection [14], motion analysis [12], and scene reconstruction [27]. Inspired by the brain's visual cortex, these networks consist of millions of neurons arranged in a series of layers that learn successively higher-level visual representations. For example, when performing facial recognition, a neuron in the first layer might detect horizontal edges, a neuron in the second layer might respond to certain curves, the third layer to an eye, the fourth layer to a whole face. Recent work has used neural networks for semantic page segmentation, suggesting that these models can be applied to synthetic documents as well as natural scenes [3, 13, 28]. In this section we provide more details on two building blocks we use in DeepFigures: ResNet-101 and OverFeat.

2.2.1 *ResNet-101.*

An important task in computer vision is object recognition: for example, given an image, determine whether it is a cat or a dog. Using the raw pixels as features poses difficulties for most traditional classification algorithms, due to the sheer volume of information and the curse of dimensionality. Instead, computer vision techniques generally extract higher level features from the image, and then run a standard machine learning classifier such as logistic regression on these features. Before neural networks, features were generally hand-engineered by researchers or practicioners; an example of one common such feature is the frequencies of edges in various regions of the image [8]. In contrast, convolutional neural networks learn their feature representations from the data. This learning is achieved by defining a broad space of possible feature extractors and then optimizing over it, typically using backpropagation and stochastic gradient descent. The architecture of the neural network corresponds to how the neurons are defined and pass information to each other and it is the neural network's architecture that defines the space of possible feature extractors we might learn.

Numerous highly successful neural network architectures have been proposed for computer vision [14, 15, 22]. Generally, with more data and more layers, neural networks tend to get increased performance. Because of this fact, large-scale datasets and optimization methods are key to neural networks' success. One problem in training neural networks with many layers is that of vanishing gradients: as gradients are propagated through successive layers, they tend to either blow up (causing parameters to quickly diverge to infinity during training) or shrink to zero, making training earlier layers difficult. Residual networks (ResNets) [14] address the problem by adding identity connections between blocks: rather than each layer receiving as input only the previous layer's output, some layers also receive the output of several layers before. These identity connections provide a path for gradients to reach earlier layers in the network undiminished, allowing much deeper networks to be trained. An ensemble of ResNet models won the ImageNet object detection competition in 2015.

Because useful image features transfer well across tasks it is common to use parts of one neural network architecture in place of components of another. ResNet-101 [14] provides one such feature extraction architecture. ResNet-101 is a 101-layer deep neural network formed by stacking "bottleneck" units consisting of a 1x1 convolutional layer, followed by a 3x3 convolutional layer that brings down the dimension of the embedding, and then another 1x1 convolutional layer that brings the dimension of the embedding back up to that of the original input. An identity connection adds the input of the bottleneck unit into the output of its last layer before passing it further down the network.

2.2.2 OverFeat. Another common task in computer vision, and the one in which we are interested in this work, is object detection: for example, determine the location of all human faces in a given image. This task can be formalized as predicting a bounding box that encloses the object while being as small as possible. Object detection is more complex than classification since rather than predicting a binary or multiclass label, the model must predict a variable-length list of bounding box coordinates that may change in size and shape. The problem can be reduced to classification by running a classifier on every possible box on the image, but due to the high computational cost of running neural networks with millions of parameters this is generally infeasible.

OverFeat [19] introduced the idea of bounding box regression. Rather than producing a class output, the model can use regression to predict bounding box coordinates directly. To enable detecting multiple objects as well as to handle objects in various locations in the image, the model is run fully-convolutionally, i.e., the entire model is run on cropped image sections centered on a uniformly spaced grid of 20x15 points.[5] For each cropped region, in order to extract the feature vectors, OverFeat uses 5 initial layers that perform convolutions and max pooling. Classification is then performed by two fully connected layers and an output layer from the feature vectors; while bounding box regression is performed by two fully connected layers and a final output layer providing 4 numbers – the coordinates for the predicted bounding box. Each class has its own output layer to provide a bounding box for that class alone. The classification result then provides a confidence for each class and every region in the grid, while the bounding box regression yields a possible bounding box for that class. Thus, for any class many bounding boxes are predicted and then later merged.

[5]Running the model at each point on a grid is significantly less computationally expensive than running the model on the same number of independent images, because the convolutional structure of network layers means much of the work on overlapping regions is redundant and can be shared; see [19] for details.

3 INDUCING FIGURE EXTRACTION LABELS

A key contribution of this paper is a novel method for inducing high-quality labels for figure extraction in a large number of scientific documents (see Table 1 for dataset statistics). The resulting dataset is critical for training statistical models for figure extraction, especially for deep neural networks, e.g., [14]. In order to induce the labels, we align the figures and tables specified using a markup languages (e.g., LaTeX) with bounding boxes in the corresponding PDF files, then use coordinates of the bounding boxes as labeled data. The following subsections provide details on how to do this alignment using two markup languages commonly used in the scientific literature: LaTeX and XML.

3.1 Aligning Figures in LaTeX Documents

Many researchers use LaTeX to typeset scientific documents, before compiling them into PDFs.[6] In LaTeX, figures and tables are specified using standard commands such as `\includegraphics`. We modify the way figures render in the compiled PDF file by adding special instructions in the header section of LaTeX source files which results in drawing a rectangle around each figure and table in the rendered PDF file. We then use the pixel-by-pixel image difference between the original and modified versions of the rendered PDF file to identify the bounding boxes of each figure, as illustrated in Fig. 1.

Unlike plain text, which may be separated by line and page breaks at the compiler's discretion, figures and tables need to be represented in contiguous blocks of space. To handle these graphical elements, LaTeX uses the concept of "floats". Floats are not part of the normal stream of text, but are instead placed at a location determined by the LaTeX compiler. Floats also include a caption to describe them and a name (e.g. "Figure 1."), allowing them to be referenced from elsewhere in body text.

Labeling figures and tables:

We add the following commands to the header section of the LaTeX source file to surround each figure and table with a bounding box in the compiled PDF file:

```
\usepackage{color}
\usepackage{floatrow}
\usepackage{tcolorbox}

\DeclareColorBox{figurecolorbox}{\fcolorbox{red}{white}}
\DeclareColorBox{tablecolorbox}{\fcolorbox{yellow}{white}}

\floatsetup[figure]{framestyle=colorbox,
    colorframeset=figurecolorbox, framearound=all,
    frameset={\fboxrule1pt\fboxsep0pt}}
\floatsetup[table]{framestyle=colorbox,
    colorframeset=tablecolorbox, framearound=all,
    frameset={\fboxrule1pt\fboxsep0pt}}
```

We use different colors for figures and tables, in order to differentiate these types automatically. Recompiling and computing the image difference between the modified and the original PDF files

[6]We use the term *LaTeX* to refer to the formal language used to describe a document's content, structure and format in TeX software distributions.

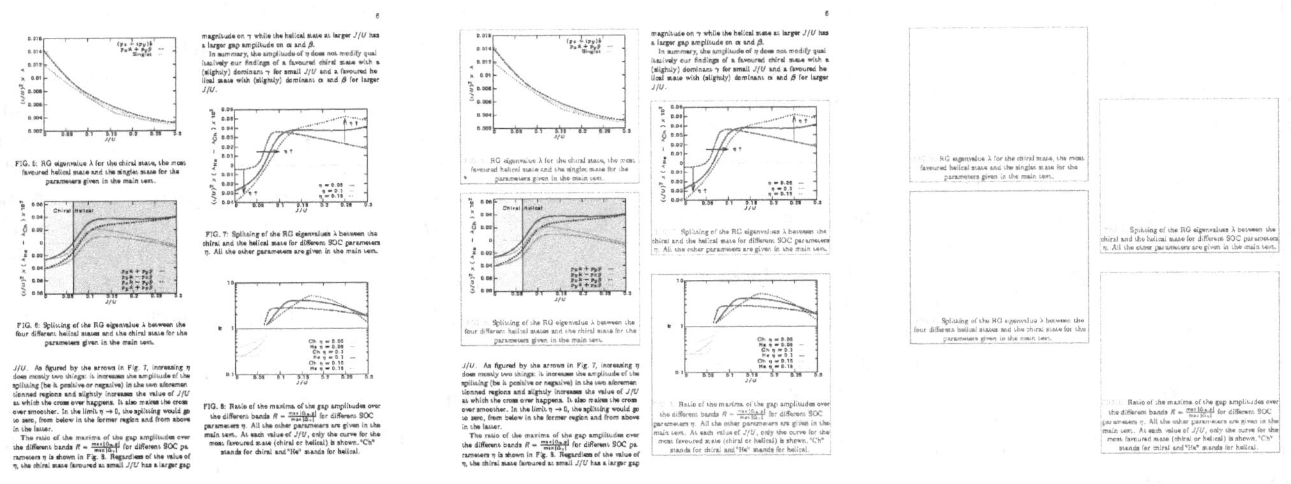

Figure 1: Modifying LaTeX source to recover figure positions. Figure bounding boxes are shown in red, figure names in green, and captions in blue. Left: original document. Middle: document compiled from modified source. Right: image difference between original and modified documents.

yield blank pages containing only the boxes.[7] We can then locate boxes by finding all connected regions of non-blank pixels and then taking the minimum and maximum x and y coordinates of each.

Labeling captions:

In order to find the coordinates of the bounding box for caption text, we modify the color of figure names and captions using the following command:

```
\usepackage[labelfont={color=green},
    textfont={color=blue}]{caption}
```

Finally, we modify the coordinates of the bounding box of each figure and table to exclude the caption, by identifying the largest rectangular region inside the float that contains no caption text. This is robust even to uncommon caption locations (e.g., above a table, or to the side of a figure).

arXiv:

In order to construct our dataset, we download LaTeX source files from arXiv,[8] a popular platform for pre-publishing research in various fields including physics, computer science, and quantitative biology. When authors make a paper submission to arXiv, they are required to upload source files if the paper is typeset using LaTeX. As of the time of writing, arXiv hosts over 900,000 papers with LaTeX source code.

[7]The added border shifts figure positions by a few pixels, so we use the same command to add white borders to figures in the original to make them align exactly.
[8]https://arxiv.org/

3.2 Aligning Figures in XML Documents

We would like our dataset to cover a diverse set of scientific domains. Although LaTeX is widely used in some fields (e.g., statistics, physics, computer science, etc.), it has been less popular in important domains such as the medical and life sciences where WYSIWYG editors (e.g., Microsoft Word) are more common. As a result, we cannot use the method described in section 3.1 to induce a large labeled dataset in these fields.

PubMed:

Fortunately, however, some publishers provide XML markup for their papers, which can also be used to induce figure extraction labels. In particular, PubMed Central Open Access Subset is a free archive of medical and life sciences research papers. The National Center for Biotechnology Information (NCBI) makes this subset available through bulk downloading. In addition to the PDF files, it provides auxiliary data to improve the user experience while reading a paper. The auxiliary data includes the paper text marked up with XML tags (including figure captions) as well as image files for all graphics.

In principle, this data can be used to induce labels for figure extraction. However, unlike LaTeX documents, the XML markup cannot be used to compile the PDF. Therefore, we propose a different approach to recover the positional information of figures.

Labeling captions:

First, for each image in the auxiliary data, we determine which page in the corresponding PDF file contains this figure by searching the PDF text (extracted by a tool such as PDFBox) for the caption text (which is also available in the auxiliary data). Since the XML and PDF text do not always match exactly (e.g., em dash in PDF vs. a hyphen in XML), we use dynamic programming to find the substring in the PDF text with smallest Levenshtein distance to the caption text in the XML file. We modify the standard Wagner-Fischer dynamic programming algorithm for edit distance [25] by setting the cost for starting (and ending) at any position in the PDF text to 0. This modification maintains the time complexity of $O(mn)$, where m and n are the string lengths.

Labeling figures:

Once we have identified the page that a figure is on, we render that page as an image and then use multi-scale template matching [2] to find the position of the figure on the page. We use the figure image as a filter and cross-correlate it with the page to produce a spatial map of image correlations. Template matching is typically done using image representations such as edge detections or oriented gradients [2], but because we do not have to deal with typical conditions present in natural images such as variations in lighting or pose, we find that template matching in raw pixel space works best. We use OpenCV's `matchTemplate` implementation with the similarity metric `CV_TM_CCOEFF_NORMED`, matching at 45 scales where the figure's largest dimension relative to the page takes up between 10% and 95% of the page.

In rare cases, the provided figure images do not match the figures as they appear in the PDF (e.g., subfigures may be laid out horizontally on the PDF but vertically in the provided image file). If template matching yields a similarity below 0.8 for any figure, we exclude the paper from our dataset to reduce the risk of inaccurate training data.

Labeling tables:

Tables are sometimes provided as images in the same way figures are. However, it is more common for tables to be represented directly in the XML with tags for each table cell. We first tried using the textual edit distance to identify table coordinates in the PDF file (similar to captions), but we found that the order of table cells often differs between PDFBox's extracted text and the XML (e.g. table cells may be extracted from the PDF in column-major order while the XML is row-major). Therefore, we instead use a bag of words similarity.

We find the token sequence in the PDF that has the highest similarity to the set of words in the XML table. We can find the optimal sequence in the PDF text efficiently by maintaining a word difference counter. For a given start position in the PDF stream, we initialize the counter to the bag of words from the XML table. For each token following this position, we decrement the counter for the word at the current position (while allowing negative counts to represent words that occur more in the PDF than in the XML). This procedure is repeated for each start position on the PDF page. The following pseudo-code illustrates our algorithm for finding the interval on the page with the lowest bag-of-words distance to the table:

```
best_dist <- math.inf
for start_word in page_words:
  diff_counter <- table_words
  cur_dist = sum(table_words)
  for end_word in page_words from start_word:
    diff_counter[end_word] -= 1
    if diff_counter[end_word] >= 0:
      cur_dist -= 1
    else:
      cur_dist += 1
    if cur_dist < best_dist:
      best_dist <- cur_dist
      store start_word and end_word positions
```

If m is the length of the XML table and n is the length of the PDF, generating or copying the initial word counter is $O(m)$ and iterating over ending words on the PDF text is $O(n)$. Both of these occur for every starting word, for a total time complexity of $O(n(n + m))$. We identify the minimum axis-aligned bounding box containing all caption tokens as the table caption region.

Dataset name	Manually-labeled CS-Large [7]	Manually-labeled PubMed	Induced labels LaTeX	Induced labels XML
# papers	346	104	242,041	791,381
# figures	952	289	1,030,671	3,064,951
# tables	282	124	164,356	1,267,464

Table 1: Number of papers, figures, and tables in the manually-labeled datasets (left) and our datasets of induced labels (right).

3.3 Comparison to Manual Annotation

In this section, we proposed a method for automatically inducing labeled data for figure extraction in scientific documents. An alternative approach is to train annotators to sift through a large number of research papers and label figure and table coordinates and their captions. While this approach typically results in high quality annotations, it is often impractical. Manual annotation is slow and expensive, and it is hard to find annotators with appropriate training or domain knowledge. With limited time and budget, the size of labeled data we can collect with this approach is modest.[9]

Scalability of induced labels:

In contrast to manual annotation, our proposed method for inducing labels is both scalable and accurate. We compare the size of our datasets with induced labels to that of manually labeled datasets in Table 1. We compare with two manually labeled datasets:

- The "CS-Large" dataset [7]: To our knowledge, this was previously the largest dataset for the task of figure extraction. Papers in this dataset were randomly sampled from computer science papers published after the year 1999 with nine citations or more.

[9] Another alternative is to use crowdsourced workers (e.g., using Amazon Mechanical Turk https://www.mturk.com/ or CrowdFlower http://www.crowdflower.com/) to do the annotation. Although crowdsourcing has been successfully used to construct useful image datasets such as ImageNet [11], [20] found that crowdsourcing figure annotations in research papers yielded low inter-annotator agreement and significant noise due to workers' lack of familiarity with scholarly documents.

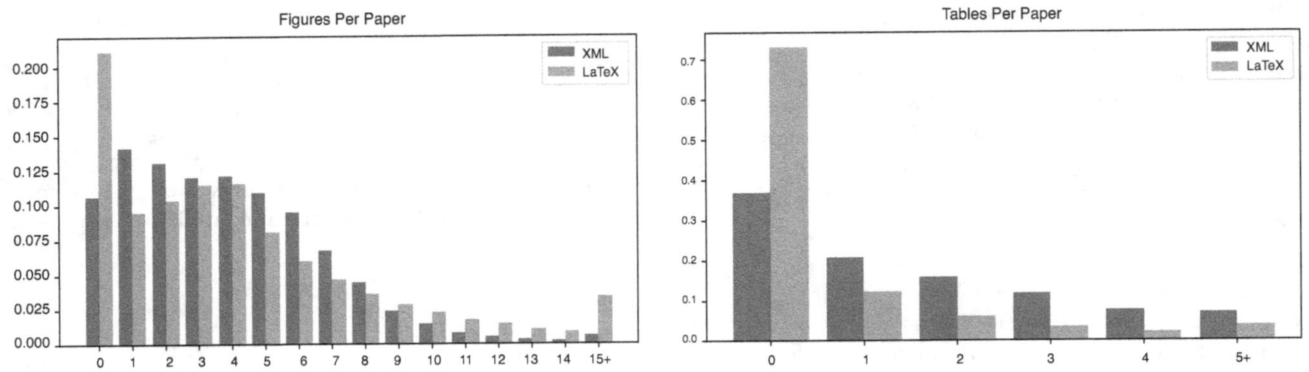

Figure 2: Distributions of figures (left) and tables (right) in our automatically generated datasets. X-axis shows number of figures/tables per paper. Y-axis shows fraction of papers with that many figures/tables. Differences are likely a result of the differing source datasets: for example, the life science papers found in PubMed may rely more on tables to convey information than math papers on arXiv.

Dataset	LaTeX		XML	
	Figures	Tables	Figures	Tables
Precision	1.00	1.00	0.97	0.94
Recall	0.95	1.00	0.91	0.94
F1	0.97	1.00	0.94	0.94

Table 2: Precision, recall and F1 score of induced labels in the "LaTeX" and "XML" datasets.

- The "PubMed" dataset: We collected this dataset by sampling papers from PubMed, and hired experts in biological sciences to annotate figures and tables, and their captions.

Both manually labeled datasets are used as test sets in our experiments (section 5). Notably, both of our datasets with induced labels "LaTeX" and "XML" are three orders of magnitude larger than "CS-Large".

Accuracy of induced labels:

In order to assess the accuracy of labels induced using our method, we collected human judgments for a sample of papers in the "LaTeX" and "XML" datasets. Table 2 reports the precision and recall of figures and tables, including captions, for 150 pages in 61 papers in the "LaTeX" dataset and 106 pages in 86 papers in the "XML" dataset. We require that the four corners of a figure (or table) and the four quadrants of its caption must be correct for each true positive data point. As shown in Table 2, the quality of induced labels are fairly high (e.g., the F1 score of induced labels ranges between 93.9% and 100%).

The following section discusses the model we developed in order to consume the induced labeled data described in this section.

4 THE DEEPFIGURES MODEL

Our system takes as input a PDF file, which we then render as a list of page images, and feed each page to our figure detection neural network. The network architecture we use for figure extraction is a slight variant of several standard neural network architectures for image classification and object detection. In particular, our model is based on TensorBox [21], applying the OverFeat detection architecture [19] to image embeddings generated using ResNet-101 [14]. This object detector then finds bounding boxes for figures in the PDF, and captions are extracted separately.

In contrast to OverFeat, which uses a relatively shallow 5-layer network to generate the spatial feature grid, we use ResNet-101 which enables higher model capacity and accuracy. Additionally, while OverFeat trained the embedding network on a classification task and then fixed those weights while training localization, learning only the weights for the final regression layer, we train the full network end-to-end, allowing the embedding network to learn features more relevant to localization and eliminating the need for pre-training.

As illustrated in Figure 3, in the network we use for figure extraction each grid cell is represented by 1024 features extracted from the ResNet-101 model, resulting in a 20x15x1024 spatial feature grid. At each grid cell, the model uses these features to predict both a bounding box and a confidence score. Boxes with confidence score above a selected threshold are returned as predictions. Figure 4 illustrates the architecture in more detail.

Matching Captions:

The OverFeat-ResNet figure detection model outputs a set of bounding boxes for figures; however, many applications, including academic search, benefit most from having a set of figure-caption pairs for the PDF. Our figure extraction pipeline extracts captions' text and bounding boxes using the same method as [7], finding paragraphs starting with a string that matches a regular expression capturing variations of "Figure N." or "Table N." and then locating the identified textual elements in the page using standard PDF processing libraries. Once we have a list of proposed captions, we match figures to captions in order to minimize the total euclidean distance between the centers of paired boxes. This is an instance of the linear assignment problem and can be solved efficiently using the Hungarian algorithm [16]. If there are more

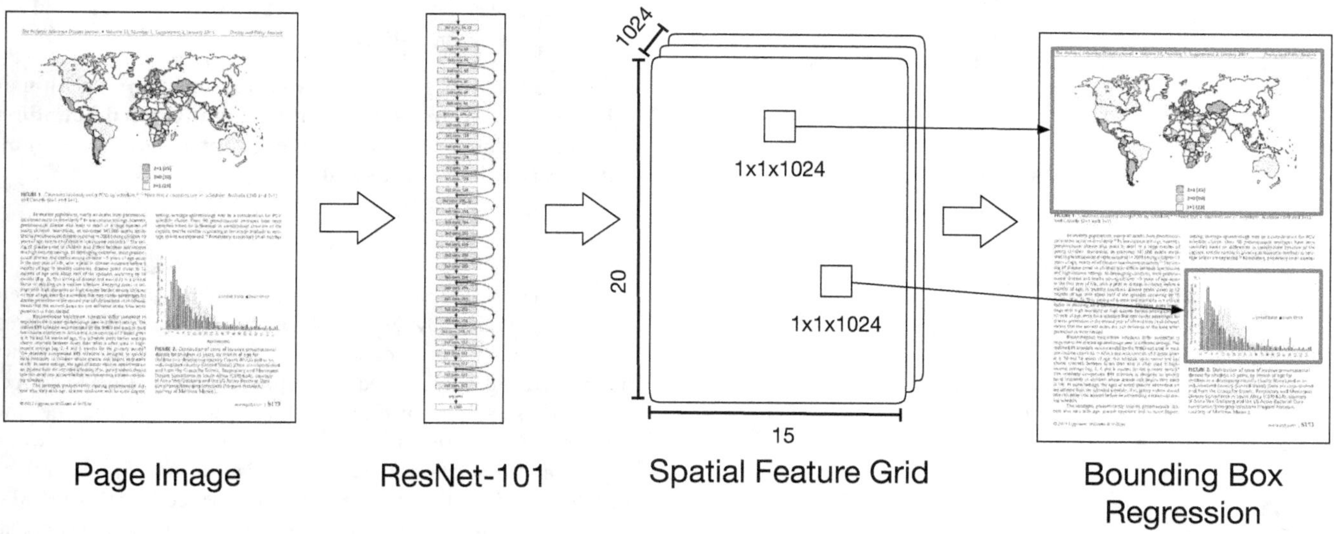

Figure 3: High-level structure of the DeepFigures model. The input to the model is a 640x480 page image. ResNet-101 is run fully-convolutionally over the image, yielding a 20x15 spatial grid of 1024-dimensional image embedding vectors. Next, regressions to predict box coordinates and confidences are run on each of the 300 grid cells, yielding 300 candidate bounding boxes. Running non-maximum suppression and filtering out predictions with confidences below a threshold yields the final predictions.

detected figures than captions or vice-versa, the algorithm picks the min(figure count, caption count) pairs that minimize total distance. See [7] for more details on matching captions.

Both of the data generation methods described in section 3 produce bounding boxes for captions as well as figures, so in principle the captions could also be detected using a neural network. In our experience, however, training the model to predict captions reduced performance. There are a few likely causes: captions are often very small along the height dimension, amplifying small absolute errors in bounding box coordinates. Similarly, captions have fewer visual cues and are much less distinct from surrounding text than figures. Finally, the baseline caption detection model from [6] performs very well. Most errors in PDFFigures 2.0 are caused by figure detection error rather than caption detection. For these reasons, we continue to use the rules-based approach for detecting captions.

To summarize how our model combines the previously mentioned components, the model generates a 20x15 spatial grid of image embedding vectors with each embedding vector having 1024 dimensions generated using ResNet-101 [14]. The feature vectors are then input into a linear regression layer with two outputs that represent the four coordinates of the bounding box. Simultaneously, the feature vectors are passed through a logistic regression layer to predict the confidence that each grid cell is at the center of a figure. Redundant boxes are eliminated via non-maximum suppression. At test time, we run inference with a confidence threshold of 50%, although this parameter may be tuned to favor precision or recall if needed.

5 EXPERIMENTS

In this section, we compare the DeepFigures model described in section 4 to PDFFigures 2.0 [7], the previous state of the art for the task of figure extraction.

Data:

We train the DeepFigures model on 4,095,622 induced figures (1,030,671 in the LaTeX dataset and 3,064,951 in the XML dataset) and 1,431,820 induced tables (164,356 in the LaTeX dataset and 1,267,464 in the XML dataset). See section 3 for more details on the two datasets.

When using any algorithmically generated dataset, the question arises of how to ensure that the model is really learning something useful, rather than simply taking advantage of some algorithmic quirk of the generating process. Therefore, we perform evaluation entirely on human annotated figures. The algorithm is trained entirely on synthetic data and tested entirely on human labeled data, so our high performance demonstrates the quality of our distantly supervised dataset.

We run evaluation on two datasets: the "CS-Large" computer science dataset introduced by [7], and a new dataset we introduce using papers randomly sampled from PubMed. Our new dataset, consisting of 289 figures and 124 tables from 104 papers, was annotated by experts in biological sciences.

Hyperparameters:

We use RMSProp as our optimizer with initial learning rate 0.001. We train for 5,000,000 steps, decaying the learning rate by a factor

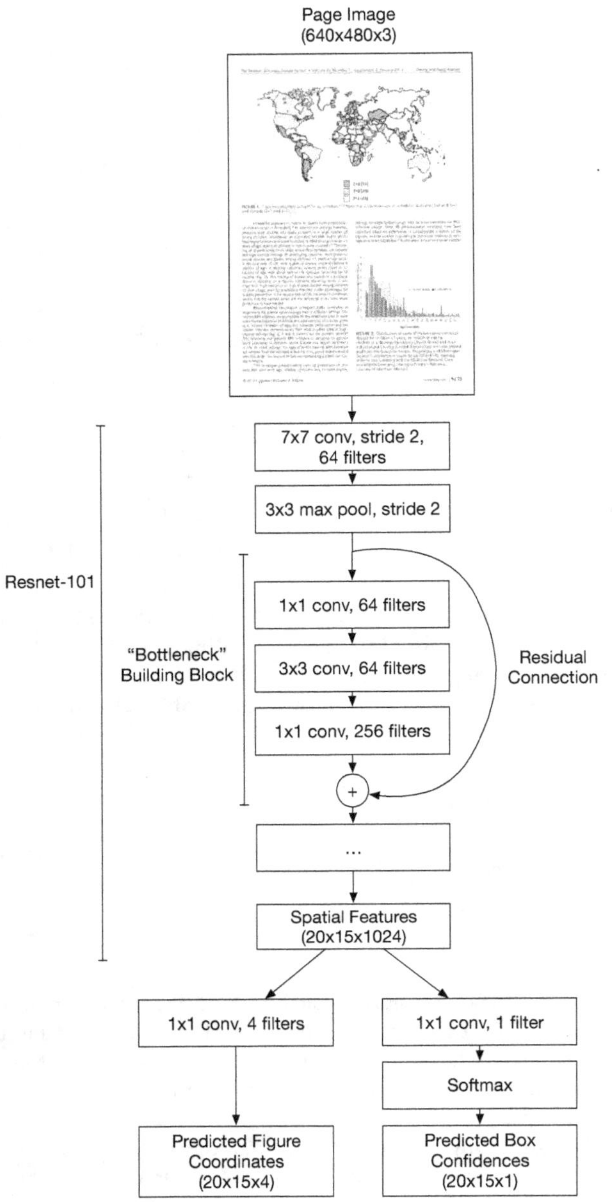

Figure 4: Architecture of the DeepFigures network expressed fully convolutionally. Note that a 1x1 convolution is equivalent to a fully connected layer run at each point on a spatial grid. Strides are 1 where not specified and all convolutional layers except those outputting predictions use ReLU activations. See [14] for the full ResNet-101 architecture.

of 2 every 330,000 steps. We use a batch size of 1 during training and did not observe significant performance gains from larger batches, likely due to the inherent parallelism in sliding window detection.

Evaluation Methodology:

Our evaluation methodology follows that of [7]. A predicted box is evaluated against a ground truth box based on Jaccard index,

System	CS-Large	PubMed
PDFFigures 2.0 [7]	**87.9%**	63.5%
DeepFigures (Ours)	84.9%	**80.6%**

Table 3: F1-scores for figure extraction systems on human labeled datasets. In keeping with [7], a predicted bounding box is considered correct if its IOU (intersection over union) with the true box is at least 0.8.

also known as intersection over union (IOU): the area of their intersection divided by the area of their union. As in [7], a predicted figure bounding box is considered correct if its IOU with the true box exceeds .80, while a predicted caption box is considered correct if its IOU exceeds .80 or if the predicted caption text matches the text from the true region extracted from the PDF. However, while [7] required annotations to include the figure number in order to be matched with predictions, we eliminate this requirement in order to simplify the human annotation task. Instead, we find the optimal assignment of predicted figures to true figures for each page, which is an instance of the linear assignment problem and can be done efficiently using the Hungarian algorithm.

Results:

As shown in Table 3, DeepFigures underperorms by 3 F1 points on "CS-Large", but achieves a 17 point improvement on the "PubMed" dataset. Given that PDFFigures 2.0 is a rule-based method that was tuned specifically for the "CS-Large" test set, it is unsurprising to see that it works better than DeepFigures for this domain.

Since DeepFigures does not use any human annotation or domain specific feature engineering, it has learned a robust model for identifying figures across a variety of domains. For example, PDFFigures 2.0 often generates false positives for graphical headers which are visually distinct from actual figures, however, allowing our model to correctly reject them.

6 EXTRACTING FIGURES IN PRODUCTION

One of the primary applications for figure extraction is academic search. The system we described for figure extraction has been deployed at scale in the Semantic Scholar search engine[10] to power the figures it serves along with other metadata from research papers. Currently, Semantic Scholar indexes more than 30 million research papers; it extracts and serves figures for 13 million of those papers, that is, the subset of papers which both allow figure extraction and have a PDF. Using a system built upon the techniques outlined in this paper, 96% of the 13 million papers were successfully extracted allowing Semantic Scholar to index 4.5 figures (or tables) for each paper on average.

The deployed system distributes the figure extraction work across numerous machines using a job queue. Each machine runs multiple worker processes which perform the following tasks:

(1) Retrieve a unique identifier for a paper from the job queue.
(2) Pull the paper down from S3.[11]

[10] www.semanticscholar.org
[11] Simple Storage Service, AWS's highly scalable object store.

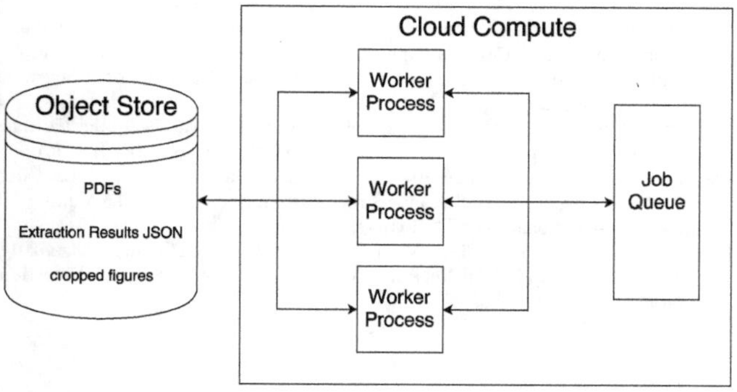

Figure 5: Deployment architecture for the Deepfigures service.

(3) Run the DeepFigures library's figure extraction code locally to detect figures and extract captions.
(4) Crop the figures out of the rendered PDFs using the detected bounding boxes.
(5) Upload the detection results and cropped images into S3 for further processing.

Once the cropped figures along with a JSON file describing the extraction results are in S3, they can be picked up by another data processing system such as Apache Spark for further transformations or indexing. In Semantic Scholar, this post-processing involves transforming the extraction results and indexing the figure metadata in Elasticsearch. From Elasticsearch, figures attached to a paper may be retrieved and their corresponding images served on the site directly from S3.

Due to the demanding computational requirements of the neural network models we use for figure detection, the use of GPU-capable machines can greatly accelerate the extraction process. The combination of I/O, network calls, rendering of PDFs, extracting captions from PDFs and neural network inference means that in order to fully utilize the GPU, CPU and network resources, it's helpful to run multiple processes extracting figures on one machine. In particular, the deployed system uses g2.xlarge instances in AWS EC2 with 8 worker processes to balance GPU and CPU requirements. Through AWS CloudFormation, the instance type is kept as a configuration option. The ability to configure the instance type, and other hardware decisions, enabled fast iteration to find a setup that properly balanced CPU, GPU and network resources. Such experimentation was crucial to finding machines with high throughput at a reasonable price.

Ultimately, the system is able to extract the figures from 15 papers per minute per machine and can scale horizontally. Running a single 12 page PDF through the whole pipeline, from queueing the paper through rendering and extraction, takes about 45 seconds. When the system is running at full speed, each paper takes around 30 seconds on average to be processed.

7 CONCLUSION

In this work, we present a novel method for inducing high-quality labels for figure extraction in scientific documents. Using this method, we contribute a dataset of 5.5 million induced labels with high accuracy, enabling researchers to develop more advanced methods for figure extraction in scientific documents.

We also introduce DeepFigures, a neural model for figure extraction trained on our induced dataset. DeepFigures has been successfully used to extract figures in 13 million papers in a large-scale academic search engine, demonstrating its scalability and robustness across a variety of domains.

Future work includes training a model to perform the full task of figure extraction end-to-end, including detecting and matching captions. This task could be aided by providing the network with additional information available from the PDF other than the rendered image, e.g. the locations of text and image elements on the page. Additionally, our data generation approaches could be extended to other information about papers such as title, authors, and sections; the distinctive visual characteristics of these elements as they appear in papers suggests neural detection models could be potentially useful.

REFERENCES

[1] Kurt D. Bollacker, Colin Evans, Praveen Paritosh, Tim Sturge, and Jamie Taylor. 2008. Freebase: a collaboratively created graph database for structuring human knowledge. In *SIGMOD*.
[2] Roberto Brunelli. 2009. *Template matching techniques in computer vision: theory and practice*. John Wiley & Sons.
[3] Kai Chen, Mathias Seuret, Marcus Liwicki, Jean Hennebert, and Rolf Ingold. 2015. Page segmentation of historical document images with convolutional autoencoders. In *ICDAR*.
[4] Sagnik Ray Choudhury, Suppawong Tuarob, Prasenjit Mitra, Lior Rokach, Andi Kirk, Silvia Szep, Donald Pellegrino, Sue Jones, and C. Lee Giles. 2013. A figure search engine architecture for a chemistry digital library. In *JCDL*.
[5] Sagnik Ray Choudhury, Shuting Wang, Prasenjit Mitra, and C. Lee Giles. 2015. Automated Data Extraction from Scholarly Line Graphs. In *GREC*.
[6] Christopher Clark and Santosh Divvala. 2015. Looking Beyond Text: Extracting Figures, Tables, and Captions from Computer Science Paper. In *AAAI, Workshop on Scholarly Big Data*.
[7] Christopher Andreas Clark and Santosh Kumar Divvala. 2016. PDFFigures 2.0: Mining figures from research papers. In *JCDL*.
[8] Navneet Dalal and Bill Triggs. 2005. Histograms of oriented gradients for human detection. In *CVPR*.
[9] Alba Garcia Seco de Herrera and Henning Müller and Stefano Bromuri. 2015. Overview of the ImageCLEF 2015 Medical Classification Task. In *CLEF*.
[10] Alba Garcia Seco de Herrera, Roger Schaer, Stefano Bromuri, and Henning Müller. 2016. Overview of the ImageCLEF 2016 Medical Task. In *CLEF*.
[11] Jia Deng, Wei Dong, Richard Socher, Li-Jia Li, Kai Li, and Li Fei-Fei. 2009. ImageNet: A large-scale hierarchical image database. In *CVPR*.
[12] Alexey Dosovitskiy, Philipp Fischer, Eddy Ilg, Philip Häusser, Caner Hazirbas, Vladimir Golkov, Patrick van der Smagt, Daniel Cremers, and Thomas Brox. 2015. FlowNet: Learning Optical Flow with Convolutional Networks. In *ICCV*.
[13] Dafang He, Scott Cohen, Brian L. Price, Daniel Kifer, and C. Lee Giles. 2017. Multi-Scale Multi-Task FCN for Semantic Page Segmentation and Table Detection. In *ICDAR*.
[14] Kaiming He, Xiangyu Zhang, Shaoqing Ren, and Jian Sun. 2016. Deep Residual Learning for Image Recognition. In *CVPR*.
[15] Alex Krizhevsky, Ilya Sutskever, and Geoffrey E. Hinton. 2012. ImageNet Classification with Deep Convolutional Neural Networks. In *NIPS*.
[16] Harold W Kuhn. 1955. The Hungarian method for the assignment problem. *Naval Research Logistics (NRL)* 2, 1-2 (1955), 83–97.
[17] Ashnil Kumar, Shane Dyer, Jinman Kim, Changyang Li, Philip HW Leong, Michael Fulham, and Dagan Feng. 2016. Adapting content-based image retrieval techniques for the semantic annotation of medical images. *Computerized Medical Imaging and Graphics* 49 (2016), 37–45.
[18] Mike Mintz, Steven Bills, Rion Snow, and Daniel Jurafsky. 2009. Distant supervision for relation extraction without labeled data. In *ACL/IJCNLP*.
[19] Pierre Sermanet, David Eigen, Xiang Zhang, Michael Mathieu, Rob Fergus, and Yann LeCun. 2014. OverFeat: Integrated Recognition, Localization and Detection using Convolutional Networks. In *ICLR*.
[20] Noah Siegel, Zachary Horvitz, Roie Levin, Santosh Divvala, and Ali Farhadi. 2016. FigureSeer: Parsing result-figures in research papers. In *ECCV*.

[21] Russell Stewart. 2017. TensorBox. https://github.com/TensorBox/TensorBox. (2017).

[22] Christian Szegedy, Wei Liu, Yangqing Jia, Pierre Sermanet, Scott Reed, Dragomir Anguelov, Dumitru Erhan, Vincent Vanhoucke, and Andrew Rabinovich. 2015. Going Deeper with Convolutions. In *CVPR*.

[23] Satoshi Tsutsui and David J. Crandall. 2017. A Data Driven Approach for Compound Figure Separation Using Convolutional Neural Networks. In *ICDAR*.

[24] Satoshi Tsutsui, Guilin Meng, Xiaohui Yao, David Crandall, and Ying Ding. 2016. Analyzing Figures of Brain Images from Alzheimer's Disease Papers. In *iConference*.

[25] Robert A Wagner and Michael J Fischer. 1974. The string-to-string correction problem. *Journal of the ACM (JACM)* 21, 1 (1974), 168–173.

[26] Jian Wu, Jason Killian, Huaiyu Yang, Kyle Williams, Sagnik Ray Choudhury, Suppawong Tuarob, Cornelia Caragea, and C. Lee Giles. 2015. PDFMEF: A Multi-Entity Knowledge Extraction Framework for Scholarly Documents and Semantic Search. In *K-CAP*.

[27] Shichao Yang, Daniel Maturana, and Sebastian Scherer. 2016. Real-time 3D scene layout from a single image using Convolutional Neural Networks. In *ICRA*.

[28] Xiao Yang, Ersin Yumer, Paul Asente, Mike Kraley, Daniel Kifer, and C. Lee Giles. 2017. Learning to Extract Semantic Structure from Documents Using Multimodal Fully Convolutional Neural Networks. In *CVPR*.

[29] Yuhai Yu, Hongfei Lin, Jiana Meng, Xiaocong Wei, and Zhehuan Zhao. 2017. Assembling Deep Neural Networks for Medical Compound Figure Detection. *Information* 8 (2017), 48.

Improving the Representation and Conversion of Mathematical Formulae by Considering their Textual Context

Moritz Schubotz[1], André Greiner-Petter[1], Philipp Scharpf[1], Norman Meuschke[1], Howard S. Cohl[2], Bela Gipp[1]
[1]Information Science Group, University of Konstanz, Germany (first.last@uni-konstanz.de)
[2]Applied and Computational Mathematics Division, NIST, U.S.A. (hcohl@nist.gov)

ABSTRACT

Mathematical formulae represent complex semantic information in a concise form. Especially in Science, Technology, Engineering, and Mathematics, mathematical formulae are crucial to communicate information, e.g., in scientific papers, and to perform computations using computer algebra systems. Enabling computers to access the information encoded in mathematical formulae requires machine-readable formats that can represent both the presentation and content, i.e., the semantics, of formulae. Exchanging such information between systems additionally requires conversion methods for mathematical representation formats. We analyze how the semantic enrichment of formulae improves the format conversion process and show that considering the textual context of formulae reduces the error rate of such conversions. Our main contributions are: (1) providing an openly available benchmark dataset for the mathematical format conversion task consisting of a newly created test collection, an extensive, manually curated gold standard and task-specific evaluation metrics; (2) performing a quantitative evaluation of state-of-the-art tools for mathematical format conversions; (3) presenting a new approach that considers the textual context of formulae to reduce the error rate for mathematical format conversions. Our benchmark dataset facilitates future research on mathematical format conversions as well as research on many problems in mathematical information retrieval. Because we annotated and linked all components of formulae, e.g., identifiers, operators and other entities, to Wikidata entries, the gold standard can, for instance, be used to train methods for formula concept discovery and recognition. Such methods can then be applied to improve mathematical information retrieval systems, e.g., for semantic formula search, recommendation of mathematical content, or detection of mathematical plagiarism.

CCS CONCEPTS

• **Information systems → Mathematics retrieval**; • **Applied computing →** *Format and notation*;

KEYWORDS

MathML; goldstandard; dataset; computer algebra systems

JCDL '18, June 3–7, 2018, Fort Worth, TX, USA

ACM ISBN 978-1-4503-5178-2/18/06...$15.00
https://doi.org/10.1145/3197026.3197058

ACM Reference Format:
Moritz Schubotz[1], André Greiner-Petter[1], Philipp Scharpf[1], Norman Meuschke[1], Howard S. Cohl[2], Bela Gipp[1]. 2018. Improving the Representation and Conversion of Mathematical Formulae by Considering their Textual Context. In *JCDL '18: The 18th ACM/IEEE Joint Conference on Digital Libraries, June 3–7, 2018, Fort Worth, TX, USA.* ACM, New York, NY, USA, 10 pages. https://doi.org/10.1145/3197026.3197058

1 INTRODUCTION

In STEM disciplines, i.e., Science, Technology, Engineering, and Mathematics, mathematical formulae are ubiquitous and crucial to communicate information in documents, such as scientific papers, and to perform computations in computer algebra systems (CAS). Mathematical formulae represent complex semantic information in a concise form that is independent of natural language. These characteristics make mathematical formulae particularly interesting features to be considered by information retrieval systems.

In the digital libraries context, major information retrieval applications for mathematical formulae include search and recommender systems as well as systems that support humans in understanding and applying mathematical formulae, e.g., by visualizing mathematical functions or providing auto completion and error correction functionality in typesetting and CAS.

However, the extensive, context-dependent polysemy and polymorphism of mathematical notation is a major challenge to exposing the knowledge encoded in mathematical formulae to such systems. The amount of mathematical concepts, e.g., mathematical structures, relations and principles, is much larger than the set of mathematical symbols available to represent these concepts. Therefore, the meaning of mathematical symbols varies in different contexts, e.g., in different documents, and potentially even in the same context. Identical mathematical formulae, even in the same document, do not necessarily represent the same mathematical concepts. Identifiers are prime examples of mathematical polysemy. For instance, while the identifier E commonly denotes energy in physics, E commonly refers to expected value in statistics.

Polymorphism of mathematical symbols is another ubiquitous phenomenon of mathematical notation. For example, whether the operator $\cdot$ denotes a scalar multiplication or a vector multiplication depends on the type of the elements that the operator is applied to. Opposed to programming languages, which handle polymorphism by explicitly providing type information about objects to the compiler, e.g., to check and call methods offered by the specific objects, mathematical symbols mostly denote such type information implicitly so that they need to be reasoned from the context.

Humans account for the inherent polysemy and polymorphism of mathematical notation by defining context-dependent meanings of mathematical symbols in the text that surrounds formulae, e.g., for identifiers, subscripts and superscripts, brackets, and invisible operators. Without such explanations, determining the meaning of symbols is challenging, even for mathematical experts. For example, reliably determining whether $[a, b]$ represents an interval or the commutator $[a, b] = ab - ba$ in ring theory requires information on whether [] represent the Dirac brackets.

Enabling computers to access the full information encoded in mathematical formulae mandates machine-readable representation formats that capture both the presentation, i.e., the notational symbols and their spacial arrangement, and the content, i.e., the semantics, of mathematical formulae. Likewise, exchanging mathematical formulae between applications, e.g., CAS, requires methods to convert and semantically enrich different representation formats. The Mathematical Markup Language (MathML) allows one to encode both presentation and content information in a standardized and extensible way (cf. Section 3).

Despite the availability of MathML, most Digital Mathematical Libraries (DML) currently exclusively use presentation languages, such as TeX and LaTeX to represent mathematical content. On the other hand, CAS, such as MAPLE, Mathematica or SageMath[1], typically use representation formats that include more content information about mathematical formulae to enable computations. The conversion between representation formats entails many conceptual and technical challenges, which we describe in more detail in Section 2. Despite the availability of numerous conversion tools, the inherent challenges of the conversion process result in a high error rate and often lossy conversion of mathematical formulae in different representation formats.

To push forward advances in research on mathematical format conversion, we make the following contributions, which we describe in the subsequent sections:

(1) We provide an openly available benchmark dataset to evaluate tools for mathematical format conversion (cf. Section 3). The dataset includes:
   - a new test collection covering diverse research areas in multiple STEM disciplines;
   - an extensive, manually curated gold standard that includes annotations for both presentation and content information of mathematical formulae;
   - tools to facilitate the future extension of the gold standard by visually supporting human annotators; and
   - metrics to quantitatively evaluate the quality of mathematical format conversions.

(2) We perform an extensive, quantitative evaluation of state-of-the-art tools for mathematical format conversion and provide an automated evaluation framework that easily allows rerunning the evaluation in future research (cf. Section 4).

(3) We propose a novel approach to mathematical format conversion (cf. Section 5). The approach imitates the human sense-making process for mathematical content by analyzing the textual context of formulae for information that helps link symbols in formulae to a knowledge base, in our case Wikidata, to determine the semantics of formulae.

[1]The mention of specific products, trademarks, or brand names is for purposes of identification only. Such mention is not to be interpreted in any way as an endorsement or certification of such products or brands by the National Institute of Standards and Technology, nor does it imply that the products so identified are necessarily the best available for the purpose. All trademarks mentioned herein belong to their respective owners.

2 BACKGROUND & RELATED WORK

In the following, we use the Riemann hypothesis (1) as an example to explain typical challenges of converting different representation formats of mathematical formulae:

$$\zeta(s) = 0 \Rightarrow \Re s = \frac{1}{2} \lor \Im s = 0. \qquad (1)$$

We will focus on the representation of the formula in LaTeX and in the format of the CAS Mathematica. LaTeX is a common language for encoding the presentation of mathematical formulae. In contrast to LaTeX, Mathematica's representation focuses on making formulae computable. Hence the content must be encoded, i.e., both the structure and the semantics of mathematical formulae must be taken into consideration.

In LaTeX, the Riemann hypothesis can be expressed using the following string:
`\zeta(s) = 0 \Rightarrow \Re s = \frac12 \lor \Im s=0.`
In Mathematica, the Riemann hypothesis can be represented as:
`Implies[Equal[Zeta[s], 0], Or[Equal[Re[s], Rational[1, 2]], Equal[Im[s], 0]]].`

The conversion between these two formats is challenging due to a range of conceptual and technical differences.

First, the grammars underlying the two representation formats greatly differ. LaTeX uses the unrestricted grammar of the TeX typesetting system. The entire set of commands can be re-defined and extended at runtime, which means that TeX effectively allows its users to change every character used for the markup, including the \ character typically used to start commands. The large degree of freedom of the TeX grammar significantly complicates recognizing even the most basic tokens contained in mathematical formulae. In difference to LaTeX, CAS use a significantly more restrictive grammar consisting of a predefined set of keywords and set rules that govern the structure of expressions. For example in Mathematica, function arguments must always be enclosed in square brackets and separated by commas.

Second, the extensive differences in the grammars of the two languages are reflected in the resulting expression trees. Similar to parse trees in natural language, the syntactic rules of mathematical notation, such as operator precedence and function scope, determine a hierarchical structure for mathematical expressions that can be understood, represented, and processed as a tree. The mathematical expression trees of formulae consist of functions or operators and their arguments. We used nested square brackets to denote levels of the tree and Arabic numbers in a gray font to indicate individual tokens in the markup. For the LaTeX representation of the Riemann hypothesis, the expression tree is:

$$\left[\zeta_1^1\ (_1^2\ s_1^3\ )_1^4\ =_1^5\ 0_1^6\ \Rightarrow_1^7\ \Re_1^8\ s_1^9\ =_1^{10}\ \left[\vdots^{11}\ 1_1^{12}\ 2_1^{13}\right]\ \lor_1^{14}\ \Im_1^{15}\ s_1^{16}\ =_1^{17}\ 0_1^{18}\right].$$

The tree consists of 18 nodes, i.e., tokens, with a maximum depth of two (for the fraction command `\frac12`). The expression tree of the Mathematica expression consists of 16 tokens with a maximum depth of five:

$$\left[{}^{19}\!\Rightarrow \left[{}^{20}\!= \left[{}^{21}\zeta\, {}^{22}s_{\mathrm{l}}\right]\, {}^{23}0_{\mathrm{n}}\right] \left[{}^{24}\!\vee \left[{}^{25}\!= \left[{}^{26}\Re\, {}^{27}s_{\mathrm{l}}\right] \left[{}^{28}\mathbb{Q}\, {}^{29}1_{\mathrm{n}}\, {}^{30}2_{\mathrm{n}}\right]\right] \left[{}^{31}\!= \left[{}^{32}\Im\, {}^{33}s_{\mathrm{l}}\right]\, {}^{34}0_{\mathrm{n}}\right]\right]\right].$$

The higher complexity of the Mathematica expression reflects that a CAS represents the content structure of the formula, which is deeply nested. In contrast, LaTeX exclusively represents the presentational layout of the Riemann hypothesis, which is almost linear.

For the given example of the Riemann hypothesis, finding alignments between the tokens in both representations and converting one representation into the other is possible. In fact, Mathematica and other CAS offer a direct import of TeX expressions, which we evaluate in Section 4.

However, aside from technical obstacles, such as reliably determining tokens in TeX expressions, conceptual differences also prevent a successful conversion between presentation languages, such as TeX, and content languages. Even if there was only one generally accepted presentation language, e.g., a standardized TeX dialect, and only one generally accepted content language, e.g., a standardized input language for CAS, an accurate conversion between the representation formats could not be guaranteed.

The reason is that neither the presentation language, nor the content language always provides all required information to convert an expression to the respective language. This can be illustrated by the simple expression: $F(a+b) = Fa + Fb$. The inherent content ambiguity of F prevents a deterministic conversion from the presentation language to a content language. F might, for example, represent a number, a matrix, a linear function or even a symbol. Without additional information, a correct conversion to a content language is not guaranteed. On the other hand, the transformation from content language to presentation language often depends on the preferences of the author and the context. For example, authors sometimes change the presentation of a formula to focus on specific parts of the formula or improve its readability.

Another obstacle to conversions between typical presentation languages and typical content languages, such as the formats of CAS, are the restricted set of functions and the simpler grammars that CAS offer. While TeX allows users to express the presentation of virtually all mathematical symbols, thus denoting any mathematical concept, CAS do not support all available mathematical functions or structures. A significant problem related to the discrepancy of the space of concepts expressible using presentation markup and the implementation of such concepts in CAS are branch cuts. Branch cuts are restrictions of the set of output values that CAS impose for functions that yield ambiguous, i.e., multiple mathematically permissible outputs. One example is the complex logarithm [7, eq. 4.2.1], which has an infinite set of permissible outputs resulting from the periodicity of its inverse function. To account for this circumstance, CAS typically restrict the set of permissible outputs by cutting the complex plane of permissible outputs. However, since the method of restricting the set of permissible outputs varies between systems, identical inputs can lead to drastically different results [5]. For example, multiple scientific publications address the problem of accounting for branch cuts when entering expressions in CAS, such as [8] for MAPLE.

Listing 1: MathML representation of the Riemann hypothesis (1) (excerpt).

```
<math><semantics><mrow>...
  <mo id="5" xref="20">=</mo>
  <mn id="5" xref="21">0</mn>
  <mo id="7" xref="19">⇒</ci>...</mrow>
<annotation-xml encoding="MathML-Content">
  <apply><implies id="19" xref="7"/>
  <apply><eq id="20" xref="5"/>...
  <apply><csymbol id="21" xref="1" cd="wikidata">Q187235...
</annotation-xml></semantics></math>
```

Our review of obstacles to the conversion of representation formats for mathematical formulae highlights the need to store *both* presentation and content information to allow for reversible transformations. Mathematical representation formats that include presentation and content information can enable the reliable exchange of information between typesetting systems and CAS.

MathML offers standardized markup functionality for both presentation and content information. Moreover, the declarative MathML XML format is relatively easy to parse and allows for cross references between presentation language (PL) and content language (CL) elements. Listing 1 represents excerpts of the MathML markup for our example of the Riemann hypothesis (1). In this excerpt, the PL token 7 corresponds to the CL token 19, PL token 5 corresponds to CL token 20, and so forth.

Combined presentation and content formats, such as MathML, significantly improve the access to mathematical knowledge for users of digital libraries. For example, including content information of formulae can advance search and recommendation systems for mathematical content. The quality of these *mathematical information retrieval systems* crucially depends on the accuracy of the computed document-query and document-document similarities. Considering the content information of mathematical formulae can improve these computations by:

(1) enabling the consideration of mathematical equivalence as a similarity feature. Instead of exclusively analyzing presentation information as indexed, e.g., by considering the overlap in presentational tokens, content information allows modifying the query and the indexed information. For example, it would become possible to recognize that the expressions $a(\frac{b}{c}+\frac{d}{c})$ and $\frac{a(b+d)}{c}$ have a distance of zero.
(2) allowing the association of mathematical tokens with mathematical concepts. For example, linking identifiers, such as E, m, and c, to energy, mass, and speed of light, could enable searching for all formulae that combine all or a subset of the concepts.
(3) enabling the analysis of structural similarity. The availability of content information would enable the application of measures, such as derivatives of the tree edit distance, to discover structural similarity, e.g., using λ-calculus. This functionality could increase the capabilities of *math-based plagiarism detection systems* when it comes to identifying obfuscated instances of reused mathematical formulae [11].

Content information could furthermore enable interactive support functions for consumers and producers of mathematical content. For example, readers of mathematical documents could be offered interactive computations and visualizations of formulae to accelerate the understanding of STEM documents. Authors of mathematical documents could benefit from automated editing suggestions, such as auto completion, reference suggestion, and sanity checks, e.g., type and definiteness checking, similar to the functionality of word processors for natural language texts.

Related Work

A variety of tools exist to convert format representations of mathematical formulae. However, to our knowledge, Kohlhase et al. presented the only study that evaluated the conversion quality of tools [26]. Unfortunately, many of the tools evaluated by Kohlhase et al. are no longer available or out of date. Watt presents a strategy to preserve formula semantics in TeX to MathML conversions. His approach relies on encoding the semantics in custom TeX macros rather than to expand the macros [27]. Padovani discusses the roles of MathML and TeX elements for managing large repositories of mathematical knowledge [15]. Nghiem et al. used statistical machine translation to convert presentation to content language [14]. However, they do not consider the textual context of formulae. We will present detailed descriptions and evaluation results for specific conversion approaches in Section 4.

Youssef addressed the semantic enrichment of mathematical formulae in presentation language. They developed an automated tagger that parses LaTeX formulae and annotates recognized tokens very similarly to Part-Of-Speech (POS) taggers for natural language [28]. Their tagger currently uses a predefined, context-independent dictionary to identify and annotate formula components. Schubotz et al. proposed an approach to semantically enrich formulae by analyzing their textual context for the definitions of identifiers [22, 24].

With their 'math in the middle approach', Dehaye et al. envision an entirely different approach to exchanging machine readable mathematical expressions. In their vision, independent and enclosed virtual research environments use a standardized format for mathematics to avoid computions and transfers between different systems. [6].

For an extensive review of format conversion and retrieval approaches for mathematical formulae, refer to [17, Chapter 2].

3 BENCHMARKING MATHML

This section presents MathMLben - a benchmark dataset for measuring the quality of MathML markup of mathematical formulae appearing in a textual context. MathMLben is an improvement of the gold standard provided by Schubotz et al. [21]. The dataset considers recent discussions of the Intrenational Mathematical Knowledge of Trust working group, in particular the idea of a 'Semantic Capture Language' [10], which makes the gold standard more robust and easily accessible. MathMLben:

- allows comparisons to prior works;
- covers a wide range of research areas in STEM literature;
- provides references to manually annotated and corrected MathML items that are compliant with the MathML standard;
- is easy to modify and extend, i.e., by external collaborators;
- includes default distance measures; and
- facilitates the development of converters and tools.

In Section 3.1, we present the test collection included in MathMLben. In Section 3.2, we present the encoding guidelines for the human assessors and describe the tools we developed to support assessors in creating the gold standard dataset. In Section 3.3, we describe the similarity measures used to assess the markup quality.

3.1 Collection

Our test collection contains 305 formulae (more precisely, mathematical expressions ranging from individual symbols to complex multi-line formulae) and the documents in which they appear.

Expressions 1 to 100 correspond to the search targets used for the 'National Institute of Informatics Testbeds and Community for Information access Research Project' (NTCIR) 11 Math Wikipedia Task [21]. This list of formulae has been used for formula search and content enrichment tasks by at least 7 different research institutions. The formulae were randomly sampled from Wikipedia and include expressions with incorrect presentation markup.

Expressions 101 to 200 are random samples taken from the NIST Digital Library of Mathematical Functions (DLMF) [7]. The DLMF website contains 9,897 labeled formulae created from semantic LaTeX source files [3, 4]. In contrast to the examples from Wikipedia, all these formulae are from the mathematics research field and exhibit high quality presentation markup. The formulae were curated by renowned mathematicians and the editorial board keeps improving the quality of the formulae's markup[2]. Sometimes, a labeled formula contains multiple equations. In such cases, we randomly chose one of the equations.

Expressions 201 to 305 were chosen from the queries of the NTCIR arXiv and NTCIR-12 Wikipedia datasets. 70% of these queries originate from the arXiv [1] and 30% from a Wikipedia dump.

All data is openly available for research purposes and can be obtained from: https://mathmlben.wmflabs.org[3].

3.2 Gold Standard

We provide explicit markup with universal, context-independent symbols in content MathML. Since the symbols from the default content dictionary of MathML[4] alone were insufficient to cover the range of semantics in our collection, we added the Wikidata content dictionary [18]. As a result, we could refer to all Wikidata items as symbols in a content tree. This approach has several advantages. Descriptions and labels are available in many languages. Some symbols even have external identifiers, e.g., from the Wolfram Functions Site, or from stack-exchange topics. All symbols are linked to Wikipedia articles, which offer extensive human-readable descriptions. Finally, symbols have relations to other Wikidata items, which opens a range of new research opportunities, e.g., for improving the taxonomic distance measure [23].

Our Wikidata-enhanced, yet standard-compliant MathML markup, facilitates the manual creation of content markup. To further support human assessors in creating content annotations, we extended

[2] http://dlmf.nist.gov/about/staff
[3] Visit https://mathmlben.wmflabs.org/about for a user guide.
[4] http://www.openmath.org/cd

Table 1: Special content symbols added to LaTeXML for the creation of the gold standard.

No	rendering	meaning	example ID
1	$[x, y]$	commutator	91
2	x_z^y	tensor	43, 208, 226
3	$x^\dagger$	adjoint	224, 277
4	x'	transformation	20
5	x°	degree	20
6	$x^{(dim)}$	contraction	225

the VMEXT visualization tool [25] to develop a visual support tool for creating and editing the *MathMLBen* gold standard.

For each formula, we saved the source document written in different dialects of LaTeX and converted it into content MathML with parallel markup using LaTeXML [12, 9]. LaTeXML is a Perl program that converts LaTeX documents to XML and HTML. We chose LaTeXML, because it is the only tool that supports our semantic macro set. We manually annotated our dataset, generated the MathML representation, manually corrected errors in the MathML, and linked the identifiers to Wikidata concept entries whenever possible. Alternatively, one could initially generate MathML using a CAS and then manually improve the markup.

Since there is no generally accepted definition of expression trees, we made several design decision to create semantic representations of the formulae in our dataset using MathML trees. In some cases, we created new macros to be able to create a MathML tree for our purposes using LaTeXML[5]. Table 1 lists the newly created macros. Hereafter, we explain our decisions and give examples of formulae in our dataset that were affected by the decisions.

- not assign Wikidata items to basic mathematical identifiers and functions like `factorial`, `\log`, `\exp`, `\times`, `\pi`. Instead, we left these annotations to the DLMF LaTeX macros, because they represent the mathematical concept by linking to the definition in the DLMF and LaTeXML creates valid and accurate content MathML for these macros [GoldID 3, 11, 19, ...];
- split up indices and labels of elements as child nodes of the element. For example, we represent `i` as a child node of `p` in `p_i` [GoldID 29, 36, 43, ...];
- create a special macro to represent tensors, such as for $T_{\alpha\beta}$ [GoldID 43], to represent upper and lower indices as child nodes (see table 1);
- create a macro for dimensions of tensor contractions [GoldID 225], e.g., to distinguish the three dimensional contraction of the metric tensor in $g^{(3)}$ from a power function (see table 1);
- chose one subexpression randomly if the original expression contained lists of expressions [GoldID 278];
- remove equation labels, as they are not part of the formula itself. For example, in

$$E = mc^2, \qquad (\star)$$

  the $(\star)$ is the ignored label;
- remove operations applied to entire equations, e.g., applying the modulus. In such cases, we interpreted the modulus as a constraint of the equation [GoldID 177];
- use additional macros (see table 1) to interpret complex conjugations, transformation signs, and degree-symbols as functional operations (identifier is a child node of the operation symbol), e.g., `*` or `\dagger` for complex conjugations [GoldID 224, 277], `S'` for transformations [GoldID 20], `30^\circ` for thirty degrees [Gold ID 30];
- for formulae with multiple cases, render each case as a separate branch [GoldID 49];
- render variables that are part of separate branches in bracket notation. We implemented the Dirac Bracket commutator [] (omitting the index `_\text{DB}`) and an anticommutator by defining new macros (see table 1). Thus, there is a distinction between a (ring) commutator `[a,b] = ab - ba` and an anti-commutator `{a,b} = ab + ba`, without further annotation of Dirac or Poisson brackets [GoldID 91];
- use the command `\operatorname{}` for multi-character identifiers or operators [GoldID 22]. This markup is necessary, because most LaTeX parsers, including LaTeXML, interpret multi-character expressions as multiplications of the characters. In general, this interpretation is correct, since it is inconvenient to use multi-character identifiers [2].

Some of these design decisions are debatable. For example, introducing a macro `\identifiername{}` to distinguish between multi-character identifiers and operators might be advantageous to our approach. However, introducing many highly specialized macros is likely not a viable approach and exaggerated. A borderline example in regard to this problem is Δx [GoldID 280]. Formulae of this form could be annotated as `\operatorname{}`, `\identifiername{}` or more generally as `\expressionname{}`. We interpret Δ as a difference applied to a variable, and render the expression as a function call.

Similar cases of overfeeding the dataset with highly specialized macros are bracket notations. For example, the bracket (Dirac) notation, e.g., [GoldID 209], is mainly used in quantum physics. The angle brackets for the Dirac notation, ⟨ and ⟩, and a vertical bar | is already interpreted correctly as "latexml - quantum-operator-product". However, a more precise distinction between a twofold scalar product, e.g., $\langle a|b\rangle$, and a threefold expectation value, e.g., $\langle a|A|a\rangle$, might become necessary in some scenarios to distinguish between matrix elements and a scalar product.

We developed a Web application to create and cultivate the gold standard entries, which is available at: https://mathmlben.wmflabs.org/. The Graphical User Interface (GUI) provides the following information for each Gold ID entry.

- **Formula Name:** the name of the formula (optional)
- **Formula Type:** either *definition, equation, relation* or *General Formula* (if none of the previous names fit)
- **Original Input TeX:** the LaTeX expression extracted from the source
- **Corrected TeX:** the manually corrected LaTeX expression
- **Hyperlink:** the hyperlink to the position of the formula in the source

[5]http://dlmf.nist.gov/LaTeXML/manual/customization/customization.latexml.html#SS1.SSS0.Px1

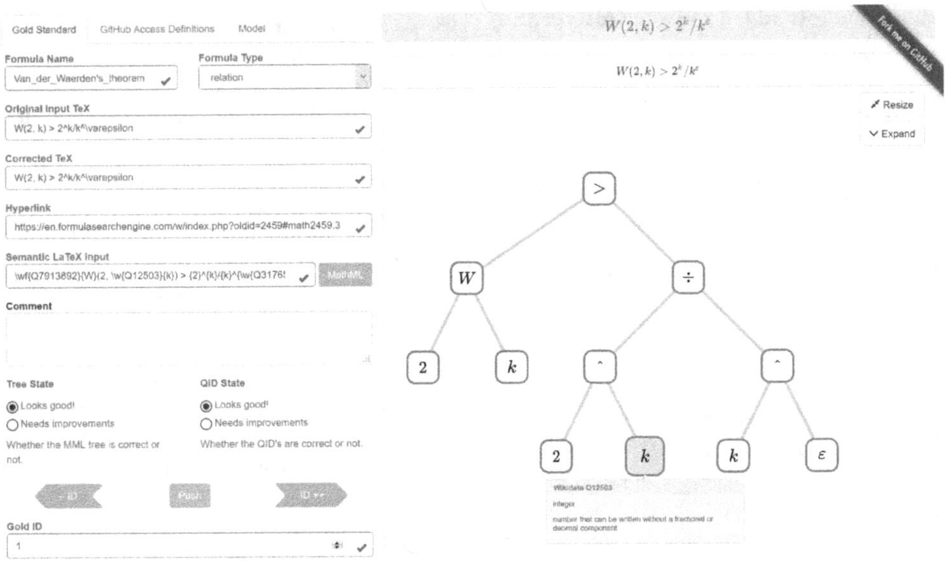

Figure 1: Graphical User Interface to support the creation of our gold standard. The interface provides several TeX input fields (left) and a mathematical expression tree rendered by the VMEXT visualization tool (right).

- **Semantic LaTeX Input:** the manually created semantic version of the corrected LaTeX field. This entry is used to generate our MathML with Wikidata annotations.
- **Preview of Corrected LaTeX:** a preview of the corrected LaTeX input field rendered as an SVG image in real time using Mathoid [20], a service to generate SVGs and MathML from LaTeX input. It is shown in the top right corner of the GUI.
- **VMEXT Preview:** the VMEXT field renders the expression tree based on the content MathML. The symbol in each node is associated with the symbol in the cross referenced presentation MathML.

Figure 1 shows the GUI that allows to manually modify the different formats of a formula. While the other fields are intended to provide additional information, the pipeline to create and cultivate a gold standard entry starts with the semantic LaTeX input field. LaTeXML will generate content MathML based on this input and VMEXT will render the generated content MathML afterwards. We control the output by using the DLMF LaTeX macros [13] and our developed extensions. The following list contains some example of the DLMF LaTeX macros.

- `\EulerGamma@{z}`: $\Gamma(z)$: gamma function,
- `\BesselJ{\nu}@{z}`: $J_\nu(z)$: Bessel function of the first kind,
- `\LegendreQ[\mu]{\nu}@{z}`: $Q_\nu^\mu(z)$: associated Legendre function of the second kind,
- `\JacobiP{\alpha}{\beta}{n}@{x}`: $P_n^{(\alpha,\beta)}(x)$: Jacobi polynomial.

The DLMF web pages, which we use as one of the sources for our dataset, were generated from semantically enriched LaTeX sources using LaTeXML. Since LaTeXML is capable to interpret semantic macros, generates content MathML that can be controlled with macros, and is easily extensible by new macros, we also used LaTeXML to generate our gold standard. While the DLMF is a compendium for special functions, we need to annotate every identifier in the formula with semantic information. Therefore, we extended the set of semantic macros.

In addition to the special symbols listed in Table 1, we created macros to semantically enrich identifiers, operators, and other mathematical concepts by linking them to their Wikidata items. As shown in Figure 1, the annotations are visualized using yellow info boxes appearing on mouse over. The boxes show the Wikidata QID, the name, and the description (if available) of the linked concept.

Aside from naming, classifying, and semantically annotating each formula, we performed three other tasks:

- correcting the LaTeX string extracted from the sources;
- checking and correcting the MathML generated by LaTeXML
- visualizing the MathMl using VMEXT

Most of the extracted formulae contained concepts to improve human readability of the source code, such as commented line breaks, `%\n`, in long mathematical expressions, or special macros to improve the displayed version of the formula, e.g., spacing macros, delimiters, and scale settings, such as `\!`, `\,` or `\>`. Since they are part of the expression, all of the tested tools (also LaTeXML) try to include these formating improvements into the MathML markup. For our gold standard, we focus on the pure semantic information and forgo formating improvements related to displaying the formula. The corrected TeX field shows the cleaned mathematical LaTeX expression.

Using the corrected TeX field and the semantic macros, we were able to adjust the MathML output using LaTeXML and verify it by checking the visualization from VMEXT.

3.3 Evaluation Metrics

To quantify the conversion quality of individual tools, we computed the similarity of each tool's output and the manually created gold standard. To define the similarity measures for this comparison, we built upon our previous work [23], in which we defined and evaluated four similarity measures: taxonomic distance, data type hierarchy level, match depth, and query coverage. The measures taxonomic distance and data type hierarchy level require the availability of a hierarchical ordering of mathematical functions and objects. For our use case, we derived this hierarchical ordering from the MathML content dictionary. The measures assign a higher similarity score if matching formula elements belong to the same taxonomic class. The match depth measure operates under the assumption that matching elements, which are more deeply nested in a formula's content tree, i.e., farther away from the root node, are less significant for the overall similarity of the formula, hence are assigned a lower weight. The query coverage measure performs a simple 'bag of tokens' comparison between two formulae and assigns a higher score the more tokens the two formulae share.

In addition to these similarity measures, we also included the tree edit distance. For this purpose, we adapted the robust tree edit distance (RTED) implementation for Java [16]. We modified RTED to accept any valid XML input and added math-specific 'shortcuts', i.e., rewrite rules that generate lower distance scores than arbitrary rewrites. For example, rewriting $\frac{a}{b}$ to ab^{-1} causes a significant difference in the expression tree: Three nodes ($\wedge, -, 1$) are inserted and one node is renamed $\div \rightarrow \cdot$. The 'costs' for performing these edits using the stock implementation of RTED are $c = 3i + r$. However, the actual difference is an equivalence, which we think should be assigned a cost of $e < 3i + r$. We set $e < r < i$.

4 EVALUATION CONTEXT-AGNOSTIC CONVERSION TOOLS

This section presents the results of evaluating existing, context-agnostic conversion tools for mathematical formulae using our benchmark dataset MathMLben (cf. Section 3). We compare the distances between the presentation MathML and the content MathML tree of a formula yielded by each tool to the respective trees of formulae in the gold standard. We use the tree edit distance with customized weights and math-specific shortcuts. The goal of shortcuts is eliminating notational-inherent degrees of freedom, e.g., additional PL elements or layout blocks, such as `mrow` or `mfenced`.

4.1 Tool Selection

We compiled a list of available conversion tools from the W3C[6] wiki, from *GitHub*, and from questions about automated conversion of mathematical LaTeX to MathML on *Stack Overflow*. We selected the following converters:

- LaTeXML: can convert generic and semantically annotated LaTeX expressions to XML/HTML/MathML. The tool is written in Perl [12] and is actively maintained. LaTeXML was specifically developed to generate the DLMF web page and can therefore parse entire TeX documents. LaTeXML also supports conversions to content MathML.
- LaTeX2MathML: is a small python project and is able to generate presentation MathML from generic LaTeX expressions[7].
- Mathoid: is a service developed using Node.js, PhantomJS and MathJax (a javascript display engine for mathematics) to generate SVGs and MathML from LaTeX input. Mathoid is currently used to render mathematical formulae on Wikipedia [20].
- SnuggleTeX: is an open-source Java library developed at the University of Edinburgh[8]. The tool allows to convert simple LaTeX expression to XHTML and presentation MathML.
- MathToWeb: is an open-source Java-based web application that generates presentation MathML from LaTeX expressions[9].
- TeXZilla: is a javascript web application for LaTeX to MathML conversion capable of handling Unicode characters[10].
- Mathematical: is an application written in C and wrapped in Ruby to provide a fast translation from LaTeX expressions to the image formats SVG and PNG. The tool also provides translations to presentation MathML[11].
- CAS: we included a prominent CAS capable of parsing LaTeX expressions.
- Part-of-Math (POM) Tagger: is a grammar-based LaTeX parser that tags recognized tokens with information from a dictionary [28]. The POM tagger is currently under development. In this paper, we use the first version. In [5], this version was used to provide translations LaTeX to the CAS MAPLE. In its current state, the program offers no export to MathML. We developed an XML exporter to be able to compare the tree provided by the POM tagger with the MathML trees in the gold standard.

4.2 Testing framework

We developed a Java-based framework that calls the programs to parse the corrected TeX input data from the gold standard to presentation MathML, and, if applicable, to content MathML. In case of the POM tagger, we parsed the input string to a general XML document. We used the corrected TeX input format instead of the originally extracted string expressions, see 3.2.

Executing the testing framework requires the manual installation of the tested tools. The POM tagger is not yet publicly available.

4.3 Results

Figure 2 shows the averaged structural tree edit distances between the presentation trees (blue) and content trees (orange) of the generated MathML files and the gold standard. To calculate the structural tree edit distances, we used the RTED [16] algorithm with costs of $i = 1$ for inserting, $d = 1$ for deleting and $r = 0$ for renaming nodes. Furthermore, the Figure shows the total number of successful transformations for the 305 expressions (black ticks). Note that we also consider differences of the presentation tree to the gold standard as deficits, because the mapping from LaTeX expressions to rendered expressions is unique (as long as the same preambles are used). A larger number indicates that more elements of an expression were misinterpreted by the parser. However, certain differences between presentation trees might be tolerable, e.g., reordering commutative

[6]https://www.w3.org/wiki/Math_Tools

[7]https://github.com/Code-ReaQtor/latex2mathml

[8]https://www2.ph.ed.ac.uk/snuggletex/documentation/overview-and-features.html

[9]https://www.mathtowebonline.com

[10]https://fred-wang.github.io/TeXZilla

[11]https://github.com/gjtorikian/mathematical

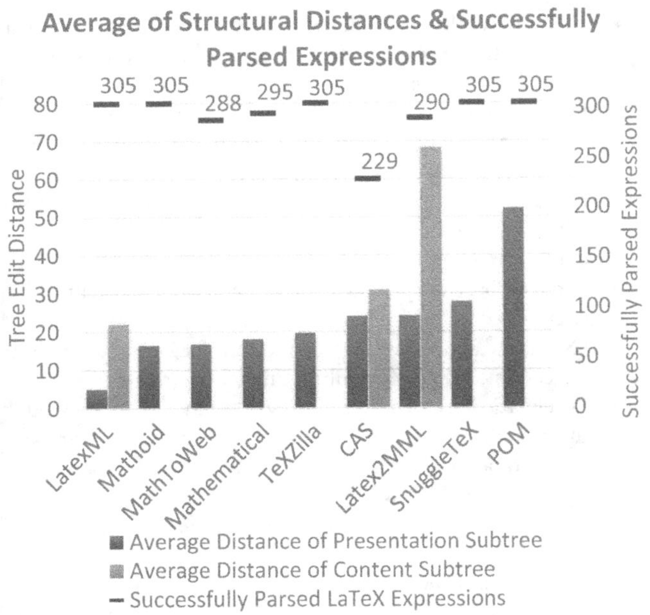

Figure 2: Overview of the structural tree edit distances (using $r = 0,\ i = d = 1$) between the MathML trees generated by the conversion tools and the gold standard MathML trees.

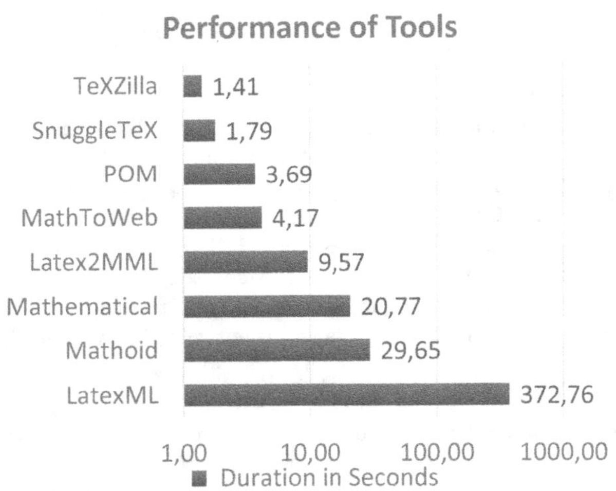

Figure 3: Time in seconds required by each tool to parse the 305 gold standard LaTeX expressions in logarithmic scale.

expressions, while differences between content trees are more critical. Also note that improving content trees may not necessarily improve presentation trees and vice versa. In case of $f(x + y)$, the content tree will change depending whether f represents a variable or a function, while the presentation tree will be identical in both cases. In contrast, $\frac{a}{b}$, ${}^{a}/_{b}$, and a/b have different presentation trees, while the content trees are identical.

Figure 3 illustrates the runtime performance of the tools. We excluded the CAS from the runtime performance tests, because the system is not primarily intended for parsing LaTeX expressions, but for performing complex computations. Therefore, runtime comparisons between a CAS and conversion tools would not be representative. We measured the times required to transform all 305 expressions in the gold standard and write the transformed MathML to the storage cache. Note that the native code of Latex2MML, Mathematical and LaTeXML were called from the Java Virtual Machine (JVM) and Mathoid was called through local web-requests, which increased the runtime of these tools. The figure is scaled logarithmically. We would like to emphasize that LaTeXML is designed to translate sets of LaTeX documents instead of single mathematical expressions. Most of the other tools are lightweight engines.

In this benchmark, we focused on the structural tree distances rather than on distances in semantics. While our gold standard provides the information necessary to compare the extracted semantic information, we will focus on this problem in future work (see Section 6).

5 TOWARDS A CONTEXT-SENSITIVE APPROACH

In this section, we present our new approach that combines textual features, i.e., semantic information from the surrounding text, with the converters to improve the outcome. Figure 4 illustrates the process of creating the gold standard, evaluating conversions, and how we plan to improve the converters with tree refinements (outside the MathMLben box). Our improvement approach includes three phases.

(1) In the first phase, the Mathematical Language Processing (MLP) approach [24] extracts semantic information from the textual context by providing identifier-definiens[12] pairs.
(2) The MLP annotations self-assess their reliability by annotate each identifier-definiens pair with its probabilities. Often, the methods do not find highly ranked semantic information. In such cases, we combine the MLP results with a dictionary-based method. In particular, we use the dictionaries from the POM tagger [28] that associate context-free semantics with the presentation tree. Since the dictionary entries are not ranked, we use them to drop unmentioned identifier-definiens pairs and choose the highest rank of the remaining pairs.
(3) Based on the chosen semantic information, we redefine the content tree by reordering the nodes and subtrees.

Currently, the implementation is too immature to release it as a semantic annotation package. Instead, we discuss the method using the following selected examples that represent typical classes of disambiguation problems:

- Invisible operator disambiguation for the times vs. apply special case.
- Parameter vs. label disambiguation for subscripts.
- Einstein notation discovery.
- Multi-character operator discovery.

Learning special notations like the examples above is subject to future work. However, we deem it reasonable to start with these examples, since our manual investigation of the tree edit distances

[12]In a definition, the *definiendum* is the expression to be defined and *definiens* is the phrase that defines the definiendum. Identifier-definiens pairs are candidates for an Identifier-definition, see [24] for a more detailed explanation.

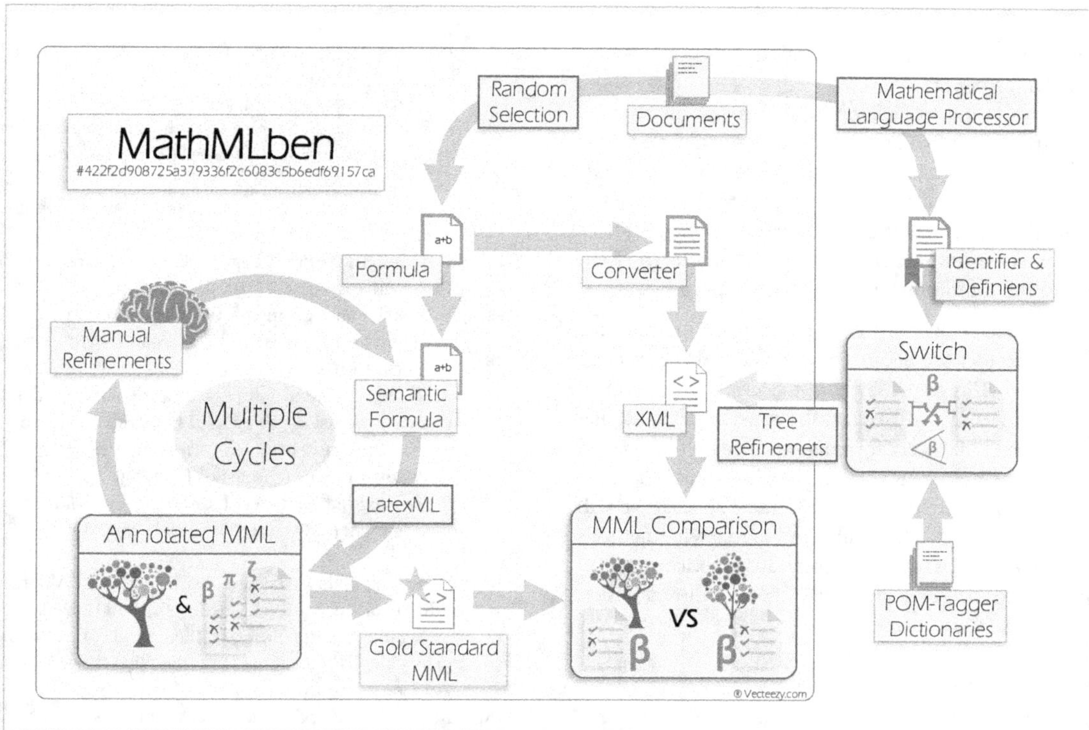

Figure 4: Mathematical language processing is the task of mapping textual descriptions to components of mathematical formulae (Part-of-Math tagging).

showed that such cases represented major reasons for errors in the content MathML tree.

Previously, the MLP software was limited to extracting information about identifiers, not general mathematical symbols. Moreover, the software was optimized for the Wikipedia dataset. We thus expanded the software for this study to enable parsing pure XHTML input as provided by the NTCIR tasks and the DLMF website. Achieving this goal required realizing a component for symbol identification. We chose the strategy of considering every simple expression that is not an identifier as a candidate for a symbol.

For first experiments we tried to improve the output by LaTeXML, since LaTeXML performs best in our tests and it was able to generate content MathML. Moreover, with the newly developed semantic macros, we are able to optimize MathML in a pre-processing step by enhance the input LaTeX expression. In consequence, we do not need to develop complex post-processing algorithms to manipulate content MathML.

As part of this study, we created a custom style sheet that fixes the following problems: (1) use of the power symbols for superscript characters unless Einstein notation was discovered, (2) interpretation of subscript indices as parameters, unless they are in text mode. For text mode, the ensemble of main symbol and subscript will be regarded as an identifier. (3) Symbols that are considered as a 'function' are applied to the following identifier, rather than being multiplied with the identifier.

First experiments using the refinement techniques have proven to be very effective. We haven chosen a small set of 10 functions for performing the refinements and to show the potential of the techniques. Of those 10 cases, with simple regular expression matching, our MLP approach found 4 cases, where the highest ranked identifier-definiens pair was 'function' for at least one identifier in the formula. In these 4 cases, the distances of the content trees decreased to zero with all previously explained refinements enabled.

While this is just a first indication for the suitability of our approach, it shows that the long chain of processing steps shows promise. Therefore, we are actively working on the presented improvements and plan to focus on the task of learning how to generate mappings from the input PL encoding to CL encoding without general rules for branch selection as we applied them so far.

6 CONCLUSION AND FUTURE WORK

We make available the first benchmark dataset to evaluate the conversion of mathematical formulae between presentation and content formats. During the encoding process for our MathML-based gold standard, we presented the conceptual and technical issues that conversion tools for this task must address. Using the newly created benchmark dataset, we evaluated popular context-agnostic LaTeX-to-MathML converters. We found that many converters simply do not support the conversion from presentation to content format, and those that did often yielded mathematically incorrect content representations even for basic input data. These results underscore the need for future research on mathematical format conversions.

Of the tools we tested, LaTeXML yielded the best conversion results, was easy to configure, and highly extensible. However, these benefits come at the price of a slow conversion speed. Due to its comparably low error rate, we chose to extend the LaTeXML output with semantic enhancements.

Unfortunately, we failed to develop an automated method to learn special notation. However, we could show that the application of special selection rules improves the quality of the content tree, i.e., allows choosing the most suitable tree from a selection of candidates. While the implementation of a few selection rules fixes nearly all issues we encountered in our test documents, the long tail of rules shows the limitations of a rule-based approach.

Future Work. We will focus our future research on methods for automated notation detection, because we consider this approach as better suited and better scalable than implementing complex systems of selection rules. We will extract the considered notational features from the textual context of formulae and use them to extend our previously proposed approach of constructing identifier name spaces [24] towards constructing notational name spaces. We will check the integrity of formed notational name spaces with methods comparable to those proposed in our previous publication [19] where we used physical units as sanity check, if semantic annotation in the domain of physics are correct.

ACKNOWLEDGMENTS

We would like to thank Abdou Youssef for sharing his Part-of-Math tagger with us and for offering valuable advice. We are also indebted to Akiko Aizawa for her advice and for hosting us as visiting researchers in her lab at the National Institute of Informatics (NII) in Tokyo. Furthermore, we thank Wikimedia Labs for providing cloud computing facilities and hosting our gold standard dataset. This work was supported by the FITWeltweit program of the German Academic Exchange Service (DAAD) as well as the German Research Foundation (DFG grant GI-1259-1).

REFERENCES

[1] A. Aizawa et al. NTCIR-11 Math-2 Task Overview. In: *Proc. 11th NTCIR Conf. on Evaluation of Information Access Technologies, Tokyo, Japan.* 2014.

[2] F. Cajori. *A history of mathematical notations.* Courier Corporation, 1928.

[3] H. S. Cohl et al. Digital Repository of Mathematical Formulae. In: *Conference on Intelligent Computer Mathematics (CICM), Coimbra, Portugal.* 2014, pp. 419–422. DOI: 10.1007/978-3-319-08434-3_30.

[4] H. S. Cohl et al. Growing the Digital Repository of Mathematical Formulae with Generic Sources. In: *CICM, Washington, DC, USA.* 2015, pp. 280–287. DOI: 10.1007/978-3-319-20615-8_18.

[5] H. S. Cohl et al. Semantic Preserving Bijective Mappings of Mathematical Formulae between Document Preparation Systems and Computer Algebra Systems. In: *CICM, Edinburgh, UK.* 2017. DOI: 10.1007/978-3-319-62075-6_9.

[6] P. Dehaye et al. Interoperability in the OpenDreamKit Project: The Math-in-the-Middle Approach. In: *CICM, Bialystok, Poland.* 2016, pp. 117–131. DOI: 10.1007/978-3-319-42547-4_9.

[7] *NIST Digital Library of Mathematical Functions.* http://dlmf.nist.gov/, Release 1.0.17 of 2017-12-22. F. W. J. Olver, et al. eds.

[8] M. England et al. Branch cuts in Maple 17. In: *ACM Comm. Comp. Algebra* (2014), pp. 24–27. DOI: 10.1145/2644288.2644293.

[9] D. Ginev, H. Stamerjohanns, and M. Kohlhase. The LaTeXML Daemon: Editable Math on the Collaborative Web. In: *LWA 2011, Magdeburg, Germany.* 2011, pp. 255–256.

[10] P. D. F. Ion and S. M. Watt. The Global Digital Mathematical Library and the International Mathematical Knowledge Trust. In: *CICM, Edinburgh, UK.* 2017, pp. 56–69.

[11] N. Meuschke et al. Analyzing Mathematical Content to Detect Academic Plagiarism. In: *Proc. CIKM.* 2017.

[12] B. Miller. LaTeXML: *A LaTeX to XML Converter.* http://dlmf.nist.gov/LaTeXML/. Accessed: 2018-01-18.

[13] B. R. Miller and A. Youssef. Technical Aspects of the Digital Library of Mathematical Functions. In: *Ann. Math. Artif. Intell.* (2003), pp. 121–136. DOI: 10.1023/A:1022967814992.

[14] M.-Q. Nghiem et al. Automatic approach to understanding mathematical expressions using mathml parallel markup corpora. In: *26th Annu. Conf. Jap. Society for Artificial Intell.* 2012.

[15] L. Padovani. On the Roles of LaTeX and MathML in Encoding and Processing Mathematical Expressions. In: *Mathematical Knowledge Management (MKM), Bertinoro, Italy.* 2003, pp. 66–79. DOI: 10.1007/3-540-36469-2_6.

[16] M. Pawlik and N. Augsten. RTED: A Robust Algorithm for the Tree Edit Distance. In: *CoRR* (2012). arXiv: 1201.0230.

[17] M. Schubotz. Augmenting Mathematical Formulae for More Effective Querying & Efficient Presentation. PhD thesis. TU Berlin, Germany, 2017.

[18] M. Schubotz. Implicit Content Dictionaries in the NIST Digital Repository of Mathematical Formulae. English. Talk presented at the OpenMath workshop CICM. Bialystok, Poland, 2016.

[19] M. Schubotz, D. Veenhuis, and H. S. Cohl. Getting the units right. In: *Workshop and Work in Progress Papers at CICM 2016, Bialystok, Poland.* 2016, pp. 146–156.

[20] M. Schubotz and G. Wicke. Mathoid: Robust, Scalable, Fast and Accessible Math Rendering for Wikipedia. In: *CICM, Coimbra, Portugal.* 2014, pp. 224–235. DOI: 10.1007/978-3-319-08434-3_17.

[21] M. Schubotz et al. Challenges of Mathematical Information Retrieval in the NTCIR-11 Math Wikipedia Task. In: *Special Interest Group on Information Retrieval (SIGIR), Santiago, Chile.* 2015, pp. 951–954. DOI: 10.1145/2766462.2767787.

[22] M. Schubotz et al. Evaluating and Improving the Extraction of Mathematical Identifier Definitions. In: *Conference and Labs of the Evaluation Forum (CLEF), Dublin, Ireland.* 2017, pp. 82–94. DOI: 10.1007/978-3-319-65813-1_7.

[23] M. Schubotz et al. Evaluation of Similarity-Measure Factors for Formulae Based on the NTCIR-11 Math Task. In: *11th NTCIR, Tokyo, Japan.* 2014.

[24] M. Schubotz et al. Semantification of Identifiers in Mathematics for Better Math Information Retrieval. In: *SIGIR, Pisa, Italy.* 2016, pp. 135–144. DOI: 10.1145/2911451.2911503.

[25] M. Schubotz et al. VMEXT: A Visualization Tool for Mathematical Expression Trees. In: *CICM, Edinburgh, UK.* 2017, pp. 340–355. DOI: 10.1007/978-3-319-62075-6_24.

[26] H. Stamerjohanns et al. MathML-aware Article Conversion from LaTeX. In: *Towards a Digital Mathematics Library. Grand Bend, Ontario, Canada.* 2009, pp. 109–120.

[27] S. M. Watt. Exploiting implicit mathematical semantics in conversion between TeX and MathML. In: *Proc. Internet Accessible Math. Commun. (IAMC)* (2002).

[28] A. Youssef. Part-of-Math Tagging and Applications. In: *CICM, Edinburgh, UK.* 2017, pp. 356–374. DOI: 10.1007/978-3-319-62075-6_25.

Citation Recommendation Using Distributed Representation of Discourse Facets in Scientific Articles

Yuta Kobayashi
Nara Institute of Science and Technology
Ikoma, Nara, Japan
kobayashi.yuta.kp1@is.naist.jp

Masashi Shimbo
Nara Institute of Science and Technology
Ikoma, Nara, Japan
shimbo@is.naist.jp

Yuji Matsumoto
Nara Institute of Science and Technology
Ikoma, Nara, Japan
matsu@is.naist.jp

ABSTRACT

Scientific articles usually follow a common pattern of discourse, and their contents can be divided into several facets, such as objective, method, and result. We examine the efficacy of using these discourse facets for citation recommendation. A method for learning multi-vector representations of scientific articles is proposed, in which each vector encodes a discourse facet present in an article. With each facet represented as a separate vector, the similarity of articles can be measured not in their entirety, but facet by facet. The proposed representation method is tested on a new citation recommendation task called *context-based co-citation recommendation.* This task calls for the evaluation of article similarity in terms of citation contexts, wherein facets help to abstract and generalize the diversity of contexts. The experimental results show that the facet-based representation outperforms the standard monolithic representation of articles.

CCS CONCEPTS

• **Information systems** → **Document representation**; **Document structure**; **Recommender systems**; *Link and co-citation analysis*; Information retrieval; • **Computing methodologies** → *Natural language processing*;

KEYWORDS

Scientific article; representation learning; natural language processing; discourse facet; co-citation analysis

ACM Reference Format:
Yuta Kobayashi, Masashi Shimbo, and Yuji Matsumoto. 2018. Citation Recommendation Using Distributed Representation of Discourse Facets in Scientific Articles. In *JCDL '18: The 18th ACM/IEEE Joint Conference on Digital Libraries, June 3–7, 2018, Fort Worth, TX, USA.* ACM, New York, NY, USA, 9 pages. https://doi.org/10.1145/3197026.3197059

JCDL '18, June 3–7, 2018, Fort Worth, TX, USA

ACM ISBN 978-1-4503-5178-2/18/06...$15.00
https://doi.org/10.1145/3197026.3197059

1 INTRODUCTION

1.1 Background

With the recent surge in the number of scientific publications, researchers are forced to spend a large amount of time finding relevant literature for their research. To reduce this workload, literature retrieval systems need to be enhanced beyond simple keyword search, in a way that enables more goal-oriented searches.

One key technology to this end is the discourse structure analysis of scientific literature [20, 25, 32, 33], which seeks to automatically classify citation contexts and the parts of body text (i.e., sentences, sections, etc.) by their functions in typical scientific discourse structure, such as Objective, Method, and Result. We call these functions *discourse facets* in this paper.

If the discourse facets of articles are correctly identified, the similarity of articles can be measured not based on their full text but on a facet-by-facet basis. For example, the similarity of two articles can be measured only in terms of methods studied, while ignoring objectives. In literature retrieval systems, this opens the possibility of answering queries such as "find an article with a different objective from the one at hand but with a similar methodology"; most likely, such queries cannot be answered by mere keyword search.

Likewise, if individual citation contexts can be classified into facets (e.g., "Is this citation made for the sake of a methodological argument?"), citation recommendation systems could take advantage of this information to make a recommendation that is consistent with the user-specified citation context.

1.2 Contributions

In this paper, we propose using the discourse facets associated with citation contexts and sections of textfor a new type of citation recommendation task, which we call *context-based co-citation recommendation* (CBCCR): Given a context in which citations should be made, as well as an article that is to be cited in that context, the system must recommend more articles to be co-cited with the given article in that context. This task requires the measurement of article similarity in light of a specific citation context. Another unique feature of CBCCR is that an evaluation dataset can be created nearly automatically from a corpus of scientific articles if we exploit the *enumerated co-citations* in them.

For CBCCR, we propose a technique for learning multi-vector distributed representations of scientific articles that takes into account the discourse facets of both text and citation graphs.

After automatically classifying all sections of the articles into three facets (Objective, Method, and Result), we train a distributed vector representation [3, 22] for each facet present in an article.

Thus, each article is represented by a set of vectors, each of which represents a single facet in that article. Since facets are represented as separate vectors, we can measure the similarity of two articles using only the vectors of a specific facet of interest: for example, how similar two articles are in terms of Method, while ignoring their similarity in Objective and Result.

Also, in CBCCR, these facets help to abstract and generalize the diversity of citation contexts. A CBCCR experiment using the constructed dataset shows that our facet-based article representations are superior to monolithic representations of articles.

1.3 Terminology

As mentioned earlier, we use the term *discourse facet* to refer to a functional role in typical discourse patterns observed in scientific articles, such as Objective, Method, and Result. To our knowledge, this term was originally introduced for the classification of citation contexts [15, 34]. Similar concepts have been referred to by various names in the literature, although the focus, granularity, and scope may vary: for example, *rhetorical status* [32] (for general sentences), or *section function* [20] (for sections), and *citation function* [33] (for citation contexts). This concept also roughly corresponds to the sections used in *structured abstracts* [13, 23, 26].

An *enumerated co-citation* is a set of citations made as a group, typically quoted in a single pair of parentheses or brackets. A *citation context* is the context in which a citation (or an enumerated co-citation) occurs. Here, the "context" merely refers to some string of words adjacent to the location of the citation. The concrete span of a context is task/method-dependent: for example, the span could be a sentence, a paragraph, or words in a fixed window around the citation.

2 RELATED WORK

2.1 Vector representation of scientific articles

In document retrieval, documents are represented as vectors of word frequency–based values, and the similarity of documents is measured by suitable operations (such as cosine) over their vectors. This "bag-of-words" vector representation has also been applied to scientific articles to capture the similarity of their contents. For example, Sugiyama and Kan [30] represented articles as vectors using a tf-idf-based method, and constructed a system that recommends articles on the basis of a list of user's past publications.

In recent years, distributed (dense) word representation [3, 22] has been attracting NLP researchers' attention due to its compatibility with neural networks. These real-valued word vectors can be used as features in a variety of NLP applications, such as machine translation [2], summarization [28], question answering [14], and text classification [18]. It has also been applied to the classification of citations in scientific articles [24].

2.2 Vector representation of citation graphs

Tracking citations provides a way to analyze the relationship between articles. Recently, the distributed representation of graphs (also called *graph embedding*) [11, 27, 31] has been rigorously pursued as a promising approach to modeling graph data including citations. It assumes that vertices capture shared similarities in local graph structure such as co-citation similarity, and vertices with similar neighborhoods will acquire similar representations. For vector representation of scientific articles, Tang et al. [31] computed the vectors of articles not from the text but from a citation graph and classified them into seven computer science conferences to which the articles were submitted: SIGIR, KDD, AAAI, CIKM, ICML, NIPS, and WWW.

In the existing methods for graph-based representation learning, the quality of vectors of the vertices and the learning time are in a trade-off relationship. In this study, we use LINE [31], which is one of the fastest graph embedding methods, as a building block in learning the facet-based representation of articles.

2.3 Capturing discourse facets in text

There have been studies on the classification of text and citation in scientific literature into discourse facets.

Kafkas et al. [20] proposed a rule-based section tagger to assign a function label (rhetorical status) to each section, i.e., Introduction & Background, Materials & Methods, Discussion, and Conclusion & Future Work. Although their rules were handcrafted, they stated that a machine-learning method was more desirable to deal with sections that are not covered by their rules.

Argumentative zoning is the task of automatically classifying sentences in scientific documents by their rhetorical status in scientific discourse [6, 12, 32], such as Aim, Background, Own, Contrast, and Basis. Teufel and Moens [32] used a naive Bayes classifier, Guo et al. [12] used naive Bayes and Support Vector Machine classifiers, and Contractor et al. [6] used a positive-unlabeled (PU) learning technique [8].

In library sciences, the use of information from citation contexts has received considerable attention. Multiple schemes have been proposed for how to classify contexts from many different points of view: by citation function [25, 33] that shows the reason for citation, by polarity (positive/negative) [5], or by importance (important/not important) [35], among others.

The facets of citation contexts have been recognized as useful information for summarizing scientific documents. A series of shared tasks on scientific document summarization continue to provide a subtask (Task 1b) for classification of citation sentences ("citances") into discourse facets: TAC 2014 [34] (CL-SciSumm Pilot 2014), CL-SciSumm 2016 [15], and CL-SciSumm 2017 [16]. Distributed word representation has also been used for facet classification recently. Munkhdalai et al. [24] used neural attention models and distributed word representation to classify citation contexts.

2.4 Co-citation analysis

Co-citation analysis [29] measures the relatedness between two articles by the number of co-citations (joint citations) they receive from articles authored by peer researchers. It is often considered a more objective (and hence reliable) indicator of relatedness than direct citations, which are made subjectively by the article authors themselves.

In co-citation analysis, the strength of individual co-citations is neglected; one joint citation from an article uniformly provides one unit of contribution to the co-citation index between cited articles. However, recent studies have suggested the need to distinguish the amount of contribution provided by individual co-citations. Gipp and Beel [10] analyzed the strength of the relationship between co-cited articles in terms of the proximity of the location of citations made in the text of an article and indicated that the strongest relationship belongs to co-citations made in the same sentence. They proposed the *co-citation proximity index* as a measure of relatedness between articles by taking the relative location of co-citations. Eto [9] pointed out that relatedness of co-cited articles is highest for those in enumerated co-citations. These findings provide the foundation of the CBCCR task we propose; the task is based on the assumption that articles in an enumerated co-citation bear high similarity, at least from a certain point of view as expressed in the citation context.

2.5 Citation recommendation

Citations are made with different motivations and in different contexts. If such a context is available, a citation recommendation system must output a list of articles that are similar to the input article not in a generic sense but in light of the specific context of citation.

Duma and Klein [7] defined a context-based citation recommendation system as one that assists the author's writing a document by suggesting other documents which are relevant to a particular context in the draft. They proposed *citation resolution* as a pilot task of context-based recommendation. In citation resolution, the system is given a citation context extracted from an article (with the actual citation hidden), as well as the list of articles collected from the References section of the same article. The system then has to choose the actual article (i.e., the one hidden from the system) cited in the given citation context from the list of articles in References.

By definition, our proposed CBCCR task (which is described in Section 3) falls into a task of context-based citation recommendation, and also bears a certain similarity to the citation resolution task. However, CBCCR departs from citation resolution in three ways. First, CBCCR deals only with enumerated co-citations but not singletons. Second, CBCCR extends the input from only a regular citation context to an enumerated co-citation context and the first article in an enumerated co-citation. Third, in CBCCR, the system has to choose articles from a large database of articles, whereas in citation resolution, the candidates are a small set of articles found in the References section of the article from which the citation context is collected. Indeed, citation resolution is not exactly a citation recommendation task, because the candidates are limited to those in References.

Of the three, the presence of a co-cited article as input is a crucial difference between CBCCR and citation resolution. As discussed in Section 2.4, co-cited articles are assumed to share high similarity from the point of view stated in the context of citation. Thus in CBCCR, the context-dependent similarity between the given article and the candidates makes a key factor in determining a recommended article. Such similarity is not a factor in citation resolution, because no co-cited articles are given to the system.

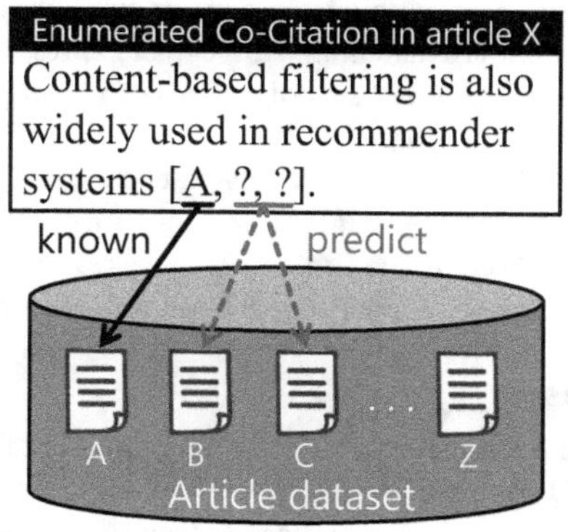

Figure 1: Context-based co-citation recommendation.

3 CONTEXT-BASED CO-CITATION RECOMMENDATION

In this section, we describe a new citation recommendation task, which we call *context-based co-citation recommendation* (CBCCR), and a dataset for this task. As mentioned earlier, CBCCR is intended as a simulation of the following scenario: A user inputs to a system a textual context of citation and a single article that she thinks is suitable to be cited in that context, and then the system suggests additional citations that are to be cited along with the input article.

3.1 Task definition

The task of CBCCR is defined as follows. The system is given a set $\mathcal{D}$ of articles (an article database), a context c of an enumerated co-citation, and the first article a_1 of the multiple articles cited in context c. The system is then required to choose from $\mathcal{D}$ the hidden articles $a_2, \ldots, a_n$ that are cited alongside a_1 in the context c. In practice, the system outputs the ranking of candidates for the hidden articles. Thus, the system is not required to determine the number n of hidden co-citations.

Figure 1 shows a schematic illustration of CBCCR. In this figure, articles A, B and C are cited by article X as an enumerated co-citation, and the article database $\mathcal{D} = \{B, C, \cdots, Z\}$ contains all articles except for A. The system is presented with A ($= a_1$) and its citation context c (= *"Content-based filtering is also widely used in recommender systems"*), and must predict B and C (a_2 and a_3, respectively) as the most suitable citations in this context, over the remaining articles $D, \ldots, Z$ in the database. The system can explore two sources of information: (1) full texts of the articles in the dataset (except for the references in the article from which the enumerated co-citation was collected[1]; i.e., article X in Figure 1), and (2) citation graphs (from which the edge $X \to B$ and $X \to C$ are excluded) to make a prediction.

CBCCR has the following advantages:

[1] References are removed from the citing article so as not to make the problem too easy. If references were present, the system would only need to choose articles from them, not from the entire repository of articles. This removal is in line with the intended scenario of the CBCCR task described at the beginning of Section 3: We assume that the user is not yet aware of the articles to cite, except for the one she has already input to the recommendation system.

- Since enumerated co-citations can be extracted automatically (e.g., by pattern matching with regular expressions over text), a large collection of sets of articles can be created without human intervention.
- Articles that are enumeratively co-cited share a citation context, which means that they are similar from a distinct point of view given by the context. This makes CBCCR as a good benchmark for context-based similarity evaluation.

3.2 Dataset

We created a dataset for CBCCR, which consists of (i) the set of the article IDs defined in the ACL Anthology[2], an open-access repository of journal, conference, and workshop articles in the field of computational linguistics/natural language processing, (ii) its citation graph, and (iii) the contexts of 1,000 enumerated co-citations in these articles coupled with the IDs of cited articles. Table 1 shows the statistics of the dataset.

To built the dataset, we first crawled the ACL Anthology for the PDF files of articles that are published in or before 2016. These PDF files were then converted to XHTML, with a customized version of the PDF rendering library Poppler[3]. From those that were successfully processed by Poppler, we finally obtained 20,496 conference/journal/workshop articles that satisfy all of the following conditions:

- The section structure of the article is correctly extracted.
- The article has a reference section at the end.
- The article has three or more sections.

These rules were designed to filter out non-conference/journal/workshop papers, such as the preface of a special issue of a journal, or the title page and the table of contents of proceedings, of which the ACL Anthology also contains a small amount. These types of articles are typically not sectioned or have only a few sections, or do not have a reference section.

In the collected articles, citation and enumerated co-citations were detected by pattern matching. Some of the patterns matched are as follows:

- `(AUTHOR1 YEAR1; AUTHOR2 YEAR2 ...)`
- `[REFERENCE_NUMBER1, REFERENCE_NUMBER2 ...]`

In addition, a citation graph was also constructed by rule-based reference matching. This citation graph is self-contained, in the sense that it only contains edges (i.e., citations) between articles included in the constructed dataset, and those of external articles are removed.

In the evaluation of CBCCR systems, edges in the citation graph from each citing article to its hidden enumeratively co-cited articles (second and subsequent citations) should be removed; otherwise, the answer can often be found merely by looking into the citation graph. However, removing the edges (citations) in all the enumerated co-citations would greatly reduce the size of the citation graph. To avoid this large collapse of citation graph, we randomly sampled 1,000 contexts out of entire 34,760 enumerated co-citation contexts in which an enumerated co-citation appears at only one place in one sentence, and used them for evaluation.

[2]http://aclweb.org/anthology/
[3]https://poppler.freedesktop.org/

Table 2 shows the histogram of the number of cited articles in 1,000 enumerated co-citation contexts in the evaluation dataset. The average number of citations in an enumerated co-citation is 2.38. Thus, for each context, the number of hidden articles is 1.38 on average.

4 FACET-BASED METHOD FOR CO-CITATION RECOMMENDATION

In this section, we describe how to learn the facet-based vector representations of articles, and how they can be used for CBCCR.

4.1 Learning article representations

Figure 2 shows the overview of learning the representations of articles. The inputs of learning model are the texts of articles in ACL Anthology, the corresponding citation graph and the text of Wikipedia. In Steps 1 to 3, the discourse facets of articles are extracted from the body text and vectorized. In Step 4, we label the edges of citation graphs according to each facet predicted by a trained classifier. Finally, in Step 5, the vector representations of the text and the graph are integrated.

4.1.1 Step 1: Learning word representations.

In the first step, the representations of words are trained, so that they can be used in the subsequent steps. To learn word representations, we use the representation learning library fastText, which provides modules for unsupervised text representation learning [4]. The vectors produced by fastText encode not only word-level information but also word n-gram and character n-gram (subword) information. We chose fastText because the use of word n-grams is advantageous to capture discriminating lexical structures [1], and the n-gram information of word and character should help learn vector representations of technical terms.

Similarly to Mikolov's skip-gram model [22], fastText learns vector representations of words in vocabulary $\mathcal{W}$ given a large training corpus. To be precise, for each sentence $S = w_1 \dots w_T$ in the corpus with $w_j \in \mathcal{W}$ for $j = 1, \dots, T$, it tries to find the vector representation for each word $w \in \mathcal{W}$ that maximizes the log-likelihood expressed by the following formula:

$$\sum_{t=1}^{T} \sum_{c \in C_t} \log p(c \mid w_t),$$

where C_t is the *context* of word w_t, which is the set of words surrounding w_t in the training sequence S, and $p(c \mid w_t)$ is the probability of observing a context word c given w_t. It is defined by

$$p(c \mid w_t) = \frac{\exp(s(w_t, c))}{\sum_{c' \in \mathcal{W}} \exp(s(w_t, c'))},$$

where $s(w, c)$ is a score function which maps a pair of words w and c to a score in $\mathbb{R}$, and is expressed by the following expression:

$$s(w, c) = \sum_{g \in \mathcal{G}_w} \langle \mathbf{z}_g, \mathbf{v}_c \rangle,$$

where $\langle \cdot, \cdot \rangle$ denotes inner product, $\mathcal{G}_w$ is the set of character n-grams appearing in w and word w itself, and $\mathbf{v}_c$ is the vector of context word c. Associating a vector representation $\mathbf{z}_g$ to each character n-gram g in word w, we represent a word by the sum of the vector representations of its n-grams.

Table 1: Statistical information of CBCCR dataset extracted from ACL Anthology.

Data	#
Articles (vertices in the citation graph)	20496
Citations (edges)	259743
Average degree of vertices	29.6
Total enumerated co-citation contexts	34760
Randomly sampled enumerated co-citation contexts (test data)	1000

Table 2: The distribution of the number of cited articles in 1,000 enumerated co-citations.

# cited articles	frequency
2	722
3	210
4	53
5	7
6	1
7+	2
Total	1000

The facet-based vector representations of articles are built through following steps. First, we extract the title and the text of each section from the dataset we built (see Section 3.2). Then, we build a corpus that combines the English Wikipedia corpus[4] and the text of the articles extracted from the ACL Anthology. We carry out unsupervised learning of word vector representations using fastText [4] with this corpus. These pre-trained word representations are used for the following classification step.

4.1.2 Step 2: Classifying sections by facet using NLMCM rules and a machine learning–based classifier.

In this step, we classify each section of the NLP articles using an annotation dataset for structured abstracts. In a preliminary classification experiment, we found that the word vectors produced by fastText were more accurate than tf-idf or Paragraph Vectors [21].

In classification, we thus use the single layer neural network classifier for text classification provided by the fastText library [18] which uses the pre-trained word vectors obtained in Step 1. We use the resource developed for structured abstracts to train the fastText classifier. A structured abstract is a summary of an article that consists of labeled sections to make it easy to comprehend. As a dataset dealing with structured abstracts, we use the National Library of Medicine Category Mappings (NLMCM) file [26], which is a dataset attached to the medical article database PubMed. The NLMCM file holds a list of 3,032 translation rules for canonicalizing various section titles appearing in structured abstracts into one of Background, Objective, Method, Results, or Conclusions.

First, we applied these rules to the section titles of the articles collected in Step 1 to obtain the facet of these sections. To simplify the model, we use only three facets. The labels of Background and Objective are merged into Objective, and Results and Conclusions are merged into Result. This simplification roughly follows the definition of citation function scheme suggested by Nanba and Okumura [25], and we use these 3 facets (Objective, Method, and Result) as the labels of section facets instead of the original five labels in NLMCM. For example, when the section title is "Introduction," it is first classified into Background based on the NLMCM rules and then classified into Objective in the three label scheme.

If none of the NLMCM rules applies to the section title, that section is left unlabeled; they are subsequently labeled by the classifier fastText [18] trained on the sections labeled by the NLMCM rules. The classifier receives as input the body text of a section, and outputs a section facet (Objective, Method or Result). In this time, each word representation is updated by the information of facet label.

Then, we estimate section facets of the 11,118 unlabeled sections by the classifier with the section titles and texts as input.

4.1.3 Step 3: Building facet vectors for each article.

In this step, we first compute the vector representations of each section in an article, which is simply the average of the vector representations of all words in the section. The word representation vectors used here are those initially trained in Step 1 and then refined for facet classification in Step 2.

We then compute the facet vectors of an article for Objective, Method, and Result by taking the average of all sections deemed as each of these facets in that article.

In the next step, we augment the citation graph by adding a discourse facet to each citation edge using a supervised classifier in the fastText library. In the final step, each facet vector of the article is updated by the graph embedding method LINE [31]. These two steps are optional for using the information of citation graphs and citation function. However, the learning classifier for citation context is necessary for predicting the citation facet of enumerated co-citation context in the CBCCR task.

4.1.4 Step 4: Classifying citations by facet (optional).

In this step, we classify citation contexts in the articles into discourse facets, and label corresponding edges in the citation graph (see Section 3.2) by the facets.

To make a training data for the citation context classifier, we combined two datasets, the Citation Function Corpus [33] annotated with 12 citation function labels and the corpus of CL-SciSumm-2017 SharedTask [16] annotated with 5 discourse facet labels. To be precise, 1,618 examples were extracted from the combined corpora,

[4]https://dumps.wikimedia.org/backup-index.html

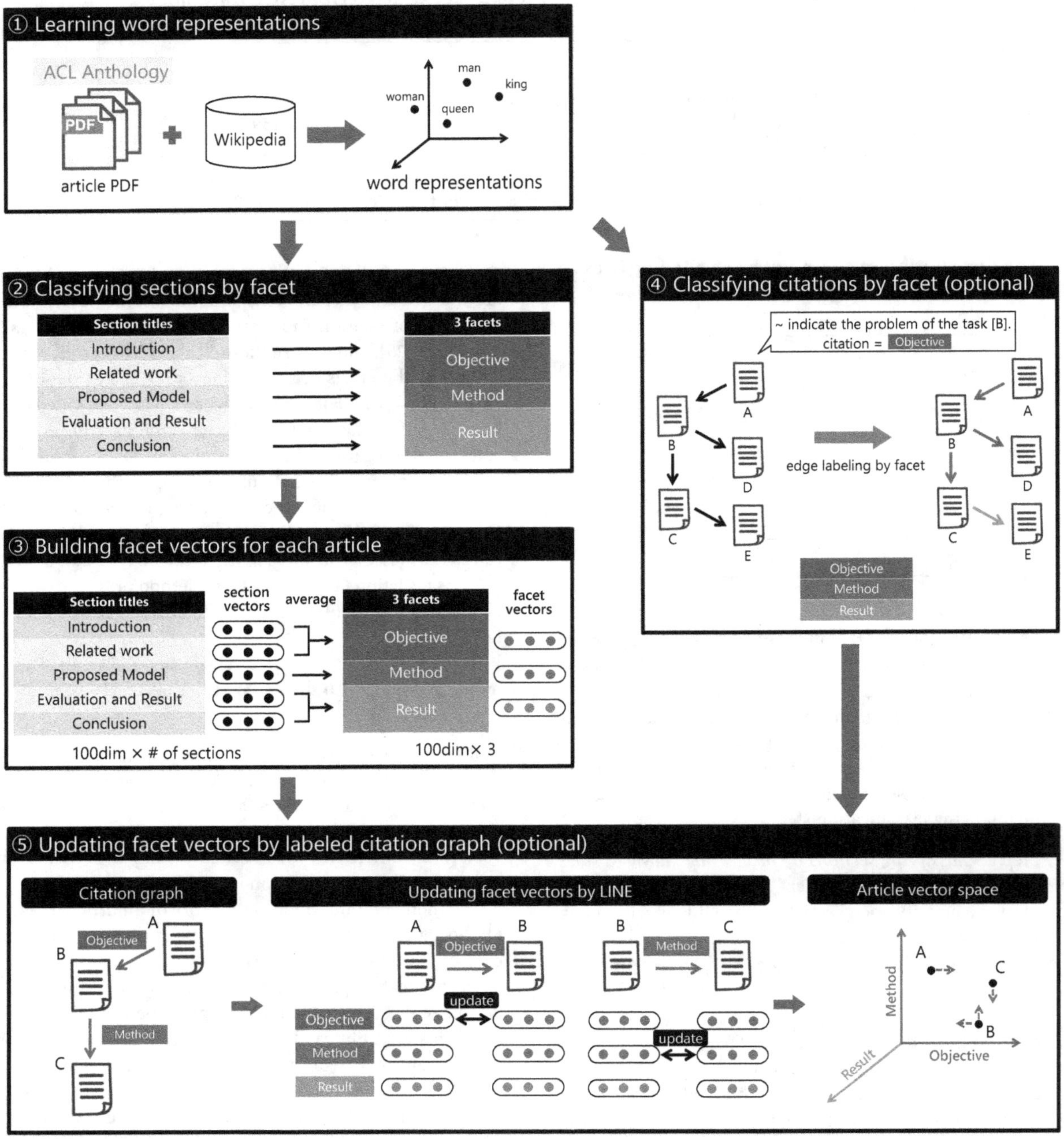

Figure 2: Overview of learning multi-vector representations of articles based on discourse facet.

such that their original function/facet labels straightforwardly correspond to the three facets used in this study. Table 4 shows the distribution of citation facets in the constructed annotation dataset.

To classify contexts into citation facets, we use the supervised classifier module of the fastText library, and train a classifier on the dataset constructed above. The input of the classifier is a citation context, and the output is one of the three citation facets, Objective, Method, and Result.

This discourse facet annotated to the citation graph is used for refining the facet vectors of articles, as we explain shortly in Step 5, where both the text information and graph information are integrated. Further, this context classifier is used subsequently in co-citation recommendation; see Section 4.2.

4.1.5 Step 5: Updating text-based facet vectors by labeled citation graphs (optional).

After the edges in the citation graph is labeled with facets in Step 4, we can refine the facet vectors obtained in Step 3 using this citation graph. Specifically, we use the graph embedding method LINE [31], which performs edge-sampling on the graph to reflect the local and global graph structure in the vector embedding of vertices.

Let us take the example depicted in Step 5 of Figure 2. The algorithm checks if there is an edge between vertices (articles) A and B, and finds that there is one and is labeled by facet "Objective." It then updates the "Object" vectors of articles A and B so that their inner product is increased. Likewise, since the edge from article B to C has the Method facet, the facet vector for Method is updated for B and C.

For each vertex k and a facet f, let $\mathbf{v}_{k,f}$ denote the facet vector of vertex k representing facet f. Updating the facet vectors is done by maximizing the following objective function for each edge (i, j) between vertices i and j on the citation graph:

$$\log \sigma \left(\langle \mathbf{v}'_{j,f}, \mathbf{v}_{i,f} \rangle \right) + \sum_{k=1}^{N} \log \sigma \left(-\langle \mathbf{v}'_{n(k),f}, \mathbf{v}_{i,f} \rangle \right),$$

where f is the facet of edge (i, j) determined in Step 4, $\sigma(\cdot)$ is the sigmoid function, $\mathbf{v}'_{j,f}$ is the complementary facet vector[5] representing the outlink from vertex j, N is the number of "negative" vertex samples, and $n(k)$ $(k = 1, \ldots, N)$ are the negative vertices sampled from all the vertices in the citation graph according to a noise distribution $P_{\text{noise}}(v)$, i.e., $n(k) \sim P_{\text{noise}}(v)$. Following the original LINE procedure, we set $P_{\text{noise}}(v) \propto d(v)^{\frac{3}{4}}$, where $d(v)$ is the out-degree of vertex v.

By following these procedures, we finally obtain a vector representations of an article that accounts for discourse facets.

4.2 Co-citation recommendation using facet-based representation

Figure 3 shows how our proposed model ranks the candidate articles using enumerated co-citation context. First, we classify the input enumerated co-citation context into a discourse facet, using the classifier learned in Section 4.1.4. Then, the similarity between the first cited article and each candidate article is calculated by their cosine similarity of the facet vector corresponding to the facet (Objective, Method, or Result) predicted by citation context classifier.

Finally, all articles are sorted in decreasing order of this similarity, and the resulting ranking list is output.

5 EXPERIMENT

5.1 Evaluation of section classification

To verify the accuracy of section facet classification by fastText, a 5-fold cross-validation was carried out using 72,721 section titles labeled by the NLMCM rules in Section 4.1.2. The number of dimensions of the word vector is 100, and the window size and the parameter of the negative sampling are both 5. The parameter of word n-gram was one of the uni-gram, bi-grams, tri-grams.

Table 3: Result of section facet classification by fastText.

fastText n-gram	Accuracy (%)
uni-gram	89.6
bi-gram	94.3
tri-gram	**96.1**

Table 4: Distribution of citation facets.

Citation facet	#
Objective	200
Method	1214
Result	204
Total	1618

Table 3 shows the cross-validation results of section facet classification with each n-gram. We confirmed that the section can be classified with a high accuracy of 96.1 percent in case of tri-grams. Hereafter, we use the word vectors and the classifier based on tri-grams.

5.2 Evaluation of citation facet classification

We performed the 5-fold cross-validation of citation facet classification by fastText with the annotated citation context dataset (Table 4) and obtained an accuracy of 90.1 percent.

5.3 Evaluation of article representations on a CBCCR task

We compared the performance of the proposed facet-based vector representations with monolithic representations (fastText and LINE) on CBCCR, using the dataset explained in Section 3.2 (see also Table 1 for the statistics of the dataset).

As the evaluation metric, we use the normalized discounted cumulative gain (nDCG) [17]. nDCG is based on the rank in the top k of the true cited article in the list of recommended articles by a system. with its score decreasing logarithmically. We set $k = 100$ in this experiment.

5.3.1 Baseline. We set two types of baseline article vectors. We used the average vector of all words in the article calculated by unsupervised fastText [18] obtained in the first step of the proposed method (see Section 4.1.1) as the text-based baseline. In addition, we compare LINE [31] as a graph-based representation vector (see Section 4.1.5). The value of negative sampling parameter is five and the window size is five. This setting is the same as that of the proposed methods, but since it does not have each component of the article, the dimension of both vectors is 300.

5.3.2 Proposed methods. We prepared facet-based vector representations in two ways. The first method, which we denote "proposed method 1: fastText + section facet", uses the representation

[5]This complementary vector is an analogue of the "context" word vectors (as opposed to the "central" word vectors) in Mikolov's distributed word representation models [22]. Complimentary vectors are used only during training, but not for co-citation recommendation; they are simply discarded after training.

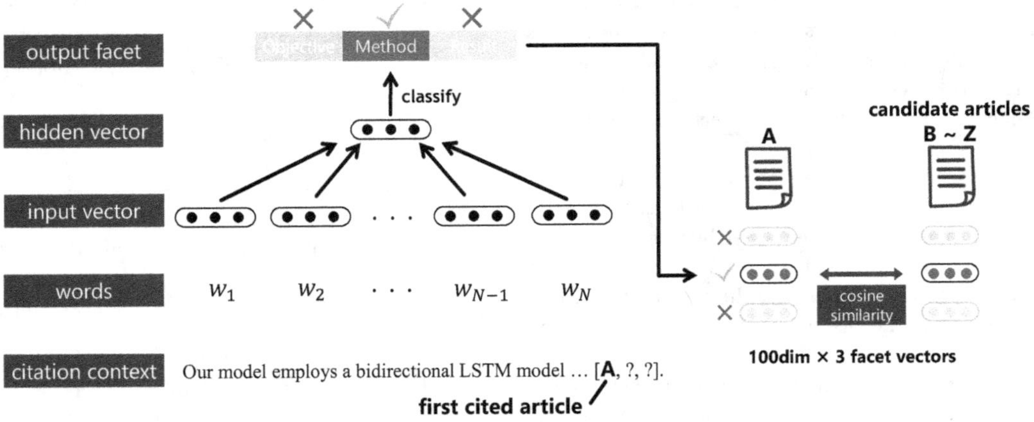

Figure 3: Co-citation recommendation using the citation context classifier and the facet-based representation of articles.

vectors obtained in Section 4.1.3. That is, it only uses Steps 1–3 to train facet vectors.

The second method, which we denote "proposed method 2: fastText + section facet + LINE + citation facet", is obtained through Steps 1–5. Thus, we further refine the vectors of the proposed method 1 with the faceted citation graph obtained in Step 4, using the graph representation learning method LINE. In Step 5 (see Section 4.1.5), the number N of negative samples per edge is set to 5.

The facet vectors in both proposed methods are set to 100 dimensions. Since we have three facets (Objective, Method, Result), an article is represented by a total of 300 dimensions; i.e., the same dimension as the baseline monolithic representations.

5.3.3 Experimental results. Table 5 shows the results of CBCCR using vector representations of the articles. We see that the accuracy of the proposed method 1 (fastText + section facet) using the information of the facet of the article improved the nDCG score compared to the baseline methods (fastText and LINE). We also observe further improvement of accuracy of proposed method 2 (fastText + section facet + LINE + citation facet), which uses not only text information but also the information of citation graphs. These results indicate that the combination of the discourse facet information of texts and citation graphs is effective for calculating the similarity between scientific articles.

6 CONCLUSION

In this study, we presented a technique for learning multi-vector representations of scientific articles, which combines the distributed representations of text and citation graphs, with each vector capturing a discourse facet (Objective, Method, and Result) within an article. In addition, we proposed a new task called *context-based co-citation recommendation* (CBCCR), which is unique in that it requires the evaluation of context-dependent similarity between articles.

We conducted experiments on our original CBCCR dataset and found that our discourse facet-based representation of articles achieves an improvement over monolithic representations.

Our future work is to utilize information from wider contexts, such as the entire section of an article in which a citation resides. We see this direction to be promising, as previous work [19] indicates that the distribution of the facets of citations differs depending on the sections in which the citations appear.

ACKNOWLEDGEMENTS

This work was partly supported by JST CREST Grant Number JPMJCR1513, Japan.

REFERENCES

[1] Awais Athar. 2011. Sentiment Analysis of Citations using Sentence Structure-Based Features. In *Proceedings of the Annual Meeting of the Association for Computational Linguistics 2011 Student Session.* 81–87.

[2] Dzmitry Bahdanau, Kyunghyun Cho, and Yoshua Bengio. 2014. Neural machine translation by jointly learning to align and translate. *arXiv preprint arXiv:1409.0473* (2014).

[3] Yoshua Bengio, Réjean Ducharme, Pascal Vincent, and Christian Janvin. 2003. A Neural Probabilistic Language Model. *Journal of Machine Learning Research* 3 (2003), 1137–1155.

[4] Piotr Bojanowski, Edouard Grave, Armand Joulin, and Tomas Mikolov. 2016. Enriching word vectors with subword information. *arXiv preprint arXiv:1607.04606* (2016).

[5] Donald O Case and Georgeann M Higgins. 2000. How can we investigate citation behavior? A study of reasons for citing literature in communication. *Journal of the Association for Information Science and Technology* 51, 7 (2000), 635–645.

[6] Danish Contractor, Yufan Guo, and Anna Korhonen. 2012. Using Argumentative Zones for Extractive Summarization of Scientific Articles. In *Proceedings of COLING 2012.* 663–678.

[7] Daniel Duma and Ewan Klein. 2014. Citation Resolution: A method for evaluating context-based citation recommendation systems. In *Proceedings of the 52nd Annual Meeting of the Association for Computational Linguistics (Volume 2: Short Papers).* 358–363.

[8] Charles Elkan and Keith Noto. 2008. Learning classifiers from only positive and unlabeled data. In *Proceedings of the 14th ACM SIGKDD international conference on Knowledge discovery and data mining.* ACM, 213–220.

[9] Masaki Eto. 2012. Spread co-citation relationship as a measure for document retrieval. In *Proceedings of the fifth ACM workshop on Research advances in large digital book repositories and complementary media.* 7–8.

[10] Bela Gipp and Joeran Beel. 2009. Citation Proximity Analysis (CPA) : A New Approach for Identifying Related Work Based on Co-Citation Analysis. In *Proceedings of the 12th International Conference on Scientometrics and Informetrics, vol. 1.* 571–575.

[11] Aditya Grover and Jure Leskovec. 2016. node2vec: Scalable feature learning for networks. In *Proceedings of the 22nd ACM SIGKDD international conference on Knowledge discovery and data mining.* 855–864.

[12] Yufan Guo, Anna Korhonen, Maria Liakata, Ilona Silins, Lin Sun, and Ulla Stenius. 2010. Identifying the Information Structure of Scientific Abstracts: An

Table 5: Result of context-based co-citation recommendation using multi-vector representations of articles.

Type of article vector representations	nDCG@100
fastText	0.44
LINE	0.46
Proposed method 1 (fastText + section facet)	0.51
Proposed method 2 (fastText + section facet + LINE + citation facet)	**0.58**

Investigation of Three Different Schemes. In *Proceedings of the 2010 Workshop on Biomedical Natural Language Processing*. 99–107.

[13] R. Brian Haynes, Cynthia D. Mulrow, Edward J. Huth, Douglas G. Altman, and Martin J. Gardner. 1990. More informative abstracts revisited. *Annals of Internal Medicine* 113, 1 (1990), 69–76.

[14] Mohit Iyyer, Jordan Boyd-Graber, Leonardo Claudino, Richard Socher, and Hal Daumé III. 2014. A neural network for factoid question answering over paragraphs. In *Proceedings of the 2014 Conference on Empirical Methods in Natural Language Processing (EMNLP)*. 633–644.

[15] Kokil Jaidka, Muthu Kumar Chandrasekaran, Sajal Rustagi, and Min-Yen Kan. 2018. Insights from CL-SciSumm 2016: the faceted scientific document summarization shared task. *International Journal on Digital Libraries* (2018). To appear. Online version available at https://doi.org/10.1007/s00799-017-0221-y.

[16] Kokil Jaidka, Devanshu Jain, and Min-Yen Kan. 2017. The CL-SciSumm shared task 2017: results and key insights. In *Proceedings of the Computational Linguistics Scientific Summarization Shared Task (CL-SciSumm 2017), organized as a part of the 2nd Joint Workshop on Bibliometric-enhanced Information Retrieval and Natural Language Processing for Digital Libraries (BIRNDL 2017)*. 1–15.

[17] Kalervo Järvelin and Jaana Kekäläinen. 2002. Cumulated gain-based evaluation of IR techniques. *ACM Transactions on Information Systems (TOIS)* 20, 4 (2002), 422–446.

[18] Armand Joulin, Edouard Grave, Piotr Bojanowski, and Tomas Mikolov. 2016. Bag of Tricks for Efficient Text Classification. *arXiv preprint arXiv:1607.01759* (2016).

[19] David Jurgens, Srijan Kumar, Raine Hoover, Dan McFarland, and Dan Jurafsky. 2016. Citation classification for behavioral analysis of a scientific field. *arXiv preprint arXiv:1609.00435* (2016).

[20] Şenay Kafkas, Xingjun Pi, Nikos Marinos, Andrew Morrison, Johanna R McEntyre, et al. 2015. Section level search functionality in Europe PMC. *Journal of biomedical semantics* 6, 1 (2015), 7.

[21] Quoc Le and Tomas Mikolov. 2014. Distributed representations of sentences and documents. In *Proceedings of the 31st International Conference on Machine Learning (ICML-14)*. 1188–1196.

[22] Tomas Mikolov, Ilya Sutskever, Kai Chen, Greg S Corrado, and Jeff Dean. 2013. Distributed representations of words and phrases and their compositionality. In *Advances in neural information processing systems*. 3111–3119.

[23] Cynthia D. Mulrow, Stephen B. Thacker, and Jacqueline A. Pugh. 1988. A proposal for more informative abstracts of review articles. *Annals of Internal Medicine* 108, 4 (1988), 613–615.

[24] Tsendsuren Munkhdalai, John Lalor, and Hong Yu. 2016. Citation analysis with neural attention models. In *Proceedings of the Seventh International Workshop on Health Text Mining and Information Analysis*. 69–77.

[25] Hidetsugu Nanba and Manabu Okumura. 1999. Towards Multi-paper Summarization Using Reference Information. In *Proceedings of the Sixteenth International Joint Conference on Artificial Intelligence*. 926–931.

[26] U.S. National Library of Medicine. Oct 26, 2015. Structured Abstracts in MEDLINE. (Oct 26, 2015). https://structuredabstracts.nlm.nih.gov/

[27] Bryan Perozzi, Rami Al-Rfou, and Steven Skiena. 2014. Deepwalk: Online learning of social representations. In *Proceedings of the 20th ACM SIGKDD international conference on Knowledge discovery and data mining*. 701–710.

[28] Alexander M Rush, Sumit Chopra, and Jason Weston. 2015. A neural attention model for abstractive sentence summarization. *arXiv preprint arXiv:1509.00685* (2015).

[29] Henry Small. 1973. Co-citation in the scientific literature: a new measure of the relationship between two documents. *Journal of American Society for Information Science* 24 (1973), 265–269.

[30] Kazunari Sugiyama and Min-Yen Kan. 2015. A Comprehensive Evaluation of Scholarly Paper Recommendation Using Potential Citation Papers. *International Journal on Digital Libraries* 16, 2 (2015), 91–109.

[31] Jian Tang, Meng Qu, Mingzhe Wang, Ming Zhang, Jun Yan, and Qiaozhu Mei. 2015. Line: Large-scale information network embedding. In *Proceedings of the 24th International Conference on World Wide Web*. 1067–1077.

[32] Simone Teufel and Marc Moens. 2002. Summarizing scientific articles: experiments with relevance and rhetorical status. *Computational linguistics* 28, 4 (2002), 410–445.

[33] Simone Teufel, Advaith Siddharthan, and Dan Tidhar. 2006. Automatic classification of citation function. In *Proceedings of the 2006 conference on empirical methods in natural language processing*. 103–110.

[34] Text Analysis Conference 2014. Text Analysis Conference 2014 Biomedical Summarization Task. https://tac.nist.gov/2014/BiomedSumm/index.html. (2014).

[35] Marco Valenzuela, Vu Ha, and Oren Etzioni. 2015. Identifying Meaningful Citations. In *Workshops at the Twenty-Ninth AAAI Conference on Artificial Intelligence*.

Biography, Ephemera, and the Future of Social Media Archiving

Catherine C. Marshall
Department of Computer Science
Texas A&M University
College Station, Texas
ccmarshall@cse.tamu.edu

ABSTRACT

Biography is a genre that intertwines history and identity. Modern biographies have relied on interviews to supplement contemporaneous sources of primary material such as letters, literary drafts, and notebooks, usually held in physical special collections acquired and curated by major research libraries. Will the addition of new digital sources such as records repositories, digital libraries, social media, and collections of ephemera change biographical research practices? I use the construction of a subject-driven collection of over 11,750 discrete digital items as a case study to demonstrate how new digital resources can extend the breadth and depth of biographical description, facilitate the rediscovery of a subject's social network, and enable formerly invisible literary influences to be foregrounded. I also explore the implications of the use of ephemera in tandem with other digital resources to ask what we might want to save in the future—including elements of today's social media platforms—and to discuss the trade-offs in making material that was once ephemeral (and difficult to access) so readily available online.

CCS CONCEPTS

• **Information systems → Digital libraries and archives** • Information systems → Social networks • Human-centered computing → Social media

KEYWORDS

Biography; Social Media; Collections; Permanence; Ephemera; Digital Libraries; Repositories; Case Study; Digital Humanities

ACM Reference format:

Catherine C. Marshall. 2018. Biography, Ephemera, and the Future of Social Media Archiving. In *Proceedings of the Joint Conference on Digital Libraries, June 3–7, 2018, Fort Worth, TX, USA (JCDL'18) ACM NY, NY, USA,* 10 pages. DOI: https://doi.org/10.1145/3197026.3197051

JCDL '18, June 3–7, 2018, Fort Worth, TX, USA

ACM ISBN 978-1-4503-5178-2/18/06...$15.00
https://doi.org/10.1145/3197026.3197051

1 INTRODUCTION

There is a growing consensus among Information Science scholars that the resources necessary to archive popular social media platforms makes such an effort impractical for a number of reasons. Most crucially, there is a murkiness inherent to the very idea of archiving social media: not only is the scale and scope immense (for example, as of 2017, Facebook surpassed two billion monthly active users using more than 100 world languages [10]), but also personalization and mutability make it difficult to define what may be involved. Not only do platform capabilities change—e.g., in 2016 Facebook introduced live video—but also many elements themselves are malleable and the experience on social media platforms is computed and highly tailored to a user's interests. In other words, every user encounters each platform in a different way. Furthermore, multi-stakeholder ownership of the platforms and their contents suggests that large-scale archiving efforts may be difficult to negotiate, especially since monetary interests, privacy, and personal identity hang in balance [24]. Indeed, the earliest comprehensive public effort to fully archive a single social media source (Twitter) has already ended [4].

Yet many researchers recognize a need to capture at least some portion of this aspect of modern life. The Internet Archive tends to take a 'low-hanging fruit' approach in an effort to save as much of the open Web as possible, including early prototypes of social media; e.g. when Friendster data was threatened by acquisition and repurposing of the platform, the Archive Team stepped in to download the user-generated content. Clifford Lynch has recently suggested a descriptive solution that recognizes the complexity of social media platforms and attempts to capture their essential core by characterizing how the algorithms present information to users [20]. In his thoughtful blog post about the amnesiac nature of today's Internet, David Rosenthal examines why different resources (including the material created within the walls of social media apps) are difficult to save [29].

A use-first approach asks, how do we think future scholars will use a resource like Facebook, Instagram, or Twitter? Where does the value of social media platforms reside? Are we attempting to document social media as a phenomenon, as cultural or historical description (as one would save newspapers), or are we saving social media content as a resource that captures contemporaneous information about individual people, institutions, events, and how they are connected? In the most comprehensive sense, would archiving social media platforms be a wholesale effort to preserve ephemeral communication? There are also important questions to resolve about who might take advantage of such an effort. Are we preserving social media for its current users or for future generations? Each use suggests a different approach and emphasis, as well as different social media platforms to consider as targets of our preservation efforts.

In the end, future use of today's social media platforms might involve all of these activities and more. Scholars and activists have already demonstrated a profound need to trace the flow of news and information within social media platforms [2]. Services such as Ancestry demonstrate individuals' desires to work with others to document their family histories using factual sources as well as family stories. Similarly, journalists use these services to retrieve or verify biographical information about their subjects. Why we save something and what we intend to do with it later crucially influences how it is kept.

In this paper, I examine a specific case of biographical research that has resulted in a collection of more than 11,750 subject-related heterogeneous items. The collection itself and the means of developing it will be explored to investigate its implications for the future of biography (literary and factual) in an era of online collections, as well as for anticipated uses of social media.

Because biography intertwines history and personal identity, it provides an obvious projected use for the type of user-contributed information that one finds on social media platforms. As a genre, biography must be factually accurate, but also must provide a valuable window onto people, places, and significant periods of time (e.g. literary movements or historical events). Biographical research is also a stress test for using the heterogeneous forms of information typically found in digital libraries and on social media platforms; multiple resources are usually required to integrate a complete description of a person in the context of the time and places they lived. Most importantly, the availability of social media platforms from a period contemporaneous with the biography's subject may help writers recover information about people who have been rendered invisible due to social forces at work during their subject's lifetime.

In this paper, I begin by providing background on the biography's subject and on the collection of contemporaneous primary material I have assembled as a basis for describing the subject's influence on a modern literary movement. Next I describe how I rediscovered the subject's social network and what the rediscovery process implies for the future use of today's social media platforms. I then examine the roles of two contrasting types of material, permanent forms of documentation and ephemera, and explore what each implies about the use of the parallel types of user-contributed material offered by social media platforms. Finally, I use common issues I have encountered to explore the implications of how social media content may influence this type of research.

2 BACKGROUND

Over the past four years, I have been collecting biographical material about Joan Harding Vollmer Burroughs, writer William S. Burroughs' wife, with the aim of writing a literary biography. As Hermione Lee's invaluable *Biography: A Very Short Introduction* asserts, biography is an investigation of identity as it is situated in history. Lee also reminds us that in different periods of time, some subjects can be rendered invisible by social forces at work. [13] This was indeed the case here. Socioeconomic status and gender influences the type of information that is available

Biographical subject. Joan Vollmer Burroughs was born in the period between the two World Wars, on February 4, 1923, in Ossining, New York, a town on the Hudson River north of New York City. Through a storied set of circumstances, while she was living near Columbia University, she fell in with and influenced a group of writers who would later be characterized as the nucleus of the Beat Movement. In 1946, one of these writers, William S. Burroughs, would become her common-law husband. An increasingly repressive trend in American politics and social thought, coupled with Burroughs' troubles with the law, resulted in the couple's move to Mexico City in 1949 with their two children. On September 6, 1951, Burroughs shot and killed his wife in what would become the most remembered single event in his long life. A variety of factors, including the circumstances of her death, led to Joan Burroughs being 'forgotten' for the next 30 years, and misrepresented for the ensuing 35 years.

Because Joan was married three times, Beat biographers have had a hard time settling on a consistent name for her. She is indexed under Vollmer, Adams (the surname of her second husband), or Burroughs. To reduce the confusion in this paper, I will refer to her by her maiden name, *Joan Vollmer*, or simply as *Joan*, since there are no other Joans in her immediate circle.

The subject-driven collection. The 11754-item collection I describe in this paper, which mainly consists of primary material, has been growing as I consult online resources (e.g. genealogy-oriented services that provide access to heterogeneous data sources, large digitized newspaper collections), request records from municipal, state, and federal archives and public and private institutions, examine relevant special collections in research libraries, and interview people from Joan's social network.

The online resources used here are broad, and many are newly available; they are expanding quickly even as I work (e.g. Ancestry.com, a heterogeneous set of repositories that is federated through search capabilities, has already added records that I had requested and received on paper from records rooms less than three years ago). Furthermore, many datasets these resources offer are available from more than one place. For example, multiple resources provide search interfaces to the US Census or the US Social Security Death Index. Some newspapers, e.g. the *Brooklyn Daily Eagle*, are available through multiple newspaper collections, albeit with important differences in coverage, scan and OCR quality, and search interfaces.

I have consulted multiple special collections in research libraries including (but not limited to) the New York Public Library's Berg Collection of English and American Literature (including the Kerouac Collection and the William S. Burroughs Papers, 1951-1972), Columbia University's William Seward Burroughs Papers, 1957-1976, and Allen Ginsberg Papers, 1943-1991, Stanford University's Allen Ginsberg Papers (1937-1994), Arizona State University's Ted Morgan papers, the University of North Carolina at Chapel Hill's collected papers of Edith Frankie Parker and Henri Cru (1887-2004), and Ohio State University Library's William S. Burroughs Papers; I verified coverage using the SNAC tool [15]. None of these special collections address Joan specifically. Instead they each have relevant material donated by the writers and letter-collectors in her social circle. These have been usefully supplemented by items from personal collections (from research colleagues and from the subject's friends and their descendants).

I have also conducted eighteen ethnographic-style interviews of relatives and friends of the subject and their descendants even though the data obtained this way must be used with care. It is difficult to find an interview subject who hasn't read a Beat biography, and shaped their own stories to conform to published anecdotes that have become the norm. Thus, these interviews must be triangulated with and prompted by other primary information. One of the reasons to write this biography (which might seem to some to cover well-trodden ground) is to take a fresh look at some of the accumulated anecdotes and received wisdom. Sixteen of the eighteen interviews were between one and three hours long; the remaining two were brief (15 minutes each due to the subjects' age and infirmity).

Collection development. Items have been retrieved or created (in the case of interview recordings, digitized records, field notes, and research notes) individually over the project's course. The items range from the mundane (municipal birth index records) to the personal (letters Joan wrote to her friends and lovers) to the revealing (newspaper stories that covered events that may have been misremembered in interviews that took place much later). Some of the items also clarified and contextualized people and events on the world or local stage that were an important part of the subject's life. Each item was stored with important metadata; individual items were dated and sourced. This metadata is vital not only for citation purposes; it is also central to the analyses necessary to piece together a biography.

At the outset, I attempted to store each item in the form it was retrieved (e.g., as a PDF file). But later the visual characteristics provided by JPEG thumbnails proved essential for determining when I'd already saved an item (over the course of four years, a researcher can and does encounter the same information multiple times. The ability to quickly assess whether an item is already part of the collection helps reduce duplication), and distinguishing at a glance between, say, a newspaper obituary, a municipal death record, or a Social Security Death Index entry. Further processing or text analysis required that I transcribe some items and extract salient information into Excel.

Focus on contemporaneous primary material. I have amassed this material with the aim of writing a book that is focused on contemporaneous evidence, rather than drawing on the many important secondary sources that have been written over the last thirty years [9,12,25,26]. Why? Because I believe the nature of biography can and will inevitably change as different kinds of primary material become more readily available. From the start, the vagaries of human memory were revealed as the contemporaneous evidence called well-accepted stories and anecdotes into question, as one might expect from recent research on human memory [18,19,27,28,31]. Forgotten events were identified and used to elicit new stories via artifact-driven interviews [7,32]. Using other analytic techniques, missing correspondence and other examples of the subject's writing were located; descendants were identified and interviewed; and much new was learned.

Figure 1 shows a typical leaf-level directory that represents a member of Joan's New York City social circle; elements of factual biography (e.g. a death record) are integrated with descriptive material (e.g. a 1944 letter written by this secondary subject).

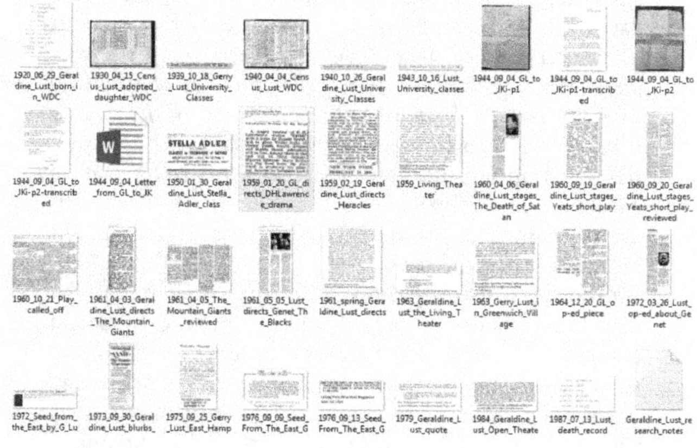

Figure 1. Documentation related to one of Joan's New York City social contacts

3 BIOGRAPHY AND SOCIAL NETWORKS

Biographical research by its nature involves collecting information about a person that reveals basic facts, the subject's essential character and beliefs, and the subject's social environment. This social network aspect is acknowledged by SNAC (Social Networks and Archival Context) [15], but SNAC is limited to the curated information in special collections as specified by their finding aids. It is only now that more data-driven biographical research is truly practical. If, in 1982, a biographer heard through an interview that a character in a novel was based on one of the subject's social contacts, one would more or less take it on faith that the person existed, and played the role he or she was said to in the subject's life. Today one can interrogate these facts and claims more extensively by gathering documentary materials from sources such as local newspapers, records from many different repositories, yearbook photos, local maps and pictures of relevant locations, and other primary material that would formerly require expensive in-person research methods. Although these methods are still desirable when they are feasible (in-person interviews and visits to places the subject lived invariably add color and depth to a biography), usually they're not possible to investigate members of the subject's social network.

Given that this is a literary biography, some of the work of identifying her social network had already been done when I began. Because Joan Vollmer is not known as a literary figure on her own, there is no "Joan Vollmer Special Collection" (aside from my own). Any papers related to her (say, letters she wrote to Allen Ginsberg) were in other special collections. Thus SNAC was used to ensure that those special collections were identified, and the relevant material was retrieved. Secondary sources (e.g. biographies of William S. Burroughs) also helped me identify Joan's social connections. Joan's social network was then extended using the three methods described below.

Connections specified by or about the subject within primary materials like letters or journals. These primary materials by or about the subject are usually in special collections or privately held personal collections. Friends' names are often mentioned in correspondence, journal entries, and other writings. For example, in a letter to Jack Kerouac from Mexico City dated July 9th, Joan refers to a friend of hers who's an astrologer: "*Sorry about your troubles with your wife, publishers, etc. I know a guy who's an astrologer, who says its [sic] a beat year for everyone, if that's any comfort.*" [11] Further research establishes who among the local group has an interest in astrology: it is bartender John Healy. Joan socialized with him often during her final summer. Often these names are incomplete and informal.

Contemporaneous primary sources. Ephemera like local newspapers might also mention social connections, mostly through co-occurrence with the subject (or the subject's immediate network). E.g. newspaper accounts of Joan's lurid death mention 13 such people who were a regular part of the Burroughs couples' Mexico City social network.

Interviews. Interviews—my own and others—revealed new social network connections from different times and places in Joan's life. E.g., Beat researcher Rob Johnson extended the Burroughs couple's social network in South Texas where they lived in the late 1940s [12]. My own interviews focused on family members, and on friends of Joan's who were not connected with the other members of the inner Beat circle (e.g. people associated with Joan's second husband, Paul Adams, a cypher to biographers).

As time passes, some social network connections dim, and others are inadvertently reinforced by interviews in which well-known anecdotes are retold. My interview with historian Bruce Mazlish, who was educated at Columbia University and hovered slightly outside of Joan's inner social circle before it was thoroughly documented, illustrated some of these effects. According to Mazlish, he was "*never part of the circle*" but he had spent some time in the apartment on 119th Street (by Columbia) that Joan had shared with Edie Parker [13].

During the course of the interview, it became clear that Mazlish was reacting to Barry Miles' biography of William S. Burroughs which had been published and promoted a few months before our interview. [25] This comprehensive secondary source suggested that he, Mazlish, may have been the father of Joan's daughter Julie Adams, a rumor he was anxious to dispel in our interview by emphasizing his distance from Joan: "*There was a young German who was part of the circle for a while. I think his name was Tobey and I don't remember the last name. He was very good-looking, y'know, tall guy and I think he, he was involved.*" Mazlish, who was in his early 90s at the time of the interview, had summoned to mind a married boyfriend of Joan's. Indeed, a tall, handsome man with a German surname and ancestry was important member of Joan's friend group during the pre-Beat era. This person is often omitted from Beat biographies, since he left Columbia before the best-documented period of the Beat Movement. His identity was resolved by contemporaneous evidence provided to me by his family, and from a letter from Jack Kerouac to Joan's roommate Edie Parker in which the mystery man was called out as part of the household, "*Take good care of Woofit, of Sweeny, and of Joanie, and of* Herbie." (Woofit and Sweeny are dogs) [6]

Table 1 shows the social distance of the people who are represented in my collection via an extended factual biography. Direct connections—1-hop—are the people the subject knew—her children, spouses, friends, and family. 2-hop connections include people the subject might not encounter directly: e.g., friends-of-friends and family-of-friends. The goal is to find the minimal information necessary to distinguish people in Joan's network from their doppelgangers, coupled with information that helps describe them and their relationship to the subject. It is also important to note when and where they became part of the subject's social network; relationships wax and wane.

Table 1. Documentation of Joan's social network.

Type	# people	related records	records/ person	missing elements	doppel-gangers
Subject	1	14	14	0%	0%
1-hop	95	797	8.39	35.79%	32.63%
2-hop	72	511	7.10	43.06%	23.61%
3-hop	10	50	5.00	10.00%	30.00%
Total	**178**	**1372**	**7.71**	**37.08%**	**28.65%**

Why is it useful to push beyond the subject's immediate social network? These people may act as indirect influences and surely help put relationships in context. More distant connections (3-hop in the table) were generally found to support communication with living relatives. Members of an extended social network are important when one is seeking overlooked primary material. Joan was a prolific letter-writer; it is only by happenstance that some of her letters came to be in special collections. It was only after I read Joan's letters held in personal collections that I realized how unrepresentative her letters to Allen Ginsberg and Jack Kerouac were (and how problematic her relationship was with both men).

Table 1 demonstrates some interesting effects of social distance: it was more difficult to gather records for factual biographies when the persons were further from the subject. In other words, it helps to know where to look and what to look for. Doppelgangers (people with the same name as the individual being addressed) often play a role in people search [22]. It's difficult to eliminate them even when a researcher is aware of distinguishing characteristics. Later in this paper, I will return to this table to address issues with doppelgangers in biographical research.

Social media platforms as a source of connections. One of the most powerful parts of social media platforms is their explicit representation of social networks. It is this aspect of Facebook that first drew me to the idea of social media platforms as a source for biographical research. When future biographers or historians are researching who their subjects (now our contemporaries) knew, it seems natural to turn to a social media platform like Facebook. In fact, the third hop connections in my research were often established by turning to Facebook: Who is the daughter (or granddaughter) of one of Joan's contemporaries? How can they be contacted? Of course various social media platforms are more useful and reliable as a source of everyday social network information, especially when they are compared to the relatively ad-hoc methods I used to find Joan's contemporaneous connections in which surnames must be inferred, and ephemeral material like correspondence or newspapers may not be readily available. Live interview subjects may forget when and where they met someone. A platform like Facebook may well prove to be useful in establishing a subject's social network.

Furthermore, the social network component perhaps the most practical part of many social media platforms to preserve. It's considered less private than actual communication or profile/personalization information. It is constrained, and in the epochal moment, static. Certainly preservation may be a limited endeavor, and this case study shows the ways in which social networks themselves may be a useful research resource.

4 PERMANENT MATERIAL

Records and other types of permanent material are useful to support factual biography, as well as to establish historical and contextual background. Access to this type of material is necessarily limited by four constraints:

- what governments and institutions collect and save;
- the ability to locate and access relevant records across many different repositories and digital libraries;
- practical concerns (tradeoffs between cost and expected benefit); and
- privacy protection (the constraints introduced by laws and policy to protect individual privacy).

The first constraint is straightforward: you can't use information that wasn't collected. Our thirst for descriptive accuracy and statistics has grown (and become more necessary) over the years. This much is evident from the detail and formal structure of records. The US Census is a good illustration, since it is information vital for allocating resources; census entries (and the surrounding sheets) may also be invaluable for biography. The census is organized by neighborhood and larger geopolitical divisions. Much can be learned about biographical subjects, although questions vary across decades.

The 1920 US Census, taken three years before Joan's birth, shows Joan's young parents living in a town outside of New York City in a middle-class neighborhood. Most of the neighbors owned their homes, were born in New York State, and spoke English. Professions varied: wheelwright, clerk, dressmaker, railroad conductor, and general contractor, among others; Joan's father was a manufacturing chemist in the textile dye industry. By 1930, the family had moved to the house in the Albany suburb where Joan grew up. The census emphasis shifted; home value and literacy were added. The neighborhood was still prosperous—doctors, lawyers, insurance agents—and the homes were relatively expensive. By 1940, the comparable census sheet reflects the effects of the Depression and a newer focus on education. Joan's childhood neighborhood had weathered the economic downturn. Home value declined, but the sparsely settled neighborhood (the Depression interrupted construction) remained middle-class. Most of the men and some women were college graduates when a college education was rarer than it is today. Thirty years of census data can provide a powerful lens for examining the subject's environment, and illustrates how perceived data needs change.

The second constraint raises some limitations with familiar information retrieval and database query technology. These technologies assume you know where to look, and the user experience is all about searching a collection. In reality, much of the work lies in finding the resource to begin with. Some resources (e.g. Ancestry or FamilySearch) offer an interface to federated search. An alert user quickly realizes just how difficult it is to rank heterogeneous search results.

The third and fourth constraints intersect information resources at the policy level. Each country, state, or municipality has its own records policy: what is collected, how it can be accessed, who can request it, and its cost. E.g., anyone can retrieve a marriage record from Palm Beach, Florida using a searchable online repository with no login. In New York City, one either must be the subject of a marriage record or wait until the end of an embargo period to get the comparable record. Access is mediated by a records clerk; proof of identity is kept on file; and payment is required.

Table 2 shows a breakdown of the collection's records and permanent material.

Table 2. Formal records and other permanent source material in biographical collection

Type	# of items	% of total
Semi-structured formal records	1546	76%
Yearbook excerpts	175	9%
ID photos and portraits	97	5%
Book excerpts	70	3%
Full documents and reports	59	3%
Magazine and journal excerpts	54	3%
Contemporaneous essays	26	1%
Total	**2027**	**100%**

About 17% of the Joan Vollmer collection consists of formal records and other permanent, fixed types of contemporaneous material (excerpts from books, magazine and journal articles, essays, documents and reports, and formal photos). As one might expect, the bulk of this material (over ¾) takes the form of semi-structured or structured records, including items such as Social Security Death Index entries and Merchant Marine ship manifests. Yearbook excerpts provide items like senior class biographies. Photos counted under this rubric include ID photos, e.g. Joan Vollmer's and William Burroughs' freshman photos from Barnard and Harvard (respectively), which were used in news coverage of the shooting. Book excerpts include descriptive primary sources (e.g. documenting social connection Gerry Lust's role in New York City's avant-garde theater). Full documents and reports includes items like a description of the Morningside Heights area in 1943 published by the New York Times Co. An advertisement for "Crotona Fast Chrome Black" from *American Dyestuff Reporter*, 1922 is counted as a journal excerpt (it's a product developed by Joan's father). Essays are less common, e.g. Joan's term paper about Nietzsche and Bergson, written on behalf of her boyfriend John Kingsland, as well as several op/ed pieces Joan contributed to publications.

Social media platforms as a source of factual information. Much research effort goes into finding and verifying "hard facts," including dates of birth and death, education, marriage, children, and work history. Will social media profiles ever prove to be a viable source for this sort of factual information? This question deserves some thought. Although existing sources are variable and not always reliable, most governmental and institutional records repositories have procedures for verifying the information they collect, and people usually contribute the information in good faith. This is not always true when people describe themselves on social media accounts. The completeness and accuracy of social media profiles cannot be guaranteed, nor can we count on the one-to-one mapping between account holders and real names.

Today social media platforms enrich user-contributed profiles and self-description with accumulated (and sometimes purchased) personalization information, some of which is based on user behavior. Because it is difficult for users to control this extended profiling, it may be easier to consider user-contributed self-description as the baseline for preservation. Although privacy concerns must be acknowledged in any case, access policies may follow the guidelines and restrictions implemented by existing records repositories, particularly those which protect their constituents via embargoes and by maintaining requestors' personal information (e.g. New York City requires a valid driver's license to be submitted with records requests).

5 EPHEMERA

Intuitively, we think of ephemera as designed to be discarded after its original intended use is over, e.g. event-related items like ticket stubs and playbills, or transient paperwork like cash register receipts and ATM reports. It's tempting to look for features that these things share: is ephemerality a property of genre (contrast, say, a yearbook with a student newspaper), material form (contrast, say, a Post-it or a receipt with a bound print book), or the importance or continuing relevance of the information conveyed (contrast, say, an "About Town" column in a local newspaper with a front-page news article)? Does ephemerality imply anything about how and whether such materials should be archived? Does it suggest limits on how such materials should be interpreted and used?

While it is tempting to make a bright-line distinction between ephemera and permanent material, and use this distinction to circumscribe the contents of collections, it is difficult—and perhaps counterproductive—to do so. Ephemera has certain properties that stem more from social norms and expectations, and less from properties of the material itself, such as genre, physical embodiment, fixity, or the information's reliability. David Levy's *Scrolling Forward* [17] provides an indispensable discussion of these issues.

Consider, for example, a student newspaper. A student newspaper is a publication, and as such, one might think it is fixed (i.e. an edition doesn't change after it is printed), but relevant only for a brief period of time. Yet universities often keep an entire run of their institution's student newspaper: the publication says a lot about the institution and its students, and may be an important source for subsequent historical research. Until recently, student newspapers were also highly local in scope: members of the Columbia University class of 1945 might not expect just anyone to read about their exploits.

Yet now any Internet user can search or browse the entire run of the Columbia *Spectator* online. It's easy to type long-ago students' names into the search box and discover something about their student years. The information that turns up may be embarrassing (perhaps the student, now a captain of industry, dressed in drag for the annual Varsity Show), trivial (e.g. perhaps the student worked as a dorm waiter), or long-forgotten. Thus the expectation of limited scope—that for the most part, other Columbia students will be reading the *Spectator* at the time and place the news was made—makes a student newspaper seem more like ephemera.

Temporal limits to relevance and accuracy might make other print reference material seem similarly ephemeral. Consider a city directory. The households in question probably don't live where they did 50 years ago. Here, too, the social expectation is that such publications will be discarded. Yet they tell us a lot: e.g., which neighborhoods were immigrant enclaves, and where people of biographical interest lived.

The Society of American Archivists confirms this intuitive definition of ephemera as *materials created for a specific, limited purpose, and generally designed to be discarded after use.* Purpose and norms are fundamental in distinguishing ephemera from other types of material.

Ephemera forms the backbone of many special collections. A famous writer's literary drafts and letters—or even her postcards and personal photos—may give the researcher flashes of interpretive insight that are unavailable to even the most attentive reader of the writer's published works.

Many of the examples proposed thusfar refer to print or physical media. Digital media may radically change our sense of ephemera. For example, we keep far more email than we do print mail (especially handwritten letters, which have all but vanished from our everyday lives). Not only that, we also keep it in a different way—normally we wouldn't have both sides of a physical correspondence—and for a different reason. Email sometimes survives simply because it is more time-consuming to curate and discard it than it is to just keep it [1]. More extreme examples may be found in personal and social media; offhand remarks contributed to Twitter or candid photos taken on smart phones may be kept beyond their intended communicative use and used in unintended ways [14].

Digitization efforts have also modified how we are able to use print ephemera: as in the earlier examples, the digitized forms of published media may be accessible to an audience that is far broader than originally intended. A researcher need not travel to a university's reading room to access a special collection, or to a small town library to access a run of a local newspaper. Some ephemera that might have been discarded or deaccessioned (e.g. local directories or out-of-date maps) are kept, and readily located. Much of the research described in this paper is based on the broader availability of ephemera.

From the user's perspective, changes to the nature of ephemera are beneficial. It used to be difficult and prohibitively expensive to visit reading rooms all over the world to consult ephemera held in multiple special collections. Biographers might travel to their subjects' hometowns to scan through old newspapers or visit collections of student work in the journalism room at a local high school. From the perspective of a biographer, historian, or social scientist, ephemera teaches us about everyday life in place at a time; it changes more quickly and reflects a more complete, personal, and informal view than material intended to be permanent. It is also an invaluable and nuanced source of information about individuals.

As the amount of ephemera kept grows, and the boundary between ephemera and intentionally permanent material becomes more porous, two issues come to the fore. The first issue stems from context and scope: place and time can become an interpretive lens for ephemera, and conversely, ephemera can augment broader, less personal information. The second issue stems from the way unexpected uses of ephemera can inadvertently compromise privacy, especially when different pieces of ephemera are extracted from large collections and brought together. As boyd and Crawford have discussed in their insightful analysis of the early days of big data, bringing together multiple data sources may have potent and unforeseen effects on an individual's privacy [3]. I often have the sense that my own efforts have violated my subject's privacy, as well as that of much of her social network.

Table 3 provides an overview of ephemera I collected as primary sources. Recall that an item refers to a unitary file, e.g., a newspaper clipping, a candid photo, a home movie clip, a directory entry, a page from a personal letter, and so on. The numbers of items reflect the type's relative prominence in the collection (but don't necessarily indicate relative value). Most of the categories are self-explanatory, although a few benefit from examples. Directory entries may point to organizational membership (e.g. in the American Mathematical Society) or link a person with a place. Candid photos may reveal activities—e.g. that William and Joan took the kids to Mexico City's central park. Photos of reference objects in historical catalogs and contemporaneous ads allow everyday things to be identified in personal photos and home movies.

Table 3. Overview of biographical ephemera

Type of ephemera	# of items	% of ephemera
Newspaper clippings or pages	6660	81%
Letters (contemporaneous)	679	8%
Directories (by the page)	414	5%
Candid photos	151	2%
Photos of places	103	1%
Photos of everyday objects	78	1%
Newsletters and excerpts	68	0%
Envelopes (contemporaneous)	34	0%
Home movie stills	29	0%
Total	**8216**	**100%**

Newspaper clippings serve three main functions: (1) they inform the biographies of members of Joan's social network; (2) they document important events (e.g. the 1947 Texas City explosion); and (3) they can drive deeper analyses to answer specific questions. For example, the arrests, fines, and crimes from a newspaper's police blotter helped show that William Burroughs 'failed the attitude test' during his 1948 arrest near Beeville, Texas.

Ephemera constitutes almost 70% of this biographical collection, or 8216 out of 11754 items. In addition to the 8216 ephemeral items and the 2027 records, there are 1511 items that fall into a liminal category of research notes, secondary material, partial analytic results, and chapter drafts. I consider these as part of the collection, but not of interest for this paper.

Comparing the sources and resources of ephemera to those for formal records is a good way to understand the changing nature of evidence. The original set of Beat biographies were largely based on interviews and a relatively small amount of primary material from special collections (some of which had not yet been donated). In addition to using a tool like SNAC, future biographers may consult digitized newspaper collections, heterogeneous public records, and repositories of many forms of cultural and historical ephemera.

Social media platforms as a source of ephemera. Necessarily ephemera will be a more controversial component of the type of user-contributed content available through most social media platforms. Usually ephemera is more closely associated with social media's communicative function rather than being a persistent and stable way of establishing an identity. Hyperlocal news (as one might find in a student newspaper) remains something that is expected to vanish quickly into a user's or institution's history and be relatively difficult to re-find. Even non-profile photos on users' accounts are curated carefully and some users object to ever being tagged in photos without their explicit consent. Social media platforms are universally acknowledged as a venue for curated self-presentation, not personal documentation. Hence if social media is to be preserved and used in any sort of historical role, this type of ephemeral material will be the most difficult aspect of the platform to handle, both from a social and technical perspective. Its complicated nature does not diminish the utility of ephemera to a researcher; however, it is unlikely that preservation of this type of content will find broad public support [24].

6 RESEARCH ISSUES

Five information-centric issues recurred repeatedly during this research: the need to disambiguate doppelgangers; assess information reliability; anticipate the variability of similar types of items (e.g. marriage records from different cities); make inferences based on missing information; and evaluate the stories of potentially unreliable narrators. These issues stem in part from the availability of online resources (e.g. digital libraries and collections of ephemera) as they are brought to bear on biography. Formerly, biography drew on curated resources from special collections; fewer factual and perspectival conflicts arose. These issues also have implications for the preservation and use of social media platforms.

Doppelgangers. Doppelgangers are a confounding (or sometimes reassuring) aspect of people search [22]. As many amateur genealogists demonstrate, it is difficult to distinguish among people with the same name. Table 1 (earlier in the paper) shows how many entities in this research had confusing doppelgangers (i.e. relevance could not be easily resolved by a crucial element like birth year). Out of 178 people in the subject's social network, 51 (or almost 29%) had doppelgangers. Sometimes this is the result of family names—a large family may reuse ancestral names in a single generation—and sometimes it's simply because a name was common. Mostly I was able to resolve these ambiguities, but a few were left unaccounted for. In Ancestry, it is possible to see the effect of such doppelgangers as misinterpretation spreads from one amateur genealogist's work to another's, especially if the correct records are difficult to find or are missing from the platform entirely.

Although the phenomenon of doppelgangers will remain a puzzle for biographers and other social media users, the availability of a subject's social network and additional contextual clues can help resolve basic confusion about identity. In this research, Facebook was often used as the bridge between past generations documented by records and members of current generations who are active social media users.

Record reliability. It is easy to think of records as being ultimately reliable, the way to resolve factual discrepancies and check the veracity of stories. But records are created by humans. Sometimes the circumstances improve reliability of the values assigned to certain attributes of the record (e.g. times on birth and death records), and sometimes they incite factual errors (e.g. ages and going-in marital status on marriage records, especially old ones, may be deliberately falsified). Records may also be falsified for the sake of self-presentation [8]. Self-presentation is easy to observe on census sheets, given data points ten years apart. Immigrants often want to assimilate and mitigate possible risks to themselves and their families. As they learn English and become more 'American', they may gradually change their place of origin to the US, especially during periods of strong anti-immigration sentiment.

In the end, it's important to remember that information originates with people. False or incorrect information can be partial (to obscure an inconvenient fact like age); it can be an aspect of self-presentation (as in the place-of-birth example above); and it can be complete and represent the assumption of a fresh identity. Sometimes errors are accidental, the result of information that is misremembered, incorrectly transcribed, or misheard. Reliability is socially enforced and often reflects the relationship between a person and an institution. This heuristic can guide our expectations of social media.

Record variability. Records covering the same type of information vary more than we've come to expect in an age of increasing uniformity and computerization. Figure 2 shows four marriage records from the first half of the 20th century; this variability holds for more recent records as well. Figure 2(a) is a note to the local judge written by the bride's father, signed in front of two named witnesses. It stands out from the others because of its informality. At first glance, the other three records appear to be very similar. But they aren't. Although Figure 2(b) is structured and regularized, it has less information than the scrap of paper shown in (a), just the couple's names, along with the judge that married them. Figure 2(c) is more narrative in form, and uses Mexican name conventions (the mother's surname follows the father's). Figure 2(d) has far more detail than the others: dates of birth rather than ages, dates of any previous divorces, communicable diseases (e.g. tuberculosis in addition to 'venereal diseases'), and consent to the marriage (Are the bride and groom sound of mind?).

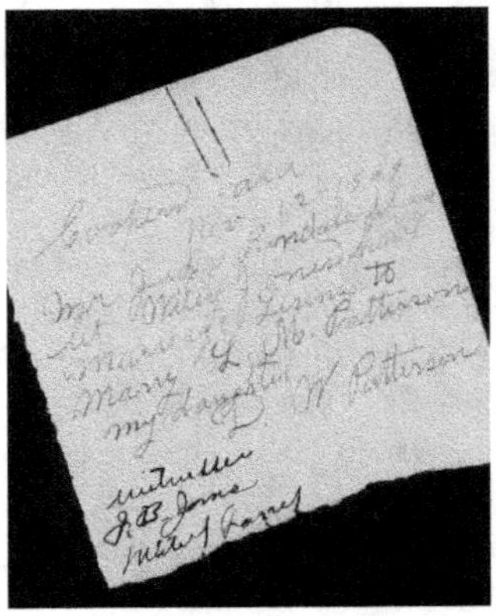

(a) Surrogate marriage record from a small town in Alabama in 1909

(b) Formal marriage record, Miller County, Arkansas, 1940.

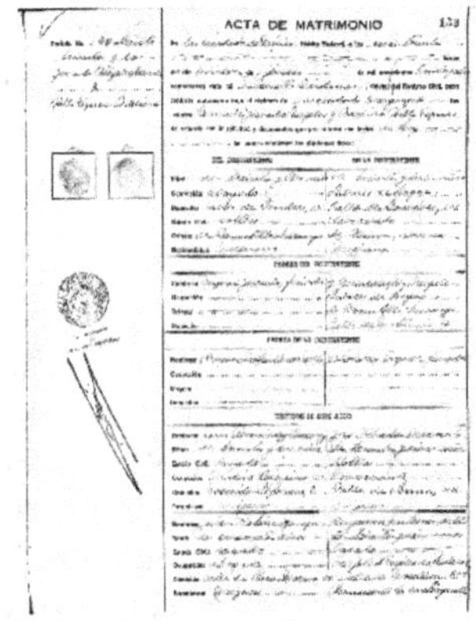

(c) Initial page of 2-pg. marriage record from Mexico City in 1938.

(d) Detailed multi-field marriage record, Steuben County, Indiana, 1938

Figure 2. Four diverse marriage records

Besides the apparent differing levels of formality, each record was obtained because the county or municipality had specific access policies that enabled me to retrieve them. Some must be obtained by writing away to a records clerk; some require carefully circumscribed types of payment (a cashier's check and a notarized request); others are online as part of a for-pay service like Ancestry; and finally some are freely available online if one knows where to look. These marriage records not only provide the researcher with different types of information; the information also may or may not be vetted (usually by requiring the parties to provide supporting records).

Witnesses to a marriage may be important members of the bride and groom's social network, so access to their names (and other information about them) often proves to be useful. If convenient strangers are witnesses, this tells us something too. Consider this aspect of the four records. Figure 2 (a) lists two witnesses with no further information about them; Figure 2(b) required no witnesses; Figure 2(c) required four witnesses with supporting information (age, profession, marital status, address, and relation to the bride and groom); and Figure 2(d) required just court officials.

In an era of social media platforms, many individuals are much better documented. Access to social media information contemporaneous with a subject is apt to provide more opportunities for triangulation, although thankfully no life is ever fully documented, nor should it be. If anything, social media platforms will underscore the problems inherent in inferring facts from missing information.

Interpreting missing information. What does it mean when a record is missing? It is difficult to interpret the absence of information. In this biographical collection, death records (and in a few cases birth records) are missing for 25 people. Sometimes this means the people are still alive (seven, according to my interviews), but the other 18 simply have no records in my collection that would suggest they are dead. Often the source for death information in the US (besides a municipally-issued or state-issued certificate) is the Social Security Death Index. The Social Security system is a relatively recent phenomenon, and it was apparently not readily adopted by some of the wealthy social elites covered by my collection. Furthermore, women frequently had fewer associated records than men: they were less apt to serve in the military (a major source of personal records) or have jobs outside the home. It is easy to see how invisible social status translates into an absence of records and vice-versa.

The people who were subject to the greatest research effort were Joan's immediate social network. If we use the social network identifiers provided by the three means explained earlier in the paper, her male friends and relatives dramatically outnumber her female friends and relatives: 63 out of 95 were male. So, too, they have a greater number of documentary records (an average of 9.56 per man as opposed to 6.09 per woman). Did female friends disappear due to lack of evidence, or did Joan simply have more male friends? It's difficult to tell at this point. Joan mentions few women in her correspondence.

Joan had no Social Security records, no passport, and nothing was recovered from a targeted Freedom of Information Act (FOIA) request. How is she documented? Via three census sheets (two US, one New York State), five marriage-and-divorce related-records (three are index-only), three miscellaneous records, and three records associated with her death. Her death record, presumably filled out with information supplied by William S. Burroughs misreports her date and place of birth. With so few records available for fact-checking, the bad information propagated to newspapers and biographies. Only one of Joan's 14 records has her real birthdate and birthplace.

It is easy to see the danger in interpreting missing records, even with background information from interviews. At least four principal entities in this research had 'missing' marriages even though they (or those immediately involved with them) had been interviewed extensively as part of other biographical efforts. Of course this shouldn't be a surprise—they were usually short-lived marriages, but they were biographically significant. The marriages were confirmed and explained when I raised them during interviews, but it is unlikely that interviewees would have brought them up without prompting. Nor is it safe to presume there's a divorce between every two marriages. In general, making reasonable inferences from missing records is only safely used to find other related information.

Unreliable narrators. Recent articles have highlighted the difficulties of relying on memory as a sole source for eyewitness testimony [31]. Over time, memories can be distorted, especially if they correspond to popular anecdotes that may be changed for the story's sake. It is easy to mix in details from evocative media portrayals of similar situations or to place oneself in a situation one has only heard about. A leading question can change the substance of a memory [18,28], and if questions go unasked, important aspects of a subject's life may be ignored.

William S. Burroughs observed in an interview with his biographer, Ted Morgan, "When I compare my memory with other people's, like [Herbert] Huncke's, when they start describing what they thought happened, and I realize how imprecise most people's memories are." [33] People often trust their own memories even if there is ample evidence that their memories are in poor alignment with events. Most of the time, this difference is unimportant: we negotiate a mutually acceptable past. But in the case of biography, the difference in competing memories may significantly change our perceptions.

Many subjects, too, can turn out to be unreliable narrators of their own lives, misrepresenting facts and events, either to control self-presentation (as is generally explored by Goffman [8]) or because the lies seem inconsequential. More crucially, misrepresentations can protect the vulnerable (e.g. the status of an illegitimate child) as well as the powerful.

7 CONCLUSION

One potential use of today's social networking platforms (especially those that use two-way connections) is in the realm of biography. At the very least, a skeletal social network is the first step in developing a connected literary biography. Similarly, some types of account profile data can be used as an initial step in developing a factual biography. Beyond those basic elements, other aspects of social media platforms might help provide historical context (e.g. local news stories, institutional pages) of the type I sought to fill out my extensive repository.

Are social connections always meaningful? Are profiles always correct and in a one-to-one correspondence with people? Certainly not. Studies show that people often have more than one account and more than one profile on any given social media platform (e.g. [23]). But detection of primary profiles seems possible, given the ways people claim to use their secondary accounts (e.g. to 'friend' accounts that might result in spam).

As common sources of ephemera disappear (e.g. small town newspapers and literary letters [5]), aspects of social media may step in to fill the void. Donor agreements can be developed so people can trade (or sell [24]) their personal data to interested parties. Sensitive information can be protected for a meaningful period (e.g. a lifetime or beyond) [30].

At their farthest reach, social media platforms also have the potential to answer other types of questions that I have imagined over the course of this project. For example, did Joan's second husband, Paul Adams, realize that his ex-wife had been shot and killed? Because Adams left Joan's social network after their marriage essentially ended in November of 1945, to learn of the shooting, it seems that either he or a close friend of his would've had to have encountered an article about it in a New York City newspaper (and realize its significance). But neither *New York Times* article about the shooting mentioned Joan's name. Furthermore, the two articles appeared on pages three and six—far enough into a daily paper that it is folly to assume they would be read carefully.

If a social media platform had been available at the time, one can imagine finding out whether Adams had encountered such an article (e.g. in his news feed), and whether he had attended to it for more than a few seconds. It would be quite a revelation. Alas, it would also be extremely creepy.

Despite the apparent utility of 'deep' social media content, preserving platform elements like network maps and profile information is more likely to be practical, especially when one considers the arguments of scholars like Clifford Lynch [20] and David Rosenthal [29]. My effort to use everyday ephemera coupled with ordinary records to supplement special collections on behalf of biography shows that it may be worthwhile to aim preservation at a middle ground, beyond platform description and short of archival completeness.

ACKNOWLEDGMENTS

I would like to thank my colleague, archivist Simon Johnson, without whom searching for these records would've been a lot more difficult and a lot less fun; William Burroughs' literary executor and son, James Grauerholz, who has been more than generous with his time and materials; and the Vollmer family, without whom I would have never known the half of it.

REFERENCES

[1] Bellotti, V., Ducheneaut, N., Howard, M., Smith, I., and Grinter, R. Quality versus quantity: e-mail-centric task management and its relation with overload. Human Computer Interaction 20, 1-2 (2005), 89-138.

[2] Bessi, A. and Ferrara, E. Social bots distort the 2016 U.S. Presidential election online discussion. *First Monday 21*, 11, Nov. 2016.

[3] boyd, d. and Crawford, K. Six Provocations for Big Data. Oxford Internet Institute, September 21, 2011.

[4] Chokshi, N. The Library of Congress No Longer Wants All the Tweets. *New York Times*, Dec. 27, 2017.

[5] Danadio, R. Literary Letters, Lost in Cyberspace. *New York Times*, Sept. 4, 2005.

[6] Edie Parker Kerouac and Henri Cru Papers (#RBC Beats Folio Z9999.1.P37), Rare Book Collection, The Wilson Library, Univ. of North Carolina at Chapel Hill.

[7] Fetterman, D. *Ethnography*. Sage, 1989.

[8] Goffman, E. *The Presentation of Self in Everyday Life*. Anchor, 1959.

[9] Grauerholz, J.W. The Death of Joan Vollmer Burroughs: What Really Happened? Proc. *Fifth Congress of the Americas*. Universidad de las Americas, Puebla, MX, 18 Oct 2001.

[10] Guynn, J. *USA Today*, "Does Facebook Speak Your Language" Sept. 29, 2016, retrieved Jan. 11, 2018.

[11] Jack Kerouac Papers, Henry W. and Albert A. Berg Collection of English and American Literature, The New York Public Library. (accessed March 15, 2017).

[12] Johnson, R. *The Lost Years of William S. Burroughs: Beats in South Texas*. Texas A&M Press, 2006.

[13] Kerouac-Parker, E. *You'll Be Okay: My Life with Jack Kerouac*. San Francisco: City Lights Books, 2007.

[14] Lampe, C., Vitak, J., Gray, R. & Ellison, N.B. Perceptions of Facebook's value as an information source. *Proc. CHI 2012*, 3195-3204.

[15] Larson, R. and Janakiraman, K. Connecting Archival Collections: The Social Networks and Archival Context Project. In *Proc TPDL11*.

[16] Lee, H. *Biography: A Very Short Introduction*. Oxford University Press, 2009.

[17] Levy, D. *Scrolling Forward*. Arcade, 2001.

[18] Loftus, E. Changing Beliefs about Implausible Events. *Journal of Experimental Psychology: Applied*, 2001.

[19] Loftus, E. Make-believe memories. *American Psychologist*, November, 2003.

[20] Lynch, C. Stewardship in the "Age of Algorithms." *First Monday 22*, 12, 4 Dec. 2017.

[21] Mannon, M. The Nature and Handling of Ephemera. *Archives Info 2*, 3, Spring 2003.

[22] Marshall, C. and Lindley, S. Searching for Myself: Motivations and Strategies for Self-Search. *Proc. CHI 2014*, pp. 3675-3684.

[23] Marshall, C. and Shipman, F. An Argument for Archiving Facebook as a Heterogeneous Personal Store. *Proc. DL'14*.

[24] Marshall, C. and Shipman, F. Exploring the ownership and persistent value of Facebook content. *Proc. CSCW15*. ACM Press, New York, 2015, 712–723.

[25] Miles, B. *Call Me Burroughs*. New York: Hachette, 2014.

[26] Morgan, T. *Literary Outlaw: The Life and Times of William S. Burroughs*. New York: Norton, 1988.

[27] Roediger, H., Bergman, E., and Meade, M. Repeated reproduction from memory. In *Bartlett, Culture, and Cognition* (A. Saito, ed.) Cambridge University Press, 2000.

[28] Roediger, H. and Gallo, D. Processes Affecting Accuracy and Distortion in Memory: An Overview. In *Memory and Suggestibility in the Forensic Interview* (Eisen, Quas, and Goodman, Eds.) Lawrence Erlbaum Associates, 2002.

[29] Rosenthal, D. The amnesiac civilization, 5 part blog post, retrieved from http://blog.dshr.org/2017/03/the-amnesiac-civilization-part-1.html.

[30] Shilton, K., Wickner, A., Oard, D., and Lin, J. Protecting Sensitive Email: Archival Views on Challenges and Opportunities. *Proc PC4DS*, August 2017.

[31] Starr, D. Remembering a Crime That You Didn't Commit. *New Yorker*, March 5, 2015.

[32] Strauss, A. and Corbin, J. *Basics of Qualitative Research*, Sage Publications, 1998.

[33] Ted Morgan Papers, MS SC MOR. Arizona State University Libraries: Special Collections (transcribed by Barry Miles, 2000; corrected by James Grauerholz, 2017.

Scraping SERPs for Archival Seeds: It Matters When You Start

Alexander C. Nwala
Old Dominion University
Norfolk, Virginia, USA
anwala@cs.odu.edu

Michele C. Weigle
Old Dominion University
Norfolk, Virginia, USA
mweigle@cs.odu.edu

Michael L. Nelson
Old Dominion University
Norfolk, Virginia, USA
mln@cs.odu.edu

ABSTRACT

Event-based collections are often started with a web search, but the search results you find on Day 1 may not be the same as those you find on Day 7. In this paper, we consider collections that originate from extracting URIs (Uniform Resource Identifiers) from Search Engine Result Pages (SERPs). Specifically, we seek to provide insight about the retrievability of URIs of news stories found on Google, and to answer two main questions: first, can one "refind" the same URI of a news story (for the same query) from Google after a given time? Second, what is the probability of finding a story on Google over a given period of time? To answer these questions, we issued seven queries to Google every day for over seven months (2017-05-25 to 2018-01-12) and collected links from the first five SERPs to generate seven collections for each query. The queries represent public interest stories: "healthcare bill," "manchester bombing," "london terrorism," "trump russia," "travel ban," "hurricane harvey," and "hurricane irma." We tracked each URI in all collections over time to estimate the discoverability of URIs from the first five SERPs. Our results showed that the daily average rate at which stories were replaced on the default Google SERP ranged from 0.21 – 0.54, and a weekly rate of 0.39 – 0.79, suggesting the fast replacement of older stories by newer stories. The probability of finding the same URI of a news story after one day from the initial appearance on the SERP ranged from 0.34 – 0.44. After a week, the probability of finding the same news stories diminishes rapidly to 0.01 – 0.11. In addition to the reporting of these probabilities, we also provide two predictive models for estimating the probability of finding the URI of an arbitrary news story on SERPs as a function of time. The web archiving community considers link rot and content drift important reasons for collection building. Similarly, our findings suggest that due to the difficulty in retrieving the URIs of news stories from Google, collection building that originates from search engines should begin as soon as possible in order to capture the first stages of events, and should persist in order to capture the evolution of the events, because it becomes more difficult to find the same news stories with the same queries on Google, as time progresses.

CCS CONCEPTS

• **Information systems → Digital libraries and archives**;

JCDL '18, June 3–7, 2018, Fort Worth, TX, USA

ACM ISBN 978-1-4503-5178-2/18/06...$15.00
https://doi.org/10.1145/3197026.3197056

KEYWORDS

Collection building; Web Archiving; Crawling; Discoverability

ACM Reference Format:
Alexander C. Nwala, Michele C. Weigle, and Michael L. Nelson. 2018. Scraping SERPs for Archival Seeds: It Matters When You Start. In *JCDL '18: The 18th ACM/IEEE Joint Conference on Digital Libraries, June 3–7, 2018, Fort Worth, TX, USA.* ACM, New York, NY, USA, 10 pages. https://doi.org/10.1145/3197026.3197056

1 INTRODUCTION AND BACKGROUND

From elections to natural disasters, web collections provide a critical source of information for researchers studying important historical events. Collections can be built automatically with focused crawlers or manually by an expert user. For example, an archivist at the National Library of Medicine collected seeds on Archive-It for the *2014 Ebola Outbreak* event [23]. Collections may also be built by multiple users. For example, the Internet Archive has on multiple occasions requested that users submit seeds via Google Docs to build collection for events such as the *2016 US Presidential Election* and the *Dakota Access Pipeline (DAPL)* event. Depending on when users begin to contribute seeds, URIs (Uniform Resource Identifiers) for early news stories may be difficult to discover via Google after one month, for as we show in this paper they can quickly fall to distant SERPs (Search Engine Result Pages).

Collection building often begins with a simple Google search to discover seeds. This can be done by issuing queries to Google and extracting URIs from the SERP (Fig. 1). For example, the following are two possible URI candidates extracted from the Google SERP (Fig. 1) to include in a collection (or seed list) about the *Hurricane Harvey* (August, 2017) event:

```
http://www.cnn.com/specials/us/hurricane-harvey
https://www.cbsnews.com/feature/hurricane-harvey/
```

A SERP provides an opportunity to generate collections for news stories and events, therefore we focused on assessing the discoverability of news stories on the Google SERP. Queries used to extract news stories are examples of *informational queries* [9], and we expect their SERP results to change as the news event evolves. We expect the SERP results for *transactional* (e.g., "samsung galaxy s3") or *navigational* (e.g., "youtube") to be less transient [18], but such queries are not the focus of our collection building effort. The URIs extracted from Google can serve as seeds: the seeds can be crawled to build collections in Archive-It, such as the Archive-It *2017 Hurricane Harvey* collection[1]. It is important to understand the behavior of Google as this will influence the collections or seeds generated from it. This is not easy because the inner workings of Google are proprietary, making it a black box. To build a representative collection about an event, it is important to capture not just a slice of

[1] https://archive-it.org/collections/9323

time, but the various stages of the events [27] - oldest to the newest. For example, on May 25, 2017, we issued the query: "healthcare bill" to Google and extracted links (Table 1, 2017-05-23 – 2017-05-25) from the SERP. Seven months later (January 5, 2017) we repeated the same operation (Table 1, 2017-12-19 – 2017-12-20). The May 2017 *healthcare bill* collection shows the initial stages of the American Health Care Act of 2017 (AHCA) by highlighting the challenges facing the passage of the bill. On the other hand, the January 2018 collection shows a different (more recent) stage of the bill, highlighting the failure of the bill and the continued existence of Obamacare. These reflect the tendency of Google to highly rank newly created URIs for these kinds of queries. We quantify this behavior by estimating the rate at which new stories occur on the Google SERP. The tendency of Google to return fresh documents can be altered by setting the custom date range parameter on the site. However, the date range information is not always available for the collections we intend to build. We explore how this parameter affects the kinds of documents returned. It is crucial to know the dynamics of finding initial stories on Google, as this would inform the time a collection building task ought to begin; if we know how fast new documents replace old documents on the Google SERP, we can plan collection building to ensure that URIs of older stories are included in the collection and not just the recent ones.

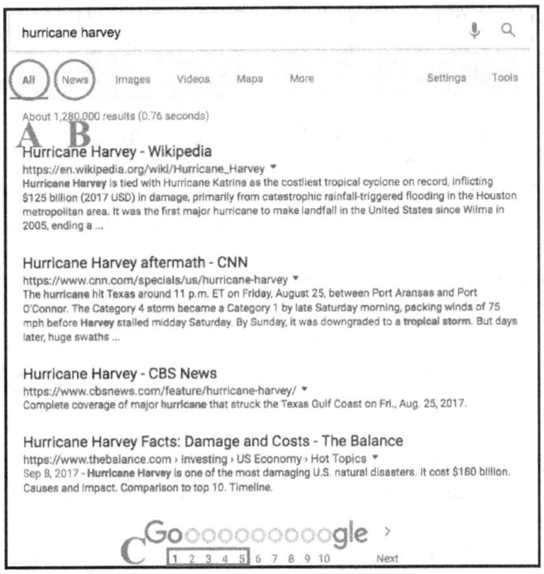

Figure 1: The Google *All* (renamed to *General*) SERP (annotation A) and *News* vertical SERP (annotation B) for query "hurricane harvey." Some links have been removed to enable showing more details. For the experiment, links were extracted from the first five pages (annotation C) of both SERPs for each query.

Accordingly, we conducted a longitudinal experiment to understand whether it is possible to retrieve a given URI of a news story over time, to gain insight about the appearance/disappearance of news stories across the pages in Google, and to identify the probability of finding the same URI of a story using the same query over time. This was achieved by issuing seven queries (Table 2) every day for over seven months (2017-05-25 to 2018-01-12), and collecting links within *h3* HTML tags from the first five pages (Fig. 1, annotation C) of the Google SERPs (Fig. 1). The queries were issued semi-automatically using a variant of the Local Stories Collection Generator [2].

The longitudinal study resulted in the following contributions that shed some light on the discoverability and behavior of news stories on Google as time progresses. First, the tendency of Google to replace older documents with new ones is well known, but not the rate at which it occurs, our findings quantify this. Given two time intervals, e.g, day 0 and day 1, if we collected a set x stories on day 0 and a set y stories on day 1, the story replacement rate on day 1 is the fraction of stories found on day 0 but not found on day 1 ($\frac{|x-y|}{|x|}$). The daily story replacement rate on the Google *General* SERP ranged from 0.21 – 0.54, the weekly rate ranged from 0.39 – 0.79, and monthly - 0.59 – 0.92. This means if you re-issued a query after one day, between 21% to 54% stories are replaced by new stories. But if you waited for one month, and issued the same query, between 59% and 92% of the original stories are replaced. The *News* vertical SERP showed a higher story replacement rates: daily - 0.31 – 0.57, weekly - 0.54 – 0.82, and monthly - 0.76 – 0.92. Second, the probability of finding the same URI of a news story with the same query declines with time. For example, the probability of finding the same URI with the same query after one day (from the initial appearance on the *General* SERP) is between 0.34 – 0.44. This probability drops rapidly after a week, to a value between 0.01 – 0.11. The probability is less for the *News* vertical (daily - 0.28 – 0.40, weekly - 0.03 – 0.14, and approximately 0 one month later). We provide two predictive models that estimate the probabilities of finding an arbitrary URI of a news story on the *General* and *News* vertical SERPs as a function of time. Third, we show that news stories do not gradually progress from page 1 to page 2, 3, etc., and then out of view (beyond the page length considered). The progression we observed is less elegant (e.g., page 5 to 1, 3 to 2). These findings are highly informative to collection building efforts that originate from Google. For example, the results suggest that collections that originate from Google should begin days after an event happens, and should continue as time progresses to capture the various stages in the evolution of the event. Our research dataset comprising of 33,432 links extracted from the Google SERPs for over seven months, as well as the source code for the application utilized to semi-automatically generate the collections, are publicly available [3].

2 RELATED WORK

Since Chakrabarti et al. first introduced the focused crawler [12] as a system of discovering topic-specific web resources, there have been many research efforts pertaining to the generation of collections with some variant of a focused crawler. Bergmark [7] introduced a method for building collections by downloading web pages and subsequently classifying them into various topics in science, mathematics, engineering and technology. Farag et al. [15] introduced the Event Focused Crawler, a focused crawler for events which uses an event model to represent documents and a similarity measure to quantify the degree of relevance between a candidate

Table 1: Rows 1 - 3: Sample collection of URIs extracted from Google on May 25, 2017 with query: "healthcare bill." This shows the initial stages of the AHCA bill, highlighting the struggles to pass the bill. Rows 4 - 6: Sample collection of URIs extracted from Google on January 5, 2018 with query: "healthcare bill." This shows the later (recent) stages of the AHCA bill, highlighting the failure of the bill which happened in September 2017.

Publication Date	Title	URI
2017-05-23	Healthcare saga shaping GOP approach to tax bill	http://thehill.com/policy/finance/334650 -healthcare-saga-shaping-gop-approach-to-tax-bill
2017-05-24	US Senate's McConnell sees tough path for passing healthcare bill	http://www.cnbc.com/2017/05/24/us-senates -mcconnell-sees-tough-path-for-passing-healthcare-bill.html
2017-05-25	Will the Republican Health Care Bill Really Lower Premiums?	http://time.com/4794400/health-care-premiums/
2017-12-19	House Republicans used lessons from failed health care bill to pass tax reform, Ryan says	https://www.pbs.org/newshour/politics/house-republicans-used -lessons-from-failed-health-care-bill-to-pass-tax-reform-ryan-says
2017-12-19	GOP tax bill also manages to needlessly screw up the healthcare system	http://www.latimes.com/business/lazarus/la-fi-lazarus-republican-tax-bill-individual-mandate-20171219-story.html
2017-12-20	How GOP tax bill's Obamacare changes will affect health care and consumers	http://www.chicagotribune.com/business/ ct-biz-obamacare-insurance-penalty-repeal-1221-story.html

URI and a collection. Klein et al. [19] demonstrated that focused crawling on the archived web results in more relevant collections than focused crawling on the live web for events that occurred in the distant past. In order to augment digital library collections with publications not already in the digital library, Zhuang et al. [32] proposed using publication metadata to help guide focused crawlers towards the homepages of authors. Klein et al. [20] also proposed a means of augmenting a digital library collection (the NASA Langley Research Center Atmospheric Science Data Center) with information discovered on the web using search engine APIs. SERPs are useful artifacts in their own right, and can be used for activities such as classifying queries as "scholarly" or "non-scholarly" [24]. This work is similar to these efforts that use focused crawlers as it relates to collection building and using search engines to discover seeds, but we do not use a focused crawler to discover URIs.

Zheng et al. [31] demonstrated that seed selection for crawlers is not a trivial problem because different seeds may result in collections that are considered "good" or "bad," and proposed different seed selection algorithms. Similarly, Schneider et al. [28] expressed the difficulty in identifying seed URIs for building thematic collections, and suggested the continuous selection of seeds for collections about unfolding events such as the 9/11 attacks, to accommodate the evolution of the events. Baroni et al. [6] presented their findings about the effectiveness of various seed selection strategies as part of a broader effort to build a large linguistically processed web-crawled corpora. They demonstrated the discovery of a variety of seeds by issuing random queries to search engine APIs. Similar to these efforts, we consider seed selection a vital part of collection building but mainly focus on the temporal considerations when selecting seeds from search engines.

Cho and Garcia-Molina [13] downloaded 720,000 pages (from 270 web servers) daily for four months to quantify the degree of change of web pages over time. They found that about 40% of all web pages changed within a week, and 50% of all the pages changed in about 50 days. Fetterly et al. [16] extended Cho and Garcia-Molina's work by downloading (once a week for 11 weeks) over 150 million web pages and assessing the degree of change of web pages. They found that the average degree of change varies significantly across top-level domains; larger pages changed more frequently than smaller pages.

In the web archiving community, link rot and content drift [17, 21] are two major reasons for collection building. Comparably, the difficultly in refinding news stories on the SERP suggests instant and persistent collection building by efforts that rely on the SERP for seed extraction or collection generation. McCown and Nelson [22] issued queries for five months to search engine web user interfaces (Google, MSN and Yahoo) and their respective APIs, and found significant discrepancies in the results found on both interfaces. They also showed how search results decay over time and modeled the decay rate. Kim and Vitor [18] studied Google, Bing, and Yahoo search engines, and showed that the top 10 results of 90% of their queries were altered within ten days. There are many more studies that examine the evolution of web pages [1, 14, 26] or the web [8, 30]. Our study is specific to news stories found in SERPs and not the evolution of the pages themselves. We sought to find out whether we could retrieve the same URI with the same query over a given period of time, instead of assessing the evolution of the content of individual web pages. This discoverability information is critical to collection building systems that utilize search engines. We tracked individual news stories to find when they were replaced by newer stories and quantified the rate at which older stories were replaced by newer stories. In addition to quantifying the rate of new stories as a function of time, we also quantify the rate of new stories for individual SERP pages. For example, we found that higher numbered pages (e.g., pages 3 - 5) have higher rates of new stories than lower numbered pages (e.g., pages 1 - 2) on Google. Our results enable understanding the dynamics of refinding news stories on SERPs and are relevant to efforts that utilize search engines to discover seeds or to build collections.

Teevan et al. [29] illustrated the tendency of users to seek to refind web pages previously seen at a rate of about 40% of all queries, and demonstrated how changes in search engine results can impede refinding links. Aula et al. [4] also studied the prevalence of the "re-find" (re-access) behavior in a group 236 experienced web users, by investigating the problems with searching and re-accessing information. Their survey showed that the users often used some strategies such as using several browser windows concurrently to facilitate re-access. Capra et al. [11] proposed a search engine use model as part of an effort to provide information to help better understand how users find, refind, and manage information on the web. There are many other studies outlining attempts to refind web resources on search engines, such the effort of Bainbridge et al. [5] to refind four copies of their published research papers on Google Scholar and ACM Digital Libary. Our research is similar to these efforts in the sense that we are interested in quantifying the likelihood of refinding URIs of news stories over time. However, the goal is not to fulfill the informational needs of particular users, but as part of an effort to extract seeds or generate collections from SERPs. Also, it is important to note that we utilize the search engine by issuing queries, it is not a known item search - we do not search for specific URIs to include in the collections we build - we let the SERP give us seeds. Instead we wish to know the rate as which the SERP produces the same URIs for the same query. Knowing the rate of new stories on the SERP for the same query indicates the ability of our collection generation process to refind previous stories and the rate at which the new stories from the SERP are included in the collection.

3 RESEARCH QUESTIONS

Before employing search engines as seed generators we sought to first assess the discoverability of news stories on SERPs (top five pages), and understand the dynamics of refinding news stories on SERPs. Our ability to build representative collections for events from SERPs is tied to the ability of retrieving old and new stories from SERPs. Our primary research question was: what is the rate at which new stories replace old stories on the SERP over time? This rate information may provide the means to approximate our ability to refind older stories about an event and the rate at which the collection we generate from SERPs receives new stories from SERPs. Similarly, if we found a URI of a news story s_0 on day d_0, what is the probability that we would find s_0 on the next day d_1, or one week later on d_7? For example, if we found a URI for a news story on the SERP on Monday, what is the probability that we would refind the same URI with the same query on Tuesday (one day later) or next Monday (one week later)?

The generalization of the first main question led to the second - what is the rate of new stories for the individual SERPs or their pages? For example, does the *General* SERP (or page 1) possess a higher new story rate than the *News* vertical SERP (or page 2)? The pages with the lowest rate of new stories may indicate the page with the highest probability of finding the initial reports of an event. Understanding the characteristics of both SERP classes could inform the choice of SERPs when extracting seeds.

Finally, we sought to gain insight about how news stories on SERPs moved across the different pages.

4 METHODOLOGY

Here we describe the generation of our dataset, the measures we extracted from the dataset, and how these measures informed our research questions.

4.1 Dataset generation, representation, and processing

Seven queries representing public interest stories were selected: "healthcare bill," "manchester bombing," "london terrorism," "trump russia," "travel ban," "hurricane harvey," and "hurricane irma." The queries represent various events that happened (or are happening) in different timelines. Consequently, the dataset extraction duration varied for the queries as outlined by Table 2. The dataset extraction process lasted from 2017-05-25 to 2018-01-12. For each query, we extracted approximately 50 links within *h3* HTML tags from the first five pages of the Google SERP from the default (*All*) and *News* vertical SERPs (Fig. 1, annotation A & B). To avoid confusion, in this research we renamed the *All* SERP to *General* SERP. The first five pages were considered in order to gain better insight about the rate of new stories across pages, as considering a few pages (e.g., 1 or 2) may present an incomplete view. In total, 73,968 (13,708 unique) URIs were collected for the *General* SERP and 77,634 (19,724 unique) for the *News* vertical SERP (Table 2).

Table 2: Dataset generated by extracting URIs from SERPs (*General* and *News* vertical) for seven queries between 2017-05-25 and 2018-01-12.

Collection (Query/ Topic)	Start date (duration in days)	News story count	
		General SERP count (unique count)	News vertical SERP count (unique count)
healthcare bill	2017-05-25 (232)	12,809 (2,559)	13,716 (3,450)
manchester bombing	2017-05-25 (232)	12,451 (1,018)	13,751 (1,799)
london terrorism	2017-06-04 (222)	10,698 (1,098)	10,450 (2,821)
trump russia	2017-06-06 (220)	12,311 (4,638)	13,728 (3,482)
travel ban	2017-06-07 (219)	12,830 (2,849)	13,439 (2,815)
hurricane harvey	2017-08-30 (135)	6,666 (685)	6,450 (2,530)
hurricane irma	2017-09-07 (127)	6,203 (861)	6,100 (2,827)
	Subtotal	73,968 (13,708)	77,634 (19,724)
	Collections Total	151,602 (33,432)	

In previous work with the Local Memory Project (LMP) [25], we introduced a local news collection generator [2]. The local news collection generator utilizes Google in order to build collections of stories from local newspapers and TV stations for US and non-US news sources. Unlike LMP, in this work we did not restrict the sources sampled to local news organization, but still utilized Google in order to discover seeds. The local news collection generator was used to scrape links from the Google SERP, and it was adapted to include the ability to extract all kinds of news stories from Google (not just from local news organizations). The Google search interface is meant for humans and not for robots and it presents a CAPTCHA when it is used too frequently in order to discourage automated searches. Consequently, the dataset collections were all generated semi-automatically with the use of the local news collection generator. The input provided to the extension was the query and the maximum number of pages to explore (five), and the output was a collection of URIs extracted from the SERPs.

The URIs collected daily from the SERPs were represented as JSON files. For a single query, two JSON files per day were generated, each file represented the URIs extracted from the *General* SERP and *News* vertical SERP. This means for a given day, a total of 14 (two per query) JSON files were generated. Each URI in a JSON file included metadata extracted from the SERP such as the *page number* and the *rank* which is the position across all SERP pages. Additionally, each file included the date the data was generated.

At the center of the analysis was the ability to track the URI of a news story over time. A URI is a unique identifier for a resource, however, URIs often have aliases (multiple URIs identifying the same resource). For example, the following pair of URIs identify the same resource:

(a) `https://www.redcross.org/donate/disaster-donations?campname=irma&campmedium=aspot`
(b) `https://www.redcross.org/donate/disaster-donations`

As a result, we transformed all URIs before matching by trimming the scheme and all parameters from the URIs, using a method suggested by Brunelle et al. [10]. The parameters in URIs often express a reference source such as `origin` and `callback`, or session parameters such as `session`. The transformed version of the URI was used to track the individual news stories. Subsequently, for each news story we recorded all the dates and pages it was observed on the SERP.

4.2 Primitive measures extraction

The following measures were extracted from the dataset and provided information to help answer our research questions.

4.2.1 *Story replacement rate, new story rate, and page level new story rate.*

Given that at time point t_0 we observed a set of URIs for news stories u_0 and at time point t_1 we observed a set of URIs for news stories u_1, then the story replacement rate at t_1 is $\frac{|u_0 - u_1|}{|u_0|}$. For example, if we observed URIs $\{a, b, c\}$ at t_0 and URIs $\{a, b, x, y\}$ at t_1, then the story replacement rate at t_1 is
$\frac{|\{a,b,c\}-\{a,b,x,y\}|}{|\{a,b,c\}|} = \frac{|\{c\}|}{|\{a,b,c\}|} = \frac{1}{3} = 0.3.$
This means that at t_1 c was replaced. Similarly, the rate of new stories going from t_0 to t_1 is $\frac{|u_1 - u_0|}{|u_1|}$. For example, if we observed URIs $\{a, b, c\}$ at t_0 and URIs $\{a, b, c, d, e\}$ at t_1, then the new story rate from t_0 to t_1 is
$\frac{|\{a,b,c,d,e\}-\{a,b,c\}|}{|\{a,b,c,d,e\}|} = \frac{|\{d,e\}|}{|\{a,b,c,d,e\}|} = \frac{2}{5} = 0.4.$
This means that at t_1 we observed new stories d and e. We calculated the story replacement and new story rates using different temporal intervals (daily, weekly, and monthly) for the individual first five pages of the *General* and *News* vertical SERPs. The daily story replacement rate indicates the proportion of stories replaced on a daily basis. This is similar to the daily new story rate because the SERP returns a similar number of results ($mean = median = mode = 10$ links and $\sigma = 0.43$). The daily new story rate approximately indicates the rate of new stories that replaced previously seen stories on the SERP on a daily basis. The higher the story replacement and new story rates, the lower the likelihood of refinding previously seen stories.

4.2.2 *Probability of finding a story.*

Given a collection of URIs for news stories for a topic (e.g., "hurricane harvey"), consider the URI for a story s_0 that was observed for the first time on page 4 of the SERP on day d_0. We represent this as $s_0^{d_0} = 4$. If we find s_0 on page 2 on the next day d_1 and then it disappears for the next two days, we represent the timeline observation of s_0 as $\{4, 2, 0, 0\}$. Therefore, given a collection (e.g., "hurricane harvey") of N URIs for news stories, the probability $P(s^{d_k})$ that the URI of a story s is seen after k days (d_k), is calculated using Eqn. 1.

$$P(s^{d_k}) = \frac{\sum_{n=1}^{N} T(s_i^{d_k})}{N}; T(s_i^{d_i}) = \begin{cases} 0 & ; \text{if } s_i^{d_i} = 0 \\ 1 & ; \text{if } s_i^{d_i} > 0 \end{cases} \tag{1}$$

The probability $P(s^{d_k} = m)$ that the URI of a story s is seen after k days (d_k) on page m, is calculated using Eqn. 2.

$$P(s^{d_k} = m) = \frac{\sum_{n=1}^{N} T(s_i^{d_k})}{N}; T(s_i^{d_i}) = \begin{cases} 0 & ; \text{if } s_i^{d_i} \neq m \\ 1 & ; \text{if } s_i^{d_i} = m \end{cases} \tag{2}$$

4.2.3 *Distribution of stories over time across pages.*

For each story URI, we recorded the dates it was observed on the SERP. For each date, we recorded the page where the story was found. The collection of stories and the date/page observations were expressed using the notation introduced in Section 4.2.2. For example, the following list of three URIs for news stories s_0, s_1, and s_2 were observed for the first time (first day - d_0) on pages, 4, 1, and 1, respectively. On the last day (d_3), the first story (s_0) was not seen on any of the pages ($s_0^{d_3} = 0$), however both the second (s_1) and third (s_2) stories were found on the first page ($s_1^{d_3} = 1$ and $s_2^{d_3} = 1$): $s_0 = \{4, 2, 0, 0\}$, $s_1 = \{1, 2, 0, 1\}$, and $s_2 = \{1, 1, 1, 1\}$.

4.2.4 *Overlap rate and recall.*

Given two sets of collections of URIs, A and B, the overlap rate $O(A, B)$ quantifies the amount of URIs common within both sets without considering the size disparities of the sets. This was calculated using the Overlap coefficient: $O(A, B) = \frac{|A \cap B|}{min(|A|, |B|)}$. The standard information retrieval recall metric $r(A, B)$ for two sets of collections A and B with respect to A, quantifies the amount of stories present in A and B (as a fraction of A) was calculated as $r(A, B) = \frac{|A \cap B|}{|A|}$.

Our dataset was generated without setting any parameters on the Google SERP. However, the Google SERP provides a date range parameter that attempts to restrict the documents returned on the SERP to documents published within the date range. For example, setting the date range to *2017-06-01* and *2017-06-30*, attempts to restrict the documents in the SERP to those published between June

Table 3: Average story replacement rate for *General* and *News* vertical SERP collections. Column markers: minimum⁻ and maximum⁺.

Collection	General SERP			News vertical SERP		
	Daily	Weekly	Monthly	Daily	Weekly	Monthly
healthcare bill	0.42	0.60	0.76	0.44	0.71	0.87
manchester bombing	0.27	0.39^-	0.59^-	0.31^-	0.54^-	0.76^-
london terrorism	0.34	0.41	0.60	0.43	0.66	0.84
trump russia	0.54^+	0.79^+	0.92^+	0.42	0.71	0.90
travel ban	0.43	0.63	0.82	0.45	0.62	0.83
hurricane harvey	0.21^-	0.41	0.67	0.49	0.77	0.91
hurricane irma	0.27	0.44	0.73	0.57^+	0.82^+	0.92^+

Table 4: Average new story rate for *General* and *News* vertical SERP collections. Column markers: minimum⁻ and maximum⁺.

Collection	General SERP			News vertical SERP		
	Daily	Weekly	Monthly	Daily	Weekly	Monthly
healthcare bill	0.42	0.58	0.62	0.44	0.70	0.82
manchester bombing	0.27	0.37^-	0.46^-	0.31^-	0.52^-	0.66^-
london terrorism	0.34	0.40	0.51	0.43	0.65	0.84
trump russia	0.54^+	0.78^+	0.83^+	0.42	0.70	0.83
travel ban	0.43	0.62	0.71	0.45	0.61	0.75
hurricane harvey	0.21^-	0.38	0.51	0.49	0.76	0.82
hurricane irma	0.27	0.41	0.61	0.57^+	0.81^+	0.91^+

1, 2017 and June 30, 2017. To assess the effect of setting the date range parameter on discovering older stories that fall within a specific timeframe, we took the following steps. First, from our original dataset, we selected five collections of stories for queries about topics that occurred before June 2017: "healthcare bill," "trump russia," "travel ban," "manchester bombing," and "london terrorism." This set of five collections was called *June-2017*. Second, we removed all stories from *June-2017* that were not published in June 2017. Third, we issued the selected five queries to the Google SERP without setting the date range to generate five additional collections (from the first five pages). This set of five collection was called *Jan-2018* (control test collection). Fourth, we issued the same five queries to the Google SERP, but this time, we set the date range to *2017-06-01* and *2017-06-30*, and extracted five collections. This set of five collections was called *Jan-2018-Restricted-to-June*. Finally, we calculated the overlap rate and recall between the *June-2017* and *Jan-2018*, as well as *June-2017* and *Jan-2018-Restricted-to-June* collections for the pairs of collections with the same query.

5 RESULTS AND DISCUSSION

Here we present the results for each of the respective measures introduced in Subsection 4.2.

5.1 Story replacement rate, new story rate, and page level new story rate

Table 3 and 4 show the average story replacment rate and new story rate, respectively over time (daily, weekly, and monthly) for both the *General* and *News* vertical SERPs. For both *General* and *News* vertical SERPs, we can see that the average story replacement rate was similar to the new story rate, and both increased with time. They also show that the story replacement and new story rates are

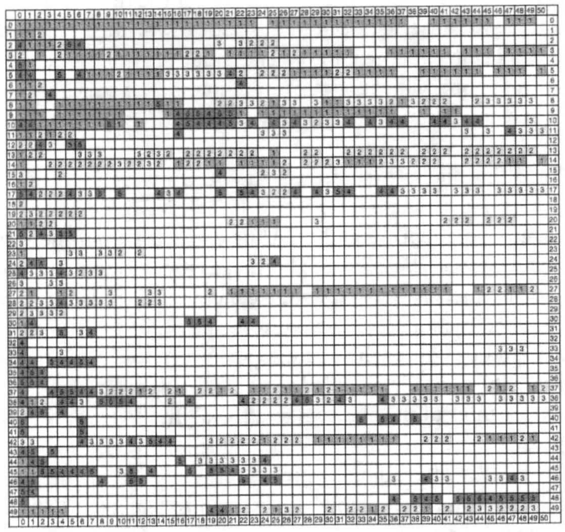

(a) Page-level temporal distribution of stories in the "manchester bombing" *General* SERP collection showing multiple page movement patterns.

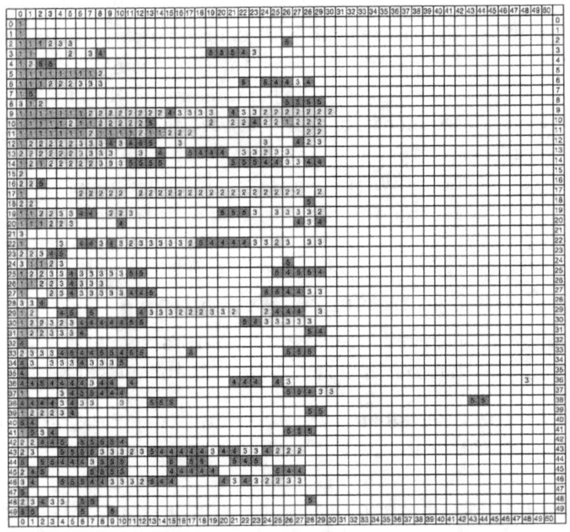

(b) Page-level temporal distribution of stories in the "manchester bombing" *News* vertical SERP collection *General* SERP collection showing multiple page movement patterns, and the shorter lifespan of *News* vertical URIs (compared to *General* SERP URIs.

Figure 2: Page-level temporal distribution of "manchester bombing" *General* and *News* vertical SERP collections showing multiple page movement patterns (Section 5.3). Stories in *General* SERP collections persist longer than stories in *News* vertical collections. Color codes - page 1, page 2, page , page 4, page 5, and blank for outside pages 1 - 5.

strongly dependent on the topic. For example, the *Hurricane Harvey* natural disaster showed a lower daily average story replacement rate (0.21) and new story rate (0.21) compared to the *Trump-Russia* event. This event maintained the highest daily (0.54), weekly (0.79), and monthly (0.92) average story replacement and new story

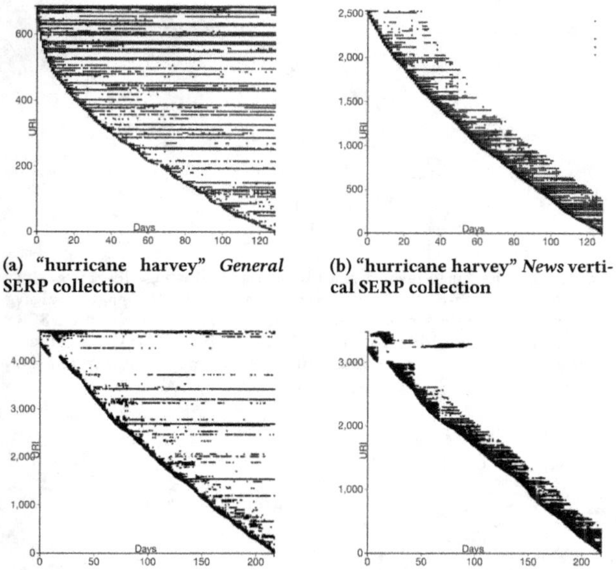

(a) "hurricane harvey" *General* SERP collection

(b) "hurricane harvey" *News* vertical SERP collection

(c) "trump russia" *General* SERP collection

(d) "trump russia" *News* vertical SERP collection

Figure 3: Temporal distributions: Stories in General SERP collections (a & c) persist longer ("longer life") than stories in *News* vertical collections (b & d). Compared to the "trump russia" *General* SERP collection, the stories in the "hurricane harvey" *News* vertical collection have a "longer life" due to a lower rate of new stories.

Table 5: Probability of finding the same story after one day, one week, and one month (from first observation) for *General* and *News* vertical SERP collections. Column markers: minimum^{-} **and** maximum^{+} **.**

Collection	General SERP			News vertical SERP		
	a day	a week	a month	a day	a week	a month
healthcare bill	0.35	0.04	0.02	0.34	0.07	0.00
manchester bombing	0.44^{+}	0.09	0.07	0.40^{+}	0.14^{+}	0.00
london terrorism	0.37	0.11^{+}	0.07	0.34	0.09	0.00
trump russia	0.39	0.01^{-}	0.01^{-}	0.36	0.10	0.00
travel ban	0.43	0.06	0.02	0.32	0.12	0.00
hurricane harvey	0.38	0.10	0.08^{+}	0.29	0.05	0.00
hurricane irma	0.34^{-}	0.07	0.05	0.28^{-}	0.03^{-}	0.00

rates (0.54 - daily, 0.78 - weekly, and 0.83 - monthly). Unlike natural disasters which have a well-defined timeframe, this on-going political event does not have a well-defined timeframe and has undergone multiple event cycles - from the firing of the FBI Director James Comey in May 2017 to the indictment of former Trump Campaign Chair Paul Manafort in October 2017. Similar to the *General* SERP, the average story replacement rate and new story rate for the *News* vertical SERP increased with time but at much faster rates. These results show us that the timing of collection building efforts that utilize SERPs is critical especially for rapidly evolving events with undefined timeframes. Since these events produce newer stories continuously, collection building must be continuous in order to capture the various cycles of the event.

Table 6: Comparison of two collections against the *June-2017* collection (documents published in June 2017). The collection *Jan-2018*, which was created (2018-01-11) without modifying the SERP date range parameter has a lower overlap than the collection (*June-2018-Restricted-to-June*) created the same day (2018-01-11) by setting the SERP date range parameter to June 2017. Even though setting the date range parameter increases finding stories with common publication dates as the date range, the recall is poor due to the fixed SERP result. Column markers: maximum **.**

Collection	Metrics	General SERP			News vertical SERP		
		June -2017	*Jan -2018*	*Jan-2018-Restricted-to-June*	*June -2017*	*Jan -2018*	*Jan-2018-Restricted-to-June*
healthcare bill	size	460	51	50	419	50	50
	overlap	1.00	0.06	0.60	1.00	0.02	0.56
	recall	1.00	0.01	0.07	1.00	0.00	0.07
manchester bombing	size	483	50	51	50	50	548
	overlap	1.00	0.04	0.82	1.00	0.00	0.50
	recall	1.00	0.00	0.08	1.00	0.00	0.05
london terrorism	size	191	50	52	50	50	172
	overlap	1.00	0.09	0.70	1.00	0.00	0.68
	recall	1.00	0.02	0.18	1.00	0.00	0.20
trump russia	size	562	50	51	50	50	524
	overlap	1.00	0.00	0.54	1.00	0.00	0.58
	recall	1.00	0.00	0.05	1.00	0.00	0.06
travel ban	size	391	50	52	50	50	370
	overlap	1.00	0.04	0.84	1.00	0.16	0.48
	recall	1.00	0.01	0.11	1.00	0.02	0.06

Figs. 4a & c show that the average story replacement rate and average new story rate differed across various pages for the *General* SERP. There was a direct relationship between page number and story replacement rate (or new story rate) - the higher the page number, the higher the story replacement rate (or new story rate), and vice versa. The direct relationship may be due to fact that higher order pages (e.g., pages 4 and 5) are more likely to receive documents from lower order pages (e.g, page 1 – 3) than the opposite. For example, the probability of going from page 1 to page 5 was 0.0239 while the probability of going from page 5 to page 1 was 0.0048. The lower order pages have the highest quality on the SERP, thus, there is high competition within documents to retain their position on a lower order page (high rank). The competition in the higher order pages is less, therefore, when documents from the lower order pages lose some rank, they may fall into the higher order pages thereby increasing the new story rate of higher order pages. The *News* vertical SERP showed an inverse relationship between the page number and the story replacement rate (or new story rate) (Fig. 4b & d) even though the probability of going from a page 1 to page 5 (0.0801) was more likely than the opposite (0.0009). This may be due to some unseen mechanism in the *News* vertical SERP.

5.2 Probability of finding a story

Table 5 shows the probability of finding the same story after one day, one week, and one month (from first observation) for *General* and *News* vertical SERP collections. The probability of finding the same URI of a news story with the same query decreased with time for both SERP collections. For the *General* SERP, the probability of the event that a given URI for a news story is observed on the SERP

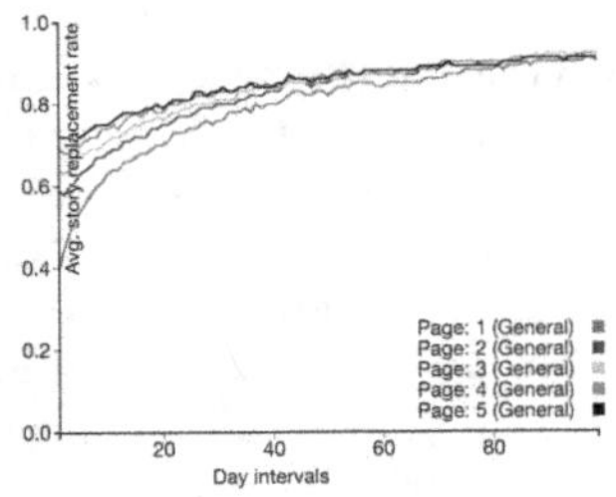

(a) The page-level avg. story replacement rates for *General* SERP collections show a direct relationship between page number and story replacement rate - the higher the page number, the higher the story replacement rate, and vice versa.

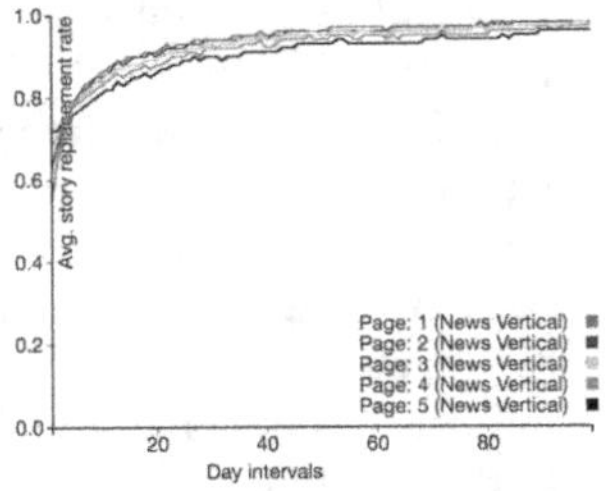

(b) The page-level avg. story replacement rates for *News* vertical SERP collections show an inverse relationship between page number and story replacement rate - the higher the page number, the lower the story replacement rate, and vice versa.

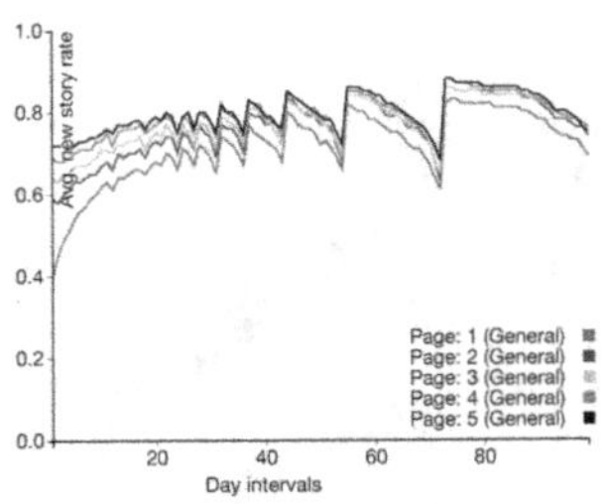

(c) Similar to the page-level avg. story replacement rate, the page-level avg. new story rate for *General* SERP collections show a direct relationship between page number and new story rate.

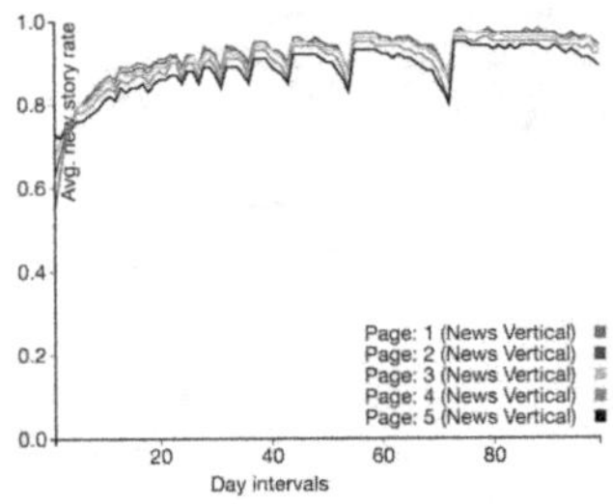

(d) Similar to the page-level avg. story replacement rate, the page-level avg. new story rate for *News* vertical SERP collections show an inverse relationship between page number and new story rate.

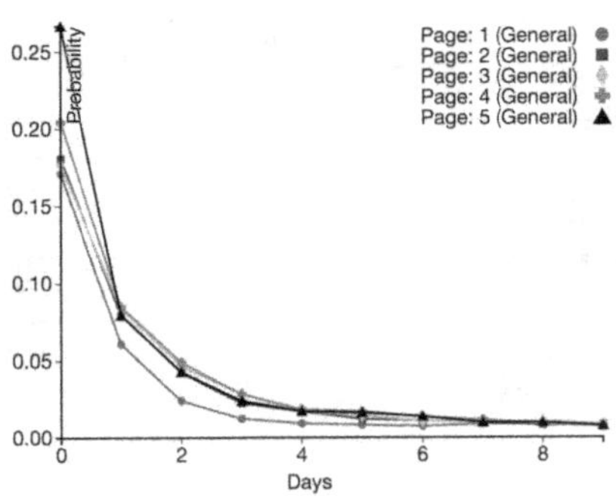

(e) Prob. of finding a story after variable number of days on pages (1-5) for *General* SERP shows direct relationship between page number and probability.

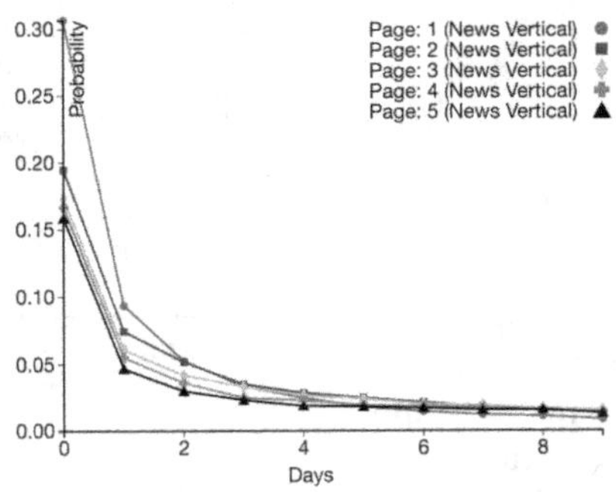

(f) Prob. of finding a story after variable number of days on pages (1-5) for *General* SERP shows inverse relationship between page number and probability.

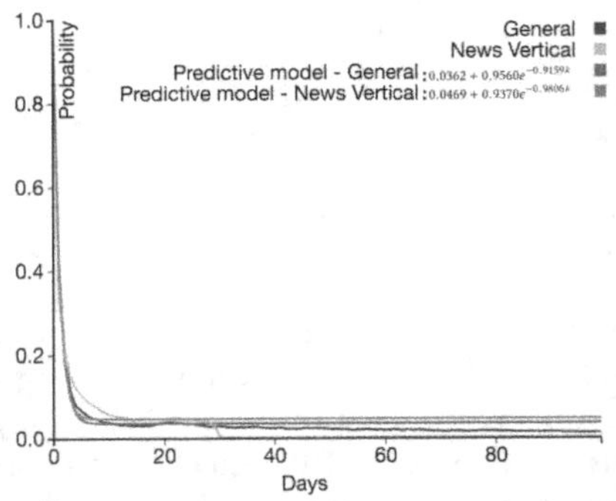

(g) Prob. of finding an arbitrary story for *General* and *News* vertical SERPs was modeled with two best-fit exponential functions. In general, the probability of finding the URI of a news story on the *General* SERP is higher (lower new story rate) than the probability of finding the same URI on the *News* vertical SERP (due to its higher new story rate).

Figure 4: a & b: Page-level new story rates for *General* and *News* vertical SERPs. c & d: Page-level story replacement rates for *General* and *News* vertical SERPs. e & f: Page-level probability of finding the URI of a story over time. g: Probability of finding an arbitrary URI of a news story was modeled with two best-fit exponential functions for both SERPs.

when the same query is issued one day after it was first observed ranged from 0.34 – 0.44. When the query was issued one week after, the probability dropped to from 0.01 – 0.11, one month after - 0.01 – 0.08. The probability of finding the same story with time is related to the rate of new stories: for a given time interval, the higher the rate of new stories, the lower the chance of observing the same story, because it is more likely to be replaced by another story. For example, compared to the *manchester bombing* collection, the *hurricane irma* collection produced a lower (0.34) probability (vs. *manchester bombing* - 0.44) of finding the same story after one day due to its higher (0.79) new story rate after one day (vs. *manchester bombing* - 0.52). The probability of observing the same news story on the *News* vertical SERP declined with time, but at a much faster rate compared to the *General* SERP. In fact, Table 5 shows that for all seven topics in the dataset, the probability of finding the same story on the *News* vertical when the query was re-issued one month after was marginal (approximately 0). This is partly because the *News* vertical SERP collections produced higher story replacement and new story rates than the *General* SERP collections.

In order to generalize the probability of finding an arbitrary URI as a function of time (days), we fitted a curve (Fig. 4g) over the union of occurrence of the URIs in our dataset with an exponential model. The probability $P_{s,sp}(k)$ of finding an arbitrary URI of a news story s on a SERP $sp \in \{General, NewsVertical\}$, after k days is predicted as follows:

$$P_{s,General}(k) = 0.0362 + 0.9560e^{-0.9159k}$$

$$P_{s,NewsVertical}(k) = 0.0469 + 0.9370e^{-0.9806k}$$

Also, similar to the story replacement and new story rates, for the *General* SERP, the results showed a direct relationship with the page number and probability of finding news stories over time (Fig. 4e). For the *General* SERP, higher order page numbers (e.g., 4 and 5) produced higher probabilities of finding the same stories compared to lower order (e.g., 1 and 2) pages. This might be because during the lifetime of a story, the probability of the story going from a lower order (high rank) page to a higher (low rank) order page is higher than the opposite - going from higher order page to lower order page (climbing in rank). For example, the probability of going from page 1 to page 5 was higher (0.0239) than the probability of going from page 5 to page 1 (0.0048). However, collections from *News* verticals showed that the lower the page number, the higher the probability of finding news stories (inverse relationship) even though the probability of falling in rank (lower order page to higher order page) is higher than the probability of climbing in rank (higher order page to lower order page).

5.3 Distribution of stories over time across pages

Fig. 3 shows how the temporal distributions differs typically between *General* and *News* vertical SERP collections. There are two dimensions in the figure: days (x-axis) and URIs of stories (y-axis). A single dot in the figure indicates that a specific story occurred at that point. The temporal distritution is a reflection of the new story rate, but at a granular (individual) story level. *General* SERP collections had lower new story rates, thus produced stories with a longer lifespan than *News* vertical SERP collections. In Fig. 3, this is represented by a long trail of dots. Since *News* vertical collections had higher story replacement and new story rates, they produced documents with shorter lifespans. For example, Fig. 3a contrasts the denser (longer lifespan) temporal distribution of the "hurricane harvey" *General* SERP collection to the sparser "trump russia" *General* SERP collection (Fig. 3c). The "trump russia" collection produced new documents on average at a rate of 0.54 (daily) to 0.83 (monthly), compared to the "hurricane harvey" collection (daily - 0.21, and monthly - 0.51). Similarly, since documents from the "trump russia" collections were rapidly replaced (story replacement rate: 0.54 – 0.92) with newer documents, they mostly did not persist on the SERP.

Fig. 2 shows how URIs moved across pages over time. The rows represent the URIs and the columns represent the pages in which the URIs were observed on a specific day. A single cell represents the page in which a URI occured on a specific day. For example, the first cell (row 0, column 0) of Fig. 2 is 1. This means the URI at row 0 was first observed on page 1. Some of the same URIs persist over time within the same page. For example Fig. 2a, row 0, shows that the highly ranked Wikipedia page[2] of the *Manchester bombing* event was seen for 24 consecutive days on the first page of the SERP, was not seen (within page 1-5) on the 25th day, and then seen for 13 consecutive days (still on page 1). Fig. 2a also shows the increase/decrease in ranks for stories. For example, in Fig. 2a, row 4, the URI[3] was first observed on page 5, the next day it increased in rank to page 1, skipping (2-4). The page-level temporal distribution also shows that some stories go directly from page 5 to 1. In contrast with *General* SERP collections, the temporal distrbution of *News* vertical collections is shorter (Fig. 2b) and reflect the higher story replacement and new story rates of *News* vertical collections.

[2]https://en.wikipedia.org/wiki/Manchester_Arena_bombing
[3]http://www.dailymail.co.uk/news/article-4578566/Evidence-Nissan-linked-Manchester-bombing.html

5.4 Overlap and recall

Table 6 shows that setting the Google date range parameter improves finding stories with respect to the set date range for both *General* and *News* vertical collection. For example, for the "healthcare bill" *General* SERP collection, the *Jan-2018* collection which was created (2018-01-11) by making a default search (without) setting the date range had an overlap rate of 0.06 with respect to the collection of documents created in June 2017 (*June-2017*). In contrast, the collection created the same day (2018-01-11) by setting the date range parameter to June 2017 (2017-06-01 to 2017-06-30) had a much higher overlap rate of 0.60. This is the case across all collection topics, especially for topics with lower new story rates (0.27 - 0.46) such as "manchester bombing" (0.82 overlap rate). The *News* vertical collections had lower overlap rates compared to the *General* SERP collections since *News* vertical collection have higher story replacement and new story rates.

Irrespective of the increase in refinding (overlap) new stories that occurs when the date range parameter is set, the recall is poor. Since the SERP only produces a fixed number of documents per page, we only get a small fraction of the documents relevant to the specified date range. The "healthcare bill" *June-2017 General* SERP collection contains 460 documents published in June 2017, collected by extracting URIs from the first five pages of the SERP. A query ("healthcare bill") issued to the SERP in January 2018, with the date range parameter set to June 2017 increased overlap (refinding stories), but did not increase the number of results - we could only extract at most approximately 50 URIs (first five page). Consequently, across all topics in Table 6, both *Jan-2018* and *Jan-2018-Restricted-to-June* collections had recall of under 0.10 except for the "london terrorism" topic (maximum recall 0.20). This reaffirms the that idea that collection building or seed selection processes that rely on the SERP must start early and persist in order to maximize recall. To further aid selection of seeds, a simple set of heuristics could identify most of the likely stable URIs (e.g., *wikipedia.org*, *nasa.gov*, *whitehouse.gov*) as well as URIs likely to quickly disappear from the top-k SERPs (e.g., *cnn.com* or *nytimes.com*, followed by a long path in the URI). The archivist could give priority to the latter URIs, knowing that the former URIs will continue to be discoverable via Google.

6 FUTURE WORK AND CONCLUSIONS

Our findings motivate the need for instant and persistent collection building. The next stage of this research is the implementation of a collection building system that extracts URIs from SERPs. The system may be triggered semi-automatically by a curator for an important event or automatically by an event detection system. An event detection system could listen to traffic in news and social media for clusters of interest, identify the events of interest, and initiate a collection building process from SERPs. In addition to the implementation of such a collection building system, it is important to investigate the kinds of collections, topics or events most suitable for SERPs. For example, this research focused on news collections, but further research is required to assess the effectiveness of using SERPs for other kinds of collections.

Collection building offers a way of preserving the historic record of important events. This involves collecting URIs of web pages that are relevant to a predefined set of topics. It is crucial for collections to capture all the stages (oldest to newest) of events and not only the recent stories. Search engines provide an opportunity to build collections or extract seeds, but tend to provide the most recent documents. As a first step toward a larger effort of generating collections from SERPs, we sought to gain insight on the dynamics of refinding stories on SERPs. Our findings illustrate the difficulty in refinding news stories as time progresses: on average, the daily rate at which stories were replaced on the Google *General* SERP ranged from 0.21 – 0.54, weekly - 0.39 – 0.79, and monthly - 0.59 – 0.92. The Google *News* vertical SERP showed even higher story replacement rates, with a daily range of 0.31 – 0.57, weekly - 0.54 – 0.82, and monthly - 0.76 – 0.92. We also showed that the probability of finding the same news story diminishes with time and is query dependent. The probability of finding the same news story with the same query again, one day after the first time the story was first seen ranged from 0.34 – 0.44. If one waited a week, or a month and issued the same query again, the probability of finding the same news story drops to 0.01 – 0.11. The probability declines even further if we used the *News* vertical SERP due to its higher story replacement and new story rates. The probability for finding the URI of a news story was further generalized through our provision of two predictive models that estimate this probability as a function of time (days). Discoverability may be improved by instructing the search engine to return documents published within a temporal range, but this information is not readily available for many events, and we discover only a small fraction of relevant documents since the count of search results are restricted. These findings collectively express the difficulty in refinding news stories with time, thus motivates the need for collection building processes that utilize the SERP to begin early and persist in order to capture the start and evolution of an event. Our research dataset comprising of 151,602 (33,432 unique) links extracted from the Google SERPs for over seven months, as well as the source code for the application utilized to semi-automatically generate the collections are publicly available [3].

ACKNOWLEDGEMENTS

This work was made possible by IMLS LG-71-15-0077-15, and help from Christie Moffat at the National Library of Medicine.

REFERENCES

[1] Eytan Adar, Jaime Teevan, Susan T Dumais, and Jonathan L Elsas. 2009. The web changes everything: understanding the dynamics of web content. In *Proceedings of the Second ACM International Conference on Web Search and Data Mining (WSDM 2009)*. 282–291.

[2] Alexander Nwala. 2016. Local Memory Project - Local Stories Collection Generator. https://chrome.google.com/webstore/detail/local-memory-project/khineeknpnogfcholchjihimhofilcfp.

[3] Alexander Nwala. 2018. Scraping SERPs for archival seeds: it matters when you start - Git Repo. https://github.com/anwala/SERPRefind.

[4] Anne Aula, Natalie Jhaveri, and Mika Käki. 2005. Information search and re-access strategies of experienced web users. In *Proceedings of the 14th international conference on World Wide Web (WWW 2005)*. 583–592.

[5] David Bainbridge, Sally Jo Cunningham, Annika Hinze, and J Stephen Downie. 2017. Writers of the Lost Paper: A Case Study on Barriers to (Re-) Finding Publications. In *International Conference on Asian Digital Libraries (ICADL 2017)*. 212–224.

[6] Marco Baroni, Silvia Bernardini, Adriano Ferraresi, and Eros Zanchetta. 2009. The WaCky wide web: a collection of very large linguistically processed web-crawled corpora. *Language resources and evaluation* 43, 3 (2009), 209–226.

[7] Donna Bergmark. 2002. Collection synthesis. In *Joint Conference on Digital Libraries (JCDL 2002)*. 253–262.

[8] Brian E Brewington and George Cybenko. 2000. How dynamic is the Web? *Computer Networks* 33, 1 (2000), 257–276.

[9] Andrei Broder. 2002. A taxonomy of web search. In *ACM SIGIR forum*, Vol. 36. 3–10.

[10] Justin F Brunelle, Michele C Weigle, and Michael L Nelson. 2015. Archiving Deferred Representations Using a Two-Tiered Crawling Approach. *International Conference on Digital Preservation (iPRES)* (2015).

[11] Robert G Capra and Manuel A Pérez-Quiñones. 2005. Using web search engines to find and refind information. *Computer* 38, 10 (2005), 36–42.

[12] Soumen Chakrabarti, Martin Van den Berg, and Byron Dom. 1999. Focused crawling: a new approach to topic-specific Web resource discovery. *Computer networks* 31, 11 (1999), 1623–1640.

[13] Junghoo Cho and Hector Garcia-Molina. 2000. The Evolution of the Web and Implications for an Incremental Crawler. In *Proceedings of the 26th International Conference on Very Large Data Bases (VLDB '00)*. 200–209.

[14] Junghoo Cho and Hector Garcia-Molina. 2003. Estimating frequency of change. *ACM Transactions on Internet Technology (TOIT)* 3, 3 (2003), 256–290.

[15] Mohamed MG Farag, Sunshin Lee, and Edward A Fox. 2017. Focused crawler for events. *International Journal on Digital Libraries (IJDL 2017)* (2017), 1–17. DOI: http://dx.doi.org/10.1007/s00799-016-0207-1

[16] Dennis Fetterly, Mark Manasse, Marc Najork, and Janet Wiener. 2003. A large-scale study of the evolution of web pages. In *Proceedings of the 12th international conference on World Wide Web (WWW 2003)*. 669–678.

[17] Shawn M. Jones, Herbert Van de Sompel, Harihar Shankar, Martin Klein, Richard Tobin, and Claire Grover. 2016. Scholarly Context Adrift: Three out of Four URI References Lead to Changed Content. *PloS one* 11, 12 (2016).

[18] Jinyoung Kim and Vitor R Carvalho. 2011. An analysis of time-instability in web search results. In *European Conference on Information Retrieval (ECIR 2011)*. 466–478.

[19] Martin Klein, Lyudmila Balakireva, and Herbert Van de Sompel. 2018. Focused Crawl of Web Archives to Build Event Collections. In *Web Science Conference (WebSci 2018)*.

[20] Martin Klein, Michael L Nelson, and Juliet Z Pao. 2007. OAI-PMH Repository Enhancement for the NASA Langley Research Center Atmospheric Sciences Data Center. In *Proceedings of the 7th International Web Archiving Workshop (IWAW 2007)*.

[21] Martin Klein, Herbert Van de Sompel, Robert Sanderson, Harihar Shankar, Lyudmila Balakireva, Ke Zhou, and Richard Tobin. 2014. Scholarly context not found: one in five articles suffers from reference rot. *PloS one* 9, 12 (2014), e115253.

[22] Frank McCown and Michael L Nelson. 2007. Agreeing to disagree: search engines and their public interfaces. In *Joint Conference on Digital Libraries (JCDL 2007)*. 309–318.

[23] National Library of Medicine. 2014. Global Health Events. https://archive-it.org/collections/4887.

[24] Alexander C Nwala and Michael L Nelson. 2016. A supervised learning algorithm for binary domain classification of Web queries using SERPs. In *Joint Conference on Digital Libraries (JCDL 2016)*. 237–238.

[25] Alexander C Nwala, Michele C Weigle, Adam B Ziegler, Anastasia Aizman, and Michael L Nelson. 2017. Local Memory Project: Providing Tools to Build Collections of Stories for Local Events from Local Sources. In *Joint Conference on Digital Libraries (JCDL 2017)*. 1–10.

[26] Christopher Olston and Sandeep Pandey. 2008. Recrawl scheduling based on information longevity. In *Proceedings of the 17th international conference on World Wide Web (WWW 2008)*. 437–446.

[27] Thomas Risse, Elena Demidova, and Gerhard Gossen. 2014. What do you want to collect from the web. In *Proceedings of the Building Web Observatories Workshop (BWOW 2014)*.

[28] Steven M Schneider, Kirsten Foot, Michele Kimpton, and Gina Jones. 2003. Building thematic web collections: challenges and experiences from the September 11 Web Archive and the Election 2002 Web Archive. *Third Workshop on Web Archives* (2003), 77–94.

[29] Jaime Teevan, Eytan Adar, Rosie Jones, and Michael AS Potts. 2007. Information re-retrieval: repeat queries in Yahoo's logs. In *Proceedings of the 30th annual international ACM SIGIR conference on Research and development in information retrieval (SIGIR 2007)*. 151–158.

[30] Antal Van den Bosch, Toine Bogers, and Maurice De Kunder. 2016. Estimating search engine index size variability: a 9-year longitudinal study. *Scientometrics* 107, 2 (2016), 839–856.

[31] Shuyi Zheng, Pavel Dmitriev, and C Lee Giles. 2009. Graph based crawler seed selection. In *Proceedings of the 18th international conference on World Wide Web (WWW 2009)*. 1089–1090.

[32] Ziming Zhuang, Rohit Wagle, and C Lee Giles. 2005. What's there and what's not?: focused crawling for missing documents in digital libraries. In *Joint Conference on Digital Libraries (JCDL 2005)*. 301–310.

A Framework for Aggregating Private and Public Web Archives

Mat Kelly
Old Dominion University
Norfolk, Virginia, USA
mkelly@cs.odu.edu

Michael L. Nelson
Old Dominion University
Norfolk, Virginia, USA
mln@cs.odu.edu

Michele C. Weigle
Old Dominion University
Norfolk, Virginia, USA
mweigle@cs.odu.edu

ABSTRACT

Personal and private Web archives are proliferating due to the increase in the tools to create them and the realization that Internet Archive and other public Web archives are unable to capture personalized (e.g., Facebook) and private (e.g., banking) Web pages. We introduce a framework to mitigate issues of aggregation in private, personal, and public Web archives without compromising potential sensitive information contained in private captures. We amend Memento syntax and semantics to allow TimeMap enrichment to account for additional attributes to be expressed inclusive of the requirements for dereferencing private Web archive captures. We provide a method to involve the user further in the negotiation of archival captures in dimensions beyond time. We introduce a model for archival querying precedence and short-circuiting, as needed when aggregating private and personal Web archive captures with those from public Web archives through Memento. Negotiation of this sort is novel to Web archiving and allows for the more seamless aggregation of various types of Web archives to convey a more accurate picture of the past Web.

CCS CONCEPTS

• **Information systems → Digital libraries and archives**; *World Wide Web*;

KEYWORDS

web archiving; memento; personalization; privacy

ACM Reference Format:

Mat Kelly, Michael L. Nelson, and Michele C. Weigle. 2018. A Framework for Aggregating Private and Public Web Archives. In *JCDL '18: The 18th ACM/IEEE Joint Conference on Digital Libraries, June 3–7, 2018, Fort Worth, TX, USA.* ACM, New York, NY, USA, 10 pages. https://doi.org/10.1145/3197026.3197045

1 INTRODUCTION

Conventional Web archives preserve publicly available content on the live Web. Some Web archives allow users to submit URIs to be individually preserved or used as seeds for an archival crawl. However, some content on the live Web may be inaccessible (e.g., beyond the crawler's capability compared to a live Web browser) or inappropriate (e.g., requires a specific user's credentials) for these crawlers and systems to preserve. For this reason and enabled by the recent influx of personal Web archiving tools, such as WARCreate, WAIL, and Webrecorder.io, individuals are preserving live Web content and personal Web archives are proliferating [20].

Personal and private captures, or mementos, of the Web, particularly those preserving content that requires authentication on the live Web, have potential privacy ramifications if shared or made publicly replayable after being preserved [21]. Given the privacy issues, strategically regulating access to these personal and private mementos would allow individuals to preserve, replay, and collaborate in personal Web archiving endeavors. Adding personal Web archives with privacy considerations to the aggregate view of the "Web as it was" will provide a more comprehensive picture of the Web while mitigating privacy violations.

This work has four primary contributions to Web archiving:

Archival Query Precedence and Short-circuiting: Allow querying of individual or subsets of archives of an aggregated set in a defined order with the series halting if a condition is met (Section 3).
TimeMap/Link Enrichment: Provide additional, more descriptive attributes to URI-Ms for more efficient querying and interaction (Section 4).
Multi-dimensional user-driven content negotiation of archives: Increase user involvement in request for URI-Ms in both temporal and other dimensions (Sections 5 and 6.1).
Public/Private Web Archive Aggregation: Introduce additional special handling of access to private Web archives for Memento aggregation using OAuth (Section 6.2).

1.1 Solutions Beyond Institutions

Personal Web archives may contain captures with personally identifiable information, such as a time sensitive statement verification Web page (Figure 1c) or a user's `facebook.com` feed (Figure 1a). A user may want to selectively share their facebook.com mementos [23] but wish to also regulate access to them [22]. Without the ability of authenticating as a user on the live Web, many public Web archives simply preserve the facebook.com login page (Figure 1b). Both captures are representative of `facebook.com`, and they may have even been captured at the same time. Users may be hesitant to share their mementos of facebook.com (or other personal or private Web pages) without a mechanism to ensure that the Web page as the user experienced it is faithfully captured and that the access of those captures can be regulated.

As a counterpoint, an individual's personal Web archive is more susceptible to disappearing without an institution's backing. Maintaining backups of archived content is unwieldy, requires diligence or automation, and is still at the mercy of hardware failures. While

JCDL '18, June 3–7, 2018, Fort Worth, TX, USA

ACM ISBN 978-1-4503-5178-2/18/06...$15.00
https://doi.org/10.1145/3197026.3197045

(a) Local Archive capture of facebook.com

(b) Internet Archive capture of facebook.com

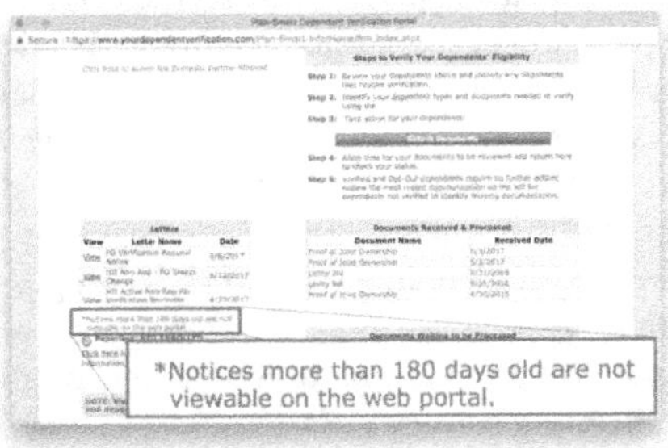

(c) Private content on the live Web that is extremely time sensitive to preserve for future access.

Figure 1: Personalized and Private Web pages.

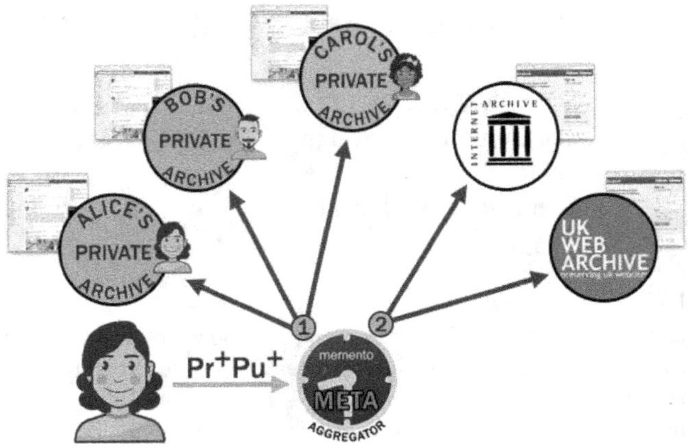

Figure 2: Archival precedence using private first then public Web archiving querying model (Pr$^+$Pu$^+$).

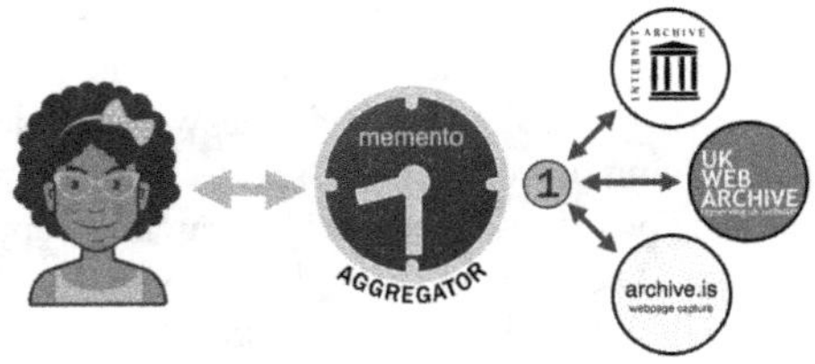

Figure 3: Conventional Memento aggregators query a set of public Web archives and do so in an equally-weighted querying model circuiting.

distributed propagation of the captures to other places may ameliorate this issue, another privacy issue remains in that distributed content may be sensitive and must be handled differently at the level of access.

To observe the more representative picture of "what I saw on the Web of the past" inclusive of private Web archive captures, we could give precedence to private Web archives over public Web archives when aggregating. For example, temporally aggregating my friends' captures (potentially residing in multiple private Web archives) with those consisting of preserved Facebook login pages (Figure 1a) from public Web archives (who are rightly not responsible for preserving my Facebook feed) may not be desirable. Instead, a user may want to instruct the aggregator to only aggregate mementos from archives with certain characteristics, e.g., a set of private Web archives, and only if no personal captures are found, look to the public Web archives for captures (Figure 2). This sort of runtime specification of archival query precedence does not currently exist. Today's Memento aggregators can only query a static set of public Web archives specified at configuration time (Figure 3).

Because more personal and private, non-institutional backed Web archives are being created, and these archives may contain sensitive data that cannot be shared without special handling, more work must to be done to address the impermanence of personal Web archives with consideration for their contents.

1.2 Enrichment of Archival Aggregates

We provide amendments to the semantics of Memento TimeMaps to encourage aggregation of mementos from more archives while still allowing for the distinction between conventional and enriched captures with additional metadata. We introduce additional *mementities* (a portmanteau of "Memento" and "entity")[1] for accessing various types of Web archives. The use of mementities could enable negotiation in additional dimensions beyond time, systematic aggregation of private captures, regulated access control to Web archives that may contain personal or private mementos, etc.

In this work (Section 4) we introduce three new types of attributes for richer TimeMaps: **content-based attributes** based on data when a URI is dereferenced, **derived attributes** requiring further analysis beyond dereferencing but useful for evaluating capture quality, and **access attributes** that guide users and software as to requirements needed to dereference mementos in private, personal, and archives with access restrictions.

Through this TimeMap enrichment, a user will be able to specify the semantics to be selective in the set of archived URIs (URI-Ms) returned in a TimeMap through a set of attributes beyond time and original URI (URI-R). This will allow the user to interact with the Memento aggregator to specify a custom subset and/or supplement the existing supporting archives in the aggregated result returned.

Conventional Memento aggregation [28] (Figure 3) is accomplished by a user requesting captures for a URI-R from a remote endpoint. The software receiving the request then relays this request to a set of Web archives with which it is configured. Once

[1]Used for distinction from the term "entity" as defined and in the now-deprecated RFC2616 describing HTTP/1.1.

```
!context ["https://oduwsdl.github.io/contexts/memento"]
!id {"uri": "http://localhost:1208/timemap/cdxj/http://facebook.com"}
!keys ["memento_datetime_YYYYMMDDhhmmss"]
!meta {"original_uri": "http://facebook.com"}
!meta {"timegate_uri": "http://localhost:1208/timegate/http://facebook.com"}
!meta {"timemap_uri": {"link_format": "http://localhost:1208/timemap/link/http://facebook.com", "json_format":
↪ "http://localhost:1208/timemap/json/http://facebook.com", "cdxj_format": "http://localhost:1208/timemap/cdxj/http://facebook.com"}}
19981212013921 {"uri": "http://archive.is/19981212013921/http://facebook.com/", "rel": "first memento", "datetime": "Sat, 12 Dec 1998
↪ 01:39:21 GMT"}
19981212013921 {"uri": "http://web.archive.org/web/19981212013921/http://facebook.com/", "rel": "memento", "datetime": "Sat, 12 Dec 1998
↪ 01:39:21 GMT"}
19981212024839 {"uri": "http://web.archive.org/web/19981212024839/http://www.facebook.com/", "rel": "memento", "datetime": "Sat, 12 Dec
↪ 1998 02:48:39 GMT"}
...
20170330231113 {"uri": "http://web.archive.org/web/20170330231113/http://www.facebook.com/", "rel": "memento", "datetime": "Thu, 30 Mar
↪ 2017 23:11:13 GMT"}
20170331013527 {"uri": "http://web.archive.org/web/20170331013527/https://www.facebook.com/", "rel": "last memento", "datetime": "Fri, 31
↪ Mar 2017 01:35:27 GMT"}
```

Figure 4: An abbreviated CDXJ TimeMap from MemGator for facebook.com.

the Web archives return a response containing their captures, the aggregator software temporally sorts the URI-Ms, adds additional Memento metadata, and returns the aggregated TimeMap to the user.

In this work we also describe a cascading hierarchical relationship between the aggregators and the mementities involved in aggregation and negotiation. We introduce a "Meta-Aggregation" concept (Section 5) to allow for a recursive relationship of one aggregator onto another, "building up" an aggregate result, potentially including supplemental information in the aggregation. Section 5.1 describes multiple scenarios where supplementing the memento aggregation using a meta-aggregator mementity would be useful. This hierarchy may also include other mementities like one to regulate access to private Web archives (identified with a URI-P) and another, a StarGate, to allow for selective negotiation (Section 6), e.g., allowing the client to request that only results from private Web archives are returned from an aggregator.

2 BACKGROUND AND RELATED WORK

2.1 Archiving and Linked Data

The Memento Framework [30] provides the constructs to interact with Web archives in the temporal dimension. An archival capture (memento) is identified by a URI-M. Memento aggregation allows identifiers for mementos (URI-Ms) from multiple Web archives to be temporally sorted using the parameters of the original live Web URI (URI-R) and a timestamp of the capture (Memento-Datetime). Memento TimeMaps contain a listing of URI-Ms for mementos of an original resource on the live Web. TimeMaps also include contextual information like the URI-R that the TimeMap represents, URIs for a Memento mementity to handle temporal content negotiation (TimeGate, i.e., URI-Gs), and identifiers for other TimeMaps (URI-Ts).

Memento TimeMaps are conventionally formatted and extend upon the Web Linking specification [24]. The syntax of the Link format applies to both information expressed in HTTP headers as well as information supplied in a TimeMap listing. Because of this, a limited set of attributes about URI-Ms is allowed within a TimeMap inclusive of `rel` and `datetime`. Additional information about a URI-M would be useful if present in a TimeMap. For example, knowing the HTTP status code of the dereferenced URI-M would reduce the amount of time needed to determine unique captures in the archive [15]. Extending TimeMaps may also provide the facility for the integration of private and public Web archives.

Alam et al. [2] defined the CDXJ format, an extension of the conventional CDX [12] archival indexing format, as an extensible means of associating additional attributes to URI-Ms. CDX files serve as indexes for Web archive files and contain many fields, like MIME-type, status code, and content-digest of the memento, which are not present in TimeMaps. MemGator [4] is an open source Memento aggregator that supports CDXJ TimeMaps (example in Figure 4) along with conventional Link-formatted and additionally JSON-formatted TimeMaps. In this work, we adapt the code for MemGator to handle additional HTTP request parameters supplied by a client as well as producing TimeMaps with the additional proposed attributes.

While these two dimensions are sufficient for the aggregation of public Web archives, additional parameters are required to express the need for privacy considerations or further steps to be executed to dereference the URI-M. Beyond the ability to express distinction in private and public mementos, it may not make sense to request public Web archive captures from an aggregator based on a variety of conditions. Some examples where expressions to distinguish captures are in isolation by URI (explicit exclusion of public captures from results) and Archival precedence (e.g., only check for captures of facebook.com in public Web archives when none are in my own).

The 'profile' link relation type [32] (discussed in Section 3) provides a standard set of semantics for processing a resource representation. We leverage and extend these semantics to allow a user to request mementos with certain properties from Web archives.

In earlier work, we developed WARCreate [18], a Google Chrome browser extension, to allow a user to capture content from their browser, even pages behind authentication, into the standard web archiving (WARC) format. We also re-packaged institutional grade Web archiving tools in WAIL [5], a native desktop application, to allow individuals to preserve, replay, and retain complete control of their captures. More recently, the Webrecorder.io service allows similar capability, including allowing the user to capture content behind authentication. But unlike WARCreate and WAIL, Webrecorder relies on the user's credentials being proxied through the service, a potentially undesirable feature with privacy ramifications.

2.2 Privacy and Security

The Snowden Archive-in-a-Box project [19] is an autonomous version of the the Snowden Digital Surveillance Archive. The project uses a Raspberry Pi single-board computer along with other hardware and a data set containing files leaked by Edward Snowden to allow browsing of the files without a user being surveilled. This use case highlights access as being the problematic factor beyond the base case of the content being sensitive. When aggregating captures from a Snowden archive with captures from other archives, requesters may wish to prevent requests from propagating to other archives via the aggregator (by specifying a privateOnly profile) or to only consult other archives when no results are returned from their instance (request precedence, both discussed in Section 3).

While little research has been performed on the aggregation of private and public captures, multiple surveys have been performed by a variety of researchers on user's perspectives on private Web archives. In particular, Marshall and Shipman [21] surveyed Web users on potential efforts for institutions to preserve their private Web contents. They particularly highlighted the need for exploration of who retains control of access of private content once it is preserved and made available.

The OAuth 2.0 Authorization Framework [10] (usage discussed in Section 4.3) provides a model for tokenization that we apply for persistent access to private Web archives. Using this model requires a secondary authorization server, implemented in this research as an additional mementity to decouple the authentication burden on the archive. This model, however, requires the archive to be aware of this additional mementity to act as a gateway to the archive.

Cushman and Kreymer [8] performed an extensive review on the security of Web archives in the context of both preservation and replay. Through technical examples on how an attacker might capture private resources, they provided approaches for mitigating each sort of attack. In related work, Brunelle et al. [6] described issues with private Web archiving on an organizational scale. Through analyzing the results of an archival crawler instance, they identified content that should not have been accessible to the crawler, which required wholesale removal of WARCs containing the information for lack of a method of selective removal.

2.3 Memento and HTTP Mechanics

Rosenthal [26] emphasized that temporal order may not be optimal for TimeMaps returned from Memento aggregators. He stated that aggregators need to develop ways of estimating usefulness of preserved content and conveying these estimates to readers. In a different work, Rosenthal [25] described the behavior of aggregators returning "Soft 403s" consisting of captures of login pages when the user likely expected content shown that was originally behind authentication.

Rosenthal [25] also described a "hints list" that an aggregator might provide based on its own experience of requesting content from archives. In this work Rosenthal also alluded to a hypothetical mechanism of the aggregator filtering content like login pages from the results and redirecting a user to a version of the TimeMap containing only captures that are not a login page.

Jones et al. [13, 31] discussed obtaining the "raw mementos" consisting of un-rewritten links in captures in a systematic way using the HTTP Link response header. By utilizing the HTTP Prefer request header [29], a user would be able to obtain a version of the memento as it appeared at the time of capture instead of a version with relative links rewritten by the archive to point back within the archive and not the live Web. An archive, in response and to confirm compliance with the request, would return the memento with the HTTP Preference-Applied response header along with the requested original version of the memento.

The HTTP Prefer header [29] allows an explicit means for a client to express their preferences of optional aspects in an HTTP Request. Van de Sompel et al. [31] highlighted that the Prefer header could be used by Web archives to allow clients to specify a request for the unaltered or un-rewritten content. Rosenthal [27] echoed Van de Sompel et al. by suggesting a list of transformations (screenshot, altered-dom, etc.) for a memento via a new HTTP header.

This work focuses on the transformation of TimeMaps, not the mementos themselves. The rewriting problem in previous work is pertinent to replay of URI-Ms whereas what we accomplish is more expressive metadata of the mementos prior to and to mitigate issues with dereferencing URI-Ms. A goal of this work is to further involve the client in the aggregation process. Interaction with the aggregators through these sort of mechanisms will be a first step in accomplishing this.

Fielding and Reschke [9] defined proactive and reactive content negotiation as that which is determined by the server as a best-guess based on metadata and a model involving communication and selection of representations, respectively. The latter may be accomplished a variety of ways inclusive of the utilization of the HTTP `300 Multiple Choices` and `406 Not Acceptable` status codes as well as the less commonly implemented HTTP Alternates header and Transparent Content Negotiation [11]. As we anticipate generating derivative TimeMaps consisting of any number of permutations of additional attributes applied on the mementos, it would be useful to associate and allow users to choose the variant they prefer using these status codes and HTTP transaction patterns.

In previous work [14], we highlighted an issue of URI-collision in the realm of personal Web archives wherein (for example) both a login page and the authenticated content of a live Web application may reside at the same URI-R (Figure 1). We [16] extended this work by identifying personalized representations of mementos and providing a mechanism to navigate between additional dimensions beyond time. As personal Web archives proliferate and are at some point aggregated into multi-archive TimeMaps (cf. a TimeMap from and containing only listings from the archive itself), it would be useful to distinguish URI-Ms that represent personalized mementos, mementos that were originally behind authentication, and mementos in personal Web archives that require additional considerations and mechanisms to access.

3 ARCHIVE QUERY PRECEDENCE AND SHORT-CIRCUITING

Private Web archives contain an inherent characteristic where exposing the metadata about an archive's contents could be sufficient to identify the archive's contents. For example, a private archive responding with a TimeMap containing URI-Ms for captures of my online bank statement would reveal where I am banking as well as where I am preserving personal banking information.

To mitigate the unnecessary revelation of potentially personal information, a client who has set up a Memento aggregator with access to their private Web archive may wish to have requests sent to public Web archives only if no results are returned from their private Web archive.

Figure 2 illustrates requests being first sent to the private archives then to public Web archives. But, it may also be desirable to allow this type of behavior to functionally coexist with conventional pipelined asynchronous archive querying. As with the Snowden Archive-in-a-Box example in Section 2, checking for the existence of captures of this content in other archives may imply interest or association with the subject matter, in some cases itself being revealing or even incriminating. To maintain privacy, a Memento aggregator with access to the Snowden archive would require special handling of requests for resources that might be contained in that archive. For example, a user may want requests for a certain URI-R to only be requested from the Snowden archive or their own personal Web archive, and not other public or private Web archives.

We propose two initial approaches to accomplish this: explicit specification by a client at the time of request and analysis of mementos with a potentially personalized representation. For the latter, we [16] identified three methods for identifying personalized representations. Of the methods proposed, but not investigated further (we opted for one of the other three), was to be able to specify additional environment variables when selecting a representation of a resource. The downside, we mentioned, was the requirement of a specialized client. The specialized "client" in this case may be the mementity responsible for determining the degree of personalization of the representation, i.e., the StarGate.

When aggregating and replaying a URI-R over time from a set of archives consisting of captures from both public and private Web archives, it may be desirable to first check for private captures prior to requesting URI-Ms from public Web archives (Figure 2). For example, in aggregating URI-Ms for `facebook.com` that include mementos of my news feed from my private archive and unauthenticated login pages from institutional public Web archives (Figure 1), the latter is less useful in observing how the page has changed over time. To maintain relevancy of the desired sort of representation, we may want to check for the existence of captures from private Web archives *first* and then, only if none are present, resort to requesting the captures consisting of a login page. This model of precedence (request priority) and short-circuiting (stop requesting captures if a condition is met) via Memento aggregators does not currently exist but could be critical in a user expressing what they expect from an aggregator beyond simply mementos for a URI-R.

In the basic model below, we express various access precedence models (henceforth *profile*) for containing boolean categorization of private and public Web archives. In each profile, order is significant and thus a simple regular expression can be used where P_u symbolizes a public Web archive endpoint, P_r a private Web archive endpoint, and the "+" superscript indicating at least one or more consecutive instances.

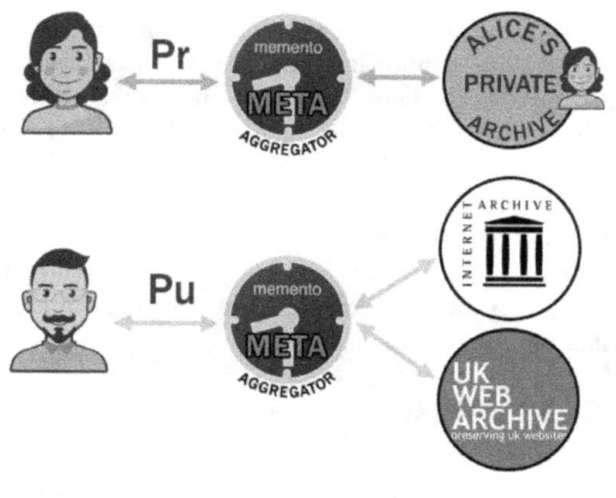

Figure 5: PrivateOnly and PublicOnly aggregation in an MMA.

```
$ curl -I
https://www.webarchive.org.uk/wayback/archive/*/http://www.example.org
HTTP/1.1 451 Unavailable For Legal Reasons
Date: Wed, 25 Oct 2017 04:39:35 GMT
Server: Apache-Coyote/1.1
Content-Type: text/html;charset=utf-8
Transfer-Encoding: chunked
Set-Cookie: JSESSIONID=823BD09DF8DD489087763640A8150023; Path=; HttpOnly
Content-Language: en
```

Figure 6: Accessing a URI-M at UKWA using curl returns an HTTP 451 status code.

$$noArchives \rightarrow \emptyset \rightarrow \{\} \quad (1)$$

$$publicOnly \rightarrow {P_u}^+ \quad (2)$$

$$privateOnly \rightarrow {P_r}^+ \quad (3)$$

$$privateFirst \rightarrow {P_r}^+{P_u}^+ \quad (4)$$

$$publicFirst \rightarrow {P_u}^+{P_r}^+ \quad (5)$$

The basic profiles pair with the syntax of the `profile` relation type [32], allowing clients to request resulting TimeMaps containing URI-Ms from a subset of archives from which the Memento mementity requests (Figure 5). The preliminary scheme for short-circuiting of subsequent requests is also boolean, e.g., requests should only be made to public Web archives when the `privateFirst` profile (Equation 4) is specified by the client when no identifiers for captures are returned from private archives. This model also assumes that the sets P_u and P_r are disjoint ($P_u \cap P_r = \emptyset$) for simplicity, but may not be the case in reality. For Web archives that contain both private and public captures, an approach toward achieving mutually exclusivity could be to separate each set of the private and public URI-Rs into an abstraction of separate collections. For example, as discussed earlier, the UK Web Archive contains captures from its legal deposit with restricted off-site access; that is, a user cannot access the mementos unless physically on location at the library (Figure 6).

4 ADDITIONAL TIMEMAP ATTRIBUTES

Aggregating private and public mementos requires the ability to distinguish captures that require special handling. To accomplish this and to provide the ability for TimeMaps to be more descriptive of the URI-Ms they contain, we extend the TimeMap syntax and semantics to allow additional attributes. In this work we introduce three new types of attributes for richer TimeMaps: **content-based attributes** based on data when dereferenced, **derived attributes** requiring further analysis beyond dereferencing but useful for evaluating capture quality, and **access attributes** that guide users and software as to requirements needed to dereference mementos in private, personal, and archives with access restrictions. In this work we focus primarily on the access attributes but define other classes of attributes for future extensibility.

4.1 Content-based Attributes

In previous work [15], we highlighted that the URI-Ms in a TimeMap for `google.com` produce nearly 85% HTTP redirects when dereferenced. Determining how many mementos exist from an archive for a URI-R is thereby impossible from a TimeMap alone. Enriching a TimeMap with information about the dereferenced capture would improve methods for determining how well (in quantity) a URI-R has been captured. HTTP data obtained when dereferencing a URI-M like status code [9], content-type [9], and Last-Modified [1] would be useful. For some of these attributes (like the aforementioned), the data may exist in the archival indexes, typically formatted as CDX. However, while many Web archives expose a Memento endpoint, few make these additional content-based attributes about the captures available through a CDX server[2]. Thus, once these attributes are discovered by dereferencing, they may be retained and expressed with the assumption that they are an accurate account of the archival record.

4.2 Derived Attributes

Other attributes about a memento may require calculation to obtain, which can be computationally and temporally expensive when performed at archival or even URI-R scale. This section briefly describes one such example of a derived attribute: Memento Damage calculation. Adding the ability for this derived attribute to be present in a TimeMap would allow for more efficient evaluation of memento quality. Brunelle et al. [7] developed a metric for determining the quality of a capture (cf. quantity in Section 4.1) when dereferencing a URI-M with a particular focus on the quantitative significance of missing embedded resources. Determining "Memento Damage" requires calculation beyond simple counting, as all resources are not equally weighted, particularly when absent. Having this information calculated and present in a TimeMap would allow a user to select the best or most complete URI-M without needing to iterate through all URI-Ms.

4.3 Access Attributes

An impetus for this research is integrating private and personal Web archives through aggregation via Memento TimeMaps. CDXJ allows additional attributes to be specified and considered when a URI-M is dereferenced. Figure 7 shows how a token may be stored in an enriched CDXJ TimeMap where the authentication procedure is discoverable at runtime. We utilize OAuth2 [10] for authorization

[2]Internet Archive does currently expose a CDX endpoint with limited fields at http://web.archive.org/cdx/search/cdx?url=example.com

```
!context ["https://oduwsdl.github.io/contexts/memento",
↪ "https://oduwsdl.github.io/contexts/damage",
↪ "https://oduwsdl.github.io/contexts/access"]
!id {
  "uri": "http://localhost:1208/timemap/cdxj/http://facebook.com"}
!meta {"...": "..."}
19981212013921 {
  "uri":
  ↪ "http://localhost:8080/20101116060516/http://facebook.com/",
  "rel": "memento",
  "datetime": "Tue, 16 Nov 2010 06:05:16 GMT",
  "status_code": 200,
  "damage": 0.24,
  "access": {
    "type": "Blake2b",
    "token": "c6ed419e74907d220c6647ef0a3a88a41..."
  }
}
```

Figure 7: An amended CDXJ record for a private capture of `facebook.com`. Line breaks added for readability.

when dereferencing URI-Ms with this field for tokenization for persistent access to private mementos.

Access control may be needed in cases where private and personal Web archives are aggregated with public Web archives via TimeMaps. An authentication procedure and subsequent tokenization will allow persistent access using a token derived from authenticating. Figure 7 shows a token being attributed on a per-URI-M basis, though a single token may be applied to all URI-Ms returned from an archive. The responsibility for attributing the token to an individual or set of mementos may lie in either the archive itself or the aggregator in this preliminary model.

4.4 Sources of Derivatives

CDXJ allows metadata fields (lines beginning with `!meta`) about the TimeMap to precede the listing of captures. Figure 4 contains metadata fields within a CDXJ TimeMap that are typically also found in a Link-formatted TimeMap, e.g., URI-R for the original resource, TimeGates, and other related TimeMaps. With the introduction of derived attributes (Section 4.2), it is critical to not just give context as to the semantics of new attributes like "damage" but also to provide guidance in generating this value.

Figure 7 provides an example where a derived attribute requiring calculation (memento damage [7]) and an access attribute are defined for guidance within the TimeMap. Definitions in the `context` utilize a URI to associate semantics of an attribute for a memento. We are still currently exploring further syntax for more expressive attributes in CDXJ TimeMaps.

5 MEMENTO META-AGGREGATOR

In this work we extend on the role of a Memento aggregator to possess additional capabilities when interacting with Web archive users, Web archives, other Memento aggregators, and other mementities. MemGator [4] allows a user to host a Memento aggregator at a location of their choosing (inclusive of the user's local machine) and configure a set of Web archives to query when starting the software. While conventional, remotely located aggregators assume that all Web archives queried are publicly accessible, a locally hosted, customizable aggregator may interface with archives that have restricted access. For example, a MemGator instance may

A = Alice's archive B = Bob's archive C = Carol's archive
I = Internet Archive R = URI-R
MMA_X = Set of archives sourced for X's MMA for R
MA = Memento aggregator at mementoweb.org

$$MMA_{Alice} = \begin{cases} \{A, B, C\}, & \text{“facebook.com”} \in R \\ \{A, C\}, & \text{“alicesembarassingphotos.net/vacation.html”} \in R \\ \{A, B, C, I\}, & \textit{otherwise} \end{cases}$$

$$MMA_{Bob} = \{B, A\}$$

$$MMA_{Carol} = \begin{cases} \{C\}, & \text{“carolsembarassingphotos.net”} \in R \\ \{MMA_{Alice}, MA\}, & \textit{otherwise} \end{cases}$$

Figure 8: A Memento Meta-Aggregator is configured to perform selective aggregation.

request mementos from a Web archive that is only accessible on the user's local area network or co-hosted on the user's machine on which the aggregator resides. Non-public archives are treated and aggregated agnostically without further consideration of their holdings. In this section we describe a mementity to account for the shortcomings of conventional Memento aggregators while also extending their standard functionality and Memento interfaces.

A Memento Meta-Aggregator (MMA) serves as a functional superset of a conventional Memento Aggregator (MA). A conventional MA provides access through identifiers to mementos (URI-Ms), TimeGates (URI-Gs), and TimeMaps (URI-Ts) from a set of Web archives. An MMA provides the ability to both supplement (Figure 9) and selectively filter the results returned from an MA with URI-Ms from additional Web archives at the request of the user or as configured with the MMA (Figure 8). In a proof-of-concept of this work, we build upon the open source MemGator to introduce these additional roles outside of the scope of the Memento aggregator mementity type to define the MMA mementity type.

Figure 9 describes a sample hierarchical relationship of mementities consisting of MMAs, MAs, and Web archive (WAs). When MA_1 receives a request for URI-Ms for a URI-R, for instance, the request is relayed to WA_1, WA_2, and WA_3 for the sets of mementos $\{a_1m_1, a_1m_2\}$, $\{a_2m_1, a_2m_2, a_2m_3\}$, and $\{a_3m_1, a_3m_2\}$, respectively. MA_1 is then responsible for combining and temporally sorting the URI-Ms then returning the aggregated TimeMap to the requesting user (or mementity). The temporal ordering within an archive corresponds to the second index (m) for convenience in the figure, however, this ordering may not hold between archives. For example, a_2m_2 is older than a_3m_1 per the temporal ordering diagram on the right side of the figure. The ordering for the mementos contained within the configured archives as requested from various mementities is displayed in the bottom portion of the figure. This figure also shows examples of an MMA obtaining results from multiple MAs (e.g., MMA_α from MA_1 and MA_2) and even MMAs referring to other MMAs for their results when queried (e.g., MMA_γ referring to MA_1, WA_5, and MMA_β with the latter referring to WA_7 and WA_8). The configuration of MMA_β is similar to the relationship of MMA_{Carol} to MMA_{Alice} in Figure 8 where a user may configure an MMA to both refer to a custom set of sources for results as well as reuse the in-place selective filtering of the sources. In this case, MMA_{Carol} would inherit the restriction of MMA_{Alice} of not sending requests for mementos of http://alicesembarassingphotos.net/vacation.html to Bob's archive.

Results from other Web archives that are aggregated with the results from an MA may be public non-aggregated Memento-compliant Web archives or private Web archives. We note that a conventional MA is not required to be present to use an MMA, because the aggregation of a static set of public Web archives may be performed by an MMA in a black box banner as if the MMA were identically configured with the same archives as the MA.

An MMA can be configured to return an aggregated TimeMap based on a set of Web archives for which it has been configured or it may be provided a set of archives to query upon request from a client. This abstraction provides a level of extensibility to current Memento aggregators for which the additional functionality may not be appropriate, scalable, or interoperable; however, providing an on-demand set of archives to query is useful in the context of personal Web archiving.

User-driven specification of aggregation parameters is particularly important for accessing personal Web archives using a Memento aggregator. If a user requests a TimeMap from a conventional Memento aggregator (Figure 3), the aggregator will request the URI-Ms from each archive with which the aggregator is configured to communicate. A user may wish to customize, prioritize, or give precedence to the archives queried (as described in Section 3). If a user hosts an aggregator themselves, the aggregator would need to be reconfigured to prevent requests for certain URI-Rs from propagating to certain archives on the basis of URI-R-archive pairs. Though this may become unwieldy, what follows is a useful example to illustrate where configuring an MMA with a core ruleset prior to considering further user-driven specification would be useful when aggregating personal and public Web archives.

5.1 MMA Archive Selection

Figure 8 abstracts the following scenario to show how an MMA can perform selective aggregation. Alice archives Web pages she views in her browser using WARCreate [18] and replays them using her local Wayback instance within WAIL [5]. Bob, Alice's acquaintance, and Carol, Alice's sister, each do the same for their own captures. Alice sets up an MMA (MMA_{Alice}) that is configured to request captures from her archive (A), Bob's archive (B), Carol's archive (C), and the Internet Archive (I). For some URI-Rs, like facebook.com, it may not make sense to aggregate Alice, Bob, and Carol's captures with those from Internet Archive, so she can specify a rule of only aggregating mementos from {A, B, C} when those URI-Rs are requested[3]. For other URI-Rs, like alicesembarrasingphotos.net, Alice may want to prevent exposing the fact that she is looking for certain old captures to Bob and the Internet Archive, but wants to also aggregate captures from Carol's archive, with whom she does not mind exposing the URI-Rs requested. She does this by creating another rule to only aggregate from archives {A,C} in those cases. By Alice controlling the MMA, she can both pre-configure the set of potential archives queried as well as provide the ability for her, Bob, or Carol to selectively aggregate from the set of archives when requesting captures for a URI-R. Were Bob uncomfortable with his aggregation requests going to Carol's archive when he used Alice's MMA, he may set up his own MMA (MMA_{Bob}) to request captures

[3]Note that MMAs do not protect the contents of an archive from being viewed, which is handled by the mementity described in Section 6.2.

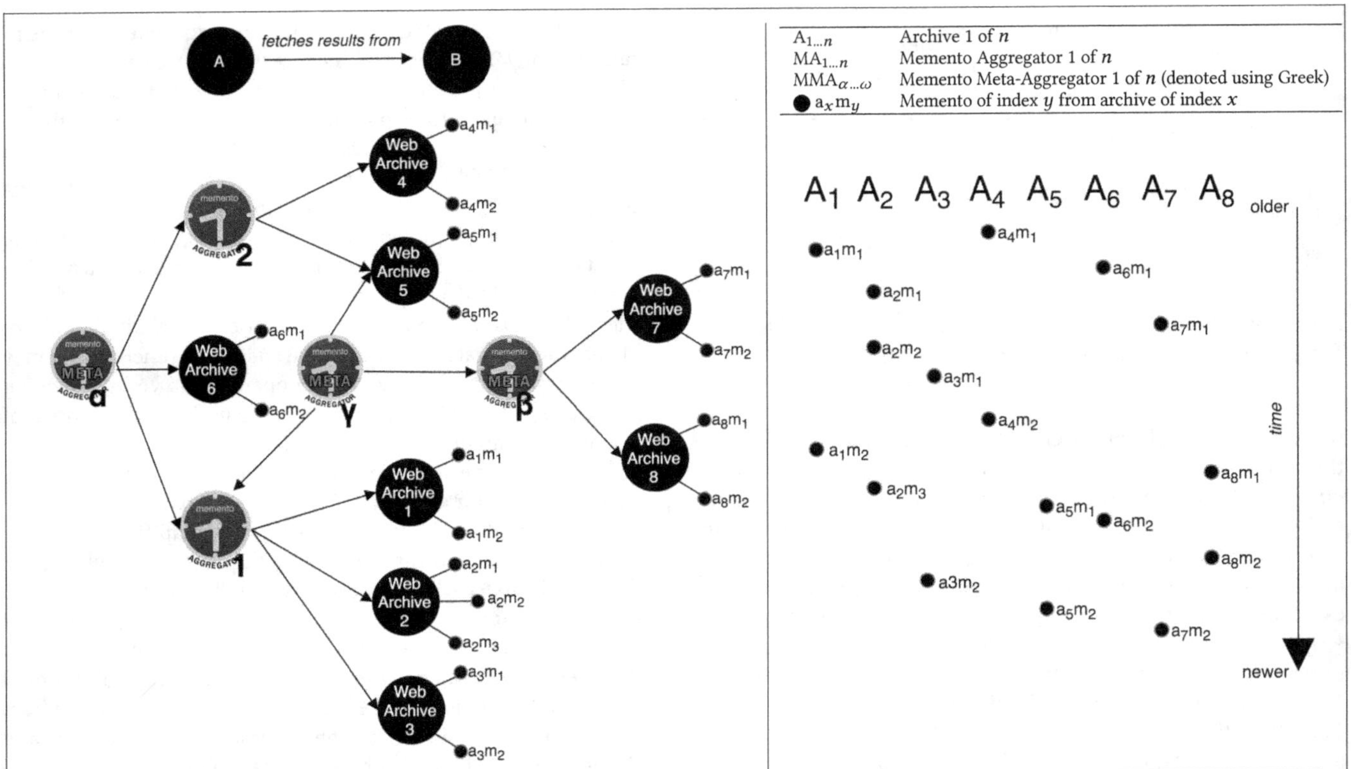

Mementity	→ Abstracted Holdings	→ Memento Holdings
MA_1	$\{A_1, A_2, A_3\}$	$\{a_1m_1, a_2m_1, a_2m_2, a_3m_1, a_1m_2, a_2m_3, m_3m_2\}$
MA_2	$\{A_4, A_5\}$	$\{a_4m1, a_4m2, a_5m_1, a_5m_2\}$
MMA_α	$\{MA_1, MA_2, A_6\} \rightarrow \{A_1, A_2, A_3, A_4, A_5, A_6\}$	$\{a_4m_1, a_1m_1, a_6m_1, a_2m_1, a_2m_2, a_3m_1, a_4m_2, a_1m_2, a_2m_3, a_5m_1, a_6m_2, a_3m_2, a_5m_2\}$
MMA_β	$\{A_7, A_8\}$	$\{a_7m_1, a_8m_1, a_8m_2, a_7m_2\}$
MMA_γ	$\{MA_1, A_5, MMA_\beta\} \rightarrow \{A_1, A_2, A_3, A_5, A_7, A_8\}$	$\{a_1m_1, a_2m_1, a_7m_1, a_2m_2, a_3m_1, a_1m_2, a_8m_1, a_2m_3, a_5m_1, a_8m_2, a_3m_2, a_5m_2, a_7m_2\}$

Figure 9: Memento Meta-Aggregators may aggregate URI-Ms from archives, Memento aggregators, and other MMAs equivalently. Shown is an example of temporally sorted captures as served from an MMA in a variety of permutations in a potentially ad hoc hierarchy.

from only his and Alice's archives without a URI-R filtering scheme like Alice's MMA. Carol also sets up an MMA (MMA_{Carol}) that defaults to using Alice's MMA and the mementoweb.org MA except when requesting URI-Rs from carolsembarrassingphotos.net.

As an endpoint, MMAs may aggregate and request access to captures to private Web archives using a token-based authorization model (e.g., using OAuth [10] as described further in Section 6.2). The query may be subsequently routed to an applicable and corresponding Web archive (private or public) after authentication has been established. MMAs may query other MMAs with the expectation that the results returned will be consistent with those from an MA with additional indicators for content beyond the scope of an MA (e.g., a flag for content from a non-aggregated or public archive). In the scenario above, Carol may want additional archives aggregated beyond the default case in Figure 8 so she can utilize the ruleset of Alice's MMA, as well as add filtering rules of her own. The filtering that an MMA performs may not be (and more likely is not) exposed to clients or other MMAs that look to it as a source for URI-Ms. Note that in the case of Carol's MMA, there exists a redundancy in that both Alice's MMA and the mementoweb.org MA will request URI-Ms from IA. While Carol's MMA may perform an operation to consolidate duplicates (i.e., a "UNIQUE" operation), time may still be wasted waiting for all archived sources to respond to requests to Carol's MMA. Carol may also only want to look to some archives if none, too few, or some other quantifier or qualifier exists in an initial set or series of archives. For advanced querying of this sort, a separate mementity exists and is described in Section 6.

5.2 User-driven Archival Specification

As in the scenario described above, a user may wish to include additional archives in the aggregation process or specify the exclusion of URI-Ms from specific archives at the time of the request. The MMA mementity type allows a user to be more descriptive in the results they would like returned compared to a conventional Memento aggregator where only a URI-R and a datetime are specified. Introducing a separate mementity instead of assigning additional roles to the existing Memento aggregator concept provides extensibility while retaining the semantic responsibilities of conventional aggregators and reusing existing infrastructure.

For a user to be able to express additional archives to be aggregated at run time requires both cooperation of the client and recipient to communicate through the same "protocol". We accomplish this using a fabricated `X-More-Archives` HTTP request header, that is consumed by a modified MemGator (serving as an MMA) to supplement the list of archives to be queried (see curl command below). Additional attributes may be specified to the MMA, for instance, if the newly supplied archive requires special handling.

```
curl -H "X-More-Archives:
↪ http://myLocalWebArchive/myCollection/timemap/*/"
  "http://mmaHost/timemap/json/http://www.themaneater.com"
```

6 STARGATE

Memento TimeGates perform content negotiation in the dimension of datetime (through the Accept-Datetime header) for a URI-R and issue an HTTP 302 redirecting to the appropriate URI-M. This work introduces negotiation with a mementity that serves as an extension to a TimeGate, a StarGate[4]. A StarGate extends the functionality of a TimeGate with additional content negotiation on other dimensions, such as those described in Section 4. This broadens archival negotiation beyond the temporal dimension into a range of others. A StarGate also acts as an endpoint to enrich a TimeMap with additional attributes about URI-Ms.

6.1 Negotiation in Other Dimensions

The Prefer HTTP header [29] provides a basis for content negotiation in other dimensions. Inclusion of the Prefer header requires defining preference in the Vary header of an HTTP response [29]. Though the specification consists of a registry of preference (of which `return=minimal` and `return=representation` are a part), Van de Sompel et al. [31] proposed the extensibility of the definition with `Prefer` values of `original-content`, `original-links`, and `original-headers`.

6.2 Authentication and Authorization through Negotiation

Figure 7 is an example CDXJ with the `access` attributes of `type` and `token`, which specify for a memento specify a previously established authentication and authorization procedure with a retained token for access persistence. In this initial work, we use an OAuth 2.0 procedure to establish these attributes but the representation is extensible and not coupled to the procedure dynamics.

Figure 10 describes the interaction flow of authentication and authorization to a private Web archive. This model uses the model described by OAuth 2.0 wherein the archive from which a capture is being requested takes on the roles of the resource owner and resource server (a fundamental pattern described in the specification), an MMA or user taking on the role of the client, and a mementity at URI-P (an identifier for an authentication mementity) taking on the role of the authorization server.

[4]"Star" here refers to common syntax for a wildcard (*)

(1) User requests captures for URI-R from MMA
(2) MMA requests URI-R from Public Web Archives $Pu_{1...n}$ and Private Web Archive Pr_1
   - $Pu_{1...n}$ each return a respective set of URI-Ms $\{\{M_1\}, \{M_2\}, \ldots\{M_n\}\}$ to MMA
   - Pr_1 returns an HTTP 401 and an identifier for an authentication mementity (URI-P)
(3) MMA returns HTTP 401, URI-P, and Pr_1 identifier to User
(4) User sends credentials and URI-R to URI-P
(5) mementity at URI-P returns a token to User
(6) User requests URI-R again from MMA with token and Pr_1 identifier
(7) MMA requests URI-R from Pr_1 along with token
   - Pr_1 returns the set of URI-Ms $\{M_{Pr}\}$ to MMA after potentially consulting mementity at URI-P for validity
(8) MMA sorts and transforms $\{\{M_1\}, \{M_2\}, \ldots\{M_n\}, \{M_{Pr}\}\}$ into a TimeMap for URI-R
(9) MMA returns TimeMap to User

Figure 10: Abstraction of the authentication to private Web archives follows a flow similar to OAuth 2.

6.3 Endpoint for Archival Aggregate Enrichment

StarGates are responsible for receiving data about URI-Ms and enriching any subsequent TimeMaps. In typical usage of Memento, the TimeGate mementity is not aware of the state of the resources it identifies. Two different approaches can be used to specify additional attributes for URI-Ms in a TimeMap: server-driven and client-driven enrichment.

In server-driven enrichment, the StarGate (or some other server-based mementity) accesses the URI-M for a URI-R in the archive and attempts to acquire the content-based attributes described in Section 4.1. These attributes are then retained by the server-based mementity and added inline to TimeMap when the respective original URI-R is requested by a client.

A client-based enrichment approach involves further user interaction of the client accessing a URI-M and a StarGate. A StarGate may provide a URI-M that acts as a proxy to the URI-M that would be requested in conventional Memento usage. By acting as a proxy, a StarGate may setup further communication between the client and StarGate when a URI-M is accessed. This may be accomplished using conventional JavaScript callbacks, a runtime executed service worker (similar to the approach for rerouting at replay-time by Alam et al. [3]).

The client-side approach also allows for distribution of the computation procedure for derived attributes (Section 4.2) with the StarGate acting as an endpoint for the result. As a safeguard to prevent malicious or miscalculated data from being served in a TimeMap, a StarGate may use a consensus model to ensure the accuracy of the result prior to associating it with a URI-M. As an example, a StarGate may change the URI-M in Figure 4 from http://web.archive.org/web/19981212013921/http://facebook.com/ to http://stargatehost/calculate/http://web.archive.org/web/19981212013921/http://facebook.com/. Upon a client accessing the latter URI, the StarGate returns a page to the client with callback information, a key to associate the calculation procedure, and a redirect to the former URI-M with additional embedded JavaScript. For clients that do not support service worker or JavaScript (e.g., curl), accessing the `stargatehost` URI will provide the same experience the client would receive if accessing the non-proxied URI-M.

7 FUTURE WORK AND CONCLUSIONS

We developed initial prototypes of the MMA[5] (extending MemGator [4]) and StarGate[6] as well as integrated a prototype of Mink [17] with the capabilities to interact with other mementities through the dynamics described in this work. Through the implementation of the concepts, mementities, and dynamics described here, users with private Web archives may aggregate their captures both with other private as well as public Web archives to get a better picture of the Web as it was without compromising the information contained in their captures. In the future, we anticipate exploring additional attributes to associate with URI-Ms as classified and described in Section 4. We also anticipate exploring the temporal and spatial ramifications of further supplementing TimeMaps and Link response headers as well as the ramifications on caching and efficient querying and aggregation of the TimeMaps by users and mementities alike. We plan on further exploring archival query precedence models (Section 3) to consider attributes of archives and their contained mementos in dimensions beyond public-private as well as more complex asynchronous models and short-circuiting techniques.

In this work we laid the foundation for aggregating private and public Web archives. We introduced conceptual Web archiving Memento entities (mementities) to facilitate a hierarchical approach toward aggregation and provided extensible means and methods to consider to further aggregate these captures for a better picture of the Web of the past. We introduced and explored archival precedence and short-circuiting of requests to archival aggregators to allow querying of individual or subsets of archives and to halt if and when a condition is met. We provided the syntax and semantics for enriching Memento TimeMaps with additional attributes to encourage them to be more expressive, particularly as required when aggregating private mementos. We introduced a model to integrate conventional live Web authentication methods with an additional mementity (StarGate) for systematic access control to private captures both from an individual user as well as from other mementities.

Acknowledgements. This work is supported by the NEH grant HK-50181-14 and IMLS grant RE-33-16-0107-16. We would also like to thank Scott Ainsworth, Sawood Alam, and Shawn Jones for preliminary reviews. Some icons adapted from the work of Agatha Krych and licensed CC-BY-SA 4.0[7].

REFERENCES

[1] Scott G. Ainsworth, Michael L. Nelson, and Herbert Van de Sompel. 2015. Only One Out of Five Archived Web Pages Existed as Presented. In *Proceedings of the 26th ACM Conference on Hypertext & Social Media*. 257–266.

[2] Sawood Alam. 2015. CDXJ: An Object Resource Stream Serialization Format. http://ws-dl.blogspot.com/2015/09/2015-09-10-cdxj-object-resource-stream.html. (September 2015).

[3] Sawood Alam, Mat Kelly, Michele C. Weigle, and Michael L. Nelson. 2017. Client-side Reconstruction of Composite Mementos Using ServiceWorker. In *Proceedings of JCDL*. 237–240.

[4] Sawood Alam and Michael L. Nelson. 2016. MemGator - A Portable Concurrent Memento Aggregator: Cross-Platform CLI and Server Binaries in Go. In *Proceedings of JCDL*. 243–244.

[5] John Berlin, Mat Kelly, Michael L. Nelson, and Michele C. Weigle. 2017. WAIL: Collection-Based Personal Web Archiving. In *Proceedings of JCDL*. 340–341.

[6] Justin F. Brunelle, Krista Ferrante, Eliot Wilczek, Michele C. Weigle, and Michael L. Nelson. 2016. Leveraging Heritrix and the Wayback Machine on a Corporate Intranet: A Case Study on Improving Corporate Archives. *D-Lib Magazine* 22, 1/2 (2016). https://doi.org/10.1045/january2016-brunelle

[7] Justin F. Brunelle, Mat Kelly, Michele C. Weigle, and Michael L. Nelson. 2015. Not All Mementos Are Created Equal: Measuring the Impact of Missing Resources. *International Journal on Digital Libraries* 16 (May 2015), 283–301. Issue 3.

[8] Jack Cushman and Ilya Kreymer. 2017. Thinking like a hacker: Security Considerations for High-Fidelity Web Archives. Presented at IIPC WAC 2017. (June 2017).

[9] R. Fielding and J. Reschke. 2014. Hypertext Transfer Protocol (HTTP/1.1): Semantics and Content. IETF RFC 7231. (June 2014).

[10] Dick Hardt. 2012. The OAuth 2.0 Authorization Framework. IETF RFC 6749. (October 2012).

[11] K. Holtman and A. Mutz. 1998. Transparent Content Negotiation in HTTP. IETF RFC 2295. (March 1998).

[12] Andy Jackson. 2015. The CDX File Format. https://iipc.github.io/warc-specifications/specifications/cdx-format/cdx-2015/. (2015).

[13] Shawn M. Jones, Herbert Van de Sompel, and Michael L. Nelson. 2016. Mementos in the Raw. http://ws-dl.blogspot.com/2016/04/2016-04-27-mementos-in-raw.html. (April 2016).

[14] Mat Kelly. 2012. *An Extensible Framework for Creating Personal Archives of Web Resources Requiring Authentication*. Master's thesis. Old Dominion University, Norfolk, Virginia, USA.

[15] Mat Kelly, Lulwah M. Alkwai, Sawood Alam, Michael L. Nelson, Michele C. Weigle, and Herbert Van de Sompel. 2017. Impact of URI Canonicalization on Memento Count. In *Proceedings of JCDL*. 303–304.

[16] Mat Kelly, Justin F. Brunelle, Michele C. Weigle, and Michael L. Nelson. 2013. A Method for Identifying Personalized Representations in the Archives . *D-Lib Magazine* 19, 11/12 (Nov/Dec 2013). http://www.dlib.org/dlib/november13/kelly/11kelly.html

[17] Mat Kelly, Michael L. Nelson, and Michele C. Weigle. 2014. Mink: Integrating the Live and Archived Web Viewing Experience Using Web Browsers and Memento. In *Proceedings of JCDL*. 469–470.

[18] Mat Kelly and Michele C. Weigle. 2012. WARCreate - Create Wayback-Consumable WARC Files from Any Webpage. In *Proceedings of JCDL*. 437–438.

[19] Evan Light. 2016. The Snowden Archive-in-a-Box: A year of travelling experiments in outreach and education. *Big Data & Society* 3, 2 (2016), 1–7.

[20] Siân E. Lindley, Catherine C. Marshall, Richard Banks, Abigail Sellen, and Tim Regan. 2013. Rethinking the Web as a Personal Archive. In *Proceedings of the 22nd International Conference on World Wide Web*. 749–760.

[21] Catherine C. Marshall and Frank M. Shipman. 2012. On the Institutional Archiving of Social Media. In *Proceedings of JCDL*. 1–10.

[22] Catherine C. Marshall and Frank M. Shipman. 2014. An Argument for Archiving Facebook As a Heterogeneous Personal Store. In *Proceedings of JCDL*. 11–20.

[23] Frank McCown and Michael L. Nelson. 2009. What Happens When Facebook is Gone?. In *Proceedings of JCDL*. 251–254.

[24] Mark Nottingham. 2017. Web Linking. IETF RFC 8288. (October 2017).

[25] David S. H. Rosenthal. 2010. The Importance of Discovery in Memento. http://blog.dshr.org/2010/12/importance-of-discovery-in-memento.html. (December 2010).

[26] David S. H. Rosenthal. 2011. Memento & the Marketplace for Archiving. http://blog.dshr.org/2011/01/memento-marketplace-for-archiving.html. (January 2011).

[27] David S. H. Rosenthal. 2016. Content negotiation and Memento. http://blog.dshr.org/2016/08/content-negotiation-and-memento.html. (August 2016).

[28] Robert Sanderson. 2012. Global Web Archive Integration with Memento. In *Proceedings of JCDL*. 379–380.

[29] J. Snell. 2014. Prefer Header for HTTP. IETF RFC 7240. (June 2014).

[30] Herbert Van de Sompel, Michael Nelson, and Robert Sanderson. 2013. HTTP Framework for Time-Based Access to Resource States – Memento. IETF RFC 7089. (December 2013).

[31] Herbert Van de Sompel, Michael L. Nelson, Lyudmila Balakireva, Martin Klein, Shawn M. Jones, and Harihar Shankar. 2016. Mementos In the Raw, Take Two. http://ws-dl.blogspot.com/2016/08/2016-08-15-mementos-in-raw-take-two.html. (August 2016).

[32] E. Wilde. 2013. The 'profile' Link Relation Type. IETF RFC 6906. (March 2013).

[5] https://github.com/machawk1/gogator

[6] https://github.com/machawk1/stargate

[7] https://github.com/machawk1/jcdl2018-artwork

My Approach = Your Apparatus?

Entropy-Based Topic Modeling on Multiple Domain-Specific Text Collections

Julian Risch
Hasso Plattner Institute, University of Potsdam
14482 Potsdam, Germany
julian.risch@hpi.de

Ralf Krestel
Hasso Plattner Institute, University of Potsdam
14482 Potsdam, Germany
ralf.krestel@hpi.de

ABSTRACT

Comparative text mining extends from genre analysis and political bias detection to the revelation of cultural and geographic differences, through to the search for prior art across patents and scientific papers. These applications use cross-collection topic modeling for the exploration, clustering, and comparison of large sets of documents, such as digital libraries. However, topic modeling on documents from different collections is challenging because of domain-specific vocabulary.

We present a cross-collection topic model combined with automatic domain term extraction and phrase segmentation. This model distinguishes collection-specific and collection-independent words based on information entropy and reveals commonalities and differences of multiple text collections. We evaluate our model on patents, scientific papers, newspaper articles, forum posts, and Wikipedia articles. In comparison to state-of-the-art cross-collection topic modeling, our model achieves up to 13% higher topic coherence, up to 4% lower perplexity, and up to 31% higher document classification accuracy. More importantly, our approach is the first topic model that ensures disjunct general and specific word distributions, resulting in clear-cut topic representations.

CCS CONCEPTS

• **Information systems → Document topic models**; *Document collection models*; • **Applied computing** → *Document searching*;

KEYWORDS

Topic modeling; Automatic domain term extraction; Entropy

ACM Reference Format:

Julian Risch and Ralf Krestel. 2018. My Approach = Your Apparatus?: Entropy-Based Topic Modeling on Multiple Domain-Specific Text Collections. In *Proceedings of The 18th ACM/IEEE Joint Conference on Digital Libraries (JCDL'18)*. ACM, New York, NY, USA, 10 pages. https://doi.org/10.1145/3197026.3197038

1 CROSS-COLLECTION TOPIC MODELS

A variety of information retrieval and data mining applications deals with unstructured text data. With unsupervised machine learning, topic models iteratively estimate probabilistic representations of topics and documents. Based on word co-occurrence frequencies, topic models cluster text documents by their latent topics and thus structure large document collections. Despite the overwhelming, unstructured amount of data, topic models thereby enable users to search for documents by topic, to explore document collections, and to extract meaningful information.

As digital libraries grow, getting an overview and keeping track of large document collections becomes even more important. However, combining the knowledge from multiple collections is challenging. Linguistic contrasts, such as domain-specific vocabulary, complicate topic modeling. Cross-collection topic models extend previous single-collection models to multiple collections. They aim to model document-topic representations despite linguistic contrasts and to reveal per-topic similarities and differences of collections.

An exemplary application of cross-collection topic modeling is the search for prior art during the patent examination process [24]. For this task, related work from any publicly available text collection, such as granted patents or scientific papers, needs to be retrieved. Patent-specific words, such as "device" or "apparatus" and paper-specific words, such as "algorithm" or "approach", hamper the effective usage of keyword-based approaches and word co-occurrence statistics.

Another field of application is bias detection in newspapers. For this task, we consider each newspaper's articles as an individual collection. We distinguish collection-independent and collection-specific words based on their frequency distribution: Collection-independent words have similar frequency across all collections, whereas collection-specific words have significantly different frequency per collection. Still, collection-specific words might occur in all collections, but they occur much more frequently in one particular collection compared to other collections. In newspapers, collection-specific words serve as a bias indicator, because these words occur more frequently in one newspaper. Further bias analysis then focuses on interpretation of these differences in language use. Similarly, cross-collection topic models can identify linguistic differences in document collections with different cultural and regional background. For example, topic modeling on traveler forum posts about different countries aims to reveal country-specific words per topic and regional and cultural differences in forum posts.

As opposed to previous work, we focus on domain-specific language and consider collections as domains with specific vocabulary. We propose a novel topic model that combines state-of-the-art cross-collection topic modeling [23] with the concept of termhood from the field of automatic domain term extraction [4]. With the help of an entropy-based termhood measure, our model

JCDL'18, June 3–7, 2018, Fort Worth, TX, USA

ACM ISBN 978-1-4503-5178-2/18/06...$15.00
https://doi.org/10.1145/3197026.3197038

ranks words according to their collection-specificity. To split the vocabulary in a set of collection-specific words and collection-independent words, the model sets an entropy threshold and estimates the proportion of collection-specific words for each dataset individually and automatically. As a consequence, the topic model guarantees a clear-cut separation of words with collection-specific and collection-independent frequency distribution. A mixture of collection-specific and collection-independent word distributions represents each latent topic. The precise distinction of collection-specific and collection-independent words is a novelty in cross-collection topic modeling. Furthermore, in order to resolve semantic ambiguity of single words, our topic model considers also multi-word phrases. We evaluate our model and a state-of-the-art approach with regard to three quality measures: topic coherence, language model perplexity, and document classification accuracy. The evaluation is based on four datasets with either two or three collections.

Section 2 presents related work in the fields of probabilistic topic models and automatic domain term extraction. We present our topic model together with the entropy-based termhood estimation, the entropy threshold definition, and the estimation procedure of the proportion of collection-specific words in Section 3. Section 4 describes the experiment setup and compares the proposed model with state-of-the-art cross-collection topic modeling. We conclude with a summarization of our contributions and paths for future work in Section 5.

2 RELATED WORK

Latent Dirichlet Allocation. Being the standard topic model for single text collections, latent Dirichlet allocation (LDA) models each document as a probability distribution over topics and each topic as a probability distribution over words [3]. Gibbs sampling [11] is used for the estimation of these latent distributions, as it is less complex to implement and achieves up to two orders of magnitude faster runtime compared to variational Bayes and expectation propagation [30]. While LDA is based on the assumption that documents with similar topic distribution exhibit similar word distribution, documents from different collections use collection-specific words and thus have different word distributions. As a consequence, LDA is not suited for modeling topics on multiple collections with domain-specific vocabulary.

Cross-Collection Latent Dirichlet Allocation. Comparative text mining extends text mining techniques to more than one document collection for the purpose of revealing collection's similarities and differences. The cross-collection mixture model (ccMix) discovers common topics across collections of news articles from different publishers and of product reviews from different companies [31]. To extend topic modeling to multiple collections, ccMix draws each word either from a topic's collection-independent or a topic's respective collection-specific word distribution. However, ccMix uses only a single, user-defined parameter as the probability that words are collection-independent or collection-specific. Therefore, ccMix cannot distinguish collection-specific and collection-independent words precisely. Instead of a single, user-defined parameter, cross-collection LDA (ccLDA) learns a probability distribution of collection-independent and collection-specific words per topic and per collection [23]. Applied to traveler forum posts about the UK, Singapore, and India, ccLDA identifies topics about "food" or "weather" alongside with collection-specific (region-specific) words per topic, such as "masala" and "seafood" or "monsoon" and "snow". An alternative to collection-specific topic distributions is proposed by Eisenstein et al.: Their approach models a background word distribution and the differences in log-frequencies from this distribution for collection-specific words [6].

More recently, supervised cross-collection topic models as extensions of LDA and ccLDA have been proposed for cross-domain learning [2, 10]. Interestingly, no topic model so far utilizes a word's frequency of occurrence across all collections in order to determine whether the word is collection-specific or not. They all lack the ability to precisely identify a word as collection-independent if it occurs with similar frequency of occurrence across all collections. Counterintuitively, in ccMix, ccLDA, and subsequent models, a word can be simultaneously part of a collection-independent and a collection-specific word distribution. In contrast, our approach guarantees a clear-cut distinction of collection-specific and collection-independent words.

Multi-Lingual and Other Cross-Collection Topic Models. Multi-lingual topic modeling deals with stronger linguistic differences between document collections. Zhang et al. model topics across different languages by incorporating a bilingual dictionary into a probabilistic topic model [32]. While their approach requires a dictionary, our experiments on multi-lingual Wikipedia articles demonstrate that we are able to model multi-lingual topics without a dictionary. LDA can be extended to multiple collections by running several LDA instances in parallel, unified by manually identifying common topics [34] or with a hierarchical model of per-topic word distributions [5]. On a newspaper dataset with different regions as collections, the hierarchical model learns a master topic across all regions and region-specific descendant topics. However, the model does not distinguish collection-specific from collection-independent words and descendant topics across different regions are almost identical for generic topics. In contrast, our approach guarantees for each topic that the collection-independent topic representation has no word in common with each collection-specific topic representation. Another contribution of Zhang et al. focuses on asymmetric and weakly-related collections, extending ccLDA with collection-specific topics [33]. In contrast, we focus on collection-specific words in common topics.

Fang et al. identify verbs, adjectives, and adverbs as differing opinion words in three news collections per topic [8]. They model only one word distribution per topic and assume that different collections share many words per topic and that only opinion words differ. This assumption does not hold for collections with strong linguistic contrasts and especially not for multi-lingual datasets. Furthermore, their model does not distinguish collection-specific and collection-independent opinion words. To the best of our knowledge, no previous work models topics on patents and scientific papers simultaneously. However, there is related work that models topics of these collections separately, such as a topic-model-based recommender system for prior art in patents [18] and a topic model on abstracts of scientific papers [11].

Automatic Term Extraction. The field of automatic (domain) term extraction (ATE) deals with the extraction of words or compounds of multiple words that are considered domain-specific terms in text documents. To this end, Kageura and Umino define termhood as "the degree that a linguistic unit is related to domain-specific concepts" [15]. Several papers address the extraction of domain-specific terms by identifying term candidates based on part-of-speech patterns and ranking them by their termhood afterwards. It is a common assumption that: "The information that a term candidate carries is also an important indicator of its termhood." [17]. Therefore, term candidates are ranked according to their termhood, which is measured with variants of term frequency-inverse document frequency (TF-IDF).

In contrast to TF-IDF, Inter-Domain Entropy (IDE) considers the distribution of a word's relative term frequency across all domains [4]. The closer this distribution is to a uniform distribution, the lower is a word's termhood. While IDE provides a ranking of words according to their termhood, the ranked list needs to be split into domain-specific and domain-independent word sets based on a threshold, which varies for different datasets. However, most previous work arbitrarily considers the top-10% or top-100 words to be specific terms or sets thresholds empirically [4, 9]. Instead of statistical information about word frequencies, Li et al. incorporate semantic information from learned latent topics into a novel termhood measure [20]. On single collections, Wilson and Chew extend the standard LDA model with different term weighting schemes [29]. Thereby, the dominance and scattering of high-frequency words can be controlled and stop word removal becomes obsolete. In our work, we combine topic modeling and domain term extraction to model multiple document collections and their linguistic characteristics.

Topic Models on Phrases. In order to reduce semantic ambiguity, text mining applications can take multi-word phrases into account (instead of single words only). For example, the unigrams "support", "vector", and "machine" have a different meaning if they are processed as a phrase and therefore topic models based on both unigrams and bigrams outperform unigram topic models at information retrieval tasks. [28]. Topical phrase mining has been applied to model medical terms [12], combined with topical change over time [14], and scaled to large datasets [7]. With a supervised approach, Kawamae et al. investigate the relationship between training labels and corresponding phrases [16]. While phrases can be modeled as a hierarchy of Pitman-Yor processes [21], Lau et al. show that also n-gram tokenization as a pre-processing step improves topic quality [19]. Recently, a data-driven approach automates phrase segmentation with robust performance at different domains [22, 26]. Hence, topic modeling and phrase segmentation can be applied in independent, automatic steps. We include automatic phrase segmentation in our proposed topic model during the pre-processing step of tokenization.

3 ENTROPY-BASED TOPIC MODELING

Our approach combines ccLDA as a cross-collection topic model with an entropy-based measure of termhood. As a result, we propose a novel topic model that splits the vocabulary in collection-specific and collection-independent words and provides more meaningful topic mixture representations of documents. Collection-specific and collection-independent words form each topic's representation and reveal commonalities and differences of the collections.

3.1 Basic Cross-Collection Model

Our model and ccLDA have in common that they both contain per-topic collection-independent word distributions φ and per-topic and per-collection collection-specific word distributions σ. Furthermore, there are per-document topic distributions θ. These three distributions have Dirichlet priors α, β, and δ. Which word w is sampled in a document depends on the document's collection c, the topic z of word w, and the binary decision variable x. x determines whether w is sampled from a collection-independent or a collection-specific word distribution. The original ccLDA samples x from a Bernoulli distribution for each occurrence of a word. As a consequence, out of two different occurrences of the same word, one occurrence might be considered collection-specific and the other collection-independent.

3.2 Extended Cross-Collection Model

The main difference compared to ccLDA is the following: ccLDA determines separately for each occurrence of a word whether this occurrence in particular is collection-specific, whereas our model determines globally whether a word is collection-specific for all its occurrences across all documents. If our model assumes that a word is collection-specific, this assumption holds for every document in which the word occurs. In contrast, if ccLDA assumes that a word is collection-specific, another occurrence of the same word in the same sentence could be considered collection-independent. Furthermore, ccLDA learns a per-topic and per-collection probability distribution from which the model randomly samples whether a particular occurrence of a word is collection-specific. In contrast, our model does not sample this property randomly but uses a precise differentiation of termhood on the vocabulary level.

According to an entropy-based termhood measure, the vocabulary is split into two sets: collection-specific and collection-independent words. With regard to this measure, x is sampled from a Bernoulli distribution ψ with the parameter γ. γ corresponds to the proportion of occurrences of collection-specific words in the entire dataset and is described together with the entropy-based termhood measure in Section 3.3. Via the Bernoulli distribution ψ and the proportion of collection-specific words γ, the entropy-based termhood measure determines the mixture of words from φ and σ across all documents. Section 4 gives examples of how this conceptual difference causes significant change in resulting topics. Figure 1 depicts the graphical model of our approach and the corresponding generative process is as follows:

(1) Draw a collection-independent multinomial word distribution φ_z from Dirichlet(β) for each topic z.
(2) Draw a collection-specific multinomial word distribution $\sigma_{z,c}$ from Dirichlet(δ) for each topic z and each collection c.
(3) For each document d, choose a collection c and draw a topic distribution θ_d from Dirichlet(α).
  (a) For each word w in d, draw a topic z from θ_d.
  (b) Draw x from Bernoulli distribution ψ according to proportion of collection-specific words γ.

(c) If $x = 0$, draw w from φ_z; else from $\sigma_{z,c}$[1].

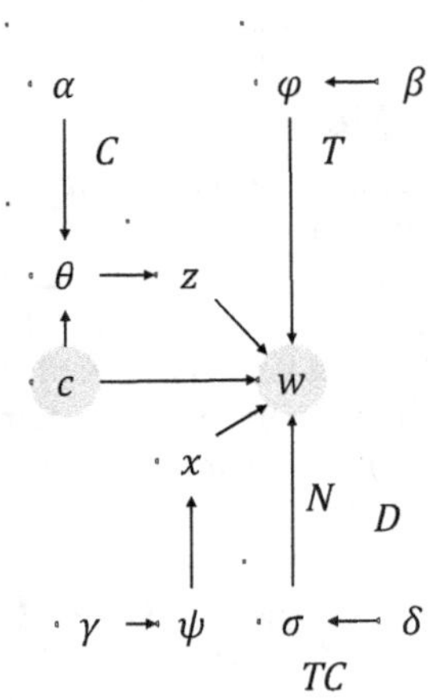

c	collection
w	word
x	determines whether w depends on σ or φ
z	topic
C	number of collections
T	number of topics
D	number of documents
N	number of words/doc.
α, β, δ	Dirichlet priors
γ	proportion of collection-specific words
θ	topic distribution
σ	collection-specific word distribution
φ	collection-independent word distribution
ψ	Bernoulli distribution of variable x

Figure 1: Graphical representation of the proposed entropy-based topic model.

3.3 Cross-Collection Word Entropy

In this paper, we distinguish collection-specific and collection-independent words based on entropy. For each word, the entropy of its frequency distribution across all collections measures the word's termhood. Intuitively, the termhood shall be low for words that are evenly distributed across documents from all collections. In contrast, the termhood shall be high for words that occur more frequently in documents of a specific collection. Together with an entropy threshold, the termhood determines whether a word is collection-specific. In our case, a random variable X represents the collection c of a given word w, where $P(X = c) = P(c|w)$ holds. In the following formulas, we consider a word w as an entry in the vocabulary and not as a particular occurrence of a word in a document. Thus, we define the normalized entropy $H(w)$ as:

$$H(w) = \frac{1}{log_2 C} \sum_{c=1}^{C} -P(c|w) \cdot log_2 P(c|w).$$

If w is uniformly distributed across all collections, $P(c|w)$ is equal for all $c \in [1, C]$ and $\sum_{c=1}^{C} -P(c|w) \cdot log_2 P(c|w)$ reaches its maximum, $log_2 C$. To obtain an entropy value in the interval of [0,1] that reaches its maximum for collection-specific words, we normalize entropy with the factor $log_2 C$. We consider $P(c|w)$ as the probability that the document's collection is c, given the occurrence of word w. Because the probability $P(c|w)$ is unknown a priori, we estimate this frequency on training documents before the topic sampling process.

3.4 Estimation of Word Probabilities

In order to estimate posterior $P(c|w)$, we estimate evidence $P(w)$, prior $P(c)$, and likelihood $P(w|c)$ on training documents:

- $P(w)$ is the probability that word w is randomly chosen from any document in the entire dataset.
- $P(c)$ is the probability that a randomly chosen word is from a document of collection c.
- $P(w|c)$ is the probability that word w occurs in a randomly chosen document of collection c.

Due to the inherent sparsity of limited training data, some words occur only once in the entire corpus. With only a single observation of such word, called hapax legomena, there is only limited knowledge about this word's true frequency distribution across collections. Although hapax legomena have been never observed in any other collection, they might have a non-zero probability of occurrence. For this reason, we use Laplace smoothing in order to create pseudocounts for unobserved words.

Based on entropy and the corresponding termhood[2], we can sort words according to their estimated collection-independence. To incorporate this sorted vocabulary into the topic model, we define an entropy threshold that splits the vocabulary in a set of collection-independent words and a set of collection-specific words. The next section describes how to estimate this threshold as a hyperparameter for arbitrary datasets automatically.

3.5 Estimation of the Entropy Threshold

We rank every word according to its entropy-based termhood. On the one hand, there are certainly collection-specific words, which occur many times in each document of one collection and never in any document of the other collection. On the other hand, there are certainly collection-independent words, which occur often and with equal frequency in each document, independently of the collection. In between, the uncertainty is highest for words with the fewest observations: hapax legomena.

We set the entropy threshold such that hapax legomena are closest to it. This threshold corresponds to the highest uncertainty whether a word is collection-specific or collection-independent. Even if a corpus contains no hapax legomenon at all, this threshold can be calculated. Imagine, there is a hapax legomenon w_{hl} that occurs exactly once in collection c_1 and never in collection c_2 in a dataset consisting of two collections. After Laplace smoothing (adding one pseudocount occurrence to each collection), w_{hl} has two occurrences in c_1 and one occurrence in c_2. Thus, we can estimate $P(c_1|w_{hl}) = \frac{2}{3}$ and $P(c_2|w_{hl}) = \frac{1}{3}$. The entropy $H_{w_{hl}}$ follows as:

$$H_{w_{hl}} = \sum_{i \in \{1,2\}} -P(c_i|w_{hl}) \cdot log_2 P(c_i|w_{hl})$$

For an arbitrary number of collections n, collections $c_1, c_2, \ldots, c_n$, $P(c_i|w_{hl}) = \frac{2}{n+1}$ for $i = 1$, and $P(c_i|w_{hl}) = \frac{1}{n+1}$ for all integers i, $1 < i \leq n$, this formula generalizes to:

$$H_{w_{hl}} = \sum_{i \in \{1,2,\ldots,n\}} -P(c_i|w_{hl}) \cdot log_2 P(c_i|w_{hl})$$

According to Zipf's law for natural language corpora, a word's frequency is inversely proportional to its rank in frequency. Thus, most words in a corpus occur exactly once and by definition are hapax legomena, having entropy value $H_{w_{hl}}$. As a consequence, we can expect this value to be the most frequent entropy value in a dataset. We show that this holds in our four evaluation datasets in Section 4.3.

[1]The conceptual difference in distinction from ccLDA is to draw w from *disjoint* φ_z and $\sigma_{z,c}$ according to *entropy-based* γ.

[2]Termhood of word w corresponds to $1 - H(w)$

If the entropy threshold is set below this most frequent value, all hapax legomena are collection-independent. If the threshold is set above this value, all hapax legomena are collection-specific. As a consequence, a small change of the entropy threshold results in a large shift of the proportion of collection-specific words. Notice that Laplace smoothing has been applied already. Otherwise, a word that occurs exactly once would be collection-specific with certainty 100%. By applying Laplace smoothing, certainty for being collection-specific ranges from 0 (inclusive) to 1 (exclusive).

Because hapax legomena have been observed once in one collection and never in any other collection, we consider them as collection-specific words. Topic representations list only the most frequent words per topic and therefore, hapax legomena typically do not appear in these representations.

$H_{w_{hl}}$ splits the vocabulary into two sets according to the entropy ranking, thus defining a set of collection-specific and a set of collection-independent words. From the sizes of these sets and word frequency observations in the training dataset, we estimate the hyperparameter γ, which corresponds to the proportion of collection-specific words in the dataset. γ is estimated by the sum of occurrences of all collection-specific words divided by the total number of occurrences of words in the dataset.

For the estimation of word distributions and topic distributions, we use Gibbs sampling based on the equations described in the original ccLDA paper [23]. Our implementation of the entropy-based cross-collection model is open-sourced online[3].

3.6 Further Considerations

Arbitrary Number of Collections. For two collections, the definition of collection-specific words is intuitive: these words occur most likely in one collection and unlikely in the other. For more than two collections, for example three, this definition is less intuitive: If a word occurs once in each of two collections but not in the third collection, is this word collection-specific? We compute the entropy of a hapax legomenon as the entropy threshold, which separates collection-specific and collection-independent words. Based on this threshold and our definition of collection-specificity, we consider words that occur once in two collections but not in the third collection as collection-independent, because their entropy is higher than the entropy of a hapax legomenon. The broader definition of collection-specificity is justified, because it considers a word as collection-specific if its frequency distribution across collections differs from a uniform distribution with larger extent than a hapax legomenon's distribution. We evaluate our model on datasets with two and with three collections in Section 4.6 and show examples for collection-specific words.

Multi-Lingual Corpora. Our entropy-based topic model is suited for multi-lingual corpora as well. If a corpus contains collections of two different languages, the linguistic differences are especially strong. In this case, collection-independent words are words that occur in documents of either language, such as named entities or loanwords. Collection-specific words are language-specific words that have no correspondence with the same spelling in the other language. Our topic model provides topic-wise language-specific and language-independent words, which makes the results of our work interesting for linguists and machine translation. In Section 4.6, we evaluate our model's multi-lingual capabilities prototypically on English, French, and German Wikipedia articles.

[3]https://hpi.de/naumann/projects/web-science/cross-collection-text-mining/entropy-based-topic-modeling.html

Table 1: Collections with their respective number of documents D and average number of words per document W/D (after stop word removal).

Dataset	Collection	D	W/D
Patents-Papers	Patents	14031	71
	Papers	16998	85
Newspapers	Guardian	30774	310
	Telegraph	30749	273
Wikipedia	English	2927	324
	French	2927	291
	German	2927	302
Traveler Forum	India	1432	199
	Singapore	1179	187
	UK	1580	288

Multi-Word Phrases. To reduce semantic ambiguity of single words, we tokenize multi-word phrases during text pre-processing. For an automatic phrase segmentation, we use the AutoPhrase algorithm of Liu et al. [26]. Therefore, we process each dataset with their phrase mining approach and segment multi-word phrases as single tokens automatically. No labeled input phrases are required.

Application to ATE. To use our model for the automatic extraction of domain terms, domains correspond to collections. As a result after training our topic model, the most frequent top-k words from the collection-specific word distribution correspond to domain terms. In the field of ATE, typical values for k are 10 to 100 [9]. An application to automatic term extraction would profit from multi-word phrases and their potential to reduce semantic ambiguity.

4 EVALUATION

To compare ccLDA with the entropy-based model, we evaluate accuracy of document classification, topic coherence, and perplexity on datasets consisting of either two or three collections from different domains.

4.1 Datasets

We present four datasets, which differ in domain, language, number of documents, average document length, and number of collections. Table 1 gives an overview of the dataset sizes.

The patents-papers dataset focuses on the domain of computer science and contains abstracts of ACM papers and U.S. patents. The patents[4] have been published by the United States Patent and Trademark Office (USPTO) between 2001 and 2016 and the papers[5] by Tang et al. [27]. We consider only those patents that contain the term "ACM" in the citations. To show that our approach generalizes to other document types, we evaluate our model on two large

[4]https://www.uspto.gov/learning-and-resources/electronic-bulk-data-products
[5]https://aminer.org/citation

Table 2: Number of topics, entropy thresholds, and respective estimated hyperparameters γ (proportion of collection-specific words).

Dataset	#Topics	Entropy	γ
Patents-Papers	260	0.918	0.632
Newspapers	155	0.918	0.184
Wikipedia	25	0.946	0.784
Traveler Forum	100	0.946	0.742

British newspapers: The Guardian and The Telegraph. The dataset of articles published in the politics category between 2010 and 2015 forms the largest dataset in our evaluation.

The third dataset consists of Wikipedia articles that have an English, a French, and a German version. We crawled English, French, and German Wikipedia articles about movies produced between 2000 and 2016. The length of such articles differs heavily, because the multi-lingual versions are no direct translations of each other. Therefore, for each triple of an English, a French, and a German Wikipedia article, we calculate the minimum number of words and reduce all three articles to this text length. If the minimum number of words is less than 300 (before stop word removal), the articles are discarded to ensure that the topic model learns only on articles of sufficient length. Longer texts make sure that there are enough topic-specific words to learn a document's topics.

From the paper that proposes ccLDA, we reuse a dataset[6] crawled from the online platform lonelyplanet.com [23]. At this platform, there are three separate forums for Singapore, India, and the UK, each having thousands of threads. Each document in Paul's dataset is the concatenation of all messages in one forum thread.

Table 2 lists the four datasets with their natural number of topics, entropy thresholds (depending on the number of collections), and proportion of collection-specific words γ. We determine the natural number of topics per dataset with a preliminary experiment following Arun et al.'s approach [1]. Their approach views LDA as a matrix factorization method and determines the natural number of topics for a given dataset by minimizing KL-Divergence of Singular value distributions. The hyperparameter γ is estimated as described in Section 3.5 and gives a first impression of the linguistic contrasts to expect in each dataset. Not surprisingly, the proportion of collection-specific words is highest in the multi-lingual Wikipedia dataset, whereas it is lowest in newspaper articles. Regarding the number of topics, patents and papers have the by far highest topical diversity.

4.2 Experimental Setup

The pre-processing consists of phrase segmentation, tokenization of multi-word phrases as single tokens[7], and removal of stop words based on stop word lists. The topic distribution priors, α, are fixed and uniform except for one background topic. According to Paul and Girju, updating α or other hyperparameters at runtime does not largely affect the sampling procedure [23]. We set β and δ to 0.01 and γ_0 and γ_1 to 1.0, corresponding to symmetric distributions with equal probability of occurrence of collection-specific and collection-independent words. The Gibbs sampling runs for a burn-in period of 200 iterations. 10 samples, separated by lags of 10 iterations, are averaged for the final result.

After the sampling process, we measure per-topic coherence separately for the collection-independent word distribution φ and each collection-specific word distribution σ. Furthermore, we measure mixed topic coherence, language model perplexity, and document classification accuracy. We split each dataset into 90% training set and 10% test set and use 10-fold cross-validation.

[6] http://cmci.colorado.edu/~mpaul/downloads/ccdata.php

[7] To ensure a fair comparison, we incorporate multi-word phrases also into the ccLDA baseline approach.

Table 3: Topic model comparison regarding accuracy (Acc), topic coherence (TC), and perplexity (Perpl).
Asterisks denote statistically significant improvement as determined by a paired two-tailed t-test at 0.05 level.

	ccLDA			Entropy-Based		
Dataset	**Acc**	**TC**	**Perpl**	**Acc**	**TC**	**Perpl**
Patents-Papers	0.61	0.404	827	0.70*	0.412*	797*
Newspapers	0.54	0.436	4151	0.61*	0.493*	4042*
Wikipedia	0.70	-	5150	0.92*	-	4955*
Traveler Forum	0.45	0.390	771	0.58*	0.413*	785

4.3 Document Classification

The evaluation of the separation of collection-specific and collection-independent words is based on a document classification task. For this task, each topic model predicts the collections of test documents given the documents' words. Rather than only outputting the most likely collection per document, topic models assign a probability to each collection. This probabilistic classification allows a more detailed evaluation regarding each topic model's degree of certainty. The document classification accuracy corresponds to the probability assigned to the correct collection normalized by the sum of probabilities assigned to all collections. We calculate the average accuracy across all test documents to obtain a document classification accuracy for each topic model. This evaluation task allows for a comparison of ccLDA and the proposed topic model.[8]

CcLDA calculates the probability $P(c|d)$ for collection c given document d as:

$$P(c|d) = \prod_{w \in d} \sum_{c} \mathbb{L}(w|\theta_d, c)$$

We use the word likelihood $\mathbb{L}(w|\theta_d, c)$ and compute the product of the likelihoods of all words in a document per collection c. The classification accuracy for document d is $\frac{P(c_{correct}|d)}{\sum_c P(c|d)}$.

Table 3 lists all evaluation results. On the Wikipedia dataset, document classification accuracy of our entropy-based model is 31% higher than ccLDA's accuracy. On the other datasets, we achieve 29% (traveler forum), 15% (patents-papers), and 13% (newspapers) higher accuracy. Especially on datasets with stronger linguistic contrasts, such as the multi-lingual Wikipedia dataset, our approach

[8] We do not consider document classification approaches as baselines, because the goal of this evaluation is to compare different cross-collection topic models.

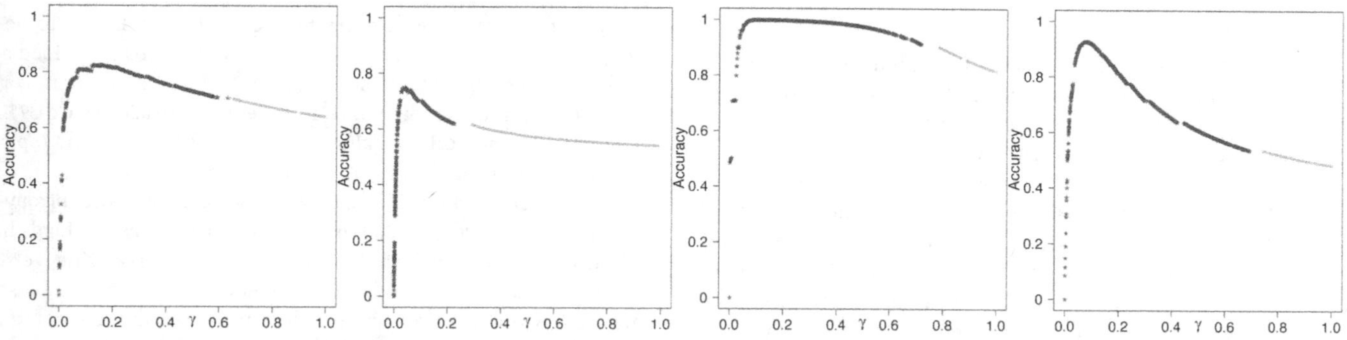

(a) Patents-Papers (b) Newspapers (c) Wikipedia (d) Traveler Forum

Figure 2: Document classification accuracy for all possible proportions of collection-specific words, γ. Collection-specific words in our entropy-based model are colored in green, collection-independent words in yellow.

outperforms ccLDA and provides a better separation of collection-specific and collection-independent words. Comparing the different datasets, both approaches achieve the highest accuracy on the Wikipedia dataset. This dataset contains many language-specific words. It confirms that language classification of Wikipedia articles is easier than, for example, classification of newspaper articles as Guardian or Telegraph articles.

Figure 2 visualizes the influence of hyperparameter γ on the document classification accuracy of our model. The number of possible, meaningful hyperparameter settings is the number of distinct entropy values for words in the entire vocabulary. Thus, vocabulary size V is an upper limit for the number of thresholds. Each possible threshold corresponds to one hyperparameter setting and splits the vocabulary into two sets of collection-specific and collection-independent words. For each possible threshold, we compute the topic model's document classification accuracy. The larger the proportion of collection-specific words, the more words our model uses to classify a document. The largest gap in each graph corresponds to hapax legomena. We can either choose to consider all hapax legomena as collection-specific words or consider all hapax legomena as collection-independent words. There is no choice in between, because all these words have the same entropy value. The smaller gaps in the graph correspond to words that occur exactly twice (dis legomena), three times (tris legomena), and so on. These words make up a large proportion of all words in the corpus, which is why their entropy value is more frequent.

Additionally, Figure 2 shows that we could achieve the highest document classification accuracy with $\gamma \approx 0.1$. However, such γ considers words as collection-specific only if they improve document classification accuracy. Incorrectly, the word's frequency distribution would not be considered. For example, consider one word that occurs in every document of one collection and never in the other collection. This single, collection-specific word achieves optimal document classification accuracy. Thus, all other words would be incorrectly considered collection-independent regardless of their frequency distribution.

4.4 Topic Coherence

The evaluation of topic coherence compares ccLDA and the entropy-based model with regard to their capability to cluster words by semantic similarity within one collection and across multiple collections. Especially, we evaluate the capability to correctly align topics of different collections despite different word distributions. For automatic evaluation of topic coherence, we use the Palmetto[9] library, which implements the C_V measure [25].

However, current topic coherence measures consider only single word distributions per topic and their topic representation in the form of top words. Current measures cannot handle multiple word distributions per topic. Therefore, we present an extension of topic coherence measures for cross-collection topic models, which we also published online. Our approach considers topic representations (which are sets of top words) of the collection-independent word distribution φ and each collection-specific word distribution σ. Per topic, we use the union of these representations as a single topic representation across the collection-independent and each collection-specific topic-word distribution. The coherence of this union can be measured with current topic coherence measures. We call this measure "mixed topic coherence", because it mixes the word distributions and thereby allows to evaluate the topical alignment of the different word distributions.

However, measuring the topic coherence based on word co-occurrences has its limitations. The C_V measure assumes that words that never co-occur in the reference dataset are not topically coherent. This assumption does not hold for datasets with strong linguistic contrast. For example, words from collections with different languages do not co-occur although they can form a coherent topic. Therefore, the C_V measure cannot evaluate topic coherence of topic models trained on our multi-lingual dataset. For all other datasets, we obtain a single coherence value per topic model by averaging all its topics' coherence values. In the evaluation, ccLDA and the proposed entropy-based model form almost equally coherent topic representations with slightly higher topic coherence of our approach, especially on the newspapers dataset (13% improvement).

[9]https://github.com/AKSW/Palmetto/

4.5 Perplexity

With test set perplexity, we evaluate a topic model's ability to generalize from training data to unseen test data. Perplexity focuses on the generative aspect of topic models to predict word probabilities for unseen documents. Lower perplexity is better.

We use the "fold-in" method used by Paul et al. for the evaluation of ccLDA to learn topic probabilities θ of test documents. "Fold-in" means that the evaluation keeps all topic model parameters fixed as they have been learned on the training data. Gibbs sampling estimates only the per-document topic distributions on the test set. This method has been introduced by Hofmann [13]. Given the topic probabilities θ_d and the collection c of a document d, the likelihood $\mathbb{L}$ of a word w in d is calculated as:

$$\mathbb{L}(w|\theta_d, c) = \sum_z P(z|\theta_d)[P(\neg x)P(w|z, \neg x) + P(x)P(w|z, c, x)].$$

In this formula, x is a binary variable that denotes whether w is collection-specific (x) or collection-independent ($\neg x$). In ccLDA, this variable depends on collection c and topic z but not on the word itself. In contrast, our model estimates x for each word in the vocabulary and thus learns the proportion of collection-specific words γ per dataset.

$P(x)$ is the probability that a collection-specific word is sampled and is equivalent to γ in our approach. $P(w|z, x)$ is the probability that in particular word w is sampled if a collection-specific word from topic z is sampled. The perplexity of a model m, with M being the total number of words in all test documents, is calculated as:

$$\mathbb{P}(m) = 2^{-\frac{1}{M}\prod_w \mathbb{L}(w|\theta_d, c)}.$$

Both models achieve comparable perplexity with slight advantages of the entropy-based model, especially on the patents-papers dataset (4% improvement). On the traveler forum dataset, ccLDA achieves lower perplexity than the entropy-based model, although this difference is not significant.

4.6 Example Topics

As an example, Table 4 shows the top-5 words of each specific and independent word distribution our model learned on the patents-papers dataset. For reasons of clarity, we limit the number of topics to 25. Topic 0, the stop word topic, correctly identifies patent-specific stop words, such as "apparatus" and paper-specific stop words, such as "approach". The word "datum", for example, is represented in the patent-specific and paper-specific word distributions, which means its collection-specific frequencies differ significantly and therefore cannot be combined in a single, collection-independent frequency. Collection-independent words, such as "method" and "system", occur with similar frequency in both collections. Another example, topic 5, deals with computer graphics (collection-independent top words) and our model shows that the focus of patents ("pixel" or "display") is rather low-level, while papers focus on high-level algorithmic problems in the context of image processing ("algorithm", "detection", "recognition"). Topic 2 is a security topic and its collection-specific words reveal that most documents about computer "attacks" are scientific papers, but no patents.

The original ccLDA is based on word co-occurrences only, which is particularly problematic if documents across collections share only few words, since they are then considered unlikely to belong to the same topic. English, French, and German Wikipedia movie articles, for example, share less than 10% of their words. For comparison, the Guardian and the Telegraph articles share 37%. As a consequence, ccLDA exhibits poor topic coherence and topic alignment across multi-lingual collections.

Table 5 compares two Indian movie topics learned by the entropy-based model and ccLDA. Both models are capable to assign English, French, and German words to respective collection-specific word distributions. However, ccLDA considers "khan" to be the most frequent word of the collection-independent distribution and the English-specific distribution. This mistake reveals ccLDA's deficiency to separate collection-specific and collection-independent words correctly. In contrast, the entropy-based model guarantees that words are either collection-specific or collection-independent. The word "bollywood" is not collection-independent, because its frequency is not uniformly distributed across all collections. Instead, the word occurs more frequently in French articles with this topic (1.1%) than in English articles (0.7%). Table 5 further indicates that ccLDA does not align topics correctly: The German-specific word distribution falsely contains sports related words and some words are not even German.

Table 6 lists two topics about the military conflict in Syria and Iraq learned by ccLDA and the entropy-based model on the newspapers dataset. The entropy-based model provides a better separation of collection-specific and collection-independent words. For example, the entropy-based model assigns "international" to both collection-specific word distributions, because the word occurs with significantly different frequencies in both collections, which also holds for "iraq", "syrian", and "assad". In both collection-specific word distributions, "assad" is the seventh most frequent word, but the difference of relative frequencies (1.2% compared to 1.4%) is comparably large so that our model represents the word with two collection-specific frequencies instead of a collection-independent frequency. In contrast, ccLDA assigns "britain" to the collection-independent and the Telegraph-specific word distribution. Representing "britain" in a collection-independent and a collection-specific distribution at the same time is inappropriate. The entropy-based model reveals that the Telegraph and The Guardian differ in usage of the words "isil" and "isis" and that the politician William Hague is mentioned more frequently in The Telegraph for this topic.

Table 7 compares transportation topics from the traveler forum corpus. In the entropy-based model, the word "luggage" occurs in the India-specific and the Singapore-specific topic representation, because it is very frequent in this topic in both collection. However, it is not collection-independent because its frequency distribution differs significantly from a uniform distribution with probabilities 0.018 in C_{India}, 0.029 in $C_{Singapore}$, and less than 0.01 in C_{UK}. In ccLDA, the word "time" is falsely collection-specific *and* collection-independent, occurring in the UK-specific, the Singapore-specific, and the collection-independent topic representation.

5 CONCLUSIONS AND FUTURE WORK

We presented a probabilistic, entropy-based topic model for multiple domain-specific text collections. Our approach incorporates

Table 4: Entropy-based model with 25 topics for the patents-papers dataset.

ID	Patent-Specific Topic Representation	**Collection-Independent Topic Representation**	Paper-Specific Topic Representation
0	datum include computer apparatus determine	**system method base provide process**	model paper approach result datum
1	task module tool script work	**software agent group activity environment**	student learning design computer learn
2	message security user electronic access_control	**key secure signature authentication encryption**	security scheme attack protocol access_control
3	circuit design test block programmable	**logic integrate gate cell delay**	test fault design circuit testing
4	server client request user content	**web_service application network system platform**	user mobile cloud architecture technology
5	pixel display render unit frame	**image color region camera method**	feature object detection recognition algorithm
6	user content template business knowledge	**system digital provide media_content base**	science computer technology community conference
7	database table result attribute schema	**query search_result retrieval xml relational**	datum algorithm database optimization mining
8	output input power second clock	**signal frequency voltage supply current**	power game low consumption circuit
9	packet queue connection protocol switch	**network route traffic communication flow**	sensor_nodes wireless protocol mobile
10	channel terminal transmit receive wireless	**communication transmission network receiver rate**	channel performance antenna interference wireless
11	partition cost constraint algorithm estimate	**cell region method route threshold**	water temperature thermal measurement study
12	display user_interface device graphical	**virtual interactive provide environment visual**	user_interface interaction human device
13	thread transaction memory request lock	**resource system application scheduling distribute**	memory parallel performance architecture processor
14	device electronic mobile user location	**customer network service product system**	market risk patient health price
15	document content input electronic feature	**text word language character annotation**	document gene semantic recognition feature
16	element entry table hash classification	**network rule set base machine**	fuzzy classification neural_network learning learn
17	item segment list matrix determine	**function method vector point space**	problem matrix equation solution linear
18	program execution instruction execute compile	**source_code language class logic type**	program programming specification formal semantics
19	object reference interface garbage pointer	**management system process policy change**	business knowledge project organization development
20	node message graph plurality leaf	**tree path number set time**	algorithm problem graph bound complexity
21	stream datum audio frame content	**video filter signal code media**	estimation algorithm noise propose scheme
22	storage memory datum device block	**system control controller volume primary**	robot vehicle design simulation robotic
23	instruction cache processor memory register	**address window bit trace set**	book guide include server learn
24	model object threedimensional modeling polygon	**surface point shape mesh flow**	simulation finite_element fluid property

Table 5: Example topics from the Wikipedia dataset.

Entropy-Based Model			ccLDA		
khan judy arjun kabir singh maya ali estevez vidya hindus			khan hitch bragg poojaclu cole vidya karan maya anjali		
English	**French**	**German**	**English**	**French**	**German**
indian	inde	adam	khan	mariage	chucky
india	indien	indien	indian	raj	team
award	portail	hochzeit	india	carter	carter
bollywood	bollywood	liebe	film	inde	spieler
love	composee	verliebt	love	kapoor	cole
kapoor	musique	tagebuch	award	ronan	spiel
mitty	kapoor	brahm	raj	sam	ella
raj	interpretee	hideko	family	amoureux	duke
english	technique	keat	shah	relation	kannibalen
role	indienne	tiger	kapoor	pierre	jennifer

Table 6: Example topics from the newspapers dataset.

Entropy-Based Model		ccLDA	
syria britain support country libya military force attack regime government british		russia country military attack britain syria support russian world international	
Telegraph	**Guardian**	**Telegraph**	**Guardian**
isil	iran	britain	force
mr_hague	iraq	isil	state
syrian	syrian	president	president
iraq	isis	force	group
air_strikes	iraqi	state	leader
refugee	international	america	power
assad	assad	british	cameron
international	western	leader	situation
oil	civilian	nation	america
stop_the_war	humanitarian	terrorist	official

Table 7: Example topics from the traveler forum dataset.

Entropy-Based Model			ccLDA		
flight airport time hour check fly arrive book leave airline			flight fly check hour airline airport arrive time luggage bag		
UK	**India**	**Singapore**	**UK**	**India**	**Singapore**
heathrow	license	taxi	ticket	mumbaus	changi
train	chandigarh	changi	train	domestic	terminal
eurostar	luggage	terminal	book	mumbai	time
london	car	luggage	time	bangkok	luggage
ticket	bike	transit	allow	international	transit
frills	drive	changi_airport	eurostar	trivandrum	the_airport
paris	reliable	the_airport	london	jet	transit_hotel
global_guide	valid	immigration	connection	air	free
paddington	storage	transit_hotel	global_guide	arrival	changi_airport
option	enfield	shuttle	travel	direct	immigration

multi-word phrases and is the first topic model that precisely distinguishes collection-specific and collection-independent words. To compare our results to the state-of-the-art in cross-collection topic modeling, ccLDA, we evaluated document classification accuracy, topic coherence, and language model perplexity. We extended topic coherence measures from single-collection to cross-collection topic models and therefore allow to consider the alignment of word distributions in the evaluation.

Experiment results demonstrate the robustness of the proposed approach on a variety of text collections across different domains. Our model outperforms ccLDA on all three quality measures on four evaluated datasets of two and three collections. Furthermore, our model provides superior topic representations due to its clear-cut separation of collection-specific and collection-independent words. This separation is achieved by splitting the vocabulary into two sets of collection-specific and collection-independent words according to an entropy-based estimation of each word's termhood. Whereas words with similar frequency across all collections are considered collection-independent, words with significantly different frequency per collection are considered collection-specific.

Possible applications are bias detection in newspaper articles or the revelation of regional and cultural differences in traveler forum posts. Furthermore, topic-based search becomes possible in patents and scientific papers with collection-specific vocabulary and in multi-lingual document collections, such as Wikipedia. While collection-specific word distributions reveal linguistic contrasts, collection-independent word distributions bridge the gap between collections by generalizing from domain-specific language.

For future work, an interesting extension of our approach is to calculate word entropy not only per corpus but per topic. This extension considers words that are collection-specific in one topic and collection-independent in another topic. Furthermore, the number of collections in our evaluation is limited to two and three. Whether this number has a crucial effect needs to be studied in more detail and besides entropy, alternative measures of skewness could be tested. Another possible path is further clustering of collection-specific words per-topic. Opinion words are one example from related work that focuses on specific groups of words. A clustering of words according to their function, role, or semantic context in a text document would be even more interesting.

REFERENCES

[1] Rajkumar Arun, Venkatasubramaniyan Suresh, C Veni Madhavan, and M Narasimha Murthy. 2010. On finding the natural number of topics with latent dirichlet allocation: Some observations. In *Proc. of the Pacific-Asia Conf. on Advances in Knowledge Discovery and Data Mining (PAKDD).* Springer, 391–402.

[2] Yang Bao, Nigel Collier, and Anindya Datta. 2013. A partially supervised cross-collection topic model for cross-domain text classification. In *Proc. of the Int. Conf. on Information and Knowledge Management (CIKM).* ACM, 239–248.

[3] David M Blei, Andrew Y Ng, and Michael I Jordan. 2003. Latent dirichlet allocation. *Journal of Machine Learning Research* 3 (2003), 993–1022.

[4] Jing-Shin Chang. 2005. Domain specific word extraction from hierarchical Web documents: A first step toward building lexicon trees from Web corpora. In *Proc. of the SIGHAN Workshop on Chinese Language Processing.* ACL, 64–71.

[5] Changyou Chen, Wray Buntine, Nan Ding, Lexing Xie, and Lan Du. 2015. Differential topic models. In *Transactions on Pattern Analysis and Machine Intelligence.* IEEE, 230–242.

[6] Jacob Eisenstein, Amr Ahmed, and Eric P Xing. 2011. Sparse additive generative models of text. In *Proc. of the Int. Conf. on Machine Learning (ICML).* ACM, 1041–1048.

[7] Ahmed El-Kishky, Yanglei Song, Chi Wang, Clare R. Voss, and Jiawei Han. 2014. Scalable Topical Phrase Mining from Text Corpora. *Proc. of the VLDB Endowment* 8, 3 (Nov. 2014), 305–316.

[8] Yi Fang, Luo Si, Naveen Somasundaram, and Zhengtao Yu. 2012. Mining contrastive opinions on political texts using cross-perspective topic model. In *Proc. of the Int. Conf. on Web Search and Data Mining (WSDM).* ACM, 63–72.

[9] Denis Fedorenko, Nikita Astrakhantsev, and Denis Turdakov. 2013. Automatic recognition of domain-specific terms: an experimental evaluation., In Proc. of the Spring Researchers Colloquium on Databases and Information Systems. *SYR-CoDIS*, 15–23.

[10] Haidong Gao, Siliang Tang, Yin Zhang, Dapeng Jiang, Fei Wu, and Yueting Zhuang. 2012. Supervised cross-collection topic modeling. In *Proc. of the Int. Conf. on Multimedia (MM).* ACM, 957–960.

[11] Thomas L Griffiths and Mark Steyvers. 2004. Finding scientific topics. *Proc. of the National Academy of Sciences (PNAS)* 101, suppl 1 (2004), 5228–5235.

[12] Yulan He. 2016. Extracting Topical Phrases from Clinical Documents. In *Proc. of the Nat. Conf. on Artificial Intelligence (AAAI).* AAAI Press, 2957–2963.

[13] Thomas Hofmann. 1999. Probabilistic latent semantic indexing. In *Proc. of the Int. Conf. on Research and Development in Information Retrieval (SIGIR).* ACM, 50–57.

[14] Shoaib Jameel and Wai Lam. 2013. An Unsupervised Topic Segmentation Model Incorporating Word Order. In *Proc. of the Int. Conf. on Research and Development in Information Retrieval (SIGIR).* ACM, 203–212.

[15] Kyo Kageura and Bin Umino. 1996. Methods of automatic term recognition: A review. *Terminology* 3, 2 (1996), 259–289.

[16] Noriaki Kawamae. 2014. Supervised N-gram Topic Model. In *Proc. of the Int. Conf. on Web Search and Data Mining (WSDM).* ACM, 473–482.

[17] Chunyu Kit. 2002. Corpus tools for retrieving and deriving termhood evidence. In *Proc. of the East Asia Forum of Terminology.* 69–80.

[18] Ralf Krestel and Padhraic Smyth. 2013. Recommending patents based on latent topics. In *Proc. of the Conf. on Recommender Systems (RecSys).* ACM, 395–398.

[19] Jey Han Lau, Timothy Baldwin, and David Newman. 2013. On Collocations and Topic Models. *ACM Transactions on Speech and Language Processing (TSLP)* 10, 3 (July 2013), 10:1–10:14.

[20] Sujian Li, Jiwei Li, Tao Song, Wenjie Li, and Baobao Chang. 2013. A novel topic model for automatic term extraction. In *Proc. of the Int. Conf. on Research and Development in Information Retrieval (SIGIR).* ACM, 885–888.

[21] Robert V. Lindsey, William P. Headden, III, and Michael J. Stipicevic. 2012. A Phrase-discovering Topic Model Using Hierarchical Pitman-Yor Processes. In *Proc. of the Joint Conf. on Empirical Methods in Natural Language Processing and Computational Natural Language Learning (EMNLP-CoNLL).* ACL, 214–222.

[22] Jialu Liu, Jingbo Shang, Chi Wang, Xiang Ren, and Jiawei Han. 2015. Mining quality phrases from massive text corpora. In *Proc. of the Int. Conf. on Management of Data (SIGMOD).* ACM, 1729–1744.

[23] Michael Paul and Roxana Girju. 2009. Cross-cultural analysis of blogs and forums with mixed-collection topic models. In *Proc. of the Conf. on Empirical Methods in Natural Language Processing (EMNLP).* ACL, 1408–1417.

[24] Julian Risch and Ralf Krestel. 2017. What Should I Cite? Cross-Collection Reference Recommendation of Patents and Papers. In *Proc. of the Int. Conf. on Theory and Practice of Digital Libraries (TPDL).* Springer, 40–46.

[25] Michael Röder, Andreas Both, and Alexander Hinneburg. 2015. Exploring the space of topic coherence measures. In *Proc. of the Int. Conf. on Web Search and Data Mining (WSDM).* ACM, 399–408.

[26] Jingbo Shang, Jialu Liu, Meng Jiang, Xiang Ren, Clare R Voss, and Jiawei Han. 2018. Automated phrase mining from massive text corpora. *IEEE Transactions on Knowledge and Data Engineering* (2018).

[27] Jie Tang, Jing Zhang, Limin Yao, Juanzi Li, Li Zhang, and Zhong Su. 2008. Arnetminer: Extraction and mining of academic social networks. In *Proc. of the Int. Conf. on Knowledge Discovery and Data Mining (SIGKDD).* ACM, 990–998.

[28] Xuerui Wang, Andrew McCallum, and Xing Wei. 2007. Topical n-grams: Phrase and topic discovery, with an application to information retrieval. In *Proc. of the Int. Conf. on Data Mining (ICDM).* IEEE, 697–702.

[29] Andrew T Wilson and Peter A Chew. 2010. Term weighting schemes for latent dirichlet allocation. In *Proc. of the Conf. of the North American Chapter of the Association for Computational Linguistics (NAACL).* ACL, 465–473.

[30] Limin Yao, David Mimno, and Andrew McCallum. 2009. Efficient methods for topic model inference on streaming document collections. In *Proc. of the Int. Conf. on Knowledge Discovery and Data Mining (SIGKDD).* ACM, 937–946.

[31] ChengXiang Zhai, Atulya Velivelli, and Bei Yu. 2004. A cross-collection mixture model for comparative text mining. In *Proc. of the Int. Conf. on Knowledge Discovery and Data Mining (SIGKDD).* ACM, 743–748.

[32] Duo Zhang, Qiaozhu Mei, and ChengXiang Zhai. 2010. Cross-lingual latent topic extraction. In *Proc. of the Annual Meeting on Association for Computational Linguistics (ACL).* ACL, 1128–1137.

[33] Jingwei Zhang, Aaron Gerow, Jaan Altosaar, James Evans, and Richard Jean So. 2015. Fast, flexible models for discovering topic correlation across weakly-related collections. In *Proc. of the Conf. on Empirical Methods in Natural Language Processing (EMNLP).* ACL, 1554–1564.

[34] Liyi Zheng, Tian Nie, Ichiro Moriya, Yusuke Inoue, Takakazu Imada, Takehito Utsuro, Yasuhide Kawada, and Noriko Kando. 2014. Comparative topic analysis of japanese and chinese bloggers. In *Proc. of the Int. Conf. on Advanced Information Networking and Applications Workshops (WAINA).* IEEE, 664–669.

WELDA: Enhancing Topic Models by Incorporating Local Word Context

Stefan Bunk
Hasso Plattner Institute
Potsdam, Germany
stefan.bunk@student.hpi.uni-potsdam.de

Ralf Krestel
Hasso Plattner Institute
Potsdam, Germany
ralf.krestel@hpi.uni-potsdam.de

ABSTRACT

The distributional hypothesis states that similar words tend to have similar contexts in which they occur. Word embedding models exploit this hypothesis by learning word vectors based on the local context of words. Probabilistic topic models on the other hand utilize word co-occurrences across documents to identify topically related words. Due to their complementary nature, these models define different notions of word similarity, which, when combined, can produce better topical representations.

In this paper we propose WELDA, a new type of topic model, which combines word embeddings (WE) with latent Dirichlet allocation (LDA) to improve topic quality. We achieve this by estimating topic distributions in the word embedding space and exchanging selected topic words via Gibbs sampling from this space. We present an extensive evaluation showing that WELDA cuts runtime by at least 30% while outperforming other combined approaches with respect to topic coherence and for solving word intrusion tasks.

CCS CONCEPTS

• **Information systems → Document topic models; Document collection models**; • **Applied computing →** *Document analysis*;

KEYWORDS

topic models, word embeddings, document representations

ACM Reference format:
Stefan Bunk and Ralf Krestel. 2018. WELDA: Enhancing Topic Models by Incorporating Local Word Context. In *Proceedings of The 18th ACM/IEEE Joint Conference on Digital Libraries, Fort Worth, TX, USA, June 3–7, 2018 (JCDL '18),* 10 pages.
https://doi.org/10.1145/3197026.3197043

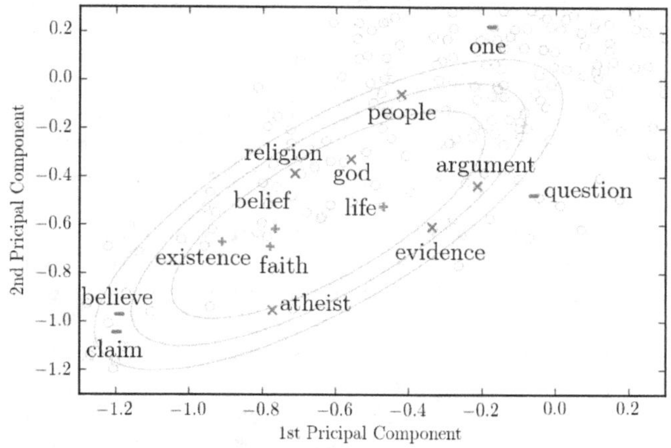

Figure 1: Illustration of an LDA topic in the word embedding space. The gray isolines show the learned probability distribution for the topic. Exchanging topic words having low probability in the embedding space (red minuses) with high probability words (green pluses), leads to a superior LDA topic.

1 INTRODUCTION

Many downstream NLP components benefit from a solid representation of documents and words, for example text categorization, part-of-speech tagging, or machine translation. One popular concept to quantify the meaning of a word is to look at the contexts in which it appears. A famous quote by Firth says: "You shall know a word by the company it keeps" [11]. In other words, if two words occur in similar contexts, they are similar. This assumption, also known as the distributional hypothesis, has driven the development of many models for text representation.

Two of these models are *word embeddings* and *topic models*. Topic modeling tries to reconstruct topics through a generative model from a collection of documents. Each document can then be represented by the topics it covers and each topic can be represented by a set of words. One of the first topic models was latent Dirichlet allocation (LDA) [7]. It models topics as probability distributions over words which makes the topics and the generative process easily interpretable by humans.

The idea of word embeddings is to assign each word in a vocabulary to a real vector in a high-dimensional vector space. This vector representation of the word is called the embedding of the word. Typically, this vector space contains 50 to 600 dimensions [18]. Although the idea is quite old [5, 24], the method has recently gained a lot of popularity in the research community [14, 15, 20]. Open-source tools such as word2vec [1] allow training on billions of words in a supervised manner. Word embeddings are a by-product, namely the internal learned weights of a neural network. Given a text, the neural network learns to predict for each word the sourrounding words. During training, a sliding window runs over the text and for

ACM ISBN 978-1-4503-5178-2/18/06...$15.00
https://doi.org/10.1145/3197026.3197043

[1]https://code.google.com/archive/p/word2vec/

each word the neural net adapts its weights to learn to predict its surrounding words. In this way, the context of a word is encoded in the learned weights of the network which then serve as vector representations for the input words.

Word embeddings and topic modeling have different origins. While the former have their roots in the neural network and deep learning community, the latter stems from Bayesian statistics which is why traditionally there is not much research combining the two methods. In this paper, we aim to explore potential synergies between these technologies. Combining the two methods seems promising due to several reasons:

(1) the two models capture different notions of similarity: the word-based embedding models focus on semantic similarity, e.g., "lecturer" and "teacher", while the document-based topic models capture relatedness, e.g., "teacher" and "school".
(2) word embedding models can more efficiently be trained on much larger corpora than standard topic models, such as LDA, thereby allowing more semantic information to be used during the topic model inference step.
(3) out-of-vocabulary (OOV) words are a problem for topic models where unseen words in new documents are typically ignored. Word embedding models do not face the same OOV problems since they are typically trained on billions of words from all domains and can incorporate new terms rather easily, while topic models are typically used to analyse domain-specific, clearly defined collections.
(4) word embeddings lack human interpretability which is where the probabilistic view of topic models can help and facilitate interpretation.

In particular, it might be useful to investigate Baroni's question whether the errors of each model type are complementary [3].

In general, there are two ways of combining these two methods: one can try to improve topic models or one can try to improve word embeddings. We focus on the former and illustrate in Figure 1 how word embeddings can help to improve topic models in our approach. The figure shows an area of a word embedding space projected two dimensions via principal component analysis (PCA). The words marked by black crosses and red minuses represent the top ten words of a topic learned by LDA. The gray dots in the background represent other words in the embedding space. When we plot the learned probability distribution for the words in the embedding space (gray isolines), we see that the words with the lowest probabilities are also the words that fit the least into the topic (the words "one", "question", "claim", and "believe"). The topic could be improved by picking words which are close in the embedding space to the existing words in the topic. In the figure, we illustrated this with the words "existence", "faith", "belief" and "life" which form a stronger topic with the rest of the words.

Further, our WELDA model can handle words that the topic model has not seen during training (OOV words). As shown by Hu et al. [12], being able to handle OOV words helps topic models significantly for tasks such as document classification. In WELDA, we can make use of the learned probability distribution for each topic in the embedding space to assign topics to unseen words in the following way: Let's assume we encounter a word previously unseen by our topic model. Instead of ignoring it — as is the default for standard topic modeling — we assign a topic probability based on the learned probability distributions in the embedding space.

2 COMPARING TOPIC MODELS AND WORD EMBEDDINGS

Topic models, as well as word embedding models, exploit the distributional hypothesis [11] which states that similar words tend to occur together. However, both models use this hypothesis to come to different conclusions. LDA works on the bag-of-words assumption, i.e., it treats a document as a whole and ignores the order of the words. When making a prediction for the next word, LDA makes a *global* prediction based on the topic distribution in the current document. Word embedding models, on the other hand, learn a word representation based only on a small, *local* context window around the word.

Both, LDA and word embeddings, can provide a vector representation for words. In LDA, this happens by taking the topic distribution for a word as the embedding in the topic space. However, this representation is not good at keeping linear relationships [19, 20]. Also, it tends to yield sparse vectors as LDA tries to keep the number of topics a word is associated with small.

The different nature of the models is also represented in the standard evaluation method for each. Word embeddings are typically evaluated using word similarity tasks or word analogy reasoning tasks. Topic models, on the contrary, are typically evaluated using topic coherence, i.e., how well the top words from the topics belong together and have a common, easily identifiable theme. When combining topic models and word embeddings, as we propose in this paper, the goal is to incorporate *a priori* semantic information about words into the topic model to increase the coherence of the topics. The assumption is that words which are close to each other in the embedding space should have a higher probability of occurring together in the same topic.

Baroni et al. [3] introduced a classification of count-based methods and prediction-based methods in distributional semantic models. Prediction-based methods try to set word vectors so that they are able to predict the context words. Count-based methods are based on counting the occurrence of words and co-occurrence with other words. Popular count-based methods typically use pointwise mutual information (PMI) and matrix transformation on the co-occurrence matrix. While word embeddings are clearly a prediction-based method, LDA constitutes a hybrid type in this classification. LDA is based on word counts and co-occurrences and treats words as discrete observations, however, the model parameters are chosen to maximize its predictive power.

Another aspect is the interpretability of the model. LDA forces the elements in a vector to sum up to one and all values must be non-negative. Thus, the embedding of a word in the topic space is easily interpretable by humans. With a word vector of [0 0 0.2 0.8] and given the meanings of a topic, a word can be interpreted, for example, as being used 20 % in *sports* and 80 % in *politics*. When working with word embeddings, a vector such as [-2.4 0.3 1.3 -0.1] is not interpretable. The arbitrary dimensions and values of a word embedding vector cannot be directly mapped to meaning by humans.

Regarding the performance, LDA operates much slower than word embeddings when the training set size is equal. LDA becomes expensive on large data sets, partially because the inference problem is NP-hard [25]. For training, the entire corpus and the topic assignments have to fit in main memory for standard implementations. In addition, when the number of documents is increased, the number of topics to represent the corpus usually needs to be increased as well which further slows down the inference. Word embeddings, on the other hand, have been successfully trained on corpora with about 100 billion words [18], thus showing that they scale to large data sets.

3 RELATED WORK

The recent popularity of word embeddings has led to a re-evaluation of topic models. There are two directions for research in this area. One type of models aim to improve word embeddings by incorporating ideas from topic modeling [9, 17, 21, 26]. The other type of models try to improve topic models by incorporating prior knowledge via word embeddings. Since we focus on the latter, we discuss related work in this area in more detail. Topic modeling for short documents, e.g. for classification, can be improved by preprocessing the short texts using word embeddings and then training a topic model on the resulting less sparse space [12]. We aim at a more general improvement of topics and therefore did a comparative evaluation with four recently proposed state-of-the-art topic models that incorporate word embeddings in one way or the other.

Gaussian LDA.. In this approach, a topic is no longer a distribution over words in the vocabulary, but a Gaussian distribution in the word embedding space [10]. Further, words are no longer atomic units but are represented by their corresponding pre-trained word embeddings. Each topic k is associated with a mean vector $\mu_k \in \mathbb{R}^M$ and a covariance matrix $\Sigma_k \in \mathbb{R}^{M*M}$, with M being the word embeddings dimensions. The prior distribution over the means is a normal distribution and the prior distribution over the covariances is an inverse Wishart distribution $\mathcal{W}^{-1}$, a distribution over symmetric positive-definite matrices. Even with some proposed performance improvements, inference in Gaussian LDA is slow and infeasible for high word embedding dimensions.

Latent Feature Topic Models (LFTM).. Nguyen et al. [22] use word embeddings to sample words not only from the multinomial topic distribution but also from the embedding space. Instead of directly sampling a word from the topic-word distribution of the chosen topic, they introduce a Bernoulli parameter $s \sim Ber(\lambda)$ to decide whether the word is sampled as usual from the topic-word distribution or from the latent feature vectors. When sampling in the embedding space, the authors need to define a distribution over all the words. This is achieved by introducing one topic vector τ_t for all topics. This topic vector lies in the same space as the word embeddings. Then, to sample in the embedding space, the model samples from a softmax-normalized multinomial word distribution. The optimization of the topic vector and the coupling between the two components make the inference difficult. As Li et al. [16] state, "the implementation is slow and infeasible when applied to a large corpus".

Nonparametric Spherical Topic Model (NSTM).. Batmanghelich et al. [4] build on top of Gaussian LDA, but argue that Gaussian distributions do not capture the distribution of words in the embedding space well. Instead, they propose the von Mises-Fisher distribution to model topics in the embedding space. The von Mises-Fisher distribution is a distribution on the hypersphere with a mean direction μ and a concentration parameter κ. The distribution is rotationally symmetric around μ. Intuitively, the von Mises-Fisher distribution is a good distribution choice because its distance function is based on cosine similarity. However, semantic relatedness between words is usually not measured by Euclidean distance in embedding models, but rather by cosine distance [19]. The length of the word vectors does not matter for the similarity. In contrast to the previous models, this model is not based on LDA but rather on hierarchical Dirichlet processes. These models allow the number of topics to be determined automatically. The authors propose an efficient parameter estimation algorithm based on stochastic variational inference. They use 50-dimensional word embeddings which they trained on Wikipedia.

Generative Topic Embedding (TopicVec). The main idea compared to LDA is to take the immediate context of a word into account and not only the bag-of-words information [16]. While LDA picks a word from one of the K multinomial topic distributions, TopicVec defines this distribution based on the context words, similar to the word2vec skip-gram architecture. For that, they encode a topic with a vector t_k in the embedding space. The authors provide a variational inference algorithm for TopicVec, which learns the topic assignments and the topic embeddings simultaneously. As the words are sampled from their context words, the architecture allows learning topics for a single document. No word collocation information over different documents is necessary. However, as no other method offers this possibility, we will evaluate TopicVec with one set of topics for all documents.

In this paper, we follow a different approach by building on top of LDA and using the information of the embedding space to resample individual topic words to incrementally improve the topics of the topic model. While other approaches suffer from long runtimes and handling large corpora, we show that combining topic models and word embeddings can be done in an efficient way.

4 WELDA – WORD EMBEDDING LATENT DIRICHLET ALLOCATION

The different definition of context in both models leads to different notions of word similarity: in topic models, words are similar if they have a high probability in the same topic; in word embedding models, words are similar if they are in the vicinity of each other in the embedding space.

4.1 Word Embeddings for Topic Modeling

We aim to combine the two methods to achieve better topic models. As word embeddings and LDA topic modeling are techniques from different backgrounds and with no inherent relationship to each other, we started with exploring how the results of one can be interpreted in the other model. To this end, we ran initial experiments on the Wikipedia corpus[2], on which we trained both a topic model and a skip-gram word embedding model with two hundred dimensions. We then evaluated the similarities between the words to understand the different strengths of both models. For embedding models, we used the cosine similarity between the two word vectors. For topic models, we built the topic distribution of a word by retrieving the word's probability in all topics in the topic-word matrix. We then normalized this probability to sum to one. To calculate the similarity between two words, we calculated the Jensen–Shannon divergence (JSD) and use $1 - JSD(P \parallel Q)$ as the similarity metric.

Even though both, word embeddings and topic models, exploit the distributional hypothesis, the correlation of word similarities is surprisingly low. We calculated the similarities of all word pairs created from the top ten words of an LDA topic model trained on Wikipedia. The similarities of word embeddings and the topic model only correlate with $R_{Pearson} = 0.30$. The results were similar when we used Hellinger distance or Bhattacharyya distance as the similarity measure for probability distributions in the topic model.

When looking at example pairs of high/low similarity in both models in Table 1[3], we see that topic models are able to detect more far-fetched, less obvious connections. This is a good property of topic models, however it sometimes makes the main theme hard to understand. Embedding models, on the other hand, assign high similarity to immediately obvious word pairs, often direct replacements or synonyms of each other.

We further evaluated both model types on a standard similarity benchmark, the WordSim-353 [1] data set. This data set contains 353 word pairs, whose similarity was assessed by thirteen to sixteen human annotators each. The subjects were asked to rate the pair from zero (totally unrelated words) to ten (very much related or identical words). The highest-rated pair was *midday – noon* (9.29) and the lowest-rated pair was *king – cabbage* (0.23). We calculated the correlation between the human ratings and the model's ratings for both the embedding and topic model using the above-mentioned similarity metrics. Embedding models excel at this task, matching the human ratings with $r_{Pearson} = 0.66$, while the topic model only achieves $r_{Pearson} = 0.49$.

To summarize, syntactic variations and more direct connectedness play a bigger role in word embedding models, while topic models often capture more loose relationships. Embedding models are good at assessing similarity between words. These observations make us believe that word embeddings can help create more coherent topic models. Our goal is to strengthen the topic themes by augmenting the top topic words with similar words from the word embedding space, but at the same time not disregarding the bag-of-words collocation information in the documents completely. In this way, we help the user understand the common theme in a topic better while still creating an overview over the entire corpus by looking at all topics.

Table 1: Examples for Different Notion of Word Similarity

		Word Embedding Similarity	
		High	Low
Topic Model Sim.	High	disease, diseases professor, lecturer poetry, prose	games, statistics war, commander rights, discriminated
	Low	catalan, galician prestige, respectability obscenity, sedition	*[completely unrelated words]*

Table 2: Notation

Symbol	Description
K	Number of topics
D	Number of documents
W_d	Number of words in document d
Θ_d	Topic distribution for document $d \sim Dirichlet(\alpha)$
Φ_k	Word distribution for topic $k \sim Dirichlet(\beta)$
Ω_k	Embedded topic distribution for topic $k \sim \mathcal{N}(\mu_k, \Sigma_k)$
$\Psi_{d,i}$	Coin toss $\sim Bernoulli(\lambda)$
$w_{d,i}$	Word in document d at position $i \sim Multinomial(\Phi_{z_{d,i}})$
$w^*_{d,i}$	Word in embedding space to replace $w_{d,i} \sim \mathcal{N}(\mu_k, \Sigma_k)$
$z_{d,i}$	Topic assignment for word $w_{d,i} \sim Multinomial(\Theta_d)$
	Hyperparameters
α, β	Dirichlet priors
λ	Resample probability
μ_k, Σ_k	Mean and variance for topic k in embedding space

4.2 Generative Model

Compared to standard LDA, WELDA incorporates knowledge from pre-computed word embeddings to estimate the final topic distributions. This ensures that words associated with a topic are also topically coherent in the embedding space. With the used notation, which is shown in Table 2, the generative view of the model is as follows:

(1) Choose number of topics K in the document collection
(2) Choose word distributions $\Phi_k \sim Dirichlet(\beta)$
(3) Fit normal distributions Ω_k to Φ_k for each topic k in the embedding space
(4) Now, for each document d:
  (a) Choose topic distribution $\Theta_d \sim Dirichlet(\alpha)$
  (b) For each position i in the document
    (i) Choose topic $z_{d,i} \sim Multinomial(\Theta_d)$
    (ii) Choose word $w \sim Multinomial(\Phi_{z_{d,i}})$
    (iii) Toss a coin $\Psi_{d,i} \sim Bernoulli(\lambda)$
    (iv) if $\Psi_{d,i} = 1$
      - Replace word w by word $w^* \sim \mathcal{N}(\mu_k, \Sigma_k)$

The crucial step is to replace words in the topic distributions by words that are topically more similar based on the learned probability distributions in the embedding space. This is achieved by the following process: in general, word embedding models are trained

[2]Complete English Wikipedia dump from June 21st, 2016
[3]High similarity indicates a similarity value in the upper quartile; low similarity in the lower quartile.

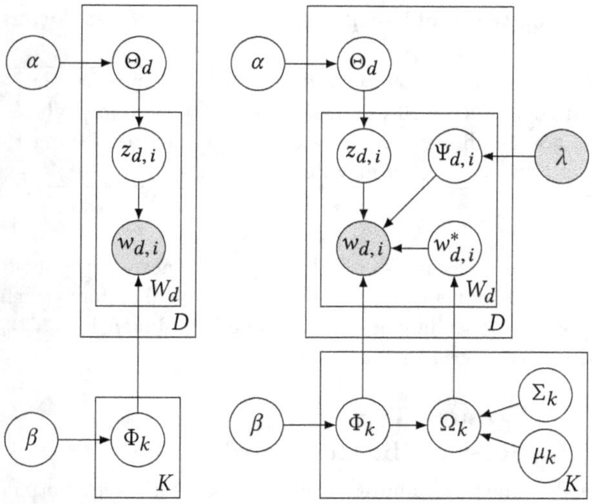

(a) LDA (b) WELDA

Figure 2: Plate notation for LDA and WELDA

on predicting words at an exact position. That means, if we look at similar words for a given word, the model predicts a word which could have been at the same position. We want to exploit this knowledge about similar words encoded in the word embedding space by transferring probability mass from general words in the topic model towards topically similar words from the embedding space. We achieve this by sampling new words from the embedding space. For this, we learn a multivariate continuous distribution in the embedding space for each topic. We use Gaussian distributions for that, but other distributions can be used as well.[4] We call each of these distributions Ω_k an *embedded topic distribution*. This embedded topic distribution is estimated from the top words of each topic Φ_k and their representation in the embedding space. While iterating over the document collection during training of the model, we selectively replace words $w_{d,i}$ in the documents with words $w^*_{d,i}$ from the embedded topic distribution. We achieve this by sampling a new word in the innermost loop of the Gibbs sampling algorithm and then proceed as if that newly sampled word appeared. These words have a high similarity in the embedding space to the top words in the topic and thus are excellent candidates to replace overly general words within the topic model. Before running Gibbs sampling, we load a pre-trained word embedding model, e.g. one learned on the English Wikipedia, but any other pre-trained embedding model would do[5].

4.3 Inference

We use the standard LDA sampling equation for our collapsed Gibbs sampler:

$$p(z_{d,i} = k | z_{-(d,i)}, \mathbf{w}) \propto \frac{\mathrm{n}^{(\mathrm{w_i})}_{-\mathrm{i,j}} + \beta}{\mathrm{n}^{(\cdot)}_{-\mathrm{i,j}} + \mathrm{W}\beta} \frac{\mathrm{n}^{(\mathrm{d_i})}_{-\mathrm{i,j}} + \alpha}{\mathrm{n}^{(\mathrm{d_i})}_{-\mathrm{i},\cdot} + \mathrm{K}\alpha} \tag{1}$$

[4]We also experimented with multivariate Gaussian mixture distributions and multivariate von Mises-Fisher distributions; see Section 5.2

[5]We also investigated the use of word embedding models trained on the topic model training data; see Section 5.3

where $\mathbf{w}$ are all words in the corpus, $n^{(w_i)}_{-i,j}$ is the number of times w_i has been assigned to topic j, and $n^{(d_i)}_{-i,j}$ is the number of times a word from document d_i has been assigned to topic j. After initializing our model by running the standard LDA algorithm until convergence to obtain stable topic assignments, we estimate Gaussian distributions in the embedding space based on the top N_{top} words of each topic. Then we run additional Gibbs sampling iterations using our collapsed Gibbs sampler but exchanging some of the words in the document based on a Bernoulli distribution. If this coin flip with success probability λ succeeds, we sample a vector from the word embedding space, based on the topic distribution of the new topic of the current word. A nearest neighbour search in the embedding space yields the nearest word w^*. Subsequently, we update the counts in the document-topic matrix and in the topic-word matrix, as if we had observed the sampled word w^* and not the word w that we actually observed in the document.

4.4 Out-of-Vocabulary Words

One of the big advantages of WELDA is its ability to cope with unseen words. In contrast to standard LDA, where words that were not observed during training are simply ignored, WELDA can handle unseen words and assign topic probabilities to them. During an inference step to assign topics to words of a new document, unseen words during training are assigned a membership probability for each topic according to the learned Gaussian distribution. Then a particular topic can be sampled for the new word using Gibbs sampling. Figure 3 (center and right) shows an example from the 20News corpus. We can identify two topics: "shipping&handling" (green) and "computers" (blue) together with their computed Gaussian distribution indicated by grey circles. If we now want to infer the topic distribution of a new document and observe a previously unseen word, e.g. "buy", we can locate this word in the embedding space and assign topic probabilities to this word. In our example, "buy" would get a higher probability in the blue "computer"-topic than in the green "shipping&handling"-topic and nearly no probability in the red topic.

4.5 Reducing Computational Complexity

In order to ensure fast learning of the model parameters we propose some simplifications. For example, we limit the number of topic words N_{top} that we consider for the estimation of the Gaussian distributions in the embedding space. This can be done without much harm, since the top 100 to 200 words of a topic are usually most indicative. Further, we use principal component analysis (PCA) to project the word vectors to a lower number of dimensions N_{pca} to speed-up the necessary nearest neighbour search. Finding the nearest neighbour becomes necessary after we obtained a sample from the embedded topic distribution and we want to find the closest word to our sample in the embedding space. The naive algorithm uses linear search and evaluates all words in the embedding space. This is expensive, especially because it happens in the innermost loop of Gibbs sampling and is therefore executed very often, approximately $\lambda \times N_{iter} \times N_{words}$ times, where N_{words} is the number of words in the entire training corpus, N_{iter} the number of Gibbs sampling iterations and λ the resampling probability. However, there are methods with a better runtime: we use either k-d trees

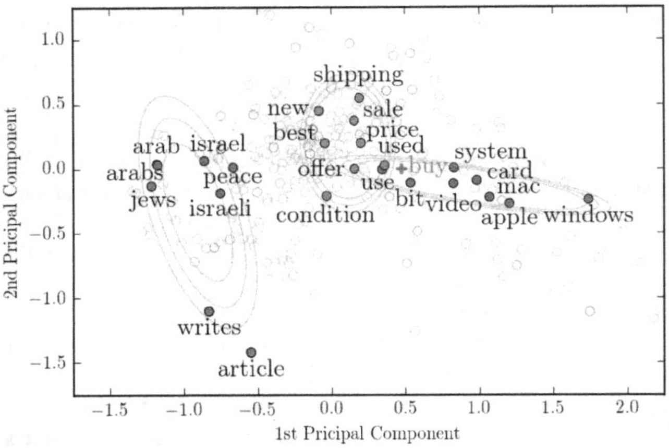

Figure 3: Illustration of three LDA topics in the word embedding space together with the grey isolines of the learned probability distributions. On the left you see two stop words assigned to the red topic. On the right you see two topics close together in the embedding space and a new word "buy", which was not in the training data.

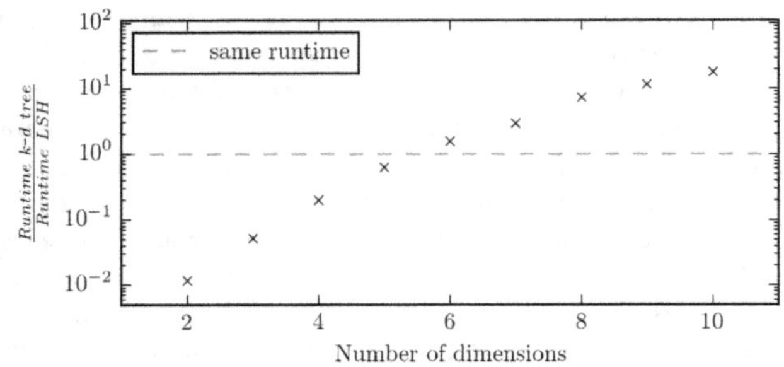

Figure 4: Performance comparison of LSH and k-d tree for the nearest neighbour word search based on the number of PCA-dimensions N_{pca}

or locality-sensitive hashing depending on the number of dimensions k of the embedding space. k-d trees by Bentley [6] arrange the points in a tree structure which allows retrieving the nearest neighbour in $O(\log k)$ on average. k-d trees are guaranteed to find the nearest neighbour. However, for high dimensions, the search degenerates to the linear search due to the curse of dimensionality. Thus we use locality-sensitive hashing (LSH) by Indyk et al. [13] for higher dimensions. LSH is an approximate method, i.e., it is not guaranteed that the nearest neighbour is found. LSH uses a hash-function based on random hyperplanes in the space to bucketize all vectors. Then, for a new vector, the same hash function is applied and only the bucket with the corresponding hash value must be checked. LSH has the opposite property, i.e., the lower the number of dimensions the longer it takes.

We therefore evaluated the runtime of the two approaches during a WELDA run. Figure 4 shows the ratio of the runtime of the k-d tree and LSH. Note the logarithmic y-axis, so the ratio actually increases almost exponentially. We see that up to five dimensions including the k-d tree is faster for looking up the nearest neighbour. For six or more dimensions, LSH is preferred. We therefore switch the algorithm depending on the number of pca-dimensions N_{pca} we use in our experiments.

Table 3: Top Words of Background Topic for 20News Corpus

would one writes like article think get know time people even good much well way make see really want apr right also going still say sure since first something back thing never take many better may things

4.6 Background Topic for Corpus-Specific Stop Words

To speed up the topic improvement process, we include a corpus-specific stop word topic to capture not only more general English-language stop words but also corpus-specific ones. We detect these stop words automatically during the initial LDA Gibbs sampling. Instead of using a symmetric Dirichlet α prior for all topics, we multiply the α_0 prior by a factor α_0^{boost}. By increasing the value of α_0 we force the first topic to appear in almost all documents. This forces LDA to put words in this topic, which occur in many documents and are rather generic. We call this first topic the *background topic* because it occurs in many documents as the generic word background for the more informative topics.

We experimented with different values of α_0^{boost}. Good results were obtained for $\alpha_0^{boost} = 15$ which led to the background topic occurring in more than 90% of all documents. Indeed, if we look at the top words from the background topic in Table 3, we find many corpus-specific stop words, such as "article" and "people".

In addition, the top-50 words in the background topic get a special treatment. Whenever one of these words occurs, we always resample the word, even if the coin toss in the WELDA algorithm failed. Note that we keep this list fixed during the WELDA iterations. The background topic changes quickly due to this approach and a robust topic emerges after a few iterations. Due to this adapted sampling technique, we differentiate between λ and λ_{act} in experiments. The former is the λ the algorithm was configured with. The latter represents the actual percentage of replacements when we also replace corpus-specific stop words. Therefore λ_{act} is always higher than λ.

This procedure helps replacing generic words from all topics, thus making the topics better. We hypothesize that WELDA has this property automatically, even without dedicated background topic replacement. This is because, by the nature of sampling, these words are more likely to be replaced as they occur more often in the documents. Also, these words are usually far away from the means of the embedded topic distributions. Thus, these words disappear from the topics during our modified Gibbs sampling. Figure 3 shows original LDA topics in the embedding space. The red topic on the left clearly contains two outliers: corpus-specific stop words ("writes" and "article"). In WELDA these words would get replaced eventually during sampling yielding more robust and stable topics. Using a dedicated background topic and always resample its words accelerates this process, since WELDA is not initialized with LDA

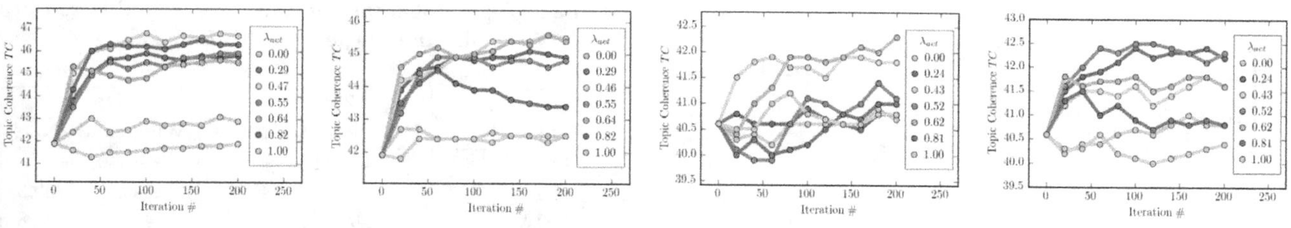

(a) With 20NEWS embeddings (b) With Wikipedia embeddings (c) With NIPS embeddings (d) With Wikipedia embeddings

Figure 5: Topic coherence for the first 200 iterations for the 20NEWS-corpus (left) and NIPS-corpus (right)

Table 4: Corpora Used for Evaluation

	20NEWS	NIPS
Documents	11,295	1,740
Words	1,395,973	2,497,017
Classes	20	*no classes*
Vocabulary Size	51,951	35,171
Words per Document	124	1,435

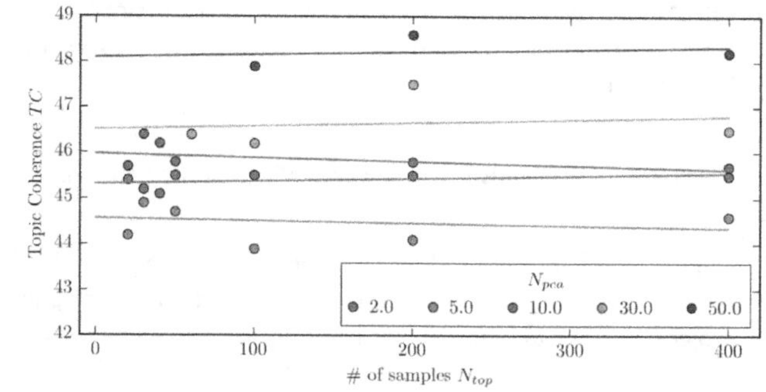

Figure 6: Influence of number of words to consider for distribution estimation N_{top} and number of dimensions for dimensionality reduction N_{pca} on topic coherence

topics that are cluttered with stop words. In Section 5.2 we show experimental results for the usage of a background topic.

5 EVALUATION

We evaluated and compared our model on two different datasets: 20NEWS and NIPS. While these datasets are rather small, most current approaches combining word embeddings and topic models have already problems processing them. To test and compare the various models, we used two different tasks: *topic coherence* and *word intrusion.*

5.1 Datasets

Some statistics of the 20NEWS[6] and NIPS[7] datasets are listed in Table 4. 20NEWS is a collection of newsgroup posts from the early 1990s. The data was downloaded from twenty different newsgroups and the name of the newsgroup is taken as the class label. The NIPS corpus is a collection of scientific papers from the proceedings of the Neural Information Processing Systems conference. The papers focus on neural computation, learning theory, algorithms and architectures, cognitive science, information theory, neuroscience, vision, speech, control and diverse applications.

We chose these two data sets because they represent two different type of corpora. The 20NEWS corpus is a general corpus with a wide range of topics. The NIPS corpus has a narrow focus with many technical terms and a lot of topical overlap. We preprocessed the corpora conducting tokenization, lowercasing, and stop word removal using a list of 150 general words from Python's nltk.

5.2 Parameter Settings

There are several configurable parameters in the algorithm that we will detail in the following.

Choice of embedded topic distribution: We tested different distributions: the performance of the *multivariate Gaussian distribution* and the *multivariate von Mises-Fisher distribution* were similar. The *Gaussian mixture model* performed well only if the initial number of topics was chosen too small, i.e. the topics generated by the original topic model were mixtures of multiple topics. With a sufficient number of topics, using mixtures of Gaussians was not necessary. In principle, WELDA can be used with any kind of multivariate distribution. Since using multivariate Gaussians allows faster training of the model with equal or exceeding quality of resulting topics, we only report results using Gaussians here.

Resampling probability $\boldsymbol{\lambda}$*:* The parameter λ decides, how often a word is resampled from the topic distributions. Thus, the parameter λ governs how much extra information from the word embeddings is leaked into the topic model. Running WELDA with $\lambda = 0.0$ corresponds to standard, unmodified LDA and will not have any effect on the model because we already start with a converged topic model. With $\lambda = 1.0$, no single word is taken from the documents, rather all words are sampled from the embedding space. Experiments showed that less then 100 iterations were necessary for the model to converge. Figure 5 displays topic coherence for the two datasets with embeddings trained on different corpora. Best topic coherence scores where achieved for $0.4 \leq \lambda \leq 0.6$. Currently we do not optimize this hyperparamter.

Number of top words for distribution estimation N_{top}*:* We are using the top words of each topic to estimate the embedded topic

[6]http://qwone.com/~jason/20Newsgroups/
[7]http://cs.nyu.edu/~roweis/data.html

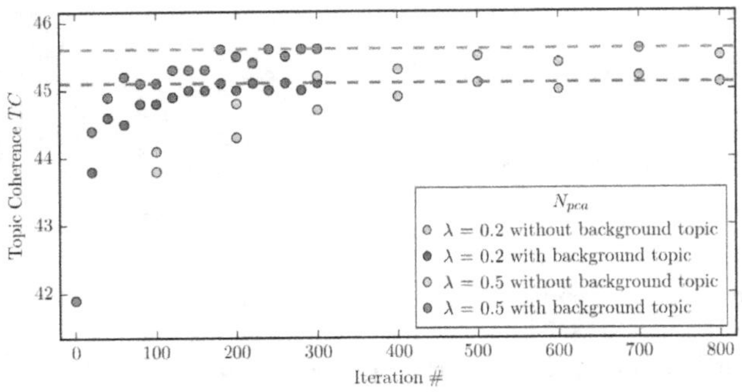

Figure 7: Comparison of WELDA with and without background topic. Background topic resampling converges faster, but not better.

distributions. Usually only the first words of a topic share a common theme.

Number of dimensions for dimensionality reduction N_{pca}: Before estimating the multivariate distribution in the embedding space, we project the high-dimensional embedding space to a lower space. There is a trade-off between the N_{pca} parameter and the N_{top} parameter. The lower the final dimension number, the fewer words we need for estimating the distribution. Fewer words are better because in this case we can use the really good top words at the start of a topic, and not the less probable ones further down the list. On the other hand, by projecting the space to a lower dimension, we throw away semantic information in the embedding space and the similarity between words becomes less reliable. In general, we expect a higher dimensionality to perform better. Best topic coherence was achieved for $N_{pca} = 50$ and $N_{top} = 200$. Figure 6 shows the influence of N_{top} and N_{pca}. Note that the regression lines added to the plot indicate that N_{top} has nearly no influence on the topic coherence measure.

Background topic: We include a dedicated background topic to capture corpus-specific stop words. This has no influence on the topic quality but on the runtime until convergence. Figure 7 shows the convergence behavior on the 20NEWS corpus with Wikipedia embeddings. While WELDA converges with a dedicated background topic after 200 iterations, at least 500 iterations are needed without.

Standard LDA parameters: As in standard LDA, the Dirichlet hyperparameters must be chosen. We use the same parameters in WELDA that we also use for the initial LDA iterations ($\alpha = \beta = 0.02$). We run LDA for 1,500 iterations [22], to ensure that the log-likelihood converges.

5.3 Topic Coherence

Topic coherence is a standard measure to evaluate topic models and measures how well the top-words in a topic fit to each other. We use the C_V metric from Röder et al. [23] which had the highest correlation with human annotators ($r_{Pearson} = 0.731$) in their experiments. We fixed the number of top words to consider for evaluation to $N = 10$ which is a common choice in the literature [2, 23]. All experiments were run with $K = 50$ topics. We tested on the 20NEWS and on the NIPS corpus. We optimized the parameters for all models on both corpora. We run WELDA for 200 iterations with Gaussian distributions and $\lambda = 0.4$. An overview of the results can be seen in Table 5. Using word embeddings learned on Wikipedia yields better results than using embeddings learned on 20NEWS or NIPS. One explanation for that is the size of the corpora, with Wikipedia having millions of documents instead of thousands. Due to the nature of the topic coherence measure (which uses Wikipedia word co-occurrence) it is also no surprise that results for the 20NEWS corpus are better. The NIPS corpus is too domain-specific to be captured by many Wikipedia articles. For NSTM, the 20NEWS corpus was to large and no results could be obtained. On both corpora (using Wikipedia embeddings), WELDA outperforms the other approaches as well as vanilla LDA significantly.

Table 5: Topic Coherence on the 20NEWS and NIPS Corpus with Wikipedia and Corpus-Specific Embeddings

Corpus:	20NEWS		NIPS	
Embeddings:	Wikipedia	20NEWS	Wikipedia	NIPS
LDA	—— 41.9 ——		—— 40.6 ——	
Gauss. LDA	38.5	40.3	39.2	39.5
LFTM	43.9	45.6	41.6	42.8
NSTM	—	—	37.5	36.8
TopicVec	48.1	46.2	43.4	**43.6**
WELDA	**48.6**	**47.4**	**44.2**	42.9

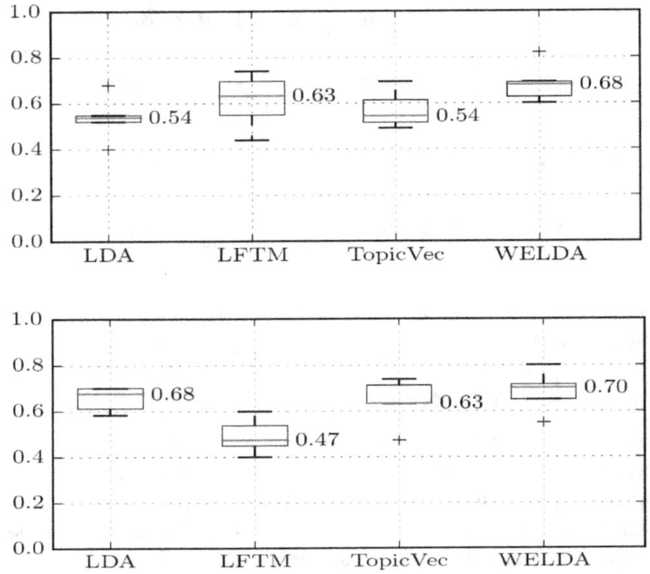

Figure 8: Word intrusion study results for model with 50 topics and 20 topics

5.4 Word Intrusion

So far we evaluated the quality of our topics using the topic coherence measure [23] to assess model quality. While the latter is cheap and many models can be evaluated, the correlation with human ratings is not perfect ($r_{Pearson} = 0.731$). Also, it is based on

Table 6: Topic Evolution from LDA to WELDA after 200 Iterations (Crossed-Out Words were Replaced by Bold Ones)

20NEWS
water power ~~use~~ air high ~~system~~ light ~~used heat time~~ **nuclear cooling temperature cycle plants**
year players baseball ~~article good writes~~ lopez ~~jewish~~ league average **hit braves season hitter**
information list mail ~~may~~ internet send anonymous ~~faq~~ email ~~use~~ **system available privacy**
israel israeli jews arab arabs ~~writes article~~ peace ~~would~~ lebanese **lebanon land israelis**
team hockey season nhl players games ~~league~~ game teams ~~year~~ **cup play**

NIPS
bayesian gaussian distribution prior posterior ~~data using~~ evidence ~~mean~~ sampling **monte carlos covariance**
kernel ~~algorithm~~ vector support loss margin ~~set~~ function ~~linear~~ examples **gerneralization svm problem**
speech recognition speaker gamma acoustic phoneme ~~time~~ vowel ~~information~~ speakers **generalization segmentation**
spike firing neurons time information neuron ~~rate~~ spikes stimulus ~~neural~~ **spiking trains**
state learning reinforcement policy action value optimal states actions ~~time~~ **reward**

co-occurrence statistics from the English Wikipedia under the assumption that this corpus contains a large number of topics and can therefore be used as a reference corpus. In the case of the 20NEWS corpus with its wide range of general topics, this assumption holds indeed. However, it is questionable for the NIPS corpus which covers a very technical, focused domain. For this reasons, we decided to conduct a manual study on the NIPS corpus in addition. We evaluated the quality of topics by the word intrusion task defined by Chang et al. [8]. In this task, a subject is presented a list of six words. Five of these six words belong to the top words of one topic of the topic model. The sixth word, called the *intruder*, was chosen randomly from another topic. The idea of this word intrusion study is the following: if the five words form a clear and coherent topic it should be simple to detect the intruder.

In our study, we picked the four best models based on topic coherence, i.e., LDA, LFTM, TopicVec and WELDA (Gaussian LDA and NSTM didn't make the cut). We tested two different scenarios: one with $K = 50$ topics and one with $K = 20$ topics. Our subject group consisted of computer science students and computer scientists familiar with the topics of the NIPS corpus. To avoid biased results, subjects were not presented with the information, whether their selection was correct [8]. Further, the underlying topic model was not displayed and we randomized the order of the samples.

We present the results for models with $K = 50$ topics and $K = 20$ topics in Figure 8. For the plots, we calculated the accuracy of each person on each topic model. Each model was evaluated by at least five persons (seven at most), resulting in at least five accuracy values. For both, $K = 20$ and $K = 50$, WELDA achieves the highest accuracy (around 70%), outperforming the other approaches and LDA significantly.

5.5 Topic Quality

Besides the quantitative evaluation results in the previous sections, we also want to report qualitative results to demonstrate the functioning of our model. Table 6 presents the top ten words of three random topics of the 20NEWS (top) and NIPS (bottom) corpora. The examples clearly show WELDA's capability to add specific, meaningful words among the top words, while at the same time downgrading overly general words.

Table 7: Runtime comparisson: 20NEWS+NIPS

Method	Runtime
Gaussian LDA	4283 min
LFTM, $\lambda = 0.6$	3753 min
NSTM	DNF
TopicVec	294 min
WELDA, $\lambda = 0.5$	206 min

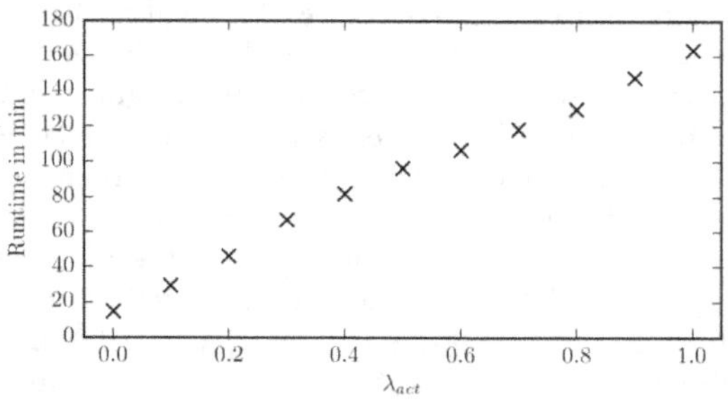

Figure 9: Runtime of WELDA on the 20NEWS corpus depending on the resampling Parameter λ with Wikipedia embeddings and $N_{pca} = 10$

5.6 Runtime

Our Experiments were conducted on a 32-core, Intel Xeon CPU E7-8837 @ 2.67GHz machine with 256 GB main memory. While some techniques have parallelized implementations available, others have not. Therefore, to ensure comparability, we ran all approaches with only a single core. We tested on 20NEWS with 200-dimensional embeddings (50-dimensional for Gaussian LDA) and on NIPS with 50-dimensional corpus-specific embeddings, both with $K = 50$ topics. We present the runtimes of the different approaches in Table 7. On both corpora, WELDA is the fastest, in total 30% faster than the second fastest approach (TopicVec) and an order of magnitude faster than Gaussian LDA and LFTM. LFTM and Gaussian LDA are very slow with 200-dimensional embeddings, making them infeasible to run on larger corpora, while NSTM did not finish at all since the 20News corpus was too large to process for NSTM.

Note that WELDA's performance largely depends on the resampling probability λ. The higher λ the more new words are sampled which leads to more nearest-neighbour searches which dominate the runtime (see Figure 9). Still, even with $\lambda = 1.0$ the runtime of WELDA on 20NEWS is with 164 min still faster than the next-fastest: TopicVec (178 min).

6 CONCLUSIONS

In this paper, we have shown that word embeddings can be used to improve topic models. We started from the distributional hypothesis and analyzed its different realization in topic models and in word embedding models. Based on this analysis, we proposed WELDA, a new type of topic model aiming to utilize the strengths of both model families. WELDA learns topic distributions for all topics in the word embedding space. These topic distributions capture and generalize the positions of the words in the embedding space. By learning an entire distribution and not only a single topic vector, we are also capturing the covariance of the word positions in the embedding space. We exchange document words by resampling words from this distribution during Gibbs sampling inference. We shift probability mass from general, low-informative words to specific, more salient words that strengthen the main theme of each topic.

Our evaluation showed improved results over state-of-the-art combined topic models on the task of detecting word intrusion and with respect to topic coherence. We could further confirm the assumption that higher dimensionality of the word embeddings leads to better performance, as more semantic regularities can be encoded in the embedding space. We experimented with using corpus-specific embeddings instead of pre-trained embeddings from Wikipedia which gave slightly worse results. Albeit lacking quality when evaluated on their own, the corpus-specific embeddings can still help to improve topic coherence, because they are learned on the same domain as the topic model. While other state-of-the-art combinations of word embeddings and topic modeling (except TopicVec) can only handle very small corpora in a reasonable amount of time, our approach is by far the fastest.

REFERENCES

[1] Eneko Agirre, Enrique Alfonseca, Keith Hall, Jana Kravalova, Marius Pas, and Aitor Soroa. 2009. A Study on Similarity and Relatedness Using Distributional and WordNet-based Approaches. In *Proceedings of the Conference of the North American Chapter of the ACL (NAACL)*. ACL, 19–27.

[2] Nikolaos Aletras and Mark Stevenson. 2013. Evaluating Topic Coherence Using Distributional Semantics. In *Proceedings of Conference on Computational Semantics (IWCS)*. ACL, 13–22.

[3] Marco Baroni, Georgiana Dinu, and German Kruszewski. 2014. Don't count, predict! A systematic comparison of context-counting vs. context-predicting semantic vectors. In *Proceedings of the Meeting of the Association for Computational Linguistics (ACL)*. ACL, 238–247.

[4] Kayhan Batmanghelich, Ardavan Saeedi, Karthik Narasimhan, and Sam Gershman. 2016. Nonparametric Spherical Topic Modeling with Word Embeddings. In *Proceedings of the Meeting of the Association for Computational Linguistics (ACL)*. ACL.

[5] Yoshua Bengio, Réjean Ducharme, Pascal Vincent, and Christian Janvin. 2003. A Neural Probabilistic Language Model. *The Journal of Machine Learning Research* 3 (2003), 1137–1155.

[6] Jon Louis Bentley. 1975. Multidimensional Binary Search Trees Used for Associative Searching. *Commun. ACM* 18, 9 (1975), 509–517.

[7] David M. Blei, Andrew Y. Ng, and Michael I. Jordan. 2003. Latent Dirichlet Allocation. *The Journal of Machine Learning Research* 3 (2003), 993–1022.

[8] Jonathan Chang, Sean Gerrish, Chong Wang, J. L. Boyd-graber, and David M Blei. 2009. Reading Tea Leaves: How Humans Interpret Topic Models. In *Advances in Neural Information Processing Systems (NIPS)*. Curran Associates, Inc., 288–296.

[9] Jianpeng Cheng, Zhongyuan Wang, Ji-Rong Wen, Jun Yan, and Zheng Chen. 2015. Contextual Text Understanding in Distributional Semantic Space. In *Proceedings of the Conference on Information and Knowledge Management (CIKM)*. ACM, 133–142.

[10] Rajarshi Das, Manzil Zaheer, and Chris Dyer. 2015. Gaussian LDA for Topic Models with Word Embeddings. In *Proceedings of the Meeting of the Association for Computational Linguistics (ACL)*. ACL, 795–804.

[11] John Rupert Firth. 1957. *Papers in linguistics, 1934-1951*. Oxford University Press.

[12] Weihua Hu and Jun'ichi Tsujii. 2016. A Latent Concept Topic Model for Robust Topic Inference Using Word Embeddings. In *Proceedings of the Meeting of the Association for Computational Linguistics (ACL)*. ACL, 380–386.

[13] Piotr Indyk and Rajeev Motwani. 1998. Approximate Nearest Neighbors : Towards Removing the Curse of Dimensionality. In *Proceedings of the Symposium on Theory of Computing (STOC)*. ACM, 604–613.

[14] Omer Levy and Yoav Goldberg. 2014. Dependency-Based Word Embeddings. In *Proceedings of the Meeting of the Association for Computational Linguistics (ACL)*. ACL, 302–308.

[15] Omer Levy and Yoav Goldberg. 2014. Linguistic regularities in sparse and explicit word representations. In *Proceedings of the Conference on Natural Language Learning (CoNLL)*. ACL, 171–180.

[16] Shaohua Li, Tat-Seng Chua, Jun Zhu, and Chunyan Miao. 2016. Generative Topic Embedding: a Continuous Representation of Documents. In *Proceedings of the Meeting of the Association for Computational Linguistics (ACL)*. ACL, 666–675.

[17] Yang Liu, Zhiyuan Liu, Tat-Seng Chua, and Maosong Sun. 2015. Topical Word Embeddings. In *Proceedings of the Conference on Artificial Intelligence (AAAI)*. AAAI Press, 2418–2424.

[18] Tomas Mikolov, Kai Chen, Greg Corrado, and Jeffrey Dean. 2013. Distributed Representations of Words and Phrases and their Compositionality. In *Advances in Neural Information Processing Systems (NIPS)*. Curran Associates, Inc., 3111–3119.

[19] Tomas Mikolov, Kai Chen, Greg Corrado, and Jeffrey Dean. 2013. Efficient estimation of word representations in vector space. *CoRR* abs/1301.3781 (2013).

[20] Tomas Mikolov, Wen-tau Yih, and Geoffrey Zweig. 2013. Linguistic regularities in continuous space word representations. In *Proceedings of the Conference of the North American Chapter of the Association for Computational Linguistics (NAACL)*, Vol. 13. ACL, 746–751.

[21] Christopher E. Moody. 2016. Mixing Dirichlet Topic Models and Word Embeddings to Make lda2vec. *CoRR* abs/1605.02019 (2016).

[22] Dat Quoc Nguyen, Richard Billingsley, Lan Du, and Mark Johnson. 2015. Improving topic models with latent feature word representations. *Transactions of the Association for Computational Linguistics (TACL)* 3 (2015), 299–313.

[23] Michael Röder, Andreas Both, and Alexander Hinneburg. 2015. Exploring the Space of Topic Coherence Measures. In *Proceedings of the Conference on Web Search and Data Mining (WSDM)*. ACM, 399–408.

[24] David E. Rumelhart, Geoffrey E. Hinton, and Ronald J. Williams. 1986. Learning representations by back-propagating errors. *Nature* 323 (Oct. 1986), 533–536.

[25] David Sontag and Daniel Roy. 2011. Complexity of Inference in Latent Dirichlet Allocation. In *Advances in Neural Information Processing Systems (NIPS)*. Curran Associates, Inc., 1008–1016.

[26] Fei Sun, Jiafeng Guo, Yanyan Lan, Jun Xu, and Xueqi Cheng. 2015. Learning Word Representations by Jointly Modeling Syntagmatic and Paradigmatic Relations. In *Proceedings of the Meeting of the Association for Computational Linguistics (ACL)*. ACL, 136–145.

AUGUR: Forecasting the Emergence of New Research Topics

Angelo A. Salatino
KMi, The Open University
Walton Hall, Milton Keynes, UK
angelo.salatino@open.ac.uk

Francesco Osborne
KMi, The Open University
Walton Hall, Milton Keynes, UK
francesco.osborne@open.ac.uk

Enrico Motta
KMi, The Open University
Walton Hall, Milton Keynes, UK
enrico.motta@open.ac.uk

ABSTRACT

Being able to rapidly recognise new research trends is strategic for many stakeholders, including universities, institutional funding bodies, academic publishers and companies. The literature presents several approaches to identifying the emergence of new research topics, which rely on the assumption that the topic is already exhibiting a certain degree of popularity and consistently referred to by a community of researchers. However, detecting the emergence of a new research area at an embryonic stage, i.e., before the topic has been consistently labelled by a community of researchers and associated with a number of publications, is still an open challenge. We address this issue by introducing *Augur*, a novel approach to the early detection of research topics. Augur analyses the diachronic relationships between research areas and is able to detect clusters of topics that exhibit dynamics correlated with the emergence of new research topics. Here we also present the *Advanced Clique Percolation Method* (ACPM), a new community detection algorithm developed specifically for supporting this task. *Augur* was evaluated on a gold standard of 1,408 debutant topics in the 2000-2011 interval and outperformed four alternative approaches in terms of both precision and recall.

ACM Reference Format:
Angelo A. Salatino, Francesco Osborne, and Enrico Motta. 2018. AUGUR: Forecasting the Emergence of New Research Topics. In JCDL '18: The 18th ACM/IEEE Joint Conference on Digital Libraries, June 3–7, 2018, Fort Worth, TX, USA, ACM, New York, NY, USA, Article 4, 10 pages. https://doi.org/10.1145/3197026.3197052

1 INTRODUCTION

The ability to promptly recognise the emergence of new research topics is an important asset for anybody involved in research, including academic publishers, researchers, institutional funding bodies and so on. Nowadays, we are experiencing a rapid growth of the number of research publications produced each year [1], and keeping up with new emerging trends is becoming progressively more challenging. In the last two decades, as very large repositories of scholarly data have become available, we have witnessed the emergence of several approaches capable of detecting novel topics and their trends [2-5]. However, these approaches are only able to detect the emergence of new topics that are already associated both with specific labels and a good number of publications. This is an important limitation since relevant stakeholders need to react as timely as possible to changes in the research landscape. For instance, academic publishers such as Springer Nature, who is funding this research, can take advantage of early intelligence to commission a pertinent book or journal. In this paper, we address this issue by introducing an innovative approach for forecasting the emergence of new research topics at a very early stage.

According to the literature, a research topic lifecycle traditionally consists of two main stages [6]. In the *initial stage*, a group of scientists agree on some basic tenets, define a conceptual framework, and begin to establish a new scientific community. Afterwards, a research area enters the *recognised phase*, one in which a substantial number of authors are active in it, producing and disseminating results. Current methods for identifying new research topics focus on these two phases.

In our recent study [7], we highlighted the existence of an *embryonic phase*, which predates the *initial stage*. In this phase, a topic has not yet been explicitly labelled and recognized by a research community, but it is already taking shape and affecting the research landscape, e.g., by fostering new collaborations between previously distant research communities. This is consistent with the well-known paradigm shift theory proposed by Kuhn [8], which states that research is pursued using a set of paradigms and when these paradigms cannot cope with certain problems, a paradigm shift can lead to the emergence of a new scientific discipline. In this phase, the relevant research communities usually start to build the foundations of the emerging new area by defining the associated challenges and paradigms, forming new collaborations, and producing seminal publications.

In our previous work [7], we showed that the emergence of new research topics is correlated with specific dynamics of already established topics, paving the way to the detection of topics at their embryonic stage. In particular, using a sample of three million papers, we compared the sections of the topic co-occurrence graphs, where new research areas are about to emerge, with a control group of subgraphs associated with established topics. The results provided evidence that the emergence of a novel research topic can be anticipated by a significant increase in the pace of collaboration between relevant research areas, which can be considered as the "ancestors" of the new topic.

In this paper, we present *Augur*, a novel approach that aims to effectively detect the emergence of new research areas by analysing topic networks and identifying clusters associated with an overall in-

JCDL '18, June 3–7, 2018, Fort Worth, TX, USA

ACM 978-1-4503-5178-2/18/06...$15.00
https://doi.org/10.1145/3197026.3197052

crease of the pace of collaboration between research areas[1]. *Augur* operates in three steps. First, it creates *evolutionary networks* describing the collaboration between research topics over time. Then it uses a novel clustering algorithm, the *Advanced Clique Percolation Method* (ACPM), to locate areas of the network that exhibit a significant increase in the pace of collaboration. Finally, it post-processes the results, merging and filtering the resulting clusters. The output of the process are clusters of existing topics (the *ancestors* of the new topic) that are nurturing a new research area that should shortly emerge. In addition, Augur also returns, for each cluster, a number of significant papers and authors, which can provide more details about the emerging research.

The main contributions of this paper are: 1) a new framework for the detection of research topics at their embryonic stage, 2) ACPM, a community detection algorithm developed for supporting this task, and 3) a gold standard composed by 1,408 debutant topics in the period 2000-2011.

The rest of the paper is organized as follows. In Section 2, we review the literature regarding the early detection of trends in research, pointing out the existing gaps. In Section 3, we describe Augur and in Section 4 we evaluate it versus four alternative approaches. Finally, in Section 5 we summarize the main conclusions and outline future directions of research.

2 LITERATURE REVIEW

Topic detection and tracking (TDT) has attracted considerable attention in the last two decades so that we can find it applied to different domains, such as social networks [9], blogs [10], and scientific literature [2, 11-16].

One of the main tasks for TDT is to analyse how topics develop in time, paying special attention to emerging topics and trends. In literature, we can find several approaches that aim to track the development of topics as well as their emergence. A classic method for identifying emerging topics, based on the identification of their rapid growth, is the burst detection algorithm of Kleinberg [17]. This approach observes the frequencies of each word and highlights the ones that occur with higher intensity over a limited period of time. However, this burst analysis is performed on every word (including stop words) and not for specific topics, therefore it must be included in a pipeline that selects relevant keywords.

Other approaches use custom metrics relying on the number of documents [12, 18] or authors [19] associated to the topic. Some other approaches perform more complex analyses, such as determining the citation patterns between documents [4, 20]. For instance, Jo, et al. [20] developed an approach that combines distributions of terms (i.e., n-grams) with the distribution of the citation graph related to publications containing that term. In particular, the authors assume that if a term is relevant for a topic, documents containing that term will have a stronger connection than randomly selected ones. Then, their algorithm identifies the set of terms having citation patterns that exhibit synergy. Similarly, He, et al. [4] combined the citation network with Latent Dirichlet Allocation (LDA) [21]. Generally, LDA is used to extract topics from a corpus, modelling topics as a multinomial distribution over words [21]. Within their study, He, et al. [4] detect topics in independent subsets of a corpus and leverage citations to connect topics in different time frames. However, these approaches suffer from time lag, as newly published papers might need some years before being cited.

Another category of approaches focus on the co-word analysis, which studies the co-occurrence of words within documents [22, 23]. Furukawa, et al. [22] proposed a method which analyses the development of conference networks to indicate the emergence of topics. In particular, using co-word analysis, they created progressive conference networks, in which nodes represent conferences and links represent their similarity in terms of keywords extracted from the papers. Then, as indicators for emerging topics, they observe conferences that are becoming similar and thus they are collapsing over each other. Di Caro, et al. [23] designed an approach for observing how topics evolve over time. After splitting the collection of documents according to different time windows, their approach selects two consecutive slices of the corpus, extracts topics using LDA and analyses how these topics change from one time window to the other. The main assumption is that by comparing the topics generated in two adjacent time windows, it is possible to observe how topics evolve as well as capture their birth and death. However, comparing two time windows implies that the new topics must appear in at least one of them, hence they have already emerged.

Another set of approaches fall into the category of overlay mapping techniques to build maps of science and enable users to assess emerging topics [24, 25]. Although these approaches provide a global perspective, the interpretation of those maps is based on visual inspection by human experts.

In brief, many approaches are capable of both tracking the development of topics over time and acknowledge their emergence. However, they focus on recognised topics, which are already associated with a good number of publications. Detecting research topics at an embryonic stage remains an open challenge.

3 AUGUR

We devote this section to presenting Augur, which is a novel approach for the effective detection of new emerging research trends. Its workflow is depicted in Figure 1, and it consists of three main stages:

i. **Creating the evolutionary networks**. Here we create semantic enhanced topic networks from publication metadata, and then convert them to evolutionary networks, which track the pace of collaboration between research topics over the last *n* years.
ii. **Clustering**. Here we detect cluster of topics that exhibit a significant increase in collaboration pace.
iii. **Post-Processing**. Here we filter and further enhance the returned clusters with information regarding influential authors and papers. This information is needed to help users to make sense of the results.

In the next sections, we will describe these stages in detail.

[1] We use the expression "collaboration between research areas" as a shortcut for "collaboration between research communities associated with specific research areas". The community of a research area is given by the authors who publish in the area in question.

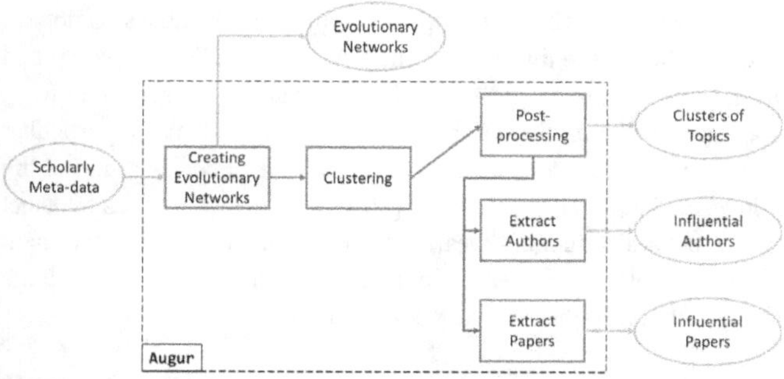

Figure 1: *Workflow of Augur. The rectangles represent the stages. The circles represent the input/output data.*

3.1 Evolutionary networks

In order to cluster the topics that exhibit an increase in collaboration pace, we first need to produce an evolutionary network for each year of the period under analysis. This is a network in which the nodes represent topics and the links represent the *pace of collaboration* (Eq. 4) of two topics in a previous time interval. In this paper, we will use a time interval of five years, since this solution was already tested successfully in Salatino, et al. [7]. Therefore, the evolutionary network of the year *t* will contain a snapshot of the interactions between topics in the year interval (*t-4, t*). For instance, an evolutionary network of the year 2000 will describe how the interaction between topics developed in the years between 1996 and 2000.

For generating the evolutionary networks, we first create a *semantic enhanced topic network* for each year of the time interval under consideration. Formally, each network is a fully weighted graph $G_{year} = (V_{year}, E_{year}, p_{year}, w_{year})$, in which V is the set of topics while E is the set of links representing the topic co-occurrences. The weight of a node in p represents the number of publications in which a topic appears in a year, while the link weights in w are equal to the number of publications in which two topics co-occur in the same year.

We generate the *semantic enhanced topic networks* by exploiting a dataset describing three million papers in the field of *Computer Science*, which have been classified using CSO[2], a large-scale ontology of research topics in Computer Science. CSO was originally created to model research topics in the Rexplore system [26], and is currently used by Springer Nature to classify proceedings in the field of *Computer Science* [27], such as the well-known LNCS series. CSO was automatically generated by applying the Klink-2 algorithm [28] to a corpus of 16 million scientific publications in the field of Computer Science.

We create the *semantic enhanced topic network* for a given year by selecting all the keywords from the publications in that year that also appear as concepts in CSO, and then aggregating keywords representing the same concept, i.e., keywords linked by a *relatedEquivalent* relationship in the ontology [28]. For instance, we aggregate keywords such as "semantic web", "semantic web technology" and "semantic web technologies" in a single semantic topic and we assign it to all publications associated with these keywords. The weight of nodes is the number of publications associated with the node keyword/s and the weight of a link is equivalent to the number of publications in which the keywords of the nodes co-occur.

In the current prototype of Augur, we have built fifteen topic networks representing topic co-occurrences in the 1995-2009 timeframe. We then produced an evolutionary network for each year in the 1999 to 2009 interval. The evolutionary network for a given year *t* is mathematically represented by the graph in Eq. 1.

$$G^{evol}_{year_t} = (V^{evol}_{year_t}, E^{evol}_{year_t}, p^{evol}_{year_t}, w^{evol}_{year_t}),\ p{:}V \rightarrow \mathbb{R}, w{:}E \rightarrow \mathbb{R} \tag{1}$$

The evolutionary graph $G^{evol}_{year_t}$ is a fully weighted graph composed by the set of vertices $V^{evol}_{year_t}$, the set of edges $E^{evol}_{year_t}$, the weights of the vertices $p^{evol}_{year_t}$ and the weights of the edges $w^{evol}_{year_t}$.

The function that maps the five semantic enhanced topic networks (*t-4, t*) to an evolutionary network is showed in Eq. 2.

$$\begin{aligned} G^{evol}_{year_t} &= f(G^{topic}_{year_t}, G^{topic}_{year_{t-1}}, G^{topic}_{year_{t-2}}, G^{topic}_{year_{t-3}}, G^{topic}_{year_{t-4}}) \\ V^{evol}_{year_t} &= unique(V^{topic}_{year_t} \cup V^{topic}_{year_{t-1}} \cup V^{topic}_{year_{t-2}} \cup V^{topic}_{year_{t-3}} \cup V^{topic}_{year_{t-4}}) \\ E^{evol}_{year_t} &= unique(E^{topic}_{year_t} \cup E^{topic}_{year_{t-1}} \cup E^{topic}_{year_{t-2}} \cup E^{topic}_{year_{t-3}} \cup E^{topic}_{year_{t-4}}) \end{aligned} \tag{2}$$

The resulting evolutionary network is composed by the unique set of topics $V^{topic}_{year_t}$ and edges $E^{topic}_{year_t}$ from the five input networks. The weight of an edge is computed as the *pace of collaboration* (Eq. 4) between two nodes while the weight of a node is computed as its *pace of growth* (Eq. 5).

In Salatino, et al. [7], we defined the pace of collaboration as the rate at which the number of publications shared by two topics changes in time and we showed that the pace of collaboration in a portion of a network is strongly correlated with the emergence of a new research area. For each edge, we first compute the *strength of collaboration* of all links in a year *t*, according to Eq. 3, and then we compute the *pace of collaboration* in a sequence of years, as showed in Eq. 4. In particular, given a link connecting node *u* and node *v*, we compute the strength of their collaboration ($\hat{w}^{topic}_{u,v}$) by normalising the weight of their link ($w^{topic}_{u,v}$) against the number of publications of both nodes (p^{topic}_u and p^{topic}_v) and then computing the harmonic mean of these two values.

$$\hat{w}^{topic}_{u,v_{year}} = HarmonicMean\left(\frac{w^{topic}_{u,v_{year}}}{p^{topic}_{v_{year}}}, \frac{w^{topic}_{u,v_{year}}}{p^{topic}_{u_{year}}}\right) \tag{3}$$

Next, with Eq. 4, we calculate the pace of collaboration ($w^{evol}_{u,v_{year}}$) as the slope of the linear regression (computed with the least-squared method) that fits the five strengths of collaboration obtained from the same link in the five topics networks. In Eq. 4, $\overline{\hat{w}^{topic}_{u,v}}$ represents the mean value of the five weights, $\overline{year}$ is the mean value of all the years $\{year_{t-4}, year_{t-3}, \ldots, year_t\}$ the topic networks refer to, and $year_{t-i}$, is the instance value from that set. If two topics do not have any co-occurrence in a year their strength of collaboration $\hat{w}^{topic}_{u,v_{year-i}}$ is zero.

$$w^{evol}_{u,v_{year}} = \frac{\sum_{i=0}^{4}(year_{t-i} - \overline{year})(\hat{w}^{topic}_{u,v_{year-i}} - \overline{\hat{w}^{topic}_{u,v}})}{\sum_{i=0}^{4}(year_{t-i} - \overline{year})^2} \tag{4}$$

The node weights in $p^{evol}_{year_t}$ represent their *pace of growth* and are computed according to Eq. 5. In particular, the weight of a given *k-th*

[2] The Computer Science Ontology http://cso.kmi.open.ac.uk

vertex ($p_{k_{year}}^{evol}$) is the slope of the line that best fits the weights of the same *k-th* vertex in the different topic networks ($p_{k_{year-i}}^{topic}$). In particular, $p_{k_{year-i}}^{topic}$ is the number of publications the *k-th* topic received in $year_{t-i}$, and $\overline{p_k^{topic}}$ is the average value of publications the same node received in that period of five years. If a topic has zero publications in a year, the weight $p_{k_{year-i}}^{topic}$ is zero.

$$p_{k_{year}}^{evol} = \frac{\sum_{i=0}^{4}(year_{t-i} - \overline{year})(p_{k_{year-i}}^{topic} - \overline{p_k^{topic}})}{\sum_{i=0}^{4}(year_{t-i} - \overline{year})^2} \quad (5)$$

3.2 Advanced Clique Percolation Method

In this phase, Augur uses the Advanced Clique Percolation Method (ACPM) for detecting clusters of topics in the evolutionary networks, which exhibit an intense activity in terms of pace of collaboration, since this dynamic was shown to be linked with the eventual emergence of new topics. ACPM is an extension of the well-known Clique Percolation Method (CPM) [29] that we specifically developed to support the Augur framework. Indeed, CPM suffers from two main limitations when addressing this task. First, it does not consider the weight of edges. Secondly, since evolutionary networks tend to be very dense, it usually returns coarse-grained and large-scale communities composed by hundreds of topics. ACPM address these issues by using also the weights and by radically redefining the concept of community, with the aim of selecting fine-grained communities even in dense networks.

ACPM consists of four steps:

1. Detecting *k-cliques* within the network;
2. Measuring pace of collaboration per *k-cliques* and filtering noise;
3. Creating the k-clique adjacency graph;
4. Locating local maxima and extracting neighbourhoods.

Algorithm 1 reports the pseudocode of the ACPM. We will now report the steps of ACPM and highlight the differences with CPM.

Step 1: Detecting k-cliques within the network. Cliques and in general, k-cliques are complete sub-graphs of order *k* in which all the nodes are connected to each other. The algorithm explores the topology of the network and detects 3-cliques (therefore k=3). This step is similar to the standard CPM.

Step 2: Measuring pace of collaboration per k-cliques and filtering noise. CPM works on binary networks (i.e., undirected and without any weight). An arbitrary network can always be converted into a binary network, simply inducing the graph that contains only the links with weight higher than a threshold *w* [29]. Indeed, with CPM, the link weights can only be used to filter the links when producing the binary network upon which locating the 3-cliques. However, filtering the network with a static threshold is not the best solution. Indeed, a link having weight below *w*, can be still be used to detect 3-cliques with an intense activity of collaboration.
Therefore, inspired by Farkas, et al. [30], we filter at the clique level rather than at the link one. After detecting the k-cliques, we compute the intensity of each clique and then remove all k-cliques having an intensity below the threshold *I*. This intensity (see Eq. 6) is computed as the harmonic mean of the weights associated to its three links (w_{ab}, w_{bc}, w_{ca}), where *a*, *b*, and *c* are the nodes of the 3-clique. In particular, this value of intensity is equivalent to the pace of collaboration of the clique, analysed in our first study [7]. This strategy allows us to detect also k-cliques containing weak links (low weights) and include them in the percolation cluster, as long as they contain edges with large weights that help them to exceed the threshold *I*.

$$PaceOfCollaboration(clique) = \frac{3}{w_{ab}^{-1} + w_{bc}^{-1} + w_{ca}^{-1}} \quad (6)$$

Step 3: Creating the k-clique adjacency graph. ACPM creates the k-clique adjacency graph $G = (V, E, W)$. *V* is the set of vertices representing the identified 3-cliques from the original graph, *E* is the set of links connecting adjacent k-cliques that share *k-1* vertices, and *W* is the set containing the node weights, i.e., the intensities of each clique computed using Eq. 6.

Step 4: Locating local maxima and extracting neighbourhoods. In this final phase, the algorithm identifies the communities within the evolutionary network. Another important difference between the standard CPM and ACPM lays in this step. CPM defines communities as connected components of the *k-clique adjacency graph*. As a result, in the presence of very dense networks, as it is the case when processing evolutionary networks, it returns very coarse-grained communities. Palla, et al. [29] suggest to monitor how communities change by trying different values of link weights *w* and tuning the value *k* for the dimension of cliques. Such analysis produces a similar effect as changing the resolution in a microscope. Increasing the threshold *w* leads the communities to shrink and fall apart, as fewer cliques will be formed. Conversely, increasing the dimension of cliques, *k*, makes the communities smaller, more cohesive and more fragmented. However, changing the values of *w* and *k* is not a good solution in this case. First, as mentioned in step 2, choosing any static threshold for *w* is not feasible. Secondly, when increasing the value of *k* (from 3 to 4 and so on), communities become too granular, preventing smaller cliques from belonging to a community.

ACPM addresses this limitation by taking advantage of the weighted *k-clique adjacency graph* produced in Step 3. It identifies the local maxima of the *k-clique adjacency graph* and then selects as communities the surrounding portion of the network.

This consists of three main steps:

1. converting the clique graph into an overlap matrix M;
2. locating local maxima in the matrix M;
3. selecting their neighbourhoods which contain all the closely related topics that show an intense collaboration.

First, ACPM converts the clique graph into an overlap matrix *M*, according to Eq. 7.

$$m_{i,j} = \begin{cases} W_j & if\ (i,j) \in E \\ W_i & if\ i = j \\ 0 & if\ (i,j) \notin E \end{cases} \qquad with\ m_{i,j} \quad \mathbb{R}^{|V|\times|V|} \tag{7}$$

For each *i* and *j* clique M reports the pace of collaboration of the *j-th* clique (W_j), if a direct link between the *i-th* and *j-th* clique exists. Since a clique is always connected with itself, the main diagonal (where *j=i*) will report the pace of collaboration of the *i-th* clique (W_i). ACPM identifies which cliques are in a local maximum by checking if the maximum value in the corresponding row is on the main diagonal.

Then, ACPM extracts the neighbourhood of a local maximum, by selecting its *ego network*. The ego network is a network consisting of a central node (*ego*), the nodes it is directly connected to (*alters*), and the ties between them [31]. In the context of this work, an ego network consists of the induced subgraph containing a given local maximum clique and the cliques that are directly connected to it. The size of an ego network is given by its *order*. When the order is 1, the ego network includes the ego node plus its immediate neighbours. The ACPM extracts the ego network of order 2, meaning that it will contain the ego node, the immediate neighbours and the neighbours of neighbours, and all the links between these cliques. We found that using order 2 allows us to better select meaningful cliques that are not directly connected to the ego node. Finally, the ACPM converts the ego networks in clusters of topics.

3.3 Post-processing

The size of the community returned in the previous step span from 10 to 200, which is arguably a very large dimension for a community of topics that is fostering a new research topic. This is because the selection of ego networks of order 2, within very dense networks, can produce very large clusters, which may also contain some topics that do not necessarily exhibit a high pace of collaboration. In addition, since ACPM returns fuzzy communities, it may happen that two (or more) clusters share a large subset of their topics, because their mutual topics had the most active collaborations in both communities. ACPM addresses these issues by post-processing the clusters.

First, for each returned cluster, Augur ranks the links by their weights in descending order and selects the first 15, which potentially embody the most active collaborations between topics. It then prunes the clusters preserving only the topics connected by the selected links. Secondly, Augur removes redundant clusters by merging clusters that have Jaccard similarity above 0.7.

Making sense

As part of helping the user in making sense of the returned cluster of topics, Augur provides a set of influential authors and papers, relevant to cluster in question.

As influential authors, Augur identifies the authors that are actively publishing in as many topics of the identified cluster as possible. This analysis is performed in the five years prior to the detection of the cluster. Similarly, as influential papers, Augur returns the papers that have been published in the previous five years, which discuss as many of the identified topics as possible. For lack of space, we will not report here the full process for the extraction of authors and papers, which will be further addressed in future work.

In sum, Augur returns as output clusters of topics exhibiting an increase in the pace of collaboration that potentially will lead to the emergence of a new topic. In addition, for each cluster, it also returns a set of influential papers and authors that can help the user in making sense of the research dynamics in question.

Algorithm 1: *Advanced Clique Percolation Method.*

```
Input  : Evolutionary Network network, Threshold threshold
Output: Communities comms
cliques← FindCliques(network, k=3);
for i ← 1 to length(cliques) do
  | poc.cliques[i]← PaceOfCollaboration(cliques[i])
end for
cliques← cliques[which(poc.cliques > threshold)];
poc.cliques← poc.cliques[which(poc.cliques > threshold)];
m← matrix(length(cliques), init=0)      // overlap mat.  initialized
  with 0
adj.mat← matrix(length(cliques), init=0)          // adjacency matrix
for i ← 1 to length(cliques) do
  for j ← 1 to length(cliques) do
    if (i ≠ j) & (SharedNodes(cliques[i],cliques[j]) == 2) then
      adj.mat[i,j]← 1 ;                    /* adjacent cliques */
      m[i,j]← poc.cliques[j]               // according to Eq.  7
    else if j == i then
      m[i,j]← poc.cliques[i];
    end if
  end for
end for
clique.graph← GraphFromAdjacencyMatrix(adj.mat);
pos.max← MaxPosition(m, mod="rowwise") // find position of max
  vals
k← 1;
for i ← 1 to length(pos.max) do
  if pos.max[i] == i then
    local.maxima[k]← i;
    k← k+1;
  end if
end for
for i ← 1 to length(local.maxima) do
  | components[i] ← EgoNetwork(clique.graph, local.maxima, order = 2);
end for
comms← ConvertComponents(components);  /* converts components
  of cliques in components of topics:  communities */
return(comms);
```

4 EVALUATION AND DISCUSSION

In this section, we present an evaluation of *Augur* on the task of forecasting the emergence of new research topics. In particular, we evaluated Augur on a gold standard extracted from historical data and compared ACPM against four other algorithms: Fast Greedy (FG), Leading Eigenvector (LE), Fuzzy C-Means (FCM), and Clique Percolation Method (CPM).

To this end, we selected topic networks from the year 1995 to 2009. We then created 11 evolutionary networks taking in consideration a time interval of five years in the period 1999-2009. For instance, the evolutionary network for 1999 considers the topic networks in the years 1995-1999, while the evolutionary network of the year 2009 considers the networks in the years 2005-2009. We then processed the evolutionary networks using the five alternative algorithms and applied the post-processing described in Section 3.3.

While Fast Greedy, Leading Eigenvector, Clique Percolation Method and ACPM directly operate on networks, Fuzzy C-Means works on a feature space and needs to know a priori the number of clusters. Therefore, before evaluating FCM, we converted the evolutionary networks to adjacency matrices so that each instance (node) got as features the nodes to which it is connected. Then, we assessed the best number of clusters, using the *elbow method*. To this end, we ran several instances of FCM, in each year, iteratively increasing the number of clusters, and we observed the number of clusters in which the curve of the squared errors of prediction (SSE) starts to bend like an elbow. We found out that the optimal number of clusters for all years was 25, so we used this value for the evaluation.

The clusters resulting from an evolutionary network in a given year (e.g., 2001) were compared with a gold standard containing the ancestors of the topics that debuted in the two following years (e.g., 2002 and 2003). In the following sections, we will describe the gold standard (Section 4.1), the method for comparing the algorithm output with the gold standard (Section 4.2), the metrics adopted to assess the performance (Section 4.3), and the results of the evaluation (Section 4.4)

The data collected during the evaluation and the gold standard are available at `http://rexplore.kmi.open.ac.uk/JCDL2018/`.

4.1 Gold Standard

Very often an evaluation is carried out to compare the results of a given algorithm against a set of results determined a priori to be correct, also known as gold standard. In the context of this study, the gold standard is composed by the debutant topics that emerged from the 2000 to 2011 and a list of related topics that can be considered as their "ancestors". We consider also their related topics since all the approaches return a cluster of ancestors linked to the future emergence of a yet unlabelled topic.

In the following, we will discuss how we selected the debutant topics and the ancestors.

Generation of debutant topics.
From Rexplore dataset, with the support of CSO, we retrieved all the topics belonging to the *Computer Science* field, which emerged in the period 2000-2011.

The simplest way to find the debut of a topic is to consider the year in which the label of the topic was used for the first time as keyword in a paper. For example, according to the Rexplore corpus, the label of the topic *Cloud Computing*, made its first appearance in the year 2006. However, considering only the year in which its label firstly appeared as the year of debut can be risky. A topic label can in fact be mentioned in few papers with some meaning and then become popular years later with a completely different meaning. It is the case of "linked data", that initially was used in the context of databases to refer to pieces of data linked to each other before being adopted by the *Semantic Web* as a specific method for publishing data using the RDF format. This label misuse can create significant noise. To tackle this problem, we select as debut year of a topic the first year in which it reaches at least 5 publications. In this way, we can be more certain that a new label is already recognised by multiple authors.

Table 1 reports the number of debutant topics per year. Unfortunately, the number of debutant topics drastically decreases in the second part of the analysed period. This is probably due to missing data in our dataset. We still included the years after 2006 in the analysis for the sake of completeness, however this issue prevents us from trusting the results of the evaluation for years after 2006. As future work, we plan to analyse other scholarly datasets to provide a gold standard that will cover also more recent years.

Table 1: *Number of topics that emerged in the years between 2000 and 2011.*

Year	2000	2001	2002	2003	2004	2005
#topics	149	194	221	216	137	241
Year	**2006**	**2007**	**2008**	**2009**	**2010**	**2011**
#topics	134	60	27	12	12	5

Extraction of related topics or ancestors.
For each debutant topic in the year of analysis we select the set of its ancestors that contributed to its creation.

Our previous study [7] showed that simply selecting the most co-occurring topics as ancestors is too simplistic. Indeed, a high co-occurrence between two topics can be due to a variety of different reasons. Therefore, we consider as ancestors only the topics that most collaborate with the debutant topic during its initial stage, specifically in its first five years of activity. For each co-occurring topic, we calculate the intensity of collaboration, as showed in Eq. 8.

$$\begin{aligned} \vec{P}_{dt} &= (p_{year}, p_{year+1}, p_{year+2}, p_{year+3}, p_{year+4}) \\ \vec{C}_{dt,rt} &= (c_{year}, c_{year+1}, c_{year+2}, c_{year+3}, c_{year+4}) \\ IoC(\vec{P}_{dt}, \vec{C}_{dt,rt}) &= \sqrt{\sum_{k=0}^{4} (p_{year+k} - c_{year+k})^2} \end{aligned} \tag{8}$$

In detail, considering $\vec{P}_{dt}$ (paper vector of the debutant topic) the non-zero vector containing the amount of papers published about the debutant topic in the first five years of activity, and $\vec{C}_{dt,rt}$ (collaboration vector of the debutant topic and its related topic) the vector containing the amount of papers in which the two topics appear together in the same five years, the intensity of collaboration $IoC(\vec{P}_{dt}, \vec{C}_{dt,rt})$ between a debutant topic and a related topic can be computed as the Euclidean distance between these two vectors.

If the distance between the collaboration vector and the paper vector of the debutant topics is close to zero, it means that the debutant topic and the related topic had a very intense relationship in the first five years of life of the debutant topic and that the related topic had a major role in shaping the debutant topic.

Then, we rank the computed values in ascending order, and select the first 25 meaningful topics, considered as influential for the debutant topic. The resulting gold standard is composed by 1,408 topics in the 2000-2011 period associated with their 35,200 ancestors.

4.2 Matching clusters with debutant topics

We assess the matching between the result set of an approach and the ancestors in the gold standard by computing the Jaccard Index between the *i-th* cluster C_i and the ancestors of the *k-th* debutant topic D_k, as showed in Eq. 9. Because a topic can have more than one label (syntactic representation) referring to it, if the cluster C_i and the debutant topic D_k contain the same topic, but with different labels, the match will fail.

To tackle this problem, we employed CSO [28] to semantically enhance Eq. 9 by including all topics SA_i that have a *same-as* relationship in CSO with the topics appearing in the cluster.

In addition, we further enhanced both sets of communities and ancestors of debutant topics using the *skos:broaderGeneric* relationship between topics [28]. In CSO, this relationship is used when a topic is broader (super-area) than another one, e.g., "semantic web" is a super-area of "linked data". We analysed four different strategies: (1) $C\ vs.D$ in which there is no semantic enhancement for both C and D except for the use of topics that are *same-as* in C – this semantic enhancement is included in all strategies; (2) $(C \cup Sup)\ vs.D$, in which clusters are enhanced with their super-areas and compared with the debutant topics; (3) $C\ vs.(D \cup Sup)$ in which we enhanced the ancestors of debutant topics with their super-areas, and (4) $(C \cup Sup)\ vs.(D \cup Sup)$ where at the same time we enhanced both set of clusters and ancestors with their super-areas.

The similarity measure $J(C_i, D_k, SA_i, EC_i, ED_k)$, in Eq. 9, combines the amount of topics matched between clusters and ancestors of debutant topics, and the topics matched using the semantic enhancement.

The similarity between the clusters and the debutant topics falls in the range 0 to 1. If similarity is very near 0 the two sets share only few topics, while for values of 0.1 to 0.4 there is already a good number of matching topics. When the similarity is near 1, that the two sets are almost identical.

$$\begin{aligned} &C_i \rightarrow i\text{-}th Cluster \\ &D_k \rightarrow k\text{-}th\, Debutant\, topic \\ &SA_i \rightarrow same\text{-}as\ of\ i\text{-}th Cluster \\ &EC_i \rightarrow super\text{-}areas\ of\ i\text{-}th\ Cluster \\ &ED_k \rightarrow super\text{-}areas\ of\ k\text{-}th\ Debutant\, topic \end{aligned} \tag{9}$$

$$J(C_i, D_k, SA_i, EC_i, ED_k) = \frac{|(C_i \cup EC_i \cup SA_i) \cap (D_k \cup ED_k)|}{|C_i \cup EC_i \cup D_k \cup ED_k|}$$

We consider a positive match between a debutant topic and a cluster only when their similarity is above a threshold *t*. Since the similarity threshold *t* cannot be defined a priori, we computed precision and recall for each method in each year, for 250 similarity thresholds, from 0 to 1.

4.3 Metrics

We assessed the performance of the five algorithms by means of precision and recall. However, since a cluster can foster the emergence of more than one new topic and similarly two or more different clusters can share the same subset of ancestors that match the same debutant topic, there is not a *direct* relationship between clusters and debutant topics. Therefore, it is important to observe this relationship from different angles (matched clusters, and matched debutant topics) and focus on the following two specific questions:

1. How good is our system in identifying portions of topic networks (clusters) that will eventually lead to the emergence of new topics? (perspective of the cluster)
2. How good is our system in identifying debutant topics that have been matched with clusters? (perspective of the debutant topics)

These two questions shape the definition of the precision and recall metrics for this task. We then define **precision** as the fraction of clusters that were successfully matched with debutant topics, and **recall** as the fraction of topics that were successfully matched with the clusters, as respectively expressed by Eq. 10 and Eq. 11.

$$Precision = \frac{|\{retrieved\, clusters\} \ltimes \{debutant\, topics\}|}{|\{retrieved\, clusters\}|} \tag{10}$$

$$Recall = \frac{|\{retrieved\, clusters\} \rtimes \{debutant\, topics\}|}{|\{debutant\ topics\}|} \tag{11}$$

The symbol ⋉ is called *left semijoin* and its operation in Eq. 9 returns the set of the clusters for which there is a match with the debutant topics. Similarly, the sign ⋊ is called *right semijoin* and in Eq. 10, it returns the set of debutant topics that received a match from the clusters.

4.4 Results

We ran the five community detection algorithms within the Augur framework and evaluated them against the gold standard. In addition, we also ran the four different strategies described in Section 4.2.

In all cases, Augur with ACPM significantly outperforms the other approaches. In Table 2 and Table 3 we report the values of precision and recall derived by applying the four strategies on the results of the five clustering algorithms for the evolutionary networks of the years 1999 and 2000. We only show the results of the years 1999 and 2000, as the behaviour in the following years is similar. The fourth strategy, which enhances both topics in the clusters and ancestors with their super-areas, returns better values of recall and precision for all approaches, being able to identify matches that other strategies would miss. Therefore, we will adopt this strategy as default in the following analysis.

Table 2: *Values of Precision and Recall obtained using the four strategies and the five approaches in the year 1999 with a similarity threshold 0.1.*

	FG		LE		FCM		CPM		ACPM	
Strat.	Pr	Re	Pr	Re	Pr	Re	Pr	Re	Pr	Re
(1)	.12	.05	.00	.00	.00	.00	**.06**	**.01**	.68	.49
(2)	.15	.07	.00	.00	.00	.00	**.06**	**.01**	.81	.59
(3)	.19	.04	.00	.00	.00	.00	.03	.00	.69	.55
(4)	**.27**	**.11**	**.00**	**.00**	**.00**	**.00**	**.06**	**.01**	**.86**	**.76**

Table 3: *Values of Precision and Recall obtained using the four strategies and the five approaches in the year 2000 with a similarity threshold 0.1.*

	FG		LE		FCM		CPM		ACPM	
Strat.	Pr	Re	Pr	Re	Pr	Re	Pr	Re	Pr	Re
(1)	.10	.01	.00	.00	.00	.00	**.05**	**.00**	.62	.39
(2)	.17	.02	.00	.00	**.96**	**.01**	**.05**	**.00**	.76	.58
(3)	.14	.02	.00	.00	.00	.00	.00	.00	.62	.48
(4)	**.21**	**.07**	**.14**	**.02**	**.96**	**.01**	**.05**	**.00**	**.78**	**.70**

Table 4, Table 5 and Table 6 report the values of precision (Pr) and recall (Re) for the five algorithms, when the matches between clusters and debutant topics respectively have similarity equal or above 0.1, 0.15 and 0.2. As we can see, the ACPM outperforms the other four clustering algorithms both in precision and recall for all the similarity thresholds.

Table 4: *Values of Precision and Recall for the five approaches along time, at similarity value of 0.10. In bold the best results.*

	FG		LE		FCM		CPM		ACPM	
Years	Pr	Re	Pr	Re	Pr	Re	Pr	Re	**Pr**	**Re**
1999	.27	.11	.00	.00	.00	.00	.06	.01	**.86**	**.76**
2000	.21	.07	.14	.02	.96	.01	.05	.00	**.78**	**.70**
2001	.13	.04	.11	.01	.00	.00	.17	.00	**.77**	**.72**
2002	.14	.04	.11	.01	.00	.00	.29	.01	**.82**	**.80**
2003	.09	.02	.20	.02	.00	.00	.08	.02	**.83**	**.79**
2004	.11	.05	.06	.00	.00	.00	.00	.00	**.84**	**.68**
2005	.07	.11	.06	.01	.00	.00	.00	.00	**.71**	**.66**
2006	.01	.01	.07	.01	.00	.00	.00	.00	**.43**	**.51**
2007	.01	.08	.00	.00	.00	.00	.00	.00	**.28**	**.44**
2008	.01	.04	.00	.00	.00	.00	.00	.00	**.15**	**.33**
2009	.00	.00	.00	.00	.00	.00	.00	.00	**.09**	**.76**

Table 5: *Values of Precision and Recall for the five approaches along time, at similarity value of 0.15. In bold the best results.*

	FG		LE		FCM		CPM		ACPM	
Years	Pr	Re	Pr	Re	Pr	Re	Pr	Re	**Pr**	**Re**
1999	.12	.06	.00	.00	.00	.00	.03	.00	**.81**	**.65**
2000	.14	.02	.00	.00	.96	.01	.00	.00	**.75**	**.55**
2001	.04	.00	.00	.00	.00	.00	.17	.00	**.73**	**.63**
2002	.07	.01	.00	.00	.00	.00	.29	.01	**.81**	**.70**
2003	.07	.01	.20	.01	.00	.00	.08	.02	**.80**	**.73**
2004	.07	.03	.06	.00	.00	.00	.00	.00	**.74**	**.58**
2005	.05	.04	.00	.00	.00	.00	.00	.00	**.68**	**.59**
2006	.00	.00	.00	.00	.00	.00	.00	.00	**.35**	**.38**
2007	.00	.00	.00	.00	.00	.00	.00	.00	**.24**	**.36**
2008	.00	.00	.00	.00	.00	.00	.00	.00	**.14**	**.25**
2009	.00	.00	.00	.00	.00	.00	.00	.00	**.07**	**.59**

Table 6: *Values of Precision and Recall for the five approaches along time, at similarity value of 0.2. In bold the best results.*

	FG		LE		FCM		CPM		ACPM	
Years	Pr	Re	Pr	Re	Pr	Re	Pr	Re	**Pr**	**Re**
1999	.08	.03	.00	.00	.00	.00	.03	.00	**.64**	**.41**
2000	.03	.00	.00	.00	.00	.00	.00	.00	**.57**	**.33**
2001	.04	.00	.00	.00	.00	.00	.17	.00	**.63**	**.44**
2002	.04	.00	.00	.00	.00	.00	.07	.01	**.70**	**.50**
2003	.02	.00	.20	.01	.00	.00	.08	.02	**.70**	**.51**
2004	.04	.02	.06	.00	.00	.00	.00	.00	**.66**	**.42**
2005	.04	.02	.00	.00	.00	.00	.00	.00	**.56**	**.43**
2006	.00	.00	.00	.00	.00	.00	.00	.00	**.30**	**.28**
2007	.00	.00	.00	.00	.00	.00	.00	.00	**.15**	**.28**
2008	.00	.00	.00	.00	.00	.00	.00	.00	**.12**	**.17**
2009	.00	.00	.00	.00	.00	.00	.00	.00	**.03**	**.24**

An analysis on the clusters revealed that Leading Eigenvector, Fuzzy C-Means, and Clique Percolation Method, returned for all years a very large cluster (above 1000 topics) and several other smaller ones (on average around 6-7 topics). The Fast Greedy method yielded few large clusters per year (with at least 300 topics) and many small ones. This confirms the difficulty of standard approaches in handling evolutionary networks, which tend to be very dense since they represent every interaction that occurred during a 5 years period. Indeed, the Fast Greedy and Leading Eigenvector algorithms try to optimise a quality function called *modularity.* During this phase, they force small communities into larger ones, offering a misleading characterisation of the underlying community structure and returning very coarse-grained clusters. Fuzzy C-Means and CPM similarly fail to correctly identify coherent clusters. As an example, Table 7 shows some statistics of the evolutionary network in the year 2000, suggesting the dense structure of the network.

Table 7: *Statistics for the evolutionary network (EN) of year 2000.*

Network parameter	EN-2000	Network parameter	EN-2000
Nodes	2263	Max degree	184
Edges	13327	Diameter	20.67
Average degree	11.77	Average clustering coefficient	0.163

Figure 2 compares the dimension of the clusters generated by CMP (left) and ACMP (right) from the evolutionary network produced in the 1996-2000 interval. In this example, CPM identifies a very large cluster containing 1,124 topics and 10,939 connections and other 53 smaller clusters. Conversely, ACPM is able to better handle the density of the evolutionary networks and detects 103 clusters of comparable dimensions. The clusters produced in the other years exhibit the same trend.

Figure 3 and Figure 4 shows precision and recall obtained respectively by ACPM and Fast Greedy (which obtained the second best results) for varying values of similarity. Each coloured line represents the values of precision and recall in a particular year.

As highlighted by Table 4-6 and Figure 3-4 the values of precision and recall are much lower in most recent years. This happens for all algorithms and is due to the aforementioned fact that the number of debutant topics in the gold standard (see Table 1) significantly decrease in the last part of the analysed period, and thus many correct clusters are unable to find a match in the gold standard.

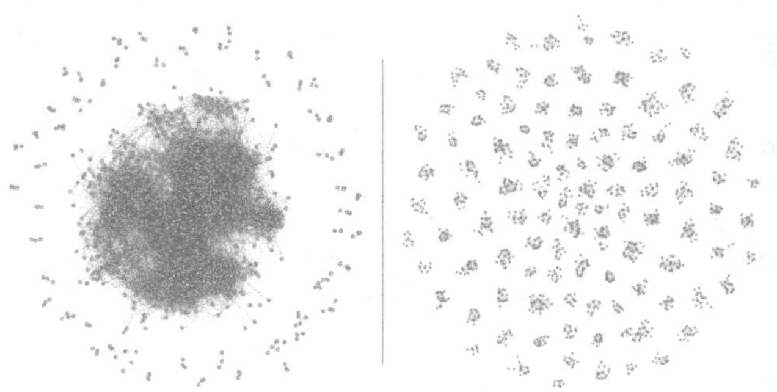

Figure 2: *On the left, we show the output of CPM in the year 2000 (54 clusters). The largest cluster counts 1,124 topics and 10,393 edges. On the right, the output of ACPM in the year 2000 (103 clusters).*

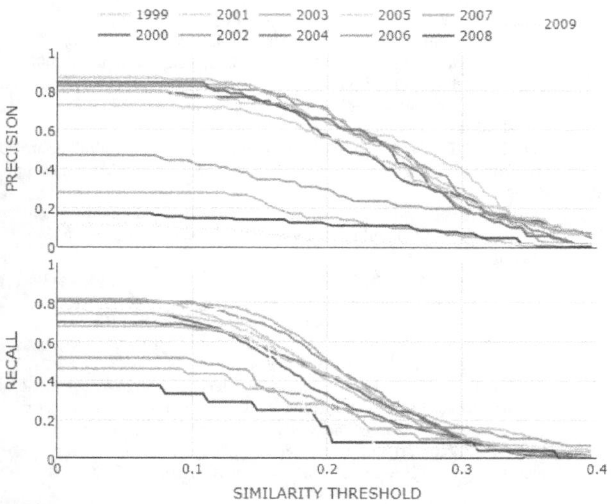

Figure 3: *Performance of the Advanced Clique Percolation Method.*

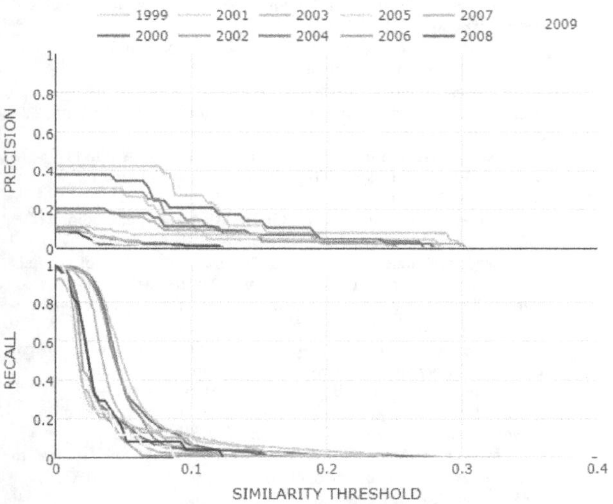

Figure 4: *Performance of Fast Greedy algorithm.*

Table 8 shows an example of a cluster produced by Augur from the topic networks in the period 1998-2002. The cluster (top-left) contains topics such as "world wide web", "query languages", "metadata", "content base retrieval", and "search engines" that exhibit a strong increment in their pace of collaboration in the period under analysis and match the ancestors of *Semantic Search*, a topic that debuted in 2003. Therefore, we considered this cluster as correctly predicting *Semantic Search* (with a similarity of 0.38). *Semantic Search* aims to improve search accuracy by understanding the contextual meaning of terms and combines research in semantic technologies and information retrieval. The topics in bold are the direct ancestors of semantic search, but, even among the other ones, we find many topics conducive to semantic search or that produced technologies adopted by this field, such as "text processing", "electronic commerce", "digital libraries", and "web browser". This is an exemplary case of the dynamics exploited by Augur, in which some topics, previously less connected, started to collaborate and moulded a novel research area that inherited their domains (e.g., "information retrieval", "digital libraries"), formats (e.g., "xml"), software (e.g., "search engines"), and applications (e.g., "content-based retrieval"). As part of the making sense process, in Table 8 we also report the top 10 authors (top-right) and the top 5 papers (bottom) relevant to this cluster.

Table 8: *Example of output produced by Augur. Top-left, we show the cluster associated with the emergence of the semantic search topic (in bold the topics that match its ancestors). Top-right, the top 10 influential authors. At the bottom, the top 5 papers.*

Cluster	Influential Authors
world wide web, query languages, metadata, content-based retrieval, information retrieval, search engines, xml, information systems, information retrieval systems, multi agent systems, intelligent agents, servers, digital libraries, electronic commerce, text processing, information management, indexing, web browsers, classification	W. Bruce Croft, Dieter Fensel, Dan Suciu, William W. Cohen, Berthier Ribeiro-Neto, Clement T. Yu, James Allan, Justin Zobel, Dragomir R. Radev, Victor Vianu

Influential Papers

- A Sheth et al. "*Managing semantic content for the Web*" (2002)
- RWP Luk et al. "*A survey in indexing and searching XML documents*" (2002)
- J Kahan et al. "*Annotea: An open RDF infrastructure for shared Web annotations*" (2002)
- R Manmatha et al. "*Modeling score distributions for combining the outputs of search engines*" (2001)
- S Dagtas et al. "*Models for motion-based video indexing and retrieval*" (2000)

5 CONCLUSIONS

In this paper, we presented Augur, a new framework to detect research topics at the embryonic stage, i.e., when they have not yet been labelled or associated with a considerable number of publications. This approach takes advantage of the results of the study presented in Salatino, et al. [7], which showed a strong correlation between the pace of collaboration in a topic network and the emergence of new research topics, a few years later. Specifically, Augur uses the Advanced Clique Percolation Method (ACPM), a novel community detection algorithm, for analysing the dynamics between existent topics and returns clusters of topics associated with the future emergence of new research areas, which are then further characterised by providing a list of significant authors and publications.

We evaluated Augur and ACPM versus four alternative approaches on a gold standard of 1,408 debutant topics in the 2000-2011 timeframe. The results show that our approach outperforms state of the art solutions and is able to successfully identify clusters that will produce new topics in the two following years.

While these results are satisfactory, our analysis presents some limitations that we plan to address in future work. In the first instance, the gold standard does not cover well the years after 2007. We thus intend to consider more up-to-date scholarly datasets and to produce a more comprehensive version of the gold standard that could be adopted by the scholarly community to further study this task. In the second instance, the current version of Augur only focuses on the pace of collaboration between topics. This single indicator may not be enough to fully understand and detect the complex dynamics behind the creation of a topic. We thus plan to investigate other kinds of dynamics that could be associated with the emergence of new research areas, such as the patterns of collaboration between prominent authors, the dynamics of citations networks, or the change in the topic distributions of high-tier scientific venues. Finally, Augur has been tested only on the field of *Computer Science*. We believe that more work is needed to evaluate it on other disciplines.

Our aim is to produce a robust approach that can be used by researchers, policy makers, and academic editors to gain a better understanding of the dynamics of academic research and detect new research trends at the earliest possible stage.

ACKNOWLEDGMENTS

We would like to thank Springer Nature for partially funding this research and Elsevier B.V. for providing us with access to their large repositories of scholarly data.

REFERENCES

[1] P. O. Larsen and M. Von Ins, "The rate of growth in scientific publication and the decline in coverage provided by Science Citation Index," *Scientometrics*, vol. 84, pp. 575-603, 2010.

[2] L. Bolelli, Ş. Ertekin, and C. L. Giles, "Topic and trend detection in text collections using latent dirichlet allocation," in *Advances in Information Retrieval*, ed: Springer, 2009, pp. 776-780.

[3] A. Duvvuru, S. Kamarthi, and S. Sultornsanee, "Undercovering research trends: Network analysis of keywords in scholarly articles," *Computer Science and Software Engineering (JCSSE), 2012 International Joint Conference on*, pp. 265-270, 2012.

[4] Q. He, B. Chen, J. Pei, B. Qiu, P. Mitra, and L. Giles, "Detecting topic evolution in scientific literature: how can citations help?," *Proceedings of the 18th ACM conference on Information and knowledge management*, pp. 957-966, 2009 2009.

[5] Y. Wu, S. Venkatramanan, and D. M. Chiu, "Research collaboration and topic trends in Computer Science based on top active authors," *PeerJ Computer Science*, vol. 2, p. e41, 2016.

[6] T. Braun, A. P. Schubert, and R. N. Kostoff, "Growth and trends of fullerene research as reflected in its journal literature," *Chemical reviews*, vol. 100, pp. 23-38, 2000.

[7] A. A. Salatino, F. Osborne, and E. Motta, "How are topics born? Understanding the research dynamics preceding the emergence of new areas," *PeerJ Computer Science*, vol. 3, p. e119, 2017/06/19 2017.

[8] T. S. Kuhn, *The structure of scientific revolutions*: University of Chicago press, 2012.

[9] M. Cataldi, L. Di Caro, and C. Schifanella, "Emerging topic detection on twitter based on temporal and social terms evaluation," in *Proceedings of the Tenth International Workshop on Multimedia Data Mining*, 2010, p. 4.

[10] M. Oka, H. Abe, and K. Kato, "Extracting topics from weblogs through frequency segments," in *Proceedings of WWW 2006 Annual Workshop on the Weblogging Ecosystem: Aggregation, Analysis, and Dynamics*, 2006.

[11] Y.-H. Tseng, Y.-I. Lin, Y.-Y. Lee, W.-C. Hung, and C.-H. Lee, "A comparison of methods for detecting hot topics," *Scientometrics*, vol. 81, pp. 73-90, 2009.

[12] S. L. Decker, B. Aleman-Meza, D. Cameron, and I. B. Arpinar, "Detection of bursty and emerging trends towards identification of researchers at the early stage of trends," University of Georgia, 2007.

[13] C. Erten, P. J. Harding, S. G. Kobourov, K. Wampler, and G. Yee, "Exploring the computing literature using temporal graph visualization," *Electronic Imaging 2004*, pp. 45-56, 2004.

[14] P. H. Lv, G.-F. Wang, Y. Wan, J. Liu, Q. Liu, and F.-c. Ma, "Bibliometric trend analysis on global graphene research," *Scientometrics*, vol. 88, pp. 399-419, 2011.

[15] X. Sun, K. Ding, and Y. Lin, "Mapping the evolution of scientific fields based on cross-field authors," *Journal of Informetrics*, vol. 10, pp. 750-761, 2016.

[16] F. Osborne, G. Scavo, and E. Motta, "A hybrid semantic approach to building dynamic maps of research communities," in *Knowledge Engineering and Knowledge Management*, ed: Springer, 2014.

[17] J. Kleinberg, "Bursty and hierarchical structure in streams," *Data Mining and Knowledge Discovery*, vol. 7, pp. 373-397, 2003.

[18] J. C. Ho, E.-C. Saw, L. Y. Lu, and J. S. Liu, "Technological barriers and research trends in fuel cell technologies: A citation network analysis," *Technological Forecasting and Social Change*, vol. 82, pp. 66-79, 2014.

[19] H. Guo, S. Weingart, and K. Börner, "Mixed-indicators model for identifying emerging research areas," *Scientometrics*, vol. 89, pp. 421-435, 2011.

[20] Y. Jo, C. Lagoze, and C. L. Giles, "Detecting research topics via the correlation between graphs and texts," *Proceedings of the 13th ACM SIGKDD international conference on Knowledge discovery and data mining*, pp. 370-379, 2007.

[21] D. M. Blei, A. Y. Ng, and M. I. Jordan, "Latent dirichlet allocation," *J. Mach. Learn. Res.*, vol. 3, pp. 993-1022, 2003.

[22] T. Furukawa, K. Mori, K. Arino, K. Hayashi, and N. Shirakawa, "Identifying the evolutionary process of emerging technologies: A chronological network analysis of World Wide Web conference sessions," *Technological Forecasting and Social Change*, vol. 91, pp. 280-294, 2015.

[23] L. Di Caro, M. Guerzoni, M. Nuccio, and G. Siragusa, "A Bimodal Network Approach to Model Topic Dynamics," *arXiv preprint arXiv:1709.09373*, 2017.

[24] K. W. Boyack, R. Klavans, and K. Börner, "Mapping the backbone of science," *Scientometrics*, vol. 64, pp. 351-374, 2005.

[25] L. Leydesdorff, I. Rafols, and C. Chen, "Interactive overlays of journals and the measurement of interdisciplinarity on the basis of aggregated journal–journal citations," *Journal of the Association for Information Science and Technology*, vol. 64, pp. 2573-2586, 2013.

[26] F. Osborne and E. Motta, "Mining semantic relations between research areas," in *The Semantic Web–ISWC 2012*, ed: Springer, 2012.

[27] F. Osborne, A. Salatino, A. Birukou, and E. Motta, "Automatic classification of springer nature proceedings with smart topic miner," in *International Semantic Web Conference*, 2016, pp. 383-399.

[28] F. Osborne and E. Motta, "Klink-2: integrating multiple web sources to generate semantic topic networks," in *The Semantic Web–ISWC 2015*, ed: Springer, 2015, pp. 408-424.

[29] G. Palla, I. Derényi, I. Farkas, and T. Vicsek, "Uncovering the overlapping community structure of complex networks in nature and society," *Nature*, vol. 435, pp. 814-818, 2005.

[30] I. Farkas, D. Ábel, G. Palla, and T. Vicsek, "Weighted network modules," *New Journal of Physics*, vol. 9, p. 180, 2007.

[31] L. C. Freeman, "Centered graphs and the structure of ego networks," *Mathematical Social Sciences*, vol. 3, pp. 291-304, 1982.

At the Nexus of Data and Collections: New Affordances in the Age of Mass-Scale Digital Libraries

J. Stephen Downie
University of Illinois
Urbana, IL USA
jdownie@illinois.edu

Elizabeth Lorang
University of Nebraska
Lincoln NE, USA
liz.lorang@unl.edu

Leen-Kiat Soh
University of Nebraska
Lincoln, NE USA
lksoh@cse.unl.edu

David Bainbridge
University of Waikato
Hamilton, NZ
davidb@waikato.ac.nz

Sandra McIntyre
HathiTrust
Ann Arbor, MI USA
mcintsan@hathitrust.org

Kevin Page
University of Oxford
Oxford, UK
kevin.page@oerc.ox.ac.uk

ABSTRACT

Within the context of mass-scale digital libraries, this panel will explore methodologies and uses for—as well as the results of—conceiving of "data as collections" and "collections as data." The panel will explore the implications of these concepts through use cases involving data mining of the HathiTrust Digital Library, particularly major projects developed at the HathiTrust Research Center. Featured will be the Workset Creation for Scholarly Analysis + Data Capsules (WCSA+DC) project, the Solr Extracted Features project, and the Image Analysis for Archival Discovery (Aida) project. Each of these projects focuses on various aspects of text, image and data mining and analysis of mass-scale digital library collections.

CCS CONCEPTS

• **Information systems → Digital libraries and archives** • Information systems → Data Mining

KEYWORDS

data mining, digital libraries, data, collections, machine learning

ACM Reference format:

J.S. Downie, E. Lorang, L.-K. Soh, D. Bainbridge, S. McIntyre, K. Page. 2018. At the Nexus of Data and Collections: New Affordances in the Age of Mass-Scale Digital Libraries. In Proceedings of the 18th ACM/IEEE-CS Joint Conference on Digital Libraries, Fort Worth, Texas USA, June 3-6, 2018 (JCDL'18), 2 pages. DOI: https://doi.org/10.1145/3197026.3205366

ACM ISBN 978-1-4503-5178-2/18/06.
DOI: https://doi.org/10.1145/3197026.3205366

1 INTRODUCTION

For much of the first twenty years of digital library development, users engaged with digital libraries through particular constructions of the libraries' materials as collections—collections typically selected, curated, and presented according to organizing principles and modes brought over from print or pre-digital environments. Now, an increasing number of large-scale digital libraries that have resulted from mass digitization projects also make their collections available as data, whether through application programming interfaces, bulk downloads, or a combined approach. Such programmatic access to digital libraries' collections expands the possibilities for locating and analyzing materials in digital libraries. These expanded possibilities have broad implications across domains, and for imagining next stages of digital library development, with regard both to the services digital libraries provide and for examining anew the constructions of collections in digital library environments. Researchers create new collections in their work, including novel assemblages of the materials, as well as datasets that express latent features in materials and collections.

This panel will consider the interplay of collections and/as data and of data and/as collections within current and emergent digital libraries and digital library services. Ultimately, the panel seeks to engage the audience in questions and conversation around imagining both collections as data and data as collections, and the potential for such data as collections to contribute, in the words of the conference theme, to knowledge and integration "across societies, disciplines, and systems."

2 PANEL OVERVIEW

Each panelist will motivate the general discussion by presenting their experiences and research related to working with collections as data or data as collections. Salient points from each presentation are summarized below.

1. The HathiTrust Digital Library was created in 2008 to provide a collaborative digital preservation repository

for university and research libraries engaged in large-scale digitization of books and book-like works. HathiTrust has grown to include 130 member libraries and 16 million volumes. Mass digitization, along with significant digitization efforts at the local institutional level, have transformed significant workflows in the research library environment, creating unique opportunities for scholarship and research, and has presented a set of key challenges. HathiTrust has worked over its first ten years to meet those challenges and to establish a basis for its corpus to be used in the widest possible ways.

2. The HathiTrust Research Center has been evolving the notion of "workset" in order to facilitate analytic access to the over 16 million volumes in the HathiTrust Digital Library. Worksets help researchers gather volumes (and other objects) into collections that will undergo computational analysis. Worksets, therefore, can play an enabling role in the transformation of digital library collections into data.
3. The Solr Extracted Feature project has turned the HTRC 5.7 billion page, 4+ TB unigram part-of-speech dataset into a searchable resource, where the generated search results can themselves be gathered together and turned into worksets [1].
4. The Aida project is taking an image-based approach to processing and analyzing large-scale, homogeneous collections of textual materials in digital libraries. The underlying principle of the team's work is that the digital images of textual materials offer significant opportunities for extending and complementing understandings of the materials that have been derived from their electronic text and textual metadata. Attention to digital images of textual materials results in new datasets that can be collected alongside datasets derived from explicitly textual features and provides new opportunities for creators of digital libraries and their users to generate additional collections out of the materials.
5. Within the WCSA+DC project, Linked Data is being used to harmonize data structures—"just enough"—to create coherent cross-corpora worksets orientated around scholars' information-seeking needs [2]. In addition to bibliographic metadata, domain-specific information is also utilised within the collection [3], and that derived from computational features [4].

3 PANELISTS

- **J. Stephen Downie** is the Associate Dean for Research and a Professor at the School of Information Sciences, University of Illinois. He is also the Illinois co-director of the HathiTrust Research Center.
- **Elizabeth Lorang**, Associate Professor, University Libraries, University of Nebraska-Lincoln and co-director of the Aida project. Her work focuses on critical analysis, application and creation of information and information structures.
- **David Bainbridge** is a Professor of Computer Science at the University of Waikato, and Director of the New Zealand Digital Library Research Project. His research interests include music information retrieval, and human computer interaction in addition to digital libraries.
- **Sandra McIntyre** is the Director of Services and Operations at HathiTrust. She manages the development and growth of HathiTrust's core portfolio of services, including preservation, discovery, access, and user and member support.
- **Dr. Kevin Page** is a senior researcher at the University of Oxford e-Research Centre. He is developing information seeking strategies for digital libraries, primarily through the use of knowledge graphs to provide contextual assistance to users.
- **Leen-Kiat Soh**, Professor, Computer Science & Engineering, University of Nebraska-Lincoln and co-director of the Aida project. His interest in this project is in intelligent image analysis, ranging from modeling and capturing structural visual cues to applying machine learning for classification tasks.

3 LEARNING OUTCOMES

- Identify gaps that exist for researchers using large-scale digital libraries for collection identification, building and segmentation.
- Explain best practices to use large-scale digital libraries in research methods.
- Describe needed tools and techniques to address these issues within the digital library community.
- Mobilize researchers, scholars and digital librarians around defining and building useful "data-collection" affordances.

REFERENCES

[1] Bainbridge, D., Downie, J.S., and Capitanu, B. Providing Pin-point Page-level Precision to 1 Trillion Tokens of Text for Workset Creation. Under review for ACM/IEEE Joint Conference on Digital Libraries 2018.

[2] Weigl, D.M., Page, K.R., Organisciak, P. and Downie, J.S., 2017, June. Information-Seeking in Large-Scale Digital Libraries: Strategies for Scholarly Workset Creation. In Digital Libraries (JCDL), 2017 ACM/IEEE Joint Conference on (pp. 1-4). IEEE.

[3] Nurmikko-Fuller, T., Page, K.R., Willcox, P., Jett, J., Maden, C., Cole, T., Fallaw, C., Senseney, M. and Downie, J.S., 2015, June. Building complex research collections in digital libraries: A survey of ontology implications. In Proceedings of the 15th ACM/IEEE-CS Joint Conference on Digital Libraries (pp. 169-172). ACM.

[4] Page, K.R., Bechhofer, S., Fazekas, G., Weigl, D.M. and Wilmering, T., 2017, June. Realising a layered digital library: exploration and analysis of the live music archive through linked data. In Digital Libraries (JCDL), 2017 ACM/IEEE Joint Conference on (pp. 1-10). IEEE.

Designing a Research Platform for Engaged Learning

Nicholas Cole (moderator)
University of Oxford
Oxford, United Kingdom
nicholas.cole@history.ox.ac.uk

Alfie Abdul-Rahman
King's College London
London, United Kingdom
alfie.abdulrahman@kcl.ac.uk

Rodney Smith
Utah Valley University
Utah, U.S.A
rodney.smith@uvu.edu

Carl Eric Scott
Utah Valley University
Utah, U.S.A
carl.scott@uvu.edu

Samuel Corry
Utah Valley University
Utah, U.S.A

Robert Johnson
University of Oxford
Oxford, United Kingdom
robert.johnson@history.ox.ac.uk

ABSTRACT

This panel addresses the opportunities and challenges of using multi-institutional collaborations and digital approaches to drive engaged-learning and archive-focused projects. It focuses in particular on the opportunities presented by the archives related to the negotiation of constitutions and international treaties.

CCS CONCEPTS

• **Information systems** → *Information retrieval*; • **Applied computing** → *Law*; • **Human-centered computing** → Interaction design;

KEYWORDS

Humanities; Data Exploration; Negotiated Texts; User Interfaces; Public Engagements

ACM Reference Format:
Nicholas Cole (moderator), Alfie Abdul-Rahman, Rodney Smith, Carl Eric Scott, Samuel Corry, and Robert Johnson. 2018. Designing a Research Platform for Engaged Learning. In *JCDL '18: The 18th ACM/IEEE Joint Conference on Digital Libraries, June 3–7, 2018, Fort Worth, TX, USA.* ACM, New York, NY, USA, 2 pages. https://doi.org/10.1145/3197026.3205367

1 INTRODUCTION

At the 2017 ACM Joint Conference on Digital Libraries (JCDL) we presented the Quill Platform (https://www.quillproject.net) [1], a framework for the study of the formal negotiations that have produced constitutions, legislation, and international treaties. In the intervening time we have launched the Negotiated Texts Network [2], which has allowed us to develop collaborations with both researchers and educators working with the records of these negotiations. These records present problems for researchers, and the Quill project is an attempt to overcome some of these challenges through digital methodologies and through the fostering of partnerships with other institutions.

In particular, the team at Oxford University have cemented a relationship with Utah Valley University (UVU), and have been working closely with staff and students from the Center for Constitutional Studies [4] based there, who have been using the Quill Project software platform to build a model of the negotiations that produced the 1895 Utah State Constitution [3]. From the point of view of the Quill Project team based at Oxford University, this collaboration has provided us with invaluable feedback on the design of our workflows and visualizations, as well as new datasets to develop and refine both our research questions and our software platform. From the point of view of UVU, the project has provided the driver for advanced undergraduate students to engage in meaningful archive-based research and to contribute substantively to a multi-institution research project.

This panel will discuss the ways in which involving undergraduates in the project through engaged-learning approach has enabled us to improve the design of the platform for both those managing the content within it and those using it for research. We will discuss the opportunities and challenges of running multi-institution collaborations of this type. We will also discuss the potential for further collaborations, which we have been exploring through the Negotiated Texts Network [2] based at The Oxford Research Centre in the Humanities, and the particular challenges posed by the records of formal negotiations.

2 PANEL OVERVIEW

The members of the panel will briefly discuss their own involvement in this project or experience with records of formal negotiations, and then the panel will discuss:

- Insights that have been generated from the two major projects to-date that have used this platform (the records of the US Federal Convention of 1787 and the 1895 Salt Lake Convention).
- The challenge of setting up a successful partnership as part of providing meaningful engaged-learning for the students involved and a genuine contribution to a research project on the other.
- The opportunities that the digital project has provided to train undergraduates on the skills needed for archival research.
- The adjustments we have been able to make to the core software platform as a result of on-going work with undergraduate-level research assistants.
- The challenges of making a transatlantic collaboration of this type work, including the lessons-learned in terms of training, contact time, supervision and work-flows.

JCDL '18, June 3–7, 2018, Fort Worth, TX, USA

ACM ISBN 978-1-4503-5178-2/18/06.
https://doi.org/10.1145/3197026.3205367

Our objective is to present both the ways in which close collaboration with between institutions has helped to enhance and shape the development of our research platform. We hope that this panel will interest an audience made up of people interested in these particular records, and in discussing the opportunities that digital projects present to enhance engaged-learning approaches for students from a variety of academic backgrounds, and the challenges of running projects that engage with students from very different institutions.

All panelists have been contacted and have agreed to participate in the panel.

2.1 Panelists

Nicholas Cole (moderator): Nicholas Cole is a Senior Research Fellow at Pembroke College Oxford and the director of the Quill Project. He studies the political thought of the eighteenth and nineteenth centuries and the history of democratic institutions. He read Ancient and Modern History at University College, Oxford, where he also completed his graduate work. Originally a historian of American political thought, his growing interest in the history of institutions and the problems that the records of their creation present led to the creation of the Quill Project in 2014. He is the co-author, along with Dr Alfie Abdul-Rahman (King's College, London) of the Quill Project's software platform. He is particularly interested in the need to develop software platforms that support humanities researchers to make better use of the resources available in archives and to support better qualitative analysis of large corpuses of written material.

Rodney Smith: Rodney Smith came to Utah Valley University from the Sandra Day O'Connor College of Law at Arizona State, where he served as the Distinguished Professor of Practice and Director of the Sports Law and Business Program. He holds a J.D. from Brigham Young University and a LL.M. and SJD from the University of Pennsylvania. His dissertation was published as a book, Public Prayer and the Constitution: A Case Study in Constitutional Interpretation. He previously served as the President at Southern Virginia University. He also served as a law school dean at Capital University, the University of Montana, and the University of Arkansas at Little Rock. He held the Herff Chair of Excellence in Law at the University of Memphis, where he emphasized constitutional law, sports law and ethics. He has taught at many law schools and has authored or co-authored four books and more than thirty articles in law journals. His work, particularly in the religious liberty area, has been widely cited by scholars and courts at all levels. He has testified before state and congressional committees, including his testimony in the proceedings that led to the confirmation of Justice Thomas to the Supreme Court. He has written numerous op-eds in major national newspapers, including USA Today and the Christian Science Monitor.

Carl Eric Scott: Carl Eric Scott has a PhD. in political science from Fordham University, and has taught political theory, American politics, and Great Books liberal arts, at a number of institutions, including Washington and Lee University, the University of Virginia, and St. John's College, Santa Fe, before coming to teach at Utah Valley University. He has written on politics, constitutionalism, film, and rock music for the National Review Online blog "Postmodern Conservative." He is the co-editor of Totalitarianism on Screen: The Art and Politics of 'The Lives of Others', published by The University of Kentucky Press, and the author of The Five Conceptions of American Liberty, an essay published by the journal National Affairs. His dissertation, The Inconstant Democratic Character, compared Plato's and Tocqueville's discussions of democratic society.

Samuel Corry: Samuel Corry is a junior at Utah Valley University, majoring in History – with an emphasis on Ancient Greek and Roman Studies – and minoring in Constitutional Studies. His interests in life are studying history, following politics (particularly Second Amendment issues), and learning and reading as much as he can. From 2013-15 Samuel served a mission for The Church of Jesus Christ of Latter-Day Saints in Northern California. His hobbies include hiking, competition shooting, writing, Krav-Maga, and spending time with family. Samuel is studying the Russian Language, Civil Rights, American Constitutionalism, and Historical Analysis. He is currently preparing himself for the LSAT with the goal of attending Law School.

Robert Johnson: Robert Johnson is the Director of the Oxford Changing Character of War Centre (CCW), Senior Research Fellow of Pembroke College, and Associate of the Department of Politics and International Relations, University of Oxford. The CCW Centre brings together academics, policy makers and armed forces professionals in the study of war, pursuing a variety of research themes including the future character of war, war and the state in a connected world, non-state warfare, strategy and war, and the moral and legal dimensions of war. Robert Johnson's primary research interests are in the history of strategy and war, and their contemporary applications.

ACKNOWLEDGMENTS

The authors would like to thank G. Mallon, K. Howarth (University of Oxford), J. Cummings, D. K. Maddox, L. Merrell, M. Nolte, C. E. Scott, and C. Sponseller (Utah Valley University) for assisting with the verification and data-entry tasks for the Quill Platform. The authors would like to thank D. Burt, D. De Roure, O. Durand, G. Mantegari, Y. Nasifoglu, and P. Willcox (University of Oxford) for participating in the data capture workshop and their helpful feedback. The authors would also like to thank D. Bobb (Bill of Rights Institute), S. Brennan (Mt Vernon), B. McCormack (Newseum), L. A. Potter (Library of Congress), and J. Silverbook (ConSource) for participating in the education and public engagement workshop and their helpful feedback.

REFERENCES

[1] N. Cole, A. Abdul-Rahman, and G. Mallon. 2017. Quill: A Framework for Constructing Negotiated Texts – with a Case Study on the US Constitutional Convention of 1787. In *Proceedings of ACM JCDL Conference*.

[2] Negotiated Texts Network. 2018. Negotiated Texts Network. (2018). https://torch.ox.ac.uk/negotiations (Accessed on: 15 Jan 2018).

[3] Utah State Legislature. 2018. 1895 Constitution for the State of Utah. (2018). https://le.utah.gov/documents/conconv/utconstconv.htm (Accessed on: 15 Jan 2018).

[4] Utah Valley University. 2017. Utah Valley University's Center for Constitutional Studies. (2017). https://www.uvu.edu/ccs/ (Accessed on: 15 Jan 2018).

Can Research Librarians make Contributions to Decision-making as Intelligence Analysts? The Prospects and Challenges

Wei Chen (moderator)
Wuhan Branch of National Science Library, Chinese Academy of Sciences
Wuhan, Hubei 430071, China
chenw@whlib.ac.cn

Jiangping Chen (moderator)
Department of Information Science, University of North Texas
Denton, Texas 76203, USA
jiangping.chen@unt.edu

Christopher Erdmann
North Carolina State University Libraries
Raleigh, North Carolina 27695, USA
ccerdman@ncsu.edu

Trevor Owens
Digital Content Management, Library of Congress
Washington, DC 20540, USA
Trevor.johnowens@gmail.com

Tao Jin
School of Library and Information Science, Louisiana State University
Baton Rouge, Louisiana 70803, USA
taojin@lsu.edu

Mark Phillips
University of North Texas Libraries
Denton, Texas 76203, USA
mark.phillips@unt.edu

ABSTRACT

This panel discusses the prospects and challenges of providing intelligence analysis services in U.S. research libraries to support decision-making at various levels.

KEYWORDS

Research librarian; decision-making; intelligence analysis

ACM Reference Format:

W. Chen, J. Chen, C. Erdmann, T. Owens, T. Jin and M. Phillips. 2018. Can Research Librarians Make Contributions to Decision-making as Intelligence Analysts? The Prospects and Challenges. In JCDL '18: The 18th ACM/IEEE Joint Conference on Digital Libraries, June 3–7, 2018, Fort Worth, TX, USA. ACM, New York, NY, USA, 2 pages. https://doi.org/10.1145/3197026.3205365

1 INTRODUCTION

Intelligence analysis, or information analysis and knowledge discovery is vital for decision-making. In a broad sense, intelligence analysis is not only related to national security, but also applicable in fields such as competitive intelligence, business intelligence, as well as research intelligence. It is a process of identifying, acquiring, analyzing, and synthesizing huge amount of data/information to provide insights and advice to decision-makers on critical decisions they must make.

From the perspective of intelligence cycle, there is a close alignment or even convergence between librarianship and intelligence analysis [1, 2]. With the wealth of data available to library and information services [3], research librarians also have opportunities to play a significant role in decision-making by providing intelligence analysis services. It seems reasonable to assume that future research librarians could be data scientists and co-investigators who are equipped with advanced data management and analysis technologies [4]. They are expected to have distinctive competencies in discovering and obtaining information from all open sources effectively, assessing quality and authenticity of information, and applying data analysis techniques to deliver neutral and reliable intelligence products and services for facilitating better decision making.

However, although a growing number of research libraries have realized the importance of expanding into nontraditional information services by enhancing analytical skills, few of them provide such services or even able to formulate a clear, concrete and operable action plans. A change of mind is necessary. Big data environments and the availabilities of analytical tools provide opportunities for research librarians to perform intelligence analysis by changing previous work process [5]. The purpose of this panel is to discuss important questions and issues as related to developing information analysis and knowledge discovery services in U.S. research libraries, especially how research librarians be trained and equipped with new data analytical technologies for intelligence analysis.

2 PANEL FORMAT

First, each panelist will briefly discuss their experience, research, or examples of projects as related to information analysis and knowledge discovery. Then, we will start an open discussion on the following questions:

JCDL '18, June 3–7, 2018, Fort Worth, TX, USA

ACM ISBN 978-1-4503-5178-2/18/06.
https://doi.org/10.1145/3197026.3205365

- How do libraries stay relevant in nowadays' digital environments? Should research libraries provide intelligence analysis services for decision-making?
- What advantages do research libraries have in providing intelligence analysis services? What challenges do they face? Such as, how can libraries establish trust from their stakeholders for such services?
- What professional competencies should research librarians possess in order to provide intelligence analysis services?
- What resources and infrastructures must be in place to support such services in research libraries?
- How could library and information science schools and programs better prepare information professionals for intelligence analysis in libraries?

Our object is to present the unique perspectives of panelists working in areas around intelligence analysis and library and information science, in the meantime engage the audience on issues we mutually find fruitful, in an effort to push new library services forward. We expect the audience to be digital library practitioners and scholars interested in competitive/business intelligence, big data analytics, knowledge management and discovery, and digital library researchers. All panelists have been contacted and have agreed to participate in the panel. We will need basic A/V equipment (e.g. microphones for speakers and a projector screen hooked up to a computer for demos).

3 PANELISTS

Wei Chen (moderator) is an Associate Professor in Wuhan Library of Chinese Academy of Sciences. His research interests mainly focus on Scientific Information Analysis, Policy Analysis, Bibliometric Analysis, Digital Library, Knowledge Management, and Information Service. He have been working as an information analyst for Chinese Academy of Sciences' Energy Strategic Information Analysis and Knowledge Integration Platform projects, which seek to provide evidence-based analytical products for decision-making.

Dr. Jiangping Chen (moderator): Dr. Chen is a Professor at Department of Information Science in College of Information at University of North Texas. She has conducted research in Intelligent Information Retrieval and Access, Digital Libraries, and Data Science and Information System. Before she started her doctoral program, she was a librarian conducting information analysis and database development in two academic libraries.

Christopher Erdmann is an author, developer and experimenter in the areas of digital libraries, social networking, library UX, interactive technologies, bibliometrics and data services in libraries. He is currently the Chief Strategist for Research Collaboration at the North Carolina State University Libraries and has previously worked for organizations such as the Harvard-Smithsonian Center for Astrophysics, European Southern Observatory, Supreme Court of the US, United Nations, University of Washington, Smithsonian (NMAH) and CNET.

Dr. Trevor Owens is a librarian, researcher, policy maker, and educator working on digital infrastructure for libraries. Owens serves as the first Head of Digital Content Management for Library Services at the Library of Congress. In addition, he teaches graduate seminars in digital history for American University's History Department and graduate seminars and digital preservation for the University of Maryland's College of Information, where he is also a Research Affiliate with the Digital Curation Innovation Center. He previously worked as a senior program administrator at the United States Institute of Museum and Library Services (IMLS). At IMLS, he led the establishment of the National Digital Platform initiative.

Dr. Tao Jin is an Associate Professor in the School of Library & Information Science at Louisiana State University. Since 2004 he has been researching, teaching, and advising in the areas of competitive intelligence, knowledge management, and business information seeking and processing. Over the years he has promoted and served for various professional organizations, such as the American Society for Information Science and Technology, Special Libraries Association, and Strategic and Competitive Intelligence Professionals. He currently sits on editorial boards of the Journal of Information and Knowledge Management, the Canadian Journal of Information and Library Science and the Journal of Intelligence.

Mark Phillips is the Associate Dean for Digital Libraries at the University of North Texas. His current research focuses on digital library infrastructure, web archiving and system for analyzing, identifying and improving metadata related to cultural heritage and digital library collections. He redesigned and rebuilt UNT's digital library. He has been involved with the development and operation of the Portal to Texas History, the UNT Digital Library and the Gateway to Oklahoma History, all hosted by the UNT Libraries.

REFERENCES

[1] Tao Jin and France Bouthillier. 2012. The Integration of Intelligence Analysis into LIS Education. *Journal of Education for Library and Information Science* 53, 2, 130-148

[2] David Shumaker, Ran Hock, and Blane Dessy. 2013. *Librarians in the Intelligence Process.* Power-point slides presented at the Understanding and Improving Intelligence Analysis: Learning from Other Disciplines Workshop, University of Mississippi, Oxford, MS

[3] Ben Showers. 2015. *Library Analytics and Metrics: Using Data to Drive Decisions and Services.* Facet Publishing, UK

[4] Jeannette Ekstrøm, Mikael Elbaek, Chris Erdmann and Ivo Grigorov. 2016. *The research librarian of the future: data scientist and co-investigator.* Retrieved from http://blogs.lse.ac.uk/impactofsocialsciences/2016/12/14/the-research-librarian-of-the-future-data-scientist-and-co-investigator/.

[5] Wei Chen, Rui Yang, Tao He, Shuo Wang, and Jiangping Chen. 2017. An Integration-based Conceptual Framework for Scientific Information Analysis, Full paper presented at *13th International Conference on Knowledge Management* (ICKM 2017: http://www.ickm.net/), October 25-27, Dallas, Texas. In. *Knowledge Discovery and Data Design Innovation* (pp. 283-300). Singapore: World Scientific.

Unobtrusive and Extensible Archival Replay Banners Using Custom Elements

Sawood Alam, Mat Kelly, Michele C. Weigle, and Michael L. Nelson
Old Dominion University
Department of Computer Science
Norfolk, Virginia, USA
{salam,mkelly,mweigle,mln}@cs.odu.edu

ABSTRACT

We compare and contrast three different ways to implement an archival replay banner. We propose an implementation that utilizes *Custom Elements* and adds some unique behaviors, not common in existing archival replay systems, to enhance the user experience. Our approach has a minimal user interface footprint and resource overhead while still providing rich interactivity and extended on-demand provenance information about the archived resources.

CCS CONCEPTS

• **Information systems → Digital libraries and archives;** • **Human-centered computing → User interface design;**

KEYWORDS

Memento; Archival Replay; Archival Banner; User Interface

ACM Reference Format:
Sawood Alam, Mat Kelly, Michele C. Weigle, and Michael L. Nelson. 2018. Unobtrusive and Extensible Archival Replay Banners Using Custom Elements. In *JCDL '18: The 18th ACM/IEEE Joint Conference on Digital Libraries, June 3–7, 2018, Fort Worth, TX, USA.* ACM, New York, NY, USA, 2 pages. https://doi.org/10.1145/3197026.3203881

1 MOTIVATION

Web archival replay systems express that a user is interacting with a *memento* (an archived representation of a resource) by adding an archival banner. Archival banners provide metadata about both the memento and original resource as well as serving to distinguish a memento from its corresponding original resource. To more accurately replicate the live web experience when viewing a memento, an archive rewrites parts of a memento's contents to ensure the embedded resources and hyperlinks are referenced to the web archive and not the live web. Any component injection in the page makes it different from the original and may consume additional screen real estate. We illustrate this in Figure 1 by archiving `example.com` in three different archives successively, resulting in cascading banners.

We propose an unobtrusive, interactive, responsive, multi-state, and extensible archival banner experience using *Custom Elements.*

ACM ISBN 978-1-4503-5178-2/18/06.
https://doi.org/10.1145/3197026.3203881

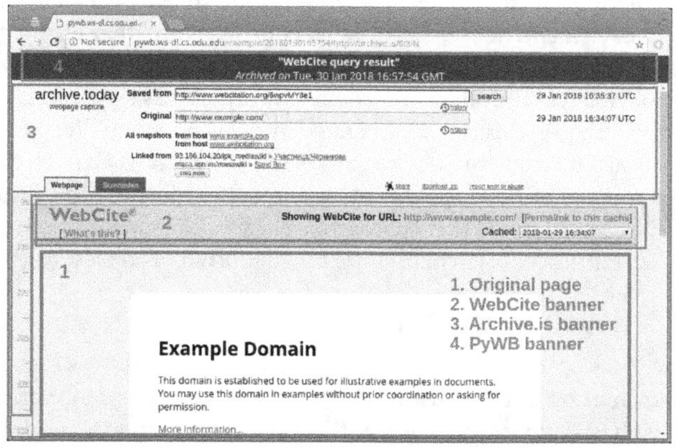

Figure 1: Three Cascading Archival Banners in a Memento

It requires minimal real estate and allows drag-and-drop repositioning in the viewport while hiding itself when not needed. In the on-demand extended mode it provides a set of interactive visualizations and provenance information that are customizable by the archive.

2 METHODOLOGY

There are three primary ways to serve an archival banner with an archived web page that shares the rendering space with the memento. Browser toolbars (e.g., the now defunct *MementoFox*) and archival emulators (e.g., *NetCapsule*) are out of scope of this work.

Inline Plain HTML Banners – This is the simplest and most commonly used approach of adding an archival banner. Many services such as the *Internet Archive, Archive-It, UK Web Archive,* and *Archive.is* use this method. *OpenWayback,* a commonly used archival replay system, supports this method. In this approach, necessary markup and style for the banner is injected directly in the archived *HTML.* While simple, it poses some serious issues, such as conflicts with the style of the memento or hiding important elements of the page, such as the header of the site.

Frame/Iframe Banners – Using *frame* or *iframe* HTML elements is another common technique to provide archival banners. This can be implemented by 1) serving both the banner and memento documents in separate *frames/iframes* of a parent page, or 2) making the banner document as the outer page and serving the memento inside an *iframe.* For example, *WebCite* uses the first approach while many archives, such as the *Portuguese Web Archive,* use the second. *PyWB,* a popular web archival replay system, uses the second approach by default, but allows using plain inline *HTML* banners. *Iframes* provide full document isolation, both style and origin. Therefore, *iframe* banners do not conflict with the position or style of other elements of the *memento*. However, their positioning is not flexible enough to place them at any arbitrary location in the viewport. Since these banners must be placed clear of the memento without any overlay possibilities, often less screen real estate is available to render mementos.

Custom Elements Banners – *Custom Elements* [4] is a recent web standard. It allows developers to define their own custom *HTML elements* in *JavaScript* using the same capabilities that native elements have. Using this approach we can hide the implementation details of the banner while injecting a minimal markup in a *memento*. By using the *Shadow DOM* [5] the style is scoped to the custom element, hence, there are no conflicts with other elements of the *memento*. Unlike an *iframe*, the origin of a *custom element* is not isolated from the main document, which has a potential security risk [3]. This can be mitigated by preventing any live-leaks in *memento* reconstruction, such as by using *ServiceWorker* [2]. Native support of *Custom Elements* is about 79% globally (as of Apr 1, 2018[1]) and rising. This approach is used by a banner introduced in *Reconstructive* [1], which is used by the *IPWB* [6] replay system.

3 RECONSTRUCTIVE BANNER

The three approaches described in Section 2 only address the implementation of the markup. However, the user experience of all three has some issues. We want to keep the experience as close to the original as possible, while still providing some means to interact with the memento and to display provenance information in an unobtrusive manner. Many current implementations load the metadata for every page, even when a user may not be interested. This results in a slow page load, poor user experience, and resource wastage of both the client and server. We only bring more data when a user asks for it. We propose the following two-state banner called *Reconstructive Banner*. It is implemented using *Custom Elements* with some UI behaviors (such as being responsive, unobtrusive, and expandable) to improve the user experience.

Floating Action Bar (FAB) – A floating bar with basic archival information and quick action buttons is placed in the bottom-right corner (as illustrated in Figure 2(a)), but draggable to any place on the page. The button shows a branding logo of the archive to highlight that it is not part of the *memento*. A similar approach was earlier used in *Mink* [7]. After a set duration of inactivity on the page, the *FAB* hides itself and reappears upon a user interaction such as mouse move or page scroll.

Expanded – When the *expand icon* in the *FAB* is clicked/tapped, it expands into a modal window with extended archival provenance information, interactive visualizations, and other metadata (as illustrated in Figure 2(b)). The *expand icon* changes to a *collapse icon* to allow restoring the *FAB* state. The expanded state does not hide or collapse automatically without an explicit user action. Both states have a *close icon* to completely remove the banner from the UI. This state may make additional resource requests to fetch some visualization libraries or data.

4 CONCLUSIONS AND FUTURE WORK

We proposed an unobtrusive and extensible method to revamp the archival replay banner UI. We implemented *Reconstructive Banner*, a responsive, multi-state, and details-on-demand archival banner using *Custom Elements* to be both more interactive and more informative to the user. We anticipate exploring the newfound and extensible abilities to archival replay banners as applicable in other archival systems.

[1]https://caniuse.com/#feat=custom-elementsv1

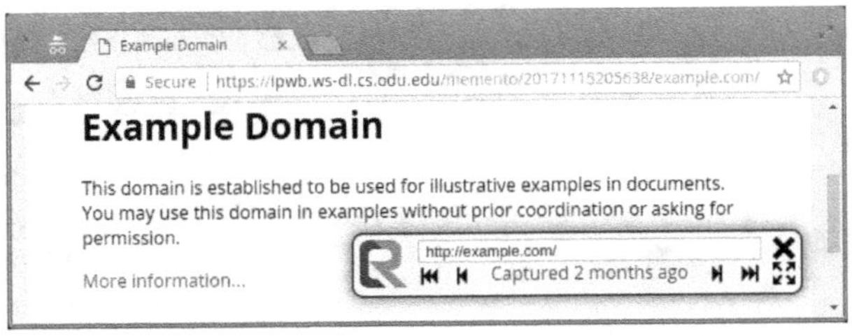

(a) Draggable Floating Action Bar (FAB): Brief Information and Quick Actions

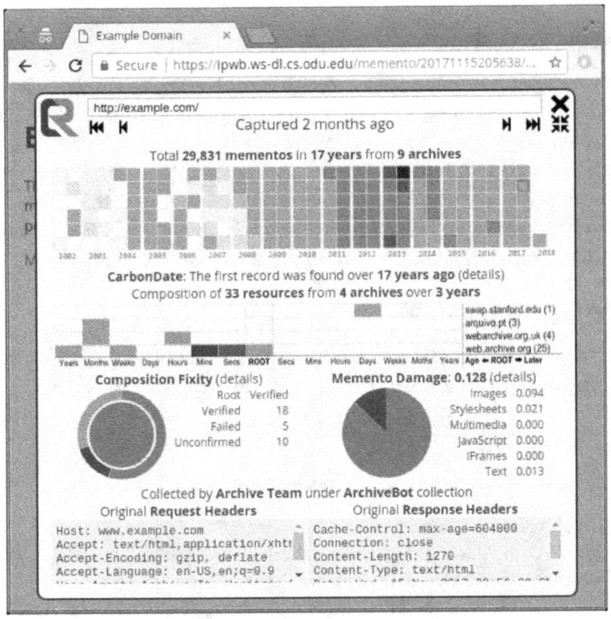

(b) Expanded: Metadata, Provenance, and Interactive Visualizations

Figure 2: Reconstructive Banner Modes

5 ACKNOWLEDGEMENTS

This work is supported in part by NSF grant III 1526700.

REFERENCES

[1] Sawood Alam. 2018. Introducing Reconstructive - An Archival Replay ServiceWorker Module. http://ws-dl.blogspot.com/2018/01/2018-01-08-introducing-reconstructive.html. (2018).
[2] Sawood Alam, Mat Kelly, Michele C. Weigle, and Michael L. Nelson. 2017. Client-side Reconstruction of Composite Mementos Using ServiceWorker. In *Proceedings of JCDL*. 237–240.
[3] John A. Berlin. 2018. *To Relive The Web: A Framework For The Transformation And Archival Replay Of Web Pages.* Master's thesis. Old Dominion University, Department of Computer Science.
[4] Domenic Denicola. 2016. Custom Elements. https://www.w3.org/TR/custom-elements/. (2016).
[5] Hayato Ito. 2017. Shadow DOM. https://www.w3.org/TR/shadow-dom/. (2017).
[6] Mat Kelly, Sawood Alam, Michael L. Nelson, and Michele C. Weigle. 2016. Inter-Planetary Wayback: Peer-To-Peer Permanence of Web Archives. In *Proceedings of TPDL*. 411–416.
[7] Mat Kelly, Michael L. Nelson, and Michele C. Weigle. 2014. Mink: Integrating the Live and Archived Web Viewing Experience Using Web Browsers and Memento. In *Proceedings of JCDL*. 469–470.

ArchiveNow: Simplified, Extensible, Multi-Archive Preservation

Mohamed Aturban, Mat Kelly, Sawood Alam, John A. Berlin,
Michael L. Nelson, and Michele C. Weigle
Old Dominion University
Department of Computer Science
Norfolk, Virginia, USA
{maturban,mkelly,salam,jberlin,mln,mweigle}@cs.odu.edu

ABSTRACT

ArchiveNow is a Python module for preserving web pages in on-demand web archives. This module allows a user to submit a URI of a web page for archiving at several configured web archives. Once the web page is captured, *ArchiveNow* provides the user with links to the archived copies of the web page. *ArchiveNow* is initially configured to use four archives but is easily configurable to add or remove other archives. In addition to pushing web pages to public archives, *ArchiveNow*, through the use of *Wget* and *Squidwarc*, allows users to generate local WARC files, enabling them to create their own personal and private archives.

CCS CONCEPTS

• Information systems → Digital libraries and archives; World Wide Web;

KEYWORDS

Web Archiving, Memento, WARC

ACM Reference Format:
Mohamed Aturban, Mat Kelly, Sawood Alam, John A. Berlin, Michael L. Nelson, and Michele C. Weigle. 2018. ArchiveNow: Simplified, Extensible, Multi-Archive Preservation. In *JCDL '18: The 18th ACM/IEEE Joint Conference on Digital Libraries, June 3–7, 2018, Fort Worth, TX, USA.* ACM, New York, NY, USA, 2 pages. https://doi.org/10.1145/3197026.3203880

1 INTRODUCTION

Preserving a web page in only a single web archive is risky. Archives may be vulnerable to security threats, or may also become temporarily or permanently unreachable. Thus, preserving web pages in multiple web archives should decrease the danger of losing archived data. Some existing work focuses on preserving web pages in multiple archives. Kelly et al. [6] built *Mink*, a Google Chrome extension that notifies a user of any available archived copies for a viewed page and suggests to archive the page in three archives. Welsh [10] developed several tools intended to archive news-related resources. For example, Welsh's *Savemy.news* (`www.savemy.news`) saves web pages in two archives. Users of this service are required to create accounts. In addition to *Savemy.news*, Welsh built three

```
% archivenow --all --cc_api_key=7e..3f http://mon
ey.cnn.com/2018/01/27/technology/future/spacex-fa
lcon-heavy-everything-you-need-to-know/index.html

{
  "uri": "http://money.cnn.com/2018/01/27/technol
  ogy/future/spacex-falcon-heavy-everything-you-n
  eed-to-know/index.html",
  "request-datetime": "20180129094723",
  "mementos": {
    "archive.org": "https://web.archive.org/web/2
    0180129094728/http://money.cnn.com/2018/01/27
    /technology/future/spacex-falcon-heavy-everyt
    hing-you-need-to-know/index.html",
    "archive.is": "https://archive.is/hr41S",
    "perma.cc": "https://perma.cc/GX8D-2NVR",
    "webcitation.org": "http://www.webcitation.or
    g/6wpUjcTO2"
  }
}
```

Figure 1: CLI example for archiving a web page in all configured web archives

separate Python libraries to interact with on-demand archiving services. *Webrecorder* [9] and *WARCreate* [7] can be used to generate WARC files [5], but the only way to use these tools is through a web browser. *ArchiveNow* can save pages in four web archives, generate WARC files, and allows customization of the set of archives used to preserve the web. ArchiveNow does not require users to have an account and can be run through the command-line (CLI), a web-based user interface (UI), a self-contained Docker container, or as a Python module. *ArchiveNow* is available for download at https://github.com/oduwsdl/archivenow.

2 MULTI-ARCHIVE PRESERVATION

ArchiveNow by default is configured to accept a URI from a user for archiving at the following four archives: the Internet Archive (IA) at `archive.org`, Archive.is (`archive.is`), Perma (`perma.cc`), and WebCite (`webcitation.org`). Figure 1 shows an example of running *ArchiveNow* to request capturing a web page by all configured archives. The value of `--cc_api_key` is an API key required by Perma. The user can select one or more archives by replacing `--all` with the corresponding archives' identifiers, such as `--ia` for IA, `--is` for Archive.is, `--wc` for WebCite, and `--cc` for Perma. Figure 2 shows the archived pages (mementos) from the four archives. In addition to running *ArchiveNow* via CLI, it can be run as a Docker container, a web service, or in Python. For example, after running "`archivenow --server`", a user can open `http://0.0.0.0:12345` in a web browser and use the UI page shown in Figure 3. A full list of options for running *ArchiveNow* is available on GitHub [1].

JCDL '18, June 3–7, 2018, Fort Worth, TX, USA

ACM ISBN 978-1-4503-5178-2/18/06.
https://doi.org/10.1145/3197026.3203880

(a) In the Internet Archive. (b) In Archive.is. (c) In WebCite. (d) In Perma.

Figure 2: The web page http://money.cnn.com/2018/01/27/technology/future/spacex-falcon-heavy-everything-you-need-to-know/index.html as it appeared on the web on January 26, 2018 is archived by four different archives using *ArchiveNow*.

Figure 3: The UI page generated by *ArchiveNow*.

3 GENERATING WARCS

ArchiveNow can also generate a WARC file using two different tools, *Wget* [3] and *Squidwarc* [2]. The WARC file format is commonly used in the web archiving community. Archived web pages stored in WARC files can be played back by tools such as OpenWayback [4] or PyWb [8]. The feature of creating WARC files by *ArchiveNow* is important especially when users are concerned about privacy. The main difference between a WARC file generated by *Squidwarc* and one generated by *Wget* is that Headless Chrome (used by *Squidwarc*) has the ability to execute JavaScript. This ability allows for the discovery of URIs of embedded resources that otherwise would not be preserved by tools that do not execute JavaScript, like *Wget*. The command "`archivenow --wget=my.warc --ia www.example.com`" downloads the web page `example.com` using *Wget* and preserves the downloaded page in a WARC file named `example.warc`. It also sends a request to IA to capture the web page. Similarly, the option `--squidwarc` can be used for preserving the web page using *Squidwarc* to generate a WARC file.

4 CONFIGURING A NEW ARCHIVE

Even though it is currently configured to save resources into four public archives, adding a new archive can be achieved by writing a new archive handler (e.g., `{identifier}_handler.py`). For example, if we want to add a new archive named "`My Archive`", we would create a file `ma_handler.py` and store it in the folder `handlers`. The "`ma`" will be the archive identifier, so to request archiving a web page (e.g., `www.example.com`) in this new archive through Python, we would write:

```
import archivenow from archivenow
archivenow.push("www.example.com","ma")
```

In `ma_handler.py`, the class name must be `MA_handler`. In addition, this class must have at least one function `push()`, which has at least one argument for passing a URI. The second argument is optional and consists of a list of key-value pairs if required by an archive to process archiving requests (e.g., an API key for *Perma*). At least two variables should be declared in the class: a boolean variable `enabled` to toggle whether requests are sent to a specified archive and a literal `name` to specify an identifier for an archive. Removing an archive can be accomplished by (1) moving the archive handler file from the folder `handlers`, (2) renaming the archive handler file to an other name that does not end with `_handler.py`, or (3) setting the variable `enabled` inside the handler file to `False`.

5 CONCLUSIONS

We introduced *ArchiveNow* for preserving web pages in multiple on-demand web archives. In addition to requesting web archives to capture a URI, *ArchiveNow* also generates WARC files for local and private archives using *Wget* and *Squidwarc*. Furthermore, *ArchiveNow* allows customization to configure new archives or remove existing configured archives. In future work, we will continue configuring new archives whenever they become available.

6 ACKNOWLEDGEMENTS

This work is supported in part by The Andrew W. Mellon Foundation (AMF) grant 11600663 and NSF grant III 1526700.

REFERENCES

[1] Mohamed Aturban. 2017. Archivenow - A Tool To Push Web Resources Into Web Archives. https://github.com/oduwsdl/archivenow. (February 2017).
[2] John Berlin. 2017. Squidwarc - A high fidelity archival crawler that uses Chrome or Chrome Headless. https://github.com/N0taN3rd/Squidwarc. (July 2017).
[3] Free Software Foundation. 2013. GNU Wget - Introduction to GNU Wget. https://www.gnu.org/software/wget/. (2013).
[4] International Internet Preservation Consortium (IIPC). 2005. OpenWayback. https://github.com/iipc/openwayback/wiki. (October 2005).
[5] ISO 28500. 2009. WARC (Web ARChive) file format. http://www.digitalpreservation.gov/formats/fdd/fdd000236.shtml. (August 2009).
[6] Mat Kelly, Michael L. Nelson, and Michele C. Weigle. 2014. Mink: Integrating the Live and Archived Web Viewing Experience Using Web Browsers and Memento . In *Proceedings of JCDL*. 469–470.
[7] Mat Kelly and Michele C Weigle. 2012. WARCreate: Create Wayback-Consumable WARC Files from Any Webpage. In *Proceedings of JCDL*. 437–438.
[8] Ilya Kreymer. 2013. PyWb - Web Archiving Tools for All. https://github.com/ikreymer/pywb. (December 2013).
[9] Ilya Kreymer. 2015. Webrecorder - a web archiving platform and service for all. https://webrecorder.io. (2015).
[10] Ben Welsh. 2016. PastPages. https://github.com/pastpages. (2016).

Influence of Service Quality on Users' Satisfaction with Mobile Library Service: A Comparison of Public and Academic Libraries

Chen Minghong
School of Information Management,
Sun Yat-sen University,
Guangzhou, China
chenmh23@mail.sysu.edu.cn

Qi Xianjun
School of Information Management,
Sun Yat-sen University,
Guangzhou, China
qixianjun@mail.sysu.edu.cn

ABSTRACT

Mobile service in libraries has become very popular in last few years. To notify the meaningful factors for the satisfaction with mobile library services, this study focuses on service quality and divides the factor into 4 sub-dimensions: resource quality, environment quality, interaction quality and outcome quality. The empirical findings revealed most sub-dimensions of service quality to be significant in explaining users' satisfaction. Moreover, it was found that, there were different perception between public and academic library user groups regarding the sub-dimensions of mobile service quality and their influences on users' satisfaction.

CCS CONCEPTS

•Information systems → Information systems applications → Digital libraries and archives

KEYWORDS

Mobile Library, Users' satisfaction, Service Quality

ACM Reference format:

Minghong Chen, Xianjun Qi. Influence of Service Quality on Users' Satisfaction with Mobile Library Service: A Comparison of Public and Academic Libraries. In JCDL '18: The 18th ACM/IEEE Joint Conference on Digital Libraries, June 3--7, 2018, Fort Worth, TX, USA. ACM, New York, NY, USA, 2 pages. https://doi.org/10.1145/3197026.3203884

1 INTRODUCTION

With advances in mobile Internet technologies and the popularity of intelligent devices, an increasing number of libraries developed and provided mobile services, involving mobile sites, text messaging services, e-books, the catalog and mobile access to databases. Mobile services which have been viewed as the extension and innovation of traditional library services allow users more conveniently to view, search and obtain information and resources of mobile libraries. However, the degree of users' satisfaction with mobile library services is relatively low at present. According to a survey conducted by the library of Wuhan University, only 20.8 percent of respondents were very satisfied with mobile services[1]. To realize the tremendous value of mobile services and strengthen the users' stickiness, it is critical to enhance the users' satisfaction, which largely depends service quality. The purpose of this study is thus to examine precisely which factors may be essential in forming satisfaction with mobile library services based on the concept of service quality and compare the different perception between users of public and academic libraries.

JCDL '18, June 3–7, 2018, Fort Worth, TX, USA

ACM ISBN 978-1-4503-5178-2/18/06.
https://doi.org/10.1145/3197026.3203884

2 RESEARCH MODEL AND HYPOTHESE

2.1 Service Quality

Previous research mainly applied LIBQUAL to measure service quality consisting of 22 core items, each measured on three levels of library service quality: minimum, perceived, and desired[2]. However, LIBQUAL which builds upon SERVQUAL may lead to poor validity resulting from the use of difference scores which are calculated by subtracting exceptions from perceptions. Given the unique characteristics of mobile library service, this study, based on Brady and Cronin's model[3], develops a multidimensional and hierarchical model to measure service quality of mobile libraries by four dimensions, i.e., resource quality, environment quality, interaction quality and outcome quality.

2.2 Resource Quality and Satisfaction

Resource quality reflects the richness, accuracy and accessibility of content provided by the mobile library services. Joo Soohyung and Choi verified the positive relationship between resource quality and user satisfaction[4]. Thus, this study hypothesizes the following:

H1. The richness of resources is positively related to user satisfaction.

H2. The accuracy of resources is positively related to user satisfaction.

H3. The accessibility of resources is positively related to user satisfaction.

2.3 Environment Quality and Satisfaction

Environment quality which reflects the basic requirement of using such services, includes mobile network and context awareness. It would be difficult for users to achieve their goals without a supportive environment. In the research of Fan and Shi[5], service quality had significant impact on the satisfaction with mobile library services. Thus, we hypothesize:

H4. The quality of mobile network is positively related to user satisfaction.

H5. The quality of context awareness is positively related to user satisfaction.

2.4 Interaction Quality and Satisfaction

Interaction quality captures the user-system interaction of the service delivery process. Although in the context of mobile services, users may not meet with the librarian face to face, the interaction between the two parties occurring through the system of mobile library is still an important component in mobile library service delivery. The ease of use of interaction is an important factor significantly influencing user satisfaction with mobile library services. Therefore, we propose the following hypotheses:
H6. Ease of use of mobile library service is positively related to user satisfaction.

2.5 Outcome quality and satisfaction

Outcome quality which is viewed as the users' fulfillment of desire, directly reflects the utilitarian value and hedonic value of the service. When users perceive usefulness and playfulness of mobile services, they would have pleasant experience and positive assessment. Accordingly, we hypothesize:
H7. Usefulness of mobile library service is positively related to user satisfaction.
H8. Playfulness of mobile library service is positively related to user satisfaction.

3 DATA COLLECTION AND ANALYSIS

3.1 Data collection

The questionnaire was developed and refined from the library service literatures. And all scale items were rephrased to relate specifically to the context of mobile library. The main survey was conducted in two public libraries and several academic libraries in Guangzhou. Total of 1000 questionnaires were distributed during three weeks. Finally, 310 valid questionnaires completed by users of public libraries and 366 valid questionnaires completed by users of academic libraries were used in the data analysis.

3.2 Empirical Analysis

We ran a confirmatory factory analysis in SmartPLS and assessed reliability, convergent validity and discriminant validity for all constructs. The analysis showed that all the CR and Cronbach's alpha exceeded the threshold values of 0.70, AVE for all constructs were above the threshold values of 0.50, suggesting good construct reliability. And all item loadings were higher than 0.70, indicating good convergent validity. In addition, the square root of the AVE was greater than the correlations for all constructs, demonstrating a satisfactory discriminant validity of the measurements.
Table 1 illustrates the results of the structural model from the PLS output. For mobile service users of public libraries, AU, AE, CA, EU, US and PL, all of which had a significant, positive effect on SA, explained 59.1% of the variance in SA. Thus, hypotheses H2, H3, H5, H6, H7 and H8 postulated in this study were supported. Meanwhile, as for mobile service users of academic libraries, RI, AU, MN, CA, US and PL, all of which had a significant, positive effect on SA, explained 59.8% of the variance in SA. The results support H1, H2, H4, H5, H7, H8 and don't support H3 and H6. Additionally, the results showed statistically differences in the impacts of four sub-dimensions of service quality on user satisfaction between the public and academic library users.

Table 1: Comparisons of user groups between public and academic libraries

Hypothesis	β1 (PBL)	Test result (PBL)	β2 (ACL)	Test result(ACL)	Δβ	Difference
H1: RI→SA	0.032	Rejected	0.111*	Supported	-0.079***	Yes
H2: AU→SA	0.146**	Supported	0.133**	Supported	0.013***	Yes
H3: AE→SA	0.135*	Supported	-0.067	Rejected	0.202***	Yes
H4: MN→SA	0.058	Rejected	0.124*	Supported	-0.066***	Yes
H5: CA→SA	0.129*	Supported	0.250***	Supported	-0.122***	Yes
H6: EU→SA	0.159*	Supported	0.034	Rejected	0.125***	Yes
H7: US→SA	0.160*	Supported	0.140*	Supported	0.020***	Yes
H8: PL→SA	0.203***	Supported	0.333***	Supported	-0.130***	Yes

Notes: (1) *p < 0.05, **p < 0.01, ***p < 0.001
(2) RI: Richness; AU: Accuracy; AE: Accessibility; MN: Mobile network; CA: Context awareness; EU: Ease of use; US: Usefulness; PL: Playfulness; SA: Satisfaction with mobile library service; PBL: Public library; ACL: Academic library

4 CONCLUSIONS

This study contributes to the literature of mobile library services by empirically examining the impacts of service quality on public and academic library users' satisfaction. The results confirm that service quality, measured by four sub-dimensions, i.e., resource quality, environment quality, interaction quality and outcome quality, is strongly related users' satisfaction, and turn out that users of public and academic library have different perception of mobile service. This study adopts the four-dimensional view to explain the service quality of mobile library and provides theoretical insights into understanding mobile library users' perceived service quality and how that influences users' satisfaction. The findings also provide implications for practitioners of mobile libraries.

5 ACKNOWLEDGMENTS

This research was supported by the NSFC projects No.71603295 and 71263006; Guangdong Natural Science Foundation, No. 2016A030313334.

REFERENCES

[1] Y. Zhao, S. Deng, T. Gao, and R. Zhou. 2016. *Research on user needs for mobile information services in Chinese university libraries: Comparison between existing user and potential users.* The Electronic Library, 34,4(2016), 617-635.
[2] P. Natesan, H. F. Ponce, and A Chavez. 2015. *When are LibQUAL+® and LibQUAL+® Lite scores psychometrically comparable?* Library & Information Science Research, 37, 1(2015),21-27.
[3] M. K. Brady and J. Cronin. 2001. *Some new thoughts on conceptualizing perceived service quality: A hierarchical approach.* Journal of Marketing, 65, 3(2001), 34-49.
[4] Joo Soohyung and Choi Namjoo. 2016. *Understanding users' continuance intention to use online library resources based on an extended expectation-confirmation model,.* The Electronic Library, 34,4(2016),554-571.
[5] X. Fan and G. Shi. 2017. *Research on the Relationship between Mobile Library Service Quality and Reader Satisfaction and Loyalty.*Library,2(2017),50-54.

Community-Driven Data Curation System for Reusability

Dong-Hoon Choi
KISTI, Korea
choid@kisti.re.kr

Eunsu Mo
KISTI, Korea
esmo@kisti.re.kr

ABSTRACT

Due to recent data explosion, scientists invest most of their efforts in the collection of data needed for research. In this paper, we address the community-driven data curation system which is essential to enhancing data understandability and reusability, thereby reducing the efforts for data collection. The curation system focuses on the interlinking between data and their related literatures to capture and organize the associations among research output. The system also focuses on domain-specific contextual information to help users understand data. A global research group in protein study has adopted the system to build a community-driven curated database and established a guideline for scientific discovery.

CCS CONCEPTS

• **Applied computing → Digital libraries and archives**

KEYWORDS

community-driven data curation, trustworthiness, reusability, data-literature interlinking

ACM Reference format:

D.H. Choi, and E. Mo. 2018. Community-Driven Data Curation System for Reusability. In Proceedings of ACM JCDL Conference, Fort Worth, USA, June 2018 (JCDL), 2 pages. DOI: https://doi.org/10.1145/3197026.3203866

1 INTRODUCTION

As open data initiatives expand, scientists invest most of their total efforts into searching data from a bunch of data sources, understanding and integrating them, and creating their own data collection [1] to solve their problems. Reducing the efforts depends on accessibility, understandability and reusability of data, which is achieved by annotating data with enough amount of metadata.

Domain-specific metadata is essential to understand and reuse data. The metadata are implied in the article that is produced from analysis of data and/or reused data. Therefore, annotation of data with domain-specific metadata involves selection of related articles and extraction of metadata from them. Data-literature interlinking(DLI) provides users with information on which data is the evidence of which article, which article cites which data, etc. This means DLI enhances data understandability and reusability. Data curation includes data management activities to enhance accessibility, quality, value, reusability, trustworthiness, etc. Trustworthiness of data has close ties with transparency and reproducibility of research articles.

To publish reusable and trustworthy data, data curation activities require collaboration with a community of experts from related domains. This paper deals with a community-driven data curation system for intrinsically disordered protein(IDP) research group. We suggest a metadata model for curated database for managing domain-specific contextual information on data and DLI, and also suggests a community-driven data curation process to improve the trustworthiness and reusability of data. In order to guarantee persistent accessibility to data, DOI is assigned to every data. Based on the metadata model and curation process, a community-driven data curation system is developed. IDP community creates PreSMoDB to establish a guideline for IDP study.

2 REQUIREMENTS FOR COMMUNITY-DRIVEN DATA CURATION SYSTEM

The requirement identified from IDP community is as follows:

Understandability of data with domain-specific metadata. Data should be provided with enough metadata to enhance the understandability. Metadata make the data understandable and easily integrated with other data from various repositories. The required metadata varies depending on the views of a creator, a deposit manager, and a reuser, respectively [2].

Trustworthiness of data via data review process. Data reusability depends largely on trustworthiness. In life science, deposit sites such as PDB [3] and GenBank [4] ensure trustworthiness through peer-review of data and then open it. The data review process is conducted by domain experts from the related subjects. Data creators submit data and required metadata necessary for review. Reviewers write a review report to give some feedback to submitters (or creators). Support of data review process is required to ensure trustworthiness of data.

Interlinking of data and related articles. Scientists survey and analyze existing related articles to define research problems. They also collect data from existing data repositories to create a data set, and analyze it to produce their own research results. DLI information becomes a key to discovery of new problems and comparison of solutions by traversing the interlinking between published data and articles related to research problems.

ACM ISBN 978-1-4503-5178-2/18/06.
https://doi.org/10.1145/3197026.3203866

Findability of data by DOI. Published data should be findable or accessible anytime and anywhere. Assignment of DOI to data ensures permanent findability of data.

3 COMMUNITY-DRIVEN CURATION PROCESS AND CURATED DB

To achieve data trustworthiness and understandability, a community-driven curation process (Fig.1) supports data verification by domain experts. In addition, DOI is assigned to approved data, ensuring findability. In the process, there is a communication path between a deposit manager and a reuser to maintain data integrity and value-addition. The deposit manager, one of research community members, is responsible for managing data and metadata. If a reuser wants to update data and metadata, he/she must ask the deposit manager to change them.

Metadata model for curated DB contains domain-specific contextual information that reflects community stakeholders' views on data. Contextual information on articles includes titles, researchers, abstract, key words, figures, tables, etc. Since DOI has been assigned to articles at publication time, DLI is modeled as relationships between data DOI and article DOI.

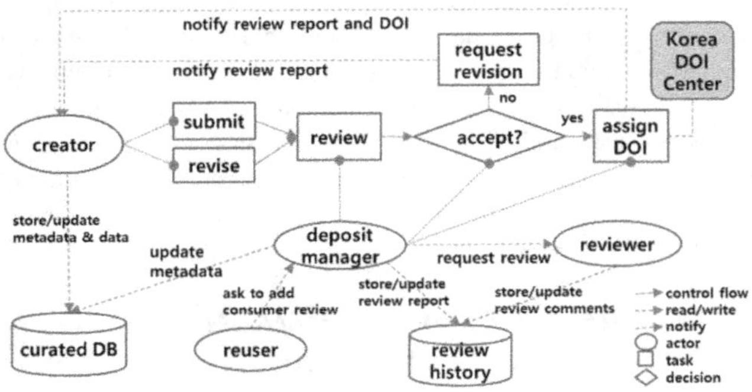

Figure 1: Community-driven data curation process.

4 DESIGN AND IMPLEMENTATION

4.1 Architecture

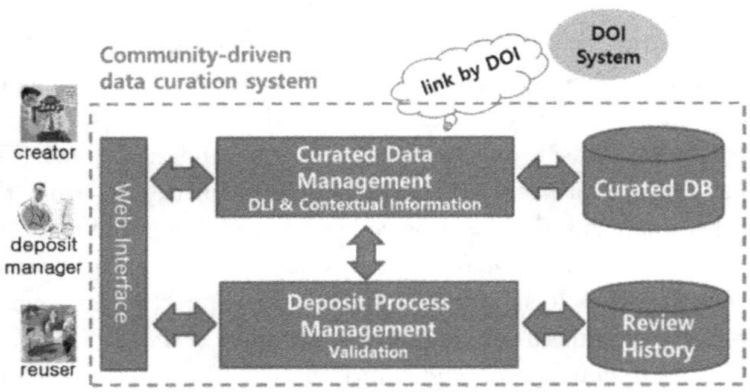

Figure 2: Data curation system architecture.

The architecture of our data curation system (Fig.2) consists of Curated Data Management(CDM) and Deposit Process Management(DPM) modules. It is supported by DOI system. DOI system guarantees accessibility to DOI-assigned data and articles. DPM manages data review tasks and their status, and CDM manages various types of metadata for contextual information. Web interface enables users to define and annotate metadata for submission, conduct peer reviews for data trustworthiness, explore DLI, and search and download data for reuse.

4.2 PreSMoDB: Application

There has been a dogma claiming that proteins only function when they have tertiary structure. According to [5], however, proteins with secondary structure can function in various ways. IDPs function like this and their active sites are called PreSMo(i.e., pre-structured motif). Since IDP and PreSMo are not deposited in PDB, researchers have to consume lots of time for detailed examination trying to figure out whether a certain discovery is new or not. In order to resolve this situation, IDP community has been created PreSMo DB(www.presmo.org) (Fig. 3).

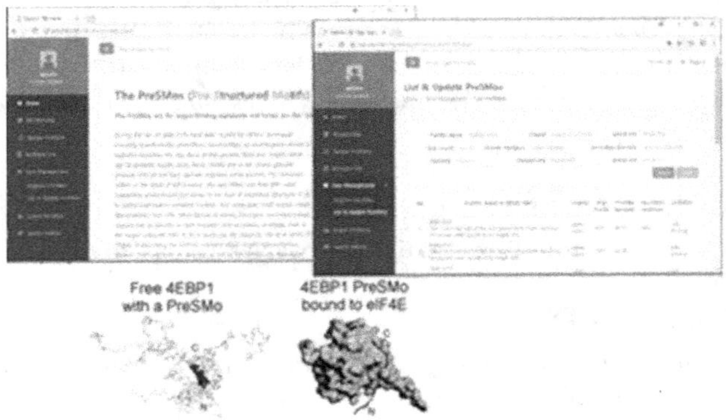

Figure 3: Example pages of PreSMoDB.

5 CONCLUSIONS

This paper has presented a community-driven data curation system and its application to PreSMoDB. PreSMoDB is evidence of breaking the rule that the function of a protein depends on its tertiary structure. We have constructed it as a guideline for scientific discovery in IDP study.

ACKNOWLEDGMENTS

This work was supported by KISTI Project K-18-L11 "Promotion of ecology for sharing scholarly information resources".

REFERENCES

[1] CrowdFlower, *2017 Data Scientist Report*, CrowdFlower 2017.
[2] Ixchel Faniel et al., "A Context-driven Approach to Data Curation for Reuse," International Digital Curation Conference, Amsterdam, February 22, 2016.
[3] RCSB PDB, http://www.rcsb.org/pdb/
[4] GenBank, http://www.ncbi.nlm.nih.gov/genbank/
[5] Hyun Lee et al. "Local Structural Elements in the Mostly Unstructured Transcriptional Activation Domain of Human p53," The Journal of Biological Chemistry, Vol. 275, No. 38, 2000, pp29426–294323.

Exploratory Investigation of Word Embedding in Song Lyric Topic Classification: Promising Preliminary Results

Kahyun Choi
School of Information Sciences
University of Illinois at Urbana Champaign
ckahyu2@illinois.edu

J. Stephen Downie
School of Information Sciences
University of Illinois at Urbana Champaign
jdownie@illinois.edu

ABSTRACT

In this work we investigate a data-driven vector representation of word embedding for the task of classifying song lyrics into their semantic topics. Previous research on topic classification of song lyrics has used traditional frequency based text representation. On the other hand, empirically driven word embedding has shown sensible performance improvment of text classification tasks, because of its ability to capture semantic relationship between words from big data. As averaging the word vectors from a short text is known to work reasonably well compared to the other comprehensive models utilizing their order, we adopt the averaged word vectors from the lyrics and user's interpretations about them, which are short in general, as the feature for this classification task. This simple approach showed promising classification accuracy of 57%. From this, we envision the potential of the data-driven approaches to creating features, such as the sequence of word vectors and doc2vec models, to improve the performance of the system.

CCS CONCEPTS

• **Information systems → Content analysis and feature selection**;

KEYWORDS

Song lyrics, Subject, Topic, Metadata, Word embedding, Classification

ACM Reference Format:

Kahyun Choi and J. Stephen Downie. 2018. Exploratory Investigation of Word Embedding in Song Lyric Topic Classification: Promising Preliminary Results. In *JCDL '18: The 18th ACM/IEEE Joint Conference on Digital Libraries, June 3–7, 2018, Fort Worth, TX, USA.* ACM, New York, NY, USA, Article 4, 2 pages. https://doi.org/10.1145/3197026.3203883

1 INTRODUCTION

The underlying topics of song lyrics have long been considered as useful metadata for the browsing and searching songs [5]. However, due to the poetic nature of lyrics it is difficult to label the songs based on their topics even for humans especially when it comes to a digital music library with big dataset. This inherent difficulty of creating a labeled dataset calls for an automatic topic labeling/classification system. However, once again training such a supervised learning system is challenging as well for the same reason: understanding the meaning of song lyrics is difficult for a machine learning algorithm, too. This problem was first addressed in [2][3], where user interpretations in addition to song lyrics were proposed as a new feature for this classification task. Because user interpretations contain richer topic-related information in a more straightforward form compared to the ambiguous song lyrics, the classification systems using user interpretations as well as the lyric text showed superior performance to its counterpart based solely on the lyrics. To this end, they collected a large amount of comments from the website, `songmeanings.com` where music lovers discuss about song lyrics and share their interpretations about them.

This paper uses a more advanced way to extract some higher level features from both the song lyrics and user interpretations. Instead of the primitive Term-Frequency (TF) representation that the preceding topic classification systems were based on, we propose to use a more advanced word embedding representation, `fastText` [1]. While the TF representation can effectively describe the simple statistics of the bag-of-words representation of a document, the independent and sparse nature of the elements of the TF vector requires the feature to be too high dimensional. Word embedding techniques can address this issue by learning a model that converts a word into a dense vector representation, which should subsequently be able to recover the other neighboring words [6]. In this way, the vector representation can encode the co-occurrence information of the words spread in the large corpus. Often, this model is represented as an artificial neural network, and consequently a deep neural network architecture is also introduced to learn this embedding more effectively.

We test out `fastText` to create the vector representation of words used in song lyrics and user interpretations. By using them we create feature vectors that are known to be more manageable and semantically meaningful. Eventually, topic classification tasks benefit from these new features.

2 EXPERIMENTS

2.1 Datasets and Preprocessing

We follow the same experimental setup used in [3]. The dataset of 800 popular songs was labeled by experts in `songfacts.com`. The balanced dataset has 8 categories in total: places, sex, ex-lover, drugs, war, parent, religion, and death. Song lyrics and user comments are collected from `songmeanings.com` where millions of user comments about meanings of song lyrics are posted.

For the word embedding, we used the word vectors trained on English Wikipedia using `fastText` [1]. The pre-trained vector is

JCDL '18, June 3–7, 2018, Fort Worth, TX, USA

ACM ISBN 978-1-4503-5178-2/18/06.
https://doi.org/10.1145/3197026.3203883

	TF	Weighted Average of Word Vectors	Average of Unique Word Vectors
Accuracy	59.00	56.60	52.00

Table 1: Classification accuracy

trained based on the skipgram model [6] and has 300 dimensions. Because this model utilizes sub-word information, it showed better performance than others in multiple tasks including human similarity judgment and word analogy tasks than `word2vec` models. As an already trained neural network model `fastText` predicts the 300 dimensional vector representation of a given word through its ordinary feedforward process.

Song lyrics and user comments were broken down into words and only alphabetic letters were kept to remove irrelevant words including typos and user IDs. Next, the words were lemmatized to group words with the same meaning and common stopwords in English were deleted.

2.2 Feature Representations and Classification

Among many classifiers, we used naïve Bayes for this preliminary experiments since it performs almost as good as Support Vector Machines (SVM) in the previous study [3] while it is faster than SVM. Considering the small size of the dataset, we excluded deep learning-based classification algorithms, although we believe that they could perform better than other classifiers once a bigger dataset is available for training. We performed 10-fold cross validation and reported the average accuracy.

Since `fastText` produces a vector per word, a document, i.e. lyrics of a song or a user comment, is represented with a sequence of vectors, whose length varies depending on the number of words. Instead of treating this sequential input data as it is, we use their weighted sum as the representative word vector, where weights are proportional to the frequency of the words. This proposed feature aggregation is based on the observation that averaging word vectors work reasonably well when classifying short texts [4].

3 RESULTS

Table 1 compares accuracy of classification systems with different feature representations. The classifier based on term frequency yielded the best accuracy, 59% [3]. When the word vectors were averaged while considering frequency of each word, the classifier performed pretty well with 56.6% accuracy. On the other hand, when frequency of words were ignored, the classification accuracy dropped to 52%. This indicates that the frequency of words still plays a role in topic classification. The confusion matrices also show how categories are confused with each other. The classification based on TF penalized "places" heavily (Figure 1) while one based on word vectors favors the category (Figure 2).

4 CONCLUSION

We took the first step towards utilizing word embedding for lyric topic classification task. Because lyrics and comments are short, averaging the word vectors kept topic information quite a lot and

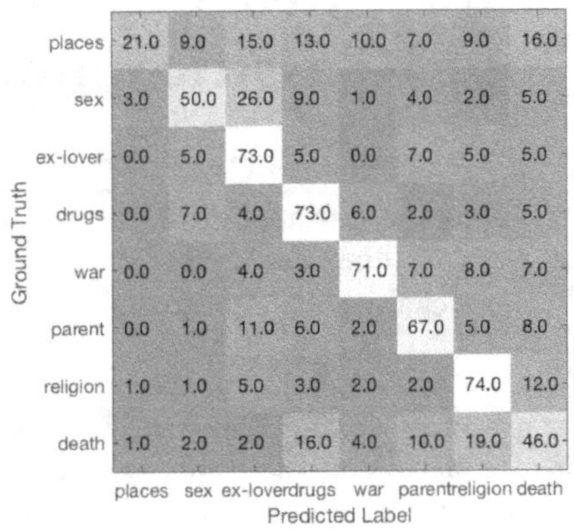

Figure 1: Confusion matrix of the classifier with TF

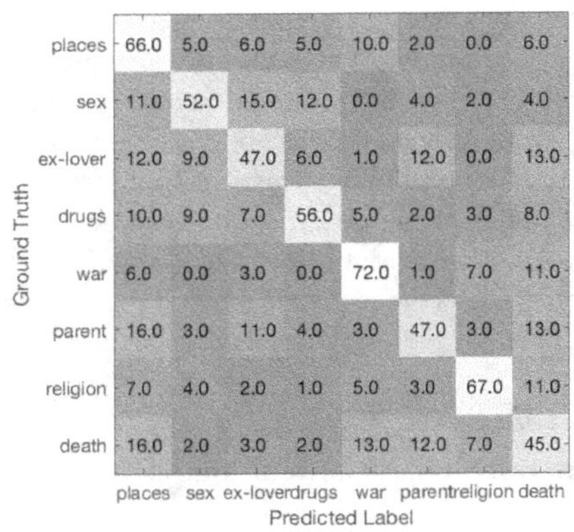

Figure 2: Confusion matrix of the classifier with averaged word vectors where frequency of words were allowed

performed well on the topic classification tasks. However, we believe that more sophisticated ways to describe song lyrics and the user interpretations can improve the classification performance. Taking sequences into account or applying `doc2vec` are among them.

REFERENCES

[1] Piotr Bojanowski, Edouard Grave, Armand Joulin, and Tomas Mikolov. 2016. Enriching Word Vectors with Subword Information. *arXiv preprint arXiv:1607.04606* (2016).

[2] Kahyun Choi, Jin Ha Lee, and J Stephen Downie. 2014. What is this song about anyway?: Automatic classification of subject using user interpretations and lyrics. *Proceedings of the 14th ACM/IEEE-CS Joint Conference on Digital Libraries* (2014), 453–454.

[3] Kahyun Choi, Jin Ha Lee, Xiao Hu, and J Stephen Downie. 2016. Music Subject Classification Based on Lyrics and User Interpretations. *Proceedings of the American Society for Information Science and Technology* (2016), 1–10.

[4] Cedric De Boom, Steven Van Canneyt, Thomas Demeester, and Bart Dhoedt. 2016. Representation learning for very short texts using weighted word embedding aggregation. *Pattern Recognition Letters* 80 (2016), 150–156.

[5] Jin Ha Lee and J Stephen Downie. 2004. Survey Of Music Information Needs, Uses, And Seeking Behaviours: Preliminary Findings. *Proceedings of the 5th International Conference on Music Information Retrieval (ISMIR)* 2004 (2004), 441–446.

[6] Tomas Mikolov, Kai Chen, Greg Corrado, and Jeffrey Dean. 2013. Efficient estimation of word representations in vector space. *arXiv preprint arXiv:1301.3781* (2013).

Can Rough Co-citation Improve the Performance of Co-citation Clustering?

Masaki Eto
Gakushuin Women's College
Tokyo, Japan
masaki.eto@gakushuin.ac.jp

ABSTRACT

Co-citation clustering is often used for mapping science in the field of bibliometrics. It may be useful to utilize information from parsing the full-text of citing documents to obtain a more precise result of the clustering. Recently, "rough co-citation," which is weak co-citation relationship and can be used to indicate new related documents, has been proposed for scientific paper searches. Applying rough co-citation to the task of clustering will be beneficial. This study aims to explore whether rough co-citation can improve the performance of co-citation clustering. A clustering experiment is conducted to evaluate the effects of using rough co-citation. The experimental results indicate that the proposed technique, which uses both the original co-citation and the rough co-citation, tends to outperform the baseline technique, which only uses the original co-citation.

CCS CONCEPTS

• **Information systems → Clustering**; Document representation; Link and co-citation analysis;

KEYWORDS

Citation context; Clustering; Co-citation; TF-IDF

ACM Reference Format:
Masaki Eto. 2018. Can Rough Co-citation Improve the Performance of Co-citation Clustering?. In *Proceedings of The 18th ACM/IEEE Joint Conference on Digital Libraries (JCDL '18)*. ACM, New York, NY, USA, 2 pages. https://doi.org/10.1145/3197026.3203908

1 INTRODUCTION

Co-citation clustering is often used for mapping science in the field of bibliometrics. It may be useful to utilize information from parsing the full-text of citing documents to obtain a more precise result of the clustering. For example, Boyack, Small, and Klavans [1] proposed a co-citation clustering technique using strong co-citation relationships based on the results of parsing the full-text of documents.

For information retrieval, not clustering, other metrics for measuring co-citation linkage based on the parsing the full-text have been developed. For example, Eto [2, 3] proposed "rough co-citation" as a weak co-citation relationship. He defined a rough co-citation relationship as "a linkage between a pair of documents cited by two other documents in a similar citation context" (Fig. 1). Additionally, he reported that rough co-citation could indicate new related documents that are not identified by the original co-citation linkages, and would, therefore, increase the success of scientific paper searches. Applying rough co-citation to the task of clustering will be beneficial.

This study aims to explore whether rough co-citation can improve the performance of co-citation clustering. Specifically, this study proposes a new co-citation clustering technique using both the original co-citation and the rough co-citation methods, and empirically evaluates the clustering results.

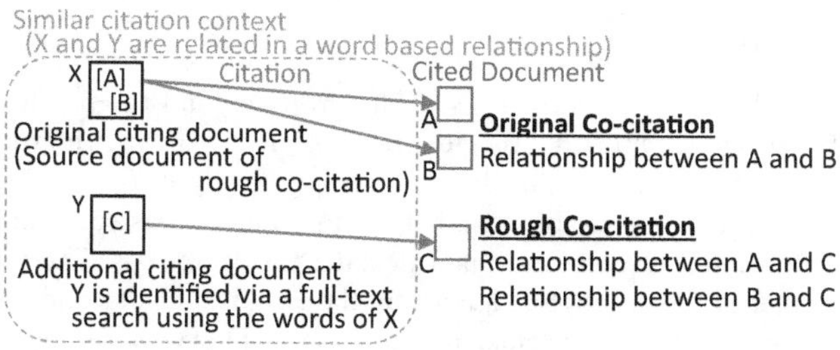

Figure 1: Example of rough co-citation relationships.

2 CO-CITATION CLUSTERING

2.1 Similarity score between documents

A co-citation-based similarity score between two documents d_i and d_j is computed as follows:

$$sim(d_i, d_j) = o\_coci(d_i, d_j) + r\_coci(d_i, d_j) \times \alpha, \quad (1)$$

where $o\_coci(d_i, d_j)$ is the frequency of the original co-citation between d_i and d_j; t is the number of top-ranked documents by a full-text search for each original citing document; $r\_coci(d_i, d_j)$ is the frequency of rough co-citation between d_i and d_j, when t documents are used as additional citing documents (Fig. 1); and α is a decay parameter for balancing the degrees of difference between the two co-citations. This study uses two t values (t = 10 and 20) and three α values (α = 0.1, 0.5, and 0.9). Furthermore, the original co-citation clustering technique is adopted as the baseline, where $sim(d_i, d_j)$ is computed by $o\_coci(d_i, d_j)$.

2.2 Clustering method

Standard hierarchical clustering using the ward method is applied to the distance matrices based on Eq. (1). Each element of a distance

ACM ISBN 978-1-4503-5178-2/18/06.
https://doi.org/10.1145/3197026.3203908

matrix is calculated as follows:

$$Distance(d_i, d_j) = exp(-sim(d_i, d_j)), \quad (2)$$

where *exp* stands for the exponential function for normalizing the value of the distance from 0 to 1. Note that the distances for the elements of the main diagonal, i.e., $i = j$, are set at 0.

3 EXPERIMENTAL SETUP

3.1 Data

This study used the Open Access Subset of PubMed Central. The test collection was constructed by selecting approximately 152,000 documents from the subset, under the condition that the documents had at least one citation linkage with another document in the subset.

The clustering experiment was conducted on 2,010 documents that were selected from all the subset documents, under the condition that each document was cited by 20 or more documents in the subset. Additionally, all documents that cited the 2,010 documents were used as the source documents of the rough co-citation (Fig. 1), and additional citing documents were specified via a TF-IDF-based full-text search (INDRI) using the title words of the source document. Note that when additional citing documents cited the same documents, these duplicates were excluded.

3.2 Evaluation criterion

To evaluate the performances of the proposed and the baseline clustering techniques, the experiment focused on internal coherence based on MeSH descriptors. Specifically, $rel(d_i, d_j)$, i.e., the degree of the relationship between d_i and d_j, was computed by the Simpson coefficient that calculates the degree based on the number of the descriptors shared by the two documents, and the clustering score was calculated as in Zhao and Karypis [4]:

$$Score = \sum_{r=1}^{k} n_r \left(\frac{1}{n_r^2} \sum_{d_i, d_j \in S_r} rel(d_i, d_j)\right), \quad (3)$$

where k denotes the number of clusters; S denotes the set of the 2,010 documents; $S_1, S_2, ..., S_k$ denote each one of the k clusters; and $n_1, n_2, ..., n_k$ denote the sizes of the corresponding clusters. This study examined five k values (k = 2, 4, 6, 8, and 10).

4 RESULTS

4.1 Statistics

In the 2,010 × 2,010 distance matrices, if an element has the value of 1, this means that no co-citation relationships were observed. Table 1 depicts the percentage of such elements in each distance matrix. As depicted in Table 1, rough co-citation can detect document relationships that cannot be identified by the original co-citation approach.

Figure 2 depicts the standard deviation values of the cluster size for each k cluster created by the proposed technique with (t, α) and the baseline technique. The value for the baseline is the highest in almost all cases, and tends to have trends different to the proposed techniques. This suggests that rough co-citation has the potential to reduce variations in cluster size.

Table 1: Elements having a value of 1 in the distance matrix.

Baseline	Proposed (t = 10)	Proposed (t = 20)
97.3%	84.5%	78.0%

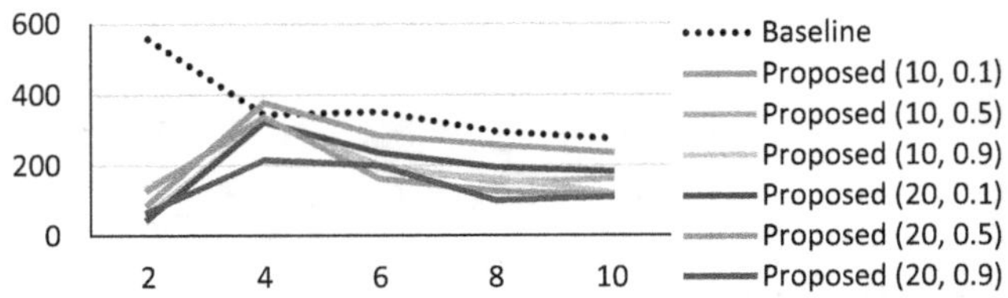

Figure 2: Standard deviation of cluster size.

4.2 Clustering score

The performance of the clustering techniques was calculated by Eq. (3). As depicted in Table 2, the maximum scores for each k value, which are indicated in bold numbers, are obtained by the scores of the proposed technique. Additionally, the scores of the baseline are the lowest scores in almost all cases. These results suggest that using rough co-citation has a positive effect on co-citation clustering.

Table 2: Clustering Score.

	2	4	6	8	10
Baseline	0.0739	0.0748	0.0752	0.0761	0.0773
Proposed (10, 0.1)	0.0749	0.0747	0.0764	0.0776	0.0782
Proposed (10, 0.5)	0.0749	**0.0769**	0.0764	0.0781	0.0785
Proposed (10, 0.9)	**0.0751**	0.0766	0.0771	0.0785	0.0785
Proposed (20, 0.1)	**0.0751**	0.0768	**0.0785**	**0.0796**	0.0797
Proposed (20, 0.5)	0.0748	0.0753	0.0763	0.0776	0.0785
Proposed (20, 0.9)	0.0750	0.0766	0.0768	0.0787	**0.0798**

5 CONCLUSIONS

This study proposes a new co-citation clustering technique. The proposed technique, which uses both the original co-citation and the rough co-citation, tends to outperform the baseline technique, which uses only the original co-citation.

A lot of work remains to be completed. One of the future tasks is to evaluate the performance of the proposed clustering technique based on the viewpoints of external isolation.

ACKNOWLEDGMENTS

This work was supported by JSPS KAKENHI Grant Number JP17K00455.

REFERENCES

[1] K.W. Boyack, H. Small, and R. Klavans. 2013. Improving the Accuracy of Co-citation Clustering Using Full Text. *Journal of the Association for Information Science and Technology*, 64(9):1759-1767.

[2] M. Eto. 2016. Rough Co-citation as a Measure of Relationship to Expand Co-citation Networks for Scientific Paper Searches, In *Proceedings of the 79th ASIS&T Annual Meeting*, Copenhagen, Denmark.

[3] M. Eto. 2017. Increasing Source Documents of Rough Co-citation to Expand Co-citation Networks for Scientific Paper Searches. ASIS&T Workshop on Informetrics and Scientometrics Research, Arlington, Virginia, USA.

[4] Y. Zhao. and G. Karypis. 2005. Hierarchical Clustering Algorithms for Document Datasets. *Data Mining and Knowledge Discovery*, 10, 141-168.

ViDeX: A Platform for Personalizing Educational Videos

Matthew Fong
University of British Columbia
mfong@ece.ubc.ca

Samuel Dodson
University of British Columbia
dodsons@mail.ubc.ca

Xueqin Zhang
University of British Columbia
xueqin@ece.ubc.ca

Ido Roll
University of British Columbia
ido.roll@ubc.ca

Sidney Fels
University of British Columbia
ssfels@ece.ubc.ca

ABSTRACT

As video-based learning is increasingly used in all sectors of education, there is a need for video players that support *active viewing* practices. We introduce a video player that allows students to mark up video with highlights, tags, and notes in order to personalize their video-based learning experience.

CCS CONCEPTS

• Information systems → Video search; • Applied computing → Interactive learning environments; Annotation;

KEYWORDS

active viewing, annotation, personalization, video-based learning

ACM Reference Format:

Matthew Fong, Samuel Dodson, Xueqin Zhang, Ido Roll, and Sidney Fels. 2018. ViDeX: A Platform for Personalizing Educational Videos. In *JCDL '18: The 18th ACM/IEEE Joint Conference on Digital Libraries, June 3–7, 2018, Fort Worth, TX, USA.* ACM, New York, NY, USA, 2 pages. https://doi.org/10.1145/3197026.3203865

1 INTRODUCTION

Video has become a popular medium for learning, especially as digital libraries [e.g., 4] and online learning platforms, such as edX, continue to grow their video collections. There are many advantages of video. For example, video allows students to control the pace of their learning by adjusting the playback speed and replaying the content as necessary. Video is now used in all sectors of education; however, video players usually encourage one-way interaction between students and content. How can digital libraries better support learning from video?

To support *active viewing* practices, we created ViDeX, a video player that allows students to personalize video with highlights, tags, and notes. By active viewing, we refer to the interactions between students and video that may suggest greater levels of learning than passively watching video from start to end. Providing students with a set of video annotation tools could better support students' different learning styles.

JCDL '18, June 3–7, 2018, Fort Worth, TX, USA

ACM ISBN 978-1-4503-5178-2/18/06.
https://doi.org/10.1145/3197026.3203865

2 PREVIOUS WORK

While there has been work on creating video players to support learning from video [e.g., 2, 3, 8], most do not allow students to add their own content to videos. In other media, students can easily personalize their learning materials. When reading a textbook, for example, many students highlight and take notes. The practice of annotating is considered a part of active reading and is associated with increases in learning outcomes [1]. While annotating is a popular and effective reading practice, most video players do not allow students to highlight, tag, or take notes within the video. By providing students with a set of tools for annotating video, ViDeX may be able to support more active viewing practices.

3 VIDEX

ViDeX is a video player designed for video-based learning. Students can annotate video in a way that is similar to marking up text using a digital reading environment, such as the Amazon Kindle platform. ViDeX is comprised of three elements: the Player, the Filmstrip, and the Transcript. In addition to these, ViDeX has a note taking area below the Filmstrip. Students can write a note that is timestamped to the current video time. Notes are organized by video time.

3.1 Player

The Player is similar to other video players in that it has a toolbar that allows students to play, navigate forwards and backwards, and adjust playback speed, closed captioning, and volume. The Player is unique in its support for creating and (re)playing video annotations. The Player toolbar also allows the student to tag, highlight, take notes, and play previously highlighted content. Clicking the "Play Highlights" button allows students to replay previously highlighted content. When this button is clicked, the playhead jumps from one highlight to the next until all highlights of a specified color have been played. The Player also displays the highlights and tags that have been created in the video to give the student a visual overview of their personalized video.

3.2 Filmstrip

The Filmstrip provides a visual overview of the video. The Filmstrip is made of thumbnails, where each thumbnail represents a part of the video. By moving their cursor across the Filmstrip, students can preview the frame corresponding to the part of the video the cursor is on. Students can click on the Filmstrip to navigate to that part of the video. Students can also select content by clicking and dragging their mouse across the thumbnails. When students make a selection, the annotation widget appears allowing them to add a highlight or

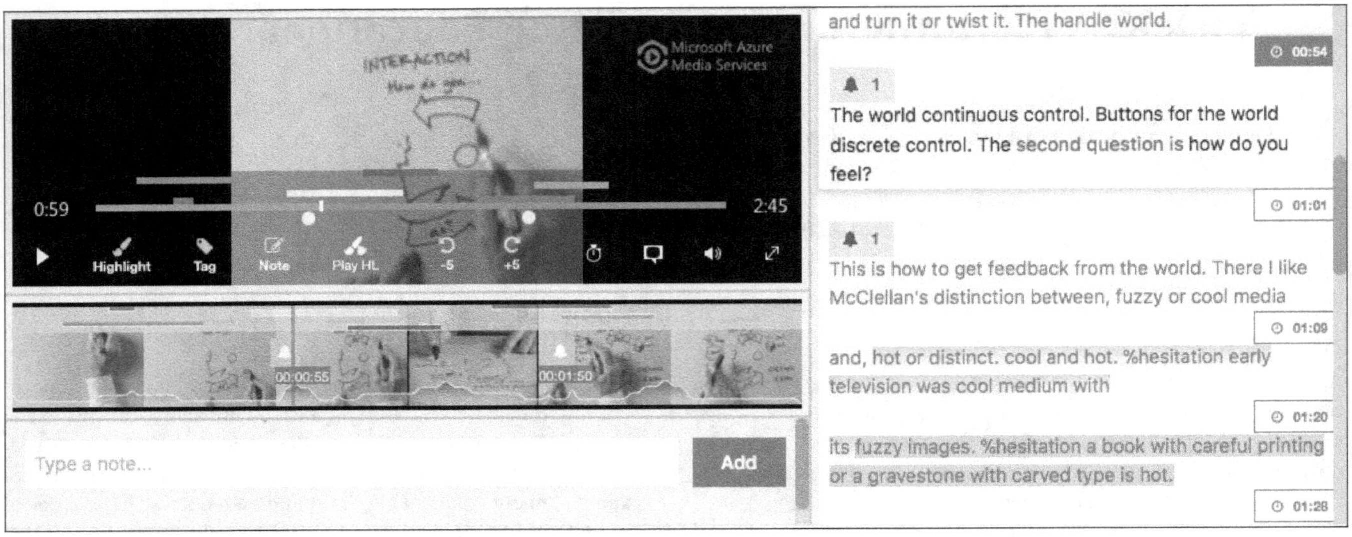

Figure 1: A screenshot of ViDeX with highlights and tags visible. The Player is displayed at the top left, the Filmstrip at the middle left, the commenting area at the bottom left, and the Transcript at the right.

tag to the specified content. Like the Player, the Filmstrip shows the highlights and tags students have added to the video. At the bottom of the Filmstrip, a graph displays the amount of times a student has watched specific parts of the video.

3.3 Transcript

A record of the spoken content of the video is provided by the Transcript. The content of the Transcript is synced with the video playback, allowing students to click content in the Transcript to navigate to that part of the video. The currently spoken word is displayed in a different color than the rest of the Transcript, acting as a text-based playhead. Students can skim the video by scrolling up and down the Transcript. Because each word in the Transcript is mapped to a time in the video, highlighting, tagging, and note taking is synced between the Player, Transcript, and Filmstrip. Students can highlight and tag by clicking and dragging across the text and using the annotation widget.

3.4 Personalization

Personalization allows students to enhance video with their own content. The video annotation tools made available to students through ViDeX may be beneficial to their video-based learning. Video annotations may support the same functions of text annotations identified by Marshall [5]. Highlighting and tagging could be used for bookmarking content to be (re)viewed, while notes may provide students with an *in situ* area to collect their thoughts and reflections when and where they occur. By providing these tools for video annotation, video players could support students as they engage in more active viewing practices.

4 FUTURE WORK

Testing ViDeX with students is needed to evaluate the usefulness and usability of video annotation and its effects on active viewing. This semester, we have deployed ViDeX in multiple undergraduate classes in multiple faculties. The analysis of log data and follow-up questionnaires and interviews will be used to identify how and why students use ViDeX. In addition to testing the latest version of ViDeX, we are working towards supporting social interactions within video by i) allowing students to share their annotations with peers and teachers and ii) the identification of consensus annotations using the "wisdom of the crowds" [7]. The former is supported by constructivist learning theory and the latter has been used for text annotations [5, 6].

Acknowledgements. This work was supported by the University of British Columbia Teaching and Learning Enhancement Fund, the Natural Sciences and Engineering Research Council of Canada, and Microsoft Corporation.

REFERENCES

[1] Thomas H Anderson and Bonnie B Armbruster. 1984. Studying. In *Handbook of Reading Research.* Pearson, New York, NY, 657–679.

[2] Elena L Glassman, Juho Kim, Andrés Monroy-Hernández, and Meredith Ringel Morris. 2015. Mudslide: A spatially anchored census of student confusion for online lecture videos. In *Proceedings of the 33rd Annual ACM Conference on Human Factors in Computing Systems.* ACM, New York, NY, 1555–1564.

[3] Juho Kim, Philip J Guo, Carrie J Cai, Shang-Wen Daniel Li, Krzysztof Z Gajos, and Robert C Miller. 2014. Data-driven interaction techniques for improving navigation of educational videos. In *Proceedings of the 27th Annual ACM Symposium on User Interface Software and Technology.* 563–572.

[4] Gary Marchionini, Barbara M Wildemuth, and Gary Geisler. 2006. The open video digital library: a Möbius strip of research and practice. *Journal of the Association for Information Science and Technology* 57, 12 (2006), 1629–1643.

[5] Catherine C Marshall. 1997. Annotation: from paper books to the digital library. In *Proceedings of the Second ACM International Conference on Digital Libraries.* ACM, New York, NY, 131–140.

[6] Frank Shipman, Morgan Price, Catherine C Marshall, and Gene Golovchinsky. 2003. Identifying useful passages in documents based on annotation patterns. In *Research and Advanced Technology for Digital Libraries,* Traugott Koch and Ingeborg Torvik Sølvberg (Eds.). Springer, Berlin, Germany, 101–112.

[7] James Surowiecki. 2004. *The wisdom of crowds: why the many are smarter than the few and how collective wisdom shapes business, economies, societies, and nations.* Doubleday, New York, NY.

[8] Sarah Weir, Juho Kim, Krzysztof Z Gajos, and Robert C Miller. 2015. Learnersourcing subgoal labels for how-to videos. In *Proceedings of the 18th ACM Conference on Computer Supported Cooperative Work & Social Computing.* 405–416.

Investigating Impact Features in Editorial Pre-Screening of Research Papers

Tirthankar Ghosal, Rajeev Verma, Asif Ekbal, Sriparna Saha, Pushpak Bhattacharyya
Indian Institute of Technology Patna
(tirthankar.pcs16,rajeev.ee15,asif,sriparna,pb)@iitp.ac.in

ABSTRACT

Editorial pre-screening is the first step in academic peer review. The deluge of research papers and the huge amount of submissions being made to journals these days makes editorial decision a very challenging task. The current work attempts to investigate certain impact factors that may have a role in the editorial decision making process. The proposed work exhibits potential for the development of an AI-assisted peer review system which could aid the editors as well as the authors in making appropriate decisions in reasonable time and thus accelerate the overall process of scholarly publishing.

CCS CONCEPTS

• **Information systems** → *Document filtering*; *Document filtering*; **Content analysis and feature selection**; *Document filtering*; • **Applied computing** → **Digital libraries and archives**;

KEYWORDS

article classification system, scope of an academic article, quality of academic article, digital libraries, citation analysis

ACM Reference Format:
Tirthankar Ghosal, Rajeev Verma, Asif Ekbal, Sriparna Saha, Pushpak Bhattacharyya. 2018. Investigating Impact Features in Editorial Pre-Screening of Research Papers. In *JCDL '18: The 18th ACM/IEEE Joint Conference on Digital Libraries, June 3–7, 2018, Fort Worth, TX, USA.* ACM, New York, NY, USA, 2 pages. https://doi.org/10.1145/3197026.3203910

1 INTRODUCTION

Peer review, despite criticisms, is still the only widely accepted method for research validation. However with the ever-expanding volume of research articles and the number of submissions made, it is increasingly becoming difficult for the editors to keep up with the pace of latest research, manually go through each submission, respond to the author(s) or forward to the expert reviewers in reasonable time. The editor is usually overwhelmed with this "burden of science". We begin our investigation on a set of accepted and desk-rejected papers along with their author-editor-reviewer interactions, made available to us by the reputed scholarly publishing house, Elsevier. Rigorous analysis of about 5,500 rejected articles from 11 different Computer Science journals led us to assert that apart from some journal specific factors, there exist at least 5 standard factors (Fig. 1) that leads to rejection from the editor's desk:

(1) Appropriateness of the article to the journal (**Scope**).
(2) **Quality**/Standard and impact of the article under review.
(3) Percentage overlap with existing articles **(Redundancy)**.
(4) **Spelling, grammar and language** of the article under review.
(5) Visually discriminative features of the article such as **template mismatch** (article not being prepared according to journal guidelines and formatting requirements), articles not having the standard components of a proper scientific communication.

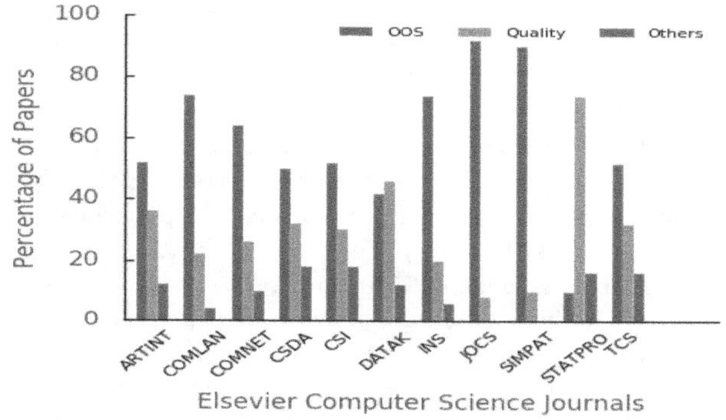

Figure 1: Analysis of Desk Rejected papers due to *out-of-scope* (OOS) and Quality(Q) for 11 different Elsevier Computer Science Journals. 500 REJECTED papers for each journal were considered in the study

Extensive study of data led us to the following 3 observations :
(1) **Addressing Scope** : *If a paper belongs to a certain domain, then majority of its bibliography would fall in that domain*
(2) **Addressing Quality** : *Better is the bibliography of a paper, higher is the prospect of quality content inside the body of the paper.*
(3) **Content** : *Some content features and location of impact/domain citations exert a "local influence" on the corresponding sections of a scientific article that greatly determines it's credibility as well as scope.*

2 DATA

We use a collection of 15,536 accepted papers from 3 different Elsevier Computer Science journals to extract information for our experiments. We also consider and review a set of 5,500 desk-rejected papers pertaining to 11 journals *viz., Artificial Intelligence* (ARTINT), *Computer Networks* (COMNET), *Theoretical Computer Science* (TCS), *Statistics and Probability Letters* (STATPRO), *Computational Statistics and Data Analysis* (CSDA), *Computer Languages, Systems and Structures* (COMLAN), *Computer Standards and Interfaces* (CSI), *Data and Knowledge Engineering* (DATAK), *Information Sciences* (INS), *Journal of Computational Science* (JOCS), and *Simulation Modelling Practice and Theory* (SIMPAT). We also went through about 7,000 author-editor-reviewer interactions of accepted, desk-rejected

JCDL '18, June 3–7, 2018, Fort Worth, TX, USA

ACM ISBN 978-1-4503-5178-2/18/06.
https://doi.org/10.1145/3197026.3203910

and rejected-after-review papers consisting of more than 2.1 million lines of review data to investigate the different causes of rejection. For the purpose of our machine learning experiments, we use a subset of these accepted and rejected papers (500 ACCEPTED+500 REJECTED articles each from ARTINT, STATPRO and COMNET). However we mine the entire accepted articles of these journals to create appropriate information and meta data repositories from which our features are derived. We generate word vectors trained on all the accepted articles of 223 Elsevier Computer Science journals which amount to 41,737,169 sentences from 400K articles. These we use to generate semantic vector representations of research articles and cluster them (Section 3).

3 FEATURE ENGINEERING

a) Scope Features: In spite of having merit, many articles are simply desk-rejected because they do not posses the content to cater to the audience of the respective journal. We extract several features from different sections of a manuscript w.r.t. the stored history information of accepted articles of the particular journal[2] :
(1) Number of keywords match (author-listed+extracted) (*KWM*)
(2) Semantic distance of a candidate article from the cluster of history accepted articles (*CD*)
(3) Overlap of bibliographic titles with history articles (*Bib-Title*)
(4) Overlap of bibliographic venues with history articles (*Bib-Conf/Jour*)
(5) Average of the number of times the authors published in the particular journal (*Auth-freq*)
We design a novel function **Citation Effect** which counts the frequency of citations within the body of the paper and employ it as a weight of (4) and (5). *In-domain* keywords, referred titles and venues have higher occurrence across all the accepted articles.
b) Quality Features: Inspired by the works on scientific impact prediction [1, 3], we extract meta information from the author profile, bibliography section and content to arrive at a set of features that to some extent plays a role in determining the quality of the prospective manuscript. **Author** credibility features are *Primary author's h-index, citation count. Average, Maximum* of *h*-indices, citation counts of all the authors (from Google Scholar). Similarly for the **Affiliation** credibility, we take the *research scores* and the *number of research articles produced* by the author-affiliated institutions from the Times Higher Education World University Rankings and Scopus.To measure the **bibliography quality** we take the citation count of the referred articles, reputation of the venues where published (CORE Computer Science rankings, h-index and SCImago Journal Rank valuesand temporal distance of the references from the submission date. **Content** features include the number of uncited references, mathematical equations, figures, and tables.

	ARTINT		STATPRO		COMNET	
R	Feature	IG	Feature	IG	Feature	IG
1	*KWM* †	0.32	*CD* †	0.30	*Auth-max-cit*	0.21
2	*Bib-Conf* †	0.28	*KWM* †	0.11	*Auth-avg-h*	0.19
3	*Bib-Title* †	0.21	*Affl-max-doc*	0.09	*Auth-avg-cit*	0.18
4	*Auth-avg-h*	0.20	*Auth-freq* †	0.07	*Auth-max-h*	0.17
5	*Venue-avg-conf*	0.16	*Math-eq*	0.06	*Bib-Title* †	0.16
6	*W-Imp-Cit-avg*	0.15	*Affl-avg-doc*	0.05	*CD* †	0.15
7	*Auth-max-cit*	0.15	*Affl-P-doc*	0.05	*KWM* †	0.14
8	*Auth-max-h*	0.14	*Bib-Jour* †	0.05	*Bib-Conf* †	0.13
9	*Affl-max-doc*	0.13	*Affl-avg-rs*	0.03	*Venue-avg-h*	0.12
10	*CD* †	0.13	*Affl-max-rs*	0.03	*W-Imp-Cit-avg*	0.11

Table 1: Feature ranking (top 10) based on Information Gain (IG), R→ Rank, Scope features(†), *Auth-avg-h→ Average of h-indices of authors, Venue-avg-conf→ Average of CORE rankings of referred conferences[A*→6,A→4,B→3,C→2,Others→1], W-Imp-Cit-avg→ Weighted average impact citation counts, Auth-max-cit→ Maximum of the citation count of the authors, Auth-max-h→ Maximum of the h-indices of the authors, Affl-max-doc→ Maximum of the research articles produced by the author affiliations, Affl-P-doc→ Research articles produced by affiliation of the primary author, Math-eq→ Number of mathematical equations in the manuscript, Affl-avg-doc→ Average of the research articles produced by the author affiliations, Affl-avg-rs→ Average of the research scores of affiliated institutions,Affl-max-rs→ Maximum of the research scores of affiliated institutions, Venue-avg-h→ Average of h-indices rankings of referred venues*

4 EXPERIMENTS AND ANALYSIS

We investigate the merit of our feature set (30 features) on 3 different journals to identify accepted and rejected articles. Table 1 provides a ranked list of top-10 performing features based on their Information Gain (IG) values. We can clearly see that *Scope* features are the most contributing ones against ARTINT, STATPRO and to some extent for COMNET. Thus validating our claim that a significant amount of desk-rejections result due to the article being *out-of-scope* of the journal concerned. We find the dominance of author's credibility for COMNET but not the affiliation. This signifies that high impact authors not only belong to premier institutions but also to non-premier institutions. The reputation of venues/conferences of bibliographic citations also has an impact thus corroborating our motivation for the quality of a research article. Artificial Intelligence is an interdisciplinary domain, hence crisp clusters could not be formed for ARTINT. However, STATPRO and COMNET have a narrow scope as compared to ARTINT. Good semantic clusters could be obtained from the accepted articles of these journals and hence outliers (distance from clusters of accepted articles) could be detected precisely. Analysis reveals that there are a limited set of specialist authors who regularly contribute to STATPRO, mostly from premier institutions. And premier institutions usually have a higher research output. Hence, affiliation and author's frequency of publication prove to be effective for STATPRO. Presence of mathematical equations in STATPRO accepted papers is another prominent feature for obvious reasons. Our approach performs with reasonable accuracy to identify accepted/desk-rejected articles (92.99% for ARTINT, 83.64% for STATPRO and 93.57% for COMNET) with Random Forest classifier.

5 CONCLUSIONS

This work is a preliminary investigation on the reasons for desk-rejections of academic manuscripts. We present important insights into the impact factors for desk-rejections across 3 different journals.

REFERENCES

[1] Yuxiao Dong, Reid A Johnson, and Nitesh V Chawla. 2016. Can scientific impact be predicted? *IEEE Transactions on Big Data* 2, 1 (2016), 18–30.

[2] Tirthankar Ghosal, Rajeev Verma, Asif Ekbal, Sriparna Saha, and Pushpak Bhattacharyya. 2018. An AI aid to the editors. Exploring the possibility of an AI assisted article classification system. *arXiv preprint arXiv:1802.01403* (2018).

[3] Luca Weihs and Oren Etzioni. 2017. Learning to Predict Citation-Based Impact Measures. In *Digital Libraries (JCDL), 2017 ACM/IEEE Joint Conference on*. IEEE, 1–10.

Generating Semantic Aspects for Queries

Dhruv Gupta
Max Planck Institute for Informatics and Graduate School of Computer Science
Saarbrücken, Germany
dhgupta@mpi-inf.mpg.de

Klaus Berberich
Max Planck Institute for Informatics and htw saar
Saarbrücken, Germany
kberberi@mpi-inf.mpg.de

Jannik Strötgen
Max Planck Institute for Informatics
Saarbrücken, Germany
jstroetge@mpi-inf.mpg.de

Demetrios Zeinalipour-Yazti
University of Cyprus
Cyprus
dzeinali@mpi-inf.mpg.de

ABSTRACT

We present an approach to explore news archives by automatically generating semantic aspects for their navigation. Given a keyword query as an input, we utilize semantic annotations present in the pseudo-relevant set of documents for generating the aspects. Our approach to generate the aspects considers the salience of the annotations by modeling their semantics as well as considering their co-occurrence in the pseudo-relevant set of documents. The generated aspects are also beneficial for representing documents in a structured manner. We show preliminary results on two news archives demonstrating the quality of the generated aspects over a testbed of more than 5,000 aspects derived from Wikipedia.

ACM Reference Format:
Dhruv Gupta, Klaus Berberich, Jannik Strötgen, and Demetrios Zeinalipour-Yazti. 2018. Generating Semantic Aspects for Queries. In *JCDL '18: The 18th ACM/IEEE Joint Conference on Digital Libraries, June 3–7, 2018, Fort Worth, TX, USA.* ACM, New York, NY, USA, 2 pages. https://doi.org/10.1145/3197026.3203900

1 INTRODUCTION

To explore news archives using only keywords offers us limited opportunities for their meaningful exploration. Nowadays, commercial search engines provide features such as *knowledge panels* [8] for queries regarding popular named entities as effective means of exploring web search results. This functionality, however, is not offered for ad-hoc keyword queries and is limited to those queries that concern popular named entities or selected search terms.

Also, users often struggle to convey their information needs clearly. A web query log analysis showed that ca. 46% of users performed query reformulation to better reflect their information needs [6]. To assist users in finding relevant documents quickly, we propose to provide semantic aspects as means of navigation. We generate these by utilizing semantic annotations present in the form of temporal expressions, disambiguated geographical locations, and other named entities in document contents.

In short, we generate aspects to informational queries as follows. First, we retrieve pseudo-relevant documents that mention the keywords present in the user's query. Second, we analyze semantic annotations in the form of temporal expressions, disambiguated geographical locations, and other named entities by considering their salience in models informed of their inherent semantics. Third, we analyze the annotations sharing different semantics by considering their co-occurrence in the set of pseudo-relevant documents.

JCDL '18, June 3–7, 2018, Fort Worth, TX, USA

ACM ISBN 978-1-4503-5178-2/18/06.
https://doi.org/10.1145/3197026.3203900

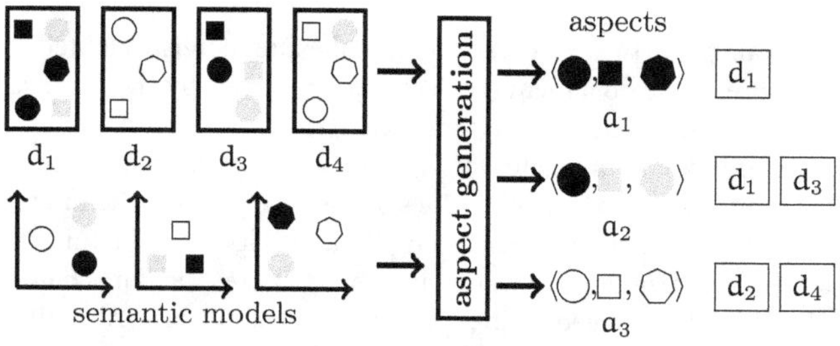

Figure 1: We generate aspects for a given set of documents by taking into account the salience of the annotations in models that are informed of their inherent semantics. We consider co-occurrence of annotations sharing different semantics. Generated aspects are also useful to provide a structured representation of documents (e.g., d_1 can be modeled as containing a_1 and a_2).

2 APPROACH

We now describe in brief the approach to generate the semantic aspects. Figure 1 gives an overall schema of our proposed approach.

Consider a news archive with documents $\mathcal{D} = \{d_1 \ldots d_N\}$. Given a keyword query q, we use a retrieval method (e.g., Okapi BM25) to obtain a set of pseudo-relevant documents $\mathcal{R} \subset \mathcal{D}$ containing the query terms. Each document $d \in \mathcal{R}$ is enriched with annotations in the form of temporal expressions, disambiguated locations, and disambiguated persons and organizations. We can therefore represent a document using these annotations and the words it contains as:

$$d = \{d_{\mathcal{W}}, d_{\mathcal{T}}, d_{\mathcal{G}}, d_{\mathcal{E}}\}. \tag{1}$$

In Equation 1, the document d is modeled as a bag-of-words $d_{\mathcal{W}}$, bag-of-temporal-expressions $d_{\mathcal{T}}$, bag-of-locations $d_{\mathcal{G}}$, and bag-of-other-named-entities $d_{\mathcal{E}}$.

Generating Semantic Aspects. An aspect represents the salience of the annotations in models that are informed of their semantics as well as the co-occurrence of annotations sharing different semantics. An aspect a consists of factors x that exhibit the aforementioned properties. Concretely, an aspect is represented as:

$$a = \langle x_{\mathcal{T}}, x_{\mathcal{G}}, x_{\mathcal{E}} \rangle. \tag{2}$$

A generated sample aspect is shown in Figure 2. In Equation 2, $x_{\mathcal{T}}$ represents a time interval of interest. We leverage the work by Gupta and Berberich [5] to generate them. In short, time intervals of interest are obtained by computing overlaps of temporal expressions (i.e., expressions that convey mentions of time that are explicit, implicit, and relative) in a time model informed of temporal

⟨ Time: [2016,2016], Entities:[WIKI:RYAN_LOCHTE][WIKI:MICHAEL_PHELPS] [WIKI:MISSY_FRANKLIN][WIKI:CONOR_DWYER][WIKI:KATIE_LEDECKY] [WIKI:ALY_RAISMAN][WIKI:SIMONE_BILES][WIKI:NATHAN_ADRIAN] [WIKI:ALEXANDER_MASSIALAS][WIKI:ANTHONY_ERVIN] [WIKI:GABBY_DOUGLAS][WIKI:SUN_YANG],Locations:[WIKI:UNITED_STATES] [WIKI:CALIFORNIA][WIKI:NEW_YORK_CITY][WIKI:LOS_ANGELES] ⟩

Figure 2: A sample generated semantic aspect for the query OLYMPIC MEDALISTS. In the aspect several famous swimmers and gymnasts are shown. The time interval signifies the 2016 Summer Olympics. While the location signifies the nationality of the athletes.

uncertainty. Furthermore, each temporal expression is weighted by the score of the document (i.e., the score returned by the retrieval method) containing the temporal expression.

In Equation 2, the factors $x_{\mathcal{G}}$ and $x_{\mathcal{E}}$ correspond to interesting locations and other named entities, respectively. These factors are identified by modeling them using their Wikipedia page links. A person, organization, or location is deemed interesting if it is highly related to other named entities present by using the Jaccard similarity. We again weight their relatedness with the document's score. We thereby give more importance to those locations and other entity factors that are present in highly relevant documents.

Finally, we determine whether the various factors having different semantics in Equation 2 co-occur frequently in some subset of the pseudo-relevant document set $\mathcal{R}$. We determine this by checking that each factor in the aspect is salient above a given threshold and is generated from the same subset of $\mathcal{R}$.

3 EVALUATION

Semantically Annotated News Archives. We consider two news archives for evaluation: (i) the New York Times Annotated Corpus, which contains news articles published during the years 1987-2007 [2]. (ii) STICS, which contains news articles crawled from the Web between the time period 2013-2016 [9]. Semantic annotations for documents were obtained by using two types of natural language processing tools. First, we obtained temporal expressions for the documents using the HeidelTime temporal tagger [12]. It provides us with resolved time intervals for explicit, implicit, and relative temporal expressions. Second, we obtained, disambiguated named entities for the documents by using AIDA as the named entity recognition and disambiguation tool [10]. By using AIDA, we are able to resolve the disambiguated locations and other named entities to their Wikipedia pages. Table 1 shows the statistics regarding the news archives and the annotations for the documents.

Testbed. In order to evaluate the quality of the generated aspects, we turned to Wikipedia. Specifically, we created a testbed of 5,122 aspects by exploiting various event tables present in Wikipedia. We selected the queries and their corresponding pages by using the Wikipedia's page on "List of lists of lists" [1]. We parsed these Wikipedia pages and additionally used external resources, such as [4], to obtain the ground-truth aspects. The query keywords and their aspects counts are shown in Table 2.

Table 1: Statistics for the news archives and contained annotations for up to 10,000 documents obtained for each evaluation query.

COLLECTION	$n_{\text{documents}}$	μ_{time}	μ_{location}	μ_{entity}
NEW YORK TIMES	1,679,374	12.50	8.65	16.25
STICS	4,075,720	10.09	5.93	10.89

Table 2: Queries with aspect counts in brackets.

Achievements [1,508]: nobel prize [114] | olympic medalists [48] | oscars [1,167] | paralympic medalists [24] | space shuttle missions [155]

Disasters [1,536]: aircraft accidents [513] | avalanches [56] | earthquakes [39] | epidemics [211] | famines [133] | genocides [35] | hailstorms [39] | landslides [85] | nuclear accidents [26] | oil spills [140] | tsunamis [88] | volcanic eruptions [171]

Politics [2,078]: assassinations [130] | cold war [81] | corporate scandals [44] | proxy wars [34] | united states presidential elections [57] | terror attacks [316] | treaties [1,057] | wars [359]

Results. We discuss initial results that measure the precision and recall of our proposed approach against a naïve baseline considering all documents returned by Okapi BM25 with disjunction operator. For the baseline, we assume each document is equivalent to an aspect (i.e., Equation 1 and 2 are identical by disregarding the bag-of-words). The preliminary results in Table 3 show that for both the news archives our approach provides both high precision and recall values than the baseline which can only outperform our method in terms of recall as it considers all the documents retrieved for the query. The smaller average size of the aspects generated ($|\mathcal{A}|$) by our method additionally reflects that many documents share similar structure that can be exploited for meaningful navigation.

Table 3: Precision and recall results for news archives.

	NEW YORK TIMES			STICS		
	AVG. $\lvert\mathcal{A}\rvert$	PRECISION	RECALL	AVG. $\lvert\mathcal{A}\rvert$	PRECISION	RECALL
OKAPI BM25	3,379	0.098	**0.152**	3,796	0.072	0.113
OUR METHOD	1,638	**0.264**	0.148	480	**0.229**	**0.134**

4 RELATED WORK

An important approach in discovering structure within text documents was given by Hearst and Plaunt [7]. Their TextTiling algorithm structures documents with sub-topics identified using only text. Koutrika et al. [11] furthermore investigated how topics contained in documents can be helpful in information consumption by generating reading orders. From the perspective of faceted search, Ben-Ytizhak et al. [3] presented methods to identify facets for document exploration. Our approach in contrast has looked at modeling the semantics underlying the annotations when measuring salience. We also take into account co-occurrence of annotations sharing different semantics when generating aspects for archive exploration.

REFERENCES

[1] List of lists of lists. en.wikipedia.org/wiki/List_of_lists_of_lists
[2] The NYT Annotated Corpus. catalog.ldc.upenn.edu/LDC2008T19
[3] Ben-Yitzhak O. et al. Beyond basic faceted search. In *WSDM'08*.
[4] Bhagavatula C. S. et al. *TabEL: Entity Linking in Web Tables*. In *ISWC'15*.
[5] Gupta D. and Berberich K. Identifying Time Intervals of Interest to Queries. In *CIKM'14*.
[6] Hearst M. A. 2009. *Search User Interfaces* (1st ed.). Cambridge University Press, New York, NY, USA.
[7] Hearst M. A. and Plaunt C. Subtopic Structuring for Full-Length Document Access. In *SIGIR'93*.
[8] Henry J.W. Providing Knowledge Panels With Search Results. (May 2 2013). US Patent App. 13/566,489.
[9] Hoffart J. et al. STICS: searching with strings, things, and cats. In *SIGIR'14*.
[10] Hoffart J. et al. Robust Disambiguation of Named Entities in Text. In *EMNLP '11*.
[11] Koutrika G. et al. Generating reading orders over document collections. In *ICDE'15*.
[12] Strötgen J. and Gertz M. Multilingual and Cross-domain Temporal Tagging. *Language Resources and Evaluation* 47, 2 (2013), 269–298.

The Navigation of Topic Space

Jim Hahn
University Library
University of Illinois at Urbana-Champaign, USA
jimhahn@illinois.edu

ABSTRACT

This poster reports on the evaluation of the topic space recommendation model, proposed here as an alternative to the personalization algorithms based on large datasets that often result in content and subject matter filter bubbles [1]. The content filter bubbles that dominate contemporary Internet media platforms have been shown to provide users more of what they already consume and exclude relevant content at the expense of user exploration and discovery. Modern algorithms have also exhibited the problematic nature of reinforcing systematic bias [2,3].

CCS CONCEPTS

• **Information systems → Digital libraries and archives**; • **Information systems → Mobile information processing systems**; • ***Information systems*** → *Content ranking*

KEYWORDS

collection navigation; bibliographic classification; browsing

ACM Reference format:

Jim Hahn. 2018. The Navigation of Topic Space. In *Proceedings of the 18th ACM/IEEE-CS Joint Conference on Digital Libraries, June 3-7, 2018 (JCDL'18) Fort Worth, Texas, USA,* ACM, New York, NY, USA 2 pages. https://doi.org/10.1145/3197026.3203892

1 INTRODUCTION

The topic space recommendation model, which was integrated into a location-based library barcode scanning mobile app module, uses a starting subject of interest exemplified within an item's bibliographic subject metadata as a query point to explore other related subject areas in a library building. Branching out from a subject starting point, the app allows users to navigate to other library collection areas not immediately near their current location in the book stacks. This paper investigated mobile information behavior within an academic undergraduate library via the Minrva mobile app, and evaluated specifically the mobile server logs of the topic space module, a collections and location-based recommendation feature of the mobile platform. The topic space recommender was designed specifically to support mobile users in the book stacks expand topic exploration while browsing [4]. After they scan a book's barcode for related recommendations, the topic space module provides users with recommendations based on their location. It has been the contention of locations-based stacks recommendations that, as users navigate the library's physical space, they also are navigating its intellectual space. This study reports trends in browsing interest via mobile recommendations, and describes the distribution of recommended topic areas. By studying the topic recommendation results over time, it is possible to identify time and topic trends on the part of mobile users that will contribute to additional theoretical insights regarding libraries as places, as well as location-based recommendations.

ACM ISBN 978-1-4503-5178-2/18/06.
https://doi.org/10.1145/3197026.3203892

2 BACKGROUND

Before the advent of Smartphones and accompanying application software, it was not possible to use server logs to determine user interactions to understand topical browsing interest in physical library book stacks. In the case of the evaluation of the topic space module in this paper, the topic space API logs recorded a user's starting location, the subjects of the start item, and recommended areas to explore that are not in the user's immediate location. This study used emerging digital technology, such as Smartphones in general and a distributed system of mobile middleware in particular, for both a service-focused collection recommendation, as well as a novel research tool to measure the topical interests of users as they navigated the physical collections of an undergraduate library.

2.1 Topic Space API

In order to generate the recommendations data required by the topic space module, research programmers created custom server side middleware that would combine several data sources for recommendations [4]. The app required data from the library catalog (e.g., VuFind) searches to filter candidate recommendations, data from an Oracle reports server in order to rank candidate recommendations based on popularity (by sum circulations), and a SQL table of the collection arrangement in the Undergraduate Library. Together these tools support recommending related items that are not nearby. The functions, with comments referencing the recommendation process are coded as follows:

```
//We form the search terms that will be used
using our custom DB table (derived from Library
of Congress Subject Headings.) String
startSearchTerms = getSearchTerms(context,
search, scannedOrManual, classifications);

//Using Vufind we take the resulting search terms
from the previous method and search all of our
available libraries. We then return a list of
starting bibIDs that relate to our search.
ArrayList bibIDs = bibID (startSearchTerms);

//We now use the starting bibIDs to create a new
list of focused search terms. We base these new
search terms off of the topics of each book as
found within Vufind. ArrayList topicSearch =
topics (bibIDs);

//This method cleans up the "topicSearch" list
and builds a final list of links to extract
information from.
ArrayList finalWebpages =
finalWebpageList(topicSearch);

//Filter out links that don't appear to be
closely related to the originally scanned book.
ArrayList filteredList =
filterList(finalWebpages);

//We now create and rank (by sum circulations) a
list of bibIDs by popularity. ArrayList
bookInfoArray = bookArray(filteredList);

//With our aggregated results from the previous
methods, we now return information about the top
two suggested Topic Spaces. ArrayList booksList =
bookList(bookInfoArray);
```

3 METHODS AND GOALS

Search log analysis has proven to be a valuable method with which to evaluate digital access and use of library resources. The study methodology was sourced from previous information science research studies in search log analysis. Three years of server logs from the API that powers the topic space module were analyzed. This study included an analysis of 18 unique mobile users of the topic space module between August 2015 and August 2017 identified in the search logs. There were 20 total book barcode scans of the topic space module on the part of this set of mobile topic space module users. The focus of this study was users' starting LC locations when they scanned library barcodes on items within the undergraduate library at the University of Illinois to understand unique users of the topic space service as a means to learn where users branched out into other areas of the library collection while browsing. The collection consists of 125,000 monographs in open stacks. The evaluation analyzed the subsequent browsing recommendations, and sought to answer the following research question: What trends can be observed in browsing interest via mobile topic space location-based browsing recommendations?

4 RESULTS

Records indicated there were 18 unique users of the topic space module (n=18) and with multiple requests to the Topic Space API (n=20) during 2015-2017. LC subclasses have a result of consequent LC ranges that the system recommended for additional browsing. Total number of records recommended are 527 (n=527 records recommended based on all starting library barcode scans.) Total recommended records for expanded browsing within each year are: n=139 in 2015, n=236 in 2016, and n=152 in 2017. Expansion of topics depends the following: 1) where a user begins; 2) the subject description of the item scanned; 3) the set of topics available within that set and more distant sets. Several starting item's LC Class provided more subsequent recommendations than did others, for example, the areas that include World History (n=127), American History (n=72), American Literature (n=63), Theory and Practice of Education (n=54), General Literature (n=45), and Sociology (n=41). Together, these starting item's LC class included 402 records, 76% of the results. The remainder of subject recommendations, those under 40 records each, also are significant to note, as taken together, these outliers included a total of 125 records, and made up 24% of the topic areas recommended. This represents the topic space recommendation model's long tail distribution of subject recommendations.

5 FINDINGS

To describe the topic distribution of long tail recommendations best, a reference to a now classic study on the power law at work here is instructive. "The theory of the Long Tail can be boiled down to this: our culture and economy is increasingly shifting away from a focus on a relatively small number of 'hits' (mainstream products and markets) at the head of the demand curve and moving toward a huge number of niches in the tail" [5]. Further study with larger datasets are required to understand whether power law distributions like the long tail model observed here will prove useful toward the design of algorithms that promote topic and content diversity within information systems.

ACKNOWLEDGEMENTS

The author sincerely appreciates the research contributions of software developers Nathaniel Ryckman & Benjamin Ryckman.

REFERENCES

[1] Eli Pariser. 2011. *The Filter Bubble: What the Internet is Hiding from You.* Penguin Press, New York, NY.

[2] Cathy O'Neil. 2016. *Weapons of Math Destruction: How Big Data Increases Inequality and Threatens Democracy.* Crown, New York, NY.

[3] Safiya Noble. 2018. *Algorithms of Oppression: How Search Engines Reinforce Racism.* NYU Press, New York, NY.

[4] Jim Hahn, Benjamin Ryckman, and Maria Lux. 2015. Topic space: Rapid prototyping a mobile augmented reality recommendation app. *Code4Lib Journal*, 30. http://journal.code4lib.org/articles/10881

[5] Chris Anderson. 2006. *The Long Tail: Why the Future of Business is Selling Less of More.* Hyperion, New York, NY. 52.

Extraction of Main Event Descriptors from News Articles by Answering the Journalistic Five W and One H Questions

Felix Hamborg, Corinna Breitinger, Moritz Schubotz, Soeren Lachnit, Bela Gipp
Department of Computer and Information Science
University of Konstanz, Germany
{firstname.lastname}@uni-konstanz.de

ABSTRACT

The identification and extraction of the events that news articles report on is a commonly performed task in the analysis workflow of various projects that analyze news articles. However, due to the lack of universally usable and publicly available methods for news articles, many researchers must redundantly implement methods for event extraction to be used within their projects. Answers to the journalistic five W and one H questions (5W1H) describe the main event of a news story, i.e., who did what, when, where, why, and how. We propose Giveme5W1H, an open-source system that uses syntactic and domain-specific rules to extract phrases answering the 5W1H. In our evaluation, we find that the extraction precision of 5W1H phrases is $p = 0.64$, and $p = 0.79$ for the first four W questions, which discretely describe an event.

CCS CONCEPTS

• **Computing methodologies** → **Information extraction** • **Information systems** → **Question answering** • Information systems → Summarization

KEYWORDS

News Event Detection, 5W1H Extraction, 5W1H Question Answering, Reporter's Questions, Journalist's Questions, 5W QA.

ACM Reference format:

F. Hamborg, C. Breitinger, M. Schubotz, S. Lachnit, B. Gipp. 2017. Extraction of Main Event Descriptors from News Articles by Answering the Journalistic Five W and One H Questions. In *Proc. of the 18th ACM/IEEE-CS Joint Conf. on Digital Libraries, Fort Worth, USA, June 2018 (JCDL'18)*, 2 p.

1 INTRODUCTION AND RELATED WORK

Extraction of a news article's main event is a fundamental analysis task required for a broad spectrum of use cases. For instance, news aggregators must identify the main event to cluster related articles [2, 3], e.g., articles reporting on the same event. Other disciplines also analyze the events reported on in articles, e.g., in so called frame analyses, social scientists identify how the media is reporting on certain events. However, no method is publicly available that extracts explicit descriptors of the main event. We define *explicit event descriptors* as the properties that occur in a text describing an event, e.g., the text phrases in a news article that enable a news reader to understand what the article is reporting on.

The clear majority of current approaches suffer from at least one of three shortcomings. First, they detect events only implicitly, e.g., by employing topic modeling, but do not extract phrases or properties that explicitly describe the article's main event [3]. The second category of approaches does not extract universally usable descriptors, but is specialized on the extraction of task-specific event properties, such as the number of protestors in a demonstration [4]. Approaches of the third category extract explicit event descriptors but are not publicly available [5].

Journalists typically answer the journalistic five W and one H questions (5W1H), i.e., *who* did *what*, *when*, *where*, *why*, and *how*, within the first few sentences of an article to inform the readers of the main event. For instance, the headline of a news article reporting on a terrorist attack in Afghanistan answers four of the 5W1H questions: "Taliban attacks German consulate in northern Afghan city of Mazar-i-Sharif with truck bomb" The highlighted phrases answer the questions who did what, where, and how; 'when' and 'why' are answered in the remainder of the article. Due to their descriptiveness of an article's main event, we focus our research on the extraction of the journalistic 5W1Hs.

2 EXTRACTION OF 5W1H PHRASES

Giveme5W1H is an open-source main event retrieval system for news articles. The system uses syntactic and domain-specific rules to extract the 5W1H phrases in a three-phase analysis pipeline depicted in Figure 1. The system builds on Giveme5W [1], and improves the extraction performance by addressing multiple of the future work directions: Giveme5W1H uses coreference resolution, question-specific semantic distance measures, combined scoring of candidates, and extracts phrases for the 'how' question.

In the first phase, *preprocessing*, Giveme5W1H performs state-of-the-art NLP, and canonicalization to bring all named entities (NE) in their normalized form. During canonicalization we parse dates written in natural language into canonical dates (TIMEX3),

This work has been supported by the Carl Zeiss Foundation.

JCDL '18, June 3–7, 2018, Fort Worth, TX, USA

ISBN 978-1-4503-5178-2/18/06.
https://doi.org/10.1145/3197026.3203899

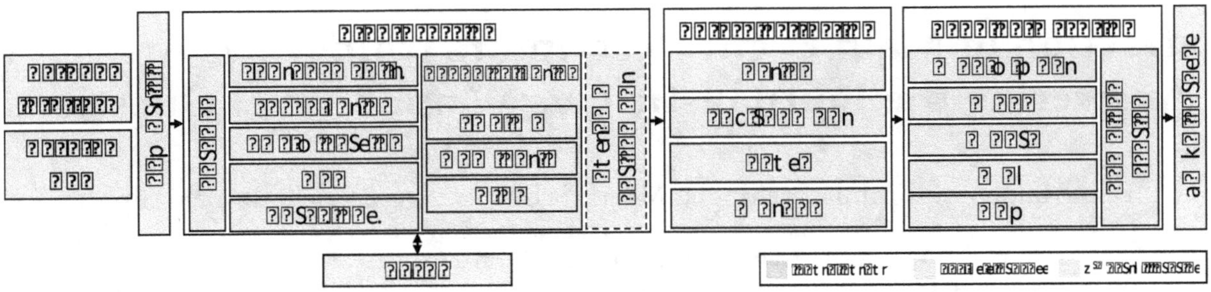

Figure 1: The three-phase analysis pipeline (1) preprocesses a news text, (2) finds candidate phrases for each of the 5W1H questions, and (3) scores these. Giveme5W1H can easily be accessed in Python and via a RESTful API.

perform geocoding, and perform NE recognition and disambiguation (NERD) to link all NEs to concepts in the YAGO graph.

The second phase, *phrase extraction*, uses four extraction chains to retrieve candidate phrases: (1) the *action* chain extracts phrases for the journalistic 'who' and 'what' questions, (2) *environment* extracts 'when' and 'where', (3) *cause* extracts 'why', and (4) *method* extracts 'how'. We extract as 'who' candidates all subjects, i.e., the first noun phrase (NP) from each sentence, and as 'what' candidates their respective predicates. To determine the 'when' candidates, we take the TIMEX3 instances, which Giveme5W1H extracts during preprocessing. Similarly, we take the geocodes as 'where' candidates. To find 'why' candidates, we look for three types of cause-effect indicators: causal conjunctions, causative adverbs, and causative verbs. We then use a set of syntax rules to find the respective causal phrase. To find 'how' candidates, we analyze copulative conjunctions, adjectives and adverbs. Often, sentences with a copulative conjunction, such as "after [the train came off the tracks]", contain a method phrase in the clause that follows the copulative conjunction. To improve extraction quality, we post-process all candidates for each question, e.g., by truncating long phrases or discarding too short phrases.

The third phase, *candidate scoring*, aims to determine the best candidate of each 5W1H question. First, we score candidates independently for each of the 5W1H questions. Therefore, we devise domain-specific scoring rules. For instance, to score 'who' candidates, we define three scoring factors, which we motivate from journalistic writing concepts, such as the inverse pyramid and journalistic hooks: the candidate shall occur in the article (1) *early* and (2) *often*, and (3) contain an *NE*. If a candidate contains an NE, we will score it higher, since in news articles, the actors involved in events are often NEs, e.g., politicians. Lastly, we perform a combined scoring that adjusts the score of a given candidate, depending on the properties of top candidates of other questions, e.g., the method by which an action was performed ('how') is usually described in the same or an adjacent sentence as the action ('what').

Giveme5W1H returns the top candidate phrase for each question, including the normalized data from canonicalization.

3 RESULTS

We use the evaluation dataset by Hamborg et al. [1], which consists of 60 articles in the categories business (*Bus*), entertainment (*Ent*), politics (*Pol*), sport (*Spo*), and tech (*Tec*). We asked three assessors to judge the relevance of each answer on a 3-point scale (non-relevant, partially relevant, and relevant). Table 1 shows the mean average generalized precision (MAgP). The MAgP over all categories and questions was 0.64. If only considering the first 4Ws, which are sufficient to uniquely represent an event, the overall MAgP was 0.79. Extracting the answers to 'why' and 'how' performed worse, since news articles often only imply causes and methods. The extraction performance is similar to state-of-the-art approaches [5], but a direct comparison is not possible due to the non-availability of methods and datasets (see Section 1).

Table 1: MAgP-Performance of Giveme5W1H

Question	Bus	Ent	Pol	Spo	Tec	Avg.
Who	.98	.88	.85	.97	.86	.91
What	.77	.67	.89	.83	.63	.75
When	.55	.91	.79	.77	.82	.77
Where	.82	.63	.85	.77	.68	.75
Why	.36	.18	.32	.33	.40	.32
How	.25	.36	.45	.27	.46	.36
Avg. all	.62	.61	.69	.66	.64	**.64**
Avg. 4W	.78	.65	.84	.83	.75	**.79**

4 CONCLUSION

We proposed *Giveme5W1H*, the first open-source system that extracts answers to the journalistic 5W1H questions, i.e., *who* did *what, when, where, why,* and *how*, to describe a news article's main event. Giveme5W1H achieved a mean average generalized precision (MAgP) of 0.64 for all questions, and an MAgP of 0.79 in answering the questions who, what, when, and where, which can uniquely represent an event. The code of Giveme5W1H and the evaluation dataset are available under an Apache 2 license on GitHub: **https://github.com/fhamborg/Giveme5W1H**

REFERENCES

[1] Hamborg, F. et al. 2018. Giveme5W: Main Event Retrieval from News Articles by Extraction of the Five Journalistic W Questions. *Proceedings of the iConference 2018* (Sheffield, UK, 2018).

[2] Hamborg, F. et al. 2017. Identification and Analysis of Media Bias in News Articles. *Proceedings of the 15th International Symposium of Information Science* (2017).

[3] Hamborg, F. et al. 2017. Matrix-based News Aggregation: Exploring Different News Perspectives. *Proceedings of the ACM/IEEE Joint Conference on Digital Libraries*. 10, 17 (2017).

[4] Oliver, P.E. and Maney, G.M. 2000. Political Processes and Local Newspaper Coverage of Protest Events: From Selection Bias to Triadic Interactions. *American Journal of Sociology*. 106, 2 (2000), 463–505.

[5] Parton, K. et al. 2009. Who, what, when, where, why?: comparing multiple approaches to the cross-lingual 5W task. *Proc. of the Joint Conf. of the 47th Annual Meeting of the ACL and the 4th Int. Joint Conference on Natural Language Processing of the AFNLP: Volume 1-Volume 1* (2009), 423–431.

Keyphrase Extraction Based on Prior Knowledge

Guoxiu He, Junwei Fang, Haoran Cui, Chuan Wu, Wei Lu
School of Information Management, Wuhan University
Wuhan, China
{guoxiu.he,junwei.fang,haoran.cui,wu.chuan,weilu}@whu.edu.cn

ABSTRACT

Keyphrase is an important way to quickly get the topic of a document by providing highly-summative information. The previous approaches for keyphrase extraction simply rank keyphrases according to statistics-based model or graph-based model, which ignore the influence of external knowledge. In this paper, we take prior knowledge, which contains controlled vocabulary of keyphrases and their prior probability, into consideration to enhance previous methods. First, we build a controlled vocabulary of keyphrases introduced by keyphrases from existing collections and a keyphrase candidate set is filtered from a given document by it. Then, we use prior probability to represent the importance of keyphrases candidate with TF-IDF and TextRank. Finally, a supervised learning algorithm is used to learn optimal weights of these three features. Experiments on four benchmark datasets show the great advantages of prior knowledge on keyphrase extraction. Furthermore, we achieve competitive performance compared with the state-of-the art methods.

CCS CONCEPTS

• **Information systems** → Information extraction; • **Computing methodologies** → Supervised learning by classification;

KEYWORDS

Keyphrase Extraction; Prior Knowledge; TF-IDF; TextRank; Supervised Learning Algorithm

ACM Reference Format:

Guoxiu He, Junwei Fang, Haoran Cui, Chuan Wu, Wei Lu. 2018. Keyphrase Extraction Based on Prior Knowledge. In *JCDL '18: The 18th ACM/IEEE Joint Conference on Digital Libraries, June 3–7, 2018, Fort Worth, TX, USA.* ACM, New York, NY, USA, 2 pages. https://doi.org/10.1145/3197026.3203869

1 INTRODUCTION

Nowadays, keyphrase extraction for documents becomes a great demand in automatically understanding the topic of academic literature which generally includes two steps: keyphrases candidate selection and keyphrases candidate ranking[2]. The first step usually uses some enlightening rules such as n-grams or noun phrases with certain part-of-speech patterns to identify potential candidates. The second step is to rank the keyphrases candidate based on their importance. Either supervised or unsupervised machine learning methods with a set of manually-defined features are used for ranking.

Existing keyphrase extraction methods consider the importance of keyphrase candidate through the frequency of keyphrases or co-occurrence relation of keyphrases within the documents only, which ignore the influence of existing knowledge of keyphrases and development trend of documents in specific domains. Ideally, when annotating keyphrases, you should consider keyphrases that have already been used for documents and are always used by specific domain.

Hence, we extract controlled vocabulary of keyphrases and their prior probability as prior knowledge and then use a supervised learning algorithm to learn optimal weights for features which are TF-IDF, TextRank and prior probability.

2 METHODOLOGY

Given a collection of N samples, the i−th sample (d_i, K_i) contains one document d_i and M_i keyphrases $K_i = \{k_{i,1}, k_{i,2}, \cdots, k_{i,M_i}\}$. Both the document d_i and keyphrase $k_{i,j}$ are sequence of words represented as $d_i = \{w_{i,1}, w_{i,2}, \cdots, w_{i,L_{d_i}}\}$ and $k_{i,j} = \{w_{i,j,1}, w_{i,j,2}, \cdots, w_{i,j,L_{k_{i,j}}}\}$, where L_{d_i} and $L_{k_{i,j}}$ denote the length of word sequence of d_i and $k_{i,j}$ respectively and w represents a word.

2.1 Keyphrase Candidate Selection

Building a controlled vocabulary of keyphrases is an important part in this work. We collect existing keyphrases from document collections and get rid of duplicates to get controlled vocabulary represented as $KV = \{k_1, k_2, \cdots, k_O\}$, where k_i is a keyphrase and O is the vocabulary size.

In addition, this paper quantifies the use of keyphrases as a prior probability of candidate keyphrases and uses them as external knowledge in keyphrase extraction. For the detailed calculation process of this probability, see the section of keyphrase candidate ranking.

The keyphrases candidate C_i of a document d_i is selected by the controlled vocabulary of keyphrases. That is, given a document d_i, candidate keyphrases are the largest match pattern of word sequence according to the controlled vocabulary of keyphrase.

2.2 Candidate Keyphrases Ranking

In order to rank keyprhases candidate, we extract prior probability combined by TF-IDF and TextRank and use a supervised learning algorithm to learn the optimal weights of them.

2.2.1 Feature Extraction. Based on keyphrases candidate C_i of document d_i, keyphrases in keyphrases candidate set need to be scored and ranked accordingly. Our method considers the importance of candidate keyphrases based on three features in a document d_i i.e. TF-IDF (TF), TextRank (TR) and Prior Probability (PP).

JCDL '18, June 3–7, 2018, Fort Worth, TX, USA

ACM ISBN 978-1-4503-5178-2/18/06.
https://doi.org/10.1145/3197026.3203869

Table 1: The Result of Experiment

Method	Inspec		Krapivin		Nus		Ke20K	
	F1@5	F1@10	F1@5	F1@10	F1@5	F1@10	F1@5	F1@10
TF-IDF[5]	0.221	0.313	0.129	0.160	0.136	0.184	0.102	0.126
TextRank[6]	0.223	0.281	0.189	0.162	0.195	0.196	0.175	0.147
RNN[5]	0.085	0.064	0.135	0.088	0.169	0.127	0.179	0.189
CopyRNN[5]	0.278	0.342	0.311	0.266	0.334	0.326	0.333	0.262
Controlled Vocabulary+TF-IDF	0.395	0.363	0.298	0.257	**0.360**	**0.303**	0.315	0.247
Controlled Vocabulary+TextRank	0.330	0.341	0.252	0.247	0.296	0.264	0.271	0.235
Prior Knowledge+TF-IDF	0.401	0.365	0.301	0.261	0.271	0.258	0.299	0.245
Prior Knowledge+TextRank	0.321	0.367	0.205	0.224	0.205	0.231	0.286	0.242
Prior Knowledge+TF-IDF+TextRank	**0.403**	**0.371**	**0.309**	0.267	0.324	0.276	**0.326**	**0.252**

Features such as *TF* ad *TR* only consider the importance of candidate keywords from the perspective of mutual information in a document, but utilization of knowledge outside the document. We introduce the use of keyphrases in the specific domain as a background feature named prior probability. According to statistics of the given collection and their keyphrases, the prior probability *PP* is defined as

$$PP_{k_i} = \frac{A_{i1} + A_{i2}}{A_{i1} + A_{i3}} \quad (A_{i1} + A_{i3} > 0)$$

Where A_{i1} represents the number of times k_i appears in documents and is also selected by the author as the keyphrase. A_{i2} represents the number of times k_i does not appear in documents but is selected as the keyphrase. A_{i3} represents the number of times k_i is in documents but not selected as a keyphrase.

In addition, in order to ensure that the magnitude difference of these three features does not affect the importance of them, they are normalized in the same way. Taking PP_{k_i} as an example, the PR_{k_i} of each candidate keyphrase do the following process:

$$PP'_{k_i} = \frac{PP_{k_i} - PP_{min}}{PP_{max} - PP_{min}}$$

where PP_{max} is the maximum and PP_{min} is the minimum.

2.2.2 *Supervised Learning Algorithm.* We use logistic regression as ranking model in this step. For a phrase k_i, TF_{k_i}, TR_{k_i} and PR_{k_i} are three features as input of model:

$$y = sigmoid(w_1 \cdot TF_{k_i} + w_2 \cdot TR_{k_i} + w_3 \cdot PR_{k_i} + b)$$

where w_1, w_2, w_3 and b are parameters will be learned by Stochastic Gradient Decline (SGD)[1] and y is the output.

3 EXPERIMENT RESULT AND ANALYSIS

We conduct experiments on four public available datasets: Inspec[3], Krapivin[4], NUS[7] and Ke20K[5]. To evaluate the performance, we adopt the F1 score, which is the primary metrics used in keyphrase extraction. To further evaluate the effectiveness of prior knowledge, we compare our methods with some baselines shown as Table 1 whose settings are same as[5].

It is observed that unsupervised learning methods such as TF-IDF and TextRank combined with the controlled vocabulary of keyphrase which is a part of prior knowledge achieve a significant improvement compared with TF-IDF and TextRank. That is, it is very important and necessary to take the external knowledge of existing keyphrases into consideration. The supervised learning algorithm based on entire prior knowledge which contains controlled vocabulary and their prior probability achieve the best performance on all dataset except Nus. The main reason is that supervised learning algorithm needs a large training set to learn the optimal weight but there are only 200 samples in Nus.

Meanwhile, our methods achieve the new state-of-the art performance on Inspec in terms of both F1@5 and F1@10, Krapivin in terms of F1@10 and Nus in terms of F1@5. And the best results obtained from our methods are comparable with the state-of-the art model named Copy Recurrent Neural Network (CopyRNN).

4 CONCLUSIONS

To the best of our knowledge, this is the first try to consider prior knowledge in keyphrase extraction. And the effectiveness of prior knowledge is introduced by the empirical analysis.

5 ACKNOWLEDGEMENTS

We would like to thank National Demonstration Center for Experimental Library and Information Science Education, Wuhan University for sharing the GPU devices. This work is partially supported by the National Natural Science Foundation of China under Grant No.71473183.

REFERENCES

[1] Yoshua Bengio, Patrice Simard, and Paolo Frasconi. 1994. Learning long-term dependencies with gradient descent is difficult. *IEEE transactions on neural networks* 5, 2 (1994), 157–166.

[2] Eibe Frank, Gordon W Paynter, Ian H Witten, Carl Gutwin, and Craig G Nevill-Manning. 1999. Domain-specific keyphrase extraction. In *IJCAI 99*, Vol. 2. Morgan Kaufmann Publishers Inc., San Francisco, CA, USA, 668–673.

[3] Anette Hulth. 2003. Improved automatic keyword extraction given more linguistic knowledge. In *EMNLP 2003*. Association for Computational Linguistics, 216–223.

[4] Mikalai Krapivin, Aliaksandr Autaeu, and Maurizio Marchese. 2009. *Large dataset for keyphrases extraction.* Technical Report. University of Trento.

[5] Rui Meng, Sanqiang Zhao, Shuguang Han, Daqing He, Peter Brusilovsky, and Yu Chi. 2017. Deep Keyphrase Generation. In *ACL 2017, Vancouver, Canada, July 30 - August 4, Volume 1: Long Papers.* 582–592.

[6] Rada Mihalcea and Paul Tarau. 2004. Textrank: Bringing order into text. In *EMNLP 2004.*

[7] Thuy Nguyen and Min-Yen Kan. 2007. Keyphrase extraction in scientific publications. *Asian Digital Libraries.* (2007), 317–326.

Seeding Strategies for Semantic Disambiguation

Extended Abstract

Annika Hinze,
David Bainbridge
University of Waikato
Hamilton, New Zealand
hinze,davidb@waikato.ac.nz

Rebekah Wilkins,
Craig Taube-Schock
University of Waikato
Hamilton, New Zealand
wilkins,cschock@waikato.ac.nz

J. Stephen Downie
University of Illinois
Urbana-Champaign, USA
jdownie@illinois.edu

ABSTRACT

Semantic disambiguation determines the meaning of words and phrases in a text, for which we use an automatically-generated Concept-in-Context (CiC) network. Words and phrases rarely belong to a single concept; disambiguation in Capisco relies on interplay between words that are in close vicinity in the text. Starting the disambiguation is a seeding process, that identifies the first concepts, which then form the context for further disambiguation steps. This paper introduces the seeding algorithm and explores seeding strategies for identifying these initial concepts in text volumes, such as books, that are stored in a digital library.

CCS CONCEPTS

• **Information systems → Information systems applications; Digital libraries and archives;**

KEYWORDS

Semantic Disambiguation, Semantic Search, Capisco

ACM Reference Format:

Annika Hinze, David Bainbridge, Rebekah Wilkins, Craig Taube-Schock, and J. Stephen Downie. 2018. Seeding Strategies for Semantic Disambiguation: Extended Abstract. In *JCDL '18: The 18th ACM/IEEE Joint Conference on Digital Libraries, June 3–7, 2018, Fort Worth, TX, USA*. ACM, New York, NY, USA, 2 pages. https://doi.org/10.1145/3197026.3203874

1 INTRODUCTION

Semantic Disambiguation determines the meaning (semantic concepts) of words and phrases in a text to allow for subsequent semantic-enhanced search or export of semantic concepts [2]. In Capisco—a semantic disambiguation technique we have devised—the interplay between words within a certain vicinity of the text is a core feature. Further we use an automatically-generated Concept-in-Context (CiC) network that is created from analyzing Wikipedia link structures. Used together, this means the approach in Capisco can also help, for example, with alleviating issues introduced by OCR-based digitizations, such as used by the HathiTrust Digital Library (HTDL). Starting the disambiguation of words and phrases in a document is a *seeding process* that identifies the first concepts, which then form the context for further disambiguation steps throughout the document. This extended abstract introduces the seeding algorithm and explores strategies for identifying these initial concepts. Note that Capisco uses neither machine learning nor natural language processing for disambiguation, but rather relies on co-occurrence of semantically-related words.

JCDL '18, June 3–7, 2018, Fort Worth, TX, USA

ACM ISBN 978-1-4503-5178-2/18/06
https://doi.org/10.1145/3197026.3203874

2 SEEDING FOR DISAMBIGUATION

The disambiguation process has two phases: seeding and full semantic analysis. Both phases use the CiC network, in which Capisco stores triples of *literal*, *concept* and *context* information. The literals refer to words or phrases (e.g., "Apple"), the concepts refers to the meaning of the literal (e.g., [Fruit] or [Computer]), and the contexts refer to the circumstances under which a literal refers to a concept (e.g, [Nutrition] or [IT]), see Figure 1. The above example is described by two triples. The full semantic analysis of terms in a document (introduced in [2]), analyses the presence of other terms in the vicinity. These may, in turn, also be ambiguous but a shared context of these terms may allow for disambiguation. This shared context is determined by the initial seeding.

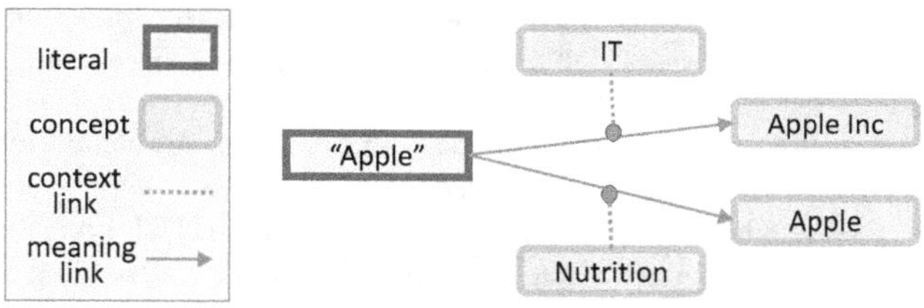

Figure 1: Example CiC triples

The seeding for the full disambiguation in Capisco starts by analyzing the stream of tokens from a corpus of text. We focus here on those produced by the OCR analysis of a text. Using the CiC network, Capisco identifies the first 100 terms, i.e., the first 100 phrases or words that can be found as literals in the CiC network. The next step determines the seed concepts by testing if any of these terms have *loose semantic connections* (vs the stronger connections identified and relied upon in the full semantic analysis). To return to our previous example: let's look at the two terms "Apple" and "Autumn" selected from the 100 terms. We seek to find if they have a loose semantic connection in the CiC network. This means that the concept [Apple] for the first term "Apple" acts as context for the concept [Autumn] and vice versa. This was identified by

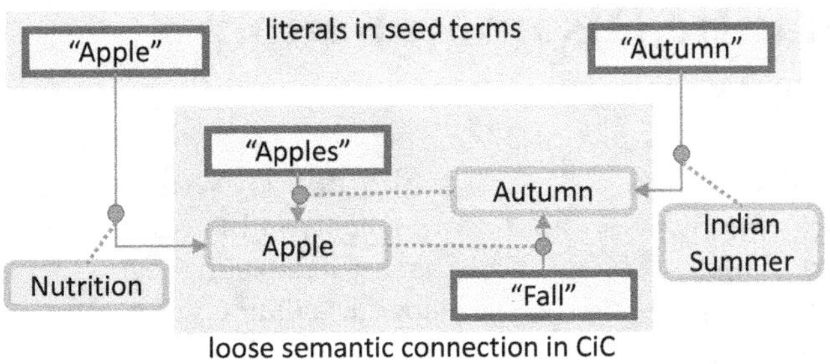

Figure 2: Example of two seed concepts [Apple] & [Autumn]

searching for all concepts for "Autumn". Figure 2 shows this constellation with the literals occurring in the document's 100 seed terms highlighted in gray and the relevant semantic connections between concepts [Apple] and [Autumn] highlighted in orange. The semantic connection is the stronger the more of those mutual connections exist between two concepts. Note that the the concept/context relationship indicating loose connection (as sufficient for seeding) does not need to be involving those two initial terms. On the other hand, strong semantic connections (suitable for disambiguation) need to use the very terms that appear in the text, but can be spread further apart through the document. The seeding phase concludes once there are either more then 10 connections between seed terms (> 20 seed concepts) or at least three pairs of connected seed terms. During the full analysis, these seed concepts and their labels are used to provide (initial) contexts for identifying the meaning of terms encountered.

Scanned books such as those provided by the HTDL typically contain a number of OCR artifacts throughout (i.e., misreading of characters, manual annotations) but often at the beginning of a volume (due to cover patterns and soiled pages). Restriction to seed terms of at least 3 char length removes errors (such as "ft" and "mm" from cover patterns being identified as [Feet] and [Metre]). Among the first clearly discernible terms in many OCR-ed documents are references to digitization (e.g., "digitized", "Internet archive"). These types of terms are well supported in Wikipedia (and thus in the CiC) and potentially create an overwhelming number of seed concepts, and therefore need to be excluded.

3 SEEDING STRATEGIES

Capisco's seeding process as described above has successfully been used for page-based disambiguation (seeding per page). As this creates a large overhead and does not carry forward any previously found seeds, it is most appropriate for documents in which each page contains distinct information (e.g., poetry, encyclopedias). For volume-based analysis discussed here, the seeding process starts at the title page.

Varied seed base: Titles often contain terms that are strongly represented in Wikipedia, which leads to a narrow set of seed concepts as they all circle around very similar topics (e.g., 9 different grammars and 12 languages among 30 seeds) for [3]. Instead of allowing each seed term to participate in more than one semantic connection, we progressed through the seed terms once a match had been found, which led to a greater variation of seed concepts.

Extracted Features: We used the 100 most significant nouns of each volume as seed terms, based on Part-of-Speech tagging on unigrams (enforces copyright protection) [4]. Term significance was identified using AntConc [1]. Unfortunately, the restriction to unigrams prevents recognition of significant terms such as "Isle of Man" [3] or person names.

Metadata: We used curated volume metadata [4] as seed terms, combining title, author and publisher information. We added any names that were provided in normalized *first-name surname* form. As this data does not contain any OCR errors and with names matching Wikipedia's naming convention, this strategy provided best results.

4 CONCLUSION

This paper explored seeding strategies for volume-based semantic disambiguation in digital libraries based on the Wikipedia linking structure. Our test results for a set of 100 out-of-copyright volumes from the HTDL is available on github (https://git.io/vN9lE).

REFERENCES

[1] Laurence Anthony. 2018. (2018). corpus analysis toolkit, at www.laurenceanthony.net/software/antconc/.

[2] Annika Hinze, Craig Taube-Schock, David Bainbridge, Rangi Matamua, and J. Stephen Downie. 2015. Improving Access to Large-scale Digital Libraries Through Semantic-enhanced Search and Disambiguation. In *ACM/IEEE JCDL'15*. ACM, 147–156.

[3] J. Kelly. 1870. *A Practical Grammar of the Antient Gaelic, Or Language of the Isle of Man, Usually Called Manks*. Quaritch, London.

[4] HathiTrust Digital Library. 2018. (2018). extracted feature set, at https://wiki.htrc.illinois.edu/display/COM/Extracted+Features+Dataset.

Which Parts of Search Results do Researchers Check when Selecting Academic Documents?

Emi Ishita
Kyushu University
Fukuoka 812-8581, Japan
ishita.emi.982@m.kyushu-u.ac.jp

Yasuko Hagiwara
Kyushu University
Fukuoka 812-8581, Japan
hagiwara_yasuko@gm.shinshu-u.ac.jp

Yukiko Watanabe
Kyushu University
Fukuoka 812-8581, Japan
watanabe.yukiko.935@m.kyushu-u.ac.jp

Yoichi Tomiura
Kyushu University
Fukuoka 819-0395, Japan
tom@inf.kyushu-u.ac.jp

ABSTRACT[1]

Our goal is to propose an alternative retrieval system of academic documents based on researcher's behavior in practice. In this study, a questionnaire survey was conducted. Question items were developed from findings in the previous observational study for researcher's behavior. From the results of 46 respondents, the top three elements checked in the search results were title, abstract, and the full-text version. They also checked structure "Introduction" in the full-text rather than other structures when they found previous research in an unfamiliar field. These results indicate that researchers use different ways for selecting documents based on the type of documents they look for.

CCS CONCEPTS

• **Information systems** → **Information retrieval**; Users • **Social and professional topics** → **User characteristics;**

KEYWORDS

Academic bibliographic system; researcher's information behavior; information retrieval system

ACM Reference format:

E. Ishita, Y. Hagiwara, Y. Watanabe, and Y. Tomiura. 2018. Which parts of search results do researchers check on selecting academic documents? In *Proceedings of ACM JCDL, June 3–7, 2018, Fort Worth, TX, USA (JCDL2018)*, 2 pages.
DOI: https://doi.org/10.1145/3197026.3203867

1 INTRODUCTION

Although some information retrieval systems for various information have been provided, bibliographic databases are still important tools for researchers [1]. Currently, bibliographic database systems not only display bibliographic information of documents as a search result, but also display links to full-text versions if they are available. Moreover, various search functions such as narrowing search results using facet functions are provided. This enables users to carry out various types of searches for academic documents. Searching for academic documents involves different behavior compared with searches in daily life. However, this behavior is influenced by the spread of search engines. For example, when researchers start to perform a document search, they use databases and search engines equally [2]. Focusing on the context of researcher's search, they change the databases to be used depending on the purpose of the search [3]. In this way, researchers are assumed to employ various search methods depending on the search environment and purpose of their search.

Our goal is to propose an alternative information retrieval system for academic documents considering a researcher's search behavior in practice and their diversity. We employ an approach to observe researcher's actual behavior and then conduct the questionnaire survey to confirm the generality of their behavior with other researchers. In this paper, we report the results of the questionnaire survey.

2 QUESTIONNAIRE SURVEY

We identified the elements that researchers checked from the research results and the order of elements checked by the observational study [4,5]. For example, the full-text version of documents is found as a new element. Some researchers use image search rather than the bibliographic database system. Moreover, the researchers' interviews in the conducted survey indicate that they checked different elements according to the type of document they were searching for. Although we recruited 10 participants for the observational survey, we conducted the questionnaire survey to confirm the generality of their behavior. We developed 14 question items based on our findings [6], inquiring the type of databases used daily, order of checked elements in research results, and frequency of use of functions of academic databases.

We obtained 88 respondents (48 researchers and 44 master's program students) from the schools of engineering in two national universities. A student in a Ph.D. program is considered as a researcher. We asked them to complete the online form survey from October 20th to November 10th, 2017. Informed consent was obtained from each respondent. In this paper, we present the responses of 48 researchers to focus on their common behavior.

JCDL '18, June 3–7, 2018, Fort Worth, TX, USA

ACM ISBN 978-1-4503-5178-2/18/06.
https://doi.org/10.1145/3197026.3203867

3 RESULTS

3.1 Elements Checked in the Search Results

Table 1 lists the elements to be confirmed in the search results (multiple answers allowed) depending on the type of document to be searched. The document to be searched could be of the following three types: to identify appropriate research methods, to find previous research in an unfamiliar field, and to learn the current research trends. Only 46 researchers who used the database (N=46) were considered. The top three elements to be confirmed were title, abstracts, and full-texts in any type. The title was the element that was the most confirmed in any case. Only when the researcher was identifying appropriate research methods was the percentage of checking the full-texts higher than that of the abstract. Titles and abstracts were revealed in previous studies as elements to be confirmed [7,8]. This result also indicates that it is common practice to check the text directly. When searching for research methods, the percentage of checking keywords was higher than others. This is considered to be because it confirms whether related methods are included in keywords. In the case of finding previous research in an unfamiliar field, the percentage of confirming the name of the journal and cited counts was higher than the other types. This indicates that these are the criteria for judging whether it is a core literature in that field. In addition, when the researchers wished to know the current research trends, the percentage of checking the publication year was high, since the publication year is important.

Table 1: Checked elements depending on the type of documents to be searched

	Research methods		Unfamiliar field		Research trends	
Title	43	93.5%	38	82.6%	39	84.8%
Abstract	37	80.4%	33	71.7%	35	76.1%
Full-text	38	82.6%	32	69.6%	32	69.6%
Publication year	9	19.6%	13	28.3%	24	52.2%
Journal title	14	30.4%	18	39.1%	17	37.0%
Author	14	30.4%	10	21.7%	13	28.3%
Number of pages	3	6.5%	3	6.5%	1	2.2%
Cited counts	10	21.7%	15	32.6%	12	26.1%
Keyword	25	54.3%	21	45.7%	20	43.5%
Research field	15	32.6%	18	39.1%	15	32.6%
Document type	15	32.6%	14	30.4%	13	28.3%
Language	5	10.9%	5	10.9%	3	6.5%
Availability	13	28.3%	13	28.3%	11	23.9%
Images	6	13.0%	6	13.0%	5	10.9%
Others	1	2.2%	1	2.2%	1	2.2%

3.2 Structures Checked in the Full-texts

Table 2 shows the percentages of each structure checked when deciding whether to carefully read the document after seeing the full-text. For example, in the research methods, the ratio of checking Method, Figure, Table, and Formula is overwhelming. To know the unfamiliar research field, the percentage of confirming Introduction was overwhelmingly larger than the others. In the investigation of the previous research, Introduction is referred to determine the position and outline of the document.

Table 2: Structures checked in the full-texts depending on the type of documents to be searched

	Research methods		Unfamiliar field		Research trends	
Introduction	28	60.9%	35	76.1%	30	65.2%
Conclusion	29	63.0%	25	54.3%	26	56.5%
Fig., Table, Formula	32	69.6%	24	52.2%	24	52.2%
Method	33	71.7%	19	41.3%	23	50.0%
References	23	50.0%	23	50.0%	18	39.1%
Related Work	17	37.0%	25	54.3%	20	43.5%
Others	2	4.3%	1	2.2%	1	2.2%

4 CONCLUSION

This result indicates that researchers checked different elements in the search results and different structures in the full-text version depending on the types of documents they were searching for. Checking the full texts seems to become more common. Thus, a seamless system providing both bibliographic data and parts of the full text could be useful. Herein, we present the results of two questions, and plan to analyze other questions with all respondents and propose an overall picture of an alternative system.

ACKNOWLEDGMENTS

This work is supported by JSPS KAKENHI Grant Number JP15H01721.

REFERENCES

[1] S. Liyana and A. Noorhidawati. 2014. How graduate students seek for information: Convenience or guaranteed result? *Malaysian Journal of Library & Information Science* 19, 2 (Mar. 2014), 1-15.

[2] Christine Wolff-Eisenberg, Alisa B. Rod, and Roger C. Schonfeld. 2016. *Ithaka S+R US Faculty Survey 2015* (Apr. 2016). DOI: https://doi.org/10.18665/sr.277685

[3] Kumaripaba Athukorala, et al. 2013. Information-seeking behaviors of computer scientists: Challenges for electronic literature search tools. *Proceedings of the Association for Information Science and Technology* 50, 1 (2013), 1-11. DOI: http://dx.doi.org/10.1002/meet.14505001041

[4] Yasuko Hagiwara, et al. 2016. A preliminary study and analysis to identify key elements in document selection. In *ISIC: Information Seeking in Context* 2016, Zadar, Croatia (Sept. 2016).

[5] Yasuko Hagiwara, et al. 2015. An experiment to identify how researchers select documents from search results. In *Proceedings of CiSAP Workshop (The annual meeting of the Consortium of iSchools Asia-Pacific)* 2015 (Dec. 2015), 8-11.

[6] Yasuko Hagiwara, et al. 2017. Identifying key elements of search results for document selection in the digital age: An Observational Study. In *Digital Libraries: Data, Information, and Knowledge for Digital Lives. ICADL 2017*, Lecture Notes in Computer Science, Vol. 10647. Springer, Cham, 237-242. DOI: https://doi.org/10.1007/978-3-319-70232-2_20

[7] M. Macedo-Rouet, J.-F. Rouet, C. Ros, and N. Vibert. 2012. How do scientists select articles in the PubMed database? An empirical study of criteria and strategies. *European Review of Applied Psychology* 62, 2 (Apr. 2012), 63-72. DOI: https://doi.org/10.1016/j.erap.2012.01.003

[8] Peiling Wang and Dagobert Soergel. 1998. A cognitive model of document use during a research project. Study I. Document selection. *Journal of the American Society for Information Science* 49, 2 (Feb. 1998), 115-133. DOI: https://doi.org/10.1002/(SICI)1097-4571(199802)49:2<115:AID-SI3>3.0.CO;2-T

Cross-language Citation Recommendation via Publication Content and Citation Representation Fusion

Zhuoren Jiang
School of Data and Computer Science
Sun Yat-sen University
Guangzhou, China
jiangzhr3@mail.sysu.edu.cn

Yao Lu
School of Data and Computer Science
Sun Yat-sen University
Guangzhou, China
luyao23@mail.sysu.edu.cn

Xiaozhong Liu*
School of Informatics and Computing
Indiana University Bloomington
Bloomington, IN, USA
liu237@indiana.edu

ABSTRACT

While citation recommendation can be important for scholars, unfortunately, because of language barrier, some scientists cannot efficiently retrieve and consume the publications hosted in a foreign language repository. In this study, we propose a novel solution, cross-language citation recommendation via Publication Content and Citation Representation Fusion (PCCRF). PCCRF can learn a representation function by mapping the publications, from various languages and repositories, to a low-dimensional joint embedding space from both content semantic and citation relation viewpoints. The proposed method can optimize the publication representations by maximizing the likelihood of observing network neighborhoods (which are generated by a semi-supervised random walk algorithm) of publications. Experimental results show that the proposed method can be promising for cross-language citation recommendation.

KEYWORDS

Citation Recommendation; Cross-language

ACM Reference Format:

Zhuoren Jiang, Yao Lu, and Xiaozhong Liu. 2018. Cross-language Citation Recommendation via Publication Content and Citation Representation Fusion. In *JCDL '18: The 18th ACM/IEEE Joint Conference on Digital Libraries, June 3–7, 2018, Fort Worth, TX, USA.* ACM, New York, NY, USA, 2 pages. https://doi.org/10.1145/3197026.3203898

1 INTRODUCTION

Language barrier could be a serious problem for the researchers (especially the junior ones who do not master English) to find an appropriate research paper. To address this problem, this paper proposes a novel solution, **Publication Content and Citation Representation Fusion (PCCRF)**. Unlike previous methods (e.g., [1]), which only focus on the textual content, in PCCRF, we address this problem by leveraging a novel cross-language citation network and representation learning. The proposed method can map a publication to a low-dimensional joint embedding space for both cross-language content semantic and citation relations. We first generate the network neighborhoods of a publication (in either source or target language) based on a semi-supervised random walk algorithm, then learn the latent publication representations by maximizing the likelihood of observing the generated neighborhoods. More importantly, PCCRF can recommend a list of ranked cross-language citations for a given paper's abstract and its monolingual citation relations (note that the query paper itself may not have any cross-language citations, but the papers cited by the query paper may have their cross-language citations). We evaluate the proposed algorithm in Chinese and English scholarly corpora, i.e., Wanfang[1] and Association for Computing Machinery (ACM) digital libraries. The results demonstrate that the proposed approach is promising to address cross-language citation recommendation.

The contribution of this paper is threefold. First, we propose a novel method to capture the publication joint representations for the cross-language content semantic and connectivity patterns of cross-language citation networks. Second, we apply the proposed embedding method for a novel cross-language citation recommendation task. An experiment on real-world bilingual scientific datasets is employed to validate the proposed approach, and the results show the potential and efficacy of our algorithm. Last but not least, the proposed methods are language independent. In other words, although in the experiment we focus on "Chinese-to-English" citation recommendation, the proposed methods can be generalized for recommending cross-language citations between any other pair of languages.

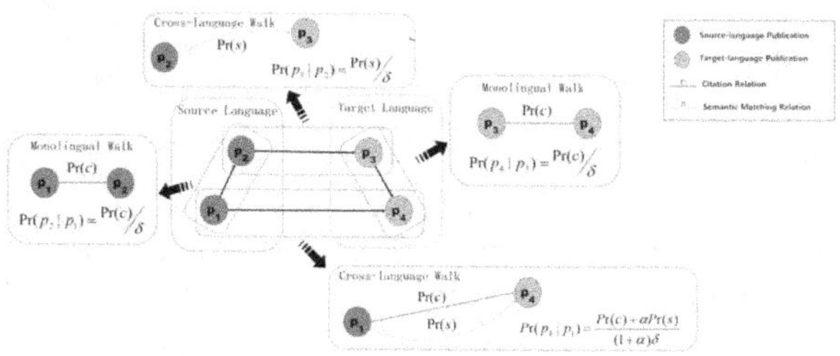

Figure 1: PCCRF random walk illustration

2 METHODOLOGY

The goal of publication representation learning is to obtain low-dimensional (compared to the publication number) dense vector (feature) representations for the publications in different languages for similarity/ranking calculation. In this work, we construct the publication representation in a graphical learning framework. However, there are two limitations left: (1) the cross-language citation

*Corresponding author

ACM ISBN 978-1-4503-5178-2/18/06.
https://doi.org/10.1145/3197026.3203898

[1] One of the biggest digital libraries in Chinese.

relations are very sparse (compare to the monolingual citations). (2) Citation networks don't utilize content semantic information.

To address these problems, as Figure 1 shows, we propose a semi-supervised random walk algorithm for flexible neighborhood sampling and cross-language content and citation fusion. Given a network $G = (P, E)$, P is the publication vertex set, E is the edge set. We can simulate a random walk of fixed length l in G with a parameter α to guide the walk. Let p_i denote the i_{th} publication in the walk, which can be generated by the following distribution:

$$Pr(p_i|p_{i-1}) = \begin{cases} \frac{Pr(c)}{\delta} & if\ \Phi(p_i, p_{i-1}) = 1 \wedge \mathbb{R}(p_i, p_{i-1}) = 1 \\ \frac{Pr(s)}{\delta} & if\ \Phi(p_i, p_{i-1}) = 0 \wedge \mathbb{R}(p_i, p_{i-1}) = 0 \\ \frac{Pr(c)+\alpha Pr(s)}{(1+\alpha)\delta} & if\ \Phi(p_i, p_{i-1}) = 0 \wedge \mathbb{R}(p_i, p_{i-1}) = 1 \end{cases} \tag{1}$$

Where $Pr(p_i|p_{i-1})$ is the normalized transition probability between p_i and p_{i-1}. $\Phi(p_i, p_{i-1}) = 1$ indicates p_i and p_{i-1} are in the same language; otherwise, $\Phi(p_i, p_{i-1}) = 0$. $\mathbb{R}(p_i, p_{i-1}) = 1$ indicates there is a citation relation between p_i and p_{i-1}; otherwise, $\mathbb{R}(p_i, p_{i-1}) = 0$. α is the fusion parameter that controls the contributions from citation and content, and δ is the normalization factor. $Pr(c) = \frac{1}{n^{cout}_{p_{i-1}}}$ is the citation probability, $n^{cout}_{p_{i-1}}$ is the out citation number of publication p_{i-1}. $Pr(s)$ is the the content semantic matching probability. We add cross-language semantic matching relations from each publication vertex (in source language corpus) to top k matched publication vertices (in target language corpus). The cross-language semantic matching calculation has two steps: (1) use machine translation (MT) to translate publication (abstract) from source language to target language[2]; (2) calculate the matching probability using language model with Dirichlet smoothing [4].

We then use $f : P \rightarrow \mathbb{R}^d$ as the mapping function from publication vertices to feature representations. Here, d specifies the number of dimensions. f is a matrix of size $|P| \times d$ parameters. Feature learning methods are based on the Skip-gram architecture [2]. For every starting publication vertex $p \in P$, we define $N_S(p) \subset P$ as a network neighborhood ("context") of vertex p generated through the proposed neighborhood sampling strategy S (semi-supervised random walk). The objective function can be formalized as:

$$\max_f \sum_{p \in P} logPr(N_S(p)|\overrightarrow{f(p)}) \tag{2}$$

Stochastic gradient ascent with negative sampling is used to optimize the model parameters of $\overrightarrow{f(\cdot)}$ [2].

Finally, we recommend the candidate cited publications in target language based on the cosine similarity of the optimized publication representations.

3 EXPERIMENT

We tested the proposed approach in a "Chinese-to-English" recommendation task. Our goal was to recommend English citations for a given Chinese paper's abstract with its Chinese citation relations. For this experiment, we collected 14,631 Chinese papers (in computer science) from the Wanfang digital library and 248,893 English papers from the ACM digital library. There were 750,557 English-cite-English relations, 11,252 Chinese-cite-Chinese relations, 27,101 Chinese-cite-English relations, and 12,403 English papers had been cited by 7,900 Chinese papers. 158,000 cross-language semantic matching relations (from Chinese to English) were generated for the proposed semi-supervised random walk algorithm.

We used ground truth cross-language citation relation (as 0 or 1 relevant scores) for evaluation. All cross-language citation relations from testing papers were removed (monolingual citation relations could be kept). To avoid evaluation bias, 10-fold cross-validation was applied.

We evaluated the performance of proposed PCCRF method against the following strong baseline algorithms: (1) Embedding Transformation (EF) [1]; (2) Item-based Collaborative Filtering (CF_I); (3) Popularity-based Collaborative Filtering (CF_P); (4) Machine Translation by Google Translation API + Language Model with Dirichlet smoothing (MT+LM); (5) DeepWalk node embedding [3] based on Citation Network (DW_C). According to Table 1, PCCRF ($\alpha = 0.25$) achieves best performance ($p < 0.0001$), in terms of all evaluation metrics.

Table 1: Measures of different cross-language citation recommendation algorithms

Algorithm	NDCG@10	P@10	MAP	MRR
EF	0.0176	0.0072	0.0185	0.0300
CF_I	0.0980	0.0330	0.0815	0.1290
CF_P	0.0041	0.0026	0.0125	0.0090
MT+LM	0.3404	0.1225	0.2831	0.3312
DW_C	0.2289	0.0938	0.1983	0.2550
PCCRF	***0.3908***†††	***0.1543***†††	***0.3312***†††	***0.4411***†††

Significant test: $^{\dagger}p < 0.01$, $^{\dagger\dagger}p < 0.001$, $^{\dagger\dagger\dagger}p < 0.0001$

4 CONCLUSION

In this study, we propose a novel problem/solution for cross-language citation recommendation by learning a joint publication representation in a network and fusing the content and citation information. Evaluation shows that: PCCRF significantly outperforms other baseline algorithms, which proves that the proposed method can efficiently integrate cross-language content and citation information for optimized publication representation.

ACKNOWLEDGMENTS

The work is supported by the National Science Foundation of China (11401601), Guangdong Province Frontier and Key Technology Innovative Grant (2015B010110003, 2016B030307003), Ministry of Science and Technology of China (2016YFB0200602), the Opening Project of State Key Laboratory of Digital Publishing Technology and the Open Project of Institute for Academic Evaluation and Development, East China Normal University (IAED2017B03).

REFERENCES

[1] Tomas Mikolov, Quoc V Le, and Ilya Sutskever. 2013. Exploiting similarities among languages for machine translation. *arXiv preprint arXiv:1309.4168* (2013).

[2] Tomas Mikolov, Ilya Sutskever, Kai Chen, Greg S Corrado, and Jeff Dean. 2013. Distributed representations of words and phrases and their compositionality. In *Advances in neural information processing systems.* 3111–3119.

[3] Bryan Perozzi, Rami Al-Rfou, and Steven Skiena. 2014. Deepwalk: Online learning of social representations. In *Proceedings of the 20th ACM SIGKDD international conference on Knowledge discovery and data mining.* ACM, 701–710.

[4] Chengxiang Zhai and John Lafferty. 2001. A study of smoothing methods for language models applied to ad hoc information retrieval. In *Proceedings of the 24th annual international ACM SIGIR conference on Research and development in information retrieval.* ACM, 334–342.

[2]As this study is not focusing on machine translation, we use Google machine translation API (https://cloud.google.com/translate) to translate the publication abstract.

Preliminary Exploration of Knowledge Curation Activities in Wikidata WikiProjects

Timothy Kanke
School of Information
Florida State University
tjk11b@my.fsu.edu

ABSTRACT

Wikidata is one of the largest knowledge curation projects on the web. Their data is used by other Wikimedia projects such as Wikipedia, as well as major search engines. This qualitative study used content analysis of discussions involving data curation and negotiation in Wikidata. Activity Theory was used as a conceptual framework for data collection and analysis of the activities, members and tools. Some of the findings map Wikidata activities to curation frameworks. An understanding of the activities in Wikidata will help inform communities wishing to contribute data to or reuse data from Wikidata, as well as inform the design of other similar online peer-curation communities, scientific research institutional repositories, digital archives, and libraries.

KEYWORDS

Online curation communities; Curation; Wikidata

ACM Reference Format:
Timothy Kanke. 2018. Preliminary Exploration of Knowledge Curation Activities in Wikidata WikiProjects. In JCDL '18: The 18th ACM/IEEE Joint Conference on Digital Libraries, June 3–7, 2018, Fort Worth, TX, USA. ACM, New York, NY, USA, 2 pages. https://doi.org/10.1145/3197026.3203878

1 INTRODUCTION

Wikidata is a free collaborative multilingual database collecting structured data for Wikimedia projects, that was launched in October 2012. It provides a centralized location for Wikimedia projects to query data allowing easier updating of information [8]. According to Wikimedia February 2018 statistics, there are more than 50,000 contributors to Wikidata with an active base of 8,000 contributors making at least 5 edits per month. Wikidata is becoming the database of structured data for other information systems such as search engines. For example, one potential use is to provide updated information about clinical drug interactions (e.g., [1]). This paper reports on the early results of an exploratory study on how editors participate in Wikidata and how they organize their work.

JCDL '18, June 3–7 2018, Fort Worth, TX, USA

ACM ISBN 978-1-4503-5178-2/18/06.
https://doi.org/10.1145/3197026.3203878

A WikiProject is a group of individuals who want to collaborate to improve Wikidata on a specific topic or a task. Since little research has been conducted on WikiProjects in Wikidata, the following literature focuses on WikiProjects in a more well-documented Wikimedia project, Wikipedia. A reason to study WikiProjects is that they help editors to find others with similar topic interests or goals of improving Wikipedia by a maintenance task. These self-selected groups tend to have distinct activities and a shared identity. WikiProjects help support collaboration by focus attention towards coordinating and completing group related tasks [3], encourage good citizenship and maintenance behaviors [7]. WikiProject communications between editors may occur in additional pages outside of the project's talk page [4]. Some advanced editors seek additional information through talk pages of users of WikiProjects [5].

This study investigated the following research questions: (1) What are some of the curation and support activities being discussed by editors in Wikidata? (2) Who are the editors participating in these activities? (3) What tools are being used to perform these activities?

2 METHODOLOGY

To address the research questions, this study used content analysis of discussions involving data curation and negotiation in Wikidata. This study used Activity Theory as a methodological and conceptual framework for data collection and analysis with a focus on the activities, members, and tools. Activity Theory provides a hierarchical structure for studying and analyzing the activities of different communities with activity being the basic unit of analysis. The activity system model focuses on collective group activities that are performed by individual subject contributions [6].

The process of data collection and analysis was as follows. First, 181 Wikidata WikiProjects were identified. 153 projects focus on topics including astronomy, music, sports, and food. The remaining nineteen projects focus on knowledge bases and meta topics. From this set of WikiProjects, a smaller subset of four projects was selected: KOS, Ontology, Freebase, and Labels and Descriptions. The talk pages were analyzed by a manual iterative process using an inductive and deductive qualitative coding technique to identify patterns and themes. An initial phase of open coding is used to organize the data followed by selective coding to define, develop, and refine the themes with attention to the relationships of the categories and concepts emerging from the data.

3 FINDINGS AND DISCUSSION

3.1 Activities

Many activities can be mapped to DCC Curation Lifecycle Model [2]. The DCC model uses the term "action" in a generalized sense while Activity Theory uses a more precise definition of action. Thus, this paper will replace "action" with "activities" to lessen confusion. Most of the activities that were identified occur in earlier stages of the DCC sequential activities. The activities are conceptualize, create or receive, appraise and select, and ingest. These activities support the goal of populating Wikidata with data from external sources such as freebase as well as original hack-a-thon content.

Several of the identified actions map to the DCC occasional activities of reappraising and dispose. Wikidata items are often created and then later expanded by many editors and bots by adding labels, descriptions in multiple languages, properties, and links to sources.

The other related activities that were identified are creating collaborative infrastructure, re-organizing collaborative infrastructure, and welcoming newcomers. Creating collaborative infrastructure include four actions: determining the scope of a project, creating work lists, determining the location of a list, and determining a location for discussion. As some WikiProjects grew in membership and data, it became necessary to reorganizing the collaborative infrastructure. For example, a talk page and table were divided into more manageable portions for each language. Welcoming newcomers is a critical issue for online communities because newcomers are a source of innovative ideas, work procedures, and resources. Actions that were identified focused on reorganizing help pages that have the potential to improve a new editor's experience.

3.2 Editors

True to the mission of Wikidata, the editors come from various Wikimedia projects including Wikipedia, Wikisource, and Wikitionary. Many editors also contribute to Wikipedia including the following languages: English, Russian, German, Dutch, Catalan, Macedonian, Oriya, Norwegian, Northern Sami, and Swedish. A few of the editors contribute to other Wikimedia projects: Wikisource and Wikitionary. Non-Wikimedia projects that were identified are OpenRefine, Schema.org, and Freebase. Some editors mention affiliation with the Wikimedia Foundation, a W3C working group, or Google. A few editors disclose their profession: librarian, professor, and software engineer.

3.3 Tools

Several tools were identified in the talk page discussions: internal communications, external hosted communications, and activity related tools. Wikimedia hosted communications include Talk pages in WikiProject, Property, Project chat, and User pages. Some editors use a WikiProject talk page to begin discussions before moving to the main project chat page. If a discussion that is relevant to a WikiProject is found to be occurring elsewhere, then there is a posting linking to that location to inform the project members. Occasionally editors use outside non-Wikimedia hosted platforms for communication and collaboration. Wikidata has a simplified user interface that lends itself to ease of contributing data, however, this simplicity may be at the cost of more advanced ontology creation tools. Some editors used Google Spreadsheet to collaborate on mapping an outside ontology to Wikidata, however, some editors expressed hesitations for collaborating on an outside resource due to privacy concerns. Bots are used to automate tasks including initial data population of properties and items from external sources. Scripts are explicitly mentioned less often than bots and are used to create constraint violation reports. Finally, Wikidata primary sources tool that is used in the process of ingesting donated data. Editors can review, edit, or reject data before importing the data.

4 CONCLUSION AND FUTURE WORK

The preliminary findings of this study identified the activities, participants, and tools used to curate knowledge. The identified activities are conceptualizing the curation process, appraising objects, ingesting objects from external sources, creating collaborative infrastructure, re-organizing collaborative infrastructure, and welcoming newcomers. Wikidata editors come from diverse backgrounds and are involved in other Wikimedia projects. Wikimedia hosts a majority of the communication, however, some WikiProjects need functionality or convenience that outside platforms provided. Future work will include expanding this study to investigate other aspects of Activity Theory including motivations, norms, rules, and roles of editors.

REFERENCES

[1] S. Ayvaz, J. Horn, O. Hassanzadeh, Q. Zhu, J. Stan, N. P. Tatonetti, and R. D. Boyce. 2015. Toward a complete dataset of drug-drug interaction information from publicly available sources. Journal of Biomedical Informatics 55, 206-217.

[2] Digital Curation Centre. 2017. Curation Reference Manual. Retrieved from http://www.dcc.ac.uk/resources/curation-reference-manual

[3] A. Forte, N. Kittur, V. Larco, H. Zhu, A. Bruckman, and R. E. Kraut. 2012. Coordination and beyond: Social functions of groups in open content production. In Proceedings of the ACM 2012 Conference on Computer Supported Cooperative Work, ACM, 417-426.

[4] M. Gilbert, J. T. Morgan, D. W. McDonald, and M. Zachry. 2013. Managing complexity: Strategies for group awareness and coordinated action in Wikipedia. In Proceedings of the 9th International Symposium on Open Collaboration, ACM, 5:1-5:10.

[5] H. Jung, S. R. Hong, P. Meas, and M. Zachry. 2015. Designing tools to support advanced users in new forms of social media interaction. In Proceedings of the 33rd Annual International Conference on the Design of Communication, ACM, 34:1-34:10.

[6] V. Kaptelinin, and B. A. Nardi. 2012. Activity theory in HCI: Fundamentals and reflections. Morgan & Claypool.

[7] A. Kittur, B. Pendleton, and R. E. Kraut. 2009. Herding the cats: The influence of groups in coordinating peer production. In Proceedings of the 5th International Symposium on Wikis and Open Collaboration, ACM, 7:1-7:9.

[8] D. Vrandecic and M. Krtotzsch. 2014. Wikidata: A free collaborative knowledgebase. Communications of the ACM, 57(10), 78-85.

Measuring Reuse of Digital Objects: Preliminary Findings from the IMLS-funded project

Extended Abstract

Elizabeth Joan Kelly
Loyola University New Orleans
USA
ejkelly@loyno.edu

Caroline Muglia
University of Southern California
USA
muglia@usc.edu

Genya O'Gara
Virtual Library of Virginia
USA
gogara@gmu.edu

Ayla Stein
UIUC
USA
astein@illinois.edu

Santi Thompson
University of Houston
USA
sathompson3@uh.edu

Liz Woolcott
Utah State University
USA
liz.woolcott@usu.edu

ABSTRACT

The first step of the Developing a Framework for Measuring Reuse of Digital Objects project involved a survey identifying how cultural heritage organizations currently assess digital library reuse, barriers to assessing reuse, and community priorities for potential solutions and next steps. This poster offers initial analysis of the survey results.

CCS CONCEPTS

• **Information systems → Digital libraries and archives**;

KEYWORDS

digital library, reuse, e-Resources, lifecycle management, usage, collection analysis, scholarly communication

ACM Reference Format:

Elizabeth Joan Kelly, Caroline Muglia, Genya O'Gara, Ayla Stein, Santi Thompson, and Liz Woolcott. 2018. Measuring Reuse of Digital Objects: Preliminary Findings from the IMLS-funded project: Extended Abstract. In *Proceedings of Joint Conference on Digital Libraries (JCDL '18)*. ACM, New York, NY, USA, 2 pages. https://doi.org/10.1145/3197026.3203871

1 INTRODUCTION

Content reuse, or how often and in what ways digital library materials are employed and repurposed, is a key indicator of the impact of digital libraries (as defined by Krystyna Matusiak)[1].

A literature review and whitepaper authored by the Digital Library Federation Assessment Interest Group (DLF-AIG) in 2015 found that traditional library analytics focus primarily on access and download statistics, which do not show how users utilize or transform unique materials from digital collections [2]. This lack of distinction, combined with nonstandard assessment approaches, makes it difficult to develop user-responsive collections or highlight the value of these materials, which in turn presents staffing, system infrastructure, and long-term funding challenges.

The grant project Developing a Framework for Measuring Reuse of Digital Objects, an Institute of Museum and Library Services (IMLS) funded project (LG-73-17-0002-17) by the DLF-AIG, is working to address this through an in-depth needs assessment of the digital library community to determine desired functionality for the construction of a reuse assessment toolkit. The development of well-defined functional requirements and use cases will serve as building blocks that go beyond use and focus on transformation.

The first step of the Developing a Framework for Measuring Reuse of Digital Objects project involved a survey identifying how cultural heritage organizations currently assess digital library reuse, barriers to assessing reuse, and community priorities for potential solutions and next steps.

2 SURVEY INFORMATION

The 19 question Qualtrics survey was distributed to 25 different listservs and advertised via the project group's website and the Digital Library Federation's social media channels. The survey remained open from September 13 – October 11, 2017.

Ten questions constitute the primary question set. Questions included those related to institution size, employment, and mission, and collection of both use and reuse data [3].

3 RESPONSES

In total, 409 surveys were started. Of those, 107 surveys were eliminated from this data set because the respondent indicated they did not agree to the IRB statement or the respondent did not answer the IRB statement agreement. In both of these scenarios, respondents were not shown any other questions in the survey. The remaining 302 surveys had at least one answer beyond the IRB agreement. This data set (which will be referred to as the total response set) represents 73.8% of all surveys started. 43% (n=130) answered all of the basic questions from the total response set.

Most respondents were from libraries in academic institutions. 30% of respondents reported being from an institution that served under-represented groups.

JCDL '18, June 3–7, 2018, Fort Worth, TX, USA

ACM ISBN 978-1-4503-5178-2/18/06.
https://doi.org/10.1145/3197026.3203871

4 ANALYSIS

4.1 Measuring Use

80% of respondents reported collecting use statistics. Google Analytics and platform specific statistics were the most commonly used data-collection tools. The three most common types of use statistics gathered were: number of visitors (12.59%), number of downloads (10.75%), and number of clicks (9.49%). The most commonly reported reasons for collecting use statistics were to "improve digital collection services" (20.19%) and "demonstrate the impact of collections on scholarship and research" (17.13%). The least commonly reported reason for collecting use statistics was to "locate pirated content for intellectual property purposes" (3.32%).

Respondents who did not collect use statistics listed the following reasons: lack of digital collections to measure, lack of staff or staff time, the need for external departments/units to collect the data, lack of priority for usage assessment, lack of tools and systems in place for gathering data, lack of policies regarding data collection, the need for concrete use cases for collecting data, uncertainty about what to do with statistics data after it has been collected, and the new or nascent stages of the respondent's digital collections.

4.2 Measuring Reuse

40% of respondents indicated that they collected reuse statistics. The most common methods for collecting reuse data were "social media metrics" (22.32%), "reverse image lookup" (13.30%) and "alert services" (13.73%). The most common kinds of reuse data collected were "digital collections and objects cited in scholarship" (19.32%) and "published or re-posted digital objects in digital media" (18.56%). The least common kinds of reuse data collected were "published data sets used in new research" (6.44%). A lack of accepted methodology or systems for gathering reuse data were the reasons provided most frequently for not gathering reuse data. Similar to the reasons for not collecting use statistics, respondents also indicated that a lack of staff or staff time was a significant barrier. Additional reasons included: institutional lack of priority for use or reuse data, difficulty in measuring reuse, uncertainty as to what reuse data was and why it should be collected, concern about privacy and patron anonymity, lack of definitions for and quantitative methods for calculating reuse, and concern that tracking reuse would be inaccurate without being able to calculate full extent of reuse.

4.3 Supporting Reuse Data Collection

In order to implement reuse assessment, respondents most commonly reported the need for the following supports: "documented standards and best practices" (14.86%), "personnel" (12.8%), "online tutorials" (12.06%), "open source tools" (11.78%), and "money" (11.68%). Additionally, respondents commented in a free text question that "research in the validity of such measurements" would be important as well as "easily implemented systems" and "better tracking tools for our implemented persistent IDs (handles, DOI)." Personnel was the most consistently rated high-need support across institutions.

4.4 Greatest Barriers to Assessment

Respondents overall expressed concern about being able to adequately measure both use and reuse in the absence of professional standards in the field. Lack of staff, time, and resources were key reasons that respondent's institutions were not pursuing more robust assessment activities. They also discussed the inability to interpret and understand data due to a lack of lack of training, understanding of statistics and data, and reliable measurements. For instance, respondents noted that the system-supplied assessment data generated by organizational content management systems differed from assessment tools like Google Analytics to such a high degree that they did not know which data to rely on. Many respondents identified the difficulty of assessing content across platforms with available tools. Additionally, the theme of not knowing what to do with the information that is gathered was expressed in several different ways. Some respondents noted that they did not know if the information they were gathering was valid or reliably interpreted and others expressed concern about not knowing how to turn that data into actionable information. Respondents also expressed that collected data may not be used or appreciated by upper administration and may even be seen as a waste of time.

5 PROGRESS

Data from the survey has been used to inform the continued work of the project. The survey results have thus far helped in developing discussion topics for the focus groups such as refining definitions and examples of use and reuse; determining necessary technology and standards for a reuse toolkit; and examining the cultural and ethical implications of reuse assessment. Data from the survey and focus groups will be used to create use cases which will then be assessed in terms of usefulness via a follow-up survey.

ACKNOWLEDGMENTS

This work is supported by the Institute of Museum and Library Services (IMLS) (LG-73-17-0002-17).

REFERENCES

[1] Krystyna K Matusiak. 2012. Perceptions of usability and usefulness of digital libraries. *International journal of humanities and arts computing* 6, 1-2 (2012), 133–147.

[2] Santi Thompson, Joyce Chapman, Jody DeRidder, Megan Hurst, Elizabeth Joan Kelly, Martha Kyrillidou, Caroline Muglia, Genya O'Gara, Ayla Stein, Rachel Trent, et al. 2015. Surveying the landscape: Use and usability assessment of digital libraries. *Digital Library Federation Assessment Interest Group, User Studies Working Group* (2015). https://doi.org/10.17605/OSF.IO/9NBQG

[3] Santi Thompson, Elizabeth Joan Kelly, Caroline Muglia, Genya O'Gara, Ayla Stein, and Liz Woolcott. 2017. Developing a Framework for Measuring Reuse of Digital Objects A Survey. *Digital Library Federation Assessment Interest Group* (2017). https://osf.io/ptvh5/

Unfolding Research Data Services: An Information Architecture Perspective*

Hammad Rauf Khan
University of North Texas
Denton, TX
United States
hammadkhan@my.unt.edu

Hsia-Ching Chang
University of North Texas
Denton, TX
United States
hsia-ching.chang@unt.edu

Jeonghyun Kim
University of North Texas
Denton, TX
United States
jeonghyun.kim@unt.edu

ABSTRACT

With the exponential growth in digital research data, libraries are beginning to find opportunities to assist researchers with planning, maintaining, sharing, and accessing data through research data services. Using a content analysis with the lens of information architecture, this study sought to better understand how these services are organized in North American academic library websites and to what extent the research data lifecycle is supported within research data services. 50 academic library websites were studied and results yielded three provisions that make up research data services: Information Access, Technical Support, and Personalized Consultation. The data lifecycle was found to be strongly supported in research data services for planning, data curation, and data access stages.

KEYWORDS

Research Data Services (RDS), Research Data Management (RDM), Data Lifecycle

ACM Reference format:

H. Khan, H.-C. Chang, J. Kim. 2018. Unfolding Research Data Services: An Information Architecture Perspective. In *Proceedings of The 18th ACM/IEEE Joint Conference on Digital Libraries, Fort Worth, Texas, USA, June 3-7 2018 (JCDL'18)*, 2 pages. https://doi.org/10.1145/3197026.3203887

1 INTRODUCTION

Scientists are attempting to address the challenges of the data deluge, while librarians are finding opportunities to help researchers plan, manage, store, preserve, and share data. Many funding agencies, including the National Science Foundation and National Institutes of Health, mandate that applicants submit a data management plan (DMP), which addresses funder policy, legal and ethical considerations, organization and documentation, data backup and security, data sharing and archiving, and data access. In response to these requirements from the funding agencies, academic libraries have begun to implement research data services (RDS), which support researchers' data management needs and challenges. In essence, research data management "consists of a number of different activities and processes associated with the data lifecycle" [2].

As the volume and complexity of digital research data increases, so does the need to address the challenges of managing it. Data management has been within the purview of librarians, as they have actively engaged in providing access to data repositories and offering services, such as data curation and now RDS. In previous research, Tenopir et al. [5] identified two major categories of RDS: informational RDS and technical RDS.

However, no significant work has been done on how RDS is organized in different academic libraries and how much of the research data lifecycle is supported within RDS. The purpose of this study is to better understand how RDS is aiding researchers in North American academic libraries. Particularly, the following two research questions guide this exploration:

RQ1. What are the provisions that make up RDS?

RQ2. To what extent does RDS support the research data lifecycle?

2 METHOD

This study adopted an innovative approach in examining RDS websites through content analysis with an information architecture (IA) perspective.

2.1 Data Collection

We focused on examining RDS websites for North American academic libraries. The sample was derived from Association of Research Libraries (ARL) member libraries that participated in the 2013 ARL survey [3]; it included a total of 50 libraries.

2.2 Data Analysis

Doing a content analysis of what is featured through the lens of IA of RDS websites could provide insight into how these services are organized and labeled. Data was recorded through the process of studying the IA, which encompasses search, organization, labeling, and navigation within the website. Using IA principles [4], we

JCDL '18, June 3–7, 2018, Fort Worth, TX, USA

ACM ISBN 978-1-4503-5178-2/18/06.
https://doi.org/10.1145/3197026.3203887

labeled how each RDS website was organized and the services offered. We also labeled how the services support each stage and/or phase of the research data lifecycle.

To assess the intercoder reliability, two independent judges coded a quarter of randomly chosen cases. The intercoder reliability was assessed by Cohen's kappa, because each judge reached coding decisions in a qualitative and nominal manner. Based on the criteria suggested by Cohen [1], substantial agreement beyond chance was obtained between the two judges (k = 0.821 for RQ1 and k = 0.781 for RQ2).

3 RESULTS AND DISCUSSION

By reviewing the contents and structure of the RDS websites, this study identified the following three emerging themes in RDS.

3.1 Information Access RDS

Information Access RDS is intended to provide access to information resources. Such RDS includes data management guides, tutorials for best practices to help researchers to manage and share data, links to funding agency requirements, links to external RDS websites, and data citation guides.

Approximately a quarter of libraries in this study have organized their RDS website as a format of LibGuide, which pulls many different types of resources on a subject or topic together in one place. Across many academic libraries, such LibGuides provide a similar organization and template design; they are often organized under categorized tabs. Many of these LibGuides heavily borrowed content and pages from other RDS LibGuides.

3.2 Technical Support RDS

Technical Support RDS involves the availability of data repositories, including institutional repositories and disciplinary repositories, as well as tools and software to assist users with creating DMPs, depositing data, and analysing/visualizing data. Technical support is extremely limited in RDS to the DMPTool, with all of the samples offering this to users, followed by 96% offering a data repository. Only 34% of the sample offers technical support for data analysis and visualization.

3.3 Personalized Consultation RDS

Personalized Consultation RDS refers to in-person assistance and/or instruction on various aspects of data management and curation. Almost all RDS websites (98%) provide some personalized consultation option. However, the consultation descriptions on the websites were vague and did not state who would provide such consultation. The RDS websites that offer specific information indicate that consultation is provided by either subject librarians (12%) or a data management team (14%).

It should be noted that 22% of libraries provide geographic information systems (GIS) within RDS. These libraries offer the option to consult specifically with a geospatial data librarian who is in charge of maps and geospatial data collection. They also provide their users the option of consulting on general research data management or the option of contacting the Library Maps, Data, or GIS department for consultation.

3.4 Data Lifecycle Alignment in RDS

Under the three RDS provisions discussed in the previous section, it is noticeable that RDS supports several stages of the research data lifecycle. Upon consulting many data lifecycle models reported in the literature, it was determined that the majority of them consider the research data lifecycle to include data planning, data acquisition, data curation, data access, and data processing.

The results showed that only 30% of the sample of North American academic libraries that provide RDS support data acquisition; the areas for data acquisition include data capture, data collection, and ownership of data. It was found that 34% of the institutions provide some form of data processing, such as tools and tips for data pre-processing, data analysis, and visualization. We also found that more than half of our sample supports data curation process and practices, such as data documentation, metadata, long-term data storage, and data deposit into repositories, whereas three-fourths of the institutions support data access, which includes licenses for research data and data citation.

From the IA investigation and content analysis of RDS provisions, this study discovered that technical support remains limited in the number of services offered. All of our samples provide data management planning, which is the highest representation of a data lifecycle stage within RDS. Additionally, this study found that the scope of current RDS activities is not comprehensive enough to provide full support for the entire research data lifecycle.

4 CONCLUSION

Research data services are critical to the progress of 21st century science in which data must be properly collected, stored, and made accessible for long-term use. This preliminary study is beneficial in understanding the composition of services provided in RDS. Information Access, Technical Support, and Personalized Consultation are all different ways in which libraries provide RDS. Based on the definitions and labeling of the three provisions of RDS, this research found that 98% of libraries provide all three options for RDS. Technical support RDS is underrepresented in the number of features offered when compared to Information Access RDS. In the future, it will be interesting to see if Technical Support RDS begins to implement more support to researchers in the analysis and visualization of data.

REFERENCES

[1] Cohen, J. 1960. A Coefficient of agreement for nominal scales. *Educational and Psychological Measurement, 20*(1), 37-46.

[2] Cox, A.M., & Pinfield, S. 2014. Research data management and libraries: Current activities and future priorities. *Journal of Librarianship and Information Science, 46*(4), 299-316.

[3] Fearon, D., Guina, B., Pralle, B., Lake, S., & Sallans, A. 2013. Research Data Management Services, SPEC KIT 334. Washington, D.C.: Association of Research Libraries.

[4] Rosenfield, L., Morville, P., & Arango, J. (2015). *Information architecture: For the webs and beyond* (4th ed.). Sebastopl, CA: O'Reilly Media.

[5] Tenopir, C., Sandusky, R. J., Allard, S., & Birch, B. (2014). Research data management services in academic research libraries and perceptions of librarians. Library & Information Science Research, 36(2), 84-90.

Signposting for Repositories

Martin Klein
Los Alamos National Laboratory
Los Alamos, NM, USA
http://orcid.org/0000-0003-0130-2097
mklein@lanl.gov

Harihar Shankar
Los Alamos National Laboratory
Los Alamos, NM, USA
http://orcid.org/0000-0003-4949-0728
harihar@lanl.gov

Herbert Van de Sompel
Los Alamos National Laboratory
Los Alamos, NM, USA
http://orcid.org/0000-0002-0715-6126
herbertv@lanl.gov

ABSTRACT

Digital repositories can often easily be navigated by humans but not by machines. We introduce Signposting, a mechanism to show machines how to maneuver repositories' objects and how to interpret their relationships. Signposting is based on standard and widely adopted web technologies - typed links and HTTP link headers.

KEYWORDS

Typed Links, Machine-Friendly Repositories, REST, HATEOS

ACM Reference Format:
Martin Klein, Harihar Shankar, and Herbert Van de Sompel. 2018. Signposting for Repositories. In *JCDL '18: The 18th ACM/IEEE Joint Conference on Digital Libraries, June 3–7, 2018, Fort Worth, TX, USA.* ACM, New York, NY, USA, 2 pages. https://doi.org/10.1145/3197026.3203879

1 INTRODUCTION

Modern digital repositories offer an impressive set of functionalities. Storage options for a variety of file types, APIs to allow for access to stored objects, fixity checking, versioning, and audit are just a few of the services frequently provided. However, while most of the common repository systems are accessible via the web, they are often lacking in adoption of common web standards. In other words, modern repositories are mostly **on the web** but not truly **of the web**. This situation becomes apparent when illustrated by an example in the realm of scholarly repositories. For a human, it is arguably fairly simple to navigate through a repository's holdings and discover an object, its core content, auxiliary content, bibliographic description, persistent identifier, and author names/identifiers. Often all of this data can be obtained without much effort by simply scanning the object's landing page. For a machine, however, the same task is much harder to accomplish, in part due to repository-specific conventions as to how to convey this information. This situation requires developers to implement heuristics in order to "interpret" the data surfaced by repositories - a proposition that does not scale and hence hinders the emergence of 3rd party value-added services in the scholarly communication landscape.

In this poster we outline the Signposting concept as a simple yet potentially powerful solution to this problem. Signposting is a standards-based approach for digital repositories in libraries, archives, and museums to expose data in a machine-friendly manner and to clarify common patterns and relationships between resources they hold.

JCDL '18, June 3–7, 2018, Fort Worth, TX, USA

ACM ISBN 978-1-4503-5178-2/18/06.
https://doi.org/10.1145/3197026.3203879

2 SIGNPOSTING PATTERNS

The core intention of Signposting[1] is to make it easier for applications to **navigate** across repository resources, not to actually **describe** them. To that end, Signposting uses a REST/HATEOS approach that consists of conveying typed links[2] in HTTP Link response headers[3] and/or the <link> element in HTML pages. These standardized technologies are easy to implement and therefore frequently used on the web. For example, motivated by LOCKSS[4] and CLOCKSS[5] use cases, Signposting has previously been explored to support preservation efforts for e-Journals [2]. Here we focus on the following, more generic but very typical usage patterns of scholarly repositories:

The *Object Identifier* pattern serves the purpose of helping machines find the identifying HTTP URI of an object. Figure 1a depicts a DOI redirecting to a landing page of a scholarly object. The landing page also links to resources that are part of the publication, such as alternate renderings of the article, all of which are identified by the same DOI. A machine that only discovers this landing page, for example by following a citation that used the URI of the landing page instead of the DOI, a scenario frequently observed [1], has no easy way to determine the identifying URI (the DOI) of the scholarly object. Similarly, it also has no convenient way of obtaining the DOI if it only discovered the PDF version of the article, for example. If, however, the repository implemented an HTTP link header pointing from the landing page and the publication representations at the DOI URI using the relation type "cite-as"[6], a machine would be able to figure out that the article and its related resources are identified by the same DOI.

The *Author Information* pattern, depicted in Figure 1b, enables machines to discover author information of repository objects. The scenario is similar to the one described above: a link is implemented with the "author" relation type[7] from the landing page and the HTTP DOI to the author identifying URI, for example, the author's ORCID URI. The below HTTP link headers that are returned in response to a HEAD/GET on the landing page convey object and author identifiers for the resource https://doi.pangaea.de/10.1594/PANGAEA.880814 hosted by the Pangaea service, one of the early adopters of the Signposting concept.

[1] http://signposting.org/
[2] https://www.iana.org/assignments/link-relations/link-relations.xhtml
[3] https://tools.ietf.org/html/rfc5988
[4] https://www.lockss.org/
[5] https://clockss.org/
[6] https://www.ietf.org/id/draft-vandesompel-citeas-02.txt
[7] https://www.w3.org/TR/html5/links.html

```
HTTP/1.1 200 OK
Server: PANGAEA/1.0
Date: Wed, 31 Jan 2018 05:58:42 GMT
Link: <https://doi.org/10.1594/PANGAEA.880814>;
rel="cite-as",
<https://orcid.org/0000-0001-5212-9808>;rel="author",
<https://orcid.org/0000-0002-9017-0083>;rel="author"
```

Bibliographic Metadata can be made discoverable by adopting the pattern shown in Figure 1c. A DOI redirects to the landing page which in turn links to bibliographic resources. If these two resources provide link headers with the relation type "describedby"[8] pointing at bibliographic resources provided by CrossRef or DataCite, a machine can easily make that connection between the DOI-identified resource and its metadata records. To make these links even more expressive and friendly to machines, they should also have a "type" attribute to convey the format of the linked metadata record. In reverse, links to the HTML page and to the HTTP DOI URI with the relation type "describes"[9] from the corresponding bibliographic resources can also be provided to support bidirectional navigation.

The *Boundary Information* pattern is related to automatically expressing the web boundary of an object. Frequently, landing pages link to related resources such as alternate renderings of the article (as seen above) and supplemental information. Clearly, these resources should be considered as being within the boundary of a publication. However, landing pages also link to other external resources such as advertisement or social media platforms, which, in turn, are not within the publication's boundary. The distinction between what falls within and what outside of the boundary is trivial for a human to make. For a machine, however, this is very hard to delineate. This pattern entails the landing page providing link headers with the relation type "item"[10] to point to in-boundary resources. In turn, these resources provide links with the relation type "collection"[11] to point back to the landing page.

The Signposting concept is not limited to these four patterns. Other examples include the expression of license information with the "license" link relation type[12] or exposing object versions with relation types such as "previous memento" and "next memento"[13].

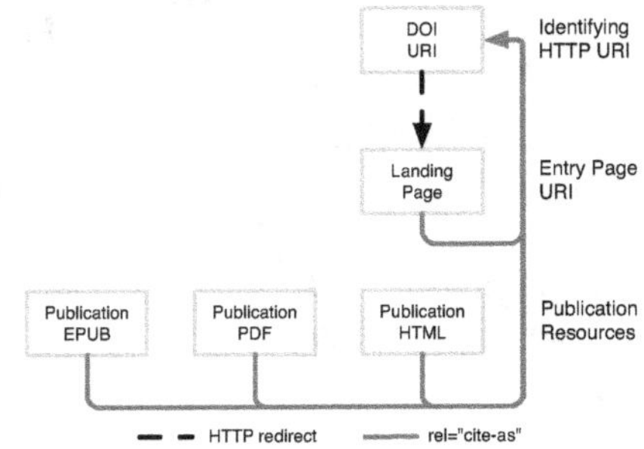

(a) Object Identifier

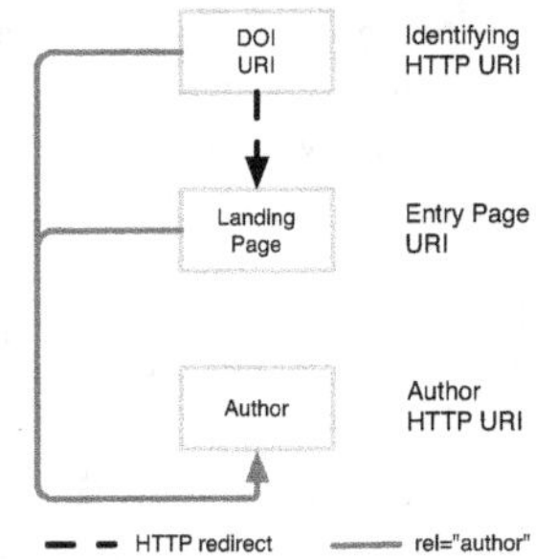

(b) Author Information

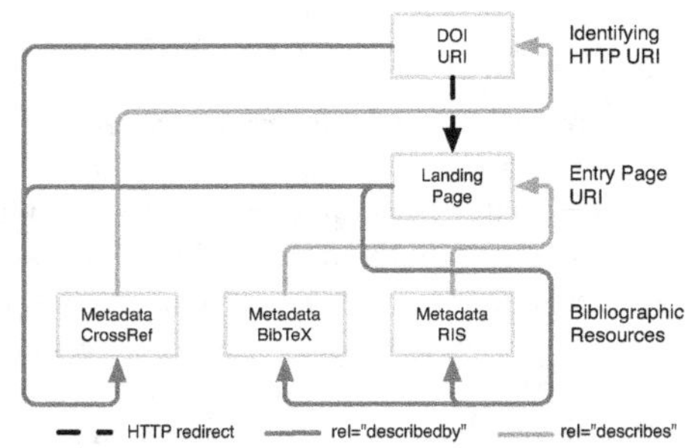

(c) Bibliographic Metadata

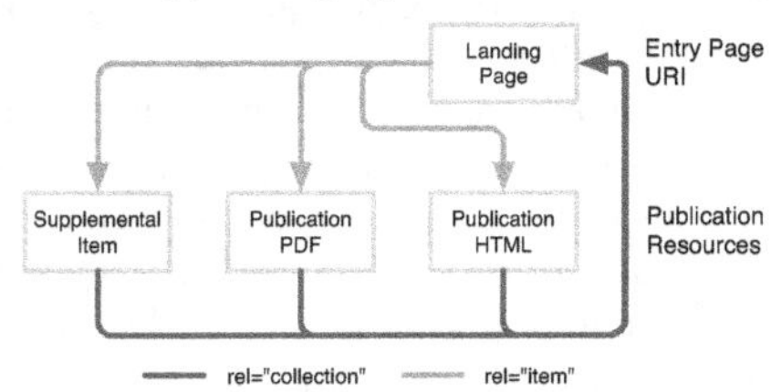

(d) Boundary Information

Figure 1: Signposting patterns

3 ACKNOWLEDGMENTS

This work is in part supported by the Andrew W. Mellon Foundation, grant number 11600663.

4 CONCLUSION

Signposting is a standard-based approach that follows the REST/HATEOS "follow-your-nose" principle to make it easier for machines to navigate across repository resources. We outline the Signposting concept on four common usage patterns and detail which link relation types should be used for the corresponding patterns. Adopting the Signposting approach helps repositories improve their web integration and increase their level of discoverability and interoperability with other systems. Ultimately, making repositories more friendly to machines will lead to applications that are beneficial for humans.

[8]https://tools.ietf.org/html/rfc6892
[9]https://tools.ietf.org/html/rfc6892
[10]https://tools.ietf.org/html/rfc6573
[11]https://tools.ietf.org/html/rfc6573
[12]https://tools.ietf.org/html/rfc4946
[13]https://tools.ietf.org/html/rfc7089

REFERENCES

[1] Herbert Van de Sompel, Martin Klein, and Shawn M. Jones. 2016. Persistent URIs Must Be Used To Be Persistent. In *Proceedings of WWW '16*. 119–120. https://doi.org/10.1145/2872518.2889352
[2] Herbert Van de Sompel, David Rosenthal, and Michael L. Nelson. 2016. Web Infrastructure to Support e-Journal Preservation (and More). (2016). http://arxiv.org/abs/1605.06154.

Robust Links in Scholarly Communication

Martin Klein
Los Alamos National Laboratory
Los Alamos, NM, USA
http://orcid.org/0000-0003-0130-2097
mklein@lanl.gov

Harihar Shankar
Los Alamos National Laboratory
Los Alamos, NM, USA
http://orcid.org/0000-0003-4949-0728
harihar@lanl.gov

Herbert Van de Sompel
Los Alamos National Laboratory
Los Alamos, NM, USA
http://orcid.org/0000-0002-0715-6126
herbertv@lanl.gov

ABSTRACT

Web resources change over time and many ultimately disappear. While this has become an inconvenient reality in day-to-day use of the web, it is problematic when these resources are referenced in scholarship where it is expected that referenced materials can reliably be revisited. We introduce Robust Links, an approach aimed at maintaining the integrity of the scholarly record in a dynamic web environment. The approach consists of archiving web resources when referencing them and decorating links to convey information that supports accessing referenced resources both on the live web and in web archives.

KEYWORDS

scholarly communication, link rot, content drift, persistence, persistent identifiers, web archiving

ACM Reference Format:
Martin Klein, Harihar Shankar, and Herbert Van de Sompel. 2018. Robust Links in Scholarly Communication. In *JCDL '18: The 18th ACM/IEEE Joint Conference on Digital Libraries, June 3–7, 2018, Fort Worth, TX, USA.* ACM, New York, NY, USA, 2 pages. https://doi.org/10.1145/3197026.3203885

1 INTRODUCTION

Our previous research [2] revealed that, increasingly, scholarly articles contain URI references to web resources such as project websites, online debates, presentations, blogs, videos, etc. Just like any other resource on the web, these referenced resources are subject to link rot and content drift, the combination of which is referred to as reference rot. As a result, over time, it becomes impossible to revisit these resources when reading a scholarly work in which they are referenced [1, 2]. These web resources that are referenced in scholarship are distinct from referenced journal articles in two ways:

(1) **Archiving:** They are not systematically archived, as is the case with journal articles through efforts such as LOCKSS[1], CLOCKSS[2], and Portico[3].
(2) **Linking:** The core assumption on which the use of persistent identifiers (PIDs) is based does not hold true for these web resources. Indeed, PID solutions rely on the custodians of PID-identified resources to keep links to their content operational. The incentive for these custodians to invest in maintaining link stability is significant because working links are crucial for accessing their collections. The creators of referenced web resources do not share that motivation. They are typically not overly concerned about the longevity of their own web resource, and definitely not about the integrity of the scholarly record. As such, a PID approach to link stability is not a realistic proposition as the custodian of the linked resource can not be expected to keep PID-based links operational.

In this poster, we present Robust Links[4], an approach aimed at increasing the integrity of the scholarly record, when references to web resources are concerned. The Robust Links concept consists of two components:

(1) **Archiving:** When referencing a web resource, pro-actively archive it using existing web archiving infrastructure.
(2) **Linking:** When linking to a web resources, decorate the link to convey information that supports to seamlessly visit the archived version of the resource when the resource itself has disappeared from the live web or when its content has drifted.

We detail both components in the following sections.

2 PRO-ACTIVE ARCHIVING

In order to make sure that referenced resources can reliably be revisited, a Memento (snapshot) of the resource should be created in one or more web archives. Ideally, this step is taken during the authoring process, while the author inspects a resource and decides to reference it. This could, for example, happen automatically when bookmarking a web resource in a reference manager[5]. But other scenarios are conceivable, such as archiving referenced resources in bulk upon submission of a manuscript to a journal/conference submission system or upon publication of the article[6]. However, our research regarding reference rot has shown that the more time has passed since authoring and referencing, the more likely it is that the referenced resource is suffering from reference rot. Therefore, the sooner a Memento of a resource is created after it was referenced, the more representative that Memento will be of what the author actually intended to reference.

[1]https://www.lockss.org/
[2]https://clockss.org/
[3]https://www.portico.org/
[4]http://robustlinks.mementoweb.org/
[5]http://hiberlink.org/zotero.html
[6]https://www.slideshare.net/martinklein0815/hiberactive

JCDL '18, June 3–7, 2018, Fort Worth, TX, USA

ACM ISBN 978-1-4503-5178-2/18/06.
https://doi.org/10.1145/3197026.3203885

Special-purpose archives such as perma.cc[7], WebCite[8], and weblock.io[9] are stepping into this problem domain and are exploring avenues to meet the challenge of operating web archives for the long term. Other established web archives such as the Internet Archive[10] and archive.is[11] also provide solutions to pro-actively create Mementos of web resources.

3 LINK DECORATION

Once a Memento is created, it would seem logical to reference the Memento rather than the live web resource. However, doing so assumes that the archive in which the Memento resides will exist forever. When the archive ceases to exist, the link to the Memento will be rotten. Also, when merely linking to the Memento, it becomes impossible to visit the live web resource. Link decoration aims at providing as many pathways as possible to visit versions of a referenced resource. The link decoration is done using HTML5 extension attributes that start with data-. The regular link, with the original URI of the reference in href is augmented with the URI of the Memento (data-versionurl) and the datetime of linking (data-versiondate). The example below shows a Robust Link to the JCDL 2018 conference website.

```
<a href="https://2018.jcdl.org/"
   data-versionurl="http://archive.is/WLgTv"
   data-versiondate="2018-02-01">JCDL 2018</a>
```

These three information elements suffice to make a reference robust:

- The original URI supports revisiting the referenced resource as it evolves over time.
- The Memento URI supports accessing the Memento that was pro-actively created.
- The combination of the original URI and the datetime of linking supports accessing a Memento of the referenced resource with an archival datetime close to the linking datetime, in any web archive, either manually or using the Memento infrastructure[12].

Use cases exist where it is appropriate to use the Memento URI as the link target (href) and the original URI as a link decoration (data-originalurl). For example, a publisher may prefer to consistently link to Mementos rather than live versions of web resources that might, over time, return the infamous "404 - Page not found". The example below shows such a Robust Link, again, for the JCDL website.

```
<a href="http://archive.is/WLgTv"
   data-originalurl="https://2018.jcdl.org/"
   data-versiondate="2018-02-01">JCDL 2018</a>
```

4 ACTIONABLE ROBUST LINKS

By utilizing legitimate HTML5 extension attributes, the above link decoration approach ensures that the information is conveyed in an interoperable machine-actionable manner. Applications (client and server) can process decorated links to offer additional functionality

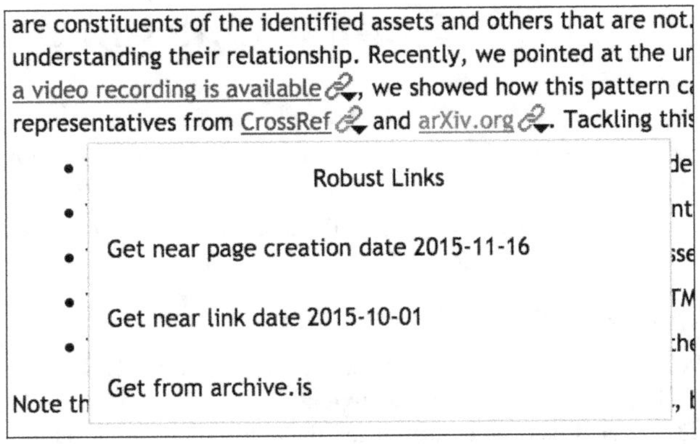

Figure 1: Actionable Robust Links

to the user. Figure 1 shows a screenshot of a section of a scholarly article [3] published in D-Lib Magazine that contains several Robust Links. These were made actionable by a few lines of JavaScript[13] embedded in the article. The JavaScript introduces the following navigation options:

- to access a Memento created in any archive closest to the date the article was published (top option),
- to access a Memento created in any archive closest to the date the link was created (middle option), and
- to access its Memento specifically created with the pro-active archiving service archive.is (bottom option).

The first option results from processing the page publication date conveyed in the paper's HTML:

```
<meta itemprop="datePublished" content="2015-11-16" />
```

while the second and third options result from the link decorations.

5 CONCLUSION

Links on the web are brittle. Archiving linked resources and decorating links are ways to make links more robust. Applications can leverage the link decorations to provide navigational paths to various versions of a referenced resource. Preferably, this includes linking to a Memento that, ideally, was created temporally close to the time of referencing the resource. The functionality that can be provided by adopting the Robust Links approach is attractive for the web in general. However, it is especially relevant for web-based scholarly communication because it helps to increase the integrity of the scholarly record.

REFERENCES

[1] Shawn M. Jones, Herbert Van de Sompel, Harihar Shankar, Martin Klein, Richard Tobin, and Claire Grover. 2016. Scholarly Context Adrift: Three out of Four URI References Lead to Changed Content. *PLoS ONE* 11, 12 (2016). https://doi.org/10.1371/journal.pone.0167475

[2] Martin Klein, Herbert Van de Sompel, Robert Sanderson, Harihar Shankar, Lyudmila Balakireva, Ke Zhou, and Richard Tobin. 2014. Scholarly Context Not Found: One in Five Articles Suffers from Reference Rot. *PLoS ONE* 9, 12 (2014). https://doi.org/10.1371/journal.pone.0115253

[3] Herbert Van de Sompel and Michael L. Nelson. 2015. Reminiscing About 15 Years of Interoperability Efforts. *D-Lib Magazine* 21, 11/12 (2015). https://doi.org/10.1045/november2015-vandesompel

[7] https://perma.cc/
[8] https://www.webcitation.org/
[9] https://weblock.io/
[10] http://web.archive.org/
[11] http://archive.is/
[12] https://tools.ietf.org/html/rfc7089
[13] https://github.com/mementoweb/robustlinks

Acquiring Web Content From In-Memory Cache

Abhinav Kumar and Zhiwu Xie
Virginia Polytechnic Institute and State University
Blacksburg, VA
{abhinavk|zhiwuxie}@vt.edu

ABSTRACT

Web content acquisition forms the foundation of value extraction of web data. Two main categories of acquisition methods are crawler-based methods and transactional web archiving or server-side acquisition methods. In this poster, we propose a new method to acquire web content from web caches. Our method provides improvement in terms of reduced penalty on HTTP transaction, flexibility to accommodate peak web server loads and minimal involvement of System Administrator to set up the system.

CCS CONCEPTS

• **Information systems** → **Digital libraries and archives**;

KEYWORDS

Web archiving, in-memory cache, Memcached

ACM Reference Format:
Abhinav Kumar and Zhiwu Xie. 2018. Acquiring Web Content From In-Memory Cache. In *JCDL '18: The 18th ACM/IEEE Joint Conference on Digital Libraries, June 3–7, 2018, Fort Worth, TX, USA.* ACM, New York, NY, USA, 2 pages. https://doi.org/10.1145/3197026.3203868

1 INTRODUCTION

Crawler-based approach has continued to dominate content acquisition for web archiving [3, 4]. This choice has significantly impacted archival quality. Lower crawling frequency results in more missing pages, but higher frequency crawling incurs higher cost and may trigger websites to restrict or even block crawlers. Although incremental crawling methods exist to adapt crawling frequency to anticipated changes [2], it is impossible both in theory and in practice to algorithmically predict every occurrence of website change. Incomplete capturing is therefore inevitable. Indeed, far from being comprehensive, existing web archives have been found to be sparsely populated [5, 7].

For web resources of high archival value, applying transactional web archiving or server-side acquisition methods may help in preserving the full web history[6]. However, since transactional archiving intercepts live HTTP request-and-response transactions, it requires the installation of server modules not prepackaged in the official software releases. System administrators from mission-critical web operations are generally suspicious of these modules. Further, archiving is invoked on each HTTP transaction, incurring a penalty on server performance [1]. On the other hand, server-side acquisition often requires the website operator to recreate historic web pages in bulk from database and content management systems, constantly needing access to backup copies of the database and file system. Very few site owners have the need or incentive to do so.

To address these problems, we proposed to acquire web content from web caches. Since the content acquisition does not sit on the critical path of the HTTP transaction, it does not directly impact server performance. We acquire all new web content from the cache since the last acquisition. The archiving is therefore of larger granularity and less chatty, bypassing the protocol bottleneck [6].

We have previously shown that this new approach can be implemented on an Apache HTTP server if the disk cache is enabled for caching HTTP responses [8]. However disk caching is less prevalent than in-memory cache in large web deployments, since caching to disk may reduce server performance. This paper demonstrates an out-of-the-box method to archive large web applications when the work load is automatically scaled and balanced among multiple servers, and Memcached is used as the page cache. We achieve this by running a low priority process that periodically polls the page cache and then persists new or updated content to a WARC file in the local file system. The frequency of the process can be adjusted to ensure archiving coverage or to improve server performance. This method does not need to alter the existing web application or install additional server modules. Our approach requires the System Administrator of the website to start the Python script and adjust the frequency of archiving. It is a small script which can be easily examined by the user.

2 IMPLEMENTATION

We demonstrate the content acquisition method using a Greek version of Wikipedia deployed on Amazon Web Service (AWS).

2.1 System Architecture

Figure 1 depicts components involved in our implementation: (1) Client, which generates HTTP requests. It interacts with the Load Balancer using HTTP GET and HTTP PUT calls; (2) Load Balancer, which equally distributes the incoming requests among all the web servers in the Autoscaling Group; (3) Web Servers in an Autoscaling Group. An Autoscaling Group helps to scale up or down depending upon the workload; (4) Database Server; (5) Object Cache server, which stores frequently used application objects and database queries; (6) HTTP Page Cache server, which caches all the HTTP GET responses. If the Web Server receives an HTTP PUT request for an existing key in the cache, this cache entry is invalidated. In our experiments, the web page URL is the key. (7) Archiving process, in the Page Cache Server.

JCDL '18, June 3–7, 2018, Fort Worth, TX, USA

ACM ISBN 978-1-4503-5178-2/18/06.
https://doi.org/10.1145/3197026.3203868

In this implementation, a typical HTTP transaction occurs in the following sequence: Client requests a web page by invoking its URL. Load Balancer receives this request and forwards it to a Web Server in the Autoscaling Group. The Web Server then checks if this URL is present in the HTTP Page Cache. If yes, it fetches the content and sends it to the Load Balancer. If the URL is not found in the HTTP Page Cache, the Web Server generates the response by fetching data from the Database and the Object Cache, caches it, and sends it to the Load Balancer. Then the Load Balancer sends the response to the client. HTTP Page Cache uses the LRU (Least Recently Used) algorithm for eviction whenever the cache is full and a new page needs to be added.

The archiving process is separated from the HTTP transaction. This is a simple Python script that runs periodically in the Memcached instance. It reads the newly added content since its last run then appends it to a WARC file on the local file system. Between two runs of the script, our system will only collect the most recently revised version of any URL. Intermediate revisions will be lost. However, ephemeral revisions that only existed for an extremely short period of time may be considered to be of low archival value since very few people would have seen them. Nevertheless, based on how frequent the web content is updated, website owners may adjust the archival interval to smaller values to avoid such archival history loss.

2.2 Hardware and Software

We use AWS EC2 (Elastic Compute Cloud) instances for computing, AWS RDS (Relational Database Services) for Database, and AWS Application Load Balancer for load balancing. The AWS EC2 instance type used for each component is shown in Figure 1. All AWS instances install Ubuntu Server 16.04 LTS (HVM), and use EBS General Purpose (SSD) Volume Type as their base image. We use Nginx Openresty version 1.11.2.5 as the Web Server. It interacts with a FastCGI server in PHP-FPM version 7.0 and a Page Cache Server using Memcached version 1.4.25. Mediawiki version 1.26 is used as the application server. The Greek Wikipedia database dump is loaded in an AWS RDS instance running MySQL 5.5.53 Engine.

2.3 Data, Workload, and Execution

We use the October 2016 Greek Wikipedia database dump with the full revision history. Server workload is generated from a Java-based REST client adapted from Yahoo Cloud Service Benchmark(YCSB). We use 10,704 of the most popular URLs based on their page view statistics. Using the monthly statistics, we verify that the URL distribution is approximately Zipfian, then generate a trace with the Zipf's constant set at 0.9898 and same GET/PUT ratio.

We run the experiment with HTTP Page Cache size of 500 MB. We then increase the workload from 10 requests per second to 100 requests per second.

We run the archiving process once every minute at low priority by assigning a 'nice' value of 19. This process can be stopped and restarted anytime.

3 RESULTS AND SUMMARY

In this experiment, when the workload increases, the Web Server CPU is the only system resource that becomes strained over time.

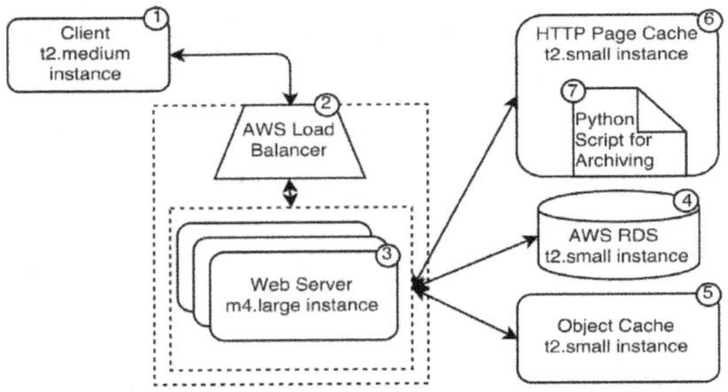

Figure 1: System components and setup

Then the autoscaling increases the number of Web Servers and cuts down the CPU load. We stop the experiment after the system repeatedly sustains 100 requests per second for 20 minutes without error with 2 Web Servers. There is no reason to believe the system cannot sustain higher loads for longer periods when the autoscaling further increases the number of Web Servers.

According to Wikipedia pageview statistics, on the busiest day in August 2016, Greek Wikipedia received a little more than 900,000 hits. This translates to about 10.5 requests per second, about one order of magnitude lower than the load sustained in this experiment. It appears to us that the proposed content acquisition method shows promise for practical use.

ACKNOWLEDGMENTS

This work is partially supported by the Institute of Museum and Library Services under Grant No.: LG-71-16-0037-16 (https://www.imls.gov/grants/awarded/lg-71-16-0037-16).

REFERENCES

[1] Justin F. Brunelle, Michael L. Nelson, Lyudmila Balakireva, Robert Sanderson, and Herbert Van de Sompel. 2013. Evaluating the SiteStory Transactional Web Archive with the ApacheBench Tool. In *Research and Advanced Technology for Digital Libraries (Lecture Notes in Computer Science)*. Springer, Berlin, Heidelberg, 204–215. https://doi.org/10.1007/978-3-642-40501-3_20

[2] Junghoo Cho and Hector Garcia-Molina. 2000. The Evolution of the Web and Implications for an Incremental Crawler. In *Proceedings of the 26th International Conference on Very Large Data Bases (VLDB '00)*. Morgan Kaufmann Publishers Inc., San Francisco, CA, USA, 200–209. http://dl.acm.org/citation.cfm?id=645926.671679

[3] Miguel Costa, Daniel Gomes, and Mário J. Silva. 2017. The evolution of web archiving. *International Journal on Digital Libraries* 18, 3 (Sept. 2017), 191–205. https://doi.org/10.1007/s00799-016-0171-9

[4] Daniel Gomes, João Miranda, and Miguel Costa. 2011. A Survey on Web Archiving Initiatives. In *Research and Advanced Technology for Digital Libraries (Lecture Notes in Computer Science)*. Springer, Berlin, Heidelberg, 408–420. https://doi.org/10.1007/978-3-642-24469-8_41

[5] Martin Klein, Herbert Van de Sompel, Robert Sanderson, Harihar Shankar, Lyudmila Balakireva, Ke Zhou, and Richard Tobin. 2014. Scholarly Context Not Found: One in Five Articles Suffers from Reference Rot. *PLOS ONE* 9, 12 (Dec. 2014), e115253. https://doi.org/10.1371/journal.pone.0115253

[6] Julien Masanès. 2006. Web Archiving: Issues and Methods. In *Web Archiving*. Springer, Berlin, Heidelberg, 1–53. https://link-springer-com.ezproxy.lib.vt.edu/chapter/10.1007/978-3-540-46332-0_1 DOI: 10.1007/978-3-540-46332-0_1.

[7] Hany M. SalahEldeen and Michael L. Nelson. 2012. Losing My Revolution: How Many Resources Shared on Social Media Have Been Lost?. In *Theory and Practice of Digital Libraries (Lecture Notes in Computer Science)*. Springer, Berlin, Heidelberg, 125–137. https://doi.org/10.1007/978-3-642-33290-6_14

[8] Zhiwu Xie, Krati Nayyar, and Edward A. Fox. 2017. Nearline Web Archiving. *Bulletin of IEEE Technical Committee on Digital Libraries* 13, 1 (April 2017). http://www.ieee-tcdl.org/Bulletin/v13n1/papers/xie.pdf

Russian Troll Hunting in a Brexit Twitter Archive

Clare Llewellyn
University Of Edinburgh
Edinburgh
C.A.Llewellyn@sms.ed.ac.uk

Laura Cram
University Of Edinburgh
Edinburgh
Laura.Cram@ed.ac.uk

Adrian Favero
University Of Edinburgh
Edinburgh
A.Favero@ed.ac.uk

Robin L Hill
University Of Edinburgh
Edinburgh
r.l.hill@ed.ac.uk

CCS CONCEPTS

• **Human-centered computing → Social networking sites;**

KEYWORDS

Social Networks, Twitter, Propaganda, Bots and Trolls

ACM Reference Format:
Clare Llewellyn, Laura Cram, Adrian Favero, and Robin L Hill. 2018. Russian Troll Hunting in a Brexit Twitter Archive. In *JCDL '18: The 18th ACM/IEEE Joint Conference on Digital Libraries, June 3–7, 2018, Fort Worth, TX, USA.* ACM, New York, NY, USA, 2 pages. https://doi.org/10.1145/3197026.3203876

1 INTRODUCTION

Twitter has identified 2,752 accounts that it believes are linked to the Internet Research Agency (IRA), a Russian company that creates online propaganda. These accounts are known to have tweeted about the US 2016 Elections and the list was submitted as evidence by Twitter to the United States Senate Judiciary Subcommittee on Crime and Terrorism. There is no equivalent officially published list of accounts from the IRA known to be active in the UK-EU Referendum debate (Brexit), but we found that the troll accounts active on the 2016 US Election also produced content related to Brexit. We found 3,485 tweets from 419 of the accounts listed as IRA accounts which specifically discussed Brexit and related topics such as the EU and migration.

We have been collating an archive of tweets related to Brexit since August 2015 and currently have over 70 million tweets. The Brexit referendum took place on the 23rd June 2016 and the UK voted to leave the European Union. We gathered the data using the Twitter API and a selection of hashtags chosen by a panel of academic experts. Currently we have in excess of fifty different hashtags and we add to the set periodically to accurately represent the evolving conversation.

JCDL '18, June 3–7, 2018, Fort Worth, TX, USA

ACM ISBN 978-1-4503-5178-2/18/06.
https://doi.org/10.1145/3197026.3203876

Twitter has closed the accounts that were documented in the Senate list meaning that these tweets are no longer available through the webpage or API. Due to Twitter's terms of service we are unable to share specific tweet text or user profile information but our findings, utilising text and metadata from derived and aggregated data, allows us to provide important insights into the behaviour of these trolls.

2 TROLLS

Social media users who attempt to manipulate opinion and spread rumors and false information are referred to as trolls [5]. A bot is an automatic content creator or republisher. Bots are common on social media and often used for legitimate purposes such as news aggregation but they are also used to influence social media conversations, repeating information on a large scale to create the impression of increased popularity [6]. When many bots tweet on a particular subject the quantity of information repetition can lead to a cascade point where humans are increasingly likely to believe and reproduce that information. Twitter has reported that the accounts described above published content created by both bots and humans. The users are 'cyborgs', accounts which are at least partially operated by humans [2]. In addition to the automatic creation of content, human trolls are instructed to produce content that spreads particular messages. The trolls are involved in astroturfing, the creation of political content accounts created with false identities (sock-puppets), in fake grassroots movements [3]. This premeditated content is produced with the aim of making real users sympathetic towards specific opinions.

3 TWEET CONTENT

When investigating troll activity relating to the South Korean 2012 election Keller et al [3], found that the trolls acted in similar and repetitive ways because the individual trolls are following central instructions. We investigated the central instructions that motivated the Brexit content production. We clustered the tweets by topic to identify commonalities at a high level. We used LDA topic modelling [1] using the Mallet toolkit [4] to cluster the tweet text content. LDA topic modelling gives a list of key words to represent each topic.

In Table 1 we can see a list of the top ten terms (where available) and a human assigned topic name. Notably, the topic words are both in english and german. We can see topics such as remaining or leaving the EU, the EU in general and the use of names or usernames of EU representatives such as Fredrica Mog. Brexit is a very common topic word but it is used in a variety of ways to push agendas relating to the US Trump election campaign and the German Chancellor Merkel, refugees and Turkey. While these topics are clearly Brexit-related they do not tell us what the trolls are saying directly about Brexit. We therefore pursued a deeper level of analysis by annotating each tweet as to whether it was directly about Brexit or about a related topic such as migration or the EU itself. To ensure reliability, we double annotated a sample of 100 randomly selected tweets, which produced an inter-annotator agreement of 0.80. We felt confident enough in the score to single annotate the remaining tweets. This gave us 1,357 tweets from 267 accounts. We then repeated the topic modelling process with the remaining tweets. In Table 2 we can see that there are still many topic words in german. It becomes apparent that the tweets were directly about Brexit but Brexit is used to push a German based agenda rather than attempting to influence British voters. We can allocate a specific topic to each tweet by using the most dominant topic as represented by the words it contains.

4 FURTHER ANALYSIS

As these accounts are cyborgs we looked at the proportion of data that was retweeted as we believed this would likely correlate with automated behaviour. A large proportion of the data is retweets (57.59%) but a substantial proportion is original content. When we looked at the hashtag topic more closely we found this was created from tweets that contained a small selection of hashtags and no other terms. These were retweets of a small number of original tweets that were created by other trolls. These tweets were all produced on the 23rd June 2016. We believe this is a likely signal of automated bot behaviour. The longitudinal nature of our set meant that we could systematically look for changes in behaviour over time. We found that the accounts were more active at certain event points; for example 11% of all of the tweets were published on the day of the referendum itself and the majority of these (97%) were retweets. Retweeting is an action that can be easily performed by bots and retweeting patterns can be indicative of bot behaviour. In addition to the specific tweet content each tweet also carries metadata which contains the user profile information. The troll accounts were created with sock-puppet personas. The tweet metadata allows us to analyse this information. These accounts are not created to look like grassroots brexit leavers or remainers but they look like conservative Americans or Germans. Our overall summary of this data is that these trolls used Brexit to promote an agenda in the US and Germany. There may be other accounts with Brexit grassroot sock-puppets but these were USA and German sock-puppet IRA controlled accounts which were occasionally used to tweet about Brexit, particularly on the day of the referendum.

Table 1: Top terms from topic modelling of tweets from IRA accounts (human defined topic name)

Topic Keywords	Name
federicamog eu_eeas meeting sabellosi press majaeuspox foreign defence hrvp syria	EU People
merkel flchtlinge erdogan deutschland trkei brexit isis schon cdu man	Merkel (Turkey)
britaininout euref brexitornot goodbyeuk brexitinout remainineu brexit	Hashtags
brexit europe trump maga people tcot usa refugee ccot pjnet	Trump
derspiegel premierministerin brexit-stress keinen merkelmussbleiben yemen hrw saudi hussainbukhaiti uae	Der Spiegel
brexit euco eucounciltvnews ukineu european doorstep council junckereu article eucopresident	EU
refugeeswelcome europe refugees refugee germany bestusatoday migrants refugeecrisis muslim breaking	Refugees
brexit merkel merkelmussbleiben deutschland girlstalkselfies frankfurt neue strker strt hnden	Merkel (Germany)
brexit refugeeswelcome remain europe refugee vote syrianrefugees blacklivesmatter leave video	Remain
brexit britain vote british leave business rtuknews article voted people	Leave

Table 2: Top terms of topic modelling of tweets annotated as about Brexit from IRA accounts (human defined name)

Topic Keywords	Name
brexit grobritannien britain farage live video ukip merkel nigel ende	Farage
brexit haben gibt brexit-stress keinen premierministerin merkelmussbleiben remain sehr	Remain
brexit bank america europa bac homebase dublin moving	Banks
brexit business britain merkel weigh beings lies economy affect rewind	Economy
brexit voted vote business article government brits whats risk trump	Voting
euco brexit ukineu eucounciltvnews european council doorstep eucopresident article junckereu	EU
goodbyeuk britaininout remainineu euref brexitornot brexit	Results
brexit merkel merkelmussbleiben frankfurt strker strt hnden sicheren frau beseitigen	Merkel
brexitornot britaininout euref brexitinout brexit giselleevns nea dskcqsp	Hashtags
brexit rtuknews people vote british leave voteleave article deal trump	Leave

REFERENCES

[1] David M Blei, Andrew Y Ng, and Michael I Jordan. 2003. Latent dirichlet allocation. *Journal of machine Learning research* 3, Jan (2003), 993–1022.

[2] Zi Chu, Steven Gianvecchio, Haining Wang, and Sushil Jajodia. 2012. Detecting automation of twitter accounts: Are you a human, bot, or cyborg? *IEEE Transactions on Dependable and Secure Computing* 9, 6 (2012), 811–824.

[3] Franziska B Keller, David Schoch, Sebastian Stier, and JungHwan Yang. 2017. How to Manipulate Social Media: Analyzing Political Astroturfing Using Ground Truth Data from South Korea.. In *ICWSM*. 564–567.

[4] Andrew Kachites McCallum. 2002. MALLET: A Machine Learning for Language Toolkit. (2002). http://mallet.cs.umass.edu.

[5] Todor Mihaylov, Georgi Georgiev, and Preslav Nakov. 2015. Finding Opinion Manipulation Trolls in News Community Forums.. In *CoNLL*. 310–314.

[6] VS Subrahmanian, Amos Azaria, Skylar Durst, Vadim Kagan, Aram Galstyan, Kristina Lerman, Linhong Zhu, Emilio Ferrara, Alessandro Flammini, and Filippo Menczer. 2016. The DARPA Twitter bot challenge. *Computer* 49, 6 (2016), 38–46.

Identification and Analysis of Converging Technology Based on Patent Co-Classification Relationship

Lucheng Lv, Tao Han, Yajuan Zhao, Xuezhao Wang, Ping Zhao
National Science Library, Chinese Academy of Sciences, Beijing, 100190, P. R. China
lvlc@mail.las.ac.cn; hant@mail.las.ac.cn; zhaoyj@mail.las.ac.cn; wangxz@mail.las.ac.cn; zhaop@mail.las.ac.cn

ABSTRACT

Patent documents are an ample source for technical knowledge, and increased dramatically in recent years. This paper aims at identifying and analyzing converging technology based on patent analysis. The identification method of Converging technology is through cluster analysis based on USPC co-occurrence matrix calculated by the cross USPC class patents of five parties during the 2005-2015 years. Finally, 161 converging technologies are identified. Converging technology is mainly distributed in the new generation of information technology, new material industry. High end equipment manufacturing industry is the most active industry in technological convergence. [1]

KEYWORDS

Patent data mining, Converging Technology, Co-Classification Analysis, Technical activity

ACM Reference Format:

Lucheng Lv, Tao Han, Yajuan Zhao, Xuezhao Wang, and Ping Zhao. 2018. Identification and Analysis of Converging Technology Based on Patent Co-Classification Relationship. In JCDL '18: The 18th ACM/IEEE Joint Conference on Digital Libraries, June 3–7, 2018, Fort Worth, TX, USA. ACM, New York, NY, USA, 2 pages. https://doi.org/10.1145/3197026.3203903

1 INTRODUCTION

Converging technology is the product of technological convergence. The identification and analysis of converging technology has positive effects on recognizing the trend of technological convergence and guiding the research direction and industrial distribution. Accordingly, there are many research papers on technological convergence. Since the concept of technological convergence was first proposed in Rosenberg's research on the evolution of the US Machine Tool Industry[1], many authors have tried to develop similar conceptions of convergence and put forward various analysis method.

Patent documents are an ample source for technical knowledge, and increase dramatically in recent years. In particular, patents have been employed for the technology driven convergence. A representative example is the paper of Geum et al.[2] which takes a quantitative approach by citation analysis and co-classification analysis to analyze the technological convergence of information technology (IT) and biotechnology(BT).

With the rapid development of the Internet, AI and robotics in recent years, the trend of technological convergence is more and more obvious. Under such an environment, what is the new converging technology? Which industries are they distributed in?

This paper aims at identifying and analyzing converging technology based on patent analysis. Research method is co-classification analysis because citation analysis has the problem of time lag. A patent classification was arranged by the examiners of a patent office according to the technical features of inventions. Since the same document may be classified in several classes, the co-classification information can be used to identify the relationships between technologies. The relevant method was later applied in a science and technology context [3]. Based on this, we assume that technologies with a high degree of co-classification are converging technologies.

2 DATASET AND METHODS

Figure 1 shows the specific process, like the following:

s1. Download 79986 quintuple patent families during the 2005-2015 years from Incopat database. Quintuple patent family means patent in family granted in China and the US, and applied in Europe, Japan and South Korea.

s2. Select the cross USPC class patents, and the number is 36880.

s3. Calculate the USPC co-occurrence matrix based on the co-occurrence relationship of USPC, and the dimension is 13512.

s4. Cluster based on the USPC co-occurrence matrix by the hierarchical clustering, and obtained 161 clusters, that is, 161 converging technologies.

s5. Interpret the converging technology and establish the mapping relationship between converging technology and strategic emerging industries and sub-industries through domain experts. The list of strategic emerging industries was released by the National Development and Reform Commission, including seven industries and related sub-industries.

s6. Draw converging technical structure map based on industrial relation of converging technology.

s7. Analyze the technical activity(TA) of converging technologies. Equation 1 is the calculation of TA. Y_n is the latest patent application year in converging technology. Y_m is the most patent application year in converging technology.

$$\mathbf{TA} = {}^{(2015 - Y_n)}/_{(2015 - Y_m)} \quad (1)$$

Figure 1: Process of the study

ACM ISBN 978-1-4503-5178-2/18/06.
https://doi.org/10.1145/3197026.3203903

3 RESULTS

Figure 2 shows the distribution of industries of converging technologies. Here are seven strategic emerging industries and one "other traditional industries" that refers to converging technologies that don't belong to the strategic emerging industries.

Figure 3 shows converging technical structure map of 161 converging technologies. Each circle represents a converging technology. The size of a circle represents the number of the quintuple patent families in the converging technologies. The color of the circle represents the industrial classification of the converging technology. The line between circles indicates that two converging technologies belong to a certain emerging sub-industry. The thickness of the lines is proportional to the number of same emerging sub-industries between two converging technology. The lines between circle of different colors represent that converging technology is cross-industry.

Figure 4 shows distribution of the average TA of industries. The smaller TA value, the more active.

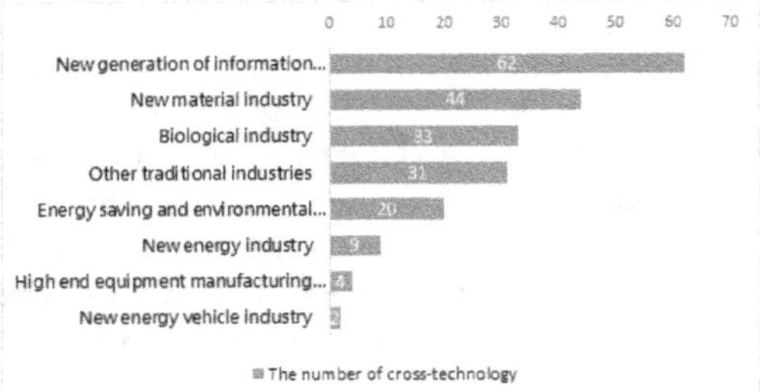

Figure 2: Distribution of industries of converging technologies

Table 1 lists 4 cross-industry and TA$\geqslant$4 cross-industry converging technologies. The column named as "Description of Technology" shows technology interpretation. The column named as "Associated Industries" shows several industries that converging technology can be used.

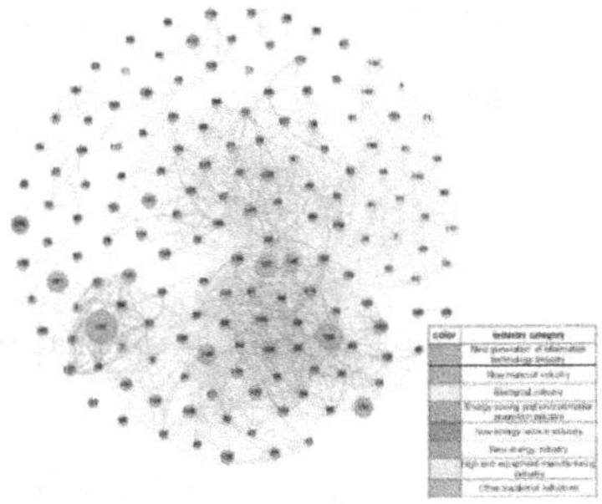

Figure 3: Converging technical structure map

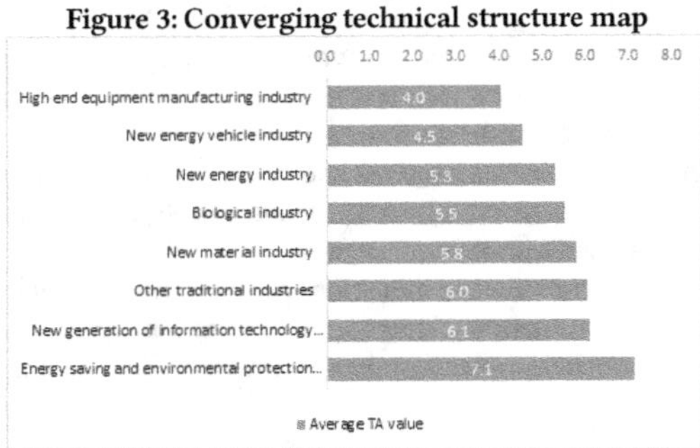

Figure 4: Distribution of the average TA value of industries

4 CONCLUSIONS

In this paper, 161 converging technologies are identified. Most of the converging technologies are converging in the same industry. The new generation of information technology, new material industry and biological industry are the top 3 industries of converging technologies. High end equipment manufacturing industry is the most active industry

Converging Tech No	Description of Technology	Associated Industries
No.65	Related manufacturing methods and process engineering of liquid crystal, light emitting diode and other display devices, semiconductor light emitting devices and so on.	Energy saving and environmental protection industry, New generation of information technology industry
No.97	The preparation of the whole carbon family and its composite materials and its application in the fields of photoelectric and heat.	New material industry, New energy industry, Energy saving and environmental protection industry
No.115	Manufacturing methods and technology of solar cell; Related manufacturing methods and technology of other photoelectric conversion elements such as solid state image sensor.	New generation of information technology industry, New energy industry
No.154	Robotics, such as control systems, visual and voice systems and so on; Power and control technology of electric vehicle/hybrid vehicle;	High end equipment manufacturing industry, New energy vehicle industry

Table 1: Cross-industry and TA$\geqslant$4 converging technologies (For lack of space, only show part of the result)

REFERENCES

[1] Rosenberg N. Technological Change in the Machine Tool Industry, 1840-1910[J]. Journal of Economic History, 1963, 23(4):414-443.

[2] Geum Y, Kim C, Lee S, et al. Technological Convergence of IT and BT: Evidence from Patent Analysis[J]. ETRI Journal, 2012, 34(3):439-449

[3] Tijssen R J W. A quantitative assessment of interdisciplinary structures in science and technology: Co-classification analysis of energy research [J]. Research Policy, 1992, 21(1):27-44

Recommending Co-authorship via Network Embeddings and Feature Engineering

The case of National Research University Higher School of Economics

Ilya Makarov, Olga Gerasimova, Pavel Sulimov, and Leonid E. Zhukov
iamakarov@hse.ru,olga.g3993@gmail.com,psulimov@hse.ru,leonid.e.zhukov@gmail.com
National Research University Higher School of Economics
Moscow, Russia

ABSTRACT

Co-authorship networks contain hidden structural patterns of research collaboration. While some people may argue that the process of writing joint papers depends on mutual friendship, research interests, and university policy, we show that, given a temporal co-authorship network, one could predict the quality and quantity of future research publications. We are working on the comparison of existing graph embedding and feature engineering methods, presenting combined approach for constructing co-author recommender system formulated as link prediction problem. We also present a new link embedding operator improving the quality of link prediction base don embedding feature space. We evaluate our research on a single university publication dataset, providing meaningful interpretation of the obtained results.

CCS CONCEPTS

• **Information systems** → **Collaborative search**; *Recommender systems*; • **Human-centered computing** → *Social networks*;

KEYWORDS

Co-authorship Networks; Recommender Systems; Machine Learning; Graph Embeddings; Link Prediction

ACM Reference Format:

Ilya Makarov, Olga Gerasimova, Pavel Sulimov, and Leonid E. Zhukov. 2018. Recommending Co-authorship via Network Embeddings and Feature Engineering: The case of National Research University Higher School of Economics. In *JCDL '18: The 18th ACM/IEEE Joint Conference on Digital Libraries, June 3–7, 2018, Fort Worth, TX, USA.* ACM, New York, NY, USA, 2 pages. https://doi.org/10.1145/3197026.3203911

1 INTRODUCTION

Modern research community has been overwhelmed by an increasing number of international conferences and journal articles, full of relevant research areas and papers. To be familiar with the new topics and small improvements in many related fields of study, it is important to keep up with current trends in respected research fields, while reading hundreds of papers may be too time-consuming. The simplest way to select the most valuable articles is to order article list, obtained from some bibliography database by keywords query, taking into account citation index or other centrality metrics for measuring influence of the author and the paper on the respected research area [7]. However, such an approach does not include the information on the author professional skills, research community, and ability to publish research results in high-impact journals.

We formulate the problem of recommending a co-author as a link prediction problem [6], in which the model should predict whether a pair of nodes in a network would have a connection and the parameters of such an edge in a given time period. A survey on link prediction applications was published in [12].

Recently, the major advancement of vectorized natural language text representations was applied to network science, suggesting new approaches in representing the learning of graph embeddings [11]. New network embedding models [1, 4, 11, 13] obtain state-of-art performance on link prediction tasks.

In this paper, we study a co-authorship recommender system based on co-authorship network where one or more of the coauthors belong to the National Research University Higher School of Economics (HSE). We use machine learning techniques to predict new edges in temporal structure of co-authorship network while extracting author and network features, providing different word [5, 15] and graph [4, 16] embeddings for network actors, their research papers and attributes.

We compare our approach with state-of-the-art algorithms for link prediction problem, and show that combined feature engineering and network emebedding outperform each approach separately.

Such obtained system could be applied for expert search [10], ranked according to research influence of co-authorship network actors, building recommender system for searching a collaborator [2, 14] or relevant research publications and future co-authors [8, 9].

2 MODEL DESCRIPTION

We extract the following information from Scopus [3]: the author list and affiliations, year, paper metadata, and keywords, used as additional node features. The whole dataset contains 8 000 papers co-authored by HSE researchers and can be easily downloaded from Scopus in *.csv format.

We filter our dataset removing 50% of existing edges preserving network connectivity. Then the existing edges were considered as positive examples, while having the same size of non-existent edges as proposed in negative sampling.

We build node embedding using standard node2vec model representing links by symmetric component-wise operator applied to the nodes embeddings (see Table 2).

JCDL '18, June 3–7, 2018, Fort Worth, TX, USA

ACM ISBN 978-1-4503-5178-2/18/06.
https://doi.org/10.1145/3197026.3203911

Table 1: Comparing ML models based on Neighbor Weighted-L2 link embedding for link prediction problem

	Precision	Accuracy	F1-score (macro)	F1-score (micro)	Logloss	ROC-AUC
Logistic Regression	0.482	0.491	0.522	0.563	1.452	0.613
Random Forest	0.812	**0.844**	**0.745**	**0.811**	**0.176**	**0.876**
Gradient Boosting	**0.852**	0.821	0.733	0.806	0.337	0.815
SVM	0.834	0.837	0.701	0.725	0.302	0.818

Table 2: Edge embeddings $g(u, v)$ computed as component-wise operator on nodes embeddings $f(u), f(v)$

Symmetry Operator	Definition
Average	$\frac{f_i(u)+f_i(v)}{2}$
Hadamard	$f_i(u) \cdot f_i(v)$
Weighted-L_1	$\lvert f_i(u) - f_i(v) \rvert$
Weighted-L_2	$(f_i(u) - f_i(v))^2$
Neighbor Weighted-L_1	$\left\lvert \frac{\sum_{w \in N(u) \cup \{u\}} f_i(w)}{\lvert N(u) \rvert + 1} - \frac{\sum_{t \in N(v) \cup \{v\}} f_i(t)}{\lvert N(v) \rvert + 1} \right\rvert$
Neighbor Weighted-L_2	$\left(\frac{\sum_{w \in N(u) \cup \{u\}} f_i(w)}{\lvert N(u) \rvert + 1} - \frac{\sum_{t \in N(v) \cup \{v\}} f_i(t)}{\lvert N(v) \rvert + 1} \right)^2$

Table 3: Comparing link embeddings for link prediction problem on Scopus dataset

	F1-score (macro)	Logloss	ROC-AUC
Average	0.563	1.321	0.553
Hadamard	0.611	0.784	0.626
Weighted-L_1	0.675	0.693	0.668
Weighted-L_2	0.705	0.597	0.774
Neighbor Weighted-L_1	0.732	0.337	0.832
Neighbor Weighted-L_2	**0.745**	**0.176**	**0.876**

3 DISCUSSION

Our new "Neighbor Weighted-L_2" operator is suggested based on the node neighborhood embedding with average pooling and showed better quality on link prediction task (see Table 3) compared to the operators presented in [4]. In Table 1 we see that Random Forest get the best AUC being competitive with XGBoost and SVM models due to sparse data in Scopus dataset after removing 50% link information and lack of ensemble methods for choosing proper negative sampling for sparse dataset.

The code for computing all the models with respect to classification and regression tasks, choosing proper edge embedding operator and tuning hyper-parameters of node embeddings is available at the paper Github http://github.com/makarovia/jcdl2018/.

We have obtained that combined approach of embedding network topology and author keywords leads to statistically significant improvement in the AUC for link prediction problem compared to structural baseline such as common neighbors measure or manually engineered graph features.

ACKNOWLEDGMENTS

This work has been funded by the Russian Academic Excellence Project '5-100'.

REFERENCES

[1] Shiyu Chang, Wei Han, Jiliang Tang, Guo-Jun Qi, Charu C. Aggarwal, and Thomas S. Huang. 2015. Heterogeneous Network Embedding via Deep Architectures. In *Proceedings of the 21th ACM SIGKDD International Conference on Knowledge Discovery and Data Mining (KDD '15)*. ACM, New York, NY, USA, 119–128. https://doi.org/10.1145/2783258.2783296

[2] Hung-Hsuan Chen, Liang Gou, Xiaolong Zhang, and Clyde Lee Giles. 2011. Collabseer: a search engine for collaboration discovery. In *Proceedings of the 11th annual international ACM/IEEE joint conference on Digital libraries*. ACM DL, New York, 231–240.

[3] Elsevier. 2018. Scopus. http://www.scopus.com/. (2018). [Online; accessed 9-January-2018].

[4] Aditya Grover and Jure Leskovec. 2016. Node2Vec: Scalable Feature Learning for Networks. In *Proceedings of the 22Nd ACM SIGKDD International Conference on Knowledge Discovery and Data Mining (KDD '16)*. ACM, New York, NY, USA, 855–864. https://doi.org/10.1145/2939672.2939754

[5] Quoc Le and Tomas Mikolov. 2014. Distributed representations of sentences and documents. In *Proceedings of the 31st International Conference on Machine Learning (ICML-14)*. ACM DL, New York, 1188–1196.

[6] Xin Li and Hsinchun Chen. 2009. Recommendation As Link Prediction: A Graph Kernel-based Machine Learning Approach. In *Proceedings of the 9th ACM/IEEE-CS Joint Conference on Digital Libraries (JCDL '09)*. ACM, New York, NY, USA, 213–216. https://doi.org/10.1145/1555400.1555433

[7] Yicong Liang, Qing Li, and Tieyun Qian. 2011. Finding relevant papers based on citation relations. In *IC on WAIM*. Springer, Springer, Berlin, 403–414.

[8] Bulanov O. Zhukov L.E. Makarov, I. 2017. Co-author Recommender System. In *Springer Proceedings in Mathematics and Statistic*. Springer, Berlin, 1–6. https://doi.org/10.1007/978-3-319-56829-4_18

[9] Ilya Makarov, Oleg Bulanov, Olga Gerasimova, Natalia Meshcheryakova, Ilia Karpov, and Leonid E. Zhukov. 2018. Scientific Matchmaker: Collaborator Recommender System. In *Analysis of Images, Social Networks and Texts*. Springer International Publishing, Cham, 404–410.

[10] David Mimno and Andrew McCallum. 2007. Expertise modeling for matching papers with reviewers. In *Proceedings of the 13th ACM SIGKDD IC*. ACM, NY, 500–509.

[11] Bryan Perozzi, Rami Al-Rfou, and Steven Skiena. 2014. DeepWalk: Online Learning of Social Representations. In *Proceedings of the 20th ACM SIGKDD International Conference on Knowledge Discovery and Data Mining (KDD '14)*. ACM, New York, NY, USA, 701–710. https://doi.org/10.1145/2623330.2623732

[12] Virinchi Srinivas and Pabitra Mitra. 2016. *Applications of Link Prediction*. Springer International Publishing, Cham, 57–61. https://doi.org/10.1007/978-3-319-28922-9_5

[13] Jian Tang, Meng Qu, Mingzhe Wang, Ming Zhang, Jun Yan, and Qiaozhu Mei. 2015. LINE: Large-scale Information Network Embedding. In *Proceedings of the 24th International Conference on World Wide Web (WWW '15)*. International World Wide Web Conferences Steering Committee, Republic and Canton of Geneva, Switzerland, 1067–1077. https://doi.org/10.1145/2736277.2741093

[14] Jie Tang, Sen Wu, Jimeng Sun, and Hang Su. 2012. Cross-domain collaboration recommendation. In *Proceedings of the 18th ACM SIGKDD international conference on Knowledge discovery and data mining*. ACM, New York, 1285–1293.

[15] Chong Wang and David M Blei. 2011. Collaborative topic modeling for recommending scientific articles. In *Proceedings of the 17th ACM SIGKDD international conference on Knowledge discovery and data mining*. ACM, ACM, NY, 448–456.

[16] Hao Wu and Kristina Lerman. 2017. Network Vector: Distributed Representations of Networks with Global Context. *CoRR* abs/1709.02448 (2017), 1–10. arXiv:1709.02448 http://arxiv.org/abs/1709.02448

On the Contribution of Word-Level Semantics to Practical Author Name Disambiguation

Mark-Christoph Müller
Heidelberg Institute for Theoretical Studies gGmbH
Heidelberg, Germany
mark-christoph.mueller@h-its.org

ABSTRACT

We demonstrate the utility of word embedding-based semantic similarity methods for Author Name Disambiguation.

CCS CONCEPTS

• **Computing methodologies** → **Lexical semantics; Supervised learning by classification;** • **Information systems** → *Similarity measures;*

KEYWORDS

Author Name Disambiguation; Digital Library; Machine Learning; Word Embeddings; Semantic Similarity

ACM Reference Format:
Mark-Christoph Müller. 2018. On the Contribution of Word-Level Semantics to Practical Author Name Disambiguation. In *JCDL '18: The 18th ACM/IEEE Joint Conference on Digital Libraries, June 3–7, 2018, Fort Worth, TX, USA.* ACM, New York, NY, USA, 2 pages. https://doi.org/10.1145/3197026.3203912

1 INTRODUCTION

For both older and more recent approaches to Author Name Disambiguation (AND), **co-author similarity** is still among the most prominent features:[1] When deciding if two identical author names observed in two publications refer to the same person, overlap between the two publications' co-authors can provide strong positive evidence. At the same time, lack of overlap between two lists of co-authors of sufficient length can provide strong negative evidence. Publication **content similarity** is another widely used AND feature. Normally, the publication *title* is taken as a proxy for publication content, because, unlike e.g. abstracts, it is always available. However, due to the nature of the AND task, content similarity is inferior to co-author similarity, and comes into play only when there is no, or only very weak, co-author evidence: Sufficiently strong co-author similarity does not require corroboration by content similarity, while sufficiently strong co-author *dissimilarity* can hardly be overruled by content similarity. In most AND approaches, content similarity is captured by means of string or n-gram matching, sometimes enhanced with TF-IDF weighting or similar methods ([2]), while methods from Natural Language Processing (NLP), in particular those based on word embeddings, have not been applied to this task, with [6] being the only exception we know of. The present work is an ongoing **follow-up study** to [6], in which we take a more focussed look at the contribution of word level semantics to AND. We limit ourselves to only six *same name groups* (or *blocks*) from the KISTI data set [4], which were selected on the basis of number of records, number of distinct authors, and average number of papers per author. We also exclude word embeddings trained on other data sources than DBLP, which is in line with our findings in [6], and we perform a more rigorous evaluation involving 50% train, 30% dev-test, and 20% eval data, with averaged results over ten randomized runs. Due to the ongoing nature of the work, we report results on dev-test only, and leave the eval data for the final evaluation. Our motivation is that automatically assessing genuine semantic similarity of publications with ambiguous author names can provide additional *positive* evidence of a nature that surface-level similarity cannot provide. As an example, consider the following example from the KISTI AND data set. Here, the name **A. Kumar** refers to the same person, but there is neither co-author nor surface-level content similarity evidence.

> A. Verma, **A. Kumar** (2004):[a]
> Articulatory class based spectral envelope representation for voice fonts.
>
> A. Karmakar, **A. Kumar**, R. K. Patney (2006):[b]
> A multiresolution model of auditory excitation pattern and its application to objective evaluation of perceived speech quality.
>
> [a]http://dblp.org/rec/conf/icmcs/VermaK04
> [b]http://dblp.org/rec/journals/taslp/KarmakarKP06

We combine advanced semantics methods from NLP with insights from the AND domain, in order to make them available to practical AND in digital libraries and other institutions.

2 FEATURES & EXPERIMENTS

We propose two simple features that are sensitive to local, single-word similarities that are observed in publication titles. For training and testing, we use a sub set of the KISTI AND data set [4]. Initially, we create instances for each of the six selected same name groups, by pairing all publication records containing the same ambiguous author name with each other, and labelling the resulting pairs as positive when the ambiguous author name in both refers to the same person, and as negative otherwise. Due to the combinatorial nature of data generation, the resulting data instances are highly skewed towards the negative class. Each training and test data instance is represented as a list of **features**. Since we want to focus on content similarity, we capture **co-author similarity** in a very simple, local manner only, by just considering the *Jaccard*

[1]See the overviews in [2, 3]. [5] is a recent paper which relies exclusively on co-author evidence.

JCDL '18, June 3–7, 2018, Fort Worth, TX, USA

ACM ISBN 978-1-4503-5178-2/18/06.
https://doi.org/10.1145/3197026.3203912

SNG	d.liu	h.lee	j.kim	r.smith	s.kumar	w.chen
# Pubs, #Authors, Mean Pubs/Author	66, 15, 4.4 (3.07)	81, 30, 2.7 (2.48)	149, 57, 2.61 (2.13)	54, 15, 3.6 (3.42)	71, 20, 3.55 (3.04)	97, 25, 3.88 (3.73)
Mean maj. BL ACC	91.74 (2.26)	95.40 (2.13)	97.76 (0.72)	87.28 (4.15)	93.00 (2.20)	93.72 (1.63)
BL 1 mean MCC	0.4986 (0.165)	0.4732 (0.151)	0.4220 (0.076)	0.3261 (0.202)	0.5686 (0.124)	0.4053 (0.110)
BL 2 mean MCC	0.5264 (0.148)	0.5315 (0.122)	0.6499 (0.099)	**0.3644** (0.190)	**0.5743** (0.126)	0.4626 (0.088)
BL 2 + Semantics mean MCC	**0.5382** (0.151)	**0.5520** (0.155)	**0.6660** (0.087)	0.3515 (0.195)	0.5666 (0.125)	**0.4766** (0.092)

Table 1: Results

similarity of the two publications' co-author name lists ca_1 and ca_2. Each list contains the initialized, non-disambiguated names of one publication's co-authors. This way, the minimum similarity is actually 0.0. Positive, and in particular negative, co-author evidence is interpretable only if both $\texttt{len}(ca_1)$ and $\texttt{len}(ca_2) >= 1$: A high co-author similarity score of two publications with e.g. three co-authors is more relevant than that of two publications with only one co-author each. Therefore, we provide $\texttt{len}(ca_1)$, $\texttt{len}(ca_2)$, and $\texttt{min}(\texttt{len}(ca_1),\texttt{len}(ca_2))$ as further features, to enable the classifier to assess the weight of the co-author similarity score. These four features are used in BL 1. ***String-level* content similarity** is represented as the IDF weighted cosine similarity of the normalized publication title token lists $tokens_1$ and $tokens_2$. Normalization includes lower-casing, stemming, and removal of stop-words. IDF weights are computed from a data set of 3.5 million publication titles from DBLP[2], from which publications contained in the KISTI data set were removed. This feature plus the features of BL 1 are used in BL 2. For representing genuine ***semantic* content similarity** of two publications, we define two novel, light-weight semantic features based on the cosine distance of the word embedding vectors of selected tokens from $tokens_1$ and $token_2$. For both features, we use one set of 200-dimensional word embeddings trained with word2vec[3] on the DBLP-derived data set mentioned above. Training was done for 50 iterations with the CBOW algorithm, using a window size of 5 and a min_count 5. For the first feature, we remove common tokens[4] from $tokens_1$ and $tokens_2$, and then select from each the token with the highest IDF score $max\_idf\_token_1$ and $max\_idf\_token_2$. We then use the pre-computed word embedding set to retrieve one vector for $max\_idf\_token_1$ and $max\_idf\_token_2$ each, and compute the feature value as the cosine distance of the two vectors: $\textbf{MaxIDFPair\_CosDist} = \texttt{CosDist}(\texttt{WE}(max\_idf\_token_1),\texttt{WE}(max\_idf\_token_2))$ For the second feature we just compute the pairwise cosine distance for *all* pairs in $tokens_1 \times tokens_2$ (again excluding identical tokens), and use the overall lowest distance as the feature value: $\textbf{Global\_MinCosDist} = \texttt{Min}(\texttt{CosDist}(\texttt{WE}(tokens_1),\texttt{WE}(tokens_2)))$ Our classifier is a simple one-layer neural network with twelve hidden units with `tanh` activation and a final two-unit `softmax` output layer, all implemented in Keras [1] and Tensorflow[5]. We use the Adam optimizer, train for 300 epochs and report the best result on dev-test reached during training.

3 RESULTS, DISCUSSION, & FUTURE WORK

The top row in Table 1 provides some basic statistics of the same name groups (averaged over ten runs, stddev given in parentheses). In order to emphasize the effect of our features and to avoid distorting effects caused by extreme variation in the mean number of publications per author, we chose the groups in such a way that there was no dominating author in each group. This is noticable in the stddev values, which are generally smaller than the mean values themselves. The second row shows the mean majority baseline accuracy, which is generally very high due to the high number of negative instances. Results are reported using the Matthews Correlation Coefficient (MCC), which is particularly suited for scoring binary classifications in highly skewed class distributions. The **BL 1** row shows that, at least for some groups, even very simple co-author features already produce reasonable results, which supports the predominant role of co-author features in AND. The differences among groups (from 0.3261 for r.smith to 0.5686 for s.kumar) can be seen as characteristics of the respective authors, who tend to have more or less recurring co-authors. The **BL 2** row shows that adding surface-based content similarity consistently (though not significantly) improves results, which is also in line with our expectations. However, the improvement varies strongly among groups, from less than 0.01 for s.kumar to more than 0.20 for j.kim. Finally, the **BL 2 + Semantics** row shows the effect of adding our similarity features. Here, improvements can only be found in four out of six groups, and the strength of the improvement is about 0.015 only. While these results show that semantic features can indeed contribute to AND, more detailed analysis of the results is required and currently under way. Also, we currently experiment with different ways of computing light-weight semantic features, including other similarity measures besides cosine, and more varied word embeddings.

[2]http://dblp.uni-trier.de/xml/

[3]https://radimrehurek.com/gensim/models/word2vec.html

[4]The non-identity constraint on the selected tokens ensures that the feature does not reproduce string-matching functionality by selecting *identical* tokens as the semantically most similar ones.

[5]http://tensorflow.org

ACKNOWLEDGMENTS

The research described in this paper was conducted in the project *SCAD – Scalable Author Name Disambiguation*, funded in part by the Leibniz Association (grant SAW-2015-LZI-2), and in part by the Klaus Tschira Foundation.

REFERENCES

[1] François Chollet. 2015. Keras. https://github.com/fchollet/keras. (2015).

[2] Anderson A. Ferreira, Marcos André Gonçalves, and Alberto H.F. Laender. 2012. A brief survey of automatic methods for author name disambiguation. *SIGMOD Record* 41, 2 (2012), 15–26.

[3] Ijaz Hussain and Sohail Asghar. 2017. A survey of author name disambiguation techniques: 2010-2016. *The Knowledge Engineering Review* 32 (2017), 1–24.

[4] In-Su Kang, Pyung Kim, Seungwoo Lee, Hanmin Jung, and Beom-Jong You. 2011. Construction of a Large-scale Test Set for Author Disambiguation. *Information Processing & Management* 47, 3 (2011), 452–465.

[5] Fakhri Momeni and Philipp Mayr. 2016. Using co-authorship networks for author name disambiguation. In *2016 IEEE/ACM Joint Conference on Digital Libraries (JCDL)*. 261–262.

[6] Mark-Christoph Müller. 2017. Semantic Author Name Disambiguation with Word Embeddings. In *2017 International Conference on Theory and Practice of Digital Libraries (TPDL)*. 300–311.

Research Paper Recommender System for University Students on the E-Book System

Chifumi Nishioka
Kyoto University Library
Kyoto, Japan
nishioka.chifumi.2c@kyoto-u.ac.jp

Hiroaki Ogata
ACCMS, Kyoto University
Kyoto, Japan
ogata.hiroaki.3e@kyoto-u.ac.jp

ABSTRACT

This paper shows a research paper recommender system for university students. The recommender system is embedded in an e-book system, which displays learning materials (e.g., slides) and is used at lectures. The recommender system suggests papers related to a learning material. The experiment revealed students do not access to recommended papers during the lecture. Instead, they access to research papers when reviewing the lecture and/or working for an assignment.

CCS CONCEPTS

• **Information systems** → **Recommender systems**; • **Human-centered computing** → *E-book readers*; • **Applied computing** → *Digital libraries and archives*;

KEYWORDS

recommender system, e-book, computer supported learning

ACM Reference Format:

Chifumi Nishioka and Hiroaki Ogata. 2018. Research Paper Recommender System for University Students on the E-Book System. In *JCDL '18: The 18th ACM/IEEE Joint Conference on Digital Libraries, June 3–7, 2018, Fort Worth, TX, USA.* ACM, New York, NY, USA, 2 pages. https://doi.org/10.1145/3197026.3203882

1 INTRODUCTION

So far, a lot of works have developed research paper recommender systems for researchers to assist in finding information. In contrast, this paper proposes a research paper recommender system for university students. The recommender system is embedded into an e-book system BookRoll [2], which displays learning materials (e.g., slides, textbooks) during lectures. It suggests research papers related to a learning material at which a student looks. The motivations of the development are two-fold: (i) Although undergraduate students are interested in research, they have almost no opportunity to know them in lectures. The recommender system provides opportunities to see how what they learn is connected with research. (ii) University libraries operate institutional repositories including research papers. Due to the recent spread of open access policies, the number of research papers in the institutional repositories has increased.

JCDL '18, June 3–7, 2018, Fort Worth, TX, USA

ACM ISBN 978-1-4503-5178-2/18/06.
https://doi.org/10.1145/3197026.3203882

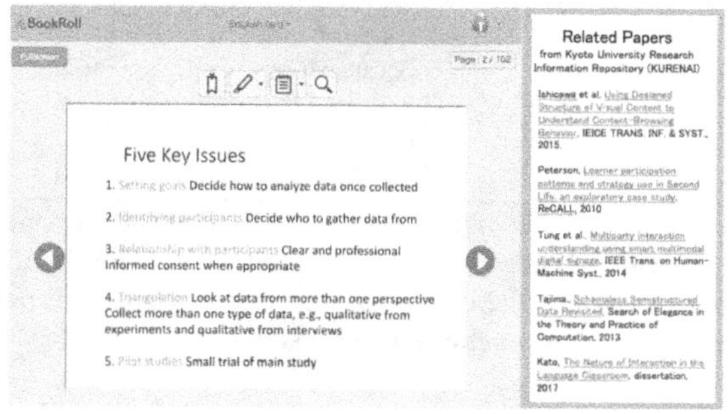

Figure 1: Research paper recommender system on the e-book system BookRoll.

We recommend research papers in the institutional repositories, in order to connect education (i.e., lectures) with research (i.e., research papers) in universities.

2 RECOMMENDER SYSTEM

As an initial step, we implement a research paper recommender system for students on an e-book system BookRoll. BookRoll is a web application that displays learning materials. The recommender system suggests research papers related to a learning material at which a student looks. Due to copyright concerns, we cannot mine full texts of research papers. Thus, we mine the research papers using only their titles. As a text mining method, we employ HCF-IDF [1], which performs well for mining titles of research papers. Research papers that have highest similarity scores to a learning material are recommended. Figure 1 shows the interface of the recommender system embedded in BookRoll.

3 EXPERIMENT

We conduct an experiment to measure how many times and why students access to recommended papers.

Procedure. We deploy the recommender system at a lecture about human interface for third-year undergraduate students on 12/13/2017. The lecture has 44 active students. We observe how many times students have accessed learning materials as well as recommended papers from 12/13/2017 to 12/20/2017. The lecture gives an assignment to students, which asks students to find three papers about human interface and summarize these papers. The deadline is 12/20/2017. After the deadline, we conduct a survey to investigate why they accessed or did not access to recommended papers.

Dataset. The learning material used in the lecture is 86-page slides in Japanese. Regarding candidate items of the recommender system, we use 107, 115 research papers written in Japanese obtained from

Question	*n*	*Result*
Q1. Are you interested in scientific research? (1: not at all – 5: very much)	44	3.36 (1.17)
Q2. Are you interested in contents of the lecture on 12/13/2017? (1: not at all – 5: very much)	44	3.57 (0.93)
Q3. Did you notice that related papers were shown at the right side of BookRoll? (Y/N)	44	56.8%
Q4. If you answer yes for Q3, did you access to recommended papers? (Y/N)	25	48.0%
Q5. If you answer yes for Q4, why did you access? (check at least one reasons)		
Because it seems interesting.	12	25.0%
Because it seems useful for the assignment.	12	75.0%
I clicked without knowing why.	12	16.7%
Q6. If you answer yes for Q4, did you find interesting and/or useful papers? (Y/N)	12	75.0%
Q7. If you answer no for Q4, why did not you access? (check at least one reasons)		
Because it seems unrelated to the contents of the lecture.	13	23.1%
Because I have no interest.	13	23.1%
Because I have no time.	13	38.5%
Another reason	13	15.4%

Table 1: The result of the survey. The first column provides question. In parentheses, answer types are given. The second column shows the number of valid answers. The third column reports the result. If the answer type is the Likert scale, mean and SD are given. If the answer type is Y/N, the result provides ratio of who answer Y. If the answer type is checkbox, the result reports ratio of who check the reason.

date	learning material	recommended papers
2017-12-13	7298	2
2017-12-14	264	3
2017-12-15	178	4
2017-12-16	237	1
2017-12-17	249	0
2017-12-18	857	21
2017-12-19	3811	17
2017-12-20	1309	24
total	14203	72

Table 2: The result of the number of accesses to learning materials and recommended papers.

our institutional repository[1]. As an external knowledge graph for HCF-IDF, we use the JST thesaurus[2].

4 RESULT AND DISCUSSION

Table 2 reports the number of accesses. In terms of the number of accesses to the learning material, please note accesses are counted for each page. Since the learning material has 86 pages and we have 44 active students, each page is accessed at on average 3.75 times. The learning material received most accesses on 12/13/2017, the lecture date. Then, the number of accesses drops and increases again towards 12/20/2017, the deadline of the assignment. Regarding the number of accesses to recommended papers, we observe few accesses on 12/13/2017. The possible reason is that students were focusing on the lecture, thus had no time to see recommended papers. Then, the number of accesses to research papers increases for the deadline of the assignment.

The result of the survey is summarized in Table 1. It shows students are fairly interested in research and the lecture (Q1 and Q2). Only 56.8% of students noticed that research papers are recommended (Q3). Thus, we need to improve the interface of the recommender system. Among students who noticed recommended papers, 48.0% of them accessed (Q4). 75.0% of students with accesses answered recommended papers were interesting or/and useful (Q6). Most reason for the access is to find useful information for the assignment (Q5). The reasons why students did not access are various (Q7). 23.1% of students without access answered that recommendations included papers unrelated to the learning material. Since research papers in the institutional repository cover many disciplines, it was difficult to retrieve only research papers about human interface in the computer science. For example, the recommender system picks a research paper about human interface in medicine. In the future, we will exploit information such as authors' affiliations (e .g., department) for improving the recommendation strategy. In free comments, we receive positive comments such as the recommender system enables to access research papers easily.

5 CONCLUSION AND FUTURE WORK

In this paper, we show a research paper recommender system for students on the e-book system BookRoll, which connects research and education in universities. In the future, we will assess how recommended papers influence on learning activities using logs recorded by BookRoll. Then, we will develop a recommendation strategy that suggests research papers, which stimulates students' learning activities.

Acknowledgments. The research is supported by Grant-in-Aid for Scientific Research (S) No. 16H06304. We appreciate Brendan Flanagan for implementation.

REFERENCES

[1] C. Nishioka and A. Scherp. 2016. Profiling vs. time vs. content: What does matter for top-k publication recommendation based on Twitter profiles?. In *JCDL*. IEEE, 171–180.

[2] H. Ogata, C. Yin, M. Oi, F. Okubo, A. Shimada, K. Kojima, and M. Yamada. 2015. E-Book-based learning analytics in university education. In *ICCE*. 401–406.

[1] https://repository.kulib.kyoto-u.ac.jp/dspace/?locale=en

[2] http://www.jst.go.jp/EN/index.html

Worksets Expand the Scholarly Utility of Digital Libraries

Kevin R. Page[1], Jacob Jett[2], Timothy W. Cole[2], Deren Kudeki[2], David Bainbridge[3], Peter Organisciak[4], J. Stephen Downie[2]

[1]Oxford e-Research Centre, Dept. of Engineering Science, University of Oxford, UK, kevin.page@oerc.ox.ac.uk
[2]School of Information Science, University of Illinois at UC, USA, {jjett2,t-cole3,dkudeki, jdownie}@illinois.edu
[3]Dept. of Computer Science, University of Waikato, Hamilton, New Zealand, davidb@waikato.ac.nz
[4]Research Methods and Information Science, University of Denver, Denver, CO USA, Peter.Organisciak@du.edu

ABSTRACT

Scholars using digital libraries and archives routinely create worksets—aggregations of digital objects—as a way to segregate resources of interest for in-depth scrutiny. To illustrate how worksets can enhance the scholarly utility of digital library content, we distill from prior user studies three key objectives for worksets (extra-digital library manipulation, intra-item properties, and robust representations), and discuss how they motivated the workset model being developed at the HathiTrust Research Center (HTRC). We describe how HTRC's implementation of its RDF-compliant workset model helps to satisfy these objectives.

CCS CONCEPTS

• **Applied computing~Digital libraries and archives** • Information systems~Retrieval tasks and goals

KEYWORDS

digital libraries, worksets, HathiTrust, semantic web, RDF

ACM Reference format:

Kevin R. Page, Jacob Jett, Timothy W. Cole, Deren Kudeki, David Bainbridge, Peter Organisciak, J. Stephen Downie. 2018. Worksets Expand the Scholarly Utility of Digital Libraries. In *Proceedings of ACM/IEEE Joint Conference on Digital Libraries, Fort Worth, TX USA, June 2018 (JCDL).* DOI: http://dx.doi.org/10.1145/3197026.3203886

1 INTRODUCTION

Worksets have been introduced as aggregations of digital data that undergo analysis for scholarly study [1-3]. In this context we draw a distinction between archives, which provide evidence for the existence of digital objects in support of an investigation or argument; and digital libraries (DL), where the digital objects and their intellectual content are collected studied, analyzed, and synthesized in support of a scholarly hypothesis. Worksets take this a step further, as an additional mechanism for creating and refining knowledge within a layered DL (as described in [4]), whereby the act of aggregation they facilitate is in of itself an intellectual product. In Section 2 we selectively describe three motivated objectives[1], which serve as specific illustrations of where worksets move beyond traditional DL functionality. In Section 3 we present key elements of an implemented workset model, and relate its utility to the requirements following from the three objectives.

2 KEY WORKSET OBJECTIVES

2.1 Objective 1: Extra-DL Resources

When working within a single DL, options to aggregate and manipulate digital objects into a workset are limited to the features and objects exposed by each DL's API or user interface. However, Fenlon et al. [5] have shown that scholars want the ability to incorporate external metadata and external digital objects within their worksets. Thus, there is a need for resource manipulation at an "extra-DL" level, to remove these single-DL constraints and to fashion worksets drawing from multiple sources, leveraging external metadata and including external resources. Realizing this objective enables inclusion of features produced by the computational analysis of workset items or tailored to domain-specific investigation of the items within a DL. In terms of [4], this illustrates the distinction between the 'collection layer' provided by the underlying DL(s), and the 'computational analysis' and 'exploratory analysis' layers realized through worksets.

2.2 Objective 2: Intra-Item Properties

As well as being a vessel for holding and manipulating extra-DL criteria, worksets must be a mechanism for processing features and/or properties *within* digital objects. These properties might be identified through computational analysis of item metadata and content, creating further metadata exposed, in turn, as criteria for forming and refining subsequent worksets. Interviews and surveys of HTRC's scholarly users [5] suggest that scholars desire a greater choice in the granularity of objects and object-metadata than is offered natively by a particular DL. For example, the default unit of granularity in the HathiTrust DL is the digitized volume; users express a preference for examining resources at the level of chapters, articles, individual pages or other textual divisions. Thus there is a need for worksets to support augmentation of item descriptions using intra-item metadata and to incorporate intra-item content.

[1] With no intended implication of comprehensive coverage.

ACM ISBN 978-1-4503-5178-2/18/06.
DOI: http://dx.doi.org/10.1145/3197026.3203886

2.3 Objective 3: Robust Representations

The representation of worksets must be adaptable into forms appropriate for different research stages and applications, while still conforming to community expectations for interoperability. For example, a scholarly analysis might require the inclusion of digital objects protected by copyright which would be required to remain within a DL's access controls. This predicates that any processing or manipulation of item content must be undertaken within a trusted infrastructure, i.e., following a non-consumptive research model. While a workset representation in a secure space can directly encapsulate restricted content, publically shared versions can only include objects by reference. Thus a workset model must be amenable to different levels of object representation according to circumstances, and offer consistency through the deterministic translation from one representation to another.

3 WORKSET IMPLEMENTATION

The implementation of worksets at the HTRC is built using a semantic web stack via an RDF-compliant ontology [2] serving as the data model for a Virtuoso triple store. This implementation realizes the aforementioned workset objectives in a number of ways, which we describe here.

Achieving Objective 1. Workset descriptions, including manifests of workset items, are maintained in a Virtuoso triple store. Each workset is stored as an individual RDF graph. Bibliographic metadata for each item in the HathiTrust DL is transformed into RDF and stored in the default graph of the triple store, with changes synchronized daily; in other respects the triple store exists as a resource decoupled from the core HathiTrust infrastructure. Items (content and metadata) referenced in a workset manifest, including any non-HathiTrust items, are linked using persistent URLs. e.g., HathiTrust volume handles. Benefits include the ability to add or subtract workset items without making tangible alterations to item metadata, and linking items and context enriching resources, e.g., granular extracted features and digital annotations, regardless of where stored (through predicates like "annotatedBy" and "hasFeaturesDataSet"). Domain-specific, computed, and extended workset-specific properties can be included simply by extending the workset graph. This affordance is inherent in the extensible and self-describing nature of RDF.

Achieving Objective 2. Our data model makes no assumptions regarding the objects which can be added to a workset. Everything is aggregated using an agnostic "gathers" predicate, with 'gatherable' resources typed accordingly (additionally/multiply typed). The use of an RDF ontology enables the easy overlay of these new information resources while retaining their domain semantics; from the semantic web perspective, as long as a source can be named (i.e., identified by a persistent global identifier, e.g., a URL) then it can be aggregated into a workset. This allows reuse of existing ontologies to describe the granularity required, e.g., schema:Article (bibliographic), fabio:Page (structural). This, in effect, reduces the effort required from scholars who wish to expand the descriptive fidelity within intra-item aggregations. Similarly, metadata for finer-grained, intra-item objects can be added by extending the graph with appropriate semantics.

Achieving Objective 3. Our workset implementation uses a 'manifest' to associate items with a workset, whereby the RDF encoding does not embed any actual item content. Depending on who, or what, is consuming the workset manifest, different localized workset formations may be realized. For example, the HTRC workset builder is a user interface for creating and refining worksets. It operates at the manifest level, fetching item metadata dynamically as needed, and never accessing item content (which is potentially in copyright). By contrast, the HTRC's Data API uses the manifest of the RDF-workset representation to fetch item content which is computationally analyzed within a secure, copyright respecting, Data Capsule [3]. As a further illustration of flexibility, since a manifest-only RDF workset representation contains no copyrighted content, it can be shared with other scholars, allowing broad reuse and recombination of worksets.

4 SUMMARY

As DLs proliferate and grow in scale, scholars require a way to both span DL boundaries and segment DLs in order to create the coherent collections of digital objects required to support their research. Appropriately modeled worksets provide a means to this end and thereby enhance DL utility. RDF is well-suited for describing worksets because of its inherent extensibility, linking, and accommodation for semantics from multiple ontologies. This latter feature facilitates workset descriptions supporting multiple domains—those operationally required for a DL alongside those specialized to the discipline of the scholar. Furthermore, standards for retrieving RDF workset descriptions from triple stores include features which facilitate on-the-fly transformation of RDF graphs, e.g., SPARQL Construct, and support operations spanning multiple DL triple stores, e.g., SPARQL Federated Query.

ACKNOWLEDGMENTS

This work supported in part by grant #41500672 from the Andrew W. Mellon Foundation; conclusions and opinions expressed are those of the authors and are not necessarily shared by the sponsor.

REFERENCES

[1] J. S. Downie, T. W. Cole, and B. Plale. 2013. Workset creation for scholarly analysis: Prototyping project. Retrieved Jan. 31, 2018 from: http://hdl.handle.net/2142/99011

[2] J. Jett, T. W. Cole, C. Maden, and J. S. Downie. 2016. The HathiTrust Research Center Workset Ontology: A Descriptive Framework for Non-Consumptive Research Collections. Journal of Open Humanities Data 2:e1. DOI: http://doi.org/10.5334/johd.3

[3] J. S. Downie, B. Plale, & T. W. Cole. 2017. Workset creation for scholarly analysis and data capsules: Laying the foundations for secure computation with copyrighted data in the HTRC. Retrieved Jan. 31, 2018 from: http://hdl.handle.net/2142/99010

[4] K. R. Page, S. Bechhofer, G. Fazekas, D. M. Weigl, & T. Wilmering. 2017. Realising a layered digital library: Exploration and analysis of the Live Music Archive through linked data. Proc. ACM/IEEE Joint Conference on Digital Libraries (JCDL). DOI: http://doi.org/10.1109/JCDL.2017.7991563

[5] K. Fenlon, M. Senseney, H. Green, S. Bhattacharyya, C. Willis, and J. S. Downie. 2014. Scholar-built collections: A study of user requirements for research in large-scale digital libraries. Proc. Am. Soc. Info. Sci. Tech., 51: 1–10. DOI: http://doi.org/10.1002/meet.2014.14505101047

Learning to Extract Comparison Points of Entity Pairs from Wikipedia Articles

Sandeep Kumar Pani
Indian Institute of technology, Kharagpur
sandeepkumarpani888@gmail.com

Naresh R
Indian Institute of technology, Kharagpur
nareshmdu@gmail.com

Pawan Goyal
Indian Institute of technology, Kharagpur
pawang@cse.iitkgp.ernet.in

Plaban Kumar Bhowmick
Indian Institute of technology, Kharagpur
plaban@gmail.com

ABSTRACT

In this paper, we present preliminary results on a novel task of extracting comparison points for a pair of entities from the text articles describing them. The task is challenging as comparison points in a typical pair of articles tend to be sparse. We presented a multi-level document analysis (viz. document, paragraph and sentence level) for extracting the comparisons. For extracting sentence level comparisons, which is the hardest task among three, we have used Convolutional Neural Network (CNN) with features extracted around ⟨ entity, aspect, value ⟩ triple. Experiments conducted on a small dataset provide encouraging performance.

CCS CONCEPTS

• **Computing methodologies → Information extraction**;

KEYWORDS

Comparison extraction; Entity comparison; Information Extraction

ACM Reference Format:

Sandeep Kumar Pani, Naresh R, Pawan Goyal, and Plaban Kumar Bhowmick. 2018. Learning to Extract Comparison Points of Entity Pairs from Wikipedia Articles. In *JCDL '18: The 18th ACM/IEEE Joint Conference on Digital Libraries, June 3–7, 2018, Fort Worth, TX, USA.* ACM, New York, NY, USA, 2 pages. https://doi.org/10.1145/3197026.3203909

1 INTRODUCTION

Automatic extraction of metadata of several forms has become one of the primary research areas in digital library. While these systems focus on extracting structured information about individual resources, extraction of information that relates multiple resources together is generally overlooked. Comparison of entities present in multiple resources is one such example. Comparisons have immense value by providing the readers concise view of differences, pros and cons of the entities or processes in focus. It is very hard to imagine book chapters in different disciplines without comparisons. Among many tasks, the researchers in different domains have to perform comparative analysis of entities and methods by analyzing multiple articles. Previous work [6] in this area uses seeded topics to get comparisons. However, extracting structured comparisons automatically from free text is an extremely challenging task and has not been explored much. There have been efforts to extract comparisons of consumer goods from product reviews [4]. The product reviews tend to be short and are very precise about different attributes of the products. Hence, these approaches are not suitable for comparison extraction from larger text body (e.g., encyclopedic description like Wikipedia articles, scientific articles) where the comparison points are immensely sparse. Furthermore, in comparison to the product reviews, the comparable descriptions in larger text body are camouflaged by the nuances of different surface representations of similar information.

In this work, our objective is to extract comparison points from a pair of Wikipedia articles describing two entities. In this respect, our paper makes the following key contributions:

- We define a novel task of generating comparison points of two entities from the respective unstructured data.
- We present a working pipeline that generates such a comparison from a large corpus without any external seed.
- We present a performance analysis of comparison extraction system with respect to a human annotated dataset.

2 NOTION OF COMPARISON

A comparison refers to a consideration or estimate of the similarities or dissimilarities between two entities, where an 'entity' refers to the main subject of the text. The 'entity' is assumed to be the subject of discussion in each sentence, but exceptions do exist. 'Aspect' refers to topic being discussed in a sentence. 'Value' describes the attributes/characteristics of the entity with respect to the aspect of the sentence. To illustrate the definitions further, we use the sentence *"Lion's prey consists of primarily mammals."*. The breakdown of this sentence would be: Entity: *Lion*, Aspect: *prey*, Value: *mammals*.

We define two sentences to be 'comparable' if

- the **focus** entities are different in semantic space but not at very large distance to be suitable objects for comparison (e.g. algae-bacteria vs. algae-mammal)
- the **aspects** are same or semantically similar (e.g., hunting, reproduction habit etc.)
- the **values** that the respective aspects assume are different (e.g., 'savannah' and 'tundra' make for good values for comparison when comparing on the attribute 'habitat'.)

JCDL '18, June 3–7, 2018, Fort Worth, TX, USA

ACM ISBN 978-1-4503-5178-2/18/06.
https://doi.org/10.1145/3197026.3203909

Table 1: Two examples of ⟨ entity, aspect, value ⟩ extraction

Sentence	Entity	Aspect	Value
1. Lion's prey consists of primarily mammals.	Lion	prey	mammals
2. Seeds and fruit form the major component of the diets of pigeons and doves.	pigeons	diets	Seeds and fruit

i.e., the comparable sentences for the two entities mention the exact same aspect (i.e., context), but can be differentiated on the values. A positive example for a comparable pair of sentences, as per our definition, can be "*Llamas typically live for 15 to 25 years, with some individuals surviving 30 years or more.*" and "*The average life expectancy of a camel is 40 to 50 years.*" A negative example for comparable pair of sentences is: "*Most baboons live in hierarchical troops.*" and "*Gorillas have a patchy distribution.*"

3 COMPARISON EXTRACTION PIPELINE

We use a pair of Wikipedia articles as our input. Our algorithm can be divided into 3 parts for deciding comparability at i) the document level, ii) paragraph level and iii) sentence level. We currently restrict our domain to biology to obtain a lexical tree with relations between all possible entities and use graph heuristics to establish comparability between documents. For such comparable entities, we use concept extraction to obtain the topic of each paragraph and then WordMover's distance [5] & Latent Semantic Indexing (LSI) to establish comparability at the paragraph level.

For a dataset consisting of 669 number of Wikipedia documents, the document level precision and recall values are 87.5% and 77.7%. For paragraph level comparability extraction, the performance of the system is 41.66% recall and 45% precision based on 836 number of paragraph pairs in the dataset. We used the response from sentence level annotations to mark the paragraph and document pairs to be comparable.

4 SENTENCE LEVEL COMPARISON

We used Open IE[1] to get the sentence structure, i.e., to extract the ⟨ entity, aspect, value ⟩ in a sentence. We then used a CNN (Convolutional Neural Network) with the following features (denoted by labels):

F1 OpenIE promises to extract the relationship between entity pairs in a sentence. This feature describes how far the verb and aspect are in the sentence.

F2 Wu-Palmer metric from Wordnet[2] to get how different the aspects between a pair of sentence were.

F3 Path-similarity from Wordnet to estimate distance of the values.

F4 We also convoluted the PMI (Pointwise Mutual Information) [1] values between the aspect and value of one sentence with another to encode how much value the 'aspects' add to the comparability of the sentences in the context of the given 'values'.

- For multi-perspective CNN [3], our input was a 0-1 classification label of whether or not 2 sentences are comparable for the training dataset. The vocabulary was built with the STS dataset[3] added to words from our training dataset.
- We used Infersent [2] for getting a sentence level representation, as it scaled well for different tasks in the NLP domain.

[1]Stanford Open Information Extraction

[2]WordNet - A Lexical Database for English

Table 2: Results for sentence-level comparison extraction

Method	Prec.	Recall	F1
- Open IE + graph similarity	0.286	0.32	0.302
- CNN (with infersent)	0.367	0.393	0.379
- Multi-perspective CNN	0.458	0.423	0.44
- CNN (with features F1,F2,F3; tuples extracted by hand)	0.461	**0.562**	0.507
- CNN (with features F2, F3; triples extracted by hand)	0.3	0.346	0.321
- CNN (features F1,F2,F3,F4; triples extracted by hand)	**0.476**	0.555	**0.513**

5 EXPERIMENTAL RESULTS

We used a human annotated dataset of 300 document pairs. The average number of comparable sentences per document is 3. This exhibits the difficulty of the task. Our final training dataset is comprised of 168 positive pairs and 264 negative pairs. Similarly, test data has 20 positive and 54 negative pairs. In both the cases, positive refers to the sentences that are labeled as comparable. Table 2 presents the results of various approaches explored in this study. It is evident from the results that adding more refined features which highlight the comparability aspect for the pair of sentences is very important. Increase in performance has been observed by using PMI-based features. For training as well as testing, we hand broke the sentence into ⟨ entity, aspect, value ⟩ and this has been reported in the table as 'triples extracted by hand'.

6 FUTURE WORK

The present system makes use of OpenIE for extraction of ⟨ entity, aspect, value ⟩. Though it works well for simpler sentences, quality of extraction has been poor for complex sentences. We intend to deploy template-based extraction of ⟨ entity, aspect, value ⟩ triples.

7 ACKNOWLEDGEMENT

This work is partially supported by *Development of National Digital Library of India as a National Knowledge Asset of the Nation* sponsored by Ministry of Human Resource Development, Government of India.

REFERENCES

[1] Gerlof Bouma. 2009. Normalized (pointwise) mutual information in collocation extraction. *Proceedings of GSCL* (2009), 31–40.
[2] Alexis Conneau, Douwe Kiela, Holger Schwenk, Loïc Barrault, and Antoine Bordes. 2017. Supervised Learning of Universal Sentence Representations from Natural Language Inference Data. *CoRR* abs/1705.02364 (2017). arXiv:1705.02364
[3] Hua He, Kevin Gimpel, and Jimmy Lin. 2015. Multi-perspective sentence similarity modeling with convolutional neural networks. In *EMNLP*. 1576–1586.
[4] Nitin Jindal and Bing Liu. 2006. Identifying Comparative Sentences in Text Documents. In *SIGIR (SIGIR '06)*. ACM, New York, NY, USA, 244–251.
[5] Matt Kusner, Yu Sun, Nicholas Kolkin, and Kilian Weinberger. 2015. From word embeddings to document distances. In *ICML*. 957–966.
[6] Xiang Ren, Yuanhua Lv, Kuansan Wang, and Jiawei Han. 2017. Comparative Document Analysis for Large Text Corpora. In *WSDM*. ACM, NY, USA, 325–334.

[3]SemEval STS Task Dataset

Challenges to Deploying Library Services in the Cloud: Data Issues Influencing IT, People, Costs, and Policy Challenges

Devendra Potnis
University of Tennessee at Knoxville
1345 Circle Park Drive, Suite 451
Knoxville, TN, 37996, USA
dpotnis@utk.edu

Reynard Regenstreif-Harms
University of Tennessee at Chattanooga
600 Douglas Street
Chattanooga, TN 37403, USA
reynard-regenstreif-harms04@utc.edu

Dwight Hunter
Chattanooga State Community College
4501 Amnicola Highway
Chattanooga, TN, 37406, USA
dwight.hunter@chattanoogastate.edu

ABSTRACT

This poster analyzes challenges to planning, deploying, and maintaining different types of library services in the cloud. We apply grounded theory principles to analyze 75 articles authored by library administrators, librarians with IT expertise, IT professionals, cybersecurity experts, and business consultants engaged in planning, deploying, and maintaining library services in the cloud. Data analysis reveals that a majority of the past literature reports challenges to implementing Software as a Service (SaaS) in libraries. The seven key areas critical to the successful implementation of SaaS in libraries are related to: (1) data, (2) authentication and privacy of patrons, (3) skills and knowledge of library staff and organizational culture, (4) IT infrastructure, (5) features of services, (6) fixed and operational costs associated with data and technology, and (7) policies and contracts.

KEYWORDS

Libraries; Cloud; Software as a Service; Challenges

ACM Reference format:

D. Potnis, Regenstreif-Harms, R., and D. Hunter. 2018. Challenges to Deploying Library Services in the Cloud: Data Issues Influencing IT, People, Costs, and Policy Challenges. In *Proceedings of ACM/IEEE Joint Conference on Digital Libraries (JCDL'18), Dallas, Texas USA, June 2018,* 2 pages. https://doi.org/10.1145/3197026.3203897

1 GOAL

In the era of budget cuts, libraries need to rely less on external information technology (IT) vendors and train librarians to design, develop, and maintain IT solutions and services [1]. The goal of this poster is to identify the key barriers to planning, deploying, and maintaining library services in the cloud and reveal the inter-relationships among these barriers, which would help libraries address the challenges to planning, deploying, and maintaining library services in the cloud. Study findings would better equip libraries for deploying services in the cloud, thereby reducing their reliance on external IT vendors and saving their scarce financial resources while better serving patrons.

JCDL '18, June 3–7, 2018, Fort Worth, TX, USA

ACM ISBN 978-1-4503-5178-2/18/06.
https://doi.org/10.1145/3197026.3203897

2 METHODS

We used a "pearl seed" approach to retrieve relevant articles on the topic of cloud computing in libraries from the following sources: (a) peer-reviewed journals (e.g., Journal of Academic Librarianship, IT and Libraries, Library Hi Tech, Online Information Review); (b) practitioner-oriented magazines (e.g., computers in libraries, ACM Transactions on Storage); and (c) professional conferences (e.g., ACM/IEEE JCDL, Computers in Libraries, Data Summit, ACRL). We focused on the experiential guidance offered by practitioners. We considered articles published from 2005 to 2016 to ensure that we captured the evolving role of cloud in offering library services. We developed MS Excel summary sheets to code all the experiences and advice shared by practitioners. The coded data was read repeatedly to identify and name patterns and themes. Each relevant publication was analyzed individually and then compared across subjects to identify patterns and common categories.

3 RESULTS

We identified seven clusters consisting of 35 challenges critical to the planning, deployment, and maintenance of library services in the cloud (see Figure 1). Data, people (i.e. library staff and patrons), policies and contracts, IT (infrastructure and features of services), and various costs associated with data, IT, and policies and contracts are the key barriers to deploying library services in the cloud. Challenges such as *configuration* belong to IT Infrastructure, Costs, and Features of Cloud Service clusters. Similarly, *security* belongs to both the data and people clusters. Figure 1 depicts factors that are correlated to each other by a double arrow. For instance, there is a correlation between institutional practices and data loss; similarly, networking is correlated with migration, access, and storage of data.

Challenges related to data seem to be correlated the most with the challenges from the remaining clusters.

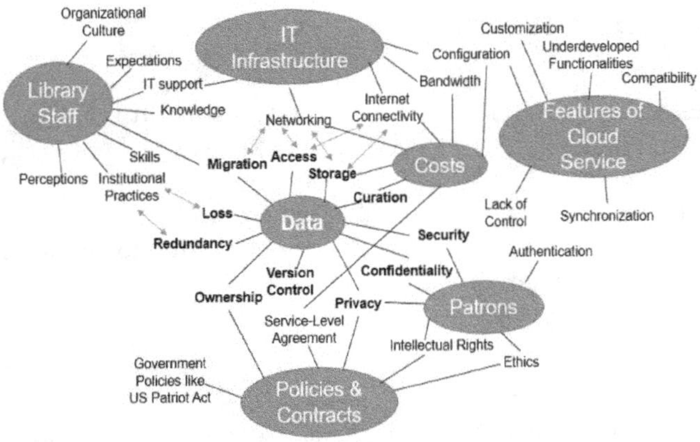

Figure 1. 35 Challenges to Deploying Library Services in the Cloud

3.1 Data

Access, storage, ownership, security, curation, confidentiality, loss, privacy, migration, and redundancy of data create challenges to using data while serving patrons using the cloud. Security and privacy are the biggest concerns of libraries using cloud, especially if libraries collect individually identifiable information such as credit card information. Once libraries release data to the cloud through a third party, they hardly have any control over it. The availability and durability of data are important when data is stored on remote hosts, creating enormous risks for privacy [2].

3.2 Patrons

The issues of authentication, confidentiality, and privacy overlap with each other for the data and patrons clusters. Sometimes where the third-party vendor stores patron data at their physical facility, they might not even inform libraries that their patrons data have been released [3]. Questions related to jurisdiction might also be raised when storing data in the cloud, which could be related to the PATRIOT Act and its successor, the FREEDOM Act.

3.3 Library Staff

The skills and knowledge of library staff, their perceptions of and expectations from ILS implementation, soft issues related to migration, institutional norms of serving patrons using the cloud, and finally, organizational culture for adopting new technological solutions are some of the key factors influencing the planning and implementation of services in the cloud. There is a significant learning curve involved in learning and building a new vocabulary of concepts to serve patrons efficiently.

3.4 IT Infrastructure

Issues related to the Internet connectivity, networking, and configuration lead to IT infrastructure challenges. Cloud-based services cannot work on low-speed Internet connections [4].

3.5 Features of Cloud Services

Libraries' lack of control over cloud-based services, the inability of libraries to customize their services they wish, issues related to synchronization and configuration, incompatibility, and underdevelopment hinder the planning and implementation of services in the cloud. There could be a feeling among librarians that they are no longer in charge of technical services.

3.6 Costs

Cloud services are neither free nor cheap. The IT budget of libraries could be affected negatively by the maintenance of cloud-based services. The operating costs of cloud computing can be expensive, including the costs of bandwidth, transition, and backup storage.

3.7 Policies and Contracts

The PATRIOT Act had a chilling effect on libraries [5]. Security policies of academic institutes could apply to cloud computing and potentially protect academic libraries from the threats arising from these services [6]. Librarians consider service level agreements (SLAs) to be the biggest concern when evaluating a cloud provider [7].

4 CONCLUSION

Although some challenges reported before 2010 have been resolved using the advancement in technology, data issues continue dominating the planning, deployment, and maintenance of library services in the cloud. Each library is different in terms of their librarians' skills, existing SLAs and their IT infrastructure needs. Libraries should interpret our findings as per their unique context, for addressing the challenges to planning and implementing services in the cloud to better serve their patrons.

REFERENCES

[1] Devendra Potnis., Reynard Regenstreif-Harms and Ed Cortez, 2016, Identifying key steps for developing mobile applications & mobile websites for libraries. *Information Technologies and Libraries*, 35, 3, 40-58. DOI: http://doi.org/10.6017/ital.v35i3.8652

[2] Marios D. Dikaiakos, George Pallis, Dimitrios Katsaros, Pankaj Mehra, and Athena Vakali. 2009, Cloud computing: Distributed internet computing for IT and scientific research. *IEEE Internet Computing* 13, 5 (Sep.-Oct. 2009(, 10-13. DOI:https://doi.org/10.1109/MIC.2009.103.

[3] Brian Hayes. 2008. Cloud computing. *Communications of the ACM* 51, 7 (Jul. 2008), 9-11. DOI:http://doi.org/10.1145/1364782.1364786.

[4] Bansode, S. and Pujari, S. 2012. Cloud computing and libraries. *Journal of Library & Information Technology* 32, 6 (Nov. 2012), 506-512. DOI:http://dx.doi.org/10.14429/djlit.32.6.2848.

[5] Eli Neiburger. 2010. User-generated content. *Library Technology Reports* 46, 8 (Nov. 2010), 13-24.

[6] Denis Galvin and Mang Sun. 2012. Avoiding the death zone: Choosing and running a library project in the cloud. *Library Hi Tech* 30, 3 (2012), 418-427. DOI:https://doi.org/10.1108/07378831211266564.

[7] Azeem Aleem and Christopher Ryan Sprott. 2012. Let me in the cloud: analysis of the benefit and risk assessment of the cloud platform. *Journal of Financial Crime* 20, 1 (2013), 6-24. DOI:https://doi.org/10.1108/13590791311287337.

Advantages of a Model-Based Library for Scientific Experiments

Susanne Putze
Digital Media Lab
University of Bremen
Germany
sputze@tzi.de

Robert Porzel
Digital Media Lab
University of Bremen
Germany
porzel@tzi.de

Rainer Malaka
Digital Media Lab
University of Bremen
Germany
malaka@tzi.de

ACM Reference Format:
Susanne Putze, Robert Porzel, and Rainer Malaka. 2018. Advantages of a Model-Based Library for Scientific Experiments. In *JCDL '18: The 18th ACM/IEEE Joint Conference on Digital Libraries, June 3–7, 2018, Fort Worth, TX, USA*. ACM, New York, NY, USA, 2 pages. https://doi.org/10.1145/3197026.3203889

1 INTRODUCTION

In many research areas, such as the material sciences, researchers plan and conduct numerous experiments. The corresponding findings are published, while the underlying data remains described haphazardly or not at all within the respective institutes and, therefore, is neither shared nor reused by the scientific community.

To address this issue, we have developed and deployed a scientific data management environment for the material sciences at various test facilities. Unlike other systems, our experiment library explicitly models every pertinent facet of the experiment and the materials tested therein - thereby supporting the initial design of the experiment, its execution and the ensuing results. Previous studies have shown that this library based on explicit models helps scientists to improve the documentation process of their experiments and helps them to embed the data management better into their research workflow. In this work we take a further look on the data collected with the explicit experiment model and investigate whether machine learning techniques can be applied to derive additional knowledge. By doing this we want to detect clusters of similar experiments, so called *experiment series*. These experiment series connect similar experiments and help to improve the expressive range of experiments and corresponding results and improve the data findability and reusability.

2 RELATED WORK

In recent years a variety of research data repositories have been developed and were made available to the scientific community. Guidelines, like the FAIR principles (i.e. Findability, Accessibility, Interoperability, and Reusability) list basic fundamentals for research data management [7]. Current data repositories represent different approaches to creating digital infrastructures for scientific data. The approaches differ along several dimensions. In some cases the approaches differ in their disciplinary scope:

- Some systems are designed as multi-domain systems, e.g. the Open Science Framework [2],
- Others are domain-specific ones focusing on a singular scientific field or type of experiment, e.g. for marine science [5] or systems biology [6].

Another dimension concerns the level of formal explication. Most systems store some meta-data about the experiments using various standards, e.g. using the Dublin Core Meta Data, but they differ in terms of modeling the content data inside explicitly or implicitly.

- One frequent approach is to store data records and their meta data in some human readable format, without having an explicit formal model of the individual entities contained in these records, e.g. PANGEA [3] or OSF [2],
- Others seek to provide structured information of the data themselves along with the published record, e.g. SEEK [8] or InfoSys [9].

Lastly, we see the genesis of the experimental records as an additional dimension to be considered.

- Most of the aforementioned systems constitute post hoc data management. That means that after the experiments have been conducted the resulting data is formated and entered into some system, e.g. [3], [2], [8] or [5].
- Currently only a few systems seek to support concurrent data management. goes a step beyond. Here the question arises of how to address the problem of involving data management as early as possible into the research workflow and to make it an integral part of it, e.g. [1] or [9].

3 EXPERIMENT LIBRARY

We developed and implemented the explicit experiment model in an iterative process with an interdisciplinary team consisting of domain experts in materials science as well as computer scientists.

Figure 1 gives an overview of the employed explicit experiment model. An experiment consists of a set of experiment settings and the tested specimen. The settings consists of different attributes, e.g. the testing machine and its parameters. The specimen includes all parameters of its production steps, e.g. the fundamental material

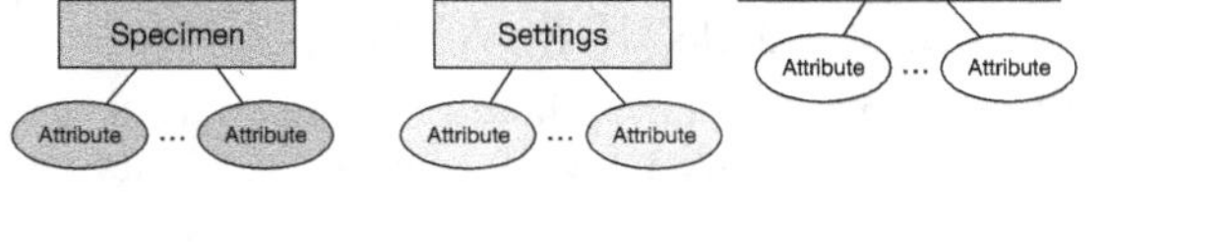

Figure 1: An explicit experiment model

JCDL '18, June 3–7, 2018, Fort Worth, TX, USA

ACM ISBN 978-1-4503-5178-2/18/06.
https://doi.org/10.1145/3197026.3203889

and its treatments. During this experiment a set of specimens are investigated and the test results are measured. Besides the raw data of the testing machine, the test results also includes a set of derived values which describe the characteristics of the material, e.g. the elastic modulus. This selection of attributes contains some which cover different types of experiment. Some attributes are common to all types of experiments while other attributes are type-specific. Each attribute may only be eligible for some types of experiments. Besides the experiment model, we added some operational data to the model, for example for user management and access rights.

The experiment model and the containing management tools are implemented as a web application with a relational data persistence layer.[1]

4 DATA COLLECTION & ANALYSIS

We evaluated our explicit experiment library with a group of experimental material scientists. They used the data documentation during their daily research to document their experiments. By this process we could collect 64 explicit experiment descriptions from 15 different research projects where in total 1704 specimens were tested. One of the benefits of this experiment library is the consistently used data model. So we are able to perform an automatic data analysis to compare several research projects without defining a joint model post-hoc. We demonstrate the benefits of the explicit model by automatic clustering experiments from our data set (spanning multiple research projects) into experiment series. An experiment series is a collection of experiments which share a number of fixed parameters and only vary in a small number of parameters (i.e. independent variables). While researchers explicitly define experiment series within one project, an automatic discovery of experiment series is able to cover entries from multiple projects.

4.1 Experiment Clustering

To detect implicit experiment series, we used an unsupervised clustering algorithm on the data set in which every experiment constitutes one sample, described by the values of its attributes. We need to consider that the attributes constitute both nominally and ordinally scaled variables. For preprocessing, we removed operational data from our data set, i.e. removing user data and access rights, ids used for data identification and timestamps. Further, we did not take rarely used attributes into account and normalized the ordinally scaled values. We applied the K-Protype algorithm[2] [4], a combination of the K-Means algorithm for numerical attributes and the K-Modes algorithm for categorical ones. Table 1 provides an overview with an exemplary chosen $k = 6$. All experiments taken within one research project are all clustered into the same cluster, but also there are clusters of experiments from multiple research projects, as the number of clusters is smaller than those of the clusters. One can now look at each discovered cluster as a hither or hidden experiment series.

1	$11_{56}, 11_{58}, 11_{59}, 11_{60}, 11_{61}, 12_{62}, 12_{63}$
2	$4_{15}, 4_{16}, 4_{54}, 4_{55}, 10_{46}, 10_{47}, 10_{48}, 10_{49}, 10_{50}, 10_{51}, 10_{52}, 10_{53}$
3	$2_{2}, 2_{7}, 2_{8}, 2_{9}, 2_{10}, 2_{11}, 2_{12}$
4	$5_{13}, 5_{14}, 5_{18}, 5_{19}, 5_{20}, 5_{21}, 5_{22}, 5_{23}, 5_{24}, 5_{25}$
5	$6_{17}, 7_{30}, 7_{32}, 13_{64}, 13_{65}, 15_{66}, 16_{67}, 16_{68}, 16_{69}, 16_{70}, 16_{71}, 16_{72}, 16_{73}, 16_{74}$
6	$1_{1}, 1_{4}, 1_{5}, 1_{6}, 1_{34}, 1_{35}, 1_{36}, 1_{37}, 1_{38}, 1_{39}, 1_{40}, 1_{41}, 1_{42}, 1_{43}$

Table 1: The elements (project_id and experiment_id) of each cluster found with $k = 6$.

5 OVERVIEW & FUTURE WORK

In this work we introduced a library for scientific experiments based on an explicit experiment model. We evaluated this library with material scientist who used the system during their daily research. Automatically clustering of the data entered show, that the explicit model helps to gain new knowledge from the data. This information might be used in future applications of experiment similarity search already during the experiment planing phase. In future, we want to continue our work on data libraries based on explicit models and collect more data across multiple institutions to apply more advanced analyzing techniques. Further, we want to extend the underlying data model and include process information into the model to achieve more precise results. Since materials have different properties dependent on the temporal order of treatments, so that the analysis of the production process can be extended with process information to get more precise experiment similarities.

REFERENCES

[1] J. Rocha da Silva, J. Aguiar Castro, Cristina Ribeiro, and J. Correia Lopes. 2014. Dendro: Collaborative Research Data Management Built on Linked Open Data. In *The Semantic Web: ESWC 2014 Satellite Events (Lecture Notes in Computer Science)*. Springer, Cham, 483–487.

[2] Center for Open Science. 2018. The Open Science Framework. https://osf.io/. (2018).

[3] H. Grobe, M. Diepenbroek, N. Dittert, M. Reinke, and R. Sieger. 2006. Archiving and Distributing Earth-Science Data with the PANGAEA Information System. In *Antarctica*. Springer, Berlin, Heidelberg, 403–406.

[4] Zhexue Huang. 1997. Clustering Large Data Sets with Mixed Numeric and Categorical Values. In *In The First Pacific-Asia Conference on Knowledge Discovery and Data Mining*. 21–34.

[5] H. Pfeiffenberger. 2017. Data Publishing Und Open Access. In *Praxishandbuch Open Access*, Söllner, K. v. and Mittermaier, B. (Eds.). De Gruyter Saur, Berlin/Boston.

[6] Natalie J. Stanford, Katherine Wolstencroft, Martin Golebiewski, Renate Kania, Nick Juty, Christopher Tomlinson, Stuart Owen, Sarah Butcher, Henning Hermjakob, Nicolas Le Novère, Wolfgang Mueller, Jacky Snoep, and Carole Goble. 2015. The Evolution of Standards and Data Management Practices in Systems Biology. *Mol. Syst. Biol.* 11, 12 (2015).

[7] M. D. Wilkinson, M. Dumontier, I. J. Aalbersberg, G. Appleton, M. Axton, A. Baak, N. Blomberg, J. Boiten, L. Bonino da Silva Santos, P. E. Bourne, J. Bouwman, A-J. Brookes, T. Clark, M. Crosas, I. Dillo, O. Dumon, S. Edmunds, C. T. Evelo, R. Finkers, A. Gonzalez-Beltran, A. J. G. Gray, P. Groth, C. Goble, J. S. Grethe, J. Heringa, P. A. C. 't Hoen, Rob Hooft, T. Kuhn, R. Kok, J. Kok, S. J. Lusher, M. E. Martone, A. Mons, A. L. Packer, B. Persson, P. Rocca-Serra, M. Roos, R. van Schaik, S. Sansone, E. Schultes, T. Sengstag, T. Slater, G. Strawn, M. A. Swertz, M. Thompson, J. van der Lei, E.v. Mulligen, J. Velterop, A. Waagmeester, P. Wittenburg, K. Wolstencroft, J. Zhao, and B. Mons. 2016. The FAIR Guiding Principles for Scientific Data Management and Stewardship. *Scientific Data* 3 (2016).

[8] K. Wolstencroft, S. Owen, O. Krebs, O. Nguyen, N. J. Stanford, M. Golebiewski, A. Weidemann, M. Bittkowski, L. An, D. Shockley, J. L. Snoep, W. Mueller, and C. Goble. 2015. SEEK: A Systems Biology Data and Model Management Platform. *BMC Systems Biology* 9 (2015), 33.

[9] T. Wuest, R. Tinscher, R. Porzel, and K.-D. Thoben. 2014. Experimental Research Data Quality In Materials Science. *International Journal of Advanced Information Technology* 4, 6 (Dec. 2014), 1–18.

[1] available here: http://www.uni-bremen.de/infosys

[2] implementation available here: https://github.com/nicodv/kmodes

Surrogator: A Tool to Enrich a Digital Library with Open Access Surrogate Resources

T Y S S Santosh, Debarshi Kumar Sanyal, Plaban Kumar Bhowmick, Partha Pratim Das
Indian Institute of Technology Kharagpur, West Bengal – 721302, India
santoshtyss@gmail.com,debarshisanyal@gmail.com,plaban@cet.iitkgp.ac.in,ppd@cse.iitkgp.ac.in

ABSTRACT

Large digital libraries often index articles without curating their digital copies in their own repositories. Examples include the National Digital Library of India (NDLI) and ACM Digital Library. Full text view generally requires subscription to libraries that host the contents. The problem is particularly severe for researchers, given high journal subscription charges. However, authors often keep a free copy in preprint servers. Sometimes a conference paper behind a paywall has a closely resembling journal version freely available on the Web. These open access surrogates are immensely valuable to researchers who cannot afford to access the original publications. We present a lightweight tool called Surrogator to automatically identify open access surrogates of access-restricted scholarly papers present in a digital library. Its focus on approximate matches makes it different from many existing applications. In this poster, we describe the design and interface of the tool and our initial experiences of using it on articles indexed in NDLI.

CCS CONCEPTS

• **Information systems** → *Search interfaces*; *Near-duplicate and plagiarism detection*; • **Applied computing** → **Digital libraries and archives**;

KEYWORDS

open access; surrogate; digital library; academic search engine

ACM Reference Format:
T Y S S Santosh, Debarshi Kumar Sanyal, Plaban Kumar Bhowmick, Partha Pratim Das. 2018. Surrogator: A Tool to Enrich a Digital Library with Open Access Surrogate Resources. In *JCDL '18: The 18th ACM/IEEE Joint Conference on Digital Libraries, June 3–7, 2018, Fort Worth, TX, USA.* ACM, New York, NY, USA, 2 pages. https://doi.org/10.1145/3197026.3203877

1 INTRODUCTION

It is common to find a digital library that indexes articles without archiving their digital copies in its own repository. Examples include the ACM Digital Library[1] and the National Digital Library of India (NDLI) [2]. For most resources, NDLI curates only metadata and directs the user to the repository that hosts the content. The repository might impose access toll on the user. The problem is particularly severe in research publications and in developing countries like India where a large section of academia cannot afford the exorbitant costs of journal subscription. Paywalls are also a handicap when scientists are outside their institutional networks.

In this poster, we present a highly customizable lightweight tool called Surrogator that identifies open access (OA) surrogates of scholarly publications. In this paper, *OA* means free to read and download and hereafter, *surrogate* means OA surrogate. Given a scholarly article, we define its *surrogate* intuitively as an article that closely resembles it in content and is written by the same authors or the same group. These surrogates may not be identical to the actual publications but prove helpful to researchers who cannot afford the published titles. For example, an extended journal paper, a technical report or a PhD thesis can be surrogates of a conference paper. Our tool is different from an academic search engine like Google Scholar[3] (hereafter, Scholar) because the latter normally tags an article with its OA copy only if the latter matches *exactly* in title and author whereas we aim at an intelligent approximate match. Manual filtering through a search engine's results can lead one to surrogates but it is an arduous process which our tool automates. Applications like OA Button[4] find OA articles but they expect a precise query like citation or DOI while our tool supports keyword-based query. We present the architecture and core algorithm of Surrogator. It is a highly extended version of [4]. This new version supports many configurable parameters and more precise comparison of articles. Our experiments suggest it can be used to identify surrogates for scholarly articles in a digital library.

2 WHAT IS A SURROGATE?

Given an article d, we define its *surrogate* article d_s as an article that is open access and satisfies one of the following properties. The properties are sorted from exact match to most inexact match, in the sense that higher the position of a property that d_s satisfies, higher is the precision of match. **Properties:** (1) d and d_s are the same articles. (2) d and d_s have the same authors, title and content but might be present in different repositories. (3) d and d_s have the same authors and slight variations in title and/or content. (4) d and d_s have slight variations in authors and same title and content. (5) d and d_s have slight variations in authors and slight variations in title and/or content. The definition of *slight variation* may vary with user requirements, document types and attributes (e.g., author lists should generally show smaller variation than title). We call surrogates in (1) and (2) above *exact matches* and the rest *near matches*.

[1] `https://dl.acm.org/`
[2] `https://ndl.iitkgp.ac.in/`
[3] `https://scholar.google.com/`
[4] `https://openaccessbutton.org/`

JCDL '18, June 3–7, 2018, Fort Worth, TX, USA

ACM ISBN 978-1-4503-5178-2/18/06.
https://doi.org/10.1145/3197026.3203877

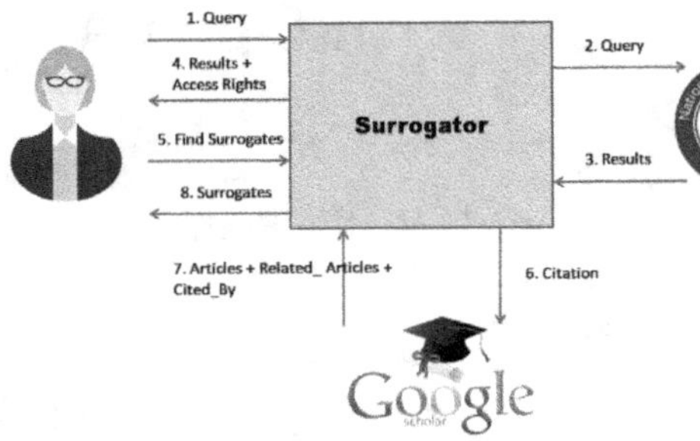

Figure 1: Surrogator: Interaction between user, Surrogator, source digital library (NDLI) and Scholar

3 SYSTEM AND ALGORITHM

System: Surrogator is implemented as a GUI-based tool in Python. Fig. 1 shows the workflow. The GUI is visible in Fig. 2. It's input comprises keywords, source name (like NDLI or Google Scholar) and a set of options (e.g., to look for exact match or near match). Surrogator forwards the query to the source, tags each retrieved result as either access-restricted or OA, and displays the tagged results. For NDLI, access permissions can be learned from the metadata of a result. For access-controlled articles, it allows the user to search for surrogates – either exact matches (on author and title) or near matches. The list of sources is controlled due to their varied interfaces which affect the page scraper. The GUI allows a user to upvote or downvote a displayed surrogate.

Algorithm: Our core algorithm to identify surrogates for a given article takes as input a citation (bibtex)[5] c and outputs a set S_c (possibly empty) of surrogate objects of c. Each surrogate object is a 3-tuple (c_i, l_i, oa_i) where c_i is a citation, l_i is a URL to its copy in a repository (might be behind a paywall), and oa_i is a URL to its OA full text. Surrogator relies heavily on Scholar due to Scholar's large coverage [1]. Surrogator first directs the query to Scholar and finds the result c' on the first page that best matches c (typically, the topmost result). If it links to an OA copy, it is returned. Otherwise, we heuristically define a search space $R = R_1 \cup R_2$ where the set R_1 is the set of articles cited by c' and R_2 the set of related articles of c' (as available in Scholar). We retain the top Q results (according to the order in Scholar) from each of R_1 and R_2 since they are huge. Then, we select the articles published within $YMAX$ years of c'. We retain only the articles with non-zero Jaccard similarity in author names ('initials lastname' when fullname is absent) with c'. We rank these articles based on a weighted average of their author similarity, cosine similarity of title (modeled as bag-of-words) and optionally, similarity of abstracts[6]. We extract abstracts from Semantic Scholar[7] since Scholar displays only part of the abstract and also throttles bulk requests. Abstracts may be compared either with cosine similarity of sentence vectors (using embeddings generated by neural networks, in our case `fastText` [2]) or Word Mover's Distance (WMD) [3]. Finally, we return the top K articles[8].

[5]Here, citation refers to a bibliographic reference normally found at the end of a paper.
[6]Weights are chosen heuristically: [without abstracts] authors: 0.6, title: 0.4; [with abstracts] authors: 0.5, title: 0.4, abstract: 0.1.
[7]`https://www.semanticscholar.org/`
[8]Q, $YMAX$, K are inputs.

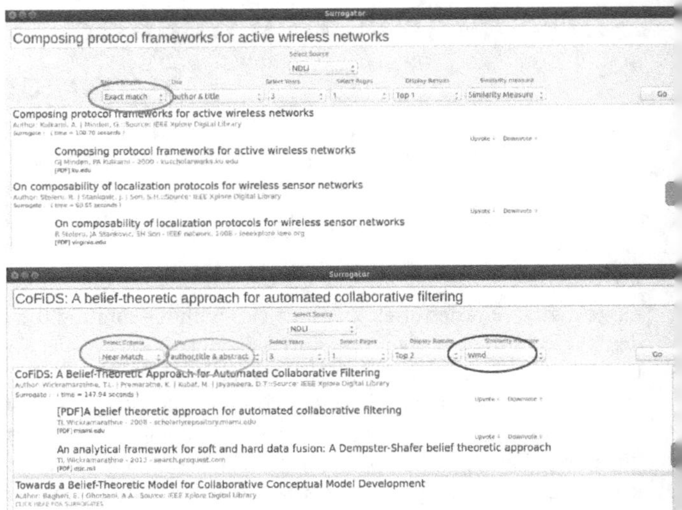

Figure 2: Surrogator retrieves exact match (top) and near match using WMD for abstract-comparison (bottom) for articles in NDLI. In both cases, $Q = 10$ (i.e., first page of Scholar results), $YMAX = 3$; $K = 1$ (top) and $K = 2$ (bottom).

4 EVALUATION

We used Surrogator on 120 references of Computer and Electrical Engineering papers. We set $Q = 10, YMAX = 3, K = 1$. Surrogator returned 76 exact match surrogates. In the remainder, it identified 44 near matches (note: for them, Scholar returns no OA copy). They were evaluated by two computer science graduates; in their overlapping choices, 31 (=70%) were marked very relevant, 6 non-relevant and the rest partially relevant[9]. Apparently, comparison of abstracts has little effect because author and title similarities already reduce the search space considerably.

5 CONCLUSION

We presented a customizable application to identify surrogates for access-restricted research publications in a digital library. Although tested on NDLI, it can be easily extended to any digital library. Comprehensive evaluation and enhancement of the tool are in progress.

ACKNOWLEDGMENTS

This work is supported by *Development of National Digital Library of India as a National Knowledge Asset of the Nation* sponsored by Ministry of Human Resource Development, Government of India.

REFERENCES

[1] G Halevi, H Moed, and J Bar-Ilan. 2017. Suitability of Google Scholar as a source of scientific information and as a source of data for scientific evaluation – Review of the Literature. *Journal of Informetrics* 11, 3 (2017), 823–834.
[2] A Joulin, E Grave, P Bojanowski, and T Mikolov. 2017. Bag of Tricks for Efficient Text Classification. In *EACL*, Vol. 2. 427–431.
[3] M Kusner, Y Sun, N Kolkin, and K Weinberger. 2015. From word embeddings to document distances. In *ICML*. 957–966.
[4] T Y S S Santosh, D K Sanyal, and P K Bhowmick. 2018. Surrogator: Enriching a digital library with open access surrogates. In *(Demo track) ACM CoDS-COMAD.*

[9]Detailed test results: `https://github.com/dksanyal/Surrogator`

Digital Library Systems in Intelligent Infrastructure for Human-Centered Communities: A Qualitative Research

Yi Shen
Virginia Polytechnic Institute and State University
yishen18@vt.edu

ABSTRACT

This poster[1] presents a socio-technical qualitative research on the strategic development of Intelligent Infrastructure for Human Centered Communities at Virginia Tech. Within such development, this study explored the future vision and projective scenarios of data infrastructure and digital libraries for smart community development. The results augment design thinking and visioning practice for digital library systems beyond traditional boundaries.

KEYWORDS

Intelligent infrastructure; smart communities; library vision and concepts; smart library scenarios; data infrastructure

ACM Reference format:

Yi Shen. 2018. SIG Proceedings Paper in word Format. In *Proceedings of ACM JCDL conference, Fort Worth, Texas USA, June 2018 (JCDL'18)*, 2 pages. https://doi.org/10.1145/3197026.3203894

1 INTRODUCTION

Today, a confluence of technological advances, such as ubiquitous mobility, networked sensors, and artificial intelligence, marks the advent of a new era with smart infrastructures. "The separation between cyber, physical, and social systems is blurring" [1]. More objects and devices are connected to digital networks, with the ability to sense their environments and both generate and communicate information. This massive number of "smart" objects, devices, and sensors will "cooperate with each other, have their own metadata, and continuously produce new data" [2].

As smart infrastructure agenda proliferates, higher education institutions are undergoing important transformations to converge intellectual domains and seek transdisciplinary solutions in this highly competitive area of global future. Virginia Tech is riding this wave of evolution by leveraging and connecting its leading programs in smart design and construction, energy, robotics and autonomous vehicle systems, ubiquitous mobility, and materials through an integrated area of development, named Intelligent Infrastructure for Human-Centered Communities (IIHCC) [3].

Academic libraries are at the nexus of big data, smart technologies, and data-driven governance and have an important role to play in accelerating and coordinating the development of smart infrastructure. As the data landscape evolves rapidly and transforms disruptively, it is critical for libraries to begin re-imagining their future and re-visioning the architecture for the age of smartness. With such goals in mind, this work raises and addresses the following timely and critical research questions: (1) What are the implications of intelligent infrastructure for digital library systems? (2) What are the future vision and anticipated scenarios for smart digital libraries? Altogether, this study presents a schematic view of how the IIHCC evolution shapes and organizes new library infrastructure and how a smart library system can mobilize the IIHCC advancement.

2 METHODS

This research employs document analysis, ethnographic participant observation, and semi-structured interviews. The document analysis covers IIHCC-relevant progress reports and stage updates as well as press release and media coverage from the spring of 2016 when the IIHCC initiative was launched throughout 2017 when this research was performed. For ethnographic participant observation, the Principal Investigator (PI) participated in various IIHCC-related town-hall meetings, information sessions, and open forums, while observing the interaction and participating in ongoing dialogue. The PI also conducted in-depth semi-structured interviews with nine stakeholders leading and charging the IIHCC planning and development. The study follows a carefully designed interview protocol by employing the qualitative methods outlined by Creswell [4] and Yin [5] and using the critical incident technique of Flanagan [6], with emphasis on typical scenarios, practical examples, and the significant experience of human subjects. Through the mixed-methods approach and triangulation of evidence, this research produces results that augment design thinking and visioning practice for digital libraries beyond traditional boundaries.

3 RESULTS AND DISCUSSION

3.1 Complex Adaptive Systems

When asked how they envision the different areas of expertise converge through IIHCC, the participants described a system view of infrastructure with "physical interdependencies" coupled with "human mediated interactions." In their views, the infrastructure building is centered around empowering communities with the structure and ability to engage in meaningful and efficient ways with their environments. Such transformation promises improved wellbeing and prosperity.

JCDL'18, June 3-7, 2018, Fort Worth, TX, USA

ACM ISBN 978-1-4503-5178-2/18/06.
https://doi.org/10.1145/3197026.3203894

Smart infrastructures, consisting of massive numbers of heterogeneous components, feature complex interactions among them and with humans. These complex systems will be "equipped with dynamic and autonomous adaptation capabilities to deal with changes in their working environments and within themselves" [7]. Data mobilization thus will be at the center of it all.

As a complex adaptive system itself, digital library should be an integral part of the infrastructure that provides intelligence in data gathering and processing. Such scenario increasingly requires the adoption of "smart design and construction" concept in library architecture that is capable of learning and analyzing human information behaviours and making recommendations for new data gathering.

3.2 Intelligent Data Infrastructure

The dynamic and diverse nature of infrastructure data requires different data management techniques and advanced processing methods. New research scenarios especially involve live streaming of traffic, energy, building, or other infrastructure data. They are often characterized by on-the-fly data processing, visual interaction, computational manipulation, and analytical capabilities. These featured scenarios are time sensitive and require rapid throughput and quick turnaround of data workflows. Typical of a self-adaptive system, the associated data infrastructure thus needs to perform context-aware and agile management of content, from automatically harvesting real time data, to algorithm-powered first level processing, to smart recommendations for further investigation, all of which constitute an intelligent data lifecycle.

The participants further anticipated a highly streamlined and cognitively magnified data platform that is equipped with high-performance processing and multispectral visualizing, sensing, and interacting capabilities. In their views, it is capable of "smart data" searching, mining, and drilling from big data. Also, the associated documentation practice needs to be flexible and reliable, speaking authentically to the data in real time and reflecting faithfully to changes on the fly, all by a living document of track records.

In this emerging enterprise, the IIHCC data infrastructure needs to be scalable and resilient in and of itself. It needs orchestration software that can integrate the diverse set of infrastructure-enabled data assets into a cohesive process, so that human agents can focus on running the business of discovery and innovation, not manually managing data bits[8].

3.3 Future Scenarios of Smart Digital Library

Three main concepts of smart digital library emerged from the interviewees' responses, including the digital octopus concept, smart village concept, and virtual assistant concept. In the digital octopus analogy, a "library in its conceptual way of being the place where data and information is generated, stored, curated, accessed" is virtually embedded everywhere in research spaces. Having the library acting like an octopus, with its "tentacles" reaching far out and its functions embedded deep in wherever data is created, all the scientists are virtually participants in this library, "building out data, curating it, and adding to the large system."

In the smart village view, where a village represents "smart construction and the city of the future," the library will be the "heart" of all the data, bridging gaps between users situated on the different spectrum and dimensionality of data workflows. It will function as a central hub for data gathering, processing, sharing, computing, and communicating. "Playing the spectrum" and encompassing different layers, the library will work to bring connections, deliver unified and personalized experience, and inspire creative synergies.

In the virtual assistant concept, the library will have specialized navigation and suggestion systems that are capable of proactively "pushing" knowledge to users and providing personalized references. Echoing the growing adoption of AI-powered virtual assistant technology, the participants expected such breakthrough to help reduce information overload and improve productivity by automatically reviewing a history of research themes and providing a global sense of the documents.

4 CONCLUSIONS

In this integrated system, users will experience live streaming of the infrastructure data and perform on-the-fly data processing, computational manipulation, and visual interaction. With relevant data and desired information automatically and systematically pushed to them, users receive personalized information summary and customized recommendations on research gaps, needed data, or new hypotheses. Scientists perform on-premises data ingestion, curation, and storage, and continuously contribute knowledge back to the system. Future digital library, whether in its conceptual form of a digital octopus, or a smart village data hub, or an intelligent virtual assistant, is an integral part of this infrastructure. It will provide intelligence in data gathering, processing, summarizing, and recommendation, and by delivering unified and personalized data solutions, it will offer an end-to-end seamless experience for users and learners throughout their journey of knowledge pursuit.

REFERENCES

[1] The ACM/IEEE International Conference on Internet of Things Design and Implementation (IoTDI). http://conferences.computer.org/IoTDI/
[2] International Workshop on Very Large Internet of Things (VLIoT 2017). https://www.ifis.uni-luebeck.de/~groppe/vliot/2017
[3] Virginia Tech Office of the Executive Vice President and Provost. 2017. Destination Areas. https://www.provost.vt.edu/destination-areas/da-overview/da-infrastructure.html
[4] John W. Creswell. 2013. Qualitative Inquiry and Research Design: Choosing among Five Approaches. London: Sage Publications.
[5] Robert K. Yin 1994. Case Study Research: Design and Methods. 2nd ed. Thousand Oaks, CA: Sage Publications.
[6] John C. Flanagan. 1954. The Critical Incident Technique. Psychological Bulletin, 51(4), 327-359.
[7] The 33rd ACM Symposium on Applied Computing: Special Track on Collective and Cooperative Systems: Aims and Scope. http://sac-cas2018.apice.unibo.it/cfp.html
[8] Gil Press. 2017.10 Predictions for the Internet of Things in 2018. Forbes.

Methodological Considerations in Developing Cultural Heritage Digital Libraries: A Community-driven Framework

Ali Shiri
University of Alberta, Canada
ashiri@ualberta.ca

ABSTRACT

We present a multi-disciplinary methodological framework that was developed to create the Digital Library North for Inuit communities in Canada's north. The framework adopts a holistic approach, taking into account existing physical and digital collections, information search behaviour of community members, culturally appropriate metadata, usability and sustainability. The methodological framework provides an empirically-supported model for developing community-focused digital libraries.

KEYWORDS

Digital libraries, Inuit communities, Canada

ACM Reference Format:

Ali Shiri. 2018. Methodological Considerations in Developing Cultural Heritage Digital Libraries: A Community-driven Framework. In JCDL '18: The 18th ACM/IEEE Joint Conference on Digital Libraries, June 3–7, 2018, Fort Worth, TX, USA. ACM, New York, NY, USA, 2 pages. https://doi.org/10.1145/3197026.3203895

1. INTRODUCTION

Lynch notes that digital libraries are not only collections of content and tools that build communities, they also allow members of communities to communicate and talk to each other [1]. Research on cultural heritage digital libraries has largely focused on such aspects as digitization, preservation, metadata, user interface design, repository, hardware and software components and interoperability [2-3]. Studies have investigated the information search behaviour of cultural heritage digital library users [4]. Fox [5] views societies as the highest-level component of a digital library, which exists to serve the information needs of its societies. European cultural heritage digital library projects point to the importance of community watch and participation in the creation and curation of digital content and call for new methodologies that cross disciplines [6]. Srinivasan argues that "acknowledging the cultural practices and belief systems of a set of users may allow systems to be more effectively created and deployed" and that involving community leaders and persuading them to join to lead the project is important [7]. However, there is limited research on multidisciplinary approaches to developing digital libraries, particularly for aboriginal and northern communities.

JCDL '18, June 3–7, 2018, Fort Worth, TX, USA

ACM ISBN 978-1-4503-5178-2/18/06.
https://doi.org/10.1145/3197026.3203893

The Digital Library North (DLN) was a three-year research project funded by the Social Sciences and Humanities Research council of Canada that developed a digital library for the Inuvialuit Settlement Region (ISR) for Inuit communities in Canada's north. This paper presents the methodological framework that was developed in order to introduce a multidisciplinary and multi-method approach to the development of a cultural heritage digital library for Inuit communities.

2. GEOGRAPHIC/CULTRAL CONTEXT

The DLN project focused on the Inuvialuit Settlement Region (ISR), comprising six communities: Paulatuk, Ulukhaktok, Sachs Harbour, Tuktoyaktuk, Inuvik and Aklavik. The ISR region was created in 1984 with the signing of the Inuvialuit Final Agreement between the Government of Canada and the Inuit of Canada's Western Arctic, in part to preserve Inuvialuit cultural identity and values and enable Inuvialuit to be 'equal and meaningful participants' in the Northern and national economy and society. The languages spoken in the ISR are Gwich'in and Inuvialuktun. The DLN project developed a digital library that could serve as a model for northern and remote regions.

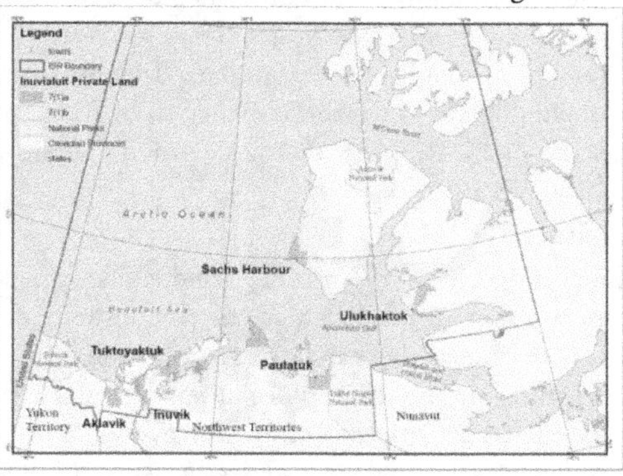

Figure 1. Inuvialuit Settlement Region (Credit: IRC)

3. METHODOLOGICAL FRAMEWORK

A detailed methodological framework was developed in order to take into account information seeking and use, digital library design, metadata design, language as well as how community engagement and partnership should be conceptualized and operationalized in a research project. This project adopted a multi-method research framework (figure 2) to identify, engage with and study northern communities as a critical success factor for developing a culturally appropriate and relevant digital library. The framework provides an inclusive and holistic framework that draws upon multiple methodologies and has actively involved numerous community leaders, members and organizations. It draws upon the approaches, methodologies and theoretical frameworks from such diverse disciplines as business, organizational information systems, social sciences, cultural anthropology, community informatics as well as LIS.

3.1 Environmental scanning

Environmental scanning is an important initial step to identify key users, communities, stakeholders and information providers. It is a method of becoming aware of the factors external to an organization that can affect the operations. In this project we have adapted existing models of environmental scanning to create a new model that suits the development of a digital library [8].

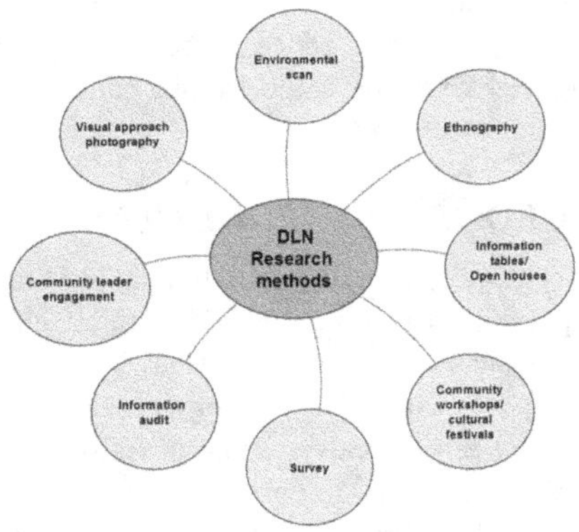

Figure 2. Digital Library North Methods

3.2 Open House: Formative usability

An open house was held at Inuvialuit Cultural Resource Centre (ICRC) to allow community members to flexibly attend the DLN usability study. The project team provided bannock and soup for participants to create a friendly and inviting environment. The use of informal ways to collect usability data allowed the DLN team to interact with a larger number of community members.

3.3 Surveys

Online and print surveys were conducted with community members in order to reach out to the remote ISR communities. The print version of the survey was distributed only in Inuvik through setting information tables at various locations (e.g. the Public Library, recreation centre) and events (Inuvialuit Day, Open Houses at ICRC and trade classes at Aurora College).

3.4 Community leader engagement

The Manager of the ICRC was instrumental in forming research partnerships with ISR communities and facilitated the involvement and participation of members, especially elders, in the focus groups and interviews. Our community partner was particularly influential in prioritizing useful types of online resources that formed parts of the content of the digital library.

3.5 Information audit

The research team conducted both formal and informal information audits to understand the overall nature of information resources within the ISR region. There are a wide variety of materials, such as language resources, oral history files, photographs of people and cultural artefacts, genealogy documents, Inuvialuktun language resources, dictionaries, materials for school children and for those studying trades, audios and videos, and meeting minutes.

3.6 Community workshops

Researchers participated in various community workshops such as mitt-making and bannock making classes. The research team also held various community demonstrations of the digital library in the six mentioned communities to familiarize them with and seek feedback on the digital library and its content.

3.7 Visual approach: Photography

Given the importance of gaining a proper understanding of the geographic, cultural, social and environmental context of the ISR region, the team made use of photography as a key data gathering method throughout the project, capturing a broad range of material culture, geographic landscapes, and cultural festivals.

4. CONCLUSION

Developing cultural heritage digital libraries for northern and indigenous communities requires a diverse methodological framework that is culturally-aware and appropriate. The key lessons learned in the DLN project include: a) environmental scanning facilitates cultural, social, political, economic, geographic and technological exploration of Inuit communities; b) community engagement and partnership is key; and c) the DLN framework allows for a more inclusive approach to the development of community-driven digital libraries and repositories for Inuit, indigenous communities.

5. REFERENCES

[1] Lynch, C. 2002. Digital collections, digital libraries & the digitization of cultural heritage information. *Microform & imaging review*, *31*(4), 131-145.

[2] Crane, G., & Wulfman, C. 2003. Towards a cultural heritage digital library. In *Proceedings of the 3rd ACM/IEEE-CS joint conference on Digital libraries* (pp. 75-86). IEEE Computer Society.

[3] Ruthven, I., & Chowdhury, G. G. (Eds.). (2015). *Cultural Heritage Information: Access and Management*. Facet.

[4] Suire, Cyrille, et al. 2016. User activity characterization in a cultural heritage digital library system. In *2016 IEEE/ACM Joint Conference on Digital Libraries (JCDL)*, (pp.257-258).

[5] Fox, E. A., Goncalves, M. A., & Shen, R. (2012). Theoretical foundations for digital libraries: The 5S (societies, scenarios, spaces, structures, streams) approach. *Synthesis Lectures on Information Concepts, Retrieval, and Services*, *4*(2), 1-180.

[6] Aparac-Jelušić, T. (2017). Digital Libraries for Cultural Heritage: Development, Outcomes, and Challenges from European Perspectives. *Synthesis Lectures on Information Concepts, Retrieval, and Services*, *9*(4), i-175.

[7] Srinivasan, R. 2007. Ethnomethodological architectures: Information systems driven by cultural and community visions. *Journal of the American Society for Information Science and Technology*, *58*(5), 723-733.

[8] Rathi, D., Shiri, A., & Cockney, C. 2017. Environmental scan: A methodological framework to initiate digital library development for communities in Canada's North. *Aslib Journal of Information Management*, *69* (1), pp. 76 - 94.

Using Social Media and Scholarly Text to Predict Public Understanding of Science

Harish Varma Siravuri
Northern Illinois University
DeKalb, Illinois
hsiravuri@niu.edu

Akhil Pandey Akella
Northern Illinois University
DeKalb, Illinois
aakella@niu.edu

Christian Bailey
Northern Illinois University
DeKalb, Illinois
cbailey10@niu.edu

Hamed Alhoori
Northern Illinois University
DeKalb, Illinois
alhoori@niu.edu

ABSTRACT

People often struggle to understand scientific texts, which leads to miscommunication and often to inaccurate and even sensationalistic reports of research. Identifying and achieving a better understanding of the factors that affect comprehension would be helpful to analyze what improves public understanding of science. In this study, we generate features from scientific text that represent some common text structures and use them to predict the semantic similarity between the scientific text and the textual content posted by the general public about the same scientific text online. In this endeavor, we built regression models to achieve this purpose and evaluated them based on their R-squared values and mean squared errors. R-squared values as high as 0.73 were observed, indicating a high chance of a relationship between certain textual features and the public's understanding of science.

KEYWORDS

Public Understanding of Science, Text Comprehension, Altmetrics

ACM Reference Format:
Harish Varma Siravuri, Akhil Pandey Akella, Christian Bailey, and Hamed Alhoori. 2018. Using Social Media and Scholarly Text to Predict Public Understanding of Science. In *JCDL '18: The 18th ACM/IEEE Joint Conference on Digital Libraries, June 3–7, 2018, Fort Worth, TX, USA*. ACM, New York, NY, USA, Article 4, 2 pages. https://doi.org/10.1145/3197026.3203890

1 BACKGROUND

1.1 Introduction

Promoting public understanding of science has always been an important consideration associated with the broader societal impact of research. Scientific literacy has been promoted as an important aspect of citizenship [6]. According to McGinn and Roth [5], scientific literacy is an important quality in promoting "good citizenship practices" such as participation in scientific laboratories, activist movements, the judicial system, and other communities. Further, scientific literacy is a significant driver of economic growth, and for this reason virtually every modern society has shown a commitment to promoting scientific study and determining the public's understanding of scientific discoveries and advances.

"The Public Understanding of Science" [1], a report published by the Royal Society, is widely considered to have given rise to the current interest in understanding and promoting scientific literacy. Interest in this area is fueled by the widely held belief that science will be the ultimate beneficiary of any gains in scientific literacy among the public [8]. In this regard, some studies investigate the relationship between textual complexity and reading comprehension [2, 9]. The existence of a similar relationship between scientific texts and public understanding of science would make it possible to identify research that is likely to be well understood by general readers.

In Conant's [3] view, there is a need to adopt scientific methodologies in order to promote critical and strategic thinking among the general public. A survey of students and teachers [10] suggests that there is a misapprehension about the purpose of scientific research among the general public. The previous study identifies the public's lack of understanding in regard to the purpose of science and offers the conclusion that the public would be well served if the purpose and place of science in society were clarified. However, merely promoting the purpose of science will not suffice: people need to read and understand scientific texts in order to understand the rationale underlying them and the relative validity of the results and their implications. Unfortunately, the vocabulary used in scientific texts is challenging to the general reader. Evans and Durant [4] proposed a two-dimensional structure for measuring civic scientific literacy, and Miller [7] suggested a three-dimensional structure to fulfill the same purpose. It is worth noting that in both of these studies, the concept for measuring civic scientific literacy includes the dimension of vocabulary as a basic scientific construct. Most previous studies focused on measuring or improving scientific comprehension rely on surveys using a sample of science students. In this study, we focused on examining readers' comprehension of the scientific text and predicting it based on various features derived from the text.

1.2 Data Collection

The data used in this study was obtained from Altmetric.com. The data includes information regarding online activity relating to 5.2

ACM ISBN 978-1-4503-5178-2/18/06.
https://doi.org/10.1145/3197026.3203890

million scholarly research outputs. Initial analysis showed that of the 5.2 million articles, over 1.7 million articles had been shared and talked about on blogs. We further randomly sampled 1% of the dataset and extracted text from the abstract section and the blog posts to build a smaller dataset consisting of 17,736 data points for further analysis. We used regular expressions to filter out texts that contained only hyperlinks to the scholarly text. Also, we removed textual content that exactly matched the title or sentences from the abstract to avoid any bias caused by social media content in which only the scholarly output is noted without an accompanying discussion of it.

2 METHODS

2.1 Feature Generation

We generated a set of five features - a target variable and four predictors - which we later used to build the regression models.

2.1.1 Target Variable. A 'comprehension score' that reflects the extent to which readers understood the scientific text. The target variable is representative of how semantically similar the text from the blogs is to the abstract. We used cosine similarity to compute the semantic similarity because the magnitude of the vectorized forms of words from either documents is significant. Using Euclidean distance instead of cosine similarity does not take this into consideration. Also, we used L2 normalization form instead of L1 normalization form for normalizing the vectors. The reason for this is we needed a single analytical solution while normalizing the vectors which could be achieved only by using L2 norm.

2.1.2 Predictors. We also generated the following four features using the scientific text to use as predictors in the regression models.

(1) Lexical diversity of the abstract - The ratio of unique word stems to the total words computed. It is an effective measure of the richness of vocabulary or verbal creativity of a text. We used Yules I measure [11] instead of a simple frequency-based measure, since it yields an unbiased result irrespective of the length of the text.
(2) Average word length - The mean of the number of characters in each word in the abstract.
(3) Average sentence length - The mean of the number of words in each sentence in the abstract.
(4) Frequency of words longer than the average word length - A measure of the number of long words that have more characters than the average word in the abstract.

2.2 Regression

Using the processed data, we built five regression models: Decision Tree Regressor, Random Forest Regressor with 100 estimators, Support Vector Regressor, KNN Regressor, and a Gradient Boost Regressor. The models used the predictors generated in 2.1.2 to to predict the the comprehension score calculated in 2.1.1. We evaluated the models based on their coefficient of determination (R squared values) and mean squared errors, as shown in Table 1.

The Decision Tree Regressor and the Random Forest Regressor were observed to perform best compared to the other models. We calculated the Gini importance of each feature for both models to determine the relative significance of each feature to the public understanding. The results are shown in Table 2.

Table 1: Coefficient of determination and mean squared errors for different models

	R Squared	Mean Squared Error
Decision Tree Regression	0.7356	0.01148
Random Forest Regression	0.6486	0.0074
Support Vector Regression	0.1202	0.0089
KNN Regression	0.0824	0.0074
Gradient Boost Regression	0.0609	0.0071

Table 2: Gini importance of each feature in respect to the Decision Tree and Random Forest Regressors

	Decision Tree	Random Forest
Lexical Diversity	0.2588	0.2657
Average Word Length	0.3122	0.2799
Average Sentence Length	0.2476	0.2622
Frequency of words longer than average word length	0.1815	0.1922

3 CONCLUSIONS AND FUTURE WORK

The results indicate the existence of a relationship between the scientific text and the public understanding of the text. The models establish a way to understand and predict how well readers are likely to comprehend a body of scientific text based solely on features derived from the text itself. In the future, we plan to augment the models using additional features and full texts instead of text drawn only from the abstract sections.

REFERENCES

[1] 1985. The Public Understanding of Science - Royal Society. (1985).
[2] Rebekah Georger Benjamin and Paula J Schwanenflugel. 2010. Text complexity and oral reading prosody in young readers. *Reading Research Quarterly* 45, 4 (2010), 388–404.
[3] James B. Conant. 1952. Science and Common Sense. *The Journal of Philosophy* 49, 1 (1952), 11–20.
[4] Geoffrey Evans and John Durant. 1995. The relationship between knowledge and attitudes in the public understanding of science in Britain. *Public Understanding of Science* 4, 1 (1995), 57–74.
[5] Michelle K. McGinn and Wolff-Michael Roth. 1999. Preparing Students for Competent Scientific Practice: Implications of Recent Research in Science and Technology Studies. *Educational Researcher* 28, 3 (1999), 14–24.
[6] Jon D. Miller. 1989. Scientific Literacy: A Conceptual and Empirical Review. *Daedalus* 112, 2 (1989), 29–48.
[7] Jon D Miller. 1998. The measurement of civic scientific literacy. *Public understanding of science* 7, 3 (1998), 203–223.
[8] Steve Miller. 2001. Public understanding of science at the crossroads. *Public Understanding of Science* 10, 1 (2001), 115–120.
[9] Sanja Stajner, Richard Evans, Constantin Orasan, and Mitkov Ruslan. 2012. What can readability measures really tell us about text complexity. In *Proceedings of the Workshop on Natural Language Processing for Improving Textual Accessibility.*
[10] Leland L. Wilson. 1954. A study of opinions related to the nature of science and its purpose in society. *Science Education* 38, 2 (1954), 159–164.
[11] G. Udny Yule. 1912. On the Methods of Measuring Association Between Two Attributes. *Journal of the Royal Statistical Society* 75, 6 (1912), 579–652.

Who Did What? Identifying Author Contributions in Biomedical Publications using Naïve Bayes

Dominika Tkaczyk
ADAPT Centre, School of Computer Science and Statistics
Trinity College Dublin, Ireland
Dominika.Tkaczyk@adaptcentre.ie

Andrew Collins
ADAPT Centre, School of Computer Science and Statistics
Trinity College Dublin, Ireland
Andrew.Collins@adaptcentre.ie

Joeran Beel
ADAPT Centre, School of Computer Science and Statistics
Trinity College Dublin, Ireland
Joeran.Beel@adaptcentre.ie

ABSTRACT

Creating scientific publications is a complex process. It is composed of a number of different activities, such as designing the experiments, analyzing the data, and writing the manuscript. Information about the contributions of individual authors of a paper is important for assessing authors' scientific achievements. Some biomedical publications contain a short section written in natural language, which describes the roles each author played in the process of preparing the article. In this paper, we present a study of authors' roles commonly appearing in these sections, and propose an algorithm for automatic extraction of authors' roles from them. In our study, we used co-clustering techniques, as well as Open Information Extraction, to semi-automatically discover the most popular roles within a corpus of contributions sections. In total 13 roles were discovered, three of which (paper revision, literature review, and interpretation) are not described by existing author role taxonomies. Discovered roles are then used to automatically build a training set for a supervised Naïve Bayes role extractor. The proposed role extractor is able to extract roles from the text with micro-averaged precision 0.68, recall 0.48 and F1 0.57.

CCS CONCEPTS

• **Information systems → Information systems applications**; *Digital libraries and archives*

KEYWORDS

document analysis, author contributions, semantic publishing

This publication has emanated from research conducted with the financial support of Science Foundation Ireland (SFI) under Grant Number 13/RC/2016. The project has also received funding from the European Union's Horizon 2020 research and innovation programme under the Marie Skłodowska-Curie grant agreement No 713567.

JCDL '18, June 3–7, 2018, Fort Worth, TX, USA

ACM ISBN 978-1-4503-5178-2/18/06.
https://doi.org/10.1145/3197026.3203907

ACM Reference format:

D. Tkaczyk, A. Collins, and J. Beel. 2018. Who Did What? Identifying Author Contributions in Biomedical Publications using Naïve Bayes. In *Proceedings of ACM JCDL, Fort Worth, Texas USA, June 2018 (JCDL'18)*, 2 pages. https://doi.org/10.1145/3197026.3203907

1 INTRODUCTION

Authorship is an important concept in scholarly communication. It allows people to credit those who have contributed to scientific discoveries, and is widely used to assess people's scientific achievements. However, authorship of papers gives only a partial picture. To evaluate researcher's achievements, it is useful to know the nature of their contributions to the authored papers.

Some biomedical publications contain sections that describe the roles each author played in performing the research and creating the paper. These sections are usually written in natural language and entitled "Authors' contributions" (Figure 1). Examples of authors' roles include: preparing the data, designing the experiments, analyzing the data, writing the manuscript.

Authors' contributions
AJ-M, HT, YS and RS carried out the IHC analysis. AJ-M, MN-M, MPU, V-MK and AM participated in study design and statistical analysis. AJ-M and MN-M drafted the manuscript. All authors read and approved the final manuscript.

Figure 1: Example of "Authors' contributions" section.

Unfortunately, authors' contributions sections, written in natural language, are unstructured and intended for humans rather than machines. Consequently, analysis of this information requires time-consuming manual work, which makes processing large collections of documents impractical. We address these issues by proposing: 1) a semi-automatic method for discovering common roles in a corpus of sections, and 2) an algorithm to automatically extract the roles from unstructured text.

2 RELATED WORK

The task of automatic extraction of author contributions directly from scientific papers has not been approached so far by researchers, to the best of our knowledge. Even though information extraction from scientific literature is a popular research area, resulting in tools such as CERMINE [1], GROBID [2], ParsCit [3], Science Parse[2] and Docear PDF Inspector [4], none of

[2] https://github.com/allenai/science-parse

them is currently able to extract author contribution information.

There is no globally accepted standard for scientific contributor roles. Typically, authors just mention the roles they believe are important. There exists a manually created taxonomy of 14 scientific contributor roles called CRediT[3]. Our study, however, does not assume any input taxonomy.

3 METHODOLOGY

A typical authors' contributions section contains several mentions of roles of individual authors. *Role mentions* are expressions of *roles* (abstract concepts) in natural language. The same abstract role (e.g. data analysis) can be expressed by many different role mentions (e.g. "X analyzed microarray sequences", "X was involved in data analysis"). In our study, we represent role mentions as 3-element tuples containing: 1) subject: "who", usually author name or initials, 2) action: activity, often a verb phrase, 3) object: "what the action was applied to", typically a noun phrase.

In the first part of the study, we used Open Information Extraction [5], as well as co-clustering techniques to semi-automatically discover roles common for biomedical publications. We analyzed a corpus of 2,000 contributions sections from PubMed Central Open Access Subset[4], with the following steps:

1. We used OpenIE to automatically extract role mentions in the form of tuples from the sections. These mentions were then cleaned, stemmed and normalized.
2. Role mentions were automatically clustered in order to find common abstract roles in the corpus. Co-clustering was applied simultaneously to actions and objects of the mentions, with the similarity based on their words and action-object co-occurrence relations (i.e. how often action and object appear together in the same role mention). The final clusters represent abstract roles, i.e. each cluster contains all the mentions of the role it represents.
3. Clusters were manually examined and corrected. This included removing some clusters and merging others. We also assigned a role name to each cluster.

In the second part of the study, we built an automated role extractor, using previously discovered roles. The extractor expects a contributions section as input. The section undergoes preprocessing: the role mentions are extracted, cleaned and normalized. Each mention is then classified into a role using a supervised Naïve Bayes classifier. The training set was automatically built from clusters resulting from the first part of the study. The classifier uses a binary bag-of-words representation, where the words are the most frequent non-stopword terms found in the training set.

4 RESULTS

During the first part of the study, 13 abstract roles were discovered: *experimenting* (1,743 instances, 17% of the entire role set), *analysis* (1,343, 16%), *study design* (1,132, 13%), *interpretation* (879, 10%), *conceptualization* (865, 10%), *paper reading* (823, 10%), *paper writing* (724, 8%), *paper review* (501, 6%), *paper drafting* (351, 4%), *coordination* (319, 4%), *data collection* (76, 1%), *paper revision* (41, 0.5%) and *literature review* (41, 0.5%). *Paper revision, literature review,* and *interpretation,* are newly discovered roles that are not included in the CRediT taxonomy.

In order to evaluate the extractor, we manually annotated a test set of 100 contributions sections. For each section, a set of author-role pairs was provided. We found three roles not discovered before: *paper approving, supervision* and *funding acquisition.* We obtained the following micro-averaged results: precision 0.68, recall 0.48, F1 0.57. Table 1 shows the results for each role.

Table 1: Precision, recall and F1 for individual roles.

Role	Precision	Recall	F1
Analysis	.91	.53	.67
Conceptualization	.75	.50	.60
Experimenting	.22	.80	.34
Study design	.77	.60	.67
Coordination	1.0	.35	.52
Data collection	.58	.56	.57
Paper drafting	.87	.54	.66
Paper writing	.61	.41	.49
Paper review	.95	.50	.66
Paper revision	.93	.31	.46
Paper reading	.81	.85	.83
Literature review	.91	.83	.87
Interpretation	.90	.51	.65

5 SUMMARY

In this paper, we presented a study of a collection of authors' contributions sections from biomedical publications. The results of our study include: 1) a set of roles semi-automatically discovered in the section corpus in an unsupervised manner, 2) an approach for automatic extraction of the roles from unstructured contributions sections. In our data, we semi-automatically discovered three author roles not included in existing taxonomies: *paper revision, literature review,* and *interpretation.* The proposed role extractor is able to extract roles directly from the text with micro-averaged precision 0.68, recall 0.48 and F1 0.57.

REFERENCES

[1] D. Tkaczyk, P. Szostek, M. Fedoryszak, P. Dendek and L. Bolikowski, "CERMINE: automatic extraction of structured metadata from scientific literature," *International Journal on Document Analysis and Recognition,* vol. 18, no. 4, pp. 317-335, 2015.

[2] P. Lopez, "GROBID: combining automatic bibliographic data recognition and term extraction for scholarship publications," *Research and Advanced Technology for Digital Libraries,* pp. 473-474, 2009.

[3] I. Councill, C. Giles and M.-Y. Kan, "ParsCit: an open-source CRF reference string parsing package," in *International Conference on Language Resources and Evaluation,* 2008.

[4] J. Beel, S. Langer, M. Genzmehr and C. Mueller, "Docear's PDF Inspector: Title Extraction from PDF Files," in *ACM/IEEE-CS Joint Conference on Digital Libraries,* 2013.

[5] G. Angeli, M. J. J. Premkumar and C. D. Manning, "Leveraging Linguistic Structure For Open Domain Information Extraction," in *ACL,* 2015.

[3] http://dictionary.casrai.org/Contributor_Roles
[4] https://www.ncbi.nlm.nih.gov/pmc/tools/openftlist/

Entity Name Extraction from Faculty Directories

João Mateus de Freitas Veneroso
Universidade Federal de Minas Gerais
Belo Horizonte, MG, Brazil
jmfveneroso@gmail.com

Berthier Ribeiro-Neto
Universidade Federal de Minas Gerais & Google Engineering
Belo Horizonte, MG, Brazil
berthier@dcc.ufmg.br
berthier@google.com

ABSTRACT

Public bibliographic databases hold invaluable data about the academic environment. However, researcher affiliation information is frequently missing or outdated. We propose a statistical data extraction method to acquire affiliation information directly from university websites and solve the name extraction task in general. Previous approaches to web data extraction either lack in flexibility, because wrappers do not generalize well across websites, or they lack in precision, because domain agnostic methods neglect useful properties of this particular application domain. Our statistical approach solves the name extraction task with a good tradeoff between generality and precision. We conducted experiments over a collection of 152 faculty web pages in multiple languages from universities in 49 countries and obtained 94.37 % precision, 97.61% recall, and 0.9596 F-measure.

KEYWORDS

Name Extraction; Information Extraction; Statistical Classifier;

ACM Reference Format:
João Mateus de Freitas Veneroso and Berthier Ribeiro-Neto. 2018. Entity Name Extraction from Faculty Directories. In *JCDL '18: The 18th ACM/IEEE Joint Conference on Digital Libraries, June 3–7, 2018, Fort Worth, TX, USA.* ACM, New York, NY, USA, 3 pages. https://doi.org/10.1145/3197026.3203902

1 INTRODUCTION

Typically, Information Extraction tasks consist of mapping unstructured or poorly structured data to a semantically well defined structure. The input is most commonly composed of a set of documents that describe a group of entities in a similar manner. The Information Extraction task consists of identifying these entities and organizing them according to a template. The most successful approaches at solving the problem of information extraction are documented in several surveys [1–5].

We are interested in the task of name extraction, particularly extracting researcher names from university websites to complement data from public databases such as the DBLP repository [1].

[1] http://dblp.uni-trier.de/.

JCDL '18, June 3–7, 2018, Fort Worth, TX, USA

ACM ISBN 978-1-4503-5178-2/18/06.
https://doi.org/10.1145/3197026.3203902

The name extraction problem is not different from a Named Entity Recognition problem, because if we are able to recognize entities we may also map them to a structured format. However, state-of-the-art named entity recognition approaches such as Conditional Random Fields do not perform so well in information extraction scenarios such as the name extraction problem, because the text in web pages is usually insufficient to provide proper contextual information about the semantic category of a word. For instance, tabular data such as the one found in most faculty directories provides minimal textual context. Our probabilistic method of label assignment resembles a Naive Bayesian classifier without the assumption of token independence. We also rely as little as possible on contextual information because it is frequently missing, noisy or inadequate in web pages.

2 IMPLEMENTATION

Before applying the classifier over the web page content, we must run the input web page through a series of preprocessing steps to clean the data as much as possible and tokenize the text. Each token is saved as an object that holds the token value and a pointer to its position in the DOM tree.

2.1 Model

Let $t = (t_1, t_2, ..., t_n)$ be a sequence of token objects obtained at the preprocessing stage, and $y = (y_1, y_2, ..., y_n)$ be a sequence of labels attributed to these tokens where y_i can be either a "Name Label" (N), meaning that token t_i is a person's name, or a "Word Label" (W), meaning that token t_i is a common word (not a person's name). Considering that each token t_i has a probability $P(t_i = y_i)$ of having label y_i, the problem of finding an optimal sequence of labels y^* for a sequence of tokens t can be written as:

$$y^* = \underset{y}{\operatorname{argmax}} P(t_1 = y_1, t_2 = y_2, ..., t_n = y_n) \tag{1}$$

We may employ the chain rule to explore the relationship between joint and conditional probabilities. For ease of exposure, consider that $P(Y_i) \equiv P(t_i = y_i)$ yielding:

$$P(Y_1, Y_2, ..., Y_n) = P(Y_1)P(Y_2|Y_1)...P(Y_n|Y_{n-1}, Y_{n-2}, ...) \tag{2}$$

The conditional probabilities $P(Y_i|Y_{i-1}, ...)$ are hard to estimate, because the joint distribution depends both on the previous labels and the previous tokens. To simplify our modeling, let us assume that the probability that token t_i has label y_i depends on the values of previous labels but is independent of the previous tokens. That is, we assume that, given a sequence of tokens {"*John*", "*Smith*"}, the conditional probability $P(\text{"}Smith\text{"}|\text{"}John\text{"} = Name)$ is equivalent to $P(\text{"}Smith\text{"}|Any\ name)$. By taking this assumption, we get:

$$P(Y_i|Y_{i-1}, Y_{i-2}, ...) \approx P(t_i|y_i, y_{i-1}, ...)P(y_i|y_{i-1}, y_{i-2}, ...) \quad (3)$$

In Equation 3, the probability $P(t_i|y_i, y_{i-1}, ...)$ depends on the current and previous labels. We make a simplifying assumption that $P(t_i|y_i, y_{i-1}, ...)$ can be approximated by $P(t_i|y_i)$. With this assumption, Equation 3 becomes:

$$P(Y_i|Y_{i-1}, Y_{i-2}, ...) \approx P(t_i|y_i)P(y_i|y_{i-1}, y_{i-2}, ...) \quad (4)$$

Finally, by replacing Equation 4 into Equation 2 and grouping together the second terms of Equation 4 to form the joint probability $P(y_1, y_2, \ldots, y_n)$, we obtain:

$$P(Y_1, \ldots, Y_n) \approx P(y_1, \ldots, y_n)P(t_1|y_1)P(t_2|y_2)\ldots P(t_n|y_n) \quad (5)$$

Equation 5 can be split into two parts: the prior: $P(y_1, y_2, \ldots, y_n)$, and the conditional token probabilities: $P(t_1|y_1)P(t_2|y_2)\ldots P(t_n|y_n)$.

2.1.1 *Prior probabilities.*

By assuming a window of size $k \leq n$ we may approximate the priors by calculating the joint probability $P(y_1, y_2, \ldots, y_k)$. We observed empirically that when a name token is found, it is very likely that the next token will also be a name. However, arbitrary sequences of non-name tokens do not alter significantly the probabilities for the next token's label. We can use this property to slide the window of k tokens over the entire sequence of tokens and estimate probabilities without deviating too much from the real distribution. We start at the beginning of the token list and calculate probabilities for each possible sequence of labels, taking the most likely one. If the first token is not a name we slide the window right by one token and repeat the process. If the first token is a name, then we extract all the tokens that are part of that name starting from the first one and slide the window right by the number of name tokens extracted.

2.1.2 *Conditional token probabilities.*

For our experiments, the conditional token probabilities were obtained by maximum likelihood estimation with Laplace smoothing to account for tokens that did not occur in the corpus. Conditional token probabilities can be made more precise by incorporating features in equation 5. We do that by changing the token conditional probabilities to:

$$P(t_i, f_1, f_2, \ldots, f_n|y_i) \approx P(t_i|y_i)P(f_1|y_i)\ldots P(f_n|y_i) \quad (6)$$

where f_i are features that are assumed to be independent. Textual features take textual clues from context words and the current token value. Structural features infer token probabilities based on the surrounding HTML structure. The textual features found to be useful in our model were: token value, token incidence and token length. The structural features found to be useful in our model were: first and second HTML parents, CSS class name, and nesting depth.

2.1.3 *Secondary estimates.*

HTML structure varies wildly between different websites, so we cannot extract useful probabilities looking at the entire collection. For example, if all names appear inside a <tr> tag in a given document it does not mean that names tend to appear inside <tr> tags rather than any other HTML tag in other documents. However for that particular document we may be able to identify other names and exclude non name tokens by knowing that tokens that occur inside <tr> tags have a higher probability of being names.

Given that the basic algorithm (without structural features) was able to extract a satisfactory number of names from a web page with sufficient precision on a first run, we may estimate probabilities for a structural feature $P(f_j|y_i)$ by looking at the extracted names. In fact, since we already attributed a label to every token in the web page, we can access the originating DOM element through the token object and estimate feature probabilities by maximum likelihood, as we did for the token conditional probabilities.

2.2 Experiments

Features	Precision	Recall	F-measure
None	91.71%	91.39%	0.9155
Textual	91.83% (0.46)	93.90% (0.15)	0.9285 (0.23)
Full	94.37% (0.05)	**97.61% (0.01)**	**0.9596 (0.01)**

Table 1: Name extraction experiment

The test collection was a set of 152 manually labeled faculty directory web pages from 49 different countries with 11,782 researcher names. We calculated the precision, recall, and f-measure for a base model with no additional features besides conditional token probabilities and priors, a model with only textual features, and a full model with textual and structural features. All measures were tested for statistical significance with a one tailed paired T-test in comparison with the base model, the t-values are presented inside parenthesis next to each measure. The measures were obtained by the averaged results of a 5 fold cross validation run.

3 CONCLUSION

Our name extraction method achieved 94.37% precision, 97.61% recall and 0.9596 F-measure over the test corpus. The model is tuned for the particular problem of name extraction, but we believe this result can be generalized to solve other data extraction problems. The algorithm is general enough to handle other types of information extraction tasks without the need for too much tinkering. The secondary estimates strategy was successful in further improving the base model. It can also be remodeled to fit other statistical classifiers since it does not rely on any particular implementation details of our strategy.

REFERENCES

[1] Alberto H. F. Laender, Berthier A. Ribeiro-Neto, Juliana S. Teixeira, and Altigran S. da Silva. A brief survey of web data extraction tools. *ACM SIGMOD Record 31(2)*, pages 84–93, 2002.

[2] Sunita Sarawagi. Information extraction. *Foundations and Trends in Databases*, 1(3):261–377, 2008.

[3] Emilio Ferrara, Pasquale De Meo, Giacomo Fiumara, and Robert Baumgartner. Web data extraction, applications and techniques: A survey. *Knowledge-Based Systems*, 70:301–323, 2014.

[4] Andreas Schulz, Jörg Lässig, and Martin Gaedke. Practical web data extraction: Are we there yet? — A short survey. *IEEE/WIC/ACM International Conference on Web Intelligence (WI), 2016*, pages 562—-567, 2016.

[5] M. I. Varlamov and D. Yu. Turdakov. A survey of methods for the extraction of information from Web resources. *Programming and Computer Software*, 42(5):279–291, 2016.

Towards A Self-Learning Library For Vibration Data

Xinyue Wang and Zhiwu Xie
Virginia Polytechnic Institute and State University
Blacksburg, VA
{xw0078|zhiwuxie}@vt.edu

ABSTRACT

Vibration data from building can reflect human activities such as human movement. Lack of relative labeled dataset has been a major challenge for conducting such analysis job. We aim to explore possibilities to produce footstep metadata automatically through machine learning techniques. In this paper, we perform an analysis on identifying human footsteps by utilizing deep neural network as a classifier.

CCS CONCEPTS

• **Information systems** → **Digital libraries and archives**; • **Computing methodologies** → *Neural networks*;

KEYWORDS

Self-learning library, footstep detection, vibration

ACM Reference Format:
Xinyue Wang and Zhiwu Xie. 2018. Towards A Self-Learning Library For Vibration Data. In *JCDL '18: The 18th ACM/IEEE Joint Conference on Digital Libraries, June 3–7, 2018, Fort Worth, TX, USA.* ACM, New York, NY, USA, Article 4, 2 pages. https://doi.org/10.1145/3197026.3203870

1 INTRODUCTION

Lack of data has been identified as one of the five grand challenges "to improve people movement or building evacuation effectiveness" [2]. Virginia Tech's Goodwin Hall offers an opportunity to address this challenge. Besides housing the College of Engineering, it is also a living laboratory that has more than 200 vibration-monitoring accelerometers embedded in more than 130 locations throughout the building. As part of an IMLS funded project to understand library big data cyberinfrastructure, we are working towards building a digital library for the collected vibration data to support multi- and cross-disciplinary exploration and discovery. This library will be used by researchers leveraging the data to conduct research ranging from crowd management, HVAC control, to human-building interactions. It needs to include high-quality metadata about the vibration. The occurrences of footsteps are of particular interest, because it forms the basis of tracking human movements. However, unlike a traditional library, it is almost impossible to generated the footstep metadata manually. The shear size of the data, its continuous accumulation, the lack of definitive information about human movements in the building all contribute to the intractability of the problem.

An analytical model has been developed to identify and localize footsteps in the building [1]. This model will continue to be validated against collected data. However, collecting more data will not automatically improve the accuracy of an analytical model. Machine learning, on the other hand, has the potential to complement the analytical model and continuously improve the metadata quality of the library. This paper reports our first attempt towards that direction.

ACM ISBN 978-1-4503-5178-2/18/06.
https://doi.org/10.1145/3197026.3203870

2 A CASE STUDY

Vibration signals from Goodwin Hall are typical time series data. Sensors collect data at sample rate varying from 792 to 8192 Hz, with sensitivity at about 1000 milli Volts/g ($g = 9.8m/s^2$). When data stream in for processing, some contiguous data segments contain footstep patterns of interest, to be labeled as footstep metadata. We aim to build a classification model which could be applied for automatic footstep detection and metadata collection.

2.1 Method

The ground truth used for the supervised learning was collected as part of the analytical model verification [1]. The data was collected during a quiet period of the building. One person walked along the 4th floor corridor, and 11 sensors deployed along the corridor picked up 162 footsteps in 65 seconds, all at the sample rate of 8192 Hz. The footsteps were then manually labeled. Though this is a small dataset, our result shows a good performance. We perform a series of data preprocessing to simulate a real life stream source.

We choose Recurrent Neural Network (RNN) because it has been proved to have better representation and classification on a multitude of time-series problems compared to shallow approaches [7].

Footstep identification is conducted in three steps: 1) prepare and transform the dataset into a stream data 2) use the RNN network to train our model; 3) evaluate the model.

2.2 Preprocessing

2.2.1 Dataset Preparation. The raw dataset contains 1) a 537401 by 11 matrix A containing the data from the 11 sensors and 2) a 162 by 1 matrix B containing the timestamp of the 162 footsteps. Although vibration data shows a footstep may last a short period of time, the original labeling assumes each footstep occurs at an exact moment, presumably the center of the waveform.

In order to label later frame-wised data, we now expand the footstep labels not just for the exact time moment but also for the time frame around it. As shown in figure 1, the original tag (vertical orange line) is located at approximately the center of the waveform

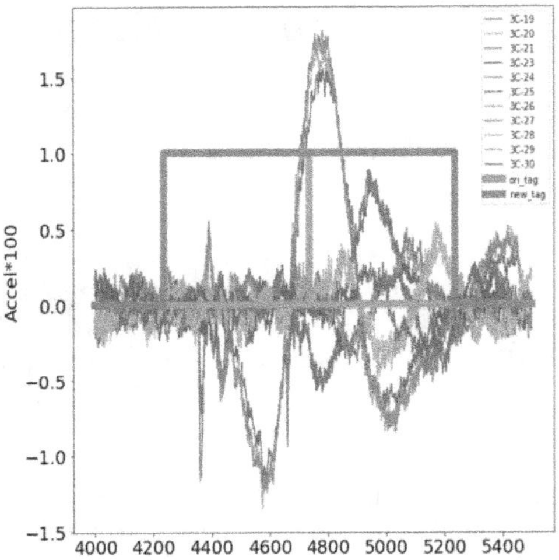

Figure 1: Sample footstep signal with tag

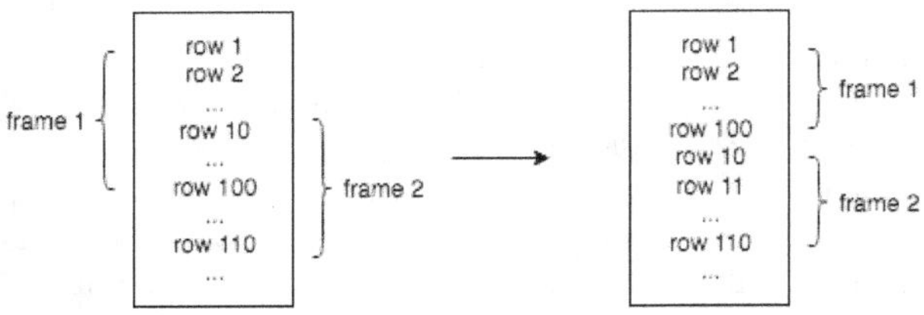

Figure 2: Order dataset by frames

of about 1000 data points (the green frame). We extend the label to cover 500 data points before and after the original label such that the whole frame is labeled as 1.

2.2.2 Stream Transformation. We transform the dataset to simulate a frame-wised stream input. The frame rate is 1 frame per 10 data points and each frame contains 100 data points, which is generally enough to cover a whole footstep. Figure 2 shows how the original data is transformed to our new stream schema.

2.2.3 Frame Labeling. We label one frame such that if more than 50 percent of points are positively labeled, then the whole frame will be labeled as positive. This results in a label dataset of 5360 rows with 1281 positive rows where the positive rate is 23.9 percent.

2.2.4 Reducing. We reduce the sample rate by 10 after we find that higher sample rate does not contribute much to the pattern identification, yet greatly increases the computation time in RNN training process.

2.3 RNN Configuration and Model Training

2.3.1 Long Short-Term Memory. Comparing to traditional recurrent unit, the Long Short-Term Memory (LSTM)[6] unit is able to easily carry information over a long distance once it detects an important feature from an input sequence at early stage[4]. Past research also shows the capability of LSTM in coping with frame wise data[5]. We therefore choose LSTM for our model building.

Table 1: Model Cross Validation Result

Folds	Train Set Score(%)	Test Set Score(%)
Fold 1	99.89	93.90
Fold 2	99.91	94.62
Fold 3	99.77	94.79

In our case, LSTM will read one frame data at a time and abstract the connections of contiguous data points in the frame with given label to produce our classifier model.

2.3.2 Training Process. We use a high level neural networks API Keras[3] as our experiment platform. We build up a Keras sequential model including one LSTM layer: abstract the connection of our dataset; and one Dense layer: bridge the output space of LSTM to our binary output space, classification result. In detail, LSTM layer firstly takes our dataset, a 5360 by 100 by 11 matrix, as input. Then a Dense layer takes the output of LSTM and output the final binary classification result as the identification for a footstep.

2.4 Model Evaluation

We use cross validation with 3 folds to evaluate our model by dividing the dataset without shifting orders. The result is shown in Table 1. Scores show the accuracy of our models on training dataset and test dataset. The score for test data shows a good performance.

3 SUMMARY AND FUTURE WORK

In this paper, we applied RNN to model a footstep identification method in an environment with relatively low noise levels. The evaluation demonstrates the superiority of RNN as a classifier without much tuning. In future work, we aim to apply our model to real life data which contains more noises to extract footstep metadata.

ACKNOWLEDGMENTS

This work is partially supported by the Institute of Museum and Library Services under Grant No.: LG-71-16-0037-16 (https://www.imls.gov/grants/awarded/lg-71-16-0037-16).

REFERENCES

[1] Sa'ed Alajlouni, Mohammad Albakri, and Pablo Tarazaga. 2018. Impact localization in dispersive waveguides based on energy-attenuation of waves with the traveled distance. 105 (2018), 361–376. https://doi.org/10.1016/j.ymssp.2017.12.007

[2] J. D. Averill. 2011. Five Grand Challenges in Pedestrian and Evacuation Dynamics. In *Pedestrian and Evacuation Dynamics*, Richard D. Peacock, Erica D. Kuligowski, and Jason D. Averill (Eds.). Springer, New York.

[3] Francois Chollet. 2015. keras. https://github.com/fchollet/keras. (2015).

[4] Junyoung Chung, Çaglar Gülçehre, KyungHyun Cho, and Yoshua Bengio. 2014. Empirical Evaluation of Gated Recurrent Neural Networks on Sequence Modeling. *CoRR* abs/1412.3555 (2014). arXiv:1412.3555 http://arxiv.org/abs/1412.3555

[5] Alex Graves and Jürgen Schmidhuber. 2005. Framewise phoneme classification with bidirectional LSTM and other neural network architectures. *Neural Networks* 18, 5 (2005), 602 – 610. https://doi.org/10.1016/j.neunet.2005.06.042 IJCNN 2005.

[6] Sepp Hochreiter and Jürgen Schmidhuber. 1997. Long Short-Term Memory. *Neural Comput.* 9, 8 (Nov. 1997), 1735–1780. https://doi.org/10.1162/neco.1997.9.8.1735

[7] Martin Längkvist, Lars Karlsson, and Amy Loutfi. 2014. A review of unsupervised feature learning and deep learning for time-series modeling. *Pattern Recognition Letters* 42 (2014), 11 – 24. https://doi.org/10.1016/j.patrec.2014.01.008

How Do People Read eBooks on Mobile Devices? Implication for Digital Reading Environment Design

Xiaoguang Wang
School of Information Management, Wuhan University, Wuhan, 430072, CHN, wxguang@whu.edu.cn

Hanghang Cheng
School of Information Management, Wuhan University, Wuhan, 430072, CHN, 2013302480047@whu.edu.cn

Jing Liu
School of Information Management, Wuhan University, Wuhan, 430072, CHN, 2012300750004@whu.edu.cn

Hongyu Wang
School of Information Management, Wuhan University, Wuhan, 430072, CHN, wanghongyu@whu.edu.cn

Chen Zhang
Office of International Affairs, Wuhan University, Wuhan, 430072, CHN, 00009694@whu.edu.cn

Abstract

The widespread use of portable devices is reshaping the reading behaviors, and thus a shift towards hyper-attention is taking place. How to use data on fine reading behavior to identify the current style of mobile reading emerges as a novel research topic. With a large-scale flipping data, this paper finds that mobile reading is a leisure-oriented and fragmented activity with obvious tidal characteristics and long tail effects, and that the book genres and user types have influence on reading behavior.

CSS CONCEPTS

• Information systems~ Digital libraries and archives

Key Word

Mobile Reading Behavior, Big Data, Data analysis

ACM Reference format:

Xiaoguang Wang, Hanghang Cheng, Jing Liu, Hongyu Wang and Chen Zhang. 2018. How Do People Read eBooks on Mobile Devices? Implication for Digital Reading Environment Design. In *Proceedings of The 18th ACM/IEEE Joint Conference on Digital Libraries, June 3–7, 2018, Fort Worth, TX, USA (JCDL '18), 2 pages.*
DOI: https://doi.org/10.1145/3197026.3203872

Introduction

Reading is a kind of social behavior, practical activity, and psychological process that derives meaning from written language and other symbols [1]. With the development of digital media and the popularity of portable devices, such as smart phone, mobile reading has become a trend. As a reading medium, mobile reading devices as a whole profoundly changes the user's reading behaviors and habits. As a result, the immersive reading characterized with deep-attention is on the wane and gives way to scanning, characterized with hyper-attention [2]. Hyper-attention features rapid shifts of user's focus among different tasks, preference for multiple information streams, a high level of stimulation and low tolerance for monotony [3].In addition, mobile reading devices can record in large amounts user's actual reading behavior data, which indicates the features and preferences of user's reading behavior, thus providing a new possibility for the study of mobile reading behavior. With analysis of a large-scale eBook flipping records, this study examines the patterns of mobile reading behaviors in the hyper-attention environment.

ACM ISBN 978-1-4503-5178-2/18/06.
https://doi.org/10.1145/3197026.3203872

Research Framework and Question

Reading ebooks on mobile device includes a serial of related activities, such as page flipping, note-taking, commenting, annotating, navigating, searching and so on. This study concentrates on the page flipping activities, which refers to the change of page number by clicking or sliding on a screen. A number of continuous page flipping forms a reading session, and the interval between two reading sessions makes a reading break. Therefore, mobile reading appears to be a discontinuous process, which consists of several reading sessions and reading breaks. The model of mobile reading is shown in Fig. 1.

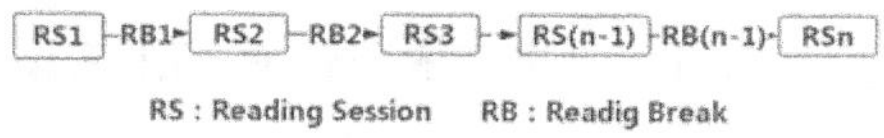

Figure 1 The model of mobile reading

In order to explore the patterns of mobile reading behaviors, we put forward three questions: (1) what are the characteristics of mobile reading behavior? Does it show a behavior pattern marked by hyper-attention as a cognitive type? (2) Does the type of books influence the behavior of mobile reading? (3) Is there any difference in mobile reading behavior of different users?

Research Method and Data

Weblog analysis is a non-intrusive way for studying internet behavior [4]. We collaborate with Baidu.com, China's largest search engine service provider, to collect user's flipping data. All the data is collected from BaiduRead, a mobile reading app with over 80 Chinese million users and 1,500,000 eBooks. We choose as samples 16 best-selling eBooks of two types according to the classification of BaiduRead, 9 ficitons (*The Devotion of Suspect X, You are My Sunshine, The Old Man and the Sea, Pride and Prejudice, The Golden Era, Border Town, Grief Grocery Store, Time Migration, Who Stole My Cheese)* and 7 professional books (*Principles of Economics, Professional JavaScript for Web Developers, The Practice of Management, Human Resource Management, Marketing, Core Java Volume 1-Fundamentals (10th Edition), Fundamental Accounting Principles*). By means of data cleaning and screening, we get 23,502,648 page flipping records and 474,929 reading sessions of 110,955 users within three months from February 25, 2017 to May 25, 2017. With the dataset, we then examine the reading duration and reading schedule, and explore the influence of book types and user's characteristics on mobile reading behavior.

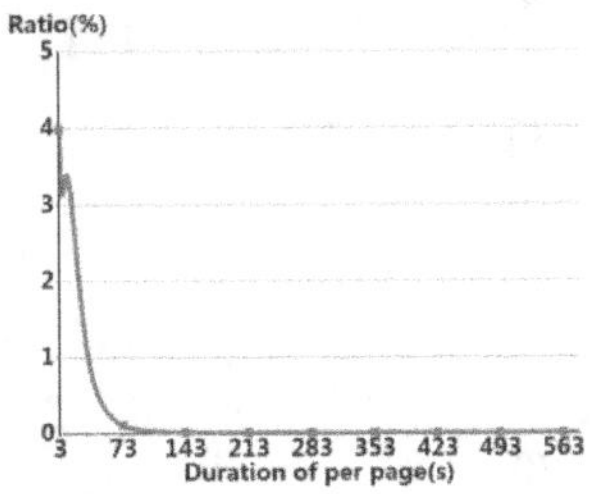

Figure 2 Distribution of page reading duration

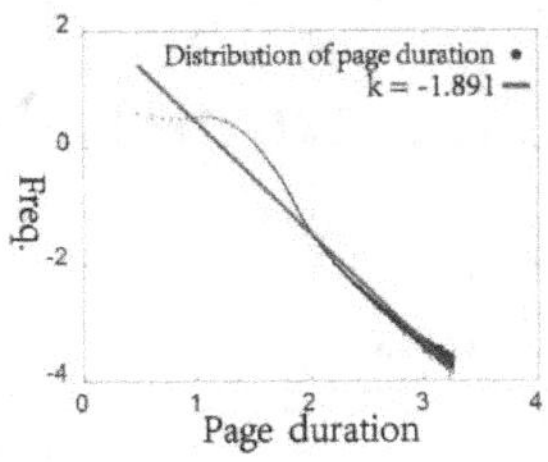

Figure 3 Power-law distribution of page reading duration

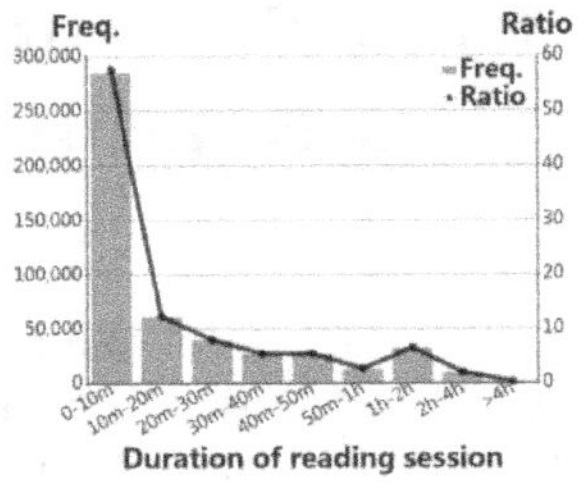

Figure 4 Distribution of reading session duration

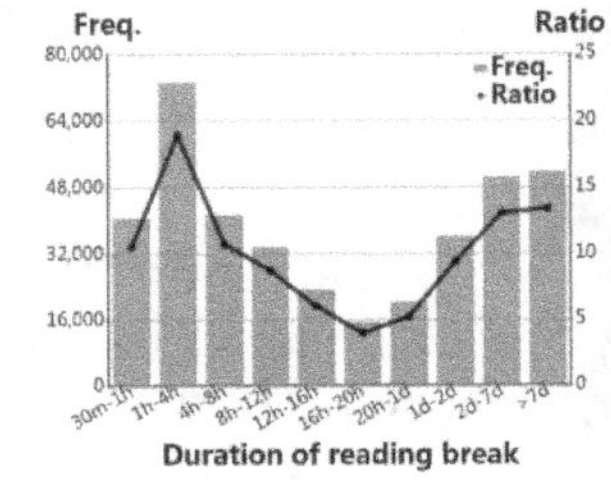

Figure 5 Distribution of reading break duration

Results

Reading Duration of per page

This study takes a range of 3s to 30 mins to be a normal reading duration of a single page. It's found that the reading duration of per page with different screen-size, font-size, column-width shows a similar distribution. As shown in Fig. 2, the reading duration of per page within 141s account for 98% based on the full sample, which conforms to the power law and the long tail effects (k=-1.887), as shown in Fig. 3. Users tend to scan quickly, so the reading duration of per page is higher in 3s to 5s; the duration of reading per page grows with interests and reaches a typical duration of around 11s. It's also found that the reading duration of per page of professional books is higher than that of fictions, and that men tend to scan while the average reading speed of women is higher. Users with high school diploma or below are apt to scan and read fast compared with other users.

Reading Session and Reading Break Duration

The distribution of reading session duration of all users also meets the power law (k=-1.484). We divide the duration of reading session and reading breaks into several spans according to users' reading habits and observe the distribution (see Fig. 4 and Fig. 5). The reading session duration of 0 to 10mins and the reading break duration of 30mins to 1h and of 1h to 4h respectively dominate the distributions. The distribution verifies that mobile reading is fragmented, yet subject to the type of books. However, the mobile reading sessions and reading breaks of users with different characteristics unexpectedly shows few difference.

Reading Schedule

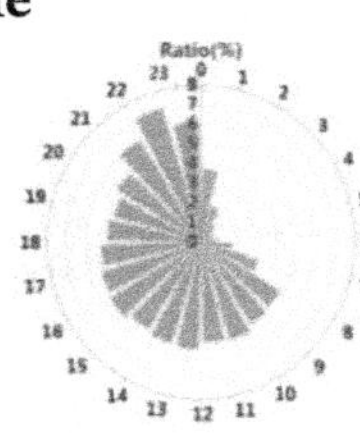

Figure 6 Distribution of reading schedule for 24 hours

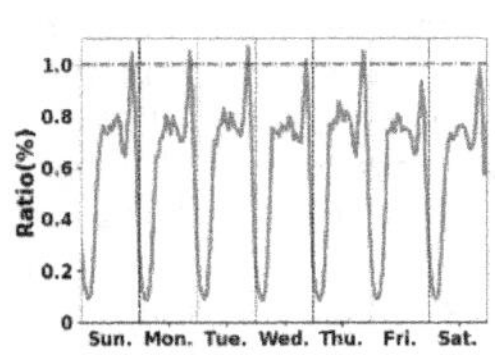

Figure 7 Weekly Distribution of Reading Schedule

Fig. 6 shows a 24-hour distribution of all users' reading time. Most of the reading is well-distributed and takes place during 8:00 to 24:00, although mostly concentrated in late night (22:00 to 24:00). It's also noticeable that most reading of fictions take place in mid-night and the reading of professional books usually take place in working hours from 8am to 6pm. At the same time, the reading of women are mostly distributed in the afternoon or at night. The reading of users below 24 years old is evenly spread throughout the day.

Fig. 7 illustrates a weekly distribution of mobile reading schedule, indicating an overt periodicity and "weekend effect" (reading less on Friday and Saturday). The reading schedule of fictions is relatively evenly-distributed within a week, while that of professional books disperses, yet mostly in working hours.

Discussion and Conclusion

This study conducts big data analysis to examine user's mobile reading behavior of eBooks, which leads to the following findings: (1) Mobile ebook reading is a leisure reading with obvious tidal characteristics, and it mainly takes place in the morning and late night; (2) mobile ebook reading is fragmented, and meets the power law and the long tail effects commonly seen in human behavior. It's a typical behavioral pattern featuring hyper-attention as cognitive characteristics; (3) the type of books and user's characteristics impact to some extent his/her mobile reading behavior.

Compared with traditional experiment-based research methods, mobile apps-aided analysis of big data provides an innovative approach to the deep understanding of fine reading behavior. Based on the findings, we put forward some suggestions, hoping to contribute to the design of eBooks apps and mobile reading environment: (1) To offer users more control and flexibility to allow them to choose reading environments and combinations of reading functions according to their preferences or reading content; (2) to reduce cognitive load to facilitate user's reading immersion.

In the future, our study will look into how users start, stop and resume reading, identify the distribution and attenuation pattern of user's attention, and explore the influence of demographic variables, such as culture background, preferences, etc., on mobile reading behavior.

References

[1] Steven R. Fischer. 2003. A history of reading. Reaktion Books, London, UK.

[2] X. Zhou. 2016. The transition from "immersive" reading to "scanning" reading. Social Sciences in China (11), 143-163.

[3] D. Nicholas, P. Huntington and A. Watkinson. 2003. Digital journals, Big Deals and online searching behaviour: a pilot study. Aslib Proceedings 55 N (1/2), 84-109.

[4] N. Katherine Hayles. 2007. Hyper and deep attention: the generational divide in cognitive modes. Profession (1), 187-199.

Clustering Analysis-Based Approach to Detecting Entity Mixture in Knowledge Bases

Haihua Xie
State Key Laboratory of Digital Publishing Technology
Peking University Founder Group Co. LTD.
Beijing, China
xiehh@founder.com.cn

Xiaoqing Lu, Zhi Tang
Institute of Computer Science & Technology
Peking University
Beijing, China
{lvxiaoqing, tangzhi}@pku.edu.cn

ABSTRACT

Entity Mixture refers to a phenomenon that the information on an entity is mistaken as attributes of another entity in information extraction during knowledge base (KB) construction and population. To improve the quality of knowledge-based services, data accuracy and validity in KBs should be enhanced. This paper presents a clustering analysis-based approach for detecting potentially mixed entities in a KB. Our approach aims at detecting the inconsistency of the attribute values of a KB instance as an indication of entity mixture occurrence. This paper also presents an experiment conducted on a data set of industrial applications to demonstrate the process of entity mixture detection. Experimental results show that our proposed methodology performs well in detecting mixed entities.

CCS CONCEPTS

• **Information systems → Information systems applications** → Digital libraries and archives

KEYWORDS

Entity Mixture; Hierarchical Clustering; Instance; Knowledge Base; Knowledge Service; Subject-Predicate-Object (SPO) Triple.

ACM Reference format:

H. Xie, X. Lu, Z. Tang. 2018. Clustering Analysis-Based Approach to Detecting Entity Mixture in Knowledge Bases. In *Proceedings of Joint Conference on Digital Libraries, Forth June 3–7, 2018, Fort Worth, TX, USA (JCDL 2018)*, 2 pages. https://doi.org/10.1145/3197026.3203896.[1]

1 Introduction

During Knowledge Base (KB) construction and population, entities with the same name may be mixed in one instance, that is, the attributes of an entity are mistakenly labeled as that of another entity, thereby causing problems in identifying entities [1]. The phenomenon of mixing attributes of different entities in one instance is called entity mixture. Eliminating entity mixture is critical to ensuring the data accuracy and validity of knowledge-based services [2]. In some cases, the inconsistency among attributes of same-name entities can be detected using straightforward reasoning methods. However, the conflicts between two triples cannot be easily detected when the attributes represented do not have direct correlations. Furthermore, the design of reasoning methods depends on the nature of the predicates in the triples. Thus, designing a general methodology for detecting entity mixture in KBs using reasoning approaches is difficult [3].

This paper introduces a clustering analysis-based approach to distinguishing mixed same-name entities in KBs. The attributes of an instance are analyzed based on their relevant descriptions in documents of a common corpus to determine whether they describe the same entity. Hierarchical clustering is performed on the set of description documents of triples of an instance. The clustering result indicates mixture, that is, if more than one cluster are obtained, mixture is assumed in triples of such instance. To test the validity of our methodology for detecting entity mixture in a KB, an experiment was conducted on a data set of industrial applications. The experimental procedure and results are presented in this paper.

2 Clustering-based Entity Mixture Detection

Entity mixture is often caused by the incorrect linking of a substance in a text to an existing instance in the KB during KB population. This problem cannot be detected and eliminated merely by information reasoning or mutual verification inside the KB, because correlations between triples with mixed entities might not exist. For instance, the inconsistency between <*ins-ID*$_1$, BirthYear, 1642> and <*ins-ID*$_1$, Granddaughter, Amanda Newton> is difficult to reason.

Our methodology is developed based on the assumption that the set of documents describing an entity must be distinguishable from that of another entity. Thus, to inspect the possibly mixed entities in an instance, the sets of documents that involve each triple of the instance are obtained. Clustering is then performed on the sets of documents to classify the triples. Therefore, the basis of clustering triples is the occurrence distribution of the attribute values of each triple in documents of a common corpus. The number of clusters in the clustering result indicates the number of entities mixed together, and no mixture exists if the number of clusters is 1. For example, when inspecting entity mixture in *ins-ID*$_1$, the sets of documents of the second to fourth triples are classified into one group, and those of the last two triples are classified into another group. Two clusters are finally obtained. Thus, two entities named Isaac Newton are mixed in *ins-ID*$_1$.

The steps to detect the existence of entity mixture in an instance of a KB are shown in Fig.1.

JCDL '18, June 3–7, 2018, Fort Worth, TX, USA

ACM ISBN 978-1-4503-5178-2/18/06.
https://doi.org/10.1145/3197026.3203896

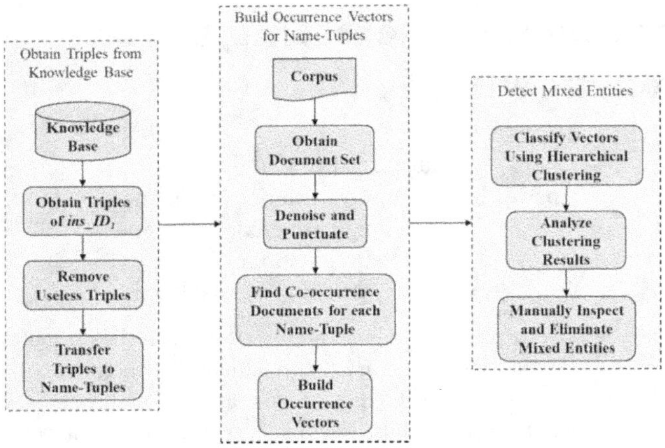

Figure 1: Workflow of Entity Mixture Detection

The core step in the workflow of entity mixture detection is clustering of occurrence vectors. Figure 2 illustrates the process of clustering occurrence vectors using hierarchical clustering.

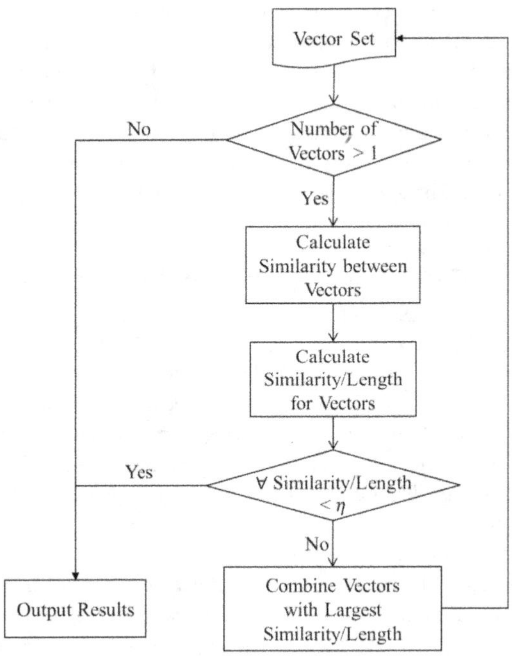

Figure 2: Process of Hierarchical Clustering

The similarity of two vectors is calculated using the following formula:

$$Similarity\,(V_1, V_2) = f_{sim}(v_{11}, v_{21}) + \ldots + f_{sim}(v_{1n}, v_{2n}) \quad (1)$$

where V_1 and V_2 are occurrence vectors, and $V_1 = \{v_{11}, \ldots v_{1n}\}$, $V_2 = \{v_{21}, \ldots v_{2n}\}$. $f_{sim}(v_{1i}, v_{2i})$ is calculated using the following formula:

$$f_{sim}(v_{1i}, v_{2i}) = \begin{cases} v_{1i} + v_{2i} & if\ v_{1i} \geq 1\ and\ v_{2i} \geq 1 \\ 0 & otherwise \end{cases} \quad (2)$$

The algorithm to combine two vectors into one vector is as follows:

$$V_{12} = \text{Combine}(V_1, V_2) = \{v_{11} + v_{21}, v_{12} + v_{22}, \ldots, v_{1n} + v_{2n}\} \quad (3)$$

The condition for terminating the clustering is

$$\forall V_i, V_j \in V_{ins}, \frac{\text{Similarity}(V_i, V_j)}{\min(\text{length}(V_i), \text{length}(V_j))} < \eta$$

where length(V_i) is equal to the number of positive elements in V_i. The similarity–length ratio of two vectors used to select vectors to combine is calculated using the following formula:

$$\text{SimilarityLengthRatio}(V_i, V_j) = \frac{\text{Similarity}(V_i, V_j)}{\min(\text{length}(V_i), \text{length}(V_j))} \quad (4)$$

The pair of vectors with the largest similarity–length ratio is selected to be combined into one vector.

An experiment is conducted on two data sets of industrial applications, one of which is a KB, and the other is a digital library of electronic books and articles (DLib). According to the workflow presented before, entity mixture detection is performed on the same-name instances and individual instances. The experimental results are shown below:

Table 1: Entity mixture detection based on different η

η	Accuracy	Recall	Strong Accuracy	Strong Recall	F Value[1]
1/8	95%	91%	90.5%	90%	90.25%
1/4	96%	100%	94%	96%	94.99%
1/2	91.5%	100%	85%	89%	86.95%
3/4	87.5%	100%	77%	81%	78.95%

[1] F value is calculated based on the strong accuracy rate and recall rate.

3 Conclusion

In summary, we present a general and automated approach to distinguishing entities based on the occurrence distribution of triples in documents of a common corpus. The approach presented in this paper is an enhancement of the methodology proposed in [3]. Experimental results show that our methodology for entity mixture detection outperforms the previous method.

ACKNOWLEDGMENTS

This work is supported by the projects of National Natural Science Foundation of China (No. 61472014, No. 61573028 and No. 61432020), the Natural Science Foundation of Beijing (No. 4142023) and the Beijing Nova Program (XX2015B010). We also thank all the anonymous reviewers for their valuable comments.

REFERENCES

[1] M. J. Cobo, M. A. Martínez, M. G. Salcedo, H. Fujita, and E. H. Viedma. Twenty-five Years at Knowledge-Based Systems: A Bibliometric Analysis. *Knowledge-Based Systems*. 2015, 80:3-13.

[2] P. Sondhi and C. Zhai. Mining Semi-Structured Online Knowledge Bases to Answer Natural Language Questions on Community QA Websites. *Proceedings of the 23rd ACM International Conference on Conference on Information and Knowledge Management (CIKM 2014)*. 2014: 341-350.

[3] H. Xie, X. Lu, Z. Tang, X. Huang. Detection of Entity Mixture in Knowledge Bases Using Hierarchical Clustering. *Fifth Conference on Natural Language Processing and Chinese Computing*. 2016:288-299.

Diversifying Citation Contexts in Academic Literature for Knowledge Recommendation

Yunhan Yang
School of Information Management
Wuhan University
Wuhan, Hubei, China

Haihua Chen
Department of Information Science
University of North Texas
Denton, Texas, USA
haihua.chen@unt.edu

Wei Lu
School of Information Management
Wuhan University
Wuhan, Hubei, China

Brenda Reyes Ayala
Department of Information Science
University of North Texas
Denton, Texas, USA

ABSTRACT

Citation contexts of an article refer to sentences or paragraphs that cite that article. Citation contexts are especially useful for recommendation and summarization tasks. However, few studies have recognized the diversity of these citation contexts, thus leading to redundant recommendation lists and abstract [3]. To address this gap, we compared several strategies that can recommend a set of diverse citation contexts by re-ranking extracted citation contexts. Diversification was achieved by combining one of two semantic distance algorithms with one of two re-ranking algorithms. Experimenting with CiteSeerX dataset, our program produced a diverse list of 10 citation contexts that could be recommended to users. We evaluated the experiment results based on a user case study of 15 articles. The case study revealed that a diversity strategy that combined the "ESA" and "MMR" led to a better reading experience for participants compared to other diversity strategies. Our study provides insights to develop better automatic academic recommendation and summarization systems.

CCS CONCEPTS

• **Computing methodologies → Semantic networks**;

KEYWORDS

Citation context, Diversity, Knowledge recommendation

ACM Reference Format:
Yunhan Yang, Haihua Chen, Wei Lu, and Brenda Reyes Ayala. 2018. Diversifying Citation Contexts in Academic Literature for Knowledge Recommendation. In *JCDL '18: The 18th ACM/IEEE Joint Conference on Digital Libraries, June 3–7, 2018, Fort Worth, TX, USA.* ACM, New York, NY, USA, Article 2, 2 pages. https://doi.org/10.1145/3197026.3203904

ACM ISBN 978-1-4503-5178-2/18/06.
https://doi.org/10.1145/3197026.3203904

1 INTRODUCTION

Citation context is a well-studied topic in information science. To diversify citation contexts, or to provide a list of citation contexts with minimum overlaps helps to obtain a comprehensive view of how a work is cited, which will also reduce the difficulty of users' choice and save them a lot of time while citing. Existing methods on diversification can be divided into three categories: (1) contentbased, selecting items that are dissimilar to each other, (2) noveltybased, selecting items that contain new information when compared to what was previously presented to the user, and (3) semantic-based, selecting items that belong to different topics [4]. However, diversification performance is far from satisfactory. For example, CiteSeerX citation contexts still contain many duplicate items.

In this paper, we proposed and evaluated four different diversification strategies. We experimented with articles related to information retrieval with between 15 and 100 citations and put them together with their citation contexts from CiteSeerX. We then tested several diverse re-ranking strategies that combined both Explicit Semantic Analysis (ESA) and WordNet as semantic distance similarity algorithms with Maximal Marginal Relevance (MMR) and DivScore as diversification ranking algorithms to select the top 10 citation contexts as diversified results. Finally, we conducted a user case study to evaluate the results.

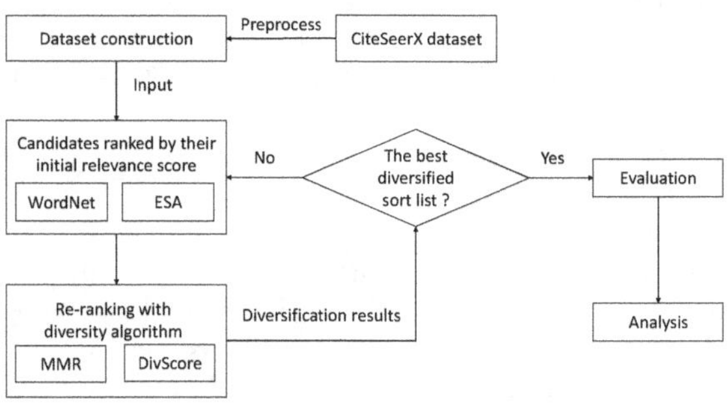

Figure 1: Figure 1: Research Design

2 METHODOLOGY

This study includes the following steps: dataset construction and pre-processing, semantic relevance calculation, ranking of candidates by initial relevance score, re-ranking, diversification evaluation, and results analysis. Figure 1 summarizes our research design.

2.1 Semantic distance calculation

In this study, we define a set of citation contexts of the cited article as $C = \{c_1, c_2, \cdots, c_n\}$. The semantic distance between them is calculated by their similarity $sim(c_i, c_j)$ based on the words using the semantic similarity algorithms ESA and WordNet. We used ESAlib tool to calculate ESA distance and NLTK to output the semantic scores of two sentences.

2.2 Re-ranking for diversification

We applied the MMR and Score Difference algorithms which belong to explicit and implicit diversification methods respectively. The former is used for iterative re-ranking, and the latter is used for single time re-ranking.

2.2.1 *MMR re-ranking for diversification.*

$$C_i = \begin{cases} \underset{c \in C}{argmax}[\lambda sim(c,q) - (1-\lambda)_{c_j \in S}^{max} sim(c, c_j)], i \neq j \\ \underset{c \in C}{argmax}[\mu * \lambda sim(c,q) - (1-\lambda)_{c_j \in S}^{max} sim(c, c_j)], i = j \end{cases}$$

In the above formula[1], C_i is the citation context with highest score in one round of iterative selection, S is the re-ranked list, λ is the coefficient: $\lambda \in [0, 1]$, μ is the penalty coefficient. S is updated after every iteration, until completing the iteration. $sim(c, q)$ is the semantic distance between each citation context and the abstract of the cited article, and $sim(c, c_j)$ semantic distance between different citation contexts.

2.2.2 *Score Difference based re-ranking for diversification.*

The Score Difference method has been widely used in document retrieval [2]. In this paper, we proposed a DivScore algorithm based on Score Difference as shown below:

ALGORITHM: DivScore Algorithm

for $1 \leq i \leq |R(q)|$ *do*

$$DivScore(C_i) = (1 - \frac{i-1}{N}) \times \mu * sim(C_i, q) + \frac{i-1}{N} \times DiffScore(C_i, C_{i-1})$$

end for

Sort C_i on $DivScore(C_i)$

where R(q) presents original citation context list of the cited paper and C_i is ranked by the correlation score. $sim(C_i, q)$ represents the correlation score between each citation context in the citing article and the abstract of the cited article. N denotes the number of citation contexts in the citation context list. $DiffScore(C_i, C_{i-1})$ represents the difference score between citation context C_i and C_{i-1}. It was calculated by $1 - sim(C_i, C_{i-1})$, penalty factor μ is set in front of $sim(C_i, q)$ when there is a similar citation context.

3 EXPERIMENTS

We randomly selected 36 cited papers with abstracts whose citation context counts were between 11 and 90 in information retrieval from CiteSeerX and pre-processed the data by removing all the punctuation and stop words. Then, the penalty coefficient of the "WordNet + MMR" strategy, the "ESA + DivScore" strategy, and the "ESA + MMR" strategy were set as 0.09, 0.45 and 0.20. We didn't consider the strategy "WordNet + DivScore" because of its poor performance. Together with the strategy using citation count only, there were four remaining diversification strategies to be evaluated.

In the evaluation phase, we presented the citation context lists generated by the four diversification strategies of 15 information retrieval articles to users. They are required to read each list and answer a few questions related to readability, diversity, and usefulness of the list to judge whether diversification is helpful in the academic writing process and which diversification strategy provided a better user experience.

4 RESULTS AND CONCLUSION

The Cohen's kappa score of the two annotators before conducting formal investigation was 0.676, was satisfactory according to Viera and Garrett's evaluation standard. We calculated the average of all respondents' score on the four strategies and three indicators (see table 1) and converted scores to 0-1 for the purpose of comparison.

Table 1: The evaluation results

Strat	Readability	Diversity	Usefulness	Overall
Strat1	0.2381	0.2857	0.0774	0.1897
Strat2	0.1905	0.2965	0.1607	0.1964
Strat3	0.3512	0.3840	0.2917	0.3371
Strat4	0.3690	0.4554	0.3452	0.3817

Notes: Strat1: Citation number (CiteSeerX); Strat2: WordNet + MMR; Strat 3: ESA + DivScore; Strat 4: ESA + MMR.

The experiment results showed that our proposed approach generated a more diverse citation context list than the original citation context list presented by CiteSeerX, which led to a better user reading experience. Moreover, among the four diversification strategies which combine "ESA", "WordNet" and "MMR", "DivScore", "ESA + MMR" performed the best.

5 ACKNOWLEDGMENTS

This work was partially supported by the NSFC 2017-2020 Projects 7167030644 and by the NSFC 2018-2020 Project 71704137.

REFERENCES

[1] Jaime Carbonell and Jade Goldstein. 1998. The use of MMR, diversity-based reranking for reordering documents and producing summaries. In *Proceedings of the 21st annual international ACM SIGIR conference on Research and development in information retrieval.* ACM, 335–336.

[2] Sadegh Kharazmi, Mark Sanderson, Falk Scholer, and David Vallet. 2014. Using score differences for search result diversification. In *Proceedings of the 37th international ACM SIGIR conference on Research & development in information retrieval.* ACM, 1143–1146.

[3] Onur Küçüktunç, Erik Saule, Kamer Kaya, and Ümit V Çatalyürek. 2015. Diversifying citation recommendations. *ACM Transactions on Intelligent Systems and Technology (TIST)* 5, 4 (2015), 55.

[4] Marialena Kyriakidi, Kostas Stefanidis, and Yannis Ioannidis. 2017. On Achieving Diversity in Recommender Systems. In *Proceedings of the ExploreDB'17.* ACM, 4.

Time-Aware Diversified Query Suggestion

Xiaojuan Zhang
School of Computer and Information Science, Southwest University
Chongqing, China
zhangxiaojuan624@gmail.com

Lin Peng
Data Intelligence, National Science Library, Chinese Academy of Sciences
Beijing, China
pengl@mail.las.ac.cn

ABSTRACT

In this paper, we study query suggestion diversification for time-aware queries, where query suggestions are diversified from multiple dimensions (e.g., topic and time). More precisely, we introduce the method of Time-aware Diversified Query Suggestion (TDQS) which ensures that the generated suggested queries indicate possible time points in which a searcher who issued the original query may be interested. Preliminary experiments on AOL query log demonstrate that our proposed method can significantly improve the diversity and relevance effectiveness for time-aware queries in comparison with two state-of-the-art methods.

CCS CONCEPTS

• **Computer systems organization → Embedded systems**; *Redundancy*; Robotics; • **Networks** → Network reliability;

KEYWORDS

time; diversification; query suggestion

ACM Reference Format:
Xiaojuan Zhang and Lin Peng. 2018. Time-Aware Diversified Query Suggestion. In *JCDL '18: The 18th ACM/IEEE Joint Conference on Digital Libraries, June 3–7, 2018, Fort Worth, TX, USA,* Jennifer B. Sartor, Theo D'Hondt, and Wolfgang De Meuter (Eds.). ACM, New York, NY, USA, Article 4, 2 pages. https://doi.org/10.1145/3197026.3203901

1 INTRODUCTION

Query suggestion diversification is a common technique for a search engine to track the problem of ambiguous queries with multi-faced aspects (subtopics), by which the recommended queries can be both relevant and diverse. However, previous work only considers a set of query suggestions representing a single time of interest to the initial query in most cases, and it may hamper the user experience if a user wants to search information in a particular time interval. We argue that time-aware query will benefit the suggested queries from diverse time periods, in particular for (a) temporally ambiguous queries that have multiple time periods in which the searcher may be interested and (b)atemporal informational queries that lack any clear time interval of interest. Hence, we introduce Time-aware Diversified Query Suggestion(TDQS), a method for studying temporally ambiguous, multi-faceted queries, where the query suggestions are diversified from multiple dimensions (e.g., topic and time).

JCDL '18, June 3–7, 2018, Fort Worth, TX, USA

ACM ISBN 978-1-4503-5178-2/18/06.
https://doi.org/10.1145/3197026.3203901

2 PROPOSED METHODS

We first generate time-aware query suggestions and then develop a probabilistic query suggestion framework model to generate a diversified ranking list of queries.

2.1 Generating Time-Aware Query Suggestion

In this step, we exploit a popular query suggestion technique proposed by Mei et al.[5] for generating time-aware query suggestions related to an input query. Moreover, we construct a query-URL bipartite graph for each day, where queries and URLs are nodes and edges that represent the click-through information from a query to a URL. Edges are weighted using click frequency-inverse query frequency(CF-IQF) within a time period t (one day in our case). For every query pair, the hitting time of a random walk is computed. The top $L = 500$ queries based on hitting time are taken and exploited as candidate queries. Based on these candidate queries, the aspects (subtopics) A_q of an input query is mined by clustering the candidate queries in a similar approach proposed in [8]. Motivated by the work of [6] , we shift and normalize the hitting time into the [0,1] range and then subtract it from 1 to get the relevance score of a query suggestion. The resultant relevance score for the original query q, a query suggestion q' for a time period t is denoted by $\widetilde{r}(q, q', t)$, and the relevance score is further smoothed using techniques from time-series analysis. Furthermore, we use the moving average method and the ϕ preceding days for each t is used as $r(q, q', t) = \frac{1}{\phi} \sum_{i=0}^{\phi-1} \widetilde{r}(q, q', t - i)$. In this paper, ϕ is set to 5.

2.2 Diversifying Query Suggestions

When aiming for temporal diversity, our objective is to determine a query suggestion list that consists of k queries related to the original query at diverse time periods and they cover different aspects of original query. Given a list of generated candidate queries Q, we iteratively choose the most probable query obtained by:

$$P(q'_{t_i}|q_t)[\alpha P_a(\overline{S}, q'_{t_i}) + (1 - \alpha)P_t(\overline{T}, t_i))] \tag{1}$$

where S is the list of selected queries to be suggested and q'_{t_i} is a candidate query from Q, and T is a time domain indicating time unites (days in our case) of queries in S. The term $P(q'_{t_i}|q_t)$ denotes the relevance of q'_{t_i} to q_t, and it equals to $r(q_t, q'_{t_i}, t)$ described above. $P_a(\overline{S}, q'_{t_i})$ and $P_t(\overline{T}, t_i)$ indicates the novelty in topic and time point level of q'_{t_i} to S, respectively. These two probabilities are controlled by α , namely they model diversity by considering in isolation the content and timestamp of the query. Totally, these three probabilities in Equation(1) are optimizing *relevance* and *diversity* of query suggestions. $P_a(\overline{S}, q'_{t_i})$ can be estimated by using the identified query aspects (subtopics). By using the set of query aspects A_q of the original query q_t, we can marginalize $P_a(\overline{S}, q'_{t_i})$ as: $P_a(\overline{S}, q'_{t_i}) = \sum_{a \in A_q} P(\overline{S}, q'_{t_i}|a)$, where a is a query aspect in A_q. By assuming that the current candidate query q'_{t_i} is independent of the queries already selected in S, $P(q_{t_i}, \overline{S}|a)$ can be derived as,

$$P(q'_{t_i}, \overline{S}|a) = P(q'_{t_i}|a) * P(\overline{S}|a) \quad (2)$$

$P(q'_{t_i}|a)$ measures the semantic coverage of q'_{t_i} with respect to a, and $P(\overline{S}|a)$ provides a measure of semantic *novelty* to the current suggestion list S for a give aspect a. To estimate these probabilities, we utilize the subtopic for each query mined from query log, and $P(q'_{t_i}|a)$ can be estimated by the semantic similarity between a and q_{t_i}. For its calculation, we represent it by the average of the cosine similarity between query terms w returned by the word2vec model[3]. This model involves learning low-dimensional representations of queries from the AOL query log by using a notion of a query as a "sentence" and terms within the query as "words". Particularly, the vector of a query is obtained by the averaging vectors of terms contained in this query. Similarly, the vector of an aspect is obtained by averaging vectors of terms consisting in this aspect. Finally, the cosine similarity between the vectors of aspect and query is used to calculate the $P(q'_{t_i}|a)$. For the estimation of $P(\overline{S}|a)$, we further assume that the queries chosen as suggestions in S are independent each other for a, and the following estimation can be given.

$$P(\overline{S}|a) \approx P(\overline{qs_1, qs_2, ..., qs_{n-1}}|a) \approx \prod\nolimits_{qs \in S} 1 - P(qs|a) \quad (3)$$

where qs is a query in S. We model the probability that the related time point t_i is relevant for a user interested in time point t using the sigmoid function interest,

$$P_t(\overline{T}, t_i) = \frac{1}{1 + e^{-\sum_{t_m \in T} |t_m - t_i|}} \quad (4)$$

where the time point t of the original query represents the particular day when this query issued. In order to get the time point t_i for the query q'_{t_i} we assume that it is possible that many users search for related information which makes the event-related queries popular if an event happens. Therefore, we set the day when one candidate query is most popular as its time point before the time point t.

3 EXPERIMENT SETUP AND RESULTS

We use AOL query log dataset in our experiment. The baselines to be compared are (1)MMR: a query suggestion diversification approach based on Maximal Marginal Relevance(MMR)[1]; (2) DQS: a diversified query suggestion model (DQS) based on query-URL bipartite graph analysis[4]. We manually selected 50 temporally ambiguous, multifaceted queries as our testing queries. Considering that we should not only measure the diversification of the suggestion but also judge whether the queries are relevant to the input query, we hire two assessors with computer science skills as relevance assessors and use a 5-grade scale (perfect=4, excellent=3, good=2, fair=1, and bad=0) to measure the relevance between the testing queries and suggested queries. Importantly, we exploit *MRR@10*[7] and

Table 1: Performance of query suggestion models. The symbols $*$, $\dagger$ in the superscript in the table indicates statistical significance (two-tailed $t-test, p < 0.05$) with respect to MMR and DQS, respectively.

Models	MRR@10	α-nDCG@10
MMR	0.5879	0.6071
DQS	0.6032	0.6234
TDQS	**0.6430***†	**0.6631***†

$\alpha - nDCG@10$ [2] to measure the ranking and diversification performance of query suggestions. It is should be noted that parameter α in Equation(1) is set to 0.6 in this paper.

We examine the query suggestion performance of the baselines as well as our TDQS model, and results in Table 1 indicate that our method (TDQS) achieves the best performance, with *MRR@10* and $\alpha - nDCG@10$ of around 0.6430 and 0.6631, respectively, and significantly outperforms all other methods.

4 CONCLUSION AND FUTURE WORK

To our best knowledge, this work reports the first attempt to return query suggestions indicating diverse interested time points to the input query. What's more, we believe that the approaches described in this paper can be applied to the context of digital libraries, and they are helpful especially when some digital libraries try to provide users with the service for returning history-oriented documents. As future work, we plan to evaluate our models on other datasets so as to verify the effectiveness of our proposal. Other future work is how query suggestion can be diversified along multiple orthogonal but not independent dimensions (e.g., topic and time)

ACKNOWLEDGMENTS

The work is supported by the National Social Science Foundation of China under Grant No.: 15 CTQ019.

REFERENCES

[1] Jaime Carbonell and Jade Goldstein. 1998. The use of MMR, diversity-based reranking for reordering documents and producing summaries. In *International ACM SIGIR Conference on Research and Development in Information Retrieval.* 335–336.

[2] Charles LA Clarke, Maheedhar Kolla, Gordon V Cormack, Olga Vechtomova, Azin Ashkan, Stefan Büttcher, and Ian MacKinnon. 2008. Novelty and diversity in information retrieval evaluation. In *Proceedings of the 31st annual international ACM SIGIR conference on Research and development in information retrieval.* 659–666.

[3] Mihajlo Grbovic, Nemanja Djuric, Vladan Radosavljevic, Fabrizio Silvestri, and Narayan Bhamidipati. 2015. Context- and Content-aware Embeddings for Query Rewriting in Sponsored Search. In *International ACM SIGIR Conference on Research and Development in Information Retrieval.*

[4] Hao Ma, Michael R Lyu, and Irwin King. 2010. Diversifying Query Suggestion Results. In *Proceedings of the 24th AAAI Conference on Artificial Intelligence*, Vol. 10.

[5] Qiaozhu Mei, Dengyong Zhou, and Kenneth Church. 2008. Query suggestion using hitting time. In *Proceedings of the 17th ACM conference on Information and knowledge management.* 469–478.

[6] Taiki Miyanishi and Tetsuya Sakai. 2013. Time-aware structured query suggestion. In *Proceedings of the 36th international ACM SIGIR conference on Research and development in information retrieval.* 809–812.

[7] Chirag Shah and W Bruce Croft. 2004. Evaluating high accuracy retrieval techniques. In *Proceedings of the 27th annual international ACM SIGIR conference on Research and development in information retrieval.* ACM, 2–9.

[8] Wei Song, Yu Zhang, Handong Gao, Ting Liu, and Sheng Li. 2011. HITSCIR system in ntcir-9 subtopic mining task. In *Proc of Ntcir.*

A Visualization Scheme for Multi-Entity Relationship

Peng Zhao
College of Computer Science
Zhejiang University
Hangzhou, China
21621130@zju.edu.cn

Yingzhen Zhu
College of Computer Science
Zhejiang University
Hangzhou, China
kikyou111@163.com

Jifang Yu
College of Computer Science
Zhejiang University
Hangzhou, China
imp_yjf@zju.edu.cn

Yin Zhang
College of Computer Science
Zhejiang University
Hangzhou, China
yinzh@zju.edu.cn

Jiangqin Wu
College of Computer Science
Zhejiang University
Hangzhou, China
wujq@zju.edu.cn

ABSTRACT

In the era of big data, huge amounts of data are generated. In the process of mining the relationship among data entities, we find that there are some similarity in these entity relationships. On this basis, this paper proposes an entity relationship model, and presents a set of visualization schemes that can display the relationship of multi entities. The scheme is applied to the visualization of Chinese herbal medicine prescription dataset and paper dataset, which accord with the model. The result is very satisfying, and proves the good applicability of the scheme.

CCS CONCEPTS

• **Information systems → information retrieval**;

KEYWORDS

data visualization, visualization scheme, Chinese herbal medicine

ACM Reference Format:

Peng Zhao, Yingzhen Zhu, Jifang Yu, Yin Zhang, and Jiangqin Wu. 2018. A Visualization Scheme for Multi-Entity Relationship. In *JCDL '18: The 18th ACM/IEEE Joint Conference on Digital Libraries, June 3–7, 2018, Fort Worth, TX, USA.* ACM, New York, NY, USA, 2 pages. https://doi.org/10.1145/3197026.3203895

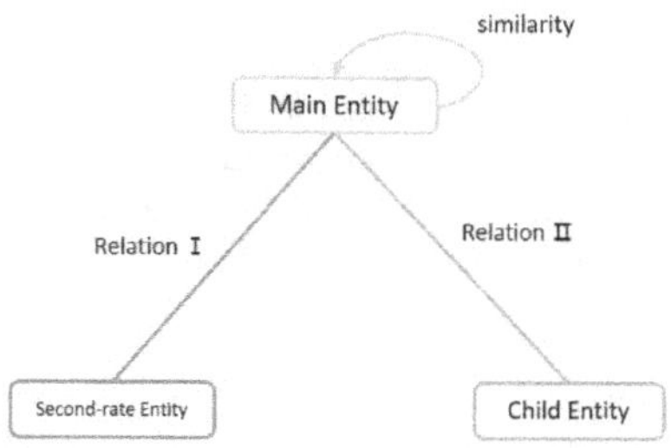

Figure 1: Model entity relation diagram.

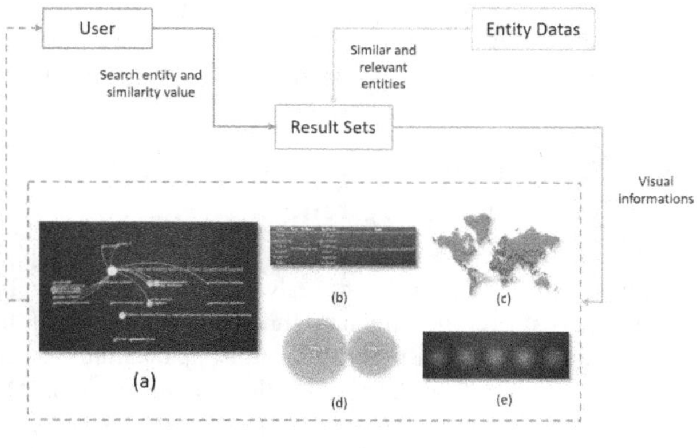

Figure 2: Visualization scheme flow chart.

1 INTRODUCTION

We sum up an entity relationship model which includes three entities: main-entity, child-entity and secondary-entity. The main-entity is composed by child-entity, relationship existed between the main-entity and secondary-entity, and the main-entities are related through relationship similarity, which is measured by the Jaccard index(between 0 and 1). Based on the relational model, we propose a set of visualization schemes. The core of the schemes is to build a visual query system to display the relationship of multi entities. Finally we construct visualization systems for the Chinese herbal medicine data set and the paper data set respectively, which conform to the model. We proved that the scheme has excellent practicability and applicability.

ACM ISBN 978-1-4503-5178-2/18/06...$15.00
https://doi.org/10.1145/3197026.3203895

2 VISUALIZATION SCHEME

As shown in figure 2, the visual query system, receiving the query entity and similarity threshold from user, through the data interface finding all the main-entities which meet the similarity threshold and the associated child-entity and secondary-entity, and returning to the drawing interface to map the entity relationship diagram. The drawing of the entity relation diagram uses the force-oriented

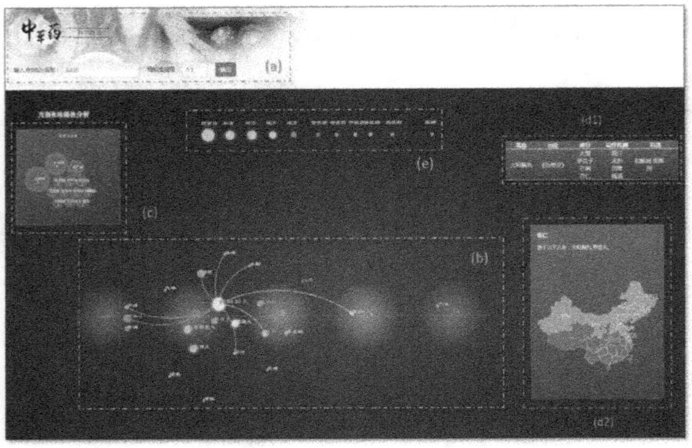

Figure 3: Interface diagram of Chinese herbal prescription query system.

layout, and the position of the class axis is added to the node. Moreover, through multi-view association[1, 2], users can interact with the system to see more detailed information of the entity nodes in the relational graph. These information are presented by bubble charts, maps, data tables, etc.

3 USE CASE

As shown in figure 3 and 4, We construct visualization systems for the Chinese herbal medicine data set and the paper data set respectively. For the Chinese herbal medicine data set, prescriptions, diseases and medicines can correspond to the main entities, the secondary entities and the child entities in the data model. And for paper data set, the papers, authors, keywords can correspond to the main entities, the secondary entities and the child entities in the data model.

3.1 Sample Analysis of Paper Collection Visualization System

As shown in figure 5,

Input "444" or "Vision-Based Analysis of Small Groups in Pedestrian Crowds", and the similarity threshold "0.5" to search in the system and we can get the entity relationship diagram (A). All the paper nodes are yellow. All of the authors' nodes are pink. Others are keyword nodes, and all keywords nodes are restricted to category axis. The color of the keyword nodes is determined by the color of the corresponding categories in the category axis. The lines connected to the searched paper node are solid, and the others are all dashed lines. In more detail, when clicking on the paper node "An Incremental DPMM-Based Method for Trajectory Clustering, Modeling, and Retrieval" in the detailed graph (A+) of (A), all the connecting nodes and lines will be highlighted, as shown in (C). (D) shows the detailed attributes information of the selected paper entity, including title, publication date, authors, keywords and link to the full-text. (B) displays a detailed description of the selected author node "Feng Zhou" in the selected relational graph and his/her address information. For (E), it is the statistical figure of the number of all papers in search results. Clicking "category 2" , we can find from (F) that all the the paper nodes belonging to category 2 in the relational graph are highlighted.

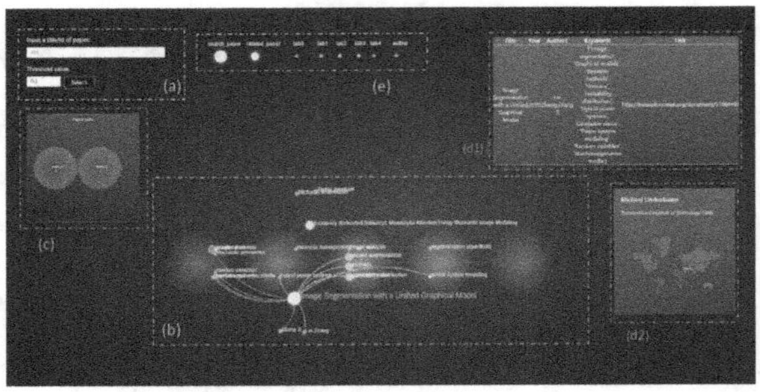

Figure 4: Visualization system interface diagram of paper dataset.

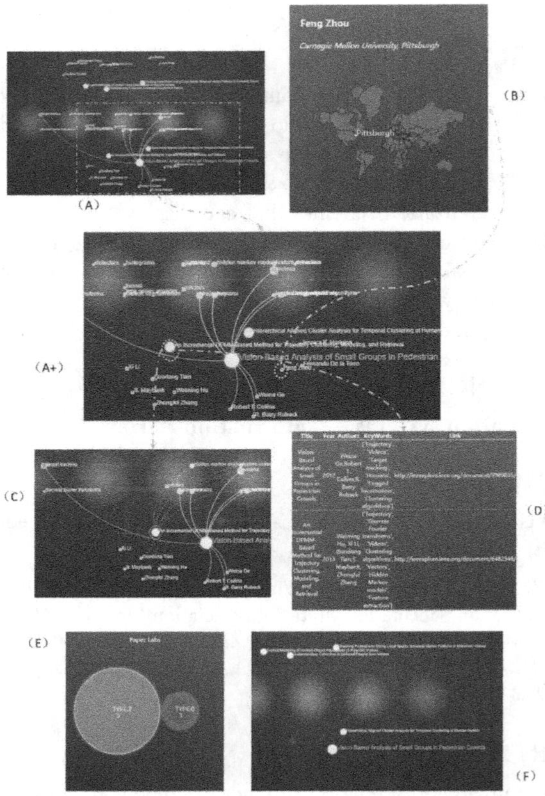

Figure 5: Paper visualization system query sample diagram.

ACKNOWLEDGMENTS

This paper is supported by Chinese Knowledge Center for Engineering Science and Technology (CKCEST), English books and books in Colleges and Universities (CADAL) and the Fundamental Research Funds for the Central Universities (2018FZA5012).

REFERENCES

[1] C. Collins and S. Carpendale. 2007. VisLink: Revealing Relationships Amongst Visualizations. *IEEE Transactions on Visualization and Computer Graphics* 13, 6 (Nov 2007), 1192–1199. https://doi.org/10.1109/TVCG.2007.70521

[2] Ben Shneiderman and Aleks Aris. 2006. Network Visualization by Semantic Substrates. *IEEE Transactions on Visualization and Computer Graphics* 12, 5 (Sept. 2006), 733–740. https://doi.org/10.1109/TVCG.2006.166

Getting Smarter: Definition, Scope, and Implications of Smart Libraries

Tara Zimmerman
University of North Texas
taradz37@gmail.com

Hsia-Ching Chang
University of North Texas
hsia-ching.chang@unt.edu

ABSTRACT

Two-dimensional The term "smart library" was coined by Aittola, Ryhanen, and Ojala in 2003, and librarians have been striving to implement smart libraries in different ways ever since. However, in the 15 years that have passed, no definitive explanation of a smart library has emerged, and it seems unclear what technologies or services truly make a library "smart." In a world of smartphones, smartwatches, and even smart homes, innovative librarians want to move toward creating next generation smart libraries, but how? Because the majority of studies relevant to smart libraries take a qualitative approach, a meta-synthesis of existing qualitative research on smart libraries has been conducted and analyzed. Three time-periods have been identified to demonstrate the transition of technology changing to meet users' needs.

KEYWORDS

Smart library; RFID; Internet of things; future libraries

ACM Reference format:
Tara Zimmerman and Hsia-Ching Chang. 2018. Getting Smarter: Definition, Scope, and Implications of Smart Libraries. In Proceedings of The 18th ACM/IEEE Joint Conference on Digital Libraries, Fort Worth, TX, USA, June 3–7, 2018 (JCDL'18), 2 pages. https://doi.org/10.1145/3197026.3203906

1 INTRODUCTION

The term "smart library" first appeared in the academic publication in 2003 [1]. To date, research on smart libraries has consisted mainly of case studies of particular libraries and innovative "smart" services they offer, ranging from library automation systems to use of artificial intelligence to full integration with a smart campus or city. While these studies have been illuminating, a key baseline of information is still missing. Librarians need a clear definition of what a smart library is, including the range of ways it can be implemented, in order to begin contemplating setting up or converting their own smart library. With that goal in mind, this study will examine what features make up a smart library and what technologies undergird it. The research questions are 1) What is the definition or the scope of a smart library?, and 2) How is a smart library implemented by using different technologies? This research will benefit the library and information science fields by synthesizing existing research and summarizing the overall findings.

ACM ISBN 978-1-4503-5178-2/18/06.
https://doi.org/10.1145/3197026.3203906

2 RESEARCH METHODOLOGY

We chose to use a meta-synthesis of relevant literature for this study. The essence of meta-synthesis is to gather existing qualitative research about smart libraries, analyze it, and summarize the findings to benefit understanding and future research [2]. The first step was to search the Academic Search Complete, EBSCOhost, Web of Knowledge, ProQuest, and ScienceDirect databases using the terms "smart library," "mobile services," "digital library," and "internet of things". In addition, Publish or Perish software tool (version 6.21.6145) was utilized to search recent publications through Google Scholar. A total of 40 articles were located and analyzed. (A list of articles used can be found at: https://goo.gl/N9Uhku.) Finding representative articles was much more difficult than anticipated, which reinforced the idea that the smart library has not been well-defined in academic literature. The definition and scope of the term "smart library" were gleaned from each article. In addition, specific uses of technology within the smart library were noted. Text analysis was applied to this information, revealing trends through the frequency of terms used. Each article was reviewed in-depth by two researchers, and its research question, methodology, and findings organized and further analyzed to identify patterns. All this information was compiled in a table to sum up the current state of research on smart libraries and to serve as a roadmap for future researchers.

3 SYNTHESIS RESULTS

Through analysis, it became clear that the evolution of understanding smart libraries over time was key. Reviewing articles chronologically as they were published highlights the change in emphasis from books to information services and eventually to knowledge infrastructure. The following three time periods have been identified to show the progression of technology changing to meet users' needs.

3.1 Library Automation (2001~2011)

Of the 40 articles reviewed, six (15%) were published between 2001 and 2011. A text analysis of the titles, definition/scope of smart library, and technology was conducted, and the word "books" appeared with more than double the frequency of any other term. For example, in 2008, Kwok, et al. [3] wrote about the large amount of human effort and time required to perform inventory management in a library, stating that RFID technologies could help to enhance library operations, "especially in book check-in, check-out, and stock checking processes." This reflects the old library paradigm. The smart libraries of this time period began automating library systems for inventory control, borrowing, returns, renewal, and tracking of library resources.

3.2 User-Centered Services (2012~2014)

Sixteen articles (40%) were published between 2012 and 2014, and the same text analysis was utilized on information from those articles. The word "service(s)" dominated, displacing "books" from first place. This is representative of a secondary phase of development of the smart library concept, the user-oriented phase. An example of this was provided by Brian, et al. [4] in 2014 when they introduced a service to patrons in which a local positioning system and embedded tags on books linked to the user's smartphone so that he/she can check in real time whether a book is available and be directed to its exact placement on a shelf. Expanding beyond automated library services, exemplary smart libraries from this era were integrating mobile apps and smartphone usage into their system, using text and email features to communicate with users, and posting videos to help remote users access their various services.

3.3 Knowledge Infrastructure (2015~2017)

Publications on the topic continued to grow, and from 2015 to present, there were 18 articles published (45%). Text analysis reveals that "information" and "knowledge" are both seen more frequently than "service(s)", while "book(s)" was much less important. This moves away from physical books and services and toward more intangible goals such as knowledge and information, which indicates a key change in what the term smart library has come to mean. For example, Jerkov, et al. [5] considered a smart library as a "knowledge broker" locating qualified sources of critical knowledge to solve specific problems. Beyond library space and place, this is the knowledge infrastructure connecting smart libraries to smart cities. A real-world example is the Stark County District Library where users can check out smart devices (e.g., radon detector, air quality monitor and electricity monitor) to experience smart home capability. Those smart home devices serve critical components of smart cities for home safety and monitoring energy consumption.

4 Discussion

A factor essential to the changing definition of smart libraries is technology, which has advanced exponentially since the first smart library articles were published. These early articles referenced artificial intelligence and basic RFID as important to facilitating smart libraries, but this understanding grew to include a broader application of RFID, which is now the standard framework for most Smart Libraries. Taking recommendations from each article and synthesizing them reveals an overall outlook for the future of smart libraries. One of the strongest overall recommendations is libraries continue developing mobile apps and websites services. Increasing engagement with users online is a major step toward building a successful smart library, and it is critical to offer patrons quick and easy remote access. A second overall recommendation is that smart librarians are a key priority in implementing a smart library. Skilled and competent staff are crucial to create a dynamic smart environment. Researchers also recommendation is to offer next generation digital features and access, using Web 2.0 and social networking services to encourage patrons to produce new knowledge.

5 CONCLUSIONS

Libraries are experiencing a need to transition resources and services to include more technology, while also honoring their primary focus of meeting user needs. This exploratory study is an examination of smart libraries, specifically how they are being defined and framed in academic literature. A meta-synthesis was chosen as the best methodology to review the articles and revealed a progression of understanding of smart libraries in articles published from 2001 through today. Over time, more libraries extended services to users by applying new technologies in innovative ways, expanding the definition of the smart library. What began as just library automation grew to include more information services and ultimately knowledge infrastructure. The corresponding growth of RFID technology to become the standard smart library framework can be seen over this time period as well. Next steps of this study are to continue seeking more articles focused on smart libraries and evidence-based library practices in realizing the concept of smart libraries in order to broaden and enrich the data and to learn more about both the benefits and risks of Smart Libraries to their communities.

REFERENCES

[1] M. Aittola, T. Ryhänen, T. Ojala. 2003. Smart Library: location-aware mobile library service. Lecture Notes in Computer Science 2795: 411-416.

[2] C. Urquhart. 2010. Systematic reviewing, meta-analysis and meta-synthesis for evidence-based library and information science. Information Research, 15(3) colis708.

[3] S.K. Kwok, C.F. Cheung, W.B. Lee, A.H.C Tsang & M.C. Tang, (2008). Development of an RFID-enabled mobile smart library system. *International Journal of Enterprise Network Management, 2*(2).

[4] A.L.A. Brian, L. Arockiam, & P.D.S.K Malarchelvi. (2014). An IoT based secured smart library system with NFC based book tracking. *International Journal of Emerging Technology in Computer Science & Electronics 11*(5), 18-21.

[5] Aleksandar Jerkov, Adam Sofronijevic, Dejana Kavaja Stanisic. 2015. Smart and sustainable library: Information literacy hub of a new city. In: Kurbanoglu S., Boustany J., Špiranec S., Grassian E., Mizrachi D., Roy L. (Eds) Information Literacy: Moving Toward Sustainability, Springer.

A Graphical Model for Topical Impact over Time

Zhiya Zuo
University of Iowa
Iowa City, IA
zhiya-zuo@uiowa.edu

Kang Zhao
University of Iowa
Iowa City, IA
kang-zhao@uiowa.edu

ABSTRACT

After being published, a document, whether it is a research paper or an online post, can make an impact when readers cite, share, or endorse it. A document may not make its greatest impact right after its publication, and some documents' impact can last a long period of time. This study develops a graphical model to capture the temporal dynamics in the impact of latent topics from a corpus of documents. Specifically, we modeled citation counts using Poisson distributions with Gamma priors. We conducted experiments on papers published in (i) D-Lib Magazine and (ii) The Library Quarterly from 2007 to 2017. Comparing with ToT, we found that our model produced more robust results on topical trends over time. The results also showed that prevalence and impact of the same topic are not correlated. Enabling better understanding and modeling of topical impact over time, this model can be used for the design of digital libraries and social media platforms, as well as evaluation of scientific contributions and policies.

CCS CONCEPTS

• **Information systems → Document topic models;** • **Applied computing → Document analysis;**

KEYWORDS

Topic models, temporal impact, text mining

ACM Reference Format:

Zhiya Zuo and Kang Zhao. 2018. A Graphical Model for Topical Impact over Time. In *JCDL '18: The 18th ACM/IEEE Joint Conference on Digital Libraries, June 3–7, 2018, Fort Worth, TX, USA.* ACM, New York, NY, USA, 2 pages. https://doi.org/10.1145/3197026.3203891

1 INTRODUCTION

Growing numbers of documents have imposed challenges on information retrieval and text mining. In the context of digital libraries, huge amounts of data have brought challenges to content searching and navigation. With a lower dimensional representation containing essential statistical characteristics for a collection of documents, information processing can be more scalable and efficient, under minimal human supervision. Topic modeling algorithms, therefore, are applied to aid the process of document/metadata annotation and labeling (e.g., [4]). In fact, there has been evidence on the effectiveness of topic modeling on such tasks [3].

JCDL '18, June 3–7, 2018, Fort Worth, TX, USA

ACM ISBN 978-1-4503-5178-2/18/06.
https://doi.org/10.1145/3197026.3203891

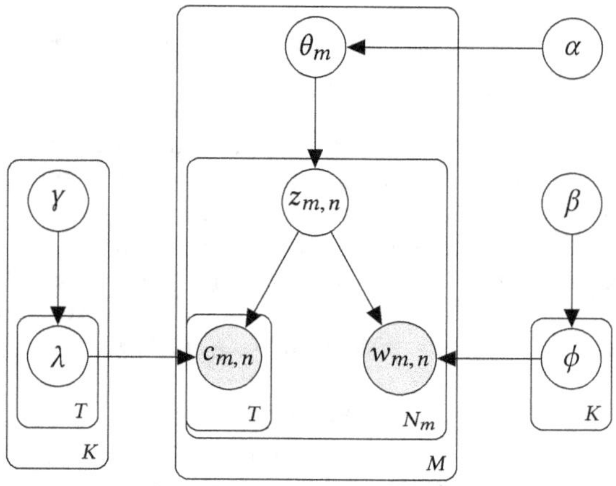

Figure 1: Graphical representation of TIoT model

While detection of latent topics among large corpora has been a remarkable success, the rise and fall of various topics are equivalently important. Blei and Lafferty [1] proposed a Markovian dynamic topic model where topics across time are dependent on their precedents. However, topics may vary in different time slices. Meanwhile, Topics over Time (ToT) model by Wang and McCallum [5] treated time as continuous variables with Beta distributions. Topics are invariant, while the shape of per topic Beta distributions portrait temporal topical prevalence. Leveraging citation data, Inheritance Topic Model (ITM) [2] aims at capturing topic evolutions.

However, none managed to explicitly model temporal dynamics of impact at topic level. While topical prevalence and evolution are helpful in identifying trend, impact can provide additional insights. Breakthrough research, for example, may not be the mainstream area, but can attract a significant amount of citations. In this study, we propose Topical Impact over Time (TIoT), to fill this gap. For academic publications, impact can be quantified by citation counts. The generative process corresponding to the graphical model in Figure 1 is as follows:

- Sample topic distributions $\boldsymbol{\theta} \sim Dirichlet(\alpha)$ for documents
- Sample word distribution $\boldsymbol{\phi} \sim Dirichlet(\beta)$ for topics
- For each document m:
  - For the nth word w_{mn}:
    - Sample a topic $z_{mn} \sim Multinomial(\boldsymbol{\theta}_m)$
    - Sample a word $w_{mn} \sim Multinomial(\boldsymbol{\phi}_{z_{mn}})$
    - Sample citations $c_t \sim Poisson(\lambda_{kt})$ for $t \in \{1..T\}$

Exact inference cannot be done on this model. We applied collapsed Gibbs sampling for approximate inference, where $\boldsymbol{\theta}$, $\boldsymbol{\phi}$, and

$\boldsymbol{\lambda}$ are integrated out. The full conditional probability for TIoT is:

$$P(z_{mn}|\mathbf{w},\mathbf{c},z_{-(mn)},\alpha,\beta,\gamma) \propto (n_{mz_{mn}}+\alpha-1)\times\frac{(n_{z_{mn}w_{mn}}+\beta-1)}{(n_{z_{mn}}+V*\beta)} \times\prod_{t=1}^{T}\left[\frac{\Gamma(\sum_d c_{dt}n_{dz_{mn}}+\gamma_1)}{\Gamma(\sum_d c_{dt}n_{dz_{mn}}+\gamma_1-c_{mt})}\frac{(n_{z_{mn}}+\gamma_2-1)^{\sum_d c_{dt}n_{dz_{mn}}\gamma_1-c_{mt}}}{(n_{z_{mn}}+\gamma_2)^{\sum_d c_{dt}n_{dz_{mn}}\gamma_1}}\right] \quad (1)$$

where n_{mz} is the number of words in m assigned to topic z; n_{zw} is the number of times word w assigned to topic z; n_z is the number of times topic z sampled; c_{dt} is the document d's citations at time t; T is the number of timestamps; K is the number of topics; M is the number of documents; N_m is the size of m. For simplicity, we assume α, β, and γ are fixed values. It is noteworthy that citations for each word are the same as their belonging documents. Since we are over-using citation information for N_m times, we will raise the last term in Equation 1 to the power of $1/N_m$ to make text and citation modality comparable, as in Wang and McCallum [5].

2 RESULTS AND DISCUSSIONS

We conducted experiments with TIoT model on two datasets: (i) D-Lib Magazine (DLM) and (ii) The Library Quarterly (TLQ). We harvested abstracts and annual citations of papers from year 2007 to 2017 from Scopus. The numbers of topics K are set to 20 for both datasets. For simplicity, we followed the convention in Wang and McCallum [5] on fixed symmetric Dirichlet ($\alpha = 50/K = 2.5$; $\beta = 0.1$) and weak gamma priors are used ($\gamma_1 = \gamma_2 = 0.005$ for all $\boldsymbol{\lambda}$). Topics presented below are extracted from one sample at the 1000th iteration of a single Gibbs sampler. We ran ToT as a baseline model with the same setting. In the following, we use ToT's Beta densities as topical prevalence and TIoT's $\boldsymbol{\lambda}$ as topical impact over time. Topics from ToT and TIoT are paired by Jensen-Shannon divergence for the purpose of comparison.

First, we show how TIoT successfully extracts the impact trend by jointly modeling topics and citations. Figure 2 shows prevalence and impact for two topics in TLQ: (i) *policy & library* (top keywords include *political, factor,* and *election*) and (ii) library service to immigrants (top keywords include *immigrants, ala,* and *library*). For *policy & library,* specifically, a steep increase in citations happened right after year 2013 - in fact, two 2013 papers in TLQ on this topic were cited by a total of over 40 times. It is also interesting to note that the 2016 U.S. presidency election may result in the small increase from 2016 to 2017. TIoT also shows the burst of impact after year 2013, where citations start to accumulate gradually for papers on *library service to immigrants.* ToT, on the other hand, failed to provide useful information with the U-shaped Beta distributions.

Finally, we emphasize that topical prevalence and impact are different aspects. To illustrate this, we show in Figure 3 that there is hardly any correlation at the two arbitrarily selected timestamps in DLIB data. In both subplots, moreover, there is at least one outlier topic with high impact but relatively low prevalence. Results are consistent for both DLIB and TLQ data.

3 CONCLUSION

This paper presented the preliminary results of TIoT model and showed its promising capability in the area of digital libraries. For

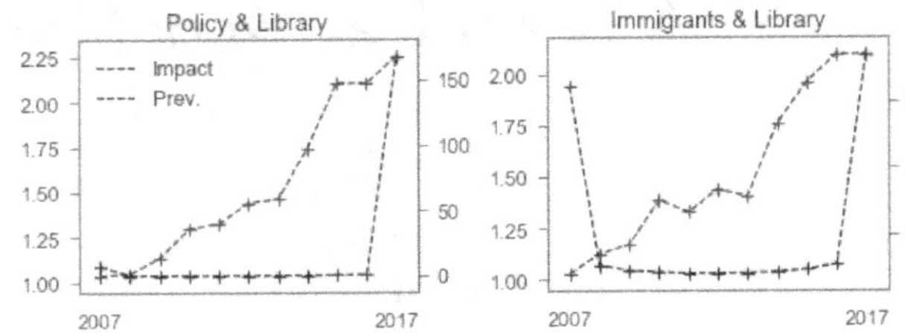

Figure 2: Two topics discovered by ToT (black) and TIoT (magenta) in TLQ dataset. Left y axes are Poisson parameters λ that measures average citation counts (i.e., impact) for that topic in each year; right y axes are Beta distribution probability densities that exhibits temporal prevalence

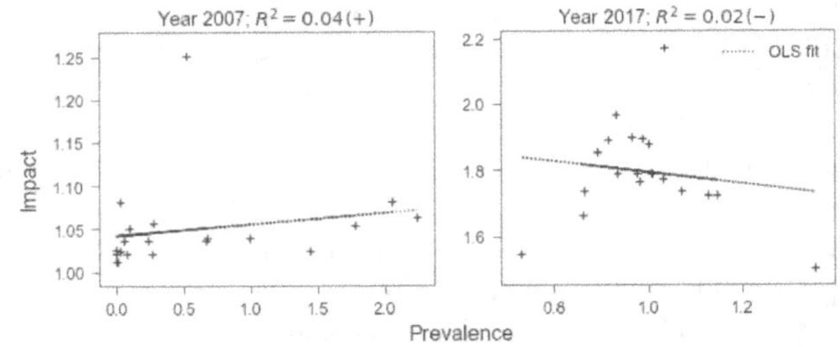

Figure 3: Correlation between topical prevalence and impact for all 20 topics in DLIB dataset in year 2007 and 2017. The dotted lines are fitted on the "+" data points by ordinal least squares. The sign of correlation is shown after R^2 value.

example, TIoT can be used for detecting trending topics and suggesting impactful papers in a bibliographical database. Annual citations, however, may increase over time, simply because of the increasing numbers of academic articles and researchers. In the future, it is important to normalize citations to make them comparable across time. Finally, it is interesting to apply TIoT on online social media and evaluate the extracted topical impact over time.

ACKNOWLEDGMENTS

The authors thank Dr. Kate Cowles and anonymous reviewers for providing valuable comments and Elsevier developer team for providing access to citation data.

REFERENCES

[1] David M. Blei and John D. Lafferty. 2006. Dynamic topic models. In *Proceedings of the 23rd international conference on Machine learning - ICML '06*. ACM Press, 113–120. https://doi.org/10.1145/1143844.1143859

[2] Qi He, Bi Chen, Jian Pei, Baojun Qiu, Prasenjit Mitra, and Lee Giles. 2009. Detecting topic evolution in scientific literature. *Proceeding of the 18th ACM conference on Information and knowledge management - CIKM '09* (2009), 957. https://doi.org/10.1145/1645953.1646076

[3] David Newman, Youn Noh, Edmund Talley, Sarvnaz Karimi, and Timothy Baldwin. 2010. Evaluating topic models for digital libraries. *Proceedings of the 10th ACM/IEEE-CS Joint Conference on Digital Libraries* (2010), 215–224. https://doi.org/10.1145/1816123.1816156

[4] Suppawong Tuarob, Line C. Pouchard, and C. Lee Giles. 2013. Automatic tag recommendation for metadata annotation using probabilistic topic modeling. *Proceedings of the 13th ACM/IEEE-CS joint conference on Digital libraries - JCDL '13* (2013), 239. https://doi.org/10.1145/2467696.2467706

[5] Xuerui Wang and Andrew McCallum. 2006. Topics over time: A non-Markov continuous-time model of topical trends. *Proceedings of the 12th ACM SIGKDD International Conference on Knowledge Discovery and Data Mining* (2006), 424–433. https://doi.org/10.1145/1150402.1150450

Providing Pin-point Page-level Precision to 1 Trillion Tokens of Text for Workset Creation

David Bainbridge
University of Waikato
Hamilton, New Zealand
davidb@waikato.ac.nz

J. Stephen Downie
University of Illinois
Urbana-Champaign, USA
jdownie@illinois.edu

Boris Capitanu
University of Illinois
Urbana-Champaign, USA
capitanu@illinois.edu

ABSTRACT

We report on the work undertaken developing a web environment that allows users to search over 1 trillion tokens of text—down to the page-level—of the HathiTrust Part-of-Speech Extracted Features Dataset to help produce worksets for scholarly analysis. We present an extended example of the web environment in use, along with details about its implementation.

KEYWORDS

Very Large Digital Libraries, Extract Feature Text Analysis, Workset Creation

ACM Reference Format:
David Bainbridge, J. Stephen Downie, and Boris Capitanu. 2018. Providing Pin-point Page-level Precision to 1 Trillion Tokens of Text for Workset Creation. In *JCDL '18: The 18th ACM/IEEE Joint Conference on Digital Libraries, June 3–7, 2018, Fort Worth, TX, USA.* ACM, New York, NY, USA, 2 pages. https://doi.org/10.1145/3197026.3203873

1 INTRODUCTION

In previous work the HathiTrust Research Centre (HTRC) has made publicly available a Part-of-Speech Unigram Extracted Feature Dataset of the full HathiTrust Digital Library (HTDL), containing over 5.7 billion pages of scanned and OCR'd content [1]. In this article we detail the work done in developing a searchable version of this resource that helps support workset creation. The implementation centres around a digital library architecture designed for large scale content with fine-grained access. In addition to metadata level field search, users can specify queries down to the page-level for words in 54 identified languages, and in the case of 6 languages, specify queries by part-of-speech. In total this constitutes over a trillion tokens of indexed text.

To illustrate the capabilities of the developed resource we start by giving an extended example of it in use: locating the pages that make reference to violins in the *Sherlock Holmes* book series. We then go on to provide details about its implementation.

ACM ISBN 978-1-4503-5178-2/18/06.
https://doi.org/10.1145/3197026.3203873

2 WORKED EXAMPLE

Figure 1 shows a snapshot of the web page that a user encounters when they first visit the developed website.[1] Notice the tabs along the top of the page. The first tab is for searching at the page level, and the second for volume-level metadata searching. In the snapshot we are looking at the third tab, through which the user can specify a combined page and volume level query. The top search box is for the volume-level metadata—*Sherlock* has been entered in this case—and the search box below that for page-level text searching—where *violin* has been entered. The final tab is for more advanced use where users can enter their query directly using a fielded Boolean query syntax. Information icons are strategically positioned throughout the search tabs to provide contextualised user help.

Below the two search boxes is an area for controlling the languages and parts-of-speech that are queried, based on the mappings from the universal POS tagset developed by Petrov et al. [2]. This part of the interface makes extensive use of check-boxes, and defaults to searching by all parts-of-speech in the English language because, at 50%, this language represents the largest proportion of the DL's content. Clicking on *Show other languages ...* expands this area of the interface to reveal the other languages available.

For the query shown in Figure 1, the checkboxes are set to perform a title-level search for *Sherlock* with pages grouped by volume, where the pages themselves include the term *violin*. Matching is case-insensitive but—given the complexities of querying across multiple languages—not stemmed. Figure 2 shows the result of performing this query. The central feature produced is the paginated result set. Above this are collated details about the search, such as how many matches were found—1,413 pages in 251 volumes—and links to share the query through email and social media platforms. Through the facets on the left, the user can further refine the query, such as restricting items to be only in the public domain.

Different to many DLs, the produced result set is not the end-result of the search interface. Beyond sharing the URL of the query, the website supports the formation of worksets. The most direct way to do this is to export the query through the actions available in the upper-left corner of the shown snapshot. From here a list of volume identifiers can be downloaded, or alternatively a more fine-grained list exported that gives volume with HTDL sequence number (effectively its page number). For authenticated users, there is also the option to publish the list of IDs resulting from the query in the HTRC registry directly.

A shopping cart feature is provided to support the formation of more intricate worksets built out of multiple queries over a period of time. The icon for this appears in the upper portion of the result set area, on the right and is used to add items from the result set to

[1] https://solr1.ischool.illinois.edu/solr-ef/index.html

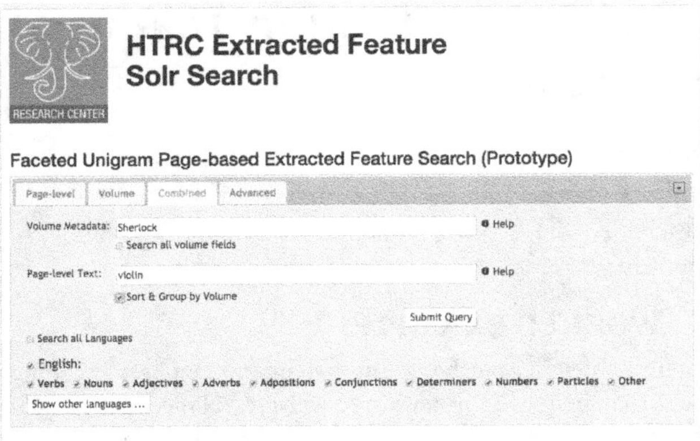

Figure 1: The Extracted Feature Solr search Page.

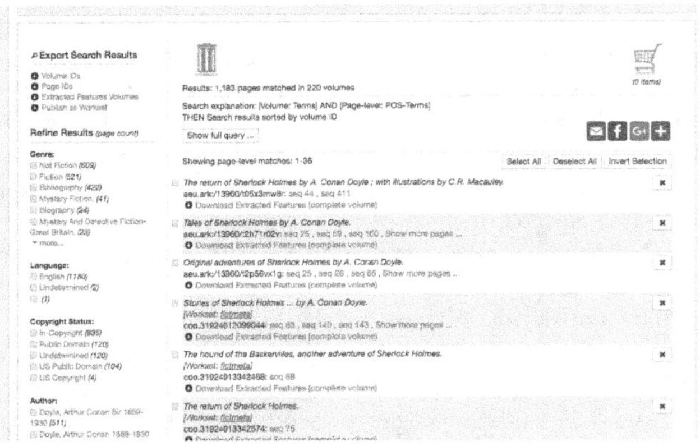

Figure 2: The Extracted Feature Solr search result set.

the cart. Complementing this, a trashcan icon (upper-left), allows the user to remove items to make it clearer to see what is left.

Three further features worthy of mention that occur within one matching item of the result set are: the *Unigram POS Page-viewer* which allows the user to view content—even in-copyright content—as a bag of words, sorted in various ways, such as alphabetically grouped by part-of-speech; the *Extracted Feature JSON Download* feature which provides a convenient, simple way to selectively download an item of interest from the the Extracted Feature dataset; and *Worksets Inclusion* which means the user can see which existing worksets an item is already in. The workset name is hyperlinked, so a user can explore this relationship further by accessing the named workset through the HTRC registry.

3 IMPLEMENTATION

Turning the 15+ million JSON Extracted Features files into a malleable, searchable resource was broken down into two key steps: transforming the data into Hadoop Sequence files, and developing a Spark framework program to ingest the documents into a Solr index. A 48 core machine was used for converting the JSON files mounted on a network disk into the Hadoop Sequence format. The process involved decompressing each JSON files (BZip2 format) on-the-fly, and then recompressing the content (again BZip2) within the formation of the Hadoop Sequence files. This process took 2 weeks to run.

The resulting files were then copied onto the Hadoop Disk File System (HDFS) operating across a 10 node, 120 core cluster machine set up to operate the Spark framework. This took slightly over a day to run, with the replication factor set to 3.

The Spark framework was where the ingest of the JSON files took place. This involved reading in the HTRC Extracted Feature JSON format and transforming it into the JSON format used by Solr for indexing. The location of the Solr server was itself separate from the machine running the Spark framework, this time a cluster computer with 2 nodes and 24 cores. The transformed JSON data was streamed to the Solr server through a dedicated switch. The Solr server was configured as a 20 core (aka shard) collection, with its replication value set to 1. The properties of the schema fields used in Solr were set to "do not store" for full-page text fields to conserve space. The ingest process took two weeks to run, and resulted in index files that cumulatively consume 7 TB.

The user interface shown in the previous section is a single-page web application. It uses AJAX calls to collect information from various servers in the HathiTrust orbit. The key call is to the Solr server. As the volume-level metadata is stored in the Solr index, this is also where it retrieves the bibliographic fields needed to present the search results. Other functionality provided by the search interface is provided through a dedicated Servlet-based server. The API to this server supports AJAX calls to access the original Extracted Feature JSON files, either individually or in Zipped format. There is also a URL shortening service provided (so long queries can be emailed out, for example) and where server-side storage of a user's session is kept, such as the items in their shopping cart.

4 CONCLUSION

The interface described here has already been used to satisfy a variety of use cases for scholars engaged with HTRC: from ones that can be satisfied with a single query term—such as on how many pages does the word *Canada* appear? (75,528,670)—through to more sophisticated ones—such as the worked example given above—and beyond.

For the most part, we have found that these use cases need to be formulated through the Advanced Query tab to provide the best response. While the worked example was constructed to give a flavour of what is possible with the interface, for instance, it is not the case that all the book titles in the *Sherlock Holmes* series include the name of the main character in it. A more accurate query is to search by author metadata and sift through the result set. This is, however, complicated by the fact that variations in how Arthur Conan Doyle's name is recorded means that an ORing of the variants (there are three) is needed, and from a "cold start" using the Advanced Query tab, what these three variations are, is not immediately apparent. In future work we seek to better support, through interactive features, the ways in which these more complex queries are constructed.

REFERENCES

[1] P. Organisciak, B. Capitanu, T. Underwood, and J. S. Downie. 2017. Access to Billions of Pages for Large-Scale Text Analysis. In *iConference Proceedings*, Vol. 2. 66–76. https://doi.org/10.9776/17014

[2] S. Petrov, D. Das, and R. McDonald. 2011. A Universal Part-of-Speech Tagset. *ArXiv e-prints* (April 2011). arXiv:cs.CL/1104.2086

MEDDLEing with Digital Library Searches: Surmounting User Model and System Misalignments through Lightweight Bespoke Proxying

David Bainbridge, Annika Hinze, Sally Jo Cunningham
University of Waikato
Hamilton, New Zealand
{davidb,hinze,sallyjo}@waikato.ac.nz

J. Stephen Downie
University of Illinois
Urbana-Champaign, USA
jdownie@illinois.edu

ABSTRACT

We document how surprisingly easy it is for user misconceptions to arise when using digital library search interfaces, and the significant unseen impact this can have on the user's interpretation of search results. Further, we detail a bespoke proxying technique we have devised called MEDDLE—for ModifiED Digital Library Environment—which is a lightweight agile technique that helps address identified pitfalls in a DL search interface that operates independently of the originating digital library.

CCS CONCEPTS

• **Human-centered computing → Web-based interaction**; • **Applied computing → Digital libraries and archives**;

KEYWORDS

Digital Library Search, Usability Issues, Bespoke Proxying

ACM Reference Format:
David Bainbridge, Annika Hinze, Sally Jo Cunningham and J. Stephen Downie. 2018. MEDDLEing with Digital Library Searches: Surmounting User Model and System Misalignments through Lightweight Bespoke Proxying. In *JCDL '18: The 18th ACM/IEEE Joint Conference on Digital Libraries, June 3–7, 2018, Fort Worth, TX, USA.* ACM, New York, NY, USA, 2 pages. https://doi.org/10.1145/3197026.3203873

INTRODUCTION

Like it or not, the phenomenal success of web search engines such as Google impacts how users interact with any search box they encounter—including the ones in our digital libraries. Given what we know about the users' "folk models" for searching [3] (i.e., expected similarity to Web search engines), in this paper we demonstrate that more can be done to align our digital libraries with this type of mental model. Extending our previous work [1], we start by presenting some worked examples to highlight the ways in which user expectation and search interfaces can disconnect. Following this, we provide implementation details of MEDDLE, the approach we have devised to help offset the effects of such misalignments. For a broader discussion of the issues, see [1].

JCDL '18, June 3–7, 2018, Fort Worth, TX, USA

ACM ISBN 978-1-4503-5178-2/18/06.
https://doi.org/10.1145/3197026.3203873

Example 1: Known-item search

Known-item searches are a common activity [2]. Using the home page of the ACM DL, however, there is a strong chance of a folk model disconnect with the interface, because the search performed is metadata only. To highlight the impact of this, consider Table 1, which shows the results of searching for articles that mention some well known DL systems.

Using the ACM DL's home page means matches are found only if the authors included the name of the system in a metadata field such as title. In the case of the "ContentDM" query, for instance, this has never occurred, so no matches are returned. Compare this to a user visiting the DL via MEDDLE—which unobtrusively redirects the query to use the full-text index—resulting in 16 articles being located. Similar improvements can be seen for the other example queries in Table 1.

Example 2: Issues of Word-wrap

Building a full-text indexed DL from PDF documents presents many challenges. In the ACM DL one such difficulty that affects some of the documents are line-wraps, where a word at the end of one line is incorrectly joined with the word that starts the next line. To illustrate the problem, we exploited the fact that we knew that many authors publishing in the ACM DL work in a "Department of Computer **Science**" at the "**University** of ..." which might place the malformed string 'ScienceUniversity" in the index.

Searching for "Department of Computer Science" as a full-text phrase returned 38,892 matches, and "Department of Computer ScienceUniversity" returned 883 matches, indicating that up to 2.22% of relevant documents are missed. Repeating the experiment with the phrase "Department of" returned 100,082 matches, in comparison to "Department of" "ScienceUniversity" which returned 2,191 matches. From this larger sample size the error rate remains broadly the same, this time 2.19%.

Employing MEDDLE to offset the word-wrap problem a user's query is intercepted, inspected, and potentially adjusted, prior to it being sent to the ACM DL server. When multiple terms are entered, MEDDLE changes the query to includes additional terms formed by concatenating adjacent words together, thereby increasing the chances of locating documents hindered by the word-wrap problem. Notwithstanding its simplicity, this heuristic works well in practice because the conjoined terms generated are unlikely to appear in

Query term	Original	Adjusted via MEDDLE
"American Memory"	1	28
"ContentDM"	0	16
"DSpace"	27	493
"Omeka"	3	22

Table 1: Comparing known-item searching in the ACM DL with and without Meddle

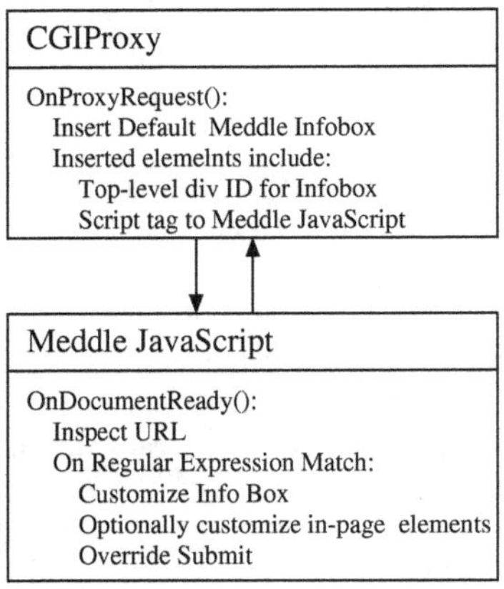

Figure 1: Overview of the Meddle software design

regular prose (with the exception of an article talking about the word-wrap problem!)

IMPLEMENTATION

Figure 1 gives an overview of the MEDDLE software design. It consists of two modules: CGIProxy and the MEDDLE JavaScript library. CGIProxy is an existing Perl module.[1] We chose it because it is a highly configurable —but more importantly—programmable proxy server solution. Used in a default installation, CGIProxy provides a RESTful interface for serving up URLs to users that have been processed through the server CGIProxy provides. A relational database (SQLite by default) is used behind the scenes to cache information to make subsequent operations more efficient.

We have customization CGIProxy to insert an HTML table—the MEDDLE Infobox—at the top of the web page that gets served up when an *OnProxyRequest()* is initiated. Initially the Infobox is rather plain, and mostly serves to highlight the fact that the page has been accessed through the MEDDLE system. The portion of HTML inserted is also marked with an *id* attribute to make it easier to access later on, and further, a *<script>* element is also introduced that binds the MEDDLE JavaScript component into the page being served up.

The JavaScript component adds an *OnDocumentReady()* handler. When the Document Object Model (DOM) is formed in the user's browser, this handler is triggered. It checks the DOM's URL with a regular expression to determine if it is a DL domain that is one that it will makes changes to (i.e., meddle with!) The procedure for changing the different DLs is modularized. For each DL, an *Adjustment()* method is provided which gets called upon a match being

[1]https://en.wikipedia.org/wiki/CGIProxy

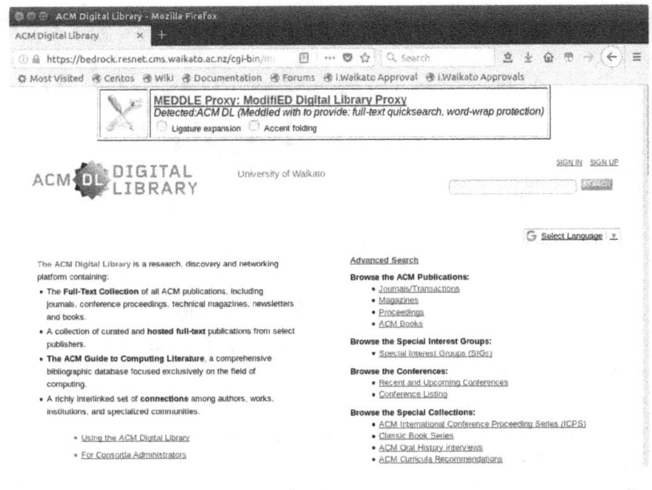

Figure 2: Example use of Meddle with the ACM Digital Library

made. Within this method, three key steps are typically taken: customization of the Infobox to include elements relevant to the given DL, changes to DOM elements in the page that has been retrieved from the DL, and overriding what to do when the Submit/Search button is pressed.

To take the ACM DL as an example, the Infobox is changed to include options for making adjustments concerning queries with accents and ligatures in them (see Figure 2). In the case where the page is the Advanced Search page, then DOM manipulation is undertaken to avoid the page defaulting to "any fields" a term that is ambiguous in the interface as it lists "full text" as one of the fields under "any fields" however our experiments with the interface has determined it is not actually included when such a search is initiated. In the case of the home page, its quick search box is changed to be a full-text query when the Search button is pressed.

CONCLUSION

The MEDDLE implementation is available, open source, through:

`http://trac.greenstone.org/browser/other-projects/meddle/trunk`

The code is intended to be exploratory. We invite others to experiment with using the technique.

REFERENCES

[1] David Bainbridge, Sally Jo Cunningham, Annika Hinze, and J. Stephen Downie. 2017. Writers of the Lost Paper: A Case Study on Barriers to (Re-) Finding Publications. In *ICADL*, Songphan Choemprayong (Ed.). Springer International Publishing, Bangkok, Thailand, 212–224.

[2] Suzanne Chapman, Shevon Desai, Kat Hagedorn, Ken Varnum, Sonali Mishra, and Julie Piacentine. 2013. Manually classifying user search queries on an academic library web site. *Journal of Web Librarianship* 7, 4 (2013), 401–421.

[3] Michael Khoo and Catherine Hall. 2012. What Would 'Google' Do? Users' Mental Models of a Digital Library Search Engine. In *Theory and Practice of Digital Libraries*, Panayiotis Zaphiris, George Buchanan, Edie Rasmussen, and Fernando Loizides (Eds.). Springer Berlin Heidelberg, Berlin, Heidelberg, 1–12.

Compiling Scholarly Profile Pages by Integrating External Authority Data

Atif Latif
ZBW - Leibniz Information Center for Economics
Kiel, Germany
A.Latif@zbw.eu

Timo Borst
ZBW - Leibniz Information Center for Economics
Kiel, Germany
T.Borst@zbw.eu

Klaus Tochtermann
ZBW - Leibniz Information Center for Economics
Kiel, Germany
K.Tochtermann@zbw.eu

ABSTRACT

Open Access (OA) Repositories provide users with barrier free access to scientific resources and play a significant role in the dissemination of scientific results and the increase of author visibility. Although these repositories are providing free resources, they are not well connected on the level of their metadata. One approach to tackle this issue is to linkup with the scattered pieces of bibliographic and biographic information residing in external sources. In this demonstration, we focus on the contributors of a repository by means of authority data that can be linked to several authority systems (WikiData,DBpedia, VIAF, ORCID, RePEc) to make repository data more diverse, interlinked and visible.

KEYWORDS

repository, linked data, authorities

ACM Reference Format:

Atif Latif, Timo Borst, and Klaus Tochtermann. 2018. Compiling Scholarly Profile Pages by Integrating External Authority Data. In *JCDL '18: The 18th ACM/IEEE Joint Conference on Digital Libraries, June 3–7, 2018, Fort Worth, TX, USA.* ACM, New York, NY, USA, 2 pages. https://doi.org/10.1145/3197026.3204473

1 INTRODUCTION

A well linked open access repository can even provide users with more innovative and unorthodox functionality, i.e. a) providing instant access to internal and external related resources in the way of recommendations[1], b) promoting persons in their role as contributors by keeping their scientific activities up to date [2] and c) fostering collaborations between institutions and contributors[3]. At the current state, these OA repositories are providing freely available scientific content, but not well connected with respect to their objects and metadata items. For example, an author may have published various articles in different repositories, but for users to locate them, they would have to visit and query any of these repositories for a collection of all the papers, potentially receiving duplicates. The same counts for biographical information, i.e. place of work, achievements etc. information which normally does not reside within a single repository, since it requires permanent maintenance and updates. From many decades libraries have used authority control files for the unique identification and better organization of bibliographic data. For instance, the Integrated Authority File (German: Gemeinsame Normdatei, also known as: Universal Authority File) or GND is an international authority file particularly used for the organization of person names, subject terms and corporate bodies from catalogues. On the other hand, Linked Open Data stresses the significance of open and machine readable structured data for unique identification, open data publishing and cross-linkage of (similar) digital resources. Both Linked Data developments and authority control converge with each other to solve the problem of unique identification and reliable linkage of resources across different domains.

2 MOTIVATION

We run our own Open Access repository named EconStor[1] which comprises of more than 150k publications from Economics, most of them being Working Papers as preprints and hosts contributions from more than 100k authors. Although the repository's items are mainly accessed through search engines (in particular Google Scholar), the application provides its own GUI with jump off pages, web statistics and a local search engine. To further promote its content, but also to normalize, to cluster and to enrich the metadata, we decided to introduce author pages into the application. These author pages will reflect both a researcher's local output in EconStor, but also his or her contextual scholarly record. Moreover, we also wanted to validate our rationale that a certain amount of EconStor authors have a valid identifier in terms of an ID, which can serve as a key for further linking and information aggregation. We are particularly focusing on authority name control identifiers due to following reasons:

- Names tend to be ambiguous. It is common that more than one person may have the same name (polysemes), or that a person may be known under different names (synonyms) which make them difficult to identify, authenticate and link to. The identifiers provide added advantage over this problem.
- Initiatives like Wikipedia, Wikidata, Freebase, VIAF and ORCID have already employed many authority control data files for the cross linkage. Linking to these these identifiers will help to enrich author information.

JCDL '18, June 3–7, 2018, Fort Worth, TX, USA

ACM ISBN 978-1-4503-5178-2/18/06.
https://doi.org/10.1145/3197026.3204473

[1] https://www.econstor.eu/

3 RELATED WORK

The enhancement of OA repositories resp. their underlying software with authority data has been a topic since years, though with no satisfying 'out-of-the-box'-solution yet. Basically, there is work on authority control by means of authority values, and/or by means of authority linking. For instance, the ePrints system, by its major release 3, supports the integration of authority values in terms of internal predefined lists kept in files or database tables[4]. While this approach requires either indexing of only internally available and used values, or external data sources to be continuously replicated into a local environment, it is cumbersome in terms of local efforts to be repeated for each local repository. In that sense, a more sustainable approach was suggested in the context of establishing a CRIS-DSpace[5], where during the submission of a publication a temporary ORCID key is assigned to the [contributor] field inside a DSpace system, so that a local researcher profile can be generated and associated with the publication(s).

4 STUDY DESIGN AND EXPERIMENT

We followed a multistage approach to link the EconStor authors with external identifiers. We used a EconStor dataset dump from April 2016 that is made available as Linked Open data. The data set consists of 111,107 publications with which 64490 authors are associated. To gauge the distribution of GND person identifier in EconStor we acquired the ECONIS database in JSON format. ECONIS is the catalogue of the German National Library of Economics and is completely integrated in the EconBiz[2] search portal. It contains more than five million title records.

4.1 Locating the GND of the authors:

In a first step, we used a Perl language script to search for all EconStor publications within an external library catalog, where authors are assigned with a GND identifier. The script returned the handle URL of those publications including author names, associated GND identifiers and other meta data elements. Afterwards, the handle URLs from the results were matched with the publications from EconStor database to retrieve the EconStor publication id and its corresponding author. In a last step, names of authors from the EconStor publication records were matched with the listed GND authors, so that the GND identifier could be added to the EconStor database. With this preprocessing, we were able to answer the following questions:

How many EconStor authors are already associated with a GND identifier (thus identifying an author on the level of a national library system)? We found that 25461 out of 64490 EconStor authors have valid GND identifiers. That is approximately 40% of total authors, who contributed to 69588 publications.

Are the most publishing EconStor author already provided with a GND Identifier? We hypothetically set the publication count number to 25 as a baseline to determine the most publishing authors in Econstor and discovered that 1121 authors have at least 25 publications. By further analysis on recent articulated GND list, we found that approximately 70% i.e., 750 out of 1121 author are associated with GND identifiers showing a good score for our repository power researchers.

[2]https://www.econbiz.de/

4.2 Locating additional identifiers:

The next step of our multistage approach is to query and connect with other external identifier. For this purpose, we repetitively SPARQL query Wikidata endpoint with EconStor author names and GND identifiers. Predominately, we choose WIKIDATA for querying, as it is considered as one of the major connecting hubs to e.g., DBpedia, VIAF, ORCID and REPEC etc. Moreover, it already connects more than 1500 sources of (national)authority data files which may lead to better external linkages. As a result of querying, we found 1780 matches to Wikidata items, 1775 matches to VIAF files, 465 matches to RePEc items, 279 DBpedia resources and 44 matches to ORCID identifiers. Further analysis on the results revealed that most of the prominent EconStor authors have external identifiers. This reconfirms our assumption that prominent authors of EconStor have scattered bibliographical and biographical information within these external identifier system, which can be actively aggregated to build a proof of concept application to showcase corresponding author profiles.

4.3 Proof of concept application

A proof of concept application is developed to showcase the initial idea of an author's profile page. On the start page, users are provided with an index page where all of the prominent authors are listed with their name as hyper-linked. When a user clicks on the link, an author's profile page is generated on the fly with biographical information collected from external identifier. In addition, bibliographical information is compiled from publication lists both from the local repository (EconStor) and a subject portal as external biblographic data source (EconBiz).

5 CONCLUSION AND FUTURE WORK

In this preliminary work, we demonstrated how to introduce author pages by means of automatic linking to other resources. The approach relies heavily on the identification of persons by linking their names to identifier systems, which originally has been an intellectual or manual cataloging workflow. We emphasized on the use of sources for authority data like GND, and showcased how Wikidata can be used as a connecting hub to find author related information. As future work, first we would like to expand the publication list of author by including other external sources, and secondly we would like to investigate the opportunities for enriching Wikidata with missing GND EconStor authors both by editorial means and by bots, the latter to bypass rather static and cumbersome library work flows.

REFERENCES

[1] Borst, T., Lehmann, M., Pianos, T., and Witt, N. (2016). Taking Libraries Cultural Content to the User - Approaches and Experiences from the EEXCESS Project. LIBER Quarterly, 26(3), 125-140.
[2] Latif, A., Afzal, M .T., Helic, D., Tochtermann, K., Maurer, Hermann A. (2010). Discovery and Construction of Authors' Profile from Linked Data (A case study for Open Digital Journal). In Proceedings of the Linked Data on the Web (LDOW2010) (Raleigh, NC, 2010).
[3] Stankovic, M., Wagner, C., Jovanovic, J. and Laublet, P. (2010). Looking for Experts? What can Linked Data do for You? In Proceedings of the Linked Data on the Web (LDOW2010) (Raleigh, NC, 2010).
[4] ePrints (2015), Authority Lists. https://wiki.eprints.org/w/Authority_Lists
[5] Bollini, A. (2016), ORCID Integration. https://wiki.duraspace.org/display/DSPACECRIS/ORCID+Integration

System for Category-driven Retrieval of Historical Events

Yasunobu Sumikawa*
University Education Center,
Tokyo Metropolitan University
ysumikawa@acm.org

Adam Jatowt
Dept. of Social Informatics,
Kyoto University
adam@dl.kuis.kyoto-u.ac.jp

ABSTRACT

In this paper, we demonstrate an online system for historical event retrieval. Our system outputs ranked events according to an input text query, time range and category relevance. It is useful for users searching not just for important past events related to input entities but events that belong to specified subset of general categories. It can be also helpful for creating datasets of events falling into specific categories or for generating specialized timelines.

KEYWORDS

Digital history, historical texts, event ranking

ACM Reference Format:

Yasunobu Sumikawa and Adam Jatowt. 2018. System for Category-driven Retrieval of Historical Events. In *JCDL '18: The 18th ACM/IEEE Joint Conference on Digital Libraries, June 3–7, 2018, Fort Worth, TX, USA.* ACM, New York, NY, USA, 2 pages. https://doi.org/10.1145/3197026.3203888

1 INTRODUCTION

Studying and analyzing history-related data can provide numerous benefits including improved comprehension of the past and support for finding meaningful connections or analogies over time. One of the common goals of teaching and spreading the knowledge of history is to allow studying how people in the past tried to solve issues and problems, and then apply the acquired knowledge for proposing creative solutions to present issues [4].

Due to the recent information explosion the amount of available data about historical events have been also increasing. Such data includes both the digitized archival documents such as news articles as well as collections of retrospective descriptions of past events (e.g., past events' lists in Wikipedia). This growth demands effective retrieval approaches to let users quickly access what they want. For example, a user (e.g., a journalist or a university student) may be interested in *health and environment* past events involving Japan that took place in the 19th century. He or she may wish to create a specialized timeline representing this particular domain (i.e., health and environment) or may just want to acquire dataset of relevant events for detailed study or as a initial data seed for more extensive retrieval. Yet, such domain-specific event collections are not immediately available on the Web [1].

*This research was performed while the first author was at Tokyo University of Science, Japan.

[1] E.g., Wikipedia generally structures important past events chronologically

JCDL '18, June 3–7, 2018, Fort Worth, TX, USA

ACM ISBN 978-1-4503-5178-2/18/06.
https://doi.org/10.1145/3197026.3203888

We propose an interactive search system for searching for historical events by category-based filtering realized through automatic event classification. Our system takes four kinds of data: text query, event category, time range and ranking method. It outputs only event descriptions that include the query terms and those that occurred within the specified time range. More importantly, the returned events are sorted based on their relevance to the selected event category or a set of categories.

Contribution: Compared to related works, the core contribution of our system is to use effective filtering for collecting category-specific range of events.

Singh *et al.* [5] proposed method for supporting historians in searching within document archives. Their approach aims at maximizing coverage and minimizing redundancy with respect to different entities and publication times of documents for a given query. For example, if a person name is given as a query, the method lists news articles reporting the person with different entities and publication times. Sumikawa and Ikejiri [6] proposed approach for temporal analogy retrieval which uses a category-based ranking method. Their search engine performs matrix multiplication to sort past events by the number of categories they share with the categories specified by the user. It assumes however the categories for all the past events are given in advance. In contrast, our search engine provides more search options and is based on automatic event classification using Support Vector Machine (SVM) classifier, thus, it can handle any collections of unlabeled past events.

2 EVENT CLASSES AND EVENT COLLECTION

Event Classes. We adopted nine broad event classes introduced and described in [3] which are based on definitions and guidelines used by Wikipedia editors. The classes are as follows: `Armed Conflicts & Attacks`, `Arts & Culture`, `Business & Economy`, `Disasters & Accidents`, `Health & Environment`, `Law & Crime`, `Politics & Elections`, `Science & Technology` and `Sport`.

Dataset. As an underlying event dataset we collected 70,987 past events from year articles in Wikipedia[2] and Wikipedia's Current Portal[3]. The timespan of the collected events ranges from AD 1 to AD 2016. On average, for all the classes, the descriptions contain 25 words, though the length can be as short as 10 words.

3 SYSTEM DESCRIPTION

Fig. 1 shows the interface of the proposed system[4]. Besides inputting the query, a user can control three options: **event category**, **time range** and **ranking method**. The input query and the selected time range act as filters preparing a subset of events that occurred in the designated time frame and that contain specified query words (typically, name of entities). When no filtering is specified (null

[2] E.g., https://en.wikipedia.org/wiki/AD_1

[3] https://en.wikipedia.org/wiki/Portal:Current_events

[4] The system can be accessed online: http://tk2-240-29917.vs.sakura.ne.jp/dataset_creation/

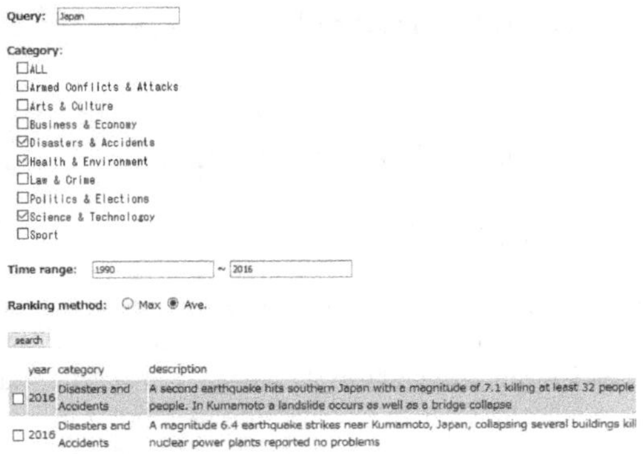

Figure 1: Snapshot of system interface.

query and unbounded time) all events stored in the database are considered. The category option allows for ranking the selected events regarding their inherent types. The ranking is based on the degree to which a dedicated classifier (described further in Sec. 3.2) judges an event to be of a particular class. Note that unlike usual approaches in information retrieval (IR) we do not focus on the topical relevance but, instead, we put special emphasis on category relevance. Hence, in the current implementation we use a condition for an event description to represent a relevant event based on simple query containment[5]. Obviously more refined approaches for topical relevance assessment (e.g., semantic ones) can be used instead.

To sum up, event descriptions that contain input query words and that describe events taking place within the specified date range are ranked based on how strongly they are recognized as belonging to the particular set of event categories. The last option, ranking method, determines the way in which the category probabilities are aggregated for ranking event descriptions.

3.1 Classifying Events

To decide event classes, we used SVM with RBF kernel equipped with the following feature groups which are described in detail in [7]: (1) TF-IDF term vectors, (2) LSA vectors (300 dimensions), (3) Doc2Vec vectors (300 dimensions), (4) VerbNet classes of verbs and ones of head verbs, (5) general entity types detected by Yodie [2] and the type of a head entity, (6) TF-IDF weighted vectors of terms captured from articles and their categories as returned by Explicit Semantic Analysis (ESA) [1] which maps target texts to Wikipedia articles. Using feature selection ($k = 2,000$) and 10-fold cross validation our classifier achieved 79.7% of F-measure (Precision of 78.4% and Recall of 79.6%). As labeled data for training we used the Wikipedia's Current Portal collecting 32,362 event descriptions.

3.2 Ranking Algorithm

Our system loads subsets of feature vectors created in Sec. 3.1 only if the occurrence time of their corresponding events matches the time frame T and if the event descriptions contain the input query Q given by the user. The system then applies SVM to the feature vectors in order to estimate to what degree each considered event is relevant to the concerned event classes. The probabilities of classes as estimated by SVM are used as confidence representation[6].

As multiple categories can be input by the user, our system aggregates membership probabilities over different categories. We provide two kinds of aggregation methods: *Max* and *Ave.* The first is the straightforward approach; it ranks events by their maximum confidence among all the selected categories. On the other hand, the second one aggregates based on computing the average confidence. The motivation behind the latter approach is that users may want to collect events belonging to more than one class. For example, the outbreak of Zika virus in 2016 caused death of many people (`Health & Environment` event) but also resulted in the decrease in the population of bees (`Disasters & Accidents` event). To return such events one needs to ensure high confidence probabilities of both the classes. Hence, we provide also an option to calculate average probability values for ranking events.

Finally, our system sorts all the events by their relevant values in descending order and returns them to the user.

More formally, the ranking algorithm is as follows:

$$E' = \{e \mid e \in E \cap \mathit{year}(e) \in T \cap Q \in w(e)\} \quad (1)$$

$$S(f, e \in E') = f(\mathit{CatRel}(FV(e))) \quad (2)$$

where function $\mathit{year}(e)$ returns a year when the event e occurred, function $w(e)$ returns words used in e and $FV(e)$ outputs a feature vector of e. E is the total set of event descriptions, while E' is the subset of E after the time range and query based filtering. For all the events, our ranking algorithm applies the higher-order function S that takes two arguments, a function f that is either *Max* or *Ave* and the set of feature vectors of e. Then, the algorithm sorts the events by the scores S as being aggregated by f.

4 CONCLUSIONS & FUTURE WORK

In this paper, we demonstrate an interactive online system for retrieving past event descriptions. Our system takes query words, time range and category relevance as an input in order to effectively collect events that related to query, that occurred at a specified time range and, most importantly, that fall into a particular event category. In the future, we plan to propose incorporating more effective methods for representing topical relevance and we plan to add historical importance scores of events.

Acknowledgments. This work was supported in part by MIC SCOPE (#171507010) and MEXT Grant-in-Aids (#17H01828 and #17K12792).

REFERENCES

[1] M.-W. Chang, L. Ratinov, D. Roth, and V. Srikumar. 2008. Importance of Semantic Representation: Dataless Classification. AAAI'08, 830–835.
[2] G. Gorrell, J. Petrak, and K. Bontcheva. 2015. Using @Twitter Conventions to Improve #LOD-Based Named Entity Disambiguation. ESWC'15, 171–186.
[3] A. Košmerlj, E. Belyaeva, G. Leban, M. Grobelnik, and B. Fortuna. 2015. Towards a Complete Event Type Taxonomy. WWW '15 Companion, 899–902.
[4] P. Lee. 2005. Historical Literacy: Theory and Research. *International Journal of Historical Learning, Teaching and Research* 5, 1 (2005), 25–40.
[5] J. Singh, W. Nejdl, and A. Anand. 2016. History by Diversity: Helping Historians Search News Archives. CHIIR '16, 183–192.
[6] Y. Sumikawa and R. Ikejiri. 2015. Mining Historical Social Issues, Vol. 39. IDT'15, 587–597.
[7] Y. Sumikawa and A. Jatowt. 2018. Classifying Short Descriptions of Past Events. ECIR'18, 729–736.

[5] This choice is partly driven by the fact that event descriptions in our dataset are very short. We also assume a user query is going to represent a named entity in most of the cases.

[6] We store the precomputed values offline for online retrieval.

Introduction to Digital Libraries

Edward Fox
Virginia Tech Department of Computer Science
Blacksburg, VA 24061 USA
fox@vt.edu

ABSTRACT

This tutorial is a thorough and deep introduction to the Digital Libraries (DL) field, providing a firm foundation: covering key concepts and terminology, as well as services, systems, technologies, methods, standards, projects, issues, and practices. It introduces and builds upon a firm theoretical foundation (starting with the '5S' set of intuitive aspects: Streams, Structures, Spaces, Scenarios, Societies), giving careful definitions and explanations of all the key parts of a 'minimal digital library', and expanding from that basis to cover key DL issues. Illustrations come from a set of case studies, including from multiple current projects, including with webpages, tweets, and social networks. Attendees will be exposed to four Morgan and Claypool books that elaborate on 5S, published 2012-2014. Complementing the coverage of '5S' will be an overview of key aspects of the DELOS Reference Model and DL.org activities. Further, use of a Hadoop cluster supporting big data DLs will be described.

CCS CONCEPTS

• **Information systems** → **Digital libraries and archives**;

KEYWORDS

Digital libraries; 5S; Big Data; Societies; Scenarios; Spaces; Structures; Streams

ACM Reference Format:

Edward Fox. 2018. Introduction to Digital Libraries. In *JCDL '18: The 18th ACM/IEEE Joint Conference on Digital Libraries, June 3–7, 2018, Fort Worth, TX, USA.* ACM, New York, NY, USA, Article 4, 2 pages. https://doi.org/10.1145/3197026.3201779

1 DL TEACHING AND LEARNING

Educational resources from an US NSF funded grant to develop DL curriculum (see http://curric.dlib.vt.edu/) will be presented, including descriptions (aimed at teachers and learners) of the more than 30 major modules and sub-modules that cover the core DL topics and related topics (e.g., those used to teach in both undergraduate and graduate courses at Virginia Tech). Most of the modules have been reviewed, revised, field tested, and used at several locations. Further, NSF TUES support has aided integration of digital library coverage in each of 3 courses: Digital Libraries, Information Retrieval, and Computational Linguistics. Part of this involved problem-project based learning, with large collections and a Hadoop cluster. Based on the above, discussion of how to learn more about DLs, and how to teach others about DLs, will be tailored to the interests of the attendees.

JCDL '18, June 3–7, 2018, Fort Worth, TX, USA

ACM ISBN 978-1-4503-5178-2/18/06.
https://doi.org/10.1145/3197026.3201779

2 TUTORIAL DESCRIPTION

2.1 Duration and Format

Half-day, on 3 June 2018.

2.2 Target Audience and Aims

Introductory or intermediate: Those new to the DL field, or coming to it from a different but related discipline, or just new to JCDL, should find this helpful, as they expand their involvement in the DL community.

This tutorial also should be of interest to those already involved in digital libraries, especially if they wish to organize/solidify their understanding and broaden their perspective, become formally grounded, or to teach a DL course.

2.3 Tutorial History

Prior related tutorials have been given at: CIKM 95; DL 98-00; ECDL 00, 01, 05-07, 10; ICADL 00-05, 07; JCDL 01-06, 08-11, 13-17; MM 96, 98, 00; SIGIR 96, 01, 05; etc.

2.4 Learning Objectives

Attendees will be able to:

- Explain 5S; compare it with DELOS/DL.org works.
- Describe core DL content/services, informally/formally.
- Describe common DL application areas, from both a user and a system perspective.
- Describe technologies that extend DL capabilities.
- Describe how to use a Hadoop cluster, with Solr, Mahout, Spark, etc., to handle large tweet and webpage collections, with clustering, classification, topic spotting, NER, etc.
- Identify modules of interest for study about DLs, or for use in DL courses, or in courses where DL content can be added.
- Learn/teach from the modules, assess understanding.
- Add to the module collection, based on special expertise.
- Apply problem-project based learning in education.

2.5 Outline

This tutorial will cover many concepts and use multiple case studies. It will touch upon international activities, including DELOS/DL.org, but will focus on what is detailed in four books about DLs [1–4], that build upon 5S, and cover:

- Introduction; Exploration; Evaluation; Integration
- Complex Objects; Annotation/Subdocuments; Ontologies

- Classification; Text Extraction; Security
- Content-based Image Retrieval; Education; Social Networks
- Bioinformatics, eScience, and Simulation DLs
- Geospatial Information

Regarding DL Teaching and Learning, the following will be covered:

- Overview of the DL curriculum project and methods
- Pedagogical and curricular recommendations
- Introduction to each of the 10 main curricular areas
- Discussion of attendee teaching/learning needs
- Discussion of modules of interest to attendees
- Discussion of problem-project based learning about DLs

3 BRIEF BIOGRAPHY

Edward Fox holds a Ph.D. and M.S. in Computer Science from Cornell, and a B.S. from M.I.T. He is a Fellow of both ACM and IEEE, cited for leadership in digital libraries and information retrieval, and serves on the IEEE Thesaurus Editorial Board. Since 1983 he has been at Virginia Tech, where he serves as Professor. He directs VT's Digital Library Research Laboratory and the Networked Digital Library of Theses and Dissertations. He was a member of the Board of CRA (the Computer Research Association). He was chair of the IEEE Technical Committee on Digital Libraries, and earlier was chair of ACM SIGIR. He was chair of the steering committee for JCDL, and is on the international advisory committee for ICADL. He has been (co-)Principal Investigator on 125 research grants/contracts. He taught over 82 tutorials and gave 66 keynote/distinguished/international invited talks. He (co-)authored 18 books, 126 journal/magazine articles, 49 books chapters, 219 refereed conference/workshop papers, 74 posters, and over 160 other publications/reports and 330 additional talks. Fox was editor for IR and DL for ACM Books, Co-Editor-in-Chief for ACM JERIC, and is on the boards of IJDL, JEMH, JIIS, J. UCS, Multimedia Tools and Applications, and PeerJ CS.

3.1 Contact information

- Dept. of Computer Science
- 114 McBryde Hall, M/C 0106
- Virginia Tech, Blacksburg, VA 24061 USA
- Tel: +1-540-231-5113 [direct], -6931[dept.]
- Mobile: +1-540-553-1856, Fax: +1-540-231-6075 [CS]
- Email: fox@vt.edu
- Website: http://fox.cs.vt.edu

4 ACKNOWLEDGMENTS

Thanks go to NSF for support through grants CCF-1032677; CMMI-1638207; DUE-0121679, 0435059, 0840719, 1141209; OCI-1032677; and IIS-0325579, 0535057, 0535060, 0910183, 0910465, 0916733, 1319578, 1619028. Thanks go to IMLS for LG-71-16-0037-16; to National Inst. of Justice for NCJ 239049, to NIH for 1R01DA039456-01, and to QNRF for support through NPRP 4-029-1-007. The opinions expressed in this document are solely those of the author.

REFERENCES

[1] E.A. Fox, M.A. Goncalves, and R. Shen. 2012. *Theoretical Foundations for Digital Libraries: The 5S (Societies, Scenarios, Spaces, Structures, Streams) Approach.* Morgan and Claypool Publishers, San Francisco. http://dx.doi.org/10.2200/S00434ED1V01Y201207ICR022

[2] E.A. Fox and J.P. Leidig. 2014. *Digital Library Applications: CBIR, Education, Social Networks, eScience/ Simulation, and GIS.* Morgan and Claypool Publishers, San Francisco. http://dx.doi.org/10.2200/S00565ED1V01Y201401ICR032

[3] E.A. Fox and R. Torres. 2014. *Digital Library Technologies: Complex Objects, Annotation, Ontologies, Classification, Extraction, and Security.* Morgan and Claypool Publishers, San Francisco. http://dx.doi.org/10.2200/S00566ED1V01Y201401ICR033

[4] R. Shen, M.A. Goncalves, and E.A. Fox. 2013. *Key Issues Regarding Digital Libraries: Evaluation and Integration.* Morgan and Claypool Publishers, San Francisco. http://dx.doi.org/10.2200/S00474ED1V01Y201301ICR026

An Introduction to Digital Humanities

Luis Meneses
Electronic Textual Cultures Laboratory
University of Victoria
Victoria, BC V8P 5C2 Canada
ldmm@uvic.ca

Richard Furuta
Center for the Study of Digital Libraries and Department of Computer Science and Engineering
Texas A&M University
College Station, TX 77843-3112 USA
furuta@cse.tamu.edu

ABSTRACT

Digital Humanities is an area of inquiry and scholarship that combines the procedural methodologies from the Sciences with the reflection that is carried out in the Humanities. Although the scope of Digital Humanities is particularly difficult to define as the field is actively evolving, some of its defining characteristics have remained constant over time. These include its new forms of scholarship involving collaborative, transdisciplinary, and computationally-engaged research, teaching, and publishing.

ACM Reference Format:

Luis Meneses and Richard Furuta. 2018. An Introduction to Digital Humanities. In JCDL '18: The 18th ACM/IEEE Joint Conference on Digital Libraries, June 3–7, 2018, Fort Worth, TX, USA. ACM, New York, NY, USA, 2 pages. https://doi.org/10.1145/3197026.3201781

KEYWORDS

Digital Humanities, tutorial, digital libraries

1 TOPICS COVERED

In this half-day tutorial, we introduce the concepts of Digital Humanities from the perspective of participants that are familiar with Digital Libraries. We focus on four core areas: concepts, the tools used, their implications, and the future of the discipline.

1.1 Concepts and Introduction

Digital Humanities has become a driving force in many universities across the world. In this topic, we will consider the question, "what are the Digital Humanities and how do they overlap with Digital Libraries?" From a topical point of view, the two areas overlap in many ways, but there also are areas of interest of interest primarily to one but not the other area. From an implementation point of view, delivery of digital libraries is often external to the institution while digital humanities are often central to the development of the identity of affected academic areas, indeed to the point of controversy.

JCDL '18, June 3–7, 2018, Fort Worth, TX, USA

ACM ISBN 978-1-4503-5178-2/18/06.
https://doi.org/10.1145/3197026.3201781

We present examples of Digital Humanities projects that help to explain what is encompassed by the area and also to help motivate an understanding of what currently is considered to be inside and outside of the scope of Digital Humanities.

1.2 Tools

The tools and software used in the Digital Humanities are the result of a close collaboration between computer scientists and humanities scholars. This collaboration makes them unique in their use and their potential contributions. We present examples of the tools commonly used in the Digital Humanities and discuss the implications that are derived from their use.

In this topic we also highlight the work that is carried out by notable scholars and research groups currently active that are known for being at the forefront of the field. Along the same lines, we provide an overview of the current trending areas of interest, along with the major conferences and publication venues. To finalize this topic, we provide a survey of the proceedings of the Digital Humanities and the Canadian Society of Digital Humanities conferences.

1.3 Implications and Discussion

As with any other scholarly field, the Digital Humanities are not free from debates. In this topic, we provide an overview of the implications and ongoing discussions in the Digital Humanities. We provide this overview using five points.

First, we analyze whether the Digital Humanities are the natural evolution of the Humanities or a new field altogether. Second, we deliberate if it is more important to do coding or to do more introspective analysis; this ongoing debate is commonly known as "more hack, less yack". Third, we discuss the impact of computers on current research methods. Fourth, we analyze the current challenges. Finally, we address a more philosophical question: Who has the important knowledge? The humanist or the technologist?

1.4 Future

In this topic we provide an overview of the future of the Digital Humanities. First, we discuss where the current methods in the discipline are heading. Second, we consider what the next big area of interest will be in the Digital Humanities. Third, we discuss the current preservation strategies and the long-term use of digital projects. Finally, we consider Open Access Scholarship.

Open Access Scholarship is gaining interest in the community as a method for disseminating scholarship: it avoids copyright issues (the author usually retains ownership) and allows research to be distributed in a faster and more convenient way.

2 TUTORIAL OUTCOMES

We expect our tutorial to have two principal participant-focused outcomes. First, by the end of the tutorial the participants should be able to articulate some of the benefits and the drawbacks of using digital tools to approach the research questions in the Humanities. And second, the participants should be able to critically interrogate the way they use the Internet to get information, produce content and interact with others.

3 EXPECTED ATTENDEE BACKGROUND

Although we won't be doing computer programming or coding in this tutorial, some degree of digital literacy is expected from participants. Given the scope of the JCDL conference, we expect that the participants will have the required background to engage in the discussions.

4 ACKNOWLEDGEMENTS

This tutorial was sponsored in part by the Digital Humanities Summer Institute (http://www.dhsi.org).

Improving Search and Retrieval in Digital Libraries by Leveraging Keyphrase Extraction Systems

Wei Jin
University of North Texas
Denton, Texas
wei.jin@unt.edu

Corina Florescu
University of North Texas
Denton, Texas
corinaflorescu@my.unt.edu

ABSTRACT

In this tutorial, we will focus on recent developments in the keyphrase extraction task using research papers as a case study. In particular, we will discuss a wide range of keyphrase extraction models ranging from the representative supervised approaches such as KEA and GenEx to more recent ones that make use of the advances in artificial intelligence. Beyond introducing the outstanding approaches in this domain, we will discuss how keyphrases can significantly improve the search and retrieval of information in digital libraries and hence, leads to an improved organization, search, retrieval, and recommendation of scientific documents. Participants will learn about existing approaches, challenges and future trends in the keyphrase extraction task, and how they can be applied to digital library applications.

CCS CONCEPTS

• **Computing methodologies** → **Artificial intelligence**; • **Natural language processing** → *Information extraction*;

KEYWORDS

Keyphrase Extraction, Information Extraction, Digital Libraries

ACM Reference Format:
Wei Jin and Corina Florescu. 2018. Improving Search and Retrieval in Digital Libraries by Leveraging Keyphrase Extraction Systems. In *JCDL '18: The 18th ACM/IEEE Joint Conference on Digital Libraries, June 3–7, 2018, Fort Worth, TX, USA.* ACM, New York, NY, USA, 2 pages. https://doi.org/10.1145/3197026.3201778

1 INTRODUCTION

Online digital libraries such as Google Scholar, CiteSeerX , ACL Anthology, ArnetMiner, and PubMed that store scientific documents or their metadata, are powerful resources for many applications that analyze scientific documents on a Web-wide scale. The current Scholarly Web contains millions of scientific documents. For example, Google Scholar is estimated to have more than 100 million documents. On one hand, these rapidly-growing scholarly document collections offer benefits for knowledge discovery, and on the other hand, finding useful information has become very challenging. Keyphrases associated with a document typically provide a high-level topic description of the document and can allow for efficient information processing. Given today's very large collections of documents, these keyphrases are extremely important not only for summarizing a document, but also for the search and retrieval of relevant information. However, these concepts are not always readily available, but they need to be gleaned from the many details in documents.

ACM ISBN 978-1-4503-5178-2/18/06.
https://doi.org/10.1145/3197026.3201778

2 EXPECTED NUMBER OF PARTICIPANTS

We expect around 20 participants to this tutorial.

3 FORMAT OF THE TUTORIAL

This tutorial is intended to unfold on a half-day program in the conference.

4 AIMS, SCOPE AND LEARNING OBJECTIVES OF THE TUTORIAL

This tutorial targets researchers who are interested in designing and applying keyphrase extraction techniques in natural language processing and information retrieval tasks such as scientific paper summarization, classification, recommendation, clustering, and search. The tutorial will introduce the problem of keyphrase extraction with focus on digital library applications, and then cover recent developments in automatically discovering and extracting keyphrases from documents, which will help handle and digest more information in less time during these "big data" times.

5 TUTORIAL OUTLINE

5.1 Motivation

We first present the need for producing research articles which provide the technological basis for worldwide collection, sharing, and dissemination of scientific discoveries. Then we motivate the need for accurate keyphrase extraction models by emphasizing our lack of ability to manually process and filter this huge amount of information. We will also show that keyphrases are particularly useful in many applications ranging from information search and retrieval [6, 11] to document summarization [10, 15], classification [12], clustering [5], recommendation [9] or simply to contextual advertisement [14].

5.2 Supervised Approaches

We introduce a previous work review on the supervised keyphrase extraction models starting with the pioneer approaches, KEA [4] and GenEx [13]. We will discuss supervised models that use features computed based on observations and statistical information and their applicability in digital library domains. For example, in scientific articles, keyphrases generally occur on positions very close to the beginning of a document and occur frequently [3]. In a scholarly domain, research papers are not isolated. Rather, they are highly inter-connected in giant citation networks, in which papers cite or are cited by other papers [2]. We will show that this information can be successfully exploited to improve the keyphrase extraction task.

5.3 Unsupervised Approaches

We describe recently developed keyphrase extraction techniques in the unsupervised line of research emphasizing those that particularly perform well on scientific papers. We first present graph-based ranking methods and centrality measures which are considered state of-the-art for unsupervised keyphrase extraction [1, 7, 8]. Then we will discuss informative features for extracting keyphrases from research papers such as the position of a phrase in the target document and the document structure and how they can be harnessed in an unsupervised framework.

5.4 Keyphrase Extraction in Digital Libraries

We analyze which class of models (supervised or unsupervised) is better suited for digital libraries. We will see that the supervised approaches typically work better than unsupervised approaches, but the requirement for large corpora with human-annotated keyphrases has lead to significant attention towards the design of unsupervised approaches. On the other hand, we will show that many of the features used to encode a candidate phrase in the supervised line of research have influenced the progress of the unsupervised approaches.

5.5 Conclusion and Future Research Directions

We conclude the tutorial by presenting some challenges and potential research directions in designing effective keyphrase extraction models in context of digital libraries.

5.6 Prerequisite Knowledge

No specific background knowledge is assumed of the audience.

6 INSTRUCTORS

6.1 Wei Jin

Dr. Wei Jin is an associate professor in the Department of Computer Science at the University of North Texas. Her research spans several related fields including large scale data mining and knowledge discovery, information retrieval and extraction, machine learning, and natural language processing. She has published broadly in the above areas and has developed advanced text mining tools for knowledge discovery from text. Wei has served on program committees of major conferences in her research areas and organized special sessions on Text and Web Mining. She is the recipient of the NSF Early Faculty Career Award. Previously, she obtained her PhD and MS degrees in Computer Science & Engineering from State University of New York at Buffalo, in 2008 and 2007, respectively. She also earned a ME degree from Institute of Computing Technology, Chinese Academy of Sciences in 2002.

6.2 Corina Florescu

Corina Florescu is a senior PhD student in the Department of Computer Science and Engineering at University of North Texas. She has explored fields like machine learning, information retrieval and natural language processing. She has focused her research efforts on summarization with applications on keyphrase extraction and her findings have been published in top conferences such as ACL and AAAI. She earned her MS degree in Computer Science from University of Bucharest, Romania in 2010.

REFERENCES

[1] Adrien Bougouin, Florian Boudin, and Béatrice Daille. 2013. Topicrank: Graph-based topic ranking for keyphrase extraction. In *International Joint Conference on Natural Language Processing (IJCNLP)*. 543–551.

[2] Cornelia Caragea, Florin Adrian Bulgarov, Andreea Godea, and Sujatha Das Gollapalli. 2014. Citation-Enhanced Keyphrase Extraction from Research Papers: A Supervised Approach. In *Proceedings of the Conference on Empirical Methods in Natural Language Processing*. 1435–1446. http://aclweb.org/anthology/D/D14/D14-1150.pdf

[3] Corina Florescu and Cornelia Caragea. 2017. PositionRank: An Unsupervised Approach to Keyphrase Extraction from Scholarly Documents. In *Proceedings of the 55th Annual Meeting of the Association for Computational Linguistics (Volume 1: Long Papers)*, Vol. 1. 1105–1115.

[4] Eibe Frank, Gordon W. Paynter, Ian H. Witten, Carl Gutwin, and Craig G. Nevill-Manning. 1999. Domain-Specific Keyphrase Extraction. In *Proceedings of the 16th International Joint Conference on Artificial Intelligence*. 668–673.

[5] Khaled M Hammouda, Diego N Matute, and Mohamed S Kamel. 2005. Corephrase: Keyphrase extraction for document clustering. In *Machine Learning and Data Mining in Pattern Recognition*. Springer, 265–274.

[6] Steve Jones and Mark S. Staveley. 1999. Phrasier: A System for Interactive Document Retrieval Using Keyphrases. In *Proceedings of the 22nd Annual International ACM SIGIR Conference on Research and Development in Information Retrieval*. 160–167. https://doi.org/10.1145/312624.312671

[7] Zhiyuan Liu, Wenyi Huang, Yabin Zheng, and Maosong Sun. 2010. Automatic keyphrase extraction via topic decomposition. In *Proceedings of the Conference on Empirical Methods in Natural Language Processing*. 366–376.

[8] Rada Mihalcea and Paul Tarau. 2004. TextRank: Bringing Order into Text. In *Proceedings of the 2004 Conference on Empirical Methods in Natural Language Processing*. 404–411. http://www.aclweb.org/anthology/W04-3252

[9] Nirmala Pudota, Antonina Dattolo, Andrea Baruzzo, Felice Ferrara, and Carlo Tasso. 2010. Automatic keyphrase extraction and ontology mining for content-based tag recommendation. *International Journal of Intelligent Systems* 25, 12 (2010), 1158–1186.

[10] Vahed Qazvinian, Dragomir R. Radev, and Arzucan Özgür. 2010. Citation Summarization Through Keyphrase Extraction. In *Proceedings of the 23rd International Conference on Computational Linguistics (COLING '10)*. 895–903.

[11] Anna Ritchie, Simone Teufel, and Stephen Robertson. 2006. How to find better index terms through citations. In *Proceedings of the Workshop on How Can Computational Linguistics Improve Information Retrieval?* ACL, 25–32.

[12] Peter Turney. 2003. Coherent keyphrase extraction via web mining. *arXiv preprint cs/0308033* (2003).

[13] Peter D Turney. 2000. Learning algorithms for keyphrase extraction. *Information Retrieval* 2, 4 (2000), 303–336.

[14] Wen-tau Yih, Joshua Goodman, and Vitor R. Carvalho. 2006. Finding Advertising Keywords on Web Pages. In *WWW'06*. 213–222.

[15] Hongyuan Zha. 2002. Generic summarization and keyphrase extraction using mutual reinforcement principle and sentence clustering. In *Proceedings of the 25th annual international ACM SIGIR conference on Research and development in information retrieval*. 113–120. https://doi.org/10.1145/564376.564398

Introduction to Machine Learning for Digital Library Applications

Rodney D. Nielsen
Human Intelligence and Language Technologies Lab
Computer Science & Engineering, UNT
Denton, TX 76207, USA
Rodney.Nielsen@UNT.edu

ABSTRACT

This tutorial begins with an overview of the major branches of machine learning (ML) and then provides more thorough coverage of deep neural networks. It covers key concepts, tools, experimental methods, applications, evaluation measures and associated issues for supervised learning (regression and classification), unsupervised learning (clustering and dimensionality reduction), semi-supervised and active learning (which combine the former approaches), and reinforcement learning. The deep neural network discussion covers convolutional neural networks (CNNs), recurrent neural networks (RNNs), word embeddings and related techniques. The discussion will be grounded on digital library (DL) - related applications and will highlight issues, techniques and tools associated with processing big data.

CCS CONCEPTS

• **Computing methodologies** → **Machine Learning** • **Information systems** → Digital libraries and archives;

KEYWORDS

machine learning, digital libraries, deep neural networks, tutorial

ACM Reference format:

Rodney D. Nielsen. 2018. Introduction to Machine Learning for Digital Library Applications. In *Proceedings of The 18th ACM/IEEE Joint Conference on Digital Libraries, Fort Worth, Texas USA, June 3-7 2018 (JCDL'18)*, 2 pages.
https://doi.org/10.1145/3197026.3201780

1 INTRODUCTION

Highlights of this tutorial include an emphasis on applications of machine learning (ML) in the digital libraries (DL) space, and an emphasis on deep neural networks, which have largely taken over vision and image processing (convolutional neural networks: CNNs) and analytics of sequence data (recurrent neural networks: RNNs).

JCDL'18, June 3–7, 2018, Fort Worth, TX, USA

ACM ISBN 978-1-4503-5178-2/18/06.
DOI: https://doi.org/10.1145/3197026.3201780

It will not just describe algorithms, but will cover good experimental design methodology and evaluation to ensure your results generalize well to new (production) data. It will also cover appropriate task-dependent evaluation measures.

2 TUTORIAL DESCRIPTION

2.1 Duration

Half day

2.2 Target Audience

Beginner to intermediate: No prior experience or knowledge of ML will be required, but those at the intermediate level in ML who have little or no experience with deep learning, CNNs, RNNs, Big Data, and or DL applications, will also benefit.

Educators, students, scientists, managers and advisors: This tutorial will be beneficial for those interested in applying ML, particularly in the area of text analysis and DL, and for educators and managers involved in ML-related decision making and advising.

Expected number of participants: ~20

2.3 Learning Objectives

Given a problem statement, you will develop the skills to:

- Recognize whether and where machine learning techniques are applicable,
- Determine which set of the ML algorithms covered in the course are applicable,
- Design a machine learning application component,
- Design and conduct appropriate machine learning experiments,
- Analyze and properly describe the outcome of ML experiments, and
- Extract key information from literature.

2.4 Outline

This tutorial is comprised of two parts: 1) a broad overview of ML's categories, associated algorithms, tools, methods and issues, and 2) an introduction to deep neural networks. It will cover a number of machine learning topics, issues, and applications at varying levels, such as the following. (Core ML topics are in regular font; cross-cutting topics are italicized; and DL-related applications are underlined – prototypical and particularly good examples have a solid underline.)

- Overview of ML and its major categories
- Supervised Learning
  - Tools
  - Regression
    - Document quality assessment in curation
  - Experimental Methods
  - Evaluation Measures
  - Classification
    - Logistic Regression
      - Spam detection
    - Nearest Neighbor
      - Authorship attribution
    - Experimental Methods
    - Evaluation Measures
    - Support Vector Machines
    - Decision Trees
    - Naïve Bayes
      - Document classification
- Unsupervised Learning
  - Clustering
    - *k*-means
      - Document clustering
    - Experimental Methods
    - Evaluation Measures
    - Expectation Maximization
    - Hierarchical Agglomerative Clustering
    - Topic Modeling
      - Document indexing
      - Keyword extraction
  - Dimensionality Reduction
    - Principle Components Analysis
    - Latent Semantic Analysis
      - Information retrieval
- Active Learning
  - Experimental Methods
  - Evaluation Measures
    - Genre classification
- Semi-supervised Learning
  - Self Training
    - Word sense disambiguation
  - Experimental Methods
  - Evaluation Measures
  - Co-Training
    - Document classification
  - Co-EM
- Reinforcement Learning
  - Experimental Methods
  - Evaluation Measures
    - Curation

Part II:

- Deep Learning
  - Deep Neural Networks
    - Perceptron
    - Hidden Layers
    - Fully-Connect Feedforward NNs
      - Document classification
    - What's new?
    - Experimental Methods
    - Evaluation Measures
    - Word Embeddings
      - Nearly all text analytics
    - Convolutional Neural Networks
      - Image classification
    - Recurrent Neural Networks
      - Authorship attribution
      - Article title generation
    - Learning from Big Data

3 BRIEF BIOGRAPHY

Rodney Nielsen is an Associate Professor in the Department of Computer Science and Engineering at the University of North Texas. He received his Ph.D. from the University of Colorado at Boulder in 2008, where he went on to work as a Research Scientist in the Institute of Cognitive Science and adjunct in the Department of Computer Science. He was also a Research Scientist at Boulder Language Technologies and a Research Collaborator at Mayo Clinic. His research interests include ML, NLP, Cognitive Science and their application to companion healthcare robots for the elderly, educational technology, and health informatics. He has over 70 peer-reviewed research publications, has sat on related advisory boards, expert panels, shared task & workshop organization boards, journal review panels, and numerous conference program committees. In addition to being the PI of federal grants totaling close to $4 million, he was the lead R&D designer and or proposal author of the artificial intelligence component of industrial contracts totaling nearly $8 million, including one which won a AAAI Innovative Applications of Artificial Intelligence award.

ACKNOWLEDGMENTS

Thanks go to support by the Institute of Education Sciences, U.S. Department of Education, Grant R305A120808 to University of North Texas, the NSF Graduate Research Fellowship Program under Grant 1144248, and the NSF under Grant 1262860. Any opinions, findings, and conclusions or recommendations expressed in this material are those of the author(s) and do not necessarily reflect the views of the National Science Foundation or the Institute of Education Sciences.

Cyberinfrastructure for Digital Libraries and Archives: Integrating Data Management, Analysis, and Publication

Weijia Xu
Texas Advanced Computing Center
The University of Texas at Austin
xwj@tacc.utexas.edu

Maria Esteva
Texas Advanced Computing Center
The University of Texas at Austin
maria@tacc.utexas.edu

Jessica Trelogan
University of Texas Library
The University of Texas at Austin
j.trelogan@austin.utexas.edu

ABSTRACT

Increasingly, digital libraries and archives need to and are using cyberinfrastructure and machine learning to meet curation, data management and researchers needs. This workshop focuses on facilitating adoption and integration between these spaces. It brings together researchers and practitioners to share visions, questions, latest advances in methodology, application experiences, and best practices.

CCS CONCEPTS

• **Information systems~Digital libraries and archives;** Information systems~Computing platforms

KEYWORDS

Digital Libraries; Archives; Cyberinfrastructure; Machine Learning

ACM Reference format:

W. Xu, M. Esteva, and J. Trelogan 2018. Cyberinfrastructure for Digital Libraries and Archives: Integrating Data Management, Analysis, and Publication In *Proceedings of The 18th ACM/IEEE Joint Conference on Digital Libraries, Fort Worth, Texas USA, June 3-7 2018 (JCDL'18)*, 2 pages. https://doi.org/10.1145/3197026.3200211

1 INTRODUCTION

Academic libraries have made significant progress accommodating data into their services and collections. This has been achieved through data management consulting services and institutional repositories for final and relatively small sized data publications. However, research data management remains challenging for large-scale data generated from complex analysis pipelines conducted in distributed computational resources [1]. More often than not, research conducted in these eco-systems involves: using multiple computational facilities, remote users with access and authorization roadblocks, data that evolves at varying time-frames, missing documentation, data transfer problems, storage scalability limitations, and data vulnerability risks. A necessary approach to meet these challenges is to use cyberinfrastructure, which refers to large shared online research environments, backed up by advanced computing resources hosted in data centers and supported by experts [2]. Coupling cyberinfrastructure and digital libraries and archives can provide the needed technical resources and the expertise required to manage and analyze data at scale, as well as new opportunities to facilitate data preservation, access, and reuse [3, 4]. However, library and archives professionals are often unfamiliar with cyberinfrastructure. In turn, cyberinfrastructure experts lack experience in traditional digital library and archives practices such as metadata, provenance, publishing, information retrieval, and digital preservation. This workshop intends to bridge the gaps between digital libraries and archives and cyberinfrastructure by inviting researchers and practitioners from both fields as well as domain experts to share their ideas, introduce theory and methods, and demonstrate successful use cases.

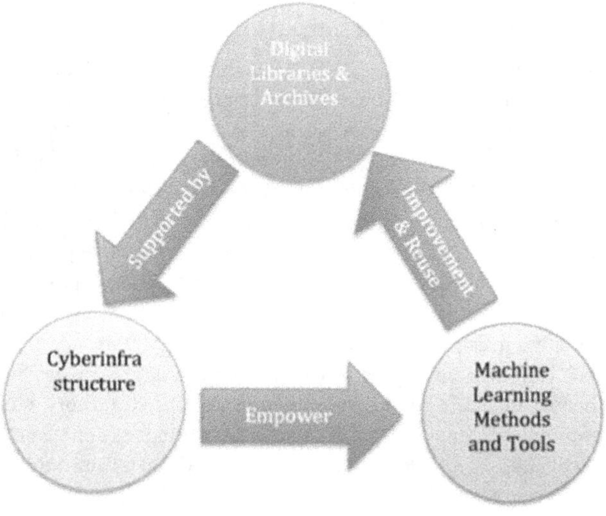

Figure 1: A Conceptual View of Cyberinfrastructure, Digital Libraries, and Machine Learning.

ACM ISBN 978-1-4503-5178-2/18/06.
https://doi.org/10.1145/3197026.3200211

2 WORKSHOP OBJECTIVES

- Bring data curators, librarians and archivists, researchers, and computational scientists together to share practical experiences at the intersection of digital libraries and cyberinfrastructure.
- Promote the usage of cyberinfrastructure within the digital library and archives community.
- Advocate adoption of best data curation practices within the computational research and cyberinfrastructure communities.
- Discuss future opportunities for cyberinfrastructure for digital libraries and archives and forge a dedicated community.

3 Workshop Structure and Format

The workshop will take a full-day with 10 ~15 presentations consisting of both invited and peer-reviewed presentations and an interactive discussion session.

3.1 Scope of Topics

We will focus on three themes: a) designing and implementing integrated data analysis and curation pipelines within open science cyberinfrastructure, b) models and methods to improve large-scale data collections access and reuse including issues of data understandibility and representation of complex datasets (ex. derived from large-scale simulations, experiments, and observational research projects) c) challenges and solutions in curating datasets beyond textual content (e.g. video, volumetric images, genomics/bio data, architectural drawings, point clouds, GIS, satellite imagery, etc.)

3.2 Workshop Participation

We expect attendance of ~50 participants. We will invite data curators and researchers with experience in the themes of this workshop to give presentations. We will also promote the workshop and call for presentations through professional list-serves (e.g. PASIG, XSEDE, NHERI, ALA, A&A, DLF, Cyverse, SIGIR, ASIST, hpc-annonunce etc.) and through TACC's and UT Libraries websites. Submissions received in response to our calls will be reviewed by the organizers and by a committee of colleagues from UT Libraries, Texas Digital Libraries, and from the Digital Curation Innovation Center at UMD. In addition we will call domain expert reviewers according to the scientific themes included in the submissions. Accepted authors will be notified in May. We will contact working groups such as EarthCube, DataOne, Planet Texas, Good Data Systems, Collections as Data, Laboratory for Image and Video Engineering, PaleoCore, Fishes of Texas, Machine Reading and others to share the call for participation and encourage attendance.

4 BIOGRAPHICAL AND CONTACT INFORMATION

Maria Esteva, maria@tacc.utexas.edu, is a researcher at the Texas Advanced Computing Center. A PhD in information science, her research focuses on large scale data curation and publication applications. She works with domain scientists modeling their research workflows to data curation and digital libraries standards, and mapping those to cyberinfrastructure with the goal of creating sustainable, understandable, and reusable data collections. She is data curator in Cyverse and DesignSafe-CI, and PI and Co-PI of two NSF funded projects: identifierservices.org and digitalrocksportal.org.

Weijia Xu, xwj@tacc.utexas.edu, is a research scientist and the manager of the Data Mining and Statistics group at the Texas Advanced Computing Center. Dr. Xu's main research interest is to enable data-driven discoveries developing new computational methods and applications that facilitate data-to-knowledge transfer. His projects have been funded through various federal and state agencies including NIH, NSF, TXDoT, USDA, and DARPA. He has over 50 peer-reviewed conference and journal publications in the fields of High Performance Computing, Big Data, and eScience.

Jessica Trelogan, j.trelogan@utexas.edu, coordinates Research Data Services at the University of Texas Libraries. She has over 20 years of experience in archaeological research, where she gained a deep understanding of the challenges involved in managing large amounts of disparate and complex data. In her role at UT Libraries, she helps connect researchers across all disciplines with the right experts, resources, and tools to manage their data throughout the lifecycle of research, from project conception to the long-term archive. In addition to consultative services and training, she manages the Texas Data Repository, a new platform for publishing and archiving UT's research data.

ACKNOWLEDGMENTS

This work was partially supported by the Extreme Science and Engineering Discovery Environment (XSEDE), which is supported by National Science Foundation grant number ACI-1548562.

REFERENCES

[1] Michener, William, Dave Vieglais, Todd Vision, John Kunze, Patricia Cruse, and Greg Janée. "DataONE: Data Observation Network for Earth—Preserving data and enabling innovation in the biological and environmental sciences." *D-Lib Magazine*17, no. 1/2 (2011): 12.

[2] Stewart, Craig A., Stephen Simms, Beth Plale, Matthew Link, David Y. Hancock, and Geoffrey C. Fox. "What is cyberinfrastructure." In Proceedings of the 38th annual ACM SIGUCCS fall conference: navigation and discovery, pp. 37-44. ACM, 2010.

[3] Si, Li, Wenming Xing, Xiaozhe Zhuang, Xiaoqin Hua, and Limei Zhou. "Investigation and analysis of research data services in university libraries." The Electronic Library 33, no. 3 (2015): 417-449.

[4] Kim, Youngseek, Benjamin K. Addom, and Jeffrey M. Stanton. "Education for eScience professionals: Integrating data curation and cyberinfrastructure." International journal of digital curation 6, no. 1 (2011): 125-138.

Web Archiving and Digital Libraries (WADL)

Martin Klein
Los Alamos National Laboratory
Research Library
Los Alamos, NM, USA
http://orcid.org/0000-0003-0130-2097
mklein@lanl.gov

Zhiwu Xie
Virginia Tech
University Libraries
Blacksburg, VA 24061 USA
http://orcid.org/0000-0002-2702-3806
zhiwuxie@vt.edu

Edward A. Fox
Virginia Tech
Dept. of Computer Science
Blacksburg, VA 24061 USA
http://orcid.org/0000-0003-1447-6870
fox@vt.edu

ABSTRACT

The 2018 edition of the Workshop on Web Archiving and Digital Libraries (WADL) will explore the integration of Web archiving and digital libraries. The workshop aims at addressing aspects covering the entire life cycle of digital resources and will also explore areas such as community building and ethical questions around web archiving.

CCS CONCEPTS

• **Information systems → Digital libraries and archives**;

KEYWORDS

Web Archiving, Community Building, Digital Preservation

ACM Reference Format:
Martin Klein, Zhiwu Xie, and Edward A. Fox. 2018. Web Archiving and Digital Libraries (WADL). In *JCDL '18: The 18th ACM/IEEE Joint Conference on Digital Libraries, June 3–7, 2018, Fort Worth, TX, USA.* ACM, New York, NY, USA, 2 pages. https://doi.org/10.1145/3197026.3200209

1 INTRODUCTION

Our understanding of the past will, to a large extent, depend on our success with Web archiving. WADL 2018 will bring together international leaders from industry, government, and academia, who focus their efforts on this important challenge. Together, we will explore the integration of Web archiving and digital libraries, over the complete digital resource life cycle: creation/authoring, uploading, publishing on the Web, crawling/collecting, compressing, formatting, storing, preserving, analyzing, indexing, supporting access, etc. The objectives of this workshop are to:

- continue to build the diverse community of people integrating Web archiving with digital libraries;
- help attendees learn about useful methods, systems, and software in this area;
- help chart future research and practice in this area, so more and higher quality Web archiving occurs;
- produce an archival publication that will help advance technology and practice; and
- promote synergistic efforts including collaborative projects and proposals.

2 RELATED WORK

The most recent related workshop, WADL 2017[1] was held in conjunction with JCDL 2017. The event was considered a great success by all participants, who voted in favor of a continuation of the workshop in 2018. Previous WADL meetings resulted in the publication of a special issue in the IEEE TCDL Bulletin such as in 2016 [3] and 2015 [2]. The workshop organizers are strongly motivated to continue this tradition with WADL 2018.

An earlier workshop, WIRE [4], focused on research of archival holdings and on making use of archives that preserve the web. The first workshop on Web Archiving and Digital Libraries, WADL 2013, led to a summary [1] after a group responded to the call for meeting[2] as part of the JCDL 2013 workshop program.

An earlier similar workshop at a prior JCDL conference took place in Ottawa in 2011[3], partly as a result of the emergence of a cooperative to explore Web archiving[4]. Broader in scope but related are the annual General Assembly meetings of the International Internet Preservation Consortium (IIPC)[5]. In addition, various sponsored programs have connected, like a closely related initiative[6] funded by the Andrew W. Mellon Foundation.

3 WORKSHOP TOPICS

WADL 2018 will cover all topics of interest, including but not limited to:

- Special Event Archiving and Collection Building
- Crawling of Dynamic and Mobile Content
- Social Media Archiving
- Archival Standards, Protocols and Systems, Tools
- Archival Metadata, Description, Classification
- Discovery of Archived Resources
- Extraction and Analysis of Archival Records
- Community Building
- Diversity in Web Archives
- Ethics in Web Archiving

ACM ISBN 978-1-4503-5178-2/18/06.
https://doi.org/10.1145/3197026.3200209

[1] http://fox.cs.vt.edu/wadl2017.html
[2] http://www.ctrnet.net/sites/default/files/JCDL2013WorkshopWebArchiving20130603.pdf
[3] http://infolab.stanford.edu/wac/
[4] http://cs.harding.edu/wag2011/
[5] http://netpreserve.org/
[6] https://library.columbia.edu/bts/web_resources_collection.html

4 WORKSHOP LOGISTICS

4.1 Audience and Attendees

Over the past few years, we have observed that the community interested in this topic is growing. Based on interest in recent years, we expect to have 20-30 attendees, including a solid representation of students. We will advertise the workshop and actively solicit submissions. All submissions will be peer-reviewed by the program committee and accepted contributions will be compiled into the WADL program. We anticipate the program to include aspects from multiple disciplines such as Computer Science, Library and Information Science, Web Science, Social Sciences, etc.

4.2 Format and Duration

We propose a full-day workshop, possibly split across two days. We anticipate invited speakers, presentations of selected papers and posters, as well as demonstrations and panels.

4.3 Special Requirements

We have an international program committee of about 15 people, in addition to the three co-chairs. We will consider running a WebEx teleconference during the workshop so that those unable to attend at the last moment will still be able to be involved. We plan to have a small poster session in addition to the usual type of activities. As in 2015 and 2016, we expect to have a special issue of IEEE TCDL Bulletin as an opportunity to publish invited contributions. In the past, the workshop has led to a call for contributions for a special issue of IJDL. The co-chairs fully intend to invest this effort in a special issue again in 2018.

5 BIOGRAPHICAL INFORMATION

Martin Klein holds a Ph.D. in Computer Science from Old Dominion University. He currently is a scientist in the Research Library at Los Alamos National Laboratory. He was program chair of DL 2014, poster chair of JCDL 2015, panel co-chair of JCDL 2016, and conference co-chair of iPres 2016. In addition, he also was co-chair of WADL 2015, 2016, and 2017 and the General Assembly of the International Internet Preservation Consortium (IIPC) in 2017 and 2018. He is an editorial board member of the International Journal on Digital Libraries (IJDL), guest editor for the Bulletin of IEEE Technical Committee on Digital Libraries, and served as a board member of the Web Archiving Collaboration at Columbia University. Martin Klein is the lead editor of the ANSI/NISO Specification Z39.99 and has published numerous journal/magazine articles and conference/workshop papers. More information can be found at: http://orcid.org/0000-0003-0130-2097.

Zhiwu Xie is a professor at Virginia Tech Libraries. He leads the IMLS-funded "Developing Library Cyberinfrastructure Strategy for Big Data Sharing and Reuse" (LCI) project, the Goodwin Hall Living Lab data management system, IMLS ETDplus, and VTechData, among others. He is deeply involved in Fedora/Hydra, APTrust, PREMIS, ResourceSync, and AltMetrics Data Quality. His research has received supported from Mellon, IBM, Amazon, and NSF XSEDE. He was a co-chair of WADL 2015, 2016, and 2017. His website is at http://scholar.lib.vt.edu/staff/zxie/.

Edward Fox holds a Ph.D. and M.S. in Computer Science from Cornell, and a B.S. from M.I.T. Since 1983 he has been at Virginia Tech, where he serves as Professor. He directs VT's Digital Library Research Laboratory and the Networked Digital Library of Theses and Dissertations. He was a member of the Board of CRA (the Computer Research Association). He was chair of the IEEE Technical Committee on Digital Libraries, and earlier was chair of ACM SIGIR. He was chair of the steering committee for JCDL, and is on the international advisory committee for ICADL. He has been (co-)Principal Investigator on over 120 research grants/contracts. He has taught over 80 tutorials and has given 66 keynote/distinguished/international invited talks. He has (co-)authored 18 books, 120 journal/magazine articles, 49 books chapters, 211 refereed conference/workshop papers, 73 posters, and over 150 other publications/reports, plus over 300 additional talks. Fox was editor for IR and DL for ACM Books. He was Co-Editor-in-Chief for ACM JERIC, and is on the boards of IJDL, JEMH, JIIS, J. UCS, Multimedia Tools & Applications, and PeerJ CS. He is a Fellow of ACM and of IEEE. His website can be found at: http://fox.cs.vt.edu.

REFERENCES

[1] Edward A. Fox and Mohamed M. Farag. 2013. Report on the Workshop on Web Archiving and Digital Libraries (WADL 2013). *ACM SIGIR Forum* 47, 2 (2013), 128–133. http://sigir.org/files/forum/2013D/p128.pdf

[2] Edward A. Fox, Zhiwu Xie, and Martin Klein. 2015. Web Archiving and Digital Libraries 2015 (WADL 2015) Overview. *Bulletin of IEEE Technical Committee on Digital Libraries* 11, 2 (2015), 1–2. http://www.ieee-tcdl.org/Bulletin/v11n2/papers/intro.pdf

[3] Edward A. Fox, Zhiwu Xie, and Martin Klein. 2017. Web Archiving and Digital Libraries (WADL) 2016: Highlights and Introduction to this Special Issue. *Bulletin of IEEE Technical Committee on Digital Libraries* 13, 1 (2017), 1–2. http://www.ieee-tcdl.org/Bulletin/v13n1/papers/intro.pdf

[4] Matthew Weber, David Lazer, and Kris Carpenter Negulescu. 2014. WIRE 2014 Workshop - Working with Internet Archives for Research. (2014). http://wp.comminfo.rutgers.edu/nsfia/

JCDL 2018 Workshop Proposal - Image Collections: Creation, Organization, Access, and Use

Wei Lu
Wuhan University
Wuhan, Hubei, China
weilu@whu.edu.cn

Jevin West
University of Washington
Washington, USA
jevinw@uw.edu

Brian O'connor
University of North Texas
Denton, Texas, USA
Brian.O'Connor@unt.edu

Krystyna Matusiak
University of Denver
Denver, Colorado, USA
Krystyna.Matusiak@du.edu

Qinghua Zhu
Nanjing University
Nanjing, Jiangsu, China
qhzhu@nju.edu.cn

Jason Lu
Cincinnati Children's Hospital Medical Center
Cincinnati, Ohio, USA
long.lu@cchmc.org

Jiangping Chen
University of North Texas
Denton, Texas, USA
Jiangping.Chen@unt.edu

ABSTRACT

We propose to have a full day workshop at JCDL 2018. This workshop will provide an opportunity for participants to exchange research ideas on image collections, including the creation, organization, access and use (COAU) of various image datasets. We expect to discuss various theories, methods, techniques, challenges, and new research directions as related to image's COAU. Especially we would like to explore innovative ideas on image annotation, retrieval, use behavior personas, processing of different types of images, and visual image metrics. The workshop will allow researchers to communicate with their peers on projects and develop new ideas through presentation and discussion. We hope to establish a community of researchers from related disciplines and explore questions critical to the future development of image's COAU. Participants of this workshop will be invited to submit a full paper to a special issue at *The Electronic Library* (http://www.emeraldinsight.com/journal/el) on Image Collections.

CCS CONCEPTS

• **Information systems** → Image search; • **Computing methodologies** → Image representations;

KEYWORDS

image collections; image annotation; image retrieval; image organization

JCDL '18, June 3–7, 2018, Fort Worth, TX, USA

ACM ISBN 978-1-4503-5178-2/18/06
https://doi.org/10.1145/3197026.3200208

ACM Reference Format:
Wei Lu, Jevin West, Brian O'connor, Krystyna Matusiak, Qinghua Zhu, Jason Lu, and Jiangping Chen. 2018. JCDL 2018 Workshop Proposal - Image Collections: Creation, Organization, Access, and Use. In *JCDL '18: The 18th ACM/IEEE Joint Conference on Digital Libraries, June 3–7, 2018, Fort Worth, TX, USA*, Jennifer B. Sartor, Theo D'Hondt, and Wolfgang De Meuter (Eds.). ACM, New York, NY, USA, 2 pages. https://doi.org/10.1145/3197026.3200208

1 INTRODUCTION

The evolution of image generating and sharing device leads to explosion of image resources. Consequently, how to effectively manage and use these image resources and to satisfy requirement of users from different areas have been challenging issues for both academia and business. There have been growing interests in image related research areas, such as image annotation and retrieval, clustering and classification, and image understanding. In addition, image research in different subject domains, such as medical disease recognition, culture image understanding, showing features of institution, and visual image metrics have drawn great attention. Major conferences such as the IEEE International Conference on Image Processing, and ACM Multimedia Conference have advanced image processing technologies.

Images are important digital objects that carry much information. Libraries and museums have been collecting and organizing images and preserving them as cultural heritages. While image collections have been developed and used by different communities. There are few opportunities for researchers and practitioners in digital libraries to interact or learn from each other on the creation organization, access and use of image collections.

We propose this workshop to bring together researchers and information practitioners on image collections, especially image organization/tagging, retrieval diversification, and understanding to exchange research ideas and promote collaboration. Our workshop is well aligned with the theme of JCDL 2018: "the fusion of different research communities, different methods, different research directions." We hope participants could develop interesting research ideas and collaborate with each other to better organize and use image collections for various purposes.

2 PROPOSED WORKSHOP FORMAT

We plan a full day workshop with the following components:

- Short introduction by the organizers.
- Presentations of papers submitted and accepted in response to an open call for research and position papers. Papers will be presented as short oral format. The number of oral presentations will be limited to at most 12 and allow for the maximum of time for interactive activities.
- Working groups focusing on relevant topics on image collections. Solicited topics are listed in Section 3.

3 POSSIBLE TOPICS

Creation of large image collections. High-quality and large-scale image datasets (LabelMe and ImageNet) play vital roles to push relevant research forward. However, existing datasets cannot cover every aspect of people's daily life. Thus, automatic dataset construction methods have emerged to create several large-scale datasets [2–4, 7–9]. Experience from the development of image collections will be valuable to develop future high-quality and large-scale image collections.

Theories and/or framework for image annotation (image tagging). Image annotation could be divided into two parts: manual annotation and automatic annotation. The former one, also named "image tagging", represents the traditional way to annotate image, it is usually processed by experts and social media users of images; The latter one represents state-of-the-art way for image annotation, that is, use computer to annotate image automatically. Currently, as the development of artificial intelligence, machine learning has been widely used in automatic image annotation. We would like to call for submission in this topic to advance research in both manual annotation and automatic annotation, and to explore new direction for development.

Image classification. Image classification mainly utilizes features of image, such as color, texture, shape and spatial relationship, to classify images into different categories according to the similarity degree of these features. The technologies in this area refer to image feature extraction, feature clustering, and so on. Image analysis, one of the vital parts of image classification, is aiming to transform digital image features to easy-to-read forms to assist image classification.

Image retrieval and image results diversification. Subtopics can be: image retrieval system construction and evaluation, content-based image retrieval, image retrieval based on semantic and visual features, and relevance feedback. As for image retrieval results diversification, information users often want to retrieve images that are both semantically relevant and visually diversity. For example, users submitting a query term like "apple" into a system may want to retrieve more diverse search results, i.e., images of apples with different shapes, colors, and textures.

Medical images. The use and role of medical imaging technologies in clinical oncology has greatly expanded from primarily a diagnostic tool to include a more central role in the context of individualized medicine over the past decade since people are paying more and more attention to healthcare [5]. However, the automatic analysis of medical images resource is still a very challenging task because the main objective of this task is not only to reach high accuracy but also to identify which parts of human body are infected by the disease[6].

Social images. The evolution of image sharing websites has led to the explosion of image resources on the Internet. Social media user often uploads their images for sharing and communication, which aims to record and transmit information. Besides, they process tagging on image for the purpose of management and description[1]. Research in social image includes social image tags, tag classification, user motivation for sharing image, user behavior and persona.

Innovative technologies on image processing and analysis. Image processing is a sub-category of signal processing, and it is one of the technologies of image classification. It also assists in feature extraction and pattern recognition. Techniques in this area include image compression, enhancement and recovery, matching, description and recognition. It has been widely used in satellite image processing, medical image processing, face detection, feature detection, face identification, microscope image processing and car barrier detection.

4 ORGANIZERS

Wei Lu, Professor, Wuhan University, China
Jevin West, Assistant Professor, University of Washington, USA
Brian O'Connor, Professor, University of North Texas, USA
Krystyna Matusiak, Associate Professor, University of Denver, USA
Qinghua Zhu, Professor, Nanjing University, China
Jason Lu, Cincinnati Children's Hospital Medical Center, USA
Jiangping Chen, Professor, University of North Texas, USA

REFERENCES

[1] Morgan Ames and Mor Naaman. 2007. Why we tag: motivations for annotation in mobile and online media. In *Proceedings of the SIGCHI conference on Human factors in computing systems*. ACM, 971–980.

[2] Yalong Bai, Kuiyuan Yang, Wei Yu, Chang Xu, Wei-Ying Ma, and Tiejun Zhao. 2015. Automatic image dataset construction from click-through logs using deep neural network. In *Proceedings of the 23rd ACM international conference on Multimedia*. ACM, 441–450.

[3] Duc-Tien Dang-Nguyen, Cecilia Pasquini, Valentina Conotter, and Giulia Boato. 2015. Raise: A raw images dataset for digital image forensics. In *Proceedings of the 6th ACM Multimedia Systems Conference*. ACM, 219–224.

[4] Jyoti Deshmukh and Udhav Bhosle. 2016. Image mining using association rule for medical image dataset. *Procedia Computer Science* 85 (2016), 117–124.

[5] Philippe Lambin, Emmanuel Rios-Velazquez, Ralph Leijenaar, Sara Carvalho, Ruud GPM van Stiphout, Patrick Granton, Catharina ML Zegers, Robert Gillies, Ronald Boellard, André Dekker, et al. 2012. Radiomics: extracting more information from medical images using advanced feature analysis. *European journal of cancer* 48, 4 (2012), 441–446.

[6] Eka Miranda, Mediana Aryuni, and E Irwansyah. 2016. A survey of medical image classification techniques. In *Information Management and Technology (ICIMTech), International Conference on*. IEEE, 56–61.

[7] Konstantin Pogorelov, Kristin Ranheim Randel, Carsten Griwodz, Sigrun Losada Eskeland, Thomas de Lange, Dag Johansen, Concetto Spampinato, Duc-Tien Dang-Nguyen, Mathias Lux, Peter Thelin Schmidt, et al. 2017. Kvasir: a multi-class image dataset for computer aided gastrointestinal disease detection. In *Proceedings of the 8th ACM on Multimedia Systems Conference*. ACM, 164–169.

[8] Fisher Yu Yinda Zhang Shuran Song and Ari Seff Jianxiong Xiao. 2015. Construction of a Large-scale Image Dataset using Deep Learning with Humans in the Loop. *arXiv preprint arXiv:1506.03365* (2015).

[9] Yan Xia, Xudong Cao, Fang Wen, and Jian Sun. 2014. Well begun is half done: Generating high-quality seeds for automatic image dataset construction from web. In *European Conference on Computer Vision*. Springer, 387–400.

Workshop Proposal on Knowledge Discovery from Digital Libraries

Hui Shi
California State Polytechnic University, Pomona USA
huishi@cpp.edu

Wu He
Old Dominion University, USA
whe@odu.edu

Guandong Xu
University of Technology Sydney, Australia
guandong.xu@uts.edu.au

OVERVIEW

The workshop is with the ACM/IEEE Joint Conference on Digital Libraries in 2018 (JCDL 2018) which will be held in Fort Worth, Texas, USA on June 3 – 7, 2018. The Joint Conference on Digital Libraries (JCDL) is a major international forum focusing on digital libraries and associated technical, practical, and social issues.

We solicit contributions on Knowledge Discovery from Digital Libraries. Knowledge is defined as facts, information, descriptions or skills acquired through experience or education. Valid, useful knowledge can help people make better predictions, support decision making and improve people's lives. Knowledge Discovery focuses on searching and extracting useful knowledge from data, databases and documents with different methodologies. The goal of Knowledge Discovery is mainly to uncover hidden relationships between data with techniques from artificial intelligence, mathematics, statistics, and algorithms.

A digital library stores and organizes a collection of digital objects, such as text, images, videos, sounds. Some of the characteristics that digital library has can make knowledge discovery easier: 1) digital library is an open platform. Users from all over the world can have access to the collection of digital library via internet; 2) digital library is an integration of a variety of information and multimedia services which allows multiple access; 3) digital library can provide fast and efficient access and user-friendly interfaces for users to retrieve information; 4) digital library usually is a large, well-organized collection that persist over time. It can contain many formats and digital objects that may be otherwise unobtainable. All the above characteristics of digital library will facilitate knowledge extraction, transformation, analyzing and presentation.

ACM Reference format:
Hui Shi, Wu He, and Guandong Xu. 2018. Workshop Proposal on Knowledge Discovery from Digital Libraries. In *Proceedings of The 18th ACM/IEEE Joint Conference on Digital Libraries, Fort Worth, Texas USA, June 3-7 2018 (JCDL'18)*, 2 pages. https://doi.org/10.1145/3197026.3200207

JCDL '18, June 3–7, 2018, Fort Worth, TX, USA

ACM ISBN 978-1-4503-5178-2/18/06.
https://doi.org/10.1145/3197026.3200207

The objectives of the workshop are to explore:

1. Advanced ways to organize and maintain Digital Libraries to facilitate Knowledge Discovery
2. Knowledge Discovery applications in Business
3. New challenges and technologies have been brought to the area of knowledge Discovery and Digital Libraries
4. Existing and novel techniques to extract and present knowledge from Digital Libraries

TOPICS OF INTERESTS

We invite original articles related to Knowledge Discovery from Library and Digital Libraries, which include but are not limited to:

- Information Visualization techniques in Knowledge Discovery from Digital Libraries
- Information extraction and text-mining approaches for semantic enrichment of Digital Libraries
- Ontology driven Knowledge Discovery from Digital Libraries
- Case-based reasoning systems for knowledge discovery from Digital Libraries
- Applications of Sematic Web in Digital Libraries
- Automatic categorization and clustering of scientific publications
- Academic recommender systems
- Applications of mining from scientific publications

SUBMISSION DETAILS

Each paper submitted to the workshop will be carefully evaluated based on originality, significance, technical soundness, and clarity of exposition and should be prepared according to the JCDL conference Authors Guidelines. It must be no longer than 10 pages and no less than 2 pages in length, including a 200-

word abstract, references and tables/figures. Authors should submit their manuscripts in PDF format to Dr. Hui Shi (huishi@cpp.edu), Dr. Wu He (whe@odu.edu) and Dr. Guandong Xu (guandong.xu@uts.edu.au) by email. Top quality papers after presented at the conference will be selected for extension and publication in Information Discovery and Delivery published by Emerald.

IMPORTANT DATES

- Paper Submission: 04/18/2018
- Author Notification: 04/30/2018
- Camera-ready Submission (for workshop proceedings): 05/15/2018
- Conference Dates: 06/03-06/07/2018
- Workshop Date: 06/06/2018 (half day)

ORGANIZERS

- Hui Shi, California State Polytechnic University, Pomona, USA
- Wu He, Old Dominion University, USA
- Guandong Xu, University of Technology Sydney, Australia

The Curative Power of Medical Data*

Daniela Gifu
Alexandru Ioan Cuza University of Iasi &
Romanian Academy - Iasi Branch,Romania
daniela.gifu@info.uaic.ro

Diana Trandabat
Alexandru Ioan Cuza University of Iasi
Romania
dtrandabat@info.uaic.ro

Kevin Bretonnel Cohen
Computational Bioscience Program U.
Colorado School of Medicine, USA
kevin.cohen@gmail.com

Jingbo Xia
Huazhong Agricultural University
R.P. China
xiajingbo.math@gmail.com

ABSTRACT

In an era when massive amounts of medical data became available, researchers working in biological, biomedical and clinical domains have increasingly started to require the help of language engineers to process large quantities of biomedical and molecular biology literature, patient data or health records. With such a huge amount of reports, evaluating their impact has long seized to be a trivial task.

Linking the contents of these documents to each other, as well as to specialized ontologies, could enable access to and discovery of structured clinical information and foster a major leap in natural language processing and health research.

CCS CONCEPTS

Applied computing → Life and medical sciences → Health informatics; *Health care information systems*; **Information systems → Information retrieval → Specialized information retrieval → Multimedia and multimodal retrieval.**

KEYWORDS

Biomedical research; medical text mining; health data analyzing.

ACM Reference format:

Daniela Gifu, Diana Trandabat, Kevin B. Cohen and Jingbo Xia. 2018. The Curative Power of Medical Data. In Proceedings of The 18th ACM/IEEE Joint Conference on Digital Libraries, Fort Worth, Texas USA, June 3-7 2018 (JCDL'18), 2 pages. https://doi.org/10.1145/3197026.3200211

1. INTRODUCTION

The interest for biomedical digital libraries, along with the continuous development of various qualitative and quantitative text analyses tools, made language technologies a natural choice for analyzing the evolution of the scientific life.

Biomedical text mining (BTM) (also called Health Informatics) is a discipline situated at the intersection of computer science, health care, information systems and linguistics. It focuses on the resources, methods and applications needed to optimize the acquisition, storage, recovery and mining of information in biomedicine. Also, BTM uses sophisticated predictive models to understand, identify and extract concepts from a large collection of scientific texts in medicine, biology, biophysics, chemistry, etc., with the aim to discover knowledge that can add value to the medical research [10].

In this context, a wide range of language resources has been developed, including complex lexicons, thesauri and ontologies that cover the entire spectrum of clinical concepts. Keizer [9] and Cornet [8] described a terminological and typology system to provide a uniform conceptual understanding.

Innovative approaches for the exploitation of biomedical data using semantic web technologies and linked data have started to be investigated by bringing together practitioners, researchers, and scholars to share examples, use cases, theories and analysis of biomedical data. A suitable forum in this direction is the MEDA 2018 Workshop, aiming at consolidating an internationally appreciated forum for scientific research in biomedical text mining, with emphasis on crowdsourcing, semantic web, knowledge integration and data linking.

2. CHALLENGES

Biomedical data analyzing is a challenging task, due to the diversity of formats and content. Most of the online information is available nowadays as unstructured documents [12], although several initiatives have been proposed to convince users to manually label their online publications using a specialized markup language[2] [11].

Among the hottest research topics covered by the biomedical research domain we can mention: crowdsourcing and collaborative

JCDL '18, June 3–7, 2018, Fort Worth, TX, USA

ACM ISBN 978-1-4503-5178-2/18/06.
https://doi.org/10.1145/3197026.3200210

[2] Medical Markup Language (MML) is a markup language proposed more than a decade ago as a set of standards facilitating the exchange of medical data between different medical information providers.

approaches in biomedicine in the era of big data [13, 18]; creating, organizing and storing biomedical data in digital libraries [2]; extracting various information from medical texts and images [14, 15]; creation of conceptual graphs, medical ontologies and specialized semantic networks [19]; applications specially designed for medicine and biology, such as medical question answering or summarization; medical search engines [4] or deep learning techniques for bioinformatics [16] or knowledge discovery using text mining [20].

Mining biomedical literature to extract the science behind it, such as concepts, patterns or relations, is a very productive research area. However, extracting non-scientific information from biomedical data has recently also seen an increasing interest, with applications ranging from identifying speculative language, to retrieval of papers with a specific writing style, in an attempt to cope with different reader preferences. Aside from mining knowledge, a new research direction tries to identify the factors that drive readers to choose one scientific article instead of another.

One of the big enablers of the recent progress in the field has been enormous growth in the amount of annotated data available. A recent publication cited 25 corpora of biomedical data that had become available within just the past five years [5], a previously unprecedented growth rate.

3 LOOKING TOWARDS THE FUTURE

One of the biggest events in science in recent years has been the spread of awareness of the problems of reproducibility of a large amount of published research [1]. It has become clear that there is considerable work to be done just to quantify the extent of this problem in natural language processing [17, 3]. With recent progress in the area of understanding some of the definitional issues involved [6], as well as a shift in the field's publication trends towards accepting work that attempts to replicate or reproduce previous work versus over-valuing innovation (recognizing, in effect, the innovative aspects of replication and reproducibility itself in the context of the current publication trends) [3], it has now become possible to systematically investigate the role of generalizability problems in failures of reproducibility in natural language processing research. It can be expected that the biomedical domain will provide a fruitful testbed for this research, due to a variety of factors related to the distributional differences between the many sublanguages of the domain and the textual genres on which most natural language processing research is evaluated, such as newswire text [21,7]. Thus, it is reasonable to expect this field to continue to grow in importance to the broader natural language processing and machine learning fields in the future.

ACKNOWLEDGMENTS

This survey was published with the support by two grants of the Romanian National Authority for Scientific Research and Innovation, UEFISCDI, project number PN-III-P2-2.1-BG-2016-0390, contract 126BG/2016 and project number PN-III-P1-1.2-PCCDI-2017-0818, contract 73PCCDI/2018 within PNCDI III.

REFERENCES

[1] Baker, M. (2016). 1,500 scientists lift the lid on reproducibility. Nature News 533, no. 7604, p. 452.

[2] Banks, M. A., & Peay, W. J. (2006). The Future of Biomedical Digital Libraries. Branco, A., Cohen, K.B., Vossen, P., Ide, N., and Calzolari, N. (2017).

[3] Replicability and reproducibility of research results for human language technology: introducing an LRE special section., pp. 1-5.

[4] Büttcher, S., Clarke, C. L., & Cormack, G. V. (2016). Information retrieval: Implementing and evaluating search engines. MIT Press.

[5] Cohen, K. B., Verspoor, K., Fort, K., Funk, C., Bada, M., Palmer, M., and E. Hunter, L.E. (2017). The Colorado Richly Annotated Full Text (CRAFT) corpus: Multi-model annotation in the biomedical domain. In Handbook of Linguistic Annotation, pp. 1379-1394. Springer, Dordrech.

[6] Cohen, K.B, Xia, J., Zweigenbaum, P., Callahan, T.J., Hargraves, O. Goss, F., Ide, N., Névéol, A., Grouin, C., and Hunter, L.E. (2018). Three dimensions of reproducibility in natural language processing. Language Resources and Evaluation Conference.

[7] Cohen, K.B., F.R. Goss, P. Zweigenbaum, and L.E. Hunter. (2017). Translational Morphosyntax: Distribution of Negation in Clinical Records and Biomedical Journal Articles. In Studies in health technology and informatics 245 , pp. 346-350.

[8] Cornet R., de Keizer N.F., Abu-Hanna A. (2006). A framework for characterizing terminological systems. In: Methods Inf Med., vol. 45, pp. 253-266.

[9] de Keizer NF, Abu-Hanna A, Zwetsloot-Schonl JHM. (2000). Understanding terminological systems I: terminology and typology. In: Methods Inf Med., vol. 39, pp. 16-21.

[10] Gifu, D. (2017). Malaria Detection System. In: Proceedings of the International Conference on Mathematical Foundations of Informatics, MFOI-2017, Cojocaru, S. and Gaindric, C., Druguş, I. (eds.), Institute of Mathematics and Computer Science, Academy of Sciences of Moldova, Chişinău, 2017, pp.74-78.

[11] Guo, J., Takada, A., Tanaka, K., Sato, J., Suzuki, M., Suzuki, T., ... & Yoshihara, H. (2004). The development of MML (Medical Markup Language) version 3.0 as a medical document exchange format for HL7 messages. Journal of medical systems, 28(6), pp. 523-533.

[12] Holzinger, Andreas; Stocker, Christof; Ofner, Bernhard; Prohaska, Gottfried; Brabenetz, Alberto; Hofmann-Wellenhof, Rainer (2013). "Combining HCI, Natural Language Processing, and Knowledge Discovery - Potential of IBM Content Analytics as an Assistive Technology in the Biomedical Field". In: Holzinger, Andreas; Pasi, Gabriella. Human-Computer Interaction and Knowledge Discovery in Complex, Unstructured, Big Data. Lecture Notes in Computer Science. Springer, pp. 13-24.

[13] Khare, R., Good, B. M., Leaman, R., Su, A. I., & Lu, Z. (2015). Crowdsourcing in biomedicine: challenges and opportunities. Briefings in bioinformatics, 17(1), pp. 23-32.

[14] Lambin, P., Rios-Velazquez, E., Leijenaar, R., Carvalho, S., van Stiphout, R. G., Granton, P., & Aerts, H. J. (2012). Radiomics: extracting more information from medical images using advanced feature analysis. In: European Journal of Cancer, 48(4), pp. 441-446.

[15] Meystre, S. M., Savova, G. K., Kipper-Schuler, K. C., & Hurdle, J. F. (2008). Extracting information from textual documents in the electronic health record: a review of recent research. In:Yearb Med Inform, 35(8), pp. 128-144.

[16] Min, S., Lee, B., & Yoon, S. (2017). Deep learning in bioinformatics. Briefings in bioinformatics, 18(5), 851-869.

[17] Pedersen, T. (2008). Empiricism is not a matter of faith. In: Computational Linguistics 34, no. 3 (2008), pp. 465-470.

[18] Shaikh, A. R., Butte, A. J., Schully, S. D., Dalton, W. S., Khoury, M. J., & Hesse, B. W. (2014). Collaborative biomedicine in the age of big data: the case of cancer. Journal of medical Internet research, 16(4).

[19] Shi, F., Chen, L., Han, J., & Childs, P. (2017). A Data-Driven Text Mining and Semantic Network Analysis for Design Information Retrieval. Journal of Mechanical Design, 139(11), 111402.

[20] Westergaard, D., Stærfeldt, H. H., Tønsberg, C., Jensen, L. J., & Brunak, S. (2018). A comprehensive and quantitative comparison of text-mining in 15 million full-text articles versus their corresponding abstracts. In: Plos Computational Biology, 14(2), e1005962.

[21] Wu, S.T., Miller, T.A., Masanz, J.J., Coarr, M., Carrell, D., Halgrim, S.R., Harris, D., and Clark, C. (2013). Negation's Not Solved: Reconsidering Negation Annotation and Evaluation. In AMIA.

JCDL 2018 Doctoral Consortium

J. Stephen Downie
University of Illinois at Urbana-Champaign
501 E. Daniel St., MC-493, Champaign, IL 61810-6211
United States of America
jdownie@illinois.edu

Oksana L. Zavalina
University of North Texas
1155 Union Circle 311068, Denton, TX 76203-5017
United States of America
oksana.zavalina@unt.edu

Sampath Jayarathna
California State Polytechnic University
3801 West Temple Avenue, Pomona, CA 91768
United States of America
ukjayarathna@cpp.edu

ABSTRACT

This is an overview of the Doctoral Consortium workshop organized and held as part of the Joint Conference on Digital Libraries 2018 conference in Fort Worth, Texas.

CCS CONCEPTS

• **General and reference → Document types**; Surveys and overviews

KEYWORDS

Doctoral research

ACM Reference format:

J.S. Downie, O.L. Zavalina, and S. Jayarathna. 2018. JCDL 2018 Doctoral Consortium. In *Proceedings of ACM JCDL'18, June 3-7, 2018, Fort Worth, TX, USA*, 2 pages.DOI: https://doi.org/10.1145/3197026.3210421

1 INTRODUCTION

The Doctoral Consortium — held annually as part of the program of the ACM/IEEE Joint Conference on Digital Libraries preceding technical program — is a workshop for Ph.D. students from all over the world who are in the early phases of their dissertation work. The goal of the Doctoral Consortium is to help students with their thesis and research plans by providing feedback and general advice in a constructive atmosphere. Students present and discuss their research in the context of a well-known and established international conference, in a supportive atmosphere with other doctoral students and an international panel of established researchers: prominent professors and experienced practitioners in the field of digital library research.

ACM ISBN 978-1-4503-5178-2/18/06.
https://doi.org/10.1145/3197026.3210421

Submissions relating to any aspect of digital library research, development, and evaluation are welcomed, including: technical advances, usage and impact studies, policy analyses, social and institutional implications, theoretical contributions, interaction and design advances, and innovative applications in the sciences, humanities, and education. Doctoral students interested in participating in the Doctoral Consortium submit the following application documents:

- an extended abstract (6-8 pages long) describing their digital library related research. This document should identify one or more significant problems, clearly formulate research questions, summarize the current knowledge of the problem domain and the state of the art of solutions, describe research methodology to be applied, present preliminary results if any, describe expected contributions of the applicant to the research area, and (for technical research) describe how the research is innovative, novel, or extends existing approaches to a problem.
- a short (one-paragraph) statement of expected benefits of participation for both the applicant and the other consortium participants, with clear discussion of expected contributions and gains
- a current Curriculum Vitae with the maximum length of 2 pages
- a 1-page signed letter from student's research supervisor that supports student's attendance at the JCDL Doctoral Consortium.

JCDL 2018 Doctoral Consortium was co-chaired by Dr. Oksana L. Zavalina (University of North Texas), Dr. J. Stephen Downie (University of Illinois at Urbana-Champaign), and Dr. Sampath Jayarathna (California State Polytechnic University). A total of 20 Doctoral Consortium submissions were received. After reviewing all submissions, 11 best submissions were selected to be presented at the full-day workshop that took place on June 3, 2018. These submissions represented various areas of digital library research conducted by Ph.D. students from 6 universities located in North America, Europe, and Asia.

The following is the list of accepted Doctoral Consortium submissions:

- "A Semantically Enriched Recommendation and Visualization Approach for Academic Literature" by

Corinna Breitinger

- "Analyzing Formula Concepts and Patterns to Improve Literature Exploration and Recommendation for STEM Documents" by Philipp Scharf
- "Automatic Mathematical Information Retrieval to Perform Translations up to Computer Algebra Systems" by Andre Greiner-Petter
- "Bootstrapping Web Archive Collections of Stories from Micro-Collections in Social Media" by Alexander Nwala
- "Digital Libraries for Experimental Data" by Susanne Putze
- "Dual Language Information Seeking in Digital Libraries" by Hani Alsalmi
- "Establishing and Verifying Fixity of Archived Web Pages" by Mohammed Aturban
- "Exploring the Implications of Artificial Intelligence in Various Aspects of Scholarly Peer Review" by Tirthankar Ghosal
- "Exploring the Knowledge Curation Work of Wikidata" by Timothy Kanke
- "Improving Collection Understanding in Web Archives" by Shawn Jones
- "Theorizing Success: Measures for Evaluating Digital Preservation Efficacy" by Stephen Abrams.

Selected applicants received complimentary JCDL conference registration and were encouraged to apply for a SIGIR-sponsored Student Travel Award to help cover some of the costs associated with travel and lodging. Experts reviewed accepted Doctoral Consortium submissions and provided comment on the content of the thesis as well as on the presentation. Accepted abstracts were distributed to participants as the workshop proceedings.

Students made 20-minute presentations on their research, focusing on the main theme of their thesis, what they have achieved so far and how they plan to continue their work. Presentations were followed by discussion and feedback from both the panel and other participants on their current research and guidance on future research directions, as well as more general questions (e.g., on the differences in Ph.D. studies in different countries). Participants are invited to publish a revised version of their extended abstracts in a special issue of the TCDL Bulletin, the publication of the IEEE-CS Technical Committee on Digital Libraries.

Author Index

www.ingramcontent.com/pod-product-compliance
Lightning Source LLC
LaVergne TN
LVHW080007210926
848481LV00011B/2960
9781450361538